Bible History
Old Testament

Alfred Edersheim

TABLE OF CONTENTS

VOLUME 3: ISRAEL IN CANAAN UNDER JOSHUA AND THE JUDGES 226

VOLUME 5: BIRTH OF SOLOMON TO REIGN OF AHAB   424

VOLUME 6: THE REIGN OF AHAB TO THE DECLINE OF THE TWO KINGDOMS   525

11

PREFACE

One of the most marked and hopeful signs of our time is the increasing attention given on all sides to the study of Holy Scripture. Those who believe and love the Bible, who have experienced its truth and power, can only rejoice at such an issue. They know that "the Word of God liveth and abideth for ever," that "not one tittle" of it "shall fail;" and that it is "able to make wise unto salvation, through faith which is in Christ Jesus."

Accordingly they have no reason to dread the results either of scientific investigation, or of searching inquiry into "those things which are most surely believed among us." For, the more the Bible is studied, the deeper will be our conviction that "the foundation of God standeth sure."

It is to help, so far as we can, the reader of Holy Scripture — not to supersede his own reading of it — that the series, of which this is the first volume, has been undertaken. In writing it I have primarily had in view those who teach and those who learn, whether in the school or in the family. But my scope has also been wider. I have wished to furnish what may be useful for reading in the family, — what indeed may, in some measure, serve the place of a popular exposition of the sacred history. More than this, I hope it may likewise prove a book to put in the hands of young men, — not only to show them what the Bible really teaches, but to defend them against the insidious attacks arising from misrepresentation and misunderstanding of the sacred text.

With this threefold object in view, I have endeavored to write in a form so popular and easily intelligible as to be of use to the Sunday-school teacher, the advanced scholar, and the Bible-class; progressing gradually, in the course of this and the next volume, from the more simple to the more detailed. At the same time, I have taken up the Scripture narrative successively, chapter by chapter, always marking the portions of the Bible explained, that so, in family or in private reading, the sacred text may be compared with the explanations furnished. Finally, without mentioning objections on the part of opponents, I have endeavored to meet those that have been raised, and that not by controversy, but rather by a more full and correct study of the sacred text itself in the Hebrew original. In so doing, I have freely availed myself not only of the results of the best criticism, German and English, but also of the aid of such kindred studies as those of Biblical geography and antiquities, the Egyptian and the Assyrian monuments, etc.

But when all has been done, the feeling grows only more strong that there is another and a higher understanding of the Bible, without which all else is vain. Not merely to know the meaning of the narratives of Scripture, but to realize their spiritual application; to feel their eternal import; to experience them in ourselves, so to speak — this is the only profitable study of Scripture, to which all else can only serve as outward preparation. Where the result is "doctrine, reproof, correction, and instruction in righteousness," the Teacher must be He, by whose "inspiration all Scripture is given." "For what man knoweth the things of a man, save the spirit of man which is in him? even so the things of God knoweth no man, but the Spirit of God." But the end of all is Christ — not only "the end of the law for righteousness to every one that believeth," but also He in whom "all the promises of God are Yea and Amen."

A. E.

Heniach Bournemouth.

INTRODUCTION

THAT the "God of Abraham, Isaac, and Jacob" is also the "God and Father of our Lord and Savior Jesus Christ," and that "they which are of faith, the same are the children of Abraham," — these are among the most precious truths of revelation. They show us not only the faithfulness of our God, and the greatness of our privileges, but also the marvelous wisdom of the plan of salvation, and its consistency throughout. For the Bible should be viewed, not only in its single books, but in their connection, and in the unity of the whole. The Old Testament could not be broken off from the New, and each considered as independent of the other. Nor yet could any part of the Old Testament be disjoined from the rest. The full meaning and beauty of each appears only in the harmony and unity of the whole. Thus they all form links of one unbroken chain, reaching from the beginning to the time when the Lord Jesus Christ came, for whom all previous history had prepared, to whom all the types pointed, and in whom all the promises are "Yea and Amen." Then that which God had spoken to Abraham, more than two thousand years before, became a blessed reality, for "the Scripture, foreseeing that God would justify the heathen through faith, preached before the gospel unto Abraham, saying, In thee shall all nations be blessed. So then they which be of faith are blessed with faithful Abraham." That this one grand purpose should have been steadily kept in view, and carried forward through all the vicissitudes of history, changes of time, and stages of civilization, — and that without requiring any alteration, only further unfolding and at last completion — affords indeed the strongest confirmation to our faith. It is also a precious comfort to our hearts; for we see how God's purpose of mercy has been always the same; and, walking the same pilgrim-way which "the fathers" had trod, and along which God had safely guided the Covenant, we rejoice to know that neither opposition of man nor yet unfaithfulness on the part of His professing people can make void the gracious counsel of God: -

"He loved us from the first of time,

He loves us to the last."

And this it is which we learn from the unity of Scripture.

But yet another and equally important truth may be gathered. There is not merely harmony but also close connection between the various parts of Scripture. Each book illustrates the other, taking up its teaching and carrying it forward. Thus the unity of Scripture is not like that of a stately building, however ingenious its plan or vast its proportions; but rather, to use a Biblical illustration, like that of the light, which shineth more and more unto the perfect day. We mark throughout growth in its progress, as men were able to bear fuller communications, and prepared for their reception. The law, the types, the history, the prophecies, and the promises of the Old Testament all progressively unfold and develop the same truth, until it appears at last in its New Testament fullness. Though all testify of the same thing, not one of them could safely be left out, nor yet do we properly understand any one part unless we view it in its bearing and connection with the others. And so when at last we come to the close of Scripture, we see how the account of the creation and of the first calling of the children of God, which had been recorded in the book of Genesis, has found its full counterpart — its fulfillment — in the book of

Revelation, which tells the glories of the second creation, and the perfecting of the Church of God. As one of the old Church teachers (St. Augustine) writes:

"Novum Testamentum in vetere latet,
Vetus in novo patet."

That in a work composed of so many books, written under such very different circumstances, by penmen so different, and at periods so widely apart, there should be "some things hard to be understood, which they that are unlearned and unstable wrest," can surely not surprise us, more particularly when we remember that it was God's purpose only to send the brighter light as men were able to bear it. Besides, we must expect that with our limited powers and knowledge we shall not be able fully to understand the ways of God. But, on the other hand, this may be safely said, that the more deep, calm, and careful our study, the more ample the evidence it will bring to light to confirm our faith against all attacks of the enemy. Yet the ultimate object of our reading is not knowledge, but experience of grace. For, properly understood, the Scripture is all full of Christ, and all intended to point to Christ as our only Savior. It is not only the law, which is a schoolmaster unto Christ, nor the types, which are shadows of Christ, nor yet the prophecies, which are predictions of Christ; but the whole Old Testament history is full of Christ. Even where persons are not, events may be types. If any one failed to see in Isaac or in Joseph a personal type of Christ, he could not deny that the offering up of Isaac, or the selling of Joseph, and his making provision for the sustenance of his brethren, are typical of events in the history of our Lord. And so indeed every event points to Christ, even as He is alike the beginning, the center, and the end of all history — "the same yesterday, and today, and for ever." One thing follows from this: only that reading or study of the Scriptures can be sufficient or profitable through which we learn to know Christ — and that as "the Way, the Truth, and the Life" to us. And for this purpose we ought constantly to ask the aid and teaching of the Holy Spirit.

A few brief remarks, helpful to the study of patriarchal history, may here find a place. In general, the Old Testament may be arranged into "The Law and the Prophets."

It was possibly with reference to this division that the Law consisted of the five books of Moses — ten being the symbolical number of completeness, and the Law with its commands being only half complete without "the Prophets" and the promises. But assuredly to the fivefold division of the Law answers the arrangement of the Psalms into five books, of which each closes with a benediction, as follows: -

Book 1: Psalm 1-41
Book 2: Psalm 42-72
Book 3: Psalm 73-89
Book 4: Psalm 90-106
Book 5: Psalm 107-150

- the last Psalm standing as a grand final benediction.

The Law or the Five Books of Moses are commonly called the Pentateuch, a Greek term meaning the "fivefold," or "five-parted" Book. Each of these five books commonly bears a title given by the Greek translators of the Old Testament (the so-called LXX.), in accordance with the contents of each: Genesis (origin, creation), Exodus (going out from Egypt), Leviticus, Numbers, and Deuteronomy (Second Law, or the Law a second time). The Jews designate each book by the first or else the most prominent word with which it begins.

VOLUME 1: THE WORLD BEFORE THE FLOOD, AND THE HISTORY OF THE PATRIARCHS

CHAPTER 1: CREATION — MAN IN THE GARDEN OF EDEN — THE FALL.
(GENESIS 1-3)

"HE that cometh unto God must believe that He is, and that He is the rewarder of them that diligently seek Him." Hence Holy Scripture, which contains the revealed record of God's dealings and purposes with man, commences with an account of the creation. "For the invisible things of Him from the creation of the world are clearly seen, being understood by the things that are made, even His eternal power and Godhead."

Four great truths, which have their bearing on every part of revelation, come to us from the earliest Scripture narrative, like the four rivers which sprung in the garden of Eden. The first of these truths is — the creation of all things by the word of God's power; the second, the descent of all men from our common parents, Adam and Eve; the third, our connection with Adam as the head of the human race, through which all mankind were involved in his sin and fall; and the fourth, that One descended from Adam, yet without his sin, should by suffering free us from the consequences of the fall, and as the second Adam became the Author of eternal salvation to all who trust in Him. To these four vital truths there might be added, as a fifth, the institution of one day in seven to be a day of holy rest unto God.

It is scarcely possible to imagine a greater contrast than between the heathen accounts of the origin of all things and the scriptural narrative. The former are so full of the grossly absurd that no one could regard them as other than fables; while the latter is so simple, and yet so full of majesty, as almost to force us to "worship and bow down," and to "kneel before the Lord our Maker." And as this was indeed the object in view, and not scientific instruction, far less the gratification of our curiosity, we must expect to find in the first chapter of Genesis simply the grand outlines of what took place, and not any details connected with creation. On these points there is ample room for such information as science may be able to supply, when once it shall have carefully selected and sifted all that can be learned from the study of earth and of nature. That time, however, has not yet arrived; and we ought, therefore, to be on our guard against the rash and unwarranted statements which have sometimes been brought forward on these subjects. Scripture places before us the successive creation of all things, so to speak, in an ascending scale, till at last we come to that of man, the chief of God's works, and whom his Maker destined to be lord of all. (Psalms 8:3-8) Some have imagined that the six days of creation represent so many periods, rather than literal days, chiefly on the ground of the supposed high antiquity of our globe, and the various great epochs or periods, each terminating in a grand revolution, through which our earth seems to have passed, before coming to its present state, when it became a fit habitation for man. There is, however, no need to resort to any such theory. The first verse in the book of Genesis simply states the general fact, that "In the beginning" — whenever that may have been — "God created the heaven and the earth." Then, in the second verse, we find earth described as it was at the close of the last great revolution, preceding the present state of things: "And the earth was without form and void; and darkness was upon the face of the deep." An almost indefinite space of time, and many changes, may therefore have intervened between the creation of heaven and earth, as mentioned in ver. 1, and the chaotic state of our earth, as described in ver. 2. As for the exact date of the first creation, it may be safely affirmed that we have not yet the knowledge sufficient to arrive at any really trustworthy conclusion.

It is of far greater importance for us, however, to know that God "created all things by Jesus Christ;" (Ephesians 3:9) and further, that "all things were created by Him, and for Him," (Colossians 1:16) and that "of Him, and through Him, and to Him are all things." (Romans 11:36. See also 1 Corinthians 8:6; Hebrews 1:2; John 1:3) This gives not only unity to all creation, but places it in living connection with our Lord Jesus Christ. At the same time we should also always bear in mind, that it is "through faith we understand that the worlds were framed by the word of God, so that things which are seen were not made of things which do appear." (Hebrews 11:3)

Everything as it proceeded from the hand of God was "very good," that is, perfect to answer the purpose for which it had been destined. "And on the seventh day God ended His work which He had made; and He rested on the seventh day from all His work which He had made. And God blessed the seventh day, and sanctified it: because that in it He had rested from all His work which God created and made." It is upon this original institution of the Sabbath as a day of holy rest that our observance of the Lord's day is finally based, the change in the precise day — from the seventh to the first of the week — having been occasioned by the resurrection of our Lord Jesus Christ, by which not only the first, but also the new creation was finally completed. (See Isaiah 65:17)

Of all His works God only "created man in His own image: in the image of God created He him." This expression refers not merely to the intelligence with which God endowed, and the immortality with which He gifted man, but also to the perfect moral and spiritual nature which man at the first possessed. And all his surroundings were in accordance with his happy state. God "put him into the garden of Eden to dress it and to keep it," and gave him a congenial companion in Eve, whom Adam recognized as bone of his bones, and flesh of his flesh. Thus as God had, by setting apart the Sabbath day, indicated worship as the proper relationship between man and his Creator, so He also laid in Paradise the foundation of civil society by the institution of marriage and of the family. (Comp. Mark 10:6, 9)

It now only remained to test man's obedience to God, and to prepare him for yet higher and greater privileges than those which he already enjoyed. But evil was already in this world of ours, for Satan and his angels had rebelled against God. The scriptural account of man's trial is exceedingly brief and simple. We are told: that "the tree of the knowledge of good and evil" had been placed "in the midst of the garden," and of the fruit of this tree God forbade Adam to eat, on pain of death. On the other hand, there was also "the tree of life" in the garden, probably as symbol and pledge of a higher life, which we should have inherited if our first parents had continued obedient to God. The issue of this trial came only too soon. The tempter, under the form of a serpent, approached Eve. He denied the threatenings of God, and deceived her as to the real consequences of eating the forbidden fruit. This, followed by the enticement of her own senses, led Eve first to eat, and then to induce her husband to do likewise. Their sin had its immediate consequence. They had aimed to be "as gods," and, instead of absolutely submitting themselves to the command of the Lord, acted independently of Him. And now their eyes were indeed opened, as the tempter had promised, "to know good and evil;" but only in their own guilty knowledge of sin, which immediately prompted the wish to hide themselves from the presence of God. Thus, their alienation and departure from God, the condemning voice of their conscience, and their sorrow and shame gave evidence that the Divine threatening had already been accomplished: "In the day that thou eatest thereof thou shalt surely die." The sentence of death which God now pronounced on our first parents extended both to their bodily and their spiritual nature — to their mortal and immortal part. In the day he sinned man died in body, soul, and spirit. And because Adam, as the head of his race, represented the whole; and as through him we should all have entered upon a very high and happy state of being, if he had remained obedient, so now the consequences of his disobedience have extended to us all; and as "by one man sin entered into the world, and death by sin," so "death passed upon all men, for that all have sinned." Nay, even "creation itself," which had been placed under his dominion, was made through his fall "subject to vanity," and came under the curse, as God said to Adam: "Cursed is the ground for thy sake; in sorrow shalt thou eat of it all the days of thy life; thorns also and thistles shall it bring forth to thee."

God, in His infinite mercy, did not leave man to perish in his sin. He was indeed driven forth from Paradise, for which he was no longer fit. But, before that, God had pronounced the curse upon his tempter, Satan, and had given man the precious promise that the seed of the woman should bruise the head of the serpent; that is, that our blessed Savior, "born of a woman," should redeem us from the power of sin and of death, through His own obedience, death, and resurrection. And even the labor of his hands, to which man was now doomed, was in the circumstances a boon.

Therefore, when our first parents left the garden of Eden, it was not without hope, nor into outer darkness. They carried with them the promise of a Redeemer, the assurance of the final defeat of the great enemy, as well as the Divine institution of a Sabbath on which to worship, and of the marriage-bond by which to be joined together into families. Thus the foundations of the Christian life in all its bearings were laid in Paradise.

There are still other points of practical interest to be gathered up. The descent of all mankind from our first parents determines our spiritual relationship to Adam. In Adam all have sinned and fallen. But, on the other hand, it also determines our spiritual relationship to the Lord Jesus Christ, as the second Adam, which rests on precisely the same grounds. For "as we have borne the image of the earthy, we shall also bear the image of the heavenly," and "as in Adam all die, even so in Christ shall all be made alive." "For as by one man's disobedience many were made sinners, so by the obedience of one shall many be made righteous." The descent of all mankind from one common stock has in times past been questioned by some, although Scripture expressly teaches that "He has made of one blood all nations, for to dwell on the face of the earth." It is remarkable that this denial, which certainly never was shared by the most competent men of science, has quite lately been, we may say, almost universally abandoned, and the original unity of the human race in their common descent is now a generally accepted fact.

Here, moreover, we meet for the first time with that strange resemblance to revealed religion which makes heathenism so like and yet so unlike the religion of the Old Testament. As in the soul of man we see the ruins of what he had been before the fall, so in the legends and traditions of the various religions of antiquity we recognize the echoes of what men had originally heard from the mouth of God. Not only one race, but almost all nations, have in their traditions preserved some dim remembrance alike of an originally happy and holy state, — a so-called golden age — in which the intercourse between heaven and earth was unbroken, and of a subsequent sin and fall of mankind. And all nations also have cherished a faint belief in some future return of this happy state, that is, in some kind of coming redemption, just as in their inmost hearts all men have at least a faint longing for a Redeemer.

CHAPTER 3: SETH AND HIS DESCENDANTS — THE RACE OF CAIN
(GENESIS 4)

THE place of Abel could not remain unfilled, if God's purpose of mercy were to be carried out. Accordingly He gave to Adam and Eve another son, whom his mother significantly called "Seth," that is, "appointed," or rather "compensation;" "for God," said she, "hath appointed me ('compensated me with') another seed instead of Abel, whom Cain slew." Before, however, detailing the history of Seth and his descendants, Scripture traces that of Cain to the fifth and sixth generations. Cain, as we know, had gone into the land of "Nod" — "wandering," "flight," "unrest," — and there built a city, which has been aptly described as the laying of the first foundations of that kingdom in which "the spirit of the beast" prevails. We must remember that probably centuries had elapsed since the creation, and that men had already multiplied on the earth. Beyond this settlement of Cain, nothing seems to have occurred which Scripture has deemed necessary to record, except that the names of the "Cainites" are still singularly like those of the "Sethites." Thus we follow the line of Cain's descendants to Lamech, the fifth from Cain, when all at once the character and tendencies of that whole race appear fully developed. It comes upon us, almost by surprise, that within so few generations, and in the lifetime of the first man, almost every commandment and institution of God should already be openly set aside, and violence, lust, and ungodliness prevail upon the earth. The first direct breach of God's arrangement of which we here read, is the introduction of polygamy. "Lamech took unto him two wives." Assuredly, "from the beginning it was not so." But this is not all. Scripture preserves to us in the address of Lamech to his two wives the earliest piece of poetry. It has been designated "Lamech's Sword-song," and breathes a spirit of boastful defiance, of trust in his own strength, of violence, and of murder. Of God there is no further acknowledgment than in a reference to the avenging of Cain, from which Lamech augurs his own safety. Nor is it without special purpose that the names of Lamech's wives and of his daughter are mentioned in Scripture. For their names point to "the lust of the eye, and the lust of the flesh," just as the occupations of Lamech's sons point to "the pride of life." The names of his wives were "Adah," that is, "beauty," or "adornment;" and "Zillah," that is, "the shaded," perhaps from her tresses, or else "sounding," perhaps from her song; while "Naamah," as Lamech's daughter was called, means "pleasant, graceful, lovely." And here we come upon another and most important feature in the history of the "Cainites." The pursuits and inventions of the sons of Lamech point to the culture of the arts, and to a settled and permanent state of society. His eldest son by Adah, "Jabal, was the father of such as dwell in tents, and of such as have cattle," that is, he made even the pastoral life a regular business. His second son, "Jubal, was the father of all such as handle the harp (or cithern), and the flute (or sackbut)," in other words, the inventor alike of stringed and of wind instruments; while Tubal-Cain, Lamech's son by Zillah, was "an instructor of every artificer in brass and iron." Taken in connection with Lamech's sword-song, which immediately follows the scriptural account of his sons' pursuits, we are warranted in designating the culture and civilization introduced by the family of Lamech as essentially godless. And that, not only because it was that of ungodly men, but because it was pursued independent of God, and in opposition to the great purposes which He had with man.

Moreover, it is very remarkable that we perceive in the Cainite race those very things which afterwards formed the characteristics of heathenism, as we find it among the most advanced nations of antiquity, such as Greece and Rome. Over their family-life might be written, as it were, the names Adah, Zillah, Naamah; over their civil life the "sword-song of Lamech," which indeed strikes the key-note of ancient heathen society; and over their culture and pursuits, the abstract of the biographies which Scripture furnishes us of the descendants of Cain. And as their lives have been buried in the flood, so has a great flood also swept away heathenism — its life, culture, and civilization from the earth, and only left on the mountaintop that ark into which God had shut up them who believed His warnings and His promises.

The contrast becomes most marked as we turn from this record of the Cainites to that of Seth and of his descendants. Even the name which Seth gave to his son — Enos, or "frail" — stands out as a testimony against the assumption of the Cainites. But especially does this vital difference between the two races appear in the words which follow upon the notice of Enos' birth: "Then began men to call upon the name of Jehovah." Of course, it cannot be supposed that before that time prayer and the praise of God had been wholly unknown in the earth. Even the sacrifices of Cain and of Abel prove the contrary. It must therefore mean, that the vital difference which had all along existed between the two races, became now also outwardly manifest by a distinct and open profession, and by the praise of God on the part of the Sethites. We have thus reached the first great period in the history of the kingdom of God — that of an outward and visible separation between the two parties, when those who are "of faith" "come out from among" the world, and from the kingdom of this world. We remember how many, many centuries afterwards, when He had come, whose blood speaketh better things than that of Abel, His followers were similarly driven to separate themselves from Israel after the flesh, and how in Antioch they were first called Christians. As that marked the commencement of the history of the New Testament Church, so this introduction of an open profession of Jehovah on the part of the Sethites, the beginning of the history of the kingdom of God under the Old Testament.

And yet this separation and coming out from the world, this "beginning to call upon the name of Jehovah," is what to this day each one of us must do for himself, if he would take up the cross, follow Christ, and enter into the kingdom of God.

CHAPTER 4: GENEALOGY OF THE BELIEVING RACE, THROUGH SETH.
(GENESIS 5)

ONE purpose of Scripture has now been fulfilled. The tendencies for evil of the Cainite race have been traced to their full unfolding, and "the kingdom of this world" has appeared in its real character. On the other hand, the race of Seth have gathered around an open profession of their faith in the promises, and of their purpose to serve God, and they have on this ground separated themselves from the Cainites. The two ways are clearly marked out, and the character of those who walk in them determined. There is, therefore, no further need to follow the history of the Cainites, and Scripture turns from them to give us an account of "the elders" who "by faith" "obtained a good report."

At first sight it seems as if the narrative here opened with only a "book," or account, "of the generations of Adam," containing here and there a brief notice interspersed; but in truth it is otherwise. At the outset we mark, as a significant contrast, that whereas we read of Adam that "in the likeness of God made He him," it is now added that "he begat a son in his own likeness, after his image." Adam was created pure and sinless in the likeness of God; Seth inherited the fallen nature of his father. Next, we observe how all the genealogies, from Adam downwards, have this in common, that they give first the age of the father at the birth of his eldest son, then the number of years which each of them lived after that event, and finally their total age at the time of death. Altogether, ten "elders" are named from the creation to the time of the flood, and thus grouped:

On examining them more closely, what strikes us in these genealogical records of the Patriarchs is, that the details they furnish are wanting in the history of the Cainites, where simply the birth of seven generations are mentioned, viz.: Adam, Cain, Enoch, Irad, Mehajael, Methusael, Lamech, and his sons. The reason of this difference is, that whereas the Cainites had really no future, the Sethites, who "called upon the name of Jehovah," were destined to carry out the purpose of God in grace unto the end. Next, in two cases the same names occur in the two races — Enoch and Lamech. But in both, Scripture furnishes characteristic distinctions between them. In opposition to the Enoch after whom Cain called his city, we have the Sethite Enoch, "who walked with God, and was not; for God took him;" and in contradistinction to the Cainite Lamech, with his boastful ode to his sword, we have the other Lamech, who called his son Noah, "saying, This same shall comfort us concerning our work and toil of our hands, because of the ground which Jehovah hath cursed." Thus the similarity of their names only brings out the more clearly the contrast of their character. Finally, as the wickedness of the one race comes out most fully in Lamech, who stands seventh in the genealogy of the Cainites, so does the godliness of the other in Enoch, who equally stands seventh in that of the Sethites.

Passing from this comparison of the two genealogies to the table of the Sethites, we are reminded of the saying, that these primeval genealogies are "monuments alike of the faithfulness of God in the fulfillment of His promise, and of the faith and patience of the fathers." Every generation lived its appointed time; they transmitted the promise to their sons; and then, having finished their course, they all "died in faith, not having received the promises, but having seen them afar off, and were persuaded of them, and embraced them, and confessed that they were strangers and pilgrims on the earth." That is absolutely all we know of the majority of them. But the emphatic and seemingly needless repetition in each case of the words, "And he died," with which every genealogy closes, tells us that "death reigned from Adam unto Moses," (Romans 5:14) with all the lessons which it conveyed of its origin in sin, and of its conquest by the second Adam. Only one exception occurs to this general rule — in the case of Enoch; when, instead of the usual brief notice how many years he "lived" after the birth of his son, we read that "he walked with God after he begat Methuselah three hundred years;" and instead of the simple closing statement that "he died," we are not only a second time told that "Enoch walked with God," but also that "he was not; for God took him." Thus both his life and his translation are connected with his "walk with God." This expression is unique in Scripture, and except in reference to Noah (Genesis 6:9) only occurs again in connection with the priest's intercourse with God in the holy place. (Malachi 2:6) Thus it indicates a peculiarly intimate, close, and personal converse with Jehovah. Alike the life, the work, and the removal of Enoch are thus explained in the Epistle to the Hebrews: "By faith Enoch was translated that he should not see death; and was not found, because God had translated him: for before his translation he had this testimony, that he pleased God." (Hebrews 11:5) His translation was like that of Elijah (2 Kings 2:10), and like what that of the saints shall be at the second coming of our blessed Lord. (1 Corinthians 15:51, 52) In this connection it is very remarkable that Enoch "prophesied" of the very thing which was manifested in his own case, "saying, Behold, the Lord cometh with ten thousands of His saints, to execute judgment upon all, and to convince all that are ungodly among them of all their ungodly deeds which they have ungodly committed, and of all their hard speeches which ungodly sinners have spoken against Him."

When Enoch was "translated" only Adam had as yet died: Seth, Enos, Cainan, Mahalaleel, and Jared were still alive. On the other hand, not only Methuselah, the son of Enoch, but also his grandson Lamech, who at the time was one hundred and thirteen years old, must have witnessed his removal. Noah was not yet born. But how deep on the godly men of that period was the impression produced by the prophecy of Enoch, and by what we may call its anticipatory and typical fulfillment in his translation, appears from the circumstance that Lamech gave to his son, who was born sixty-nine years after the translation of Enoch, the name of Noah — "rest" or "comfort" — "saying, This same shall comfort us concerning our work and toil of our hands, because of the ground which Jehovah hath cursed." Evidently Lamech felt the burden of toil upon an earth which God had cursed, and looked forward to a gracious deliverance from the misery and corruption existing in consequence of it, by the fulfillment of the Divine promise concerning the Deliverer. In longing hope of this he called his son Noah. A change, indeed, did come; but it was by the destruction of that sinful generation, and by the commencement of a new period in the covenant-history. We mark that, in the case of Noah, Scripture no longer mentions, as before, only one son; but it gives us the names of the three sons of Noah, to show that henceforth the one line was to divide into three, which were to become the founders of human history.

It is most instructive, also, to notice that Enoch, who seems to have walked nearest to God, only lived on earth altogether three hundred and sixty-five years — less than half the time of those who preceded and who succeeded him. An extraordinary length of life may be a blessing, as affording space for repentance and grace; but in reference to those most dear to God, it may be shortened as a relief from the work and toil which sin has brought upon this world. Indeed, the sequel will show that the extraordinary duration of life, though necessary at the first, yet by no means proved a source of good to a wicked and corrupt generation.

CHAPTER 5: THE UNIVERSAL CORRUPTION OF MAN — PREPARATION FOR THE FLOOD.
(GENESIS 6)

IT is a remarkable circumstance that all nations should have preserved in their traditions notices of the extraordinary length to which human life was at the first protracted. We can understand that knowledge of such a fact would be most readily handed down. But we should remember, that before the "flood" the conditions of vigor, constitution, climate, soil, and nourishment were quite different from those on which the present duration of life depends. A comparison between the two is therefore impossible, for the best of all reasons, that we have not sufficient knowledge of the primitive state of matters. But this we can clearly see, that such long continuance of life was absolutely necessary, if the earth was to be rapidly peopled, knowledge to advance, and, above all, the worship of God and faith in that promise about a Deliverer which He had revealed, to be continued. As it was, each generation could hand down to remote posterity what it had learned during the centuries of its continuance. Thus Adam was alive to tell the story of Paradise and the fall, and to repeat the word of promise, which he had heard from the very mouth of the Lord, when Lamech was born; and though none of the earlier "fathers" could have lived to see the commencement of building the ark, which took place in the year 1536 from the creation, yet Lamech died only five years before "the flood," and his father Methuselah — the longest-lived man — in the very year of the deluge. If we try to realize how much information even in our own days, when intercourse, civilization, and the means of knowledge have so far advanced, can be gained from personal intercourse with the chief actors in great events, we shall understand the importance of man's longevity in the early ages of our race.

But, on the other hand, it was possible to pervert this long duration of life to equally evil purposes. The rare occurrence, during so many centuries, of death with its terrors would tend still more to blunt the conscience; the long association of evil men would foster the progress of corruption and evil; and the apparently indefinite delay of either judgment or deliverance would strengthen the bold unbelief of scoffers. That such was the case appears from the substance of Lamech's prophecy; from the description of the state of the earth in the time of Noah, and the unbelief of his contemporaries; and from the comparison by our Lord (Matthew 24:37- 39; Luke 17:26) between "the days of Noe" and those of "the coming of the Son of man," when, according to St. Peter (2 Peter 3:3, 4), there shall be "scoffers, walking after their own lusts, and saying, Where is the promise of His coming? for since the fathers fell asleep, all things continue as they were from the beginning of creation."

The corruption of mankind reached its highest point when even the difference between the Sethites and the Cainites became obliterated by intermarriages between the two parties, and that from sensual motives. We read that "the sons of God saw the daughters of men that they were fair; and they took them wives of all which they chose." At that time the earth must have been in a great measure peopled, and its state is thus described, "And God saw that the wickedness of man was great in the earth, and that every imagination of the thoughts of his heart was only evil continually." This means more than the total corruption of our nature, as we should now describe it, and refers to the universal prevalence of open, daring sin, and rebellion against God, brought about when the separation between the Sethites and the Cainites ceased. With the exception of Noah there was none in that generation "to call upon the name of Jehovah." "In those days there were 'giants' (in Hebrew: Nephilim) in the earth . . . . the same were the mighty men (or heroes) which were of old, the men of renown." Properly speaking, these Nephilim were "men of violence," or tyrants, as Luther renders it, the root of the word meaning, "to fall upon." In short, it was a period of violence, of might against right, of rapine, lust, and universal unbelief of the promise. With the virtual extinction of the Sethite faith and worship no further hope remained, and that generation required to be wholly swept away in judgment.

And yet, though not only the justice of God, but even His faithfulness to His gracious promise demanded this, the tender loving-kindness of Jehovah appears in such expressions as these: "It repented Jehovah that He had made man on the earth, and it grieved Him" — literally, "it pained into His heart." The one term, of course, explains the other. When we read that God repented, it is only our human way of speaking, for, as Calvin says, "nothing happens by accident, or that has not been foreseen." It brings before our minds "the sorrow of Divine love over the sins of man," in the words of Calvin, "that when the terrible sins of man offend God, it is not otherwise than as if His heart had been wounded by extreme sorrow." The consequence was, that God declared He would destroy "from the face of the earth both man and beast," — the latter, owing to the peculiar connection in which creation was placed with man, as being its lord, which involved it in the ruin and punishment that befell man. But long before that sentence was actually executed, God had declared, "My Spirit shall not always strive with man," — or rather, "dwell with man," "bear rule," or "preside," among them, — "for that he also is flesh," or, as some have rendered it, "since in his erring," or aberration, he has become wholly "carnal, sensual, devilish;" "yet his days shall be an hundred and twenty years;" that is, a further space of a hundred and twenty years would in mercy be granted them, before the final judgments should burst. It was during these hundred and twenty years that "the long-suffering of God waited," "while the ark was a preparing, wherein few, that is, eight souls, were saved by water."

For, to the universal corruption of that generation, there was one exception — Noah. It needs no more than simply to put together the notices of Noah, in the order in which Scripture places them: "But Noah found grace in the eyes of Jehovah;" and again: "Noah was a just man, and perfect" — as the Hebrew word implies, spiritually upright, genuine, inwardly entire and complete, one whose heart had a single aim — "in his generations," or among his contemporaries; and lastly, "Noah walked with God," — this expression being the same as in the case of Enoch. The mention of his finding grace in the eyes of Jehovah precedes that of his "justice," which describes his moral bearing towards God; while this justice was again the outcome of inward spiritual rectitude, or of what under the fuller light of the New Testament we would designate a heart renewed by the Holy Spirit. The whole was summed up and completed in an Enoch-like walk with God. The statement that Noah found grace is like the forth-bursting of the sun in a sky lowering for the storm. Three times the sacred text repeats it, that the earth was corrupt, adding that it was full of violence, just as if the watchful eye of the Lord, who "looked upon the earth," had been searching and trying the children of men, and was lingering in pity over it, before judgment was allowed to descend.

Nor was this all. Even so, "the long-suffering of God waited" for one hundred and twenty years, "while the ark was a preparing;" and during this time, especially, Noah must have acted as "a preacher of righteousness." The building of the ark commenced when Noah was four hundred and eighty years old; that is, before any of his three sons, Shem, Ham, and Japheth, had been born, — in fact, just twenty years before the birth of Shem. Thus the great faith of Noah appeared not only in building an ark in the midst of a scoffing and unbelieving generation, and that against all human probability of its ever being needed, and one hundred and twenty years before it was actually required, but in providing room for "his sons" and his "sons' wives," while as yet he himself was childless! Indeed, the more we try to realize the circumstances, the more grand appears the unshaken confidence of the patriarch. The words in which God announced His purpose were these: "The end of all flesh is come before Me," — that is, as some have explained it, the extreme limit of human depravity; — "for the earth is filled with violence through them," — that is, violence proceeding from them ("from before their faces"), — "and, behold, I will destroy them with the earth." Noah and his family were alone to be preserved, and that by means of an "ark," — an expression which only occurs once more in reference to the ark of bulrushes in which Moses was saved. (Exodus 2:3-5) Noah was to construct his ark of "gopher," most likely cypress wood, and to "pitch it within and without with pitch." The ark was to be three hundred cubits long, fifty broad, and thirty high; that is, reckoning the cubit at one foot and a half, four hundred and fifty feet long, seventy-five broad, and forty-five high. As the wording of the Hebrew text implies, there was all around the top, one cubit below the roof, an opening for light and for air (rendered in our version "window"), in which, it has been suggested, some translucent substance like our glass may have been inserted. Here there seems also to have been a regular "window," which is afterwards specially referred to (ch. 8:6). The door was to be in the side of the ark, which was arranged in three stories of rooms (literally "cells"), or the accommodation of all the animals in the ark, and the storage of food. For "of every living thing" Noah was to bring with him into the ark, — seven pairs, in the case of "clean beasts," and one pair of those that were not clean. Then, when the appointed time for it came, God would "bring a flood of waters upon the earth, to destroy all flesh, wherein is the breath of life, from under heaven." But with Noah God would "establish" His "covenant," that is, carry out through him His purpose in the covenant of grace, which was to issue in the birth of the Redeemer. Accordingly, Noah, his wife — for here there is no trace of polygamy, — his sons, and his sons' wives were to go into the ark, and there to be kept alive during the general destruction of all around.

Thus far the directions of Scripture. Much needless ingenuity has been wasted on a calculation of the exact space in the ark, of its internal arrangements, and of the accommodation it contained for the different species of animals then existing. Such computations are essentially unreliable, as we can neither calculate the exact room in the ark, nor yet the exact number of species which required to be accommodated within its shelter. Scripture, which sets before us the history of God's kingdom, never gratifies such idle and foolish inquiries. But of this we may be quite sure, that the ark which God provided was literally and in every sense quite sufficient for the purposes for which it was intended, and that these purposes were fully secured. It may perhaps help us to realize this marvelous structure if we compare it to the biggest ship known — the Great Eastern, whose dimensions are six hundred and eighty feet in length, eighty-three in breadth, and fifty-eight in depth; or else if we describe it as nearly half the size of St. Paul's Cathedral in London. It should be borne in mind that the ark was designed not for navigation, but chiefly for storage. It had neither masts, rudder, nor sails, and was probably flat at the bottom, resembling a huge floating chest. To show how suitable its proportions were for storage, we may mention that a Dutchman, Peter Jansen, built in 1604 a ship on precisely the same proportions (not, of course, the same figures), which was found to hold one-third more lading than any other vessel of the same tonnage.

All other questions connected with the building of the ark may safely be dismissed as not deserving serious discussion. But the one great fact would stand out during that period: Noah preaching righteousness, warning of the judgment to come, and still exhibiting his faith in his practice by continuing to provide an ark of refuge. To sum up Noah's life of faith, Noah's preaching of faith, and Noah's work of faith in the words of Scripture: "By faith Noah, being warned of God of things not seen as yet, moved with fear, prepared an ark to the saving of his house; by the which he condemned the world, and became heir of the righteousness which is by faith." (Hebrews 11:7).

CHAPTER 6: THE FLOOD
(GENESIS 7-8:15)

THERE is a grandeur and majestic simplicity about the scriptural account of "The Flood" which equally challenges and defies comparison. Twice only throughout the Old Testament is the event again referred to — each time in the grave, brief language befitting its solemnity. In Psalm 29:10 we read: "Jehovah sitteth upon the flood; yea, Jehovah sitteth King for ever," — a sort of Old Testament version of "Jesus Christ, the same yesterday, and today, and for ever." Then, if we may carry out the figure, there is an evangelical application of this Old Testament history in Isaiah 54:9, 10: "For this is as the waters of Noah unto Me: for as I have sworn that the waters of Noah should no more go over the earth; so have I sworn that I would not be wroth with thee, nor rebuke thee. For the mountains shall depart, and the hills be removed; but My kindness shall not depart from thee, neither shall the covenant of My peace be removed, saith Jehovah that hath mercy on thee."

The first point in the narrative of "The Flood" which claims our attention is an emphatic mention, twice repeated, of Noah's absolute obedience, "according unto all that Jehovah commanded him." (Genesis 6:22; 7:5) Next, we mark a "solemn pause of seven days" before the flood actually commenced, when "all the fountains of the great deep were broken up, and the windows of heaven were opened;" in other words, the floodgates alike of earth and heaven thrown wide open. The event happened "in the sixth hundredth year of Noah's life, in the second month, the seventeenth day of the month;" that is, if we calculate the season according to the beginning of the Hebrew civil year, about the middle or end of our month of November. Then Noah and his wife, his three sons — Shem, Ham, and Japheth — and their wives, and all the animals, having come into the ark, "Jehovah shut him in," and for forty days and forty nights "the rain was upon the earth," while, at the same time, the fountains of the great deep were broken up. The flood continued for one hundred and fifty days, when it began to subside. The terrible catastrophe is thus described: "And the flood was forty days upon the earth; and the waters increased, and bare up the ark, and it was lift up above the earth. And the waters prevailed, and were increased greatly upon the earth; and the ark went upon the face of the waters. And the waters prevailed exceedingly upon the earth; and all the high hills, that were under the whole heaven, were covered. Fifteen cubits upward did the waters prevail; and the mountains were covered. And all flesh died that moved upon the earth, both of fowl, and of cattle, and of beast, and of every creeping thing that creepeth upon the earth, and every man: all in whose nostrils was the breath of life, of all that was in the dry land, died. And every living substance was destroyed which was upon the face of the ground, both man, and cattle, and the creeping things, and the fowl of the heaven; and they were destroyed from the earth: and Noah only remained alive, and they that were with him in the ark."

The remarks of a recent writer on this subject are every way so appropriate that we here reproduce them: "The narrative is vivid and forcible, though entirely wanting in that sort of description which in a modern historian or poet would have occupied the largest space. We see nothing of the death-struggle; we hear not the cry of despair; we are not called upon to witness the frantic agony of husband and wife, and parent and child, as they fled in terror before the rising waters. Nor is a word said of the sadness of the one righteous man who, safe himself, looked upon the destruction which he could not avert. But an impression is left upon the mind with peculiar vividness from the very simplicity of the narrative, and it is that of utter desolation. This is heightened by the repetition and contrast of two ideas. On the one hand, we are reminded no less than six times in the narrative (Genesis 6, 7, 8) who the tenants of the ark were, the favored and rescued few; and, on the other hand, the total and absolute blotting out of everything else is not less emphatically dwelt upon" (Genesis 6:13, 17; 7:4, 21-23).

We will not take from the solemnity of the impressive stillness, amid which Scripture shows us the lonely ark floating on the desolate waters that have buried earth and all that belonged to it, by attempting to describe the scenes that must have ensued. Only the impression is left on our minds that the words "Jehovah shut him in," may be intended to show that Noah, even if he would, could not have given help to his perishing contemporaries. At the end of the one hundred and fifty days it is said, in the peculiarly touching language of Scripture, "God remembered Noah, and every living thing, and all the cattle that was with him in the ark." A drying wind was made to pass over the earth, the flood "was restrained," "and the waters returned from the earth continually." On the seventeenth day of the seventh month, that is, exactly five months after Noah had entered it, the ark was found to be resting "upon the mountains of Ararat," — not necessarily upon either the highest peak, which measures seventeen thousand two hundred and fifty feet, nor yet, perhaps, upon the second highest, which rises to about twelve thousand feet, but upon that mountain range. Still the waters decreased; and seventy-three days later, or on the first day of the tenth month, the mountain-tops all around became visible. Forty days more, and Noah "sent forth a raven," which, finding shelter on the mountain-tops, and food from the floating carcasses, did not return into the ark. At the end of seven days more "he sent forth a dove from him to see if the waters were abated from off the face of the ground," that is, from the low ground in the valleys. "But the dove found no rest for the sole of her foot, and she returned unto him into the ark." Yet another week, and he sent her forth a second time, when she returned again in the evening, bearing in her mouth an olive-leaf. It is a remarkable fact, as bearing indirect testimony to this narrative, that the olive has been ascertained to bear leaves under water. A third time Noah put forth the messenger of peace, at the end of another week, and she "returned not again unto him any more." "No picture in natural history," says the writer already quoted, "was ever drawn with more exquisite beauty and fidelity than this. It is admirable alike for its poetry and its truth." On the first day of the first month, in the sixth hundredth and first year, "the waters were dried up from off the earth; and Noah removed the covering of the ark, and looked, and, behold, the face of the ground was dry. And in the second month, on the twenty-seventh day of the month, was the earth dried," — just one year and ten days after Noah had entered the ark.

Thus far the scriptural narrative. It has so often been explained that the object of the Bible is to give us the history of the kingdom of God, not to treat of curious or even scientific questions, that we can dismiss a matter too often discussed of late in an entirely unbecoming spirit, in these words of a recent writer: "It is a question among theologians and men of science whether the flood was absolutely universal, or whether it was universal only in the sense of extending over all the part of the world then inhabited. We do not here enter into this controversy; but we may notice the remarkable fact that the district lying to the east of Ararat, where the ark rested, bears traces of having at one time been under water.

It is a peculiarly depressed region, lying lower than the districts around, and thus affording peculiar facilities for such a submersion."

But there is another matter connected with the flood so marked and striking as to claim our special attention. It is that the remembrance of the flood has been preserved in the traditions of so many nations, so widely separated and so independent of each other, that it is impossible to doubt that they have all been derived from one and the same original source. As might be expected, they contain many legendary details, and they generally fix the locality of the flood in their own lands; but these very particulars mark them as corruptions of the real history recorded in the Bible, and carried by the different nations into the various countries where they settled. Mr. Perowne has grouped these traditions into those of Western Asia, including the Chaldean, the Phoenician, that of the so-called "Sibylline Oracles," the Phrygian, the Syrian, and the Armenian stories; then those of Eastern Asia, including the Persian, Indian, and Chinese; and, thirdly, those of the American nations — the Cherokee, and the various tribes of Mexican Indians, with which — strange though it may seem — he groups those of the Fiji Islands. To these he adds, as a fourth cycle, the similar traditions of the Greek nations. But the most interesting of all these traditions is the Chaldean or Babylonian, which deserves more than merely passing notice.

Though it needs not such indirect confirmations to convince us of the truth of the narratives in the Bible, it is very remarkable how all historical investigations, when really completed and rightly applied, confirm the exactness of what is recorded in the Holy Scriptures. But their chief value to us must always be this, that they tell us of that Ark which alone rides on the waters of the deluge, and preserves for ever safe them who are "shut in" there by the hand of Jehovah.

CHALDEAN NARRATIVE OF THE DELUGE

In general we may say that we have two Chaldean accounts of the flood. The one comes to us through Greek sources, from Berosus, a Chaldean priest in the third century before Christ, who translated into Greek the records of Babylon. This, as the less clear, we need not here notice more particularly. But a great interest attaches to the far earlier cuneiform inscriptions, first discovered and deciphered in 1872 by Mr. G. Smith, of the British Museum, and since further investigated by the same scholar. These inscriptions cover twelve tablets, of which as yet only part has been made available. They may broadly be described as embodying the Babylonian account of the flood, which, as the event took place in that locality, has a special value. The narrative is supposed to date from two thousand to two thousand five hundred years before Christ. The history of the flood is related by a hero, preserved through it, to a monarch whom Mr. Smith calls Izdubar, but whom he supposes to have been the Nimrod of Scripture. There are, as one might have expected, frequent differences between the Babylonian and the Biblical account of the flood. On the other hand, there are striking points of agreement between them, which all the more confirm the scriptural account, as showing that the event had become a distinct part of the history of the district in which it had taken place. There are frequent references to Erech, the city mentioned in Genesis 10:10; allusions to a race of giants, who are described in fabulous terms; a mention of Lamech, the father of Noah, though under a different name, and of the patriarch himself as a sage, reverent and devout, who, when the Deity resolved to destroy by a flood the world for its sin, built the ark. Sometimes the language comes so close to that of the Bible that one almost seems to read disjointed or distorted quotations from Scripture. We mention, as instances, the scorn which the building of the ark is said to have called forth on the part of contemporaries; the pitching of the ark without and within with pitch; the shutting of the door behind the saved ones, the opening of the window, when the waters had abated; the going and returning of the dove since "a resting-place it did not find," the sending of the raven, which, feeding on corpses in the water, "did not return;" and, finally, the building of an altar by Noah. We sum up the results of this discovery in the words of Mr. Smith:

"Not to pursue this parallel further, it will be perceived that when the Chaldean account is compared with the Biblical narrative, in their main features the two stories fairly agree; as to the wickedness of the antediluvian world, the Divine anger and command to build the ark, its stocking with birds and beasts, the coming of the deluge, the rain and storm, the ark resting on a mountain, trial being made by birds sent out to see if the waters had subsided, and the building of an altar after the flood. All these main facts occur in the same order in both narratives, but when we come to examine the details of these stages in the two accounts, there appear numerous points of difference; as to the number of people who were saved, the duration of the deluge, the place where the ark rested, the order of sending out the birds, and other similar matters."

We conclude with another quotation from the same work, which will show how much of the primitive knowledge of Divine things, though mixed with terrible corruptions, was preserved among men at this early period:

"It appears that at that remote age the Babylonians had a tradition of a flood which was a Divine punishment for the wickedness of the world; and of a holy man, who built an ark, and escaped the destruction; who was afterwards translated and dwelt with the gods. They believed in hell, a place of torment under the earth, and heaven, a place of glory in the sky; and their description of the two has, in several points, a striking likeness to those in the Bible. They believed in a spirit or soul distinct from the body, which was not destroyed on the death of the mortal frame; and they represent this ghost as rising from the earth at the bidding of one of the gods, and winging its way to heaven."

CHAPTER 7: AFTER THE FLOOD — NOAH'S SACRIFICE — NOAH'S SIN — NOAH'S DESCENDANTS.
(GENESIS 8:15-9:28.)

RIGHTLY considered, the destruction of "all flesh" by the deluge was necessary for its real preservation. Death was needful for its new life. The old world was buried in the flood, that a new order of things might rise from its grave. For, manifestly, after the mixing up of the Sethite with the Cainite race, an entirely new commencement required to be made if the purpose of God in grace was to be carried to its goal. Hence, also, God once more pronounced upon Noah the blessing of fruitfulness which he had spoken to Adam, and gave him dominion over creation, yet, as we shall see, with such modifications as the judgment that had just passed, and the new state of things which had commenced, implied.

It deserves our notice that, even after the earth was quite dry, Noah awaited the express command of God before leaving the ark. His first act after that was to build "an altar unto Jehovah," and there to offer "burnt-offerings" "of every clean beast, and of every fowl." Nor was it merely in gratitude and homage to God, but also in spiritual worship that he thus commenced his life anew, and consecrated earth unto Jehovah. In bringing an animal sacrifice Noah followed the example of Abel; in calling upon the name of Jehovah he once again and solemnly adopted the profession of the Sethites. But there was this difference between his and any preceding sacrifice, that now for the first time we read of building an altar. While Paradise was still on earth, men probably turned towards it as the place whence Jehovah held intercourse with man. But when its site was swept away in the flood, God, as it were, took up His throne in heaven, and from thence revealed Himself unto men and held intercourse with them. (See also Genesis 11:5, 7) And the truth, that our hearts and prayers must rise upwards to Him who is in heaven, was symbolized by the altar on which the sacrifice was laid. Scripture significantly adds, that "Jehovah smelled a sweet savor," or rather "a savor of rest," "of satisfaction;" in other words, He accepted the sacrifice. "And Jehovah said in His heart," that is, He resolved, "I will not again curse the ground for man's sake, for (or because) the imagination of man's heart is evil from his youth." Both Luther and Calvin have remarked on the circumstance that men's universal sinfulness, which formerly had been the cause of the judgment of the flood, should now be put forward as the reason for not again cursing the ground. But in fact this only marks another difference between the state of man before and after the flood. If we may so say, God now admitted the fact of universal sinfulness as existing, and made it an element of His future government. He looked upon man as a miserable and wretched sinner, with whom in His compassion and long-suffering He would bear, delaying His second and final judgment till after He should have accomplished all that He had promised to do for the salvation of men. Putting aside Israel, as God's special people, the period between Noah and Christ may be described, in the words of St. Paul, as "the times of this ignorance" which "God winked at," (Acts 17:30) or as those when "through the forbearance of God" sins were passed over. (Romans 3:25, see marginal rendering)

Having thus explained the fundamental terms on which the Lord would deal with the nations of the earth during the period between the flood and the coming of the Savior, that is, during the Jewish dispensation, we proceed to notice, in the words which God addressed to Noah, some other points of difference between the former and the new state of things. First of all, the gracious announcement that, while the earth remained, seed-time and harvest, cold and heat, summer and winter, day and night were not to cease, implies not only His purpose to spare our earth, but also that man might henceforth reckon upon a regular succession of seasons, and that he was to make this earth for the present his home, to till it, and to possess it. Hence it was quite another matter when Noah became an "husbandman," from what it had been when Cain chose to be "a tiller of the ground." Next, as already stated, God renewed the blessing of fruitfulness in much the same terms in which He had spoken it originally to Adam, and once more conferred dominion over the lower creation. But in this new grant there was this essential difference — that man's dominion would now be one of force, and not, as formerly, of willing subjection. If God had at the first brought "every beast" and "every fowl" before Adam, as it were, to do homage to him, and to receive from him their names, it was now said to Noah and to his descendants, "The fear of you and the dread of you shall be upon every beast of the earth; . . . into your hand are they delivered."

Perhaps we ought also to notice in this connection that, whatever may have been the common practice before, now for the first time the use of animal food was expressly permitted, with the exception of the blood, and that probably for the reason afterwards mentioned in the case of sacrifices, that the blood was the seat of life. (Leviticus 17:11, 14) Another and most important change is marked by the solemn prohibition of murder, with this addition, that "whoso sheddeth man's blood, by man shall his blood be shed." Such crimes were no longer to be avenged directly by God Himself, but He delegated His authority to man. (Romans 8:1, 2) As Luther rightly says, "In these words the civil magistracy is instituted, and the Divine right of bearing the sword." For when it is added, as a reason why murder should be punished with death, that God made man in His own image, it seems to convey that vengeance might not be taken by any one at his own will, but that this belonged to those who on earth represented the authority of God, or were His delegates; whence also they are called in Psalm 82:6, "gods," or rather "Elohim." And, as Luther rightly argues, "If God concedes to man the power over life and death, assuredly this carries with it authority over that which is less than life, such as goods, family, wife, children, servants, and land." Thus the words spoken by the Lord to Noah contain the warrant and authority of those who are appointed rulers and judges over us. In later times the Jews have been wont to speak of what they called the seven Noachic commandments, which, according to them, were binding upon all Gentile proselytes. These were a prohibition (1) of idolatry, (2) of blasphemy, (3) of murder,

(4) of incest, (5) of robbery and theft, (6) of eating blood and strangled animals, and (7) an injunction of obedience to magistrates. (Comp. also Acts 15:20)

In confirmation of what God had spoken, He "established" His "covenant" with Noah and his sons, and in "token" thereof "set," or "appointed," His "bow in the cloud." It may have been so, that the rainbow was then seen for the first time, although this does not necessarily follow from the words of Scripture. They only tell us that henceforth the rainbow was to be a "token" or visible symbol to man of God's promise no more to destroy all flesh by a flood, and also that He Himself would "look upon it" as such, so that He might "remember the everlasting covenant between God and every living creature." The symbol of the rainbow was therefore to be both a sign and a seal of God's promise. And we can readily understand how impressive, whenever a storm burst upon the earth, this symbol would have appeared to those who had witnessed the flood. In the poetical language of a

German writer, "The rainbow, caused by the influence of the sun upon the dark clouds, would show to man, that what was from heaven would penetrate that which rose from earth; and as it spanned the gulf between heaven and earth, it would seem to proclaim peace between God and man; while even the circumstance that it bounded the horizon would symbolize, how the covenant of mercy extended to earth's utmost bounds."

From this scene of intercourse between Noah and God we have to pass to an event in his history, alas, of a very different character. When Noah — with his three sons, Shem, Ham, and Japheth — left the ark to become an husbandman, he planted a vineyard, as Jewish legend has it, from a slip of the vine that had strayed out of Paradise. But it may boldly be asserted that, except the forbidden fruit itself, none has brought more sin, ruin, and desolation upon our earth. Whether Noah was unacquainted with the intoxicating property of the vine, or neglected proper moderation, the sad spectacle is presented of the aged patriarch, so lately rescued from the flood, not only falling a victim to drunkenness, but exposing himself in that state to the impious and vile conduct of his son Ham. As Luther says, "Ham would not have mocked his father, when overcome with wine, if he had not long before cast from his soul that reverence which, according to God's command, children should cherish towards their parents." It is a relief to find the other sons of Noah, so far from sharing their brother's sin, reverently defending their father from the unnatural vileness of Ham. As we might have expected, the conduct of the brothers received meet reward, — the curse descended on Ham, while a blessing, suited to each, was given to Shem and Japheth. But, in the words of the patriarch, the curse lights specially upon Canaan, the son of Ham, not to the exclusion of his other sons, but probably because as Noah had suffered from his son, so Ham was to experience his punishment in his son; and Canaan may have been specially singled out, either because he fully entered into the spirit of his father, or more probably because of the later connection between Israel and the Canaanites, in whom they would see alike the spirit and the curse of Ham fully realized. In connection with this we mark, that, twice before (Genesis 9:18, 22), when Ham is mentioned, it is added that he was "the father of Canaan."

Shem, Ham, and Japheth, who were to repeople the earth, seem to have impressed their own characteristics on their descendants. Their very names are symbolical and prophetic. Shem means splendor or glory, Ham burning heat, and Japheth enlargement. Bearing this in mind, we listen to the words of the patriarch:

"Cursed be Canaan,
A servant of servants shall he be to his brethren;"

and we know that this has been the fate of the children of Ham, or the races of Africa; while, strangely, the name of Canaan has been interpreted as meaning "he who is subject." Again,

"Blessed be Jehovah, the God of Shem,
And Canaan shall be their slave:"

a prophecy most signally fulfilled when Israel took possession of the land of Canaan; and, lastly,

"God (Elohim) shall enlarge Japheth (enlargement);
And he shall dwell in the tents of Shem,
And Canaan shall be their slave."

This latter prophecy consists of three parts. It promises from God, as the God of power, that enlargement to Japheth which is the characteristic of his descendants, the European nations. And it adds that Japheth (not, as some have read it, God) shall dwell in the tents of

Shem, that is, as St. Augustine has said, "in the churches which the apostles, the sons of the prophets, reared;" thus referring to the blessing which was to flow to all nations through the Hebrew race. Lastly, Canaan was to be the servant of Japheth, as seen in the subjection to Greece and Rome, of Tyre and Carthage, the ancient centers of wealth and merchandise, and of Egypt, the empire of might and of the oldest civilization.

But the words spoken to Shem, the ancestor of the Hebrew race, deserve special notice. The blessing here begins quite differently from that of Japheth. It opens with a thanksgiving to God, for, as Luther says, "Noah sees it to be such that he cannot express it in words, therefore he turns to thanksgiving." Then, the blessing of Shem is not outward, but spiritual; for Jehovah is to be the God of Shem. To speak in an anticipatory figure, Shem's portion, in the widest sense, is that to be hereafter assigned to Levi, amongst the Jews; and Japheth is to dwell in his tents, — in other words, Israel is to be the tribe of Levi to all nations. More than that, whereas Elohim is to give enlargement to Japheth, Jehovah the covenant-God is to be the God of Shem. Thus the primitive promise to Adam is now both further defined and enlarged. The promised Deliverer is to come through Shem, as the ancestor of the chosen race, in the midst of whom Jehovah is to dwell; and through Shem, Japheth is to share in the coming spiritual blessing. Here, then, is clearly defined the separation of the Jews and the Gentiles, and the mission of each: the one from Jehovah, the other from Elohim; the one in the Church, the other in the world.

CHAPTER 8: GENEALOGY OF NATIONS — BABEL — CONFUSION OF TONGUES
(GENESIS 10-11:10)

IT was the Divine will, that after the flood the whole earth should be repeopled by the descendants of Noah. For this purpose they must, of course, have separated and spread, so as to form the different nations and tribes among whom the world should be apportioned. Any attempted unity on their part would not only be contrary to the Divine purpose, but also, considering the universal sinfulness of man, prove dangerous to themselves, and even be untrue, since their inward separation had already appeared in the different characters and tendencies of Ham and his brothers. But before recording the judgment by which the Divine purpose was enforced, Scripture gives us the genealogy of the different nations, and this with a threefold object — to show how the earth was all peopled from the descendants of Noah; to define the relation of Israel towards each nationality; and, best of all, to register, as it were, their birth in the book of God, thereby indicating, that, however "in time past He suffered all nations to walk in their own ways," (Acts 14:6) they also were included in the purposes of mercy, and intended finally to "dwell in the tents of Shem."

In accordance with the general plan on which Holy Scripture is written, we read after the prophecy of Noah, which fixed the future of his sons, no more of that patriarch than that he "lived after the flood three hundred and fifty years," and that he died at the age of nine hundred and fifty years. Regarding the division of earth among his three sons, it may be said generally, that Asia was given to Shem, Africa to Ham, and Europe to Japheth. In the same general manner a modern scholar has traced all existing languages to three original sources, themselves, no doubt, derived from a primeval spring, which may have been lost in the "confusion of tongues," though its existence is attested by constant and striking points of connection between the three great families of languages. The more we think of the allotment of Europe, Asia, and Africa among the three sons of Noah, the more clearly do we see the fulfillment of prophecy regarding them. As we run our eye down the catalogue of nations in Genesis 10, we have little difficulty in recognizing them; and beginning with the youngest, Japheth, we find of those known to the general reader, the Cymry of Wales and Brittany (Gomer), the Scythians (Magog), the Medes (Madai), the Greeks (Ionians, Javan), and the Thracians (Tiras). Among their descendants, the Germans, Celts, and Armenians have been traced to the three sons of Gomer. It is not necessary to follow this table farther, though all will remember Tarshish, or Spain, and the Kittim, or "inhabitants of the isles."

Passing next to Shem (ver. 21), we notice that he is called "the father of all the children of Eber," because in Eber the main line divided into that of Peleg, from whom the race of Abraham sprang, and the descendants of Joktan (ver. 25). The descendants of Shem are exclusively Asiatic nations, among whom we only notice Asshur or Assyria, and Uz, as the land which gave birth to Job.

We have reserved Ham for the last place, because of the connection of his story with the dispersion of all nations. His sons were Cush or Ethiopia, Mizraim or Egypt, Phut or Libya, and Canaan, which, of course, we know. It will be noticed, that the seats of all these nations were in Africa, except that of Canaan, whose intrusion into the land of Palestine was put an end to by Israel. But yet another of Ham's descendants had settled in Asia. Nimrod, the founder of the Babylonian empire, the conqueror of Assyria, and the builder of Nineveh (ver. 11), was the son of Cush. Altogether this "mighty one in the earth," who founded the first world-empire, reminds us of Cain and of his descendant Lamech. Leaving out of view the possible meaning of his name, which some have explained as being "we will rebel," boastful violence and rebellion certainly constitute the characteristics of his history. Most strangely have the Assyrian tablets of the royal successors of Nimrod been made to furnish an explanation of his description as "a mighty hunter" — for this is the title given in them to the great conquering warrior-monarchs, as "hunting the people." Thus we gather the full meaning of the expression, "he began to be a mighty one in the earth." From Babylon, which was "the beginning of his kingdom," Nimrod "went out into Assyria" (ver. 11, marginal rendering), "and builded Nineveh" — the remarkable circumstance here being that each time four cities are mentioned in connection with Nimrod: first, the four cities of his Babylonian empire, of which Babel was the capital, and then the four cities of his conquered Assyrian empire, of which Nineveh was the capital. Now all this tallies in the most striking manner with what we read in ancient history, and with those Assyrian monuments which within our own lifetime have by the labors of Layard and Loftus been exhumed from their burial of many centuries, to give witness for the Bible. For, first, we now know that the great Asiatic empire of Babylon was of Cushite origin. Nay, even the name Nimrod occurs in the list of Egyptian kings. Secondly, we are made aware that Babel was the original seat of the empire; and, strangest of all, that the earliest Babylonian kings bore a title which is supposed to mean "four races," in reference to "the quadruple groups of capitals" of Babylonia and Assyria. Lastly, we know that, as stated in the Bible, "the Babylonian empire extended its sway northwards" to Assyria, where Nineveh was founded, which in turn succeeded to the empire once held by Babel. In all these respects, therefore, the latest historical investigations have most strikingly confirmed the narrative of Scripture.

Of the magnificence of Babel, the capital of the empire of Nimrod, "the mighty hunter," it is difficult to convey an adequate conception, without entering into details foreign to our purpose. But some idea of it may be formed from its extent, which according to the lowest computation, covered no less than one hundred square miles, or about five times the size of London; while the highest computation would make it cover two hundred square miles, or ten times the extent of London! Such was the world-city, the first "beginning" of which at least Nimrod had founded. No wonder that the worldly pride of that age should have wished to make such a place the world-capital of a world-empire, whose tower "may reach unto heaven!" The events connected with the discomfiture of their plan took place in the days of Peleg, the grandson of Shem. (Genesis 10:25) As Peleg was born one hundred years after the flood, and lived two hundred and thirty-nine years, there must have been already a considerable population upon the earth.

If evidence were required that the flood had indeed destroyed sinners but not sin, it would be found in the bearing and language of men in the days of Nimrod and Peleg. After leaving the ark, they had "journeyed eastward" (ch. 11:2) till they reached the extensive well-watered plain of Shinar, where they settled. Being still all "of one language and of one speech," they resolved to build themselves there "a city, and a tower whose top may reach unto heaven," for the twofold purpose of making themselves "a name," and lest they "be scattered abroad upon the face of the whole earth." Such words read singularly like those which a Nimrod would employ, and they breathe the spirit of "Babylon" in all ages. Assuredly their meaning is: "Let us rebel!" — for not only would the Divine purpose of peopling the earth have thus been frustrated, but such a world-empire would in the nature of it have been a defiance to God and to the kingdom of God, even as its motive was pride and ambition. A German critic has seen in the words "let us make us a name" — in Hebrew, sheen — a kind of counterfeit of the Shem in whom the promises of God centered, or, if one might so express it, the setting up of an anti-Christ of worldly power. Something of this kind seems certainly indicated in what God says of the attempt (ver. 6): "And this they begin to do: and now nothing will be restrained from them which they have imagined to do." These words seem to imply that the building of Babel was only intended as the commencement of a further course of rebellion. The gathering of all material forces into one common center would have led to universal despotism and to universal idolatry, — in short, to the full development of what as anti-Christ is reserved for the judgment of the last days. We read, that "Jehovah came down to see the city and the tower," that is, using our human modes of expression, to take judicial cognizance of man's undertaking. In allusion to the boastful language in which the builders of Babel and of its tower had in their self-confidence stated their purpose: "Go to, let us make brick," etc. (ver. 3), Jehovah expressed His purpose of defeating their folly, using the same words: "Go to, let us go down, and there confound their language." And by this simple means, without any outward visible interference, did the Lord arrest the grandest attempt of man's rebellion, and by confounding their language, "scattered them abroad from thence upon the face of all the earth." "Therefore is the name of it called Babel, or confusion." What a commentary does this history afford to the majestic declarations of the second Psalm!

Of the tower of Babel no certainly ascertained remains have as yet been discovered. It has commonly been identified with the ruins called Birs Nimrud, about six miles to the south-west of the site of ancient Babylon. Birs Nimrud is "a pyramidical mound, crowned apparently by the ruins of a tower, rising to the height of one hundred and fifty-five and a half feet above the level of the plain, and in circumference somewhat more than two thousand feet." Its distance from Babylon, however, seems opposed to the idea that these are the ruins of the tower spoken of in Scripture. But even so, Birs Nimrud can only be a few centuries younger than the tower of Babel; and its construction enables us to judge what the appearance of the original tower must have been. Birs Nimrud faced north-east, and formed a sort of "oblique pyramid, built in seven receding stages. The platform on which these stages rested was of crude brick; the stages themselves of burnt brick, painted in different colors in honor of gods or planets — each stage as it was placed on the other receding, so as to be considerably nearer the back of the building, or the south-west." The first stage, painted black in honor of Saturn, was a square of two hundred and seventy-two feet, and twenty-six feet high; the second stage, orange colored, in honor of Jupiter, was a square of two hundred and thirty feet, and twenty-six high; the third stage, bright red, in honor of Mars, was a square of one hundred and eighty-eight feet, and also twenty-six high; the fourth stage, golden, for the Sun, was one hundred and forty-six feet square, and fifteen high; the fifth stage, pale yellow, for Venus, was one hundred and four feet square, and fifteen high; the sixth stage, dark blue, for Mercury, was sixty-two feet square, and fifteen high; and the seventh stage, silver, for the Moon, was twenty feet square, and fifteen high. The whole was surmounted by a chapel, which must have nearly covered the whole top. The whole height, as already stated, was one hundred and fifty-three feet; or about one-third that of the great pyramid of Egypt, which measures four hundred and eighty feet. It is also interesting to notice, how exactly what we know of early Babylonian architecture tallies with what we read in Scripture: "Let us make brick, and burn them thoroughly. And they had brick for stone, and slime (or rather, bitumen) had they for mortar." The small burnt bricks, laid in bitumen, are still there; not only in the tower, but in the still existing ruins of the ancient palace of Babel, which was coeval with the building of the city itself.

Holy Scripture does not inform us whether "the tower" was allowed to stand after the dispersion of its builders; nor yet does it furnish any details as to the manner in which "Jehovah did there confound the language of all the earth." All this would have been beyond its purpose. But there, at the very outset, when the first attempt was made to found, in man's strength, a vast kingdom of this world, which God brought to naught by confounding the language of its builders, and by scattering them over the face of the earth, we see a typical judgment, of which the counterpart in blessing was granted on the day of Pentecost; when, by the outpouring of the Holy Spirit, another universal kingdom was to be founded, the first token of which was that gift of tongues, which pointed forward to a reunion of the nations, when the promise would be fulfilled that they should all be gathered into the tents of Shem!

CHAPTER 9: THE NATIONS AND THEIR RELIGION — JOB

A MODERN German writer has well said: "The birth of heathenism may be dated from the moment when the presumptuous statement was uttered, 'Go to, let us build a city and a tower whose top may reach unto heaven, and let us make us a name.'" Even Josephus, the ancient Jewish historian, regards Nimrod as the father of heathenism, the characteristic of which is to find strength and happiness in sin, and not in God. Its essential principle is to reject all that is not seen, and to cling to that which is temporal. Thus we also may be heathens in heart, even though we are not such in mind, and do not worship stocks or stone. Indeed, it is very remarkable, that neither nation nor tribe has ever been discovered which did not acknowledge and worship some superior Being; and yet from the most savage barbarians to the most refined philosopher, they have all been destitute of the knowledge of the one living and true God. The only exception in the world has been that of Israel, to whom God specially revealed Himself; and even Israel required constant teaching, guidance, and discipline from on high to keep them from falling back into idolatry. Idolatry is the religion of sight in opposition to that of faith. Instead of the unseen Creator, man regarded that which was visible — the sun, the moon, the stars — as the cause and the ruler of all; or he assigned to everything its deity, and thus had gods many and lords many; or else he converted his heroes, real or imaginary, into gods. The worship of the heavens, the worship of nature, or the worship of man — such is heathenism and idolatry. And yet all the while man felt the insufficiency of his worship, for behind these gods he placed a dark, immovable, unsearchable Fate, which ruled supreme, and controlled alike gods and men. It was indeed a terrible exchange to make — to leave our heavenly Father and His love for such delusions and disappointments. The worst of it was, that man gradually became conformed to his religion. He first imputed his own vices to his gods, and next imitated the vices of his gods. Assuredly, the heathen nations were the younger son in the parable (Luke 15:12), who had left his father's house with the portion of goods that belonged to him — heathen science, art, literature, and power — to find himself at the last driven to eat the husks on which the swine do feed, and yet not able to satisfy the cravings of his hunger! Blessed be God for that revelation of Himself in Christ Jesus, which has brought the prodigal back to the Father's home and heart!

But even so, God did not leave Himself without a witness. The inward searching of man after a God, the accusing voice of his conscience, the attempt to offer sacrifices, and the remnants of ancient traditions of the truth among men — all seemed to point upward. And then, as all were not Israel who were of Israel, so God also had at all times His own, even among the Gentile nations. Job, Melchizedek, Rahab, Ruth, Naaman, may be mentioned as instances of this. It will be readily understood that the number of those "born out of season," as it were, from among the Gentiles, must have been largest the higher we ascend the stream of time, and the nearer we approach the period when early traditions were still preserved in their purity in the earth. The fullest example of this is set before us in the book of Job, which also gives a most interesting picture of those early times.

Two things may be regarded as quite settled about the book of Job. Its scene and actors are laid in patriarchal times, and outside the family or immediate ancestry of Abraham. It is a story of Gentile life in the time of the earliest patriarchs. And yet anything more noble, grand, devout, or spiritual than what the book of Job contains is not found, "no, not in Israel." This is not the place to give either the history of Job, or to point out the depth of thought, the vividness of imagery, and the beauty and grandeur of language with which it is written. It must suffice to take the most rapid survey of the religious and social life which it sets before us. Without here referring to the sayings of Elihu, Job had evidently perfect knowledge of the true God; and he was a humble, earnest worshipper of Jehovah. Without any acquaintance with "Moses and the prophets," he knew that of which Moses and the prophets spoke. Reverent, believing acknowledgment of God, submission, and spiritual repentance formed part of his experience, which had the approval of God Himself. Then Job offered sacrifices; he speaks about the great tempter; he looks for the resurrection of the body; and he expects the coming of Messiah.

We have traced the barest outlines of the religion of Job. The friends who come to him, if they share not his piety, at least do not treat his views as something quite strange and previously unheard. This, then, is a blessed picture of at least a certain class in that age. How far culture and civilization must have advanced in those times we gather from various allusions in the book of Job. Job himself is a man of great wealth and high rank. In the language of a recent writer:

"The chieftain lives in considerable splendor and dignity. . . . Job visits the city frequently, and is there received with high respect as a prince, judge, and distinguished warrior. (Job 29:7,9) There are allusions to courts of justice, written indictments, and regular forms of procedure. (Job 13:26; 31:28) Men had begun to observe and reason upon the phenomena of nature, and astronomical observations were connected with curious speculations upon primeval traditions. We read of mining operations, great buildings, ruined sepulchers. . . . Great revolutions had occurred within the time of the writer; nations, once independent, had been overthrown, and whole races reduced to a state of misery and degradation."

Nor ought we to overlook the glimpses of social life given us in this history. While, indeed, there was violence, robbery, and murder in the land, there is happily also another side to the picture. "When I went out to the gate through the city, when I prepared my seat in the street, the young men saw me, and hid themselves; and the aged arose and stood up." Along with such becoming tribute of respect paid to worth, we find that the relationship between the pious rich and the poor is thus described: "When the ear heard me, then it blessed me; and when the eye saw me, it gave witness to me: because I delivered the poor that cried, and the fatherless, and him that had none to help him. The blessing of him that was ready to perish came upon me, and I caused the widow's heart to sing for joy." Assuredly there is nothing in all this which we could wish to see altered even in New Testament times! But the more terrible in contrast must have been the idolatry and the corruption of the vast majority of mankind; an idolatry which they had probably inherited from before the flood, and which soon attained gigantic proportions, and a corruption which went on ever increasing during the "times of this ignorance."

CHAPTER 10: THE CHRONOLOGY OF THE EARLY HISTORY OF THE BIBLE — COMMENCEMENT OF THE HISTORY OF GOD'S DEALINGS WITH ABRAHAM AND HIS SEED

BEFORE further proceeding with our history some brief explanation may be desirable of the chronological table given in this volume, and in general of the early chronology of the Bible. It will be noticed, first, that the years are counted from "B.C.," that is, from "before Christ;" the numbers, of course, becoming smaller the farther we come down from the creation of the world, and the nearer we approach the birth of our Savior. Thus, if the year of creation be computed at 4004 before Christ, the deluge, which happened 1656 years later, would fall in the year 2348 B.C. Further, it will be observed that we have given two chronological tables of the same events, which differ by many hundreds of years — the one "according to Hales," the other "according to Ussher," which latter is that of "the dates in the margin of English Bibles," and, we may add, corresponds with the Hebrew text of the Old Testament. The explanation of the difference between them is that our calculations of Biblical dates may be derived from one of three sources. We have, in fact, the five books of Moses in three different forms before us. First, we have the original Hebrew text of the Old Testament; next, there exists a translation of it in Greek, completed long before the time of our Lord, which was commonly used by the Jews at the time of Christ, for which reason also it is generally quoted in the New Testament. This version is known as that of the "LXX," or "Seventy," from the supposed number of translators. Finally, we have the Samaritan Pentateuch, or that in use among the Samaritans. Now, as the genealogies differ in these three in regard to the ages of the patriarchs, the question arises which of them should be adopted? Each in turn has had its defenders, but the most learned critics are now almost unanimous in concluding, as indeed we might have expected, that the Hebrew text contains the true chronology. Of the other two, the Samaritan is so untrustworthy that for practical purposes we may leave it entirely out of view. The Septuagint chronology differs from that of the Hebrew text in prolonging the ages of the patriarchs, partially before the deluge, but chiefly between the deluge and the calling of Abraham, — the result being that the flood is thrown five hundred and eighty-six years later than in the Hebrew text; and the birth of Abraham yet other eight hundred and seventy-eight years — the total difference amounting to no less than one thousand two hundred and forty-five years! It is not difficult to guess the reason why the Greek translators had thus altered the original numbers. It was evidently their wish to throw the birth of Abraham as late as possible after the flood. Of these two chronologies, that of the Hebrew text may, for convenience sake, be designated as the short, and that of the "LXX" as the long chronology; and, in a general way, it may be said that (with certain modifications which it would take too long to explain) Hales has adopted the long, or Greek, and Ussher the short, or Hebrew chronology.

This may suffice on a matter which has engaged only too much discussion. It is far more important to think of the kingdom of God, the history of which is given us in the Holy Scriptures; for now we are at the beginning of its real appearance. If God had at the first dealt with mankind generally, then with one part of the race, and lastly with one division of nations, He now chose and raised up for Himself a peculiar people, through whom His purposes of mercy towards all men were to be carried out. This people was to be trained from its cradle until it had fulfilled its mission, which was when He came who was the Desire of all nations. Three points here claim our special attention: -

1. The election and selection of what became the people of God. Step by step we see in the history of the patriarchs this electing and separating process on the part of God. Both are marked by this twofold characteristic: that all is accomplished, not in the ordinary and natural manner, but, as it were, supernaturally; and that all is of grace. Thus Abram was called alone out of his father's house — he was elected and selected. The birth of Isaac, the heir of the promises, was, in a sense, supernatural; while, on the other hand, Ishmael, the elder son of Abram, was rejected. The same election and selection appears in the history of Esau and Jacob, and indeed throughout the whole patriarchal history. For at the outset the chosen race was to learn what is the grand lesson of all Scriptures that everything comes to us from God, and is of grace, — that it is not man's doing, but God's working; not in the ordinary manner, but by His special interposition. Nor should we fail to mark another peculiarity in God's dealings. To use a New Testament illustration, it was the grain of mustard-seed which was destined to grow into the tree in whose branches all the birds of the air were to find lodgment. In Abram the stem was cut down to a single root. This root first sprang up into the patriarchal family, then expanded into the tribes of Israel, and finally blossomed and bore fruit in the chosen people. But even this was only a means to an end. Israel had possessed, so to speak, the three crowns separately. It had the priesthood in Aaron, the royal dignity in David and his line, and the prophetic office. But in the "last days" the triple crown of priest, king, and prophet has been united upon Him Whose it really is, even JESUS, a "Prophet like unto Moses," the eternal priest "after the order of Melchizedek," and the real and ever reigning "Son of David." And in Him all the promises of God, which had been given with increasing clearness from Adam onwards to Shem, then to Abraham, to Jacob, in the law, in the types of the Old Testament, and, finally, in its prophecies have become "Yea and amen," till at the last all nations shall dwell in the tents of Shem.

2. We mark a difference in the mode of Divine revelation in the patriarchal as compared with the previous period. Formerly, God had spoken to man, either on earth or from heaven, while now He actually appeared to them, and that specially as the Angel of Jehovah, or the Angel of the Covenant. The first time Jehovah "appeared" unto Abram was when he entered the land of Canaan, in obedience to that Divine call which singled him out to become the ancestor of the people of God. (Genesis 12:7) After that a fresh appearance of Jehovah, and of the Angel of the Covenant, in whom He manifested Himself, marked each stage of the Covenant history. And this appearance was not only granted to Abraham and to Hagar, to Jacob, to Moses, to Balaam, to Gideon, to Manoah and to his wife, and to David, but even towards the close of Jewish history this same Angel of Jehovah is still found pleading for rebellious, apostate Israel in these words: "O Jehovah of Hosts, how long wilt Thou not have mercy on Jerusalem?" (Zechariah 1:12) The more carefully we follow His steps, the more fully shall we be convinced that He was not an ordinary Angel, but that Jehovah was pleased to reveal Himself in this manner under the Old Testament. We shall have frequent occasion to return to this very solemn subject. Meantime it may be interesting to know that of old the Jews also regarded Him as the Shechinah, or visible presence of God, — the same as appeared in the pillar of the cloud and of fire, and afterwards in the temple, in the most holy place; while the ancient Church almost unanimously adored in Him the Son of God, the Second Person of the blessed Trinity. We cannot conceive any subject more

profitable, or likely to be fraught with greater blessing, than reverently to follow the footsteps of the Angel of Jehovah through the Old Testament.

3. The one grand characteristic of the patriarchs was their faith. The lives of the patriarchs prefigure the whole history of Israel and their Divine selection. In the words of a recent German writer, amidst all varying events, the one constant trait in patriarchal history was "faith which lays hold on the word of promise, and on the strength of this word gives up that which is seen and present for that which is unseen and future." Thus "Abraham was the man of joyous, working faith; Isaac of patient, bearing faith; Jacob of contending and prevailing faith." But all lived and "died in faith, not having received the promises, but having seen them afar off, and were persuaded of them, and embraced them, and confessed that they were strangers and pilgrims in the earth." And it is still so. Without ignoring the great privilege of those who are descended from Abraham, yet, in the true sense, only "they which are of faith, the same are the children of Abraham;" "and if ye be Christ's, then are ye Abraham's seed, and heirs according to the promise." To adapt the words of a German poet:

"What marks each one within the fold
Is faith that does not see;
And yet, as if it did behold,
Trusts, unseen Lord, to Thee!"

CHAPTER 11: THE CALLING OF ABRAM — HIS ARRIVAL IN CANAAN, AND TEMPORARY REMOVAL TO EGYPT
(GENESIS 11:27-13:4)

WITH Abram an entirely new period may be said to begin. He was to be the ancestor of a new race in whom the Divine promises were to be preserved, and through whom they would finally be realized. It seemed, therefore, necessary that, when Abram was called, he should forsake his old home, his family, his country, and his people. Not to speak of the dangers which otherwise would have beset his vocation, a new beginning required that he should be cut off from all that was "behind." Had he remained in Ur of the Chaldees, he would at best only have been a new link in the old chain. Besides, the special dealings of God, and Abram's faith and patience, as manifested in his obedience to the Divine command, were intended to qualify him for being the head of the new order of things, "the father of all who believe." Lastly, it was intended that the history of Abram, as that of his seed after him, should prepare the way for the great truths of the Gospel, and exhibit as in a figure the history of all who through faith and patience inherit the promises.

Hitherto, God had only interposed, as in the flood, and at the confounding of tongues, to arrest the attempts of man against His purposes of mercy. But when God called Abram, He personally and actively interfered, and this time in mercy, not in judgment. The whole history of Abram may be arranged into four stages, each commencing with a personal revelation of Jehovah. The first, when the patriarch was called to his work and mission; (Genesis 12-14) the second, when he received the promise of an heir, and the covenant was made with him; (Genesis 15, 16) the third, when that covenant was established in the change of his name from Abram to Abraham, and in circumcision as the sign and seal of the covenant; (Genesis 17-21) the fourth, when his faith was tried, proved, and perfected in the offering up of Isaac. (Genesis 22-25:11) These are, so to speak, the high points in Abram's history, which the patriarch successively climbed, and to which all the other events of his life may be regarded as the ascent.

Descending the genealogy of Shem, Abram stands tenth among "the fathers" after the flood. He was a son — apparently the third and youngest — of Terah, the others being Haran and Nahor. The family, or perhaps more correctly the tribe or clan of Terah, resided in Chaldea, which is the southern part of Babylonia. "Ur of the Chaldees," as recently again discovered, was one of the oldest, if not the most ancient, among the cities of Chaldea. It lies about six miles away from the river Euphrates, and, curious to relate, is at present somewhere near one hundred and twenty-five miles from the Persian Gulf, though it is supposed, that at one time it was actually washed by its waters, the difference being accounted for by the rapid deposit of what becomes soil, or of alluvium, as it is called. Thus Abram must in his youth have stood by the seashore, and seen the sand innumerable, to which his posterity in after ages was likened. Another figure, under which his posterity is described, must have been equally familiar to his mind. It is well known that the brilliancy of a starlit sky in the East, and especially where Abram dwelt, far exceeds anything which we witness in our latitudes. Possibly this may have first led in those regions to the worship of the heavenly bodies. And Abram must have been the more attracted to their contemplation, as the city in which he dwelt was "wholly given" to that idolatry; for the real site of Ur has been ascertained from the circumstance that the bricks still found there bear the very name of Hur on them. Now this word points to Hurki, the ancient moon-god, and Ur of the Chaldees was the great "Moon-city," the very center of the Chaldean moon-worship! The most remarkable ruins of that city are those of the old moon-temple of Ur, which from the name on the bricks are computed to date from the year 2000 before Christ. Thus bricks that are thirty-eight centuries old have now been brought forward to bear witness to the old city of Abraham, and to the tremendous change that must have passed over him when, in faith upon the Divine word, he obeyed its command.

Jewish tradition has one or two varying accounts to show how Abram was converted from the surrounding idolatry, and what persecutions he had to suffer in consequence. Scripture does not indulge our fancy with such matters; but, true to its uniform purpose, only relates what belongs to the history of the kingdom of God. We learn, however, from Joshua 24:2, 14, 15, that the family of Terah had "in old time, on the other side of the flood," or of Euphrates, "served other gods;" and we can readily understand what influence their surroundings must, in the circumstances, have exercised upon them. It was out of this city of Ur that God called Abram. Previously to this, Haran, Abram's eldest brother, had died. We read, that "Terah took Abram, his son, and Lot the son of Haran his son's son, and Sarai his daughter-in-law, his son Abram's wife, and they went forth with them from Ur of the Chaldees, to go into the land of Canaan; and they came unto Haran, and dwelt there." The words which we have italicized leave no room for doubt, that the first call of God had come to Abram long before the death of Terah, and when the clan were still at Ur. (Comp. Acts 7:2) From the circumstance that Haran is afterwards called "the city of Nahor," (Genesis 24:10; comp. 27:43) we gather that Nahor, Abraham's brother, and his family had also settled there, though perhaps at a later period, and without relinquishing their idolatry. It is a remarkable confirmation of the scriptural account, that, though this district belongs to Mesopotamia, and not to Chaldea, its inhabitants are known to have for a long time retained the peculiar Chaldean language and worship. Haran has preserved its original name, and at the time of the Romans was one of the great battle-fields on which that power sustained a defeat from the Parthians.

The journey from Ur, in the far south, had been long, wearisome, and dangerous; and the fruitful plains around Haran must have held out special inducements for a pastoral tribe to settle. But when the Divine command came, Abram was "not disobedient unto the heavenly vision." Perhaps the arrival and settlement of Nahor and his family, bringing with them their idolatrous associations, may have formed an additional incentive for departing. And so far, God had in His providence made it easier for Abram to leave, since his father Terah had died in Haran, at the age of two hundred and five years. The second call of Jehovah to Abram, as given in Genesis 12:1-3, consisted of a fourfold command, and a fourfold promise. The command was quite definite in its terms: "Get thee out of thy country, and from thy kindred, and from thy father's house, unto a land that I will shew thee;" leaving it, however, as yet undecided which was to be the place of his final settlement. This uncertainty must have been an additional and, in the circumstances, a very serious difficulty in the way of Abram's obedience. But the word of promise reassured him. It should be distinctly marked, that on this, as on every other occasion in Abram's life, his faith determined his obedience. Accordingly, we read, "By faith Abraham, when he was called to go out into a place which he should after receive for an inheritance, obeyed; and he went out, not knowing whither he went." (Hebrews 11:8) The promise upon which he trusted assured to him these four things: "I will make of thee a great nation;" "I will bless thee," with this addition (in ver. 3), "and thou shalt be a blessing, and I will bless them that bless thee, and curse him that curseth thee;" "I will make thy name great ;" and, lastly, "In thee shall all families of the earth be blessed."

When we examine these promises more closely, we at once perceive how they must have formed yet another trial of Abram's faith; since he was not only going, a stranger into a strange land, but was at the time wholly childless. The promise that he was to "be a blessing," implied that blessing would, so to speak, be identified with him; so that happiness or evil would flow from the relationship in which men would place themselves towards Abram. On the other hand, from the peculiar terms "them that bless thee," in the plural, and "him that curseth thee," in the singular, we gather that the Divine purpose of mercy embraced many, "of all nations, kindreds, and tongues." Lastly, the great promise, "In thee shall all families of the earth be blessed," went far beyond the personal assurance, "I will make thy name great." It resumed and made more definite the previous promises of final deliverance, by fixing upon Abram as the spring whence the blessing was to flow. Viewed in this light, all mankind appear as only so many families, but of one and the same father; and which were to be again united in a common blessing in and through Abram. Repeated again and again in the history of Abram, this promise contained already at the outset the whole fullness of the Divine purpose of mercy in the salvation of men. Thus was the prediction to be fulfilled: "God shall enlarge Japheth, and he shall dwell in the tents of Shem," as is shown by St. Peter in Acts 3:25, and by St. Paul in Galatians 3:8, 14.

Abram was seventy-five years old "when he departed out of Haran," accompanied by Lot and his family. Putting aside the various traditions which describe his prolonged stay at Damascus, and his supposed rule there, we learn from Scripture that Abram entered the land of promise, as many years afterwards his grandson Jacob returned to it, leaving on his right the majestic Lebanon, and on his left the pastures of Gilead and the mountain-forests of Bashan. Straight on he passed over hills and through valleys, till he reached the delicious plain of Moreh, or rather the spreading terebinth-tree of Moreh, in the valley of Sichem. Travelers have spoken in the most enthusiastic terms of this vale. "All at once," writes Professor Robinson, "the ground sinks down to a valley running towards the west, with a soil of rich, black vegetable mold. Here a scene of luxuriant and almost unparalleled verdure burst upon our view. The whole valley was filled with gardens of vegetables, and orchards of all kinds of fruits, watered by several fountains, which burst forth in various parts, and flow westward in refreshing streams. It came upon us suddenly, like a scene of fairy enchantment. We saw nothing to compare with it in all Palestine." Another traveler says: "Here there are no wild thickets; yet there is always verdure, always shade, — not of the oak, the terebinth, or the garoub-tree, but of the olive-grove, so soft in color, so picturesque in form, that for its sake we can willingly dispense with all other wood." Such was the first resting-place of Abram in the land of promise, in the plain, or rather in the wood of Moreh, which probably derived its name from the Canaanitish proprietor of the district. For, as shown by the remark of the sacred writer, "and the Canaanite was then in the land," the country was not tenantless, but occupied by a hostile race; and if Abram was to enter on its possession, it must once more be by faith in the promises.

Here it was that Jehovah actually "appeared" unto Abram, under some visible form or other; and now for the first time in sight of the Canaanite was the promise conveyed, "unto thy seed will I give this land." It is added that Abram "there builded an altar unto Jehovah who appeared unto him." Thus, the soil on which Jehovah had been seen, and which He had just promised to Abram, was consecrated unto the Lord; and Abram's faith, publicly professed in the strange land, grasped Jehovah's promise, solemnly given.

From Shechem, Abram removed, probably for the sake of pasturage, southwards to a mountain on the east of Bethel, pitching his tent between Bethel and Ai. This district is, in the words of Robinson, "still one of the finest tracts for pasturage in the whole land." In the glowing language of Dean Stanley: "We here stand on the highest of a succession of eminences, . . . its topmost summit resting, as it were, on the rocky slopes below, and distinguished from them by the olive-grove, which clusters over its broad surface above. From this height, thus offering a natural base for the patriarchal altar, and a fitting shade for the patriarchal tent, Abram and Lot must be conceived as taking the wide survey of the country . . such as can be enjoyed from no other point in the neighborhood." What met their astonished gaze from this point will be described in the following chapter. Meantime, we note that here, also, Abram "builded an altar unto Jehovah;" and, though He does not seem to have visibly appeared unto him, yet the patriarch called upon the name of Jehovah. After a residence, probably of some time, Abram continued his journey, "going on still toward the south," — a pilgrim and a stranger "in the land of promise;" his possession of it only marked by the altars which he left on his track.

A fresh trial now awaited the faith of Abram. Strong as it always proved in what concerned the kingdom of God, it failed again and again in matters personal to himself. A famine was desolating the land, and, as is still the case with the Bedouin tribes under similar circumstances, Abram and his family "went down into Egypt," which has at all times been the granary of other nations. It does not become us to speculate whether this removal was lawful, without previous special directions from God; but we know that it exposed him to the greatest danger. As we must not underrate the difficulties of the patriarchs, so neither must we overrate their faith and their strength. Abram "was a man of like passions with us," and of like weaknesses. When God spoke to him he believed, and when he believed then he obeyed. But God had said nothing as yet to him, directly, about Sarai; and, in the absence of any special direction, he seems to have taken the matter into his own hands, after the manner of those times and countries. From Genesis 20:13 we learn that when he first set out from his father's house, an agreement had been made between the two, that Sarai was to pass as his sister, because, as he said, "the fear of God" was not among the nations with whom they would be brought in contact; and they might slay Abram for his wife's sake. The deceit — for such it really was — seemed scarcely such in their eyes, since Sarai was so closely related to her husband that she might almost be called his sister. In short, as we all too oftentimes do, it was deception, commencing with self-deception; and though what he said might be true in the letter, it was false in the spirit of it. But we must not imagine that Abram was so heartless as to endanger his wife for the sake of his own safety. On the contrary, it seemed the readiest means of guarding her honor also; since, if she were looked upon as the sister of a mighty chief, her hand would be sought, and certain formalities have to be gone through, which would give Abram time to escape with his wife. This is not said in apology, but in explanation of the matter.

Ancient Egyptian monuments here again remarkably confirm the scriptural narrative. They prove that the immigration of distinguished foreigners, with their families and dependents, was by no means uncommon. One of them, dating from the time of Abram, represents the arrival of such a "clan," and their presentation and kindly reception by Pharaoh. Their name, appearance, and dress show them to be a pastoral tribe of Semitic origin. Another ancient tablet records how such foreigner attained the highest dignities in the land. So far, then, Abram would meet with a ready welcome. But his device was in vain, and Sarai "was taken into the house of Pharaoh." As the future brother-in-law of the king, Abram now rapidly acquired possessions and wealth. These presents Abram could, of course, not refuse, though they increased his guilt, as well as his remorse and sense of shame. But he had committed himself too deeply to retrace his steps; and the want of faith, which had at the first given rise to his fears, may have gone on increasing. Abram had given up for a time the promised land, and he was now in danger of losing also the yet greater promise. But Jehovah did not, like Abram, deny her who was to be the mother of the promised seed. He visited "Pharaoh and his house with great plagues," which by-and-by led to their ascertaining the true state of the case — possibly from Sarai herself. Upon this the king summoned Abram, and addressed him in words of reproach, which Abram must have the more keenly felt that they came from an idolater. Their justice the patriarch acknowledged by his silence. Yet the interposition of God on behalf of Abram induced Pharaoh to send him away with all his possessions intact; and, as the wording of the Hebrew text implies, honorably accompanied to the boundary of the land.

It is a true remark, made by a German writer, that while the occurrence of a famine in Canaan was intended to teach Abram that even in the promised land nourishment depended on the blessing of the Lord, — in a manner teaching him beforehand this petition, "Give us this day our daily bread," — his experience in Egypt would also show him that in conflict with the world fleshly wisdom availed nothing, and that help came only from Him who "suffered no man to do them wrong: yea, He reproved kings for their sakes; saying, Touch not Mine anointed, and do My prophets no harm," (Psalm 105:14, 15) thus, as it were, conveying to Abram's mind these two other petitions: "Lead us not into temptation, but deliver us from evil." And so Abram once more returned to Bethel, "unto the place where his tent had been at the beginning; unto the place of the altar which he had made at the first: and there Abram called on the name of Jehovah." In one respect this incident is typical of what afterwards befell the children of Israel. Like him, they went into Egypt on account of a famine; and, like him, they left it under the influence of "fear of them which fell" upon the Egyptians — yet laden with the riches of Egypt.

CHAPTER 12: THE SEPARATION OF ABRAM AND LOT — ABRAM AT HEBRON — SODOM PLUNDERED — LOT RESCUED — THE FLEETING WITH MELCHIZEDEK
(GENESIS 13, 14)

HITHERTO Abram had been accompanied by Lot in all his wanderings. But a separation must take place between them also. For Abram and his seed were to be kept quite distinct from all other races, so that the eye of faith might in future ages be fixed upon the father of the faithful, as on him from whom the promised Messiah was to spring. Like so many of God's most marked interpositions, this also was brought about by what seemed a series of natural circumstances, and probably Abram himself was ignorant of the Divine purpose in what at the time must have been no small trial to him. The increase of their wealth, and especially of their herds and flocks in Egypt, led to disputes between the herdsmen of Abram and of Lot, which were the more painful that, as the Bible notes, "the Canaanite and the Perizzite dwelled then in the land," and must have been witnesses to this "strife" between "brethren." To avoid all occasion of it, Abram now proposed a voluntary separation, allowing Lot, though he was the younger and the inferior, the choice of district — and this not merely from generosity, but in faith, leaving it to the Lord to determine the bounds of his habitation.

As the two stood on that highest ridge between Bethel and Ai, the prospect before them was indeed unrivaled. Looking back northwards, the eye would rest on the mountains which divide Samaria from Judaea; westwards and southwards, it would range over the later possession of Benjamin and Judah, till in the far distance it descried the slope on which Hebron lay. But the fairest vision was eastward: in the extreme distance, the dark mountains of Moab; at their foot, the Jordan, winding through a valley of untold fertility; and in the immediate foreground, the range of hills above Jericho. As the patriarchs gazed upon it, the whole cleft of the Jordan valley was rich with the most luxuriant tropical vegetation, the sweetest spot of all being around the Lake of Sodom, at that time probably a sweetwater lake, the "circuit" of the plain resembling in appearance, but far exceeding in fertility and beauty, the district around the Sea of Galilee. In this "round" of Jordan, and by the waters of Sodom, rich cities had sprung up, which, alas! were also the seat of the most terrible corruption. As Lot saw this "round" or district, fair like Paradise, green with perennial verdure, like the part of Egypt watered by the Nile, his heart went out after it, unmindful of, or not caring to inquire into, the character of its inhabitants. The scene might well have won the heart of any one whose affections were set on things beneath. Lot's heart was so set; and he now vindicated by his choice the propriety of his being separated from Abram. Assuredly their aims went asunder, as the ways which they took. Yet, even thus, God watched over Lot, and left him not to reap the bitter fruit of his own choice.

Nor was Abram left in that hour without consolation. As most he needed it when alone, and with apparently nothing but the comparatively barren hills of Judaea before him, Jehovah once more renewed to him, and enlarged the promise of the land, far as his eye could range, bestowing it upon Abram and his "seed for ever." For the terms of this promise were not made void by the seventy years which Judah spent in the captivity of Babylon, nor yet are they annulled by the eighteen centuries of Israel's present unbelief and dispersion. The promise of the land is to Abram's "seed for ever." The land and the people God has joined together; and though now the one lies desolate, like a dead body, and the other wanders unresting, as it were a disembodied spirit, God will again bring to each other in the days when His promise shall be finally established. So Abram must have understood the word of Jehovah. And when, so to speak, he now took possession by faith of the promised land, he was directed to walk through it. In the course of these wanderings he reached Hebron, one of the most ancient cities of the world, where in the wood of one, Mamre, he pitched his tent under a spreading terebinth, and built an altar unto Jehovah. This place seems through the rest of his life to have continued one of the centers of his movements.

Meanwhile Lot had taken up his abode in a district which, like the rest of Canaan at the time of Joshua's conquest, was subdivided among a number of small kings, each probably ruling over a city and the immediately surrounding neighborhood. For twelve years had this whole district been tributary to Chedorlaomer. In the thirteenth year they rebelled; and, in the fourteenth, the hordes of Chedorlaomer and of his three confederates swept over the intervening district, carrying desolation with them, till they encountered the five allied monarchs of the "round of Jordan," in the vale of Siddim, the district around what afterwards became the Dead Sea. Once more victory attended the invaders — two of the Canaanitish kings were killed, the rest fled in wild confusion; Sodom and Gomorrah were plundered, and their inhabitants — Lot among them — carried away captives by the retreating host. This was the first time — at least in Scripture history — that the world-kingdom, as founded by Nimrod, was brought into contact with the people of God, and that on the soil of Palestine. For Chedorlaomer and his confederates occupied the very land and place where afterwards the Babylonian and Assyrian empires were. It became necessary, therefore, that Abram should interfere. God had given him the land, and here was its hereditary enemy; and God now called and fitted him, though but a stranger and a pilgrim on its soil, to become its deliverer; while alike the mode and the circumstances of this deliverance were to point forward to those realities of which it was the type.

One who had escaped from the rout brought Abram tidings of the disaster. He immediately armed his own trained servants, three hundred and eighteen in number; and being joined by Aner, Eshcol, and Mamre, the chieftains to whom the district around Hebron belonged, followed in pursuit of Chedorlaomer and his allies. Probably, as is common in such warfare, victory had made them careless. They may have feasted, or their bands, laden with captives and spoil, may have been straggling, and without order. Certainly they were ignorant of any coming danger, when Abram, having divided his force, fell upon them, in the dead of night, from several sides at the same time, inflicted a great slaughter, and pursued them to close by Damascus. All the spoil and all the captives, among them Lot also, were rescued and brought back. As the returning host of Abram entered the valley of Shaveh, close under the walls of what afterwards became Jerusalem, they were met by two persons bearing very different characters, and coming from opposite directions. From the banks of Jordan the new king of Sodom, whose predecessor had fallen in battle against Chedorlaomer, came up to thank Abram, and to offer him the spoils he had won; while from the heights of Salem — the ancient Jerusalem — the priest-king Melchizedek descended to bless Abram, and to refresh him with "bread and wine." This memorable meeting seems to have given the valley its name, "the king's dale;" and here, in later times, Absalom erected for himself a monumental pillar.(2 Samuel 18:18) But now a far different scene ensued, and one so significant in its typical meaning as to have left its impress alike on the prophecies of the Old and in the fulfillment of the New Testament. Melchizedek appears like a meteor in the sky — suddenly, unexpectedly, mysteriously, — and then as suddenly disappears. Amid the abundance of genealogical details of that period we know absolutely nothing of his descent; in the roll of kings and their achievements, his name and reign, his birth and death remain unmentioned. Considering the position which he occupies towards Abram, that silence must have been intentional, and its intention typical; that is, designed to point forward to corresponding realities in Christ. Still more clearly than its silence does the information which Scripture furnishes about Melchizedek show the deep significance of his personality. His name is "King of Righteousness," his government that of the "Prince of Peace;" he is a priest," neither in the sense in which Abram was, nor yet "after the order of Aaron," his priesthood being distinct and unique; he blesses Abram, and his blessing sounds like a ratification of the bestowal of the land upon the patriarch; while Abram gives "him tithes of all." There is in this latter tribute an acknowledgment of Melchizedek both as king and priest — as priest in giving him "tithes," and as king in giving him these tithes of all the spoil, as if he had royal claim upon it; while Abram himself refuses to touch any of it, and his allies are only allowed to "take their portion."

This is not the place to discuss the typical meaning of this story; yet the event and the person are too important to pass them unnoticed. Twice again we meet Melchizedek in Scripture: once in the prophecy of Psalm 110:4: "Thou art a priest for ever after the order of Melchizedek;" the other time in the application of it all to our blessed Savior, in Hebrews 7:3. That Melchizedek was not Christ Himself is evident from the statement that he was "made like unto the Son of God" (or "likened unto" Him, Hebrews 7:3); while it equally appears from these words, and from the whole tenor of Scripture, that he was a type of Christ. In fact, we stand here at the threshold of two dispensations. The covenant with Noah had, so to speak, run its course, or rather was merging into that with Abram. As at the commencement of the New Testament, John gave testimony to Jesus, and yet Jesus was baptized by John; so here Melchizedek gave testimony to Abram, and yet received tithes from Abram. If we add, that in our view Melchizedek was probably the last representative of the race of Shem in the land of Canaan, which was now in the hands of the Canaanites, who were children of Ham, as well as that he was the last representative of the faith of Shem, in the midst of idolatry — being a "priest of the most high God," — the relation between them will become more clear. It was the old transferred to the new, and enlarged in it; it was the rule and the promise of Shem, solemnly handed over to Abram by the last representative of Shem in the land, who thus gave up his authority in the name of "the most high God, possessor of heaven and earth," "which hath delivered" Abram's enemies into his hands. It has been well observed, that "Abram's greatness consisted in his hopes, that of Melchizedek in his present possession." Melchizedek was both a priest and a king, — Abram only a prophet; Melchizedek was recognized as the rightful possessor of the country, which as yet was only promised to Abram. True, the future will be infinitely greater than the present, — but then it was as yet future. Melchizedek owned its reality by blessing Abram, and transferring his title, as it were, to him; while Abram recognized the present, by giving tithes to Melchizedek, and bending to receive his blessing. Thus Melchizedek, the last representative of the Shemitic order, is the type of Christ, as the last representative of the Abrahamic order. What lay in germ in Melchizedek was to be gradually unfolded — the priesthood in Aaron, the royalty in David — till both were most gloriously united in Christ. Melchizedek was, however, only a shadow and a type; Christ is the reality and the antitype.

It is for this reason that Scripture has shut to us the sources of historical investigation about his descent and duration of life, that by its silence it might point to the heavenly descent of Jesus. For the same reason also Abram, who so soon afterwards vindicated his dignity and position in the language of superiority with which he declined the king of Sodom's offer of the spoils, bent lowly before Melchizedek, that in his blessing he might receive the spiritual inheritance which he now bequeathed him. Nor will the attentive reader fail to remark the language in which Melchizedek spake of God as "the most high," and the "possessor of heaven and earth" — terms which Abram adopted, but to which he added the new name of "Jehovah," as that of "the most high God, the possessor of heaven and earth" — a name which indicated that covenant of grace of which Abram was to be the representative and the medium. It is quite in accordance with this whole transaction that Abram put aside the offer of the king of Sodom: "Give me the persons, and take the goods to thyself." Assuredly, it had not been as an ally of the king of Sodom, but to vindicate his position, and that of all connected with him, that the Lord had summoned Abram to the war, and given him the victory. And so these figures part, never to meet again: the king of Sodom to hasten to the judgment, already lingering around him; the king of Salem to wait for the better possession promised, which indeed was already commencing.

CHAPTER 13: THE TWOFOLD PROMISE OF "A SEED" TO ABRAHAM — ISHMAEL — JEHOVAH VISITS ABRAHAM — THE DESTRUCTION OF SODOM — ABRAHAM'S SOJOURN AT GERAR — HIS COVENANT WITH ABIMELECH

(GENESIS 15-20, 21:22-34)

HIGH times of success and prosperity are only too often followed by seasons of depression. Abram had indeed conquered the kings of Assyria, but his very victory might expose him to their vengeance, or draw down the jealousy of those around him. He was but a stranger in a strange land, with no other possession than a promise, — and not even an heir to whom to transmit it. In these circumstances it was that "Jehovah came unto Abram in a vision," saying, "I am thy shield, and thy exceeding great reward" — that is, Myself am thy defense from all foes, and the source and spring whence thy faith shall be fully satisfied with joy. It was but natural, and, as one may say, childlike, that Abram should in reply have opened up before God all his wants and his sorrow, as he pointed, not in the language of doubt, but rather of question, to his own childless state, which seemed to leave Eliezer, his servant, his only heir. But Jehovah assured him that it was to be otherwise than it seemed; nay, that his seed should be numberless as the stars in the sky. "And he believed in Jehovah: and He counted it to him for righteousness." The remark stands solitary in the narrative, as if to call attention to a great fact; and its terms indicate, on the part of Abram, not merely faith in the word, but trustfulness in the person of Jehovah as his Covenant-God. Most touching and sublime is the childlikeness of that simple believing without seeing, and its absolute confidence. Ever since, through thousands of years, it has stood out as the great example of faith to the church of God. And from this faith in the living God sprang all the obedience of Abram. Like the rod of Aaron, his life budded and blossomed and bore fruit "within the secret place of the Most High."

To confirm this faith Jehovah now gave to Abram a sign and a seal, which yet were such once more only to his faith. He entered into a covenant with him. For this purpose the Lord directed Abram to bring an heifer, a she- goat, and a ram, each of three years old, also a turtle-dove and a young pigeon. These sacrifices — for they were all representatives of the kinds afterwards used as sacrifices — were to be divided, and the pieces laid one against the other, as the custom was in making a covenant, the covenanting parties always passing between them, as it were to show that now there was no longer to be division, but that what had been divided was to be considered as one between them. But here, at the first, no covenanting party appeared at all to pass between the divided sacrifices. All day long, as it seemed to Abram, he sat watching lonely, only driving from the carcasses the birds of prey which came down upon them. So it seemed to the eye of sense! Presently even gathered around, and a deep sleep and a horror of great darkness fell upon Abram. The age of each sacrificed animal, the long, lonely day, the birds of prey swooping around, and the horror that had come with the night, all betokened what Jehovah now foretold: how for three generations the seed of Abram should be afflicted in Egypt; but in the fourth, when the measure of the iniquity of the present inhabitants of Canaan would be full, they were to return, and enter on the promised possession of the land. As for Abram himself, he was to go "to his fathers in peace." Then it was that the covenant was made; not, as usually, by both parties passing between the divided sacrifice, but by Jehovah alone doing so, since the covenant was that of grace, in which one party alone — God — undertook all the obligations, while the other received all the benefits.

For the first time did Abram see passing between those pieces the smoking furnace and the burning lamp — the Divine brightness enwrapt in a cloud, just as Moses saw it in the bush, and the children of Israel on their wilderness march, and as it afterwards dwelt in the sanctuary above the mercy-seat, and between the cherubim. This was the first vision vouchsafed to Abram, the first stage of the covenant into which God entered with him, and the first appearance of the glory of the Lord. At the same time, what may be called the personal promise to Abram was also enlarged, and the boundaries of the land clearly defined as stretching from the Nile in the west, to the Euphrates in the east, an extent, it may be here observed, which the Holy Land has never yet attained, not even in the most flourishing days of the Hebrew monarchy.

Precious as the promise of God to Abram had been, it had still left one point undetermined — who the mother of the promised seed was to be. Instead of waiting for the direction of God in this respect also, Sarai seems in her impatience to have anticipated the Lord; and, as we always do when taking things into our own hands, in a manner contrary to the mind of God, as well as to her own sorrow and disappointment. Ten years had elapsed since Abram had entered Canaan, when Sarai, despairing of giving birth to the heir of the promise, followed the common custom of those days and countries, and sought a son by an alliance between her husband and Hagar, her own Egyptian maid. The consequences of her folly were dispeace in her home, then reproaches, and the flight of Hagar. What else might have followed it is difficult to tell, had not the Lord in mercy interposed. None less than the Angel of the Covenant Himself appeared to the fugitive slave, as she rested by a fountain in the wilderness that led down into her native Egypt. He bade her return to her mistress, promised to the son whom she was to bear that liberty and independence of bearing which has ever since characterized his descendants, and gave him the name of Ishmael — the Lord heareth, — as it were thus binding him alike by his descent, and by the Providence that had watched over him, to the God of Abram. Hagar also learned there for the first time to know Him as the God who seeth, the living God, whence the fountain by which she had sat henceforth bore the name of "The Well of the Living, who beholdeth me." So deep are the impressions which a view of the Lord maketh, and so closely should we always connect with them the events of our lives.

Hagar had returned to Abram's house, and given birth to Ishmael. And now ensued a period which we must regard as of most sore trial to Abram's faith. Full thirteen years elapsed without apparently any revelation on the part of God. During this time Ishmael had grown up, and Abram may almost insensibly have accustomed himself to look upon him as the heir, even though in all probability he knew that he had not been destined for it. Abram was now ninety-nine years old, and Sarai stricken in years. For every human hope and prospect must be swept away, and the heir be, in the fullest sense, the child of the promise, that so faith might receive directly from God that for which it had waited. It was in these circumstances that Jehovah at last once more appeared in visible form to Abram, — this time to establish and fulfill the covenant which He had formerly made. Hence also now the admonition: "Walk before Me, and be thou perfect," which follows but can never precede the covenant. In token of this established covenant, God enjoined upon Abram and his descendants the rite of circumcision as a sign and a seal; at the same time changing the worse than that, they fell into the most grievous and abominable sin, the issue of which was the birth of the ancestors of Israel's hereditary enemies — Moab and Ammon. (Deuteronomy 23:3, 4) But even this is not all. Whether from a dislike to a neighborhood so lately visited by such judgments, or in quest of better pasturage for his flocks, Abraham left the district of Mamre, and traveled in a south-easterly direction, where he settled in the territory of Abimelech, king of Gerar, in the land of the Philistines. Abimelech seems to have been a royal title, like that of Pharaoh. (Comp. Genesis 26:1, 8) But in this instance, as we gather from Scripture, the possessor of this title was far different from the king of Egypt. In fact, he appears to have been not merely true and upright in character, but to have feared the Lord. Accordingly, when Abraham was once more guilty of the same dissimulation as formerly in Egypt, passing off his wife for his sister from fear for his own life, God directly communicated to Abimelech in a dream the real state of matters. Upon this, Abimelech hastened to amend the wrong he had, unwittingly, so nearly committed. In comparison to the Gentile king, Abraham occupies indeed an unfavorable position. He is unable to vindicate his conduct on other grounds than what amounts to a want of faith. But, as God had informed Abimelech, Abraham, despite his weakness, was "a prophet;" and in that capacity, as already quoted, "He suffered no man to do them wrong; yea, He reproved kings for their sakes, saying, Touch not Mine anointed, and do My prophets no harm." The alliance with Abraham which Abimelech had sought by marriage, was shortly afterwards concluded by a formal covenant between the two, accompanied by a sacrifice of the sacred number of seven ewe lambs. (Genesis 21:22) To show that this was intended not as a private but as a public alliance, Abimelech came accompanied by his chief captain, or phichol, (Comp. Genesis 26:26) at the same time expressly stating it as the motive in the public step which he took, that God was with Abraham in all that he did. In similar manner, the sympathy on these points between Abimelech and his people had formerly been shown, when the king had communicated to "all his servants" what God had told him about Abraham, "and the men were sore afraid." In these circumstances we do not wonder that Abraham should have made the land of the Philistines the place of lengthened residence, pitching his tent close by Beersheba, "the well of the oath," with Abimelech, or rather "the well of the seven" ewe lambs, — and there he once more "called on the name of Jehovah, the everlasting God."

CHAPTER 14: BIRTH OF ISAAC — ISHMAEL SENT AWAY — TRAIL OF ABRAHAM'S FAITH IN THE COMMAND TO SACRIFICE ISAAC — DEATH OF SARAH — DEATH OF ABRAHAM
(GENESIS 21-25:18)

AT last the time had come when the great promise to Abraham should receive its fulfillment. The patriarch was in his hundredth and Sarah in her ninetieth year when Isaac was born to them. Manifestly, it had been the Divine purpose to protract as long as possible the period before that event; partly to exercise and mature Abraham's faith, and partly that it should appear the more clearly that the gift of the heir to the promises was, in a manner, supernatural. As we have seen, the very name of their child was intended to perpetuate this fact; and now Sarah also, in the joyousness of her heart, said, "God hath made me to laugh, so that all that hear will laugh with me," — literally, "Laughter has God prepared for me; every one that heareth it will (joyously) laugh with me." Thus, as Abraham's laughter had been that of faith in its surprise, so the laughter of Sarah was now in contrast to that of her former weakness of trust, one of faith in its gratitude. But there might be yet a third kind of laughter, — neither of faith, nor even of unbelief, but of disbelief: the laughter of mockery, and it also would receive its due recompense. According to God's direction (Genesis 17:12), Abraham had circumcised Isaac on the eighth day. When the period for weaning him arrived, the patriarch made, after the manner of those times, a great feast. We can scarcely say what the age of the child was, — whether one year, or, as Josephus implies, three years old. In either case, Ishmael must have been a lad, springing into manhood — at least fifteen, and possibly seventeen years of age. "And Sarah saw the son of Hagar, the Egyptian, which she had born unto Abraham, mocking," — literally, "that he was a mocker." As a German writer observes: "Isaac, the object of holy laughter, serves as the target of his unholy wit and profane banter. He does not laugh; he makes merry. 'What! this small, helpless Isaac, the father of nations!' Unbelief, envy, and pride in his own carnal pre-eminence, — such were the reasons of his conduct. Because he does not understand, 'Is anything too hard for Jehovah?' therefore he finds it laughable to connect such great issues with so small a beginning." It was evidently in this light that the apostle viewed it, when describing the conduct of Ishmael in these words. "As then he that was born after the flesh persecuted him that was born after the Spirit." (Galatians 4:29) On this ground, and not from jealousy, Sarah demanded that the bondwoman and her son should be "cast out." But Abraham, who seems to have misunderstood her motives, was reluctant to comply, from feelings of paternal affection quite natural in the case, till God expressly directed him to the same effect. The expulsion of Ishmael was necessary, not only from his unfitness, and in order to keep the heir of the promise unmixed with others, but also for the sake of Abraham himself, whose faith must be trained to renounce, in obedience to the Divine call, everything, — even his natural paternal affection. And in His tender mercy God once more made the trial easier, by bestowing the special promise that Ishmael should become "a nation." Therefore, although Hagar and her son were literally cast forth, with only the barest necessaries for the journey — water and bread, — this was intended chiefly in trial of Abraham's faith, and their poverty was only temporary. For, soon afterwards we read in

Scripture, that, before his death, Abraham had enriched his sons (by Hagar and Keturah) with "gifts;" (Genesis 25:6) and at his burying Ishmael appears, as an acknowledged son, by the side of Isaac, to perform the last rites of love to their father. (Genesis 25:9)

Thus "cast out," Hagar and her son wandered in the wilderness of Beersheba, probably on their way to Egypt. Here they suffered from what has always been the great danger to travelers in the desert — want of water. The lad's strength failed before that of his mother. At length her courage and endurance also gave way to utter exhaustion and despondency. Hitherto she had supported the steps of her son; now she let him droop "under one of the shrubs," while she went "a good way off," not to witness his dying agony, yet still remaining within reach of him. To use the pictorial language of Scripture, "She lift up her voice and wept." Not her cry, however, but that of Abraham's son went up into the ears of the Lord; and once more was Hagar directed to a well of water, but this time by an "angel of God," not, as before, by the "Angel of Jehovah." And now also, to strengthen her for the future, the same assurance concerning Ishmael was given to Hagar which had previously been made to Abraham. This promise of God has been abundantly fulfilled. The lad dwelt in that wide district between Palestine and Mount Horeb, called "the wilderness of Paran," which to this day is the undisputed dominion of his descendants, the Bedouin Arabs.

Bitter as the trial had been to "cast out" Ishmael, his son, it was only a preparation for a far more severe test of Abraham's faith and obedience. For this — the last, the highest, but also the steepest ascent in Abraham's life of faith — all God's previous leadings and dealings had been gradually preparing and qualifying him. But even so, it seems to stand out in Scripture alone and unapproached, like some grand mountain-peak, which only one climber has ever been called to attain. No, not one; for yet another and far higher mountain peak, so lofty that its summit reacheth into heaven itself, has been trodden by the "Seed of Abraham," Who has done all, and far more than Abraham did, and Who has made that a blessed reality to us which in the sacrifice of the patriarch was only a symbol. And, no doubt, it was when on Mount Moriah — the mount of God's true "provision" — Abraham was about to offer up his son, that, in the language of our blessed Lord (John 8:56), he saw the day of Christ, "and was glad."

The test, trial, or "temptation" through which Abraham's faith had now to pass, that it might be wholly purified as "gold in the fire," came in the form of a command from God to bring Isaac as a burnt-offering. Nothing was spared the patriarch of the bitterness of his sorrow. It was said with painful particularity: "Take now thy son, thine only son, whom thou lovest;" and not a single promise of deliverance was added to cheer him on his lonely way. The same indefiniteness which had added such difficulty to Abraham's first call to leave his father's house marked this last trial of the obedience of his faith. He was only told to get him "into the land of Moriah," where God would further tell him upon which of the mountains around he was to bring his strange "burnt-offering." Luther has pointed out, in his own terse language, how to human reason it must have seemed as if either God's promise would fail, or else this command be of the devil, and not of God. From this perplexity there was only one issue — to bring "every thought into captivity to the obedience of Christ." And Abraham "staggered not" at the word of God; doubted it not; but was "strong in faith," "accounting" — yet not knowing it — "that God was able to raise up Isaac even from the dead; from whence he also received him in a figure." For we must not detract from the trial by importing into the circumstances our knowledge of the issue. Abraham had absolutely no assurance and no knowledge beyond that of his present duty. All he had to lay hold upon was the previous promise, and the character and faithfulness of the covenant God, who now bade him offer this sacrifice. Sharp as the contest must have been, it was brief. It lasted just one night; and next morning, without having taken "counsel with flesh and blood," Abraham, with his son Isaac and two servants, were on their way to "the land of Moriah." We have absolutely no data to determine the exact age of Isaac at the time; but the computation of Josephus, that he was twenty-five years old, makes him more advanced than the language of the Scripture narrative seems to convey to our minds. Two days they had traveled from Beersheba, when on the third the "mountains round about Jerusalem" came in sight. From a gap between the hills, which forms the highest point on the ordinary road, which has always led up from the south, just that one mountain would be visible on which afterwards the temple stood. This was "the land of Moriah," and that the hill on which the sacrifice of Isaac was to be offered! Leaving the two servants behind, with the assurance that after they had worshipped they would "come again" — for faith was sure of victory, and anticipated it, — father and son pursued their solitary road, Isaac carrying the wood, and Abraham the sacrificial knife and fire. "And they went both of them together. And Isaac spake unto Abraham his father, and said, My father: and he said, Here am I, my son. And he said, Behold the fire and the wood: but where is the lamb for a burnt-offering? And Abraham said, My son, God will provide himself a lamb for a burnt-offering: so they went both of them together." Nothing further is said between the two till they reach the destined spot. Here Abraham builds the altar, places on it the wood, binds Isaac, and lays him upon the altar. Already he has lifted the sacrificial knife, when the Angel of Jehovah, the Angel of the Covenant, arrests his hand. Abraham's faith has now been fully proved, and it has been perfected. "A ram caught in the thicket" will serve for "a burnt-offering in the stead of his son;" but to Abraham all the previous promises are not only repeated and enlarged, but "confirmed by an oath," "that by two immutable things, in which it was impossible for God to lie," he "might have a strong consolation." "For when God made promise to Abraham, because He could swear by no greater, He sware by Himself." (Hebrews 6:13) This "oath" stands out alone and solitary in the history of the patriarchs; it is afterwards constantly referred to (Genesis 24:7; 26:3; 50:24; Exodus 13:5, 11; 33:1, etc.), and, as Luther observes, it became really the spring whence all flowed that was promised "by oath" unto David, in Psalm 89:35; 110:4; 132:11. No wonder Abraham called the place "Jehovah Jireh," "Jehovah seeth," or "Jehovah provideth," which means that He seeth for us, for, as even the term implieth, His providence, or providing, is just His seeing for us, what, where, and when we do not see for ourselves. As we remember that on this mountain-top the temple of the Lord afterwards stood, and that from it rose the smoke of accepted sacrifices, we can understand all the better what the inspired writer adds by way of explanation: "As it is said to this day, In the mount where Jehovah is seen," — where He seeth and is seen, — whence also the name of Moriah is derived.

But before passing from this event, it is necessary to view it in its bearings upon Abraham, upon Isaac, and even upon the Canaanites, as well as in its higher typical or symbolical application. It is very remarkable that a German writer who has most strenuously opposed the truth of this scriptural narrative, has been compelled to some extent to admit the deeper bearing of this history on the faith of Abraham. He writes: "Hitherto even Isaac, that precious gift so long promised, had been only a natural blessing to Abraham. A son like any other, although the offspring of Sarah, he had been born and educated in his house. Since his birth Abraham had not been called to bear for him the pangs of a soul struggling in faith, and yet every blessing becomes only spiritual and truly lasting, if we appropriate it in the contest of faith." At God's bidding Abraham had necessarily given up country, kindred, and home, and then his paternal affection towards Ishmael. It yet remained to give up even Isaac after the flesh, so as to receive him again spiritually; to give up not merely "his only son, the goal of his longing, the hope of his life, the joy of his old age" — all that was dearest to him; but the heir of all the promises, and that in simple, absolute faith upon God, and in perfect confidence, that God could raise him even from the dead. Thus was the promise purged, so to speak, from all of the flesh that clung to it; and thus Abraham's faith was perfected, and his love purified. Upon Isaac, also, the event had a most important bearing. For when he resisted not his father, and allowed himself to be bound and laid on the altar, he entered into the spirit of Abraham, he took upon himself his faith, and thus showed himself truly the heir to the promises. Nor can we forget how this surrender of the first-born was the first of that dedication of all the first-born unto God, which afterwards the law demanded, and which meant that in the first-born we should consecrate all and everything unto the Lord. Perhaps the lesson which the Canaanites might learn from the event will seem to some quite secondary, as compared with these great truths. Yet we must bear in mind, that all around cruel human sacrifices were offered on every hill, when God gave His sanction to a far different offering, by for ever substituting animal sacrifices for that surrender of the best beloved which human despair had prompted for an atonement for sin. And yet God Himself gave up His beloved, His own only begotten Son for us, — and of this the sacrifice of Isaac was intended to be a glorious type; and as Abraham received this typical sacrifice again from the dead "in a figure," so we in reality, when God raised up His own Son, Jesus Christ, from the dead, and has made us sit together with Him in heavenly places.

After the offering up of Isaac, Abraham lived many years; yet scarcely any event worth record in Scripture occurred during their course. The first thing we afterwards read is the death of Sarah, at the age of one hundred and twenty-seven. She is the only woman whose age is recorded in Scripture, the distinction being probably due to her position towards believers, as stated in 1 Peter 3:6. Isaac was at the time thirty-seven years old, and Abraham once more resident in Hebron. The account of Abraham's purchase of a burying-place from "the children of Heth" is exceedingly pictorial. It also strikingly exhibits alike Abraham's position in the land as a stranger and a pilgrim, and yet his faith in his future possession thereof. The treaty for the field and cave of. Machpelah (either "the double" cave, or else "the separated place," or "the undulating spot"), which Abraham wished to purchase for "a burying-place," was carried on in public assembly, "at the gate of the city," as the common Eastern fashion is. The patriarch expressly acknowledged himself "a stranger and a sojourner" among "the children of Heth;" and the sacred text emphatically repeats again and again how "Abraham stood up, and bowed himself to the people of the land." On the other hand, they carry on their negotiations in the true Eastern fashion, first offering any of their own sepulchers, since Abraham was confessedly among them "a prince of God" (rendered in our version "a mighty prince"), then refusing any payment for Machpelah, but finishing up by asking its fullest value, in this true oriental manner: "My lord, hearken unto me: the land is worth four hundred shekels of silver (about fifty guineas); what is that betwixt me and thee?" In contrast, Abraham truly stands out prince-like in his courtesy and in his dealings. And so the field and cave were secured to him — a "burying-place," Abraham's only "possession" in a land that was to be his for ever! But even in this purchase of a permanent family burying-place, Abraham showed his faith in the promise; just as, many centuries later, the prophet Jeremiah showed his confidence in the promised return of Judah from Babylon, by purchasing a field in Anathoth. (Jeremiah 32:7, 8) In this cave of

Machpelah lie treasured the remains of Abraham and Sarah, of Isaac and Rebekah, of Leah also, and the embalmed bodies of Jacob and perhaps Joseph. No other spot in the Holy Land holds so much precious dust as this; and it is, among all the so-called "holy places," the only one which to this day can be pointed out with perfect certainty. Since the Moslem rule, it has not been accessible to either Christian or Jew. The site over the cave itself is covered by a Mahomedan sanctuary, which stands enclosed within a quadrangular building, two hundred feet long, one hundred and fifteen wide, and fifty or sixty high, the walls of which are divided by pilasters, about five feet apart, and two and a half feet wide. This building, with its immense stones, one of which is no less than thirty-eight feet long, must date from the time of David or of Solomon. The mosque within it was probably anciently a church; and in the cave below its floor are the patriarchal sepulchers.

Three years after the death of Sarah, Abraham resolved to fill the gap in his own family and in the heart of Isaac, by seeking a wife for his son. To this we shall refer in connection with the life of Isaac. Nothing else remains to be told of the third-eight years which followed the death of Sarah. We read, indeed, that Abraham "took a wife," Keturah, and that she bore him six sons, but we are not sure of the time when this occurred. At any rate, the history of these sons is in no wise mixed up with that of the promised seed. They became the ancestors of Arab tribes, which are sometimes alluded to in Holy Writ. And so, through the impressive silence of so many years as make up more than a generation, Scripture brings us to the death of Abraham, at the "good old age" of one hundred and seventy-five, just seventy-five years after the birth of Isaac. To quote the significant language of the Bible, he" was gathered to his people," an expression far different from dying or being buried, and which implies reunion with those who had gone before, and a firm and assured belief in the life to come. And as his sons Isaac and Ishmael, both aged men, stand by his sepulcher in the cave of Machpelah, we seem to hear the voice of God speaking it unto all times: "These all died in faith, not having received the promises, but having seen them afar off, and were persuaded of them, and embraced them, and confessed that they were strangers and pilgrims on the earth." (Hebrews 11:13)

CHAPTER 15: THE MARRIAGE OF ISAAC — BIRTH OF ESAU AND JACOB — ESAU SELLS HIS BIRTHRIGHT — ISAAC AT GERAR — ESAU'S MARRIAGE

(GENESIS 24; 25:19-26:35)

THE sacred narrative now turns to the history of Isaac, the heir to the promises, still marking in its course the same dealings on the part of God which had characterized the life of Abraham. Viewed in connection with the Divine promises, the marriage of Isaac would necessarily appear a subject of the deepest importance to Abraham. Two things were quite firmly settled in the mind of the patriarch: Isaac must on no account take a wife from among the Canaanites around, — he must not enter into alliance with those who were to be dispossessed of the land; and Jehovah, who had so often proved a faithful God, and in obedience to whose will he now refused what might have seemed highly advantageous connections, would Himself provide a suitable partner for Isaac. These two convictions determined Abraham's conduct, as they also guided that of "his eldest servant," whom Abraham commissioned to execute his wishes, and who, in general, seems to have been deeply imbued with the spirit of his master.

Some time before (Genesis 22:20) Abraham had been informed that his brother Nahor, whom he left behind in Haran, had been blessed with numerous descendants. To him the patriarch now dispatched "his servant, the elder of his house, who ruled over all that was his" — generally supposed to have been Eliezer of Damascus (Genesis 15:2), though at that time he must, like his master, have been far advanced in years. But before departing, he made him swear by Jehovah — since this matter concerned the very essence of the covenant — to avoid every alliance with the Canaanites, and to apply to his "kindred." And when the servant put before him the possibility, that the execution of this wish might render it necessary for Isaac to return to the land whence Abraham had come, the patriarch emphatically negatived the suggestion, as equally contrary to the Divine will, while his faith anticipated no difficulty, but calmly trusted the result in God's hands. In all this Abraham had no fresh revelation from heaven; nor needed he any. He only applied to present circumstances what he had formerly received as the will of God, just as in all circumstances of life we need no fresh communication from above — only to understand and to apply the will of God as revealed to us in His holy word.

The result proved how true had been Abraham's expectations. Arrived at Haran, Abraham's servant made it a matter of prayer that God would "prosper his way," for even when in the way of God's appointment, we must seek and ask His special blessing. There, as he stood outside the city by the well to which, according to the custom of the East, the maidens would resort at even to draw water for their households, it naturally occurred to him to connect in his prayer a mark of that religious courtesy, hospitality, and kindness to which he had been accustomed in his master's house, with the kindred of Abraham, and hence with the object of his journey. His prayer was scarcely finished when the answer came. "Before he had done speaking" (Comp. Daniel 9:20, 21) Rebekah, the daughter of Bethuel, the son of Nahor, Abraham's brother, came to the well by which the stranger stood with his camels. Her appearance was exceedingly prepossessing ("the damsel was very fair to look upon"), and her bearing modest and becoming. According to the sign on which he had fixed in his own mind, he asked her for water to drink; and according to the same sign, she exceeded his request by drawing for his camels also. But even so Abraham's servant did not yield to his first impressions; only at the literality of the answer to his prayer, "the man wondering at her, held his peace, to know whether Jehovah had made his way prosperous or not." Before asking further who her kindred were, and seeking their hospitality, he rewarded her kindness by splendid presents. But when the answers of Rebekah showed him that Jehovah had actually led him straight "to the house of his master's brethren," the man, fairly overcome by his feelings, "bowed down his head, and worshipped Jehovah."

The description of what now ensued is not only exceedingly graphic, but true to the life. It is said that Rebekah "ran and told her mother's house," that is, evidently to the female portion of the household. Next, Laban, Rebekah's brother, seeing the jewels and hearing her tale, hastens to invite the stranger with true Eastern profusion of welcome. But the terms in which Laban, partially at least an idolater, addressed Abraham's servant: "Thou blessed of Jehovah," remind us how easily the language of Abraham — in other words, religious language, is picked up by those who have really no claim to use it. The servant of Abraham, on the other hand, is quite like his master in his dignified bearing and earnestness of purpose. Before accepting hospitality at the hands of Bethuel and Laban, he will have an answer to the commission on which he has been sent, nor can persuasions or entreaty prevail on him to prolong his stay, even over the following day. With the full consent of Rebekah, the caravan returns to Canaan. Once more it is evening when the end of the journey is reached. It so happens that Isaac has "gone out to meditate in the field" — an expression which implies religious communion with God, probably in connection with this very marriage — when he meets the returning caravan. Rebekah receives her future husband with the becoming modesty of an Eastern bride, and the heart-happiness of the son of promise is secured to him in union with her whom the Lord Himself had "provided" as his wife. Isaac was at the time of his marriage forty years old.

In the quiet retirement of his old age Abraham not only witnessed the married happiness of his son, but even lived fifteen years beyond the birth of Esau and Jacob. As for Isaac, he had settled far from the busy haunts of the Canaanites, at the well Lahai-Roi a retreat suited to his quiet, retiring disposition. For twenty years the union of Isaac and Rebekah had remained unblessed with children, to indicate that here also the heir to the promises must be a gift from God granted to expectant faith. At last Jehovah listened to Isaac's "entreaty," "for his wife," or rather, literally, "over against his wife," for, as Luther strikingly remarks: "When I pray for any one, I place him right in view of my heart, and neither see nor think of anything else, but look at him alone with my soul;" and this is true of all intercessory prayer. Rebekah was now to become the mother of twin sons. But even before their birth a sign occurred which distressed her, and induced her "to inquire of Jehovah" its meaning, though we know not in what precise manner she did this. The answer of God indicated this at least quite clearly, that of her children "the elder shall serve the younger;" that is, that, contrary to all usual expectation, the firstborn should not possess the birthright which the Divine promise had conveyed to the family of Abraham. The substitution of the younger for the elder son was indeed in accordance with God's previous dealings, but it seemed strange where the two were sons of the same parents. It is not only reasonable, but quite necessary for the understanding of the subsequent history, to believe that Rebekah communicated the result of her inquiry to her husband, and that afterwards both Esau and Jacob were also made acquainted with the fact. This alone fully accounts for the conduct of Jacob and of his mother in seeking to appropriate the birthright, contrary to what would otherwise have been the natural arrangement. When the two children were born, the red and hairy appearance of the elder procured for him the name of Esau, or "hairy;" while the younger was called Jacob, or he "who takes hold by the heel," because "his hand took hold by Esau's heel" — a name which afterwards was adapted to mean "a supplanter,"(Genesis 27:36) since he who takes hold by the heel "trips up" the other.

The appearance of the children did not belie their character when they grew up. The wild disposition of Esau, which found occupation in the roaming life of a hunter, reminds us of Ishmael; while Jacob, gentle and domestic, sought his pleasures at home. As is so often the case, Isaac and Rebekah made favorites of the sons who had the opposite of their own disposition. The quiet, retiring Isaac preferred his bold, daring, strong, roaming elder son; while Rebekah, who was naturally energetic, felt chiefly drawn to her gentle son Jacob. Yet at bottom Esau also was weak and easily depressed, as appeared in his tears and impotent reproaches when he found himself really deprived of the blessing; while Jacob, too, like his mother, impetuous, was ever ready to take matters into his own hands. We repeat it, that all parties must at the time have been aware that, even before the birth of the children, the word of God had designated Jacob as heir of the promises. But Isaac's preference for Esau made him reluctant to fall in with the Divine arrangement; while the impetuosity of Rebekah and of Jacob prompted them to bring about in their own way the fulfillment of God's promise, instead of believingly waiting to see when and how the Lord would do it. Thus it came that Jacob, watching his opportunities, soon found occasion to take advantage of his brother. One day Esau returned from the chase "faint" with hunger. The sight of a mess of lentils, which to this day is a favorite dish in Syria and Egypt, induced him, unaccustomed and unable as he was to control the desires of the moment, to barter away his birthright for this "red" pottage. The circumstances become the more readily intelligible when we remember, besides the unbridled disposition of Esau, that, as Lightfoot has pointed out, it was a time of commencing famine in the land. For, immediately afterwards (Genesis 26:1), we read that "there was a famine in the land," greater even than that at the time of Abraham, and which compelled Isaac for a season to leave Canaan. From this event, so characteristic and decisive in his history, Esau, after the custom of the East, obtained the name of Edom, or "red," from the color of "the mess of pottage" for which he had sold his birthright.

In regard to the conduct of the two brothers in this matter, we must note, that Scripture in no way excuses nor apologizes for that of Jacob. According to its wont, it simply states the facts, and makes neither comment nor remark upon them. That it leaves to "the logic of facts;" and the terrible trials which were so soon to drive Jacob from his home, and which kept him so long a bondsman in a strange land, are themselves a sufficient Divine commentary upon the transaction. Moreover, it is very remarkable that Jacob never in his after-life appealed to his purchase of the birthright. But so far as Esau is concerned only one opinion can be entertained of his conduct. We are too apt to imagine that because Jacob wronged or took advantage of Esau, therefore Esau was right. The opposite of this is the case. When we ask ourselves what Jacob intended to purchase, or Esau to sell in the "birthright," we answer that in later times it conveyed a double share of the paternal possessions. (Deuteronomy 21:17) In patriarchal days it included "lordship" over the rest of the family, and especially succession to that spiritual blessing which through Abraham was to flow out into the world (Genesis 27:27, 29), together with possession of the land of Canaan and covenant-communion with Jehovah. (Genesis 28:4) What of these things was spiritual, we may readily believe, Esau discredited and despised, and what was temporal, but yet future, as his after conduct shows, he imagined he might still obtain either by his father's favor or by violence. But that for the momentary gratification of the lowest sensual appetites he should have been ready to barter away such unspeakably precious and holy privileges, proved him, in the language of the Epistle to the Hebrews (Hebrews 12:16), to have been "a profane person," and therefore quite unfitted to become the heir of the promises. For profanity consists in this: for the sensual gratification or amusement of the moment to give up that which is spiritual and unseen; to be careless of that which is holy, so as to snatch the present enjoyment, — in short, practically not to deem anything holy at all, if it stands in the way of present pleasure. Scripture puts it down as the bitter self-condemnation which Esau, by his conduct, pronounced upon himself: "and he did eat and drink, and rose up, and went his way; thus Esau despised his birthright."

Before farther following the history of Isaac's trials and joys, it seems desirable to make here a few general remarks, for the purpose of explaining the conduct alike of Isaac and of Jacob, and its bearing on the history of the covenant. It has been common to describe Abraham as the man of faith, Isaac as the model of patient bearing, and Jacob as the man of active working; and in the two latter cases to connect the spiritual fruits, which were the outcome of their faith, with their natural characters also. All this is quite correct; but, in our opinion, it is necessary to take a broader view of the whole matter. Let it be borne in mind, that God had both made and established His covenant with Abraham. The history of Isaac and Jacob, on the other hand, rather represents the hindrances to the covenant. These are just the same as we daily meet in our own walk of faith. They arise from opposite causes, according as in our weakness we either lag behind, or in our haste go before God. Isaac lagged behind, Jacob tried to go before God; and their history exhibits the dangers and difficulties arising from each of these causes, just as, on the other hand, God's dealings with them show how mercifully, how wisely, and yet how holily He knew to remove these hindrances out of the way, and to uproot these sins from their hearts and lives. Accordingly, we shall consider the history of Isaac and Jacob as that of the hindrances of the covenant and of their removal.

Viewed in this light we understand all the better, not only Jacob's attempt to purchase the "birthright" — as if Esau had had the power of selling it! — but what followed that transaction? It seems that a grievous famine induced Isaac to leave his settlement, and it naturally occurred to him in so doing to follow in the wake of his father Abraham, and to go into Egypt. But when he had reached Gerar, the residence of Abimelech, king of the Philistines, where Abraham had previously sojourned, "Jehovah appeared unto him," and specially directed him to remain there, at the same time renewing to him the promises He had made to Abraham. Both in this direction and in the renewal of blessing we recognize the kindness of the Lord, Who would not expose Isaac to the greater trials of Egypt, and would strengthen and encourage his faith. Apparently, he had on reaching Gerar not said that Rebekah was his wife; and when he was, at last, "asked" about it, the want of courage which had prompted the equivocation, ripened into actual falsehood. Imitating in this the example of Abraham, he passed off his wife as his sister. But here also the kindness of the Lord interposed to spare him a trial greater than he might have been able to bear. His deceit was detected before his wife had been taken by any one; and an order given by Abimelech — whether the same who ruled at the time of Abraham, or his successor — secured her future safety. The famine seems now to have become so intense, that Isaac began to till land for himself. And God blessed him with an unusually large return — still further to encourage his faith amidst its trials. Commonly, even in very fruitful parts of Palestine, the yield is from twenty-five to fifty times that which had been sown; and in one small district, even eighty times that of wheat, and one hundred times that of barley. But Isaac at once "received an hundredfold" — to show him that even in a year of famine God could make the most ample provision for His servant. The increasing wealth of Isaac excited the envy of the Philistines. Disputes arose, and they stopped up the wells which Abraham had digged. At last, even Abimelech, friendly as he was, advised him to leave the place. Isaac removed to the valley of Gerar. But there also similar contentions arose; and Isaac once more returned to Abraham's old settlement at Beersheba. Here Jehovah again appeared unto him, to confirm, on his re-entering the land, the promises previously made. Beersheba had also its name given it a second time. For Abimelech, accompanied by his chief captain and his privy councilor, came to Isaac to renew the covenant which had formerly been there made between the Philistines and Abraham. Isaac was now at peace with all around. Better still, "he built an altar" in Beersheba, "and called upon the name of Jehovah." But in the high day of his prosperity fresh trials awaited him. His eldest son Esau, now forty years old, took two Canaanitish wives, "which were a grief of mind unto Isaac and to Rebekah." Assuredly, if Isaac had not "lagged far behind," he would in this have recognized the final and full unfitness of Esau to have "the birthright." But the same tendency which had hitherto kept him at best undecided, led, ere it was finally broken, to a further and a far deeper sorrow than any he had yet experienced.

CHAPTER 16: ISAAC'S BLESSING OBTAINED BY JACOB DECEITFULLY — ESAU'S SORROW — EVIL CONSEQUENCES OF THEIR ERROR TO ALL THE MEMBERS OF THEIR FAMILY — JACOB IS SENT TO LABAN — ISAAC RENEWS AND FULLY GIVES HIM THE BLESSING OF ABRAHAM

(GENESIS 27-28:9)

IF there is any point on which we should anxiously be on our guard, it is that of "tempting God." We do so tempt the Lord when, listening to our own inclinations, we put once more to the question that which He has already clearly settled. Where God has decided, never let us doubt, nor lag behind. But if anything might be described as clearly settled by God, it was, surely, the calling of Jacob and the rejection of Esau. It had been expressly foretold in prophecy even before the children were born; and Esau had also afterwards proved himself wholly unfit to be the heir of the promise, first by his light-minded profanity, and next by his alliance with the Canaanites, than which nothing could have more directly run counter to the will of God, and to the purposes of the covenant. Despite these clear indications, Isaac did lag behind, reluctant to follow the direction of God. In truth, he had thrown his natural affections as a makeweight into the scale. As we shall presently show, Isaac hesitated, indeed, to allot unto Esau the spiritual part of the blessing; but what he regarded as the natural rights of the first-born appeared to him inalienable, and these he meant now formally to recognize by bestowing upon him the blessing.

A German writer aptly observes: "This is one of the most remarkable complications of life, showing in the clearest manner that a higher hand guides the threads of history, so that neither sin nor error can ultimately entangle them. Each one weaves the threads which are committed to him according to his own views and desires; but at last, when the texture is complete, we behold in it the pattern which the Master had long devised, and towards which each laborer had only contributed one or another feature." At the time of which we write Isaac was one hundred and thirty-seven years old — an age at which his half-brother Ishmael had died, fourteen years before; and though Isaac was destined to live yet forty-three years longer (Genesis 35:28), the decay of his sight, and other infirmities, brought the thought of death very near to him. Under these circumstances he resolved formally to bestow the privileges naturally belonging to the first-born upon Esau. With this, however, he coupled, as a sort of preliminary condition, that Esau should bring and prepare for him some venison. Possibly he regarded the finding of the game as a sort of providential sign, and the preparation of it as a token of affection. There would be nothing strange in this, for those who believe in God, and yet for some reason refuse implicitly to follow His directions, are always on the outlook for some "sign" to justify them in setting aside the clear intimations of His will. But Rebekah had overheard the conversation between her husband and her son. Probably she had long been apprehensive of some such event, and on the outlook for it. And now the danger seemed most pressing. Another hour, and the blessing might for ever be lost to Jacob. Humanly speaking, safety lay in quick resolution and decided action. It mattered not what were the means employed, if only the end were forming an alliance with him whom Abraham had, by God's command, "cast out!" Thus the spiritual incapacity and unfitness of Esau appeared at every step, even where he tried to act kindly and dutifully.

To conclude, by altering and adapting the language of a German writer: After this event Isaac lived other forty-three years. But he no more appears in this history. Its thread is now taken up by Jacob, on whom the promise has devolved. Scripture only records that Isaac was gathered to his fathers when one hundred and eighty years old, and full of days, and that he was buried in the cave of Machpelah by Esau and Jacob, whom he had the joy of seeing by his death-bed as reconciled brothers. When Jacob left, his father dwelt at Beersheba. The desire to be nearer to his father's burying-place may have been the ground of his later settlement in Mamre, where he died. (Genesis 35:27-29) Rebekah, who at parting had so confidently promised to let Jacob know whenever Esau's anger was appeased, may have died even before her favorite son returned to Canaan. At any rate the promised message was never delivered, nor is her name mentioned on Jacob's return.

CHAPTER 17: JACOB'S VISION AT BETHEL — HIS ARRIVAL AT THE HOUSE OF LABAN — JACOB'S DOUBLE MARRIAGE AND SERVITUDE — HIS FLIGHT FROM HARAN — PURSUIT OF LABAN, AND RECONCILIATION WITH JACOB

(GENESIS 28:10-31:55)

IT had been a long and weary journey that first day when Jacob left his home at Beersheba. More than forty miles had he traveled over the mountains which afterwards were those of Judah, and through what was to become the land of Benjamin. The sun had set, and its last glow faded out from the gray hills of Ephraim, when he reached "an uneven valley, covered, as with gravestones, by large sheets of bare rock, — some few here and there standing up like the cromlechs of Druidical monuments." Here, close by a wild ridge, the broad summit of which was covered by an olive grove, was the place where Abraham had first rested for some time on entering the land, and whence he and Lot had, before their separation, taken a survey of the country. There, just before him, lay the Canaanitish Luz; and beyond it, many days' journey, stretched his weary course to Haran. It was a lonely, weird place, this valley of stones, in which to make his first night's quarters. But perhaps it agreed all the better with Jacob's mood, which had made him go on and on, from early morning, forgetful of time and way, till he could no longer pursue his journey. Yet, accidental as it seemed — for we read that "he lighted upon a certain place," — the selection of the spot was assuredly designed of God. Presently Jacob prepared for rest. Piling some of the stones, with which the valley was strewed, he made them a pillow, and laid him down to sleep. Then it was, in his dream, that it seemed as if these stones of the valley were being builded together by an unseen hand, step upon step, "a ladder" — or, probably more correctly, "a stair." Now, as he watched it, it rose and rose, till it reached the deep blue star-spangled sky, which seemed to cleave for its reception. All along that wondrous track moved angel-forms, "ascending and descending upon it;" and angel-light was shed upon its course, till quite up on the top stood the glorious Jehovah Himself, Who spake to the lonely sleeper below: "I am Jehovah, the God of Abraham thy father, and the God of Isaac." Silent in their ministry, the angels still passed up and down the heaven-built stairs, from where Jacob lay to where Jehovah spake. The vision and the words which the Lord spoke explain each other, the one being the symbol of the other. On that first night, when an outcast from his home, and a fugitive, heavy thoughts, doubts, and fears would crowd around Jacob; when, in every sense, his head was pillowed on stones in the rocky valley of Luz, Jehovah expressly renewed to him, in the fullest manner, the promise and the blessing first given to Abraham, and added to it this comfort, whatever might be before him: "I am with thee, and will keep thee in all places whither thou goest, and will bring thee again into this land; for I will not leave thee until I have done that which I have spoken to thee of." And what Jacob heard, that he also saw in symbolic vision. The promise was the real God-built stair, which reached from the lonely place on which the poor wanderer lay quite up to heaven, right into the very presence of Jehovah; and on which, all silent and unknown by the world, lay the shining track of angel-ministry. And so still to each one who is truly of Israel is the promise of that mysterious "ladder" which connects earth with heaven. Below lies poor, helpless, forsaken man; above, stands Jehovah Himself, and upon the ladder of promise which joins earth to heaven, the angels of God, in their silent, never-ceasing ministry, descend, bringing help, and ascend, as to fetch new deliverance. Nay, this "ladder" is Christ, for by this "ladder" God Himself has come down to us in the Person of His dear Son, Who is, so to speak, the Promise become Reality, as it is written: "Hereafter ye shall see heaven open, and the angels of God ascending and descending upon the Son of Man." (John 1:51)

"And Jacob awaked out of his sleep, and he said, Surely Jehovah is in this place, and I knew it not." Quite another fear now came upon him from that of loneliness or of doubt. It was awe at the conscious presence of the ever-watchful, ever-mindful covenant-God which made him feel, as many a wanderer since at such discovery: "How dreadful is this place! This is none other but the house of God, and this is the gate of heaven." And early next morning Jacob converted his stony pillow into a memorial pillar, and consecrated it unto God. Henceforth this rocky valley would be to him no more the Canaanitish Luz, but Beth-el, "the house of God;" just as John the Baptist declared that God could of such stones raise up children to Abraham. At the same time Jacob vowed a vow, that when God had fulfilled His promise, and brought him back again "in peace," he would, on his part also, make the place a Beth-el, by dedicating it to God, and offering unto the Lord a tenth of all that He should give him, which also he did. (Genesis 35:6, 7)

No further incident worth recording occurred till Jacob reached the end of his journey in "the land of the people of the East." Here he found himself at a "well," where, contrary to the usual custom, three flocks were already in waiting, long before the usual evening time for watering them. Professor Robinson has made this personal observation, helpful to our understanding of the circumstances: "Over most of the cisterns is laid a broad and thick flat stone, with a round hole cut in the middle, forming the mouth of the cistern. This hole we found in many cases covered with a heavy stone, which it would require two or three men to roll away." We know not whether these flocks were kept waiting till sufficient men had come to roll away the stone, or whether it was the custom to delay till all the flocks had arrived. At any rate, when Jacob had ascertained that the flocks were from Haran, and that the shepherds knew Laban, the brother of Rebekah, and when he saw the fair Rachel, his own cousin, coming with her flock, he rolled away the stone himself, watered his uncle's sheep, and in the warmth of his feelings at finding himself not only at the goal of his journey, but apparently God-directed to her whose very appearance could win his affections, he embraced his cousin. Even in this little trait the attentive observer of Jacob's natural character will not fail to recognize "the haste" with which he always anticipated God's leadings. When Laban, Rachel's father, came to hear of all the circumstances, he received Jacob as his relative. A month's trial more than confirmed in the mind of that selfish, covetous man the favorable impression of Jacob's possible use to him as a shepherd, which his first energetic interference at the "well" must have produced. With that apparent frankness and show of liberality under which cunning, selfish people so often disguise their dishonest purposes, Laban urged upon Jacob to name his own "wages." Jacob had learned to love Rachel, Laban's younger daughter. Without consulting the mind of God in the matter, he now proposed to serve Laban seven years for her hand. This was just the period during which, among the Hebrews, a Jewish slave had to serve; in short, he proposed becoming a bondsman for Rachel. With the same well-feigned candor as before, Laban agreed: "It is better that I give her to thee, than that I should give her to another man (to a stranger)." The bargain thus to sell his daughter was not one founded on the customs of the time, and Laban's daughters themselves felt the degradation which they could not resist, as appears from their after statement, when agreeing to flee from their father's home: "Are we not counted of him strangers? for he has sold us." (Genesis 31:14, 15)

The period of Jacob's servitude seemed to him rapidly to pass, and at the end of the seven years he claimed his bride. But now Jacob was to experience how his sin had found him out. As he had deceived his father, so Laban now deceived him. Taking advantage of the Eastern custom that a bride was always brought to her husband veiled, he substituted for Rachel her elder sister Leah. But, as formerly, God had, all unknown to them, overruled the error and sin of Isaac and of Jacob, so He did now also in the case of Laban and Jacob. For Leah was, so far as we can judge, the one whom God had intended for Jacob, though, for the sake of her beauty, he had preferred Rachel. From Leah sprang Judah, in whose line the promise to Abraham was to be fulfilled. Leah, as we shall see in the sequel, feared and served Jehovah; while Rachel was attached to the superstitions of her father's house; and even the natural character of the elder sister fitted her better for her new calling than that of the somewhat petulant, peevish, and self-willed, though beautiful younger daughter of Laban. As for the author of this deception, Laban, he shielded himself behind the pretense of a national custom, not to give away a younger before a first born sister. But he readily proposed to give to Jacob Rachel also, in return for other seven years of service. Jacob consented, and the second union was celebrated immediately upon the close of Leah's marriage festivities, which in the East generally last for a week. It were an entire mistake to infer from the silence of Scripture that this double marriage of Jacob received Divine approbation. As always, Scripture states facts, but makes no comment. That sufficiently appears from the lifelong sorrow, disgrace, and trials which, in the retributive providence of God, followed as the consequence of this double union.

The sinful weakness of Jacob appeared also in his married life, in an unkind and unjust preference for Rachel, and God's reproving dealings in that He blessed the "hated" wife with children, while he withheld from Rachel a boon so much desired in a family where all that was precious stood connected with an heir to the promises. At the same time, this might also serve to teach again the lesson, given first to Abraham and then to Isaac, how especially in the patriarchal family this blessing was to be a direct gift from the Lord. (See also Psalm 127:3) Leah bore in rapid succession four sons, whom she significantly named Reuben (" behold! a son"), saying, "Surely Jehovah hath looked upon my affliction;" Simeon ("hearing"), "Because Jehovah hath heard that I was hated;" Levi ("cleaving," or "joined"), in the hope "Now this time will my husband cleave to me;" and Judah ("praised," viz., be Jehovah), since she said: "Now will I praise Jehovah." It deserves special notice, that in the birth of at least three of these sons, Leah not only recognized God, but specially acknowledged Him as Jehovah, the covenant-God.

We do not suppose that Rachel, who had no children of her own, waited all this time without seeking to remove what she enviously and jealously regarded as her sister's advantage. Indeed, the sacred text nowhere indicates that the children of Jacob were born in the exact succession of time in which their names are recorded. On the contrary, we have every reason to suppose that such was not the case. It quite agrees with the petulant, querulous language of Rachel, that she waited not so long, but that so soon as she really found herself at this disadvantage compared with her sister, she persuaded her husband to make her a mother through Bilhah, her own maid, as Sarah had done in the case of Hagar. Thus the sins of the parents too often reappear in the conduct of their successors. Instead of waiting upon God, or giving himself to prayer, Jacob complied with the desire of his

Rachel, and her maid successively bore two sons, whom Rachel named "Dan," or "judging," as if God had judged her wrong, and "Naphtali," or "my wrestling," saying: "With great wrestling have I wrestled with my sister, and I have prevailed." In both instances we mark her gratified jealousy of her sister; and that, although she owned God, it was not as Jehovah, but as Elohim, the God of nature, not the covenant-God of the promise.

Once again the evil example of a sister, and its supposed success, proved infectious. When Leah perceived that she no longer became as before, a mother, and probably without waiting till both Rachel's adopted sons had been born, she imitated the example of her sister, and gave to Jacob her own maid Zilpah as wife. Her declension in faith further appears also in the names which she chose for the sons of Zilpah. At the birth of the eldest, she exclaimed, "Good fortune cometh," and hence called him "Gad," or "good fortune;" the same idea being expressed in the name of the second, Asher, or "happy." Neither did Leah in all this remember God, but only thought of the success of her own device. But the number of children now granted to the two sisters neither removed their mutual jealousies, nor restored peace to the house of Jacob. Most painful scenes occurred; and when at length Leah again gave birth to two sons, she recognized, indeed, God in their names, but now, like her sister, only Elohim, not Jehovah; while she seemed to see in the first of them a reward for giving Zilpah to her husband, whence the child's name was called Issachar ("he gives," or "he brings reward"); while she regarded her last-born son, Zebulun, or "dwelling," as a pledge that since she had borne him six sons, her husband would now dwell with her!

It has already been stated that we must not regard the order in which the birth of Jacob's children is mentioned as indicating their actual succession. They are rather so enumerated, partly to show the varying motives of the two sisters, and partly to group together the sons of different mothers. That the scriptural narrative is not intended to represent the actual succession of the children appears also from the circumstance, that the birth of an only daughter, Dinah ("judgment") is mentioned immediately after that of Zebulun. The wording of the Hebrew text here implies that Dinah was born at a later period ("afterwards"), and, indeed, she alone is mentioned on account of her connection with Jacob's later history, though we have reason to believe that Jacob had other daughters (See Genesis 37:35, and 46:7), whose names and history are not mentioned.

And now at last better thoughts seem to have come to Rachel. When we read that in giving her a son of her own, "God hearkened to her," we are warranted in inferring that believing prayer had taken in her heart the former place of envy and jealousy of her sister. The son whom she now bore, in the fourteenth year of Jacob's servitude to Laban, was called Joseph, a name which has a double meaning: "the remover," because, as she said, "God hath taken away my reproach," and "adding," since she regarded her child as a pledge that God — this time "Jehovah" — "shall add to me another son." The object of Jacob's prolonged stay with his father-in-law was now accomplished. Fourteen years' servitude to Laban left him as poor as when first he had come to him. The wants of his increasing family, and the better understanding now established in his family, must have pointed out to him the desirableness of returning to his own country. But when he intimated this wish to his father-in-law, Laban was unwilling to part with one by whom he had so largely profited. With a characteristic confusion of heathen ideas with a dim knowledge of the being of Jehovah, Laban said to Jacob (we here translate literally): "If I have found grace in thy sight (i.e. tarry), for I have divined (ascertained by magic), and Jehovah hath blessed me for thy sake." The same attempt to place Jehovah as the God of Abraham by the side of the god of

Nahor — not denying, indeed, the existence of Jehovah, but that He was the only true and living God — occurs again later when Laban made a covenant with Jacob. (Genesis 31:53) It also frequently recurs in the later history of Israel. Both strange nations and Israel itself, when in a state of apostasy, did not deny that Jehovah was God, but they tried to place Him on a level with other and false deities. Now, Scripture teaches us that to place any other pretended God along with the living and true One argues as great ignorance, and is as great a sin, as to deny Him entirely.

In his own peculiar fashion Laban, with pretended candor and liberality, now invited Jacob to name his wages for the future. But this time the deceiver was to be deceived. Basing his proposal on the fact that in the East the goats are mostly black and the sheep white, Jacob made what seemed the very modest request, that all that were spotted and speckled in the flock were to be his share. Laban gladly assented, taking care to make the selection himself, and to hand over Jacob's portion to his own sons, while Jacob was to tend the flocks of Laban. Finally, he placed three days' journey betwixt the flocks of Jacob and his own. But even so, Jacob knew how, by an artifice well understood in the East, to circumvent his father-in- law, and to secure that, though ordinarily "the ringstraked, speckled, and spotted" had been an exception, now they were the most numerous and the strongest of the flocks. And the advantage still remained on the side of Jacob, when Laban again and again reversed the conditions of the agreement. (Genesis 31:7) This clearly proved that Jacob's artifice could not have been the sole nor the real reason of his success. In point of fact, immediately after the first agreement with Laban, the angel of God had spoken to Jacob in a dream, assuring him that, even without any such artifices, God would right him in his cause with Laban. (Genesis 31:12, 13) Once more, then, Jacob acted, as when in his father's house. He "made haste;" he would not wait for the Lord to fulfill his promise; he would use his own means — and employ his cunning and devices — to accomplish the purpose of God, instead of committing his cause unto Him. And as formerly he had had the excuse of his father's weakness and his brother's violence, so now it might seem as if he were purely on his defense, and as if his deceit were necessary for his protection — the more so as he resorted to his device only in spring, not in autumn, so that the second produce of the year belonged chiefly to his father-in-law.

The consequences proved very similar to those which followed his deceit in his father's house. The rapidly growing wealth of Jacob during the six years of this bargain so raised the enmity and envy of Laban and of his sons, that Jacob must have felt it necessary for his own safety to remove, even if he had not received Divine direction to that effect. But this put an end to all hesitancy; and having communicated his purpose to his wives, and secured their cordial consent, he left secretly, while Laban was away at the sheep-shearing, which would detain him some time. Three days elapsed before Laban was informed of Jacob's flight. He immediately pursued after him, "with his brethren," his anger being further excited by the theft of his household gods, or "teraphim," which Rachel, unknown, of course, to Jacob, had taken with her. On the seventh day Laban and his relatives overtook Jacob and his caravan in Mount Gilead. The consequences might have been terrible, if God had not interposed to warn Laban in a dream, not to injure nor to hurt Jacob. Being further foiled in his search after the missing teraphim, through the cunning of his own daughter, Laban, despite his hypocritical professions of how affectionate their leave-taking might have been if Jacob had not "stolen away," stood convicted of selfishness and unkindness. In fact, if the conduct of Jacob, even in his going away, had been far from straightforward, that of Laban was of the most unprincipled kind. However, peace was restored between them, and a covenant made, in virtue of which neither party was to cross for hostile purposes the memorial pillar which they erected, and to which Laban gave a Chaldee and Jacob a Hebrew name, meaning "the heap of witness."

Hypocritically as in the mouth of Laban the additional name of Mizpah sounds, which he gave to this pillar, it is a very significant designation to mark great events in our lives, especially our alliances and our undertakings. For Mizpah means "watchtower," and the words which accompanied the giving of this name were:

"Jehovah watch between me and thee, when we are absent one from another."

CHAPTER 18: JACOB AT MAHANAIM — THE NIGHT OF WRESTLING — RECONCILIATION BETWEEN JACOB AND ESAU — JACOB SETTLES AT SHECHEM — JACOB PROCEEDS TO BETHEL TO PAY HIS VOW — DEATH OF RACHEL — JACOB SETTLES AT HEBRON

(GENESIS 32-36)

WE are now nearing what may be described as the high point in the spiritual history of Jacob. Quite different as the previous history of Abraham had been from that of Jacob, yet, in some sense, what Mount Moriah was to Abraham, that the fords of Jabbok became to his grandson: a place of trial and of decision, — only that while the one went to it, the other only left it, with a new name, and all that this implied.

One dreaded meeting was past, and its apprehended dangers averted. Jacob had in his fear "stolen away" from Laban. He had been pursued as by an enemy, but God had brought peace out of it all. Standing by his "Mizpah," he had seen Laban and his confederates disappearing behind the range of Gilead, their spears and lances glistening in the sunlight, as they wound through the pine and oak forests which cover the mountain side. One enemy was now behind him; but another and far more formidable had yet to be encountered. In dealing with Laban, Jacob could justly plead his long service and the heartless selfishness of his employer. But what could he say to Esau in excuse or palliation of the past? How would he meet him? and did his brother still cherish the purpose of revenge from which he had fled twenty years ago? To these questions there was absolutely no answer, except the one which faith alone could understand: that if he now returned to his own country, and faced the danger there awaiting him, it was by the express direction of the Lord Himself. If so, Jacob must be safe. Nor was he long in receiving such general assurance of this as might strengthen his faith. Leaving the mountains of Gilead, Jacob had entered the land of promise, in what afterwards became the possession of Gad. A glorious prospect here opened before him. Such beauty, fruitfulness, freshness of verdure, and richness of pasturage; dark mountain forests above, and rich plains below, as poor Palestine, denuded of its trees, and with them of its moisture — a land of ruins — has not known these many, many centuries! And there, as he entered the land, "the angels of God met him." Twenty years before they had, on leaving it, met him at Bethel, and, so to speak, accompanied him on his journey. And now in similar pledge they welcomed him on his return. Only then, they had been angels ascending and descending on their ministry, while now they were "angel hosts" to defend him in the impending contest, whence also Jacob called the name of that place Mahanaim, "two hosts," or "two camps." And if at Bethel he had seen them in a "dream," they now appeared to him when waking, as if to convey yet stronger assurance.

Such comfort was, indeed, needed by Jacob. From Mahanaim he had sent to his brother Esau a message intended to conciliate him. But the messengers returned without any reply, other than that Esau was himself coming to meet his brother, and that at the head of a band of four hundred men. This certainly was sufficiently alarming, irrespective of the circumstance that since Esau was (as we shall presently show) just then engaged in a warlike expedition against Seir, the four hundred men with whom he advanced, had probably gathered around his standard for plunder and bloodshed, just like those wild Bedouin tribes which to this day carry terror wherever they appear. Even to receive no reply at all would, in itself, be a great trial to one like Jacob. Hitherto he had by his devices succeeded in removing every obstacle, and evading every danger. But now he was absolutely helpless, in face of an enemy from whom he could neither retreat nor escape. It is said in the sacred text: "Then Jacob was greatly afraid and distressed." The measures to which he resorted prove this. He divided his caravan into two bands, in the hope that if Esau attacked the one, the other might escape during the fray. The result thus aimed at was very doubtful, and, at the best, sad enough. Jacob must have deeply felt this, and he betook himself to prayer. Mingling confession of his utter unworthiness with entreaty for deliverance from the danger before him, he successively pleaded before God His express command to return to Canaan, His past mercies, and His gracious promises, at the same time addressing God as Jehovah, the covenant-God of Abraham and of Isaac. Not one of these pleas could fail. That cry of despair was the preparation for what was to follow: Jacob was now learning to obtain, otherwise than by his own efforts, that which Jehovah had promised to give.

We know, with almost perfect certainty, the exact spot where the most important transaction in the life of Jacob took place. It was at the ford of Jabbok, the confluence of the two streams which flow from the East into Jordan, between the Sea of Galilee and the Dead Sea, and almost midway between these two points. Indeed, there is only one ford of Jabbok "practicable," "and even here," as a recent traveler records, "the strong current reached the horse's girths." The beauty and richness of the whole district is most striking — park-like scenery alternating with sweet glades, covered with rich crops; "trees and shrubs grouped in graceful variety;" then peeps into the great Jordan valley, with its almost tropical vegetation, and of the hills of Palestine beyond. Looking down upon the ford, the brook Jabbok is almost invisible from the thicket of oleander which covers its banks; while on the steeper sides, up either way, forests of oak and of evergreen oak merge into the darker pine. It was night in this solitude. Overhead shone the innumerable stars — once the pledge of the promise to Abraham. The impressive silence was only broken by the rushing of Jabbok, and the lowing of the flocks and herds, as they passed over the brook, or the preparations for transporting the women, children, and servants. Quite a large number of the cattle and sheep Jacob now sent forward in separate droves, that each, as it successively came to Esau as a gift from his brother, might tend to appease his feelings of anger, or satisfy the cupidity of his followers. At last they were all gone, each herdsman bearing a message of peace. The women also and children were safely camped on the south side of Jabbok. Only Jacob himself remained on the northern bank. It was a time for solitude — "and Jacob was left alone," quite alone, as when first he left his father's house. There on the oleander banks of Jabbok occurred what has ever since been of the deepest significance to the church of God. "There wrestled with him a man till the breaking of day." That "Man" was the Angel of Jehovah in Whom was His Presence. "And when He saw that He prevailed not against him, He touched the hollow of his thigh; and the hollow of Jacob's thigh was out of joint, as he wrestled with Him." The contest by wrestling must now have become impossible. But a far other contest ensued. "And He said, Let Me go, for the day breaketh. And he (Jacob) said, I will not let Thee go, except Thou bless me." Jacob had now recognized the character of his opponent and of the contest, and he sought quite another victory, and by quite other means than before. He no longer expected to prevail in his own strength. He asked to be blessed by Him with whom he had hitherto only wrestled, that so he might prevail. That blessing was given. But first the Lord brought before him what had been his old name as expressive of his old history — Jacob, "the cunning, self-helpful supplanter;" then He bestowed on him a new name, characteristic of his new experience and better contest by prayer: Israel, "a prince with God." In that new character would he have "power with God and men," and "prevail" against all enemies. But the mysterious name of the Angel he must not yet know; for "the mystery of godliness" was not to be fully revealed till all the purposes for which Jacob was to become Israel had been fulfilled. And now "He blessed him there." "And Jacob called the name of the place Peniel (the face of God): for I have seen God face to face, and my soul has recovered. And as he passed over Penuel the sun rose upon him, and he halted upon his thigh. Therefore the children of Israel eat not of the sinew which shrank, which is upon the hollow of the thigh, unto this day." And "to this day," literally, is this custom observed among "the children of Israel."

Now what was the meaning of this solemn transaction? Assuredly, it was symbolical — but of what? It was a real transaction, but symbolical of Jacob's past, present, and future. The "man" who wrestled with Jacob "until the breaking of day" was Jehovah. Jacob had, indeed, been the believing heir to the promises, but all his life long he had wrestled with God — sought to attain success in his own strength and by his own devices. Seeming to contend with man, he had really contended with God. And God had also contended with him. At last farther contest was impossible. Jacob had become disabled, for God had touched the hollow of his thigh. In the presence of Esau Jacob was helpless. But before he could encounter his most dreaded earthly enemy, he must encounter God, with Whom he had all along, though unwittingly, contended by his struggles and devices. The contest with Esau was nothing; the contest with Jehovah everything. The Lord could not be on Jacob's side, till he had been disabled, and learned to use other weapons than those of his own wrestling. Then it was that Jacob recognized with whom he had hitherto wrestled. Now he resorted to other weapons, even to prayer; and he sought and found another victory, even in the blessing of Jehovah and by His strength. Then also, truly at "the breaking of day," he obtained a new name, and with it new power, in which he prevailed with God and man. Jacob, indeed, "halted upon his thigh;" but he was now Israel, a prince with God. And still to all ages this contest and this victory, in despair of our own efforts, and in the persevering prayer, "I will not let Thee go except Thou bless me," have been and are a most precious symbol to the children of God. May we not also add, that as the prophet Hosea pointed to it as symbolical of Israel's history (Hosea 12:4), so it shall be fully realized when "they shall look upon Me Whom they have pierced, and they shall mourn?" (Zechariah 12:10)

As Jacob passed over Jabbok in the early morn, the glittering of spears and lances in the sunlight, among the dark pine forests, betokened the approach of Esau with his four hundred men. But Jacob had nothing more to fear: the only real contest was over. It was necessary, when Jacob returned to take possession of the land and of the promises, that all that was past in his history should be past — it was so! Never, after that night, did Jacob again contend with carnal weapons; and though the old name of Jacob reappears again and again by the side of his new designation, it was to remind both him and us that Jacob, though halting, is not dead, and that there is in us always the twofold nature, alike of Jacob and of Israel. What now followed we cannot tell better than in the words of a recent German writer: "Jacob, who in his contest with the Angel of Jehovah had prevailed by prayer and entreaty, now also prevails by humility and modesty against Esau, who comes to meet him with four hundred men." As already hinted, Esau had probably been just engaged in that warlike expedition to Mount Seir, which resulted in his conquest of the land, where he

93

afterwards settled. (Genesis 36:6, 7) This accounts for his appearance at the head of an armed band. Possibly, he may, at the same time, have wished to have the revenge of giving anxiety to his brother, and of showing him the contrast between their respective positions; or he may to the last have been undecided how to act towards his brother. At any rate, under the overruling guidance of God, and "overcome by the humility of Jacob, and by the kindliness of his own heart, Esau fell upon the neck of his brother, embraced and kissed him. With reluctance he accepted the rich presents of Jacob, and he offered to accompany him to the end of his journey with his armed men — a proposition which Jacob declined in a friendly spirit. Thus the two brothers, long separated in affection, were reconciled to each other. Their good understanding remained undisturbed till the day of their death."

There was nothing in Jacob's language to his brother which, when translated from Eastern to our Western modes of conduct and expression, is inconsistent with proper self-respect. If he declined the offer of an armed guard, it was because he felt he needed not an earthly host to protect him. Besides, it was manifestly impossible for cattle and tender children to keep up with a Bedouin warrior band. While Esau, therefore, returned to Mount Seir, there to await a visit from his brother, Jacob turned in a north-westerly direction to Succoth, a place still east of Jordan, and afterwards in the possession of the tribe of Gad. Here he probably made a lengthened stay, for we read that "he built him an house, and made booths for his cattle," whence also the name of Succoth, or "booths." At last Jacob once more crossed the Jordan, "and came in peace to the city of Shechem, which is in the land of Canaan." The words seem designedly chosen to indicate that God had amply fulfilled what Jacob had asked at Bethel: to "come again in peace." (Genesis 28:21) But great changes had taken place in the country. When Abram entered the land, and made this his first resting-place, there was no city there, and it was only "the place of Shechem." (Genesis 12:6) But now the district was all cultivated and possessed, and a city had been built, probably by "Hamor the Hivite," the father of Shechem, who called it after his son. (Comp. Genesis 4:17) From "the children of Hamor" Jacob bought the field on which he "spread his tent." This was "the portion" which Jacob afterwards gave to his son Joseph (Genesis 48:22), and here the "bones of Joseph, which the children of Israel brought out of Egypt," were, at least at one time, buried. (Joshua 24:32) Far more interesting than this, we know that by the well which Jacob there dug, sat, many centuries afterwards, "David's greater Son," to tell the poor sinning woman of Samaria concerning the "well of water springing up unto everlasting life" — the first non-Jewess blessed to taste the water of which "whosoever drinketh" "shall never thirst." (John 4:14) Here Jacob erected an altar, and called it El-elohe-Israel, "God, the God of Israel."

But his stay at Shechem was to prove a fresh source of trial to Jacob. Dinah, his daughter, at that time (as we gather) about fifteen years of age, in the language of the sacred text, "went out to see the daughters of the land," or, as Josephus, the Jewish historian, tells us, to take part in a feast of the Shechemites. A more terrible warning than that afforded by the results of her thoughtless and blameworthy participation in irreligious and even heathen festivities could scarcely be given. It led to the ruin of Dinah herself, then to a proposal of an alliance between the Hivites and Israel, to which Israel could not, of course, have agreed; and finally to vile deceit on the part of Simeon and Levi, for the purpose of exacting bloody revenge, by which the whole male population of Shechem were literally exterminated. How deeply the soul of Jacob recoiled from this piece of Eastern cruelty, appears from the fact, that even on his deathbed, many years afterwards, he reverted to it in these words: -

"Simeon and Levi are brethren;

Their swords are weapons of iniquity.
O my soul, come not thou into their council;
Unto their assembly, mine honor, be not thou united!" (Genesis 49:5, 6)

But one, though undesigned, consequence of the crime proved a further blessing to Jacob. It was quite clear that he and his family must remove from the scene of Simeon's and Levi's treachery and cruelty. Then it was that God directed Jacob to return to Beth-el, and fulfill the promise which he had there made on fleeing from the face of Esau his brother. About ten years must have elapsed since the return of Jacob from Mesopotamia, and yet he had not paid his vows unto the Lord! From what follows, we infer that, in all probability, the reason of this delay had been that the family of Jacob had not been purged from idolatry, and that hitherto Jacob had been too weak to remove from his household what must have rendered his appearance at Beth-el morally impossible. But now we read, that "he said unto his household, and to all that were with him, Put away the strange gods that are among you, and be clean, and change your garments" (this as a symbol of purification): "and let us arise, and go up to Bethel." And all the teraphim and idolatrous "charms" were buried deep down below a terebinth-tree "which was by Shechem." A touching incident is recorded immediately on their arrival at Beth-el. "Deborah, Rebekah's nurse, died, and she was buried beneath Beth-el, under an oak, and the name of it was called Allon-bachuth (the oak of weeping)." Thus Deborah's long and faithful service in the household of Isaac, and the family-mourning over the old, tried family friend, are deemed worthy of perpetual memorial in the Book of God! But from the circumstance that Deborah died in the house of Jacob, we infer not only that her mistress Rebekah was dead, but that there must have been some intercourse between Isaac and Jacob since his return to Canaan. Most probably Jacob had visited his aged parent, though Scripture does not mention it, because it in no way affects the history of the covenant. At Bethel God again appeared to Jacob; and while He once more bestowed on him the name of Israel and the covenant-promises previously given, Jacob also paid his vow unto the Lord, and on his part likewise renewed the designation of the place as Beth-el.

From Bethel they continued their journey towards Mamre, the place of Isaac's residence. On the way, some distance from Ephrath, "the fruitful," which in later times was called Bethlehem, "the house of bread," (Micah 5:2) Rachel died in giving birth to Jacob's twelfth son. His mother wished to call her child Ben-oni, "the son of my sorrow;" but his father named him Benjamin, which has been variously interpreted as meaning "son of the right hand," "son of days, i.e. of old age," and "son of happiness," because he completed the number of twelve sons. From Jeremiah 31:15, we gather that Rachel actually died in Ramah. "Jacob set a pillar upon her grave." As the oak, or rather the terebinth, of Deborah was still known at the time of the Judges, when Deborah's greater namesake dwelt under its shadow, "between Ramah and Bethel in Mount Ephraim," (Judges 4:5) so the pillar which marked Rachel's grave was a landmark at the time of Samuel. (1 Samuel 10:2, 3) Another crime yet stained the family of Jacob at Migdal Eder, "the watchtower of the flock," in consequence of which Reuben was deprived of the privileges of the firstborn. (Genesis 49:4) At last Jacob came to his journey's end, "unto Isaac his father, unto Mamre, unto the city of Arbah, which is Hebron, where Abraham and Isaac sojourned." Here Scripture pauses to record, by way of anticipation, the death of Isaac, at the age of one hundred and eighty years, although that event took place twelve years after Jacob's arrival at Hebron; and, indeed, Isaac had lived to share his son's sorrow, when Joseph was sold into Egypt, having only died ten years before Jacob and his sons settled in Egypt. But the course of sacred history has turned from Isaac, and, in fact, Jacob himself is now but a secondary actor in its events. The main interest henceforth centers in Joseph, the elder son of Rachel, with whose life the progress of sacred history is identified.

CHAPTER 19: JOSEPH'S EARLY LIFE — HE IS SOLD BY HIS BRETHREN INTO SLAVERY — JOSEPH IN THE HOUSE OF POTIPHAR — JOSEPH IN PRISON

(GENESIS 37-39)

FOR the proper understanding of what follows, it is necessary to bear in mind that what may be called the personal history of the patriarchs ceases with Jacob; or rather that it now merges into that of the children of Israel — of the family, and of the tribes. The purpose of God with the patriarchs as individuals had been fulfilled, when Jacob had become father of the twelve, who were in turn to be the ancestors of the chosen people. Hence the personal manifestations of God to individuals now also ceased. To this there is only a solitary exception, when the Lord appeared unto Jacob as he went into Egypt, to give him the needful assurance that by His will Israel removed from Canaan, and that in His own good time He would bring them back to the land of promise. By way of anticipation, it may be here stated that this temporary removal was in every respect necessary. It formed the fulfillment of God's prediction to Abram at the first making of the covenant (Genesis 15:12-17); and it was needful in order to separate the sons of Jacob from the people of the land. How readily constant contact with the Canaanites would have involved even the best of them in horrible vices appears from the history of Judah, when, after the selling of Joseph, he had left his father's house, and, joining himself to the people of the country, both he and his rapidly became conformed to the abominations around. (Genesis 38) It was necessary also as a preparation for the later history of Israel, when the Lord God would bring them out from their house of bondage by His outstretched arm, and with signs and wonders. As this grand event was to form the foundation and beginning of the history of Israel as a nation, so the servitude and the low estate which preceded it were typical, and that not only of the whole history of Israel, but of the Church itself, and of every individual believer also, whom God delivers from spiritual bondage by His mighty grace. Lastly, all the events connected with the removal into Egypt were needful for the training of the sons of Israel, and chiefly for that of Joseph, if he were to be fitted for the position which God intended him to occupy. Nor can we fail to recognize, that, although Joseph is not personally mentioned in the New Testament as a type of Christ, his history was eminently typical of that of our blessed Savior, alike in his betrayal, his elevation to highest dignity, and his preserving the life of his people, and in their ultimate recognition of him and repentance of their sin. Yet, though "known to God" were all these "His works from the beginning," all parties were allowed, in the free exercise of their own choice, to follow their course, ignorant that all the while they were only contributing their share towards the fulfillment of God's purposes. And in this lies the mystery of Divine Providence, that it always worketh wonders, yet without seeming to work at all — whence also it so often escapes the observation of men. Silently, and unobserved by those who live and act, it pursues its course, till in the end all things are seen "to work together" for the glory of God, and "for good to them that love God, that are the called according to His purpose."

The scriptural history of Joseph opens when he is seventeen years of age. Abundant glimpses into the life of the patriarchal family are afforded us. Joseph is seen engaged in pastoral occupations, as well as his brethren. But he is chiefly with the sons of Bilhah and Zilpah, the maids of Leah and Rachel. Manifestly also there is ill feeling and jealousy on the part of the sons of Leah towards the child of Rachel. This must have been fostered by the difference in their natural disposition, as well as by the preference which Jacob showed for the son of his beloved wife. The bearing of the sons of Jacob was rough, wild, and lawless, without any concern for their father's wishes or aims. On the other hand, Joseph seems to have united some of the best characteristics of his ancestors. Like Abraham, he was strong, decided, and prudent; like Isaac, patient and gentle; like Jacob, warmhearted and affectionate. Best of all, his conduct signally differed from that of his brethren. On the other hand, however, it is not difficult to perceive how even the promising qualities of his natural disposition might become sources of moral danger. Of this the history of Joseph's ancestors had afforded only too painful evidence. How much greater would be the peril to a youth exposed to such twofold temptation as rooted dislike on the part of brothers whom he could not respect, and marked favoritism on that of his father! The holy reticence of Scripture — which ever tells so little of man and so much of God — affords us only hints, but these are sufficiently significant. We read that "Joseph brought unto his father" the "evil report" of his brethren. That is one aspect of his domestic relations. Side by side with it is the other: "Now Israel loved Joseph more than all his children." Even if "the coat of many colors," which he gave to "the son of his old age," had been merely a costly or gaudy dress, it would have been an invidious mark of favoritism, such as too often raises bitter feelings in families. For, as time is made up of moments, so life mostly of small actions whose greatness lies in their combination. But in truth it was not a "coat of many colors," but a tunic reaching down to the arms and feet, such as princes and persons of distinction wore, and it betokened to Joseph's brothers only too clearly, that their father intended to transfer to Joseph the right of the first-born. We know that the three oldest sons of Leah had unfitted themselves for it — Simeon and Levi by their cruelty at Shechem, and Reuben by his crime at the "watch-tower of the flock." What more natural than to bestow the privilege on the first-born of her whom Jacob had intended to make his only wife? At any rate, the result was that "his brethren hated him," till, in the expressive language of the sacred text, "they could not get themselves to address him unto peace," that is, as we understand it, to address to him the usual Eastern salutation: "Peace be unto thee!"

It needed only an occasion to bring this state of feeling to an outbreak, and that came only too soon. It seems quite natural that, placed in the circumstances we have described, Joseph should have dreamt two dreams implying his future supremacy. We say this, even while we recognize in them a distinct Divine direction. Yet Scripture does not say, either, that these dreams were sent him as a direct communication from God, or that he was directed to tell them to his family. The imagery of the first of these dreams was taken from the rustic, that of the second from the pastoral life of the family. In the first dream Joseph and his brothers were in the harvest-field — which seems to imply that Jacob, like his father Isaac, had tilled the ground — and Joseph's sheaf stood upright, while those of his brothers made obeisance. In the second dream they were all out tending the flock, when the sun and moon and the eleven stars made obeisance to Joseph. The first of these dreams was related only unto his brethren, the second both to his father and to his brothers. There must have been something peculiarly offensive in the manner in which he told his dreams, for we read not only that they hated him yet the more for his dreams," but also "for his words." Even Jacob saw reason to reprove him, although it is significantly added that he observed the saying. As we now know it, they were prophetic dreams; but, at the time, there were no means of judging whether they were so or not, especially as Joseph had so "worded" them, that they might seem to be merely the effect of vanity in a youth whom favoritism had unduly elated. The future could alone show this; but, meantime, may we not say that it was needful for the sake of Joseph himself that he should be removed from his present circumstances to where that which was holy and divine in him would grow, and all of self be uprooted? But such results are only obtained by one kind of training — that of affliction.

The sons of Jacob were pasturing their flocks around Shechem, when the patriarch sent Joseph to inquire of their welfare. All unconscious of danger the lad hastened to execute the commission. Joseph found not his brethren at Shechem itself, but a stranger directed him to "Dothan," the two wells, whither they had gone. "Dothan was beautifully situated, about twelve miles from Samaria. Northwards spread richest pasture-lands; a few swelling hills separated it from the great plain of Esdraelon. From its position it must have been the key to the passes of Esdraelon, and so, as guarding the entrance from the north, not only of Ephraim, but of Palestine itself. On the crest of one of those hills the extensive ruins of Dothan are still pointed out, and at its southern foot still wells up a fine spring of living water. Is this one of the two wells from which Dothan derived its name? From these hills Gideon afterwards descended upon the host of Midian. It was here that Joseph overtook his brethren, and was cast into the dry well. And it was from that height that the sons of Jacob must have seen the Arab caravan slowly winding from Jordan on its way to Egypt, when they sold their brother, in the vain hope of binding the word and arresting the hand of God."

But we are anticipating. No sooner did his brothers descry Joseph in the distance, than the murderous plan of getting rid of him, where no stranger should witness their deed, occurred to their minds. This would be the readiest means of disposing alike of "the dreamer" and of his "dreams." Reuben alone shrunk from it, not so much from love to his brother as from consideration for his father. On pretense that it would be better not actually to shed their brother's blood, he proposed to cast him into one of those cisterns, and leave him there to perish, hoping, however, himself secretly to rescue and to restore him to his father. The others readily acceded to the plan. A Greek writer has left us a graphic account of such wells and cisterns. He describes them as regularly built and plastered, narrow at the mouth, but widening as they descend, till at the bottom they attain a width sometimes of one hundred feet. We know that when dry, or covered with only mud at the bottom, they served as hiding-places, and even as temporary prisons. (Jeremiah 38:6; Isaiah 24:22) Into such an empty well Joseph was now cast, while his brothers, as if they had finished some work, sat down to their meal. We had almost written, that it so happened — but truly it was in the providence of God, that just then an Arab caravan was slowly coming in sight. They were pursuing what we might call the world-old route from the spice district of Gilead into Egypt — across Jordan, below the Sea of Galilee, over the plain of Jezreel, and thence along the sea-shore. Once more the intended kindness of another of his brothers well-nigh proved fatal to Joseph. Reuben had diverted their purpose of bloodshed by proposing to cast Joseph into "the pit," in the hope of being able afterwards to rescue him. Judah now wished to save his life by selling him as a slave to the passing Arab caravan. But neither of them had the courage nor the uprightness frankly to resist the treachery and the crime. Again the other brothers hearkened to what seemed a merciful suggestion. The bargain was quickly struck. Joseph was sold to "the Ishmaelites" for twenty shekels — the price, in later times, of a male slave from five to twenty years old (Leviticus 27:5), the medium price of a slave being thirty shekels of silver, or about four pounds, reckoning the shekel of the sanctuary, which was twice the common shekel (Exodus 21:32), at two shillings and eight-pence. Reuben was not present when the sale was made. On his return he "rent his clothes" in impotent mourning. But the others dipped Joseph's princely raiment in the blood of a kid, to give their father the impression that Joseph had been "devoured by a wild beast." The device succeeded. Jacob mourned him bitterly and "for many days," refusing all the comfort which his sons and daughters hypocritically offered. But even his bitterest lamentation expressed the hope and faith that he would meet his loved son in another world — for, he said: "I will go down into the grave (or into Sheol) unto my son, mourning."

Except by an incidental reference to it in the later confession of his brothers (Genesis 42:21), we are not told either of the tears or the entreaties with which Joseph vainly sought to move his brethren, nor of his journey into Egypt. We know that when following in the caravan of his new masters, he must have seen at a distance the heights of his own Hebron, where, all unsuspecting, his father awaited the return of his favorite. To that home he was never again to return. We meet him next in the slave-market. Here, as it might seem in the natural course of events, "Potiphar, an officer of Pharaoh, captain of the guard, an Egyptian, bought him off the hands of the Ishmaelites." The name Potiphar frequently occurs on the monuments of Egypt (written either Pet-Pa-Ra, or Pet-P-Ra), and means: "Dedicated to Ra," or the sun. According to some writers, "at the time that Joseph was sold into Egypt, the country was not united under the rule of a single native line, but governed by several dynasties, of which the fifteenth dynasty of Shepherd-kings was the predominant one, the rest being tributary to it." At any rate, he would be carried into that part of Egypt which was always most connected with Palestine. Potiphar's office at the court of Pharaoh was that of "chief of the executioners," most probably (as it is rendered in our Authorized Version) captain of the king's body-guard. In the house of Potiphar it went with Joseph as formerly in his own home. For it is not in the power of circumstances, prosperous or adverse, to alter our characters. He that is faithful in little shall also be faithful in much; and from him who knoweth not how to employ what is committed to his charge, shall be taken even that he hath. Joseph was faithful, honest, upright, and conscientious, because in his earthly, he served a heavenly Master, Whose presence he always realized. Accordingly "Jehovah was with him," and "Jehovah made all that he did to prosper in his hand." His master was not long in observing this. From an ordinary domestic slave he promoted him to be "overseer over his house, and all that he had he put into his hand." The confidence was not misplaced. Jehovah's blessing henceforth rested upon Potiphar's substance, and he "left all that he had in Joseph's hand; and he knew not ought that he had, save the bread which he did eat." The sculptures and paintings of the ancient Egyptian tombs bring vividly before us the daily life and duties of Joseph. "The property of great men is shown to have been managed by scribes, who exercised a most methodical and minute supervision over all the operations of agriculture, gardening, the keeping of live stock, and fishing. Every product was carefully registered, to check the dishonesty of the laborers, who in Egypt have always been famous in this respect. Probably in no country was farming ever more systematic. Joseph's previous knowledge of tending flocks, and perhaps of husbandry, and his truthful character, exactly fitted him for the post of overseer. How long he filled it we are not told."

It is a common mistake to suppose that earnest religion and uprightness must necessarily be attended by success, even in this world. It is, indeed, true that God will not withhold any good thing from those whose Sun and Shield He is; but then success may not always be a good thing for them. Besides, God often tries the faith and patience of His people — and that is the meaning of many trials. Still oftener are they needed for discipline and training, or that they may learn to glorify God in their sufferings. In the case of Joseph it was both a temptation and a trial by which he was prepared, outwardly and inwardly, for the position he was to occupy. The beauty which Joseph had inherited from his mother exposed him to wicked suggestions on the part of his master's wife, which will surprise those least who are best acquainted with the state of ancient Egyptian society. Joseph stood quite alone in a heathen land and house. He was surrounded only by what would blunt his moral sense, and render the temptation all the more powerful. He had also, as compared with us, a very imperfect knowledge of the law of God in its height and depth. Moreover, what he had seen of his older brothers would not have elevated his views. Still, he firmly resisted evil, alike from a sense of integrity towards his master, and, above all, from dread "of this great wickedness and sin against God." Yet it seemed only to fare the worse with him for his principles. As so often, the violent passion of the woman turned into equally violent hatred, and she maliciously concocted a false charge against him. We have reason to believe that Potiphar could not in every respect have credited the story of his wife. For the punishment awarded in Egypt to the crime of which she accused him, was far more severe than that which Joseph received. Potiphar consigned him to the king's prison, of which, in his capacity as chief of the body-guard, he was the superintendent. How bitterly it fared there with him at the first, we learn from these words of Psalm 105:17,18 -

"He sent before them a man:
Sold for a slave was Joseph,
They afflicted with fetters his feet,
The iron entered into his soul."

The contrast could scarcely be greater than between his former prophetic dreams and his present condition. But even so Joseph remained steadfast. And, as if to set before us the other contrast between sight and faith, the sacred text expressly states it: "But" — a word on which our faith should often lay emphasis — "Jehovah was with Joseph, and showed him mercy, and gave him favor in the sight of the keeper of the prison." By-and-by, as his integrity more and more appeared, the charge of the prisoners was committed unto him; and as "what he did Jehovah made to prosper," the whole management of the prison ultimately passed into Joseph's hands. Thus, here also Jehovah proved Himself a faithful covenant-God. A silver streak was lining the dark cloud. But still must "patience have her perfect work."

CHAPTER 20: JOSEPH IN PRISON — THE DREAM OF PHARAOH'S TWO OFFICERS — THE DREAM OF PHARAOH — JOSEPH'S EXALTATION — HIS GOVERNMENT OF EGYPT
(GENESIS 40, 41; 47:13-26)

ELEVEN years had passed since Joseph was sold into Egypt, and yet the Divine promise, conveyed in his dreams, seemed farther than ever from fulfillment. The greater part of this weary time had probably been spent in prison, without other prospect than that of such indulgence as his services to "the keeper of the prison" might insure, when an event occurred which, for a brief season, promised a change in Joseph's condition. Some kind of "offense" — real or imaginary — had, as is so often the case in the East, led to the sudden disgrace and imprisonment of two of Pharaoh's chief officers. The charge of "the chief of the butlers" — or chief of the cupbearers — and of "the chief of the bakers" naturally devolved upon "the captain of the guard," — a successor, as we imagine, of Potiphar, since he appointed Joseph to the responsible post of their personal attendant. They had not been long in prison when, by the direct leading of Divine Providence, both dreamed in the same night a dream, calculated deeply to impress them. By the same direct guidance of Providence, Joseph was led to notice in the morning their anxiety, and to inquire into its cause. We regard it as directly from God, that he could give them at once and unhesitatingly the true meaning of their dreams.

We are specially struck in this respect with the manner in which Joseph himself viewed it. When he found them in distress for want of such "interpreter" as they might have consulted if free, he pointed them straight to God: "Do not interpretations belong to God?" thus encouraging them to tell, and at the same time preparing himself for reading their dreams, by casting all in faith upon God. In short, whether or not he were eventually enabled to understand their dreams, he would at least not appear like the Egyptian magicians — he would not claim power or wisdom; he would own God, and look up to Him.

We say it the more confidently, that Joseph's interpretation came to him directly from God, that it seems so easy and so rational. For, it is in the supernatural direction of things natural that we ought most to recognize the direct interposition of the Lord. The dreams were quite natural, and the interpretation was quite natural — yet both were directly of God. What more natural than for the chief butler and the chief baker, three nights before Pharaoh's birthday, on which, as they knew, he always "made a feast unto all his servants," to dream that they were each again at his post? And what more natural than that on such an occasion Pharaoh should consider, whether for good or for evil, the case of his absent imprisoned officers? Or, lastly, what more natural than that the chief butler's consciousness of innocence should suggest in his dream that he once more waited upon his royal master; while the guilty conscience of the chief baker saw only birds of prey eating out of the basket from which he had hitherto supplied his master's table?

Here, then, it may be said, we have all the elements of Joseph's interpretation to hand, just as we shall see they were equally obvious in the dreams which afterwards troubled Pharaoh. Yet as then none of the magicians and wise men of Egypt could read what, when once stated, seems so plainly written, so here all seems involved in perplexity till God gives light.

As already stated, the two dreams were substantially the same. In each case the number three, whether of clusters in the vine from which the chief butler pressed the rich juice into Pharaoh's cup, or of baskets in which the chief baker carried the king's bakemeat, pointed to the three days intervening before Pharaoh's birthday. In each case also their dreams transported them back to their original position before any charge had been brought against them, the difference lying in this: that, in the one dream, Pharaoh accepted the functions of his officer; while, in the other, birds which hover about carcasses ate out of the basket. It is also quite natural that, if the chief butler had a good conscience towards his master, he should have been quite ready at the first to tell his dream; while the chief baker, conscious of guilt, only related his when encouraged by the apparently favorable interpretation of his colleague's. Perhaps we ought also to notice, in evidence of the truthfulness of the narrative, how thoroughly Egyptian in all minute details is the imagery of these dreams. From the monuments the growth and use of the vine in Egypt, which had been denied by former opponents of the Bible, have been abundantly proved. From the same source we also learn that bakery and confectionery were carried to great perfection in Egypt, so that we can understand such an office as a royal chief baker. Even the bearing of the baskets furnishes a characteristic trait: as in Egypt men carried loads on their heads, and women on their shoulders.

The event proved the correctness of Joseph's interpretation. On Pharaoh's birthday-feast, three days after their dreams, the chief butler was restored to his office, but the chief baker was executed. When interpreting his dream, Joseph had requested that, on the chief butler's restoration, he, who had himself suffered from a wrongful charge, should think on him, who, at first "stolen away out of the land of the Hebrews," had so long been unjustly kept in apparently hopeless confinement. This wording of Joseph's petition seems to indicate that, at most, he only hoped to obtain liberty; and that probably he intended to return to his father's house. So ignorant was he as yet of God's further designs with him! But what was a poor Hebrew slave in prison to a proud Egyptian court official? It is only like human nature that, in the day of his prosperity, "the chief butler did not remember Joseph, but forgot him!"

Two other years now passed in prison — probably more dreary and, humanly speaking, more hopeless than those which had preceded. At length deliverance came, suddenly and unexpectedly. This time it was Pharaoh who dreamed successively two dreams. In the first, seven fat kine were feeding among the rich "marsh-grass" on the banks "of the Nile." But presently up came from "the river" seven lean kine, which devoured the well-favored, without, however, fattening by them. The second dream showed one stalk of corn with seven ears, "full and good," when up sprang beside it another stalk, also with seven ears, but "blasted with the east wind;" "and the thin ears devoured the seven good ears." So vivid had been the dream that it seemed to Pharaoh like reality — "and Pharaoh awoke, and, behold, it was a dream." Only a dream! and yet the impression of its reality still haunted him, so that he sent for "the magicians of Egypt, and all the wise men thereof" to interpret his dreams. But these sages were unable to suggest any explanation satisfactory to the mind of Pharaoh; for we can scarcely believe that they did not attempt some interpretation. In this perplexity, his memory quickened by Oriental terror at his master's disappointment, the chief of the cup-bearers suddenly remembered his own and the chief baker's dreams just two years before, and Joseph's interpretation of them. The event becomes all the more striking and also natural if we may take the date literally as "at the end of two full years," or on the third anniversary of that birthday of Pharaoh.

Before proceeding, we notice some of the particulars which give the narrative its vivid coloring, and at the same time wonderfully illustrate its historical truthfulness. And, first of all, we again mark the distinctly Egyptian character of all. The "river" is "the Nile," the sacred stream of Egypt, on which its fertility depended — and Pharaoh stands on its banks. Then the term which we have rendered "marsh-grass," or "reed-grass," is certainly an Egyptian word for which there is no Hebrew equivalent, because that to which it applied was peculiar to the banks of the Nile. Next, the whole complexion of the dreams is Egyptian, as we shall presently show. Moreover, it is remarkable how closely recent independent inquiries have confirmed the scriptural expressions about "the magicians" and "the wise men" of Egypt. It has been always known that there was a special priestly caste in Egypt, to whom not only the religion but the science of the country was entrusted. But of late we have learned a great deal more than this. We know not only that magic formed part and parcel of the religion of Egypt, but we have actually restored to us their ancient magical Ritual itself! We know their incantations and their amulets, with a special reference to the dead; their belief in lucky and unlucky days and events, and even in the so-called "evil eye." But what is most to our present purpose, we know that the care of the magical books was entrusted to two classes of learned men, whose titles exactly correspond to what, for want of better designation, is rendered as "magicians," or perhaps "scribes," and "wise men!" It was before this assemblage, then, of the wisest and most learned, the most experienced in "magic," and the most venerable in the priesthood, that Pharaoh vainly related his dreams. Most wise truly in this world, yet most foolish; most learned, yet most ignorant! What a contrast between the hoary lore of Egypt and the poor Hebrew slave fetched from prison: they professedly claiming, besides their real knowledge, supernatural powers; he avowedly, and at the outset, disclaiming all power on his part, and appealing to God! A grander scene than this Scripture itself does not sketch; and what an illustration of what was true then, true in the days of our Lord, true in those of St. Paul, and to the end of this dispensation: "Where is the wise? where is the scribe? where is the disputer of this world? Hath not God made foolish the wisdom of this world?"

And yet when we hear the interpretation through the lips of Joseph, how simple, nay, how obvious does it appear, quite commanding Pharaoh's implicit conviction. Clearly, the two dreams are one — the first bearing on the pastoral, the other on the agricultural life of Egypt. The dreams are about the flocks and the crops. In both cases there is first sevenfold fatness, and then sevenfold leanness, such as to swallow up the previous fatness, and yet to leave no trace of it. The second dream illustrates the first; and yet the first bears already its own interpretation. For the kine were in Egypt reverenced as symbol of Isis, the goddess of earth as the nourisher; and in the hieroglyphics the cow is taken to mean earth, agriculture, and nourishment. And then these kine were feeding by the banks of that Nile, on whose inundations it solely depended whether the year was to be one of fruitfulness or of famine. Equally Egyptian is the description of the stalk with many ears, which is just one of the kinds of wheat still grown in Egypt. But, we repeat it, obvious as all this now seems to us, the wise men of Egypt stood speechless before their monarch! And what a testimony, we again say, for God, when Joseph is "brought hastily out of the dungeon!" To the challenge of Pharaoh: "I have heard of thee, to wit: Thou hearest a dream to interpret it" — that is, thou only requirest to hear, in order to interpret a dream, — he answers, simply, emphatically, but believingly: "Ah, not I" ("not to me," "it does not belong to me"), "God will answer the peace of Pharaoh;" i.e., what is for the peace of the king. Nor can we omit to notice one more illustration of the accuracy of the whole narrative, when we read that, in preparation for his appearance before Pharaoh, Joseph "shaved himself." This we know from the monuments was peculiarly Egyptian under such circumstances; whereas among the Hebrews, for example, shaving was regarded as a mark of disgrace.

The interpretation, so modestly yet so decidedly given by Joseph, that the dreams pointed to seven years of unprecedented fruitfulness followed by an equal number of famine, so grievous that the previous plenty should not be known, approved itself immediately to the mind of Pharaoh and "of all his servants." With this interpretation Joseph had coupled most sagacious advice, for the source of which, in so trying a moment, we must look far higher than the ingenuity of man. (See Matthew 10:18, 19) He counseled the king to exact in the years of plenty a tax of one-fifth of the produce of the land, and to have it stored under royal supervision against the seven years of famine. Viewed as an impost, this was certainly not heavy, considering that they were years of unexampled plenty; viewed as a fiscal measure, it was most beneficial as compared with what we may suppose to have been previously a mere arbitrary system of taxation, which in reality was tyrannical exaction; while at the same time it would preserve the people from absolute destruction. Lastly, regarded in the light of a higher arrangement, it is very remarkable that this proportion of giving, on the part of Pharaoh's subjects, afterwards became the basis of that demanded from Israel by Jehovah, their heavenly King. We can scarcely wonder that Pharaoh should have at once appointed such a council or to superintend the arrangements he had proposed. In point of fact he naturalized him, made him his grand vizier, and publicly proclaimed him "ruler over all the land." Once more every trait in the description is purely Egyptian. Pharaoh gives him his signet, which "was of so much importance with the ancient Egyptian kings, that their names were always enclosed in an oval which represented an elongated signet." He arrays him "in vestures of byssus," the noble and also the priestly dress; he puts the chain, or "the collar of gold"# "about his neck," which was always the mode of investiture of high Egyptian officials; he makes him ride "in the second chariot which he had," and he has it proclaimed before him: "Avrech," that is, "fall down," "bend the knee," or "do obeisance." To complete all, on his naturalization Joseph's name is changed to Zaphnath-paaneah, which most probably means "the supporter of life," or else "the food of the living," although others have rendered it "the savior of the world," and the Rabbis, but without sufficient reason, "the revealer of secrets." Finally, in order to give him a position among the highest nobles of the land, Pharaoh "gave him to wife Asenath" (probably "she who is of Neith," the Egyptian goddess of wisdom), "the daughter of Poti-pherah ("dedicated to the sun"), priest of On," that is, the chief priest of the ancient ecclesiastical, literary, and probably also political capital of the land, "the City of the Sun." This is the more noteworthy, as the chief of the priesthood was generally chosen from among the nearest relatives of Pharaoh. Yet in all this story there is really nothing extraordinary. As Egypt depends for its produce entirely on the waters of the Nile, the country has at all times been exposed to terrible famines; and one which lasted for exactly seven years is recorded in A.D. 1064-1071, the horrors of which show us the wisdom of Joseph's precautionary measures. Again, so far as the sudden elevation of Joseph is concerned, Eastern history contains many such instances, and indeed, a Greek historian tells us of an Egyptian king who made the son of a mason his own son-in-law, because he judged him the cleverest man in the land. What is remarkable is the marvelous Divine appointment in all this, and the equally marvelous Divine choice of means to bring it about.

Joseph was exactly thirty years old on his elevation, the same age, we note, on which our blessed Lord entered on His ministry as "the Savior of the world," "the Supporter of life," and "the Revealer of secrets." The history of Joseph's administration may be traced in a few sentences. During the seven years of plenty, "he gathered corn as the sand of the sea, very much, until he left numbering," a notice which remarkably agrees with "the representations of the monuments, which show that the contents of the granaries were accurately noted by scribes when they were filled." Then, during the years of famine, he first sold corn to the people for money. When all their money was exhausted, they proposed of their own accord to part with their cattle to Pharaoh, and lastly with their land. In the latter case exception was made in favor of the priestly caste, who derived their support directly from Pharaoh. Thus Pharaoh became absolute possessor of all the money, all the cattle, and all the land of Egypt, and that at the people's own request. This advantage would be the greater, if there had been any tendency to dissatisfaction against the reigning house as an alien race. Nor did Joseph abuse the power thus acquired. On the contrary, by a spontaneous act of royal generosity he restored the land to the people on condition of their henceforth paying one-fifth of the produce in lieu of all other taxation. Besides the considerations already stated in favor of such a measure, it must be borne in mind that in Egypt, where all produce depends on the waters of the Nile, a system of canals and irrigation, necessarily kept up at the expense of the State, would be a public necessity. But the statement of Scripture, which excepts from this measure of public taxation "the land of the priests only, which became not Pharaoh's," remarkably tallies with the account of secular historians.

Two things here stand out in the history of Joseph. The same gracious Hand of the Lord, which, during his humiliation, had kept him from sin, disbelief, and despair, now preserved him in his exaltation from pride, and from lapsing into heathenism, to which his close connection with the chief priest of Egypt might easily have led him. More than that, he considered himself "a stranger and a pilgrim" in Egypt. His heart was in his father's home, with his father's God, and on his father's promises. Of both these facts there is abundant evidence. His Egyptian wife bore him two sons "before the years of famine came." He gave to both of them Hebrew, not Egyptian names. By the first, Manasseh, or "he that maketh forget," he wished to own the goodness of God, who had made him forget his past sorrow and toil. By the second, Ephraim, or "double fruitfulness," he distinctly recognized that, although Egypt was the land in which God had caused him "to be fruitful," it was still, and must ever be, not the land of his joy but that of his "affliction!" If it be asked why, in his prosperity, Joseph had not informed his father of his life and success, we answer, that in such a history safety lay in quiet waiting upon God. If Joseph had learned the great lesson of his life, it was this, that all in the past had been of God. Nor would He now interfere with further guidance on His part. The Lord would show the way, and lead to the end. But as for him, he believed, and therefore made no haste. Thus would God be glorified, and thus also would Joseph be kept in perfect peace, because he trusted in Him.

CHAPTER 21: THE SONS OF JACOB ARRIVE IN EGYPT TO BUY CORN — JOSEPH RECOGNIZES HIS BROTHERS — IMPRISONMENT OF SIMEON — THE SONS OF JACOB COME A SECOND TIME, BRINGING BENJAMIN WITH THEM — JOSEPH TRIES HIS BRETHREN — HE MAKES HIMSELF KNOWN TO THEM — JACOB AND HIS FAMILY PREPARE TO DESCEND INTO EGYPT

(GENESIS 42-45)

WE are now approaching a decisive period in the history of the house of Israel. Yet once again everything seems to happen quite naturally, while in reality everything is supernatural. The same causes which led to a diminution of rain in the Abyssinian mountains, and with it of the waters of the Nile, brought drought and famine to Palestine. It is quite in character that, in such straits, the wild, lawless sons of Jacob should have stood helplessly despondent, while the energies of their father were correspondingly roused. "Why do ye look one upon another? . . . I have heard that there is corn in Egypt: get you down thither, and buy for us from thence." The ten sons of Jacob now departed on this errand. But Benjamin, who had taken the place of Joseph in his father's heart, was not sent with them, perhaps from real fear of "mischief" by the way, possibly because his father did not quite trust the honest intentions of his sons. The next scene presents to us the Hebrew strangers among a motley crowd of natives and foreigners, who had come for corn; while Joseph, in all the state of the highest Egyptian official, superintends the sale. In true Eastern fashion the sons of Jacob make lowest obeisance before "the governor over the land." Of course they could not have recognized in him, who looked, dressed, and spoke as an Egyptian noble, the lad who, more than twenty years before, had, in "the anguish of his soul," "besought" them not to sell him into slavery. The same transformation had not taken place in them, and Joseph at once knew the well-remembered features of his brethren. But what a change in their relative positions! As he saw them bending lowly before him, his former dreams came vividly back to him. Surely, one even much less devout than Joseph would, in that moment, have felt that a Divine Hand had guided the past for a Divine purpose. Personal resentment or pique could not have entered into his mind at such a time. If, therefore, as some have thought, severity towards his brethren partially determined his conduct, this must have been quite a subordinate motive. At any rate, it is impossible to suppose that he cherished any longer feelings of anger, when shortly afterwards, on their expression of deep penitence, "he turned himself about from them and wept." But we prefer regarding Joseph's conduct as consistent throughout. The appearance of his brothers before him seemed to imply that God had not meant to separate him from his family, nor yet that he should return to them, but that they should come to him, and that he had been sent before to keep them alive. But for such a re-union of the family it was manifestly needful, that their hearts and minds should have undergone an entire change from that unscrupulous envy which had prompted them to sell him into slavery. This must be ascertained before he made himself known to them. Moreover, its reality must be tested by the severest trial to which their altered feelings could be subjected.

Thus viewing it, we can understand the whole conduct of Joseph. Of course, his first object would be to separate the sons of Jacob from the crowd of other purchasers, so as to deal specially with them, without, however, awakening their suspicions; his next to ascertain the state of matters at home. Then he would make them taste undeserved sorrow by the exercise of an arbitrary power, against which they would be helpless — even as Joseph had been in their hands. Thus they might see their past sin in their present sorrow. All these objects were attained by one and the same means. Joseph charged them with being spies, who, on pretense of buying corn, had come to find out the defenseless portions of the land. The accusation was not unreasonable in the then state of Egypt, nor uncommon in Eastern countries. It was not only that this afforded a pretext for dealing separately with them, but their answer to the charge would inform Joseph about the circumstances of his family. For, naturally, they would not only protest their innocence, but show the inherent improbability of such an imputation. Here no argument could be more telling than that they were "all one man's sons," since no one would risk the lives of all his children in so dangerous a business. But this was not enough for Joseph. By reiterating the charge, he led them to enter into further details, from which he learned that both his father and Benjamin were alive. Still their reference to himself as one "who is not," seemed to imply persistence in their former deceit, and must have strengthened his doubts as to their state of mind. But now experience of violence would show them not only their past guilt, but that, however God might seem to delay, He was the avenger of all wrong. More than that, if Benjamin were placed relatively to them in the same circumstances of favoritism as Joseph had been; and if, instead of envying and hating him, they were prepared, even when exposed through him to shame and danger, not only to stand by him, but to suffer in his stead, then they had repented in the truest sense, and their state of mind was the opposite of what it had been twenty years ago. Proceeding on this plan, Joseph first imprisoned all the ten, proposing to release one of their number to fetch Benjamin, in order to test, as he said, the truthfulness of their statements.

This excessive harshness was probably intended to strike terror into their hearts; and, at the end of three days, he so far relented as to retain only one of their number as a hostage; at the same time encouraging them both by the statement that, in so doing, his motive was "fear of God," and by the assurance that, once satisfied of their innocence, he cherished no evil design against them. The reference to "fear of God" on the part of an Egyptian, and this apparent shrinking from needless rigor, must have cut them to the heart, as it brought out in contrast their own implacable conduct towards Joseph. Simeon was chosen to remain behind as hostage, because he was the next oldest to Reuben, who was not detained, since he had endeavored to save the life of Joseph. This also must have contributed to remind them of their former wrong; and, for the first time, they avow to one another their bitter guilt in the past, and how God was now visiting it. So poignant were their feelings that, in the presence of Joseph, they spoke of it, in their own Hebrew, ignorant that Joseph, who had conversed with them through an interpreter, understood their words. Joseph was obliged hastily to withdraw, so as not to betray himself; but he wavered not in his purpose. Simeon was bound before their eyes, and the rest were dismissed; but each with ample provender for the journey, besides the corn they had bought, and with the purchase-money secretly restored to them.

The terror with which the unexpected turn of events had inspired them was deepened when, at their first night's quarters, one of them discovered the money in his sack. But, as before, the impression was wholesome. They traced in this also the avenging hand of God: "What is this that God hath done unto us?"

The narrative which, on their return, they had to tell their father was sufficiently sad. But the discovery they now made, that the money which they had paid had been secretly put back into each man's sack, seemed to imply some deep design of mischief, and filled Jacob and his sons with fresh fears. If the condition of their again appearing before the ruler of Egypt was, that they must bring Benjamin with them, then he, who had already lost two sons, would refuse to expose to such a risk his darling, the last remaining pledge of his Rachel. Reuben, indeed, volunteered the strange guarantee of his own two sons: "Slay my two sons, if I bring him not to thee." But this language was little calculated to reassure the heart of Jacob. For a time it seemed as if Jacob's former sorrow was to be increased by the loss of Simeon, and as if Joseph and his family were never again to meet.

If we ask ourselves why Joseph should have risked this, or added to his father's sorrow, we answer, to the first question, that, since Joseph now knew the circumstances of his family, and had Simeon beside him, he could at any time, on need for it appearing, have communicated with his father. As to the second difficulty, we must all feel that this grief and care could not be spared to his father if his brothers were to be tried, proved, and prepared for their mission. And did it not seem as if Joseph had rightly understood the will of God in this matter, since the heart of his brethren had been at once touched to own their past sin and the Hand of God?

Could he not then still further commit himself to God in well-doing, and trust Him? Nay, could he not also trust Jacob's faith to bear up under this trial? At most it would be short, and how blessed to all the fruits expected from it! Once more the event proved the correctness of his views. As the stock of provisions, which the sons of Jacob had brought, became nearly exhausted, a fresh application to the royal granaries of Egypt was absolutely necessary. This time it was Judah who offered himself in surety for Benjamin. His language was so calm, affectionate, and yet firm, as to inspire Jacob with what confidence can be derived from the earnest, good purpose of a true man. But he had higher consolation — that of prayer and faith: "God Almighty give you mercy before the man, that he may send away your other brother, and Benjamin." Yet, even if God had otherwise appointed, — if He saw fit to take from him his children, his faith would rise to this also: "And I, if I am bereaved, I am bereaved!" — good is the will of the Lord, and he would bow before it.

It is touching, as it were, to watch the trembling hands of the old man as he makes feeble attempts to ward off the wrath of the dreaded Egyptian. It was a famine-year, and, naturally, there would be scarcity of the luxuries which were usually exported from the East to Egypt. Let them, then, take a present of such dainties to the Egyptian — "a little balm, and a little honey, spices, and myrrh, nuts, and almonds." As for the money which had been put back into their sacks, it might have been an oversight. Let them take it again with them, along with the price of what corn they were now to purchase. And so let them go forth in the name of the God of Israel — Benjamin, and all the rest. He would remain behind alone, as at the fords of Jabbok, — no, not alone; but in faith and patience awaiting the issue. Presently the ten brothers, with more anxious hearts than Joseph ever had on his way to Egypt or in the slave-market, are once more in the dreaded presence of the Egyptian. Joseph saw the new-comers, and with them what he judged to be his youngest brother, whom he had left in his home a child only a year old. Manifestly, it was neither the time nor the place to trust himself to converse with them. So he gave his steward orders to take them to his house, and that they should dine with him at noon. Joseph had spoken in Egyptian, which seems to have been unknown to the sons of Jacob. When they saw themselves brought to the house of Joseph, it immediately occurred to them that they were to be charged with theft of the former purchase-money. But the steward with kindly words allayed the fears which made them hesitate before entering "at the door of the house."

The sight of Simeon, who was at once restored to them, must have increased their confidence. Presently preparations were made for the banquet. It was a deeply trying scene for Joseph which ensued when he met his brethren on his return home. Little could they imagine what thoughts passed through his mind, as in true Oriental fashion they laid out the humble presents his father had sent, and lowly "bowed themselves to him to the earth." His language ill concealed his feelings. Again and again he inquired for his father, and as they replied: "Thy servant our father is in good health; he is yet alive," they again "bowed clown their heads, and made obeisance." But when he fastened his eyes on Benjamin, his own mother's son, and had faltered it out, so unlike an Egyptian: "God be gracious unto thee, my son," he was obliged hastily to withdraw, "for his bowels did yearn upon his brother." Twenty-two years had passed since he had been parted from his brother, and Benjamin now stood before him — a youth little older than he when his bitter bondage in prison had commenced. Would they who had once sacrificed him on account of jealousy, be ready again to abandon his brother for the sake of selfishness? At the banquet a fresh surprise awaited the sons of Jacob. Of course, after the Egyptian fashion, Joseph ate by himself, and the Egyptians by themselves; he as a member of the highest caste, and they from religious scruples. We know from secular history that the Egyptians abstained from certain kinds of meat, and would not eat with the knives and forks, nor from the cooking utensils which had been used by those of any other nation. But it must have seemed unaccountable, that at the banquet their places were arranged exactly according to their ages. How could the Egyptian have known them, and what mysterious circumstances surrounded them in his presence? Yet another thing must have struck them. In their father's house the youngest of their number, the son of Rachel, had been uniformly preferred before them all. And now it was the same in the Egyptian palace! If the Egyptian ruler "sent messes unto them from before him," "Benjamin's mess was five times so much as any of theirs." Why this mark of unusual distinction, as it was regarded in ancient times?

However, the banquet itself passed pleasantly, and early next morning the eleven, gladsome and thankful, were on their way back to Canaan. But the steward of Joseph's house had received special instructions. As before, each "bundle of money" had been restored in every man's sack. But, besides, he had also placed in that of Benjamin, Joseph's own cup, or rather his large silver bowl. The brothers had not traveled far when the steward hastily overtook them. Fixing upon the eleven the stain of base ingratitude, he charged them with stealing the "bowl" out of which "his lord drank, and whereby, indeed, he divined." Of course this statement of the steward by no means proves that Joseph actually did divine by means of this "cup." On the contrary, such could not have been the case, since it was of course impossible to divine, out of a cup that had been stolen from him, that it was stolen (ver. 15)! But, no doubt, there was in Joseph's house, as in that of all the great sages of Egypt, the silver bowl, commonly employed for divination, in which unknown events were supposed to appear in reflection from the water, sometimes after gems or gold (with or without magical inscriptions and incantations) had been cast into the cup, to increase the sheen of the broken rays of light. Similar practices still prevail in Egypt.

The charge of treachery and of theft so took the brothers by surprise, that, in their conscious innocence, they offered to surrender the life of the guilty and the liberty of all the others, if the cup were found with any of them. But the steward had been otherwise instructed. He was to isolate Benjamin from the rest. With feigned generosity he now refused their proposal, and declared his purpose only to retain the guilty as bondsman. The search was made, and the cup found in the sack of Benjamin. Now the first great trial of their feelings ensued. They were all free to go home to their own wives and children; Benjamin alone was to be a bondsman. The cup had been found in his sack! Granting that, despite appearances, they knew him to be innocent, why should they stand by him? At home he had been set before them as the favorite; nay, for fear of endangering him, their father had well nigh allowed them all, their wives and their children, to perish from hunger. In Egypt, also, he, the youngest, the son of another mother, had been markedly preferred before them. They had formerly got rid of one favorite, why hesitate now, when Providence itself seemed to rid them of another? What need, nay, what business had they to identify themselves with him? Was it not enough that he had been put before them everywhere; must they now destroy their whole family, and suffer their little ones to perish for the sake of one who, to say the best, seemed fated to involve them in misery and ruin? So they might have reasoned. But so they did not reason, nor, indeed, did they reason at all; for in all matters of duty reasoning is ever dangerous, and only absolute, immediate obedience to what is right, is safe. "They rent their clothes, and laded every man his ass, and returned to the city."

The first trial was past; the second and final one was to commence. In the presence of Joseph, "they fell before him on the ground" in mute grief. Judah is now the spokesman, and right well does his advocacy prefigure the pleading of his great Descendant. Not a word does he utter in extenuation or in plea. This one thought only is uppermost in his heart: "God hath found out the iniquity of thy servants." Not guilty indeed on this charge, but guilty before God, who hath avenged their iniquity! How, then, can they leave Benjamin in his undeserved bondage, when not he, but they have really been the cause of this sorrow? But Joseph, as formerly his steward, rejects the proposal as unjust, and offers their liberty to all except Benjamin. This gives to Judah an opening for pleading, in language so tender, graphic, and earnest, that few have been able to resist its pathos. He recounts the simple story, how the great Egyptian lord had at the first inquired whether they had father or brother, and how they had told him of their father at home, and of the child of his old age who was with him, the last remaining pledge of his wedded love, to whom the heart of the old man clave. Then the vizier had asked the youth to be brought, and they had pleaded that his going would cost the life of his father. But the famine had compelled them to ask of their father even this sacrifice. And the old man had reminded them of what they knew only too well: how his wife, the only one whom even now he really considered such, had borne him two sons; one of those had gone out from him, just as it was now proposed Benjamin should go, and he had not seen him since, and he had said: "Surely he is torn in pieces." And now, if they took this one also from him, and mischief befell him, his gray hairs would go down with sorrow to the grave. What the old man apprehended had come to pass, no matter how. But could he, Judah, witness the grief and the death of his old father? Was he not specially to blame, since upon his guarantee he had consented to part with him? Nay, he had been his surety; and he now asked neither pardon nor favor, only this he entreated, to be allowed to remain as bondsman instead of the lad, and to let him go back with his brethren. He besought slavery as a boon, for how could he "see the evil" that should "come on his father?"

Truly has Luther said: "What would I not give to be able to pray before the Lord as Judah here interceded for Benjamin, for it is a perfect model of prayer, nay, of the strong feeling which must underlie all prayer." And, blessed be God, One has so interceded for us, Who has given Himself as our surety, and become a bondsman for us. (Psalm 40:6, 7; Philippians 2:6-8) His advocacy has been heard; His substitution accepted; and His intercession for us is ever continued, and ever prevails. The Lord Jesus Christ is "the Lion of the tribe of Judah, the Root of David," and "hath prevailed to open the book, and to loose the seven seals thereof."

The last trial was now past. Indeed, it had been impossible to continue it longer, for Joseph "could not refrain himself." All strangers were hastily removed, and Joseph, with all tenderness of affection and delicacy of feeling, made himself known to them as the brother whom they had sold into Egypt, but whom in reality God had sent before for the purpose not only of saving their lives, but of preserving their posterity, that so His counsel of mercy with the world might be accomplished. Then let them not be grieved, for God had overruled it all. Three times must he speak it, and prove his forgiveness by the most loving marks, before they could credit his words or derive comfort from them. But one object Joseph had now in view: to bring his father and all his family to be near him, that he might nourish them; for as yet only two out of the seven years of famine had passed. And in this purpose he was singularly helped by Divine Providence. Tidings of what had taken place reached Pharaoh, and the generous conduct of his vizier pleased the king. Of his own accord he also proposed what Joseph had intended; accompanying his invitation with a royal promise of ample provision, and sending "wagons" for the transport of the women and children. On his part, Joseph added rich presents for his father. When the eleven returned, first alone, to their father, and told him all, "the heart of Jacob fainted, for he believed them not." Presently, as he saw the Egyptian "wagons" arriving, a great reaction took place. "The spirit of Jacob their father revived." The past, with its sorrows and its sin, seemed blotted out from his memory. Once more it was not, as before, Jacob who spoke, but "Israel" (the prince with God and man) who said, "It is enough, Joseph my son is yet alive: I will go and see him before I die."

CHAPTER 22: DEPARTURE OF JACOB AND HIS FAMILY INTO EGYPT — JACOB'S INTERVIEW WITH PHARAOH — HIS LAST ILLNESS AND COMMAND TO BE BURIED IN CANAAN — ADOPTION OF EPHRAIM AND MANASSEH AMONG THE SONS OF ISRAEL

(GENESIS 46-48)

A DIFFICULT path lay before the patriarch Jacob. As yet he had had no direct intimation from God that he should remove with his family to Egypt. But, on the other hand, God's dealings with Joseph, the invitation of Pharaoh, and the famine in Canaan served to point it out as the period of which God had spoken to Abram (Genesis 15:13), when his seed should leave Canaan, and become strangers and enslaved in a land that was not theirs. He knew that two things must take place before the return of Israel to, and their final possession of the promised land. "The iniquity of the Amorites" must be "full," and the family of Israel must have grown into a nation. The former was still future, and as for the latter it is easy to see that any further stay in Canaan would have been hindering and not helpful to it. For at the time Canaan was divided among numerous independent tribes, with one or more of whom the sons of Jacob, as they increased in numbers, must either have coalesced or entered into warfare. Still more dangerous to their religion would have been their continuance among and intercourse with the Canaanites. It was quite otherwise in Egypt. Thither they went professedly as sojourners, and for a temporary purpose. The circumstance that they were shepherds, and as such "an abomination to the Egyptians," kept them separate, alike politically, religiously, and socially, from the rest of the people, and, indeed, caused them to be placed in a district by themselves. Yet "the land of Goshen" was the best for the increase of their substance in flocks and herds. These may be designated as the outward reasons for their removal into Egypt at that time; the higher and spiritual bearings of the event have already been stated.

The assurance which Jacob needed for his comfort was granted him, as he reached Beersheba, the southern boundary of the promised land. There the patriarch offered "sacrifices unto the God of his father Isaac," and there the faithful Lord spake to him "in the visions of the night." His words gave Jacob this fourfold assurance, that God was the covenant-God, and that Jacob need not fear to go down into Egypt; that God would there make of him a great nation, in other words, that the transformation from the family to the nation should take place in Egypt; that God would go down with him; and, lastly, that He would surely bring him up again. And each of these four assurances was introduced by an emphatic I, to indicate the personal and direct source of all these blessings. Thus strengthened, Israel pursued his journey in confidence of spirit.

As so often in Scripture, a very important lesson is conveyed to us in this connection, though in a manner to escape superficial observation. It has been repeatedly remarked, that the Bible does not furnish the history of individuals as such, but gives that of the kingdom of God. This appears most clearly in the list, which is introduced at this stage, of "the names of the children of Israel which came into Egypt." Manifestly, it is not to be taken as literally the catalogue of those who companied with Jacob on his journey to Egypt. For one thing, some of them, such as Joseph himself, and his sons Ephraim and Manasseh, and their children, if at the time they had any, were already in Egypt. Then, some of the grandsons and great-grandsons of Jacob, mentioned in this catalogue, must have been born after the sons of Jacob came into Egypt; while, on the other hand, there must have been others who are not mentioned, since it is impossible to imagine that all the families of those whose further descendants are not named became extinct. But if the principle is kept in view, that only what concerns the kingdom of God is recorded, then all becomes plain. We now regard this not as a biographical list, but as a genealogical table, drawn up with a special object in view. That object is, to enumerate first the ancestors of the tribes of Israel, and then such of their descendants as founded the separate and distinct "families" in each tribe. Accordingly this genealogical table contains, besides the names of such descendants of Jacob as literally went with him into Egypt, also those of such as became "heads of houses." This appears quite clearly from a comparison with Numbers 26, where the "families" of Israel are specially enumerated. Among their founders not one single name appears that had not been previously given in the earlier table. Certain names, however, have dropped out in the second table, viz., that of a son of Simeon, and of one of Asher, and those of three sons of Benjamin — no doubt, either because they became extinct, or else because they were removed from their places through some judgment. Nor does it seem strange to find the names of the future heads of families beforehand enumerated in this catalogue. Do we not similarly read, that in Abraham yet unborn generations of Levi had given tithes to Melchizedek? Indeed, Scripture constantly expresses itself on this wise. Thus we read that God said to Abraham, to Isaac, and to Jacob: "I will give thee the land," when, as yet, they were but strangers and pilgrims in it; and, many centuries before the event took place: "In thee shall all nations of the earth be blessed;" while to Jacob himself God spake: "I will bring thee up again," from Egypt. For with God nothing is, in the real sense, future. "He seeth the end from the beginning." But when the sacred text sums up the genealogical table with the statement that "all the souls" were "threescore and ten," we think of the significance of the number, seven times ten, seven being the sacred covenant number, and ten that of perfectness.

On his journey Jacob sent Judah in advance, to inform Joseph of his arrival. He hastened to receive his father in the border-land of Goshen. Their meeting, after so long a parting, was most affectionate and touching. The Hebrew expression, rendered in our Authorized Version: "Joseph . . . presented himself unto him," implies extraordinary splendor of appearance. But when in the presence of his Hebrew father, the great Egyptian lord was once more only the lad Joseph. He "fell on his neck, and wept on his neck a good while." It now became the duty of Joseph to inform Pharaoh of the actual arrival of his family in Egypt, so as to obtain at the same time a fresh welcome, and a temporary concession of the land of Goshen for their settlement. For this purpose Joseph went first alone to the king, and next introduced five of his brothers. Both he and they laid stress on the fact that by occupation the family were shepherds. This would secure their stay in Goshen, as the district was most suitable for pasturage, and at the same time most remote and most isolated from the great bulk of the people. For the Egyptian monuments show that shepherds were considered as the lowest class or caste, probably because their nomadic habits were so opposed to the settled civilization of the country. Another point which the sons of Jacob were specially to bring out before Pharaoh was this, that they had come only "to sojourn," not to settle in the land, so that, as they had arrived at the first upon the express invitation of the king, they might be at liberty freely to depart when the time for it came. It is of importance to notice this in connection with the wrong afterwards done in the forcible detention of their descendants. It happened as Joseph had expected. Pharaoh assigned to them a dwelling-place "in the best of the land," that is, in the portion most suitable, in fact, in almost the only district suitable for pasturage — in the borderland between Canaan and Egypt, the land of Goshen, or of Rameses, as it is sometimes called from the city of that name. A careful and able scholar has thus expressed himself on the subject: "The land of Goshen lay between the eastern part of the ancient Delta, and the western border of Palestine; it was scarcely a part of Egypt Proper, was inhabited by other foreigners besides the Israelites, and was in its geographical names rather Semitic than Egyptian; it was a pasture-land, especially suited to a shepherd people, and sufficient for the Israelites, who there prospered, and were separate from the main body of the Egyptians."

Before settling him in Goshen, Joseph presented his father to Pharaoh, who received him with the courtesy of an Eastern monarch, and the respect which the sight of age, far exceeding the ordinary term of life in Egypt, would ensure. In acknowledgment of Pharaoh's kindness, "Jacob blessed" him; and in answer to the question about his age, compared "the days of the years" of his own "pilgrimage" with those of his fathers. Abraham had lived one hundred and seventy-five, Isaac one hundred and eighty years; while Jacob was at the age of only one hundred and thirty, apprehending the approach of death. Compared to theirs, his days had not only been "few" but "evil," full of trial, sorrow, and care, ever since his flight from his father's house. Yet, however differing in outward events, the essential character of their lives was the same. His and theirs were equally a "pilgrimage." For,

"these all died in faith, not having received the promises, but having seen them afar off, and were persuaded of them, and embraced them, and confessed that they were strangers and pilgrims on the earth. For they that say such things declare plainly that they seek a country, ... a better country, that is, a heavenly: wherefore God is not ashamed to be called their God: for He hath prepared for them a city." (*Hebrews 11:13, 14, 16*)

And in such wise also must each of our lives, whatever its outward history, be to us only a "pilgrimage."

But seventeen more years were granted to Israel in his quiet retirement of Goshen. Feeling that now the time of his departure had really come, he sent for Joseph. It was not to express weak regrets, nor even primarily to take such loving farewell as, under such circumstances, might be proper and fitting. Israel, as he is here again characteristically named, was preparing for another great act of faith. On his dying bed, he still held fast by the promises of God concerning the possession of Canaan, and all that was connected with it; and he exacted an oath from his son to bury him with his fathers, in the cave of Machpelah. Having obtained this solemn promise, it is said, "he bowed himself in worship over the head of the bed."

One thing still remained to be done. As yet the sons of Joseph had not been formally adopted into the family of Israel. But the two oldest of them, Manasseh and Ephraim, were to become heads of separate tribes; for Joseph was to have this right of the firstborn — two portions in Israel. Therefore, when, shortly after his interview with his father, Joseph was informed that the last fatal sickness had come upon him, he hastened to bring his two sons that they might be installed as co-heirs with the other sons of Jacob. In this Joseph signally showed his faith. Instead of seeking for his sons the honors which the court of Egypt offered them, he distinctly renounced all, to share the lot of the despised shepherd race. For the first time we here find the blessing accompanied with the laying on of hands.

But Jacob's eyes were dim, and when Joseph had brought his two sons close to his father, placing Manasseh, as the eldest, to his father's right hand, and Ephraim, as the younger, to his left, he ascribed it to failure of sight when Israel crossed his hands, laying the right on Ephraim and the left on Manasseh. But Jacob had been "guiding his hands wittingly." In fact, he had done it prophetically. The event proved the truth of this prophecy. At the time of Moses, indeed, Manasseh still counted twenty thousand men more than Ephraim. (Numbers 26:34, 37) But this comparative relationship was reversed in the days of the Judges; and ever afterwards Ephraim continued, next to Judah, the most powerful tribe in Israel. What, however, chiefly impresses us is, to see how intensely all the feelings, remembrances, and views of the dying man are intertwined with his religion. No longer does he cherish any hard thoughts about his "evil" days in the past. His memory of former days is now only of the gentleness and the goodness of God, Who had led him all through his pilgrimage. His feelings come out most fully in the words of blessing which he spake: "The God, before Whose face walked my fathers, Abraham and Isaac; the God Who pastured me from my existence on unto this day; THE ANGEL Who redeemed me from all evil, bless the lads; and let my name, and the name of my fathers, Abraham and Isaac, be named upon them, and let them increase to a multitude in the midst of the land." In this threefold reference to God as the covenant-God, the Shepherd and the Angel-Redeemer, we have a distinct anticipation of the truth concerning the blessed Trinity.

The blessing having been spoken, "Jacob gave to his son Joseph," as a special gift, "that parcel of ground" by Sychar (John 4:5), the ancient Shechem, which he had originally bought of "the children of Heth;" (Genesis 33:19) but which, as he prophesied, he — that is, his descendants — would have to take again with sword and bow out of the hand of the Amorite. In this possession of Joseph, many centuries later, rested the Redeemer-Shepherd, when, even in His weariness, He called and pastured His flock. (John 4) But as for Jacob, the last assurance which he gave to his son was emphatically to repeat this confession of his faith: "Behold, I die: but God shall be with you, and bring you again unto the land of your fathers." For men pass away, but the word and purpose of the Lord abide for ever!

CHAPTER 23: THE LAST BLESSING OF JACOB — DEATH OF JACOB — DEATH OF JOSEPH
(GENESIS 49:1)

THE last scene had now come, and Jacob gathered around his dying couch his twelve sons. The words which he spake to them were of mingled blessing and prediction. Before him, in prophetic vision, unrolled, as it were, pictures of the tribes of which his sons were to be the ancestors; and what he saw he sketched in grand outlines. It is utterly impossible to regard these prophetic pictures as exact representations of any one definite period or even event in the history of Israel. They are sketches of the tribes in their grand characteristics, rather than predictions, either of special events, or of the history of Israel as a whole. And to them applies especially the description which one has given of prophetic visions generally, that "they are pictures drawn without perspective," — that is, such that you cannot discern the distance from you of the various objects. Two other general remarks may be helpful to the reader. It will be observed that, generally, in the "blessing" spoken, the name of the ancestor seems to unfold the future character and history of the tribe. Secondly, as against all cavilers, it may be said deliberately, that these words of blessing must have been spoken by Jacob himself. When we attempt to imagine them as spoken at any other period in the history of Israel, we find ourselves surrounded by insuperable difficulties. For these words can only apply to the tribes as Jacob viewed them. They could not have been written at any other period, since in that case every later writer would have said something quite inapplicable to one or other of the tribes, so that he could not have used this precise language concerning them all. With these brief prefatory remarks we address ourselves to the words of "blessing:"

Reuben, my firstborn thou,

My might and the firstling of my strength,

Pre-eminence of dignity and pre-eminence of power -

Such should have been the position of Reuben, as the firstborn, had it not been for the "upboiling" of his passions and his consequent sin. Hence Jacob continues:

Upboiling like water,

Thou shalt not have the pre-eminence,

Because thou wentest up thy father's bed,

Then defiledst thou it -

He went up my couch!

The sons next in age to Reuben were Simeon and Levi. Their wanton cruelty at Shechem, from which Jacob recoiled with horror even on his death-bed, had made them "brethren," or companions in evil. As they had united for evil, so God would scatter them in Israel, so that they should not form independent and compact tribes. In point of fact, we know that even at the second numbering of Israel (Numbers 26:14), Simeon had sunk to be the smallest tribe. In the last blessing of Moses (Deuteronomy 33), no mention at all is made of Simeon. Nor does this tribe seem to have obtained any well-defined portion in the land, but only to have held certain cities within the possession of Judah. (Joshua 19:1-9) Lastly, we know that such of the families of Simeon as largely increased and became powerful, afterwards left the Holy Land, and settled outside its boundaries. (1 Chronicles 4:38-43) The tribe of Levi also received not any possession in Israel; only that their scattering was changed from a curse into a blessing by their election to the priesthood. This scattering of two tribes was the significant answer which God in His righteous providence made to their ancestors' attempt at vindicating the honor of their race by carnal means and weapons.

Simeon and Levi are brethren;
Instruments of violence are their swords;
Into their council come not thou, oh my soul,
Unto their assembly be not thou united, mine honor;
For in their anger they slew men,
And in their self-will they hamstrung oxen.
Cursed be their anger, for it was fierce,
And their wrath, for it was cruel.
I will divide them in Jacob,
And scatter them in Israel.

The three older brothers being thus dispossessed, and Joseph receiving the twofold territorial portion, the other privileges of the birthright are solemnly transferred to Judah. He is to be the leader, "the lion." As the lion is king of the forest, so was Judah to have royal sway, through David onwards to the Son of David, the Shiloh, unto Whom, as "the Lion of the tribe of Judah," all nations should render homage and obedience. Similarly, fullness of earthly riches was to distinguish the lot of Judah, these earthly blessings being themselves emblems of the spiritual riches dispensed in the portion of Judah. The whole description here is full of Messianic allusions, which were afterwards taken up in the prophecy of Balaam (Numbers 23:24; 24:9, 17); then applied to David (Psalm 89:20-37); and from him carried forward in prophecy, through Psalm 72, Isaiah 9, 11, to Ezekiel 21:27, and Zechariah 9:9, till they were finally realized in Jesus Christ, "sprung out of Juda," (Hebrews 7:14) "our peace, who hath made both one," (Ephesians 2:14) and who "must reign till He hath put all enemies under His feet," (1 Corinthians 15:25) "the Lion of the tribe of Judah, the Root of David," Who "hath prevailed." (Revelation 5:5)

In the blessing upon Judah we note, for the first time, how the prophetic significance of the name unfolds and appears:

Judah thou! Thy brethren shall praise thee!
Thy hand in the neck of thine enemies,
Thy father's sons shall bow down before thee.
A lion's whelp is Judah;
From the prey, my son, thou art gone up:
He stoopeth down, he coucheth like a lion ,
And like a lioness — who shall rouse him?
The scepter shall not depart from Judah,
Nor the ruler's staff from between his feet,
Until Shiloh come,
And to Him willing obedience of the nations!
He bindeth unto the vine his foal,
And unto the choice vine his ass's colt;
He washeth his garments in wine,
And in the blood of grapes his raiment;
Sparkling his eyes from wine,
And white his teeth from milk.

As local illustrations of this richness of the portion of Judah, the reader will remember that the best wine in Palestine grew near Hebron and Engedi (Numbers 13:23, etc.; Song of Solomon 1:14), and that some of the best pasture-land was south of Hebron, about Tekoa and Carmel. (1 Samuel 25:2; 2 Chronicles 26:10; Amos 1:1)

The next blessing also connects itself with the name of Zebulun, or "dwelling," although it requires to be borne in mind, in further illustration of the fact that it was not intended as a literal prediction, that the possessions of the tribe of Zebulun, so far as we can judge from Joshua 19:10-16, never actually touched the Mediterranean nor the Sea of Galilee, nor yet literally bordered on Zidon:

Zebulun — by the coast of seas shall he dwell,
And that, by the coast of ships,
And his side towards Zidon.

The name of Issachar, "reward," or "hire," is also emblematical of the character of the tribe, as, in its rich portion of Lower Galilee, it preferred labor with quietude, to power and domination:

Issachar is a bony ass,
Crouching between the folds.
He saw rest, that it was a boon,
And the land, that it was pleasant,
And he bent his shoulder to bear,
And became a tributary servant.

The allusion in the case of Dan, or "judgment," is again to the name. Although Dan was only the son of a bondmaid, he should not be behind his brethren, but "give judgment" to his people, that is, to Israel — the reference being possibly to such men as Samson, though also generally to the character of the tribe. There is another mysterious and most important allusion here, to which we shall immediately advert:

Dan shall give judgment to his people,
As one of the tribes of Israel.
Dan shall be a serpent by the way,
An adder in the path,
Which biteth the heels of the horse
So that backwards falleth his rider.

We shall not presume to offer an authoritative explanation of this comparison of Dan to a serpent, and to that kind of adder which, being of the color of the sand, remains unobserved till it has given its deadly bite. We only put it as a suggestion, whether this may not contain an allusion to apostasy or to the Antichrist , at the same time noting that the name of Dan is omitted from the list of the tribes in Revelation 7:5-8.

It is also significant that, immediately after the mention of these contests in connection with Dan, Jacob bursts forth in a prayer, intended, as says Calvin, not only to express his own personal faith and hope, but his confidence for his descendants. Quite the oldest Jewish commentary, or rather paraphrase, puts it this way: "My soul waiteth not for the deliverance of Gideon, the son of Joash, for it was only temporal; nor for that of Samson, for it was but transient; but for the redemption by the Messiah, the Son of David, which in Thy word Thou hast promised to send to Thy people, the children of Israel; for this, Thy salvation, my soul waiteth."

For Thy salvation wait I, oh Jehovah!

In reference to Gad, we have a threefold allusion to a kindred word, signifying oppression. To the prediction itself we cannot attach any definite historical fulfillment:

Gad — a press presseth upon him,

But he presseth on their heel.

In the case of Asher, the reference is evidently to the most fertile possession of that tribe, extending from Mount Carmel to the land of Tyre, the district richest in corn and oil (1 Kings 5:11):

Out of Asher fatness: his bread -

And he yieldeth royal dainties.

The allusion as to Naphtali is to the graceful agility and fleetness of the people, and also to their mental ability and quickness:

Naphtali is a hind let loose -

He uttereth words of beauty.

At last Jacob comes to the name of his loved son Joseph. Then it seems as if his whole heart were indeed overflowing. First, he sketches his fruitfulness, like that of a fruit-free "planted by rivers of water," (Psalm 1:3) whose boughs run over the wall (Comp. Psalm 80:8-11); then he describes his strength, as derived from God Himself; and, lastly, he pours forth richest blessings, richer far than any his ancestors had bestowed:

Son of a fruit-tree (a fruitful bough) is Joseph,

Son of a fruit-tree by a well,

Whose daughters (branches) spread over the wall.

The archers harass him,

They shoot at him, and hate him;

But his bow abideth in firmness,

And the arms of his hands remain supple

From the Hands of the Strong One of Jacob,

From thence, from the Shepherd, from the Rock of Israel,

From the God of thy father — may He help thee!

And from the Almighty -

may He bless thee!

Blessings of heaven from above!

Blessings of the deep that lieth beneath!

Blessings of the breasts and of the womb!

The blessings of thy father exceed

The blessings of my ancestors

Unto the bound of the everlasting hills —

May they come on the head of Joseph,

And on the crown of the head of him who is separated among

his brethren!

The allusions to Benjamin will be understood by a reference to Ehud (Judges 3:15), to Judges 5:14; 20:16; 1 Chronicles 8:40; 12:2; 2 Chronicles 14:8; 17:17, and to the history of Saul and of Jonathan:

Benjamin — a wolf who ravins:

In the morning he devoureth prey,

And at even he divideth spoil!

And now, having spoken these his last blessings, Jacob once more charged his sons to bury him in the cave of Machpelah. Then he gathered up his feet into the bed, laid him peacefully down, and without sigh or struggle yielded up the ghost, and was "gathered unto his people."

Such was the end of Jacob — the most pilgrim-like of the pilgrim fathers. His last wishes were obeyed to the letter. The first natural outburst of grief on the part of Joseph past, he "commanded his servants, the physicians, to embalm his father" — either to do the work themselves or to superintend it. Forty days the process lasted, and seventy days, as was their wont, the Egyptians mourned.

At the end of that period Joseph, as in duty bound, applied to Pharaoh, though not personally, since he could not appear before the king in the garb of mourning, craving permission for himself and his retinue to go up and bury his father in the land of Canaan. The funeral procession included, besides Joseph and "all his house," "his brethren, and his father's house," also "all the servants of Pharaoh, the elders of his house, and all the elders of the land of Egypt," — that is, the principal state and court officials, under a guard of both "chariots and horsemen." So influential and "very great a company" would naturally avoid, for fear of any collisions, the territory of the Philistines, through which the direct road from Egypt lay. They took the circuitous route through the desert and around the Dead Sea — significantly, the same which Israel afterwards followed on their return from Egypt — and halted on the Eastern bank of Jordan, at Goren-ha-Atad, "the buckthorn threshing-floor," or perhaps "the threshing-floor of Atad." The account of the funeral, as that of the embalming, and indeed every other allusion, is strictly in accordance with what we learn from Egyptian monuments and history. The custom of funeral processions existed in every province of Egypt, and representations of such are seen in the oldest tombs. As a German scholar remarks: "When we look at the representations upon the monuments, we can almost imagine that we actually see the funeral train of Jacob." At Goren-ha-Atad other mourning rites were performed during seven days. The attention of the inhabitants of the district was naturally attracted to this "grievous mourning of the Egyptians," and the locality henceforth bore the name of Abel Mizraim, literally "meadow of the Egyptians," but, by slightly altering the pronunciation: "mourning of the Egyptians." Here the Egyptians remained behind, and none but the sons and the household of Jacob stood around his grave at Machpelah.

On their return to Egypt an unworthy suspicion seems to have crossed the minds of Joseph's brethren. What if, now that their father was dead, Joseph were to avenge the wrong he had sustained at their hands? But they little knew his heart, or appreciated his motives. The bare idea of their cherishing such thoughts moved Joseph to tears. Even if bitter feelings had been in his heart, was he "in the place of God" to interfere with His guidance of things? Had it not clearly appeared that, whatever evil they might have thought to do him, "God meant it unto good?" With such declarations, and the assurance that he would lovingly care for them and their little ones, he appeased their fears.

Other fifty-four years did Joseph live in Egypt. He had the joy of seeing his father's blessing commence to be fulfilled. Ephraim's children of the third generation, and Manasseh's grandchildren "were brought up upon his knees." At the good old age of one hundred and ten years, as he felt death approaching, he gathered "his brethren" about him. Joseph was full of honors in Egypt; he had founded a family, than which none was more highly placed. Yet his last act was to disown Egypt, and to choose the lot of Israel — poverty, contempt, and pilgrimage: to renounce the present, in order to cleave unto the future. It was a noble act of faith, true like that of his fathers! His last words were these: "I die: and God will surely visit you, and bring you out of this land unto the land which He swore to Abraham, to Isaac, and to Jacob." And his last deed was to take a solemn oath of the children of Israel, to carry up his bones with them into the land of promise. In obedience to his wishes they embalmed his body, and laid it in one of those Egyptian coffins, generally made of sycamore wood, which resembled the shape of the human body. And there, through ages of suffering and bondage, stood the figure-like coffin of Joseph, ready to be lifted and carried thence when the sure hour of deliverance had come. Thus Joseph, being dead, yet spake to Israel, telling them that they were only temporary sojourners in Egypt, that their eyes must be turned away from Egypt unto the land of promise, and that in patience of faith they must wait for that hour when God would certainly and graciously fulfill His own promise.

When at the close of this first period of the Covenant-history we look around, we feel as if now indeed "the horror of great darkness" were fast falling upon Israel, which Abraham had experienced as he was shown the future of his descendants. (Genesis 15:12) Already personal intercourse between heaven and earth had ceased. From the time that Jacob had paid his vow in Bethel (Genesis 35:15), no personal manifestation of God, such as had often gladdened his fathers and him, was any more vouchsafed, except on his entrance into Egypt (Genesis 46:2-4), and then for a special purpose. Nor do we read of any such during the whole eventful and trying life of Joseph. And now long centuries of utter silence were to follow. During all that weary period, with the misery of their bondage and the temptation of idolatry around constantly increasing, there was neither voice from heaven nor visible manifestation to warn or to cheer the children of Israel in Egypt. One mode of guidance was for a time withdrawn. Israel had now only the past to sustain and direct them. But that past, in its history and with its promises, was sufficient. Besides, the torch of prophecy, which the hands of dying Jacob had held, cast its light into the otherwise dark future. Nay, the fact that Joseph's life, which formed the great turning-point in Israel history, had been allowed to pass without visible Divine manifestations to him and to them was in itself significant. For even as his unburied body seemed to preach and to prophesy, so his whole life would appear like a yet unopened or only partially opened book, — a grand unread prophecy, which the future would unfold. And not merely the immediate future, as it concerned Israel; but the more distant future as it concerns the whole Church of God. For, although not the person of Joseph, yet the leading events of his life are typical of the great facts connected with the life and the work of Him who was betrayed and sold by His brethren, but whom "God exalted with His right hand to be a Prince and a Savior."

VOLUME 2: THE EXODUS AND THE WANDERINGS IN THE WILDERNESS

PREFACE

THE period covered by the central books of the Pentateuch is, in many respects, the most important in Old Testament history, not only so far as regards Israel, but the Church at all times. Opening with centuries of silence and seeking Divine forgetfulness during the bondage of Egypt, the pride and power of Pharaoh are suddenly broken by a series of miracles, culminating in the deliverance of Israel and the destruction of Egypt's host.

In that Paschal night and under the blood-sprinkling, Israel as a nation is born of God, and the redeemed people are then led forth to be consecrated at the Mount by ordinances, laws, and judgments. Finally, we are shown the manner in which Jehovah deals with His people, both in judgment and in mercy, till at the last He safely brings them to the promised inheritance.

In all this we see not only the history of the ancient people of God, but also a grand type of the redemption and the sanctification of the Church. There is yet another aspect of it, since this narrative exhibits the foundation of the Church in the Covenant of God, and also the principles of Jehovah's government for all time. For, however great the difference in the development, the essence and character of the covenant of grace are ever the same. The Old and New Testaments are essentially one — not two covenants but one, gradually unfolding into full perfectness, "Jesus Christ Himself being the chief corner stone" of the foundation which is alike that of the apostles and prophets. (Ephesians 2:20)

There is yet a further consideration besides the intrinsic importance of this history. It has, especially of late, been so boldly misrepresented, and so frequently misunderstood, or else it is so often cursorily read — neither to understanding nor yet to profit — that it seemed desirable to submit it anew to special investigation, following the sacred narrative consecutively from Chapter to Chapter, and almost from Section to Section. In so doing, I have endeavored to make careful study of the original text, with the help of the best critical appliances. So far as I am conscious, I have not passed by any real difficulty, nor yet left unheeded any question that had a reasonable claim to be answered. If this implied a more detailed treatment, I hope it may also, with God's blessing, render the volume more permanently useful. Further, it has been my aim, by the aid of kindred studies, to shed additional light upon the narrative, so as to render it vivid and pictorial, enabling readers to realize for themselves the circumstances under which an event took place. Thus I have in the first two chapters sought to read the history of Israel in Egypt by the light of its monuments, and also to portray the political, social, and religious state of the people prior to the Exodus. Similarly, when following the wanderings of Israel up to the eastern bank of the Jordan, I have availed myself of the best recent geographical investigations, that so the reader might, as it were, see before him the route followed by Israel, the scenery, and all other accessories.

It need scarcely be said, that in studying this narrative the open Bible should always be at hand. But I may remind myself and others, that the only real understanding of any portion of Holy Scripture is that conveyed to the heart by the Spirit of God. And, indeed, throughout, my great object has been, not to supersede the constant and prayerful use of the Bible itself, but rather to lead to those Scriptures, which alone "are able to make wise unto salvation through faith which is in Christ Jesus?"

A.E.
HENIACH, BOURNEMOUTH
February — 1876.

CHAPTER 1: EGYPT AND ITS HISTORY DURING THE STAY OF THE CHILDREN OF ISRAEL, AS ILLUSTRATED BY THE BIBLE & ANCIENT MONUMENTS
(EXODUS 1:1-7)

THE devout student of history cannot fail to recognize it as a wonderful arrangement of Providence, that the beginning and the close of Divine revelation to mankind were both connected with the highest intellectual culture of the world. When the apostles went forth into the Roman world, they could avail themselves of the Greek language, then universally spoken, of Grecian culture and modes of thinking. And what Greece was to the world at the time of Christ, that and much more had Egypt been when the children of Israel became a God-chosen nation. Not that in either case the truth of God needed help from the wisdom of this world. On the contrary, in one sense, it stood opposed to it. And yet while history pursued seemingly its independent course, and philosophy, science, and the arts advanced apparently without any reference to revelation, all were in the end made subservient to the furtherance of the kingdom of God. And so it always is. God marvelously uses natural means for supernatural ends, and maketh all things work together to His glory as well as for the good of His people.

It was, indeed, as we now see it, most important that the children of Israel should have been brought into Egypt, and settled there for centuries before becoming an independent nation. The early history of the sons of Jacob must have shown the need alike of their removal from contact with the people of Canaan, and of their being fused in the furnace of affliction, to prepare them for inheriting the land promised unto their fathers. This, however, might have taken place in any other country than Egypt. Not so their training for a nation. For that, Egypt offered the best, or rather, at the time, the only suitable opportunities. True, the stay there involved also peculiar dangers, as their after history proved. But these would have been equally encountered under any other circumstances, while the benefits they derived through intercourse with the Egyptians were peculiar and unique. There is yet another aspect of the matter. When standing before King Agrippa, St. Paul could confidently appeal to the publicity of the history of Christ, as enacted not in some obscure corner of a barbarous land, but in full view of the Roman world "For this thing was not done in a corner." (Acts 26:26) And so Israel's bondage also and God's marvelous deliverance took place on no less conspicuous a scene than that of the ancient world-empire of Egypt.

Indeed, so close was the connection between Israel and Egypt, that it is impossible properly to understand the history of the former without knowing something of the latter. We shall therefore devote this preliminary chapter to a brief description of Egypt. In general, however historians may differ as to the periods when particular events had taken place, the land itself is full of reminiscences of Israel's story. These have been brought to light by recent researches, which almost year by year add to our stock of knowledge. And here it is specially remarkable, that every fresh historical discovery tends to shed light upon, and to confirm the Biblical narratives.

Yet some of the principal arguments against the Bible were at one time derived from the supposed history of Egypt! Thus while men continually raise fresh objections against Holy Scripture, those formerly so confidently relied upon have been removed by further researches, made quite independently of the Bible, just as an enlarged knowledge will sweep away those urged in our days. Already the Assyrian monuments, the stone which records the story of Moab, (2 Kings 3) the temples, the graves, and the ancient papyri of Egypt have been made successively to tell each its own tale, and each marvelously bears out the truth of the Scripture narrative. Let us see what we can learn from such sources of the ancient state of Egypt, so far as it may serve to illustrate the history of Israel.

The connection between Israel and Egypt may be said to have begun with the visit of Abram to that country. On his arrival there he must have found the people already in a high state of civilization. The history of the patriarch gains fresh light from monuments and old papyri. Thus a papyrus (now in the British Museum), known as The Two Brothers. and which is probably the oldest work of fiction in existence, proves that Abram had occasion for fear on account of Sarai. It tells of a Pharaoh, who sent two armies to take a fair woman from her husband and then to murder him. Another papyrus (at present in Berlin) records how the wife and children of a foreigner were taken from him by a Pharaoh. Curiously enough, this papyrus dates from nearly the time when the patriarch was in Egypt. From this period also we have a picture in one of the tombs, representing the arrival of a nomad chief, like Abram, with his family and dependents, who seek the protection of the prince. The newcomer is received as a person of distinction. To make the coincidence the more striking — though this chief is not thought to have been Abram, he is evidently of Semitic descent, wears a "coat of many colors," is designated Hyk, or prince, the equivalent of the modem Sheich, or chief of a tribe, and even bears the name of, Ab-shah, "father of sand," a term resembling that of, Ab-raham, the "father of a multitude."

Another Egyptian story — that of Sancha, "the son of the sycamore," — reminds us so far of that of Joseph, that its hero is a foreign nomad, who rises to the highest rank at Pharaoh's court and becomes his chief counselor. These are instances how Egyptian history illustrates and confirms that of the Bible. Of the forced employment of the children of Israel in building and repairing certain cities, we have, as will presently be shown, sufficient confirmation in an Egyptian inscription lately discovered. We have also a pictorial representation of Semitic captives, probably Israelites, making bricks in the manner described in the Bible; and yet another, dating from a later reign, in which Israelites — either captives of war, or, as has been recently suggested, mercenaries who had stayed behind after the Exodus — are employed for Pharaoh in drawing stones, or cutting them in the quarries, and in completing or enlarging the fortified city of Rameses, which their fathers had formerly built. The builders delineated in the second of these representations are expressly called Aperu, the close correspondence of the name with the designation Hebrew, even in its English form, being apparent. Though these two sets of representations date, in all probability, from a period later than the Exodus, they remarkably illustrate what we read of the state and the occupations of the children of Israel during the period of their oppression. Nor does this exhaust the bearing of the Egyptian monuments on the early history of Israel. In fact, we can trace the two histories almost contemporaneously — and see how remarkably the one sheds light upon the other.

In general, our knowledge of Egyptian history is derived from the monuments, of which we have already spoken, from certain references in Greek historians, which are not of much value, and especially from the historical work of Manetho, an Egyptian priest who wrote about the year 250 B.C. At that time the monuments of Egypt were still almost intact. Manetho had access to them all; he was thoroughly conversant with the ancient literature of his country, and he wrote under the direction and patronage of the then monarch of the land. Unfortunately, however, his work has been lost, and the fragments of it preserved exist only in the distorted form which Josephus has given them for his own purposes, and in a chronicle, written by a learned Christian convert of the third century (Julius Africanus). But this latter also has been lost, and we know it only from a similar work written a century later (by Eusebius, bishop of Caesarea), in which the researches of Africanus are embodied. Such are the difficulties before the student! On the other hand, both Africanus and Eusebius gathered their materials in Egypt itself, and were competent for their task; Africanus, at least, had the work of Manetho before him; and, lastly, by universal consent, the monuments of Egypt remarkably confirm what were the undoubted statements of Manetho. Like most heathen chronologies, Manetho's catalogue of kings begins with gods, after which he enumerates thirty dynasties, bringing the history down to the year 343 B.C.

Now some of these dynasties were evidently not successive, but contemporary, that is, they present various lines of kings who at one and the same time ruled over different portions of Egypt. This especially applies to the so-called 7th, 8th, 9th, 10th, and 11th dynasties. It is wholly impossible to conjecture what period of time these may have occupied. After that we have more solid ground. We know that under the 12th dynasty the whole of Egypt was united under one sway. As we gather from the monuments, the country was in a very high state of prosperity and civilization. At the beginning of this dynasty we suppose the visit of Abram to have taken place. The reign of this 12th dynasty lasted more than two centuries, and either at its close or at the beginning of the 13th dynasty we place the accession and rule of Joseph.

From the fourth king of the 13th to the accession of the 18th dynasty Egyptian history is almost a blank. That period was occupied by the rule of the so-called Hyksos, or Shepherd kings, a foreign and barbarous race of invaders, hated and opposed by the people, and hostile to their ancient civilization and religion. Although Josephus represents Manetho as assigning a very long period to the reign of "the Shepherds," he gives only six names. These and these only are corroborated by Egyptian monuments, and we are warranted in inferring that these alone had really ruled over Egypt. The period occupied by their reign might thus amount to between two and three centuries, which agrees with the Scripture chronology. "The Shepherds" were evidently an eastern race, and probably of Phoenician origin. Thus the names of the two first kings in their list are decidedly Semitic (Salatis, "mighty," "ruler," and Beon, or Benon, "the son of the eye," or, the "beloved one"), and there is evidence that the race brought with it the worship of Baal and the practice of human sacrifices -both of Phoenician origin. It is important to keep this in mind, as we shall see that there had been almost continual warfare between the Phoenicians along the west coast of Palestine and the Hittites, and the native Egyptian kings, who, while they ruled, held them in subjection. This constant animosity also explains why, not without good reason, "every shepherd was an abomination" unto the real native Egyptians. (Genesis 46:34) — It also explains why the Shepherd kings left the Israelitish shepherds unmolested in the land of Goshen, where they found them. Thus a comparison of Scripture chronology with the history of Egypt, and the evidently peaceful, prosperous state of the country, united under the rule of one king, as described in the Bible, lead us to the conclusion that Joseph's stay there must have taken place at the close of the 12th, or, at latest, at the commencement of the 13th dynasty. He could not have come during the rule of the Hyksos, for then Egypt was in a distracted, divided, and chaotic state; and it could not have been later, for after the Shepherd kings had been expelled and native rulers restored, no "new king," no new dynasty, "arose up over Egypt." On the other hand, the latter description exactly applies to a king who, on his restoration, expelled the Hyksos. And here the monuments of Egypt again afford remarkable confirmation of the history of Joseph. For one thing, the names of three of the Pharaohs of the 13th dynasty bear a striking resemblance to that given by the Pharaoh of the Bible to Joseph (Zaphnath-paaneah). Then we know that the Pharaohs of the 12th dynasty stood in a very special relationship to the priest city of On, (Genesis 41:45) and that its high-priest was most probably always a near relative of Pharaoh. Thus the monuments of that period enable us to understand the history of Joseph's marriage. But they also throw light on a question of far greater importance — how so devout and pious a servant of the Lord as Joseph could have entered into such close relationship with the priesthood of Egypt. Here our knowledge of the most ancient religion of Egypt enables us to furnish a complete answer.

Undoubtedly, all mankind had at first some knowledge of the one true God, and a pure religion inherited from Paradise. This primeval religion seems to have been longest preserved in Egypt. Every age indeed witnessed fresh corruptions, until at last that of Egypt became the most abject superstition. But the earliest Egyptian religious records, as preserved in that remarkable work, The Ritual for the Dead, disclose a different state of things. There can be no doubt that, divested of all later glosses, they embodied belief in "the unity, eternity, and self-existence of the unknown Deity," in the immortality of the soul, and in future rewards and punishments, and that they inculcated the highest duties of morality. The more closely we study these ancient records of Egypt, the more deeply are we impressed with the high and pure character of its primeval religion and legislation. And when the children of Israel went into the wilderness, they took, in this respect also, with them from Egypt many lessons which had not to be learned anew, though this one grand fundamental truth had to be acquired, that the Deity unknown to the Egyptians was, Jehovah, the living and the true God. We can therefore understand how such close connection between Joseph and the Egyptian priesthood was both possible and likely.

But this is not all. Only under a powerful native ruler could the redivision of the land and the rearrangement of taxation, which Joseph proposed, have taken place. Moreover, we know that under the rule of the last great king of this native dynasty (the 13th) a completely new system of Nile-irrigation was introduced, such as we may well believe would have been devised to avoid another period of famine, and, strangest of all, a place by the artificial lake made at that time bears the name Pi-aneh, "the house of life," which is singularly like that given by Pharaoh to Joseph. If we now pass over the brief 14th dynasty and the Hyksos period, when we may readily believe Israel remained undisturbed in Goshen, we come to the restoration of a new native dynasty (the so-called 18th). After the "Shepherds" (Exodus 1:9, 10) had been expelled, the Israelitish population, remaining behind in the borderland of Goshen, would naturally seem dangerously large to the "new king," the more so as the Israelites were kindred in descent and occupation to the "Shepherds," and had been befriended by them. Under these circumstances a wise monarch might seek to weaken such a population by forced labor. For this purpose he employed them in building fortress-cities, such as Pithom and Raamses, (Exodus 1:11) Raamses bears the name of the district in which it is situated, but Pithom means "the fortress of foreigners," thus indicating its origin. Moreover, we learn from the monuments that this "new king" (Aahmes I.) employed in building his fortresses what are called the Fenchu — a word meaning "bearers of the shepherd's staff," and which therefore would exactly describe the Israelites.

The period between the "new king" of the Bible (Aahmes I.) and Thothmes II. (the second in succession to him), when we suppose the Exodus to have taken place, quite agrees with the reckoning of Scripture. Now this Thothmes II. began his reign very brilliantly. But after a while there is a perfect blank in the monumental records about him. But we read of a general revolt after his death among the nations whom his father had conquered. Of course, one could not expect to find on Egyptian monuments an account of the disasters which the nation sustained at the Exodus, nor how Pharaoh and his host had perished in the Red Sea. But we do find in his reign the conditions which we should have expected under such circumstances, viz., a brief, prosperous reign, then a sudden collapse; the king dead; no son to succeed him; the throne occupied by the widow of the Pharaoh, and for twenty years no attempt to recover the supremacy of Egypt over the revolted nations in Canaan and east of the Jordan. Lastly, the character of his queen, as it appears on the monuments, is that of a proud and bitterly superstitious woman, just such as we would have expected to encourage Pharaoh in "hardening his heart" against Jehovah. But the chain of coincidences does not break even here. From the Egyptian documents we learn that in the preceding reign — that is, just before the children of Israel entered the desert of Sinai — the Egyptians ceased to occupy the mines which they had until then worked in that peninsula. Further, we learn that, during the latter part of Israel's stay in the wilderness, the Egyptian king, Thothmes III., carried on and completed his wars in Canaan, and that just immediately before the entry of Israel into Palestine the great confederacy of Canaanitish kings against him was quite broken up. This explains the state in which Joshua found the country, so different from that compact power which forty years before had inspired the spies with such terror; and also helps us to understand how, at the time of Joshua, each petty king just held his own city and district, and how easily the fear of a nation, by which even the dreaded Pharaoh and his host had perished, would fall upon the inhabitants of the land (compare also Balaam's words in Numbers 23:22; 24:8). We may not here follow this connection between the two histories any farther. But all through the troubled period of the early Judges down to Barak and Deborah, Egyptian history, as deciphered from the monuments, affords constant illustration and confirmation of the state of Canaan and the history of Israel, as described in the Bible. Thus did Providence work for the carrying out of God's purposes, and so remarkably does He in our days raise up witnesses for His Word, where their testimony might least have been expected.

We remember that Abram was at the first driven by famine into Egypt. The same cause also led the brothers of Joseph to seek there corn for their sustenance. For, from the earliest times, Egypt was the great granary of the old world. The extraordinary fertility of the country depends, as is well known, on the annual overflow of the Nile, caused in its turn by rains in the highlands of Abyssinia and Central Africa. So far as the waters of the Nile cover the soil, the land is like a fruitful garden; beyond it all is desolate wilderness. Even in that "land of wonders," as Egypt has been termed, the Nile is one of the grand outstanding peculiarities. Another, as we have seen, consists in its monuments. These two landmarks may conveniently serve to group together what our space will still allow us to say of the country and its people.

The name of the country, Egypt (in Greek Ai-gyptos), exactly corresponds to the Egyptian designation Kah-Ptah, "the land of Ptah" — one of their gods — and from it the name of Copts seems also derived. In the Hebrew Scriptures its name is Mizraim, that is, "the two Mazors," which again corresponds with another Egyptian name for the country, Chem (the same as "the land of Ham" Psalm 105:23, 27), both Mazor and Chem meaning in their respective languages the red mud or dark soil of which the cultivated part of the country consisted. It was called "the two Mazors," probably because of its ancient division into Upper and Lower Egypt. The king of Upper Egypt was designated by a title whose initial sign was a bent reed, which illustrates such passages as 2 Kings 18:21; Isaiah 36:6; Ezekiel 29:6; while the rulers of Lower Egypt bore the title of "bee," which may be referred to in Isaiah 7:18. The country occupies less than 10,000 square geographical miles, of which about 5,600 are at present, and about 8,000 were anciently, fit for cultivation. Scripture history has chiefly to do with Lower Egypt, which is the northern part of the country, while the most magnificent of the monuments are in Upper, or Southern, Egypt.

As already stated, the fertility of the land depends on the overflowing of the Nile, which commences to rise about the middle of June, and reaches its greatest height about the end of September, when it again begins to decrease. As measured at Cairo, if the Nile does not rise twenty-four feet, the harvest will not be very good; anything under eighteen threatens famine. About the middle of August the red, turbid waters of the rising river are distributed by canals over the country, and carry fruitfulness with them. On receding, the Nile leaves behind it a thick red soil, which its waters had carried from Central Africa, and over this rich deposit the seed is sown. Rain there is none, nor is there need for it to fertilize the land. The Nile also furnishes the most pleasant and even nourishing water for drinking, and some physicians have ascribed to it healing virtues. It is scarcely necessary to add that the river teems with fish. Luxuriously rich and green, amidst surrounding desolation, the banks of the Nile and of its numerous canals are like a well-watered garden under a tropical sky. Where climate and soil are the best conceivable, the fertility must be unparalleled.

The ancient Egyptians seem to have also bestowed great attention on their fruit and flower gardens, which, like ours, were attached to their villas. On the monuments we see gardeners presenting handsome bouquets; gardens traversed by alleys, and adorned with pavilions and colonnades; orchards stocked with palms, figs, pomegranates, citrons, oranges, plums, mulberries, apricots, etc.; while in the vineyards, as in Italy, the vines were trained to meet across wooden rods, and hang down in rich festoons. Such was the land on which, in the desolate dreariness and famine of the wilderness, Israel was tempted to look back with sinful longing! When Abram entered Egypt, his attention, like that of the modern traveler, must have been riveted by the Great Pyramids. Of these about sixty have been counted, but the largest are those near the ancient Memphis, which lay about ten miles above Cairo. Memphis — in Scripture Noph (Isaiah 19:13; Jeremiah 2:16; 46:14, 19; Ezekiel 30:13, 16) was the capital of Lower, as Thebes that of Upper, Egypt, the latter being the Pathros of Scripture. (Isaiah 11:11; Jeremiah 44:1, 15) It is scarcely possible to convey an adequate idea of the pyramids. Imagine a structure covering at the base an area of some 65,000 feet, and slanting upwards for 600 feet; or, to give a better idea than these figures convey "more than half as long on every side as Westminster Abbey, eighty feet higher than the top of St. Paul's, covering thirteen acres of ground, and computed to have contained nearly seven million tons of solid masonry?

We cannot here enter on the various purposes intended by these wonderful structures, some of which, at any rate, were scientific. Not far from the great pyramids was the ancient On, connected with the history of Joseph, and where Moses probably got his early training, But all hereabout is full of deepest interest — sepulchers, monuments, historical records, and sites of ancient cities. We are in a land of dreams, and all the surroundings bear dreamy outlines; gigantic in their proportions, and rendered even more gigantic by the manner in which they are disposed. Probably the most magnificent of these monuments in Upper Egypt, the Pathros of Scripture — are those of its capital, Thebes, the No, or No Amon of the Bible. (Jeremiah 46:25; Ezekiel 30:14-16; Nahum 3:8) It were impossible in brief space to describe its temple. The sanctuary itself was small, but opposite to it a court opened upon a hall into which the great cathedral of Paris might be placed, without touching the walls on either side! One hundred and forty columns support this hall, the central pillars being sixty-six feet high, and so wide that it would take six men with extended arms to embrace one of them. The mind gets almost bewildered by such proportions. All around, the walls bear representations, inscriptions, and records — among others, those of Shishak, who captured Jerusalem during the reign of Rehoboam. But the temple itself is almost insignificant when compared with the approach to it, which was through a double row of sixty or seventy ram-headed sphinxes, placed about eleven feet apart from each other. Another avenue led to a temple which enclosed a lake for funeral rites; and yet a third avenue of sphinxes extended a distance of 6,000 feet to a palace. These notices are selected to give some faint idea of the magnificence of Egypt.

It would be difficult to form too high an estimate of the old-world culture and civilization, here laid open before us. The laws of Egypt seem to have been moderate and wise; its manners simple and domestic; its people contented, prosperous, and cultured. Woman occupied a very high place, and polygamy was almost the exception. Science, literature, and the arts were cultivated; commerce and navigation carried on, while a brave army and an efficient fleet maintained the power of the Pharaohs. Altogether the country seems old in its civilization, when alike the earliest sages of Greece and the lawgivers of Israel learned of its wisdom. But how different the use which Israel was to make of it from that to which the philosophers put their lore! What was true, good, and serviceable was to enter as an element into the life of Israel. But this life was formed and molded quite differently from that of Egypt. Israel as a nation was born of God; redeemed by God; brought forth by God victorious on the other side the flood; taught of God; trained by God; and separated for the service of God. And this God was to be known to them as Jehovah, the living and the true God. The ideas they had gained, the knowledge they had acquired, the life they had learned, even the truths they had heard in Egypt, might be taken with them, but, as it were, to be baptized in the Red Sea, and consecrated at the foot of Sinai.

Quite behind them in the far distance lay the Egypt they had quitted, with its dreamy, gigantic outlines. As the sand carried from the desert would cover the land, so did the dust of superstition gradually bury the old truths. We are ready to admit that Israel profited by what they had seen and learned. But all the more striking is the final contrast between Egyptian superstition, which ultimately degraded itself to make gods of almost everything in nature, and the glorious, spiritual worship of the Israel of God. That contrast meets us side by side with the resemblance to what was in Egypt, and becomes all the more evident by the juxtaposition. Never is the religion of Israel more strikingly the opposite to that of Egypt than where we discover resemblances between the two; and never are their laws and institutions more really dissimilar than when we trace an analogy between them. Israel may have adopted and adapted much from Egypt, but it learned only from the Lord God, who, in every sense of the expression, brought out His people with a mighty hand, and an outstretched arm!

NOTE ON THE BOOK OF EXODUS

For a clearer understanding, a general outline of the Book of Exodus may here be given. Like Genesis (see Hist. of the Patriarchs, Introd. p. 15.), it consists of two great parts, the first describing the redemption of Israel, and the second the consecration of Israel as the People of God. The first part (ch. 1-15:21) appropriately ends with "the Song of Moses;" while, similarly, the second part closes with the erection and consecration of the Tabernacle, in which Jehovah was to dwell in the midst of His people, and to hold fellowship with them. Again, each of these two parts may be arranged into seven sections (seven being the covenant number), as follows:

PART I:

THE SEVEN SECTIONS OF PART II ARE AS FOLLOWS:

The reader will note these parts and sections in his Bible, and mark what grandeur and unity there is in the plan of the Book of Exodus, and how fully it realizes the idea of telling the story of the kingdom of God.

CHAPTER 2: THE CHILDREN OF ISRAEL IN EGYPT — THEIR RESIDENCES, OCCUPATIONS, SOCIAL ARRANGEMENTS, CONSTITUTION, AND RELIGION — "A NEW KING WHO KNEW NOT JOSEPH."

(EXODUS 1. TO END.)

THREE centuries and a half intervened between the close of the Book of Genesis and the events with which that of Exodus opens. But during that long period the history of the children of Israel is almost an entire blank.

The names of their families have come down to us, but without any chronicle of their history; their final condition at the time of the Exodus is marked, but without any notice of their social or national development. Except for a few brief allusions scattered through the Old Testament, we should know absolutely nothing of their state, their life, or their religion, during all that interval. This silence of three and a half centuries is almost awful in its grandeur, like the loneliness of Sinai, the mount of God. Two things had been foretold as marking this period, and these two alone appear as outstanding facts in the Biblical narrative. On the boundary of the Holy Land the Lord had encouraged Israel:

"Fear not to go down into Egypt; for I will there make of thee a great nation." (Genesis 46:3)

And the Book of Exodus opens with the record that this promise had been fulfilled, for

"the children of Israel were fruitful, and increased abundantly, and multiplied, and waxed exceeding mighty; and the land was filled with them." (Exodus 1:7)

Yet another prediction, made centuries before to Abram, was to be fulfilled. His seed was to be "a stranger in a land not theirs," to be enslaved and afflicted. (Genesis 15:13-16) And as the appointed centuries were drawing to a close, there "arose up a new king over Egypt," who "evil entreated our fathers." (Acts 7:19) Thus, in the darkest period of their bondage, Israel might have understood that, as surely as these two predictions had been literally fulfilled, so would the twofold promise also prove true, "I will bring thee up again," and that "with great substance." And here we see a close analogy to the present condition of the Jews. In both cases the promised future stands in marked contrast to the actual state of things. But, like Israel of old, we also have the "more sure word of prophecy," as a "light that shineth in a dark place until the day dawn." The closing years of the three and a half centuries since their entrance into Egypt found Israel peaceful, prosperous, and probably, in many respects, assimilated to the Egyptians around. "The fathers" had fallen asleep, but their children still held undisturbed possession of the district originally granted them. The land of Goshen, in which they were located, is to this day considered the richest province of Egypt, and could, even now, easily support a million more inhabitants than it numbers.

Goshen extended between the most eastern of the ancient seven mouths of the Nile and Palestine. The borderland was probably occupied by the more nomadic branches of the family of Israel, to whose flocks its wide tracts would afford excellent pasturage; while the rich banks along the Nile and its canals were the chosen residence of those who pursued agriculture. Most likely such would also soon swarm across to the western banks of the Nile, where we find traces of them in various cities (Exodus 12) of the land. There they would acquire a knowledge of the arts and industries of the Egyptians. It seems quite natural that, in a country which held out such inducements for it, the majority of the Israelites should have forsaken their original pursuits of shepherds, and become agriculturists. To this day a similar change has been noticed in the nomads who settle in Egypt. Nor was their new life entirely foreign to their history. Their ancestor, Isaac, had, during his stay among the Philistines, sowed and reaped. (Genesis 26:12) Besides, at their settlement in Egypt, the grant of land — and that the best in the country — had been made to them "for a possession," a term implying fixed and hereditary proprietorship. (Genesis 47:11, 27) Their later reminiscences of Egypt accord with this view. In the wilderness they looked back with sinful longing to the time when they had cast their nets into the Nile, and drawn them in weighted with fish; and when their gardens and fields by the waterside had yielded rich crops -"the cucumbers, and the melons, and the leeks, and the onions, and the garlic." (Numbers 11:5)

And afterwards, when Moses described to them the land which they were to inherit, he contrasted its cultivation with their past experience of Egypt, "where thou sowedst thy seed, and wateredst it with thy foot, as a garden of herbs." (Deuteronomy 11:10) As further evidence of this change from pastoral to agricultural pursuits, it has also been remarked that, whereas the patriarchs had possessed camels, no allusion is made to them in the narrative of their descendants. No doubt this change of occupation served a higher purpose. For settlement and agriculture imply civilization, such as was needed to prepare Israel for becoming a nation.

In point of fact, we have evidence that they had acquired most of the arts and industries of ancient Egypt. The preparation of the various materials for the Tabernacle, as well as its construction, imply this. Again, we have such direct statements, as, for example, that some of the families of Judah were "carpenters" (1 Chronicles 4:14), "weavers of fine Egyptian linen" (ver. 21), and "potters" (ver. 23). These must, of course, be regarded as only instances of the various trades learned in Egypt. Nor was the separation between Israel and the Egyptians such as to amount to isolation. Goshen would, of course, be chiefly, but not exclusively, inhabited by Israelites. These would mingle even in the agricultural districts, but, naturally, much more in the towns, with their Egyptian neighbors. Accordingly, it needed the Paschal provision of the blood to distinguish the houses of the Israelites from those of the Egyptians; (Exodus 12:13) while Exodus 3:22 seems to imply that they were not only neighbors, but perhaps, occasionally, residents in the same houses. This also accounts for the "mixed multitude" that accompanied Israel at the Exodus, and, later on, in the wilderness, for the presence in the congregation of offspring from marriages between Jewish women and Egyptian husbands. (Leviticus 24:10)

While the greater part of Israel had thus acquired the settled habits of a nation, the inhabitants of the border-district between Goshen and Canaan continued their nomadic life. This explains how the tribes of Reuben, Gad, and Manasseh possessed so much larger flocks than their brethren, as afterwards to claim the wide pasture-lands to the east of Jordan. (Numbers 32:1-4) We have, also, among the records of "ancient stories," (1 Chronicles 4:22) a notice of some of the descendants of Judah exercising lordship in Moab, and we read of a predatory incursion into Gath on the part of some of the descendants of Ephraim, which terminated fatally. It is but fair to assume that these are only instances, mentioned, the one on account of its signal success, the other on that of its failure, and that both imply nomadic habits and incursions into Canaan on the part of those who inhabited the border-land.

But whether nomadic or settled, Israel preserved its ancient constitution and religion, though here also we notice modifications and adaptations, arising from their long settlement in Egypt. The original division of Israel was into twelve tribes, after the twelve sons of Jacob, an arrangement which continued, although the sons of Joseph became two tribes (Ephraim and Manasseh), since the priestly tribe of Levi had no independent political standing. These twelve tribes were again subdivided into families (or rather clans), mostly founded by the grandsons of Jacob, of which we find a record in Numbers 26., and which amounted in all to sixty. From Joshua 7:14 we learn that those "families" had at that time, if not earlier, branched into "households," and these again into what is described by the expression "man by man" (in the Hebrew, Gevarim). The latter term, however, is really equivalent to our "family," as appears from a comparison of Joshua 7:14 with vers. 17, 18. Thus we have in the oldest times tribes and clans, and in those of Joshua, if not earlier, the clans again branching into households (kin) and families. The "heads" of those clans and families were their chiefs; those of the tribes, "the princes." (Numbers 1:4, 16, 44; 2:3; etc.; 7:10) These twelve princes were "the rulers of the congregation." (Exodus 34:31; Numbers 7:2; 30:1; 31:13; 32:2; 34:18) By the side of these rulers, who formed a hereditary aristocracy, we find two classes of elective officials, (Deuteronomy 1:9-14) as "representatives" of "the congregation." (Numbers 27:2) These are designated in Deuteronomy 29:10 as the "elders" and the "officers," or, rather, "scribes." Thus the rule of the people was jointly committed to the "princes," the "elders," and the "officers." The institution of "elders" and of "scribes" had already existed among the children of Israel in Egypt before the time of Moses. For Moses" gathered the elders of Israel together," to announce to them his Divine commission, (Exodus 3:16; 4:29) and through them he afterwards communicated to the people the ordinance of the Passover. (Exodus 12:21) The mention of "scribes" as "officers" occurs even earlier than that of elders, and to them, as the lettered class, the Egyptian taskmasters seem to have entrusted the superintendence of the appointed labors of the people. (Exodus 5:6, 14, 15, 19)

From the monuments of Egypt we know what an important part "the scribes" played in that country, and how constantly their mention recurs. Possibly, the order of scribes may have been thus introduced among Israel. As the lettered class, the scribes would naturally be the intermediaries between their brethren and the Egyptians. We may, therefore, regard them also as the representatives of learning, alike Israelitish and Egyptian. That the art of writing was known to the Israelites at the time of Moses is now generally admitted. Indeed, Egyptian learning had penetrated into Canaan itself, and Joshua found its inhabitants mostly in a very advanced state of civilization, one of the towns bearing even the name of Kirjath-sepher, the city of books, or Kirjath-sannah, which might almost be rendered "university town." (Joshua 15:15, 49) In reference to the religion of Israel, it is important to be in mind that, during the three and a half centuries since the death of Jacob, all direct communication from Heaven, whether by prophecy or in vision, had so far as we know, wholly ceased. Even the birth of Moses was not Divinely intimated. In these circumstances the children of Israel were cast upon that knowledge which they had acquired from "the fathers," and which, undoubtedly, was preserved among them. It need scarcely be explained, although it shows the wisdom of God's providential arrangements, that the simple patriarchal forms of worship would suit the circumstances in Egypt much better than those which the religion of Israel afterwards received. Three great observances here stand out prominently. Around them the faith and the worship alike of the ancient patriarchs, and afterwards of Israel, may be said to have clustered. They are: circumcision, sacrifices, and the Sabbath. We have direct testimony that the rite of circumcision was observed by Israel in Egypt. (Exodus 4:24-26; Joshua 5:5) As to sacrifices, even the proposal to celebrate a great sacrificial feast in the wilderness, (Exodus 8:25-28) implies that sacrificial worship had maintained its hold upon the people. Lastly, the direction to gather on the Friday two days provision of manna, (Exodus 16:22) and the introduction of the Sabbath command by the word "Remember," (Exodus 20:8) convey the impression of previous Sabbath observance on the part of Israel. Indeed, the manner in which many things, as, for example, the practice of vows, are spoken of in the law, seems to point back to previous religious rites among Israel.

Thus far for those outward observances, which indicate how, even during those centuries of silence and loneliness in Egypt, Israel still cherished the fundamental truths of their ancestral religion. But there is yet another matter, bearing reference not to their articles of belief or their observances, but to the religious life of the family and of individuals in Israel. This appears in the names given by parents to their children during the long and hard bondage of Egypt. It is well known what significance attaches in the Old Testament to names. Every spiritually important event gave it a new and characteristic name to a person or locality. Sometimes — as in the case of Abram, Sarai, and Jacob — it was God Himself Who gave such new name; at others, it was the expression of hearts that recognized the special and decisive interposition of God, or else breathed out their hopes and experiences, as in the case of Moses' sons. But any one who considers such frequently recurring names among "the princes" of Israel, as Eliasaph (my God that gathers), Elizur (my God a rock), and others of kindred import, will gather how deep the hope of Israel had struck its roots in the hearts and convictions of the people. This point will be further referred to in the sequel. Meantime, we only call attention to the names of the chiefs of the three families of the Levites: Eliasaph (my God that gathers), Elizaphan (my God that watcheth all, around), and Zuriel (my rock is God) — the Divine Name (El) being the same by which God had revealed Himself to the fathers.

Besides their own inherited rites, the children of Israel may have learned many things from the Egyptians, or been strengthened in them. And here, by the side of resemblance, we also observe marked contrast between them. We have already seen that, originally, the religion of the Egyptians had contained much of truth, which, however, was gradually perverted to superstition. The Egyptians and Israel might hold the same truths, but with the difference of understanding and application between dim tradition and clear Divine revelation. Thus, both Israel and the Egyptians believed in the great doctrines of the immortality of the soul, and of future rewards and punishments. But, in connection with this, Israel was taught another lesson, far more difficult to our faith, and which the ancient Egyptians had never learned, that God is the God of the present as well as of the future, and that even here on earth He reigneth, dispensing good and evil. And perhaps it was owing to this that the temporal consequences of sin were so much insisted upon in the Mosaic law. There was no special need to refer to the consequences in another life. The Egyptians, as well as Israel, acknowledged the latter, but the Egyptians knew not the former. Yet this new truth would teach Israel constantly to realize Jehovah as the living and the true God. On the other hand, the resemblances between certain institutions of Israel and of Egypt clearly prove that the Law was not given at a later period, but to those who came out from Egypt, and immediately upon their leaving it. At the same time, much evil was also acquired by intercourse with the Egyptians. In certain provisions of the Pentateuch we discover allusions, not only to the moral corruptions witnessed, and perhaps learned, in Egypt, but also to the idolatrous practices common there. Possibly, it was not the gorgeous ritual of

Egypt which made such deep impression, but the services constantly there witnessed may have gradually accustomed the mind to the worship of nature. As instances of this tendency among Israel, we remember the worship of the golden calf, (Exodus 32) the warning against sacrificing unto the "he-goat," (Leviticus 17:7) and the express admonition, even of Joshua (24:14), to "put away the strange gods" which their "fathers served on the other side of the flood." To the same effect is the retrospect in Ezekiel 20:5-8, in Amos 5:26, and in the address of Stephen before the Jewish council. (Acts 7:43) Yet it is remarkable that, although the forms of idolatry here referred to were all practiced in Egypt, there is good reason for believing that they were not, so to speak, strictly Egyptian in their origin, but rather foreign rites imported, probably from the Phoenicians. Such then was the political, social, and religious state of Israel, when, their long peace was suddenly interrupted by tidings that Aahmes I. was successfully making war against the foreign dynasty of the Hyksos. Advancing victoriously, he at last took Avaris, the great stronghold and capital of the Shepherd kings, and expelled them and their adherents from the country. He then continued his progress to the borders of Canaan, taking many cities by storm. The memorials of the disastrous rule of the Shepherds were speedily removed; the worship which they had introduced was abolished, and the old Egyptian forms were restored. A reign of great prosperity now ensued.

Although there is difference of opinion on the subject, yet every likelihood (as shown in the previous chapter) seems to attach to the belief that the accession of this new dynasty was the period when the "king arose who knew not Joseph."7 For reasons already explained, one of the first and most important measures of his internal administration would necessarily be to weaken the power of the foreign settlers, who were in such vast majority in the border province of Goshen. He dreaded lest, in case of foreign war, they might join the enemy, "and get them up out of the land." The latter apprehension also shows that the king must have known the circumstances under which they had at first settled in the land. Again, from the monuments of Egypt, it appears to have been at all times the policy of the Pharaohs to bring an immense number of captives into Egypt, and to retain them there in servitude for forced labors. A somewhat similar policy was now pursued towards Israel. Although allowed to retain their flocks and fields, they were set to hard labor for the king. Egyptian "taskmasters" were appointed over them, who "made the children of Israel serve with rigor," and did "afflict them with their burdens." A remarkable illustration of this is seen in one of the Egyptian monuments. Laborers, who are evidently foreigners, and supposed to represent Israelites, are engaged in the various stages of brickmaking, under the superintendence of four Egyptians, two of whom are apparently superior officers, while the other two are overseers armed with heavy lashes, who cry out, "Work without fainting!" The work in which the Israelites were employed consisted of brickmaking, artificial irrigation of the land, including, probably, also the digging or restoring of canals, and the building, or restoring and enlarging of the two "magazine-cities"8 of Pithom and Raamses, whose localities have been traced in Goshen, and which served as depots both for commerce and for the army. According to Greek historians it was the boast of the Egyptians that, in their great works, they only employed captives and slaves, never their own people. But Aahmes I had special need of Israelitish labor, since we learn from an inscription, dating from his twenty-second year, that he was largely engaged in restoring the temples and buildings destroyed by the "Shepherds."

But this first measure of the Pharaohs against Israel produced the opposite result from what had been expected. So far from diminishing, their previous vast growth went on in increased ratio, so that the Egyptians "were sorely afraid 9 (alarmed) because of the children of Israel." (Exodus 1:12) Accordingly Pharaoh resorted to a second measure, by which all male children, as they were born, were to be destroyed, probably unknown to their parents. But the two Hebrew women, who, as we suppose, were at the head of "the guild" of midwives, do not seem to have communicated the king's order to their subordinates. At any rate, the command was not executed. Scripture has preserved the names of these courageous women, and told us that their motive was "fear of God" (in the Hebrew with the article, "the God," as denoting the living and true God). And as they were the means of "making" or upbuilding the houses of Israel, so God "made them houses." It is true that, when challenged by the king. they failed to speak out their true motive; but, as St. Augustine remarks, "God forgave the evil on account of the good, and rewarded their piety, though not. their deceit."

How little indeed any merely human device could have averted the ruin of Israel, appears from the third measure which Pharaoh now adopted. Putting aside every restraint, and forgetting, in his determination, even his interests, the king issued a general order to cast every Jewish male child, as it was born, into the Nile. Whether this command, perhaps given in anger, was not enforced for any length of time, or the Egyptians were unwilling permanently to lend themselves to such cruelty, or the Israelites found means of preserving their children from this danger, certain it is, that, while many must have suffered, and all needed to use the greatest precautions, this last ruthless attempt to exterminate Israel also proved vain. Thus the two prophecies had been fulfilled. Even under the most adverse circumstances Israel had so increased as to fill the Egyptians with alarm; and the "affliction" of Israel had reached its highest point. And now the promised deliverance was also to appear. As in so many instances, it came in what men would call the most unlikely manner.

CHAPTER 3: THE BIRTH, AND THE TRAINING OF MOSES, BOTH IN EGYPT AND IN MIDIAN, AS PREPARATORY TO HIS CALLING
(EXODUS 2)

TO the attentive reader of Scripture it will not seem strange — only remarkable — that the very measure which Pharaoh had taken for the destruction of Israel eventually led to their deliverance. Had it not been for the command to cast the Hebrew children into the river, Moses would not have been rescued by Pharaoh's daughter, nor trained in all the wisdom of Egypt to fit him for his calling. Yet all throughout, this marvelous story pursues a natural course; that is, natural in its progress, but supernatural in its purposes and results.

A member of the tribe of Levi, and descendant of Kohath,(Exodus 6:20; Numbers 26:59) Amram by name, had married Jochebed, who belonged to the same tribe. Their union had already been blessed with two children, Miriam and Aaron, when the murderous edict of Pharaoh was issued. The birth of their next child brought them the more sorrow and care, that the "exceeding fairness" of the child not only won their hearts, but seemed to point him out as destined of God for some special purpose. In this struggle of affection and hope against the fear of man, they obtained the victory, as victory is always obtained, "by faith." There was no special revelation made to them, nor was there need for it. It was a simple question of faith, weighing the command of Pharaoh against the command of God and their own hopes. They resolved to trust the living God of their fathers, and to brave all seeming danger. It was in this sense that "by faith Moses, when he was born, was hid three months of his parents, because they saw he was a proper child; and they were not afraid of the king's commandment." Longer concealment at home being impossible, the same confidence of faith now led the mother to lay the child in an ark made, as at that time the light Nile-boats used to be, of "bulrushes," or papyrus — a strong three-cornered rush, that grew to a height of about ten or fifteen feet.

The "ark" — a term used in Scripture only here and in connection with the deliverance of Noah by an "ark" — was made tight within by "slime" — either Nile-mud or asphalt — and impenetrable to water by a coating of "pitch." Thus protected, the "ark," with its precious burden, was deposited among "the flags" in the brink, or lip of the river, just where Pharaoh's daughter was wont to bathe, though the sacred text does not expressly inform us whether or not this spot was purposely chosen. The allusion in Psalm 78:12 to the "marvelous things" done "in the field of Zoan," may perhaps guide us to the very scene of this deliverance. Zoan, as we know, was the ancient Avaris, the capital of the Shepherd kings, which the new dynasty had taken from them. The probability that it would continue the residence of the Pharaohs, the more so as it lay on the eastern boundary of Goshen, is confirmed by the circumstance that in those days, of all the ancient Egyptian residences, Avaris or Zoan alone lay on an arm of the Nile which was not infested by crocodiles, and where the princess therefore could bathe. There is a curious illustration on one of the Egyptian monuments of the scene described in the rescue of Moses. A noble lady is represented bathing in the river with four of her maidens attending upon her, just like the daughter of Pharaoh in the story of Moses. But to return — the discovery of the ark, and the weeping of the babe, as the stranger lifted him, are all true to nature. The princess is touched by the appeal of the child to her woman's feelings. She compassionates him none the less that he is one of the doomed race. To have thrown the weeping child into the river would have been inhuman. Pharaoh's daughter acted as every woman would have done in the circumstances. To save one Hebrew child could be no very great crime in the king's daughter. Moreover, curiously enough, we learn from the monuments, that just at that very time the royal princesses exercised special influence — in fact, that two of them were co-regents. So when, just at the opportune moment, Miriam, who all along had watched at a little distance, came forward and proposed to call some Hebrew woman to nurse the weeping child — this strange gift, bestowed as it were by the Nile, god himself on the princess, — she readily consented. The nurse called was, of course, the child's own mother, who received her babe now as a precious charge, entrusted to her care by the daughter of him who would have compassed his destruction.

So marvelous are the ways of God. One of the old church-writers has noted that "the daughter of Pharaoh is the community of the Gentiles," thereby meaning to illustrate this great truth, which we trace throughout history, that somehow the salvation of Israel was always connected with the instrumentality of the Gentiles. It was so in the history of Joseph, and even before that; and it will continue so until at the last, through their mercy, Israel shall obtain mercy. But meanwhile a precious opportunity was afforded to those believing Hebrew parents to mold the mind of the adopted son of the princess of Egypt. The three first years of life, the common eastern time for nursing, are often, even in our northern climes, where development is so much slower, a period decisive for after life. It requires no stretch of imagination to conceive what the child Moses would learn at his mother's knee, and hear among his persecuted people. When a child so preserved and so trained found himself destined to step from his Hebrew home to the court of Pharaoh — his mind full of the promises made to the fathers, and his heart heavy with the sorrows of his brethren, — it seems almost natural that thoughts of future deliverance of his people through him should gradually rise in his soul. Many of our deepest purposes have their root in earliest childhood, and the lessons then learnt, and the thoughts then conceived, have been steadily carried out to the end of our lives.

Yet, as in all deepest life-purpose, there was no rashness about carrying it into execution. When Jochebed brought the child back to the princess, the latter gave her adopted son the Egyptian name "Moses," which, curiously enough, appears also in several of the old Egyptian papyri, among others, as that of one of the royal princes. The word means "brought forth" or "drawn out," "because," as she said in giving the name, "I drew him out of the water."

But for the present Moses would probably not reside in the royal palace at Avails. St. Stephen tells us (Acts 7:22) that he "was instructed in all the wisdom of the Egyptians." In no country was such value attached to education, nor was it begun so early as in Egypt. No sooner was a child weaned than it was sent to school, and instructed by regularly appointed scribes. As writing was not by letters, but by hieroglyphics, which might be either pictorial representations, or symbols (a scepter for a king, etc.), or a kind of phonetic signs, and as there seem to have been hieroglyphics for single letters, for syllables, and for words, that art alone must, from its complication, have taken almost a lifetime to master it perfectly. But beyond this, education was carried to a very great length, and, in the case of those destined for the higher professions, embraced not only the various sciences, as mathematics, astronomy, chemistry, medicine, etc., but theology, philosophy, and a knowledge of the laws. There can be no doubt that, as the adopted son of the princess, Moses would receive the highest training. Scripture tells us that, in consequence, he was "mighty in his words and deeds," and we may take the statement in its simplicity, without entering upon the many Jewish and Egyptian legends which extol his wisdom, and his military and other achievements.

Thus the first forty years of Moses' life passed. Undoubtedly, had he been so minded, a career higher even than that of Joseph might have been open to him. But, before entering it, he had to decide that one great preliminary question, with whom he would cast in his lot — with Egypt or with Israel, with the world or the promises. As so often happens, the providence of God here helped him to a clear, as the grace of God to a right, decision. In the actual circumstances of Hebrew persecution it was impossible at the same time "to be called the son of Pharaoh's daughter" and to have part, as one of them, "with the people of God." The one meant "the pleasures of sin" and "the treasures of Egypt" — enjoyment and honors, the other implied "affliction" and "the reproach of Christ" -or suffering and that obloquy which has always attached to Christ and to His people, and at that time especially, to those who clung to the covenant of which Christ was the substance.

But "faith," which is "the substance of things hoped for, the evidence of things not seen," enabled Moses not only to "refuse" what Egypt held out, but to "choose rather the affliction," and, more than that, to "esteem the reproach of Christ greater riches than the treasures of Egypt," because "he had respect unto the recompense of the reward." (Hebrews 11:24-26) In this spirit "he went out unto his brethren, and looked on their burdens." (Exodus 2:11)

But his faith, though deep and genuine, was as yet far from pure and spiritual. The ancient Egyptians were noted for the severity of their discipline, and their monuments represent the "taskmasters" armed with heavy scourges, made of tough bending wood, which they unmercifully used. The sight of such sufferings, inflicted by menials upon his brethren, would naturally rouse the utmost resentment of the son of the Princess Royal. This, together with the long-cherished resolve to espouse the cause of his brethren, and the nascent thought of becoming their deliverer, led him to slay an Egyptian, whom he saw thus maltreating "an Hebrew, one of his brethren." Still it was not an access of sudden frenzy, for "he looked this way and that way," to see "that there was no man" to observe his deed; rather was it an attempt to carry out spiritual ends by carnal means, such as in the history of Moses' ancestors had so often led to sin and suffering. He would become a deliverer before he was called to it of God; and he would accomplish it by other means than those which God would appoint. One of the fathers has rightly compared this deed to that of Peter in cutting off the ear of the high-priest's servant; at the same time also calling attention to the fact, that the heart both of Moses and Peter resembled a field richly covered with weeds, but which by their very luxuriance gave promise of much good fruit, when the field should have been broken up and sown with good seed.

In the gracious dispensation of God, that time had now come. Before being transplanted, so to speak, Moses had to be cut down. He had to strike root downwards, before he could spring upwards. As St. Stephen puts it, "his brethren understood not how that God, by his hand, would give them deliverance" — what his appearance and conduct among them really meant; and when next he attempted to interfere in a quarrel between two Hebrews, the wrong-doer in harsh terms disowned his authority, and reproached him with his crime. It was now evident that the matter was generally known. Presently it reached the ears of Pharaoh. From what we know of Egyptian society, such an offense could not have remained unpunished, even in the son of a princess, and on the supposition that she who had originally saved Moses was still alive, after the lapse of forty years, and that the then reigning Pharaoh was her father. But, besides, Moses had not only killed an official in the discharge of his duty, he had virtually taken the part of the Hebrews, and encouraged them to rebellion. That Moses commanded such position of influence that Pharaoh could not at once order his execution, but "sought to slay him," only aggravated the matter, and made Moses the more dangerous. Open resistance to Pharaoh was of course impossible. The sole hope of safety now seemed to lie in renouncing all further connection with his people. That or flight were the only alternatives. On the other hand, flight might further provoke the wrath of the king, and it was more than doubtful whether any of the neighboring countries could, under such circumstances, afford him safe shelter. It was therefore, indeed, once more an act of "faith" when Moses "forsook Egypt, not fearing the wrath of the king, for he endured" (or remained steadfast, viz., to his choice and people), "as seeing the Invisible One," that is, as one who, instead of considering the king of Egypt, looked by faith to the King invisible. (1 Timothy 1:17)

Like Jacob of old, and Joseph under similar circumstances, Moses must now go into a strange land. All that Egypt could teach him, he had acquired. What he still needed could only be learned in loneliness, humiliation, and suffering. Two things would become manifest in the course of his history. That which, in his own view, was to have freed his people from their misery, had only brought misery to himself. On the other hand, that which seemed to remove him from his special calling, would prepare the way for its final attainment. And so it often happens to us in the most important events of our lives, that thus

142

we may learn the lessons of faith and implicit self-surrender and that God alone may have the glory.

Disowned by his people, and pursued by the king, the gracious Providence of God prepared a shelter and home for the fugitive. Along the eastern shore of the Red Sea the Midianites, descended from Abraham through Keturah, (Genesis 25:2-4) had their settlements, whence, as nomads, they wandered, on one side to the southern point of the peninsula of Sinai, and on the other, northward, as far as the territory of Moab. Among the Midianites it happened to Moses, as of old to Jacob on his flight. At the "well" he was able to protect the daughters of Reuel, "the priest of Midian," against the violence of the shepherds, who drove away their flocks. Invited in consequence to the house of Reuel, he continued there, and eventually married Zipporah, the daughter of the priest. This, and the birth of his two sons, to which we shall presently refer, is absolutely all that Moses himself records of his forty years' stay in Midian.

But we are in circumstances to infer some other and important details. The father-in-law of Moses seems to have worshipped the God of Abraham, as even his name implies: Reuel, the "friend of El" the latter the designation which the patriarchs gave to God, as El Shaddai, "God Almighty." (Exodus 6:3) This is further borne out by his after-conduct. (Exodus 18) Reuel is also called Jethro and Jether, (Exodus 3:1; 4:18) which means "excellency," and was probably his official title as chief priest of the tribe, the same as the Imam of the modern Arabs, the term having a kindred meaning.

But the life of Moses in the house of Reuel must have been one of humiliation and loneliness. From her after-conduct (Exodus 4:25) we infer that Zipporah was a woman of violent, imperious temper, who had but little sympathy with the religious convictions of her husband. When she first met him as "an Egyptian," his bravery may have won her heart. But further knowledge of the deepest aims of his life might lead her to regard him as a gloomy fanatic, who busied his mind with visionary schemes. So little indeed does she seem to have had in common with her husband that, at the most trying and noble period of his life, when on his mission to Pharaoh, he had actually to send her away. (Exodus 18:2, 3) Nor could there have been much confidence between Moses and his father-in-law. His very subordinate position in the family of Jethro (3:1); the fact of his reticence in regard to the exact vision vouchsafed him of God (4:18); and the humble manner in which Moses was sent back into Egypt (ver. 20), all give a saddening view of the mutual relations. What, however, all this time were the deepest feelings and experiences of his heart, found expression in the names which he gave to his two sons. The elder he named Gershom (expulsion, banishment), "for he said, I have been a stranger in a strange land" (Exodus 2:22) the second he called Eliezer, "my God is help" (18:4). Banished to a strange land, far from his brethren and the land of promise, Moses longs for his real home. Yet this feeling issues not in despondency, far less in disbelief or distrust. On the contrary, "the peaceable fruits of righteousness," springing from the "chastening" of the Lord, appear in the name of his second son; "for the God of my fathers," said he, "is mine help, and delivered me from the sword of Pharaoh." The self-confidence and carnal zeal manifest in his early attempt to deliver his brethren in Egypt have been quenched in the land of his banishment, and in the school of sorrow. And the result of all he has suffered and learned has been absolute trustfulness in the God of his fathers, the God of the promises, Who would surely fulfill His word.

CHAPTER 4: THE CALL OF MOSES — THE VISION OF THE BURNING BUSH -THE COMMISSION TO PHARAOH AND TO ISRAEL - AND THE THREE "SIGNS," AND THEIR MEANING
(EXODUS 2:23; 4:17)

WHEN God is about to do any of His great works, He first silently prepares all for it. Not only the good seed to be scattered, but the breaking up of the soil for its reception is His. Instrumentalities, unrecognized at the time, are silently at work; and, together with the good gift to be bestowed on His own, He grants them the felt need and the earnest seeking of it. Thus prayers and answers are, as it were, the scales of grace in equipoise.

It was not otherwise when God would work the great deliverance of His people from Egypt. Once more it seemed as if the clouds overhead were just then darkest and heaviest. One king had died and another succeeded; but the change of government brought not to Israel that relief which they had probably expected. Their bondage seemed now part of the settled policy of the Pharaohs. Not one ray of hope lit up their sufferings other than what might have been derived from faith. But centuries had passed without any communication or revelation from the God of their fathers!

It must therefore be considered a revival of religion when, under such circumstances, the people, instead of either despairing or plotting rebellion against Pharaoh, turned in earnest prayer unto the Lord, or, as the sacred text puts it, significantly adding the definite article before God, (Exodus 2:23) "cried" "unto the God," that is, not as unto one out of many, but unto the only true and living God. This spirit of prayer, now for the first time appearing among them, was the first pledge and harbinger, indeed, the commencement of their deliverance. (Exodus 3:7; Deuteronomy 26:7) For though only "a cry," so to speak, spiritually inarticulate, no intervening period of time divided their prayer from its answer. "And God heard their groaning, and God remembered His covenant with Abraham, with Isaac, and with Jacob. And God looked upon the children of Israel, and God had respect unto them" — literally, He "knew them," that is, recognized them as the chosen seed of Abraham, and, recognizing, manifested His love towards them.

The southern end of the peninsula of Sinai, to which the sacred narrative now takes us, consists of a confused mass of peaks (the highest above 9,000 feet), some of dark green porphyry, but mostly red granite of different hues, which is broken by strips of sand or gravel, intersected by wadies or glens, which are the beds of winter torrents, and dotted here and there with green spots, chiefly due to perennial fountains. The great central group among these mountains is that of Horeb, and one special height in it Sinai, the "mount of God." Strangely enough it is just here amidst this awful desolateness that the most fertile places in "the wilderness" are also found. Even in our days part of this plateau is quite green. Hither the Bedouin drive their flocks when summer has parched all the lower districts. Fruit-trees grow in rich luxuriance in its valleys, and "the neighborhood is the best watered in the whole peninsula, running streams being found in no less than four of the adjacent valleys." It was thither that Moses, probably in the early summer, drove Reuel's flock for pasturage and water. Behind him, to the east, lay the desert; before him rose in awful grandeur the mountain of God. The stillness of this place is unbroken; its desolateness only relieved by the variety of coloring in the dark green or the red mountain peaks, some of which "shine in the sunlight like burnished copper." The atmosphere is such that the most distant outlines stand out clearly defined, and the faintest sound falls distinctly on the ear. All at once truly a "strange sight" presented itself. On a solitary crag, or in some sequestered valley, one of those spiked, gnarled, thorny acacia trees, which form so conspicuous a feature in the wadies of" the desert," of which indeed they are. The only timber tree of any size," stood enwrapped in fire, and yet "the bush was not consumed."

At view of this, Moses turned aside "to see this great sight." And yet greater wonder than this awaited him. A vision which for centuries had not been seen now appeared; a voice which had been silent these many ages again spoke. "The Angel of Jehovah" (ver. 2), who is immediately afterwards Himself called "Jehovah" and "God" (vers. 4, 5), spake to him "out of the midst of the bush." His first words warned Moses to put his shoes from off his feet, as standing on holy ground; the next revealed Him as the same Angel of the Covenant, who had appeared unto the fathers as "the God of Abraham, the God of Isaac, and the God of Jacob." The reason of the first injunction was not merely reverence, but it was prompted by the character of Him who spoke. For in the East shoes are worn chiefly as protection from defilement and dust, and hence put off when entering a sanctuary, in order, as it were, not to bring within the pure place defilement from without. But the place where Jehovah manifests Himself — whatever it be — is "holy ground," and he who would have communication with Him must put aside the defilement that clings to him. In announcing Himself as the God of the fathers, Jehovah now declared the continuity of His former purpose of mercy, His remembrance of Israel, and His speedy fulfillment of the promises given of old. During these centuries of silence He had still been the same, ever mindful of His covenant, and now, just as it might seem that His purpose had wholly failed, the set time had come, when He would publicly manifest Himself as the God of Abraham, Isaac, and Jacob.

The same truth was symbolically expressed by the vision of the burning bush. Israel, in its present low and despised state, was like the thorn bush in the wilderness (comp. Judges 9:15), burning in the fiery "furnace of Egypt," (Deuteronomy 4:20) but "not given over unto death," because Jehovah, the Angel of the Covenant, was "in the midst of the bush" — a God who chastened, but did "not consume." And this vision was intended not only for Moses, but for all times. It symbolizes the relationship between God and Israel at all times, and similarly that between Him and His Church. For the circumstances in which the Church is placed, and the purpose of God towards it, continue always the same. But this God, in the midst of the flames of the bush, is also a consuming fire, alike in case of forgetfulness of the covenant on the part of His people, (Deuteronomy 4:24) and as "a fire" that "burneth up His enemies round about." (Psalm 97:3) This manifestation of God under the symbol of fire, which on comparison will be seen to recur through all Scripture, shall find its fullest accomplishment when the Lord Jesus shall come to judge -"His eyes as a flame of fire, and on His head many crowns." (Revelation 19:12)

But as for Moses, he "hid his face; for he was afraid to look upon God." The vision vouchsafed, and the words which accompanied it, prepare us for the further communication which the Lord was pleased to make to His servant. He had heard the cry of His people; He knew their sorrows, and He had come to deliver and bring them into the Land of Promise, "a good land," it is added, "and a large," a land "flowing with milk and honey" -large and fruitful enough to have been at the time the territory of not fewer than six Canaanitish races (ver. 8). Finally, the Lord directed Moses to go to Pharaoh in order to bring His people out of Egypt.

Greater contrast could scarcely be conceived than between the Moses of forty years ago and him who now pleaded to be relieved from this work. If formerly his self-confidence had been such as to take the whole matter into his own hands, his self-diffidence now went the length of utmost reluctance to act, even. as only the Lord's messenger and minister. His first and deepest feelings speak themselves in the question, "Who am I, that I should go unto Pharaoh, and that I should bring forth the children of Israel out of Egypt?" (ver. 11). But the remembrance of former inward and outward failure was no longer applicable, for God Himself would now be with him. In token of this he was told, "When thou hast brought forth the people out of Egypt, ye shall serve God upon this mountain." Evidently this "token" appealed to his faith, as indeed every "sign" does, whence their misunderstanding by those "who are not of the household of faith" (comp. Matthew 12:38, 39; Luke 16:31). Similarly, long afterwards, a distantly future event — the birth of the Virgin's Son — was to be a sign to the house of Ahaz of the preservation of the royal line of David. (Isaiah 7:10-14) Was it then that underneath all else God saw in the heart of Moses a want of realizing faith, and that He would now call it forth? This first difficulty, on the part of Moses, had been set aside. His next was: What should he say in reply to this inquiry of Israel about God? "What is His Name?" (ver. 13). This means, What was he to tell them in answer to their doubts and fears about God's purposes towards them? For, in Scripture, the name is regarded as the manifestation of character or of deepest purpose, whence also a new name was generally given after some decisive event, which for ever after stamped its character upon a person or place.

In answer to this question, the Lord explained to Moses, and bade him tell Israel, the import of the name Jehovah, by which He had at the first manifested Himself, when entering into covenant with Abraham. (Genesis 15:7) It was, "I am that I am" — words betokening His unchangeable nature and faithfulness. The "I am" had sent Moses, and, as if to remove all doubt, he was to add' "the God of your fathers, of Abraham, Isaac, and Jacob." "This," the Lord declares, "is my Name for ever, and this is my memorial to all generations;" in other words, as such He would always prove Himself, and as such He willeth to be known and remembered, not only by Israel, but "to all generations." Here, then, at the very outset, when the covenant with Abraham was transferred to his seed, the promise also, which included all nations in its blessing, was repeated. In further preparation for his mission, God directed Moses on his arrival in Egypt to "gather" the elders of Israel together, and, taking up the very words of Joseph's prophecy when he died, (Genesis 1:24) to announce that the promised time had come, and that God had "surely visited" His people. Israel, he was told, would hearken to his voice; not so Pharaoh, although the original demand upon him was to be only to dismiss the people for a distance of three days' journey into the wilderness. Yet Pharaoh would not yield, "not even by a strong hand" (ver. 19) — that is, even when the strong hand of God would be upon him. But, at the last, the wonder-working power of Jehovah would break the stubborn will of Pharaoh; and when Israel left Egypt it would not be as fugitives, but, as it were, like conquerors laden with the spoil of their enemies.

Thus the prediction clearly intimated that only after a long and severe contest Pharaoh would yield. But would the faith of Israel endure under such a trial? This is probably the meaning of Moses' next question, seemingly strange as put at this stage:

"But, behold, they will not believe me, nor hearken unto my voice: for they will say, Jehovah hath not appeared unto thee." (Exodus 4:1)

To such doubts, whether on the part of Israel, of Pharaoh, or of the Egyptians, a threefold symbolical reply was now furnished, and that not only to silence those who might so object, but also for the encouragement of Moses himself. This reply involved the bestowal of power upon Moses to work miracles. We note that here, for the first time in Old Testament history, this power was bestowed upon man, and that the occasion was the first great conflict between the world and the Church. These miracles were intended to be like "a voice" from heaven, bearing direct testimony to the truth of Moses' commission. So we read in Exodus 4:8 of Israel "hearkening unto" and "believing" "the voice" of the signs, and in Psalm 105:27 (marginal reading) that Moses and Aaron "shewed the words of His signs among them." But while this was the general purpose of the three signs now displayed — first to Moses himself — each had also its special reference. The first to Pharaoh, the second to Israel, and the third to the might of Egypt.

In the first sign Moses was bidden to look at the rod in his hand. It was but an ordinary shepherd's staff, At God's command he was to cast it on the ground, when presently it was changed into a serpent, from which Moses fled in terror. Again God commands, and as Moses seized the serpent by the tail, it once more "became a rod in his hand." The meaning of this was plain. Hitherto Moses had wielded the shepherd's crook. At God's command he was to cast it away; his calling was to be changed, and he would have to meet "the serpent" — not only the old enemy, but the might of Pharaoh, of which the serpent was the public and well-known Egyptian emblem. "The serpent was the symbol of royal and divine power on the diadem of every Pharaoh" — the emblem of the land, of its religion, and government.

At God's command, Moses next seized this serpent, when it became once more in his hand the staff with which he led his flock — only that now the flock was Israel, and the shepherd's staff the wonder-working "rod of God." (Exodus 4:20) In short, the humble shepherd, who would have fled from Pharaoh, should, through Divine strength, overcome all the might of Egypt.

The second sign shown to Moses bore direct reference to Israel. The hand which Moses was directed to put in his bosom became covered with leprosy; but the same hand, when a second time he thrust it in, was restored whole. This miraculous power of inflicting and removing a plague, universally admitted to come from God, showed that Moses could inflict and remove the severest judgments of God. But it spoke yet other "words" to the people. Israel, of whom the Lord had said unto Moses, "Carry them in thy bosom," (Numbers 11:12) was the leprous hand. But as surely and as readily as it was restored when thrust again into Moses' bosom, so would God bring them forth from the misery and desolateness of their state in Egypt, and restore them to their own land.

The third sign given to Moses, in which the water from the Nile when poured upon the ground was to become blood, would not only carry conviction to Israel, but bore special reference to the land of Egypt. The Nile, on which its whole fruitfulness depended, and which the Egyptians worshipped as divine, was to be changed into blood. Egypt and its gods were to be brought low before the absolute power which God would manifest.

These "signs," which could not be gainsaid, were surely sufficient. And yet Moses hesitated. Was he indeed the proper agent for such a work? He possessed not the eloquence whose fire kindles a nation's enthusiasm and whose force sweeps before it all obstacles. And when this objection also was answered by pointing him to the need of direct dependence on Him who could unloose the tongue and open eyes and ears, the secret reluctance of Moses broke forth in the direct request to employ some one else on such a mission. Then it was that "the anger of the Lord was kindled against Moses." Yet in His tender mercy He pitied and helped the weakness of His servant's faith. For this twofold purpose God announced that even then Aaron was on his way to join him, and that he would undertake the part of the work for which Moses felt himself unfit. Aaron would be alike the companion and, so to speak, "the prophet" of Moses. (Exodus 7:1) As the prophet delivers the word which he receives, so would Aaron declare the Divine message committed to Moses. "AND MOSES WENT." (Exodus 4:18)

Two points yet require brief explanation at this stage of our narrative. For, first, it would appear that the request which Moses was in the first place charged to address to Pharaoh was only for leave "to go three days journey into the wilderness," whereas it was intended that Israel should for ever leave the land of Egypt. Secondly, a Divine promise was given that Israel should "not go empty," but that God would give the people favor in the sight of the Egyptians, and that every woman should "borrow of her neighbor," so that they would "spoil the Egyptians."

At the outset, we observe the more than dutiful manner in which Israel was directed to act towards Pharaoh. Absolutely the king, Pharaoh had no right to detain the people in Egypt. Their fathers had avowedly come not to settle, but temporarily "to sojourn," (Genesis 47:4) and on that understanding they had been received. And now they were not only wrongfully oppressed, but unrighteously detained. But still they were not to steal away secretly, nor yet to attempt to raise the standard of rebellion.

Nor was the Divine power with which Moses was armed to be at the first employed either in avenging their past wrongs or in securing their liberty.

On the contrary, they were to apply to Pharaoh for permission to undertake even so harmless an expedition as a three days pilgrimage into the wilderness to sacrifice unto God — a request all the more reasonable, that Israel's sacrifices would, from a religious point of view, have been "an abomination" to the Egyptians, (Exodus 8:62) and might have led to disturbances. The same almost excess of regard for Pharaoh prompted that at the first only so moderate a demand should be made upon him. It was infinite condescension to Pharaoh's weakness, on the part of God, not to insist from the first upon the immediate and entire dismissal of Israel. Less could not have been asked than was demanded of Pharaoh, nor could obedience have been made more easy. Only the most tyrannical determination to crush the rights and convictions of the people, and the most daring defiance of Jehovah, could have prompted him to refuse such a request, and that in face of all the signs and wonders by which the mission of Moses was accredited. Thus at the first his submission was to be tried where it was easiest to render it, and where disobedience would be "without excuse."

There might have been some plea for such a man as Pharaoh to refuse at once and wholly to let those go who had so long been his bondsmen; there could be absolutely none for resisting a demand so moderate and supported by such authority. Assuredly such a man was ripe for the judgment of hardening; just as, on the other hand, if he had at the first yielded obedience to the Divine will, he would surely have been prepared to receive a further revelation of His will, and grace to submit to it. And so God in His mercy always deals with man. "He that is faithful in that which is least, is faithful also in much and he that is unjust in the least, is unjust also in much." The demands of God are intended to try what is in us. It was so in the case of Adam's obedience, of Abraham's sacrifice, and now of Pharaoh; only that in the latter case, as in the promise to spare Sodom if even ten righteous men were found among its wicked inhabitants, the Divine forbearance went to the utmost verge of condescension. The same principle of government also appears in the New Testament, and explains how the Lord often first told of "earthly things," that unbelief in regard to them might convince men of their unfitness to hear of "heavenly things." Thus the young ruler (Matthew 19:16) who believed himself desirous of inheriting eternal life, and the scribe who professed readiness to follow Christ, (Matthew 8:19) had each only a test of "earthly things" proposed, and yet each failed in it. The lesson is one which may find its application in our own ease — for only "then shall we know if we follow on to know the Lord."

The second difficulty about the supposed direction to Israel to "borrow jewels of silver, and jewels of gold, and raiment," and so to "spoil the Egyptians," (Exodus 3:22) rests upon a simple misunderstanding of the text. Common sense even would indicate that, under the circumstances in which the children of Israel, at the last, left the land, no Egyptian could have contemplated a temporary loan of jewels, soon to be repaid. But, in truth, the word rendered in our Authorized Version by "borrowing," does not mean a loan and is not used in that sense in a single passage in which it occurs throughout the Old Testament. It always and only means "to ask" or to request." This "request," or "demand" — as, considering the justice of the case, we should call it — was readily granted by the Egyptians. The terror of Israel had fallen on them, and instead of leaving Egypt as fugitives, they marched out like a triumphant host, carrying with them "the spoil" of their Divinely conquered enemies.

It is of more importance to notice another point. Moses was the first to bear a Divine commission to others. He was also the first to work miracles. Miracles present to us the union of the Divine and the human. All miracles pointed forward to the greatest of all miracles, "the mystery of godliness, into which angels desire to look; "the union of the Divine with the human" in its fullest appearance in the Person of the God-Man. Thus in these two aspects of his office, as well as in his mission to redeem Israel from bondage and to sanctify them unto the Lord, Moses was an eminent type of Christ.

"Wherefore" let us "consider the Apostle and High Priest of our profession, Christ Jesus; who was faithful to Him that appointed Him, as also Moses was faithful in all his house — as a servant, for a testimony of those things which were to be spoken after; but Christ as a Son over His own house; whose house are we, if we hold fast the confidence and the rejoicing of the hope firm unto the end." (Hebrews 3:1, 2, 5, 6)

CHAPTER 5: MOSES RETURNS INTO EGYPT — THE DISMISSAL OF ZIPPORAH -MOSES MEETS AARON — THEIR RECEPTION BY THE CHILDREN OF ISRAEL — REMARKS ON THE HARDENING OF PHARAOH'S HEART

(EXODUS 15:17-31)

SCRIPTURE-HISTORY is full of seemingly strange contrasts. Unintelligible to the superficial observer, the believing heart rejoices to trace in them, side by side, the difference between what appears to the eye of man and what really is before God; and then between the power of God, and the humbleness of the means and circumstances through which He chooses to manifest it. The object of the one is to draw out our faith, and to encourage it in circumstances which least promise success; that of the other, to give all the glory to God, and ever to direct our eye from earth to heaven. So it was, when, in the days of His flesh, neither Israel nor the Gentiles recognized the royal dignity of Christ in Him who entered Jerusalem, "meek, and riding upon an ass and the colt of an ass." And so it also appeared, when, in the simple language of Scripture, "Moses took his wife and his sons, and set them upon an, ass, and he returned to the land of Egypt: and Moses took the rod of God in his hand." (Exodus 4:20)

What a contrast! He who bears in his hand the rod of God is dismissed in this mean manner — his wife and sons, and all their goods laden on one ass, and himself humbly walking by their side! Who would have recognized in this humble guise him who carried that by which he would smite down the pride of Pharaoh and the might of Egypt?

On his return from "the mount of God," Moses had simply announced to his father-in-law his purpose of revisiting Egypt Probably Jethro had not sufficient enlightenment for Moses to communicate to him the Divine vision. Besides, the relations between them at the time (as we gather even from the manner in which Jethro allowed him to depart) seem not to have been such as to invite special confidence; possibly, it might have only raised hindrances on the part of Jethro or of Zipporah. But it was an indication that God furthered his way, when alike his father-in-law and his wife so readily agreed to an expedition which, in the circumstances, might have been fraught with great danger. And this was not all. After he had resolved to go, but before he actually set out, God encouraged him by the information that all the men were dead who had sought his life. Again, while on his journey, He gave him threefold strengthening for the work before him. First, He pointed him to the Divine rod in his hand, with which he was to attest by miracles his mission to Pharaoh. (Exodus 4:21) Secondly, lest he should be discouraged by the failure of these signs to secure Pharaoh's submission, God not only foretold the hardening of the king's heart, but by saying, "I will harden his heart" (ver. 21), proved that that event also was under His own immediate control and direction. Lastly, in the message which he was to bear to Pharaoh a double assurance was conveyed (vers. 22, 23). Jehovah demanded freedom for the people, because "Israel is my son, even my firstborn," and He threatened, in case of Pharaoh's refusal, "to slay" his "son," even the king's "firstborn." So terrible a threat was to prove the earnestness of the Divine demand and purpose. On the other hand, the tide given to Israel implied that God would not leave "His firstborn" in the bondage of

Egypt. In the contest with Pharaoh Jehovah would surely prevail. That precious relationship between God and His people, which was fully established in the covenant at Mount Sinai, (Exodus 19:5) might be said to have commenced with the call of Abraham. Israel was "the son of God" by election, by grace, and by adoption (Deuteronomy 32:18; Isaiah 64:8; Jeremiah 3:4; Malachi 1:6; 2:10) As such, the Lord would never withdraw His love from him, (Hosea 11:1; Jeremiah 31:9-20) but pity him even as a father his children; (Psalm 103:13) and, although He would chasten the people for their sins, yet would He not withdraw His mercy from them. Such a relationship is nowhere else in the Old Testament indicated as subsisting between God and any other nation. But it is exceedingly significant that Israel is only called "the firstborn." For this conveys that Israel was not to be alone in the family of God, but that, in accordance with the promise to Abraham, other sons should be born into the Father's house. Thus even the highest promise spoken to Israel included in it the assurance of future blessing to the Gentiles.

And yet he who was to declare Israel the heir to this precious legacy was himself at the time living in neglect of the sign of that very covenant! His own second son had not been circumcised according to the Divine commandment (Genesis 17:14) — whether from neglect, owing to faith discouraged, or, more probably, as we gather from the subsequent conduct of Zipporah, on account of his wife's opposition, which in his depressed circumstances he could not overcome. But judgment must begin at the house of God; and no one is fit to be employed as an instrument for God who in any way lives in neglect of His commandments. God met even His chosen servant Moses as an enemy. His life was in imminent danger, and Zipporah had to submit, however reluctantly, to the ordinance of God. But her mood and manner showed that as yet she was not prepared to be Moses' helpmate in the work before him. He seems to have understood this, and to have sent her and the children back to his father-in-law. Only at a later period, when he had "heard of all that God had done for Moses and for Israel His people," did Jethro himself bring them again to Moses. (Exodus 18:1-7)

Thus purged from the leaven of sin, Moses continued his journey. Once more God had anticipated His servant's difficulties; we might almost say, the fulfillment of His own promises. Already He had directed Aaron "to go into the wilderness to meet Moses." At the mount of God the two brothers met, and Aaron willingly joined the Divine mission of Moses. Arrived in Egypt, they soon "gathered together all the elders of the children of Israel." At hearing of the gracious tidings which Aaron announced, and at sight of "the signs" with which he attested them, it is said, "they bowed their heads and worshipped." Then God had not forsaken His people whom He foreknew! So then, not Moses' unbelieving fears (4:1), but God's gracious promise (3:18), had in this respect also been amply realized. Neither their long stay in Egypt nor their bondage had extinguished their faith in the God of their fathers, or their hope of deliverance. However grievously they might afterwards err and sin, the tidings that "Jehovah had visited" His people came not upon them as strange or incredible. More than that, their faith was mingled with humiliation and worship.

Before we pass to an account of the wonders by which Moses was so soon to prove before Pharaoh the reality of his mission, it may be convenient here briefly to consider a very solemn element in the history of these transactions — we mean, the hardening of Pharaoh's heart. Not that we can ever hope fully to understand what touches the counsels of God, the administration of His government, the mysterious connection between the creature and the Creator, and the solemn judgments by which He vindicates His power over the rebellious. But a reverent consideration of some points, taken directly from the text itself, may help us at least, like Israel of old, to "bow our heads and worship." We have already noticed, that before Moses had returned into Egypt, (Exodus 4:21) God had declared of Pharaoh, "I will harden his heart," placing this phase in the foreground, that Moses might be assured of God's overruling will in the matter. For a similar purpose, only much more fully expressed, God now again announced to Moses, before the commencement of the ten plagues, (Exodus 7:3)

"I will harden Pharaoh's heart, and multiply My signs and My wonders in the land of Egypt."

These are the two first statements about the hardening of Pharaoh's heart. In both cases the agency is ascribed to God; but in both cases the event is yet future, and the announcement is only made in order to explain to Moses what his faith almost needed to know.

Twice ten times in the course of this history does the expression hardening occur in connection with Pharaoh. Although in our English version only the word "harden" is used, in the Hebrew original three different terms are employed, of which one (as in Exodus 7:3) literally means to make hard or insensible, the other (as in 10:1) to make heavy, that is, unimpressionable, and the third (as in 14:4), to make firm or stiff, so as to be immovable. Now it is remarkable, that of the twenty passages which speak of Pharaoh's hardening, exactly ten ascribe it to Pharaoh himself, and ten to God, and that in both cases precisely the same three terms are used. Thus the making "hard," "heavy," and "firm" of the heart is exactly as often and in precisely the same terms traced to the agency of Pharaoh himself as to that of God. As a German writer aptly remarks, "The effect of the one is the hardening of man to his own destruction; that of the other, the hardening of man to the glory of God."

Proceeding further, we find that, with the exception of the two passages (Exodus 4:21; 7:3) in which the Divine agency in hardening is beforehand announced to Moses for his instruction, the hardening process is during the course of the actual history, in the first place, traced only to Pharaoh himself. Thus, before the ten plagues, and when Aaron first proved his Divine mission by converting the rod into a serpent, (Exodus 7:10) "the heart of Pharaoh was hardened," that is, by himself (vers. 13, 14).

Similarly, after each of the first five plagues (7:22; 8:15; 8:19; 8:32; 9:7) the hardening is also expressly attributed to Pharaoh himself. Only when still resisting after the sixth plague do we read for the first time, that "the Lord made firm the heart of Pharaoh" (9:12). But even so, space for repentance must have been left, for after the seventh plague we read again (9:34) that "Pharaoh made heavy his heart;" and it is only after the eighth plague that the agency is exclusively ascribed to God. Moreover, we have to consider the progress of this hardening on the part of Pharaoh, by which at last his sin became ripe for judgment. It was not only that he resisted the demand of Moses, even in view of the miraculous signs by which his mission was attested; but that, step by step, the hand of God became more clearly manifest, till at last he was, by his own confession, "inexcusable." If the first sign of converting the rod into a serpent could in a certain manner be counterfeited by the Egyptian magicians, yet Aaron's rod swallowed up theirs (7:12). But after the third plague, the magicians themselves confessed their inability to carry on the contest, declaring, "This is the finger of God" (8:9). If any doubt had still been left upon his mind, it must have been removed by the evidence presented after the fifth plague (9:7), when "Pharaoh sent, and, behold, there was not one of the cattle of the Israelites dead." Some of the Egyptians. at least, had profited by this lesson, and on the announcement of the seventh plague housed their cattle from the predicted hail and fire (9:20, 21). Lastly, after that seventh plague, Pharaoh himself acknowledged his sin and wrong (9:27), and promised to let Israel go (ver. 28). Yet after all, on its removal, he once more hardened his heart (ver. 35)!

Can we wonder that such high-handed and inexcusable rebellion should have been ripe for the judgment which appeared in the Divine hardening of his heart? Assuredly in such a contest between the pride and daring of the creature and the might of the Lord God, the truth of this Divine declaration had to be publicly manifested:

"Even for this purpose have I raised thee up, that I might show My power in thee, and that My name might be declared throughout all the earth." (Romans 9:17)

For the long-suffering and patience of God will not always wait. It is indeed most true, that "God hath no pleasure in the death of the wicked, but rather that he be converted and live;" (Ezekiel 33:11) and that He "will have all men come to the knowledge of the truth and be saved." (1 Timothy 2:4, 2 Peter 3:9)

But "he that being often reproved hardeneth his neck, shall suddenly be destroyed, and then without remedy." (Proverbs 29:1)

The same manifestation of God which to the believing is "a savor of life unto life," is to those who resist it "a savor of death unto death." As one has written, "the sunlight shining upon our earth produces opposite results according to the nature of the soil." In Scripture language: (Hebrews 6:7, 8) "the earth which drinketh in the rain that cometh oft upon it, and bringeth forth herbs meet for them by whom it is dressed, receiveth blessing from God: but that which beareth thorns and briars is rejected, and is nigh unto cursing; whose end is to be burned." Or, as a German writer puts it, "It is the curse of sin that it makes the hard heart ever harder against the gracious drawing of the Divine love, patience, and long-suffering."

Thus they who harden themselves fall at last under the Divine judgment of hardening, with all the terrible consequences which it involves.

Hitherto we have only traced this as it appears in the course of Pharaoh's history. There are, however, deeper bearings of the question, connected with the Divine dealings, the sovereignty, and the power of God. For such inquiries this is obviously not the place. Suffice it to draw some practical lessons. First and foremost, we learn the insufficiency of even the most astounding miracles to subdue the rebellious will, to change the heart, or to subject a man unto God. Our blessed Lord Himself has said of a somewhat analogous case, that men would not believe even though one rose from the dead. (Luke 16:31) And His statement has been only too amply verified in the history of the world since His own resurrection. Religion is matter of the heart, and no intellectual conviction, without the agency Of the Holy Spirit, affects the inmost springs of our lives. Secondly, a more terrible exhibition of the daring of human pride, the confidence of worldly power, and the deceitfulness of sin than that presented by the history of this Pharaoh can scarcely be conceived. And yet the lesson seems to have been overlooked by too many! Not only sacred history but possibly our own experience may furnish instances of similar tendencies; and in the depths of his own soul each believer must have felt his danger in this respect, for "the heart is deceitful above all things, and desperately wicked." Lastly, resistance to God must assuredly end in fearful judgment. Each conviction suppressed, each admonition stifled, each loving offer rejected, tends towards increasing spiritual insensibility, and that in which it ends. It is wisdom and safety to watch for the blessed influences of God's Spirit, and to throw open our hearts to the sunlight of His grace.

CHAPTER 6: MOSES AND AARON DELIVER THEIR MESSAGE TO PHARAOH — INCREASED OPPRESSION OF ISRAEL — DISCOURAGEMENT OF MOSES — AARON SHOWS A SIGN — GENERAL VIEW AND ANALYSIS OF EACH OF THE TEN "STROKES," OR PLAGUES

(Exodus 5-12:30)

THE predicted trial was soon to come. Provoked through the daring of man, who would measure his strength against that of the living God, it was to establish two facts for all ages and to all mankind. In sight of Egypt (Exodus 7:5) and of Israel (10:2) it was to evidence that God was Jehovah, the only true and the living God, far above all power of men and of gods. (Exodus 9:14) This was one aspect of the judgments which were to burst upon Egypt. (Romans 9:17) The other was, that He was the faithful Covenant-God, who remembered His promises, and would bring out His people "with a stretched-out arm and with great judgments," to take them to Himself for a people, and to be to them a God (4:1-8). These are the eternal truths which underlie the history of Israel's deliverance from Egypt. How Israel had understood and taught them to their children, appears from many passages of Scripture, especially from Psalm 78 and 105. Nor is their application less suited to our wants. It exhibits alike the Law and the Gospel — the severity and the goodness of God — and may be summed up in that grand proclamation unto all the world: "Jehovah reigneth." (Psalm 99:1)

The sacred narrative here consists of two parts, the one preparatory, so far as all parties in this history are concerned — Pharaoh, Israel, and Moses; the other describing the successive "signs" in which Jehovah manifested Himself and His power, and by which He achieved both the deliverance of Israel and His judgments upon Pharaoh and Egypt. And here we shall notice successive progress, externally in the character of the Plagues sent by God, and internally in their effect upon Pharaoh and his people. Twice, before the plagues laid low the pride of Egypt, Moses and Aaron had to appear before Pharaoh, once with a simple message (5:1-5), the second time both with a message and a sign to attest their mission (6:10-13; 7:8-13). In this also we mark the Divine condescension and goodness. If at the first interview the king could say,

"Who is Jehovah, that I should obey His voice to let Israel go? I know not Jehovah, neither will I let Israel go" (Exodus 5:2),

it became impossible to urge this plea, when, at the king's challenge, "Shew a miracle for you" (7:9), Aaron's rod was changed into a serpent. This proved beyond doubt that Jehovah was God, and that he had commissioned His servants, since they wielded His power. The only question still possible was, whether the gods whom Pharaoh served were equal to the Lord. For this purpose the king summoned his magicians, who imitated, in a certain way, the miracle of Aaron. But even so, the inferiority of their power was proven when" Aaron's rod swallowed up their rods." This assuredly — even taking their own profession of miracle-working — should have been sufficient to indicate to Pharaoh that "Jehovah, He is God" — had his hardness of heart admitted of such conviction. But as between Moses' and

Aaron's first and second interview with Pharaoh important events occurred, it may be well briefly to record them again in their order.

After the first interview, in which Moses and Aaron had simply delivered the Divine command, Pharaoh, who had pleaded ignorance of Jehovah (that is, of His Deity and claims), professed to regard the demand of Moses as a mere pretense to procure a series of holidays for the people. They were "vain words" (5:9) "to let the people from their works" (ver. 4). As "the people of the land" — that is, the Israelites, the laboring class — were "many," to "make them rest from their burdens" (ver. 5) would inflict great damage upon the king. To prevent their having either time or inclination to listen to such suggestions, the king ordered that, while the old amount of work should continue to be exacted, the straw needful for making the sun-dried bricks (such as we find on the monuments of Egypt) should no longer be supplied. The time requisite for gathering "stubble instead of straw" prevented, of course, their fulfilling their "daily tasks."

The punishment then fell upon the Israelitish "officers," or rather "scribes," whom the Egyptian "taskmasters" had set over the work and held responsible for it. An appeal to Pharaoh only explained the cause of his increased severity, and the "officers" of a people which but lately had acknowledged that God had visited them, not seeing that visitation, but rather seemingly the opposite, ventured in their unbelief to appeal to Jehovah against Moses and Aaron! So rapidly do the results of a faith which cometh only by the hearing of the ear give way before discouragements.

As for Moses, the hour of his severest trial had now come. With the words of Israel's complaint he went straight to the Lord, yet, as St. Augustine remarks, not in the language of contumacy or of anger, but of inquiry and prayer. To his question, "Lord, wherefore hast Thou so evil entreated this people?" (5:22) — as so often to our inquiries into God's "Wherefore" -no reply of any kind was made. "What I do thou knowest not now, but thou shalt know hereafter." To us, indeed, the "need be" of making the yoke of Egypt as galling as possible seems now evident, as we remember how the heart of the people clung to the flesh-pots of Egypt, even after they had tasted the heavenly manna; (Numbers 11) and the yet higher "need be for it," since the lower Israel's condition and the more tyrannical Pharaoh's oppression, the more glorious the triumph of Jehovah, and the more complete the manifestation of His enemy's impotence. But in Moses it only raised once more, at this season of depression, the question of his fitness for the work which he had undertaken. For when Satan cannot otherwise oppose, he calls forth in us unbelieving doubts as to our aptitude or call for a work. The direction which Moses now received from God applies, in principle, to all similar cases. It conveyed a fresh assurance that God would certainly accomplish His purpose; it gave a fuller revelation of His character as Jehovah, with the special promises which this implied (6:2-8); and it renewed the commission to Moses to undertake the work, accompanied by encouragements and assurances suitable in the circumstances.

One point here claims special attention, not only on account of the difficulties which it presents to the general reader, but also because its lessons are so precious. When, on the occasion just referred to, God said to Moses (Exodus 6:2, 3),

"I am Jehovah and I appeared unto Abraham, unto Isaac, and unto Jacob in El Shaddai (God Almighty), but as to My name Jehovah was I not known to them,"

It cannot, of course, mean, that the patriarchs were ignorant of the special designation Jehovah, since it frequently occurs in their history. To understand this passage aright, we must bear in mind the meaning of the expression "name" as applied to God, and that of the term "Jehovah." By the "name of God" we are of course to understand not a mere appellation of God, but that by which He makes Himself known to man. Now Scripture teaches us that we only know God in so far as He manifests, or reveals Himself. Hence the peculiar name of God indicates the peculiar manner in which He had manifested Himself, or, in other words, the character, of His dealings at the time. Now the character of God's dealings — and therefore His name — was in patriarchal times unquestionably El Shaddai (Genesis 17:1; 35:11; 48:3). But His manifestation as Jehovah -the dealings by which, in the sight of all men, He made Himself known as such — belonged not to that, but to a later period. For the term "Jehovah" literally means, "He who is," which agrees with the explanation given by God Himself. "He who is that He is." (Exodus 3:14) As here used, the word "to be" refers not to the essential nature of God, but to His relationship towards man. In that relationship God manifested Himself, and He was known as Jehovah — as "He who is that He is," in other words, as unchangeable — when, after centuries of silence, and after the condition of Israel in Egypt had become almost hopeless, He showed that He had not forgotten His promise given to the fathers, that He had all along been preparing its fulfillment; and that neither the resistance of Pharaoh nor the might of Egypt could stay His hand. Viewed in this light, the distinction between the original El Shaddai manifestation to the patriarchs and the Jehovah knowledge vouchsafed to the children of Israel becomes both clear and emphatic.

But to return. The first interview of Moses with Pharaoh had served to determine the relationship of all parties in reference to the Divine command. It had brought out the enmity of Pharaoh, ripening for judgment; the unbelief of Israel, needing much discipline; and even the weakness of Moses. There, at the outset of his work, even as the Lord Jesus at the commencement of His ministry, he was tempted of the adversary, and overcame by the word of God. Yet how great in this also, is the difference between the type and the Antitype!

Still, though hardly fought, the contest was gained, and Moses and Aaron confronted a second time the king of Egypt. On this occasion Aaron, when challenged by Pharaoh, proved his fight to speak in the name of God. He cast down his rod, and it became a serpent, and although "the magicians of Egypt" "did in like manner with their enchantments," the superiority of Aaron appeared when his "rod swallowed up their rods." Without here entering into the general question of magic before the coming of our Lord, or of the power which the devil and his agents may have wielded on earth before our Savior subdued his might, and led captivity captive, there was really nothing in what the Egyptian magicians did that Eastern jugglers do not profess to this day. To make a serpent stiff and to look like a rod, and then again suddenly to restore it to life, are among the commonest tricks witnessed by travelers. St. Paul mentions the names of Jannes and Jambres as those who "withstood Moses," (2 Timothy 3:8) and his statement is not only confirmed by Jewish tradition, but even referred to by the Roman writer Pliny. Both their names are Egyptian, and one of them occurs in an ancient Egyptian document. In this connection it is also important to notice, that the Hebrew term for "the serpent," into which Aaron's rod was changed, is not that commonly used, but bears a more specific meaning. It is not the same term as that for the serpent (nachash) by which Moses was to accredit his mission before his own people, (Exodus 4:3, 4) but it indicated the kind of serpent (tannin) specially used by Egyptian conjurers, and bore pointed reference to the serpent as the great symbol of Egypt. Hence also the expression "dragon," which is the proper rendering of the word, is frequently in Scripture used to denote Egypt. (Psalm 74:13; Isaiah 27:1; 51:9; Ezekiel 29:3;

32:2) Accordingly Pharaoh should have understood that, when Aaron's rod swallowed up the others, it pointed to the vanquishment of Egypt, and the executing of judgment "against all the gods of Egypt." (Exodus 12:12) Willfully to shut his eyes to this, and to regard Aaron and Moses as magicians whom his own equaled in power, was to harden his heart, and to call down those terrible plagues which ushered in the final judgment upon Pharaoh and his people.

Before describing in detail the plagues of Egypt, a few general remarks will be helpful to our understanding of the subject.

1. The plagues were miraculous — yet not so much in themselves as in the time, the manner, and the measure in which they came upon Egypt. None of them was wholly unknown in Egypt, but had visited the land at some time or other, and in some measure. As so often, the Lord here employed ordinary natural events. The supernaturalness of the plagues consisted in their severity, their successive occurrence, their coming and going at the word of Moses, their partial extent, and the unusual seasons and manner in which they appeared.

2. We mark in them a regular arrangement and steady progress. Properly speaking, there were only nine plagues (3 X 3), the tenth "stroke" being in reality the commencement of judgment by Jehovah Himself, when He went out "into the midst of Egypt" to slay its firstborn. Of these nine, the first three were in connection with that river and soil which formed the boast of Egypt, and the object of its worship. They extended over the whole country, and at the third the magicians confessed, "This is the finger of God." By them the land was laid low in its pride and in its religion. The other six came exclusively upon the Egyptians, as the Lord had said: "I will put a division between My people and thy people," "to the end that thou mayest know that I am Jehovah in the midst of the land." If the first three plagues had shown the impotence of Egypt, the others proved that Jehovah reigned even in the midst of Egypt. Finally, the three last "strokes" were not only far more terrible than any of the others, but intended to make Pharaoh know "that there is none like Me in all the earth." (Exodus 9:14)

To show that Jehovah, He is God, that He was such in the midst of Egypt, and finally, that there was none like Him in the midst of all the earth — or, that Jehovah was the living and the true God — such was the threefold object of these "strokes."

3. In reference to the duration of these strokes, the interval between them, and the length of time occupied by all, we know that the first plague lasted seven days, (Exodus 7:25) and that the killing of the firstborn and the Passover occurred in the night of the fourteenth, Abib (or Nisan), corresponding to about the beginning of April. In reference to the seventh plague (that of the hail), we have this statement to guide us as to its time: (Exodus 9:31, 32) the flax and the barley was smitten, for the barley was in the ear, and the flax was boiled (or in blossom). But the wheat and the rice (or rather the spelt) were not smitten: for they were not grown." This would fix the time as about the end of January or the beginning of February, giving an interval of at least eight weeks between the seventh and the tenth stroke, or, if we might take this as an average, of more than two weeks between each plague. Computed at this rate, the first "stroke" would have fallen in September or October, that is, after the cessation of the annual overflow of the Nile. But this seems unlikely, not only because the red coloring ordinarily appears in the river at the commencement of its increase, but because the expressions (7:19, 21) seem to imply that the river was then at its rise (and not on the decrease), and especially because just before this the Israelites are represented as gathering "stubble" for their bricks, which must have been immediately after

the harvest, or about the end of April. Hence it seems more likely (as most interpreters suppose) that the first "stroke" fell upon Egypt about the middle of June, in which case from the first "plague" an interval of about ten months would have elapsed prior to the slaying of the firstborn. All this time did the Lord deal with Egypt, and Pharaoh was on his trial! There is, as we have already indicated, a terrible irony about "the plagues" of Egypt, since in the things in which Egypt exalted itself it was laid low.

We seem to hear it throughout,

"He that sitteth in the heavens shall laugh. The Lord shall have them in derision." (Psalm 2:4) This will appear more clearly as we briefly consider each of the "strokes."

The first "stroke," or "Plague." Early in the morning, during the rise of the Nile, Pharaoh went down to the river to offer unto its waters the customary Divine worship. Probably, he was accompanied by his wise men and magicians. Here he was confronted by Moses with the message of God. On his refusal to listen, Moses smote, as he had threatened the waters with the rod of God, and the Nile, in all its branches, canals, cisterns, and reservoirs, becomes red, like blood. Such a change of color in the Nile was by no means uncommon, or Pharaoh would scarcely have quite hardened his heart against the miracle. In ordinary times this appearance of the river arises partly from the red earth, which the swollen waters carry with them, and partly from the presence of small cryptogamic plants and animalcules (infusoria).

The supernaturalness of the event lay in its suddenness, in its appearance at the command of Moses, and in the now altered qualities of the water. "The fish that was in the river died" — thus depriving the people of one of the main staples of their food; — "and the river stank, and the Egyptians could not drink of the water of the river," thus cutting off the main supply of their drink. Somehow the magicians, however, contrived to imitate this miracle, probably on some of the water that had been drawn before "the rod" had smitten the river. And so for seven days, throughout the whole land of Egypt, the blood-like, un-drinkable water in every household "vessel of wood" or of earthenware, and in the large stone troughs which stood for general use in the corners of streets and on village-roads, bore testimony for Jehovah. And the Egyptians had to dig round about the river, that their drinking-water might be filtered for use. But "Pharaoh turned and went into his house, neither did he set his heart to this also." The second "stroke" or "plague" — that of the frogs — was also in connection with the river Nile. At the same time it must be remembered that the frog was also connected with the most ancient forms of idolatry in Egypt, so that what was the object of their worship once more became their curse. Here also a natural occurrence, not uncommon in Egypt, rendered Pharaoh's unbelief not impossible. After the annual inundation of the Nile the mud not uncommonly produces thousands of frogs — called by the Arabs to this day by the name corresponding to the term used in the Bible. These frogs "are small, do not leap much, are much like toads, and fill the whole country with their croaking. They are rapidly consumed by the, ibis, which thus preserves the land from the stench described in Exodus 8:14. The supernaturalness of the visitation lay in their extraordinary number and troublsomeness (8:3), and in their appearance at the bidding of Moses. The magicians here also succeeded in imitating Moses upon a small scale. But apparently they were wholly unable to remove the plague, and Pharaoh had to ask the intercession of Moses, at the same time promising to let the people go. To give the king yet further proof that "the stroke" was not natural but of God, Moses left Pharaoh the option of himself fixing what time he pleased for their removal: "Glory over me: when shall I entreat for thee?" (8:9) — that is, let me not fix a time, but let me yield to thee the glory of fixing the exact time for the cessation of the plague. "But when Pharaoh saw that there was respite (literally, enlargement, breathing-space), he made heavy his heart."

The third stroke, as always the third in each of the three series of plagues, came unannounced to Pharaoh, and consisted, not exactly of what we call "lice," but rather of a kind of small insects, scarcely visible, but which penetrate everywhere and cause the most intense inconvenience. Sir S. Baker describes this visitation of vermin, which is not uncommon after the rice-harvest, in almost the words of Scripture: "It is as though the very dust were turned into lice." The "plague" came when Aaron, as directed by God, had smitten the dust of the earth with his rod. As twice before the river, so now the fertile soil, which the Egyptians also worshipped, became their curse. In vain the magicians tried to imitate this miracle. Their power was foiled. But, to neutralize the impression, they "said unto Pharaoh, This is the finger of Elohim" (8:19) — the result of the power of a God. He has done this. Therefore, being in no way due to Moses and Aaron, it cannot confirm their demand. We are vanquished, yet not by Moses and Aaron, but by a Divine power equally superior to them and to us. Therefore "Pharaoh's heart was hardened" ("made firm" and insensible).

And now in the second series of plagues commenced the distinction between the Egyptians and Israel, the latter being exempted from "the strokes," to show that it was not "the finger of Elohim merely," but that He was "Jehovah in the midst of the land" of Egypt (8:22). For the same reason, Moses and Aaron were not used as instruments in the fourth and fifth plagues. They were simply announced to Pharaoh by the messengers of Jehovah, but inflicted by God Himself, to show that they came directly from His hand.

The fourth stroke consisted of swarms of so-called dog-flies, which not only infested the houses, but "corrupted the land" by depositing everywhere their eggs. This "plague" (Psalm 78:45) is to this day most troublesome, painful, and even dangerous, as these animals fasten upon every uncovered surface, especially the eyelids and corners of the eyes, and their bites cause severe inflammation. it was announced to Pharaoh, as he went to the river early in the morning (8:20), as has been suggested, probably "with a procession, in order to open the solemn festival which was held one hundred and twenty days after the first rise" of the Nile (i.e. about the end of October or early in November). Although it wrung from Pharaoh consent for the people to go, yet on its removal, "he hardened his heart at this time also" — perhaps because in this and the next plague he did not see the instrumentality of Moses, and therefore fell back upon the theory of the magicians about "the finger of Elohim." The fifth stroke was a very grievous murrain (not uncommon in Egypt, which has been supposed to have been of the same kind as the "cattle-plague" in our own country, only far more extensive. But although Pharaoh ascertained, by special inquiry, that Israel had been exempted from this plague, his heart was hardened.

The sixth stroke was again made to descend by the instrumentality of Moses and Aaron. As the third in the second series, it came without any warning to the king. Moses and Aaron were directed to take "ashes of the furnace" — probably in reference to the great buildings and pyramids in which Egypt took such pride — and to "sprinkle it up towards heaven; and it became a boil breaking forth with blains upon man and upon beast" (9:10). Such "burning turnouts breaking into pustulous ulcers," but exclusively confined to man, are not uncommon in the valley of the Nile. Even the magicians seem now to have yielded (ver. 11), but the judgment of hardening had already come upon Pharaoh.

The sixth plague had struck not only the pride and the possessions of the Egyptians, but their persons. But the three which now followed in rapid succession, stroke upon stroke, were far more terrible than any that had preceded, and indeed represented "all" God's "plagues" (ver. 14). They were ushered in by a most solemn warning, unheeded by him who was nigh unto destruction (vers. 15-18). The reason why God did not at once destroy Pharaoh and his people is thus stated by the Lord Himself:

(Exodus 9:15, 16) "For now if I had stretched forth My hand and smitten thee and thy people with the pestilence, then hadst thou been cut off from the earth. But now, in very deed for this cause have I let thee stand (made thee stand, raised thee up), (Romans 9:17) for to show in thee My power (perhaps, to let thee see or experience it — this is the first reason; the second) and that My Name may be declared throughout all the earth."

That this actually was the result we gather from Exodus 15:14. Nay, the tidings spread not only among the Arabs, but long afterwards among the Greeks and Romans, and finally, through the Gospel, among all nations of the earth.

Only one day for thought and repentance was granted to Pharaoh (9:18) before the seventh stroke descended. It consisted of such hail as had never been seen in Egypt, mingled with thunder and fiery lightning. The cattle in Egypt are left out to graze from January to April, and such of the Egyptians as gave heed to the warning of Moses withdrew their cattle, and servants into shelter, and so escaped the consequences; the rest suffered loss of men and beasts. That some "among the servants of Pharaoh" "feared the word of Jehovah" (9:20) affords evidence of the spiritual effect of these "strokes." Indeed Pharaoh himself now owned, "I have sinned this time" (ver. 27). But this very limitation, and the hardening of his heart when the calamity ceased, show that his was only the fear of consequences, and, as Moses had said, "that ye will not yet fear Jehovah Elohim" (ver. 30).

A very decided advance is to be marked in connection with the eighth stroke. For Moses and Aaron, on the ground of Pharaoh's former confession of sin, brought this message from God to him: "How long wilt thou refuse to humble thyself before Me?" (Exodus 10:3)

Similarly, "Pharaoh's servants," warned by previous judgments, now expostulated with the king (10:7), and he himself seemed willing to let the male Israelites go for a short season, provided they left their families and flocks behind. On the other hand, the hardening of Pharaoh's heart had also so far advanced, that, on Moses' refusal to submit to conditions, the king burst into such daring taunts as (vers. 10, 11): "So be it! Jehovah be with you as I will let go you and your little ones. Look! for evil is before your faces" (i.e. your intentions are evil; or, perhaps, it may be rendered. See to it! for beware, danger is before you). "Not so! Go then, ye men, for that ye are seeking" (the language evidently ironical). And they were driven out from Pharaoh's presence.

And thus it came, that when "Moses stretched forth his rod over the land of Egypt, Jehovah brought an east wind upon the land all that day, and all that night; and when it was morning the east wind brought the locusts." Once more they were natural means which the Lord used. For the plague of locusts was common in Egypt; yet even the heathen used to regard this as a special visitation of God. In Scripture it serves as the emblem of the last judgments coming upon our earth. (Revelation 9:3-10) This "plague," so much dreaded at all times, came now slowly, from far-off Arabia, upon the doomed land, more grievous than such visitation had ever been known, and to the utter destruction of every green thing still left in Egypt — Goshen alone being again excepted. Pharaoh felt it, and for the first time not only confessed his sin, but asked forgiveness, and entreated that "this death" might be taken away (10:16, 17). Not for want of knowledge, then, did Pharaoh harden himself after that. Yet now also it was not repentance, but desire for removal of "this death," that had influenced Pharaoh. No sooner had his request been granted, than his rebellion returned.

Once more unannounced came the ninth stroke, more terrible than any that had preceded. A thick darkness covered the whole land, except Goshen. There was this peculiar phenomenon about it, that, not only were the people unable to see each other, but "neither rose any from his place for three days." It was literally, as Scripture has it, a "darkness which might be felt" — the darkness of a great sand-storm, such as the Chamsin or southwest wind sometimes brings in early spring, only far more severe, intense, and long. Let us try to realize the scene. Suddenly and without warning would the Chamsin rise, The air, charged with electricity, draws up the fine dust and the coarser particles of sand till the light of the sun is hid, the heavens are covered as with a thick veil, and darkness deepens into such night that even artificial light is of no avail. And the floating dust and sand enter every apartment, pervade every pore, find their way even through closed windows and doors. Men and beasts make for any kind of shelter, seek refuge in cellars and out-of-the-way places from the terrible plague. And so, in utter darkness and suffering, three weary nights and long days pass, no one venturing to stir from his hiding. Once more, Pharaoh now summoned Moses. This time he would let all the people go, if only they would leave their flocks behind as pledge of their return. And when Moses refused the condition, the king

"said unto him, Get thee from me, take heed to thyself; see my face no more; for in that day thou seest my face thou shalt die" (10:28).

It was a challenge which sounded not strange in Moses' ears, for before this interview God had informed him what would happen, and directed that Israel should prepare to leave. And Moses now took up the kings challenge, and foretold how after those terrible three days darkness "at midnight," Jehovah Himself would "go out into the midst of Egypt," and smite every firstborn of man and beast. Then would rise through the night a great lamentation over the land, from the chamber of the palace, where Pharaoh's only son lay a-dying, to that of the hut where the lowliest maidservant watched the ebbing tide of her child's life.

But in Goshen all these three days was light and festive joy. For while thick darkness lay upon Egypt, the children of Israel, as directed by God, had already on the tenth of the month — four days before the great night of woe — selected their Paschal lambs, and were in waiting for their deliverance. And alike the darkness and the light were of Jehovah — the one symbolical of His judgments, the other of His favor.

CHAPTER 7: THE PASSOVER AND ITS ORDINANCES — THE CHILDREN OF ISRAEL LEAVE EGYPT — THEIR FIRST RESTING-PLACE THE PILLAR OF CLOUD AND OF FIRE — PURSUIT OF PHARAOH PASSAGE THROUGH THE RED SEA — DESTRUCTION OF PHARAOH AND HIS HOST — THE SONG "ON THE OTHER SIDE."

(EXODUS 12-15:21)

EVERY ordinance had been given to Israel about the Paschal feast, and observed by them. On the tenth day of the month, Abib (the month of ears, so called, because in it the ears of wheat first appear), or, as it was afterwards called, Nisan, (Esther 3:7; Nehemiah 2:1) the "Passover" sacrifice was chosen by each household.

This was four days before the "Passover" actually took place — most probably in remembrance of the prediction to Abraham, (Genesis 15:16) that "in the fourth generation" the children of Israel should come again to the land of Canaan. The sacrifice might be a lamb or a kid of goats, but it must be "without blemish, a male of the first year." Each lamb or kid should be just sufficient for the sacrificial meal of a company, so that if a family were too small, it should join with another. The sacrifice was offered "between the evenings" by each head of the company, the blood caught in a basin, and some of it "struck" "on the two side-posts and the upper door-post of the houses" by means of "a branch of hyssop." The latter is not the hyssop with which we are familiar, but most probably the caper, which grows abundantly in Egypt, in the desert of Sinai, and in Palestine. In ancient times this plant was regarded as possessing cleansing properties. The direction, to sprinkle the entrance, meant that the blood was to be applied to the house itself, that is, to make atonement for it, and in a sense to convert it into an altar. Seeing this blood, Jehovah, when He passed through to smite the Egyptians, would "pass over the door," so that it would "not be granted the destroyer to come in" unto their dwellings. (Exodus 12:23) Thus the term "Passover," or Pascha, literally expresses the meaning and object of the ordinance.

While all around the destroyer laid waste every Egyptian household, each company within the blood-sprinkled houses of Israel was engaged in the sacrificial meal. This consisted of the Paschal lamb, and "unleavened bread with," or rather "upon, bitter herbs," as if in that solemn hour of judgment and deliverance they were to have set before them as their proper meal the symbol of all the bitterness of Egypt, and upon it the sacrificial lamb and unleavened bread to sweeten and to make of it a festive supper. For everything here was full of deepest meaning. The sacrificial lamb, whose sprinkled blood protected Israel, pointed to Him whose precious blood is the only safety of God's people; the hyssop (as in the cleansing of the leper, and of those polluted by death, and in Psalm 51:7) was the symbol of purification; and the unleavened bread that "of sincerity and truth," in the removal of the "old leaven" which, as the symbol of corruption, pointed to "the leaven of malice and wickedness." (1 Corinthians 5:7, 8) More than that, the spiritual teaching extended even to details. The lamb was to be "roast," neither eaten "raw," or rather not properly cooked (as in the haste of leaving), nor yet "sodden with water" — the latter because nothing of it was to pass into the water, nor the water to mingle with it, the lamb and the lamb alone being the food of the sacrificial company. For a similar reason it was to be roasted and served up whole — complete, without break or division, not a bone of it being broken, (Exodus 12:46) just as not even a bone was broken of Him who died for us on the cross. (John 19:33, 36) And this undividedness of the Lamb pointed not only to the entire surrender of the Lord Jesus, but also to our undivided union and communion in and with Him. (1 Corinthians 10:17) So also none of this lamb was to be kept for another meal, but that which had not been used must be burnt. Lastly, those who gathered around this meal were not only all Israelites, but must all profess their faith in the coming deliverance; since they were to sit down to it with loins girded, with shoes on their feet and a staff in their hand, as it were, awaiting the signal of their redemption, and in readiness for departing from Egypt.

A nobler spectacle of a people's faith can scarcely be conceived than when, on receiving these ordinances, "the people bowed the head and worshipped" (12:27). Any attempt at description either of Israel's attitude or of the scenes witnessed when the Lord, passing through the land "about midnight," smote each firstborn from the only son of Pharaoh to the child of the maidservant and the captive, and even the firstborn of beasts, would only weaken the impression of the majestic silence of Scripture. Such things cannot be described — at least otherwise than by comparison with what is yet to follow. Suffice then, that it was a fit emblem of another "midnight," when the cry shall be heard: "Behold, the Bridegroom cometh." (Matthew 25:6) In that midnight hour did Jehovah execute "judgment against all the gods of Egypt," (Exodus 12:12) showing, as Calvin rightly remarks, how vain and false had been the worship of those who were now so powerless to help. That was also the night of Israel's birth as a nation "of their creation and adoption as the people of God." (Isaiah 43:15) Hence the very order of the year was now changed. The month of the Passover(Abib) became henceforth the first of the year. The Paschal supper was made a perpetual institution, with such new rules as to its future observance as would suit the people when settled in the land; and its observance was to be followed by a "feast of unleavened bread," lasting for seven days, when all leaven should be purged out of their households.

Finally, the fact that God had so set Israel apart in the Paschal night and redeemed them to Himself, was perpetuated in the injunction to "sanctify" unto the Lord "all the firstborn both of man and of beast." (Exodus 13:1-7) When at last this "stroke" descended upon Egypt, Pharaoh hastily called for Moses and Aaron. In that night of terror he dismissed the people unconditionally, only asking that, instead of the curse, a "blessing" might be left behind (12:32).

"And the Egyptians were urgent upon the people that they might send them out of the land in haste, for they said, We be all dead men." Ere the morning had broken, the children of Israel were on their march from Rameses, around which most of them had probably been congregated. Their "army" consisted in round numbers of "600,000 on foot — men, beside children" (12:37), or, as we may compute it, with women and children, about two millions.

This represents a by no means incredible increase during the four hundred and thirty years that had elapsed since their settlement in Egypt, even irrespective of the fact that, as Abraham had had three hundred and eighteen "trained servants born in his own 73 house," (Genesis 14:14) and therefore afterwards circumcised (Genesis 17:13), whom he could arm against the invaders of Sodom, so the sons of Jacob must have brought many with them who were afterwards incorporated in the nation.

With these two millions of Israelites also went up a mixed multitude of varied descent, drawn in the wake of God's people by the signs and wonders so lately witnessed — just as a mixed crowd still follows after every great spiritual movement, a source of hindrance rather than of help to it, (Numbers 11:4) ever continuing strangers, and at most only fit to act as "hewers of wood and drawers of water." (Deuteronomy 29:11) But a precious legacy of faith did Israel bear, when they took with them out of Egypt the bones of Joseph, (Exodus 13:19) which all those centuries had waited for the fulfillment of God's promise. As Calvin aptly writes: "In all those times of adversity the people could never have forgotten the promised redemption. For if, in their communings, the oath which Joseph had made their fathers swear had not been remembered, Moses could in no wise have been aware of it." Such a sight had never been witnessed in the land of Egypt as when the nation, so delivered, halted for their first night-quarters at Succoth, or, "booths." The locality of this and the following station, Etham, cannot be exactly ascertained; nor is this the place to discuss such questions. Succoth may have been fixed upon as the general rendezvous of the people, while at Etham they had reached "the edge of the wilderness," which divides Egypt from Palestine. The straight road would have brought them shortly into the land of the Philistines, face to face with a warlike race, against which even Egypt could often scarcely stand. Of course they would have contested the advance of Israel. To such test God in His mercy would not expose a people so unprepared for it, as was Israel at that time. Accordingly, they were directed to "turn" southward, and march to "Pi-hahiroth, between Migdol and the sea," where they were to encamp.

Two events, as we understand it, marked Etham, the second stage of their journey. It was apparently here, at the edge of the wilderness, (Exodus 13:21) that Jehovah first "went before" His people "by day in a pillar of cloud, to lead them the way; and by night in a pillar of fire, to give them light, to go by day and night," that is, to enable them at all times to march onward. In Exodus 13:17, 18, we read that "God (Elohim) led the people," but now Jehovah, as it were, took command (ver. 21), and, by a sensible sign of His Presence, ensured their safety. This pillar was at the same time one "of fire and of the cloud" (14:24), "of light" and "of cloud and darkness" (ver. 20). Ordinarily, by day only the cloud was visible, but by night the fire, which the cloud had enwrapped, shone out. (Numbers 9:15, 16) In this cloud Jehovah was visibly present in the "Angel" of the covenant; (Exodus 14:19) there the glory of Jehovah appeared (16:10; 40:34; Numbers 16:42); thence He spoke to Moses and to Israel; and this was the Shechinah, or visible Presence, which afterwards rested upon the Most Holy Place. And this pledge and symbol of His visible Presence appears once more in the description of the last days, only then "upon every dwelling-place of Mount Zion." (Isaiah 4:5)

Secondly, it was probably from Etham, as they turned southwards, that tidings were carried to Pharaoh, which made him hope that Israel had, by this sudden backward movement, "entangled" themselves as in a net, and would fall a ready prey to his trained army. (Exodus 14:2-4) Perhaps now also, for the first time, he realized that the people had "fled" (ver. 5) -not merely gone for a few days to offer sacrifice, as they might have done, close by Etham, but left entirely and forever. The sacred text does not necessarily imply that from Etham to Pi-hahiroth there was only one day's march. Indeed, opinions as to the exact locality of each of the stages to the Red Sea are still divided, though the general route is sufficiently ascertained. While Israel thus pursued their journey, Pharaoh quickly gathered his army, the principal strength of which lay in its "six hundred chosen chariots." Each of these was drawn by two fiery, trained horses, and contained two warriors, one bearing the shield and driving, the other fully armed. A most formidable array it would have been under any circumstances; much more so to an untrained multitude, encumbered with women and children, and dispirited by centuries of slavery to those very Egyptians, the flower of whose army they now saw before them.

It must have been as the rays of the setting sun were glinting upon the war chariots, that the Israelites first descried the approach of Pharaoh's army. It followed in their track, and came approaching them from the north. There was no escape in that direction. Eastward was the sea; to the west and south rose mountains. Flight was impossible; defense seemed madness. Once more the faith of Israel signally failed, and they broke into murmuring against Moses. But the Lord was faithful. What now took place was not only to be the final act of sovereign deliverance by God's arm alone, nor yet merely to serve ever afterwards as a memorial by which Israel's faith might be upheld, but also to teach, by the judgments upon Egypt, that Jehovah was a righteous and holy Judge.

There are times when even prayer seems unbelief, and only to go forward in calm assurance is duty. "Wherefore criest thou unto Me? Speak unto the children of Israel that they go forward." Yet this forward movement was to be made only after Moses had stretched the rod of God over the sea, and the Angel of the Lord gone behind the host, casting the light of the pillar upon Israel's path, while, with the darkness of the cloud, he kept Egypt apart from them. Then blew the "strong east wind all that night," as never it had swept across those water before. They divided, and formed on each side a wall, between which Israel passed dry-shod.

When the host of Egypt reached the seashore, night had probably fallen, and the Israelites were far advanced on the dry bed of the sea. Their position would be seen by the fire from the cloud which threw its light upon the advancing multitude. To follow where they had dared to go, seemed dictated by military honor, and victory within easy reach. Yet, read in the light of what was to follow, it sounds like Divine irony that "the Egyptians pursued and went in after them in the midst of the sea." And so the long night passed. The gray morning light was breaking on the other side of the waters, when a fiercer sun than that about to rise on the horizon east its glare upon the Egyptians. "Jehovah looked unto" them "through the pillar of fire and of the cloud, and troubled the host of the Egyptians." It was the fire of His Divine Presence, bursting suddenly through the pillar of the cloud, which threw them into confusion and panic. The wheels of their chariots became clogged, the sand beneath them seemed to soften under the fiery glow, and they drove heavily. With that light from the fiery cloud, the conviction flashed upon them that it was Jehovah who fought for Israel and against them. They essayed immediate flight. But already Moses had, at God's command, once more stretched his hand over the sea. In that morning watch, the wind veered round; the waters returned, and Pharaoh, with the flower of his host, sank, buried beneath the waves. Thus, in the language of Scripture,

"Jehovah shook off the Egyptians in the midst of the sea." (Exodus 14:27)

Incidental confirmations of this grand event are not wanting. Throughout the Old Testament, it is constantly appealed to, and forms, so to speak, the foundation on which God rests His claim upon His people. Local tradition also has preserved its memory. Nor has anything yet been urged to shake our faith in the narrative. Although the exact spot of the passage through the Red Sea is matter of discussion, yet all are agreed that it must have taken place near Suez, and that the conditions are such as to make it quite possible for the host of Israel to have safely crossed during that night. Moreover, it is a curious fact, illustrating the history of Pharaoh's overthrow, that, according to Egyptian documents, seventeen years elapsed after the death of Thothmes II (whom we regard as the Pharaoh of this narrative) before any Egyptian expedition was undertaken into the Peninsula of Sinai, and twenty-two years before any attempt was made to recover the power over Syria which Egypt seems to have lost. And thus, also, it was that Israel could safely pursue their march through the wilderness, which had hitherto been subject to the Egyptians.

But Moses and the children of Israel sang on the other side of the sea a song of thanksgiving and triumph, which, repeated every Sabbath in the Temple, when the drink-offering of the festive sacrifice was poured out, reminded Israel that to all time the kingdom was surrounded by the hostile powers of this world; that there must always be a contest between them; and that Jehovah would always Himself interpose to destroy His enemies and to deliver His people. Thus that great event is really not solitary, nor yet its hymn without an echo. For all times it has been a prophecy, a comfort, and a song of anticipated sure victory to the Church. And so at the last, they who stand on the "sea of glass mingled with fire," who have "gotten the victory," and have "the harps of God," "sing the song of Moses, the servant of God, and the song of the Lamb."

CHAPTER 8: THE WILDERNESS OF SHUR — THE SINAITIC PENINSULA — ITS SCENERY AND VEGETATION — ITS CAPABILITIES OF SUPPORTING A POPULATION — THE WELLS OF MOSES -THREE DAYS MARCH TO MARAH — ELIM ROAD TO THE WILDERNESS OF SIN — ISRAEL'S MURMURING — THE MIRACULOUS PROVISION OF THE QUAILS — THE MANNA

(EXODUS 15:22; 16)

WITH the song of triumph on the other side the sea, the first part of the Book of Exodus ends. Israel has now become a nation. God has made it such by a twofold deliverance. He has, so to speak, "created" it for Himself. It only remains that this new-born people of God shall be consecrated to Him at the mount. And the second part of Exodus describes their wilderness-journey to Sinai, and their consecration there unto God. In this also it may serve to us as the pattern of heavenly things on our passage through the wilderness to the mount.

As Israel looked in the morning light across the now quiet sea, into which Jehovah had so lately shaken the pursuers of His people, their past danger must have seemed to them greater than ever. Along that defile, the only practicable road, their enemies had followed them. Assuredly the sea was the only pathway of safety to them, and in that sea they had been baptized unto Moses, and unto Moses' God. And now, as they turned towards the wilderness, there seemed to stand before them, and to extend all along their line of vision, east and north, a low range of bare limestone hills, that bounded the prospect, rising like a wall. Accordingly they called this the wilderness of Shur, or of "the wall." (Exodus 15:22) This then was the wilderness, fresh, free, and undisputed! But this also was that "great and terrible wilderness," so full of terror, danger, and difficulty, (Deuteronomy 8:15; 32:10) through which they must now pass. Under the shadow of that mass of rocky peaks, along the dry torrent-beds which intersect them, through the unbroken stillness of that scenery, of which grandeur and desolateness are the characteristics, led their way. A befitting road to such a sanctuary as Sinai! But what contrast in all around to the Egypt they had left behind only a few hours!

When we think of the desert through which Israel journeyed, we must not picture to ourselves a large, flat, sandy tract, wholly incapable of cultivation. In fact it is in almost every particular quite the contrary. That tract of land which bears the name of the Peninsula of Sinai, extends between the Gulf of Suez on the west, and that of Akaba (or the Persian Gulf) on the east. Its configuration is heart-shaped, the broader part lying towards Palestine, the narrower, or apex, stretching southwards into the sea. It really consists of three distinct portions. The northern, called the Wilderness of Tih, or, "of the Wandering," is pebbly, high table-land, the prevailing color being that of the gray limestone. Next comes a broad belt of sandstone and yellow sand, the only one in the desert of the Exodus. To the south of it, in the apex of the peninsula, lies the true Sinaitic range.

This portion bears the name of the Tor, and consists in the north chiefly of red sandstone, and in the center of red granite and green porphyry. The prevailing character of the scenery is that of an irregular mass of mountains, thrown together in wild confusion. The highest peak rises to about 9,000 feet. Between these wind what seem, and really are, torrent-beds, filled, perhaps, for a very short time in winter, but generally quite dry. These are called Wadies, and they form the highway through the wilderness. Here and there, where either a living spring rises, or the torrent has left its marks, or where the hand of man is at work, cultivated patches, fair and fruitful, are found; palm-trees spring up, even gardens and fields, and rich pasture ground. But, generally, the rocky mountain-sides are bare of all vegetation, and their bright coloring gives the scenery its peculiar character. The prevailing tints are red and green; but this is varied by what seems a purple, rose, or crimson-colored stream poured down the mountain side, while, occasionally, the green of the porphyry deepens into black. Over all this, unbroken silence prevails, so that the voice is heard in the pure air at extraordinary distances. Besides the cultivated or fruitful spots already mentioned, and tiny rock-flowers, and aromatic herbs, the vegetation of the wilderness consists chiefly of the caper-plant, the hyssop of the Bible, which springs from the clefts of the rocks and hangs down in gay festoons; the "thorn," a species of acacia; another species of the same tree, the Shittim-wood of Scripture, of which the framework of the Tabernacle was made; the white broom, or juniper of Scripture; and the tamarisk, which, at certain seasons of the year, produces the natural manna. This leads us to say, that it were a mistake to suppose that the wilderness offered no means of support to those who inhabited it. Even now it sustains a not inconsiderable population, and there is abundant evidence that, before neglect and ravages had brought it to its present state, it could, and did, support a very much larger number of people. There were always Egyptian colonies engaged in working its large copper, iron, and turquoise mines, and these settlers would have looked well to its springs and cultivated spots. Nor could the Israelites, any more than the modern Bedouin, have had difficulty in supporting, in the desert, their numerous herds and flocks. These would again supply them with milk and cheese, and occasionally with meat. We know from Scripture that, at a later period, the Israelites were ready to buy food and water from the Edomites, (Deuteronomy 2:6) and they may have done so from passing caravans as well. Similarly, we gather from such passages as Leviticus 8:2, 26, 31; 9:4; 10:12; 24:5; Numbers 7:13, and others, that they must have had a supply of flour, either purchased, or of their own sowing and reaping, during their prolonged stay in certain localities, just as the modern Bedouin still cultivate what soil is fit for it.

Such was the wilderness on which Israel now entered. During the forty years that Moses had tended the flocks of Jethro, its wadies and peaks, its pastures and rocks must have become well known to him. Nor could the Israelites themselves have been quite ignorant of its character, considering the constant connection between Egypt and the desert. We are therefore the more disposed to attach credit to those explorers who have tried to ascertain what may have been the most likely route taken by the children of Israel. This has of late years been made the subject of investigation by scholars thoroughly qualified for the task. Indeed, a special professional survey has been made of the Desert of Sinai. The result is, that most of the stations on the journey of Israel have been ascertained, while, in reference to the rest, great probability attaches to the opinion of the explorers.

The first camping-place was, no doubt, the modern Ayun Musa (Wells of Moses), about half an hour from the sea-shore. Even now the care of the foreign consuls has made this a most pleasant green and fresh summer retreat. One of the latest travelers has counted nineteen wells there, and the clumps of palm-trees afford a delightful shade. There is evidence that, at the time of Moses, the district was even more carefully cultivated than now, and its water-supply better attended to. Nor is there any doubt as to the next stage in Israel's wilderness-journey. The accounts of travelers quite agree with the narrative of the

Bible. Three days' journey over pebbly ground through desert wadies, and at last among bare white and black limestone hills, with nothing to relieve the eye except, in the distance, the "shur," or wall of rocky mountain which gives its name to the desert, would bring the weary, dispirited multitude to the modern Hawwarah, the "Marah" of the Bible. Worse than fatigue and depression now oppressed them, for they began to suffer from want of water. For three days they had not come upon any spring, and their own supplies must have been well-nigh exhausted. When arrived at Hawwarah they found indeed a pool, but, as the whole soil is impregnated with nitre, the water was bitter (Marah) and unfit for use. Luther aptly remarks that, when our provision ceases, our faith is wont to come to an end. It was so here. The circumstances seemed indeed hopeless. The spring of Hawwarah is still considered the worst on the whole road to Sinai, and no means have ever been suggested to make its waters drinkable. But God stilled the murmuring of the people, and met their wants by a miraculous interposition. Moses was shown a tree which he was to cast into the water, and it became sweet. Whether or not it was the thorny shrub which grows so profusely at Hawwarah, is of little importance. The help came directly from heaven, and the lesson was twofold.

"There He made for them a statute and an ordinance, and there He proved them." (Exodus 15:25)

The "statute," or principle, and "the ordinance," or fight, was this, that in all seasons of need and seeming impossibility the Lord would send deliverance straight from above, and that Israel might expect this during their wilderness-journey. This "statute" is, for all times, the principle of God's guidance, and this "ordinance" the right or privilege of our heavenly citizenship. But He also ever "proves" us by this, that the enjoyment of our right and privilege is made to depend upon a constant exercise of faith.

From Hawwarah, or Marah, a short march would bring Israel to a sweet and fertile spot, now known as Waddy Gharandel, the Elim of Scripture, "where were twelve wells of water, and threescore and ten palm-trees; and they encamped there by the waters." This spot was suitable for a more lengthened encampment. In point of fact, we find that quite a month passed before their next stage in the wilderness of Sin. (Exodus 16:1) Even now this valley, watered by a perennial stream, has rich pasturage for cattle, and many shrubs and trees. Here, and in the neighborhood, the flocks and herds would find good sustenance, and the people rest. Leaving Elim, the character of the scenery changes. Instead of dreary level plains of sand, as hitherto, we are now entering among the mountains, and the bright green of the caper-plant forms a striking contrast to the red sandstone of the rocks. Hitherto the route of Israel had been directly southward, and in pursuing it, they had successively skirted the Tih, and near Elim a belt of sand. But now the host was to enter on the Sinaitic range itself. From Numbers 33:10, we know that from Elim their journey first brought them again to the shore of the "Sea of Weeds." The road which they would follow would be from Wady Gharandel through the Wady Taiyebeh, in a south westerly direction. Here the sandstone again gives place to chalk hills and rocks. Where the road descends to the sea (at Ras Abu Zenimeh) it would touch, probably, the most dreary, flat, and desolate place in the whole wilderness. This spot was the next camping-ground of the children of Israel after Elim. From the shore of the Red Sea the next halting-place brought them into the Wilderness of Sin itself. (Numbers 33:11) That name applies to the whole extensive sandy plain, which runs along the shore of the Red Sea, from the camping-place of Israel to the southern end of the Sinaitic Peninsula. On leaving the Wilderness of Sin, (Numbers 33:12-14) we read of two stations, Dophkah and, Alush, before the Israelites reached Rephidim.

The Wilderness of Sin, the modern El Markha, is a dreary, desolate tract, which obtains its name from a long ridge of white chalk hills.

In this inhospitable desert, the provisions which Israel had brought from Egypt, and which had now lasted a month, began to fail. Behind them, just above the range of chalk cliffs, they would see, in the distance, the purple streaks of those granite mountains which form the proper Sinaitic group. To the west lay the sea, and across it, in the dim mist, they could just descry the rich and fertile Egypt, which they had for ever left behind. Once more their unbelief broke forth. True, it was only against Moses that their murmurs rose. But in reality their rebellion was against God. To show this, and thereby "to prove them, whether they would walk in the law of God or no," (Exodus 16:4) that is, follow Him implicitly, depending upon, and taking such provision as He sent, and under the conditions that He dispensed it, God would now miraculously supply their wants. Bread and meat would be given them, both directly sent from God, yet both so given that, while unbelief was inexcusable, it should still be possible. To show the more clearly that these dealings were from the Lord, they were bidden "come near before Jehovah," and "behold the glory of Jehovah," as it "appeared in the cloud." (Exodus 16:9, 10) That Presence ought to have prevented their murmuring, or rather changed it into prayer and praise. And so it always is, that, before God supplies our wants, He shows us that His presence had been near, and He reveals His glory. That Presence is in itself sufficient; for no good thing shall be wanting to them that trust in Him.

As evening gathered around the camp, the air became darkened. An extraordinary flight of quails, such as at that season of the year passes northward from the warmer regions of the interior, was over the camp. It is a not uncommon occurrence that, when wearied, these birds droop and settle down for rest, so as to be easily clubbed with sticks, and even caught by the hand. The miraculousness chiefly consisted in the extraordinary number, the seasonable arrival, and the peculiar circumstances under which these quails came. But greater wonder yet awaited them on the morrow. While passing through the Wady Gharandel they might have observed that the tamarisk, when pricked by a small insect, exuded drops of white, sweet, honey-like substance, which melted in the sun. This was the natural manna (a name perhaps derived from the Egyptian), which, in certain districts, is found from the middle of May to about the end of July. But "can God furnish a table in the wilderness?" Can He command the clouds from above, and open the doors of heaven? Can He rain down manna upon them to eat? That would indeed be to give them of the corn of heaven! Truly, this were angels' food, the provision, direct from God, "the bread of heaven!" (Psalm 78:19-27; 105:40)

The Lord did this, and far more. As in the evening, He had "caused an east wind to blow in the heavens; and by His power He brought in the south wind; He rained flesh also upon them as dust, and feathered fowls like as the sand of the sea, so, in the morning, as the dew that had lain rose in white vapor, and was carried towards the blue sky, there lay on the face of the ground "a small round thing, as small as the hoar frost." "It was like coriander seed, white; and the taste of it was like wafers made with honey." (Exodus 16:21)

The children of Israel said, Manna! What is that? It was manna, and yet it was not manna; not the manna which the wilderness produced, and yet in some respects like it; it was the manna from heaven, the bread which God gave them to eat. Thus it recalls our present condition. We are in the wilderness, yet not of the wilderness; our provision is like the wilderness food, yet not the wilderness manna; but, above all, it is sent us directly from God.

Such assuredly must have been the lessons which Israel was, and which we to this day are, called to learn. The very resemblance in some points of the natural to the heaven-sent manna would suggest a truth. But the difference between them was even greater and more patent than their likeness. On this point let there be no mistake. Israel could never have confounded the heaven-sent with the natural manna. The latter is seen in but a few districts of the desert, and only at certain seasons at most during three months; it is produced by the prick of an insect from the tamarisks; it is not the least like coriander-seed; nor yet capable of being baked or seethed (16:23); and the largest produce for a whole year throughout the Peninsula amounts to about 700 lbs., and would therefore not have sufficed to feed the host of Israel even for one day, far less at all seasons and during all the years of their wanderings! And so, in measure, it is still with the provision of the believer. Even the "daily bread" by which our bodies are sustained, and for which we are taught to pray, is, as it were, manna sent us directly from heaven. Yet our provision looks to superficial observers as in so many respects like the ordinary manna, that they are apt to mistake it, and that even we ourselves in our unbelief too often forget the daily dispensation of our bread from heaven.

There is yet another point in which the miraculous provision of the manna, continued to Israel during all the forty years of their wilderness-journey, resembles what God's provision to us is intended to be. The manna was so dispensed that "he that gathered much had nothing over, and he that gathered little had no lack; they gathered every man according to his eating." (Exodus 16:18)

For this marks the true purpose of God's giving to us, whichever interpretation of the verse just quoted we adopt' whether we regard it as describing the final result of each man's work, that, however much or little he had gathered, it was found, when measured, just sufficient for his want; or understand it to mean that all threw into a common store what they had gathered, and that each took from it what he needed.

By two other provisions did God sanctify His daily gift. First, the manna came not on the Sabbath. The labor of the previous day provided sufficient to supply the wants of God's day of holy rest. But on ordinary days the labor of gathering the bread which God sent could not be dispensed with. What was kept from one day to the other only "bred worms and stank" (16:20). Not so on the Lord's day. This also was to be to them "a statute" and an "ordinance" of faith, that is, a principle of God's giving and a rule of their receiving. Secondly, "an omer full of manna" was to be "laid up before Jehovah" in a "golden pot." Together with "Aaron's rod that budded, and the tables of the covenant," it was afterwards placed in the Holiest of all, within the ark of the covenant, overshadowed by "the cherubim of glory." (Hebrews 9:4)

Thus, alike in the "rain of bread from heaven," in the ordinance of its ingathering, and in the Sabbath law of its sanctified use, did God prove Israel — even as He now proves us, whether we will "walk in His law or no." (Exodus 16:4)

CHAPTER 9: REPHIDIM — THE DEFEAT OF AMALEK AND ITS MEANING — THE VISIT OF JETHRO AND ITS SYMBOLICAL IMPORT
(EXODUS 17, 18)

A SWEET spot or grander scenery can scarcely be imagined than Wady Feiran. Here we are at last among those Sinaitic mountains which rise in such fantastic shapes and exhibit every variety of coloring. Following the windings of Wady Feiran we come upon a wide fertile plain, seemingly all shut in by mountains. This is Rephidim, the battle-field where Israel, fighting under the banner of Jehovah, defeated Amalek. The place is too full of interest to be cursorily passed by.

Just before reaching the plain of Rephidim, the children of Israel would, on their way from the Wilderness of Sin, pass a large, bare, outstanding rock. This, according to an Arab tradition, to which considerable probability attaches, is the rock which Moses smote, and whence the living water gushed. Now we know that, when Israel reached that spot, they must have been suffering from thirst, since, all the way from the Red Sea, these three days, they would not have passed a single spring, while their march in early May through that wilderness must have been peculiarly hot and weary. Again, it is quite certain that they must have passed by that rock, and under its shadow they would in all likelihood halt. For at that moment the valley of Rephidim before them with its living springs was held by Amalek, who, as the modern Bedouin would do in similar circumstances, had gathered around their wells and palms, waiting to attack the enemy as he came up thirsty, weary, and way-worn. Here then probably was the scene of the miracle of the smitten rock. Beyond it lay the battle-field of Rephidim.

Before following the Biblical narrative, let us try to realize the scene. Advancing from the rock just described upon that broad plain, we seem to be in a sort of dreamy paradise, shut in by strange walls of mountains. As the traveler now sees Rephidim, many a winter's storm has carried desolation into it. For this is the region of sudden and terrific storms, when the waters pour in torrents down the granite mountains, and rush with wild roar into the wadies and valleys, carrying with them every living thing and all vegetation, uprooting palms, centuries old, and piling rocks and stones upon each other in desolate grandeur. At present the stillness of the camp at night is often broken by the dismal howl of wolves, which in winter prowl about in search of food, while in the morning the mark of the leopard's foot shows how near danger had been. But in the days of the Exodus Rephidim and its neighborhood were comparatively inhabited districts. Nothing, however, can have permanently changed the character of the scenery. Quite at the north of the valley are groves of palms, tamarisks and other trees, offering delicious shade. Here the voice of the bulbul is heard, and, sweeter still to the ear of the traveler, the murmur of living water. This beautiful tract, one of the most fertile in the peninsula, extends for miles along the valley. To the north, some 700 feet above the valley, rises a mountain (Jebel Tahuneh), which, not without much probability, is regarded as that on which Moses stood when lifting up to heaven his hand that held the rod, while in the valley itself Israel fought against Amalek. As a sort of background to it we have a huge basin of red rock, gneiss and porphyry, above which a tall mountain-peak towers in the far distance. Turning the other way and looking south, across the battle-field of Rephidim, the majestic Mount Serbal, one of the highest in the Peninsula (6,690 feet), bounds the horizon. On either side of it two valleys run down to Rephidim. Between them is a tumbled and chaotic mass of mountains of all colors and shapes. Lastly, far away to the south-east from where Moses stood, he must have descried through an opening among the hills, the blue range of Sinai.

But before us lies the highland valley of Rephidim itself, nearly 1,500 feet above the level of the sea. Here in close proximity, but in striking contrast to sweet groves and a running river, are all around fantastic rocks of gorgeous diversity of color, white boulders, walls of most lovely pink porphyry, from the clefts of which herbs and flowers spring and wind, and gray and red rocks, over which it literally seems as if a roseate stream had been poured. In this spot was the fate of those who opposed the kingdom of God once and, viewing the event prophetically, for ever decided. Wonderful things had Israel already experienced. The enemies of Jehovah had been overthrown in the Red Sea; the bitter waters of Marah been healed; and the wants of God's people supplied in the wilderness. But a greater miracle than any of these — at least one more palpable — was now to be witnessed, for the purpose of showing Israel that no situation could be so desperate but Jehovah would prove "a very present help in trouble." That this was intended to be for all time its meaning to Israel, appears from the name Massah and Meribah, temptation and chiding, given to the place, and from the after references to the event in Deuteronomy 6:16; Psalms 68:15; 105:41, and especially in Psalm 114:8. The admonition (Psalm 115:8) "Harden not your heart, as in Meribah, as in the day of Massah in the wilderness, when your fathers tempted Me, proved Me, and saw My work," refers, however, primarily, to a later event, recorded in Numbers 20:2, and only secondarily to the occurrence at Rephidim. At the same time it is true, that when the children of Israel chode with Moses on account of the want of water in Rephidim, it was virtually a tempting of Jehovah. Judgment did not, however, at that time follow. Once more would God prove Himself, and prove the people. Moses was directed to take with him of the elders of Israel, and in their view to smite the rock in Horeb (that is, "dry," "parched"). God would stand there before him — to help and to vindicate His servant. And from the riven side of the parched rock living waters flowed — an emblem this of the "spiritual rock which followed them;" an emblem also to us — for "that Rock was Christ." (1 Corinthians 10:4)

It was probably while the advanced part of the host were witnessing the miracle of the Smitten Rock that Amalek fell upon the worn stragglers, "and smote the hindmost, — even all that were feeble," — when Israel was "faint and weary." (Deuteronomy 25:18) It was a wicked deed, for Israel had in no way provoked the onset, and the Amalekites were, as descendants of Esau, closely related to them. But there is yet deeper meaning attaching both to this contest and to its issue. For, first, we mark the record of God's solemn determination "utterly to put out the remembrance of Amalek from under heaven," (Exodus 17:14) and His proclamation of "war of Jehovah with Amalek from generation to generation" (17:16). Secondly, we have in connection with this the prophetic utterance of Balaam to this effect: (Numbers 24:20) "Amalek the first-fruits of the heathen" (the beginning of the Gentile power and hostility), "but his latter end even to destruction;" while, lastly, we notice the brief but deeply significant terms in which Scripture accounts for the cowardly attack of Amalek: (Deuteronomy 25:18) "he feared not God."

The contest of Amalek therefore must have been intended, not so much against Israel simply as a nation, as against Israel in their character as the people of God. It was the first attack of the kingdoms of this world upon the kingdom of God, and as such it is typical of all that have followed. Strange as it may sound, in such a contest God will not fight for

Israel as at the Red Sea. Israel itself must also fight, though success will be granted only so long as their fight is carried on under the banner of God. That banner was the rod which Moses had received, and with which he was to perform miracles. This rod represented the wonder-working Presence of Jehovah with His people as their Shepherd, their Ruler and their Leader. Yet in the fight which Israel waged, it was not enough simply to stretch forth the rod as over the Red Sea. The hand that holds the rod must also be lifted up to heaven — the faith that holds the symbol of God's wonder-working presence must rise up to heaven and draw down in prayer the pledged blessing, to give success to Israel's efforts, and ensure victory to their arms. Thus we understand this history. Moses chose a band to fight against Amalek, placing it under the command of Hoshea, a prince of the tribe of Ephraim, (Numbers 13:8, 16; Deuteronomy 32:44) whose name, perhaps, from that very event, was changed to Joshua (Jehovah is help).

In the mean time Moses himself took his position on the top of a hill, with the rod of God in his hand. So long as this rod was held up Israel prevailed, but when Moses' hands drooped from weariness, Amalek prevailed. Then Aaron and Hur — the latter a descendant of Judah, and the grandfather of Bezaleel, who seems to have held among the laity a position akin to that of Aaron (Exodus 24:14) — stayed the hands of Moses until the going down of the sun, and the defeat of Amalek was complete.

This holding up of Moses' hands has been generally regarded as symbolical of prayer. But if that were all, it would be difficult to understand why it was absolutely needful to success that his hands should be always upheld, so that when they drooped, merely from bodily weariness, Amalek should have immediately prevailed. Moreover, it leaves unexplained the holding up of the rod towards heaven. In view of this difficulty it has been suggested by a recent commentator, that the object of holding up the hands was not prayer, but the uplifting of the God-given, wonder-working rod, as the banner of God, to which, while it waved above them, and only so long, Israel owed their victory. With this agrees the name of the memorial-altar, which Moses reared to perpetuate the event -Jehovah-nissi, "the Lord my banner." But neither does this explanation quite meet the statements of Scripture. Rather would we combine both the views mentioned. The rod which Moses held up was the banner of God -the symbol and the pledge of His presence and working; and he held it up, not over Israel, nor yet over their enemies, but towards heaven in prayer, to bring down that promised help in their actual contest. And so it ever is.

Amalek opposes the advance of Israel; Israel must fight, but the victory is God's; Israel holds the rod of almighty power in the hand of faith; but that rod must ever be uplifted toward heaven in present application for the blessing secured by covenant-promise.

If the attack of Amalek represented the hostility of the world to the kingdom of God, the visit of Jethro, which followed Israel's victory, equally symbolized the opposite tendency. For Jethro came not only as Moses' father-in-law to bring back his wife and children — although even this would have expressed his faith in Jehovah and the covenant-people, — but he "rejoiced for all the goodness which Jehovah had done to Israel." More than that, he professed,

"Now I know that Jehovah is greater than all gods; for He has shown Himself great in the thing wherein they (the Egyptians) had dealt proudly against them (the Israelites)" (Exodus 18:11).

As this acknowledgment of God led Jethro to praise Him, so his praise found expression in burnt-offerings and sacrifices, after which Jethro sat down with Moses and Aaron, and the elders of Israel, to the sacrificial meal of fellowship with God and with each other. Thus

Jethro may be regarded as a kind of first fruits unto God from among the Gentiles, and his homage as an anticipating fulfillment of the promise; (Isaiah 2:3) "And many people shall go and say, Come ye, and let us go up to the mountain of Jehovah, to the house of the God of Jacob; and He will teach us of His ways, and we will walk in His paths."

A very marked advantage was immediately derived from the presence of Jethro. Just as after the conversion of the Gentiles to Christianity, the accumulated learning and research of heathenism were to be employed in the service of the Gospel, so here the experience of Jethro served in the outward arrangements of the people of God. Hitherto every case in dispute between the people had been brought to Moses himself for decision. The consequence was, that Moses was not only in danger of "wearing away," from the heaviness of the work, but the people also (18:18), since the delay which necessarily ensued was most tedious, and might easily have induced them to take justice into their own hands. Now the advice which Jethro offered was to teach the people "ordinances and laws," and to "shew them the way wherein they must walk, and the work they must do." Whatever questions arose to which the ordinances, laws, and directions, so taught them, would find a ready application, were to be considered "small matters," which might be left for decision to subordinate judges, whom Moses should "provide out of all the people — able men, such as fear God, men of truth, hating covetousness" (ver. 21). Whatever came not within range of a mere application of these known laws were "great matters," which Moses should reserve for his own decision, or rather, "bring the causes unto God." And this wise advice was given so modestly and with such express acknowledgment that it only applied "if God command" him so, that Moses heard in it the gracious direction of God Himself. Nor would it be possible to imagine a more beautiful instance of the help which religion may derive from knowledge and experience, nor yet a more religious submission of this world's wisdom to the service and the will of God, than in the advice which Jethro gave, and the manner in which he expressed it. From Deuteronomy 1:12-18 we learn that Moses carried out the plan in the same spirit in which it was proposed. The election of the judges was made by the people themselves, and their appointment was guided, as well as their work directed, by the fear and the love of the Lord.

CHAPTER 10: ISRAEL AT THE FOOT OF MOUNT SINAI — THE PREPARATIONS FOR THE COVENANT — THE "TEN WORDS?" AND THEIR MEANING

(EXODUS 19-20:17)

IT was the third month after leaving Egypt when the children of Israel reached that innermost mountain-group from which the Peninsula of Sinai derives its name. Roughly speaking, the whole district occupies about twice the area of Yorkshire.

Running through it, like roads, pass very many wadies, all seemingly leading up to the grand central sanctuary, where God was about to give His law to His people. This mountain district bears in Scripture two distinct names — Horeb and Sinai — the former applying probably to the whole group, the latter to one special mountain in it. The meaning of the name Horeb is probably "mountain of the dried-up ground," that of Sinai "mountain of the thorn." At present the whole Sinaitic group is known by the designation of Jebel Musa. It forms "a huge mountain-block, about two miles in length and one mile in breadth, with a narrow valley on either side,... and a spacious plain at the north-eastern end."

That plain, at present known as Er Rahah, is computed to be capable of accommodating a host of two millions. Right before it rises Jebel Musa, from which protrudes a lower bluff, visible from all parts of the plain. This is the modern Ras Sufsafeh (Willow-head), and was in all probability the Sinai upon which the Lord came down, and whence He spake" the ten words." In that case the plain of Er Rahah must have been that on which Israel stood, and the mound in front, on the ascent to Ras Sufsafeh, the spot where Moses "separated from the elders who had accompanied him so far on his ascent."

On leaving Rephidim the main body of the Israelites would pass through what is known as Wady es Sheikh, a broad open valley, containing tamarisk trees, and "cut right through the granitic wall." As a turn in the road is reached, "the journey lies entirely through granite rocks, the sharp, rugged outlines of which, as well as the increasing height and somber gray coloring of the mountains, impart much more solemn grandeur to the scenery." A late eloquent traveler thus describes the approach to Sinai: "At each successive advance these cliffs disengaged themselves from the intervening and surrounding hills, and at last they stood out — I should rather say, the columnar mass, which they form, stood out — alone against the sky.

On each side the infinite complications of twisted and jagged mountains fell away from it. On each side the sky compassed it round, as though it were alone in the wilderness. And to this great mass we approached through a wide valley, a long-continued plain, which, enclosed as it was between two precipitous mountain ranges of black and yellow granite, and having always at its end this prodigious mountain-block, I could compare to nothing else than the immense avenue through which the approach was made to the great Egyptian temples."

As we try to realize the scene presented at the giving of the Law, we can well understand how "all the people that was in the camp trembled." (Exodus 19:16) The vast plain of Er Rahah, and all the neighboring valleys and glens, were dotted with the tents of Israel. No more suitable camping-ground could have been found than this, the best-watered neighborhood in the whole peninsula, where "running streams are found in no less than four of the adjacent valleys." The plain itself is nearly 5,000 feet above the level of the sea. Right in front, cut off by intervening valleys from all around, rises the Horeb group (its highest point 7,363 feet), and from it projects into the valley, like some gigantic altar or pulpit, the lower bluff of Ras Sufsafeh (6,830 feet) — "the nether part of the mount" — that Sinai from which the voice of the living God was heard. In front is the mound on which Moses parted from the elders. So abruptly does Sufsafeh rise, "that you may literally stand under it and touch its base," and so thoroughly is the mountain range separated from all around, that there could be no difficulty whatever in "setting bounds unto the people round about," to prevent their going up into the mount, or even touching the border of it. (Exodus 19:12) Behind Sufsafeh, on some peak or cleft, Moses was forty days with the Lord, and descending into the adjacent valley, he would — as the members of the Ordnance Survey record they had frequently experienced — hear the sound from the camp without being able to see what passed in it.

But now as the people gazed on it, "Mount Sinai was altogether on smoke." (Exodus 19:18) That vast isolated mountain-block — two miles in length and one in breadth — seemed all on fire! As "the smoke of a furnace" it rose to heaven, "and the whole mount quaked greatly," and "there were thunders and lightnings" and "the voice of the trumpet exceeding loud." But, more awful than any physical signs, "Jehovah came down upon Mount Sinai," "and Jehovah called Moses to the top of the mount," and God Himself "spake all these words" of the commandments. For three days had the people been preparing by continued sanctification, and now they stood in readiness at the foot of, although shut off from, the mountain. But even so, "when the people saw it, they removed, and stood afar off. And they said unto Moses, Speak thou with us, and we will hear, but let not God speak with us, lest we die." (Exodus 20:18, 19) This outward sanctification of Israel had been preceded by inward and spiritual preparation. As always, the demand and the command of God had been preceded by His promise. For He ever gives what He asks. It is, as St. Augustine beautifully expresses it, "Give what Thou commandest, and command what Thou wilt." Arrived at the foot of Mount Sinai, Moses had gone up to a lower peak, as if to ask the commands of his Lord, and Jehovah had spoken to him from the top of the mountain. He was directed, before the people prepared to receive the Law, to remind them of their gracious deliverance from Egypt, of the judgments of God's hand, and of the mercy and kindness which they had received. For as "on eagle wings had Jehovah borne them, God's dealings being compared to the eagle, who spreads his strong pinions under the young birds when they take their first flight, lest, weary or faint, they be dashed on the rocks (comp. Deuteronomy 32:11). Yet all this mercy — Moses was to tell Israel -was but the pledge of far richer grace. For now would the Lord enter into covenant with them. And if Israel obeyed His voice, and kept the covenant, then, in His own words, "Ye shall be to Me a precious possession from among all nations for Mine is all the earth. And ye shall be unto Me a kingdom of priests and a holy nation." (Exodus 19:5, 6)

The promise thus conveyed was both special and universal; and it described alike the character of God's people and their destination. All the earth was God's, not only by right of creation and possession, but as destined yet to own Him its Lord. Herein lay a promise of universal blessing to all mankind, and with this the mission of Israel was closely bound up. But while all the earth was the Lord's, Israel was to be His "precious possession from among all nations," His choice treasure — for this the Hebrew expression implies — or, as St. Paul (Titus 2:14) and St. Peter (1 Peter 2:9) explain it, "a peculiar people." The manner in which this dignity would appear, is explained by the terms in which Israel is described as "a kingdom of priests and a holy nation." The expression "kingdom of priests" means a kingdom whose citizens are priests, and as such possess royal dignity and power, or, in the language of St. Peter, "a royal priesthood." So far as Israel was concerned, the outward and visible theocracy, which God established among them, was only the means by which this end was to be obtained, just as their observing the covenant was the condition of it. But the promise itself reached far beyond the Old Covenant, and will only be fulfilled in its completeness when "the Israel of God" — whom already the Lord Jesus, "the First-begotten of the dead and the Prince of the kings of the earth," "hath made kings and priests unto God and His Father" (Revelation 1:5, 6; 5:10) — shall share with Him His glory and sit with Him on His throne. Thus the final object of the royal priesthood of Israel were those nations, from among whom God had chosen His people for a precious possession. Towards them Israel was to act as priests. For, just as the priest is the intermediary between God and man, so Israel was to be the intermediary of the knowledge and salvation of God to all nations. And this their priesthood was to be the foundation of their royalty, A still more solemn description of Israel, and of us who are called "the Israel of God," is that of "holy nation." As Calvin rightly observes, "This designation was not due to the piety or holiness of the people, but because God distinguished them by peculiar privileges from all others. But this sanctification implies another, viz., that they who are so distinguished by God's grace should cultivate holiness, so that in turn they sanctify God."

The Hebrew term for "holy" is generally supposed to mean "separated, set apart." But this is only its secondary signification, derived from the purpose of that which is holy. Its primary meaning is to be splendid, beautiful, pure, and uncontaminated. God is holy — as the Absolutely Pure, Resplendent, and Glorious One. Hence this is symbolized by the light. God dwelleth in light that is unapproachable; (1 Timothy 6:16) He is "the Father of light, with Whom is no variableness, neither shadow of turning" — light which never can grow dimmer, nor give place to darkness. (James 1:17) Christ is the light that shineth in the darkness of our world, "the true light which lighteth every man." (John 1:5, 9) And Israel was to be a holy people as dwelling in the light, through its covenant-relationship to God. It was not the selection of Israel from all other nations that made them holy, but the relationship to God into which it brought the people. The call of Israel, their election and selection, were only the means. Holiness itself was to be attained through the covenant, which provided forgiveness and sanctification, and in which, by the discipline of His law and the guidance of His Holy Arm, Israel was to be led onward and upward. Thus, if God showed the excellence of His name or His glory in creation, (Psalm 8) the way of His holiness was among Israel. (Psalm 77:13; Psalm 104; Psalm 103)

This detailed consideration of what Moses was charged to say, will help us to understand both the preparations for the covenant, and the solemn manner in which it was inaugurated. When Moses intimated to the people the gracious purpose of God, they declared their readiness to obey what God had spoken. But as the Lord could only enter into covenant with the people through the mediation of Moses, on account of their weakness and sinfulness, He spoke in a thick cloud with His servant before them all, so that they might see and hear, and for ever afterwards believe. As previously indicated, the outward preparations of the people were twofold. First, they underwent certain purifications, symbolical of inward cleansing. Secondly, bounds were set round Sinai, so that none might break through nor touch the mountain. Then, on the third day, Moses led forth the men, and placed them "at the nether part of the mount," "that burned with fire." There God proclaimed His holy and eternal law amidst portentous signs, which indicated that He was great and terrible in His holiness, and a jealous God, though the fire of His wrath and zeal was enwrapt in a dense cloud.

The revelation of God's will, which Israel heard from Mount Sinai, is contained in the ten commandments, or, as they are called in the Hebrew original, "the ten words." These were prefaced by this declaration of what Jehovah was and what He had done:

"I am Jehovah thy God, which have brought thee out of the land of Egypt, out of the house of bondage." (Exodus 20:2)

This (as Calvin says) "to prepare the souls of the people for obedience." The "ten words" were afterwards written on two tables of stone, which were to be kept within the ark of the covenant, "the mercy-seat" being significantly placed over them. (Exodus 25:16; 40:20) It is not easy to say how they were arranged on these two tables, but not improbably the first four "words" with "the Preface" (in ver. 1) may have occupied the first, and the other six commandments the second Table of the Law. But we only know for certain, that "the tables were written on both their sides, on the one side and on the other were they written. And the tables were the work of God, and the writing was the writing of God, graven upon the tables."

Considering more closely these "ten words", of the covenant," we notice, first, their number, ten, as that of completeness. Next, we see that the fifth commandment (to honor our parents) forms a transition from the first to the second table — the first table detailing our duties towards God; the second those towards man. But our duty to our parents is higher than that towards men generally; indeed, in a certain sense is Divine, just as the relationship to an earthly father symbolizes that to our Father in heaven. Hence the command is to honor, whereas our duty to men only requires us to love them. Again, almost all the commands are put in a negative form ("thou shalt not"), implying that transgression, not obedience, is natural to us. But "the commandment is exceeding broad," and requires a corresponding right state of mind. Accordingly we find that the law of the ten commandments is summed up in this. "Thou shalt love the Lord thy God with all thy heart, and with all thy soul, and with all thy strength; and thy neighbor as thyself." Lastly, the first five "words" have always some reason or motive attached to them. Not so those of the second table, which are mostly put quite generally, to show that such commands as, not to kill, not to commit adultery, not to steal, not to bear false witness, are intended to apply to all possible cases, and not only to friends or fellow-citizens.

Passing from general considerations to particulars, we find that the "first word" not only forbids all idolatry in thought, word, and deed, but enjoins to love, fear, serve, and cleave to the Lord. (Deuteronomy 6:5, 13; 10:12, 20) The second word shows the manner in which the Lord will be served — more particularly, not under any image or by any outward representation. As Calvin remarks, it condemns "all fictitious worship which men have invented according to their own minds," and not according to the word of God. The third word forbids the profaning of the name of Jehovah, in which He has manifested His glory, by using it either for untruth or in vain words, that is, either in false or idle swearing, in cursing, in magic, or such like. The fourth word, which implies a previous knowledge of the Sabbath on the part of Israel, enjoins personal, domestic, and public rest from all manner of labor on God's holy day, which is to be spent in His service and for His glory. The fifth word directs honor to parents as (in the language of Luther) "the vicars of God," and hence implies similar reverence towards all God's representatives, especially magistrates and rulers. The Second Table progresses from outward deed (in the sixth, seventh, and eighth "words") to speech (ninth commandment), and finally to thought and desire. The sixth, seventh, and eighth words apply equally to what may injure our own life, chastity, or property, and those of others. The ninth word should be literally translated: "Thou shalt not answer against thy neighbor as a false witness" (or "as a witness of falsehood"). Comparing this with the statement in Deuteronomy 5:20, where the expression is "a witness of vanity," we gather that not only all untrue, but all unfounded statements against our neighbor are included in this commandment. Lastly, the tenth word sounds the inmost depths of our hearts, and forbids all wrong and inordinate desires in reference to anything that is our neighbor's.

Such law was never given by man; never dreamed of in his highest conceptions. Had man only been able to observe it, assuredly not only life hereafter but happiness and joy here would have come with it. As it was, it brought only knowledge of sin. Yet, for ever blessed be God: "The law was given by Moses, but grace and truth came by Jesus Christ." (John 1:17)

CHAPTER 11: CIVIL & SOCIAL ORDINANCES OF ISRAEL AS THE PEOPLE OF GOD — THEIR RELIGIOUS ORDINANCES IN THEIR NATIONAL ASPECT — THE "COVENANT MADE BY SACRIFICE" AND THE SACRIFICIAL MEAL OF ACCEPTANCE

(EXODUS 20:18-24:12)

THE impression produced upon the people by the phenomena accompanying God's revelation of His law was so deep, that they entreated that any further Divine communication might be made through the mediatorship of Moses. As Peter, when the Divine power of the Lord Jesus suddenly burst upon him, (Luke 5:8) felt that he, a sinful man, could not stand in the presence of his Lord, so were the children of Israel afraid of death, if they continued before God. But such feelings of fear have nothing spiritual in themselves. While Moses acceded to their request, he was careful to explain that the object of all they had witnessed had not been the excitement of fear (Exodus 20:20), but such searching of heart as might issue, not in slavish apprehension of outward consequences, but in that true fear of God, which would lead to the avoidance of sin.

And now Moses stood once more alone in the "thick darkness, where God was." The ordinances then given him must be regarded as the final preparation for that covenant which was so soon to be ratified. (Exodus 24) For, as the people of God, Israel must not be like the other nations. Alike in substance and in form, the conditions of their national life, the fundamental principles of their state, and the so-called civil rights and ordinances which were to form the groundwork of society, must be Divine. To use a figure: Israel was God's own possession. Before hallowing and formally setting it apart, God marked it out, and drew the boundary lines around His property. Such was the object and the meaning of the ordinances, (Exodus 20:22; 23) which preceded the formal conclusion of the covenant, recorded in Exodus 24: Accordingly the principles and "judgments" (21:1), or rather the "rights" and juridical arrangements, on which national life and civil society in Israel were based, were not only infinitely superior to anything known or thought of at the time, but such as to embody the solid and abiding principles of national life for all times.

And in truth they underlie all modern legislation, so that the Mosaic ordinances are, and will remain, the grand model on which civil society is constructed.

Without entering into details, we note the general arrangement of these ordinances. They were preceded by a general indication of the manner in which Israel was to worship God. (Exodus 20:22-26) As God had spoken to Israel "from heaven," so they were not to make any earthly representation of what was heavenly. On the other hand, as God would "come unto" them — from heaven to earth, and there hold intercourse with them, the altar which was to rise from earth towards heaven was to be simply "an altar of earth" (ver. 24), or if of stones, of such as were in the condition in which they had been found in the earth. Moreover, as the altar indicated that place on earth where God would appear for the purpose of blessing Israel, it was only to be reared where God recorded His name, that is, where He appointed it. In other words, their worship was to be regulated by His manifestation in grace, and not by their own choice or preferences. For grace lies at the foundation of all praise and prayer.

The sacrifices and worship of Israel were not to procure grace; grace had been the originating cause of their worship. And so it ever is. "We love Him, because He first loved us," and the gift of His dear Son to us sinners is free and unconditional on the part of the Father, and makes our return unto Him possible. And because this grace is free, it becomes man all the more to serve God with holy reverence, which should show itself even in outward demeanor (ver. 26).

"The judgments" next communicated to Moses determined, first, the civil and social position of all in Israel relatively to each other (Exodus 21:1; 23:12), and then their religious position relatively to the Lord (23: 13-19)."

The Divine legislation begins, as assuredly none other ever did, not at the topmost but at the lowest rung of society. It declares in the first place the personal rights of such individuals as are in a state of dependence — male (21:2-6) and female slaves (vers. 7-11). This is done not only with a sacred regard for the rights of the person, but with a delicacy, kindness, and strictness beyond any code ever framed on this subject. If slavery was still tolerated, as a thing existent, its real principle, that of making men chattels and property, was struck at the root, and the institution became, by its safeguards and provisions, quite other from what it has been among any nation, whether ancient or modern.

Then follow "judgments" guarding life (vers. 12-14), with crimes against which, the maltreatment and the cursing of parents (vers. 15, 17), and man-stealing (ver. 16), are put on a level. It is the sanctity of life, in itself, in its origin, and in its free possession, which is here in question, and the punishment awarded to such crimes is neither intended as warning nor as correction, but strictly as punishment, that is, as retribution. From the protection of life, the law passes to that of the body against all injuries, whether by man (vers. 18-27)or by beast (vers. 28-32). The principle here is, so far as possible, compensation, coupled with punishment in grave offenses.

Next, the safety of property is secured. But before entering upon it, the Divine law, Divine also in this, protects also the life of a beast. (Exodus 21:33-36) Property is dealt with under various aspects. First, we have the theft of cattle — most important to guard against among an agricultural people — a different kind of protection being wisely allowed to owners by day and by night (22:1-4). Then, damage to fields or their produce is considered (vers. 5, 6). After that, loss or damage of what had been entrusted for safe keeping (vers. 7-15), and along with it loss of honor (vers. 16, 17) are dealt with.

The statutes which follow (vers. 18-30) are quite different in character from those which had preceded. This appears even from the omission of the "if," by which all the previous ordinances had been introduced. In truth, they do not contemplate, as the others, any possible case, but they state and ordain what must never be allowed to take place. They are beyond the province of ordinary civil legislation, and concern Israel as being specially the people of Gad. As such they express what Jehovah expects from His own people, bound to Him by covenant. And this, perhaps, is the most wonderful part of the legislation, regulating and ordering what no civil rule has ever sought to influence. As before, the series of statutes begins by interdicting what is contrary to the God-consecrated character of the nation. Thus, at the outset all magic is exterminated (ver. 18), and with it all unnatural crimes (ver. 19), and idolatrous practices (ver. 20). In short, as before in worship, so now in life, heathenism, its powers, its vileness, and its corruptions are swept aside. On the other hand, in opposition to all national exclusiveness, the stranger (though not the strange god) is to be kindly welcomed (ver. 21); widows and the fatherless are not to be "humiliated" (vers. 22-24); those in temporary need not to be vexed by usury (vers. 25-27); God as the supreme

Lawgiver is not to be reviled, nor yet are those appointed to rule under Him to be cursed (ver. 28); the tribute due to the Lord as King is to be cheerfully given (vers. 29, 30); and the holy dignity of His people not to be profaned even in their daily habits (ver. 31).

Again, nothing that is untrue, unloving, or unjust is to be said, done, or attempted (23:1-3), and that not merely in public dealings, but personal dislike is not to influence conduct. On the contrary, all loving help is to be given even to an enemy in time of need (vers. 4, 5); the poor and persecuted are not to be unjustly dealt with; no bribe is to be taken, "for the gift maketh open eyes blind, and perverteth the causes of the righteous," and the same rule is to apply to the stranger as to Israel (vers. 6-9). Finally in this connection, the seventh year's and the seventh day's rest are referred to, not so much in their religious character as in their bearing upon the poor and the workers (vers. 10-12).

Passing from the statutes fixing the civil and social position of all in Israel to their religious position relatively to Jehovah, (Exodus 23:13-19) we have first of all an injunction of the three great annual feasts. Although strictly religious festivals, they are here viewed, primarily, not in their symbolical and typical meaning (which is universal and eternal), but in their national bearing: the paschal feast as that of Israel's deliverance from Egypt, the feast of weeks as that "of harvest, the first fruit of thy labors," and the feast of tabernacles as that of final "ingathering" (vers. 14-17). Of the three ordinances which now follow (vers, 18-19), the first refers to the Paschal sacrifice (comp. Exodus 12:15,20; 13:7; 34:25), and the second to the feast of first fruits or of weeks. From this it would follow, that the prohibition to "seethe a kid in its mother's milk" (ver. 19)must, at least primarily, have borne some reference to the festivities of the week of tabernacles; perhaps, as the learned Rabbinical commentator Abarbanel suggests, because some such practices were connected with heathen, idolatrous rites at the time of the ingathering of fruits.

The "judgments" which the Lord enjoins upon His people are appropriately followed by promises (23:20-33), in which, as their King and Lord, He undertakes their guidance and protection, and their possession of the land He had assigned to them. First and foremost, assurance is given them of the personal presence of Jehovah in that ANGEL, in Whom is the Name of the Lord (ver. 20). This was no common angel, however exalted, but a manifestation of Jehovah Himself, prefigurative of, and preparatory to His manifestation in the flesh in the Person of our Lord and Savior Jesus Christ. For all that is here said of Him is attributed to the Lord Himself in Exodus 13:21; while in Exodus 33:14, 15, He is expressly designated as "the Face" of Jehovah ("My Face" — in the Authorized Version "My presence"). Accordingly, all obedience is to be shown to His guidance, and every contact with idolatry and idolaters avoided. In that case the Lord would fulfill every good and gracious promise to His people, and cause them to possess the land in all its extent.

Such were the terms of the covenant which Jehovah made with Israel in their national capacity. when the people had ratified them by acceptance, (Exodus 24:3) Moses wrote all down in what was called "the book of the covenant" (24:7). And now the covenant itself was to be inaugurated by sacrifice, the sprinkling of blood, and the sacrificial meal. This transaction was the most important in the whole history of Israel. By this one sacrifice, never renewed, Israel was formally set apart as the people of God; and it lay at the foundation of all the sacrificial worship which followed. Only after it did God institute the Tabernacle, the priesthood, and all its services. Thus this one sacrifice prefigured the one sacrifice of our Lord Jesus Christ for His Church, which is the ground of our access to God and the foundation of all our worship and service. Most significantly, an altar was now built at the foot of Mount Sinai, and surrounded by twelve pillars, "according to the twelve tribes of Israel" Ministering youths — for as yet there was no priesthood — offered the burnt, and sacrificed the peace offerings unto Jehovah. Half of the blood of the sacrifices was put into basins, with the other half the altar was sprinkled, thus making reconciliation with God. Then the terms of the covenant were once more read in the hearing of all, and the other half of the blood, by which reconciliation had been made, sprinkled on the people with these words: "Behold the blood of the covenant which Jehovah hath made with you upon all these words (or terms)."

As a nation Israel was now reconciled and set apart unto God — both having been accomplished by the "blood of sprinkling." Thereby they became prepared for that fellowship with Him which was symbolized in the sacrificial meal that followed. (Exodus 24:9-11) There God, in pledge of His favor, fed His people upon the sacrifices which He had accepted. The sacrificial meal meant the fellowship of acceptance; its joy was that of the consciousness of this blessed fact. And now Moses and Aaron, and his two sons (the future priests), along with seventy of the elders of Israel, went up into the mount, "and did eat and drink" at that sacrificial meal, in the seen presence of the God of Israel, not indeed under any outward form, (Deuteronomy 4:12-15) but with heaven's own brightness underneath the Shechinah. Thus "to see God, and to eat and drink," was a foretaste and a pledge of the perfect blessedness in beholding Him hereafter. It was also a symbol and a type of what shall be realized when, as the Alleluia of the "great multitude" proclaims the reign of the "Lord God omnipotent," the gladsome, joyous bride of the Lamb now made ready for the marriage, and adorned with bridal garments, hears the welcome sound summoning her to "the marriage supper of the Lamb." (Revelation 19:6-9)

CHAPTER 12: THE PATTERN SEEN ON THE MOUNTAIN — THE TABERNACLE, THE PRIESTHOOD, AND THE SERVICES IN THEIR ARRANGEMENT AND TYPICAL MEANING — THE SIN OF THE GOLDEN CALF — THE DIVINE JUDGMENT — THE PLEA OF MOSES — GOD'S GRACIOUS FORGIVENESS — THE VISION OF THE GLORY OF THE LORD VOUCHSAFED TO MOSES

(Exodus 24:12; 25-33)

NEVER assuredly have we stronger proof of the Divine origin of what we call grace, and of the weakness and unprofitableness of human nature, than in the reaction which so often follows seasons of religious privilege. Readers of the New Testament will recall many instances of this in the Gospel-history, and will remember how our Lord, ever and again, at such times took His disciples aside into some desert place for quietness and prayer. But perhaps the saddest instance of how near the great enemy lingers to our seasons of spiritual enjoyment, and how great our danger of giddiness, when standing on such heights, is furnished by the history of Israel, immediately after the solemn covenant had been ratified.

Now that God had set apart His reconciled people unto Himself, it was necessary to have some definite place where He would meet with, and dwell among them, as also to appoint the means by which they should approach Him, and the manner in which he would manifest Himself to them. To reveal all this, as well as to give those "tables of stone," on which the commandments were graven, God now called Moses once more "up into the mount." Accompanied by "Joshua, his minister," he obeyed the Divine behest, leaving the rule of the people to Aaron and Hur. For six days he had to wait, while "the glory of Jehovah abode upon the mount" On the seventh, Moses was summoned within the bright cloud, which, to the children of Israel beneath, seemed "like a devouring fire", Joshua probably remaining near, but not actually with him. "Forty days and forty nights" "Moses was in the mount," without either eating bread or drinking water. (Deuteronomy 9:9) The new revelation which he now received concerned the Tabernacle which was to be erected, the priesthood which was to serve in it, and the services which were to be celebrated. Nay, it extended to every detail of furniture, dress, and observance. And for what was needful for this service, the free-will offerings of Israel were to be invited. (Exodus 25:1-8)

We have it upon the highest authority, that, not only in its grand outlines, but in all minutest details, everything was to be made "after the pattern" which God showed to Moses on the mount. (Exodus 25:9) And so we also read in Acts 7:44, and Hebrews 8:5; 9:23, teaching us, that Moses was shown by God an actual pattern or model of all that he was to make in and for the sanctuary. This can convey only one meaning. It taught far more than the general truth, that only that approach to God is lawful or acceptable which He has indicated. For, God showed Moses every detail to indicate that every detail had its special meaning, and hence could not be altered in any, even the minutest, particular, without destroying that meaning, and losing that significance which alone made it of importance. Nothing here was intended as a mere ornament or ceremony, all was symbol and type. As symbol, it indicated a present truth; as type, it pointed forward (a prophecy by deed) to future spiritual realities, while, at the same time, it already conveyed to the worshipper the first-fruits, and the earnest of their final accomplishment in "the fullness of time." We repeat, everything here had a spiritual meaning — the material of which the ark, the dresses of the priesthood, and all else was made; colors, measurements, numbers, vessels, dresses, services, and the priesthood itself — and all proclaimed the same spiritual truth, and pointed forward to the same spiritual reality, viz., God in Christ in the midst of His Church. The Tabernacle was "the tent of meeting" (Ohel Moed) where God held intercourse with His people, and whence He dispensed blessing unto them. The priesthood, culminating in the high-priest, was the God-appointed mediatorial agency through which God was approached and by which He bestowed His gifts; the sacrifices were the means of such approach to God, and either intended to restore fellowship with God when it had been dimmed or interrupted, or else to express and manifest that fellowship. But alike the priesthood, the sacrifices, and the altar pointed to the Person and the work of the Lord Jesus Christ. So far as the Tabernacle itself was concerned, the court with the altar of burnt-offering was the place by which Israel approached God; the Holy Place that in which they held communion with God; and the Most Holy Place that in which the Lord Himself visibly dwelt among them in the Shechinah, as the covenant-God, His Presence resting on the mercy-seat which covered the Ark.

It is most instructive to mark the order in which the various ordinances about the Tabernacle and its furniture were given to Moses. First, we have the directions about the Ark, as the most holy thing in the Most Holy Place; (Exodus 25:10-22) then, similarly, those about the table of shewbread and the golden candlestick (25:23-40), not only as belonging to the furniture of the Holy Place, but because spiritually the truths which they symbolized — life and light in the Lord — were the outcome of God's Presence between the cherubim. After that, the dwelling itself is described, and the position in it of Ark, table, and candlestick. (Exodus 26)

Then only comes the altar of burnt-offering, with the court that was to surround the sanctuary (27:1-19). We now enter, as it were, upon a different section, that of ministry. here directions are first given about the burning of the lamps on the seven-branched candlestick (27:20, 21); after which we have the institution of, and all connected with, the priesthood. (Exodus 28; 29) The last, because the highest, point in the ministry is that about the altar of incense and its service (30:1-10). This symbolized prayer, and hence could only come in after the institution of the mediatorial priesthood. Thus far it will be noticed, that the arrangement is always from within outwards — from the Most Holy Place to the court of the worshippers, symbolizing once more that all proceeds from Him Who is the God of grace, Who, as already quoted in the language of St. Augustine, "gives what He commands," and that the highest of all service, to which everything else is subservient, or rather to which it stands related as the means towards the end, is that of fellowship in prayer — the worshipful beholding of God.

These directions are followed by some others strictly connected with the character of Israel as the people of God. Israel is His firstborn among the nations, (Exodus 4:22, 23) and, as such, must be redeemed, like the firstborn son of a family, (Exodus 22:29; 34:20; Numbers 3:12, 13, 16) to indicate, on the one hand, that the people are really His own property, and that the life entrusted to them belongeth to Him and, on the other hand, to express that, in the firstborn, all the family is hallowed to God. (Romans 11:16) This was the import of the "atonement money." (Exodus 30:11-6)

But even so, each approach to Him needed special washing — hence the laver (30:17-21). Again, within Israel, the priests were to be the sacred representatives of the people. As such, they, and all connected with their service, must be anointed with a peculiar oil, symbolical of the Holy Spirit, all counterfeit of which was to be visited with such punishment as reminds us of that following upon the sin against the Holy Ghost (vers. 22-33). Lastly, the material for the highest symbolical service, that of incensing, is described (vers. 34-38). The whole section closes by designating the persons whom the Lord had raised up for doing all the work connected with the preparation of His Sanctuary. (Exodus 31:1-11)

The institutions thus made were, in reality, the outcome and the consequences of the covenant which the Lord had made with Israel. As "a sign" of this covenant between Jehovah and the children of Israel, (Exodus 31:17) God now ordered anew the observance of the Sabbath (31:12-17) — its twofold provision of rest and of sanctification (ver. 15) being expressive of the civil and the religious aspects of that covenant, and of their marvelous combination. Thus furnished with all needful directions, Moses finally received, at the Hand of the Lord, the "two tables of testimony," "written with the finger of God" (ver. 18).

While these sacred transactions were taking place on the mount, a far different scene was enacted below in the camp of Israel. Without attempting the foolish and wrongful task of palliating the sin of making the Golden Calf, (Exodus 32:1-6) it is right that the matter should be placed in its true light. The prolonged absence of Moses had awakened peculiar fears in the people. They had seen him pass more than a month ago into the luminous cloud that covered the mount.

"And the sight of the glory of Jehovah was like a devouring fire on the top of the mount in the eyes of the children of Israel." (Exodus 24:17)

What more natural than for those who waited, week after week, in unexplained solitude, within sight of this fire, to imagine that Moses had been devoured by it. Their leader was gone, and the visible symbol of Jehovah was high up on the mountain top, like "a devouring fire." They must have another leader; that would be Aaron. But they must also have another symbol of the Divine Presence. One only occurred to their carnal minds, besides that which had hitherto preceded them. It was the Egyptian Apis, who, under the form of a calf, represented the powers of nature. To his worship they had always been accustomed; indeed, its principal seat was the immediate neighborhood of the district in Egypt where, for centuries, they and their fathers had been settled. Probably, this also was the form under which many of them had, in former days, tried, in a perverted manner, to serve their ancestral God, combining the traditions of the patriarchs with the corruptions around them (compare Joshua 24:14; Ezekiel 20:8; 23:3, 8). It is quite evident that Israel did not mean to forsake Jehovah, but only to serve Him under the symbol of Apis. This appears from the statement of the people themselves on seeing the Golden Calf: (Exodus 32:4) "This is thy God," and from the proclamation of Aaron (32:5): "To-morrow is a feast to Jehovah."

Their great sin consisted in not realizing the Presence of an unseen God, while the fears of their unbelief led them back to their former idolatrous practices, unmindful that this involved a breach of the second of those commandments so lately proclaimed in their hearing, and of the whole covenant which had so solemnly been ratified. Some expositors have sought to extenuate the guilt of Aaron by supposing that, in asking for their golden ornaments to make "the calf," he had hoped to enlist their vanity and covetousness, and so to turn them from their sinful purpose. The text, however, affords no warrant for this hypothesis. It is true that Aaron was, at the time, not yet in the priesthood, and also that his proclamation of "a feast to Jehovah" may have been intended to bring it out distinctly, that the name of Jehovah was still, as before, acknowledged by Israel. But his culpable weakness — to say the least of it — only adds to his share in the people's sin. Indeed, this appears from Aaron's later confession to Moses, (Exodus 32:21-24) than which nothing more humiliating is recorded, even throughout this sad story. Perhaps, however, it was well that, before his appointment to the priesthood, Aaron, and all after him, should have had this evidence of natural unfitness and unworthiness, that so it might appear more clearly that the character of all was typical, and in no way connected with the worthiness of Aaron or of his house.

While Israel indulged in the camp in the usual licentious dances and orgies which accompanied such heathen festivals yet another trial awaited Moses. It had been God Himself Who informed Moses of the "quick" apostasy of His people (32:7, 8), accompanying the announcement by these words: "Now therefore let Me alone, that My wrath may wax hot against them, and that I may consume them. and I will make of thee a great nation" (ver. 10). One of the fathers has already noticed, that the Divine words, "Now therefore let Me alone," seemed to imply a call to Moses to exercise his office as intercessor for his people. Moreover, it has also been remarked, that the offer to make of Moses a nation even greater than Israel, (Deuteronomy 9:14) was, in a sense, a real temptation, or rather a trial of Moses' singleness of purpose and faithfulness to his mission. We know how entirely Moses stood this trial, and how earnestly, perseveringly, and successfully he pleaded for Israel with the Lord (vers. 11-14). But one point has not been sufficiently noticed by commentators. When, in announcing the apostasy of Israel, God spake of them not as His own but as Moses' people — "thy people, whom thou broughtest out of the land of Egypt" (ver. 7) — He at the same time furnished Moses with the right plea in his intercession, and also indicated the need of that severe punishment which was afterwards executed, lest Moses might, by weak indulgence, be involved in complicity with Israel's sin. The latter point is easily understood. As for the other, we see how Moses, in his intercession, pleaded the argument with which God had furnished him.

Most earnestly did he insist that Israel was God's people, since their deliverance from Egypt had been wholly God-wrought. Three special arguments did he use with God, and these three may to all time serve as models in our pleading for forgiveness and restoration after weaknesses and falls. These arguments were: first, that Israel was God's property, and that His past dealings had proved this (ver. 11); secondly, that God's own glory was involved in the deliverance of Israel in the face of the enemy (ver. 12); and, thirdly, that God's gracious promises were pledged for their salvation (ver. 13). And such pleas God never refuses to accept (ver. 14). But, although informed of the state of matters in the camp of Israel, Moses could have been scarcely prepared for the sight which presented itself, when, on suddenly turning an eminence, the riotous multitude, in its licentious merriment, appeared full in view. The contrast was too great, and as 'Moses' wrath waxed hot, he cast the tables out of his hands, and brake them beneath the mount" (ver. 19). It is not necessary to suppose that what follows in the sacred text is related in the strict order of time.

Suffice it, that, after a short but stern reproof to Aaron, Moses took his station "in the gate of the camp," summoning to him those who were "on the side of Jehovah." All the sons of Levi obeyed, and were directed to go through the camp and "slay every man his brother, and every man his companion, and every man his neighbor" (ver. 27). On that terrible day no less than 3,000 men fell under the sword of Levi. As for the Golden Calf, its wooden framework was burnt in the fire and its gold covering ground to powder, and strewed upon the brook which descended from Sinai. Of this Israel had to drink, in symbol that each one must receive and bear the fruits of his sin, just as, later on, the woman suspected of adultery was ordered to drink the water into which the writing of the curses upon her sin had been washed. (Numbers 5:24)

There is one point here which requires more particular inquiry than it has yet received. As commonly understood, the slaughter of these 3,000 stands out as an unexplained fact. Why just these 3,000? Did they fall simply because they happened to stand by nearest, on the principle, as has been suggested, of decimating an offending host; and why did no one come to their aid? Such indiscriminate punishment seems scarcely in accordance with the Divine dealings. But the text, as it appears to us, furnishes hints for the right explanation. When Moses stood in the camp of Israel and made proclamation for those who were on Jehovah's side, we read that "he saw that the people were naked" (ver. 25), or unreined, licentious (comp. ver. 6; 1 Corinthians 10:7, 8). In short, there stood before him a number of men, fresh from their orgies, in a state of licentious attire, whom even his appearance and words had not yet sobered into quietness, shame, and repentance. These, as we understand it, still thronged the open roadway of the camp, which so lately had resounded with their voices; these were met by the avenging Levites, as, sword in hand, they passed from gate to gate, like the destroying angel through Egypt on the Paschal night; and these were the 3,000 which fell on that day, while the vast multitude had retired to the quietness of their tents in tardy repentance and fear, in view of him whose presence among them betokened the nearness of that holy and jealous God, Whose terrible judgments they had so much cause to dread.

Thus ended the day of Moses' return among his people. On the morrow he gathered them to speak, not in anger but in sorrow, of their great sin. Then returning from them to the Lord, he entreated forgiveness for his brethren, with an intensity and self-denial of love (vers. 31, 32), unequaled by that of any man except St. Paul.

Thus far he prevailed, that the people were not to be destroyed, nor the covenant to cease; but God would not personally go in the midst of a people so incapable of bearing His holy Presence; He would send a created angel to be henceforth their leader. And still would this sin weight the scale in the day of visitation, which the further rebellion of this people would only too surely bring. The first words of the final sentence, that their carcasses were to fall in the wilderness, (Numbers 14:29) were, so to speak, already uttered in this warning of the Lord on the morrow of the slaughter of the 3,000: "Nevertheless in the day when I visit I will visit their sin upon them." "Thus," in the language of Scripture (ver. 35), "Jehovah smote the people, because they made the calf, which Aaron made."

That the Lord would not go personally with Israel because of their stiffneckedness, was, indeed, felt to be "evil tidings." (Exodus 33:4) The account of the people's repentance and of God's gracious forgiveness (Exodus 33) forms one of the most precious portions of this history. The first manifestation of their godly sorrow was the putting away of their "ornaments," not only temporarily but permanently. Thus we read:" The children of Israel stripped themselves of their ornaments from the mount Horeb onward" (33:6). Israel was, so to speak, in permanent mourning, ever after its great national sin. Next, as the Lord would not personally be in the midst of Israel, Moses removed the tent — probably his own -outside the camp, that there he might receive the Divine communications, when "the cloudy pillar descended," "and Jehovah talked with Moses." Moses called this "the tent of meeting" (rendered in the Authorized Version "the tabernacle of the congregation:" ver. 7). It is scarcely necessary to say, that this was not "the Tabernacle" (as the Authorized Version might lead one to infer), since the latter was not yet constructed.

To this "tent of meeting" all who were of the true Israel, and who regarded Jehovah not merely as their national God, but owned Him personally and felt the need of Him, were wont to go out. This must not be looked upon as either a protest or an act of separation on their part, but as evidence of true repentance and of their desire to meet with God, who no longer was in the camp of Israel. Moreover, all the people, when they saw the cloudy pillar descend to Moses, "rose up and worshipped." Altogether, this was perhaps the period of greatest heart-softening during Israel's wanderings in the wilderness.

And God graciously had respect to it. He had already assured Moses that he stood in special relationship to Him ("I know thee by name"), and that his prayer for Israel had been heard ("thou hast also found grace in My sight"). But as yet the former sentence stood, to the effect that an angel, not Jehovah Himself, was to be Israel's future guide. Under these circumstances Moses now entreated Jehovah to show him His way, that is, His present purpose in regard to Israel, adding, that if God would bring them into the Land of Promise, He would "consider that this is Thy people," and hence He their God and King. This plea also prevailed, and the Lord once more promised that His own presence would go with them, and that He Himself would give them the rest of Canaan (ver. 14; comp. Deuteronomy 3:20; Hebrews 4:8). And Moses gave thanks by further prayer, even more earnest than before, for the blessing now again vouchsafed (vers. 15, 16).

But one thing had become painfully evident to Moses by what had happened. However faithful in his Master's house, (Hebrews 3:5) he was but a servant; and a servant knoweth not the will of his master. The threat of destruction if Jehovah remained among Israel, and the alternative of sending with them an angel, must have cast a gloom over his future mediatorship. It was, indeed, only that of a servant, however highly favored, not of a son. (Hebrews 3:5, 6) Oh, that he could quite understand the Being and character of the God of Israel — see, not His likeness, but His glory! (Exodus 33:18) Then would all become clear, and, with fuller light, joyous assurance fill his heart. That such was the real meaning of Moses' prayer, "Show me Thy glory" (ver. 18), appears from the mode in which the Lord answered it. "And He said, I will make all My goodness pass before thee, and I will proclaim the Name of Jehovah before thee." Then was Moses taught, that the deepest mystery of Divine grace lay not in God's national, but in His individual dealings, in sovereign mercy, "And I will be gracious to whom I will be gracious, and will show mercy on whom I will show mercy" (ver. 19). Yet no man could see the face, the full outshining of Jehovah. Neither flesh nor spirit, so long as it dwelt in the flesh, could bear such glory. While that glory passed by, God would hold Moses in a clift of the rock, perhaps in the same in which a similar vision was afterwards granted to Elijah, (1 Kings 19:9) and there He would support, or "cover" him with His hand. Only "the back parts" — the after-glory, the luminous reflection of what Jehovah really was — could Moses bear to see. But what Moses witnessed, hid in the clift of the rock, and Elijah, the representative of the prophets, saw more clearly, hiding his face in his mantle, while he worshipped, appears fully revealed to us in the Face of Jesus Christ, in Whom "the whole fullness of the Godhead dwelleth bodily."

CHAPTER 13: MOSES A SECOND TIME ON THE MOUNT — ON HIS RETURN HIS FACE SHINETH — THE REARING OF THE TABERNACLE — ITS CONSECRATION BY THE SEEN PRESENCE OF JEHOVAH

(EXODUS 34-50)

THE covenant relationship between God and Israel having been happily restored, Moses was directed to bring into the mount other two tables -this time of his own preparing — instead of those which he had broken, that God might once more write down the "ten words." (Exodus 34:1-4) Again he passed forty days and forty nights on Sinai without either eating or drinking (34:28). The communications which he received were preceded by that glorious vision of Jehovah's brightness, which had been promised to him. What he saw is nowhere told us; only what he, heard, when Jehovah" proclaimed" before him what Luther aptly designates as "the sermon about the name of God." It unfolded His inmost being, as that of love unspeakable — the cumulation of terms being intended to present that love in all its aspects. And, in the words of a recent German writer "Such as Jehovah here proclaimed, He also manifested it among Israel at all times, from Mount Sinai until He brought them into the land of Canaan; and thence till He cast them out among the heathen. Nay, even now in their banishment, He is 'keeping mercy for thousands, who turn to the Redeemer that has come out of Zion.'"

When Moses thus fully understood the character of Jehovah, he could once more plead for Israel, now converting into a plea for forgiveness even the reason which had seemed to make the presence of Jehovah among Israel dangerous — that they were a stiff-necked people (ver. 9). In the same manner had the Lord, in speaking to Noah, made the sin of man, which had erst provoked judgment, the ground for future forbearance. (Genesis 6:5, 6; Genesis 8:21) And the Lord now graciously confirmed once more His covenant with Israel. In so doing He reminded them of its two conditions, the one negative, the other positive, but both strictly connected, and both applying to the time when Moses should be no more, and Israel had entered on possession of the Promised Land. These two conditions were always to be observed, if the covenant was to be maintained. The one was avoidance of all contact with the Canaanites and their idolatry (vers. 11-16); the other, observance of the service of Jehovah in the manner prescribed by Him (vers. 17-26).

Another confirmation of the Divine message which Moses bore from the mount, appeared on his return among Israel. All unknown to himself, the reflection of the Divine glory had been left upon him, and "the skin of his face shone (shot out rays) because of His (God's) talking with him."

As Aaron and the children of Israel were afraid of this reflection of the Divine glory, Moses had to use a coveting for his face while speaking to them, which he only removed when conversing with the Lord. It is to this that the apostle refers (2 Corinthians 3:7) when he contrasts the Old Testament glory on the face of Moses, which "was to be done away" at any rate at the death of Moses — and which was connected with what, after all, was "the ministration of death," with "the ministration of the Spirit" and its exceeding and enduring glory. Moreover, the veil with which Moses had to cover his face was symbolical of the veil covering the Old Testament, which is only "done away in Christ" (2 Corinthians 3:13, 14).

Everything was now ready for the construction of the Tabernacle and of all requisite for its services. We can understand how, especially in view of the work before them, the Sabbath rest should now be once more enjoined. (Exodus 35:2, 3) Then a proclamation was made for voluntary contributions of all that was needful, to which the people responded with such "willing offerings" (35:29), that soon not only "sufficient" but "too much" "for all the work" was gathered. (Exodus 36:5-7) The amount of gold and silver actually used is expressly mentioned in Exodus 38:24-26. The sum total of the gold amounts in present value to at least 131,595l., and that of the silver to about 75,444l., or both together to 207,039l., And it must be borne in mind, that this sum does not indicate the whole amount offered by Israel — only that actually employed. In regard to the silver, either less of it was offered or none at all may have been required, since the 75,444l. in silver represent the exact amount of the "ransom money" (Exodus 30:12) which every Israelite had to pay on their being first numbered (38:26). Nor was it only gold, silver, and other material which the people brought. All "wise-hearted" men and women "whose heart the Lord stirred up" — that is, all who understood such work, and whose zeal was kindled by love for God's sanctuary — busied themselves, according to their ability, under the direction of Bezaleel, the grandson of Hur, and Aholiab, of the tribe of Daniel But what chiefly impresses us in the sacred narrative is the evidence of spiritual devotion, which appeared alike in the gifts and in the labor of the people.

"And Moses did look upon all the work, and, behold, they had done it as Jehovah had commanded, even so had they done it: and Moses blessed them." (Exodus 39:43)

Under such willing hands, the whole work was completed within an almost incredibly short period. On comparing Exodus 19:1, which fixes the arrival of Israel at Mount Sinai as in the third month (of the first year), with Exodus 40:2, which informs us that the Tabernacle was ready for setting up "on the first day of the first month" (of the second year), we find that an interval of nine months had elapsed. From this, however, must be deducted twice forty days, during which Moses was on the mount, as well as the days when Israel prepared for the covenant, and those when it was ratified and the law given, and also the interval between Moses' first and second stay on the mountain. Thus the whole of the elaborate work connected with the Tabernacle and its services must have been done within six months. And now that "the Tabernacle was reared up, Moses first placed within the Most Holy Place the Ark holding "the testimony," and covered it with the mercy-seat; next, he ranged in the Holy Place, to the north, the table of shewbread, setting "the bread in order upon it before the Lord;" then, to the south, "the candlestick," lighting its lamps before the Lord; and finally "the golden altar" "before the veil" of the Most Holy Place, "and he burnt sweet incense thereon." All this being done, and the curtain at the entrance to the Tabernacle hung up, (Exodus 40:28) the altar of burnt-offering was placed "by the door of the Tabernacle," and "the laver" between it and that altar, although probably not in a straight line, but somewhat to the side of the altar of burnt-offering. And on the altar smoked the burnt and the meat-offering, and the laver was filled with water, in which Moses, and Aaron, and his sons washed their hands and their feet.

All was now quite in readiness means, ordinances, and appointed channels of blessing, and all was in waiting. One thing only was needed; but upon that the meaning and the efficacy of everything else depended. But God was faithful to His promise. As in believing expectancy Israel looked up, "the cloud covered the tent of the congregation, and the glory of Jehovah filled the Tabernacle." Outside, visible to all, rested "upon the tent" that Cloud and Pillar, in which Jehovah had hitherto guided them, and would continue so to do. For, as the cloud by day and the appearance of fire by night tarried over the Tabernacle, the children of Israel "abode in their tents," "and journeyed not." But "when it was taken up," then Israel's camp was speedily broken up, and, journeying, they followed their Divine Leader (comp. Numbers 9:15-23). A constant, visible, and guiding Presence of Jehovah this among His professing people, resting above the outer tent that covered the Tabernacle. But within that Tabernacle itself there was yet another and unapproachable Presence. For "the glory of Jehovah filled the Tabernacle. And Moses was not able to enter into the tent of the congregation, because the cloud abode thereon, and the glory of Jehovah filled the Tabernacle." (Exodus 40:34, 35) Presently it withdrew within the Most Holy Place, into which none could enter but the high-priest once a year, and that on the day and for the purpose of atonement, and where it rested between the cherubim of glory, above the mercy-seat, that covered the ark with the testimony. For "the way into the holiest of all was not yet made manifest." "But Christ being come an high-priest of good things to come, by a greater and more perfect tabernacle, not made with hands, that is to say, not of this building; neither by the blood of goats and calves, but by His own blood He entered in once into the holy place, having obtained eternal redemption for us." (Hebrews 9:8, 11, 12)

CHAPTER 14: ANALYSIS OF THE BOOK OF LEVITICUS — THE SIN OF NADAB & ABIHU — JUDGMENT UPON THE BLASPHEMER.
(LEVITICUS)

THE Book of Exodus was intended to tell how the Lord God redeemed and set apart for Himself "a peculiar people." Accordingly, it appropriately closes with the erection of the Tabernacle and the hallowing of it by the visible Presence of Jehovah in the Holy Place. It yet remained to show the other aspect of the covenant. For the provisions and the means of grace must be accepted and used by those for whom they are designed, and the "setting apart" of the people by Jehovah implied, as it's converse, consecration on the part of Israel. And this forms the subject matter of the Book of Leviticus, which a recent German writer has aptly described as "the code regulating the spiritual life of Israel, viewed as the people of God."

To sum up its general contents — it tells us in its first Part (1-16.) how Israel was to approach God, together with what, symbolically speaking, was inconsistent with such approaches; and in its second Part (17-27.) how, having been brought near to God, the people were to maintain, to enjoy, and to exhibit the state of grace of which they had become partakers. Of course, all is here symbolical, and we must regard the directions and ordinances as conveying in an outward form so many spiritual truths. Perhaps we might go so far as to say, that Part 1 of Leviticus exhibits, in a symbolical form, the doctrine of justification, and Part that of sanctification; or, more accurately, the manner of access to God, and the holiness which is the result of that access.

It has already been pointed out, that the Book of Leviticus consists of two Parts; the one ending with chapter 16; the other, properly speaking, with chapter 25; chapter 26 being a general conclusion, indicating the blessings of faithful adherence to the covenant, while chapter 27, which treats of vowing unto the Lord, forms a most appropriate appendix. At the close of the book itself, (Leviticus 26:46) and of the chapter which, for want of a better name, we have termed its appendix (27:34), we find expressions indicating the purpose of the whole, and that the book of Leviticus forms in itself a special and independent part of the Pentateuch. We repeat it, the Book of Leviticus is intended for Israel as the people of God; it is the statute-book of Israel's spiritual life; and, on both these grounds, it is neither simply legal, in the sense of ordinary law, nor yet merely ceremonial, but throughout symbolical and typical. Accordingly, its deeper truths apply to all times and to all men.

Part 1 (1-16.), which tells Israel how to approach God so as to have communion with Him, appropriately opens with a description of the various kinds of sacrifices. (Leviticus 1-7) It next treats of the priesthood.

(Leviticus 8-10) The thoroughly symbolical character of all, and hence the necessity of closest adherence to the directions given, are next illustrated by the judgment which befell those who offered incense upon "strange fire." (Leviticus 10:1-6) From the priesthood the sacred text passes to the worshippers. (Leviticus 11-15) These must be clean — personally (11:1-47), in their family-life, (Leviticus 12) and as a congregation. (Leviticus 13-15) Above and beyond all is the great cleansing of the Day of Atonement, (Leviticus 16) with which the first part of the book, concerning access to God, closes.

The Second Part of the Book of Leviticus, which describes, in symbolical manner, the holiness that becometh the people of God, treats, first, of personal holiness, (Leviticus 17) then of holiness in the family, (Leviticus 18) of holiness in social relations, (Leviticus 19, 20) and of holiness in the priesthood. (Leviticus 21, 22) Thence the sacred text proceeds to holy seasons. (Leviticus 23, 24) As the duty of close adherence to the Divine directions in connection with the priesthood had been illustrated by the judgment upon Nadab and Abihu, (Leviticus 10:1-6) so now the solemn duty, incumbent on all Israel, to treat the Name of Jehovah as holy, is exhibited in the punishment of one who had blasphemed it. (Leviticus 24:10-end) Finally, Leviticus 25 describes the holiness of the land. Thus Part II. treats more especially of consecration. As Part I., describing access to God, had culminated in the ordinance of the Day of Atonement, so Part II. in that of the Jubilee Year. Lastly, Leviticus 26 dwells on the blessing attaching to faithful observance of the covenant; while Leviticus 27, reaching, as it were, beyond ordinary demands and consecrations, speaks of the free-will offerings of the heart, as represented by vows.

It now only remains to describe the two illustrative instances already referred to — the one connected with the priesthood, the other with the people. Aaron and his sons had just been solemnly consecrated to their holy office, and the offering, which they had brought, consumed in view of the whole people by fire from before Jehovah, to betoken His acceptance thereof. (Leviticus 9) All the more did any transgression of the Lord's ordinance, especially if committed by His priests, call for signal and public punishment. But, Nadab and Abihu, the two eldest sons of Aaron, attempted to offer "strange fire before Jehovah, which He commanded them not." (Leviticus 10:1)

Some writers have inferred from the prohibition of wine or of any strong drink to the priests during the time of their ministry, which immediately follows upon the record of this event (10:8-11), that these two had been under some such influence at the time of their daring attempt. The point is of small importance, comparatively speaking. It is not easy to say what the expression "strange fire" exactly implies. Clearly, the two were going to offer incense on the golden altar (ver. 1), and as clearly this service was about to be done at a time not prescribed by the Lord. For a comparison of vers. 12 and 16 shows that it took place between the sacrifice offered by Aaron (Leviticus 9) and the festive meal following that sacrifice; whereas incense was only to be burnt at the morning and evening sacrifices. Besides, it may be, that they also took "strange fire" in the sense of taking the burning coals otherwise than from the altar of burnt-offering. In the ceremonial for the Day of Atonement the latter is expressly prescribed, (Leviticus 16:12) and it is a fair inference that the same direction applied to every time of incensing. At any rate, we know that such was the invariable rule in the Temple at the time of Christ.

But Nadab and Abihu were not allowed to accomplish their purpose. The same fire, which a little ago had consumed the accepted sacrifice, (Leviticus 9:24) now struck them, "and they died before Jehovah," that is, in front of His dwelling-place, most probably in the court (comp. Leviticus 1:5), just as they were about to enter the Holy Place. Thus, on the very day of their consecration to the priesthood, did the oldest sons of Aaron perish, because they had not sanctified the Lord in their hearts, but had offered Him a worship of their own devising, instead of that holy incense consumed by fire from off the altar, which symbolized prayer, offered up on the ground of accepted sacrifice. And this twofold lesson did the Lord Himself teach in explanation of this judgment (10:3). So far as the priesthood was concerned — "I will sanctify Myself in those who stand near to Me, and" (so far as all the people were concerned) "before all the people I will glorify Myself." In other words, if those who had been consecrated to Him would not sanctify Him in heart and life, He would sanctify Himself in them by judgments (comp. also Ezekiel 38:16), and thus glorify His Name before all, as the Holy One, Who cannot with impunity be provoked to anger.

So deeply was Aaron solemnized, that, in the language of Scripture, he "held his peace." Not a word of complaint escaped his lips; nor yet was a token of mourning on his part, or on that of his sons, allowed to cast the shadow of personal feelings, or of latent regret, upon this signal vindication of Divine holiness (10:6). Only their "brethren, the whole house of Israel" were permitted to "bewail this burning (of His anger) which Jehovah hath kindled."

The history of the judgment upon the blasphemer (Leviticus 24:10-14) was inserted in the portion of Leviticus where it stands, either because it happened at the time when the laws there recorded were given, or else because it forms a suitable introduction to, and illustration of, the duty of owning Jehovah, which finds its fullest outward expression in the rest of the Sabbatical and in the arrangements of the Jubilee Year, enjoined in Leviticus 25. It also affords another instance of the dangers accruing to Israel from the presence among them of that "mixed multitude" which had followed them from Egypt. (Exodus 12:38) There seems no reason to doubt the Jewish view, that the latter occupied a separate place in the camp; the children of Israel being ranged according to their tribes, "every man by his own standard, with the ensign of their father's house." (Numbers 2:2) But as the blasphemer was only the son of a Danite mother — Shelomith, the daughter of Dibri — his father having been an Egyptian, he would not have been entitled to pitch his tent among the tribe of Daniel.

Hebrew tradition further states, that this had been the cause of the quarrel, when the blasphemer" went out among the children of Israel; and this son of the Israelitish woman and a man of Israel strove together in the camp." Finally, it adds, that the claim to dwell among the Danites having been decided by Moses against him, the man "blasphemed the Name (of Jehovah), and cursed." Whatever truth, if any, there be in this tradition, the crime itself was most serious. If even cursing one's parents was visited with death, what punishment could be too severe upon one who had "reviled" Jehovah, and "cursed!" But just because the case was so solemn, Moses did not rashly adjudicate in it (comp. the corresponding delay in Numbers 15:34)

"They put him inward to determine about them (i.e. about blasphemers), according to the mouth (or command) of Jehovah." Then by Divine direction the blasphemer was taken without the camp; those who had heard his blasphemy laid "their hands upon his head," as it were to put away the blasphemy from themselves, and lay it on the head of the guilty (comp. Deuteronomy 21:6); and the whole congregation shared in the judgment by stoning him.

But the general law which decreed the punishment of death upon blasphemy (Leviticus 24:16) was to apply to native Israelites as well as to the stranger, as indeed all crimes that carried retributive punishment -specially those against the life or the person — were to be equally visited, whether the offender were a Jew or a foreigner. This is the object of the repetition of these laws in that connection. (Leviticus 24:17-22) For Jehovah was not a national deity, like the gods of the heathen; nor were Israel's privileges those of exceptional favor in case of offenses; but Jehovah was the Holy One of Israel, and holiness became His house for ever.

CHAPTER 15: ANALYSIS OF THE BOOK OF NUMBERS — THE NUMBERING OF ISRAEL — AND THAT OF THE LEVITES — ARRANGEMENT OF THE CAMP, AND ITS SYMBOLICAL IMPORT — THE MARCH

(NUMBERS 1-4; 10:1-11)

THE Book of Numbers reads almost like a chronicle of the principal events during the thirty-eight years which elapsed between Israel's stay in the wilderness of Sinai, and their arrival on the borders of Canaan.

What took place during the journey to Mount Sinai had been intended to prepare the people for the solemn events there enacted. Similarly, the thirty-eight years wanderings which followed were designed to fit Israel for entering on possession of the Land of Promise. The outward history of the people during that period exhibited, on the one hand, the constant care and mercy of Jehovah, and on the other, His holiness and His judgments; while the laws and ordinances given them were needful for the organization of the commonwealth of Israel in its future relations. A brief analysis of the whole book will show the connection of all.

In general, the Book of Numbers seems to consist of three parts, the first, (Numbers 1-10:10) detailing the preparations for the march from Sinai; the second, (Numbers 10:11-21) The history of the journeyings of Israel through the wilderness; and the third, (Numbers 22-26) the various occurrences on the east of the Jordan. If we examine each of these parts separately, we find that Part 1 consists of four sections, detailing — 1. The numbers and the outward arrangement of each of the tribes, (Numbers 1, 2) and the appointment of the Levites to their service (3, 4.); 2. Laws concerning the higher and spiritual order of the people, culminating in the priestly blessing (5, 6.); 3. The three last occurrences before leaving Mount Sinai (7, 8, 9:1-14); 4. The signals for the march in the wilderness (9:15 -10: 10).

Part II tells the history of the wanderings of Israel, in their three stages 1. From Sinai to Paran, near Kadesh, detailing all that happened there (10:10-14); 2. From the announcement of the death of the generation which had 125 come out from Egypt to the re-assembling of the people at Kadesh in the fortieth year after the Exodus (15-19); 3. The march from Kadesh to Mount Hor, with the events during its course (20, 21). Lastly, Part III. consists of five sections detailing -

Before leaving the encampment at Mount Sinai, God directed Moses and Aaron to take a census of all who constituted the host of Israel in the language of Scripture. "All that are able to go forth to war," "their armies," (Numbers 1:3) that is, "every male from twenty years old and upwards." In this they were to be assisted by one delegate from each tribe, "every one head of the house of his fathers" (1:4); or, as they are designated in ver. 16, "the called (representatives) of the congregation, princes of their paternal tribes, heads of thousands in Israel."

The latter expression indicates that the census was taken on the plan proposed by Jethro, (Exodus 18:21, 25) by which Israel was arranged into thousands, hundreds, fifties, and tens. This also accounts for the even numbers assigned to each tribe as the final result of the numbering, Manifestly, the census was made on the basis of the poll taken, nine months before, for the purpose of the "atonement money." (Exodus 30:11-16) This poll had yielded a total of 603,550, (Exodus 38:26) which is precisely the same number as that in Numbers 1:46. Probably, therefore, the census was substantially only a re-arrangement and registration of the people according to their tribes, in thousands, hundreds, fifties, and tens, made with the co-operation of the hereditary rulers of the tribes. The above number of men capable of bearing arms would, if we may apply modern statistical results, imply a total population of upwards of two millions. Thirty-eight years later, just before entering upon possession of the land, a second census was taken, (Numbers 26) which yielded a total number of 601,730 capable of bearing arms (26:51), thus showing a decrease of 1820 during the years of wandering in the wilderness. Arranging these two census according to the tribes, and placing them side by side, we gather some interesting information:

First Census (Exodus 30; Numbers 1)

Second Census (Numbers 26)

A comparison of the foregoing figures will show, that, while some of the tribes remarkably increased, others equally remarkably decreased, during the thirty-eight years' wanderings. Thus, for example, Issachar increased nineteen per cent., Benjamin and Asher twenty-nine per cent., and Manasseh about sixty-three per cent.; while Reuben decreased six per cent., Gad twelve per cent., Naphtali fifteen per cent., and Simeon almost sixty-three per cent. Some interpreters have connected the large decrease in the latter tribe with the judgment following upon the service of Baal Peor; the fact that Zimri, a prince of the tribe of Simeon, had been such a notable offender (Numbers 25:6-14) leading to the inference that the tribe itself had been largely implicated in the sin.

It has already been noted, that the Levites were taken for the ministry of the sanctuary in place of the firstborn of Israel. (Numbers 3:11, 12) The number of the latter amounted to 22,273. (Numbers 3:43) But this statement is not intended to imply that, among all the Jewish males, amounting to upwards of a million of all ages — from the grandfather to the infant lately born — there were only 22,273 "firstborns." The latter figure evidently indicates only the number of the firstborn since the departure from Egypt. With reference to those born previously to the Exodus we are expressly told: (Numbers 3:13; 8:17) "all the firstborn are Mine; on the day that I smote all the firstborn of Egypt I hallowed unto Me all the firstborn in Israel."

Hence the fresh hallowing of the firstborn of Israel, and their subsequent numbering with a view to the substitution of the Levites for them, must have dated from after the Paschal night. Thus the 22,273 firstborn sons, for whom the Levites were substituted, represent those born after the departure from Egypt. If this number seems proportionally large, it should be remembered that the oppressive measures of Pharaoh would tend to diminish the number of marriages during the latter part of Israel's stay in Egypt, while the prospect of near freedom would, in a corresponding manner, immensely increase them. Besides, it is a well-known fact that even now the proportion of boys to girls is very much greater among Jews than among Gentiles. Viewed in this light, the account of Scripture on this subject presents no difficulties to the careful reader.

As already explained, the Levites were not numbered with the other tribes, but separately, (Numbers 3:15) and appointed ministers to Aaron the priest "for the service of the Tabernacle," in room of the firstborn of Israel (3:5-13). Not being regarded as part of the host, they were counted "from a month old and upward," the number of their males amounting to 22,000, which at the second census (after the thirty-eight years' wanderings) had increased to 23,000. (Numbers 3:39; 26:62) This has been computed to imply about 13,000 men, from twenty years and upwards — a number less than half that of the smallest of the other tribes (Benjamin, 35,400).

With this computation agrees the statement (Numbers 4:48) that the number of Levites "from thirty years old and upwards, even unto fifty years old, every one that came to do the service of the ministry," amounted in all to 8,580.

The same proportion between Levi and the rest of the people seems to have continued in after times, as we gather from the results of the census taken by King David, (1 Chronicles 23:3) when Levi had only increased from 23,000 to 38,000, while the rest of the tribes had more than doubled. The Levites were arranged into families after their ancestors, Gershon, Kohath, and Merari, the three sons of Levi. (Numbers 3:14-43) The Gershonites (again subdivided into two families, and amounting to 7,500), under their leader Eliasaph — "My God that gathers" — had charge of "the Tabernacle," or rather of "the dwelling-place;" of "the tent," of "the covering thereof;" and of "the hanging (or curtain) for the door of the tent of meeting;" as also of "the hangings of the court" (in which the Tabernacle stood); of the curtain for its door; and of all the cordage necessary for these "hangings."

We have been particular in translating this passage, because it proves that the common view, which places the curtains "of fine twined linen, and blue, and purple, and scarlet," (Exodus 26:1) outside the boards that constituted the framework of the Tabernacle, is entirely erroneous. Evidently these hangings, and not the boards, constituted "the Tabernacle," or rather "the dwelling" — "the tent," outside the framework, consisting of the eleven curtains of goats' hair, (Exodus 26:7) and "the covering" of the whole being twofold — one "of rams' skins dyed red," and another "of badgers' skins." (Exodus 26:14)

Whilst the Gershonites had charge of "the dwelling," "the tent," and the hangings of the outer court, the care of the "boards of the dwelling," with all that belonged thereto, and of "the pillars of the court round about" — in short, of all the outer solid framework of the Tabernacle and of the court — devolved upon the Merarites, under their chief, Zuriel ("My Rock is God"). Finally, the most important charge — that of the contents and vessels of the sanctuary — was committed to the Kohathites, under their chief Elizaphan ("My God watcheth round about").

Viewed as a whole, the camp of Israel thus formed a threefold square — a symbolical design, further developed in the Temple of Solomon, still more fully in that of Ezekiel, and finally shown in all its completeness in "the city that lieth foursquare."

The innermost square — as yet elongated and therefore not perfect in its width (or comprehension), nor yet having the perfect form of a cube, except so far as the Most Holy Place itself was concerned (which was a cube) — was occupied by "the dwelling," covered by "the tent," and surrounded by its "court." Around this inner was another square, occupied by the ministers of the Tabernacle in the East, or at the entrance to the court, by Moses, Aaron, and his sons; in the South by the Kohathites, who had the most important Levitical charge; in the West by the Gershonites; and in the North by the Merarites. Finally, there was a third and outermost square, which formed the camp of Israel. The eastern or most important place here was occupied by Judah, bearing the standard of the division. With Judah were Issachar and Zebulon (the sons of Leah), the three tribes together a host of 186,400 men. The southern place was held by Reuben, with the standard of that division, camped probably nearest to Zebulon, or at the south-eastern corner. With Reuben were Simeon and Gad (the sons of Leah and of Zilpah, Leah's maid), forming altogether a host of 151,450 men. The western post was occupied by Ephraim, with the standard of his division, being probably camped nearest to Gad, or at the south-western corner. With Ephraim were Manasseh and Benjamin (in short, the three descendants of Rachel), forming altogether a host of 108,100 men. Lastly, the northern side was occupied by Dan, with his standard, camping probably nearest to Benjamin, or at the north-western corner. With Dan were Asher and Naphtali (the sons of Bilhah and Zilpah), forming altogether a host of 157,600 men. This was also the order of march, Judah with his division leading, after which came Reuben, with his division, then the sanctuary with the Levites in the order of their camping, the rear consisting of the divisions of Ephraim and of Daniel. The sacred text does not specially describe the banners carried by the four leading tribes. According to Jewish tradition they bore as emblems "the likeness of the four living creatures," seen by Ezekiel in his vision of the Chariot, (Ezekiel 1:10) the color of the standard being the same as that of the precious stones on the high-priest's breastplate, on which the names of the standard-bearing tribes were graven. (Exodus 28:15-21) In that case Judah would have had on its standard a lion on a blood-red ground (the sardian stone or sard); Reuben the head of a man on a ground of dark red color (the ruby or carbuncle); Ephraim the head of a bullock on a ground of hyacinth (the ligury, according to some, Ligurian amber); and Dan an eagle on a ground of bright yellow, like gold (the ancient chrysolith, perhaps our topaz). This, supposing the names to have been graven in the order in which the tribes camped. But Josephus and some of the Rabbis range the names on the breastplate in the same order as on the ephod of the high-priest, (Exodus 28:10) that is, "according to their birth." In that case Reuben would have been on the sardian stone or sard, Judah on the ruby or carbuncle, Dan on a sapphire, or perhaps lapis-lazuli (blue), and Ephraim on an onyx, or else a beryl, the color of the banners, of course, in each case corresponding. Altogether the camp is supposed to have occupied about three square miles.

The direction either for marching or for resting was, as explained in a former chapter, given by the Cloud in which the Divine Presence was. But for actual signal to move, two silver trumpets were to be used by the sons of Aaron. A prolonged alarm indicated the commencement of the march. At the first alarm the eastern, at the second the southern part of the camp was to move forward, then came the Tabernacle and its custodians, the western, and finally the northern part of the camp, Naphtali closing the rear. On the other hand, when an assembly of the people was summoned, the signal was only one blast of the trumpets in short, sharp tones. In general, and for all times, the blast of these silver trumpets, whether in war, on festive, or on joyous occasions, had this spiritual meaning: "ye shall be remembered before Jehovah your God." (Numbers 10:1-10) In other words, Israel was a host, and as such summoned by blast of trumpet. But Israel was a host of which Jehovah was Leader and King, and the trumpets that summoned this host were silver trumpets of the sanctuary, blown by the priests of Jehovah. Hence these their blasts brought Israel as the Lord's host in remembrance before their God and King.

CHAPTER 16: THE OFFERINGS OF THE PRINCES — THE SETTING APART OF THE LEVITES — SECOND OBSERVANCE OF THE PASSOVER
(NUMBERS 7-9)

THREE other occurrences are recorded, before the camp of Israel broke up from Mount Sinai, although they may not have taken place in the exact order in which, for special reasons, they are told in the sacred text. These events were: the offering of certain gifts on the part of "the princes" of Israel: (Numbers 7) the actual setting apart of the Levites to the service for which they had been already previously designated; (Numbers 7) and a second observance of The Passover." (Numbers 9:1-14) The offerings of the princes of Israel commenced immediately after the consecration of the tabernacle. (Leviticus 8:10-9:1; Numbers 7:1) But their record is inserted in Numbers 7, partly in order not to interrupt the consecutive series of Levitical ordinances, which naturally followed upon the narrative of the consecration of the tabernacle, (Leviticus 11-end of book) and partly because one of the offerings of the princes bore special reference to the wilderness-journey, which was then about to be immediately resumed. Probably these offerings may have been brought on some of the days on which part of the Levitical ordinances was also proclaimed. We know that the presentation of gifts by the princes occupied, altogether, the mornings of twelve, or rather of thirteen days.

On the first day (Numbers 7:1-9) they brought in common "six covered wagons and twelve oxen," for the transport of the Tabernacle during the journeyings of the children of Israel. Four of these wagons with eight oxen were given to the Merarites, who had charge of the heavy framework and of the pillars; the other two wagons and four oxen to the Gershonites, who had the custody of the hangings and curtains. As for the vessels of the sanctuary, they were to be carried by the Kohathites on their shoulders. Then, during the following twelve days "the princes" offered successively each the same gift, that so "there might be equality," anticipating in this also the New Testament principle. (2 Corinthians 8:14) Each offering consisted of a "silver charger," weighing about four and a half pounds, a "silver bowl," weighing about two and a quarter pounds, both of them full of fine flour mingled with oil for a meat-offering, and a "golden spoon," about a third of a pound in weight, "full of incense." These gifts were accompanied by burnt, sin, and peace-offerings, which no doubt were sacrificed each day, as the vessels were presented in the sanctuary. And as they brought their precious offerings, with humble confession of sin over their sacrifices, with thanksgiving and with prayer, the Lord graciously signified His acceptance by speaking unto Moses "from off the mercy-seat," "from between the cherubim." (Numbers 7:89)

The second event was the formal setting apart of the Levites, (Numbers 8:5, etc.) which was preceded by a significant direction to Aaron in reference to the lighting of the seven-branched candlestick in the sanctuary.

To make the meaning of this symbol more clear, it was added, "the seven lamps shall give light over against the candlestick" — that is, each of the seven lamps (the number being also significant) shall be so placed as to throw its light into the darkness over against it. Each separately — and yet each as part of the one candlestick in the Holy Place, and burning the same sacred oil, was to shed light into the darkness over against the candlestick. For the light on the candlestick was symbolical of the mission of Israel as the people of God, and the Levites were really only the representatives of all Israel, having been substituted instead of their firstborn. (Numbers 3:11-13) On this account, also, the Levites were not specially "hallowed," as the priests had been, but only "cleansed" for their ministry, and after that presented to the Lord.

The first part of this symbolical service consisted in sprinkling on them "water of sin" (rendered in our Authorized Version "water of purifying"), alike to confess the defilement of sin and to point to its removal. After that they were to shave off all their hair and to wash their clothes. The Levites were now "unsinned" (8:21), so far as their persons were concerned. Then followed their dedication to the work.

For this purpose the Levites were led "before the Tabernacle" (8:9), that is, probably into the outer court, bringing with them two young bullocks — the one for a burnt, the other for a sin-offering, and each with its meat-offering. The people, through their representatives — the princes — now laid their hands upon them, as it were to constitute them their substitutes and representatives. Then Aaron took them "before Jehovah" (ver. 10), that is, into the Holy Place, and "waved them for a wave-offering of the children of Israel" — probably by leading them to the altar and back again — after which, the Levites would lay their hands upon the sacrifices which were now offered by Aaron, who so "made an atonement for them" (ver. 21). The significance of all these symbols will be sufficiently apparent. "And after that, the Levites went in to do service in the Tabernacle of the congregation" (ver. 22).

The third event recorded was a second celebration of the Passover on the anniversary of Israel's deliverance from Egypt — "in his appointed season, according to all the rites of it, and according to all the ceremonies thereof." (Numbers 9:3) We specially mark how the Lord now again directed all — the injunction to "keep the Passover" being expressly repeated here, perhaps to obviate the possibility of such a misunderstanding as that the Passover was not to be observed from year to year. Again, when certain men, "defiled by a dead body," complained that they had thereby been excluded from the feast, Moses would not decide the matter himself, but brought their case before God. The direction given was, that, under such or similar circumstances, the Passover should be observed exactly a month later, it being at the same time added, to guard against any willful, not necessary, neglect, that whoever omitted the ordinance without such reason should "be cut off from among His people." (Numbers 9:13) For, as the significance of symbolical rites depended upon their entirety, so that if any part of them, however small, had been omitted, the whole would have been nullified, so, on the other hand, Israel's compliance with the prescribed rites required to be complete in every detail to secure the benefits promised to the obedience of faith. But not to receive these benefits was to leave an Israelite outside the covenant, or exposed to the Divine judgment. More than that, being caused by unbelief or disobedience, it involved the punishment due to open rebellion against God and His Word.

CHAPTER 17: DEPARTURE FROM SINAI — MARCH INTO THE WILDERNESS OF PARAN — AT TABERAH AND KIBROTH-HATTAAVAH

(NUMBERS 10:29-11)

AT length, on the twentieth day of the second month, the signal for departure from Sinai was given. The cloud which had rested upon the Tabernacle moved; the silver trumpets of the priests summoned "the camps" of Israel to their march, and as the Ark itself set forward, Moses, in joyous confidence of faith, spake those words of mingled prayer and praise which, as they marked the progress of Israel towards the Land of Promise, have ever been the signal in every forward movement of the Church:

Arise, O Jehovah, let Thine enemies be scattered:

Let them also that hate Thee flee before Thee.

The general destination of Israel was, in the first place, "the wilderness of Paran," a name known long before. (Genesis 14:6; 21:21) This tract may be described as occupying the whole northern part of the Sinaitic peninsula, between the so-called Arabah on the east, and the wilderness of Shur in the west, (Genesis 16:7; Exodus 15:22) which separates Philistia from Egypt.

Here Israel was, so to speak, hedged in by the descendants of Esau — on the one side by the Edomites, whose country lay east of the Arabah, and on the other by the Amalekites, while right before them were the Amorites. The whole district still bears the name Badiet et Tih, "the desert of the wanderings." Its southern portion seems, as it were, driven in wedgeways into the Sinaitic peninsula proper, from which it is separated by a belt of sand. Ascending from the so-called Tot, which had been the scene of the first year of Israel's pilgrimage and of the Sinaitic legislation, the Tih might be entered by one of several passes through the mountains which form its southern boundary. The Et Tih itself "is a limestone plateau of irregular surface." It may generally be described as "open plains of sand and gravel... broken by a few valleys," and is at present "nearly waterless, with the exception of a few springs, situated in the larger wadies," which, however, yield rather an admixture of sand and water than water... "The ground is for the most part hard and unyielding, and is covered in many places with a carpet of small flints, which are so worn and polished... as to resemble pieces of black glass." In spring, however, there is a scanty herbage even here, while in the larger wadies there is always sufficient for camels, and even "a few patches of ground available for cultivation." Such was "that great and terrible wilderness, wherein were fiery serpents, and scorpions, and drought, where there was no water," (Deuteronomy 8:15) through which Jehovah their God safely led Israel!

A still earlier retrospect on the part of Moses brings the events about to be described most vividly before us. Addressing Israel, he reminds them: (Deuteronomy 1:19) "when we departed from Horeb, we went through all that great and terrible wilderness, which ye saw by the way of the mountain of the Amorites, as Jehovah our God commanded us; and we came to Kadesh-barnea."

This "mountain of the Amorites" is the most interesting spot in the whole Et Tih, or "wilderness of the wanderings." Arrived there, it seemed as if Israel were just about to take possession of the Promised Land. Thence the spies went forth to view the land. But here also the sentence was spoken which doomed all that unbelieving, faint-hearted generation to fall in the wilderness, and thither Israel had to return at the end of their forty years wanderings to start, as it were, anew on their journey of possession. "The mountain of the Amorites" is a mountain plateau in the north-east of the Et Tih, about seventy miles long, and from forty to fifty broad, which extends northward to near Beersheba. It contains many spots known to us from patriarchal history, and also celebrated afterwards. According to the description of travelers, we are here, literally, in a land of ruins, many of them dating far back, perhaps from the time of the Exodus, if not earlier.

Even the old name of the Amorites is still everywhere preserved as 'Amir and 'Amori. It leaves a peculiar impression on the mind to find not only the old Scripture names of towns continued these thousands of years, but actually to hear the wells which Abraham and Isaac had dug still called by their ancient names! About half way towards Beersheba the whole character of the scenery changes. Instead of the wilderness we have now broad valleys, with many and increasing evidences of former habitation all around. Indeed, we are now in the Negeb, or "south country" (erroneously rendered "the south" in our Authorized Version), which extends from about Kadesh to Beersheba. If "certain primeval stone remains" found throughout the Sinaitic peninsula have been regarded by the latest travelers as marking the journeyings, or rather the more prolonged settlements of Israel in "the wilderness," there is one class of them which deserves special attention. These are the so-called "Hazeroth," or "fenced enclosures," consisting of "a low wall of stones in which thick bundles of thorny acacia are inserted, the tangled branches and long needle-like spikes forming a perfectly impenetrable hedge around the encampment" of tents and cattle which they sheltered. These "Hazeroth," so frequently referred to in Scripture, abound in this district.

Such then was the goal and such the line of march before Israel, when, on that day in early summer, the Ark and the host of the Lord moved forward from the foot of Sinai. At the reiterated request of Moses, Hobab, the brother-in-law of Moses, had consented to accompany Israel, and to act as their guide in the wilderness, in the faith of afterwards sharing "what goodness Jehovah" would do unto His people. (Numbers 10:32) This we learn from such passages as Judges 1:16; 1 Samuel 15:6; 27:10; 30:9. Although the pillar of cloud was the real guide of Israel in all their journeying, yet the local knowledge of Hobab would manifestly prove of the greatest use in indicating springs and places of pasturage. And so it always is. The moving of the cloud or its resting must be our sole guide; but under its direction the best means which human skill or knowledge can suggest should be earnestly sought and thankfully used.

For three days Israel now journeyed without finding "a resting-place." By that time they must have fairly entered upon the "great and terrible wilderness." The scorching heat of a May sun reflected by such a soil, the fatigues of such a march, with probably scarcity of water and want of pasturage for their flocks — all combined to depress those whose hearts were not strong in faith and filled with longing for the better country. Behind and around was the great wilderness, and, so far as could be seen, no "resting-place" before them! In truth, before inheriting the promises, Israel had now to pass through a trial of faith analogous to that which Abraham had undergone. Only as in his case each victory had been marked by increasing encouragements, in theirs each failure was attended by louder warnings, until at last the judgment came which deprived that unbelieving generation of their share in the enjoyment of the promise. Three days journey under such difficulties, and "the people were as they who complain of evil in the ears of Jehovah." (Numbers 11:1)

But as this really reflected upon His guidance, it displeased the Lord, and a fire, sent by Jehovah, "consumed in the ends of the camp." At the intercession of Moses "the fire was quenched." But the lesson which might have been learned, and the warning conveyed in the judgment which had begun in the uttermost parts of the camp, remained unnoticed. Even the name Taberah (burning), with which Moses had intended to perpetuate the memory of this event, was unheeded. Possibly, the quenching of the fire may have deadened their spiritual sensibility, as formerly the removal of the plagues had hardened the heart of Pharaoh and of his people. And so Taberah soon became Kibroth-hattaavah, and the fire of wrath that had burned in the uttermost parts raged fiercely within the camp itself.

The sin of Israel at Kibroth-hattaavah was due to lust, and manifested itself in contempt for God's provision and in a desire after that of Egypt.

The "mixed multitude" which had come up with Israel were the first to lust. From them it spread to Israel. The past misery of Egypt — even its cruel bondage — seemed for the moment quite forgotten, and only the lowest thoughts of the abundant provision which it had supplied for their carnal wants were present to their minds. This impatient question of disappointed lustfulness, "Who shall give us flesh to eat?" repeated even to weeping, can only be accounted for by such a state of feeling. But if it existed, it was natural that God's gracious provision of manna should also be despised. As if to mark their sin in this the more clearly, scripture here repeats its description of the manna, and of its miraculous provision. (Numbers 11:7-9) When Moses found "the weeping" not confined to any particular class, but general among the people (11:10), and that "the anger of Jehovah was kindled greatly," his heart sank within him. Yet, as has been well observed, he carried his complaint to the Lord in prayer, and therefore his was not the language of unbelief, only that of utter depression. Rightly understood, these words of his, "Have I conceived all this people? have I begotten them?" implied that not he but God was their father and their provider, (Exodus 4:22; Isaiah 63:16) and that therefore he must cast their care upon the Lord. But even so the trial of Moses had in this instance become a temptation, although God gave him "with the temptation a way of escape."

Two things would the Lord do in answer to the appeal of Moses. First, He would, in His tender mercy, support and encourage His servant, and then manifest His power and holiness. With this twofold purpose in view, Moses was directed to place seventy of the elders of Israel — probably in a semi-circle — around the entrance to the Tabernacle. These "elders" were henceforth to help Moses in bearing the burden of the people. He had wished help, and he was now to receive it, although he would soon experience that the help of man was vain, and God alone the true helper. And then, to show in sight of all men that He had appointed such help, yet only as a help to Moses, God" came down in a cloud," spake unto Moses, and then put of his spirit upon these "elders." In manifestation of this new gift "they prophesied," by which, however, we are to understand not the prediction of future events, but probably that "speaking in the spirit" which in the New Testament also is designated as "prophesying." (1 Corinthians 12; 14) Further, lest in the mind of the people this should be connected with any miraculous power inherent in Moses, the same spirit descended, and with the same effect, upon two (Eldad and Medad) who had been "written," that is, designated for the office, but who for some reason had been prevented from appearing at the door of the Tabernacle. The lesson, it was evident, was required, for even Joshua had misunderstood the matter. When he found that Eldad and Medad prophesied "in the camp," he deemed the authority of his master compromised, and wished to "forbid them," since these men had not received the gift through Moses. We are here reminded of the similar conduct of John, who would have forbidden one "casting out devils" in the name of Christ, because he followed not with the other disciples, and of the Lord's rebuke of such mistaken zeal, (Mark 9:38; Luke 9:49) — a mistake too often repeated, and a rebuke too much forgotten in the Christian Church at all times. Far different were the feelings of Moses. As a faithful servant, he emphatically disclaimed all honor for himself, and only expressed the fervent wish that the same spiritual gifts might be shared by all the Lord's people.

One thing was still required. God would manifest His power in providing for the wants of the people, and His holiness in taking vengeance on their lust. The lesson was specially needed, for even Moses had, when first told, questioned the full promise of providing for the whole people flesh sufficient to last for a month. (Numbers 11:18-23) And now the Lord again showed how easily He can bring about supernatural results by what we call natural means. As explained in a former chapter, in spring the quails migrate in immense numbers from the interior of Africa northwards. An east wind, blowing from the Arabian Gulf, now drove them, in vast quantities, just over the camp of Israel. Here they fell down exhausted by the flight, and lay, to the distance of a day's journey "on this side and on that," in some places two cubits high. It is the same lesson which we have so often learned in this history. The "wind" which brought the quails" went forth from the Lord," and the number brought was far beyond what is ordinarily witnessed, although such a flight and drooping of birds are by no means uncommon. And so God can, by means unthought of, send sudden deliverances unexpectedly, even to one like Moses. But as for Israel, they had now their wishes more than gratified. The supply of flesh thus provided sufficed not only for the present, but was such that the greater part of it was preserved for after use (11:32). Thus had God shown the folly of those who murmured against His provision or questioned His ability. It still remained to punish the presumption and sin of their conduct. "While the flesh was yet between their teeth, ere it was chewed, the wrath of Jehovah was kindled against the people, and Jehovah smote the people with a very great plague. And he called the name of that place Kibroth-hattaavah (the graves of lust): because there they buried the people that lusted." But how deeply the impression of this judgment sunk into the hearts of the godly in Israel appears from such passages as Psalm 78:26-31, while its permanent lesson to all times is summed up in these words:

"He gave them their request; but sent leanness into their soul." (Psalm 106:15)

CHAPTER 18: MURMURING OF MIRIAM AND AARON — THE SPIES SENT TO CANAAN — THEIR "EVIL REPORT" — REBELLION OF THE PEOPLE, AND JUDGMENT PRONOUNCED UPON THEM — THE DEFEAT OF ISRAEL — "UNTO HORMAH"

(NUMBERS 12-14)

HITHERTO the spirit of rebellion on the part of the people had been directed against Jehovah Himself. If Moses had lately complained of continual trials in connection with those to whom he stood in no way closely related, (Numbers 11:12) he was now to experience the full bitterness of this,

"A man's foes shall be they of his own household." (Matthew 10:36)

From Kibroth-hattaavah Israel had journeyed to Hazeroth, a station the more difficult to identify from the commonness of such "fenced enclosures" in that neighborhood. Here Miriam and — apparently at her instigation, — Aaron also "spake against Moses," as it is added, "because of the Ethiopian woman whom he had married," referring most likely to a second marriage which Moses had contracted after the death of Zipporah.

For the first time we here encounter that pride of Israel after the flesh and contempt for all other nations, which has appeared through-out their after history, and in proportion as they have misunderstood the spiritual meaning of their calling. Thus, as Calvin remarks, Miriam and Aaron now actually boasted in that prophetic gift, which should have only wrought in them a sense of deep humility. (Numbers 12:2) But Moses was not like any ordinary prophet, although in his extreme meekness he would not vindicate his own position (12:3). He "was faithful," or approved, "to Him that appointed him," (Hebrews 3:2, 5) not merely in any one special matter, but "in all the house" of Jehovah, that is, in all pertaining to the kingdom of God. And the Lord now vindicated His servant both by public declaration, and by punishing Miriam with leprosy. At the entreaty of Aaron, who owned his sister's and his own guilt, and at the intercession of Moses, this punishment was indeed removed. But the isolation of Miriam from the camp of Israel would teach all, how one who had boasted in privileges greater than those of others might be deprived even of the ordinary fellowship of Israel's camp.

The seven days of Miriam's separation were past, and Israel again resumed the march towards the Land of Promise. They had almost reached its boundary, when the event happened which not only formed the turning-point in the history of that generation, but which, more than any other, was typical of the future of Israel. For as that generation in their unbelief refused to enter the Land of Promise when its possession lay open before them, and as they rebelled against God and cast off the authority of Moses, so did their children reject the fulfillment of the promises in Christ Jesus, disown Him whom God had exalted a Prince and a Savior, and cry out: "Away with Him! away with Him!" And as the carcasses of those who had rebelled fell in the wilderness, so has similar spiritual judgment followed upon the terrible cry: "His blood be upon us and upon our children!" But, blessed be God, as mercy was ultimately in store for the descendants of that rebellious generation, so also, in God's own time, will Israel turn again unto the Lord and enjoy the promises made unto the fathers.

The scene of this ever-memorable event was "the wilderness of Paran," or, to define the locality more exactly, Kadesh-barnea. (Numbers 13:26; Deuteronomy 1:19) The spot has first been identified by Dr. Rowlands and Canon Williams, and since so fully described by Professor Palmer, that we can follow the progress of events, step by step. Kadesh is the modern 'Ain Gadis, or spring of Kadesh, and lies in that north-eastern plateau of the wilderness of Paran, which formed the stronghold of the Amorites. A little north of it begins the Negeb or "south country" of Palestine, which, as already explained, reaches to about Beersheba, and where the Promised Land really begins.

The district is suited for pasturage, and contains abundant traces of former habitation, and, in the north, also evidence of the former cultivation of vines. Here, and not, as is usually supposed, in the neighborhood of Hebron, we must look for that valley of Eshcol, whence the spies afterwards on their return brought the clusters of grapes, as specimens of the productiveness of the country, Kadesh itself is the plain at the foot of the cliff whence the 'Ain Gadis springs.

To the east is a ridge of mountains, to the west stretches a wide plain, where the Canaanites had gathered to await the advance of Israel. Hence, if the spies were to "get up this Negeb" ("south country "), they had "to go up by the mountain," (Numbers 13:17, 22) in order to avoid the host of Canaan. In so doing they made a detour, passing south of 'Ain Gadis, through what is called in Scripture the wilderness of Zin (13:21), from which they ascended into the mountains. Thus much seems necessary to understand the localization of the narrative.

But to return. From Deuteronomy 1:22, we gather that the proposal of sending spies "to search out the land" had originally come from the people. By permission of the Lord, Moses had agreed to it, (Numbers 13:1) adding, however, a warning to "be of good courage" (Numbers 13:20), lest this should be associated with fear of the people of the land. Twelve persons, seemingly the most suitable for the work, — spiritually and otherwise — were chosen from "the rulers "of the tribes.

Of these we only know Caleb and Joshua, the "minister of Moses," whose name Moses had formerly changed from Hoshea, which means "help," to Joshua, or "Jehovah is help." Detailed and accurate directions having been given them, the spies left the camp of Israel "at the time of the first-ripe grapes," that is, about the end of July. Thus far they were successful. Eluding the Canaanites, they entered Palestine, and searched the land to its northernmost boundary., "unto Rehob, as men come to Hamath," that is, as far as the plain of Coele-Syria. On their way back, coming from the north, they would of course not be suspected. Accordingly they now descended by Hebron, and explored the route which led into the Negeb by the western edge of the mountains. "In one of these extensive valleys - perhaps in Wady Hanein, where miles of grape-mounds even now meet the eye — they cut the gigantic cluster of grapes, and gathered the pomegranates and figs, to show how goodly was the land which the Lord had promised for their inheritance."

After forty days absence the spies returned to camp. The report and the evidence of the fruitfulness of the land which they brought, fully confirmed the original promise of God to Israel. (Exodus 3:8) But they added: (Numbers 13:28) "Only that the people is strong which occupieth the land, and the cities fortified, very great, and also descendants of the Anak have we seen there," whom, in their fear, they seem to have identified (ver. 33) with the Nephilim of the antediluvian world.

This account produced immediate terror, which Caleb sought in vain to allay. His opposition only elicited stronger language on the part of the other "spies," culminating in their assertion, that, even if Israel were to possess the land, it was one "that eateth up its inhabitants," that is, a country surrounded and peopled by fierce races in a state of constant warfare for its possession. Thus the most trustworthy and the bravest from among their tribes, with only the exception of Caleb and of Joshua (whose testimony might be set aside on the ground of his intimate relationship to Moses), now declared their inability either to conquer or to hold the land, for the sake of which they had left the comforts of Egypt and endured the hardships and dangers of "the great and terrible wilderness. A night of complete demoralization followed — the result being open revolt against Moses and Aaron, direct rebellion against Jehovah, and a proposal to elect a fresh leader and return to Egypt! In vain Moses and Aaron "fell on their faces" before God in sight of all the congregation; in vain Joshua and Caleb "rent their clothes" in token of mourning, and besought the people to remember that the Presence of Jehovah with them implied certain success. The excited people only "spake" of stoning them, when of a sudden "the glory of Jehovah visibly appeared in the tent of meeting to all the children of Israel." (Numbers 14:10) Almost had the Lord destroyed the whole people on the spot, when Moses again interposed — a type of the great Leader and Mediator of His people. With pleadings more urgent than ever before, he wrestled with God — his language in its intensity consisting of short, abrupt sentences, piled, as it were, petition on petition, but all founded on the glory of God, on His past dealings, and especially on the greatness of His mercy, repeating in reference to this the very words in which the Lord had formerly condescended to reveal His inmost Being, when proclaiming His "Name" before Moses. (Exodus 33:17, 19) Such plea could not remain unheeded; it was typical of the great plea and the great Pleader. But as, when long afterwards Israel called down upon themselves and their children the blood of Jesus, long and sore judgments were to befall the stiffnecked and rebellious, even although ultimately all Israel should be saved, so was it at Kadesh. According to the number of days that the spies had searched the land, were to be the years of their wanderings in the wilderness, and of all that generation which had come out from Egypt, at the age of twenty and upwards, not one was to enter the Land of Promise, but their carcasses were to fall in that wilderness, with the exception of Caleb and Joshua. But as for the other ten searchers of the land, quick destruction overtook them, and they "died by the plague before Jehovah."

This commencement of Divine judgment, coupled as it was with abundant evidence of its reality — especially in the immediate destruction of the ten spies, while Caleb and Joshua were preserved alive — produced an effect so strange and unlooked for, that we could scarcely understand it, but for kindred experience in all ages of the Church. It was now quite plain to Israel what they might, and certainly would have obtained, had they only gone forward. Yesterday that Land of Promise — in all its beauty and with all its riches — so close at hand as to be almost within sight of those mountain ranges, was literally theirs. Today it was lost to them. Not one of their number was even to see it. More than that, their carcasses were to fall in that wilderness! All this simply because they would not go forward yesterday! Let them do so today. If they had then done wrong, let them do the opposite today, and they would do right. Moreover, it was to Israel that God had pledged His word, and as Israel, He would have brought them into the land. They were Israel still let them now go forward and claim Israel's portion. But it was not so; and never is so in kindred circumstances. The wrong of our rebellion and unbelief is not turned into right by attempting the exact opposite. His still the same spirit, which prompted the one, that influences the other. The obedience which is not of simple faith is of self-confidence, and only another kind of unbelief and self-righteousness. It is not the doing of this or that, nor the circumstance of outwardly belonging to Israel, which secures victory over the enemy, safety, or possession of the land. It is that "Jehovah is among us." (Numbers 14:42) And the victory is ever that of faith. Not a dead promise to the descendants of Jacob after the flesh, but the presence of the living God among His believing Israel secured to them the benefits of the covenant. And Israel's determination to go up on the morrow, and so to retrieve the past, argued as great spiritual ignorance and unfitness, and involved as much rebellion and sin, as their former faint-heartedness and rebellion at the report of the spies.

In vain Moses urged these considerations on the people. The people "presumed to go up to the head of the mountain," although Moses and the Ark of the Covenant of Jehovah remained behind in the camp.

From Kadesh it is only about twenty miles to Hormah, to which place their enemies afterwards "smote and discomfited them." As we know from the descriptions of travelers, increasing fertility, cultivation, and civilization must have met the host as it advanced into the Negeb. The Israelites were in fact nearing what they must have felt home-ground — sacred to them by association with Abraham and Isaac. For a little to the north of Hormah are the wells of Rehoboth, Sitnah, and Beersheba, which Abraham and Isaac had dug, the memory of which is to this day preserved in the modern names of Ruheibeh, Shutneh, and Bir Seba. Abraham himself had "journeyed toward the Negeb, and dwelled between Kadesh and Shur," (Genesis 20:1) and Isaac had followed closely in his footsteps. (Genesis 26:17-end) And of the next occupants of the land, the Amorites, we find almost constantly recurring mementoes, and nowhere more distinctly than in the immediate neighborhood of Hormah. From Judges 1:17, we know that that city, or probably rather the fort commanding it, had originally borne the name of Zephath, which simply means "watch-tower." The name Hormah, or "banning," was probably given it on a later occasion, when, after the attack of the king of Arad, Israel had "vowed the vow" utterly to destroy the cities of the Canaanites (Numbers 21:1-3). But, as Dr. Rowlands and Canon Williams have shown, the name Zephath has been preserved in the ruins of Sebaita, while Professor Palmer has discovered, close by, the ancient "watch-tower," which was a strong fort on the top of a hill commanding Sebaita. It is intensely interesting, amid the ruins of later fortifications, to come upon these primeval remains, which mark not only the ancient site of Zephath, but may represent the very fort behind which the Amorites and Canaanites defended themselves against Israel, and whence they issued to this war. As if to make it impossible to mistake this "mountain of the Amorites," the valley north of Sebaita bears to this day the name Dheigat el 'Amerin, or Ravine of the Amorites, and the chain of mountains to the south-west of the fort that of Ras Amir, "head" or top "of the Amorites."

Israel had presumed to go up into this mountain-top without the presence of Jehovah, without the Ark of the Covenant, and without Moses. Yesterday they had been taught the lesson that their seeming weakness would be real strength, if Jehovah were among them. To-day they had in bitter experience to find out this other and equally painful truth — that their seeming strength was real weakness. Smitten and discomfited by their enemies, they fled "even unto Hormah."

CHAPTER 19: THE THIRTY-EIGHT YEARS IN THE WILDERNESS — THE SABBATH-BREAKER — THE GAINSAYING OF KORAH AND OF HIS ASSOCIATES — MURMURING OF THE PEOPLE; THE PLAGUE, & HOW IT WAS STAYED — AAKON'S ROD BUDDING, BLOSSOMING, AND BEARING FRUIT

(NUMBERS: 33:19-37; 16, 17; DEUTERONOMY 1:46-11:15)

MORE than thirty-seven years of "wanderings" were now to be passed in "the wilderness of Paran," until a new generation had risen to enter on possession of the Land of Promise. Of that long period scarcely more than one single record is left us in Scripture. As a German writer observes, The host of Israel, being doomed to judgment, ceased to be the subject of sacred history, while the rising generation, in whom the life and hope of Israel vow centered, had, as yet, no history of its own. And so we mark all this period rather by the death of the old than by the life of the new, and the wanderings of Israel by the graves which they left behind, as their carcasses fell in the wilderness.

Still, we may profitably gather together the various notices scattered in Scripture. First, then, we learn that Israel "abode in Kadesh many days," (Deuteronomy 1:46) and that thence their direction was "towards the Red Sea." (Deuteronomy 2:1) Their farthest halting-place from Kadesh seems to have been Ezion-gaber, which, as we know, lay on the so-called Elanitic Gulf of the Red Sea. Thence they returned, at the end of the forty years wanderings, once more to "the wilderness of Zin, which is Kadesh." (Numbers 33:36) The "stations" on their wanderings from Kadesh to Ezion-geber are marked in Numbers 33:18-35. There are just seventeen of them, after leaving Rithmah — a name derived from retem, a broom-bush, and which may therefore signify the valley of the broom-bushes. If we rightly understand it, this was the original place of the encampment of Israel near Kadesh. In point of fact, there is a plain close to 'Ain Gadis or Kadesh which to this day bears the name of Abu Retemet. As for Kadesh itself — or the Holy Place, the place of "sanctifying" — which originally bore the name En-Mishpat, "well of judgment," (Genesis 14:7) we imagine that it derived its peculiar name from the events that there took place, the additional designation of Barnea — Kadesh Barnea — either marking a former name of the place, or more probably meaning "the land of moving to and fro."

We presume that the encampment in "the broom-valley" was in all probability determined by the existence and promise of vegetation there, which, no doubt, was due to the presence of watercourses. Indeed, an examination of the names of the seventeen stations occupied by Israel during their wanderings shows, that all the encampments were similarly selected in the neighborhood of water and vegetation. Thus we have Rimmon-parez, "the pomegranate breach" — perhaps the place where Korah's rebellion brought such terrible punishment; Libnah, "whiteness," probably from the white poplar trees growing there; Rissah, "dew;" Mount Shapher, "the mount of beauty," or "of goodliness;" Mithcah, "sweetness," in reference to the water; Hashmonah, "fatness," "fruitfulness," where to this day there is a pool full of sweet living water, with abundant vegetation around; Bene-jaakan, or, as in Deuteronomy 10:6, Beeroth Bene-jaakan, "the wells of the children of Jaakan," probably the wells which the Jaakanites had dug on their expulsion by the

Edomites from their original homes; (Genesis 36:27; 1 Chronicles 1:42) Jotbathah, "goodness;" and Ebronah, probably "fords." The other names are either derived from peculiarities of scenery, or else from special events, as Kehelathah, "assembling;" Makheloth, "assemblies;" Haradah, "place of terror," etc.

The first impression which we derive, alike from the fewness of these stations, and from their situation, is, that the encampments were successively occupied for lengthened periods. More than that, we infer from the peculiar wording of some expressions in the original, that, during these thirty-eight years, the people were scattered up and down, the Tabernacle with the Levites forming, as it were, a kind of central camp and rallying-place. It is also quite certain that, at that period, the district in which the wanderings of Israel lay was capable of supporting such a nomadic population with their flocks and herds. Indeed, the presence of water, if turned to account, would always transform any part of that wilderness into a fruitful garden. In this respect the knowledge of irrigation, which the Israelites had acquired in Egypt, must have been of special use. Lastly, the people were not quite isolated. Not only were they near what we might call the direct highway between the East and Egypt, but they were in contact with other tribes, such as the Bene-jaakan. Deuteronomy 2:26-29 seems to imply that at times it was possible to purchase provisions and water, while Deuteronomy 2:7 shows that Israel had not only "lacked nothing" during "these forty years," but that they had greatly increased in substance and wealth. Such passages as Deuteronomy 8:14, etc.; 29:5; and Nehemiah 9:21 prove in what remarkable manner God had cared for all the wants of His people during that period; and there can be no doubt that in the prophetic imagery of the future, especially by Isaiah, there is frequent retrospect to God's gracious dealings with Israel in the wilderness.

Brief as is the record of these thirty-eight years, it contains a notice of two events, both in rebellion against the Lord. The first gives an account of a man who had openly violated the Divine law by gathering "sticks upon the Sabbath day." (Numbers 15:32-36) Although the punishment of death had been awarded to such a "presumptuous sin," (Exodus 31:14; 35:2) the offender was, in the first place, "put in ward," partly to own the Lord by specially asking His direction, since only the punishment itself but not its mode had been previously indicated, and partly perhaps to impress all Israel with the solemnity of the matter. Due observance of the Lord's day was, indeed, from every point of view, a question of deepest importance to Israel, and the offender was, by Divine direction, "brought without the camp, and stoned with stones, and he died." We are not told at what particular period of the wanderings of Israel this event had occurred. It is apparently inserted as an instance and illustration, immediately after the warning against" presumptuous sins" (literally, "sins with a hand uplifted," viz., against Jehovah). These sins in open contempt of God's word involved the punishment of being "cut off" from the people of the Lord.

Nor have we any precise date by which to fix the other and far more serious instance of rebellion on the part of Korah and of his associates, (Numbers 16) in which afterwards the people, as a whole, were implicated. (Numbers 16:41-50) There is, however, reason to suppose that it occurred at an early period of "the wanderings" — perhaps, as already suggested, at Rimmon-parez. The leaders of this rebellion were Korah, a Levite -descendant of Izhar, the brother of Amram, (Exodus 6:18) and therefore a near relative of Aaron — and three Reubenites, Dathan, Abiram, and On. But as the latter is not further mentioned, we may suppose that he early withdrew from the conspiracy. These men gained over to their side no fewer than two hundred and fifty princes from among the other tribes, all of them members of the national representative council, and "men of renown," or, as we should express ilk well-known leading men. Thus the movement assumed very large proportions, and evidenced wide-spread disaffection and dissatisfaction.

The motives of this conspiracy seem plain enough. They were simply jealous and disappointed ambition, though the rebels assumed the language of a higher spirituality. As descended from a brother of Aaron, Korah disliked, and perhaps coveted, what seemed to him the supremacy of Aaron, for which he could see no valid reason. He had also a special grievance of his own. True, he was one of that family of the Kohathites to whom the chief Levitical charge in the sanctuary had been committed; but then the Kohathites numbered four families, (Numbers 3:27) and the leadership of the whole was entrusted not to any of the older branches, but to the youngest, the Uzzielites (Numbers 3:30). Was there not manifest wrong and injustice in this, probably affecting Korah personally? It speaks well for the Levites as a whole, that, notwithstanding all this, Korah was unable to inveigle any of them in his conspiracy. But close to the tents of the Kohathites and of Korah was the encampment of the tribe of Reuben, who held command of the division on the south side of the camp. Possibly — and indeed the narrative of their punishment seems to imply this — the tent of Korah and those of the Reubenitic princes, Dathan, Abiram, and On, were contiguous. And Reuben also had a grievance; for was not Reuben Jacob's first-born, who should therefore have held the leadership among the tribes? It was not difficult to kindle the flame of jealousy in an Eastern breast. What claim or right had Moses, or rather the tribe of Levi whom he represented, to supremacy in Israel? Assuredly this was a grievous wrong and an intolerable usurpation, primarily as it affected Reuben, and secondarily all the other tribes. This explains the ready participation of so many of the princes in the conspiracy, the expostulation of Moses with Korah (16:8-11), and his indignant appeal to God against the implied charges of the Reubenites (ver. 15). Indeed, the conspirators expressly stated these views as follows (ver. 3), "Sufficient for you!" — that is, You, Moses and Aaron, have long enough held the priesthood and the government; "for the whole congregation, all are holy, and in the midst of them Jehovah. And why exalt ye yourselves over the convocation of Jehovah?" It will be observed that the pretense which they put forward to cover their selfish, ambitious motives was that of a higher spirituality, which recognized none other than the spiritual priesthood of all Israel. But, as we shall presently show, their claim to it was not founded on the typical mediatorship of the high-priest, but on their standing as Israel after the flesh.

The whole of this history is so sad, the judgment which followed it so terrible — finding no other parallel than that which in the New Testament Church overtook Ananias and Sapphira — and the rebellion itself is so frequently referred to in scripture, that it requires more special consideration. The rebellion of Korah, as it is generally called, from its prime mover, was, of course, an act of direct opposition to the appointment of God. But this was not all. The principle expressed in their gainsaying (ver. 3) ran directly counter to the whole design of the old covenant, and would, if carried out, have entirely subverted its typical character. It was, indeed, quite true that all Israel were holy and priests, yet not in virtue of their birth or national standing, but through the typical priesthood of Aaron, who "brought them nigh" and was their intermediary with God. Again, this priesthood of Aaron, as indeed all similar selections — such as those of the place where, and the seasons when God would be worshipped, of the composition of the incense, or of the sacrifices -although there may have been secondary and subordinate reasons for them, depended in the first place and mainly upon God's appointment.

"Him whom the Lord hath chosen will He cause to come near unto Him" (6:5); "whom the Lord doth choose, he shall be holy" (ver. 7).

Every other service, fire, or place than that which God had chosen, would, however well and earnestly intended, be "strange" service, "strange" fire, and a "strange" place. This was essential for the typical bearing of all these arrangements. It was God's appointment, and not the natural fitness of a person or thing which here came into consideration. If otherwise, they would have been natural sequences, not types — constituting a rational rather than a Divine service. It was of the nature of a type that God should appoint the earthly emblem with which He would connect the spiritual reality. The moment Israel deviated in any detail, however small, they not only rebelled against God's appointment, but destroyed the meaning of the whole by substituting the human and natural for the Divine. The types were, so to speak, mirrors of God's own fitting, which exhibited, as already present, future spiritual realities with all their blessings. In Christ all such types have ceased, because the reality to which they pointed has come.

This digression seemed necessary, alike for the proper understanding of the history of Korah and for that of the typical arrangements of the Old Testament. But to return. On the morning following the outbreak of the rebellion, Korah and his two hundred and fifty associates presented themselves, as Moses had proposed, at the door of the Tabernacle. Here "they took every man his censer, and put fire in them, and laid incense thereon." Indeed, Korah had gained such influence, that he was now able to gather there "all the congregation" as against Moses and Aaron. Almost had the wrath of God, whose glory visibly appeared before all, consumed "this congregation" in a moment, when the intercession of Moses and Aaron once more prevailed. In these words: "O God, the God of the spirits of all flesh, shall one man sin, and wilt Thou be wroth with all the congregation?" (as Calvin remarks) Moses made his appeal "to the general grace of creation," praying that, "as God was the Creator and Maker of the world, He would not destroy man whom He had created, but rather have pity on the work of His hands." And so there is a plea for mercy, and an unspeakable privilege even in the fact of being the creatures of such a God!

Leaving the rebels with their censers at the door of the Tabernacle -perhaps panic-struck — Moses next repaired to the tents of Dathan and Abiram, accompanied by the elders, and followed by the congregation. On the previous day the two Reubenites had refused to meet Moses, and sent him a taunting reply, suggesting that he only intended to blind the people.

And now when Dathan and Abiram, with their wives and children, came out and stood at the door of their tents, as it were, to challenge what Moses could do, the people were first solemnly warned away from them. Then a judgment, new and unheard of, was announced, and immediately executed. The earth opened her mouth and swallowed up these rebels and their families, with all that appertained to them, that is, with such as had taken part in their crime. As for Korah, the same fate seems to have overtaken him. But it is an emphatic testimony alike to the truth of God's declaration, that He punisheth not men for the sins of their fathers, (Jeremiah 31:30; Ezekiel 18:19, 20) and to the piety of the Levites, that the sons of Korah did not share in the rebellion of their father, and consequently died not with him. (Numbers 26:11) More than this, not only were Samuel and afterwards Heman descendants of Korah, (1 Samuel 1:1; 1 Chronicles 6:33-38) but among them were some of those "sweet singers of Israel," whose hymns, Divinely inspired, were intended for the Church at all times. And all the Psalms "of the sons of Korah" have this common characteristic, which sounds like an echo of the lesson learned from the solemn judgment upon their house, that their burden is praise of the King Who is enthroned at Jerusalem, and longing after the services of God's sanctuary. But as for "the two hundred and fifty men that offered incense," "there came out a fire from the Lord and consumed" them, as, on a former occasion, it had destroyed Nadab and Abihu. (Leviticus 10:2) Their censers, which had been "hallowed," by being presented before the Lord, (Numbers 16:37) were converted into plates for covering the altar of burnt offering, that so they might be a continual "memorial unto the children of Israel" of the event and its teaching.

This signal judgment of God upon the rebels had indeed struck the people who witnessed it with sudden awe, but it led not to that repentance (Psalm 4:4) which results from a change of heart. The impression passed away, and "on the morrow" nothing remained but the thought that so many princes of tribes, who had sought to vindicate tribal independence, had been cut off for the sake of Moses! It was in their cause, the people would argue, that these men had died; and the mourning in the tents of the princes, the desolateness which marked what had but yesterday been the habitations of Korah, Dathan, and Abiram, would only give poignancy to the feeling that with this event a yoke of bondage had been for ever riveted upon the nation. For they recognized not the purpose and meaning of God; this would have implied spiritual discernment; only that, if judgment had proceeded from Jehovah, it had come, if not at the instigation of, yet in order to vindicate Moses and Aaron. In their ingratitude they even forgot that, but for the intercession of these two, the whole congregation would have perished in the gainsaying of Korah. So truly did that generation prove the justice of the Divine sentence that none of their number should enter into the land of Canaan, and so entirely unfit did their conduct (as of old that of Esau) show them for inheriting the promises!

But as for Moses and Aaron, when the congregation was once more gathered against them with this cruel and unjust charge on their lips, "Ye have killed the people of Jehovah," they almost instinctively "faced towards the tent of meeting," as the place whence their help came and to which their appeal was now made. Nor did they look in vain.

Denser and more closely than before did the cloud cover the tabernacle, and from out of it burst visibly the luminous glory of Jehovah. And as Moses and Aaron entered the court of the tabernacle, "Jehovah spake unto Moses, saying, Get you up from among this congregation, and I will consume them as in a moment. And they fell upon their faces." But what was Moses to plead? He knew that "already" was "wrath gone forth from Jehovah," and "the plague" had "begun." What could he now say? In the rebellion at Mount Horeb, (Exodus 32:31) again at Kadesh, (Numbers 14:13, etc.) and but the day before at the gainsaying of Korah, he had exhausted every argument. No similar plea, nor indeed any plea, remained. Then it was, in the hour of deepest need, when every argument that even faith could suggest had been taken away, and Israel was, so to speak, lost, that the all-sufficiency of the Divine provision in its vicarious and mediatorial character appeared. Although as yet only typical, it proved all sufficient.

The incense kindled on the coals taken from the altar of burnt-offering, where the sacrifices had been brought, typified the accepted mediatorial intercession of our great High Priest. And now, when there was absolutely no plea upon earth, this typical pleading of His perfect righteousness and intercession prevailed. Never before or after was the Gospel so preached under the Old Testament as when Aaron, at Moses' direction, took the censer, and, having filled it from the altar, "ran into the midst of the congregation," "and put on incense, and made an atonement for the people" (16:47).

And as he stood with that censer "between the dead and the living," "the plague," which had already swept away not less than 14,700 men, "was stayed." Thus if Korah's

215

assumption of the priestly functions had caused, the exercise of the typical priesthood now removed, the plague.

But the truth which God now taught the people was not to be exhibited only in judgment. After the storm and the earthquake came the "still, small voice," and the typical import of the Aaronic priesthood was presented under a beautiful symbol. By direction of God, "a rod" for each of the twelve tribes, bearing the respective names of their princes, was laid up in the Most Holy Place, before the Ark of the Covenant.

And on the morrow, when Moses entered the sanctuary, "behold the rod of Aaron for the house of Levi had budded, and brought forth buds, and bloomed blossoms, and yielded almonds." The symbolical teaching of this was plain. Each of these "rods" was a ruler's staff, the emblem of a tribe and its government. This was the natural position of all these princes of Israel. But theirs as well as Aaron's were rods cut off from the parent-stem, and therefore incapable of putting forth verdure, bearing blossom, or yielding fruit in the sanctuary of God. By nature, then, there was absolutely no difference between Aaron and the other princes; all were equally incapable of the new life of fruitfulness. What distinguished Aaron's rod was the selection of God and the miraculous gift bestowed upon it. And then, typically in the old, but really in the new dispensation, that rod burst at the same time into branches, into blossom, and even into fruit — all these three combined, and all appearing at the same time. And so these princes "took every man his rod," but Aaron's rod was again brought before the Ark of the Covenant, and kept there "for a token." Nor was even the choice of the almond, which blossoms first of trees, without its deep meaning. For the almond, which bursts earliest into flower and fruit, is called in Hebrew "the waker" (shaked, comp. Jeremiah 1:11,12). Thus, as the "early waker," the Aaronic priesthood, with its buds, blossoms, and fruit, was typical of the better priesthood, when the Sun of Righteousness would rise "with healing in His wings."

CHAPTER 20: THE SECOND GATHERING OF ISRAEL IN KADESH — THE SIN OF MOSES AND AARON — EMBASSY TO EDOM — DEATH OF AARON -RETREAT OF ISRAEL FROM THE BORDERS OF EDOM — ATTACK BY THE CANAANITISH KING OF ARAD
(NUMBERS 20; 21:1-3)

IT was indeed most fitting that, at the end of the thirty-seven years wanderings, Israel should once more gather at Kadesh. There they had been scattered, when the evil report which the spies had brought led to their unbelief and rebellion; and thence had the old generation carried, as it were, its sentence of death back into the wilderness, till during these long and weary years its full terms had been exhausted. And now a new generation was once more at Kadesh. From the very spot where the old was broken off was the fresh start to be made. God is faithful to His purpose; He never breaks off. If the old was interrupted, it had been by man's unbelief and rebellion, not by failure on the part of God; and when He resumed His work, it was exactly where it had been so broken off. And man also must return to where he has departed from God, and to where sentence has been pronounced against him, before he enters on his new journey to the Land of Promise. But what solemn thoughts might not have been expected in this new generation, as they once more stood ready to resume their journeying on the spot where that of their fathers had been arrested. As He had sanctified His Name in Kadesh by judgment, would they now sanctify it by their faith and willing obedience?

Besides Joshua and Caleb, to whom entrance into the land had been specially promised, only three of the old generation still remained. These were Miriam, Moses, and Aaron. And now, just at the commencement of this fresh start, as if the more solemnly to remind them of the past, Miriam, who had led the hymn of thanksgiving and triumph on their first entering the desert, (Exodus 15:31) was taken away. Only Moses and Aaron were now left — weary, wayworn pilgrims, to begin a new journey with new pilgrims, who had to learn afresh the dealings of Jehovah. And this may help us to understand what happened at the very outset of their pilgrimage. Israel was in Kadesh, or rather in the desert of Zin, the name Kadesh applying probably to the whole district as well as to a special locality. So large a number of people gathered in one place would naturally soon suffer from want of water. Let it also be remembered, that that generation knew of the wonders of the Lord chiefly by the hearing of the ear, but of His judgments by what they had seen of death sweeping away all who had come out of Egypt. In the hardness of their hearts it now seemed to them as if the prospect before them were hopeless, and they destined to suffer the same fate as their fathers. Something of this unbelieving despair appears in their cry, "Would God that we had died when our brethren died before Jehovah" (Numbers 20:3) — that is, by Divine judgment, during these years of wandering. The remembrance of the past with its disappointments seems to find expression in their complaints (20:5). It is as if they contrasted the stay of their nation in Egypt, and the hopes awakened on leaving it, with the disappointment of seeing the good land almost within their grasp, and then being turned back to die in the wilderness! And so the people broke forth in rebellion against Moses and against Aaron.

217

Feelings similar to theirs seem to have taken hold even on Moses and Aaron — only in a different direction. The people despaired of success, and rebelled against Moses and Aaron. With them as leaders they would never get possession of the Land of Promise. On the other hand, Moses and Aaron also despaired of success, and rebelled, as it were, against the people. Such an unbelieving people, rebelling at the very outset, would never be allowed to enter the land. The people felt as if the prospect before them were hopeless, and so did Moses and Aaron, although on opposite grounds. As we have said, the people rebelled against Moses and Aaron, and Moses and Aaron against the people. But at bottom, the ground of despair and of rebellion, both on the part of the people and of Moses, was precisely the same. In both cases it was really unbelief of God. The people had looked upon Moses and not upon God as their leader into the land, and they had despaired. Moses looked at the people as they were in themselves, instead of thinking of God who now sent them forward, secure in His promise, which He would assuredly fulfill. This soon appeared in the conduct and language of Moses. By Divine direction he was to stand in sight of the people at "the rock before their eyes" with "the rod from before Jehovah" — no doubt the same with which the miracles had been wrought in Egypt, and under whose stroke water had once before sprung from the rock at Rephidim. (Exodus 17:6)

It is generally thought that the sin of Moses, in which Aaron shared, consisted in his striking the rock — and doing so twice — instead of merely speaking to it, "and it shall give forth its water;" and also, in the hasty and improper language which he used on the occasion, "Hear now, ye rebels, must we fetch you water out of this rock?" But it seems difficult to accept this view. On the one hand, we can scarcely imagine that unbelief should have led Moses to strike, rather than to speak to the rock, as if the former would have been more efficacious than the latter. On the other hand, it seems strange that Moses should have been directed to "take the rod," if he were not to have used it, the more so as this had been the Divinely sanctioned mode of proceeding at Rephidim. (Exodus 17:6)

Lastly, how, in that case, could Aaron have been implicated in the sin of Moses? Of course, the striking the rock twice was, as we read in Psalm 106:32, 33, evidence that they had "angered" Moses, and that "his spirit was provoked." This also showed itself in his language, which Scripture thus characterizes, "he spake unadvisedly with his lips" — or, as the word literally means, "he babbled." Be it observed, that Moses is not anywhere in Scripture blamed for striking instead of speaking to the rock, while it is expressly stated that the people "angered him also at the waters of strife, so that it went ill with Moses for their sakes."

The other aspect of the sin of Moses was afterwards expressly stated by the Lord Himself, when He pronounced on Moses and Aaron the sentence that they should not "bring this congregation into the land," which He had given them, on this ground:

"Because ye believed Me not, to sanctify Me in the eyes of the children of Israel" (20:12).

Thus in their rebellion against Moses and Aaron, the people had not believed that Jehovah would bring them into the land which He had given them; while, in their anger at the people, Moses and Aaron had not believed God, to sanctify Him in His power and grace in the eyes of the children of Israel. Israel failed as the people of God; Moses as their mediator. Hitherto Moses had, under every provocation, been faithful as a steward over his charge, and pleaded with God and prevailed, because he believed. Now for the first time Moses failed, as we all fail, through unbelief, looking at the sin of the people, and thence inferring the impossibility of their inheriting the promises, instead of looking at the grace and power of God which made all things possible, and at the certainty of the promise. Unlike Abraham in similar circumstances, "he staggered at the promises." And having through unbelief failed as mediator of the people, his office was to cease, and the conduct of Israel into the land to devolve upon another.

It is only in this sense that we can accept the common statement, that the sin of Moses was official rather than personal. For these two — office or work, and person — cannot be separated either as regards responsibility or duty. Rather would we think of Moses and Aaron as aged pilgrims, worn with the long way through the wilderness, and footsore with its roughnesses and stones, whose strength momentarily failed when the weary journey was once more resumed, and who in their weariness stumbled at the rock of offense. Yet few events possess deeper pathos than this "babbling" at the waters of Meribah. Its true parallel is found not in the Old but in the New Testament. It is true that, in similar circumstances, Elijah also despaired of Israel, and was directed to "the mount of God," there to learn the same lesson as Moses — before, like him, he was unclothed of his office. But the full counterpart to the temptation of Moses is presented in the history of John the Baptist, when doubting, not the Person but the mode of working of the Messiah, and despairing, from what he saw and heard, of the fulfillment of the promise at that time and among that generation, he sent his disciples on that memorable embassy, just before he also was unclothed of his office. This is not the place to follow the subject further. Suffice it to point out, on the one hand, Moses, Elijah, John the Baptist, and, on the other, Joshua, Elisha, and our blessed Lord, as the types and antitypes presented to us in Scripture.

Before leaving Kadesh, Moses sent messengers to the king of Edom, and also, as we learn from Judges 11:17, to the king of Moab, whose dominions lay on the north of Edom, asking permission for Israel to pass through their countries.

A glance at the map will show that this would have been the most direct route, if Palestine was to be entered from the other side Jordan at Jericho. Certainly it was the easiest route, as it avoided contact with those who held the Negeb, or south country, who thirty-seven years before had met Israel in hostile conflict and signally defeated them. (Numbers 14:44, 45) But in vain Moses urged upon Edom the claims of national kinship, Israel's past sufferings in Egypt, and their marvelous deliverance and guidance by The Angel of Jehovah. In vain also did he limit his request to permission to use the ordinary caravan road -"the king's highway" — without straying either to the right or the left, adding the promise of payment for the use of the wells. (Numbers 20:14-17) The children of Esau not only absolutely refused, but hastily gathered an army of observation on their borders. Meantime, while the messengers of Moses had gone on their embassy, the camp of Israel had moved forward to what may be described as "the uttermost of the border" of Edom. A day's journey eastward from Kadesh, through the wide and broad Wady Murreh, suddenly rises a remarkable mountain, quite isolated and prominent, which Canon Williams describes as "singularly formed," and the late Professor Robinson likens to "a lofty citadel." Its present name Moderah preserves the ancient Biblical Moserah, which, from a comparison of Numbers 20:22-29 with Deuteronomy 10:6, we know to have been only another designation for Mount Hor. In fact, "Mount Hor" or Hor-ha-Hor ("mountain, the mountain") just means" the remarkable mountain." This was the natural route for Israel to take, if they hoped to pass through Edom by the king's highway — the present Wady Ghuweir, — which would have led them by way of Moab, easily and straight, to the other side of Jordan. It was natural for them here to halt and await the reply of the king of Edom. For while Moderah lies at the very boundary, but still outside Edom, it is also at the entrance to the various wadies or roads, which thence open east, south, and south-west so that the children of Israel might thence take any route which circumstances would indicate. Moreover, from the height of Moderah they would be able to observe any hostile movement that might be directed against them, whether from the east by Edom, or from the north and west by the Amalekites and Canaanites. From what has been said, it will be gathered that we regard this as the Mount Hor where Aaron died.

Thus speedily, within a day's journey of the place of his sin, was the Divine sentence upon Aaron executed. There is a solemn grandeur about this narrative, befitting the occasion and in accordance with the locality. In the sight of all the congregation these three, Moses, Aaron, and Eleazar, went up the mount. In his full priestly dress walked Aaron to his burial. He knew it, and so did all in that camp, who now, for the last time, reverently and silently looked upon the venerable figure of him who, these forty years, had ministered unto them in holy things.

There was no farewell. In that typical priesthood all depended on the unbroken continuance of the office, not of the person. And hence on that mountain-top Aaron was first unclothed of his priestly robes, and Eleazar, his son, formally invested with them. Thus the priesthood had not for a moment ceased when Aaron died. Then, not as a priest but simply as one of God's Israel, was he "gathered unto his people." But over that which passed between the three on the mount has the hand of God drawn the veil of silence. And so the new priest, Eleazar, came down from the solemn scene on Mount Hor to minister amidst a hushed and awe-stricken congregation. "And when all the congregation saw that Aaron was dead, they mourned for Aaron thirty days, even all the house of Israel."

Serious tidings were now in store for Israel. The messengers returned from Edom bringing absolute refusal to the request of passage through that country. Not only so, but the large army of Edom was assembling on the frontier, close to the camping-ground of Israel. If, according to the Divine command, Edom was not to be attacked, then Israel must rapidly retreat. The ordinary route from Mount Hor "to compass the land of Edom," so as to advance northwards, by the east of Edom, would have led Israel straight down by the Wady El-Jeib, and so through the northern part of the Arabah. But this route touched the western boundary of Edom, just where, as we gather from the Scriptural narrative, the army of Edom was echeloned. To avoid them, it became therefore necessary, in the first place, to retrace their steps again through part of the Wady Murreh, in order thence to strike in a south-easterly direction through what are now known as "the mountains of the 'Azazimeh," the ancient dukedom of Teman, or Mount Paran. By this detour Israel would strike the Arabah far south of where the army of Edom awaited them, passing through the modern Wadies Ghudhaghidh and 'Adbeh. In point of fact, we learn from Deuteronomy 10:7 that Gudgodah and Jotbath were the two stations reached next after the retreat from Mount Hor. But just at the point where the host of Israel would turn southwards from Wady Murreh, they were also in almost a straight line for the territory of the king of Arad. Of course, he would be informed that Israel had been refused a passage through Edom, and, finding them on the flank of his territory, would naturally imagine that they intended to invade it. "And the Canaanitish king of Arad, which dwelt in the Negeb" (or south country), "heard tell that Israel came by the way of the spies" (or, more probably, "the way of the merchants," the caravan road); "then he fought against Israel, and took of them prisoners" having probably fallen on their rearguard.

The event is mentioned for this twofold reason: to show the unprovoked enmity of Canaan against Israel, and the faithfulness of God. For Israel at that time "vowed a vow" utterly to destroy the cities of the Canaanites. And God hearkened and heard. Many years afterwards He gave the prayed-for victory, (Jude 1:17) when the name of Hormah or ban — utter destruction — given in prophetic anticipation of God's faithfulness, became a reality.

CHAPTER 21: JOURNEY OF CHILDREN OF ISRAEL IN "COMPASSING" LAND OF EDOM — THE "FIERY SERPENTS" AND THE "BRAZEN SERPENT" — ISRAEL ENTERS THE LAND OF THE AMORITES — VICTORIES OVER SIHON AND & OG, — THE KINGS OF THE AMORITES AND OF BASHAN — ISRAEL CAMPS IN "LOWLANDS OF MOAB" CLOSE BY THE JORDAN

(NUMBERS 21:3-35; 33:35-49; DEUTERONOMY 2, 3)

THE opposition of Edom and the unprovoked attack of the Canaanite king of Arad must have convinced Israel that the most serious difficulties of their march had now commenced. It was quite natural that, during the thirty-eight years when they were scattered up and down in the Sinaitic peninsula, their powerful neighbors should have left them unmolested, as the wandering Bedouin are at this day. But when Israel again gathered together and moved forward as a host, then the tidings of the marvelous things which God had done for them, communicated with all the circumstantiality common in the east, would excite mingled terror and a determination to resist them. The latter probably first; the former as resistance was seen to be vain, and the God of Israel realized as stronger than all other national deities. Eastern idolaters would naturally thus reason; and the knowledge of this will help our understanding of the Scriptural narrative.

The general direction of Israel's march, in order to "compass" the land of Edom, was first to the head of the Elanitic Gulf of the Red Sea, or the Gulf of 'Akabah. Thence they would, a few hours north of Ezion-geber (the giant's backbone), enter the mountains, and then pass northwards, marching to Moab "by the road which runs between Edom and the limestone plateau of the great eastern desert" (comp. Deuteronomy 2:8).

Probably they were prepared to contend for every fresh advance which they made northwards. But the first part of their journey was otherwise trying. That deep depression of the Arabah through which they marched — intensely hot, bare of vegetation, desolate, rough, and visited by terrible sandstorms — was pre-eminently "that great and terrible wilderness," of which Moses afterwards reminded the people. (Deuteronomy 1:19) What with the weariness of the way, the want of water, and of all food other than the manna, "the soul of the people was much discouraged," "and the people spake against God and against Moses." The judgment of "fiery serpents" which the Lord, "in punishment, sent among the people," and of which so many died bore a marked resemblance to all His former dealings. Once more He did not create a new thing for the execution of His purpose, but only disposed sovereignly of what already existed. Travelers give remarkable confirmation and illustrations of the number and poisonous character of the serpents in that district. Thus one writes of the neighborhood of the gulf: "The sand on the shore showed traces of snakes on every hand. They had crawled there in various directions. Some of the marks appeared to have been made by animals which could not have been less than two inches in diameter. My guide told me that snakes were very common in these regions." Another traveler on exactly the route of the children of Israel states: "In the afternoon a large and very mottled snake was brought to us, marked with fiery spots and spiral lines, which evidently belonged, from the formation of its teeth, to one of the most poisonous species... The Bedouins say that these snakes, of which they have great dread, are very numerous in this locality." From the fact that the brazen serpent is also called "fiery" (a Saraph), we infer that the expression describes rather the appearance of these "fire-snakes" than the effect of their bite.

Two things are most marked in this history, the speedy repentance of Israel, couched in unwonted language of humility, (Numbers 21:7) and the marvelous teaching of the symbol, through which those who had been mortally bitten were granted restoration to life and health. Moses was directed to make a fiery serpent of brass, and to set it upon a pole, and whosoever looked upon it was immediately healed. From the teaching of our Lord (John 3:14, 15) we know that this was a direct type of the lifting up of the Son of Man, "that whosoever believeth in Him should not perish, but have eternal life." The simplicity of the remedy — only to look up in faith, its immediateness and its completeness as well as the fact that this was the only but also the all-sufficient remedy for the deadly wound of the serpent — all find their counterpart in the Gospel. But for the proper understanding both of the type and of the words of our Lord, we must inquire in what manner Israel would view and understand the lifting up of the brazen serpent and the healing that flowed from it. Undoubtedly, Israel would at once connect this death through the fiery serpents with the introduction of death into Paradise through the serpent.

And now a brazen serpent was lifted up, made in the likeness of the fiery serpent, yet without its poisonous bite. And this was for the healing of Israel. Clearly then, the deadly poison of the fiery serpent was removed in the uplifted brazen serpent! All this would carry back the mind to the promise given when first the poisonous sting of the serpent was felt, that the Seed of the Woman should bruise the head of the serpent, and that in so doing His own heel should be bruised. In this sense even the apocryphal Book of Wisdom (16:6) designates the brazen serpent "a symbol of salvation." And so we are clearly taught that "God sending His own Son in the likeness of sinful flesh, and for sin, condemned sin in the flesh;" (Romans 8:3) that

"He hath made Him to be sin for us, who knew no sin; (2 Corinthians 5:21)
and that
"His own self bare our sins in His own body on the tree." (1 Peter 2:24)

The precious meaning of the type is thus deduced by Luther from the three grand peculiarities of this "symbol of salvation:" "First, the serpent which Moses made at the command of God had to be of brass or copper, that is, red, and like those fiery serpents, which were red, and burning in their bite — yet without poison. Secondly, the brazen serpent had to be set up on a pole for a sign" (comp. Colossians 2:14, etc.). "Thirdly, those who would be healed of the fiery serpents bite must look up to the brazen serpent, lifted up on the pole" (perceive, and believe), "else they could not recover nor live." Similarly a modern German critic thus annotates John 3:14:

"Christ is the antitype of this serpent, inasmuch as He took upon Himself and vicariously bore sin, the most noxious of all noxious powers."

It is of the deepest interest to follow the march of the children of Israel, when every day's journey brought them nearer to the Land of Promise as their goal. To them it was not, as to us, a land of ruins and of memories, but of beauty and of hope. To a people who had all their lives seen and known nothing but "the wilderness," the richness, fertility, and varied beauty of Palestine, as it then was, must have possessed charms such as we can scarcely imagine. Then every step in advance was, so to speak, under the direct leading of God, and, in a sense, a miracle, while every such leading and miracle was itself a pledge of others yet to follow. The researches of modern travelers enable us almost to company with Israel on this their march. As already stated, the wonderful tenacity with which old names keep their hold in the far East helps us to discover the exact spots of Biblical scenes; while, on the other hand, descriptions of the localities throw most vivid light on the Scriptural narratives, and afford evidence of their trustworthiness.

The reader ought to remember that the route which lay before Israel was in part the same as that still traversed by the great caravans from Damascus to Mecca. The territories which they successively passed or entered were occupied as follows. First, Israel skirted along the eastern boundary of Edom, leaving it on their left. The western boundary of Edom, through which Israel had sought a passage when starting from Kadesh, (Numbers 20:18) would from its mountainous character and few passes have been easily defended against the Israelites. But it was otherwise with the eastern line of frontier, which lay open to Israel, had they not been Divinely directed not to fight against Edom. (Deuteronomy 2:4-6) This, however, explains the friendly attitude which the Edomites found it prudent to adopt along their eastern frontier, (Deuteronomy 2:29) although their army had shortly before been prepared to fight on the western. At Ije Abarim, "the ruins," or "the hills of the passages," or "of the sides" -perhaps "the lateral hills" the Israelites were approaching the wilderness which lay to the east of Moab.

The brook or Wady Zared (Numbers 21:12) here forms the boundary between Edom and Moab. But as Israel had been also commanded not to fight against Moab, (Deuteronomy 2:9) they left their territory equally untouched, and, continuing straight northwards, passed through the wilderness of Moab, until they reached the river Arnon, the modern Wady Moab, which formed the boundary between the Moabites and the Amorites. The territory of the Amorites stretched from the Arnon to the Jabbok. It had originally belonged to the Moabites; (Numbers 21:26) but they had been driven southwards by the Amorites. No command of God prevented Israel from warring against the Amorites, and when Sihon, their king, refused to give them a free passage through his territory, they were Divinely directed to that attack which issued in the destruction of Sihon, and the possession of his land by Israel.

At the brook Zared — on the southern boundary of Moab — the Israelites had already been in a line with the Dead Sea, leaving it, of course, far on their left. The river Arnon also, which formed the boundary between Moab and the Amorites, flows into the Dead Sea almost opposite to Hazazon-tamar, or En-gedi. This tract, which now bears the name of el-Belkah, is known to the reader of the Old Testament as the land Gilead, while in New Testament times it formed the province of Perea. Lastly, the district north of the Jabbok and east of the Jordan was the ancient Bashan, or the modern Hauran. The fact that the country north of the Arnon had, before its possession by the Amorites, been so long held by Moab explains the name "Fields of Moab" (rendered in the Authorized Version "country of Moab," Numbers 21:20)as applied to the upland hills of Gilead, just as the western side of Jordan similarly bore the name of "the plains of Moab," or rather "the lowlands of Moab." (Numbers 22:1) The children of Israel were still camped on the south side of the Arnon when they sent the embassy to Sihon, demanding a passage through his territory. Canon Tristram has given a most vivid description of the rift through which the Arnon flows. Its width is calculated at about three miles from crest to crest, and its depth at 2,150 feet from the top of the southern, and at 1,950 from that of the northern bank. Of course, the army of Israel could not have passed the river here, but higher up, to the east, "in the wilderness." (Numbers 21:13) They probably waited until the messengers returned from Sihon. How high their courage and confidence in God had risen, when tidings arrived that Sihon with all his army was coming to meet them, appears even from those extracts of poetic pieces which form so marked a peculiarity of the Book of Numbers, and which read like stanzas of war-songs by the camp-fires. From the banks of the Arnon the route of Israel was no doubt northward till they reached Bamoth or Bamolh Baal, "the heights of Baal," (Numbers 21:19) one of the stations afterwards taken up by Balak and Balaam. (Numbers 22:41) "And from Bamoth (they marched) to the valley, which is in the fields of Moab (on the plateau of Moab), on the height of Pisgah, and looks over to the face of the wilderness," that is, over the tract of land which extends to the north-eastern shore of the Dead Sea. (Numbers 21:20)

From this plateau on the mountains of the Abarim, of which Pisgah and Nebo were peaks, Israel had its first view of the Land of Promise, and especially of that mysterious Sea of Salt whose glittering surface and deathlike surroundings would recall such solemn memories and warnings. At last then the goal was in view! The decisive battle between Sihon and Israel was fought almost within sight of the Dead Sea. The victory at Jahaz, in which Sihon was smitten "with the edge of the sword" — that is, without quarter or sparing, — gave Israel possession of the whole country, including Heshbon and "all the daughters thereof" — or daughter-towns, — from the Arnon to the upper Jabbok (the modern Nahr Amman). The latter river formed the boundary between the Amorites and the Ammonites. Beyond this the Amorites had not penetrated, because "the border of the children of Ammon was strong." (Numbers 21:24) And Israel also forbore to penetrate farther, not on the same ground as the Amorites, but because of an express command of God. (Deuteronomy 2:19) Leaving untouched therefore the country of Ammon, the Israelites next moved northward, defeated Og, king of Bashan, and took possession of his territory also, and of the mountains of Gilead. The whole country east of the Jordan was now Israel's, and the passage of that river could not be disputed.

Before actually entering upon their long-promised inheritance, some great lessons had, indeed, yet to be learned. An event would take place which would for ever mark the relation between the kingdom of God and that of this world. The mission of Moses, the servant of the Lord, must also come to an end, and the needful arrangements be made for possessing and holding the land of Palestine. But all these belong, strictly speaking, to another period of Israel's history. When the camp was pitched in Shittim, "on this side Jordan by Jericho," waiting for the signal to cross the boundary line, the wanderings of the children of Israel were really at an end.

VOLUME 3: ISRAEL IN CANAAN UNDER JOSHUA AND THE JUDGES

PREFACE

THE history of Israel as a nation may be said to commence with their entrance into their own land. All previous to this — from the Paschal night on which Israel was born as a people to the overthrow of Sihon and of Og, the last who would have barred Israel's way to their home — had been only preparatory. During the forty years' wanderings the people had, so to speak, been welded together by the strong hand of Jehovah. But now, when the Lion of Judah couched by the banks of Jordan, Israel was face to face with its grand mission, and the grand task of its national life commenced: to dispossess heathenism, and to plant in its stead the kingdom of God (Psalm 80:8-11), which was destined to strike root and to grow, till, in the fullness of time, it would extend to all nations of the world.

Accordingly, when the camp of Israel was pitched at Shittim, a new period commenced. Its history records, first, certain events which had to take place immediately before entering the Land of Promise; next, the conquest, and then the apportionment of the land among the tribes of Israel; and, lastly, in the time of the Judges, side by side, the unfolding of Israel's religious and national condition, and the assertion of those fundamental principles which underlay its very existence as a God-called people. These principles are: — The special relationship of Israel as the people of God towards Jehovah, and Jehovah's special dealings towards them as their King.

The history of the wilderness period had, indeed, been shaped by this two-fold relationship, but its consequences appeared more clearly under Joshua, and most fully in the time of the Judges. When not only Moses, but Joshua, and even the elders who had been his contemporaries had passed away, the people, now settled in the land, were left free to develop those tendencies which had all along existed. Then ensued that alternation of national apostasy and judgment, and of penitent return to God and deliverance, which constitutes, so to speak, the framework on which the Book of Judges is constructed. This part of Israel's history attained alike its highest and its lowest point in Samson, with whom the period of the Judges appropriately closes. For, the administration of Samuel forms only the transition to, and preparation for the establishment of royalty in Israel. But the spiritual import of the whole history of that period is summed up in these words of Holy Scripture (Psalm 44:2-4):

"Thou didst drive out the heathen with Thy hand, and plantedst them: Thou didst afflict the people, and cast them out. For they got not the land in possession by their own sword, neither did their own arm save them, but Thy right hand, and Thine arm, and the light of Thy countenance, because Thou hadst a favor unto them. Thou art my King, O God: command deliverances for Jacob."

The Books of Joshua and of the Judges form the two first portions of what in the Hebrew Canon are designated as the "Former Prophets." This, not because their narratives are largely connected with the rise and activity of the prophets, nor yet because their authors were prophets, but rather because the character and contents of these books are prophetic.

They give the history of Israel from the prophet's point of view — not a succinct and successive chronicle of the nation, but a history of the Kingdom of God in Israel. This also explains its peculiarities of form and style. For, neither are the Judges, for example, mentioned in the order of their succession, nor must it be supposed that they ruled over all the tribes of Israel. Similarly, there are evidently large blanks left in the history of the times, and while some events or reigns of considerable duration are only cursorily mentioned, very detailed and circumstantial narratives are given of persons and occurrences, which only occupied the scene for a comparatively short period. But as, from the frequent references to authorities, and from their evident knowledge of details, the writers of these books must have had at command ample material for a full history, we conclude that the selection, Divinely guided, was made in accordance with the "Spirit of Prophecy," to mark the progress of the Kingdom of God in connection with Israel.

From what has been said it will be readily understood, that the history traced in this volume offers peculiar difficulties — from its briefness, its abruptness, its rapid transitions, the unusual character of its incidents, and its sudden and marked Divine interpositions. These difficulties are not so much exegetical or critical — although such are certainly not wanting — but rather concern the substance of the narratives themselves, and touch the very essence of Holy Scripture. For myself, I am free to confess that I entered on my present undertaking, I shall not say with apprehension but with great personal diffidence. I knew, indeed, that what appears a difficulty might find its full and satisfactory solution, even though I were not able to indicate it, and that a narrative might have its Divine meaning and spiritual purpose, even though I should fail to point it out. Yet I imagine that most readers of the Books of Joshua and Judges will in some measure understand and sympathize with my feelings. All the more is it now alike duty and privilege, at the close of these investigations, to express it joyously and thankfully, that the more fully these narratives are studied, the more luminous will they become; the more will their Divine meaning appear; and the more will they carry to the mind conviction of their truthfulness, and to the heart lessons of their spiritual import. Perhaps I may be allowed in illustration of these statements to point to my study of the characters of Balaam and Joshua, and of the histories of Gideon, of Jephthah, and especially of Samson.

From this circumstance, and faithful to the plan, which I proposed to myself in this series, of gradually leading a reader onwards, the sacred narrative has received in this volume more full treatment — the discussion of such textual questions as fell within its scope, being, however, chiefly thrown into the footnotes. Many questions, indeed, on which I could have earnestly wished to enter, lay quite outside the purport of the present series, and had therefore reluctantly to be left aside. These concern chiefly the antiquity and the authenticity of these books of Holy Scripture. I venture to think, that a great deal yet remains to be said on these points — the chief defect of former treatises lying, in my opinion, in this, that they rather busy themselves with refuting the arguments of opponents, than bring forward what I would call the positive evidence. That such positive evidence abundantly exists, a somewhat careful study has increasingly convinced me. I am not ashamed to own my belief that, notwithstanding confident assertions of writers on the opposite side, we may trustfully and contentedly walk in "the old paths;" and the present volume is intended as a reverent contribution, however inadequate, towards the better understanding of what, I verily believe, "holy men of old spake as they were moved by the Spirit," and that, "for doctrine, for reproof, for correction, for instruction in righteousness."

Alfred Edersheim
Loders Vicarage, Bridport
February 23, 1877

CHAPTER 1: ISRAEL ABOUT TO TAKE POSSESSION OF THE LAND OF PROMISE — DECISIVE CONTEST SHOWING THE REAL CHARACTER OF HEATHENISM — CHARACTER AND HISTORY OF BALAAM.

(NUMBERS 22)

THE wilderness-life and the early contests of Israel were over. Israel stood on the threshold of the promised possession, separated from it only by the waters of Jordan. But, before crossing that boundary-line, it was absolutely necessary that the people should, once and for all, gain full knowledge of the real character of heathenism in its relation to the kingdom of God. Israel must learn that the heathen nations were not only hostile political powers, opposing their progress, but that heathenism itself was in its nature antagonistic to the kingdom of God. The two were incompatible, and therefore no alliance could ever be formed with heathenism, no intercourse cultivated, nor even its presence tolerated. This was the lesson which, on the eve of entering Palestine, Israel was to learn by painful experience in connection with the history of Balaam. Its importance at that particular period will readily be understood. Again and again was the same lesson taught throughout the history of Israel, as each alliance or even contact with the kingdoms of this world brought fresh sorrow and trouble. Nor is its application to the Church of God, so far as concerns the danger of commixture with, and conformity to the world, less obvious. And so the history of Balak and of Balaam has, besides its direct lessons, a deep meaning for all times.

With the decisive victories over Sihon and over Og, all who could have barred access to the Land of Promise had been either left behind, or else scattered and defeated. And now the camp of Israel had moved forward, in the language of Scripture, to "the other side Jordan from Jericho." Their tents were pitched in rich meadow-land, watered by many streams, which rush down from the neighboring mountains — Arboth, or lowlands of Moab, as the country on this and that side the river was still called, after its more ancient inhabitants.

As the vast camp lay scattered over a width of several miles, from Abel Shittim, "the meadow of the acacias," in the north, to Beth Jeshimoth, "the house of desolations," on the edge of the desert, close to the Dead Sea, in the south (Numbers 33:49), it might have seemed as if the lion of Judah were couching ready for his spring on the prey. But was he the lion of Judah, and were the promises of God to him indeed "yea and amen?" A fiercer assault, and one in which heathenism would wield other arms than those which had so lately been broken in their hands, would soon decide that question.

We can perceive many reasons why Moab, though apparently not immediately threatened, should, at that special moment, have come forward as the champion and representative of heathenism (Numbers 22:1- 3). True, Israel had left their land untouched, restrained by express Divine command from invading it (Deuteronomy 2:9). But their close neighborhood was dangerous. Besides, had not all that land north of the Arnon, which Israel had just wrested from the Amorites, been till lately Moabitish — the very name of Moab still lingering on mountain-plateau and lowland plains; and might not Moab again have what once it held? But there was far more involved than either fear or cupidity suggested.

The existence alike of heathen nations and of heathenism itself depended on the issue. There can be no doubt that the prophetic anticipation of the song of Moses (Exodus 15:14-16) had already in great part been fulfilled. "The nations" had "heard" of God's marvelous doings for Israel, and were afraid; "the mighty men of Moab, trembling" had taken "hold upon them." Among the wandering tribes of the east, tidings, especially of this kind, travel fast. Jethro had heard them long before (Exodus 18:1), and the testimony of Rahab (Joshua 2:9) shows how fear and dread had fallen upon the inhabitants of the land. Force of arms had been tried against them. The Amorites, who had been able to wrest from Moab all the land north of the Arnon, had boldly marched against Israel under the leadership of Sihon their king, and been not only defeated but almost exterminated. A similar fate had befallen the brave king of Bashan and his people. There could be no question that so far Jehovah, the God of Israel, had proved true to His word, and stronger than the gods of the nations who had been subdued. Farther progress, then, in the same direction might prove fatal alike to their national existence, their national deities, and their national religion.

In trying to realize the views and feelings of heathenism under such circumstances, we must beware of transporting into them our modern ideas. In our days the question is as to the acknowledgment or else the denial of Jehovah God. In those days it turned upon the acknowledgment or the opposite of Jehovah as the only true and living God, as this is expressed in the first commandment. Heathenism would never have thought of denying the existence or power of Jehovah as the national God of the Hebrews (see, for example, 1 Kings 20:23; 2 Kings 18:25, 33-35). What it controverted was, that Jehovah was the only God — all others being merely idols, the work of men's hands. Prepared as they were to acknowledge Jehovah as the national Deity of the Hebrews, the question before them would be, whether He or their gods were the more powerful. It was a point of the deepest interest to them, since, if anything were known of Jehovah, it would be this, that He was "a jealous God," and that the rites by which He was worshipped were so different from theirs, as to involve an entire change, not only of religion, but of popular habits and manners. From what has been stated, it will be understood why, in attempting to break the power of Israel, whose God had hitherto — whether from accident, fate, or inherent power — proved Himself superior to those of the nations, the king of Moab had, in the first place, recourse to "divination," and why he was so specially anxious to secure the services of Balaam.

Balaam, or rather Bileam, the son of Beor, belonged apparently to a family of magicians who resided at Pethor, possibly, as has been suggested, a city of professional soothsayers or students of that craft, but certainly situated in "Aram" or Mesopotamia, and on the banks of the Euphrates (Numbers 22:5; 23:7; Deuteronomy 23:4). His name, which means "devourer," or "swallower up," and that of his father, which means "burner up," or "destroyer" — whether given them at birth, or, as is so common in the East, from their supposed characteristics — indicate alike the claims which they put forth and the estimate in which they were popularly held. If, as has been conjectured, Balak, the king of Moab, was of Midianitish origin (his father having been a Midianitish usurper), it becomes all the more intelligible that in his peculiar circumstances he would apply for advice and help to the Midianites; that he would ally himself with them; and that through them he would come to know of, and along with them send for, Balaam (Numbers 22:4, 7, etc.).

At any rate, those Midianite wanderers of the desert which stretched between Mesopotamia and the dominions of Moab would, like modern Bedawin under similar circumstances, not only know of the existence of a celebrated magician like Balaam, but probably greatly exaggerate his power. Moreover, being themselves unable to attack Israel, they would nevertheless gladly make common cause with Moab, and that, although for the present their territory was not directly threatened, any more than that of the Moabites. This explains the alliance of Moab and Midian and their common embassy to Balaam.

The object in view was twofold. As already explained, the success of Israel as against the nations, or rather that of Israel's God against their deities, might, in their opinion, arise from one of two causes. Either their own national deities — Chemosh and Baal — had not been sufficiently propitiated — sufficient influence or power had not been brought to bear upon them; or else Jehovah was really stronger than they. In either case Balaam would bring invaluable, and, if he only chose to exert it, sure help. For, according to heathen views, a magician had absolute and irresistible power with the gods; power was inherent in him or in the incantations which he used. And herein lay one of the fundamental differences between heathenism and the Old Testament, between magic and miracles. In the former it was all of man, in the latter it was shown to be all of God. No prophet of the Lord ever had or claimed power, like the magicians; but in every case the gracious influence was specially, and for that time, transmitted directly from God. Only the God-Man had power in Himself, so that His every contact brought health and life. And in the Christian dispensation also, however much of the supernatural there may be experienced and witnessed, nothing is magical; there is no mere exercise of power or of authority; but all is conveyed to us through the free promises of God, and in the dispensation of His grace.

But to return. Supposing that Jehovah were really superior to Chemosh and Baal, the king of Moab and his associates would none the less desire the aid of Balaam. For it was a further principle of heathenism, that national deities might be induced to transfer their blessing and protection from one nation to another. Thus the ancient Romans were wont, when laying siege to a foreign city, solemnly to invite its special gods to come out to them and join their side, promising them in return not only equal but higher honors than they had hitherto enjoyed. And if something of this kind were now needful — if influence was to be exerted on the God of the Israelites, who was so capable of it as Balaam, both from his profession as a dealer with the gods, and from his special qualifications? And this leads up to the principal personage in this history, to his character, and to the question of his religion.

What has been said of the knowledge which the king of Moab must have possessed of Jehovah's dealings in reference to Israel (Exodus 15:14-16) applies, of course, with much greater force to Balaam himself. As a professional magician, belonging to a family of magicians, and residing at one of their chief seats, it was alike his duty and his interest to acquaint himself with such matters. Moreover, we ought not to forget that, in the place of his residence, traditions of Abraham would linger with that Eastern local tenacity which we have already had so frequent occasion to notice. Indeed, we have positive evidence that Balaam's inquiries had gone back far beyond the recent dealings of Jehovah to His original covenant-relationship towards His people. A comparison of the promise of God to Abraham in Genesis 13:16 with the mode of expression used by Balaam in Numbers 23:10; still more — the correspondence between Genesis 49:9 and Numbers 23:24, 24:9 in his description of Judah; but most of all, the virtual repetition of the prophecy Genesis 49:10 in Numbers 24:17, prove beyond doubt that Balaam had made himself fully acquainted with the promises of Jehovah to Israel. That a professional soothsayer like Balaam should have been quite ready, upon a review of their whole history, to acknowledge Jehovah as the national God of Israel, and to enter — if the expression may be allowed — into professional relationship with such a powerful Deity, seems only natural in the circumstances. This explains his conduct in speaking to and of Jehovah, and apparently owning Him. But in all this Balaam did not advance a step beyond the mere heathen point of view, any more than Simon Magus when, "beholding the miracles and signs which were done," "he was baptized;" (Acts 8:13) nor did his conduct bring him nearer to the true service of Jehovah than were those seven sons of Sceva to that of Christ, when they endeavored to cast out evil spirits in the name of the Lord Jesus (Acts 19:13, 14). In fact, Scripture designates him uniformly by the word Kosem, which is the distinctive term for heathen soothsayers in opposition to prophets of the Lord. And with this his whole conduct agrees. Had he possessed even the most elementary knowledge of Jehovah as the only true and living God, or the most rudimentary understanding of His covenant-purposes, he could not, considering his acquaintance with previous prophecy, have for a moment entertained the idea of allying himself with Balak against Israel. On the other hand, if, according to his view of the matter, he could have succeeded in making the God of Israel, so to speak, one of his patron-deities, and if, upon his own terms, he could have become one of His prophets; still more, if he could have gained such influence with Him as to turn Him from His purpose regarding Israel, then would he have reached the goal of his ambition, and become by far the most powerful magician in the world. Thus, in our opinion, from the time when we first meet him, standing where the two roads part, to the bitter end of his treachery, when, receiving the reward of Judas, he was swept away in the destruction of Midian, his conduct was throughout consistently heathen, and his progress rapid in the downward course.

Where the two roads part! In every great crisis of history, and, we feel persuaded, in the great crisis of every individual life, there is such a meeting and parting of the two ways — to life or to destruction. It was so in the case of Pharaoh, when Moses first brought him the summons of the Lord to let His people go free, proving his authority by indubitable signs. And Balaam stood at the meeting and parting of the two ways that night when the ambassadors of Balak and the elders of Midian were for the first time under his roof. That embassy was the crisis in his history. He had advanced to the knowledge that Jehovah, the God of Israel, was God. The question now came: Would he recognize Him as the only true and living God, with Whom no such relationship could exist as those which heathenism supposed; towards Whom every relationship must be moral and spiritual, not magical — one of heart and of life service, not of influence and power? To use New Testament language, in his general acknowledgment of Jehovah, Balaam had advanced to the position described in the words: "he that is not against us is for us" (Luke 9:50). But this is only, as it were, the meeting and parting of the two roads. The next question which comes is far deeper, and decisive, so far as each individual is concerned. It refers to our relationship to the Person of Christ. And in regard to this we read: "He that is not with Me is against Me" (Matthew 12:30).

As always in such circumstances, God's great mercy and infinite patience and condescension were not wanting to help Balaam in the crisis of his life. There could, at least, be no doubt on two points. Balak's avowed wish had been, by the help of Balaam, to "smite" Israel and "drive them out of the land" (Numbers 22:6); and his expressed conviction, "he whom thou blessest is blessed, and he whom thou cursest is cursed." Now, not to speak of the implied magical power thus attributed to him, Balaam must have known that Balak's intention ran directly counter to Jehovah's purpose, while the words, in which the power of blessing and cursing was ascribed to Balaam, were not only a transference to man of what belonged to God alone, but must have been known to Balaam as the very words in which Jehovah had originally bestowed the blessing on Abraham:

"I will bless them that bless thee, and curse him that curseth thee" (Genesis 12:3).

That Balaam so knew these words appears from his own quotation of them in Numbers 24:9. The proposal of Balak therefore ran directly counter to the fundamental purpose of God, as Balaam knew it — and yet he could hesitate even for a single moment! But this is not all. In His infinite long-suffering, not willing that any should perish, God even now condescended to Balaam. He had proposed to the ambassadors of Balak that they should "lodge" with him that night, and that on the morrow he would make his reply, as Jehovah would speak unto him. And Jehovah did condescend to meet Balaam in his own way, and that night fully communicated to him His will. The garbled and misrepresenting account of it, which Balaam in the morning gave to his guests, finally marked his choice and decided his fate.

But why did Jehovah God appear to, or deal with such an one as Balaam? Questions like these ought, with our limited knowledge of God's purposes, not always to be entertained. In the present instance, however, we can suggest at least some answer. Of God's purpose, so far as Balaam's personal condition was concerned, we have already spoken. But a wider issue was here to be tried. Balak had sent for Balaam in order through his magic to destroy Israel, or rather to arrest and turn aside the wonder-working power of Jehovah. It was, therefore, really a contest between heathenism and Israel as the people of God, which would exhibit and decide the real relationship between Israel and the heathen world, or in other words, between the Church of God and the kingdoms of this world. And as formerly God had raised up Pharaoh to be the instrument of bringing down the gods of Egypt, so would He now decide this contest through the very man whom Balak had chosen as its champion — using him as a willing instrument, if he yielded, or as an unwilling, if he rebelled, but in any case as an efficient instrument for carrying out His own purposes. It is in this manner that we regard God's meeting Balaam, and His speaking both to him and through him.

Three brief but emphatic utterances had God in that first night made to Balaam:

"Thou shalt not go with them; thou shalt not curse the people: for they are blessed" (Numbers 22:12).

Of these Balaam, in his reply to the ambassadors next morning, had deliberately suppressed the last two (22:13). Yet they were the most important, as showing the utter hopelessness of the undertaking, and the utter powerlessness of any man to control or influence the purpose of God. He thus withheld knowledge of the utmost importance for understanding alike the character of the true God and that of His true servants, who simply obey, but do not seek to control, His will. But even in what he did repeat of God's message there was grievous misrepresentation. For this statement, "Jehovah refuses to give me leave to go with you" (22:13), implied an ungrounded arbitrariness on the part of God; confirmed Balak in his heathen views; and perhaps encouraged him to hope for better results under more favorable circumstances. As for Balaam himself, we may be allowed to infer, that he misunderstood God's appearance to, and conversation with him, as implying a sort of league with, or acknowledgment of him, while all the time he had irrevocably departed from God, and entered the way of sin and of judgment. Accordingly, we find Balaam thenceforth speaking of Jehovah as "my God," and confidently assuming the character of His servant. At the same time, he secured for himself the presents of Balak, while, in his reply, he took care not to lose the favor of the king, but rather to make him all the more anxious to gain his aid, since he was owned of Jehovah, Who had only refused a leave which on another occasion He might grant.

It was under these circumstances that a second embassy from Balak and Midian, more honorable than the first, and with almost unlimited promises, came again to ask Balaam "to curse this people" (ver. 17). The king had well judged. With no spiritual, only a heathen acknowledgment of Jehovah, covetousness and ambition were the main actuating motives of Balaam. In the pithy language of the New Testament (2 Peter 2:15), he "loved the wages of unrighteousness." But already his course was sealed. Refusing to yield himself a willing, he would now be made the unwilling instrument of exalting Jehovah. And thus God gave him leave to do that on which he had set his heart, with this important reservation, however: "But yet the word which I shall say unto thee, that shalt thou do." Balaam, whose blinded self-satisfaction had already appeared in his profession to the ambassadors, that he could "not go beyond the word of Jehovah his God," understood not the terrible judgment upon himself implied in this "let him alone," which gave up the false prophet to his own lusts. He had no doubt been so far honest, although he was grossly and willfully ignorant of all that concerned Jehovah, when he proposed to consult God a second time, whether he might curse Israel. And now it seemed as if God had indeed inclined to him. Balaam was as near reaching the ideal of a magician, and having "power," as was Simon Magus when he offered the apostles money to bestow on him the power of imparting the Holy Ghost.

It was no doubt on account of this spirit of deluded self satisfaction, in which next morning he accompanied the ambassadors of Balak, that "God's anger was kindled because he went," and that "the angel of Jehovah stood in the way for an adversary against him" — significantly, the angel of the covenant with a drawn sword, threatening destruction. The main object of what happened to him on the journey was, if possible, to arouse Balaam to a sense of his utter ignorance of, and alienation from Jehovah. And so even "the dumb ass, speaking with man's voice, forbad the madness of the prophet" (2 Peter 2:16).

We know, indeed, that animals are often more sensitive to the presence or nearness of danger than man — as it were, perceive what escapes our senses. But in this case the humiliating lesson was, that while the self-satisfied prophet had absolutely seen nothing, his ass had perceived the presence of the angel, and, by going out of the way, or falling down, saved the life of his master; and that, even so, Balaam still continued blinded, perverse, and misunderstanding, till God opened the mouth of the dumb animal, so that with man's voice it might forbid the madness of the prophet. To show Balaam himself as he really was, and the consequences of his conduct; and to do so in the strongest, that is, in this case, in the most humiliating manner, such was the object of the apparition of the angel, and of the human language in which Balaam heard the ass reproving him.

But even this produced no real effect — only an offer on the part of Balaam to get him back again, if it displeased the angel of Jehovah (22:34). The proposal was as blundering, and argued as deep ignorance, as his former readiness to go with the ambassadors. For the question was not simply one of going or not going, but of glorifying God, and acknowledging the supremacy of His covenant-purpose. Balaam might have gone and returned without doing this; but Jehovah would now do it Himself through Balaam. And already the elders of Moab and Midian had hurried on along with Balaam's own servants, to announce the arrival of the prophet. Presently from the lonely, terrible interview with the angel was he to pass into the presence of the representative of that heathenism against which the drawn sword in the angel's hand was really stretched out.

CHAPTER 2: THE "PROPHECIES" OF BALAAM — THE END OF BALAAM — PARALLEL BETWEEN BALAAM AND JUDAS
(NUMBERS 22:36-31:1-20)

THE meeting between the king of Moab and the soothsayer took place at Ir Moab, the "city" or capital of Moab, close by its northern boundary. It commenced with gentle reproaches on the part of the monarch, which, Eastern-like, covered large promises, to which the soothsayer replied by repeating his old profession of being only able to speak the word that God would put in his mouth. There is no need of assuming hypocrisy on his part; both monarch and soothsayer acted quite in character and quite consistently. From Ir Moab they proceeded to Kirjath Huzoth, "the city of streets," the later Kiriathaim.

Here, or in the immediate neighborhood, the first sacrifices were offered, Balaam as well as "the princes" taking part in the sacrificial meal. Next morning, Balak took the soothsayer to the lofty heights of Mount Attarus, to Bamoth Baal "the heights of Baal," so-called because that plateau was dedicated to the service of Baal. The spot, which also bears the names of Baal-meon, Beth Baal-meon, and Beth-meon, commands a magnificent view. Although "too far recessed to show the depression of the Dead Sea," the view northwards stretches as far as Jerusalem, Gerizim, Tabor, Hermon, and Mount Gilead. But, although the eye could sweep so far over the Land of Promise, he would, from the conformation of the mountains, only see "the utmost part of the people," (Numbers 22:41) that is, the outskirts of the camp of Israel.

In accordance with the sacred significance which, as Balaam knew, attached to the number seven in the worship of Jehovah, seven altars were now built on the heights of Baal, and seven bullocks and seven rams offered upon them — a bullock and a ram on each altar. Leaving Balak and the princes of Moab by the altars, Balaam went forth in the regular heathen manner, in the hope of meeting Jehovah (Numbers 23:3), which is explained by Numbers 24:1 as meaning "to seek auguries," such as heathen soothsayers saw in certain natural appearances or portents. And there, on the top of "a bare height," God did meet Balaam, not in auguries, but by putting "a word in Balaam's mouth." As the man shared not in it otherwise than by being the outward instrument of its communication, this "word" was to him only "a parable," and is designated as such in Scripture. Never before so clearly as in presence of the powers of heathenism, assembled to contend against Israel, did Jehovah show forth His almighty power, alike in making use of an instrument almost passive in His hand, and in disclosing His eternal purpose.

FIRST "PARABLE" OF BALAAM

From Aram brought me Balak,
The king of Moab from the mountain of the east -
Come, curse me Jacob, And come, threaten Israel!
How shall I curse whom God doth not curse,
And how shall I threaten whom Jehovah threatens not
For, from the top of the rocks I see him,
And from the hills I behold him:
Lo, a people dwelling alone,
And not reckoning itself among the nations (the Gentiles)!

Who can count the dust of Jacob,

And the number of the fourth part of Israel?

Let me die the death of the righteous.

And let my latter end be like his!

Two things will be noted, without entering into special criticism. First, as to the form of this parable: each thought is embodied in two sentences, with rapid, almost abrupt, transitions from one thought to the other. Secondly, the outward and inward separation of Israel (the former as symbol of the latter) is singled out as the grand characteristic of God's people — a primary truth this of the Old Testament, and, in its spiritual application, of the New Testament also. But even in its literality it has proved true in the history of Israel of old, and still applies to them, showing us that Israel's history is not yet finished; that God has not forgotten His people; and that a purpose of mercy yet awaits them, in accordance with His former dealings. Such a people Balaam could not curse. On the contrary, he could only wish that his death should be like theirs whom God's ordinances and institutions kept separate outwardly, and made righteous inwardly, referring in this, of course, to Israel not as individuals, but in their totality as the people of God. In the language of a German critic, "The pious Israelite could look back with calm satisfaction, in the hour of his death, upon a life rich in proofs of the blessing, forgiving, protecting, delivering, saving mercy of God. With the same calm satisfaction would he look upon his children, and children's children, in whom he lived again, and in whom also he would still take part in the high calling of his nation, and in the ultimate fulfillment of the glorious promise which it had received from God.... And for himself, the man who died in the consciousness of possessing the mercy and love of God, knew also that he would carry them with him as an inalienable possession, a light in the darkness of Sheol. He knew that he would be 'gathered to his fathers' — a thought which must have been a very plenteous source of consolation, of hope, and of joy."

THE SECOND "PARABLE" OF BALAAM

It was but natural that Balak should have been equally surprised and incensed at the words of the soothsayer. The only solution he could suggest was, that a fuller view of the camp of Israel might change the disposition of the magician. "Come, I pray thee, with me unto another place, from whence thou mayest see them (viz., in their totality); only the end (utmost part) of them seest thou, but the whole of them thou seest not — and from thence curse me them." The station now selected was on the field of the watchers," on the top of Pisgah, affording not only a full view of the camp, but of the Land of Promise itself. Here Moses, not long afterwards, took his farewell prospect of the goodly heritage which the Lord had assigned to His people. The same formalities as before having been gone through, in regard to altars and sacrifices, Balaam once more returned to Balak with the following message:

Rise up, Balak, and hear,

Hearken to me, son of Zippor!

Not man is God that He should lie,

Nor a son of man that He should repent!

Hath He said, and shall He not do it,

Hath He spoken, and shall He not fulfill it?

Behold, to bless, I have received -

And He hath blessed, and I cannot turn it back!

He beholdeth not iniquity in Jacob,

And He looketh not upon distress in Israel:

Jehovah his God is with him,
And the king's jubilee in the midst of him.
God bringeth them out of Egypt -
As the unwearied strength of the buffalo is his.
For, no augury in Jacob, no soothsaying in Israel,
According to the time it is said to Jacob and to Israel what God doeth.
Behold, the people, like a lioness it riseth,
And like a lion it raiseth itself up -
He shall not lie down, till he has eaten the prey,
And drink the blood of the slain.

The meaning of this second "parable" needs no special explanation. Only it will be noticed, that the progress of thought is successively marked by four lines — the last two always expressing the ground, or showing the foundation of the two first. The center couplet is the most important. It marks for ever, that the Covenant-Presence of God in Israel, or, as we should now express it, that the grace of God, is the ultimate cause of the forgiveness of sins, and that the happy realization of Jehovah as the King is the ground of joy. Whenever and wherever that Presence is wanting only unforgiven sin is beheld; wherever that shout is not heard only misery is felt.

THE THIRD "PARABLE" OF BALAAM

In his despair Balak now proposed to try the issue from yet a third locality. This time a ridge somewhat farther north was selected — "the top of Peor that looketh toward Jeshimon." A third time seven altars were built and sevenfold sacrifices offered. But there was a marked difference in the present instance. Balaam went no more "as at other times to seek for auguries" (Numbers 24:1). Nor did Jehovah now, as formerly (23:5, 16), "put a word in his mouth." But "the Spirit of God came upon him" (24:2), in the same manner as afterwards upon Saul (1 Samuel 19:23) — he was in the ecstatic state, powerless and almost unconscious, or, as Balaam himself describes it, with his outward eyes shut (ver. 3), and "falling," as if struck down, while seeing "the vision of the Almighty," and "having his (inner) eyes opened" (ver. 4).

Saith Balaam, the son of Beor,
And saith the man with closed eye,
Saith he, hearing the words of God,
Beholding the vision of the Almighty: he beholdeth -
falling down — and with open eyes!
How good are thy tabernacles, Jacob,
Thy dwellings, O Israel -
Like (watered) valleys they stretch, like gardens by a river,
Like aloes Jehovah planted, like cedars by the waters.
Flow waters from his twin buckets — and his seed by many waters,
Higher than Agag shall be his king — and his kingdom be exalted.
God brings him from Egypt — his the unwearied strength of the buffalo -
He shall eat the nations (Gentiles) his enemies — and their bones
shall he gnaw — and his arrows shall he split.
He coucheth, lieth down like a lion and like a lioness - who shall rouse him?
Blessed he that blesseth thee, and cursed he that curseth thee!

We can scarcely wonder that the bitter disappointment of Balak should now have broken forth in angry reproaches. But Balaam had not yet finished his task. Before leaving the king he must deliver another part of the message, which he had already received from Jehovah, but not yet spoken.

"Come, I will advise thee what this people shall do to thy people in the latter days" (24:14).

PROPHETIC MESSAGE THROUGH BALAAM IN FOUR "PARABLES"

First "parable," descriptive first of the "latter days," and then referring to
Moab, as the representative of heathenism:
Saith Balaam, the son of Beor,
and saith the man with closed eye,
Saith he, hearing the words of God, and knowing the knowledge of
the Most High,
Beholding the vision of the Almighty: he beholdeth — falling down
- and with open eyes:
I behold Him, but not now — I descry Him, but not nigh!
Cometh a Star from Jacob, and rises a Sceptre from Israel,
And dasheth the two sides of Moab, and overthroweth the sons of
tumult.
And Edom shall be a possession, and a possession shall be Seir
- his enemies —
And Israel is doing mighty things!
And shall come from Jacob (a ruler)
And shall destroy what remaineth out of the cities.

Second "parable" against Amalek — as the representative of heathenism in its first contest against Israel:
And he beheld Amalek, and he took up his parable, and said:
First of the Gentiles Amalek — and his latter end even unto
destruction.

Third "parable" in favor of the Kenites as the friends and allies of Israel:
And he beheld the Kenites, and he took up his parable, and said:
Durable thy dwelling-place, and placed on the rock thy nest.
For shall Kajin be for destruction,
Until Assbur shall lead thee away?

Fourth "parable" concerning the Assyrian empire, and the kingdoms of
this world, or prophecy of "the end," appropriately beginning with a
"woe:"
And he took up his parable, and said:
Woe! who shall live when God putteth this?
And ships from the side of Chittim — and afflict Asshur, and
afflict Eber -
And he also unto destruction!

This latter may, indeed, be characterized as the most wonderful of prophecies. More than a thousand years before the event, not only the rising of the great world-empire of the West is here predicted, with its conquest of Asshur and Eber (i.e, of the descendants of Eber) (Genesis 10:21), but far beyond this the final destruction of that world-empire is foretold! In fact, we have here a series of prophecies, commencing with the appearance of the Messiah and closing with the destruction of Anti-Christ. To this there is no parallel in Scripture, except in the visions of Daniel. No ingenuity of hostile criticism can take from, or explain away the import of this marvelous prediction.

And now the two parted — the king to go to his people, the soothsayer, as we gather from the sequel, to the tents of Midian. But we meet Balaam only too soon again. One who had entered on such a course could not stop short of the terrible end. He had sought to turn away Jehovah from His people, and failed. He would now endeavor to turn the people from Jehovah. If he succeeded in this, the consequences to Israel would be such as Balak had desired to obtain. By his advice (Numbers 31:16; Revelation 2:14) the children of Israel were seduced into idolatry and all the vile abominations connected with it.

In the judgment which ensued, not fewer than 4,000 Israelites perished, till the zeal of Phinehas stayed the plague, when in his representative capacity he showed that Israel, as a nation, abhorred idolatry and the sins connected with it, as the greatest crime against Jehovah. But on "the evil men and seducers" speedy judgment came. By God's command the children of Israel were avenged of the Midianites. In the universal slaughter of Midian, Balaam also perished. The figure of Balaam stands out alone in the history of the Old Testament. The only counterpart to it is that of Judas, the traitor. Balaam represented the opposition of heathenism; Judas that of Judaism. Both went some length in following the truth; Balaam honestly acknowledged the God of Israel, and followed His directions: Judas owned the Messianic appearance in Jesus, and joined His disciples. But in the crisis of their inner history, when that came which, in one form or another, must be to every one the decisive question — each failed. Both had stood at the meeting and parting of the two ways, and both chose that course which rapidly ended in their destruction. Balaam had expected the service of Jehovah to be quite other from what he found it; and, trying to make it such as he imagined and wished, he not only failed, but stumbled, fell, and was broken. Judas, also, if we may be allowed the suggestion, had expected the Messiah to be quite other than he found Him; disappointment, perhaps failure in the attempt to induce Him to alter His course, and an increasingly widening gulf of distance between them, drove him, step by step, to ruin. Even the besetting sins of Balaam and of Judas — covetousness and ambition — are the same. And as, when Balaam failed in turning Jehovah from Israel, he sought — only too successfully — to turn Israel from the Lord; so when Judas could not turn the Christ from His purpose towards His people, he also succeeded in turning Israel, as a nation, from their King. In both instances, also, for a moment a light more bright than before was cast upon the scene. In the case of Balaam we have the remarkable prophetic utterances, reaching far beyond the ordinary range of prophetic vision; at the betrayal of Judas, we hear the prophetic saying of the High-priest going far beyond the knowledge of the time, that Jesus should die, not only for His own people, but for a ruined world. And, lastly, in their terrible end, they each present to us most solemn warning of the danger of missing the right answer to the great question — that of absolute and implicit submission of mind, heart, and life to the revealed Covenant-Will of God.

CHAPTER 3: THE SECOND CENSUS OF ISRAEL — THE "DAUGHTERS OF ZELOPHEHAD" — APPOINTMENT OF MOSES' SUCCESSOR — SACRIFICIAL ORDINANCES — THE WAR AGAINST MIDIAN — ALLOCATION OF TERRITORY EAST OF THE JORDAN — LEVITICAL AND CITIES OF REFUGE.

(NUMBERS 26-36)

BEFORE describing the closing scene of Moses' life, we may here conveniently group together brief notices of the events intervening between the judgment of "the plague" on account of Israel's sin (Numbers 25) and the last discourses of Moses recorded in the Book of Deuteronomy.

1. A second census of Israel was taken by Divine direction (Numbers 26). The arrangements for it were in all probability the same as those at the first census, thirty-eight years before (Numbers 1). The "plague" had swept away any who might yet have remained of the old doomed generation, which had come out of Egypt. At any rate, none such were now left (Numbers 26:64). This may have been the reason for taking a new census. But its main object was in view of the approaching apportionment of the land which Israel was so soon to possess. Accordingly, the census was not taken as before (Numbers 1), according to the number of individuals in each tribe, but according to "families." This corresponded in the main with the names of the grandsons and great-grandsons of Jacob, enumerated in Genesis 46. In reference to the future division of the land, it was arranged that the extent of the "inheritance" allotted to each tribe should correspond to its numbers (Numbers 26:52-54). But the exact locality assigned to each was to be determined "by lot" (vers. 55, 56), so that each tribe might feel that it had received its "possession" directly from the Lord Himself.

The proposed division of the land brought up a special question of considerable importance to Israel. It appears that one Zelophehad, of the tribe of Manasseh, and of the family of Gilead, had died — not in any special judgment, but along with the generation that perished in the wilderness. Having left no sons, his daughters were anxious to obtain a "possession," lest their father's name should be "done away from among his family" (Numbers 27). By Divine direction, which Moses had sought, their request was granted, and it became "a statute of judgment" in Israel — a juridical statute — that daughters, or in their default — the nearest kinsman, should enter upon the inheritance of those who died without leaving sons.

In all such cases, of course the children of those who obtained the possession would have to be incorporated, not with the tribe to which they originally belonged, but with that in which their "inheritance" lay. Thus the "name" of a man would not "be done away from among his family." Nor was this "statute" recorded merely on account of its national bearing, but for higher reasons. For this desire to preserve a name in a family in Israel sprang not merely from feelings natural in such circumstances, but was connected with the hope of the coming Messiah. Till He appeared, each family would fain have preserved its identity. Several instances of such changes from one tribe to another, through maternal inheritance, are recorded in Scripture (comp. 1 Chronicles 2:34, 35; Numbers 32:41, and

Deuteronomy 3:14, 15, and 1 Chronicles 2:21-23; and notably, even in the case of priests, Ezra 2:61, 62, and Nehem. 7:63 and 64).

2. God intimated once more to Moses his impending death, before actual entrance into the Land of Promise (Numbers 27:12-14). In so doing, mention of the sin which had caused this judgment was repeated, to show God's holiness and justice, even in the case of His most approved servants. On the other hand, this second reminder also manifested the faithfulness of the Lord, Who would have his servant, as it were, set his house in order, that he might meet death, not at unawares, but with full consciousness of what was before him. It is touching to see how meekly Moses received the sentence. Faithful to the end in his stewardship over God's house, his chief concern was, that God would appoint a suitable successor, so "that the congregation of the Lord be not as sheep which have no shepherd" (vers. 15-17). To this office Joshua, who had the needful spiritual qualifications, was now set apart by the laying on of Moses' hands, in presence of Eleazar the priest and of the congregation. Yet only part of Moses'" honor" — so much as was needful to ensure the obedience of Israel — was put upon Joshua, while his public movements were to be directed by "the judgment of the Urim" and Thummim. Thus did God not only vindicate the honor of His servant Moses, but also show that the office which Moses had filled was, in its nature, unique, being typical of that committed in all its fullness to the Great Head of the Church.

3. Now that the people were about to take possession of the land, the sacrificial ordinances were once more enjoined, and with full details. The daily morning and evening sacrifice had already been previously instituted in connection with the altar of burnt-offering (Exodus 29:38-42). To this daily consecration of Israel were now added the special sacrifices of the Sabbath — symbolical of a deeper and more special dedication on God's own day. The Sabbatic and the other festive sacrifices were always brought in addition to the daily offering. Again, the commencement of every month was marked by a special sacrifice, with the addition of a sin-offering, while the blast of the priests' trumpets was intended, as it were, to bring Israel's prayers and services in remembrance before the Lord. If the beginning of each month was thus significantly consecrated, the feast of unleavened bread (from the 15th to the 21st of Abib), which made that month the beginning of the year, was marked by the repetition on each of its seven days of the sacrifices which were prescribed for every "new moon." The Paschal feast (on the 14th of Abib) had no general congregational sacrifice, but only that of the lamb for the Paschal supper in each household. Lastly, the sacrifices for the feast of weeks were the same as those for the feast of unleavened bread, with the addition of the two "wave loaves" and their accompanying sacrifices prescribed in Leviticus 23:7-21. This concluded the first festive cycle in the year.

The second cycle of feasts took place in the seventh or sacred month — seven being the sacred number, and that of the covenant. It began with new moon's day when, besides the daily, and the ordinary new moon's offerings, special festive sacrifices were brought (Numbers 29:1-6). Then on the 10th of that month was the "Day of Atonement," while on the 15th commenced the feast of tabernacles, which lasted seven days, and was followed by an octave. All these feasts had their appropriate sacrifices.

The laws as to sacrifices appropriately close with directions about "vows" (Numbers 30). In all the ordinances connected with the sacred seasons, the attentive reader will mark the symbolical significance attaching to the number seven — alike in the feasts themselves, in their number, their sacrifices, and in that of the days appointed for holy convocation. Indeed, the whole arrangement of time was ordered on the same principle, ascending from the Sabbath of days, to the Sabbath of weeks, of months, of years, and finally to the Sabbath of Sabbatic years, which was the year of Jubilee. And thus all time pointed forward and upward to the "Sabbatism," or sacred rest, that remaineth for "the people of God" (Hebrews 4:9).

4. All that has hitherto been described occurred before the expedition against Midian, by which Israel was "avenged" for the great sin into which they had by treachery been seduced. That expedition which was accompanied by Phinehas, whose zeal had formerly stayed the plague (Numbers 25:7, 8), was not only completely successful, but executed all the Divine directions given. The Midianites seem to have been taken by surprise, and made no resistance. The five kings of Midian, or rather the five chieftains of their various tribes (comp. Numbers 25:15), all of whom seem to have been tributaries of Sihon (comp. Joshua 13:21), were killed, as well as the great bulk of the population, and "their cities," and "tent-villages" (erroneously rendered in the Authorised Version "goodly castles") "burnt with fire." Besides a large number of prisoners, immense booty was taken. To show their gratitude for the marvelous preservation of the people, who had probably surprised their enemies in one of their wild licentious orgies, the princes offered as an "oblation" to the sanctuary all the golden ornaments taken from the Midianites. The value of these amounted, according to the present standard of money, to considerably upwards of 25,000l.

The destruction of the power of Midian, who might have harassed them from the east, secured to Israel the quiet possession of the district east of Jordan, which their arms had already conquered. All along, from the river Arnon in the south, which divided Israel from Moab, to the river Jabbok and far beyond it, the land of Gilead and of Bashan, their borders were safe from hostile attacks.

The accounts of travelers are unanimous in describing that district as specially suited for pastoral purposes. We read of magnificent park like scenery, of wide upland pastures, and rich forests, which everywhere gladden the eye. No wonder that those of the tribes which had all along preserved their nomadic habits, and whose flocks and herds constituted their main possessions and their wealth, should wish to settle in those plains and mountains. To them they were in very truth the land of promise, suited to their special wants, and offering the very riches which they desired. The other side Jordan had little attraction for them; and its possession would have been the opposite of advantageous to a strictly pastoral people. Accordingly, "the children of Gad," and "the children of Reuben" requested of Moses:

"Let this land be given unto thy servants for a possession, and bring us not over Jordan" (Numbers 32:5).

If this proposal did not actually imply that those tribes intended henceforth quietly to settle down, leaving their brethren to fight alone for the conquest of Palestine proper, it was at least open to such interpretation. Moses seems to have understood it in that sense. But, if such had been their purpose, they would not only have separated themselves from the Lord's work and leading, but, by discouraging their brethren, have re-enacted, only on a much larger scale, the sin of those unbelieving spies who, thirty-eight years before, had brought such heavy judgment upon Israel. And the words of Moses prevailed. Whether from the first their real intentions had been right, or the warning of Moses had influenced them for good, they now solemnly undertook to accompany their brethren across Jordan, and to stand by them till they also had entered on their possession. Until then they would only restore the "folds" for their sheep, and rebuild the destroyed cities, to afford safe dwelling-places for their wives and children, and, of course, for such of their number as were either left behind for defense, or incapable of going forth to war.

On this express promise, their request was granted, and the ancient kingdoms of Sihon and of Og were provisionally assigned to Reuben, Gad, and half the tribe of Manasseh, which latter had made special conquests in Gilead (Numbers 32:39). But the actual division of the district among these tribes was left over for the period when the whole country should be allocated among the children of Israel (Joshua 13).

5. The arrangements preparatory to possession of the land appropriately concluded with two series of ordinances. The first of these (Numbers 33:50-34:56) directed the extermination of the Canaanites and of all traces of their idolatry, re-enjoining, at the same time, the partition of the now purified land, by lot, among the tribes of Israel (Numbers 33:50-56).

Next, the boundary lines of Palestine were indicated, and the persons named who were to superintend the partition of the country (Numbers 34). This duty was intrusted to Eleazar the high-priest, and to Joshua, along with ten representative "priests", one from each of the ten tribes, Reuben and Gad having already received their portion on the other side Jordan. The second series of ordinances now enacted (Numbers 35, 36) was, if not of greater importance, yet of even deeper symbolical meaning. According to the curse that had been pronounced upon Levi, that tribe was destined to be "divided in Jacob" (Genesis 49:7). But, in the goodness of God, this was now converted into a blessing alike to Levi and to all Israel. The Levites, the special property and election of the Lord, were to be scattered among all the other tribes, to recall by their presence everywhere the great truths which they symbolized, and to keep alive among the people the knowledge and service of the Lord. On the other hand, they were not to be quite isolated, but gathered together into cities, so that by fellowship and intercourse they might support and strengthen one another. For this purpose forty-eight cities were now assigned to the Levites — of course not exclusive of any other inhabitants, but "to dwell in," that is, they were to have as many houses in them as were required for their accommodation. Along with these houses certain "suburbs," also, or "commons" for their herds and flocks, were to be assigned them — covering in extent on each side a distance of 1000 cubits (1500 feet) round about their cities (Numbers 35:4). Besides, around this inner, another outer circle of 2000 cubits was to be drawn in every direction. These were to be the fields and vineyards of the Levites (ver. 5).

The number of these cities in each tribe varied according to the size of its territory. Thus Judah and Simeon had to furnish nine cities, Naphtali only three, and each of the other tribes four (Joshua 21). Lastly, the thirteen Levitical cities in the territories of Judah, Simeon, and Benjamin were specially assigned to the priests, the descendants of the house of Aaron, while six of the Levitical cities — three east and three west of the Jordan — were set apart as "cities of refuge," for the unintentional manslayer. It is interesting to notice, that even the number of the Levitical cities was significant. They amounted in all to forty-eight, which is a multiple of four, the symbolical number of the kingdom of God in the world, and of twelve, the number of the tribes of Israel.

In regard to the "cities of refuge," for the protection of the unintending manslayer, it must not be imagined that the simple plea of unintentional homicide afforded safety. The law, indeed, provided that the country both east and west of the Jordan should be divided in three parts — each with its "city of refuge," the roads to which were always to be kept in good repair. But, according to the sacred text (Numbers 35:25, comp. Joshua 20:4), a homicide would, on arriving at the gates of a city of refuge, first have to plead his cause before the elders of that city, when, if it approved itself to their minds, they would afford, him provisional protection. If, however, afterwards, the "avenger of blood" claimed his extradition, the accused person would be sent back under proper protection to his own city, where the whole case would be thoroughly investigated. If the homicide was then proved to have been unintentional, the accused would be restored to the "city of refuge," and enjoy its protection, till the death of the high priest set him free to return to his own city.

As for the duty of "avenging blood," its principle is deeply rooted in the Old Testament, and traced up to the relation in which God stands to our world. For, the blood of man, who is God's image, when shed upon earth, which is God's property, "crieth" unto God (Genesis 4:10) — claims payment like an unredeemed debt. Hence the expression "avenger of blood," which should be literally rendered "redeemer of blood." On the other hand, the symbolical meaning of the cities of refuge will readily be understood. There — in the place of God's merciful provision — the manslayer was to find a refuge, sheltered, as it were, under the wings of the grace of God, till the complete remission of the punishment at the death of the high priest — the latter symbolically pointing forward to the death of Him Whom God has anointed our great High Priest, and Who "by His one oblation of Himself once offered," hath made "a full, perfect, and sufficient sacrifice, oblation, and satisfaction" for the sins of the world.

CHAPTER 4: DEATH AND BURIAL OF MOSES.
(DEUTERONOMY 3:23-29; NUMBERS 27:15-23; DEUTERONOMY 34)

ALL was now ready, and Israel about to cross the Jordan and take possession of the Promised Land! It was only natural — one of those traits in the history of the great heroes of the Bible, so peculiarly precious, as showing in their weakness their kinship to our feelings — that Moses should have longed to share in what was before Israel. Looking back the long vista of these one hundred and twenty years — first of life and trial in Egypt, then of loneliness and patient faith while feeding the flocks of Jethro, and, lastly, of labor and weariness in the wilderness, it would indeed have been strange, had he not wished now to have part in the conquest and rest of the goodly land. He had believed in it; he had preached it; he had prayed for it; he had labored, borne, fought for it. And now within reach and view of it must he lay himself down to die?

Scripture records (Deuteronomy 3:23-26), with touching simplicity, what passed between Moses and his Heavenly Father. "And I entreated grace from the Lord at that time, saying: Lord Jehovah, Thou hast begun to show Thy servant Thy greatness and Thy strong hand. For what God is there in heaven or in the earth which doeth like Thy doings and like Thy might? Oh, that I might now go over and see the good land which is on the other side Jordan, this goodly mountain and the Lebanon! And Jehovah was wroth with me on account of you, and hearkened not unto me. And God said to me: Let it now suffice thee — continue not to speak to Me any more on this matter."

The deep feelings of Moses had scarcely bodied themselves in the language of prayer. Rather had it been the pouring forth of his inmost desires before his Father in heaven — a precious privilege which His children possess at all times. But even so Moses had in this also, though but "as a steward" and "afar off," to follow Him whose great type he was, and to learn the peaceful rest of this experience, after a contest of thought and wish: "Nevertheless, not my will, but Thine be done." And it was the good will of God that Moses should lay himself down to rest without entering the land. Although it came in punishment of Israel's and of Moses' sin at the waters of Meribah, yet it was also better that it should be so — better for Moses himself. For on the top of Pisgah God prepared something better for Moses than even entrance into the land of earthly promise.

And now calmly, as a father setteth his house in order, did Moses prepare for his departure. During his life all his thoughts had been for Israel; and he was faithful even unto the death. His last care also had been for the people whom he had loved, and for the work to which he had been devoted — that Jehovah would provide for His congregation "a shepherd" "who may lead them out and bring them in" (Numbers 27:16, 17). Little else was left to be done. In a series of discourses, Moses repeated, and more fully re-stated, to Israel the laws and ordinances of God their King. His last record was "a song" of the mercy and truth of God (Deuteronomy 32); his last words a blessing upon Israel (Deuteronomy 33). Then, amid the respectful silence of a mourning people, he set out alone upon his last pilgrim-journey. All the way up to the highest top of Pisgah the eyes of the people must have followed him. They could watch him as he stood there in the sunset, taking his full view of the land — there to see for himself how true and faithful Jehovah had been. Still could they descry his figure, as, in the shadows of even, it moved towards a valley apart.

After that no mortal eye ever beheld him, till, with Elijah, he stood on the mount of transfiguration. Then indeed was the longing wish of Moses, uttered many, many centuries before, fulfilled far beyond his thinking or hoping at the time. He did stand on "the goodly mountain" within the Land of Promise, worshipping, and giving testimony to Him in "Whom all the promises are yea and amen." It was a worthy crowning this of such a life. Not the faithful steward of Abraham, Eliezer of Damascus, when he brought to his master's son the God-given bride, could with such joy see the end of his faithful stewardship when the heir entered on his possession, as this "steward over God's house," when on that mountain he did homage to "the Son in His own house."

But to Israel down in the valley had Moses never so preached of the truth and faithfulness of Jehovah, and of His goodness and support to His people, as from the top of Pisgah. There was a strange symbolical aptness even in the ascent of the mount, 4,500 feet up, which is "rapid" but "not rugged."

Standing on the highest crest, the prospect would, indeed, seem almost unbounded. Eastwards, stretching into Arabia, rolls a boundless plain — one waving ocean of corn and grass. As the eye turns southwards, it ranges over the land of Moab, till it rests on the sharp outlines of Mounts Hor and Seir, and the rosy granite peaks of Arabia. To the west the land descends, terrace by terrace, to the Dead Sea, the western outline of which can be traced in its full extent. Deep below lies that sea, "like a long strip of molten metal, with the sun mirrored on its surface, waving and undulating in its further edge, unseen in its eastern limits, as though poured from some deep cavern beneath." Beyond it would appear the ridge of Hebron, and then as the eye traveled northwards, successively the sites of Bethlehem and of Jerusalem. The holy city itself would be within range of view — Mount Moriah, the Mount of Olives; on the one side of it the gap in the hills leading to Jericho, while on the other side, the rounded heights of Benjamin would be clearly visible. Turning northwards, the eye follows the winding course of Jordan from Jericho, the city of palm-trees, up the stream. Looking across it, it rests on the rounded top of Mount Gerizim, beyond which the plain of Esdraelon opens, and the shoulder of Carmel appears. That blue haze in the distance is the line of "the utmost sea." Still farther northwards rise the outlines of Tabor, Gilboa, the top of snow-clad Hermort, and the highest range of Lebanon. In front are the dark forests of Ajalon, Mount Gilead, then the land of Bashan and Bozrah.

"And Jehovah shewed Moses all the land of Gilead, unto Dan, and all Naphtali, and the land of Ephraim, and Manasseh, and all the land of Judah, unto the utmost sea, and the Negeb, and the plain of the valley of Jericho, the city of palm-trees, unto Zoar" (Deuteronomy 34:1-3).

Such was the prospect which, from that mountain-top, spread before Moses. And when he had satiated his eyes upon it, he descended into that valley apart to lay him down to rest. Into the mysterious silence of that death and burial at the hands of Jehovah we dare not penetrate. Jewish tradition, rendering the expression (Deuteronomy 34:5) literally, has it that "Moses the servant of Jehovah died there... at the mouth of Jehovah," or, as they put it, by the kiss of the Lord. But from the brief saying of Scripture (Jude 9) may we not infer that although Moses also received in death the wages of sin, yet his body passed not through corruption, however much "the devil," contending as for his lawful prey, "disputed" for its possession, but was raised up to be with Elijah the first to welcome the Lord in His glory? For "men bury a body that it may pass into corruption. If Jehovah, therefore, would not suffer the body of Moses to be buried by men, it is but natural to seek for the reason in the fact that He did not intend to leave him to corruption."

But "there arose not a prophet since in Israel like unto Moses, whom Jehovah knew face to face, in all the signs and the wonders, which Jehovah sent him to do in the land of Egypt to Pharaoh, and to all his servants, and to all his land, and in all that mighty hand, and in all the great terror which Moses showed in the sight of all Israel" (Deuteronomy 34:10-12).

"and Moses verily was faithful in all his house, as a servant, for a testimony of those things which were to be spoken after; but Christ as a Son over His own house; whose house are we, if we hold fast the confidence and the rejoicing of the hope firm unto the end" (Hebrews 3:5, 6).

CHAPTER 5: THE CHARGE TO JOSHUA — DESPATCH OF THE TWO SPIES TO JERICHO — RAHAB.

(JOSHUA 1, 2)

A WIDE, rich plain at the foot of the mountains of Moab, carpeted with wild flowers springing in luxuriant beauty, watered by many rivulets and rills, here and there covered by acacia trees, where birds of brightest plumage carol, and beyond, to the south, by the banks of streams, where scented oleanders rise to a height of twenty-five feet, their flower-laden boughs bending like those of the willow — such is Abel-Shittim, "the meadow of acacias." Beyond it are the fords of Jordan, and the western heights; in the distance southwards, the hills of Judaea, on which the purple light rests. Climate and vegetation are tropical, on the eastern even more than on the western banks of the Jordan. Many memories hallow the place Somewhere here must Elijah have smitten the waters of Jordan, that they parted, ere the fiery chariot wrapt him from the companionship of Elisha. In this district also was the scene of John's baptism, where the Savior humbled Himself to fulfill all righteousness. And on this "meadow of acacias" did an early summer shed its softness when, about the month of March, forty years after the Exodus, the camp of Israel kept thirty days' solemn mourning for Moses (Deuteronomy 34:8). Behind them rose that mountain-top, from which "that saint of God" had seen his last of Israel and of the goodly land, which they were so soon to possess; before them lay the Land of Promise which they were presently to enter.

Such a leader as Moses had been would Israel never more see; nor yet one with whom God had so spoken, "mouth to mouth," as a man with his friend. A feeling of loneliness and awe must have crept over the people and over their new leader, Joshua, like that which Elisha felt, when, alone, he turned him back with the mantle of Elijah that came to him from heaven, to test whether now also the waters would divide at the bidding of the Lord God of Elijah. And the faithful Covenant-God was with Joshua, as he waited, not unbelievingly, but expectantly, in that mourning camp of Abel-Shittim, for a fresh message from God. Though he had been previously designated by God, and set apart to the leadership, it was well he should so wait, not only for his own sake, but also "that the people might afterwards not hesitate gladly to follow his leadership, who had not moved a foot without the leading of God." And in due time the longed-for direction came: not in doubtful language, but renewing alike the commission of Joshua and the promises to Israel. Far as the eye could reach, to the heights of Anti-Lebanon in the extreme distance, to the shores of the Great Sea, to the Euphrates in the East — all was theirs, and not a foeman should withstand them, for God would "not fail nor forsake" their leader. Only two things were requisite: that, in his loving obedience, the word and commands of God should be precious to Joshua; and that in strong faith he should be "very courageous." This latter command was twice repeated, as it were to indicate alike the inward courage of faith and the outward courage of deed.

That this call had found a response in the hearts not only of Joshua, but also of the people, appears from the answer of Reuben, Gad, and the half tribe of Manasseh, when reminded of their obligation to share in the impending warfare of their brethren. While professing their readiness to acknowledge in all things the authority of Joshua, they also expressly made the latter conditional on the continued direction of Jehovah, and re-echoed the Divine admonition to be "strong and of a good courage." So much does success in all we undertake depend on the assurance of faith!

"For he that wavereth is like a wave of the sea driven with the wind and tossed. For let not that man think that he shall receive anything of the Lord" (James 1:6, 7).

Thus directed and encouraged, Joshua gave orders that the people should provide themselves with the necessary victuals to begin, if occasion should offer, their forward march on the third day. In point of fact, however, it was at least five days before that movement could be made. For Joshua had deemed it prudent to adopt proper preparatory measures, although, or rather just because he was assured of Divine help, and trusted in it. Accordingly he had sent, unknown to the people, two spies "to view the land and Jericho." The reason of this secrecy lay probably both in the nature of their errand, and in the sad remembrance of the discouragement which evil report by the spies had formerly wrought among the people (Numbers 14:1). As the two spies stealthily crept up the eight miles of country from the western bank of the Jordan to "the city of palm trees," they must have been struck with the extraordinary "beauty and luxuriance of the district. Even now there is a bright green oasis of several miles square which marks the more rich and populous groves of Jericho."

Its vegetation is most rich and rare; almost every tree is tenanted by the bulbul or Palestinian nightingale, with the "hopping thrush," "the gorgeous Indian blue kingfisher, the Egyptian turtle-dove, and other singing birds of Indian or Abyssinian affinity." "On the plain above are the desert larks and chats, while half an hour's walk takes us to the Mount of Temptation, the home of the griffon, where beautifully plumed partridges, rock-swallows, rock-doves, and other birds abound. But, beyond all others, Jericho is the home of the lovely sun-bird,.... resplendent with all the colors of the humming-bird" — its back brilliant green, its throat blue, and its breast purple, "with a tuft of rich red, orange, and yellow feathers at each shoulder." The little streams — which Elisha healed from its after curse — swarms with fish, while climate and prospect are equally delicious in that early summer-like spring, when the spies visited it. And what the wealth and beauty of this plain must have been when it was crowded with feathery palms, and scented balsam gardens, we learn from the descriptions of Josephus (Ant. xv. 4, 2). This paradise of Canaan was guarded by the fortress of Jericho — one of the strongest in the whole land. Behind its walls and battlements immense wealth was stored, partly natural and partly the result of civilization and luxury. This appears even from the character and value of the spoil which one individual — Achan — could secrete from it (Joshua 7:21).

As the spies neared the city, the setting sun was casting his rays in richest variegated coloring on the limestone mountains which surrounded the ancient Jericho like an amphitheater, rising closest, and to the height of from 1200 to 1500 feet, in the north, where they bear the name of Quarantania, marking the traditional site of the forty days of our Lord's temptation; and thence stretching with widening sweep towards the south. Friend or ally there was none in that city, whose hospitality the two Israelites might have sought. To have resorted to a khan or inn would have been to court the publicity which most of all they wished to avoid. Under these circumstances, the choice of the house of Rahab, the harlot, was certainly the wisest for their purpose. But even so, in the excited state of the public mind, when, as we know (Joshua 2:11), the terror of Israel had fallen upon all, the arrival of two suspicious-looking strangers could not remain a secret. So soon as the gates were shut, and escape seemed impossible, the king sent to make captives of what he rightly judged to be Israelitish spies. But Rahab had anticipated him. Arriving at the same conclusion as the king, and expecting what would happen, she had "hid them" — perhaps hastily — "with the stalks of flax which she had laid in order upon the roof," after the common Eastern fashion of drying flax on the flat roofs of houses. By the adroit admission of the fact that two men, previously unknown to her, had indeed come, to which she added the false statement that they had with equal abruptness left just before the closing of the gates, she succeeded in misleading the messengers of the king. The story of Rahab sounded likely enough; she had seemingly been frank, nor was there any apparent motive for untruthfulness on her part, but quite the opposite, as the same danger threatened all the inhabitants of Jericho. As Rahab had suggested, the messengers "pursued quickly" in the supposed wake of the Jewish emissaries, which would have been "the way to Jordan, unto the fords," by which they must return to the camp of Israel, and the gates were again shut, to make escape from Jericho impossible, if, after all, they had not quitted the city.

Thus far the device of Rahab had succeeded. So soon as night settled upon the city, she repaired to the roof, and acquainted the spies, who were ignorant of any danger, with what had taken place. At the same time she explained the motives of her conduct. They must indeed have listened with wonder, not unmingled with adoring gratitude, as she told them how they, in Canaan, had heard what Jehovah had done for Israel at the Red Sea, and that, by His help, the two powerful kings of the Amorites had been "utterly destroyed." The very language, in which Rahab described the terror that had fallen upon her countrymen, was the same as that uttered prophetically forty years before, when Moses and the children of Israel sang the new song on the other side of the Red Sea, Exodus 15:14-16 (comp. Exodus 23:27; Deuteronomy 2:25; 11:25). But the effect of this knowledge of Jehovah's great doings differed according to the state of mind of those who heard of them. In the Canaanites it called forth the energy of despair in resisting Israel, or rather Israel's God. But in Rahab's heart it awakened far other feelings. She knew that Jehovah had given to Israel the land — and far better than even this, that "Jehovah your God, He is God in heaven above and in earth beneath." Knowing God's purpose, she would shelter the spies, and so further their errand; knowing that He alone was God, she and all near and dear to her must not take part in the daring resistance of her countrymen, but seek safety by separating themselves from them and joining the people of God. And so she implored mercy for herself and her kindred in the day when Jehovah would surely give Israel the victory. Such a request could not be refused, evidenced as its genuineness had been by her "works." The two spies solemnly acceded to it, but on condition that she would prove true to the end, helping on their work by still keeping their mission secret, and evidencing her faith by gathering on the day of trial all her kindred within her house. That house should be distinguished from all other dwellings in Jericho by exhibiting the same "scarlet cord," with which she let down the spies over the city wall upon which her house was built. All throughout, this story is full of deepest symbolical meaning. And in truth, one, prepared so to act, was in heart "an Israelite indeed," and her household already belonged to the "household of faith."

We are now in circumstances to appreciate the faith by which the harlot Rahab perished not with them that were disobedient, when she had "received the spies with peace," a faith which, as St. James argues, evidenced itself "by works" (James 2:25). In so doing, it is not necessary either to represent her in her former life as other than she really was, or even to extenuate her sin in returning a false answer to the king of Jericho. Nor, on the other hand, do we wish to exaggerate the spiritual condition to which she had attained.

Remembering who, and what, and among whom she had been all her life-time, her emphatic confession, that Jehovah, the God of Israel, "He is God in heaven above, and in earth beneath;" her unwavering faith in the truth of His promises, which moved her to self-denying action at such danger and sacrifice, and supported her in it; her separation from her countrymen; her conduct towards the spies at the risk of her life — all show her to have had that faith which "is the substance of things hoped for, the evidence of things unseen;" not a "dead faith," "without works," but one which "wrought with her works, and by works was made perfect." And He Who "giveth more grace" to them who wisely use what they have, marvelously owned and blessed this "first-fruits" from among the Gentiles. Her history, which, in all its circumstances, bears a remarkable analogy to that of the woman of Samaria (John 4), is recorded for the instruction of the Church. And, as in the case of the Hebrew midwives who had preserved Israel (Exodus 1:21), God also "made her a house." She became the wife of Salmon, a prince of the tribe of Judah, and from her sprang in direct line both David (Ruth 4:21) and David's Lord (Matthew 1:4).

But as for the two Israelitish spies, they hid themselves, according to Rahab's advice, for three days among the limestone caves and grottoes which abound in Mount Quarantania, while their pursuers vainly searched for them in the opposite direction of the fords of Jordan. When the fruitless pursuit had ceased, they made their way back to Joshua, expressing to him their conviction, as the result of their mission: "Truly Jehovah hath delivered into our hands all the land; for even all the inhabitants of the country do faint because of us."

CHAPTER 6: MIRACULOUS PARTING OF THE JORDAN, AND THE PASSAGE OF THE CHILDREN OF ISRAEL — GILGAL AND ITS MEANING — THE FIRST PASSOVER ON THE SOIL OF PALESTINE.

(JOSHUA 3-5:12)

THE morrow after the return of the spies, the camp at Shittim was broken up, and the host of Israel moved forward. It consisted of all those tribes who were to have their possessions west of the Jordan, along with forty thousand chosen warriors from Reuben, Gad, and the half tribe of Manasseh. A short march brought them to the brink of Jordan. Strictly speaking, the Jordan has a threefold bank; the largest at the water's edge, which, in spring, is frequently inundated, owing to the melting of snow on Hermon; a middle bank, which is covered with rich vegetation, and an upper bank, which overhangs the river. The people now halted for three days, first to await the Divine direction as to the passage of the river, and then to prepare for receiving in a proper spirit the manifestation of Divine power about to be manifested in the miraculous parting of Jordan. For, as one has remarked, the expression used by Joshua, "the living God is among you" (Joshua 3:10), does not merely imply the presence of God among Israel, but, as the event proved, the operations by which He shows Himself both living and true.

All that was to be done by Israel was Divinely indicated to Joshua, and all was done exactly as it had been directed. First, proclamation was made throughout Israel to "sanctify" themselves, and that not only outwardly by symbolic rites, but also inwardly by turning unto the Lord, in expectant faith of "the wonders" about to be enacted. These were intimated to them beforehand (Joshua 3:5, 13).

Thus passed three days. It was "the tenth day of the first month" (Joshua 4:19), the anniversary of the day on which forty years before Israel had set apart their Paschal lambs (Exodus 12:3), that the miraculous passage of the Jordan was accomplished, and Israel stood on the very soil of the promised land. Before the evening of that anniversary had closed in, the memorial stones were set up in Gilgal. All between those two anniversaries seemed only as a grand historical parenthesis. But the kingdom of God has no blanks or interruptions in its history; there is a grand unity in its course, for Jehovah reigneth. With feelings stirred by such remembrances, and the expectancy of the great miracle to come, did Israel now move forward. First went the Ark, borne by the priests, and, at a reverent distance of 2000 cubits, followed the host. For, it was the Ark of the Covenant which was to make a way for Israel through the waters of Jordan, and they were to keep it in sight, so as to mark the miraculous road, as it was gradually opened to them. It is to this that the Divine words refer (Joshua 3:4): "that ye may know," or rather come to know, recognize, understand, "the way by which ye must go: for ye have not passed this way heretofore." With the exception of Caleb and Joshua, none, at least of the laity, had been grown up at the time, and seen it, when the Lord parted the waters of the Red Sea at the Exodus. Then it had been the uplifted wonder-working rod of Moses by which the waters were parted. But now it was the Ark at whose advance they were stayed. And the difference of the means was quite in accordance with that of the circumstances. For now the Ark of the Covenant was the ordinary symbol of the Divine Presence among Israel; and God commonly employs the ordinary means of grace for the accomplishment of His marvelous purposes of mercy.

It was early spring, in that tropical district the time of early harvest (Joshua 3:15), and the Jordan had overflown its lowest banks. As at a distance of about half a mile the Israelites looked down, they saw that, when the feet of those who bore the Ark touched the waters, they were arrested." Far up "beyond where they stood, at the city of Adam that is beside Zarethan," did the Divine Hand draw up the waters of Jordan, while the waters below that point were speedily drained into the Dead Sea. In the middle of the river-bed the priests with the Ark halted till the whole people had passed over dryshod. Then twelve men, who had previously been detailed for the purpose, took up twelve large stones from where the priests had stood in the river-bed, to erect them a solemn memorial to all times of that wondrous event.

Only after that did the priests come up from Jordan. And when "the soles of the priests' feet were lifted up unto the dry land" (literally, were detached, viz., from the clogging mud, "upon the dry"), "the waters of Jordan returned unto their place, and flowed over all his banks, as before." It must have been towards evening when the rest of the march was accomplished — a distance of about five miles — and Israel's camp was pitched at what afterwards became Gilgal, "in the east border of Jericho," about two miles from the latter city.

The object and meaning of this "notable miracle" are clearly indicated in the sacred text. We know that it was as absolutely necessary in the circumstances as formerly the cleaving of the Red Sea had been. For, at that season of the year, and with the means at their disposal, it would have been absolutely impossible for a large host with women and children to cross the Jordan. But, besides, it was fitting that a miracle similar to that of the Exodus from Egypt should mark the entrance into the Land of Promise; fitting also, that the commencement of Joshua's ministry should be thus Divinely attested like that of Moses (Joshua 3:7). Finally, it would be to Israel a glorious pledge of future victory in the might of their God (ver. 10), while to their enemies it was a sure token of the judgment about to overtake them (Joshua 5:1).

Two things yet remained to be done, before Israel could enter upon the war with Canaan. Although the people of God, Israel had been under judgment for nearly forty years, and those born in the wilderness bore not the covenant mark of circumcision. To renew that rite in their case was the first necessity, so as to restore Israel to its full position as the covenant-people of God.

After that, a privilege awaited Israel which for thirty-eight years they had not enjoyed. Probably the Passover at the foot of Sinai (Numbers 9:1) had been the last, as that feast would not have been observed by the people in their uncircumcision. But at Gilgal their reproach was "rolled away," and the people of God renewed the festive remembrance of their deliverance from Egypt. Truly, that first Passover on the soil of Palestine had a twofold meaning. Even the circumstances recalled its first celebration. As the night of the first Passover was one of terror and judgment to Egypt, so now, within view of the festive camp of Gilgal,

"Jericho was straitly shut up because of the children of Israel: none went out, and none came in" (Joshua 6:1).

And now also the Divine wilderness-provision of the "manna which had clung to them with the tenacity of all God's mercies," ceased on, "the morrow after they had eaten of the old corn of the land: neither had the children of Israel manna any more; but they did eat of the fruits of the land of Canaan that year." And so also have miraculous gifts ceased in the Church, because their continuance has become unnecessary. Similarly will our manna-provision for daily life-need cease, when we at the last enter upon the land of promise, and for ever enjoy its fruits!

CHAPTER 7: THE "PRINCE OF THE HOST OF JEHOVAH" APPEARS TO JOSHUA — THE MIRACULOUS FALL OF JERICHO BEFORE THE ARK OF JEHOVAH.

(JOSHUA 5:13; 6:27)

AT first sight it may seem strange, that, when such fear had fallen upon the people of the land, any attempt should have been made to defend Jericho. But a fuller consideration will help us not only to understand this, but also by-and-by to see special reasons, why this one fortress should have been miraculously given to Israel. Not to mention motives of honor, which would at least have some influence with the men of Jericho, it was one of the main principles of heathenism, that each of their "gods many" was limited in his activity to one special object. But what the Canaanites had heard of Jehovah showed Him to be the God of nature, who clave the Red Sea and arrested the waters of Jordon, and that He was so far also the God of battles, as to give Israel the victory over the Amorite kings. But was His strength also the same as against their gods in reducing strong fortresses? Of that at any rate they had no experience. Trivial as such a question may sound in our ears, we have evidence that it was seriously entertained by heathendom. To mention only one instance, we know that a similar suggestion was made at a much later period, not by obscure men, but by the servants and trusted advisers of Ben-hadad, and that it was acted upon by that monarch in the belief that "Jehovah is God of the hills, but he is not God of the valleys" (1 Kings 20:28). At any rate, it was worth the trial, and Jericho, as already stated, was the strongest fortress in Canaan, and the key to the whole country.

This latter consideration could not but have weighed on the mind of Joshua, as from the camp of Gilgal he "viewed the city." As yet no special direction had been given him how to attack Jericho, and, assuredly, the people whom he commanded were untrained for such work. While such thoughts were busy within him, of a sudden, "as he lifted up his eyes and looked, there stood over against him," not the beleaguered city, but "a man with his sword drawn in his hand." Challenged by Joshua: "Art thou for us, or for our adversaries?" the strange warrior replied: "No! But I am the Captain (or Prince) of the host of Jehovah, now I am come." Here His speech was interrupted — for Joshua fell on his face before Him, and reverently inquired His commands. The reply: "Loose thy shoe from off thy foot, for the place whereon thou standest is holy," must have convinced Joshua that this Prince of the host of Jehovah was none other than the Angel of the Covenant, Who had spoken to Moses out of the burning bush (Exodus 3:4), and Who was co-equal with Jehovah. Indeed, shortly afterwards, we find Him expressly spoken of as Jehovah (Joshua 6:2).

So then the mission of Joshua was substantially the continuation and completion of that of Moses. As at the commencement of the latter, the Angel of the Covenant had appeared and spoken out of the burning bush, so He now also appeared to Joshua, while the symbolical act of "loosing the shoe off his foot," in reverent acknowledgment of the Holy One of Israel, recalled the vision of Moses, and at the same time connected it with that of his successor. Having assured Joshua of complete victory, the Angel of Jehovah gave him detailed directions how Israel was to compass Jericho, under the leadership of the Ark of the Lord, and how, when the wall of the city had fallen, the people were to act. Implicit obedience of what in its nature was symbolical, was absolutely requisite, and Joshua communicated the command of the Lord both to priests and people.

And now a marvelous sight would be witnessed from the walls of Jericho. Day by day, a solemn procession left the camp of Israel. First came lightly armed men, then followed seven priests blowing continually, not the customary silver trumpets, but large horns, the loud sound of which penetrated to the far distance, such as had been heard at Sinai (Exodus 19:16, 19; 20:18). The same kind of horns were to be used on the first day of the seventh month (Leviticus 23:24), and to announce the year of Jubilee (Leviticus 25:9).

Thus heralded, came the Ark of Jehovah, borne by the priests, and after it "the rereward" of Israel. So they did for six days, each day once encompassing the walls of Jericho, but in solemn silence, save for the short sharp tones, or the long-drawn blasts of the priests' horns. The impression made by this long, solemn procession, which appeared and disappeared, and did its work, in solemn silence, only broken by the loud shrill notes of the horns, must have been peculiar. At length came the seventh day. Its work began earlier than on the others — "about the dawning of the day." In the same order as before, they encompassed the city, only now seven times. "And it came to pass at the seventh time, when the priests blew with the trumpets, Joshua said unto the people, Shout; for Jehovah hath given you the city." "And it came to pass, when the people heard the sound of the trumpet, and the people shouted with a great shout, that the wall fell down flat, so that the people went up into the city, every man straight before him, and they took the city." As for Jericho itself, Joshua had by Divine command declared it "cherem," or "devoted" to Jehovah (Joshua 6:17). In such cases, according to Leviticus 27:28, 29, no redemption was possible, but, as indicated in Deuteronomy 13:16, alike the inhabitants and all the spoil of the city was to be destroyed, "only the silver, and the gold, and the vessels of brass and of iron" being reserved and "put into the treasury of the house of Jehovah" (Joshua 6:24; comp. Numbers 31:22, 23, 50-54). This was not the ordinary sentence against all the cities of Canaan. In all other cases the inhabitants alone were "smitten with the edge of the sword" (Joshua 8:26; 10:28; comp. Deuteronomy 2:34; 3:6; 8:2; 20:16), while the cattle and the spoil were preserved. But in the case of Jericho, for reasons to be afterwards stated, the whole city, with all that it contained, was cherem. Only Rahab, "and her father's household, and all that she had," were saved from the general wreck.

It lies on the surface of the Scriptural narrative that "a notable miracle," unparalleled in history, had in this case been "wrought" by Jehovah for Israel. As a German writer puts it: It would have been impossible to show it more clearly, that Jehovah had given the city to Israel. First, the river was made to recede, to allow them entrance into the land; and now the walls of the city were made to fall, to give them admission to its first and strongest city. Now such proofs of the presence and help of Jehovah, so soon after Moses' death, must have convinced the most carnal among Israel, that the same God who had cleft the Red Sea before their fathers was still on their side. And in this light must the event also have been viewed by the people of Canaan. But, besides, a deeper symbolical meaning attached to all that had happened. The first and strongest fortress in the land Jehovah God bestowed upon His people, so to speak, as a free gift, without their having to make any effort, or to run any risk in taking it.

A precious pledge this of the ease with which all His gracious promises were to be fulfilled. Similarly, the manner in which Israel obtained possession of Jericho was deeply significant. Evidently, the walls of Jericho fell, not before Israel, but before the Ark of Jehovah, or rather, as it is expressly said in Joshua 6:8, before Jehovah Himself, whose presence among His people was connected with the Ark of the Covenant. And the blast of those jubilee-horns all around the doomed city made proclamation of Jehovah, and was, so to speak, the summons of His kingdom, proclaiming that the labor and sorrow of His people were at an end, and they about to enter upon their inheritance. This was the symbolical and typical import of the blasts of the jubilee-horns, whenever they were blown. Hence also alike in the visions of the prophets and in the New Testament the final advent of the kingdom of God is heralded by the trumpet-sound of His angelic messengers (comp. 1 Corinthians 15:52; 1 Thessalonians 4:16; Revelation 20 and 21). But, on the other hand, the advent of the kingdom of God always implies destruction to His enemies. Accordingly, the walls of Jericho must fall, and all the city be destroyed. Nor will the reader of this history fail here also to notice the significance of the number seven — seven horns, seven priests, seven days of compassing the walls, repeated seven times on the seventh day! The suddenness of the ruin of Jericho, which typified the kingdom of this world in its opposition to that of God, has also its counterpart at the end of the present dispensation. For "the day of the Lord cometh as a thief in the night; and when they shall say, Peace and safety, then sudden destruction cometh upon them, as travail upon a woman with child; and they shall not escape."

Lastly, it was fitting that Jericho should have been entirely devoted unto the Lord; not only that Israel might gain no immediate spoil by what the Lord had done, but also because the city, as the firstfruits of the conquest of the land, belonged unto Jehovah, just as all the first, both in His people and in all that was theirs, was His — in token that the whole was really God's property, Who gave everything to His people, and at Whose hands they held their possessions. But, to indicate the state of heart and mind with which Israel compassed the city, following the Ark in solemn silence, we recall this emphatic testimony of Scripture (Hebrews 11:30):

"By faith the walls of Jericho fell down, after they were compassed about seven days."

In this instance also, as just before the Lord cleft the Red Sea, and again afterwards, when in answer to Jehoshaphat's prayer God destroyed the heathen combination against His people, the Divine call to them was, "Stand ye still" (in expectant faith) "and see the salvation of Jehovah" (Exodus 14:13, 2 Chronicles 20:17). And so it ever is to His believing people in similar circumstances.

CHAPTER 8: UNSUCCESSFUL ATTACK UPON AI — ACHAN'S SIN, AND JUDGEMENT — AI ATTACKED A SECOND TIME AND TAKEN.
(JOSHUA 7-8:29)

THE conquest of Jericho without fight on the part of Israel had given them full pledge of future success. But, on the other hand, also, might it become a source of greatest danger, if the gracious promises of God were regarded as national rights, and the presence of Jehovah as secured, irrespective of the bearing of Israel towards Him. It was therefore of the utmost importance, that from the first it should appear that victory over the enemy was Israel's only so long as the people were faithful to the covenant of their God.

In their progress towards the interior of the land, the fortress next to be taken was Ai. Broken up as the country seems to have been into small territories, each under an independent chieftain or "king," who reigned in his fortified city and held sway over the district around, a series of sieges rather than of pitched battles was to be expected. Ai, situated on a conical hill about ten miles to the west of Jericho, was a comparatively smaller city, numbering only 12,000 inhabitants (Joshua 8:25). Yet its position was exceedingly important. Southwards it opened the road to Jerusalem, which is only a few hours distant; northwards it commanded access to the heart of the country, so that, as we find in the sequel, a victorious army could march thence unopposed into the fertile district of Samaria.

Moreover, the fate of Ai virtually decided also that of Bethel. The latter city, ruled by another independent "king," lay to the west of Ai, being separated from it by a high intervening hill. This hill, about midway between Bethel and Ai, possessed special interest. It was the site of Abram's altar, when he first entered the land (Genesis 12:8). Here also had the patriarch stood with Lot, overlooking in the near distance the rich luxuriance of the Jordan valley, when Lot made his fatal choice of residence (Genesis 13:4, 10). Standing on this hill, a valley is seen to stretch westward to Bethel, while eastward, around Ai, "the wadys which at first break down steeply... descend gradually for about three quarters of a mile, before taking their final plunge to the Jordan valley. The gently sloping ground is well studded with olive trees." This rapid sketch of the locality will help us to realize the events about to be recorded.

The advance now to be made by Israel was so important, that Joshua deemed it a proper precaution to send "men to view Ai." Their report satisfied him that only an army-corps of about 3000 men was requisite to take that city. But the expedition proved far from successful. The men of Ai issued from the city, and routed Israel, killing thirty-six men, pursuing the fugitives as far as "Shebarim" ("mines," or perhaps "quarries" where stones are broken), and smiting them "in the going down," that is, to about a mile's distance, where the wadys, descending from Ai, take "their final plunge" eastwards. Viewed in any light, the event was terribly ominous. It had been Israel's first fight west of the Jordan — and their first defeat. The immediate danger likely to accrue was a combination of all their enemies round about, and the utter destruction of a host which had become dispirited. But there was even a more serious aspect than this. Had God's pledged promises now failed? or, if this could not even for a moment be entertained, had the Lord given up His gracious purpose, His covenant with Israel, and the manifestation of His "Name" among all nations, connected therewith?

Feelings like these found expression in Joshua's appeal to God, when, with rent clothes and ashes upon their heads, he and the elders of Israel lay the livelong day, in humiliation and prayer, before the Lord, while in the camp "the hearts of the people" had "melted and became as water." We require to keep in view this contrast between the impotent terror of the people and the praying attitude of their leaders, to realize the circumstances of the case; the perplexity, the anxiety, and the difficulties of Joshua, before we judge of the language which he used. It fell indeed far short of the calm confidence of a Moses; yet, in its inquiry into the reason of God's dealings, which were acknowledged, faith, so to speak, wrestled with doubt (Joshua 7:7), while rising fear was confronted by trust in God's promises (ver. 9). Best of all, the inward contest found expression in prayer. It was therefore, after all, a contest of faith, and faith is "the victory over the world."

Strange, that amidst this universal agitation, one should have remained unmoved, who, all the time, knew that he was the cause of Israel's disaster and of the mourning around. Yet his conscience must have told him that, so long as it remained, the curse of his sin would follow his brethren, and smite them with impotence. It is this hardness of impenitence — itself the consequence of sin — which, when properly considered, vindicates, or rather demonstrates, the rightness of the Divine sentence afterwards executed upon Achan. His sin was of no ordinary character. It had not only been a violation of God's express command, but daring sacrilege and profanation. And this under circumstances of the most aggravated character. Besides, Joshua had, just before the fall of Jericho, warned the people of the danger to themselves and to all Israel of taking "of the accursed thing" (Joshua 6:18). So emphatic had been the ban pronounced upon the doomed city, that it was extended to all time, and even over the whole family of any who should presume to restore Jericho as a fortress (6:26).

And, in face of all this, Achan had allowed himself to be tempted! He had yielded to the lowest passion. One of those Babylonish garments, curiously woven with figures and pictures (such as classical writers describe), a massive golden ornament, in the shape of a tongue, and a sum of silver, amounting to about 25l in a city the walls of which had just miraculously fallen before the Lord, had induced him to commit this daring sin! More than that, when it had come true, as Joshua predicted (6:18), that such theft would "make the camp of Israel a curse, and trouble it," Achan had still persisted in his sin.

It will be remembered that, forty years before, at the brink of the Red Sea, "the Lord said unto Moses: Wherefore criest thou unto Me? speak unto the children of Israel, that they go forward!" (Exodus 14:15). As then, so now, when Joshua and the elders of Israel lay on their faces before the Lord, not prayer, but action was required. In the one case it was not exercise of faith to pray where obedience was called for; nor yet, in the other, had prayer any meaning, nor could it expect an answer, while sin remained unremoved. And so it ever is. The cause of Israel's disaster lay, not in want of faithfulness on the part of the Lord, but on that of Israel. Their sin must now be searched out, and "the accursed" be "destroyed from among them." For, although the sin of Achan was that of an individual, it involved all Israel in its guilt. The sinner was of Israel, and his sin was in Israel's camp. It is needless here to discuss the question, how one guilty of sin should involve in its consequences those connected with him, whether by family or social ties. It is simply a fact, admitting no discussion, and is equally witnessed when God's law in nature, and when His moral law is set at defiance. The deepest reason of it lies, indeed, in this, that the God of nature and of grace is also the founder of society; for, the family and society are not of man's devising, but of God's institution, and form part of His general plan. Accordingly, God deals with us not merely as individuals, but also as families and as nations. To question the rightness of this would be to question alike the administration, the fundamental principles, and the plan of God's universe. But there is reason for devout thankfulness, that we can, and do recognize the presence of God in both nature and in history. The highest instance of the application of this law, is that which has rendered our salvation possible. For just as we had sinned and destroyed ourselves through our connection with the first Adam, so are we saved through the second Adam — the Lord from heaven, Who has become our Substitute, that in Him we might receive the adoption of children.

The tidings, that the sin of one of their number had involved Israel in judgment, must have rapidly spread through the camp of Israel. But even this knowledge and the summons to sanctify themselves, that on the morrow the transgressor might be designated by the Lord, did not move Achan to repentance and confession. And now all Israel were gathered before the Lord. First approached the princes of the twelve tribes. Each name of a tribe had been written separately, when "the lot" that "came up," or was drawn, bore the name of Judah.

Thus singled out, the heads of the various clans of Judah next presented themselves, when the lot designated that of Zarhi. And still the solemn trial went on, with increasing solemnity, as the circle narrowed, when successively the families of Zabdi, and finally, among them, the household of Achan was singled out by the hand of God. All this time had Achan kept silence. And now he stood alone before God and Israel, that guilty one who had "troubled" all. Would he at the last confess, and "give glory to Jehovah" by owning Him as the God who seeth and knoweth all sin, however deeply hidden? It was in the language of sorrow, not of anger, that Joshua adjured him. It wrung from Achan a full admission of his crime. How miserable the whole thing must have sounded in his own ears, when he had put the facts of his sin into naked words; how paltry the price at which he had sold himself, when it was brought into the broad sunlight and "laid out before the Lord," in the sight of Joshua and of all Israel. One thing more only remained to be done. They led forth the wretched man, with all his household, and all that belonged to them, and all Israel stoned him. And then they burned the dead body, and buried all beneath a heap of stones, alike as a memorial and a warning. But the valley they called that of "Achor," or trouble — while the echoes of that story sounded through Israel's history to latest times, in woe and in weal, for judgment and for hope (Isaiah 65:10; Hosea 2:15).

The sin of Israel having been removed, God once more assured Joshua of His presence to give success to the undertaking against Ai. In pledge thereof He was even pleased to indicate the exact means which were to be used in reducing the city. A corps of 30,000 men was accordingly detailed, of whom 5000 were placed in ambush on the west side of Ai, where, under shelter of the wood, their presence was concealed from Ai, and, by the intervening hill, from Bethel. While the main body of the Israelites under Joshua were to draw away the defenders of Ai by feigned flight, this corps was at a given signal to take the city, and after having set it on fire, to turn against the retreating men. Such was the plan of attack, and it was closely adhered to. "The ambush" lay on the west of Ai, while the main body of the host pitched north of the city, a valley intervening between them and Ai. Next, Joshua moved into the middle of that valley. Early the following morning the king of Ai discovered this advance of the Israelitish camp, and moved with his army to the "appointed place," right in front of "the plain," which, as we know from the description of travelers, was covered by olive trees.

The battlefield was well chosen, since Ai occupied the vantage-ground on the slope, while an advance by Israel would be checked and broken by the olive plantation which they would have to traverse. Joshua and all Israel now feigned a retreat, and fled in an easterly direction towards the wilderness. Upon this, all the people that were in Ai, in their eager haste to make the victory decisive, "allowed themselves to be called away" to pursue after Israel, till they were drawn a considerable distance from the city.

The olive plantation now afforded those who had lain in ambush shelter for their advance. The preconcerted signal was given. Joshua, who probably occupied a height apart, watching the fight, lifted his spear. As the outposts of the ambush saw it, and reported that the signal for their advance had been given, a rush would be made up the steep sides of the hill towards the city. But the signal would also be perceived and understood by the main army of Israel, and they now anxiously watched the result of movements which they could not follow. They had not long to wait. Above the dark green olive trees, above the rising slopes, above the white walls, curled slowly in the clear morning air the smoke of the burning city. Something in the attitude and movements of Israel must have betrayed it, for "the men of Ai looked behind them," only to see that all was lost, and no means of escape left them. And now the host of Israel "turned again," while those who had set Ai on fire advanced in an opposite direction. Between these two forces the men of Ai were literally crushed. Not one of them escaped from that bloody plain and slope. The slaughter extended to the district around. Finally, the king of Ai was put to death, and his dead body "hanged upon a tree till eventide."

But of what had been Ai "they made a Tel (or heap) for ever." Never was Scripture saying more literally fulfilled than this. For a long time did modern explorers in vain seek for the site of Ai, where they knew it must have stood. "The inhabitants of the neighboring villages," writes Canon Williams, to whom the merit of the identification really belongs, "declared repeatedly and emphatically that this was Tel, and nothing else. I was satisfied that it should be so when, on subsequent reference to the original text of Joshua 8:28, I found it written, that 'Joshua burnt Ai, and made it a Tel for ever, even a desolation unto this day!' There are many Tels in modern Palestine, that land of Tels, each Tel with some other name attached to it to mark the former site. But the site of Ai has no other name 'unto this day.' It is simply et-Tel — the heap 'par excellence.'"

CHAPTER 9: SOLEMN DEDICATION OF THE LAND AND OF ISRAEL ON MOUNTS EBAL AND GERIZIM — THE DECEIT OF THE GIBEONITES

(JOSHUA 8:30, 9:1-27)

BY the miraculous fall of Jericho God had, so to speak, given to His people the key to the whole land; with the conquest of Ai they had themselves entered, in His strength, upon possession of it. The first and most obvious duty now was, to declare, by a grand national act, in what character Israel meant to hold what it had received of God. For, as previously explained, it could never have been the Divine object in all that had been, or would be done, merely to substitute one nation for another in the possession of Palestine; but rather to destroy the heathen, and to place in their room His own redeemed and sanctified people, so that on the ruins of the hostile kingdom of this world, His own might be established. To mark the significance of the act by which Israel was to declare this, it had before been prescribed by Moses as a first duty (Deuteronomy 27:2), and detailed directions given for it (Deuteronomy 27). The act itself was to consist of three parts. The law — that is, the commands, "statutes," and "rights," contained in the Pentateuch — was to be written on "great stones," previously covered with "plaster," in the manner in which inscriptions were made on the monuments of Egypt. Then sacrifices were to be offered on an altar of "whole stones." The memorial stones were to be set up, and the sacrifices offered on Mount Ebal. But the third was to be the most solemn part of the service. The priests with the Ark were to occupy the intermediate valley, and six of the tribes (Simeon, Levi, Judah, Issachar, Joseph, and Benjamin) — those which had sprung from the lawful wives of Israel — were to stand on Mount Gerizim, while the other six (of whom five had sprung from Leah's and Rachel's maids, Reuben being added to them on account of his great sin, Genesis 49:4) were placed on Mount Ebal.

Then, as the priests in the valley beneath read the words of blessing, the tribes on Mount Gerizim were to respond by an Amen; and as they read the words of the curses, those on Mount Ebal were similarly to give their solemn assent — thus expressly taking upon themselves each obligation, with its blessing in the observance, and its curse in the breach thereof. An historical parallel here immediately recurs to our minds. As, on his first entrance into Canaan, Abraham had formally owned Jehovah by rearing an altar unto Him (Genesis 12:7), and as Jacob had, on his return, paid the vow which he had recorded at Bethel (Genesis 35:7), so Israel now consecrated its possession of the land by receiving it as from the Lord, by recording His name, and by taking upon itself all the obligations of the covenant.

A glance at the map will enable us to realize the scene. From Ai and Bethel the direct route northwards leads by Shiloh to Shechem (Judges 21:19). The journey would occupy altogether about eleven hours. Of course, Israel could not have realized at the time that they were just then traveling along what would become the great highway from Galilee to Jerusalem, so memorable in after-history. Leaving the sanctuary of Shiloh a little aside, they would climb a rocky ridge. Before them a noble prospect spread. This was the future rich portion of Ephraim: valleys covered with corn, hills terraced to their tops, the slopes covered with vines and olive-yards. On wards the host moved, till it reached a valley, bounded south and north by mountains, which run from west to east. This was the exact spot on which Abram had built his first altar (Genesis 12:7); here, also, had Jacob's first settlement been (Genesis 33:19). Not a foe molested Israel on their march right up the middle of the land, partly, as previously explained, from the division of the land under so many petty chieftains, but chiefly because God had a favor unto them and to the work to which they had set their hands. Travelers speak in rapturous terms of the beauty of the valley of Shechem, even in the present desolateness of the country. It is a pass which intersects the mountain-chain, that runs through Palestine from south to north. To the south it is bounded by the range of Gerizim, to the north by that of Ebal. From where the priests with the Ark took up their position on the gentle rise of the valley, both Gerizim and Ebal appear hollowed out, forming, as it were, an amphitheater, while the "limestone strata, running up in a succession of ledges to the top of the hills, have all the appearance of benches."

Here, occupying every available inch of ground, were crowded the tribes of Israel: men, women, and children, "as well the strangers, and he that was born among them." As they stood close together, the humblest in Israel by the side of the "officers," "elders," and "judges," all eagerly watching what passed in the valley, or solemnly responding to blessing or curse, a scene was enacted, the like of which had not before been witnessed upon earth, and which could never fade from the memory. It is noteworthy that, on Mount Ebal, whence came the responses to the curses, the great stones were set up on which "the law" was written, and that there also the sacrifices were offered. This is in itself characteristic. Perhaps even the circumstance is not without significance, that they who stood on Mount Ebal must have had their view bounded by the mountains of Benjamin. Not so they who occupied Gerizim, the mount whence came the responses to the blessings. For the view which greeted those who at early morn crowded the top of the Mount of Blessings, was only second to that vouchsafed to Moses from the summit of Pisgah. If less in extent than the latter, it was more distinct and detailed.

All Central Palestine lay spread like a map before the wondering gaze of Israel. Tabor, Gilboa, the hills of Galilee rose in succession; in the far-distance snow-capped Hermon bounded the horizon, with sweet valleys and rich fields intervening. Turning to the right, they would descry the Lake of Galilee, and follow the cleft of the Jordan valley, marking beyond it Bashan, Ajalon, Gilead, and even Moab; to their left, the Mediterranean from Carmel to Gaza was full in view, the blue outline far away dimly suggesting thoughts of the "isles of the Gentiles," and the blessings in store for them. as far as the eye could reach — and beyond it, to the uttermost bounds of the earth — would the scene which they witnessed in that valley below be repeated; the echo of the blessings to which they responded on that mount would resound, till, having wakened every valley, it would finally be sent back in songs of praise and thanksgiving from a redeemed earth. And so did Israel on that spring morning consecrate Palestine unto the LORD, taking sea and lake, mountain and valley — the most hallowed spots in their history — as witnesses of their covenant.

From this solemn transaction the Israelites moved, as we gather from Joshua 9:6, to Gilgal, where they seem to have formed a permanent camp. The mention of this place in Deuteronomy 11:30, where it is described as "beside the oaks of Moreh," that is, near the spot of Abram's first altar (Genesis 12:7), implies a locality well-known at the time, and, as we might almost conjecture from its after history, a sort of traditional sanctuary.

This alone would suffice to distinguish this Gilgal from the first encampment of Israel east of Jericho, which only obtained its name from the event which there occurred. Besides, it is impossible to suppose that Joshua marched back from Shechem to the banks of Jordan (9:6; 10:6, 7, 9, 15, 43), and, again, that he did so a second time, after the battles in Galilee, to make apportionment of the land among the people by the banks of Jordan (14:6). Further, the localization of Gilgal near the banks of Jordan would be entirely incompatible with what we know of the after-history of that place. Gilgal was one of the three cities where Samuel judged the people (1 Samuel 7:16); here, also, he offered sacrifices, when the Ark was no longer in the tabernacle at Shiloh (1 Samuel 10:8; 13:7-9; 15:21); and there, as in a central sanctuary, did all Israel gather to renew their allegiance to Saul (1 Samuel 11:14). Later on, Gilgal was the great scene of Elisha's ministry (2 Kings 2:1), and still later it became a center of idolatrous worship (Hosea 4:15; 9:15; 12:11; Amos 4:4; 5:5). All these considerations lead to the conclusion, that the Gilgal, which formed the site of Joshua's encampment is the modern Jiljilieh, a few miles from Shiloh, and about the same distance from Bethel — nearly equi-distant from Shechem and from Jerusalem.

In this camp at Gilgal a strange deputation soon arrived. Professedly, and apparently, the travelers had come a long distance. For their garments were worn, their sandals clouted, their provisions dry and moldy, and the skins in which their wine had been were rent and "bound up" (like purses), as in the East wine-bottles of goat's skin are temporarily repaired on a long journey.

According to their own account, they lived far beyond the boundaries of Palestine, where their fellow-townsmen had heard what the Lord had done in Egypt, and again to Sihon and to Og, wisely omitting from the catalogue the miraculous passage of Jordan and the fall of Jericho, as of too recent date for their theory. Attracted by the name of Jehovah, Israel's God, who had done such wonders, they had been sent to make "a league" with Israel. It must have been felt that the story did not sound probable — at least, to any who had learned to realize the essential enmity of heathenism against the kingdom of God, and who understood that so great a change as the report of these men implied could not be brought about by "the hearing of the ear." Besides, what they proposed was not to make submission to, but a league with, Israel: by which not merely life, but their land and liberty, would be secured to them. But against any league with the inhabitants of Canaan, Israel had been specially warned (Exodus 23:32; 34:12; Numbers 33:55; Deuteronomy 7:2). What if, after all, they were neighbors? The suspicion seems to have crossed the minds of Joshua and of the elders, and even to have been expressed by them, only to be set aside by the protestations of the pretended ambassadors. It was certainly a mark of religious superficiality and self-confidence on the part of the elders of Israel to have consented on such grounds to "a league." The sacred text significantly puts it: "And the men (the elders of Israel) took of their victuals (according to the common Eastern fashion of eating bread and salt with a guest who is received as a friend), but they asked not counsel at the mouth of Jehovah."

Their mistake soon became apparent. Three days later, and Israel found that the pretended foreigners were in reality neighbors! Meanwhile, the kings or chieftains who ruled in Western Palestine had been concerting against Israel a combined movement of their forces from "the hills," or highlands of Central Palestine, from "the valleys," or the Shephelah (low country), between the mountain-chain and the sea, and "from the coasts of the great sea over against Lebanon," that is, from Joppa northwards by the sea-shore. The existence of the small confederate republic of Gibeon with its three associate cities in the midst of small monarchies throws a curious light upon the state of Palestine at the time; and the jealousy which would naturally exist between them helps to explain alike the policy of the Gibeonites, and the revenge which the Canaanitish kings were shortly afterwards preparing to take. The history of the republic of Gibeon is interesting.

"Gibeon was a great city, as one of the royal cities.... greater than Ai, and all the men thereof were mighty" (Joshua 10:2).

Its inhabitants were "Hivites" (11:19). Afterwards Gibeon fell to the lot of Benjamin, and became a priest-city (18:25; 21:17). When Nob was destroyed by Saul, the tabernacle was transported to Gibeon, where it remained till the temple was built by Solomon (1 Chronicles 16:39; 21:29; 1 Kings 3:4; 2 Chronicles 1:3). It lay about two hours to the north-west of Jerusalem, and is represented by the modern village of el-Jib. Its three associate towns were Chephirah, about three hours' west from Gibeon, the modern Kefir; Beeroth, about ten miles north of Jerusalem, the modern el-Bireh — both cities afterwards within the possession of Benjamin; and Kirjath-Jearim, "the city of groves," probably so called from its olive, fig, and other plantations, as its modern representative, Kuriet-el-Enab, is from its vineyards. The latter city, which was afterwards allotted to Judah, is about three hours from Jerusalem; and there the Ark remained from the time of its return from the Philistines to that of David (1 Samuel 7:2; 2 Samuel 6:2; 1 Chronicles 13:5, 6).

When the people learned the deceit practiced upon them, they "murmured against the princes;" but the latter refused to break their solemn oath, so far as it insured the lives and safety of the Gibeonites. If they had sworn rashly and presumptuously "by Jehovah, God of Israel," it would have only added another and a far more grievous sin to have broken their oath; not to speak of the effect upon the heathen around. The principle applying to this, as to similar rash undertakings, is, that a solemn obligation, however incurred, must be considered binding, unless its observance involve fresh sin. But in this instance it manifestly did not involve fresh sin. For the main reason of the destruction of the Canaanites was their essential hostility to the kingdom of God. The danger to Israel, accruing from this, could be avoided in a solitary instance. With a view to this, the Gibeonites were indeed spared, but attached as "bond-men" to the sanctuary, where they and their descendants performed all menial services (Joshua 9:23). Nor, as the event proved, did they ever betray their trust, or lead Israel into idolatry. Still, as a German writer observes, the rashness of Israel's princes, and the conduct of the Gibeonites, conveys to the church at all times solemn warning against the devices and the deceit of the world, which, when outward advantage offers, seeks a friendly alliance with, or even reception into, the visible kingdom of God.

CHAPTER 10: THE BATTLE OF GIBEON — CONQUEST OF THE SOUTH OF CANAAN — THE BATTLE OF MEROM — CONQUEST OF THE NORTH OF CANAAN — STATE OF THE LAND AT THE CLOSE OF THE SEVEN-YEARS' WAR.

(JOSHUA 10-12)

THE surrender of Gibeon would fill the kings of Southern Canaan with dismay. It was, so to speak, treason within their own camp; it gave Israel a strong position in the heart of the country and within easy reach of Jerusalem; while the possession of the passes leading from Gibeon would throw the whole south of Canaan open to their incursion. In the circumstances it natural that the chieftains of the south would combine, in the first place, for the retaking of Gibeon. The confederacy, which was under the leadership of Adoni-Zedek, king of Jerusalem, embraced Hoham, King of Hebron (about seven hours' south of Jerusalem); Piram, king of Jarmuth, the present Jarmuk, about three hours' to the south-west of Jerusalem; Japhia, king of Lachish, and Debir, king of Eglon, both cities close to each other, and not far from Gaza, to the south-west of Hebron.

The march of the combined kings was evidently rapid, and the danger pressing, for it seems to have found the Gibeonites wholly unprepared, and their entreaty to Joshua for immediate succor was of the most urgent kind. That very night Joshua marched to their relief with "all the people of war, that is, the mighty men of valor."

The relieving army came upon the enemy as "suddenly" as they had appeared in sight of Gibeon. It was probably very early in the morning when Joshua and his warriors surprised the allied camp. Gibeon lay in the east, surrounded, as in a semicircle, north, west, and south, by its three confederate cities. The five kings had pushed forward within that semicircle, and camped in the "open ground at the foot of the heights of Gibeon." Animated by the assurance which God had expressly given Joshua: "Fear them not: for I have delivered them into thine hand; there shall not a man of them stand before thee," the host of Israel fell upon them with an irresistible rush. The Canaanites made but a short stand before their unexpected assailants; then fled in wild confusion towards the pass of Upper Beth-horon, "the house of caves." They gained the height before their pursuers, and were hurrying down the pass of the Nether Beth-horon, when a fearful hailstorm, such as not unfrequently sweeps over the hills of Palestine, burst upon them. It was in reality "the Lord" who, once more miraculously employing natural agency, "cast down great stones from heaven upon them;" "and they were more which died from the hailstones than they whom the children of Israel slew with the sword."

It was but noon; far behind Israel in the heaven stood the sun over Gibeon, and before them over Ajalon in the west hung the crescent moon. The tempest was extinguishing day and light, and the work was but half done. In the pass to Nether Beth-horon Israel might be readily divided; at any rate, the enemy might escape before their crushing defeat had assured safety to Gibeon, and given the south of Palestine to Israel. Now, or never, was the time to pursue the advantage. Oh, that the sun would once more burst forth in his brightness; oh, that the all too short day were protracted "until the people had avenged themselves upon their enemies!" Then it was that Joshua burst into that impassioned prayer of faith, which is quoted in the sacred text from the "Book of Jasher," — or "Book of the Pious," — apparently, as we infer from 2 Samuel 1:18, a collection of poetical pieces, connected with the sublimest scenes in the history of the heroes of the kingdom of God. In this instance the quotation begins, as we take it, Joshua 10:12, and ends with ver. 15. This is proved by the insertion in ver. 15 of a notice, which in the historical narrative occurs only in ver. 43. For it is evident that Joshua did not return to Gilgal immediately after the battle of Gibeon (ver. 21), but pursued the war as described in the rest of ch. 10, till the whole south of Palestine was reduced. Thus verses 12-15 are a quotation from "the Book of the Pious," inserted within the Book of Joshua, the narrative of which is resumed in ver. 16. The quotation reads as follows:

"Then spake Joshua to Jehovah,
In the day Jehovah gave the Amorite before the sons of Israel,
And he spake in the sight of Israel.
Sun, on Gibeon rest still,
And moon, on the valley of Ajalon!
And still rested the sun, And the moon stood,
Till the people were avenged on their foes.
(Is not this written in the 'Book of the Pious?')
And the sun stood in mid-heaven,
And hasted not to go — like (as on) a complete day.
And there was not like that day, before or after,
That Jehovah hearkened to the voice of man — For Jehovah warred for Israel!
And Joshua returned, and all Israel with him to the camp, to Gilgal."

And God hearkened to the voice of Joshua. Once more the sun burst forth, and the daylight was miraculously protracted till Israel was avenged of its enemies. Onwards rolled the tide of fugitives, hotly pursued by Israel, through the pass of Nether Beth-horon to Azekah, and thence to Makkedah. Here tidings were brought to Joshua, that the five kings had hid themselves in one of the caves with which that district abounds. But Joshua would not be diverted from his object. He ordered large stones to be rolled to the mouth of the cave, and its entrance to be guarded by armed men, while the rest of the army followed the enemy and smote their "rearguard." Only broken remnants of the fugitives found shelter in the "fenced cities." Joshua himself had camped before the city of Makkedah. Thither the pursuing corps returned, and thence the war was afterwards carried on (10:21, 29). On the morning after the victory, the five confederate kings were brought from their hiding-place. In a manner not uncommon in ancient times, Joshua made his captains put their feet upon the necks of the prostrate kings, who had so lately gone forth boastfully in all the pride and. pomp of war. But the lesson which Israel was to learn from their victory was not one of self-confidence in their supposed superiority, but of acknowledgment of God and confidence in Him: "Fear not, nor be dismayed, be strong and of good courage: for thus shall Jehovah do to all your enemies against whom ye fight."

The death of these five kings proved only the beginning of a campaign which may have lasted weeks, or even months, for we find that successors of these five kings afterwards shared their fate. In the end, the whole south of Canaan was in the hands of Israel, though some of the cities taken appear to have been afterwards again wrested from them, and occupied by the Canaanites. The extent of the conquest is indicated (10:41) by a line drawn south and north, westwards — "from Kadesh-barnea even unto Gaza" — and eastwards, "from the district of Goshen unto Gibeon."

The campaign thus finished in the south had soon to be renewed in the north of Canaan. The means, the help, and the result were the same as before. Only, as the danger was much greater, from the multitude of Israel's opponents — "even as the sand that is upon the sea-shore," — and from their formidable mode of warfare ("horses and chariots very many"), hitherto unknown to Israel, the Lord once more gave express assurance of victory: "I will deliver them up all slain before Israel." At the same time He enjoined "to hough (or hamstring) their horses, and burn their chariots with fire," lest Israel should be tempted to place in future their trust in such weapons. The allied forces of the northern enemy were under the leadership of Jabin, king of Hazor, which "beforetimes was the head of all those kingdoms." They consisted not only of the three neighboring "kings" (or chieftains) of Madon, Shimron, and Achshaph, but of all the kings "in the north and (on the mountain" (of Naphtali, Joshua 20:7), of those in the Arabah, south of the Lake of Gennesaret, of those "in the plains," or valleys that stretched to the Mediterranean, and in "the heights of Dor," at the foot of Mount Carmel — in short, of all the Canaanite tribes from the Mediterranean in the south-west up to Mizpeh "the view") under Mount Hermon in the far north-east.

With the rapidity and suddenness which characterized all his movements, Joshua fell upon the allied camp by the Lake Merom (the modern el-Huleh), and utterly routed the ill-welded mass of the enemy. The fugitive Canaanites seem to have divided into three parts, one taking the road north-west to "Zidon the Great," another that west and south-west to the "smelting-pits by the waters" (Misrephoth-Maim), and the third that to the east leading to the valley of Mizpeh. In each direction they were hotly pursued by the Israelites. One by one all their cities were taken. Those in the valleys were burnt, but those on the heights, with the exception of Hazor, left standing, as requiring only small garrisons for their occupation. Altogether the war in the south and north must have occupied at least seven years, at the end of which the whole country was in the possession of Israel, from the "smooth mountain (Mount Halak) that goeth up to Seir," — that is, the white chalk mountains in the chain of the Azazimeh, in the Negeb — as far north as "Baal-gad," the town dedicated to "Baal" as god of "fortune," the Caesarea Philippi of the Gospels (11:16-18). More than that, Joshua also drove the Anakim, who had inspired the spies with such dread, from their original seats in the mountains, and in and around Hebron, Debir, and Anab into the Philistine cities of Gaza, Gath, and Ashdod. From ch. 15:14 we infer that they shortly afterwards returned, but were conquered by that veteran hero, Caleb.

To sum up all, we find that the wars under Joshua put Israel into possession of Canaan and broke the power of its inhabitants, but that the latter were not exterminated, nor yet all their cities taken by Israel (13:1-6; 17:14, etc.; 18:3, 23:5, 12). Indeed, such a result could scarcely have been desirable, either in reference to the country or to Israel, while, from Exodus 23:28-30 and Deuteronomy 7:22, we know that from the beginning it had not been the Divine purpose. But there was also a higher object in this. It would teach that a conquest, begun in the power of God and in believing dependence on Him, must be completed and consolidated in the same spirit. Only thus could Israel prosper as a nation. Canaan had been given to Israel by God, and given to their faith. But much was left to be done which only the same faith could achieve. Any conformity to the heathen around, or tolerance of heathenism, any decay of the spirit in which they had entered the land, would result not only in weakness, but in the triumph of the enemy. And so it was intended of the Lord. The lesson of all this is obvious and important. To us also has our Joshua given entrance into Canaan, and victory over our enemies — the world, the flesh, and the devil. We have present possession of the land. But we do not yet hold all its cities, nor are our enemies exterminated. It needs on our part constant faith; there must be no compromise with the enemy, no tolerance of his spirit, no cessation of our warfare. Only that which at first gave us the land can complete and consolidate our possession of it.

CHAPTER 11: DISTRIBUTION OF THE LAND — UNCONQUERED DISTRICTS — TRIBES EAST OF THE JORDAN — "THE LOT" — TRIBES WEST OF THE JORDAN — THE INHERITANCE OF CALEB — DISSATISFACTION OF THE SONS OF JOSEPH — THE TABERNACLE AT SHILOH — FINAL DIVISION OF THE LAND.

(JOSHUA 13-21)

THE continuance of unsubdued races and districts soon became a source of danger, although in a direction different from what might have been anticipated. Sufficient had been gained by a series of brilliant victories to render the general tenure of the land safe to Israel. The Canaanites and other races were driven to their fastnesses, where for the time they remained on the defensive. On the other hand, a nation like Israel, accustomed to the nomadic habits of the wilderness, would scarcely feel the need of a fixed tenure of land, and readily grow weary of a desultory warfare in which each tribe had separately to make good its boundaries. Thus it came that Joshua had grown old, probably ninety or a hundred years, while the work intrusted to him was far from completed. In the far south and along the sea-shore the whole district from the brook of Egypt to Ekron was still held, in the south-west and south-east, by the Geshurites and the Avites, while the territory farther north from Ekron to Gaza was occupied by the five lords of the Philistines (Joshua 13:2, 3).

According to the Divine direction, all these, though not descended from Canaan (Genesis 10:14), were to be "counted to the Canaanites," that is, treated as such. Traveling still farther northwards along the sea-shore, the whole "land of the Canaanites" or of the Phoenicians far up to the celebrated "cave" near Sidon, and beyond it to Aphek and even "to the borders of the Amorites" was still unconquered. Thence eastward across Lebanon as far as Baal-gad and "the entering into Hamath," and again back from Mount Lebanon, across country, to the "smelting-pits on the waters," was subject to the Sidonians or Phoenicians. Yet all this belonged by Divine gift to Israel. That it was still unoccupied by them, and that Joshua was now old, constituted the ground for the Divine command to make immediate distribution of the land among the tribes. It was as if, looking to His promise, God would have bidden Israel consider the whole land as theirs, and simply go forward, in faith of that promise and in obedience to His command.

It will be remembered that only nine and a half tribes remained to be provided for, since "unto the tribe of Levi He gave none inheritance," other than what came from the sanctuary, while Reuben, Gad, and half Manasseh had had their portions assigned by Moses east of the Jordan.

That territory was bounded by Moab along the south-eastern shores of the Dead Sea, while the eastern border of Reuben and Gad was held by Ammon. Both these nations were by Divine command not to be molested by Israel (Deuteronomy 2:9, 19). The southernmost and smallest portion of the district east of the Jordan belonged to Reuben. His territory extended from the river Arnon, in the south, to where Jordan flowed into the Dead Sea, and embraced the original kingdom of Sihon. Northward of it, the Ammonites had once held possession, but had been driven out by Sihon. That new portion of Sihon's kingdom was given not to Reuben but to Gad. The territory of that tribe ran along the Jordan as far as the

Lake of Gennesaret — the upper portion (from Mahanaim) narrowing almost into a point. North of this was the possession of the half tribe of Manasseh, which embraced the whole of Bashan. It occupied by far the largest extent of area. But from its position it also lay most open to constant nomadic incursions, and possessed comparatively few settled cities.

The division of the land among the nine and a half tribes was, in strict accordance with Divine direction (Numbers 26:52-56; 33:54; 34:2-29), made by Eleazar, Joshua, and one representative from each of the ten tribes. It was decided by the "lot," which probably, however, only determined the situation of each inheritance, whether north or south, in. land or by the sea-shore, not its extent and precise boundaries. These would depend upon the size of each tribe. In point of fact, the original arrangements had in some cases to be afterwards modified, not as to tribal localization, which was unalterably fixed by the Divine lot, but as to extent of territory. Thus Judah had to give up part of its possession to Simeon (Joshua 19:9), while Dan, whose portion proved too small, obtained certain cities both from Judah and from Ephraim. As regards the lot, we may probably accept the Rabbinical tradition, that two urns were set out, one containing the names of the ten (or rather nine and a half) tribes, the other the designation of the various districts into which the country had been arranged, and that from each a lot was successively drawn, to designate first the tribe, and then the locality of its inheritance.

This is not the place, however interesting the task, to describe the exact boundaries and cities of each tribe. We can only attempt the most general outline, which the reader must fill up for himself. Beginning in the far south, at Kadesh in the wilderness, and along the borders of Edom, we are within the territory of Simeon; north of it, bounded on the west by the land of the Philistines, and on the east by the Dead Sea, is the possession of Judah; beyond it, to the east, that of Benjamin, and to the west, that of Dan; north of Dan we reach Ephraim, and then Manasseh, the possession of Issachar running along the east of these two territories, and ending at the southern extremity of the Lake of Gennesaret; by the shore of that lake and far beyond it is the territory of Naphtali, first a narrow slip, then widening, and finally merging into a point. Asher occupied the seaboard, north of Manasseh; while, lastly, Zebulon is as it were wedged in between Issachar, Manasseh, Asher, and Naphtali.

It only remains briefly to notice the incidents recorded in connection with the territorial division of the land.

1. It seems that before the first lot was drawn in the camp at Gilgal, Caleb, the son of Jephunneh, came forward with a special claim. It will be remembered, that of the twelve princes sent from Kadesh only he and Joshua had brought "a good report of the land," in the spiritual sense of the expression, as encouraging the people to go forward. And when the Divine sentence doomed that rebellious generation to death in the wilderness, Caleb and Joshua alone were excepted. Strictly speaking, no more than this might have been implied in the promise by Moses, now claimed by Caleb: "Surely the land whereon thy feet have trodden shall be thine inheritance" (Joshua 14:9), since to have survived was to obtain the inheritance.

But there seems to have been more than merely a promise of survival, although it alone is mentioned in Numbers 14:24, 30. For we infer from the words and the attitude of Caleb, and from the similar privileges afterwards accorded to Joshua (19:49, 50), that Moses had, by direction of the Lord, given these two a right of special and personal choice. This on account of their exceptional faithfulness, and as the sole survivors of the generation to whom the land had been given. It was as if the surviving proprietors might choose their portion, before those who, so to speak, were only next of kin had theirs allotted to them. Of this Caleb now reminds Joshua, and in words of such vigorous faith, as make us love still better the tried old warrior of Jehovah. Appearing at the head of "the house of fathers," in Judah, of which he was the head, he first refers to the past, then owns God's faithfulness in having preserved him to the age of eighty-five, with strength and courage undiminished for the holy war.

From 14:9 we infer that, when the twelve spies distributed themselves singly over the land, for the purposes of their mission, Caleb specially "searched" that "mountain," which was the favorite haunt of the dreaded Anakim. If this be so, we discover a special meaning and special faith on the part of Caleb, when he, rather than Joshua, attempted to "still the people before Moses, and said, Let us go up at once" (Numbers 13:30). In that case there was also special suitableness in the Divine bestowal made then and there:

"Surely the land whereon thy feet have trodden shall be thine inheritance" (Joshua 14:9, 12).

But even if otherwise, the courage and faith of the old warrior shine only the more brightly, as, recalling the terror formerly inspired by the Anakim and the strength of their cities, he claims that very portion for his own. Yet his courage bears no trace of self-sufficiency, only of believing dependence upon the Lord. "If so be Jehovah will be with me, and I shall drive them out" (ver. 12).

The claim thus made was immediately acknowledged, Joshua adding his blessing on Caleb's proposed undertaking. But it was some time later that the expedition was actually made, when Caleb offered the hand of his daughter, Achsah, as the prize of taking the great stronghold of Debir, the ancient Kirjath-sepher, or "book-city," — probably the fortified depository of the sacred books of the Anakim. The prize was won by a near kinsman, Othniel, who, after the death of Joshua, was the first "judge" of Israel (Judges 3:9). The history of the campaign, with its accompanying incidents, is inserted in Joshua 15:13-19, because, both geographically and historically, it fits into that part of the description of the inheritance of Judah.

2. The first signs of future weakness and disagreement appeared so early as when the lot designated the possession of the children of Joseph (Ephraim and half the tribe of Manasseh). Theirs was the richest and most fertile in the land, including the plain of Sharon, capable of producing almost boundless store, and of becoming the granary of the whole land. On that ground then no complaint could be made. Nor could any reasonable objection be taken to the size of their lot, provided they were prepared to go forward in faith and occupy it as against the Canaanites, who still held the principal towns in the valley, all the way from Bethshean by the Jordan to the plain of Jezreel and farther. But the children of Joseph were apparently afraid of such encounter because of the iron chariots of their enemies. Equally unwilling were they to clear the wooded heights of Ephraim, which connect the range north of Samaria with Mount Carmel, and where the Perizzites and the Rephaim had their haunts. Rather did they clamor for an additional "portion" (17:14). Their demands were, of course, refused; Joshua turning the boastful pride in which they had been made into an argument for action on their part against the common enemy (ver.18). But this murmuring of the children of Joseph, and the spirit from which it proceeded, gave sad indications of dangers in the near future. National disintegration, tribal jealousies, coupled with boast-fullness and unwillingness to execute the work given them of God, were only too surely foreboded in the conduct of the children of Joseph.

3. If such troubles were to be averted, it was high time to seek a revival of religion. With that object in view, "the whole congregation of the children of Israel" were now gathered at

Shiloh, and the tabernacle set up there (18:1). The choice of Shiloh was, no doubt, Divinely directed (Deuteronomy 12:11). It was specially suitable for the purpose, not only from its central situation — about eight hours' north of Jerusalem, and five south of Shechem — but from its name, which recalled rest and the promised rest-giver (Genesis 49:10). Then Joshua solemnly admonished the assembled people as to their "slackness" in taking possession of the land which Jehovah had given them. To terminate further jealousies, he asked the people to choose three representatives from each of the seven tribes whose inheritance had not yet been allotted. These were to "go through the land and describe it," that is, to make a general estimate and valuation, rather than an accurate survey, "with reference to their inheritance," that is, in view of their inheriting the land. After their return to Shiloh these twenty-one delegates were to divide the land into seven portions, when the lot would assign to each tribe the place of its inheritance.

4. The arrangement thus made was fully carried out. After its completion Joshua, who, like Caleb, had received a special promise, was allowed to choose his own city within his tribal inheritance of Ephraim. Finally, the cities of refuge, six in number; the Levitical cities, thirty-five in number; and the thirteen cities of the priests, the sons of Aaron, were formally set aside.

Thus, so far as the Lord was concerned, He "gave unto Israel all the land which He sware to give unto their fathers; and they possessed it, and dwelt therein. And Jehovah gave them rest round about, according to all that He sware unto their fathers: and there stood not a man of all their enemies before them; Jehovah delivered all their enemies into their hand. There failed not ought of any good thing Jehovah had spoken unto the house of Israel; all came to pass" (Joshua 21:43-45).

CHAPTER 12: RETURN OF THE TWO AND A HALF TRIBES TO THEIR HOMES — BUILDING OF AN ALTAR BY THEM — EMBASSY TO THEM — JOSHUA'S FAREWELL ADDRESSES — DEATH OF JOSHUA — REVIEW OF HIS LIFE AND WORK.
(JOSHUA 22-24)

YET another trial awaited Joshua, ere he put off the armor and laid him down to rest. Happily, it was one which he rather dreaded than actually experienced. The work given him to do was ended, and each of the tribes had entered on its God-given inheritance. And now the time had come for those faithful men who so truly had discharged their undertaking to recross Jordan, and "get unto to the land of their possession." These many years had the men of Reuben, Gad, and Manasseh fought and waited by the side of their brethren. And now that God had given them rest, Joshua dismissed the tried warriors with a blessing, only bidding them fight in their own homes that other warfare, in which victory meant loving the Lord, walking in His ways, keeping His commandments, and cleaving unto and serving Him.

It must have been with a heavy heart that Joshua saw them depart from Shiloh. It was not merely that to himself it would seem like the beginning of the end, but that misgivings and fears could not but crowd upon his mind.

They parted from Shiloh to comparatively far distances, to be separated from their brethren by Jordan, and scattered amid the wide tracts, in which their nomadic pastoral life would bring them into frequent and dangerous contact with heathen neighbors. They were now united to their brethren; they had fought by their side; would this union continue? The very riches with which they departed to their distant homes (22:8) might become a source of danger. They had parted with Jehovah's blessing and monition from the central sanctuary at Shiloh. Would it remain such to them, and they preserve the purity of their faith at a distance from the tabernacle and its services? Joshua remembered only too well the past history of Israel; he knew that even now idolatry, although publicly non-existent, had still its roots and fibers in many a household as a sort of traditional superstition (24:23). Under such circumstances it was that strange tidings reached Israel and Joshua. Just before crossing Jordan the two and a half tribes had built an altar that could be seen far and wide, and then departed without leaving any explanation of their conduct. At first sight this would have seemed in direct contravention of one of the first principles of Israel's worship. Place, time, and manner of it were all God-ordained and full of meaning, and any departure therefrom, even in the slightest particular, destroyed the meaning, and with it the value of all. More especially would this appear an infringement of the express commands against another altar and other worship (Leviticus 17:8, 9; Deuteronomy 12:5-7), to which the terrible punishment of extermination attached (Deuteronomy 13:12-18). And yet there was something so strange in rearing this altar on the western side of the Jordan, and not on the eastern, and in their own possession, that their conduct, however blameworthy, might possibly bear another explanation than that of the great crime of apostasy.

It was an anxious time when the whole congregation gathered, by their representatives, at Shiloh, not to worship, but to consider the question of going to war with their own brethren and companions in arms, and on such grounds. Happily, before taking decided action, a deputation was sent to expostulate with the two and a half tribes. It consisted of ten princes, representatives, each of a tribe, and all "heads of houses of their fathers," though, of course, not the actual chiefs of their tribes. At their head was Phinehas, the presumptive successor to the high priesthood, to whose zeal, which had once stayed the plague of Peor, the direction might safely be left. We are not told how they gathered the representatives of the offending tribes, but the language in which, as recorded, the latter were addressed, is quite characteristic of Phinehas.

The conduct of the two and a half tribes had been self-willed and regardless of one of the first duties — that of not giving offense to the brethren, nor allowing their liberty to become a stumbling-block to others. For a doubtful good they had committed an undoubted offense, the more unwarranted, that they had neither asked advice nor offered explanation. Phinehas could scarcely help assuming that they had "committed unfaithfulness towards the God of Israel." He now urged upon them the remembrance, yet fresh in their minds, of the consequences of the sin of Peor, and which had, alas! still left its bitter roots among the people. If, on account of their uncleanness, they felt as if they needed nearer proximity to the altar, he invited them back to the western side of the Jordan where the other tribes would make room for them. But if they persisted in their sin, he reminded them how the sin of the one individual, Achan, had brought wrath on all the congregation. If so, then the rest of Israel must take action, so as to clear themselves of complicity in their "rebellion."

In reply, the accused tribes protested, in language of the most earnest expostulation, that their conduct had been wholly misunderstood. So far from wishing to separate from the tabernacle and worship of Jehovah, this great altar had been reared as a witness to all ages that they formed an integral part of Israel, lest in the future they might be debarred from the service of Jehovah. That, and that alone, had been their meaning, however ill expressed. The explanation thus offered was cause of deep thankfulness to the deputies and to all Israel. Thus, in the good providence of God, this cloud also passed away.

A twofold work had been intrusted to Joshua: to conquer the land (Joshua 1:8), and to divide it by inheritance among the people (1:6). Both had been done, and in the spirit of strength, of courage, and of believing obedience enjoined at the outset (1:7). Unlike his great predecessor and master, Moses, he had been allowed to finish his task, and even to rest after its completion. And now he had reached one hundred and ten years, the age at which his ancestor Joseph had died (Genesis 50:26). Like a father who thinks of and seeks to provide for the future of his children after his death; like Moses when he gathered up all his life, his mission, and his teaching in his last discourses; as the Apostle Peter, when he endeavored that Christians might "be able after his Exodus to have these things always in remembrance," so did Joshua care for the people of his charge. On two successive occasions he gathered all Israel, through their representative "elders," to address to them last words. They are in spirit and even in tenor singularly like those of Moses, as indeed he had no new truth to communicate.

The first assembly must have taken place either in his own city of Timnath-serah, or else at Shiloh. The address there given had precisely the same object as that afterwards delivered by him, and indeed may be described as preparatory to the latter.

Probably the difference between the two lies in this, that the first discourse treated of the future of Israel rather in its political aspect, while the second, as befitted the circumstances, chiefly dwelt on the past mercies of Jehovah, and urged upon the people decision in their spiritual choice. Both discourses are marked by absence of all self-exaltation or reference to his own achievements. It is the language of one who, after long and trying experience, could sum up all he knew and felt in these words: "As for me and my house, we will serve Jehovah." The first discourse of Joshua consisted of two parts (23:2-13, and 14-16), each beginning with an allusion to his approaching end, as the motive of his admonitions. Having first reminded Israel of all God's benefits and of His promises, in case of their faithfulness, he beseecheth them: "Take heed very much to your souls to love Jehovah your God" (ver. 11), the danger of an opposite course being described with an accumulation of imagery that shows how deeply Joshua felt the impending danger. Proceeding in the same direction, the second part of Joshua's address dwells upon the absolute certainty with which judgment would follow, as surely as formerly blessing had come.

The second address of Joshua, delivered to the same audience as the first, was even more solemn. For, this time, the assembly took place at Shechem, where, on first entering the land, Israel had made solemn covenant by responding from Mounts Ebal and Gerizim to the blessings and the curses enunciated in the law. And the present gathering also was to end in renewal of that covenant. Moreover, it was in Shechem that Abraham had, on entering Canaan, received the first Divine promise, and here he had built an altar unto Jehovah (Genesis 12:6, 7). Here also had Jacob settled after his return from Mesopotamia, and purged his household from lingering idolatry, by burying their Teraphim under an oak (Genesis 33:20; 35:2, 4). It was truly a "sanctuary of Jehovah" (Joshua 24:26), and they who came to it, "gathered before God" (ver.1). In language the most tender and impressive, reminding us of Stephen's last speech before the Sanhedrim (Acts 7), Joshua recalled to them the mercies of God (Joshua 24:2-13), specially in those five great events: the calling of Abraham, the deliverance from Egypt, the defeat of the Amorites and of the purpose of Balaam, the miraculous crossing of Jordan and taking of Jericho, and finally, the Divine victory given them over all the nations of Canaan. On these grounds he now earnestly entreated them to make decisive choice of Jehovah as their God.

And they replied by solemnly protesting their determination to cleave unto the Lord, in language which not only re-echoed that of the preface to the ten commandments (Exodus 20:2; Deuteronomy 5:6), but also showed that they fully responded to Joshua's appeals. To bring the matter to a clear issue, Joshua next represented to them that they could not serve Jehovah (24:19) — that is, in their then state of heart and mind — "in their own strength, without the aid of grace; without real and serious conversion from all idols; and without true repentance and faith." To attempt this were only to bring down judgment instead of the former blessing. And when the people still persevered in their profession, Joshua, having made it a condition that they were to put away the strange gods from among them and "direct" their hearts "unto Jehovah, God of Israel," made again solemn covenant with them. Its terms were recorded in a document which was placed within the book of the Law, and in memory there of a great stone was set up under the memorable tree at Shechem which had been the silent witness of so many solemn transactions in the history of Israel.

With this event the history of Joshua closes. Looking back upon it, we gather the lessons of his life and work, and of their bearing upon the future of Israel. Born a slave in Egypt, he must have been about forty years old at the time of the Exodus. Attached to the person of Moses, he led Israel in the first decisive battle against Amalek (Exodus 17:9, 13), while Moses, in the prayer of faith, held up to heaven the God-given "rod."

It was no doubt on that occasion that his name was changed from Oshea, "help," to Jehoshua, "Jehovah is help" (Numbers 13:16). And this name is the key to his life and work. Alike in bringing the people into Canaan, in his wars, and in the distribution of the land among the tribes — from the miraculous crossing of Jordan and taking of Jericho to his last address — he was the embodiment of his new name: "Jehovah is help!" To this outward calling his character also corresponded. It is marked by singleness of purpose, directness, and decision. There is not indeed about him that elevation of faith, or comprehensiveness of spiritual view which we observed in Moses. Witness Joshua's despondency after the first failure at Ai. Even his plans and conceptions lack breadth and depth. Witness his treaty with the Gibeonites, and the commencing disorganization among the tribes at Shiloh. His strength always lies in his singleness of purpose. He sets an object before him, and unswervingly follows it. So in his campaigns: he marches rapidly, falls suddenly upon the enemy, and follows up the victory with unflagging energy. But there he stops — till another object is again set before him, which he similarly pursues. The same singleness, directness, and decision, rather than breadth and elevation, seem also to characterize his personal religion.

There is another remarkable circumstance about Joshua. The conquest and division of the land seem to have been his sole work. He does not appear to have even ruled as a judge over Israel. But so far also as the conquest and division of the land were concerned, his work was not complete, nor, indeed, intended to be complete. And this is characteristic of the whole Old Testament dispensation, that no period in its history sees its work completed, but only begun and pointing forward to another yet future, till at last all becomes complete in the "fullness of time" in Christ Jesus. Thus viewed, a fresh light is cast upon the name and history of Joshua. Assuredly Joshua did not give "rest" even to his own generation, far less to Israel as a nation. It was rest begun, but not completed — a rest which even in its temporal aspect left so much unrest; and as such it pointed to Christ. What the one Joshua could only begin, not really achieve, even in its outward typical aspect, pointed to, and called for the other Joshua, the Lord Jesus Christ, in Whom and by Whom all is reality, and all is perfect, and all is rest for ever. And so also it was only after many years that Oshea became Joshua, while the name Joshua was given to our Lord by the angel before His birth (Matthew 1:21). The first became, the second was Joshua. And so the name and the work of Joshua pointed forward to the fullness in Christ, alike by what it was and by what it was not, and this in entire accordance with the whole character and object of the Old Testament.

CHAPTER 13: SUMMARY OF THE BOOK OF JUDGES — JUDAH'S AND SIMEON'S CAMPAIGN — SPIRITUAL AND NATIONAL DECAY OF ISRAEL — "FROM GILGAL TO BOCHIN."

(JUDGES 1-3:4)

IF evidence were required that each period of Old Testament history points for its completion to one still future, it would be found in the Book of Judges. The history of the three and a half centuries which it records brings not anything new to light, either in the life or history of Israel; it only continues what is already found in the Book of Joshua, carrying it forward to the Books of Samuel, and thence through Kings, till it points in the dim distance to the King, of Israel, the Lord Jesus Christ, Who gives perfect rest in the perfect kingdom. In the Book of Joshua we see two grand outstanding facts, one explaining the outer, the other the inner history of Israel. As for the latter, we learn that ever since the sin of Peor, if not before, idolatry had its hold upon the people. Not that the service of the Lord was discarded, but that it was combined with the heathen rites of the nations around. But as true religion was really the principle of Israel's national life and unity, "unfaithfulness" towards Jehovah was also closely connected with tribal disintegration, which, as we have seen, threatened even in the time of Joshua. Then, as for the outer history of Israel, we learn that the completion of their possession of Canaan was made dependent on their faithfulness to Jehovah. Just as the Christian can only continue to stand by the same faith in which, in his conversion to God, he first had access to Him (Romans 5:2), so Israel could only retain the land and complete its conquest by the same faith in which they had at first entered it. For faith is never a thing of the past. And for this reason God allowed a remnant of those nations to continue in the land "to prove Israel by them" (Judges 3:1), so that, as Joshua had forewarned them (Joshua 23:10-16, comp. Judges 2:3), "faithfulness" on their part would lead to sure and easy victory, while the opposite would end in terrible national disaster.

Side by side with these two facts, there is yet a third, and that the most important: the unchanging faithfulness of the Lord, His unfailing pity and lovingkindness, according to which, when Israel was brought low and again turned to Him, He

"raised them up judges,... and delivered them out of the hand of their enemies all the days of the judge" (Judges 2:18).

The exhibition of these three facts forms the subject-matter of Israel's history under the Judges, as clearly indicated in Judges 2:21, 3:4. Accordingly, we must not expect in the Book of Judges a complete or successive history of Israel during these three and half centuries, but rather the exhibition and development of those three grand facts. For Holy Scripture furnishes not — like ordinary biography or history — a chronicle of the lives of individuals, or even of the successive history of a period, save in so far as these are connected with the progress of the kingdom of God. Sacred history is primarily that of the kingdom of God, and only secondarily that of individuals or periods. More particularly is this the reason why we have no record at all of five of the Judges — not even that Jehovah had raised them up.

For this cause also some events are specially selected in the sacred narrative, which, to the superficial reader, may seem trivial; sometimes even difficult or objectionable. But a more careful study will show that the real object of these narratives is, to bring into full view one or other of the great principles of the Old Testament dispensation. For the same reason also we must not look for strict chronological arrangement in the narratives. In point of fact, the Judges ruled only over one or several of the tribes, to whom they brought special deliverance. Accordingly, the history of some of the Judges overlaps each other, their reign having been contemporaneous in different parts of the land. Thus while in the far east across Jordan the sway of the children of Ammon lasted for eighteen years, till Jephthah brought deliverance (Judges 10:6-12:7), the Philistines at the same time oppressed Israel in the far southwest. This circumstance renders the chronology of the Book of Judges more complicated.

The Book of Judges divides itself into three parts: a general introduction (1-3:6), a sketch of the period of the Judges (3:7-16:31), arranged in six groups of events (3:7-11; 3:12-31; 4, 5; 6-10:5; 10:6-12:15; 13-16), and a double Appendix (17-21). The two series of events, recorded in the latter, evidently took place at the commencement of the period of the Judges. This appears from a comparison of Judges 18:1 with 1:34, and again of Judges 20:28 with Joshua 22:13 and 24:33. The first of the two narratives is mainly intended to describe the religious, the second the moral decadence among the tribes of Israel. In these respects they throw light upon the whole period. We see how soon, after the death of Joshua and of his contemporaries, Israel declined — spiritually, in combining with the heathen around, and mingling their idolatrous rites with the service of Jehovah; and nationally, the war with the Canaanites being neglected, and the tribes heeding on every great occasion only their private interests and jealousies, irrespective of the common weal (5:15-17, 23; 8:1-9), until "the men of Ephraim" actually levy war against Jephthah (12:1-6), and Israel sinks so low as to deliver its Samson into the hands of the Philistines (15:9-13)!

Side by side with this decay of Israel we notice a similar decline in the spiritual character of the Judges from an Othniel and a Deborah down to Samson. The mission of these Judges was, as we have seen, chiefly local and always temporary, God raising up a special deliverer in a time of special need. It is quite evident that such special instruments were not necessarily always under the influence of spiritual motives. God has at all periods of history used what instruments He pleased for the deliverance of His people — a Darius, a Cyrus, a Gamaliel, and in more modern times often what appeared the most unlikely, to effect His own purposes. Yet in the history of the Judges it seems always the best and most religious whom the locality or period affords who is chosen, so that the character of the Judges affords also an index of the state of a district or period. And in each of them we mark the presence of real faith (Hebrews 11), acting as the lever-power in their achievements, although their faith is too often mingled with the corruptions of the period. The Judges were Israel's representative men — representatives of its faith and its hope, but also of its sin and decay. Whatever they achieved was "by faith." Even in the case of Samson, all his great deeds were achieved in the faith of God's gift to him as a Nazarite, and when "the Spirit of the Lord came upon him." Hence the Judges deserved to be enrolled in the catalogue of Old Testament "worthies." Besides, we must not forget the necessary influence upon them of the spirit of their age. For we mark in the Bible a progressive development, as the light grew brighter and brighter unto the perfect day. In truth, if this were not the case, one of two inferences would follow. Either we would be tempted to regard its narratives as partial, or else be driven to the conclusion that these men could not have been of the period in which they are placed, since they had nothing in common with it, and hence could neither have been leaders of public opinion, nor even been understood by it.

From these brief preliminary observations we turn to notice, that there were altogether twelve, or rather, including Deborah (Judges 4:4), thirteen Judges over Israel. Of only eight of these are any special deeds recorded. The term Judge must not, however, be regarded as primarily referring to the ordinary judicial functions, which were discharged by the elders and officers of every tribe and city. Rather do we regard it as equivalent to leader or ruler. The period of the Judges closes with Samson. Eli was mainly high priest, and only in a secondary sense "Judge," while Samuel formed the transition from the Judges to royalty. With Samson the period of the Judges reached at the same time its highest and its lowest point. It is as a Nazarite, devoted to God before his birth, that he is "Judge," and achieves his great feats — and it is as a Nazarite that he falls and fails through selfishness and sin. In both respects he is the representative of Israel — God-devoted, a Nazarite people, and as such able to do all things, yet falling and failing through spiritual adultery. And thus the period of the Judges ends as every other period. It contains the germ of, and points to something better; but it is imperfect, incomplete, and fails, though even in its failure it points forward. Judges must be succeeded by kings, and kings by the King — the true Nazarite, the Lord Jesus Christ.

The period between the death of Joshua and the first "Judge" is summarized in Judges 1-3:6. It appears, that under the influence of Joshua's last address, deepened no doubt by his death, which followed soon afterwards, the "holy war" was resumed. In this instance it was purely aggressive on the part of Israel, whereas formerly, as a matter of fact, the attack always came from the Canaanites (except in the case of Jericho and of Ai). But the measure of the sin of the nations who occupied Palestine was now full (Genesis 15:13-16), and the storm of judgment was to sweep them away. For this purpose Israel, to whom God in His mercy had given the land, was to be employed — but only in so far as the people realized its calling to dedicate the land unto the Lord. On the ruins of what not only symbolized, but at the time really was the kingdom of Satan, the theocracy was to be upbuilt. Instead of that focus whence the vilest heathenism overspread the world, the kingdom of God was to be established, with its opposite mission of sending the light of truth to the remotest parts of the earth. Nor can it be difficult to understand how, in such circumstances, at such a time, and at that period of religious life, any compromise was impossible — and every war must be one of extermination.

Before entering on this new "war," the children of Israel asked Jehovah, no doubt through the Urim and Thummim, which tribe was to take the lead. In reply, Judah was designated, in accordance with ancient prophecy (Genesis 49:8). Judah, in turn, invited the co-operation of Simeon, whose territory had been parceled out of its own. In fact, theirs were common enemies. The two tribes encountered and defeated the Canaanites and Perizzites in Bezek, a name probably attaching to a district rather than a place, and, as the word seems to imply, near the shore of the Dead Sea. In the same locality Adoni-bezek appears to have made a fresh stand, but with the same disastrous result. On that occasion a remarkable, though most cruel retaliation overtook him. As chieftain of that district he must have been equally renowned for his bravery and cruelty. After a custom not uncommon in antiquity, the many chieftains whom he had subdued were kept, like dogs, "for lengthened sport," under the banqueting table of the proud conqueror in a mutilated condition, their thumbs and great toes cut off, in token that they could never again handle sword and bow, nor march to war.

It need scarcely be said, that the Mosaic law never contemplated such horrors. Nevertheless the allied tribes now inflicted mutilation upon Adoni-bezek. The victors carried him to Jerusalem, where he died. On that occasion the city itself, so far as it lay within the territory of Judah, was taken and burnt. But the boundary line between Judah and Benjamin ran through Jerusalem, the Upper City and the strong castle, which were held by the Jebusites, being within the lot of Benjamin. In the war under Joshua, the Jebusites had foiled Judah (Joshua 15:63). Now also they retired to their stronghold, whence the Benjamites did not even attempt to dislodge them (Judges 1:21). From Jerusalem the tribes continued their victorious march successively to "the mountain," or highlands of Judah, then to the Negeb, or south country, and finally to the Shephelah, or lowlands, along the sea-shore. Full success attended the expedition, the tribes pursuing their victories as far south as the utmost borders of the ancient kingdom of Arad, where, as their fathers had vowed (Numbers 21:2), they executed the ban upon Zephath or Hormah. The descendants of Hobab (Judges 4:11) the Kenite the brother-in-law of Moses, who had followed Israel to Canaan (Numbers 10:29), and had since pitched their tents near Jericho, now settled in this border land, as best suited to their nomadic habits and previous associations (Judges 1:8-11, 16). The campaign ended with the incursion into the Shephelah, where Judah wrested from the Philistines three out of their five great cities. This conquest, however, was not permanent (14:19; 16:1), nor were the inhabitants of the valley driven out, "because they had chariots of iron."

But the zeal of Israel did not long continue. In fact, all that follows after the campaign of Judah and Simeon is a record of failure and neglect, with the single exception of the taking of Bethel by the house of Joseph. Thus the tribes were everywhere surrounded by a fringe of heathenism. In many parts, Israelites and heathens dwelt together, the varying proportions among them being indicated by such expressions as that the "Canaanites dwelt among" the Israelites, or else the reverse. Sometimes the Canaanites became tributary. On the other hand, the Amorites succeeded in almost wholly driving the tribe of Dan out of their possessions, which induced a considerable proportion of the Danites to seek fresh homes in the far north (Judges 18).

Israel was settling down in this state, when their false rest was suddenly broken by the appearance among them of "the Angel of Jehovah." No Divine manifestation had been vouch-safed them since the Captain of Jehovah's host had stood before Joshua in the camp at Gilgal (Joshua 5:13-15). And now, at the commencement of a new period, and that one of spiritual decay, He "came" from Gilgal to Bochim, not to announce the miraculous fall of a Jericho before the ark of Jehovah, but the continuance of the heathen power near them in judgment upon their unfaithfulness and disobedience. "From Gilgal to Bochim!" There is much in what these names suggest — and that even although Gilgal may have been the permanent camp, where leading representatives of the nation were always assembled, to whom "the Angel of Jehovah" in the first place addressed Himself, and Bochim, or "weepers," the designation given afterwards to the meeting-place by the ancient sanctuary (either Shechem or more probably Shiloh), where the elders of the people gathered to hear the Divine message.

And truly what had passed between the entrance into Canaan and that period might be thus summed up: "From Gilgal to Bochim!" The immediate impression of the words of the Angel of Jehovah was great. Not only did the place become Bochim, but a sacrifice was offered unto Jehovah, for wherever His presence was manifested, there might sacrifice be brought (comp. Deuteronomy 12:5; Judges 6:20, 26, 28; 13:16; 2 Samuel 24:25).

But, alas! the impression was of but short continuance. Mingling with the heathen around, "they forsook Jehovah, and served Baal and Ashtaroth." Such a people could only learn in the school of sorrow. National unfaithfulness was followed by national judgments.

Yet even so, Jehovah, in His mercy, ever turned to them when they cried, and raised up "deliverers." In the truest sense these generations "had not known all the wars of Canaan" (Judges 3:1). For the knowledge of them is thus explained in the Book of Psalms (Psalm 44:2, 3):

"Thou didst drive out the heathen with Thy hand, and plantedst them; Thou didst afflict the nations, and east them out. For they got not the land in possession by their own sword, neither did their own arm save them: but Thy right hand, and Thine arm, and the light of Thy countenance, because Thou hadst a favor unto them."

This lesson was now to be learned in bitter experience by the presence and power of the heathen around:

"to prove Israel by them, to know whether they would hearken unto the commandments of Jehovah, which He commanded their fathers by the hand of Moses" (Judges 3:4).

CHAPTER 14: OTHNIEL — EHUD — SHAMGAR
(JUDGES 3:5-31)

THE first scene presented in the history of the Judges is that of Israel's intermarriage with the heathen around, and their doing "evil in the sight of Jehovah," forgetting Him, and serving "Baalim and the groves." And the first "judgment" on their apostasy is, that they are "sold" by the Lord into the hand of "Chushan-rishathaim, king of Mesopotamia," or rather of "Aram-naharaim," "the highland by the two streams" (Euphrates and Tigris). Curiously enough, there is an ancient Persian tradition, according to which the monarchs of Iran, who held dominion "by the streams," waged war against Egypt, Syria, and Asia Minor. Of their heroes, who are described as Cushan, or from the land of Chusistan (= Scythians, Parthians?), the most notable is Rustan or Rastam, a name evidently akin to Rishathaim. And so ancient heathen records once more throw unexpected light upon the historical narratives of the Old Testament. The oppression had lasted full eight years when Israel "cried unto Jehovah." The deliverer raised up for them was Othniel, the younger brother of Caleb, whose bravery had formerly gained him the hand of his wife (1:12-15). But his success now was not due to personal prowess.

"The Spirit of Jehovah was upon him, and he judged Israel, and went out to war." For the first time in the Book of Judges we meet here the statement, that "the Spirit of Jehovah" "was upon," or "clothed," or else "came upon" a person.

We naturally connect the expression with what we read of "the manifold gifts of the Spirit" as these are detailed in Isaiah 11:2, which were distributed to each as God pleased, and according to the necessity of the time (1 Corinthians 12:11). But, in thinking of these influences, we ought to bear two things in mind. First: although, in each case, the influence came straight from above — from the Spirit of God — for the accomplishment of a special purpose, it was not necessarily, as under the New Testament dispensation, a sanctifying influence. Secondly: this influence must not be regarded as the same with the abiding presence of the Holy Spirit in the heart. This also belongs to the New Testament dispensation. In short, these gifts of the Holy Spirit were miraculous, rather than gracious — like the gifts in the early Church, rather than as "the promise of the Father." In the case of Othniel, however, we note that the Spirit of God "was upon" him, and that, under His influence, "he judged" Israel, even "before he went out to war." And so, while ancient Jewish tradition in all other instances paraphrases the expression, "the Spirit of the Lord," by "the spirit of strength," in the case of Othniel — "the lion of God" — it renders it: "the spirit of prophecy." A war so undertaken must have been successful, and "the land had rest forty years."

The next judgment to rebellious Israel came likewise from the east. Quite on the eastern boundary of Reuben and of Gad lay the land of Moab. One of the chieftains of its tribes, Eglon, now allied himself with the old enemies of Israel, Ammon and Amalek, the former occupying the territory south of Reuben, the latter the districts in the far south-west, below Philistia. Eglon swept over the possessions of the trans-Jordanic tribes, crossed the river, and made Jericho, which was probably rebuilt as a town, though not as a fortress, his capital. Having thus cut the land, as it were, into two, and occupied its center and garden, Eglon reduced Israel for eighteen years to servitude. At the end of that period the people once more "cried unto the Lord," and "the Lord raised them up a deliverer," although Holy Scripture does not say that in his mode of deliverance he acted under the influence of the Spirit of the Lord. In the peculiar circumstances of the case this silence is most significant.

The "deliverer" was "Ehud (probably, the praised one), the son of Gera, a Benjamite, a man left-handed," or, as the original has it, "shut up" or "weak" "as to his right hand." The conspiracy against Eglon was well planned. Ehud placed himself at the head of a deputation charged to bring Eglon "a present," or, more probably, the regular tribute, as we gather from the similar use of the word in 2 Samuel 8:2, 6; 17:3, 4. But Ehud carried under his raiment a two-edged dagger, a cubit long; according to the LXX translation, about three-quarters of a foot. The tribute was delivered, no doubt with many protestations of humility and allegiance on the part of Ehud, and the deputation graciously dismissed.

It was needful for his plan, and probably in accordance with his wish to involve no one else in the risk, that the rest should be done by Ehud alone. Having seen his fellow-countrymen safely beyond "the quarries that were by Gilgal," or, rather, as the term implies, beyond "the terminal columns" (always objects of idolatrous worship), that divided the territory of Eglon from that of Israel, he returned to the king, whose confidence his former appearance had no doubt secured. The narrative here is exceedingly graphic. The king is no longer in the palace where the deputation had been received, but in his "upper chamber of cooling," a delicious summer-retreat built out upon the end of the flat roof. Ehud professes to have "a secret errand," which had brought him back when his companions were gone.

All the more that he does not ask for the withdrawal of the king's attendants does Eglon bid him be "Silent!" in their presence, which, of course, is the signal for their retirement. Alone with the king, Ehud saith, in a manner not uncommon in the East: "I have a message from God unto thee," on which Eglon, in token of reverence, rises from his seat. This is the favorable moment, and, in an instant, Ehud has plunged his dagger up to the hilt into the lower part of his body, with such force that the blade came out behind. Not pausing for a moment, Ehud retires, closes and locks the doors upon the murdered king, and escapes beyond the boundary.

Meanwhile the king's attendants, finding the room locked, have waited, till, at last, they deem it necessary to break open the doors. The horror and confusion consequent upon the discovery of the murder have given Ehud still further time. And now the preconcerted signal is heard. The shrill blast of the trumpet in Seirath (perhaps the "hairy" or "wooded") wakes the echoes of Mount Ephraim. All around from their hiding troop the men of Israel. The first object is to haste back towards Jericho and take the fords of Jordan, so as to allow neither help to come, nor fugitives to escape; the next to destroy the garrison of Moab. In both, Israel are successful, and, "at that time" — of course, not on that precise day — 10,000 of Moab are slain, all of them, as we should say, fine men and brave soldiers. "And the land had rest fourscore years."

Ancient history, both Greek and Roman, records similar stories, and, where the murderer has been a patriot, elevates him to the highest pinnacle of heroism. Nay, even Christian history records like instances, as in the murder of Henry III and Henry IV of France, the former, even in its details, so like the deed of Ehud. But strikingly different from the toleration, and even commendation, of such deeds by the Papacy is the judgment of the Old Testament. Its silence is here severest condemnation. It needed not cunning and murder to effect deliverance. Not one word of palliation or excuse is said for this deed. It was not under the influence of "the Spirit of Jehovah" that such deliverance was wrought, nor is it said of Ehud, as of Othniel, that he "judged Israel." Even Jewish tradition compares Ehud to the "ravening wolf" which had been the early emblem of his tribe, Benjamin (Genesis 49:27).

It must have been during this period of eighty years' rest, that another danger at least threatened Benjamin. This time it came from an opposite direction — from the west, where the Philistines held possession. "After" Ehud (3:31), that is, after his example, a notable exploit was performed by Shamgar ("the name of a stranger"?). Under the impulse of sudden sacred enthusiasm, he seized, as the first weapon to hand, an ox-goad, commonly used to urge on the oxen in ploughing. The weapon is formidable enough, being generally about eight feet long, and six inches round at the handle, which is furnished with an iron horn to loosen the earth off the plough, while the other end is armed with a long iron spike. With this weapon he slew no fewer than 600 Philistines, whom, probably, panic seized on his appearance. The exploit seems to have been solitary, and we read neither of further war, nor yet of Shamgar's rule, only that for the time the danger of a Philistine incursion was averted.

CHAPTER 15: THE OPPRESSION OF JABIN AND SISERA — DEBORAH AND BARAK — THE BATTLE OF TAANACH — THE SONG OF DEBORAH
(JUDGES 4, 5)

DARKER and darker are the clouds which gather around Israel, and stranger and more unexpected is the deliverance wrought for them. It had begun with Othniel, truly a "lion of God." But after the "lion of God" came one left-handed, then a woman, then the son of an idolater, and then an outlaw of low birth, as if it were ever to descend lower and lower, till the last stage is reached in the Nazarite, Samson, who, as Nazarite, is the typical representative of Israel's calling and strength, and, as Samson, of Israel's weakness and spiritual adultery. Yet each period and each deliverance has its characteristic features and high points. The narrative opens as if to resume the thread of Israel's continuous history, only temporarily broken by Ehud's life: "And the children of Israel continued to do evil in the eyes of Jehovah — and Ehud was dead." This furnished a long wished-for opportunity.

It had been about a century before when a Jabin ("the prudent" or "understanding," — no doubt the monarch's title, like Pharaoh or Abimelech) had marshaled the chieftains of Northern Palestine against Joshua, and been signally defeated (Joshua 11:1-10). Since then his capital had been restored and his power grown, till now it seemed the fitting moment to recover his ancient empire. As we understand the narrative, the hosts of Jabin had swept down from Hazor in the far north, and occupied the possessions of Naphtali, Zebulun, and Issachar. While Jabin himself continued in his capital, his general, Sisera ("mediation," "lieutenant"?) held the southern boundary of the annexed provinces, making his headquarters at Harosheth ha Gojim — "the smithy of the nations" — perhaps so called from being the arsenal where his iron war-chariots, armed with scythes, were made. The site of this place is probably somewhere in the neighborhood of Bethshean, which afterwards formed the southernmost point of Galilee. Evidently it must have been south of Mount Tabor, to which Barak afterwards marched from Kedron, in the north of Naphtali. For, irrespective of the utterly helpless state of the country, as described in Judges 5:6, Sisera would not have allowed Barak to turn his flank or to march on his rear. The occupation of the north of Palestine by Sisera had lasted twenty years. Relief must have seemed well-nigh hopeless. On the one hand, the population was wholly disarmed (Judges 5:8); on the other, Sisera had no less than nine hundred war-chariots — means of attack which Israel most dreaded. But as often before, so now, suffering led Israel to cry unto the Lord — and help was soon at hand.

One of the most painful circumstances in the history of the Judges is the utter silence which all this time seems to envelop Shiloh and its sanctuary. No help comes from the priesthood till quite the close of this period. Far away in Mount Ephraim God raised up a woman, on whom He had poured the spirit of prophecy. It is the first time in this history that we read of the prophetic gift. The sacred text conveys, that she exercised it in strict accordance with the Divine law, for it is significantly added in connection with it, that "she judged Israel at that time." Deborah, "the bee," is described as a "burning woman." The meeting-place for all in Israel who sought judgment at her hands was between Ramah and

Bethel, under a palm-tree, which afterwards bore her name. Thence she sent for Barak ("lightning,") the son of Abinoam ("my father" — God — "is favor"), from the far north, from Kadesh in Naphtali. His ready obedience proved his preparedness. But when Deborah laid on him the Divine command "gradually to draw" an army of 10,000 men to Mount Tabor, Barak shrank from it, unless Deborah would accompany him.

This evidently proved distrust in the result of the undertaking, which in turn showed that he looked for success to the presence of man, rather than entirely to the power of God. Accordingly, he must learn the folly of attaching value to man; and Deborah predicted, that not Israel's leader, but a woman, wholly unconnected with the battle, would have the real triumph.

Accompanied by Deborah, Barak now returned to Kadesh, whither he summoned the chiefs of Naphtali and Zebulon. All plans being concerted, the combatants converged in small companies, from all roads and directions, "on foot," towards the trysting-place. About six or eight miles east of Nazareth rises abruptly a beautifully-shaped conical mountain, about 1,000 feet high.

This is Mount Tabor ("the height"), its sloping sides covered with trees, and affording from its summit one of the most extensive and beautiful prospects in Palestine. Here the army under Barak and Deborah gathered. Tidings soon reached the head-quarters of Sisera. His chariots could of course only fight to advantage in the valleys, and he naturally marched north-west to the plain of Jezreel or Esdraelon. This has ever been, and will prove in the final contest (Revelation 16:16), the great battle-field of Israel. It was now the first of many times that its fertile soil was to be watered with the blood of men.

Sisera had chosen his position with consummate skill. Marching in almost straight line upon the plain of Megiddo, his army was now posted at its entrance, resting upon the ancient Canaanitish town of Taanach (Judges 5:19, comp. Joshua 12:21). Behind, and at his left flank, were the mountains of Manasseh, before him opened the basin of the valley, merging into the plain of Esdraelon, watered by the Kishon. Into this plain must Barak's army descend "on foot," badly armed, without experienced officers, without cavalry or chariots — and here his own 900 war-chariots would operate to best advantage. It was not even like one of those battles in which mountaineers hold their own fastnesses, or swoop down on their enemies in narrow defiles. On the contrary, all seemed to tell against Israel — but this, that God had previously promised to draw Sisera and his army to the river Kishon, and to deliver them into Barak's hand. Then once more did the Lord appear as "a man of war," and fight on the side of His people. It is said: "And Jehovah discomfited," or rather, "threw into confusion, Sisera and all his chariots, and all his host." The expression is the same as when Jehovah fought against Egypt (Exodus 14:25), and again when before Gibeon Joshua bade sun and moon stand still (Joshua 10:10). It indicates the direct interference of the Lord through terrible natural phenomena; (comp. also its use in 2 Samuel 22:15; Psalm 18:14; 144:6). As we gather from Judges 5:20-22, a fearful storm swept down from heaven in face of the advancing army. The battle must have drawn towards Endor, where its fate was finally decided (Psalm 83:9, 10). Presently the war-chariots were thrown into confusion, and instead of being a help became a source of danger. The aftrighted horses carried destruction into the ranks of the host. Soon all were involved in a common panic. A scene of wild confusion ensued. It was impossible to retreat, and only in one direction could flight be attempted. And now the waters of Kishon had swollen into a wild torrent which swept away the fugitives!

To escape capture, Sisera leaped from his chariot, and fled on foot northwards towards Hazor. Already he had passed beyond Kadesh, and almost reached safety. There the boundary of Naphtali was marked by what was known as "the oakwood at the twin tents of wandering" (Elon be-Zaanannim; comp. Joshua 19:33). Here Heber the Kenite had pitched his tent, having separated from his brethren, who had settled in the extreme south at Arad (Judges 1:16). Living quite on the boundary of Jabin's dominion, and not being really Israelites, the clan of Heber had been left unmolested and "there was peace between Jabin, king of Hazor, and the house of Heber the Kenite."

Only outward, not real peace! There is something wild and weird about the appearance of these Kenites on the stage of Jewish history. Originally an Arab tribe they retain to the last the fierceness of their race. Though among Israel, they never seem to amalgamate with Israel, and yet they are more keenly Israelitish than any of the chosen race.

In short, these stranger-converts are the most intense in their allegiance to the nation which they have joined, while at the same time they never lose the characteristics of their own race. We mark all this, for example, in the appearance of Jehonadab, the son of Rechab (2 Kings 10:15), and again much later during the troubles that befell Judah in the time of Jeremiah (Jeremiah 35). Jael, "the chamois," the wife of Heber, was among the Kenites what Deborah, the "torch-woman," was in Israel, only with all the characteristics of her race developed to the utmost. At her tent-door she meets the fugitive Sisera. She disarms his suspicions; she invites him to rest and security; she even sacrifices the sacred rights of hospitality to her dark purpose. There is something terrible and yet grand about that fierce woman, to whom every other consideration is as nothing, so that she may avenge Israel and destroy its great enemy. All seems lawful to her in such an undertaking; every means sanctified by the end in view. She has laid the worn warrior to rest; she has given him for refreshment of the best her tent affords. And now, as he lies in heavy sleep, she stealthily withdraws one of the long iron spikes to which the tent-cords are fastened, and with a heavy hammer once, again, and yet a third time, strikes it into his temples. It is not long before Barak — a "lightning" in pursuit as in battle — has reached the spot. Jael lifts aside the tent-curtain and shows him the gory corpse. In silence Barak turns from the terrible spectacle. But the power of Jabin and his dominion are henceforth for ever destroyed.

There is, as it seems to us, not a word in Scripture to express its approbation of so horrible a deed of deceit and violence — no, not even in the praise which Deborah in her song bestows upon Jael. It was not like Deborah's war, nor like Barak's battle, but strictly Kenite. Her allegiance to the cause of the people of God, her courage, her zeal, were Israelitish; their fanatical, wild, unscrupulous manifestation belonged to the race from which she had sprung, to the traditions amidst which she had been nurtured, and to the fiery blood which coursed in her veins — they were not of God nor of His word, but of her time and race. Heathen history tells of similar deeds, and records them with highest praise; Scripture with solemn silence. Yet even so Jehovah reigneth, and the fierce Arab was the sword in His hand!

1. "Then sang Deborah and Barak on that day, saying:

2. For the loose flowing of the long hair, For the free dedication of the people, Praise ye Jehovah!

3. Hear O kings, hearken O rulers, I — to Jehovah will I sing, Will psalmody to Jehovah, the God of Israel!

4. Jehovah, when Thou didst come forth from Seir, When Thou marchedst from out the fields of Edom, The earth trembled, also the heavens dropped, Even the clouds dropped water.

5. The mountains quaked before Jehovah — This Sinai before Jehovah, the God of Israel.

6. In the days of Shamgar, the son of Anath, In the days of Jael, the highways ceased, And they who went on paths, went by roundabout ways.

7. Deserted was the open country in Israel — deserted — Till I arose, Deborah, I arose a mother in Israel!

8. Chose they new gods — Then war at the gates — If shield was seen or spear Among forty thousand in Israel!

9. My heart towards the rulers of Israel, Those who freely vowed (dedicated) themselves among the people. Praise ye Jehovah!

10. Ye that ride on white she-asses, Ye that sit on coverings Ye that walk by the way — consider!

11. From the noise (sound, voice) of the archers between the draw-wells — There they rehearse the righteous deeds of Jehovah, The mighty deeds of His open country in Israel — Then went down to the city gates the people of Jehovah!

PART II

12. Awake, awake, Deborah, Awake, awake — utter the song; Arise, Barak, and lead captive thy captives, son of Abinoam!

13. Then went down a remnant of the mighty, of the people, Jehovah went down for me among the heroes!

14. From out of Ephraim — his root in Amalek; After thee: Benjamin among thy nations — From Machir come down they who bear rule, From Zebulon who draw out with the staff of the writer.

15. But the princes of Issachar were with Deborah — And Issachar the foundation of Barak, Pouring on foot into the valley! By the brooks of Reuben great resolves of heart

16. Why abodest thou among the folds To hear the flutes of the flocks? By the brooks of Reuben great ponderings of heart!

17. Gilead dwells on the other side Jordan! And Dan, who pass upon ships? Asher sitteth by the sea-shore, And by its bays resteth!

18. Zebulon a people that jeoparded its life unto death, And Naphtali on the heights of the field!

19. Came kings — warred — Then warred the kings of Canaan, In Taanach, by the waters of Megiddo — Spoil of silver took they none!

20. From heaven warred, The stars out of their paths warred against Sisera!

21. The river Kishon swept them away, River of encounters, River Kishon! March forth my soul in strength!

22. Then clattered the hoofs of the horse From the racing and chasing of his mighty.

23. Curse ye Meroz, saith the Angel of Jehovah, Curse ye — cursed its inhabitants, For they came not to the help of Jehovah, The help of Jehovah against the mighty!

PART III.

24. Blessed among women, Jael, The wife of Heber, the Kenite, Among women in the tent blessed!

25. Water asked he — milk she gave, In the cup of the noble brought she thickened milk

26 Her hand to the tent-nail sendeth forth, And her right hand to the ponderous hammer of workmen — Hammers she Sisera, shivers his head, Cleaves and pierces his temple!

27. Between her feet he winds — he falls — he lies — Between her feet he winds — he falls — Where he winds there he falls desolated!

28. High up through the window spies — anxiously she calls, The mother of Sisera — cut through the lattice: 'Why tarrieth his chariot to come, Why linger the steps of his war-chariots?'

29. The wise of her princesses answer — Nay, she herself answers her words to herself: 'Are they not finding — dividing spoil —

30. A maiden-twain maidens to the head of the warriors — Spoil of dyed garments to Sisera, Spoil of dyed garments — many-colored kerchief — A dyed garment, twain many-colored kerchiefs for the necks of the prey!'

31. So perish all Thine enemies, Jehovah — And let those who love Him be like the going forth of the sun in his strength! And the land had rest forty years.

CHAPTER 16: MIDIANITISH OPPRESSION — THE CALLING OF GIDEON — JUDGMENT BEGINS AT THE HOUSE OF GOD — THE HOLY WAR — THE NIGHT-BATTLE OF MOREH
(JUDGES 6-7:22)

WITH the calling of Gideon commences the second period in the history of the Judges. It lasted altogether less than a century. During its course events were rapidly hastening towards the final crisis. Each narrative is given with full details, so as to exhibit the peculiarity of God's dealings in every instance, the growing apostasy of Israel, and the inherent unfitness even of its best representatives to work real deliverance.

The narrative opens, as those before, with a record of the renewed idolatry of Israel. Judgment came in this instance through the Midianites, with whom the Amalekites and other "children of the east" seem to have combined. It was two hundred years since Israel had avenged itself on Midian (Numbers 31:3-11). And now once more, from the far east, these wild nomads swept, like the modern Bedawin, across Jordan, settled in the plain of Jezreel, and swooped down as far as Gaza in the distant south-west. Theirs was not a permanent occupation of the land, but a continued desolation. No sooner did the golden harvest stand in the field, or was stored into garners, than they unexpectedly arrived. Like the plague of locusts, they left nothing behind. What they could not carry away as spoil, they destroyed. Such was the feeling of insecurity to life and property, that the people made them "mountain-dens, and caves, and strongholds," where to seek safety for themselves and their possession. Seven years had this terrible scourge impoverished the land, when the people once more bethought themselves of Jehovah, the God of their fathers, and cried unto Him. This time, however, before granting deliverance, the Lord sent a prophet to bring Israel to a knowledge of their guilt as the source of their misery. The call to repentance was speedily followed by help.

1. The calling of Gideon. — Far away on the south-western border of Manasseh, close by the boundary of Ephraim, was the little township of Ophrah, belonging to the family of Abiezer (Joshua 17:2; 1 Chronicles 7:18), apparently one of the smallest clans in Manasseh (Judges 6:15). Its head or chief was Joash — "Jehovah strength," or "firmness."

As such he was lord of Ophrah. In such names the ancient spiritual faith of Israel seems still to linger amidst the decay around. And now, under the great oak by Ophrah, suddenly appeared a heavenly stranger. It was the Angel of Jehovah, the Angel of the Covenant, Who in similar garb had visited Abraham at Mamre (Genesis 18). Only there He had come, in view of the judgment about to burst, to confirm Abraham's faith — to enter into fellowship with him, while here the object was to call forth faith, and to prove that the Lord was ready to receive the vows and prayers of His people, if they but turned to Him in the appointed way. This may also explain, why in the one case the heavenly visitor joined in the meal, while in the other fire from heaven consumed the offering (comp. Judges 13:16; 1 Kings 18:38; 2 Chronicles 7:1).

Close by the oak was the winepress of Joash, and there his son Gideon was beating out the wheat with a stick. Alike the place and the manner of threshing were quite unusual, and only accounted for by the felt need for secrecy, and the constant apprehension that at an unexpected moment some wild band of Midianites might swoop down upon him. If, as we gather from the Angel's salutation, Gideon was a strong hero, and if; as we infer from his reply, remembrances and thoughts of the former deeds of Jehovah for Israel had burned deep into his heart, we can understand how the humiliating circumstances under which he was working in his father's God-given possession, in one of the remotest corners of the land, must have filled his soul with sadness and longing.

It is when "the strong warrior" is at the lowest, that the Messenger of the Covenant suddenly appears before him. Not only the brightness of His face and form, but the tone in which He spake, and still more His words, at once struck the deepest chords in Gideon's heart. "Jehovah with thee, mighty hero!" Then the speaker was one of the few who looked unto Jehovah as the help-giver; and he expressed alike belief and trust! And was there not in that appellation "mighty warrior" a sound like the echo of national expectations — like a call to arms? One thing at least the Angel immediately gained. It was — what the Angel of His Presence always first gains — the confidence of Gideon's heart. To the unknown stranger he pours forth his inmost doubts, sorrows, and fears. It is not that he is ignorant of Jehovah's past dealings, nor that he questions His present power, but that he believes that, if Jehovah had not withdrawn from Israel, their present calamities could not have rested upon them. The conclusion was right and true, so far as it went; for Israel's prosperity or sufferings depended on the presence or the absence of Jehovah. Thus Gideon's was in truth a confession of Israel's sin, and of Jehovah's justice. It was the beginning of repentance. But Gideon had yet to learn another truth — that Jehovah would turn from His anger, if Israel only turned to Him; and yet another lesson for himself: to put personal trust in the promise of God, based as it was on His covenant of love, and that whether the outward means to be employed seemed adequate or not.

But Gideon was prepared to learn all this; and, as always, gradually did the Lord teach His servant, both by word, and by the sight with which He confirmed it. The reply of the Angel could leave no doubt on the mind of Gideon that a heavenly messenger was before him, Who promised that through him Israel should be saved, and that simply because He sent him. It is not necessary to suppose that Gideon understood that this messenger from heaven was the Angel of the Covenant. On the contrary, the revelation was very gradual. Nor do the questions of Gideon seem strange — for such they are rather than doubts. Looking around at his tribe, at his clan, and at his own position in it, help through him seemed most unlikely, and, if we realize all the circumstances, was so. Only one conclusive answer could be returned to all this: "I shall be with thee." The sole doubt now left was: Who was this great I AM? — and this Gideon proposed to solve by "asking for a sign," yet not a sign to his unbelief, but one connected with worship and with sacrifice. Jehovah granted it. As when Moses sought to know God, He revealed not His being but His character and His ways (Exodus 33:18; 34:6), so now He revealed to Gideon not only Who had spoken to him, but also that His "Name" was "Jehovah, Jehovah God, merciful and gracious, longsuffering, and abundant in goodness and truth, keeping mercy for thousands, forgiving iniquity, and transgression, and sin."

It would be almost fatal to the proper spiritual understanding of this, as of other Biblical narratives, if we were to transport into it our present knowledge, ideas, and views. Remembering the circumstances of the nation, of Gideon, and of Israel; remembering also the stage of spiritual knowledge attainable at that period, and the difficulty of feeling really sure Who the speaker was, we can understand Gideon's request (6:1-17): "Work for me a sign that THOU (art He) Who art speaking with me." It is difficult to imagine what special sign Gideon was expecting. Probably he had formed no definite idea. Suffice it, he would bring a sacrificial gift; the rest he would leave to Him. And he brought of the best. It was a kid of the goats, while for the "cakes," to be offered with it, he took a whole ephah of flour, that is, far more than was ordinarily used. But he does all the ministry himself; for no one must know of it. To dispense with assistance, he puts the meat and the cakes in the "bread-basket," "and the broth in a pot." Directed by the Angel, he spreads his offering on a rock.

Then the Angel touches it with the end of His staff; fire leaps out of the rock and consumes the sacrifices; and the Angel has vanished out of his sight. There was in this both a complete answer to all Gideon's questions, and also deep symbolic teaching. But a fresh fear now fills Gideon's heart. Can one like him, who has seen God, live? To this also Jehovah gives an answer, and that for all times: "Peace to thee — fear not — thou shalt not die!" And in perpetual remembrance thereof — not for future worship — Gideon built an altar there, and attached to it the name, "Jehovah-Peace!"

2. One part was finished, but another had to begin. Jehovah had called — would Gideon be ready to obey? For judgment must now begin at the house of God. No one is fit for His work in the world till he has begun it in himself and in his own house, and put away all sin and rebellion, however hard the task. It was night when the command of Jehovah came. This time there was neither hesitation nor secrecy about Gideon's procedure. He obeyed God's directions literally and immediately. Taking ten of his servants, he first threw down the altar of Baal, and cut down the Asherah — the vile symbol of the vile service of Astarte — that was upon it.

One altar was destroyed, but another had to be raised. For, the altar of Jehovah could not be reared till that of Baal had been cast down. It was now built, and that not in some secret hiding-place, but on "the top of this defense" — either on the top of the hill on which the fort stood, or perhaps above the place where the people were wont to seek shelter from the Midianites. Upon this altar Gideon offered his father's "second bullock of seven years old" — the age being symbolical of the time of Midian's oppression — at the same time using the wood of the Asherah in the burnt-sacrifice. Such a reformation could not, and was not intended to be hidden. The Baal's altar and its Asherah were indeed Joash's, but only as chief of the clan. And when on the following morning the Abiezrites clamored for the death of the supposed blasphemer, Joash, whose courage and faith seem to have been re-awakened by the bold deed of his son, convinced his clan of the folly of their idolatry by an unanswerable argument, drawn from their own conduct. "What!" he exclaimed, in seeming condemnation, "will ye strive for Baal? Or will ye save him? He that will strive for him let him die until the morrow! If he be a god, let him strive for himself, because he has thrown down his altar. And they called him on that day Jerubbaal ('let Baal strive'), that is to say, Let the Baal strive with him, because he has thrown down his altar."

3. The Holy War. — Gideon had now purified himself and his house, and become ready for the work of the Lord. And yet another important result had been secured. The test to which Baal had been put had proved his impotence. Idolatry had received a heavy blow throughout the land. In Ophrah at least the worship of Jehovah was now alone professed. Moreover, the whole clan Abiezer, and, beyond it, all who had heard of Gideon's deed, perpetuated even in his name, were prepared to look to him as their leader. The occasion for it soon came. Once more the Midianitish Bedawin had swarmed across Jordan; once more their tents covered the plain of Jezreel. Now or never — now, before their destructive raids once more began, or else never under Gideon — must Israel arise! Yet not of his own purpose did he move. In the deeply expressive language of Scripture: "The Spirit of

Jehovah clothed Gideon," like a garment round about, or rather like an armor. Only after that he blew the trumpet of alarm. First, his own clan Abiezer "was called after him." Next, swift messengers bore the tidings all through Manasseh, and that tribe gathered. Other messengers hastened along the coast (to avoid the Midianites) through Asher northwards to Zebulun and Naphtali, and they as well as Asher, which formerly had not fought with Barak, obeyed the summons.

All was ready — yet one thing more did Gideon seek. It was not from unbelief, nor yet in weakness of faith, that Gideon asked a sign from the Lord, or rather a token, a pledge of His presence. Those hours in the history of God's heroes, when, on the eve of a grand deed of the sublimest faith, the spirit wrestles with the flesh, are holy seasons, to which the superficial criticism of a glib profession, that has never borne the strain of utmost trial, cannot be applied without gross presumption. When in such hours the soul in its agony is seen to cast its burden upon the Lord, we feel that we stand on holy ground. It is like a stately ship in a terrific gale, every beam and timber strained to the utmost, but righting itself at last, and safely reaching port. Or rather it is like a close following of Jesus into the Garden of Gethsemane — with its agony, its prayer, and its victory. In substance, though not in its circumstances, it was the same struggle as that which was waged in the night when Jacob prayed: "I will not let Thee go except Thou bless me;" the same as when, many centuries afterwards, the Baptist sent his disciples to ask Jesus: "Art Thou He, or do we wait for another?"

The "sign" was of Gideon's own choosing, but graciously accorded him by God. It was twofold. On the first night the fleece of wool spread on the ground it was to be full of dew, but the ground all around dry. This, however, might still admit of doubt, since a fleece would naturally attract the dew. Accordingly, the next night the sign was reversed, and the fleece alone remained dry, while the ground all around was wet with dew. The symbolical meaning of the sign is plain. Israel was like that fleece of wool, spread on the wide extent of the nations. But, whereas all the ground around was dry, Israel was filled with the dew, as symbol of the Divine blessing (Genesis 27:28; Deuteronomy 33:13; Proverbs 19:12; Isaiah 26:19; Hosea 14:5; Micah 5:7.). And the second sign meant, that it was equally of God, when, during Israel's apostasy, the ground all around was wet, and the fleece of Jehovah's flock alone left dry.

4. The battle: "For Jehovah and for Gideon!" — The faith which had made such trial of God was to be put to the severest trial. Israel's camp was pitched on the height; probably on a crest of Mount Gilboa, which seems to have borne the name of Gilead. At its foot rose "the spring Harod" — probably the same which now bears the name Jalood. Beyond it was the hill Moreh (from the verb "to indicate," "to direct"), and north of it, in the valley, lay the camp of Midian, 135,000 strong (Judges 8:10), whereas the number of Israel amounted to only 22,000. But even so they were too many — at least for Jehovah "to give the Midianites into their hand, lest Israel vaunt themselves against Me, saying, Mine own hand hath saved me." In accordance with a previous Divine direction (Deuteronomy 20:8), proclamation was made for all who were afraid, to "turn and wind about from Mount Gilead."

Still, Gideon must have been surprised, when, in consequence, he found himself left with only 10,000 men. But even these were too many. To "purify them" (as by refining — for such is the meaning of the word), Gideon was now to bring them down to the spring Harod, where those who were to go to battle would be separated from the rest. All who lapped the water with the tongue out of their hands (out of the hollow hand), as a dog lappeth water, were to go with Gideon, the rest to return, each to his own place. Only three hundred were now left, and with these God declared He would save, and deliver the Midianites into Gideon's hand. If we ask about the rationale of this means of distinction, we conclude, of course, that it indicated the bravest and most ardent warriors, who would not stoop to kneel, but hastily quenched their thirst out of the hollow of their hands, in order to hasten to battle. But Jewish tradition assigns another and deeper meaning to it. It declares that the practice of kneeling was characteristic of the service of Baal, and hence that kneeling down to drink when exhausted betrayed the habit of idolaters. Thus the three hundred would represent those in the host of Israel — "all the knees which have not bowed unto Baal" (1 Kings 19:18). They who had been selected now "took victuals from the people in their hands, and the trumpets" — the rest were sent away.

That night the small company of Israel occupied an advanced position on the brow of the steep mountain, that overhangs the valley of Jezreel. Effectually concealed, probably by the shelter of wood or vineyards, the vast straggling camp of Midian spread right beneath them. That night came the Divine command to Gideon to go down to the camp, for God had given it into his hand. And yet, alike in condescension to Gideon's weakness, and to show how thoroughly the Lord had prepared the victory, He first allowed him to ascertain for himself the state of matters in the camp of Midian. Quietly Gideon and his page Phurah ("the branch") crept from rock to rock, over where the last patrol of the advance-guard kept watch around the camp-fire.

Here they overheard the tale of a strange dream. Alike the dream and its interpretation are peculiarly Eastern and in character. Both would make the deepest impression on those sons of the desert, and, communicated to the next patrol, as the first watch was relieved by the second, must have prepared for that panic which, commencing with the advance-guard, was so soon to spread through the whole camp of Midian. The dream was simply this: "Behold, a loaf of barley-bread rolled itself into the camp of Midian, and it came to the tent (the principal one, that of the general), and struck it, and it fell, and it turned from above and it was fallen!" To which his neighbor (comrade) replied: "This is nothing else but the sword of Gideon, the son of Joash, a man of Israel; given hath the God into his hand Midian and all his camp." So wondrous seemed the dream and its interpretation, that, when Gideon and his armor-bearer heard it, they bent in silent worship, assuredly knowing that God had given them the victory. In truth, with the tale of this dream the miracle of the victory had already begun.

There is such pictorialness and such truthfulness of detail about all this narrative, that we almost seem to see the events enacted before us. That camp of Bedouins, like locusts in numbers — with their wives, children, and camels, like the sand by the seashore; then the watchfire by which alone they keep guard; the talk over the camp-fire; the dream so peculiarly Bedouin, and its rapid interpretation, no less characteristically Eastern — and yet the while all ordered and arranged of God — while that small band of three hundred Israelites lies concealed on the neighboring height, and Gideon and his "young man," are close by, behind the great shadows which the watch-fire casts, hidden perhaps in the long grass! Then the dream itself! It was all quite natural, and yet most unnatural. The Midianites — especially the advanced-guard, that lay nearest to Israel, could not be ignorant that Gideon and his host occupied yonder height. Fame would spread, probably exaggerate, the "mighty valor" of Gideon, and the valor of his followers — while the diminished numbers of Gideon would, of course, not be known, as they had retired by circuitous routes. Moreover, the Midianites must also have been aware that this was to Israel a religious war; nor can they have been ignorant of the might of Jehovah. The fears which all this inspired appear in the interpretation of the dream. But the dream itself was the result of the same feelings. Barley-bread was deemed the poorest food; yet a loaf of this despised provision of slaves rolls itself into Midian's camp, strikes the tent of the leader, turns it upside down, and it falls! Here is a dream-picture of Israel and its victory — all quite natural, yet marvelously dreamed and told just at that particular time. And still, often do dreams, excited by natural causes, link themselves, in God's appointment, to thoughts that come supernaturally.. We have throughout this history marked how often what seemed to happen quite naturally, was used by God miraculously, and how the supernatural linked itself to what, more or less, had its counterpart in the ordinary course of nature. It had been so in the history of Moses and of Israel; it was so when Joshua defeated the allied kings before Gibeon, and when Barak encountered the invincible chariots of Sisera. In each case it was the Lord, Who gave miraculous victory through terrific tempest. So also it had been in an hour, when thoughts of Israel's past and present must have burned deepest into the heart of Gideon, that the Angel stood before him, even as it was by means most natural that God separated from the rest the three hundred who had not bent the knee to Baal, and who alone were to go to the holy war. Thoughts like these do not detract from, they only make the supernatural the more marvelous. Yet they seem also to bring it nearer to us, till we feel ourselves likewise within its circle, and can realize that even our "daily bread" comes to us straight from heaven! Gideon and Phurah have returned to the waiting host. In whispered words he has told what they had witnessed. And now the three hundred are divided into three companies. It is not the naked sword they grasp, for in that night not Israel, but Jehovah is to fight. In one hand each man holds a trumpet, in the other, concealed in a pitcher, a burning torch. Each is to do exactly as the leader. Silently they creep round to three different parts of Midian's camp. The guard has just been relieved, and the new watchers have settled quietly by the watch-fire. Suddenly a single trumpet is heard, then three hundred — here, there, everywhere the sound of war is raised. The night is peopled with terrors. Now with loud crash three hundred pitchers are broken; three hundred torches flash through the darkness; three hundred voices shout: "The sword for Jehovah and for Gideon!" Then is the enemy all around the camp! No one can say in what numbers. Again and again rings the trumpet-sound; wave the torches. The camp is roused. Men, women, children, camels rush terror-stricken through the dark night. No one knows but that the enemy is in the very midst of them, and that the neighbor whom he meets is an Israelite, for all around still sounds the war-trumpet, flash the torches, and rises the war-cry. Each man's sword is turned against his neighbor. Multitudes are killed or trampled down, and their cries and groans increase the terror of that wild night. A hopeless panic ensues, and ere morning-light, the site of the camp and the road of the fugitives towards Jordan are strewed with the slain.

CHAPTER 17: FARTHER COURSE OF GIDEON — THE EPHOD AT OPHRAH — DEATH OF GIDEON — CONSPIRACY OF ABIMELECH — THE PARABLE OF JOTHAM — RULE AND END OF ABIMELECH

(JUDGES 7:23-9:57)

THE tide of battle had rolled towards the Jordan. The fugitives seem to have divided into two main bodies. The quickest, under the leadership of Zebah and Zalmunna, succeeded in crossing the Jordan, and hastened towards the wilderness, while the main body of the army, encumbered with women and cattle, fled in a south-easterly direction, trying to gain the more southern fords of the Jordan within the possession of Issachar, and almost in a straight line with that of Ephraim. The two kings were the object of Gideon's own pursuit, in which he was joined by those of Naphtali, Asher, and Manasseh, who had shortly before been dismissed from the battle. To overtake the other body of fugitives, Gideon summoned the Ephraimites, directing them to occupy "the waters," or tributaries of Jordan, unto Beth-barah (the house of springs) and the Jordan. The success of Ephraim was complete. A great battle seems to have been fought (Isaiah 10:26), in which the leaders of the Midianites, Oreb and Zeeb ("the raven" and "the wolf") were taken and slain. The Ephraimites continued the pursuit of the fugitives to the other side of the Jordan, bringing with them to Gideon the gory heads of Oreb and Zeeb. Strange and sad, that their first meeting with Gideon after this victory should have been one of reproaches and strife, on account of their not having been first summoned to the war — strife, springing from that tribal jealousy which influenced for such evil the whole history of Ephraim. Nor was the reply of Gideon much more satisfactory than their noisy self-assertion (8:1-3). To us at least it savors more of the diplomacy of an Oriental, than the straightforward bearing of the warrior of God.

While Ephraim occupied "the waters" and the fords of the Jordan, Gideon himself had crossed the river at the spot where Jacob of old had entered Canaan on his return from Padan-Aram. "Faint yet pursuing," the band reached Succoth; but its "princes" refused even the most useful provisions to Gideon's men. The people of the neighboring Penuel acted in the same heartless manner — no doubt from utter lack of interest in the cause of God, from cowardice, and, above all, from scorn for the small band of 300, with which Gideon had gone in pursuit of the flower of Midian's army. They had calculated the result by the outward means employed, but were destined soon to feel the consequences of their folly. Making a detour eastwards, through the wilderness, Gideon advanced on the rear of Midian, and fell unexpectedly upon the camp at Karkor, which was held by 15,000 men under the command of Zebah and Zalmunna ("sacrifice" and "protection refused"). The surprise ended in defeat and flight, the two Midianite leaders being made prisoners and taken across Jordan. On his way, Gideon "taught the men of Succoth," by punishing their rulers — seventy-seven in number, probably consisting of either seven, or else five "princes," and of seventy or else seventy-two elders — while in the case of Penuel, which seems to have offered armed resistance to the destruction of its citadel, "the men of the city" were actually slain.

The fate of Gideon's princely captives did not long remain doubtful. It seems that he would have spared their lives, if they had not personally taken part in the slaughter of his brothers, which may have occurred at the commencement of the last campaign, and while the Midianites held Jezreel — possibly under circumstances of treachery and cruelty, prompted perhaps by tidings that Gideon had raised the standard of resistance. It may have been to investigate the facts on the spot, that Gideon had brought back the two princes, or he may have only heard of it on his return. At any rate, the two Midianites not only confessed, but boasted of their achievement. By the law of retaliation they were now made to suffer death, although the hesitation of Gideon's son spared them the humiliation of falling by the hand of a young lad.

The deliverance of Israel was now complete. It had been wrought most unexpectedly, and by apparently quite inadequate means. In the circumstances, it was natural that, in measure as the people failed to recognize the direct agency of Jehovah, they should exalt Gideon as the great national hero. Accordingly, they now offered him the hereditary rule over, at least, the northern tribes. Gideon had spiritual discernment and strength sufficient to resist this temptation. He knew that he had only been called to a temporary work, and that the "rule" which they wished could not be made hereditary. Each "judge" must be specially called, and qualified by the influence of the Holy Spirit. Besides, the latter was not, as since the ascension of our Blessed Savior, a permanent indwelling of the Holy Spirit as a Person, but consisted in certain effects produced by His agency. The proposal of Israel could therefore only arise from carnal misunderstanding, and must be refused.

But Gideon himself was not proof against another temptation and mistake. God had called him not only to temporal, but to spiritual deliverance of Israel. He had thrown down the altar of Baal; he had built up that of Jehovah, and offered on it accepted sacrifice. Shiloh was deserted, and the high priest seemed set aside. Ophrah had been made what Shiloh should have been, and Gideon had taken the place of the high priest. All this had been by express Divine command — and without any reference to the services of the tabernacle. Moreover, Gideon's office had never been recalled. Should it not now be made permanent, at least, in his own person? The keeping of Israel's faith had been committed to his strong hand; should he deliver it up to the feeble grasp of a nominal priesthood which had proved itself incapable of such a trust? It was to this temptation that Gideon succumbed when he asked of the people the various golden ornaments, taken as spoil from the enemy. The gold so obtained amounted to seventeen thousand shekels — or nearly the weight of fifty pounds. With this Gideon made an ephod, no doubt with the addition of the high-priestly breastplate and its precious gems, and of the Urim and Thummim. Here, then, was the commencement of a spurious worship. Presently, Israel went to Ophrah, "a whoring after it," while to Gideon himself and to his house this "thing became a snare."

In truth, the same spiritual misunderstanding which culminated in Gideon's arrogating to himself high-priestly functions, had appeared almost immediately after that night-victory of Jehovah over Midian. Even his reply to the jealous wrangling of Ephraim does not sound like the straightforward language of one who had dismissed the thousands of Israel to go to battle with only three hundred. Again, there is what at least looks like petty revenge about his dealings with Succoth and Penuel; while it is difficult to understand upon what principle, other than that of personal retaliation, he had made the lives of Zebah and Zalmunna wholly dependent upon their conduct towards his own family. And the brief remarks of Scripture about the family-life of Gideon, after he had made the ephod, only tend to confirm our impressions. But, meantime, for "forty years in the days of Gideon," "the country was in quietness," and, however imperfect in its character, the service of Jehovah seems to have been, at least outwardly, the only one professed. Matters changed immediately upon his death. Presently the worship of Baalim becomes again common, and especially that of the "Covenant-Baal" (Baal-berith). There is a sad lesson here. If Gideon had made a spurious ephod, his people now chose a false "covenant-god." And, having first forsaken the Covenant-Jehovah, they next turned in ingratitude from their earthly deliverer, "neither showed they kindness to the house of Jerubbaal." Thus sin ever brings its own punishment.

Not far from Ophrah, but in the territory of Ephraim, was the ancient Shechem, connected with so much that was most solemn in the history of Israel. We know the long-standing tribal jealousy of Ephraim and their desire for leadership. Moreover, as we learn from Judges 9:28, Shechem seems to have retained among its inhabitants the lineal representatives of Hamor, the original "prince" and founder of Shechem in the days of Jacob (Genesis 33:19; 34:2; comp. Joshua 24:32). These would represent, so as speak, the ancient feudal heathen aristocracy of the place, and, of course, the original worshippers of Baal. As perhaps the most ancient city in that part of the country, and as the seat of the descendants of Hamor, Shechem seems to have become the center of Baal worship. Accordingly we find there the temple of the "Covenant-Baal" (Judges 9:4). Possibly the latter may have been intended to express and perpetuate the union of the original heathen with the more modern Israelitish, or "Shechem" part of the population. Here then were sufficient elements of mischief ready: tribal jealousy; envy of the great and ancient Shechem towards little Ophrah; hatred of the rule of the house of Gideon; but, above all, the opposition of heathenism. It is very characteristic of this last, as the chief motive at work, that throughout all the intrigues against the house of Gideon, he is never designated by his own name, but always as Jerubbaal — he that contended against Baal. Contending against Baal had been the origin of Gideon's power; and to the heathen mind it seemed still embodied in that Jehovah-Ephod in the possession of Gideon's sons at Ophrah. The present rising would in turn be the contending of Baal against the house of Gideon, and his triumph its destruction. It only needed a leader. Considering the authority which the family of Gideon must still have possessed, none better could have been found than one of its own members.

Gideon had left no fewer than seventy sons. If we may judge from their connivance at the worship of Baal around, from the want of any recognized outstanding individuality among them, and especially from their utter inability to make a stand even for life against an equal number of enemies, they must have sadly degenerated; probably were an enervated, luxurious, utterly feeble race. There was one exception, however, to this; one outside their circle, and yet of it — Abimelech, not a legitimate son of Gideon's, but one by "a maid-servant," a native of Shechem. Although we know not the possible peculiarities of the case, it is, in general, quite consistent with social relations in the East, that Abimelech's slave-mother should have had influential connections in Shechem, who, although of an inferior grade, could enter into dealings with "the citizens" of the place. Abimelech seems to have possessed all the courage, vigor, and energy of his father; only coupled, alas! with restless ambition, reckless unscrupulousness, and daring impiety. His real name we do not know; for Abimelech, father-king, or else king-father, seems to have been a by-name, probably suggested by his natural qualifications and his ambition.

The plot was well contrived by Abimelech. At his instigation his mother's relatives entered into negotiations with the "citizens" or "householders" of Shechem. The main considerations brought to bear upon them seem to have been: hatred of the house of Gideon, and the fact that Abimelech was a fellow-townsman. This was sufficient. The compact was worthily ratified with Baal's money. Out of the treasury of his temple they gave Abimelech seventy shekels. This wretched sum, somewhere at the rate of half-a-crown a person, sufficed to hire a band of seventy reckless rabble for the murder of Gideon's sons. Such was the value which Israel put upon them! Apparently unresisting, they were all slaughtered upon one stone, like a sacrifice — all but one, Jotham ("Jehovah [is] perfect"), who succeeded in hiding himself, and thus escaped.

This is the first scene. The next brings us once more to "the memorial by the vale" which Joshua had set up, when, at the close of his last address, the people had renewed their covenant with Jehovah (Joshua 24:26, 27). It was in this sacred spot that "the citizens of Shechem and the whole house of Millo" were now gathered to make Abimelech king! Close by, behind it, to the south, rose Gerizim, the Mount of Blessings. On one of its escarpments, which tower 800 feet above the valley, Jotham, the last survivor of Gideon's house, watched the scene. And now his voice rose above the shouts of the people.

In that clear atmosphere every word made its way to the listeners below. It was a strange parable he told, peculiarly of the East, that land of parables, and in language so clear and forcible, that it stands almost unique. It is about the Republic of Trees, who are about to elect a king. In turn the olive, the fig tree, and the vine, the three great representatives of fruit-bearing trees in Palestine, are asked. But each refuses; for each has its own usefulness, and inquires with wonder: "Am I then to lose" my fatness, or my sweetness, or my wine, "and to go to flutter above the trees?"

The expressions are very pictorial, as indicating, on the one hand, that such a reign could only be one of unrest and insecurity, a "wavering" or "fluttering" above the trees, and that, in order to attain this position of elevation above the other trees, a tree would require to be uprooted from its own soil, and so lose what of fatness, sweetness, or refreshment God had intended it to yield. Then, these noble trees having declined the offer, and apparently all the others also, the whole of the trees next turn to the thornbush, which yields no fruit, can give no shadow, and only wounds those who take hold of it, which, in fact, is only fit for burning. The thornbush itself seems scarcely to believe that such a proposal could seriously be made to it. "If in truth" (that is, "truly and sincerely") "ye anoint me king over you, come, put your trust in my shadow; but if not (that is, if you fear so to do, or else find your hopes disappointed), let fire come out of the thornbush and devour the cedars of Lebanon." The application of the parable was so evident, that it scarcely needed the pungent sentences in which Jotham in conclusion set before the people their conduct in its real character.

Jotham had not spoken as a prophet, but his language was prophetic. Three years, not of kingdom, but of rule, and the judgment of God, which had been slumbering, began to descend. Scripture marks distinctly both the Divine agency in the altered feeling of Shechem towards Abimelech, and its import as boding judgment.

The course of events is vividly sketched. First, the citizens post "liers in wait" in all the mountain passes, in the vain hope of seizing Abimelech. The consequence is universal brigandage. This device having failed, they next invite, or at least encourage the arrival among them of a freebooting adventurer with his band. It is the season of vintage, and, strange and terrible as it may sound, a service, specially ordered by Jehovah, is observed, but only to be prostituted to Baal. According to Leviticus 19:24, the produce of the fourth year's fruit planting was to be brought as "praise-offerings" (Hillulim) to Jehovah. And now these men of Shethem "made praise offerings" (Hillulim), but went with them into the house of Baal-berith. At the sacrificial feast which followed, wine soon loosened the tongues. It is an appeal to Baal as against the house of Jerubbaal; a revolt of old Shechem against modern Shechem; in favor of the old patrician descendants of Hamor against Abimelech and his lieutenant Zebul. This insulting challenge, addressed in true Oriental fashion to the absent, is conveyed by secret messengers to Abimelech.

That night he and his band move forward. Divided into four companies, they occupy all the heights around Shechem. Ignorant how near was danger, Gaal stands next morning in the gate with his band, in the same spirit of boastfulness as at the festival of the previous night. He is still, as it were, challenging imaginary foes. Zebul is also there. As Abimelech's men are seen moving down towards the valley, Zebul first tries to lull Gaal's suspicions. And now they are appearing in all directions — from the mountains, "from the heights of the land," and one company "from the way of the terebinth of the magicians."

Zebul now challenges Gaal to make good his boasting. A fight ensues in view of the citizens of Shechem, in which Gaal and his band are discomfited, and he and his adherents are finally expelled from the town. If the Shechemites had thought thus to purchase immunity, they were speedily undeceived. Abimelech was hovering in the neighborhood, and, when the unsuspecting people were busy in their fields, he surprised and slaughtered them, at the same time occupying the city, which was razed to the ground and sowed with salt. Upon this the citizens of the tower, or of Millo, sought refuge in the sacred precincts of "the hall of the god Berith." But in vain. Abimelech set it on fire, and 1000 persons perished in the flames. Even this did not satisfy his revenge. He next turned his forces against the neighboring town of Thebez. Reduced to the utmost straits, its inhabitants fled to the strong tower within the city. Thither Abimelech pursued them. Almost had the people of Thebez shared the fate of the citizens of Millo, when Abimelech's course was strangely arrested. From the top of the tower a woman cast down upon him an "upper millstone." As the Rabbis put it, he, that had slaughtered his brothers upon a stone, was killed by a stone. Abimelech died as he had lived. Feeling himself mortally wounded, ambitious warrior to the last, he had himself run through by the sword of his armor-bearer, to avoid the disgrace of perishing by the hand of a woman. But his epitaph, and that of the men of Shechem who had perished by his hand, had been long before written in the curse of Jotham.

CHAPTER 18: SUCCESSORS OF ABIMELECH — CHRONOLOGY OF THE PERIOD — ISRAEL'S RENEWED APOSTASY, AND THEIR HUMILIATION BEFORE JEHOVAH — OPPRESSION BY THE AMMONITES — JEPHTHAH — HIS HISTORY AND VOW — THE SUCCESSORS OF JEPHTHAH

(JUDGES 10-12)

THE sudden and tragic end of Abimelech seems to have awakened repentance among the people. It is thus that we explain the mention of his name (10:1) in connection with three judges, who successively ruled over the northern tribes. The first of these was Tola ("scarlet-worm"), the son of Puah (probably "red dye") and grandson of Dodo, a man of Issachar. His reign lasted twenty-three years, and was followed by that of Jair ("Enlightener"), who judged twenty-two years. The family notice of the latter indicates great influence, each of his thirty sons appearing as a "chief" (riding on "ass-colts"), and their property extending over thirty out of the sixty cities (1 Kings 4:13; 2 Chronicles 2:23) which formed the ancient Havoth-Jair, or circuits of Jairs (Numbers 32:41; Deuteronomy 3:14).

These forty-five years of comparative rest conclude the second period in the history of the Judges. The third, which commences with fresh apostasy on the part of Israel, includes the contemporaneous rule of Jephthah and his successors — Ibzan, Elon, and Abdon (12:8-15) — in the north and east, and of Samson in the south and west. While in the north and east Jephthah encountered the Ammonites, Samson warred against the Philistines in the south-west. The oppression of Ammon over the eastern and northern tribes lasted eighteen years (10:8, 9); the rule of Jephthah six years (12:7); that of his three successors twenty-five years — covering in all a period of forty-nine years. On the other hand, the oppression of the Philistines lasted in all forty years (13:1), during twenty years of which (15:20) Samson "began to deliver Israel" (13:5), the deliverance being completed only twenty years later under Samuel, when the battle of Ebenezer was gained (1 Samuel 7). Thus Abdon, Jephthah's last successor in the north, must have died nine years after the battle of Ebenezer. These dates are of great importance, not only on their own account, but because they show us the two parallel streams of Israel's history in the north and the south. Again, the coincidence of events in the south with those in the north casts fresh light upon both. Thus, as Eli's high-priestly administration, which in a general sense is designated as "judging Israel," lasted forty years (1 Samuel 4:18), and his death took place about twenty years and seven months before the victory of Samuel over the Philistines (1 Samuel 6:1; 7:2), it is evident that the first twenty years of Eli's administration were contemporary with that of Jair in the east, while the last twenty were marked by the Philistine oppression, which continued forty years. In that case Samson must have been born, and have grown up during the high priesthood of Eli, and most of his exploits, as judging Israel for twenty years, taken place under Samuel, who gained the battle of Ebenezer, and so put an end to Philistine oppression, a short time after the death of Samson. In connection with this we may note, that Samuel's period of judging is only mentioned after the battle of Ebenezer (1 Samuel 7:15).

There is another and very important fact to be considered. The terrible fate which overtook the house of Gideon, culminating in the death of Abimelech, seems for ever to have put an end to the spurious ephod-worship of Jehovah, or to that in any other place than that He had chosen, or through any other than the Levitical priesthood. Accordingly, the sanctuary of Shiloh and its ministers now come again, and permanently, into prominent notice. This not only in the case of Eli and Samuel, but long before that. This appears from the sacred text. For when, previous to the calling of Jephthah, the children of Israel repented, we are told that they "cried unto the Lord," and that the Lord spake unto them, to which they in turn made suitable reply (Judges 10:10, 11, 15). But the peculiar expressions used leave no doubt on our mind, that the gathering of Israel before the Lord had taken place in His sanctuary at Shiloh, and the answer of Jehovah been made by means of the Urim and Thummim (comp. Judges 1:1).

For clearness' sake, it may be well to explain, that Judges 10:6-18 forms a general introduction, alike to the history of Jephthah and his successors, and to that of Samson. In ver. 6 seven national deities are mentioned whom Israel had served, besides the Baalim and Ashtaroth of Canaan. This in opposition to the sevenfold deliverance (vers. 11, 12) which Israel had experienced at the hands of Jehovah. Then follows, in ver. 7, a general reference to the twofold contemporaneous oppression by the Ammonites in the east and north, and by the Philistines in the south and west. In ver. 8 the account of the Ammonites' oppression commences with the statement, that "they ground down and bruised the children of Israel that year," and in a similar manner for eighteen years. In fact, the Ammonites, in their successful raids across the Jordan, occupied districts of the territory of Judah, Benjamin, and Ephraim, which bordered either on the Dead Sea or on the fords of Jordan.

Next, we have in verses 10-15 an account of Israel's humiliation and entreaty at Shiloh, and of the Lord's answer by the Urim and Thummim. Finally, ver. 16 informs us, how the genuineness of their repentance appeared not in professions and promises, but in the putting away of all "strange gods," and that when there was no immediate prospect of Divine help. After this, to reproduce the wonderful imagery of Scripture: "His soul became short on account of the misery of Israel." That misery had lasted too long; He could not, as it were, be any longer angry with them, nor bear to see their suffering. For, as a German writer beautifully observes: "The love of God is not like the hard and fast logical sequences of man; it is ever free.... The parable of the prodigal affords a glimpse of the marvelous 'inconsistency' of the Father, who receives the wanderer when he suffered the consequences of his sin.... Put away the strange gods, and the withered rod will burst anew into life and verdure." And such is ever God's love — full and free. For, in the words of the author just quoted: "Sin and forgiveness are the pivots of all history, specially of that of Israel, including in that term the spiritual Israel."

Now, indeed, was deliverance at hand. For the first time these eighteen years that Ammon had camped in Gilead, the children of Israel also camped against them in Mizpeh, or, as it is otherwise called (Joshua 13:26; 20:8), in Ramath-Mizpeh or Ramoth-Gilead (the modern Salt), a city east of the Jordan, in an almost direct line from Shiloh. The camp of Israel could not have been better chosen. Defended on three sides by high hills, Mizpeh lay "on two sides of a narrow ravine, half way up, crowned by a (now) ruined citadel," which probably at all times defended the city.

"Ramoth-Gilead must always have been the key of Gilead, at the head of the only easy road from the Jordan, opening immediately on to the rich plateau of the interior, and with this isolated cone rising close above it, fortified from very early times, by art as well as by nature." All was thus prepared, and now the people of Gilead, through their "princes," resolved to offer the supreme command to any one who had already begun to fight against the children of Ammon — that is, who on his own account had waged warfare, and proved successful against them. This notice is of great importance for the early history of Jephthah.

Few finer or nobler characters are sketched even in Holy Scripture than Jephthah, or rather Jiphthach ("the breaker through"). He is introduced to us as "a mighty man of valor" — the same terms in which the angel had first addressed Gideon (6:12). But this "hero of might" must first learn to conquer his own spirit. His history is almost a parallel to that of Abimelech — only in the way of contrast. For, whereas Abimelech had of his own accord left his father's house to plan treason, Jephthah was wrongfully driven out by his brothers from his father's inheritance. Abimelech had appealed to the citizens of Shechem to help him in his abominable ambition; Jephthah to the "elders of Gilead" for redress in his wrong, but apparently in vain (11:7). Abimelech had committed unprovoked and cruel murder with his hired band; Jephthah withdrew to the land of Tob, which, from 2 Samuel 10:6, 8, we know to have been on the northern boundary of Peraea between Syria and the land of Ammon. There he gathered around him a number of freebooters, as David afterwards in similar circumstances (1 Samuel 22:2); not, like Abimelech, to destroy his father's house, but, like David, to war against the common foe. This we infer from Judges 10:18, which shows that, before the war between Gilead and Ammon, Jephthah had acquired fame as contending against Ammon. This life of adventure would suit the brave Gileadite and his followers; for he was a wild mountaineer, only imbued with the true spirit of Israel. And now, when war had actually broken out, "the elders of Gilead" were not in doubt whom to choose as their chief. They had seen and repented their sin against Jehovah, and now they saw and confessed their wrong towards Jephthah, and appealed to his generosity. In ordinary circumstances he would not have consented; but he came back to them, as the elders of Gilead had put it, because they were in distress. Nor did he come in his own strength. The agreement made with the elders of Israel was solemnly ratified before Jehovah.

He that has a righteous cause will not shrink from having it thoroughly sifted. It was not because Jephthah feared the battle, but because he wished to avoid bloodshed, that he twice sent an embassy of remonstrance to the king of Ammon. The claims of the latter upon the land between the Arnon and the Jabbok were certainly of the most shadowy kind. That country had, at the time of the Israelitish conquest, belonged to Sihon, king of the Amorites. True, the Amorites were not its original owners, having wrested the land from Moab (Numbers 21:26). Balak might therefore have raised a claim; but, although he hired Balaam to protect what still remained of his kingdom against a possible attack by Israel, which he dreaded, he never attempted to recover what Israel had taken from the Amorites, although it had originally been his. Moreover, even in dealing with the Amorites, as before with Edom and Moab, whose territory Israel had actually avoided by a long circuit, the utmost forbearance had been shown. If the Amorites had been dispossessed, theirs had been the unprovoked attack, when Israel had in the first place only asked a passage through their country. Lastly, if 300 years' undisputed possession of the land did not give a prescriptive right, it would be difficult to imagine by what title land could be held. Nor did Jephthah shrink from putting the matter on its ultimate and best ground. Addressing the Ammonites, as from their religious point of view they could understand it, he said: "And now Jehovah God of Israel hath dispossessed the Amorites from before His people, and shouldest thou possess it? Is it not so, that which Chemosh thy god giveth thee to possess, that wilt thou possess; and all that which Jehovah our God shall dispossess before us, that shall we possess?" We do not wonder that of a war commenced in such a spirit we should be told: "And the Spirit of the Lord came upon Jephthah." Presently Jephthah passed all through the land east of the Jordan, and its people obeyed his summons.

We are now approaching what to many will appear the most difficult part in the history of Jephthah — perhaps among the most difficult narratives in the Bible. It appears that, before actually going to war, Jephthah solemnly registered this vow: "If thou indeed givest the children of Ammon into mine hand — and it shall be, the outcoming (one), that shall come out from the door of my house to meet me on my returning in peace from the children of Ammon, shall be to Jehovah, and I will offer that a burnt offering." We know that the vow was paid. The defeat of the Ammonites was thorough and crushing. But on Jephthah's return to his house the first to welcome him was his only daughter — his only child — who at the head of the maidens came to greet the victor. There is a terrible irony about those "timbrels and dances," with which Jephthah's daughter went, as it were, to celebrate her own funeral obsequies, while the fond father's heart was well-nigh breaking. But the noble maiden was the first to urge his observance of the vow unto Jehovah. Only two months did she ask to bewail her maidenhood with her companions upon the mountains. But ever after was it a custom for the maidens in Israel to go out every year for four days, "to praise the daughter of Jephthah."

Such is the story; but what is its meaning? What did Jephthah really intend by the language of his vow; and did he feel himself bound by it in the literal sense to offer up his daughter as a burnt sacrifice? Assuredly, we shall make no attempt either to explain away the facts of the case, or to disguise the importance of the questions at issue. At the outset we are here met by these two facts: that up to that period Jephthah had both acted and spoken as a true worshipper of Jehovah, and that his name stands emblazoned in that roll of the heroes of the faith which is handed down to us in the Epistle to the Hebrews (11:32). But it is well-nigh impossible to believe that a true worshipper of Jehovah could have either vowed or actually offered a human sacrificed — not to speak of the sacrifice being that of his own and only child. Such sacrifices were the most abhorrent and opposed to the whole spirit and letter of the Law of God (Leviticus 18:21; 20:2-5; Deuteronomy 12:31; 18:10), nor do we find any mention of them till the reigns of the wicked Ahaz and Manasseh. Not even Jezebel had ventured to introduce them; and we know what thrill of horror ran through the onlookers, when the heathen king of Moab offered his son an expiatory sacrifice on the walls of his capital (2 Kings 3:26, etc.). But the difficulty becomes well-nigh insuperable, when we find the name of Jephthah recorded in the New Testament among the heroes of the faith. Surely, no one guilty of such a crime could have found a place there! Still, these are considerations which, though most important, are outside the narrative itself, and in any truthful investigation the latter should, in the first place, be studied by itself.

In so doing we must dismiss, as irrelevant and untruthful, such pleas as the roughness of those times, the imperfectness of religious development, or that of religious ignorance on the part of the outlaw Jephthah, who had spent most of his life far from Israel. The Scripture sketch of Jephthah leaves, indeed, on the mind the impression of a genuine, wild, and daring Gilead mountaineer — a sort of warrior-Elijah. But, on the other hand, he acts and speaks throughout as a true worshipper of Jehovah. And his vow, which in the Old Testament always expresses the highest religious feeling (Genesis 28:20; 1 Samuel 1:11; Psalm 116:14; Isaiah 19:21), is so sacred because it is made to Jehovah. Again, in his embassy to the king of Ammon, Jephthah displays the most intimate acquaintance with the

Pentateuch, his language being repeatedly almost a literal quotation from Numbers 20. He who knew so well the details of Scripture history could not have been ignorant of its fundamental principles. Having thus cleared the way, we observe:

1. That the language of Jephthah's vow implied, from the first, at least the possibility of some human being coming out from the door of his house, to meet him on his return. The original conveys this, and the evident probabilities of the case were strongly in favor of such an eventuality. Indeed, Jephthah's language seems to have been designedly chosen in such general terms as to cover all cases. But it is impossible to suppose that Jephthah would have deliberately made a vow in which he contemplated human sacrifice; still more so, that Jehovah would have connected victory and deliverance with such a horrible crime.

2. In another particular, also, the language of Jephthah's vow is remarkable. It is, that "the outcoming (whether man or beast) shall be to Jehovah, and I will offer that a burnt-offering." The great Jewish commentators of the Middle Ages have, in opposition to the Talmud, pointed out that these two last clauses are not identical. It is never said of an animal burnt-offering, that it "shall be to Jehovah" — for the simple reason that, as a burnt-offering, it is such. But where human beings are offered to Jehovah, there the expression is used, as in the case of the first-born among Israel and of Levi (Numbers 3:12, 13). But in these cases it has never been suggested that there was actual human sacrifice.

3. It was a principle of the Mosaic law, that burnt sacrifices were to be exclusively males (Leviticus 1:3).

4. If the loving daughter had devoted herself to death, it is next to incredible that she should have wished to spend the two months of life conceded to her, not with her broken-hearted father, but in the mountains with her companions.

5. She bewails not her "maiden age," but her "maidenhood" — not that she dies so young, but that she is to die unmarried. The Hebrew expression for the former would have been quite different from that used in Scripture, which only signifies the latter. But for an only child to die unmarried, and so to leave a light and name extinguished in Israel, was indeed a bitter and heavy judgment, viewed in the light of pre-Messianic times. Compare in this respect especially such passages as Leviticus 20:20 and Psalm 78:63. The trial appears all the more withering when we realize, how it must have come upon Jephthah and his only child in the hour of their highest glory, when all earthly prosperity seemed at their command. The greatest and happiest man in Israel becomes in a moment the poorest and the most stricken. Surely, in this vow and sacrifice was the lesson of vows and sacrifices taught to victorious Israel in a manner the most solemn.

6. It is very significant that in 11:39 it is only said, that Jephthah "did with her according to his vow" — not that he actually offered her in sacrifice, while in the latter case the added clause, "and she knew no man," would be utterly needless and unmeaning. Lastly, we may ask, Who would have been the priest by whom, and where the altar on which, such a sacrifice could have been offered unto Jehovah?

On all these grounds — its utter contrariety to the whole Old Testament, the known piety of Jephthah, the blessing following upon his vow, his mention in the Epistle to the Hebrews, but especially the language of the narrative itself — we feel bound to reject the idea of any human sacrifice. In what special manner, besides remaining unmarried, the vow of her dedication to God was carried out, we do not feel bound to suggest. Here the principle, long ago expressed by Clericus, holds true: "We are not to imagine that, in so small a volume as the Old Testament, all the customs of the Hebrews are recorded, or the full history of all that had taken place among them. Hence there are necessarily allusions to many things which cannot be fully followed out, because there is no mention of them elsewhere."

Yet another trial awaited Jephthah. The tribal jealousy of Ephraim, which treated the Gileadites (more especially the half tribe of Manasseh) as mere runaways from Ephraim, who had no right to independent tribal action, scarcely to independent existence — least of all to having one of their number a "Judge," now burst into a fierce war. Defeated in battle, the Ephraimites tried to escape to the eastern bank of the Jordan; but Gilead had occupied the fords. Their peculiar pronunciation betrayed Ephraim, and a horrible massacre ensued.

Six years of rest — "then died Jephthah the Gileadite, and was buried in one of the cities of Gilead." We know not the locality, nor yet the precise place where he had lived, nor the city in which his body was laid. No father's home had welcomed him; no child was left to cheer his old age. He lived alone, and he died alone. Truly, as has been remarked, his sorrow and his victory are a type of Him Who said: "Not my will, but Thine be done." It almost seems as if Jephthah's three successors in the judgeship of the eastern and northern tribes were chiefly mentioned to mark the contrast in their history. Of Ibzan of Bethlehem, of Elon the Zebulonite, and of Abdon the Pirathonite, we know alike the dwelling and the burying-place. They lived honored, and died blessed — surrounded, as the text emphatically tells us, by a large and prosperous number of descendants. But their names are not found in the catalogue of worthies whom the Holy Ghost has selected for our special example and encouragement.

CHAPTER 19: MEANING OF THE HISTORY OF SAMSON — HIS ANNUNCIATION AND EARLY HISTORY — THE SPIRIT OF JEHOVAH "IMPELS HIM" — HIS DEEDS OF FAITH
(JUDGES 13-15)

THERE is yet another name recorded in the Epistle to the Hebrews among the Old Testament "worthies," whose title to that position must to many have seemed at least doubtful. Can Samson claim a place among the spiritual heroes, who "through faith subdued kingdoms, wrought righteousness, obtained promises?" The question cannot be dismissed with a summary answer, for if, as we believe, the Holy Spirit pronounced such judgment on his activity as a judge, then careful and truthful study of his history must bear it out. But then also must that history have been commonly misread and misunderstood. Let it be remembered, that it is of Samson's activity as a Judge, and under the impulse of the Spirit of God, we are writing, and not of every act of his life. In fact, we shall presently distinguish two periods in his history; the first, when he acted under the influence of that Spirit; the second, when, yielding to his passions, he fell successively into sin, unfaithfulness to his calling, and betrayal of it, followed by the desertion of Jehovah and by His judgment. And, assuredly, the language of the Epistle to the Hebrews could not apply to the period of Samson's God-desertion and of his punishment, but only to that of his first activity or of his later repentance.

It was in the days of Eli the high priest. Strange and tangled times these, when once again principles rather than men were to come to the front, if Israel was to be revived and saved. The period of the Judges had run its course to the end. The result had been general disorganization, an almost complete disintegration of the tribes, and decay of the sanctuary. But now, just at the close of the old, the new was beginning; or rather, old principles were once more asserted. In Eli the Divine purpose concerning the priesthood, in Samson that concerning the destiny and mission of Israel, were to reappear. In both cases, alike in their strength and in their weakness — in the faithfulness and in the unfaithfulness of its representatives. The whole meaning of Samson's history is, that he was a Nazarite. His strength lay in being a Nazarite; his weakness in yielding to his carnal lusts, and thereby becoming unfaithful to his calling. In both respects he was not only a type of Israel, but, so to speak, a mirror in which Israel could see itself and its history. Israel, the Nazarite people — no achievement, however marvelous, that it could not and did not accomplish! Israel, unfaithful to its vows and yielding to spiritual adultery — no depth of degradation so low, that it would not descend to it! The history of Israel was the history of Samson; his victories were like theirs, till, like him, yielding to the seductions of a Delilah, Israel betrayed and lost its Nazarite strength. And so also with Samson's and with Israel's final repentance and recovery of strength. Viewed in this light, we can not only understand this history, but even its seeming difficulties become so many points of fresh meaning. We can see why his life should have been chronicled with a circumstantiality seemingly out of proportion to the deliverance he wrought; and why there was so little and so transient result of his deeds. When the Spirit of God comes upon him, he does supernatural deeds; not in his own strength, but as a Nazarite, in the strength of God, by Whom and for Whom he had been set apart before his birth. All this showed the meaning and power of the Nazarite; what deliverance God could work for His people even by a single Nazarite, so that, in the language of prophecy, one man could chase a thousand! Thus also we understand the peculiar and almost spasmodic character of Samson's deeds, as also the reason why he always appears on the scene, not at the head of the tribes, but alone to battle.

If the secret of Samson's strength lay in the faithful observance of his Nazarite vow, his weakness sprung from his natural character. The parallel, so far as Israel is concerned, cannot fail to be seen. And as Samson's sin finally assumed the form of adulterous love for Delilah, so that of his people was spiritual unfaithfulness. Thus, if the period of the Judges reached its highest point in Samson the Nazarite, it also sunk to its lowest in Samson the man of carnal lusts, who yielded his secret to a Delilah. As one has put it: "The strength of the Spirit of God bestowed on the Judges for the deliverance of their people was overcome by the power of the flesh lusting against the Spirit." Yet may we, with all reverence, point from Samson, the Nazarite for life, to the great antitype in Jesus Christ, the "Nazarite among His brethren," (Genesis 49:26) in Whom was fulfilled that "which was spoken by the prophets, He shall be called a Nazarite" (Matthew 2:23).

And it is at any rate remarkable that ancient Jewish tradition, in referring to the blessing spoken to Dan (Genesis 49:17, 18), applies this addition: "I have waited for Thy salvation, Jehovah," through Samson the Danite, to the Messiah.

1. Samson's birth. According to the chronological arrangement already indicated, we infer that Samson was born under the pontificate of Eli, and after the commencement of the Philistine oppression, which lasted forty years. If so, then his activity must have begun one or two years before the disastrous battle in which the ark fell into the hands of the Philistines, and in consequence of which Eli died (1 Samuel 4:18).

While in the east and north the Ammonites oppressed Israel, the same sin had brought on the west and south of Palestine the judgment of Philistine domination. Then it was, that once more the Angel of Jehovah came, to teach the people, through Samson, that deliverance could only come by recalling and realizing their Nazarite character as a priestly kingdom unto Jehovah; and that the Lord's Nazarite, so long as he remained such, would prove all-powerful through the strength of his God. The circumstances connected with the annunciation of Samson were supernatural. In the "secluded mountain village" of Zorah, the modern Surah, about six hours west of Jerusalem, within the possession of Dan, lived Manoah ("resting") and his wife. Theirs, as we judge from the whole history, was the humble, earnest piety which, despite much apostasy, still lingered in Israel.

It is to be observed that, like Sarah in the Old, and the mother of the Baptist in the New Testament, Manoah's wife was barren. For the child about to be born was not only to be God-devoted but God-given — and that in another sense even from his contemporary, Samuel, who had been God-asked of his mother. But in this case the Angel of the Covenant Himself came to announce the birth of a child, who should be "a Nazarite unto God from the womb," and who as such should "begin to deliver Israel out of the hand of the Philistines." Accordingly, He laid on the mother, and still more fully on the unborn child, the Nazarite obligations as these are detailed in Numbers 6:1-8, with the exception of that against defilement by contact with the dead, which evidently would have been incompatible with his future history.

The appearance of the Angel and His unnamedness had carried to the woman thoughts of the Divine, though she regarded the apparition as merely that of a man of God. Manoah had not been present; but in answer to his prayer a second apparition was vouchsafed. It added nothing to their previous knowledge, except the revelation of the real character of Him Who had spoken to them. For, when Manoah proposed to entertain his guest, he learned that He would not eat of his food, and that His name was "Wonderful." The latter, of course, in the sense of designating His character and working, for, as in the parallel passage, Isaiah 9:6, such names refer not to the being and nature of the Messiah, but to His activity and manifestation — not to what He is, but to what He does. As suggested by the Angel, Manoah now brought a burnt-offering unto Jehovah — for, wherever He manifested Himself, there sacrifice and service might be offered. And when the Angel "did wondrously;" when fire leaped from the altar, and the Angel ascended in the flame that consumed the burnt-offering, then Manoah and his wife, recognizing His nature, fell worshipping on the ground. No further revelation was granted them; but when Manoah, in the spirit of the Old Testament, feared lest their vision of God might render it impossible for them to live on earth, his wife, more fully enlightened, strove to allay such doubts by the inference, that what God had begun in grace He would not end in judgment. An inference this, applying to all analogous cases in the spiritual history of God's people. And so months of patient, obedient waiting ensued, when at last the promised child was born, and obtained the name of Samson, or rather (in the Hebrew) Shimshon. His calling soon appeared, for as the child grew up under the special blessing of the Lord, "the Spirit of Jehovah began to impel him in the camp of Dan, between Zorah and Eshtaol."

2. About an hour south-west from Zorah, down the rocky mountain-gorges, lay Timnath, within the tribal possession of Dan, but at the time held by the Philistines. This was the scene of Samson's first exploits.

The "occasion" was his desire to wed a Philistine maiden. Against such union, as presumably contrary to the Divine will (Exodus 34:16; Deuteronomy 7:3), his parents remonstrated, not knowing "that it was of Jehovah, for he was seeking an occasion from (or on account of) the Philistines." Strictly speaking, the text only implies that this "seeking occasion on account of the Philistines" was directly from the Lord; his proposed marriage would be so only indirectly, as affording the desired occasion. Here then we again come upon man's individuality — his personal choice, as the motive power of which the Lord makes use for higher purposes. We leave aside the question, whether or not Samson had, at the outset, realized a higher Divine purpose in it all, and mark two points of vital importance in this history. First, whenever Samson consciously subordinated his will and wishes to national and Divine purposes, he acted as a Nazarite, and "by faith;" whenever national and Divine purposes were made subservient to his own lusts, he failed and sinned. Thus we perceive throughout, side by side, two elements at work: the Divine and the human; Jehovah and Samson; the supernatural and the natural — intertwining, acting together, influencing each other, as we have so often noticed them throughout the course of Scripture history. Secondly, the influences of the Spirit of God upon Samson come upon him as impulses from without — sudden, mighty, and irresistible by himself and by others.

The misunderstanding and ignorance of Samson's motives on the part of his parents cannot fail to recall a similar opposition in the life of our Blessed Lord, even as, reverently speaking, this whole history foreshadows, though "afar off," that of our great Nazarite. But to return. Yielding at last to Samson, his parents, as the custom was, go with him to the betrothal at Timnath. All here and in the account of the marriage is strictly Eastern, and strictly Jewish. Nay, such is the tenacity of Eastern customs, that it might almost serve as descriptive of what would still take place in similar circumstances. But, under another aspect, we are here also on the track of direct Divine agency, all unknown probably to

Samson himself. To this day "vineyards are very often far out from the villages, climbing up rough wadies and wild cliffs." In one of these, precisely in the district where he would be likely to meet wild beasts, Samson encountered a young lion. "And the Spirit of Jehovah came mightily upon him," or "lighted upon him," the expression being notably the same as in 1 Samuel 10:10; 11:6; 16:13; 18:10. Samson rent him, as he would have torn a kid. This circumstance became "the occasion against the Philistines." For, when soon afterwards Samson and his parents returned once more for the actual marriage, he found a swarm of bees in the dried skeleton of the lion. The honey, which he took for himself and gave to his parents, became the occasion of a riddle which he propounded, after a custom usual in the East, to the "thirty companions" who acted as "friends of the bridegroom." The riddle proved too hard for them. Unwilling to bear the loss incurred by their failure — each "a tunic" and a "change-garment," these men threatened Samson's wife and her family with destruction.

The woman's curiosity had from the first prompted her to seek the answer from her husband. But now her importunity, quickened by fear, prevailed. Of course, she immediately told the secret to her countrymen, and Samson found himself deceived and betrayed by his wife. But this was the "occasion" sought for. Once more "the Spirit of Jehovah lighted upon Samson." There was not peace between Israel and the Philistines, only an armed truce. And so Samson slew thirty men of them in Ashkelon, and with their spoil paid those who had answered his riddle. In his anger at her treachery he now forsook for a time his bride, when her father, as it were in contempt, immediately gave her to the first of the "bridegroom's friends."

This circumstance gave "occasion" for yet another deed. Samson returns again to his wife. Finding her the wife of another, he treats this as Philistine treachery against Israel, and declares to his father-in-law and to others around: "This time I am blameless before the Philistines when I do evil unto them."

The threatened "evil" consists in tying together, two and two, three hundred jackals, tail to tail, with a burning torch between them, and so sending the maddened animals into the standing corn of the Philistines, which was just being harvested, into their vineyards, and among their olives. The destruction must have been terrible, and the infuriated Philistines took vengeance not upon Samson, but upon his wife and her family, by burning "her and her father with fire." This was cowardly as well as wicked, upon which Samson "said unto them, If (since) ye have done this, truly when I have been avenged upon you, and after that I will cease." The result was another great slaughter. But Samson, knowing the cowardice of his countrymen, felt himself now no longer safe among them, and retired to "the rock-cleft (rock-cave) Etam" ("the lair of wild beasts").

Samson's distrust had not been without sufficient ground. Afraid to meet Samson in direct conflict, the Philistines invaded the territory of Judah and spread in Lehi. Upon this, his own countrymen, as of old, not understanding "how that God by his hand would deliver them," actually came down to the number of 3000, to deliver Samson into the hand of the Philistines. Another parallel this, "afar off," to the history of Him whom His people delivered into the hands of the Gentiles! Samson offered no resistance, on condition that his own people should not attack him. Bound with two new cords, he was already within view of the hostile camp at Lehi; already he heard the jubilant shout of the Philistines, when once more "the Spirit of Jehovah came mightily upon him." Like flax at touch of fire, "flowed his bonds from off his hands."

This sudden turn of affairs, and manifestation of Samson's power, caused an immediate panic among the Philistines. Following up this effect, Samson seized the weapon readiest to hand, the jawbone of an ass, and with it slew company after company, "heap upon heap," till, probably in various encounters, no less than 1000 of the enemy strewed the ground. Only one more thing was requisite. All "this great deliverance" had evidently been given by Jehovah. But had Samson owned Him in it; had he fought and conquered "by faith," and as a true Nazarite? Once more it is through the operation of natural causes, supernaturally overruled and directed, that Samson is now seen to have been the warrior of Jehovah, and Jehovah the God of the warrior. Exhausted by the long contest with the Philistines and the heat of the day, Samson sinks faint, and is ready to perish from thirst. Then God cleaves first, as it were, the rock of Samson's heart, so that the living waters of faith and prayer gush forth, before He cleaves the rock at Lehi. Such plea as his could not remain unheeded. Like that of Moses (Exodus 32:31), or like the reasoning of Manoah's wife, it connected itself with the very covenant purposes of Jehovah and with His dealings in grace. After such battle and victory Samson could not have been allowed to perish from thirst; just as after our Lord's victory, He could not fail to see of the travail of His soul and be satisfied; and as it holds true of the Christian in his spiritual thirst, after the great conquest achieved for him:

"He that spared not His own Son, but delivered Him up for us all, how shall He not with Him also freely give us all things?" (Romans 8:32)

Then, in answer to Samson's prayer, "God clave the hollow place which is in Lehi," probably a cleft in the rock, as erst He had done at Horeb (Exodus 17:6) and at Kadesh (Numbers 20:8, 11). But the well which sprang thence, and of which, in his extremity, Samson had drunk, ever afterwards bore the significant name En-hakkore, the well of him that had called — nor had called in vain!

CHAPTER 20: THE SIN AND FALL OF SAMSON — JEHOVAH DEPARTS FROM HIM — SAMSON'S REPENTANCE, FAITH, AND DEATH
(JUDGES 16)

THE closing verse of Judges 15 marks also the close of this period of Samson s life. Henceforth it is a record of the terrible consequences, first of using God's gift, intrusted for the highest and holiest purposes, for self-indulgence, and then of betraying and losing it. And this betrayal and loss are ever the consequence of taking for self what is meant for God, just as in the parable of the prodigal son the demand for the portion of goods which belonged to him is followed by the loss of all, by want and misery. And here, in this its second stage, the history of Samson closely follows that of Israel. As Israel claimed for self, and would have used for self the gifts and calling of God; as it would have boasted in its Nazarite-strength and trusted in it, irrespective of its real meaning and the object of its bestowal, so now Samson. He goes down to Gaza, one of the fortified strongholds of the Philistines, not impelled by the Spirit of Jehovah, but for self-indulgence, confident and boastful in what he regards as his own strength.

Nor does that strength yet fail him, at least outwardly. For God is faithful to His promise, and so long as Samson has not cast away His help, it shall not fail him. But already he is on the road to it, and the night at Gaza must speedily be followed by the story of Delilah. Meanwhile, the men of Gaza and Samson must learn another lesson — so far as they are capable of it. All night the guards are posted by the gates to wait for the dawn, when, as they expect, with the opening of the gates, Samson will leave the city, and they take him prisoner. During the night, however, they may take their sleep; for are not the gates strong and securely fastened? But, at midnight, Samson leaves the city, carrying with him its gates, and putting them down on "the top of a hill which faces towards Hebron," that is, at a distance of about half an hour to the south-east of Gaza.

Samson had once more escaped the Philistines; but the hour of his fall was at hand. To regard the God-intrusted strength as his own, and to abuse it for selfish purposes, was the first step towards betraying and renouncing that in which it really lay. Samson had ceased to be a Nazarite in heart before he ceased to be one outwardly. The story of Delilah is too well known to require detailed repetition.

Her very name — "the weak" or "longing one" — breathes sensuality, and her home is in the valley of Sorek, or of the choice red grape. The Philistine princes have learned it at last, that force cannot prevail against Samson, until by his own act of unfaithfulness he has deprived himself of his strength. It is the same story as that of Israel and its sin with Baal-Peor. The same device is adopted which Balaam had suggested for the ruin of Israel, and, alas! with the same success. The five princes of the Philistines promise each to give Delilah 1000 and 100 shekels, or 5500 in all, about 700 pounds, as the reward of her treachery. Three times has Samson eluded her persistency to find out his secret. Each time she has had watchers in an adjoining apartment ready to fall upon him, if he had really lost his strength. But the third time he had, in his trifling with sacred things, come dangerously near his fall, as in her hearing he connected his strength with his hair. And yet, despite all warnings, like Israel of old, he persisted in his sin.

At last it has come. He has opened all his heart to Delilah, and she knows it. But Scripture puts the true explanation of the matter before us, in its usual emphatic manner, yet with such manifest avoidance of seeking for effect, that only the careful, devout reader will trace it. The facts are as follows: When Samson betrays his secret to Delilah, he says (16:17): "If I be shaven, then my strength will go from me," whereas, when the event actually takes place, Scripture explains it: "He wot not that Jehovah was departed from him." In this contrast between his fond conceit about his own strength and the fact that it was due to the presence of Jehovah, lies the gist of the whole matter. As one writes: "The superhuman strength of Samson lay not in his uncut hair, but in this, that Jehovah was with him. But Jehovah was with him only so long as he kept his Nazarite vow." Or, in the words of an old German commentary: "The whole misery of Samson arose from this, that he appropriated to himself what God had done through him. God allows his strength to be destroyed, that in bitter experience he might learn, how without God's presence he was nothing at all. And so our falls always teach us best." But, as ever, sin proves the hardest taskmaster. Every indignity is heaped on fallen Samson. His eyes are put out; he is loaded with fetters of brass, and set to the lowest prison work of slaves. And here, also, the history of Samson finds its parallel in that of blinded Israel, with the judgment of bondage, degradation, and suffering, consequent upon their great national sin of casting aside their Nazarite vow.

But, blessed be God, neither the history nor its parallel stops here. For "the gifts and callings of God are without repentance." The sacred text expressly has it: "And the hair of his head began to grow, as it was shorn" — that is, so soon as it had been shorn. Then began a period of godly sorrow and repentance, evidenced both by the return of God to him, and by his last deed of faith, in which for his people he sacrificed his life; herein also following the great Antitype, though "afar off." We imagine, that "the lad" who led him to the pillars on which the house of Dagon rested was a Hebrew, cognizant of Samson's hopes and prayers, and who, immediately after having placed him in the fatal position, left the temple, and then carried the tidings to Samson's "brethren" (16:31).

It is a high day in Gaza. From all their cities have the princes of the Philistines come up; from all the country around have the people gathered. The temple of the god Dagon — the fish-god, protector of the sea — is festively adorned and thronged. Below, the lords of the Philistines and all the chief men of the people are feasting at the sacrificial meal; above, along the roof, the gallery all around is crowded by three thousand men and women who look down on the spectacle beneath. It is a feast of thanksgiving to Dagon, of triumph to Philistia, of triumph against Jehovah and His people, and over captive Samson. The image of Dagon — the body of a fish with the head and hands of a man — which less than twenty years before had fallen and been broken before the ark of Jehovah (1 Samuel 5:4), stands once more proudly defying the God of Israel. And now the mirth and revelry have reached their highest point: Samson is brought in, and placed in the middle of the temple, between the central pillars which uphold the immense roof and the building itself. A few words whispered to his faithful Hebrew servant, and Samson's arms encircle the massive pillars. And then an unuttered agonizing cry of repentance, of faith from the Nazarite, once more such, who will not only subordinate self to the nation and to his calling, but surrender life itself! Blind Samson is groping for a new light — and the brightness of another morning is already gilding his horizon. With all his might he bows himself. The pillars reel and give way. With one terrible crash fall roof and gallery, temple and image of Dagon; and in the ruins perish with Samson the lords of the Philistines and the flower of the people.

It has been told in Zorah. Gaza and Philistia are hushed in awe and mourning. Samson's brethren and his father's house come down. From the ruins they search out the mangled body of the Nazarite. No one cares to interfere with them. Unmolested they bear away the remains, and lay them to rest in the burying-place of Manoah his father.

And so ends the period of the judges. Samson could have had no successor — he closed an epoch. But already at Shiloh a different reformation was preparing; and with different weapons will repentant Israel, under Samuel, fight against the Philistines, and conquer!

CHAPTER 21: SOCIAL AND RELIGIOUS LIFE IN BETHLEHEM IN THE DAYS OF JUDGES — THE STORY OF RUTH — KING DAVID'S ANCESTORS
(THE BOOK OF RUTH)

YET another story of a very different kind from that of Samson remains to be told. It comes upon us with such sweet contrast, almost like a summer's morning after a night of wild tempest. And yet without this story our knowledge of that period would be incomplete. It was "in the days when the judges judged" — near the close of that eventful period. West of the Jordan, Jair and Eli held sway in Israel, while east of the river the advancing tide of Ammon had not yet been rolled back by Jephthah, the Gileadite. Whether the incursions of the Ammonites had carried want and wretchedness so far south into Judah as Bethlehem (Judges 10:9), or whether it was only due to strictly natural causes, there was a "famine in the land," and this became, in the wonder-working Providence of God, one of the great links in the history of the kingdom of God.

Bearing in mind the general characteristics of the period, and such terrible instances of religious apostasy and moral degeneracy as those recorded in the two Appendices to the Book of Judges (Judges 17-21), we turn with a feeling of intense relief to the picture of Jewish life presented to us in the Book of Ruth. Sheltered from scenes of strife and semi-heathenism, the little village of Bethlehem had retained among its inhabitants the purity of their ancestral faith and the simplicity of primitive manners.

Here, embosomed amidst the hills of Judah, where afterwards David pastured his father's flocks, and where shepherds heard angels hail the birth of "David's greater Son," we seem to feel once again the healthful breath of Israel's spirit, and we see what moral life it was capable of fostering alike in the individual and in the family. If Boaz was, so to speak, the patriarch of a village, in which the old Biblical customs were continued, the humblest homes of Bethlehem must have preserved true Israelitish piety in its most attractive forms. For, unless the Moabitess Ruth had learned to know and love the land and the faith of Israel in the Bethlehemite household of Elimelech, transported as it was for a time into the land of Moab, she would not have followed so persistently her mother-in-law, away from her own home, to share her poverty, to work, if need be, even to beg, for her. And from such ancestry, nurtured under such circumstances, did the shepherd king of Israel spring, the ancestor and the type of the Lord and Savior of men. These four things, then, seem the object of the Book of Ruth: to present a supplement by way of contrast to the Book of Judges; to show the true spirit of Israel; to exhibit once more the mysterious connection between Israel and the Gentiles, whereby the latter, at the most critical periods of Israel's history, seem most unexpectedly called in to take a leading part; and to trace the genealogy of David. Specially perhaps the latter two. For, as one has beautifully remarked: If, as regards its contents, the Book of Ruth stands on the threshold of the history of David, yet, as regards its spirit, it stands, like the Psalms, at the threshold of the Gospel. Not merely on account of the genealogy of Christ, which leads up to David and Boaz, but on account of the spirit which the teaching of David breathes, do we love to remember that Israel's great king sprang from the union of Boaz and Ruth, which is symbolical of that between Israel and the Gentile world.

Everything about this story is of deepest interest — the famine in Bethlehem, "the house of bread," evidently caused, as afterwards its removal, by the visitation of God (Ruth 1:6); the hints about the family of Elimelech; even their names: Elimelech, "my God is king;" his wife, Naomi, "the pleasant," and their sons Mahlon (or rather Machlon) and Chilion (rendered by some "the weak," "the faint;" by

The family is described as "Ephrathites of Bethlehem-judah." The expression is apparently intended to convey, that the family had not been later immigrants, but original Jewish settlers — or, as the Jewish commentator have it, patrician burghers of the ancient Ephrath, or "fruitfulness" (Genesis 35:19; 48:7; comp. 1 Samuel 17:12; Micah 5:2). At one time the family seems to have been neither poor nor of inconsiderable standing (Ruth 1:19-21; 2; 3). But now, owing to "the famine," Ephrath was no longer "fruitfulness," nor yet Bethlehem "the house of bread;" and Elimelech, unable, on account of the troubles in the west, to go for relief either into Philistia or into Egypt, migrated beyond Jordan, and the reach of Israel's then enemies, to "sojourn" in Moab.

There is no need to attempt excuses for this separation from his brethren and their fate on the part of Elimelech, nor for his seeking rest among those hereditary enemies of Israel, outside Palestine, on whom a special curse seems laid (Deuteronomy 23:6). We have only to mark the progress of this story to read in it the judgment of God on this step. Of what befell the family in Moab, we know next to nothing. But this we are emphatically told, that Elimelech died a stranger in the strange land. Presently Machlon and Chilion married Moabite wives — Machlon, Ruth (Ruth 4:10); Chilion, Orpah.

So other ten years passed. Then the two young men died, each childless, and Naomi was left desolate indeed. Thus, as one has remarked: "The father had feared not to be able to live at home. But scarcely had he arrived in the strange land when he died. Next, the sons sought to found a house in Moab; but their house became their grave. Probably, they had wished not to return to Judah, at least till the famine had ceased — and when it had ceased, they were no more. The father had gone away to have more, and to provide for his family — and his widow was now left without either children or possession!" Similarly, we do not feel it needful to attempt vindicating the marriage of these two Hebrew youths with Moabite wives. For there really was no express command against such unions. The instances in Scripture (Judges 3:6; 1 Kings 11:1; Nehemiah 13:23), which are sometimes quoted as proof to the contrary, are not in point, since they refer to the marriage of Hebrews in the land of Israel, not to that of those resident outside its boundaries (comp. Deuteronomy 7:3), and in the case of such marriages this is evidently an important element.

And now tidings reached Moab, that "Jehovah had visited his people to give them bread." Naomi heard in it a call to return to her own land and home. According to eastern fashion, her daughters-in-law accompanied her on the way. When Naomi deemed that duty of proper respect sufficiently discharged, she stopped to dismiss them — as she delicately put it — to their "mother's" houses, with tenderly spoken prayer, that after all their sorrow the God of Israel would give them rest in a new relationship, as they had dealt lovingly both with the dead and with her. Closely examined, her words are found to convey, although with most exquisite delicacy, that, if her daughters-in-law went with her, they must expect to remain for ever homeless and strangers. She could offer them no prospect of wedded happiness in her own family, and she wished to convey to them, that no Israelite in his own land would ever wed a daughter of Moab. It was a noble act of self-denial on the part of the aged

Hebrew widow by this plain speaking to strip herself of all remaining comfort, and to face the dark future, utterly childless, alone, and helpless. And when one of them, Orpah, turned back, though with bitter sorrow at the parting, Naomi had a yet more trying task before her. Ruth had, indeed, fully understood her mother-in-law's meaning; but there was another sacrifice which she must be prepared to make, if she followed Naomi. She must not only be parted from her people, and give up for ever all worldly prospects, but she must also be prepared to turn her back upon her ancestral religion. But Ruth had long made her choice, and the words in which she intimated it have deservedly become almost proverbial in the church. There is such ardor and earnestness about them, such resolution and calmness, as to lift them far above the sphere of mere natural affection or sense of duty. They intimate the deliberate choice of a heart which belongs in the first place to Jehovah, the God of Israel (1:17), and which has learned to count all things but loss for the excellency of this knowledge. Although the story of Ruth has been invested with romance from its sequel, there is nothing romantic about her present resolve. Only the sternest prose of poverty is before her. Not to speak of the exceedingly depressing influence of her language (1:13, 20, 21), Naomi had been careful to take from her any hope of a future, such as she had enjoyed in the past. In truth, the choice of Ruth is wholly unaccountable, except on the ground that she felt herself in heart and by conviction one of a Hebrew household — an Israelitish woman in soul and life, and that although she should in a sense be disowned by those with whom she had resolved to cast in her lot.

There was stir in the quiet little village of Bethlehem — especially among the women — when Naomi unexpectedly returned after her long absence, and that in so altered circumstances. The lamentations of the widow herself made her even repudiate the old name of Naomi for Mara ("bitter"), for that "Jehovah" had "testified against," and "Shaddai" afflicted her. Whether or not Naomi and her acquaintances really understood the true meaning of this "testifying" on the part of Jehovah, certain it is, that the temporary excitement of her arrival soon passed away, and the widow and her Moabite companion were left to struggle on alone in their poverty. Apparently no other near relatives of Elimelech were left, for Boaz himself is designated in the original as "an acquaintance to her husband," though the term indicates also relationship. And thus through the dreary winter matters only grew worse and worse, till at last early spring brought the barley-harvest.

It was one of those arrangements of the law, which, by its exquisite kindness and delicacy — in such striking contrast to the heathen customs of the time — shows its Divine origin, that what was dropped, or left, or forgotten in the harvest, was not to be claimed by the owner, but remained, as a matter of right, for the poor, the widows, and emphatically also for the "stranger." As if to confute the later thoughts of Jewish narrowness, "the stranger" alone is mentioned in all the three passages where this command occurs (Leviticus 19:9, 10; 23:22; Deuteronomy 24:19-22).

Thus would the desolate share in Israel's blessings — and that as of Divine right rather than of human charity, while those who could no longer work for others might, as it were, work for themselves. Yet it must have been a bitter request, when Ruth, as if entreating a favor, asked Naomi's leave to go and glean in the fields, in the hope that she might "find favor" in the sight of master and reapers, so as not to be harshly spoken to, or roughly dealt with. And this was all — all that Ruth had apparently experienced of the "blessedness of following the Lord," for Whose sake she had left home and friends! But there is a sublimeness in the words of Scripture which immediately follow — a carelessness of effect, and yet a startling surprise characteristic of God's dealings. As Ruth went on her bitter errand, not knowing whither, Scripture puts it: — "her hap happened the portion of field belonging to Boaz" — the same Divine "hap" by which sleep fled from Ahasuerus on that decisive night; the same "hap" by which so often, what to the careless onlooker seems a chance "occurrence," is sent to us from God directly.

The whole scene is most vividly sketched. Ruth has come to the field of Boaz; she has addressed herself to "the servant that was set over the reapers," and obtained his leave to "glean" after the reapers, and to "gather in the sheaves." From early morn she has followed them, and, as the overseer afterwards informs Boaz (2:7), "her sitting in the house," whether for rest or talk, had been "but little."

And now the sun is high up in the heavens, when Boaz comes among his laborers. In true Israelitish manner he salutes them: "Jehovah with you!" to which they respond, "Jehovah bless thee!" He could not but have known "all the poor" (in the conventional sense) in Bethlehem, and Ruth must have led a very retired life, never seeking company or compassion, since Boaz requires to be informed who the Moabite damsel was. But though a stranger to her personally, the story of Ruth was well known to Boaz. Seen in the light of her then conduct and bearing, its spiritual meaning and her motives would at once become luminous to Boaz. For such a man to know, was to do what God willed. Ruth was an Israelite indeed, brave, true, and noble. She must not go to any other field than his; she must not be treated like ordinary gleaners, but remain there, where he had spoken to her, "by the maidens," so that, as the reapers went forwards, and the maidens after them to bind the sheaves, she might be the first to glean; she must share the privileges of his household; and he must take care that she should be unmolested.

It is easier, even for the children of God, to bear adversity than prosperity, especially if it come after long delay and unexpectedly. But Ruth was "simple" in heart; or, as the New Testament expresses it, her "eye was single," and God preserved her. And now, in the altered circumstances, she still acts quite in character with her past. She complains not of her poverty; she explains not how unused she had been to such circumstances; but she takes humbly, and with surprised gratitude, that to which she had no claim, and which as a "stranger" she had not dared to expect. Did she, all the while, long for a gleam of heaven's light — for an Israelitish welcome, to tell her that all this came from the God of Israel, and for His sake? It was granted her, and that more fully than she could have hoped. Boaz knew what she had done for man, and what she had given up for God. Hers, as he now assured her, would be recompense for the one, and a full reward of the other, and that from Jehovah, the God of Israel, under Whose wings she had come to trust. And now for the first time, and when it is past, the secret of her long-hidden sorrow bursts from Ruth, as she tells it to Boaz: "Thou hast consoled me, and spoken to the heart of thine handmaid."

What follows seems almost the natural course of events — natural, that Boaz should accord to her the privileges of a kinswoman; natural also, that she should receive them almost unconscious of any distinction bestowed on her — keep and bring home part even of her meal to her mother-in-law (2:18), and still work on in the field till late in the evening (ver. 17). But Naomi saw and wondered at what Ruth's simplicity and modesty could have never perceived. Astonished at such a return of a day's gleaning, she had asked for details, and then, without even waiting to hear her daughter's reply, had invoked God's blessing on the yet unknown dispenser of this kindness. And so Ruth the Moabitess has begun to teach the language of thanksgiving to her formerly desponding Hebrew mother! But when she has told her story, as before to Boaz, so now to Naomi its spiritual meaning becomes luminous.

In her weakness, Naomi had murmured; in her unbelief, she had complained; she had deemed herself forsaken of God and afflicted. All the while, however she and hers might have erred and strayed, God had never left off His kindness either to the living or to the dead! And it is only after she has thus given thanks, that she explains to the astonished Ruth: "The man is near unto us — he is one of our redeemers" (comp. Leviticus 25:25; Deuteronomy 25:5). Still even so, no further definite thoughts seem to have shaped themselves in the mind of either of the women. And so Ruth continued in quiet work in the fields of Boaz all the barley-harvest and unto the end of the wheat-harvest, a period of certainly not less than two months.

But further thought and observation brought a new resolve to Naomi. The two months which had passed had given abundant evidence of the utter absence of all self-consciousness on the part of Ruth, of her delicacy and modesty in circumstances of no small difficulty. If these rare qualities must have been observed by Naomi, they could not have remained unnoticed by Boaz, as he daily watched her bearing. Nor yet could Ruth have been insensible to the worth, the piety, and the kindness of him who had been the first in Israel to speak comfort to her heart. That, in such circumstances, Naomi, recognizing a true Israelitess in her daughter-in-law, should have sought "rest" for her — and that rest in the house of Boaz, was alike to follow the clear indications of Providence, and what might be called the natural course of events. Thus, then, all the actors in what was to follow were prepared to take their parts. The manner in which it was brought about must not be judged by our western notions, although we are prepared to defend its purity and delicacy in every particular. Nor could Naomi have well done otherwise than counsel as she did. For the law which fixed on the next-of-kin the duty of redeeming a piece of land (Leviticus 25:25), did not connect with it the obligation of marrying the childless widow of the owner, which (strictly speaking) only devolved upon a brother-in-law (Deuteronomy 25:5); although such seems to have been the law of custom in Bethlehem, and this, as we believe, in strict accordance with the spirit and object, if not with the letter of the Divine commandment. Thus Naomi had no legal claim upon Boaz — not to speak of the fact, of which she must have been aware, that there was a nearer kinsman than he of Elimelech in Bethlehem. Lastly, in accordance with the law, it was not Naomi but Ruth who must lay claim to such marriage (Deuteronomy 25:7, 8).

Yet we should miss the whole spirit of the narrative, if, while admitting the influence of other matters, we were not to recognize that the law of redemption and of marriage with a childless widow, for the purpose of "not putting out a name in Israel," had been the guiding principle in the conduct of all these three — Naomi, Ruth, and Boaz. And, indeed, of the value and importance of this law there cannot be fuller proof than that furnished by this story itself — bearing in mind that from this next-of-kin-union descended David, and, "according to the flesh," the Lord Jesus Christ, the Son of David.

Keeping all this in view, we proceed to gather up the threads of our story. By the advice of her mother-in-law, Ruth puts off alike her widow's and her working dress. Festively arrayed as a bride — though, assuredly, not to be admired by Boaz, since the transaction was to take place at night — she goes to the threshing-floor, where, as the wind sprang up at even, Boaz was to winnow his barley. Unobserved, she watcheth where he lies down, and, softly lifting the coverlet, lays herself at his feet. At midnight, accidentally touching the form at his feet, Boaz wakes with a start — and "bent down, and, behold a woman lying at his feet!" In reply to his inquiry, the few words she speaks — exquisitely beautiful in their womanly and Scriptural simplicity — explain her conduct and her motive. Two things here require to be kept in mind: Boaz himself sees nothing strange or unbecoming in what Ruth has done; on the contrary, he praises her conduct as surpassing all her previous claims to his respect. Again, the language of Boaz implies that Ruth, although daring what she had felt to be right, had done it with the fear which, in the circumstances, womanly modesty would prompt. We almost seem to hear the low whispered tones, and the tremor of her voice, as we catch the gentle, encouraging words of Boaz' reply: "My daughter," and as he stills the throbbing of her heart with his kindly-spoken, fatherly: "Fear not!" No thought but of purity and goodness, and of Israel's law intruded on the midnight converse of those who were honored to become the ancestors of our Lord.

And now he, on his part, has explained to Ruth, how there is yet a nearer kinsman, whose claims must first be set aside, if the law is to be strictly observed. And, assuredly, if observance of the law of redemption, with all that it implied in Israel, had not been the chief actuating motive of Boaz and Ruth, there would have been no need first to refer the matter to the nearer kinsman, since there could be no possible hindrance to the union of those whose hearts evidently belonged to each other.

The conduct of each party having been clearly determined, they lie down again in silence. What remained of the short summer's night soon passed. Before the dawn had so far brightened that one person could have recognized another, she left the threshing-floor, bearing to her mother the gift of her kinsman, as if in pledge that her thoughts had been understood by him, and that her hope concerning the dead and the living would be realized.

The story now hastens to a rapid close. Early in the morning Boaz goes up to the gate, the usual place for administering law, or doing business. He sits down as one party to a case; calls the unnamed nearer kinsman, as he passes by, to occupy the place of the other party, and ten of the elders as witnesses or umpires — the number ten being not only symbolical of completeness, but from immemorial custom, and afterwards by law, that which constituted a legal assembly. To understand what passed between Boaz and the unnamed kinsman, we must offer certain explanations of the state of the case and of the law applying to it, different from any hitherto proposed. For the difficulty lies in the sale of the property by Naomi — nor is it diminished by supposing that she had not actually disposed of, but was only offering it for sale. In general we may here say, that the law (Numbers 27:8, 11) does not deal with any case precisely similar to that under consideration. It only contemplates one of two things, the death of a childless man, when his next-of-kin (speaking broadly) is bound to marry his widow (Deuteronomy 25:5); or else a forced sale of property through poverty, when the next-of-kin of the original proprietor may redeem the land (Leviticus 25:25). It is evident, that the former must be regarded as a duty, the latter as a privilege attaching to kinship, the object of both being precisely the same, the preservation of the family (rather than of the individual) in its original state. But although the law does not mention them, the same principle would, of course, apply to all analogous cases. Thus it might, for example, be, that a man would marry the widow, but be unable to redeem the property. On the other hand, he never could claim to redeem property without marrying the widow, to whom as the representative of her dead husband the property attached. In any case the property of the deceased husband was vested in a childless widow. In fact, so long as the childless widow lived, no one could have any claim on the property, since she was potentially the heir of her deceased husband. All authorities admit, that in such a case she had the use of the property, and a passage in the Mishnah (Yebam. iv. 3) declares it lawful for her to sell possessions, though it does seem very doubtful whether the expression covers the sale of her deceased husband's land. Such, however, would have been in strict accordance with the principle and the spirit of the law. In the case before us then, the property still belonged to Naomi, though in reversion to Ruth as potentially representing Elimelech and Machlon, while the claim to be married to the next-of-kin could, of course, in the circumstances, only devolve upon Ruth. Thus the property still held by Naomi went, in equity and in law, with the hand of Ruth, nor had any one claim upon the one without also taking the other. No kinsman had performed the kinsman's duty to Ruth, and therefore no kinsman could claim the privilege of redemption connected with the land. With the hand of Ruth the land had, so to speak, been repudiated. But as the kinsman had virtually refused to do his part, and Naomi was unable to maintain her property, she disposed of it, and that quite in the spirit of the law. There was no wrong done to any one. The only ground for passing the land to a kinsman would have been, that he would preserve the name of the dead. But this he had virtually refused to do. On the other hand, it was still open to him to redeem the land, if, at the same time, he would consent to wed Ruth. It would have been the grossest injustice to have allowed the privilege of redeeming a property to the kinsman who refused to act as kinsman. Instead of preserving a name in Israel, it would in reality have extinguished it for ever.

This was precisely the point in discussion between Boaz and the unnamed kinsman. Boaz brought, first, before him the privilege of the kinsman: redemption of the land. This he accepted. But when Boaz next reminded him, that this privilege carried with it a certain duty towards Ruth, and that, if the latter were refused, the former also was forfeited, he ceded his rights to Boaz. The bargain was ratified according to ancient custom in Israel by a symbolical act, of which we find a modification in Deuteronomy 25:9. Among all ancient nations the "shoe" was a symbol either of departure (Exodus 12:11), or of taking possession (comp. Psalm 60:8).

In this instance the kinsman handed his shoe to Boaz — that is, ceded his possession to him. Alike the assembled elders, and those who had gathered around to witness the transaction, cordially hailed its conclusion by wishes which proved, that "all the city knew that Ruth was a virtuous woman," and were prepared to receive the Moabitess as a mother in Israel, even as Thamar had proved in the ancestry of Boaz. It had all been done in God and with God, and the blessing invoked was not withheld. A son gladdened the hearts of the family of Bethlehem. Naomi had now a "redeemer," not only to support and nourish her, nor merely to "redeem" the family property, but to preserve the name of the family in Israel. And that "redeemer" — a child, and yet not a child of Boaz; a redeemer-son, and yet not a son of Naomi — was the father of Jesse. And so the story which began in poverty, famine, and exile leads up to the throne of David. Undoubtedly this was the main object for which it was recorded: to give us the history of David's family; and with his genealogy, traced not in every link but in symbolical outline, the Book of Ruth appropriately closes. It is the only instance in which a book is devoted to the domestic history of a woman, and that woman a stranger in Israel. But that woman was the Mary of the Old Testament.

VOLUME 4: THE HISTORY OF ISRAEL UNDER SAMUEL, SAUL, AND DAVID

PREFACE

THE history of Israel, viewed as the Theocracy, or Kingdom of God, consists of three periods:

First, that under the guidance of Prophets (from Moses to Samuel); Secondly, that under the rule of Kings (from Saul to the Babylonish Captivity); and, Thirdly, that under the reign of High-Priests (from Ezra to the birth of Jesus Christ).

Thus the Theocracy had passed through its full typical development in all its stages, when He came, to Whom they all pointed: Jesus Christ, the Prophet, King, and High-priest of the Kingdom of God. The period described in the present volume closes one of these stages, and commences another. The connecting link between them was Samuel — who alone fully realized the mission of the Judges, and who was also Divinely appointed to inaugurate the new institution of royalty in Israel. That royalty next appeared in its twofold possibility — or, as we might express it, in its negative and positive aspects. Saul embodied the royal ideal of the people, while David represented the Scriptural ideal of royalty in its conscious subjection to the will of the Heavenly King. Saul was, so to speak, the king after Israel's, David after God's own heart. But with the actual introduction of monarchy the first period had come to an end, and a new era begun, which was intended to continue till the third and last preliminary stage was reached, which prepared the way for the Advent of Him, Who was the fulfillment of the typical meaning of all.

From what has been said it will be inferred that the period about to be described must have witnessed the birth of new ideas, and the manifestation of new spiritual facts; otherwise spiritual advancement would not have kept pace with outward progress. But it is in the rhythm of these two that the real meaning of Scripture history lies, marking, as it does, the pari passu inner and outer development of the kingdom of God. On the other hand, the appearance of new ideas and spiritual facts would necessarily bring out in sharper contrast the old that was passing away, and even lead to occasional antagonism. Of course, these new ideas and facts would not at first be fully understood or realized. They rather pointed towards a goal which was to be reached in the course of history. For nothing could be more fatal to the proper understanding of Holy Scripture, or of the purposes of God in His dealings with His ancient people, than to transport into olden times the full spiritual privileges, the knowledge of Divine truth, or even that of right and duty, which we now enjoy. It is not to do honor, but dishonor, to the Spirit of God to overlook the educational process of gradual development, which is not only a necessity of our nature, but explains our history. A miracle of might could, indeed, have placed the age of Samuel on the same spiritual level with that of the New Testament, at least so far as regards the communication of the same measure of truth. But such an exhibition of power would have eliminated the moral element in the educational progress of Israel, with the discipline of wisdom, mercy, and truth which it implied, and, indeed, have rendered the whole Old Testament history needless.

What has been stated will lead the student to expect certain special difficulties in this part of the history. These concern, in our opinion, the substance more than the form or letter of the text, and raise doctrinal and philosophical rather than critical and exegetical questions. The calling and later rejection of Saul; his qualification for the work by the influence of the

Spirit of God, and afterwards the sending of a spirit of evil from the Lord; in general, the agency of the Spirit of God in Old Testament times, as distinguished from the abiding Presence of the Comforter under the Christian dispensation, and, in connection with it, the origin and the character of the Schools of the Prophets and of prophetic inspiration — these will readily occur to the reader as instances of what we mean. As examples of another class of difficulties, he will recall such questions as those connected with the ban upon Amalek, the consultation of the witch of Endor, and in general with the lower moral standpoint evidently occupied by those of that time, even by David himself. Such questions could not be passed over. They are inseparably connected with the Scriptural narratives, and they touch the very foundations of our faith. In accordance with the plan of progressive advance which I set before myself in the successive volumes of this Bible History, I have endeavored to discuss them as fully as the character of this work allowed. Whether or not I may always succeed in securing the conviction of my readers, I can at least say, that, while I have never written what was not in accordance with my own conscientious conviction, nor sought to invent an explanation merely in order to get rid of a difficulty, my own reverent belief in the authority of the Word of God has not in any one case been the least shaken. It sounds almost presumptuous to write down such a confession. Yet it seems called for in clays when the enumeration of difficulties, easily raised, owing to the distance of these events, the great difference of circumstances, and the necessary scantiness of our materials of knowledge — whether critical, historical, or theological, — so often takes the place of sober inquiry; and high-sounding phrases which, logically tested, yield no real meaning, are substituted for solid reasoning.

As in the course of this volume I have strictly kept by the Biblical narratives to be illustrated, I may perhaps be allowed here to add a bare statement of three facts impressed on me by the study of early Old Testament history.

First, I would mark the difference between the subjective and objective aspects of its theology. However low, comparatively speaking, may have been the stage occupied by Israel in their conceptions of, and dealings with God, yet the manifestations of the Divine Being are always so sublime that we could not conceive them higher at any later period. As we read their account we are still as much overawed and solemnized as they who had witnessed them. In illustration, we refer to the Divine manifestations to Elijah and Elisha. In fact, their sublimeness increases in proportion as the human element, and consequently the Divine accommodation to it, recedes. Secondly, even as regards man's bearing towards the Lord, the Old Testament never presents what seems the fundamental character of all ancient heathen religions. The object of Israel's worship and services was never to deprecate, but to pray. There was no malignant deity or fate to be averted, but a Father Who claimed love and a King Who required allegiance. Lastly, there is never an exhibition of mere power on the part of the Deity, but always a moral purpose conveyed by it, which in turn is intended, to serve as germ of further spiritual development to the people. We are too prone to miss this moral purpose, because it is often conveyed in a form adapted to the standpoint of the men of that time, and hence differs from that suited to our own.

Of course, there are also many and serious critical and exegetical questions connected with such portions of the Bible as the two Books of Samuel and the first Book of Chronicles. To these I have endeavored to address myself to the best of my power, so far as within the scope of a volume like this. Whether or not I may have succeeded in this difficult task, I am at least entitled to address a caution to the reader. Let him not take for granted that bold assertions of a negative character, made with the greatest confidence, even by men of undoubted learning and ability, are necessarily true. On the contrary, I venture to say, that their trustworthiness is generally in inverse ratio to the confidence with which they are made. This is not the place to furnish proof of this, — and yet it seems unfair to make a charge without illustrating it at least by one instance. It is chosen almost at random from one of the latest works of the kind, written expressly for English readers, by one of the ablest Continental scholars, and the present leader of that special school of critics. The learned writer labors to prove that the promise in Genesis 3:15 "must lose the name of, 'Proto-Evangelism,' which it owes to a positively incorrect view" of the passage. Accordingly he translates it: "I will put enmity between thee (the serpent) and the woman, and between thy seed and her seed: this (seed) shall lie in wait for thy head, and thou shalt lie in wait for his heel" — or, as he explains it: "man aims his attack at the head of the serpent, while it tries to strike man in the heel." It may possibly occur to ordinary readers that it scarcely needed what professes to be a record of Divine revelation to acquaint us with such a fact. Very different are the views which the oldest Jewish tradition expresses on this matter. But this is not the point to which I am desirous of directing attention. Dr. Kuenen supports his interpretation by two arguments.

First, he maintains that the verb commonly rendered "bruise," means "to lie in wait for," "according to the Septuagint and the Targum of Onkelos," — and that accordingly it cannot bear a Messianic reference.

Secondly, he, of course, implies that it is used in this sense by Onkelos in the passage in question. Now, the answer to all this is very simple, but quite conclusive.

First, the Hebrew verb referred to is always used in the Targumim for "bruise," or "rub off," as will be seen by a reference to Levy's well-known Dictionary of the Targumim, Vol. 2, pp. 462b, 463a.

Secondly, neither the word nor the rendering in question occurs in the Targum Onkelos, nor anything at all like it (as implied in the language of Kuenen); while, Thirdly, it is used, not indeed in the Targum Onkelos, but in the so-called Targum (Pseudo-) Jonathan and in the Jerusalem Targum (which in the whole of this history closely follow Jewish traditionalism), but in the sense of "bruise," with evident mystic reference — and what is more, with express mention of its application to Messiah the King!

I will not be so rash as to say, *Ex una disce omnes*, but this instance may at least point the moral to our caution. In conclusion, I can only repeat the apostolic assurance, as in this sense also expressive of the feelings with which I close the present part of my investigations:

"NEVERTHELESS THE FIRM FOUNDATION OF GOD STANDETH!"
ALFRED EDERSHEIM
LODERS VICARAGE, BRIDPORT.

CHAPTER 1: PURPORT AND LESSONS OF THE BOOKS OF SAMUEL — ELI — HANNAH'S PRAYER AND VOW — THE BIRTH OF SAMUEL — DEDICATION OF THE CHILD — HANNAH'S SONG.

(2 SAMUEL 1-2:11)

ONCE more, after long and ominous silence, the interest of the sacred story turns towards the Tabernacle which God had pitched among men, and the Priesthood which He had instituted. The period of the Judges had run its full course, and wrought no deliverance in Israel. In this direction, evidently, help or hope was not to be looked for. More than that, in the case of Samson, it had appeared how even the most direct aid on the part of God might be frustrated by the self-indulgence of man. A new beginning had again to be made; but, as we have hitherto noticed in all analogous cases in sacred history, not wholly new, but one long foreshadowed and prepared.

Two great institutions were now to be prominently brought forward and established, both marking a distinct advance in the history of Israel, and showing forth more fully than before its typical character. These two institutions were the Prophetic Order and the Monarchy. Both are connected with the history of Samuel. And this explains alike why the books which record this part of sacred history bear the name of Samuel, and why they close not with the death of David, as might have been expected in a biography or in a history of his reign, but with the final establishment of his kingdom (2 Samuel 20). At the close of 2 Samuel four chapters (21-24.) are added as a sort of appendix, in which various events are ranged, not chronologically, but in accordance with the general plan and scope of the work, which is: to present Israel as the kingdom of God, and as under the guidance of the spirit of prophecy. This also explains two other peculiarities. In a work compiled with such an object constantly in view, we do not expect, nor do we find in it, a strictly chronological arrangement of events. Again, we notice large gaps in the history of Samuel, Saul, and David, long periods and important facts being omitted, with which the author must have been acquainted — and to which, indeed, in some instances, he afterwards expressly refers, — while other periods and events are detailed at great length. All these peculiarities are not accidental, but designed, and in accordance with the general plan of the work. For, we must bear in mind, that as in the case of other parts of Holy Scripture, so in the Books of Samuel, we must not look for biographies, as of Samuel, Saul, and David, nor yet expect merely an account of their administration, but a history of the kingdom of God during a new period in its development, and in a fresh stage of its onward movement towards the end. That end was the establishment of the kingdom of God in Him to Whom alike the Aaronic priesthood, the prophetic order, and Israel's royalty were intended to point. These three institutions were prominently brought forward in the new period which opens in the books of Samuel. First, we have in the history of Eli a revival of the interest attaching to the priesthood. Next, we see in Samuel the real commencement of the Old Testament prophetic order. Not that the idea of it was new, or the people unprepared for it. We can trace it so early as in Genesis 20:7 (comp. Psalm 105:15); and we find not only Moses (Deuteronomy 34:10), but even Miriam (Exodus 15:20; Numbers 12:2) designated by the title of prophet;

while the character and functions of the office (if "office" and not "mission" be the correct term) are clearly defined in Deuteronomy 13:1-5; 18:9-22.

And although Joshua was not himself a prophet, yet the gift of prophecy had not ceased in his time. In proof we point not only to Deborah (Judges 4:4), but also to other instances (Judges 6:8). But on the other hand, the order of prophets as such evidently began with Samuel. The same remarks apply to the institution of royalty in Israel. It had been contemplated and prepared for from the first. Passing from the promise to Abraham (Genesis 17:6, 16), with its prophetic limitation to Judah (Genesis 49:10), we find the term kingdom applied to Israel, as marking its typical destiny (Exodus 19:6), centering of course in the King (Numbers 24:17, 19). And as the character of the prophetic order, so that of this royalty also was clearly defined in Deuteronomy 17, while from Judges 8:23 we learn, that the remembrance and expectation of this destiny were kept alive in Israel. It was, however, during the period which we are about to describe, that royalty was first actually introduced in Israel. It appeared, if we may so express it, in Saul in its negative, and in David in its, positive aspect; and to the latter all the promises and types applied which were connected with its establishment. Nor is it without the deepest significance in this respect that in the books of Samuel the designation "Jehovah of Hosts," occurs for the first time, and that Hannah, who was the first to use this title in her prayer (1 Samuel 1:11), prophesied of that King (2:10) in Whom all Israel's hopes were fulfilled, and Whose kingdom is the subject of grateful praise alike by the Virgin-mother, and by the father of the Baptist (Luke 2).

But to turn to the history itself. Once more the Sanctuary had been restored to its former and God-destined position, and Eli the high-priest judged in Israel. Once more God had visibly interposed to own the institution of Nazarites, which, more than any other, symbolized Israel's spiritual calling of voluntary self-surrender to God.

Alone, and unaided by man, the Nazarite Samson had made war for God against the Philistines. In the miraculous strength supplied from on high, he had prevailed against them. But neither priest nor Nazarite of that time had realized the spirituality of their calling. Both had been raised up to show what potentiality for good there was in God's institutions; and both were removed to prove that even God's institutions were powerless, except by a continuous and living connection with Him on Whose presence and blessing depended their efficacy. But already God was preparing other instrumentalities — a prophet, who should receive and speak His Word, and another Nazarite, voluntarily devoted to God by his mother, and who would prevail not in the strength of his own arm, but by the power of prayer, and by the influence of the message which he brought from God. That prophet, that Nazarite was Samuel His birth, like that of Samson, was Divinely announced; but, in accordance with the difference between the two histories this time by prophecy, not as before, by angelic message. Samuel was God-granted, Samson God-sent; Samuel was God-dedicated, Samson was God-demanded. Both were Nazarites; but the one spiritually, the other outwardly; both prevailed-but the one spiritually, the other outwardly. The work of Samson ended in self-indulgence, failure, and death; that of Samuel opened up into the royalty of David, Israel's great type-king.

Up in Mount Ephraim, due west from Shiloh, lay Ramah, "the height," or by its full name, Ramathaim Zophim, "the twin heights of the Zophites." From Joshua 21:20, we know that, amongst others, certain districts within the tribal possession of Ephraim were assigned to the Levitical families which descended from Kohath.

One of these — that of Zophai or Zuph (1 Chronicles 6:25, 35) — had given its name to the whole district, as "the land of Zuph" (1 Samuel 9:5). From this family sprang Elkanah, "the God-acquired," or "purchased," a name which characteristically occurs in the Old Testament only in Levitical families. It was not in accordance with what "was from the first," that Elkanah had two wives, Hannah ("favor," "grace") and Peninnah ("pearl," or "coral"). Perhaps the circumstance that Hannah was not blessed with children may have led to this double marriage. "Yearly" — as has been inferred from the use of the same peculiar expression in Exodus 13:10 — "at the Feast of the Passover," the one above all others to which families as such were wont to "go up" (Luke 2:41), Elkanah came to Shiloh with his household for the twofold purpose of "worshipping" and of "sacrificing" peace-offerings according to the law (Exodus 23:15; 34:20; Deuteronomy 16:16).

Although, Eli being old, the chief direction of the services devolved upon his unworthy sons, Hophni and Phinehas, yet these were joyous occasions (Deuteronomy 12:12; 16:11; 27:7), when the whole household would share in the feast upon the thank-offering. At that time Elkanah was wont to give to Peninnah and to her children their "portions;" but to Hannah he gave "a portion for two persons," as if to indicate that he loved her just as if she had borne him a son. Whether from jealousy or from malevolence, Peninnah made those joyous seasons times of pain and bitter emotion to Hannah, by grieving and trying to make her dissatisfied and rebellious against God. And so it happened each year: Hannah's sorrow, as time passed, seeming ever more hopeless. In vain Elkanah tried to comfort her by assurance of his own affection. The burden of her reproach, still unrolled from her, seemed almost too heavy to bear.

It was surely in the noble despair of faith — as if in her own way anticipating the New Testament question: "Lord, to whom shall we go?" — that Hannah rose from the untasted sacrificial feast, with the resolve to cast upon the Lord the burden she could not bear. It was early evening in spring time, and the aged high-priest Eli (a descendant not of Eleazar, but of Ithamar, to whom the high-priesthood seems to have been transferred from the elder branch of the Aaronic family, comp. Josephus' Antiquities, 5. 11. 5) sat at the entrance probably to the holy place, when a lonely woman came and knelt towards the sanctuary. Concealed by the folds of the curtain, she may not have noticed him, though he watched every movement of the strange visitor. Not a sound issued from her lips, and still they moved faster and faster as, unburdening the long secret, she poured out her heart in silent prayer.

And now the gentle rain of tears fell, and then in spirit she believingly rose to the vow that the child she sought from the Lord should not be cherished for the selfish gratification of even a mother's sacred love. He would, of course, be a Levite, and as such bound from his twenty-fifth or thirtieth year to service when his turn for it came. But her child should wholly belong to God. From earliest childhood, and permanently, should he be attached to the house of the Lord. Not only so — he should be a Nazarite, and that not of the ordinary class, but one whose vow should last for life (Numbers 6:2; comp. Judges 13:5).

It leaves on us the twofold sad impression that such prayerful converse with God must have been rare in Shiloh, and that the sacrificial feasts were not infrequently profaned by excesses, when such a man as Eli could suspect, and roughly interrupt Hannah's prayer on the supposition of her drunkenness. But Eli was a man of God; and the modest, earnest words which Hannah spake soon changed his reproof into a blessing. And now Hannah comes back to those she had left at the sacrificial feast. The brief absence had transformed her, for she returns with a heart light of sorrow and joyous in faith. Her countenance and bearing are changed. She eats of the erst untasted food, and is gladsome. She has already that for which to thank God, for she is strong in faith.

Another morning of early worship, and the family return to their quiet home. But God is not unmindful of her. Ere another Passover has summoned the worshippers to Shiloh, Hannah has the child of her prayers, whom significantly she has named Samuel, the God-answered (literally: heard of God — Exauditus a Deo). This time Hannah accompanied not her husband, though he paid a vow which he seems to have made, if a son were granted; no, nor next time. But the third year, when the child was fully weaned, she presented herself once more before Eli. It must have sounded to the old priest almost like a voice from heaven when the gladsome mother pointed to her child as the embodiment of answered prayer: "For this boy have I prayed; and Jehovah gave me my asking which I asked of Him. And now I (on my part) make him the asked one unto Jehovah all the days that he lives: he is 'the asked one' unto Jehovah!" And as she so vowed and paid her vow, one of the three bullocks which they had brought was offered a burnt-offering, symbolic of the dedication of her child. Once more Hannah "prayed;" this time not in the language of sorrow, but in that of thanksgiving and prophetic anticipation. For was not Samuel, so to speak, the John the Baptist of the Old Testament? and was it not fitting that on his formal dedication unto God, she should speak words reaching far beyond her own time, and even furnishing what could enter into the Virgin-mother's song?

"And Hannah prayed and said:

1 "My heart rejoiceth in Jehovah — Uplifted my horn in Jehovah, Wide opened my mouth upon my foes For I rejoice in Thy salvation!

2 None holy as Jehovah — for none is beside Thee, Nor is there rock as our God! 3 Multiply not speech lofty, lofty — (Nor) insolence come out of your mouth, For God of all knowledge is Jehovah, And with Him deeds are weighed.

4 Bow-heroes are broken, And the stumbling girded with strength.

5 "The full hire themselves out for bread And the hungry cease — Even till the barren bears seven, And the many-childed languisheth away! 6 Jehovah killeth and maketh alive, He bringeth down to Sheol, and bringeth up.

7 Jehovah maketh poor and maketh rich, He layeth low and lifteth up. 8 He lifteth from the dust the weak, And from the dunghill raiseth the poor To make them sit down with nobles. And seats of honor will He assign them — For Jehovah's are the pillars of the earth, And He hath set on them the habitable world.

9 The feet of His saints will He keep, And the wicked in darkness shall be put to silence, For not by strength shall man prevail!

10 Jehovah — broken they that strive with Him, Above him (over such) in the heavens shall He thunder; Jehovah shall judge the ends of the earth, And give strength to His King, And lift on high the horn of His Anointed!"

And so the child and his parents parted — where parting is ever best: leaving him "ministering unto the Lord." But yearly, as they came up to the twice-loved service in Shiloh, they saw again the child, still serving in the courts of the Lord's house, "girded with a linen ephod." And the gift they brought him each year from home was that with which Hannah's love best liked to connect her absent child — "a little Meil," or priestly robe in which to do his service. She had made him "the God-asked," and present or absent he was ever such in her loving thoughts. But, as Eli had prayed, instead of the "asked one," who was "asked" for Jehovah, three sons and two daughters gladdened Hannah's heart. "But the boy Samuel grew up with Jehovah" (1 Samuel 2:21).

CHAPTER 2: THE SIN OF ELI'S SONS — ELI'S WEAKNESS — A PROPHET'S MESSAGE — SAMUEL'S FIRST VISION — HIS CALL TO THE PROPHETIC OFFICE.

(1 SAMUEL 2:12-3:21)

QUITE another scene now opens before us, and one which, as it shows the corruptness of the priestly family, also argues a very low religious state among the people. The high-priest Eli was "very old," and the administration of the sanctuary was left in the hands of his two sons, Hophni and Phinehas. The energy, amounting almost to severity, which, even in his old age, Eli could display, as in his undeserved reproof of Hannah, was certainly not exercised towards his sons. They were "sons of Belial," and, "knew not Jehovah" in His character and claims. Their conduct was scandalous even in a decrepid age, and the unblushing frankness of their vices led "the people of the Lord to transgress," by "bringing into contempt" the sacrificial services of the sanctuary.

The main element of hope and the prospect of a possible revival lay in the close adherence of the people to these services. But the sons of Eli seemed determined to prove that these ordinances were mainly designed for the advantage of the priesthood, and therefore not holy, of Divine significance, and unalterably fixed. Contrary to the Divine institution, "the priest's right," as he claimed it, was to take, if necessary by force, parts of the sacrifices before these had really been offered unto the Lord (Leviticus 3:3- 5; comp. 7:30-34).

Nor was this all. The open immorality of the high-priest's sons was as notorious as their profanity. The only step which the aged high-priest took to put an end to such scandals was mild expostulation, the truisms of which had only so far value as they expressed it, that in offenses between man and man, Elohim would, through the magistracy, restore the proper balance, but who was to do that when the sin was against Jehovah? Such remonstrances could, of course, produce no effect upon men so seared in conscience as to be already under sentence of judicial hardening (ver. 25).

But other and more terrible judgments were at hand. They were solemnly announced to Eli by a prophet (comp. Judges 13:6), since by his culpable weakness he shared the guilt of his sons. As so often in His dealings with His own people, the Lord condescended to reason, not only to exhibit the rightness of His ways, but to lay down principles for all time for the guidance of His church. Had He not dealt in special grace with the house of Aaron? He had honored it at the first by special revelation; He had singled it out for the privilege of ministering unto Him at the altar; for the still higher function of presenting in the incense the prayers of His people; and for that highest office of "wearing the ephod" in the solemn mediatorial services of the Day of Atonement. Moreover, He had made ample provision for all their wants. All this had been granted in perpetuity to the house of Aaron (Exodus 29:9). It had been specially confirmed to Phinehas on account of his zeal for the honor of God (Numbers 25:13). But even the latter circumstance, as well as the nature of the case, indicated that the whole rested on a moral relationship, as, indeed, the general principle holds true: "Them that honor Me I will honor, and they that despise Me shall be lightly esteemed." In accordance with this, Eli and his house would become subjects of special judgment: none of his descendants, so long as they held office, should attain old age (1 Samuel 2:31); in punishment of their own insolence of office they would experience constant humiliation (ver. 32); another and more faithful line of priests should fill the highest office (ver. 35); and the deposed family would have to seek at their hands the humblest places for the sake of the barest necessaries of life (ver. 36). Thus justice would overtake a family which, in their pride of office, had dared to treat the priesthood as if it were absolutely their own, and to degrade it for selfish purposes. As for the chief offenders, Hophni and Phinehas, swift destruction would overtake them in one day; and their death would be the sign of the commencement of those judgments, which were to culminate in the time of Solomon (1 Kings 2:27; comp. Josephus' Antiq. 5. 11, 5; 8. 1, 3).

But, uncorrupted by such influences around, "the child Samuel grew, and was in favor both with Jehovah and with men," — in this respect also the type of the "faithful Priest," the great Prophet, the perfect Nazarite (Luke 2:52). It was in many respects as in the days of the Son of man. "The word of Jehovah" by prophetic revelation "was precious," it was rare, and prophetic "vision was not spread."

Meanwhile Samuel had grown into a youth, and was, as Levite, "ministering unto Jehovah before Eli." But as yet, beyond humble, faithful walk before God, heart-fellowship with Him, and outward ministrations in His sanctuary, Samuel had not other knowledge of Jehovah, in the sense of personal revelation or reception of His message (3:7). The sanctuary in Shiloh had become permanent, and we are warranted in inferring that "the dwelling," which formerly was adapted to Israel's wanderings, had lost somewhat of its temporary character. The "curtains" which in the wilderness had formed its enclosure, had no doubt been exchanged for buildings for the use of the priesthood in their ministry and for the many requirements of their services. Instead of the "veil" at the entrance to the outer court there would be doors, closed at even and opened to the worshippers in the morning. The charge of these doors seems to have devolved upon Samuel, who as "minister" and guardian lay by night within the sacred enclosure, in the court of the people — or, at least, close to it, as did the priests on duty in later times. The aged high-priest himself seems to have lain close by, probably in one of the rooms or halls opening out upon the sanctuary.

It was still night, though the dawn was near. The holy oil in the seven-branched candlestick in the holy place was burning low, but its light had not yet gone out, when a voice calling Samuel by his name wakened him from sleep. As Eli's eyes had begun to "wax dim," so that he would require the aid of the young Levite on ministry, it was natural to infer that it was the voice of the aged high-priest that had called him. But it was not so, and Samuel again laid him down to rest. A second time the same voice called him, and a second time he repaired in vain to Eli for his commands. But when yet a third time the call was repeated, the high-priest understood that it was not some vivid dream which had startled the youth from his sleep, but that a voice from heaven commanded his attention. There is such simplicity and child-like faith, such utter absence of all intrusive curiosity, and such entire self-forgetfulness on the part of Eli, and on that of Samuel such complete want of all self-consciousness, as to render the surroundings worthy of the scene about to be enacted. Samuel no longer seeks sleep; but when next the call is heard, he answers, as directed by his fatherly teacher: "Speak, for Thy servant heareth." Then it was that not, as before, merely a voice, but a vision was granted him, when Jehovah repeated in express terms, this time not in warning prediction, but as the announcement of an almost immediate event, the terrible judgment impending upon Eli and his sons.

With the burden of this communication upon him, Samuel lay still till the gray morning light; nor, whatever thoughts might crowd upon him, did the aged high-priest seek to intrude into what might pass between that Levite youth and the Lord, before Whom he had stood for so many years in the highest function of the priestly office, and into Whose immediate Presence in the innermost sanctuary he had so often entered. Suffice it, the vision and the word of Jehovah had passed from himself — passed not to his sons and successors in the priesthood, but to one scarce grown to manhood, and whose whole history, associated as it was with that very tabernacle, stood out so vividly before him. This itself was judgment. But what further judgment had the voice of the Lord announced to His youthful servant?

And now it was morning, and Samuel's duty was to open the gates of the sanctuary. What was he to do with the burden which had been laid upon him? In his reverence for his teacher and guide, and in his modesty, he could not bring himself unbidden to speak of that vision; he trembled to repeat to him whom most it concerned the words which he had heard. But the sound of the opening gates conveyed to Eli, that whatever might have been the commission to the young prophet, it had been given, and there could be no further hesitation in asking its import. Feeling that he and his family had been its subject, and that, however heavy the burden, it behooved him to know it, he successively asked, entreated, and even conjured Samuel to tell it in all its details. So challenged, Samuel dared not keep back anything. And the aged priest, however weak and unfaithful, yet in heart a servant of the Lord, received it with humiliation and resignation, though apparently without that resolve of change which alone could have constituted true repentance (1 Samuel 3:17, 18).

By the faithful discharge of a commission so painful, and involving such self-denial and courage, Samuel had stood the first test of his fitness for the prophetic office. Henceforth "the word of the Lord" was permanently with him. Not merely by isolated commissions, but in the discharge of a regular office, Samuel acted as prophet in Israel. A new period in the history of the kingdom of God had commenced; and all Israel, from Dan to Beer-sheba, knew that there was now a new link between them and their Heavenly King, a living center of guidance and fellowship, and a bond of union for all who were truly the Israel of God.

CHAPTER 3: EXPEDITION AGAINST THE PHILISTINES — THE TWO BATTLES OF EBENEZER — DEATH OF ELI'S SONS, AND TAKING OF THE ARK — DEATH OF ELI — JUDGMENT ON THE PHILISTINE CITIES — THE RETURN OF THE ARK.

(1 SAMUEL 4-7:1)

TIME had passed; but in Shiloh it was as before. Eli, who had reached the patriarchal age of ninety-seven, was now totally blind, and his sons still held rule in the sanctuary. As for Samuel, his prophetic "word was to all Israel." Some effect must have been produced by a ministry so generally acknowledged. True, it did not succeed in leading the people to repentance, nor in teaching them the spiritual character of the relationship between God and themselves, nor yet that of His ordinances in Israel.

But whereas the conduct of Eli's sons had brought the sanctuary and its services into public contempt (1 Samuel 2:17), Samuel's ministry restored and strengthened belief in the reality of God's presence in His temple, and in His help and power. In short, it would tend to keep alive and increase historical, although not spiritual belief in Israel. Such feelings, when uncombined with repentance, would lead to a revival of religiousness rather than of religion; to confidence in the possession of what, dissociated from their higher bearing, were merely externals; to a confusion of symbols with reality; and to such a reliance on their calling and privileges, as would have converted the wonder-working Presence of Jehovah in the midst of His believing people into a magic power attaching to certain symbols, the religion of Israel into mere externalism, essentially heathen in its character, and the calling of God's people into a warrant for carnal pride of nationality. In truth, however different in manifestation, the sin of Israel was essentially the same as that of Eli's sons. Accordingly it had to be shown in reference to both, that neither high office nor yet the possession of high privileges entitles to the promises attached to them, irrespective of a deeper relationship between God and His servants.

It may have been this renewed, though entirely carnal confidence in the Presence of God in His sanctuary, as evidenced by the prophetic office of Samuel, or else merely a fresh outbreak of that chronic state of warfare between Israel and the Philistines which existed since the days of Samson and even before, that led to the expedition which terminated in the defeat at Eben-ezer. At any rate, the sacred text implies that the Philistines held possession of part of the soil of Palestine; nor do we read of any recent incursion on their part which had given them this hold. It was, therefore, as against positions which the enemy had occupied for some time that "Israel went out to battle" in that open "field," which from the monument erected after the later deliverance under Samuel (1 Samuel 7:12), obtained the name of Eben-ezer, or stone of help The scene of action lay, as we know, in the territory of Benjamin, a short way beyond, Mizpeh, "the look out," about two hours to the north-west of Jerusalem. The Philistines had pitched a short way off at Aphek, "firmness," probably a fortified position. The battle ended in the entire defeat of Israel, with a loss of four thousand men, not fugitives, but in the "battle-array" itself.

They must have been at least equal in numbers to the Philistines, and under favorable circumstances, since at the council of war after their defeat, "the elders of Israel" unhesitatingly ascribed the disaster not to secondary causes, but to the direct agency of Jehovah. It was quite in accordance with the prevailing religious state that, instead of inquiring into the causes of God's controversy with them, they sought safety in having among them "the ark of the covenant of the Lord," irrespective of the Lord Himself and of the terms of His covenant. As if to mark, in its own peculiarly significant manner, the incongruity of the whole proceeding, Scripture simply puts together these two things in their sharp contrast: that it was "the ark of the covenant of Jehovah of Hosts, which dwelleth, between the cherubim," and that "Hophni and Phinehas were there with the ark of the covenant of God" (1 Samuel 4:4).

Such an event as the removal of the ark from the sanctuary, and its presence in the camp, had never happened since the settlement of Israel in Canaan. Its arrival, betokening to their minds the certain renewal of miraculous deliverances such as their fathers had experienced, excited unbounded enthusiasm in Israel, and caused equal depression among the Philistines. But soon another mood prevailed.

Whether we regard ver. 9 as the language of the leaders of the Philistines, addressed to their desponding followers, or as the desperate resolve of men who felt that all was at stake, this time they waited not to be attacked by the Israelites. In the battle which ensued, and the flight of Israel which followed, no less than thirty thousand dead strewed the ground. In the number of the slain were Hophni and Phinehas, and among the booty the very ark of God was taken! Thus fearfully did judgment commence in the house of Eli; thus terribly did God teach the lesson that even the most sacred symbol connected with His immediate Presence was in itself but wood and gold, and so far from being capable of doing wonders, might even be taken and carried away. Tidings of this crashing defeat were not long in reaching Shiloh. Just outside the gate of the sanctuary, by the way which a messenger from the battlefield must come, sat the aged high-priest. His eyes were "stiffened" by age, but his hearing was keen as he waited with anxious heart for the expected news. The judgment foretold, the presence of his two sons with the army in the field, the removal of the ark, without any Divine authority, at the bidding of a superstitious people, must have filled him with sad misgivings. Had he been right in being a consenting party to all this? Had he been a faithful father, a faithful priest, a faithful guardian of the sanctuary? And now a confused noise as of a tumult reached him. Up the slopes which led to Shiloh, "with clothes rent and earth upon his head," in token of deepest meaning, ran a Benjamite, a fugitive from the army. Past the high-priest he sped, without stopping to speak to him whose office had become empty, and whose family was destroyed. Now he has reached the market-place; and up and down those steep, narrow streets fly the tidings. They gather around him; they weep, they cry out in the wildness of their grief, and "the noise of the crying" is heard where the old man sits alone still waiting for tidings. The messenger is brought to him. Stroke upon stroke falls upon him the fourfold disaster: "Israel is fled!" "a great slaughter among the people!" "thy two sons are dead!" "the ark of God is taken!" It is this last most terrible blow, rather than anything else, which lays low the aged priest. As he hears of the ark of God, he falls backward unconscious, and is killed in the fall by "the side of the gate" of the sanctuary. Thus ends a judgeship of forty years!

Yet another scene of terror. Within her house lies the wife of Phinehas, with the sorrows and the hopes of motherhood upon her. And now these tidings have come into that darkened chamber also. They gather around her as the shadows of death. In vain the women that are about try to comfort her with the announcement that a son has been born to her. She answers not, neither regards it. She cannot forget her one great sorrow even in this joy that a man is born into the world. She has but one word, even for her new-born child: "Ichabod," "no glory." To her he is Ichabod — for the glory is departed from Israel. And with that word on her lips she dies. The deepest pang which had wrought her death was, as in the case of her father-in-law, that the ark, the glory of Israel, was no more. Two have died that day in Shiloh of grief for the ark of God — the aged high-priest and the young mother; two, whose death showed at least their own fidelity to their God and their heart-love for His cause and presence.

But although such heavy judgment had come upon Israel, it was not intended that Philistia should triumph. More than that, in the hour of their victory the heathen must learn that their gods were not only wholly powerless before Jehovah, but merely idols, the work of men's hands. The Philistines had, in the first place, brought the ark to Ashdod, and placed it in the temple of Dagon as a votive offering, in acknowledgment of the victory which they ascribed to the agency of their national god. Had not the ark of God been brought into the camp of Israel, and had not the God of Israel been defeated and led captive in His ark through the superior power of Dagon? But they were soon to feel that it was not so; and when on the morn of its arrival at Ashdod, the priests opened the temple doors, they found the statue of their god thrown upon its face in front of the ark. It might have been some accident; and the statue, with its head and bust of a bearded man, and body in the form of a fish, was replaced in the cella at the entrance of the temple. But next morning the head and hands, which were in human form, were found cut off and lying on the threshold, as if each entrant should in contempt tread upon these caricatures of ideal humanity; and nothing but the Dagon itself, the fish-body, was left, which once more lay prostrate before the ark.

But this was not all. If the gods of Philistia were only vanity, the power and strength in which the people may have boasted, were likewise to appear as unavailing before the Lord. He "laid waste" the people of Ashdod — as we infer from 1 Samuel 6:4, 11, 18 — by that terrible plague of southern countries, field-mice, which sometimes in a single night destroy a harvest, and are known to have driven whole tribes from their dwelling-places. While thus the towns and villages around Ashdod were desolated, the inhabitants of that city itself and of its neighborhood, suffered from another plague, possibly occasioned by the want caused by famine, in the form of an epidemic — probably a malignant skin disease, — highly infectious and fatal in its character.

As we gather from the context, Philistia consisted at that time of a federation of five "cities," or cantons, under the oligarchical rule of "lords," or princes, with this provision, that no great public measure (such as the removal of the ark, which had been placed at Ashdod by common decree) might be taken without the consent of all. Accordingly, on an appeal of the people of Ashdod, the lords of the Philistines ordered the removal of the ark to Gath, probably judging, that the calamities complained of were due rather to natural causes than to its presence. But in Gath the same consequences also followed; and when on its further transportation to Ekron the public sufferings were even greater and more sudden than before, the cry became universal to return the ark to the land of Israel.

The experience of these seven months during which the ark had been in their land, not only convinced the lords of the Philistines of the necessity of yielding to the popular demand, but also made them careful as to the manner of handling the ark when returning it to its place. Accordingly they resolved to consult their priests and soothsayers on this question: "What shall we do in reference to the ark of Jehovah — instruct us with what we shall send it to its place?" The reply was to this effect, that if the ark were returned it should be accompanied by a "trespass-offering" in expiation of their wrong (Leviticus 6:5; Numbers 5:7), — consisting, according to common heathen custom, of votive offerings in gold, representing that wherein or whereby they had suffered. Never perhaps did superstition more truly appear in its real character than in the advice which these priests pressed upon their people. Evidently they were fully acquainted with the judgments which the God of Israel had executed upon the Egyptians when hardening their hearts, and with solemn earnestness they urge the return of the ark and a trespass-offering. And yet they are not quite sure whether, after all, it was not mere chance that had happened to them; and they propose a curious device by which to decide that question (1 Samuel 6:7-9).

The advice of the priests was literally followed. The ark, with its trespass-offerings, was placed on a new cart, which had never served profane purposes. To this were attached two milch cows, on whom never yoke of other service had been laid, and from whom their calves had just been taken.

No force was to be used to keep them from returning to their calves; no guidance to be given what road to take. And, behold, it happened as the priests had suggested it would, if it were God Who had smitten them. "Though lowing as they went" for their calves, the kine took the straight road to the nearest Israelitish border-city, Beth-shemesh ("the house of the Sun"), followed by the wondering lords of the Philistines. The boundary was reached, and the Philistines waited to see what would happen. About fourteen miles west of Jerusalem, on the northern boundary of the possession of Judah, about two miles from the great Philistine plain, and seven from Ekron, lay the ancient "sun city," Beth-shemesh. It was one of those allotted by Joshua to the priests (Joshua 21:16), though, of course, not exclusively inhabited by them. To reach it from Ekron, the great plain has first to be traversed. Then the hills are crossed which bound the great plain of Philistia. Ascending these, and standing on the top of a steep ridge, a valley stretches beneath, or rather "the junction of two fine plains." This is "the valley of Beth-shemesh," where on that summer afternoon they were reaping the wheat-harvest (1 Samuel 6:13); and beyond it, on, "the plateau of a low swell or mound," was the ancient Beth-shemesh itself.

A fit place this to which to bring the ark from Philistia, right in view of Zorah, the birth-place of Samson. Here, over these ridges, he had often made those incursions which had carried terror and destruction to the enemies of Israel. The sound of the approaching escort — for, no doubt, the Philistine "lords" were accompanied by their retainers, and by a multitude eager to see the result — attracted the attention of the reapers below. As, literally, "they lifted up their eyes" to the hill whence it slowly wound down, the momentary fear at seeing the Philistine escort gave place first to astonishment and then to unbounded joy, as they recognized their own ark heading the strange procession. Now it had reached the boundary — probably marked by a "great stone" in the field of Joshua.

The Philistines had remained reverently within their own territory, and the unguided kine stood still by the first landmark in Israel. The precious burden they brought was soon surrounded by Beth-shemites. Levites were called to lift it with consecrated hands, and to offer first the kine that had been devoted by the Philistines to the service of the Lord, and then other "burnt-offerings and sacrifices" which the men of Beth-shemesh had brought. But even so, on its first return to the land, another lesson must be taught to Israel in connection with the ark of God. It was the symbol to which the Presence of Jehovah in the midst of His people attached. Alike superstition and profanity would entail judgment at His Hand. What the peculiar desecration or sin of the Beth-shemites may have been, either on that day of almost unbounded excitement, or afterwards, we cannot tell. Suffice it that it was something which the people themselves felt to be incompatible with the "holiness" of Jehovah God (ver. 20), and that it was punished by the death of not less than seventy persons. In consequence the ark was, at the request of the Beth-shemites, once more removed, up the heights at the head of the valley to the "city of forest-trees," Kirjath-jearim, where it was given in charge to Abinadab, no doubt a Levite; whose son Eleazar was set apart to the office of guardian, not priest, of the ark. Here this sacred symbol remained, while the tabernacle itself was moved from Shiloh to Nob, and from Nob to Gibeon, till David brought it, after the conquest of Jerusalem, into his royal city (2 Samuel 6:2, 3, 12). Thus for all this period the sanctuary was empty of that which was its greatest treasure, and the symbol of God's Personal Presence removed from the place in which He was worshipped.

CHAPTER 4: SAMUEL AS PROPHET — THE GATHERING AT MIZPEH — BATTLE OF EBEN-EZER; ITS CONSEQUENCES — SAMUEL'S ADMINISTRATION — THE DEMAND FOR A KING.

(1 SAMUEL 7, 8)

PERHAPS the most majestic form presented, even among the heroes of Old Testament history, is that of Samuel, who is specially introduced to us as a man of prayer (Psalm 99:6). Levite, Nazarite, prophet, judge — each phase of his outward calling seems to have left its influence on his mind and heart. At Shiloh, the contrast between the life of self-denial of the young Nazarite and the unbridled self-indulgence of Eli's sons must have prepared the people for the general acknowledgment of his prophetic office. And Nazarite — God-devoted, stern, unbending, true to his calling, whithersoever it might direct him, — such was ever the life and the character of Samuel!

It needed such a man in this period of reformation and transition, when all the old had signally failed, not through inherent weakness, but through the sin of the people, and when the forms of the new were to be outlined in their Divine perfectness. The past, the present, and the future of the people seemed to meet in his history; and over it the figure of the life-Nazarite cast its shadow, and through it the first voice from the prophetic order was heard in Israel.

The sanctuary, destitute of the ark, and tended by a decrepit priesthood, over which the doom had been pronounced, had apparently fallen into utter disregard. The ark, carried captive into Philistia, but having proved a conqueror there, had indeed been restored to Israel, but was rather a witness of the past than the symbol of present help. The only living hope of Israel centered in the person of Samuel. Although, since the death of Eli, no longer attached to the sanctuary, which indeed his mission to a certain extent set aside, his spiritual activity had not been interrupted. Known and owned as prophet, he closely watched, and at the proper time decisively directed the religious movement in Israel. That decisive hour had now come.

Twenty years had passed since the return of the ark — a period, as we gather from the subsequent history, outwardly of political subjection to the Philistine, and spiritually of religious depression, caused by the desolateness of their sanctuary, and the manifest absence of the Lord from among His people. It was no doubt due to the influence of Samuel that these feelings led them towards the Lord. In the language of Scripture, they "lamented after Jehovah." But this was only preparatory. It was Samuel's work to direct to a happy issue the change which had already begun. His earnest message to all Israel now was: "If with all your hearts you are returning to Jehovah," — implying in the expression that repentance was primarily of the heart, and by the form of the Hebrew verb, that that return had indeed commenced and was going on — "put away the strange gods (Baalim, ver. 4), and the Ashtaroth, and make firm your hearts towards Jehovah" — in opposition to the former vacillation and indecision — "and serve Him alone." To Israel so returning with their whole heart, and repenting alike by the removal of their sin, and by exercising lively faith, Jehovah would, as of old, prove a Savior — in the present instance, from the Philistines.

The words of Samuel produced the marks of at least full outward repentance. The next step was to call the people to one of those solemn national gatherings, in which, as on former occasions (Joshua 23:2, etc.; 24:1, etc.), they would confess national sins and renew national obligations towards Jehovah. On its mountain height, Mizpeh, the "look out" of Benjamin, was among those ancient sanctuaries in the land, where, as in Shechem (Joshua 24:26), in Gilgal (Joshua 5:2-12, 15), and in Bethel (Judges 20:18, 23, 26; 21:2), the people were wont to assemble for solemn deliberation (Judges 11:11; 20:1). But never before, since the days of Moses, had Israel so humbled itself before the Lord in confession of sin. It was thus that Samuel would prepare for his grand act of intercession on their behalf, and it was under such circumstances that he publicly exercised, or more probably that he began his office of "judge" (1 Samuel 8:6), in its real meaning, by setting right what was wrong within Israel, and by becoming the means of their deliverance from the enemy.

The assembly had met in Mizpeh, not with any thought of war, far less in preparation for it. In fact, when Israel in Mizpeh heard of the hostile approach of the Philistines, "they were afraid" (ver. 7). But as rebellion had caused their desertion, so would return bring them help from the Lord. As so generally in this history, all would happen naturally in the ordinary succession of cause and effect; and yet all would be really and directly of God in the ordering and arrangement of events. Israel must not go to war, nor must victory be clue to their own prowess. It must be all of God, and the Philistines must rush on their own fate. Yet it was quite natural that when the Philistines heard of this grand national gathering at Mizpeh, after twenty years of unattempted resistance to their rule, they should wish to anticipate their movements; and that, whether they regarded the assembly as a revival of distinctively national religion or as preparatory for war. Similarly, it was natural that they would go on this expedition not without serious misgivings as to the power of the God of Israel which they had experienced during the stay of the ark in their land; and that in this state of mind they would be prepared to regard any terrible phenomenon in nature as His interposition, and be affected accordingly.

All this actually took place, but its real causes lay deeper than appeared on the surface. While Israel trembled at the approach of the Philistines, Samuel prayed, and "Jehovah answered him." The great thunder-storm on that day, which filled the Philistines with panic, was really the Lord's thundering. It was a wild mass of fugitives against which Israel went out from Mizpeh, and whom they pursued and smote until under the broad meadows of Beth-car, "the house of the lamb." And it was to mark not only the victory, but its cause and meaning, that Samuel placed the memorial-stone on the scene of this rout, between "the look out" and Shen, "the tooth," probably a rocky crag on the heights down which the Philistines were hurled in their flight. That stone he named "Eben-ezer, saying, Hitherto hath Jehovah helped us."

Helped — but only "hitherto!" For all Jehovah's help is only "hitherto" — from day to day, and from place to place — not unconditionally, nor wholly, nor once for all, irrespective of our bearing. But even so, the outward consequences of this Philistine defeat were most important. Although their military possession of certain posts, and their tenure of these districts still continued (comp. 1 Samuel 10:5; 13:4, 11-21; 14:21), yet the advancing tide of their incursions was stemmed, and no further expeditions were attempted such as that which had been so signally defeated. More than that. In the immediate vicinity of the field of battle, all the cities which the Philistines had formerly taken from Israel, "with the coasts thereof," — that is, with their surroundings — were restored to Israel, along the whole line extending north and south from Ekron to Gath. Moreover, "the Amorites," or

Canaanitish tribes in that neighborhood, had withdrawn from their alliance with the Philistines: "And there was peace between Israel and the Amorites."

Similarly, order was introduced into the internal administration of the land, at least so far as the central and the southern portions of it were concerned. Samuel had his permanent residence in Ramah, where he was always accessible to the people. But, besides, "he went from year to year in circuit" — to Bethel, thence to Gilgal, returning by Mizpeh to his own home. In each of these centers, sacred, as we have seen, perhaps from time immemorial, he "judged Israel," — not in the sense of settling disputes between individuals, but in that of the spiritual and national administration of affairs, as the center and organ of the religious and political life of the people.

We have no means of judging how long this happy state of things lasted. As usually, Holy Scripture furnishes not details even of the life and administration of a Samuel. It traces the history of the kingdom of God. As we have no account of events during the twenty years which preceded the battle of Eben-ezer (1 Samuel 7:2), so we are left in ignorance of those which followed it. From the gathering at Mizpeh, with its consequences, we are at once transported to Samuel's old age. He is still "the judge;" the same stern, unbending, earnest, God-devoted man as when in the full vigor of manhood. But he has felt the need of help in matters of detail; and his two sons are now made "judges," with residence in Beer-sheba, the ancient "well of the seven," or "of the oath," on the southern boundary of the land. Their office seems to have been chiefly, if not exclusively, that of civil administration, for which in the border district, and so near a nomadic or semi-nomadic population, there must have been ample need.

Unfortunately, they were quite unlike their father. Although not guilty of the wicked practices of Eli's sons, yet among a pastoral and nomadic population there would be alike frequent opportunity for, and abundant temptation to, bribery; nor would any other charge against a judge so quickly spread, or be so keenly resented as this.

Soon the murmurs became a complaint; and that loud enough to bring about a meeting of that most ancient and powerful institution in Israel, "the eldership," or local and tribal oligarchy. Probably it was not merely discontent with this partial administration of justice that led to the proposal of changing the form of government from a pure theocracy to hereditary monarchy. Other causes had long been at work. We know that a similar proposal had been made to Gideon (Judges 8:22), if not to Jephthah (Judges 11:6). Although in both instances these overtures had been declined, the feeling which prompted it could only have gained strength. An hereditary monarchy seemed the only means of combining the tribes into one nation, putting an end to their mutual jealousies, and subordinating tribal to national interests. All nations around had their kings; and whether for war or in peace, the want of a strong hand wielding a central power for the common good must have been increasingly felt.

Moreover, the ancient God-given constitution of Israel had distinctly contemplated and provided for a monarchy, when once the people had attained a settled state in the land. It must be admitted that, if ever, circumstances now pointed to this as the proper period for the change. The institution of "judges," however successful at times and in individuals, had failed as a whole. It had neither given external security nor good government to the people. Manifestly, it was at an end. Samuel must soon die; and what after him? Would it not be better to make the change under his direction, instead of leaving the people in charge of two men who could not even keep their hands from taking bribes? Many years had elapsed since the battle of Mizpeh, and yet the Philistines were not driven out of the land. In fact, the present administration held out no prospect of any such result. This then, if ever was the proper time to carry out the long-desired and much-needed reform.

It cannot be denied that there was much force in all these considerations; and yet we find that not only Samuel resented it, but that God also declared it a virtual rejection of Himself. The subject is so important as to require careful consideration.

First, as to the facts of the case. The "elders of Israel" having formally applied to Samuel: "Make us now a king to judge us, like all the nations," on the ground of his own advanced age and the unfitness of his sons, "the thing was evil in the eyes of Samuel as they spake it, Give us a king to judge us." But instead of making an immediate reply, Samuel referred the matter to the Lord in prayer. The view which Samuel had taken was fully confirmed by the Lord, Who declared it a rejection of Himself, similar to that of their fathers when they forsook Him and served other gods. Still He directed His prophet to grant their request, with this twofold proviso: to "bear strong testimony against them" in reference to their sin in this matter, and to "declare to them the right of the king," — not, of course, as God had fixed it, but as exercised in those heathen monarchies, the like of which they now wished to inaugurate in Israel. Samuel having fully complied with the Divine direction, and the people still persisting in their request, the prophet had now only to await the indication from on high as to the person to be appointed king — till which time the deputies of Israel were dismissed to their homes.

Keeping in view that there was nothing absolutely wrong in Israel's desire for a monarchy (Deuteronomy 17:14, etc.; comp. even Genesis 17:6, 16; 35:11), nor yet, so far as we can judge, relatively, as concerned the time when this demand was made, the explanation of the difficulty must lie in the motives and the manner rather than in the fact of the "elders," request. In truth, it is precisely this — the "wherefore" and the "how," not the thing itself, — not that they spake it, but "as they spake it," which was "evil in the eyes of Samuel." Israel asked "a king" to "judge" them, such as those of all the nations. We know what the term "judge" meant in Israel. It meant implicit reliance for deliverance from their enemies on an individual, specially God-appointed — that is, really on the unseen God. It was this to which the people had objected in the time of Gideon, and which they would no longer bear in the days of Samuel. Their deliverance was unseen, they wanted it seen; it was only certain to faith, but quite uncertain to them in their state of mind; it was in heaven, they wanted it upon earth; it was of God, they wanted it visibly embodied in a man. In this aspect of the matter, we quite understand why God characterized it as a rejection of Himself, and that in reference to it He directed Samuel to "bear strong testimony against them."

But sin is ever also folly. In asking for a monarchy like those around them, the people were courting a despotism whose intolerable yoke it would not be possible for them to shake off in the future (1 Samuel 8:18). Accordingly, in this respect Samuel was to set before them "the right of the king" (vers. 9, 11), that is, the royal rights, as claimed by heathen monarchs. But whether from disbelief of the warning, or the thought that, if oppressed, they would be able to right themselves, or, as seems to us, from deliberate choice in view of the whole case, the "elders" persisted in their demand. And, truth to say, in the then political circumstances of the land, with the bond of national unity almost dissolved, and in the total failure of that living realization of the constant Presence of the Divine "Judge," which, if it had existed, would have made His "reign" seem the most to be desired, but, when wanting, made the present state of things appear the most incongruous and undesirable, their choice seems to us only natural. In so doing, however, they became openly unfaithful to their calling, and renounced the principle which underlay their national history. Yet even so, it was but another phase in the development of this history, another stage in the progress towards that end which had been viewed and willed from the first.

CHAPTER 5: THE CALLING OF SAUL — OCCASION OF HIS INTERVIEW WITH SAMUEL — SAMUEL COMMUNES WITH SAUL — SAUL IS ANOINTED KING — THE THREE "SIGNS " — THEIR DEEPER SIGNIFICANCE.

(1 SAMUEL 9-10:16)

THE Divine direction for which prophet and people were to wait was not long withheld. It came, as so often, through a concurrence of natural circumstances, and in the manner least expected. Its object, if we may venture to judge, was to embody in the person of the new king the ideal which Israel had had in view in making their demand for a monarchy. He should possess all the natural attractions and martial qualities which the people could desiderate in their king; he should reflect their religious standpoint at its best; but he should also represent their national failings and the inmost defect of their religious life: that of combining zeal for the religion of Jehovah, and outward conformity to it, with utter want of real heart submission to the Lord, and of true devotedness to Him.

Thus viewed, we can understand alike the choice of Saul at the first, his failure afterwards, and his final rejection. The people obtained precisely what they wanted; and because he who was their king so corresponded to their ideal, and so reflected the national state, he failed. If, therefore, it is with a feeling of sadness that we follow this story, we must remember that its tragic element does not begin and end with Saul; and that the meaning of his life and career must be gathered from a deeper consideration of the history of his people. In truth, the history of Saul is a summary and a reflection of that of Israel. A monarchy such as his must first succeed, and finally fail when, under the test of trials, its inmost tendencies would be brought to light. Such a reign was also necessary, in order to bring out what was the real meaning of the people's demand, and to prepare Israel for the king of God's election and selection in the person of David.

Of all the tribes in Israel perhaps the most martial, although the smallest, was that of Benjamin. The "family" of Abiel was, indeed, not famous for wealth or influence. But it must have occupied a prominent place in Benjamin for the manly qualities and the military capacity of its members, since within a narrow circle it numbered such men as Saul, Jonathan, and Abner. The whole of this history gives such sketches of primitive life in Israel as to prove that it was derived from early and authentic sources.

Kish, the father of Saul, and Ner, the father of Abner, were brothers, the sons of Abiel (comp. 1 Samuel 14:51). The former is described in the text as "a hero of might," by which, as in the case of Boaz, who is similarly designated (Ruth 2:1), were meant in those times men stalwart, strong, and true, worthy representatives and, if need were, defenders of their national rights and of their national religion. Such, no doubt, was also the father of Abner. And yet there was exquisite simplicity about the family-life of these great, strong men. Kish had lost his she-asses — a loss of some consequence in times of such poverty that a man would consider "the fourth part of a shekel," or a sus — about 6 and 1/2d. of our money — as quite an adequate gift to offer a "seer" in return for consulting him (1 Samuel 9:8). To find, if possible, the straying animals, Saul, the only son of Kish, as we infer from the text, was sent in company with a servant. Saul, "the asked-for," was not only "choice and goodly," like all his race, but apparently as handsome as any man in the land, and taller than any by head and shoulders. In any country and age this would tell in favor of a popular leader, but especially in ancient times, and more particularly in Israel at that period.

From his home at Gibeah Saul and his servant passed in a north-westerly direction over a spur of Mount Ephraim. Thence they turned in their search north-eastward to "the land of Shalishah," probably so called from the circumstance that three Wadys met there, and then eastwards to the land of Shaalim — probably "the hollow," the modern Salem. Having traversed another district, which is called "the land of Yemini," — either "the right hand," or else "of Benjamin," though apparently not within the territory of Benjamin — they found themselves in the district of Zuph, where Samuel's home at Ramah was.

For three days had the two continued their unsuccessful search, when it occurred to Saul that their long absence might cause his father more anxiety than the straying of the she-asses. But before returning home, Saul's servant suggested that since they were just in view of the city where "the seer" lived, they might first consult him as to "the way" they "should go" in order to find the she-asses.

Having ascertained that the seer was not only in the city, but that the people had had "a sacrifice" on the "height" outside, where, as we know (1 Samuel 7:17), Samuel had built an altar, the two hastened on, in the hope of finding him in the city itself, before he went up "to bless," or speak the prayer of thanksgiving, with which the sacrificial meal would begin. For, amidst the guests gathered there, the two strangers could have little expectation of finding access to the president of the feast. They had just entered the city itself, and were "in the gate," or wide place inside the city-entrance, where the elders used to sit and popular assemblies gathered, when they met Samuel coming from an opposite direction on his way to the "Bamah," or sacrificial "height." To Saul's inquiry for "the seer's house," Samuel replied by making himself known. He had expected him — for the day before the Lord had expressly intimated it to him. Indeed, Samuel had prepared for it by ordering the choicest piece of that which was to be eaten of the sacrifice to be set aside for his guest — so sure was he of his arrival. And now when he saw before him in the gate the stateliest and finest-looking man in all Israel, the same voice which had led him to expect, indicated that this was the future leader of God's people.

The bearing of Samuel towards Saul was precisely such as the circumstances required. Moreover, it was consistent throughout, and dignified. An entirely new office, involving the greatest difficulties and responsibilities, was most unexpectedly to be almost thrust upon Saul; an office, besides, the reality of which would not only be soon tested by such enemies as the Philistines, but to which he had neither family nor personal claims, and which would be sure to excite tribal jealousies and personal envies. To prepare Saul, it was necessary to call forth in him expectations, it might be vague, of great things; to inspire him with absolute confidence in Samuel as the medium through whom God spake; and finally, by converse on the deepest concerns of Israel, to bring out what lay inmost in his heart, and to direct it to its proper goal. Accordingly, Samuel invited Saul first to the feast and then to his house, at the outset intimating that he would tell him all that was in his heart (ver. 19). This assuredly could not have reference to the finding of the she-asses, since he immediately informed Saul about them, as evidence that he was "a seer," whose words must, therefore, be received as a message coming from God. Mysterious as was the allusion to what was in Saul's heart, the remark which accompanied his intimation of the finding of the she-asses sounded even more strange. As if treating such a loss as a very small matter, he added (ver. 20). "And whose is all that is desirable in Israel? Is it not thine and thy father's house?"

The remark was so strange both in itself and as coming from "the seer," that Saul, feeling its seeming incongruity, could only answer by pointing to the fact that Benjamin was the smallest tribe, and his own family among the least influential in it. Saul was undoubtedly aware that Israel had demanded and were about to receive from Samuel a king. His reply leaves the impression on us, that, although, probably he did not exactly formulate it in his own mind, yet Samuel's words had called up in him thoughts of the kingdom. Else why the reference to the size of his tribe and the influence of his family? And this was exactly what Samuel had wished: gradually to prepare him for what was coming. Apparently the "seer" made no answer to what Saul had said. But at the sacrificial feast he pursued the same course towards his guest. To the Ephraimites there assembled he was, of course, unknown. But even they must have been surprised at finding that, while the mass of the people feasted outside, among the thirty principal guests who were bidden into "the parlor," not only was the chief place given to this stranger, but that the principal portion of the sacrifice had, as a mark of special honor, been reserved for him.

The feast was past, and Saul followed his host to his house. There on the flat roof, so often the scene of private converse in the East, Samuel long "communed" with Saul, no doubt of "all that was in his heart;" not, indeed, of the office about to be conferred on him, but of the thoughts which had been called up in Saul that day: of Israel's need, of Israel's sin, of Israel's help, and of Israel's God. After such "communing," neither of them could have found much sleep that night. It was gray dawn when they rose; and as the morning broke, Samuel called up to Saul on the roof that it was time to depart. He himself convoyed him through the town; then, sending forward the servant, he stopped to deliver the message of God. Taking a vial of oil, he "anointed" Saul, thus placing the institution of royalty on the same footing as that of the sanctuary and the priesthood (Exodus 30:23, etc., Leviticus 8:10, etc.), as appointed and consecrated by God and for God, and intended to be the medium for receiving and transmitting blessing to His people. And with this, a kiss, in token of homage (Psalm 2:12), and the perhaps not quite unexpected message: "Is it not that Jehovah hath anointed thee to be prince over His inheritance?" Saul was appointed the first king in Israel.

In order to assure Saul of the Divine agency in all this, Samuel gave him three signs. Each was stranger than the other, and all were significant of what would mark the path of Israel's king. After leaving Samuel, coming from Ephraim, he would cross the northern boundary of Benjamin by the grave of Rachel. There he would meet two men who would inform him of the finding of the she-asses and of his father's anxiety on his account.

This, as confirming Samuel's words, would be a pledge that it was likewise by God's appointment he had been anointed king. Thus the first sign would convey that his royalty was of God. Then as he passed southwards, and reached "the terebinth Tabor," three men would meet him, coming from an opposite direction, and "going up to God, to Bethel," bearing sacrificial gifts.

These would salute him, and, unasked, give him a portion of their sacrificial offerings — two loaves, probably one for himself, another for his servant. If, as seems likely, these three men belonged to "the sons of the prophets," the act was even more significant. It meant homage on the part of the godly in Israel, yet such as did not supersede nor swallow up the higher homage due to God — only two loaves out of all the sacrificial gifts being presented to Saul. To Saul this, then, would indicate royalty in subordination to God. The last was the strangest, but, rightly understood, also the most significant sign of all. Arrived at Gibeah Elohim, his own city, or else the hill close by, where the Philistines kept a garrison, he would, on entering the city, meet "a band of prophets" coming down from the Bamah, or sacrificial height, in festive procession, preceded by the sound of the nevel, lute or guitar, the thof, or tambourine (Exodus 15:20), the flute, and the chinnor or hand-harp, themselves the while "prophesying."

Then "the Spirit of Jehovah" would "seize upon him," and he would "be turned into another man." The obvious import of this "sign," in combination with the others, would be: royalty not only from God and under God, but with God. And all the more significant would it appear, that Gibeah, the home of Saul, where all knew him and could mark the change, was now held by a garrison of Philistines; and that Israel's deliverance should there commence by the Spirit of Jehovah mightily laying hold on Israel's new king, and making of him another man. When all these "signs happen to thee," added the prophet, "do to thyself what thy hand findeth" (as circumstances indicate, comp. Judges 9:33); concluding therefrom: "for God is with thee."

The event proved as Samuel had foretold. Holy Scripture passes, indeed, lightly over the two first signs, as of comparatively less importance, but records the third with the more full detail. It tells how, immediately on leaving Samuel, "God turned to Saul another heart" (ver 9); how, when he met the band of prophets at Gibeah (ver. 10, not "the hill," as in our Authorised Version), "the Spirit of Elohim" "seized" upon him, and he "prophesied among them;" so that those who had so intimately known him before exclaimed in astonishment: "What is this that has come unto the son of Kish? Is Saul also among the prophets?" Upon which "one from thence," more spiritually enlightened than the rest, answered: "And who is their father?" implying that, in the case of the other prophets also, the gift of prophecy was not of hereditary descent. Thus the proverb arose: "Is Saul also among the prophets?" to indicate, according to circumstances, either a sudden and almost incredible change in the outward religious bearing of a man, or the possibility of its occurrence.

But there are deeper questions here which must, at least briefly, be answered. Apparently, there were already at that time prophetic associations, called "schools of the prophets." Whether these owed their origin to Samuel or not, the movement received at least a mighty impulse from him, and henceforth became a permanent institution in Israel. But this "prophesying" must not be considered as in all cases prediction. In the present instance it certainly was not such, but, as that of the "elders" in the time of Moses (Numbers 11:25), an ecstatic state of a religious character, in which men unreservedly poured forth their feelings. The characteristics of this ecstatic state were entire separation from the circumstances around, and complete subjection to an extraordinary influence from without, when thoughts, feelings, words, and deeds were no longer under personal control, but became, so to speak, passive instruments. Viewing it in this light, we can understand the use made of music, not only by true prophets, but even among the heathen. For the effect of music is to detach from surrounding circumstances, to call forth strong feelings, and to make us yield ourselves implicitly to their influence.

In the case of the prophets at Gibeah and in that of Saul, this ecstatic state was under the influence of the "Spirit of Elohim." By this, as in the case of the judges, we are, however, not to understand the abiding and sanctifying Presence of the Holy Ghost dwelling in the heart as His temple. The Holy Ghost was peculiarly "the gift of the Father" and "of the Son," and only granted to the Church in connection with, and after the Resurrection of our Blessed Lord.

Under the Old Testament, only the manifold influences of the Spirit were experienced, not His indwelling as the Paraclete. This appears not only from the history of those so influenced, and from the character of that influence, but even from the language in which it is described. Thus we read that the Spirit of Elohim "seized upon" Saul, suddenly and mightily laid hold on him, — the same expression being used in Judges 14:6, 19; 15:14; 1 Samuel 16:13; 18:10. But although they were only "influences" of the Spirit of Elohim, it need scarcely be said that such could not have been experienced without deep moral and religious effect. The inner springs of the life, thoughts, feelings, and purposes must necessarily have been mightily affected. It was so in the case of Saul, and the contrast was so great that his fellow-townsmen made a proverb of it. In the language of Holy Scripture, his "heart," that is, in Old Testament language, the spring of his feeling, purposing, and willing, was "turned into another" from what it had been, and he was "turned into another man," with quite other thoughts, aims, and desires than before. The difference between this and what in the New Testament is designated as "the new man," is too obvious to require detailed explanation. But we may notice these two as important points: as in the one case it was only an overpowering influence of the Spirit of Elohim, not the abiding Presence of the Paraclete, so the moral effects produced through that influence were not primary, but secondary, and, so to speak, reflex, while those of the Holy Ghost in the hearts of God's people are direct, primary, and permanent.

The application of these principles to "the spiritual gifts" in the early Church will readily occur to us. But perhaps it is more important to remember that we are always — and now more than ever — prone to confound the influences of the Spirit of God with His abiding Presence in us, and to mistake the undoubted moral and religious effects, which for a time may result from the former, for the entire inward change, when "all old things have passed away," and, "all things have become new," and are "of Christ." Yet the one is only the reflex influence of the spirit of man, powerfully influenced by the Spirit of Elohim; the other the direct work of the Holy Ghost on the heart.

One of the effects of the new spiritual influence which had come upon Saul was, that when his uncle, Ner, met him upon the Bamah, or high place (ver. 14), probably joining him in his worship there to find out the real meaning of a change which he must have seen more clearly than any other, and which it would readily occur to him to connect with the visit to Samuel, he forbore to gratify a curiosity, probably not unmixed with worldly ambition and calculations.

But yet another charge had Samuel given to Saul before parting (ver. 8), and that not only a charge, but a life-direction, a warning, and a test of what was in him. That he understood it, is evident from 1 Samuel 13:7, 8. But would he submit to it, or rather to God? That would be to him the place and time when the two ways met and parted — and his choice of either one or the other would be decisive, both so far as his life and his kingdom were concerned.

CHAPTER 6: SAUL CHOSEN KING AT MIZPEH — HIS COMPARATIVE PRIVACY — INCURSION OF NAHASH — RELIEF OF JABESH-GILEAD — POPULAR ASSEMBLY AT GILGAL — ADDRESS OF SAMUEL.

(1 SAMUEL 10:17-12:25.)

IN answer to the people's demand, Saul had been selected as their king. The motives and views which underlay their application for a king were manifest. They had been clearly set before the representatives of Israel by Samuel; and they had not gainsaid the correctness of his statement. They wanted not only a king, but royalty like that of the nations around, and for the purpose of outward deliverance; thus forgetting God's dealings in the past, disclaiming simple trust in Him, and disbelieving the sufficiency of His leadership. In fact, what they really wanted was a king who would reflect and embody their idea of royalty, not the ideal which God had set before them. And no better representative of Israel could have been found than Saul, alike in appearance and in military qualification; nor yet a truer reflex of the people than that which his character and religious bearing offered. He was the typical Israelite of his period, and this neither as regarded the evil-disposed or "sons of Belial," nor yet, of course, the minority of the truly enlightened, but the great body of the well-disposed people. If David was the king "after God's own heart," Saul was the king after the people's own heart. What they had asked, they obtained; and what they obtained, must fail; and what failed would prepare for what God had intended.

But as yet the choice of Saul had been a secret between the messenger of the Lord and the new king. As in every other case, so in this, God would give the person called to most difficult work every opportunity of knowing His will, and every encouragement to do it. For this purpose Samuel had first called up great thoughts in Saul; then "communed" with him long and earnestly; then given him undoubted evidence that the message he bore was God's; and, finally, embodied in one significant direction alike a warning of his danger and guidance for his safety. All this had passed secretly between the two, that, undisturbed by influences from without, Saul might consider his calling and future course, and this in circumstances most favorable to a happy issue, while the transaction was still, as it were, between God and himself, and before he could be led astray by the intoxicating effect of success or by popular flattery.

And now this brief period of preparation was past, and what had been done in secret must be confirmed in public. Accordingly Samuel summoned the people — no doubt by their representatives — to a solemn assembly "before Jehovah" in Mizpeh. Here the first great victory over the Philistines had been obtained by prayer (7:5), and here there was an "altar unto Jehovah" (ver. 9). As so often before, the lot was solemnly cast to indicate the will of God. But before so doing, Samuel once more presented to the people what the leadership of the Lord had been in the past, and what their choice of another leadership implied. This not with the view of annulling the proposed establishment of royalty, but with that of leading the people to repentance of their sin in connection with it. But the people remained unmoved. And now the lot was drawn.

It fell on Saul, the son of Kish. But although he had come to Mizpeh, he could not be found in the assembly. It was a supreme moment in the history of Israel when God had indicated to His people, gathered before Him, their king by name. In circumstances so urgent, inquiry by the Urim and Thummim seemed appropriate. The answer indicated that Saul had concealed himself among the baggage on the outskirts of the encampment. Even this seems characteristic of Saul. It could have been neither from humility nor modesty — both of which would, to say the least, have been here misplaced. It is indeed true that this was a moment in which the heart of the bravest might fail, and that thoughts of what was before him might well fill him with anxiety.

Saul must have known what would be expected of him as king. Would he succeed in it? He knew the tribal and personal jealousies which his election would call forth. Would he be strong enough to stand against them? Such questions were natural. The only true answer would have been a spiritual one. Unable to give it, Saul withdrew from the assembly. Did he wonder whether after all it would come to pass or what would happen, and wait till a decision was forced upon him? The people, at any rate, saw nothing in his conduct that seemed to them strange; and so we may take it that it was just up to the level of their own conceptions, though to us it appears very different from what a hero of God would have done.

And so the newly-found king was brought back to the assembly. And when Samuel pointed to him as he stood there, "from his shoulders upward" overtopping every one around, the people burst into a shout: "Let the king live!" For thus far Saul seemed the very embodiment of their ideal of a king. The transaction was closed by Samuel explaining to the people, this time not "the right of the king" (1 Samuel 8:9, 11), as claimed among other heathen nations whom they wished to imitate, but "the right of the kingdom" (10:25), as it should exist in Israel in accordance with the principles laid down in Deuteronomy 17:14-20. This was put in writing, and the document solemnly deposited in the tabernacle.

For the moment, however, the establishment of the new monarchy seemed to bring no change. Saul returned to his home in Gibeah, attended indeed on his journey, by way of honor, by "a band whom Elohim had touched in their hearts," and who no doubt "brought him presents" as their king. But he also returned to his former humble avocations. On the other hand, "the sons of Belial" not only withheld such marks of homage, but openly derided the new king as wanting in tribal influence and military means for his office. When we bear in mind that these represented a party, possibly belonging to the great tribes of Judah and Ephraim, so strong as openly to express their opposition (1 Samuel 11:12), and sufficiently numerous not to be resisted by those who thought otherwise, the movement must have been formidable enough to dictate as a prudential measure the retirement of Saul till the time when events would vindicate his election. And so complete was that privacy, that even the Philistine garrison in Gibeah remained in ignorance of the fact of Saul's new office, and of what it implied; and that in the east, across the Jordan, the Ammonite king who waged war with Israel was apparently wholly unaware of any combined national movement on the part of the people, or of any new center of union and resistance against a common enemy.

This expedition on the part of Nahash, king of the Ammonites, to which we have just referred, is otherwise also of interest, as showing that the desire of Israel after a king must have sprung from other and deeper motives than merely the age of Samuel, or even the conduct of his sons. From 1 Samuel 12:12 it appears that the invasion by Nahash commenced before Israel's demand for a king, and was, indeed, the cause of it; thus proving that, as Samuel charged them, distrust of their heavenly Leader was the real motive of their movement. The expedition of Nahash had no doubt been undertaken to renew the claims which his predecessor had made, and to avenge the defeat which Jephthah had inflicted upon him (Judges 11:13, 33). But Nahash had penetrated much farther into Israelitish territory than his predecessor. His hordes had swarmed up the lovely rich valley of the Jabesh, laying bare its barley-fields and olive plantations, and wasting its villages; and they were now besieging the capital of Gilead — Jabesh-gilead — which occupied a commanding position on the top of an isolated hill overhanging the southern crest of the valley. In their despair, the people of Jabesh offered to surrender, but Nahash, in his insolence, insisted that he would thrust out their right eyes, avowedly to "lay it as a shame upon all Israel." Terrible as these conditions were, the "elders" of Jabesh saw no means of resisting, and only begged seven days' respite, to see whether any were left in Israel able and willing to save them. In the foolhardiness of his swagger, Nahash consented, well assured that if Israel were, as he fully believed, incapable of a combined movement for the relief of Jabesh, the whole land would henceforth be at his mercy, and between Philistia in the west and Ammon in the east, Israel — their land and their God — would lie helpless before the heathen powers.

It is, to say the least, a curious coincidence that Jabesh was the only town in Israel which had not taken part in the exterminating warfare against the tribe of Benjamin (Judges 21:9). But it was not on that ground, but because tidings had no doubt reached them of the new royal office in Israel, that their messengers went straight to Gibeah. It was evening when Saul returned home "behind the oxen," with which he had been working, to find Gibeah strangely moved.

The tidings which the men of Jabesh had brought had filled the place with impotent lamentation, not roused the people to action. So low had Israel sunk! But now, as he heard it, once more "the Spirit of Elohim seized upon Saul." He hewed in pieces the "yoke of oxen" with which he had just returned, and sent — probably by the messengers from Jabesh — these pieces throughout the land, bidding those know who had no higher thoughts than self, that thus it would be done to their oxen who followed not after Saul and Samuel in the general war against Ammon.

This, if ever, was the time when the Divine appointment of Saul must be vindicated; and to indicate this he conjoined with himself Samuel, the venerated prophet of God, so long the judge of Israel. It is said that "the terror of Jehovah" fell upon the people. From all parts of the land armed men trooped to the trysting-place at Bezek, within the territory of Issachar, near to Bethshan, and almost in a straight line to Jabesh. Three hundred thousand from Israel, and thirty thousand from Judah, (for that territory was in part held by the Philistines), had obeyed the summons of Saul. It was not an army, but a ban — a landsturm — an armed rising of the people.

From the brow of the hill on which Bethshan lay, in the plain of Jezreel, you might look across Jordan and see Jabesh-gilead on its eminence. A very few hours would bring relief to the beleaguered city, and so they bade them know and expect. A feigned promise of subjection on the morrow made Nahash and his army even more confident than before. And what, indeed, had they to fear when all Israel lay so helplessly prostrate?

It was night when Saul and the armed multitude which followed him broke up from Bezek. Little did he know how well the brave men of Jabesh would requite the service; how, when on that disastrous day on Mount Gilboa he and his sons would fall in battle, and the victorious Philistines fasten their dead bodies to the walls of Bethshan, these brave men of Jabesh would march all night and rescue the fallen heroes from exposure (1 Samuel 31:8-13). Strange that Saul's first march should have been by night from Bethshan to Jabesh, the same route by which at the last they carried his dead body at night.

But no such thoughts disturbed the host as they crossed the fords of the Jordan, and swarmed up the other bank. A few hours more, and they had reached the valley of the Jabesh. Following the example of Gideon (Judges 7:16), Saul divided the people "into three companies." From the rear and from either flank they fell upon the unsuspecting Ammonites when most secure — "in the morning watch," between three and six o'clock. A general panic ensued; and before the rout was ended not two of the enemy were left together. The revulsion of popular feeling toward Saul was complete. They would even have killed those who had formerly derided the new monarchy. But Saul refused such counsel. Rather did Samuel make different use of the new state of feeling. On his proposal the people followed him and Saul to Gilgal, to which place so many sacred memories clung. Here they offered thank and peace-offerings, and greatly rejoiced as they renewed "the kingdom," and, in the sense of real and universal acknowledgment, "made Saul king before Jehovah."

Although all his lifetime Samuel never ceased to judge Israel, yet his official work in that capacity had now come to an end. Accordingly he gave a solemn and public account of his administration, calling alike the Lord and His anointed to witness of what passed between him and the people. Leaving his sons to bear the responsibility of their own doings, he challenged any charge against himself. But, as a faithful servant of the Lord, and ruler in Israel, he went further. Fain would he bring them to repentance for their great sin in the manner wherein they had demanded a king. One by one he recalled to them the "righteous doings" of Jehovah in the fulfillment of His covenant-promises in the past.

In contrast to this never-failing help, he pointed to their unbelief, when, unmindful of what God had done and distrustful of what He would do, they had, on the approach of serious danger, virtually said concerning His leadership, "Nay, but a king shall reign over us." And God had granted their desire. But upon their and their king's bearing towards the Lord, not upon the fact that they had now a king, would the future of Israel depend. And this truth, so difficult for them to learn, God would now, as it were, prove before them in a symbol. Did they think it unlikely, nay, well-nigh impossible, to fail in their present circumstances? God would bring the unlikely and seemingly incredible to pass in a manner patent to all. Was it not the time of wheat-harvest, when in the east not a cloud darkens the clear sky? God would send thunder and rain to convince them, by making the unlikely real, of the folly and sin of their thoughts in demanding a king.

So manifest a proof of the truth of what Samuel had said, and of the nearness of God and of His personal interposition, struck terror into the hearts of the people, and led to at least outward repentance. In reply to their confession and entreaty for his continued intercession, Samuel assured then, that he would not fail in his duty of prayer for them, nor yet God, either in His faithfulness to His covenant and promises, or in His justice and holiness if they did wickedly.

And so the assembly parted — Israel to their tents, Saul to the work of the kingdom which lay to his hands, and Samuel to the far more trying and difficult duty of faithfully representing and executing the will of God as His appointed messenger in the land.

CHAPTER 7: SAUL MARCHES AGAINST THE PHILISTINES — POSITION OF THE TWO CAMPS — JONATHAN'S FEAT OF ARMS — SAUL RETREATS TO GILGAL — TERROR AMONG THE PEOPLE — SAUL'S DISOBEDIENCE TO THE DIVINE COMMAND, AND REJECTION OF HIS KINGDOM.

(1 SAMUEL 13)

AT Gilgal Saul had been accepted by the whole people as their king, and it now behooved him to show himself such by immediately taking in hand as his great work the liberation of the land from Israel's hereditary enemy the Philistines.

For this purpose he selected from the armed multitude at Gilgal three thousand men, of whom two thousand under his own command were posted in Michmash and in Mount Bethel, while the other thousand advanced under Jonathan to Gibeah of Benjamin (or Gibeah of Saul). Close to this, a little to the north, at Geba, the Philistines had pushed forward an advanced post, perhaps from Gibeah, to a position more favorable than the latter. Unable, with the forces at his disposal, to make a regular attack, it seems to have been Saul's purpose to form the nucleus of an army, and meanwhile to blockade and watch the Philistines in Geba. So far as we can judge, it does not appear to have lain within his plan to attack that garrison, or else the enterprise would have been undertaken by himself, nor would it have caused the surprise afterwards excited by Jonathan's success.

As it is of considerable importance for the understanding of this history to have a clear idea of the scene where these events took place, we add the most necessary details. Geba, the-post of the Philistines, lay on a low conical eminence, on the western end of a ridge which shelves eastwards towards the Jordan. Passing from Geba northwards and westwards we come to a steep descent, leading into what now is called the Wady-es-Suweinit. This, no doubt, represents the ancient "passage of Michmash" (1 Samuel 13:23). On the opposite steep brow, right over against Geba, lies Michmash, at a distance of barely three miles in a north-westerly direction. This Wady-es-Suweinit is also otherwise interesting. Running up in a north-westerly direction towards Bethel, the ridge on either side the wady juts out into two very steep rock-covered eminences — one south-west, towards Geba, the other northwest, towards Michmash. Side wadys, trending from north to south behind these two eminences, render them quite abrupt and isolated. These two peaks, or "teeth," were respectively called Bozez, "the shining," and Seneh, either "the tooth-like," "the pointed," or perhaps "the thorn," afterwards the scene of Jonathan's daring feat of arms (1 Samuel 14:1-13). Bethel itself lies on the ridge, which runs in a north-westerly direction from Michmash. From this brief sketch it will be seen that, small as Saul's army was, the Philistine garrison in Geba was, to use a military term, completely enfiladed by it, since Saul with his two thousand men occupied Michmash and Mount Bethel to the north-east, north, and north-west, threatening their communications through the Wady-es-Suweinit with Philistia, while Jonathan with his thousand men lay at Gibeah to the south of Geba.

But the brave spirit of Jonathan could ill brook enforced idleness in face of the enemy. Apparently without consultation with his father, he attacked and "smote" the Philistine garrison in Geba. The blow was equally unexpected by Philistine and Israelite. In view of the preparations made by the enemy, Saul now retired to Gilgal — probably not that in which the late assembly had been held, but the other Gilgal near Jericho.

Hither "the people were called together after Saul." But the impression left on us is, that from the first the people were depressed rather than elated, frightened rather than encouraged by Jonathan's feat of arms. And no wonder, considering not only the moral unpreparedness of the people, but their unfitness to cope with the Philistines, alike so far as arms and military training were concerned. The hundreds of thousands who had followed Saul to Jabesh were little better than an undisciplined mob that had seized any kind of weapons. Such a multitude would be rather a hindrance than a help in a war against disciplined infantry, horsemen, and war-chariots. In fact, only three thousand of them were fit to form the nucleus of an army, and even they, or what at last remained of them to encounter the Philistines, were so badly equipped that they could be truthfully described as without either "sword or spear" (13:22).

The army with which the Philistines now invaded the land was the largest and best appointed, which they had yet brought into the field. Avoiding the former mistake of allowing their opponents to take them in flank by camping in Michmash, the Philistines now occupied that post themselves, their line extending thither from Beth-aven.

From their position at Gilgal the Israelites could see that mighty host, and under the influence of terror rapidly melted away. Some passed across the Jordan, the most part hid themselves in the caves and pits and rocks with which the whole district around the position of the Philistines abounds. The situation was indeed becoming critical in the extreme. Day by day the number of deserters increased, and even those who yet remained "behind him," "were terrified."

And still Saul waited from day to day for that without which he had been told he must not move out of Gilgal, and which now was so unaccountably and, as it would seem to a commander, so fatally delayed! It will be remembered that on parting from Saul, immediately after his anointing, Samuel had spoken these somewhat mysterious words (1 Samuel 10:7, 8): "And it shall be when these signs shall come unto thee, do for thyself as thine hand shall find, for Elohim is with thee. And when thou goest down before me to Gilgal, — and behold I am going down to thee, — to offer burnt-offerings and to sacrifice sacrifices of peace-offerings, seven days shalt thou tarry till I come to thee, and shew thee what thou shalt do."

The first part of Samuel's injunction — to do as his hand should find — Saul had followed when making war against Nahash. It is the second part which sounds so mysterious. It will be remembered that, immediately after the defeat of Nahash, Saul and the people had, on the suggestion of Samuel, gone to Gilgal, there to "renew the kingdom." Manifestly that visit to Gilgal could not have been meant, since, so far from having to wait seven days for the arrival of Samuel, the prophet had accompanied Saul thither. It can, therefore, only have been intended to apply to this retreat of Saul upon Gilgal in preparation for his first great campaign against the Philistines.

And what to us sounds so mysterious in the language of Samuel may not have been so at the time to Saul. During that communing on the roof of Samuel's house, or afterwards, the two may have spoken of a great war against the Philistines, and of the necessity of gathering all Israel in preparation for it to Gilgal, not only for obvious military reasons, but as the place where the "reproach of Israel had first been rolled away (Joshua 5:9), and whence appropriately the re-conquest of the land should commence by sacrifices and seeking the direction of the Lord.

But even if at the time when first uttered by Samuel it had seemed mysterious to Saul, there could be no doubt that the injunction applied to the circumstances in which the king and his followers now found themselves. What should he do? Day by day passed without tidings of Samuel, and still his followers decreased, and the hearts of those who remained waxed more feeble. Yet Saul did wait the full seven days which Samuel had appointed. But when the seventh day was drawing to a close he forbore no longer; and although, as he said, most reluctantly, he had the sacrifices offered, no doubt by the regular priesthood (comp. 2 Samuel 24:,5; 1 Kings 3:4; 8:63).

No sooner had the sacrifices been offered, than on a sudden Samuel himself appeared — as we understand it, before the full term which he had set for his arrival had actually been passed. Whether simply to brave it, or, as seems to us more likely, from real ignorance of the import of what he had done, Saul went to meet and salute Samuel. But the prophet came as God's messenger. He denounced the folly of Saul, and his sin in disobeying the express command of the Lord, and intimated that, had he stood the test, his kingdom, or royal line, would have been established, whereas now his throne would pass to a worthier successor. Not, therefore, his personal rejection, nor even that of his title to the throne, but only that of his "kingdom," or line, as unfit to be "captains" over "Jehovah's people" — such was the sentence which Samuel had to announce on that day.

The "folly" of Saul's conduct must, indeed, have been evident to all. He had not waited long enough, and yet too long, so far as his following was concerned, which, after the sacrifice, amounted to only about six hundred men (1 Samuel 13:15). On the other hand, the only motive which, even politically speaking, could have brought numbers to his ranks or fired them with courage, was a religious belief in the help of Jehovah, of which Saul's breach of the Divine command and the defection of Samuel would threaten to deprive Israel. But still there are questions involved in the Divine punishment of Saul which require most earnest attention, not only for the vindication, but even for the proper understanding of this history. To the first question which arises, why Samuel thus unduly delayed his journey to Gilgal, apparently without necessary reason, we can, in fairness, only return the answer, that his delay seems to have been intentional, quite as much as that of our blessed Lord, after He had heard of the sickness of Lazarus, and when He knew of his death (John 11:6, 14, 15). But if intentional, its object can only have been to test the character of Saul's kingdom. Upon this, of course, the permanency of that kingdom would depend. We have already seen that Saul represented the kind of monarchy which Israel wished to have established. Saul's going down to Gilgal to offer sacrifices, and yet not offering them properly; his unwillingness to enter on the campaign without having entreated the face of Jehovah, and yet offending Him by disobedience; his waiting so long, and not long enough; his trust in the help of Jehovah, and yet his distrust when his followers left him; his evident belief in the absolute efficacy of sacrifices as an outward ordinance irrespective of the inward sacrifice of heart and will — are all exactly representative of the religious state of Israel. But although Israel had sought, and in Saul obtained a monarchy "after their own heart," yet, as Samuel had intimated in Gilgal (12:14, 20- 22, 24), the Lord, in His infinite mercy, was willing to forgive and to turn all for good, if Israel would only "fear the Lord and serve Him in truth." Upon this conversion, so to speak, of Israel's royalty into the kingdom of God the whole question turned. For, either Israel must cease to be the people of the Lord, or else the principle on which its monarchy was founded must become spiritual and Divine; and consequently any government that contravened this must be swept away to give place to another. If it be asked, what this Divine principle of monarchy was to be, we have no hesitation in answering, that it was intended to constitute a kingdom in which the will of the earthly should be in avowed subjection to that of the heavenly King. This was right in itself; it was expressive of the covenant-relationship by which Jehovah became the God of Israel, and Israel the people of Jehovah; and it embodied the typical idea of the kingdom of God, to be fully realized in the King of the Jews, Who came not to do His own will, but that of His Father in heaven, even to the bitter agony of the cup in Gethsemane and the sufferings of Golgotha. Saul was the king after Israel's own heart (1 Samuel 12:13); David the king after God's own heart, not because of his greater piety or goodness, but because, despite his failings and his sins, he fully embodied the Divine idea of Israel's kingdom; and for this reason also he and his kingdom were the type of our Lord Jesus Christ and of His kingdom.

In what has been said the second great difficulty, which almost instinctively rises in our minds on reading this history, has in part been anticipated. It will easily be understood that this great question had, if ever, to be tested and decided at the very commencement of Saul's reign, and before he engaged in any great operations, the success or failure of which might divert the mind. If to be tried at all, it must be on its own merits, and irrespective of results. Still, it must be admitted, that the first feeling with most of us is that, considering the difficulties of Saul's position, the punishment awarded to him seems excessive. Yet it only seems, but is not such. Putting aside the idea of his personal rejection and dethronement, neither of which was implied in the words of Samuel, the sentence upon Saul only embodied this principle, that no monarchy could be enduring in Israel which did not own the supreme authority of God. As Adam's obedience was tested in a seemingly small matter, and his failure involved that of his race, so also in the case of Saul. His partial obedience and his anxiety to offer the sacrifices as, in his mind, in themselves efficacious, only rendered it the more necessary to bring to the foreground the great question of absolute, unquestioning, and believing submission to the will of the Heavenly King. Saul's kingdom had shown itself not to be God's kingdom, and its continuance was henceforth impossible. However different their circumstances, Saul was as unfit for the inheritance of the kingdom, with the promises which this implied and the typical meaning it bore, as Esau had been for the inheritance of the first-born, with all that it conveyed in the present, in the near, and in the distant future.

CHAPTER 8: CAMPS OF ISRAEL AND OF THE PHILISTINES — JONATHAN AND HIS ARMOR-BEARER — PANIC AMONG THE PHILISTINES, AND FLIGHT — SAUL'S RASH VOW — THE "LOT" CAST AT AJALON — CESSATION OF THE WAR.

(1 SAMUEL 13:15-14:46)

WHEN, after Samuel's departure, Saul with his six hundred men marched out of Gilgal, he found the Philistines occupying the range at Michmash which he had formerly held. With such weak following as he could command, it was wise on his part to take up a position in the "uttermost part of Gibeah" (14:2), that is, as we gather from the context, to the north of the town itself, and on the outskirts of Geba and its district (13:16). Geba is only about an hour and a quarter north of Gibeah. We may therefore suppose Saul's camp to have been about two miles to the north of the latter city, and to have extended towards Geba. His head-quarters were under a pomegranate tree at a place called Migron — probably a "land-slip;" and there, besides his principal men, he had the then occupant of the high-priesthood, Ahiah, the son of Ahitub, an elder brother of Ichabod, "wearing an ephod," or discharging the priestly functions.

From Geba itself Michmash, which lay on the opposite ridge, was only divided by the intervening Wady-es-Suweinit. How long the Israelites had lain in that position we are not informed. But we are told that "the spoilers," or rather "the destroyers," "went out of the camp of the Philistines in three bands" (13:17), — one "facing" in a north-easterly direction by Ophrah towards the district of Shual, the "fox-country," the other "facing" westwards towards Bethhoron, and the third south-eastwards, "the way to the district that overlooketh the valley of Zeboim" ("raveners," viz., wild beasts) "toward the wilderness" (of Judah).

Thus the only direction left untouched was south and south-west, where Saul and Jonathan held the strong position of Gibeah-Geba. If the intention had been to draw them thence into the open, it failed. But immense damage must have been inflicted upon the country, while a systematic raid was made upon all smithies, so as to render it impossible not only to prepare weapons, but so much as to have the means of sharpening the necessary tools of husbandry.

In these circumstances it is once more the noble figure of Jonathan which comes to the foreground. Whatever fitness he might have shown for "the kingdom," had he been called to it, a more unselfish, warm-hearted, genuine, or noble character is not presented to us in Scripture than that of Jonathan. Weary of the long and apparently hopeless inactivity, trustful in Jehovah, and fired by the thought that with Him there was "no hindrance to save, by much or by little," he planned single-handed an expedition against the Philistine outpost at Michmash. As he put it, it was emphatically a deed of faith, in which he would not take counsel either with his father or with any of the people, only with God, of Whom he would seek a sign of approbation before actually entering on the undertaking. The sole companion whom he took was, as in the case of Gideon (Judges 7:9, 10), his armor-bearer, who seems to have been not only entirely devoted to his master, but like-minded. In the Wady-es-Suweinit, which, as we have seen, forms "the passage" between the ridge of Geba, where Jonathan was, and that of Michmash, now occupied by the Philistines, were the two conical heights, or "teeth of rock," called Bozez and Seneh. One of these, as we gather from the text, faced Jonathan and his armor-bearer toward the north over against Michmash. This we suppose to have been Bozez, "the shining one," probably so called from its rocky sides and top. It is figuratively described in the text as cast like metal. Here, on the top of a sharp, very narrow ledge of rock, was the Philistine outpost. The "tooth of rock" opposite, on which Jonathan and his armor-bearer "discovered" themselves to their enemies, was Seneh, "the thornlike," or "pointed," or else "the tooth."

All around there was thick wood, or rather forest (14:25), which stretched all the way towards Bethel (2 Kings 2:23, 24). Standing on the extreme point of Seneh, the Philistines would probably only see Jonathan, with, at most, his armor-bearer; but they would be ignorant what forces might lurk under cover of the trees. And this was to be the sign by which Jonathan and his companion were to discern whether or not God favored their enterprise. If, when they "discovered" themselves to the Philistines, these would challenge them to stay and await their coming over to fight, then Jonathan and his companion would forbear, while, if the challenge were the other way, they would infer that Jehovah had delivered them into their hand. The one, of course, would argue courage on the part of the Philistines, the other the want of it. What followed is graphically sketched in the sacred text. From the point of "the thorn," or "tooth of the rock," Jonathan "discovered" himself to the Philistines. This open appearance of the Hebrews was as startling as unexpected, nor could the Philistines have imagined that two men alone would challenge a post. Manifestly the Philistine post had no inclination to fight an unknown enemy; and so with genuine Eastern boastfulness they heaped abuse on them, uttering the challenge to come up. This had been the preconcerted signal; and, choosing the steepest ascent, where their approach would least be looked for, Jonathan and his armor-bearer crept up the ledge of the rock on their hands and feet. Up on the top it was so narrow that only one could stand abreast. This we infer not only from the language of the text, but from the description of what ensued. As Jonathan reached the top, he threw down his foremost opponent, and the armor-bearer, coming up behind, killed him. There was not room for two to attack or defend in line. And so twenty men fell, as the text expresses it, within "half a furrow of a yoke of field," — that is, as we understand it, within the length commonly ploughed by a yoke of oxen, and the width of about half a furrow, or more probably half the width that would be occupied in ploughing a furrow.

All this time it would be impossible, from the nature of the terrain, to know how many assailants were supporting Jonathan and his armor-bearer. This difficulty would be still more felt in the camp and by those at a little farther distance, since it would be manifestly impossible for them to examine the steep sides of Bozez, or the neighboring woods. The terror, probably communicated by fugitives, who would naturally magnify the danger, perhaps into a general assault, soon became a panic, or, as the text expresses it, a "terror of Elohim." Presently the host became an armed rabble, melting away before their imaginary enemy, and each man's sword in the confusion turned against his neighbor. At the same time the Hebrew auxiliaries, whom cowardice or force had brought into the camp of the Philistines, turned against them, and the noise and confusion became indescribable.

From the topmost height of Gibeah the outlook, which Saul had there posted, descried the growing confusion in the Philistine camp. Only one cause could suggest itself for this. When Saul mustered his small army, he found that only Jonathan and his armor-bearer were missing. But the king sufficiently knew the spirit of his son not to regard as impossible any undertaking on his part, however seemingly desperate. What was he to do? One thing alone suggested itself to him. He would take counsel of the Lord by the well-known means of the Urim and Thummim.

But while preparations were making for it, the necessity of its employment had evidently ceased. It was not a sudden commotion, but an increasing panic among the Philistines that was observed. Presently Saul and his men, as they came to battle, found that the enemy himself had been doing their work. And now it became a rout. The Hebrews from the Philistine camp had joined the pursuers, and, as the well-known notes of the trumpet wakened the echoes of Mount Ephraim, the men who were in hiding crept out of their concealment and followed in the chase. And so the tide of battle rolled as far as Beth-aven.

But, though the battle was chiefly pursuit of the fleeing foe, already "the men of Israel were distressed," or rather "pressed," by weariness and faintness. For quite early in the day, and in the absence of Jonathan, Saul had yielded to one of his characteristic impulses. When he ascertained the real state of matters as regarded the Philistines, he put the people under a vow — to which, either by an "Amen," or else by their silence they gave assent — not to taste food until the evening, till he had avenged himself of his enemies. It need scarcely be said, that in this Saul acted without Divine direction. More than that, it is difficult to discern in it any religious motive, unless it were, that the enemies on whom Saul wished personally to be avenged were also the hereditary foes of Israel. And yet in the mind of Saul there was no doubt something religious about this rash vow. At any rate the form in which his impetuous Eastern resolve was cast, was such, and that of a kind which would peculiarly commend itself to an Israelite like Saul. Foolish and wrong as such a vow had been, still, as Israel had at least by their silence given consent, it lay as a heavy obligation upon the people. However faint, none dared break the fast during that long and weary day, when they followed the enemy as far as the western passes of Ajalon that led down into the Philistine plains. But Jonathan had not known it, till one told him of his father's vow after he had paused in the forest to dip his staff into honey that had dropped from the combs of wild bees. For such an offense Jonathan was certainly not morally responsible. Considering how small an amount of nourishment had helped him in his weariness, he could only deplore the rashness of his father, whose vow had, through the faintness which it entailed on the people, defeated the very object he had sought.

At last the weary day closed in Ajalon, and with it ended the obligation upon the people. The pursuit was stopped; and the people, ravenous for food, slew the animals "on the ground," felling them down, and eating the meat without being careful to remove the blood. It is true that, when Saul heard of it, he reproved the people for the sin which this involved, and took immediate steps to provide a proper slaughtering-place. Still this breach of an express Divine command (Leviticus 19:26) must in fairness be laid to the charge of Saul's rash vow. Nor could the building of a memorial-altar on the spot be regarded as altering the character of what had taken place that day.

Night was closing around Ajalon. The place, the circumstances, nay, his very vow, could not but recall to Saul the story of Joshua, and of his pursuit of the enemies of Israel (Joshua 10:12, 13). His proposal to follow up the Philistines was willingly taken up by the people, who had meanwhile refreshed themselves and were eager for the fray. Only the priests would first ask counsel of God. But no answer came, though sought by Urim and Thummim. Some burden must lie upon Israel, and Saul with his usual rashness would bring it to the test with whom lay the guilt, at the same time swearing by Jehovah that it should be avenged by death, even though it rested on Jonathan, the victor of that day, who had "wrought this great salvation in Israel," nay, who "had wrought with God" that day. But the people, who well knew what Jonathan had done, listened in dull silence. It must have been a weird scene as they gathered around the camp fire, and the torches cast their fitful glare on those whose fate the lot was to decide. First it was to be between all the people on the one side, and Saul and Jonathan on the other. A brief, solemn invocation, and the lot fell upon Saul and his son. A second time it was cast, and now it pointed to Jonathan. Questioned by his father, he told what he had done in ignorance. Still Saul persisted that his vow must be fulfilled. But now the people interposed. He whom God had owned, and who had saved Israel, must not die. But the pursuit of the Philistines was given up, and the campaign abruptly closed. And so ended in sorrow and disappointment what had been begun in self-willed disobedience to God and distrustfulness of Him.

CHAPTER 9: THE WAR AGAINST AMALEK — SAUL'S DISOBEDIENCE, AND ITS MOTIVES — SAMUEL COMMISSIONED TO ANNOUNCE SAUL'S REJECTION — AGAG HEWN IN PIECES.

(1 SAMUEL 14:47-52; 15)

THE successful war against the Philistines had secured Saul in possession of the throne. Henceforth his reign was marked by wars against the various enemies of Israel, in all of which he proved victorious.

These expeditions are only indicated, not described, in the sacred text, as not forming constituent elements in the history of the kingdom of God, however they may have contributed to the prosperity of the Jewish state. The war against Amalek alone is separately told (ch. 15), alike from its character and from its bearing on the kingdom which God would establish in Israel. Along with these outward successes the sacred text also indicates the seeming prosperity of Saul, as regarded his family-life. It almost appears as if it had been intended to place before us, side by side in sharp contrast, these two facts: Saul's prosperity both at home and abroad, and his sudden fall and rejection, to show forth that grand truth which all history is evolving: Jehovah reigneth!

Israel's oldest and hereditary enemies were the Amalekites. Descended from Esau (Genesis 36:12, 16; 1 Chronicles 1:36; comp. Josephus' Antiq. 2., 1, 2), they occupied the territory to the south and south-west of Palestine. They had been the first wantonly to attack Israel in the wilderness, (Exodus 17:8, etc.), and "war against Amalek from generation to generation," had been the Divine sentence upon them.

Besides that first attack we know that they had combined with the Canaanites (Numbers 14:43-45), the Moabites (Judges 3:22, 13), and the Midianites (Judges 7:12) against Israel. What other more direct warfare they may have carried on, is not expressly mentioned in Scripture, because, as frequently observed, it is not a record of the national history of Israel. But from 1 Samuel 15:33 we infer that, at the time of which we write, they were not only in open hostility against Israel, but behaved with extreme and wanton cruelty. Against this unrelenting hereditary foe of the kingdom of God the ban had long been pronounced (Deuteronomy 25:17-19). The time had now arrived for its execution, and Samuel summoned Saul in the most solemn manner to this work. It was in itself a difficult expedition. To be carried out in its full sweep as a "ban," it would, in Saul's then state of mind, have required peculiar self-abnegation and devotion. Looking back upon it from another stage of moral development and religious dispensation, and in circumstances so different that such questions and duties can never arise, and that they seem immeasurably far behind, as the dark valley to the traveler who has climbed the sunlit height, or as perhaps events and phases in our own early history, many things connected with the "ban" may appear mysterious to us. But the history before us is so far helpful as showing that, besides its direct meaning as a judgment, it had also another and a moral aspect, implying, as in the case of Saul, self-abnegation and real devotedness to God.

Thus viewed, the command to execute the "ban" upon Amalek was the second and final test of Saul's fitness for being king over God's people. The character of this kingdom had been clearly explained by Samuel at Gilgal in his address to king and people (1 Samuel

12:14, 20, 21, 24). There is evidently an internal connection between the first (1 Samuel 13:8-14) and this second and final trial of Saul. The former had brought to light his want of faith, and even of simple obedience, and it had been a test of his moral qualification for the kingdom; this second was the test of his moral qualification for being king. As the first trial, so to speak, developed into the second, so Saul's want of moral qualification had ripened into absolute disqualification — and as the former trial determined the fate of his line, so this second decided his own as king. After the first trial his line was rejected; after the second his own standing as theocratic king ceased. As God-appointed king he was henceforth rejected; Jehovah withdrew the sanction which He had formerly given to his reign by the aid of His power and the Presence of His Spirit. Henceforth "the Spirit of Jehovah departed from Saul" (1 Samuel 16:14), and he was left, in the judgment of God, to the influence of that evil spirit to whom his natural disposition and the circumstances of his position laid him specially open (comp. Matthew 12:43-45).

In view of the great moral trial which this expedition against Amalek would involve, Samuel had been careful to make it clear that the call to it came by Divine authority, reminding the king that he had been similarly sent to anoint him (1 Samuel 15:1). From the circumstance that Saul seems to have marched against Amalek, not with a chosen host, but to have summoned the people as a whole to execute the "ban," we infer that he had understood the character of his commission. Moving from Telaim ("the place of lambs"), probably in the eastern part of the south country, he came to "the city of Amalek," which is not named, where he "laid an ambush in the valley."

Before proceeding farther, he found means to communicate with that branch of the tribe of the Kenites who, from ancient times, had been on terms of friendship with Israel (Numbers 10:29; Judges 1:16).

In consequence they removed from among the Amalekites. Then a general slaughter began, which is described as "from Havilah," in the south-east, on the boundaries of Arabia, to the wilderness of Shur "over against," or eastward of Egypt. Every Amalekite who fell into their hands was destroyed, with the notable exception, however, of Agag, their king. And as they spared him, so also "the best of the sheep, and of the oxen, and of those of the second sort, and the (wilderness-) fed lambs, and all that was good."

The motives for the latter are, of course, easily understood; not so that for sparing Agag. Did they wish to have in his person a sort of material guarantee for the future conduct of Amalek, — or did it flatter the national as well as the royal vanity to carry with them such a captive as Agag, — or did they really wish a sort of alliance and fraternity with what remained of Amalek? All these motives may have operated. But of the character of the act as one of rebellion and disobedience there could be no doubt, in view of the direct Divine command (15:3).

If in the case of Saul's first failure it was difficult to withhold sympathy, however clearly his sin and unfitness for the theocratic kingdom appeared, it is not easy even to frame an excuse for his utterly causeless disregard of so solemn a command as that of "the ban." All Jewish history, from Achan downwards, rose in testimony against him; nay, remembering his proposal to kill even Jonathan, when he had unwittingly infringed his father's rash vow, Saul stood convicted out of his own mouth! Nor was there any tangible motive for his conduct, nor anything noble or generous either about it, or about his after-bearing towards Samuel. Rather, quite the contrary. What now follows in the sacred narrative is tragic, grand, and even awful. The first scene is laid at night in Samuel's house at Ramah. It is God Who speaketh to the aged seer. "It repenteth Me that I have made Saul king, for he has returned from after Me, and My Word he has not executed" (literally, set up). "And it kindled in Samuel" (intense feeling, wrath), "and he cried unto Jehovah the whole night."

It is one of the most solemn, even awful thoughts — that of the Divine repentance, which we should approach with worshipful reverence. God's repentance is not like ours, for, "the Strength of Israel will not lie, nor repent; for He is not a man that He should repent." Man's repentance implies a change of mind, God's a change of circumstances and relations. He has not changed, but is ever the same; it is man who has changed in his position relatively to God. The Saul whom God had made king was not the same Saul whom God repented to have thus exalted; the essential conditions of their relationship were changed. God's repentance is the unmovedness of Himself, while others move and change. The Divine finger ever points to the same spot; but man has moved from it to the opposite pole. But as in all repentance there is sorrow, so, reverently be it said, in that of God. It is God's sorrow of love, as, Himself unchanged and unchanging, He looks at the sinner who has turned from Him. But, although not wholly unexpected, the announcement of this change on the part of Saul, and of his consequent rejection, swept like a terrible tempest over Samuel, shaking him in his innermost being. The greatness of the sin, the terribleness of the judgment, its publicity in the sight of all Israel, who knew of his Divine call, and in whose presence Samuel, acting as Divine messenger, had appointed him, — all these thoughts "kindled within him" feelings which it would be difficult to analyze, but which led to a "cry" all that long night, if perchance the Lord would open a way of deliverance or of pardon. With the morning light came calm resolve and the terrible duty of going in search of Saul on this errand of God. Nor did the stern Nazarite now shrink from aught which this might imply, however bitterly he might have to suffer in consequence. Saul had returned to Gilgal, as if in his infatuation he had intended to present himself in that place of so many sacred memories before the God Whose express command he had just daringly set aside. By the way he had tarried at Carmel, where he "had set him up a monument" of his triumph over Agag. And now as Samuel met him, he anticipated his questions by claiming to have executed Jehovah's behest.

But the very bleating of the sheep and lowing of the oxen betrayed his failure, and the excuse which he offered was so glaringly untrue, that Samuel interrupted him to put the matter plainly and straightforwardly in its real bearing: "Was it not when thou wast small in thine own eyes thou becamest head of the tribes of Israel?" — implying this as its counterpart: Now that thou art great in thine own eyes, thou art rejected, for it was God Who appointed thee, and against Him thou hast rebelled.

Once more Saul sought to cloak his conduct by pretense of greater religiousness, when Samuel, in language which shows how deeply the spiritual meaning of ritual worship was understood even in early Old Testament times, laid open the mingled folly and presumption of the king, and announced the judgment which the Lord had that night pronounced in his hearing.

And now the painful interest of the scene still deepens. If there had been folly, hypocrisy, and meanness in Saul's excuses, there was almost incredible weakness also about his attempt to cast the blame upon the people. Evidently Saul's main anxiety was not about his sin, but about its consequences, or rather about the effect which might be produced upon the people if Samuel were openly to disown him. He entreated him to go with him, and when Samuel refused, and turned to leave, he laid such hold on the corner of his mantle that he rent it. Not terrified by the violence of the king, Samuel only bade him consider this as a sign of how Jehovah had that day rent the kingdom from him. At last the painful scene ended. Saul gave up the pretense of wishing Samuel's presence from religious motives, and pleaded for it on the ground of honoring him before the elders of his people. And to this Samuel yielded. Throughout it had not been a personal question, nor had Samuel received directions about Saul's successor, nor would he, under any circumstances, have fomented discord or rebellion among the people. Besides, he had other and even more terrible work to do ere that day of trial closed. And now the brief service was past, and Samuel prepared for what personally must have been the hardest duty ever laid upon him. By his direction Agag was brought to him. The unhappy man, believing that the bitterness of death, its danger and pang were past, and that probably he was now to be introduced to the prophet as before he had been brought to the king, came "with gladness." So far as Agag himself was concerned, these words of Samuel must have recalled his guilt and spoken its doom: "As thy sword has made women childless, so be thy mother childless above (ordinary) women."

But for Israel and its king, who had transgressed the "ban" by sparing Agag, there was yet another lesson, whatever it might cost Samuel. Rebellious, disobedient king and people on the one side, and on the other Samuel the prophet and Nazarite alone for God — such, we take it, was the meaning of Samuel having to hew Agag in pieces before Jehovah in Gilgal.

From that day forward Samuel came no more to see Saul. God's ambassador was no longer accredited to him; for he was no longer king of Israel in the true sense of the term. The Spirit of Jehovah departed from him. Henceforth there was nothing about him royal even in the eyes of men — except his death. But still Samuel mourned for him and over him; mourned as for one cut off in the midst of life, dead while living, a king rejected of God. And still "Jehovah repented that He had made Saul king over Israel."

CHAPTER 10: SAMUEL MOURNS FOR SAUL — HE IS DIRECTED TO THE HOUSE OF JESSE — ANOINTING OF DAVID — PREPARATION OF DAVID FOR THE ROYAL OFFICE — THE "EVIL SPIRIT FROM THE LORD" UPON SAUL — DAVID IS SENT TO COURT — WAR WITH THE PHILISTINES — COMBAT BETWEEN DAVID AND GOLIATH — FRIENDSHIP OF DAVID AND JONATHAN.

(1 SAMUEL 16-18:4)

IF the tragic events just recorded, and the share which Samuel had in them, had left on the mind a lingering feeling as of harshness or imperiousness on the part of the old prophet, the narrative which follows must remove all such erroneous impressions. So far from feeling calm or satisfied under the new state of things which it had been his duty to bring about, Samuel seems almost wholly absorbed by sorrow for Saul personally, and for what had happened; not unmixed, we may suppose, with concern for the possible consequences of his rejection.

It needed the voice of God to recall the mind of the prophet to the wider interests of the theocracy, and to calm him into complete submission by showing how the difficulties which he anticipated had been provided for. A new king had already been fixed upon, and the duty was laid on Samuel to designate him for that office. Accordingly Samuel was now sent to anoint one of the sons of Jesse to be Saul's successor. From the first, and increasingly, Samuel's public career had been difficult and trying. But never before had his faith been so severely tested as by this commission. He who had never feared the face of man, and who so lately had boldly confronted Saul at Gilgal, now spake as if afraid for his life, in case Saul, who no doubt was already under the influence of the "evil spirit," or rather the spirit of evil, should hear of what might seem an attempt to dethrone him. But, as always in such circumstances, the fears, which weakness suggested, proved groundless. As in the case of Saul, so in that of David, it was not intended that the anointing should be followed by immediate outward consequences. Hence there was no need for publicity; on the contrary, privacy served important purposes. The chief present object seems to have been a solemn call to David to prepare himself, as having been set apart for some great work.

Besides, in view of the meaning of this symbol, and of its results in Saul and David (1 Samuel 16:13), the anointing may be regarded as an ordinance in connection with the gift of the Spirit of God, Who alone qualified for the work. In view of all this, God directed Samuel to combine the anointing of Jesse's son with a sacrificial service at Bethlehem, the home of Jesse. Only the latter, or public service, required to be made generally known. Many reasons will suggest themselves why the other part of Samuel's commission should have remained secret, probably not fully understood by Jesse, or even by David himself.

The narrative also affords some interesting glimpses into the history of the time. Thus we infer that Samuel had been in the habit of visiting various places in the land for the purpose of sacrifice and instruction. The former was quite lawful, so long as the ark was not in its central sanctuary. On the other hand, it needs no comment to show the importance of such periodical visits of the prophet at a time when religious knowledge was necessarily so scanty, and the means of grace so scarce. It helps us to understand how religion was kept alive in the land. Again, the narrative implies that the family of Jesse must have occupied a leading place in Bethlehem, and been known as devoted to the service of the Lord. Nor do we wonder at this, remembering that they were the immediate descendants of Boaz and Ruth.

As we follow Samuel to Bethlehem, we seem to mark the same primitive simplicity and life of piety as of old. When the, "elders" hear of Samuel's coming, they go to meet him, yet with fear lest the unexpected visit betoken some unknown sin resting on their quiet village. This apprehension is removed by Samuel's explanation, and they are invited to attend the "sacrifice." But the sacrificial meal which usually followed was to be confined to Jesse and his family, in whose house, as we infer, Samuel was a welcome guest. It would appear that Samuel himself was not acquainted with all that was to happen, the Lord reserving it for the proper moment to point out to His servant who was to be Israel's future king. And this, as we judge, partly because the aged prophet had himself a lesson to learn in the matter, or rather to unlearn what of the ideas of his time and people unconsciously clung to him.

All this appears from the narrative. One by one the sons of Jesse were introduced to Samuel. The manly beauty of Eliab, the eldest, and his rank in the family, suggested to the prophet that he might be "Jehovah's anointed." But Samuel was to learn that Jehovah's judgment was, "not as what man seeth" (looketh to), "for man looketh to the eyes but Jehovah looketh to the heart."

And so the others followed in turn, with a like result. Evidently, Samuel must have expressed it to Jesse that on that day one of his family was to be chosen by Jehovah, but for what purpose seems not to have been known to them. Nor did Jesse himself, nor even David, apparently understand what was implied in the rite of anointing. No words of solemn designation were uttered by the prophet, such as Samuel had spoken when he anointed Saul (1 Samuel 10:1). Besides, as Saul was the first king anointed, and as none had been present when it took place, we may reasonably suppose that alike the ceremony and its meaning were unknown to the people. Both Jesse and David may have regarded it as somehow connected with admission to the schools of the prophets, or more probably as connected with some work for God in the future, which at the proper time would be pointed out to them. And thus was David in this respect also a type of our Lord, Whose human consciousness of His calling and work appears to have been, in a sense, progressive; being gradually manifested in the course of His history.

But to return. The seven sons of Jesse had successively passed before Samuel, yet he was not among them whom the prophet had been sent to anoint. But for all that his mission had not failed: he had only learned to own the sovereignty of God, the failure of his own judgment, and the fact that he was simply a passive instrument to carry out, not his own views, but the will of the Lord. For, the youngest of the family still remained. So unlikely did it seem to his father that he could be called to any great work, that he had been left in the field to tend the sheep. But when, at the bidding of Samuel, he came, his very bearing and appearance seemed to speak in his favor. In the language of the text, "he was reddish, and fair of eyes, and goodly to look at." And now the command to anoint him was given, and immediately and unquestioningly obeyed by Samuel.

The sacrifice past, and the sacrificial meal over, Samuel returned to Ramah, and David to his humble avocation in his father's household. And here also we love to mark the print of our Lord's footsteps, and to see in the history of David the same humble submission to a lowly calling, and faithful discharge of menial toil, and the same subjectness to his parents, as we adoringly trace in the life of Him Who humbled Himself to become David's son. But there was henceforth one difference in the life of the son of Jesse. From the day of his anointing forward, "the Spirit of Jehovah seized upon David," as formerly upon Saul, to qualify him by might and by power for the work of "God's anointed." But from Saul, who was no longer the king of God's appointment, had the Spirit of Jehovah departed, not only as the source of "might and of power," but even as "the Spirit of a sound mind." At his anointing, the Spirit then given him had made him "another man" (1 Samuel 10:6, 10). But Saul had resisted and rebelled, nor had he ever turned from his pride and disobedience in repentance to the Lord. And now the Spirit of God not only departed from him, but in judgment God sent an "evil spirit," or rather "a spirit of evil," to "terrify" Saul. Not that God ever sends a spirit who is evil. The angels whom God sends are all good, though their commission may be in judgment to bring evil upon us.

As one has rightly remarked, "God sends good angels to punish evil men, while to chastise good men, evil angels claim the power." The "evil spirit" sent from God was the messenger of that evil which in the Divine judgment was to come upon Saul, visions of which now affrighted the king, filled him with melancholy, and brought him to the verge of madness — but not to repentance. It is thus also that we can understand how the music of David's harp soothed the spirit of Saul, while those hymns which it accompanied — perhaps some of his earliest Psalms — brought words of heaven, thoughts of mercy, strains of another world, to the troubled soul of the king.

Had he but listened to them, and yielded himself not temporarily but really to their influence! But he was now the old Saul, only sensibly destitute of the Divine help, presence, and Spirit, and with all the evil in him terribly intensified by the circumstances. He had all the feelings of a man cast down from his high estate through his own sin, disappointed in his hopes and ambition, and apprehensive that at any moment the sentence of rejection, pronounced against him, might be executed, and that "better" one appear to whom his kingdom was to be given. And now an angel of evil from the Lord affrighted him with thoughts and visions of what would come to pass. For man can never withdraw himself from higher influences. As one of the fathers has it, "When the Spirit of the Lord departs, an evil spirit takes His place. And this should teach us to pray with David: 'Take not Thy Holy Spirit from me.'"

Yet, in the wonder-working providence of God, this very circumstance led David onwards towards his destination. The quiet retirement of the shepherd's life was evidently of deepest importance to him immediately after his anointing. We can understand what dangers — inward and outward — would have beset a sudden introduction to publicity or rush into fame. On the other hand, humble avocations, retirement, thought, and lonely fellowship with God would best develop his inner life in constant dependence upon God, and even call out those energies and that self-reliance which, in conjunction with the higher spiritual qualifications, were so necessary in his after-calling. Nor was it time lost even so far as his outward influence was concerned. It was then that the Spirit-helped youth acquired in the neighboring country, and far as Eastern story would carry it, the reputation of "a mighty, valiant man, and a man of war," when, all unaided and unarmed, he would slay "both the lion and the bear" that had attacked the flock which he tended. But, above all, it is to this period of inward and spiritual preparation in solitary communion with God that we trace the first of those Psalms which have for ever made "the sweet singer," in a sense, the "shepherd" of all spiritual Israel. And here also we love to connect the plains and the shepherds of Bethlehem, who heard angels hymning the birth of our dear Lord, with His great ancestor and type, and to think how in those very plains the shepherd-king may have watched his flock in the quiet of the starlit night, and poured forth in accents of praise what is the faith and hope of the Church in all times. No doubt this talent of David also, though probably only viewed as a worldly gift, became known in the neighborhood. And so, when the courtiers of Saul suggested music as the well-known remedy in antiquity for mental disturbances, such as those from which the king suffered through the "evil spirit," one of the servant-men in attendance, probably a native of the district around Bethlehem, could from personal knowledge recommend David as "cunning in playing,... knowing of speech, ... and Jehovah is with him."

The words, seemingly casually spoken, were acted upon, and David was sent for to court. He came, bringing such gifts as the primitive habits of those times suggested to Jesse as fitting for a loyal subject to offer to his monarch. And as he stood before Saul in all the freshness of youth, with conscience clear, and in the Spirit-holpen vigor of a new life — so like the ideal of what Saul might have become, like him even in stature — the king's past and better self seems to have come back to him, "the king loved David greatly," and took him into his service. And God's blessing rested on it: for, when the king heard, as it were, the sound of the rushing wings of the spirit of evil, and almost felt the darkness as he spread them over him, then, as David's hands swept the harp of praise, and it poured forth its melody of faith and hope, it seemed as if heaven's light fell on those wings, and the evil spirit departed from Saul. And thus we learn once more the precious lesson, how "God moves in a mysterious way His wonders to perform."

What, if the result alone had been announced, would have seemed impossible, and hence miraculous in its accomplishment, was brought about by a chain of events, each linked to the other by natural causation. It is this naturalness, in many cases, of the supernatural which most shows that "Jehovah reigneth." What He has promised in His grace that He bringeth about in His providence. Next to inward humility and strength in dependence on the Lord, perhaps the most important lessons which David could learn for his future guidance would be those which at the court of Saul, and yet not of the court, he would derive from daily observation of all that passed in the government, standing in so near and confidential relationship to the king as to know all — the good and the evil, the danger and the difficulty — and yet being so wholly independent as to remain unbiased in his estimate of persons and judgment of things.

So time passed. But in the intervals of calmness, when Saul needed not the ministry of David, the young Bethlehemite was wont to return to his father's home and to his humble avocations, — to find in quiet retirement that rest and strength which he needed (1 Samuel 17:15). And now once more had the dark cloud of war gathered over the land. It was again Israel's hereditary enemy the Philistines, who, probably encouraged by their knowledge of Saul's state, had advanced as far into Judah as the neighborhood of Bethlehem. About ten miles to the south-west of that city lay Shochoh (or Sochoh), the modern Shuweikeh. Here a broad wady, or valley, marking a water-course, runs north for about an hour's distance. This is the modern Wady-es-Sumt, the valley of the acacias, the ancient valley of Elah, or of the terebinth. At the modern village of Sakarieh, the ancient Shaarim, the wady divides, turning westwards towards Gath, and northwards by the Wady Surar towards Ekron. Shochoh and Ephes-Dammim, the modern Damum, about three miles north-east of Shochoh, between which two points the Philistine camp was pitched, lay on the southern slope of the wady, while the host of Israel was camped on the northern slope, the two being separated by the deep part of the wady. But no longer did the former God-inspired courage fire Israel. The

Spirit of God had departed from their leader, and his followers seemed to share in the depression which this consciousness brought. In such a warfare, especially among Easterns, all depended on decision and boldness. But unbelief makes cowards; and Saul and his army were content with a merely defensive position, without venturing to attack their enemies. Day by day the two armies gathered on the opposite slopes, only to witness what was for Israel more than humiliation, even an open defiance of their ability to resist the power of Philistia — by implication, a defiance of the covenant-people as such, and of Jehovah, the covenant-God, and a challenge to a fight between might in the flesh and power in the Spirit. And truly Israel, under the leadership of a Saul, was ill prepared for such a contest. But herein also lay the significance of the Philistine challenge, and of the manner in which it was taken up by David, as well as of his victory. It is not too much to assert that this event was a turning-point in the history of the theocracy, and marked David as the true king of Israel, ready to take up the Philistine challenge of God and of His people, to kindle in Israel a new spirit, and, in the might of the living God, to bring the contest to victory.

Forty days successively, as the opposing armies had stood marshaled in battle-array, Goliath of Gath — a descendant of those giants that had been left at the time of Joshua (Joshua 11:21, 22) — had stepped out of the ranks of the Philistines to challenge a champion of Israel to single combat, which should decide the fate of the campaign, and the subjection of either Israel or the Philistines. Such challenges were common enough in antiquity. But it indicated a terrible state of things when it could be thrown down and not taken up, — a fearful "reproach" when an "uncircumcised Philistine" could so "defy the armies of the living God" (1 Samuel 17:8-10, 26, 36). And yet as Goliath left the ranks of his camp, and "came down" (ver. 8) into the valley that separated the two hosts, and, as it were, shook his hand in scorn of high heaven and of Israel, not a man dared answer; till at last the Philistine, rendered more and more bold, began to cross the wady, and "came up" the slopes towards where Israel stood (ver. 25), when at sight of him they "fled," and "were sore afraid."

For, where the realizing sense of God's presence was wanting, the contest would only seem one of strength against strength. In that case, the appearance and bearing of the Philistine must have been sufficiently terrifying to Orientals. Measuring about nine feet nine inches, he was covered front and back by a coat of mail of brass, consisting of scales overlapping each other, such as we know were used in ancient times, but weighing not less than about one hundred and fifty-seven pounds.

That armor, no doubt, descended to his legs, which were cased in "greaves of brass," while a helmet of the same material defended his head. As weapons of offense he carried, besides the sword with which he was girded (ver. 51; 21:9), an enormous javelin of brass, which, after the manner of the ancient soldiers, was slung on his back, and a spear, the metal head of which weighed about seventeen or eighteen pounds.

Such was the sight which David beheld, when sent by his father to the army to inquire after the welfare of his three elder brothers, who had followed Saul into the war, and at the same time, in true Oriental fashion, to carry certain provisions to them, and to bring a present from the dairy produce to their commanding officer. The description of what follows is so vivid that we can almost see the scene. All is truly Oriental in its cast, and truly Scriptural in its spirit.

David, who had never been permanently in Saul's service, had, on the outbreak of the war, returned to his home. When he now arrived at the "trench" which ran round the camp, to trace and defend it, the army of Israel was being put in battle-array against that of the Philistines on the opposite hill.

In true Oriental fashion, they were raising a shout of defiance while not venturing on an attack. David left his baggage with the keeper of the baggage, and ran forward to the foremost ranks, where, as he knew, the position of Judah, and therefore of his brothers, must be (Numbers 2:3; 10:14). While conversing with them, the scene previously described was re-enacted. As Goliath approached nearer and nearer, the order of battle was dissolved before him. It is quite characteristic that these fear-stricken Israelites should have tried to excite one another by dwelling on the insult offered to Israel, and the rewards which Saul had promised to the victorious champion of his people. Quite characteristic also, from what we know of him, was the bearing of David. We need not attempt to eliminate from the narrative the personal element, as we may call it, in the conduct of David. God appeals to outward motives, even in what is highest — such as the loss or gain of our souls, — and the tale of what was "to be done" to him who wrought such deliverance in Israel might well fire a spirit less ardent than that of David to realize Israel's great need. But what was so distinctive in David — who probably knew Saul too well confidently to expect the literal fulfillment of his promises — was the spiritual response to the challenge of the Philistine which sprung unbidden to his lips (ver. 26), and which, when the hour for personal action came, was felt to be a deep reality to which his faith could confidently appeal (vers. 36, 37). Truly we seem to breathe another atmosphere than that hitherto in the camp of Israel; nor could his public career be more appropriately begun, who was to pasture Israel according to the integrity of his heart, and to lead them "by the skillfulness of his hands" (Psalm 78:70-72).

And here we have another instance of the prefigurative character of the history of David. As "the brothers" and near kinsfolk of our blessed Lord misunderstood His motives, and could not enter into the spirit of His work, so Eliab, when he imputed to David a dissatisfied ambition that could not rest contented with humble avocations, and when he characterized his God-inspired courage and confidence as carnal, and a delight in war and bloodshed for its own sake (ver. 28). But it was too late to arrest David by such objections. Putting them aside, as making a man an offender for a word, but without retaliating by convicting Eliab of his own uncharitableness, worldliness, and unbelief, David turned away to repeat his inquiries. Tidings of the young champion, who had displayed quite another banner against the Philistine than that of Saul, were soon brought to the king. In the interview which followed, the king bade the shepherd think of his youth and inexperience in a contest with such a warrior as Goliath. Yet he seems to speak like one who was half convinced by the bearing and language of this strange champion, and easily allowed himself to be persuaded; not so much, we take it, by the account of his prowess and success in the past as by the tone of spiritual assurance and confidence in the God of Israel with which he spake.

Once more thoughts of the past must have crowded in upon Saul. There was that in the language of this youth which recalled the strength of Israel, which seemed like the dawn of another morning, like a voice from another world. But if he went to the combat, let it be at least in what seemed to Saul the most fitting and promising manner — arrayed in the king's own armor — as if the whole meaning of David's conduct — nay, of the combat itself and of the victory — had not lain in the very opposite direction: in the confessed inadequacy of all merely human means for every such contest, and in the fact that the victory over Goliath must appear as the Lord's deliverance, achieved through the faith of a personal, realizing, conscious dependence on Him. And so Saul's armor must be put aside as that which had "not been proved" in such a contest, of which the champion of the Lord had never made trial in such encounters — and of which he never could make trial. A deep-reaching lesson this to the Church and to believers individually, and one which bears manifold application, not only spiritually, but even intellectually. The first demand upon us is to be spiritual; the next to be genuine and true, without seeking to clothe ourselves in the armor of another.

A few rapid sketches, and the narrative closes. Goliath had evidently retired within the ranks of the Philistines, satisfied that, as before, his challenge had remained unanswered. And now tidings that a champion of Israel was ready for the fray once more called him forth. As he advanced, David waited not till he had crossed the wady and ascended the slope where Israel's camp lay, but hastened forward, and picked him five stones from the dry river-bed in the valley. And now the Philistine had time to take, as he thought, the full measure of his opponent. Only a fair-looking, stout, unarmed shepherd-youth, coming against him with his shepherd's gear, as if he were a dog! Was this, then, the champion of Israel? In true Eastern fashion, he advanced, boasting of his speedy and easy victory; in true heathen spirit the while cursing and blaspheming the God in Whose Name David was about to fight. But David also must speak. To the carnal confidence in his own strength which Goliath expressed, David opposed the Name — that is, the manifestation — of Jehovah Zevaoth, the God of heaven's hosts, the God also of the armies of Israel. That God, Whom Goliath had blasphemed and defied, would presently take up the challenge. He would fight, and deliver the giant into the hand of one even so unequal to such contest as an unarmed shepherd. Thus would "all the earth" — all Gentile nations — see that there was a God in Israel; thus also would "all this assembly" (the kahal, the called) — all Israel — learn that too long forgotten lesson which must underlie all their history, that "not by sword or spear, saith Jehovah: for Jehovah's is the war, and He gives you into our hands."

Words ceased. Slowly the Philistine giant advanced to what seemed easy victory. He had not even drawn the sword, nor apparently let down the visor of his helmet, — for was not his opponent unarmed? and a well-directed thrust of his spear would lay him bleeding at his feet. Swiftly the shepherd ran to the encounter. A well-aimed stone from his sling — and the gigantic form of the Philistine, encased in its unwieldy armor, mortally stricken, fell heavily to the ground, and lay helpless in sight of his dismayed countrymen, while the unarmed David, drawing the sword from the sheath of his fallen opponent, cut off his head, and returned to the king with the gory trophy. All this probably within less time than it has taken to write it down. And now a sudden dismay seized on the Philistines. Their champion and pride so suddenly swept down, they fled in wild disorder. It was true, then, that there was a God in Israel! It was true that the war was Jehovah's, and that He had given them into Israel's hand! Israel and Judah raised a shout, and pursued the Philistines up that ravine, through that wady, to Shaarim, and beyond it to the gates of Gath, and up that other wady to Ekron. But while the people returned to take the spoil of the Philistine tents, David had given a modest account of himself to the jealous king and his chief general; had won the generous heart of Jonathan; and had gone to lay up the armor of the Philistine as his part of the spoil in his home. But the head of the Philistine he nailed on the gates of Jerusalem, right over in sight of the fort which the heathen Jebusites still held in the heart of the land.

CHAPTER 11: SAUL'S JEALOUSY, AND ATTEMPTS UPON DAVID'S LIFE — DAVID MARRIES MICHAL — RIPENING OF SAUL'S PURPOSE OF MURDER — DAVID'S FLIGHT TO SAMUEL — SAUL AMONG THE PROPHETS — DAVID FINALLY LEAVES THE COURT OF SAUL.

(1 SAMUEL 18:4-20:42)

THE friendship between Jonathan and David, which dated from the victory over Goliath, and the modest, genuine bearing of the young conqueror, is the one point of light in a history which grows darker and darker as it proceeds. We can imagine how a spirit so generous as that of Jonathan would be drawn towards that unaffected, brave youth, so free from all self-consciousness or self-seeking, who would seem the very embodiment of Israelitish valor and piety. And we can equally perceive how gratitude and admiration of such real nobleness would kindle in the heart of David an affection almost womanly in its tenderness. Ancient history records not a few instances of such love between heroes, ratified like this by a "covenant," and betokened by such gifts as when Jonathan put on David his "mantle," his "armor-coat," and even his arms, — but none more pure and elevated, or penetrated, as in this instance, by the highest and best feelings of true piety.

There can be no doubt that this friendship was among the means which helped David to preserve that loyalty to Saul which was the grand characteristic of his conduct in the very trying period which now ensued. How these trials called out his faith, and consequently his patience; how they drew him closer to God, ripened his inner life, and so prepared him for his ultimate calling, will best appear from a comparison of the Psalms which date from this time. The events, as recorded in the sacred text, are not given in strict chronological order, but rather in that of their internal connection. As we understand it, after David's victory over Goliath, he was taken into the permanent employ of Saul. This and his general success in all undertakings, as well as his prudence and modesty, which, at least during the first period, disarmed even the jealousy of Saul's courtiers, are indicated in general terms in 1 Samuel 18:5. But matters could not long progress peacefully. On the return of the army from the pursuit of the Philistines, the conquerors had, after the custom of the times, been met in every city through which they passed by choruses of women, who, with mimic dances, sung antiphonally the praise of the heroes, ascribing the victory over thousands to Saul, and over ten thousands to David.

It was quite characteristic of the people, and it implied not even conscious preference for David, least of all danger to Saul's throne. But it sufficed to kindle in Saul deep and revengeful envy. Following upon what the spirit of evil from the Lord had set before him as his own fate, sealed as it was by his solemn rejection from the kingdom and the conscious departure of the Spirit of God, the popular praise seemed to point out David as his rival. And every fresh success of David, betokening the manifest help of God, and every failure of his own attempts to rid himself of this rival, would only deepen and embitter this feeling, and lead him onwards, from step to step, until the murderous passion became all engrossing, and made the king not only forgetful of Jehovah, and of what evidently was His purpose, but also wholly regardless of the means which he used. Thus Saul's dark passions were ultimately concentrated in the one thought of murder. Yet in reality it was against Jehovah that he contended rather than against David. So true is it that all sin is ultimately against the Lord; so bitter is the root of self; and so terrible the power of evil in its constantly growing strength, till it casts out all fear of God or care for man. So true also is it that "he that hateth his brother is a murderer," in heart and principle. On the other hand, these constant unprovoked attempts upon the life of David, regardless of the means employed, till at last the whole forces of the kingdom were used for no other purpose than to hunt down an innocent fugitive, whose only crime was that God was with him, and that he had successfully fought the cause of Israel, must have had a very detrimental effect upon the people. They must have convinced all that he who now occupied the throne was unfit for the post, while at the same time they could not but demoralize the people in regard to their real enemies, thus bringing about the very results which Saul so much dreaded.

It deserves special notice, that Saul's attempts against the life of David are in the sacred text never attributed to the influence of the spirit of evil from the Lord, although they were no doubt made when that spirit was upon him. For God never tempts man to sin; but he sinneth when he is drawn away by his own passion, and enticed by it. If proof were needed that the spirit whom God sent was not evil in himself, it would be found in this, that while formerly David's music could soothe the king, that power was lost when Saul had given way to sin. On the first occasion of this kind, Saul, in a maniacal fit, twice poised against David the javelin, which, as the symbol of royalty, he had by him (like the modern scepter); and twice "David turned (bent) aside from before him."

The failure of his purpose only strengthened the king's conviction that, while God had forsaken him, He was with David. The result, however, was not repentance, but a feeling of fear, under which he removed David from his own presence, either to free himself of the temptation to murder, or in the hope, which he scarcely yet confessed to himself, that, promoted to the command over a thousand men, David might fall in an engagement with the Philistines. How this also failed, or rather led to results the opposite of those which Saul had wished, is briefly marked in the text.

With truest insight into the working of such a mind, the narrative traces the further progress of this history. Perhaps to test whether he really cherished ambitious designs, but with the conscious wish to rid himself of his dreaded rival, Saul now proposed to carry out his original promise to the conqueror of Goliath, by giving David his eldest daughter Merab to wife, at the same time professing only anxiety that his future son-in-law should fight "the battles of Jehovah." The reply given might have convinced him, that David had no exaggerated views of his position in life. It is idle to ask why Saul upon this so rapidly transferred Merab to one who is not otherwise known in history.

The affection of Michal, Saul's younger daughter, for David, promised to afford Saul the means of still further proving David's views, and of bringing him to certain destruction. The plan was cleverly devised. Taught by experience, David took no further notice of the king's personal suggestion of such an alliance.

At this the courtiers were instructed secretly to try the effect of holding out a prospect so dazzling as that of being the king's son-in-law. But the bait was too clumsily put, — or rather it failed to take, from the thorough integrity of David. Next came not the suggestion merely, but a definite proposal through the courtiers, to give the king as dowry within a certain specified time a pledge that not less than a hundred heathen had fallen in "the Lord's battles." If the former merely general admonition to fight had not led to David's destruction, a more definite demand like this might necessitate personal contests, in which, as Saul imagined, every chance would be against David's escape. But once more the king was foiled. David, who readily entered on a proposal so much in harmony with his life-work, executed within less than the appointed time double the king's requirements, and Michal became his wife.

And still the story becomes darker and darker. We have marked the progress of murderous thought in the king's mind, from the sudden attack of frenzy to the scarcely self-confessed wish for the death of his victim, to designed exposure of his life, and lastly to a deliberate plan for his destruction. But now all restraints were broken through. Do what he might, David prospered, and all that Saul had attempted had only turned out to the advantage of the son of Jesse. Already he was the king's son-in-law; Michal had given her whole heart to him; constant success had attended those expeditions against the heathen which were to have been his ruin; nay, as might be expected in the circumstances, he had reached the pinnacle of popularity. One dark resolve now settled in the heart of the king, and cast it shadow over every other consideration. David must be murdered. Saul could no longer disguise his purpose from himself, nor keep it from others. He spoke of it openly — even to Jonathan, and to all around him. So alarming had it become, that Jonathan felt it necessary to warn David, who, in his conscious integrity, seemed still unsuspicious of real danger. Yet Jonathan himself would fain have believed that his father's mood was only the outcome of that dreadful disease of which he was the victim. Accordingly, almost within hearing of David, who had secreted himself near by, he appealed to his father, and that in language so telling and frank, that the king himself was for the moment won. So it had been only frenzy — the outburst of the moment, but not the king's real heart-purpose — and David returned to court!

The hope was vain. The next success against the Philistines rekindled all the evil passions of the king. Once more, as he yielded to sin, the spirit of evil was sent in judgment — this time from Jehovah. As Saul heard the rushing of his dark pinions around him, it was not sudden frenzy which seized him, but he attempted deliberate murder. What a contrast: David with the harp in his hand, and Saul with his spear; David sweeping the chords to waken Divine melody in the king's soul, and the king sending the javelin with all his might, so that, as it missed its aim, it stuck in the wall close by where David had but lately sat. Meanwhile David escaped to his own house, apparently unwilling even now to believe in the king's deliberate purpose of murder. It was Saul's own daughter who had to urge upon her husband the terrible fact of her father's planned crime and the need of immediate flight, and with womanly love and wit to render it possible. How great the danger had been; how its meshes had been laid all around and well nigh snared him — but chiefly what had been David's own feelings, and what his hope in that hour of supreme danger: all this, and much more for the teaching of the Church of all ages, we gather from what he himself tells us in the fifty-ninth Psalm.

The peril was past; and while the cowardly menials of Saul — though nominally of Israel, yet in heart and purpose, as in their final requital, "heathens" (Psalm 59:6, 8) — prowled about the city and its walls on their terrible watch of murder, "growling" like dogs that dare not bark to betray their presence, and waiting till the dawn would bring their victim, lured to safety, within reach of their teeth, Michal compassed the escape of her husband through a window — probably on the city-wall. In so doing she betrayed, however, alike the spirit of her home and that of her times. The daughter of Saul, like Rachel of old (Genesis 31:19), seems to have had Teraphim — the old Aramaean or Chaldean household gods, which were probably associated with fertility. For, despite the explicit Divine prohibition and the zeal of Samuel against all idolatry, this most ancient form of Jewish superstition appears to have continued in Israelitish households (comp. Judges 17:5; 18:14; 1 Samuel 15:23; Hosea 3:4; Zechariah 10:2). The Teraphim must have borne the form of a man; and Michal now placed this image in David's bed, arranging about the head "the plait of camel's hair," and covering the whole "with the upper garment" (as coverlet), to represent David lying sick.

The device succeeded in gaining time for the fugitive, and was only discovered when Saul sent his messengers a second time, with the peremptory order to bring David in the bed. Challenged by her father for her deceit, she excused her conduct by another falsehood, alleging that she had been obliged by David to do so on peril of her life.

Although we are in no wise concerned to defend Michal, and in general utterly repudiate, as derogatory to Holy Scripture, all attempts to explain away the apparent wrong-doing of Biblical personages, this instance requires a few words of plain statement. First, it is most important to observe, that Holy Scripture, with a truthfulness which is one of its best evidences, simply relates events, whoever were the actors, and whatever their moral character. We are somehow prone to imagine that Holy Scripture approves all that it records, at least in the case of its worthies — unless, indeed, the opposite be expressly stated. Nothing could be more fallacious than such an inference. Much is told in the Bible, even in connection with Old Testament saints, on which no comment is made, save that of the retribution which, in the course of God's providence, surely follows all wrong-doing. And here we challenge any instance of sin which is not followed by failure, sorrow, and punishment. It had been so in the case of Abraham, of Isaac, and of Jacob; and it was so in that of David, whose every attempt to screen himself by untruthfulness ended in failure and sorrow. Holy Scripture never conceals wrong-doing — least of all seeks to palliate it. In this respect there is the most significant contrast between the Bible and its earliest (even pre-Christian) comments. Those only who are acquainted with this literature know with what marvelous ingenuity Rabbinical commentaries uniformly try, not only to palliate wrong on the part of Biblical heroes, but by some turn or alteration in the expression, or suggestion of motives, to present it as actually right. But we must go a step further. He who fails to recognize the gradual development of God's teaching, and regards the earlier periods in the history of God's kingdom as on exactly the same level as the New Testament, not only most seriously mistakes fundamental facts and principles, but misses the entire meaning of the preparatory dispensation. The Old Testament never places truth, right, or duty on any lower basis than the New. But while it does not lower, it does not unfold in all their fullness the principles which it lays down. Rather does it adapt the application of truths, the exposition of rights, and the unfolding of duties, to the varying capacities of each age and stage. And this from the necessity of the case, in highest wisdom, in greatest mercy, and in the interest of the truth itself. The principle: "When I was a child, I spake as a child, I understood as a child, I thought as a child," applies to the relation between the Old and the New Testament standpoint, as well as to all spiritual and even intellectual progress. The child is ignorant of all the bearings of what he learns; the beginner of the full meaning and application of the axioms and propositions which he is taught. Had it been otherwise in spiritual knowledge, its acquisition would have been simply impossible.

Here also we have to distinguish between what God sanctioned and that with which He bore on account of the hardness of the heart of those who had not yet been spiritually trained in that "time of ignorance," which "God overlooked." To come to the particular question in hand. Nothing could be more clear in the Old Testament than the Divine insistence on truthfulness. He Himself condescends to be His people's example in this. The command not to lie one to another (Leviticus 19:11) is enforced by the consideration, "I am Jehovah," and springs as a necessary sequence from the principle: "Be ye holy, for I Jehovah your God am holy." It is scarcely requisite to add, that in no other part of Holy Scripture is this more fully or frequently enforced than in the Book of Psalms. And yet, when occasion arose, David himself seems not to have scrupled to seek safety through falsehood, though with what little success appears in his history. It appears as if to his mind untruth had seemed only that which was false in the intention or in its object, not that which was simply untrue in itself, however good the intention might be, or however desirable the object thereby sought. And in this connection it deserves notice, how among the few express moral precepts which the New Testament gives — for it deals in principles rather than in details; it gives life, not law, — this about lying recurs with emphatic distinctness and frequency.

As might almost have been anticipated, David's destination in his flight was Ramah. To tell Samuel, who had anointed him, all that had happened; to ask his guidance, and seek refreshment in his company, would obviously suggest itself first to his mind. For greater safety, the two withdrew from the city, to "Naioth," "the dwellings," which seems to have been a block of dwellings within a compound, occupied by an order of prophets, of which Samuel was the "president," and, we may add, the founder. Not that "prophetism" (if the term may be used) commenced with Samuel.

In the sense of being the bearers of God's message, the patriarchs are called "prophets" (Genesis 20:7; Psalm 105:15). But in its strict sense the term first applied to Moses (Numbers 11:25; Deuteronomy 34:10; Hosea 12:13). Miriam was a prophetess (Exodus 15:20; comp. Numbers 12:2). In the days of the Judges there were prophets (Judges 4:4; 6:8). At the time of Eli, prophetic warning came through a "man of God" (1 Samuel 2:27); and although "the word of God" (or prophecy) "was rare" in those days (1 Samuel 3:1), yet it came not upon the people as a strange and unknown manifestation (comp. also 1 Samuel 9:9). Here, however, we must make distinction between the prophetic gift and the prophetic office. The latter, so far as appears, began with Samuel. A further stage is marked in the days of Elijah and Elisha. Then they were no longer designated "prophets," as at the time of Samuel, but "sons of the prophets," or "disciples" (1 Kings 20:35; 2 Kings 4:38; 6:1). Lastly, whereas we read of only one prophetic community, Naioth, in the time of Samuel, and that close to his residence at Ramah, there were several such in the days of Elisha, in different parts of the country — as at Gilgal, Bethel, and Jericho. Whether there was a continuous succession in this from Samuel to Elijah can scarcely be determined, though the probability seems in its favor (comp. 1 Kings 18:13).

It is of more importance to understand the difference between "prophets" and "sons of the prophets," the circumstances under which these orders or unions originated, and the peculiar meaning attached to this prophetic calling. The first point seems sufficiently clear. The "sons of the prophets" were those who of set purpose devoted themselves to this work, and were, on the one hand, disciples of prophets, and on the other, the messengers or ministers to carry out their behests. Dedication and separation to the work (symbolized even by a common abode, and by a distinctive appearance and dress), religious instruction, and, above all, implicit obedience, are the historical features of those "sons of the prophets." Quite other was the "union," "company," or rather "congregation of prophets" (1 Samuel 19:20) near Ramah.

There is no evidence of their having all permanently dedicated themselves to the office; the contrary seems rather implied. No doubt from among them sprung those who were afterwards "seers," such as Gad, Nathan, and Iddo; but the majority seem to have joined the union under a temporary constraining influence of the mighty Spirit of God. And although, as we gather from many passages of Holy Scripture (as 1 Samuel 22:5; 1 Chronicles 29:29, and other passages in the Books of Kings), they were occupied with the composition and the study of sacred history, and no doubt with that of the law also, as well as with the cultivation of hymnology, it would be a great mistake to regard them as a class of students of theology, or to represent them as a monastic order.

In point of fact, the time of Samuel, and that of Elijah and Elisha, were great turning-points, periods of crisis, in the history of the kingdom of God. In the first, the tabernacle, the priesthood, and the God-appointed services had fallen into decay, and, for a time, may be said to have been almost in abeyance. Then it was that God provided other means of grace, by raising up faithful, devoted men, who gathered into a living sanctuary, filled not by the Shechinah, but by the mighty Spirit of God. Under the direction of a Samuel, and the influence of a "spiritual gift," — like those of apostolic days — their presence and activity served most important purposes. And, as in apostolic days, the spiritual influence under which they were seems at times to have communicated itself even to those who were merely brought into contact with them. This, no doubt, to prove its reality and power, since even those who were strangers to its spiritual purpose, and unaffected by it, could not resist its might, and thus involuntarily bore witness to it. And something analogous to this we also witness now in the irresistible influence which a spiritual movement sometimes exercises even on those who are and remain strangers to its real meaning.

Thus far as regards "the congregation of prophets" in the days of Samuel. In the time of Elijah, Israel — as distinct from Judah — was entirely cut off from the sanctuary, and under a rule which threatened wholly to extinguish the service of God, and to replace it by the vile and demoralizing rites of Baal. Already the country swarmed with its priests, when God raised up Elijah to be the breaker-up of the way, and Elisha to be the restorer of ancient paths. The very circumstances of the time, and the state of the people, pointed out the necessity of the revival of the ancient "order," but now as "sons of the prophets" rather than as prophets. Nor did this change of designation imply a retrogression. What on superficial inquiry seems such, is, on more careful consideration, often found to mark real progress. In earliest patriarchal, and even in Mosaic times, the communications between Jehovah and His people were chiefly by Theophanies, or Personal apparitions of God; in the case of the prophets, by inspiration; in the New Testament Church, by the indwelling of the Holy Ghost. It were a grievous mistake to regard this progress in the spiritual history of the kingdom of God as a retrogression. The opposite is rather the case. And somewhat similarly we may mark, in some respects, an advance in the succession of "sons of the prophets" to the order of "prophetics," or "prophesiers," as we may perhaps designate them by way of distinction. "But all these things worketh one and the self-same Spirit, dividing to every man" (and to every period in the Church's history) "severally as He will," and adapting the agencies which He uses to the varying necessities and spiritual stages of His people.

What has been stated will help to explain how the three embassies which Saul sent to seize David in the Naioth were in turn themselves seized by the spiritual influence, and how even Saul, when attempting personally to carry out what his messengers had found impossible, came yet more fully and manifestly than they under its all-subduing power.

It proved incontestably that there was a Divine power engaged on behalf of David, against which the king of Israel would vainly contend, which he could not resist, and which would easily lay alike his messengers and himself prostrate and helpless at its feet. If, after this, Saul continued in his murderous designs against David, the contest would manifestly be not between two men, but between the king of Israel and the Lord of Hosts, Who had wrought signs and miracles on Saul and his servants, and that in full view of the whole people. It is this latter consideration which gives such meaning to the circumstances narrated in the sacred text, that the common report, how the spiritual influence had subdued and constrained Saul, when on his murderous errand against David, led to the renewal of the popular saying: "Is Saul also among the prophets?" For all Israel must know it, and speak of it, and wonder as it learns its significance.

Thus at the end, as at the beginning of his course, Saul is under the mighty influence of the Spirit of God — now to warn, and, if possible, to reclaim, as formerly to qualify him for his work. And some result of this kind seems to have been produced. For, although David fled from Naioth on the arrival of Saul, we find him soon again near the royal residence (20:1), where, indeed, he was evidently expected by the king to take part in the festive meal with which the beginning of every month seems to have been celebrated (vers. 5, 25, 27). The notice is historically interesting in connection with Numbers 10:10; 28:11-15, as also that other one (1 Samuel 20:6, 29), according to which it appears to have been the practice in those days of religious unsettledness for families to have had a yearly "sacrifice" in their own place, especially where, as in Bethlehem, there was an altar (comp. 16:2, etc.).

But, whatever had passed, David felt sure in his own mind that evil was appointed against him, and that there was but a step between him and death. Yet on that moral certainty alone he did not feel warranted to act. Accordingly he applied to Jonathan, whom he could so fully trust, expressly placing his life, in word as in deed, in his hands, if he were really guilty of what the king imputed to him (ver. 8). With characteristic generosity, Jonathan, however, still refused to believe in any settled purpose of murder on the part of his father, attributing all that had passed to the outbursts of temporary madness. His father had never made a secret of his intentions and movements. Why, then, should he now be silent, if David's suspicions were well founded? The suggestion that Jonathan should excuse David's absence from the feast by his attendance on the yearly family-sacrifice at Bethlehem, for which he had asked and obtained Jonathan's leave, was well calculated to bring out the feelings and purposes of the king. If determined to evil against David, he would in his anger at the escape of his victim, and his own son's participation in it, give vent to his feelings in language that could not be mistaken, the more so, if, as might be expected, Jonathan pleaded with characteristic warmth on behalf of his absent friend. But who could be trusted to bring tidings to David as he lay in hiding, "or" tell him "what" Saul would "answer" Jonathan "roughly" — or, in other words, communicate the details of the conversation?

To discuss the matter, unendangered by prying eyes and ears, the two friends betook themselves "to the field." The account of what passed between them — one of the few narratives of this kind given in Scripture — is most pathetic. It was not merely the outflowing of personal affection between the two, or perhaps it would not have been recorded at all. Rather is it reported in order to show that, though Jonathan had never spoken of it, he was fully aware of David's future destiny; more than that, he had sad presentiment of the fate of his own house. And yet, in full view of it all, he believingly submitted to the will of God, and still lovingly clave to his friend! There is a tone of deep faith toward God, and of full trust in David, in what Jonathan said. Far more fully and clearly than his father does he see into the future, alike as regards David and the house of Saul. But there is not a tinge of misunderstanding of David, not a shadow of suspicion, not a trace of jealousy, not a word of murmur or complaint. More touching words, surely, were never uttered than this charge which Jonathan laid on David as his part of their covenant, in view of what was to come upon them both: "And not only if I am still alive — not only shalt thou do with me the mercy of Jehovah" (show towards me Divine mercy) "that I die not; but thou shalt not cut off thy mercy from my house — not even" (at the time) "when Jehovah cutteth off the enemies of David, every one from the face of the earth" (20:14, 15).

The signal preconcerted between the friends was, that on the third day David should lie in hiding at the same spot where he had concealed himself "in the day of business" — probably that day when Jonathan had formerly pleaded with his father for his friend (19:2-7) — beside the stone Ezel, perhaps "the stone of demarcation," marking a boundary. Jonathan was to shoot three arrows. If he told the lad in attendance that they lay nearer than he had run to fetch them, David might deem himself safe, and come out of hiding. If, on the contrary, he directed him to go farther, then David should conclude that his only safety lay in flight. The result proved that David's fears had been too well grounded. Saul had evidently watched for the opportunity which the New Moon's festival would offer to destroy his hated rival. On the first day he noticed David's absence, but, attributing it to some Levitical defilement, made no remark, lest his tone might betray him. But on the following day he inquired its reason in language which too clearly betokened his feelings. It was then that Jonathan repeated the false explanation which David had suggested. Whether or not the king saw through the hollowness of the device, it certainly proved utterly unavailing. Casting aside all restraint, the king turned on his son, and in language the most insulting to an Oriental, bluntly told him that his infatuation for David would cause his own and his family's ruin. To the command to send for him for the avowed purpose of his murder, Jonathan with characteristic frankness and generosity replied by pleading his cause, on which the fury of the king rose to such a pitch, that he poised his javelin against his own son, as formerly against David.

Jonathan had left the feast in moral indignation at the scene which had taken place before the whole court. But deeper far was his grief for the wrong done to his friend. That day of feasting became one of fasting to Jonathan. Next morning he went to give the preconcerted signal of danger. But he could not so part from his friend. Sending back the lad to the city with his bow, quiver, and arrows, the two friends once more met, but for a moment. There was not time for lengthened speech; the danger was urgent. They were not unmanly tears which the two wept, "till David wept loudly."

The parting must be brief — only just sufficient for Jonathan to remind his friend of their covenant of friendship in God, to Whose care he now commended him. Then Jonathan retraced his lonely way to the city, while David hastened on his flight southward to Nob. Only once again, and that in sadly altered circumstances, did these two noblest men in Israel meet.

CHAPTER 12: DAVID AT NOB — OBSERVED BY DOEG — FLIGHT TO GATH — DAVID FEIGNS MADNESS — THE CAVE OF ADULLAM — SHELTER IN MOAB — RETURN TO THE LAND OF ISRAEL — JONATHAN'S LAST VISIT — PERSECUTIONS BY SAUL.

(1 SAMUEL 21-23)

AMIDST the many doubts which must have beset the mind of David, one outstanding fact, however painful, was at least clear. He must henceforth consider himself an outlaw, whom not even the friendship of a Jonathan could protect. As such he must seek some shelter — best outside the land of Israel, and with the enemies of Saul. But the way was far, and the journey beset by danger. On all accounts — for refreshment of the body, for help, above all, for inward strengthening and guidance — he would first seek the place whither he had so often resorted (1 Samuel 22:15) before starting on some perilous undertaking.

The Tabernacle of the Lord was at that time in Nob, probably the place that at present bears a name which some have rendered "the village of Esau" (or Edom) — reminding us of its fatal celebrity in connection with Doeg the Edomite. The village is on the road from the north to Jerusalem — between Anathoth and the Holy City, and only about one hour north-west from the latter. Here Ahimelech (or Ahiah, 1 Samuel 14:3), the great-grandson of Eli, ministered as high-priest — a man probably advanced in years, with whom his son Abiathar (afterwards appointed high-priest by David, 1 Samuel 30:7) was, either for that day or else permanently, conjoined in the sacred service.

Nob was only about an hour to the south-east of Gibeah of Saul. Yet it was not immediately on parting with Jonathan that David appeared in the holy place. We can readily understand that flight along that road could not have been risked by day — nor, indeed, anywhere throughout the boundaries of the district where Saul's residence was. We therefore conclude that David lay in hiding all that night. It was the morning of a Sabbath when he suddenly presented himself, alone, unarmed, weary, and faint with hunger before the high-priest. Never had he thus appeared before Ahimelech; and the high-priest, who must, no doubt, have been aware of dissensions in the past between the king and his son-in-law, was afraid of what this might bode. But David had a specious answer to meet every question and disarm all suspicion. If he had come unarmed, and was faint from hunger, the king's business had been so pressing, and required such secrecy, that he had avoided taking provisions, and had not even had time to arm himself. For the same reasons he had appointed his followers to meet him at a trysting-place, rather than gone forth at the head of them.

In truth, David's wants had become most pressing. He needed food to support him till he could reach a place of safety. For he dared not show himself by day, nor ask any man for help. And he needed some weapon with which, in case of absolute necessity, to defend his life. We know that it was the Sabbath, because the shewbread of the previous week, which was removed on that day, had to be eaten during its course.

It affords sad evidence of the decay into which the sanctuary and the priesthood had fallen, that Ahimelech and Abiathar could offer David no other provisions for his journey than this shewbread; which, according to the letter of the law, only the priests might eat, and that within the sanctuary (Leviticus 24:9). But there was the higher law of charity (Leviticus 19:18), which was rightly regarded as overruling every merely levitical ordinance, however solemn (comp. Matthew 12:5; Mark 2:25). If it was as David pretended, and the royal commission was so important and so urgent, it could not be right to refuse the necessary means of sustenance to those who were engaged on it, provided that they had not contracted any such levitical defilement as would have barred them from access to the Divine Presence (Leviticus 15:18). For, viewed in its higher bearing, what were the priests but the representatives of Israel, who were all to be a kingdom of priests? This idea seems indeed implied in the remark of David (21:5): "And though the manner" (the use to which it is put) "be not sacred, yet still it will be made" (become) "sacred by the instrument," — either referring to himself as the Divine instrument about to be employed, or to the "wallet" in which the bread was to be carried, as it were, on God's errand. By a similar pretense, David also obtained from the high-priest the sword of Goliath, which seems to have been kept in the sanctuary wrapt in a cloth, behind the ephod, as a memorial of God's victory over the might of the heathen. Most important of all, David, as we infer from 22:10, 15, appears to have "inquired of the Lord," through the high-priest — whatever the exact terms of that inquiry may have been. In this also there was nothing strange, since David had done so on previous occasions, probably before entering on dangerous expeditions (22:15).

But already David's secret was betrayed. It so happened in the Providence of God, that on this special Sabbath, one of Saul's principal officials, the "chief over the herdsmen," was in Nob, "detained before Jehovah." The expression implies that Doeg was obliged to remain in the sanctuary in consequence of some religious ceremony — whether connected with his admission as a proselyte, for he was by birth an Edomite, or with a vow, or with some legal purification. Such a witness could not be excluded, even if David had chosen to betray his secret to the priest. Once committed to the fatal wrong of his falsehood, David had to go on to the bitter end, all the while feeling morally certain that Doeg was his enemy, and would bring report of all to Saul (22:22). His feelings as connected with this are, as we believe, expressed in Psalm 7.

At first sight it may seem strange that on his further flight from Nob, David should have sought shelter in Gath, the city of Goliath, whom he had killed in single combat. On the other hand, not only may this have been the place most readily accessible to him, but David may have imagined that in Gath, especially, the defection of such a champion from the hosts of Saul would be hailed as a notable triumph, and that accordingly he would find a welcome in seeking its protection. The result, however, proved otherwise. The courtiers of Achish, the king, — or, to give him his Philistine title, the Abimelech (my father king) of Gath (comp. Genesis 20:2; 26:8) — urged on him the high position which David held in popular estimation in Israel, and his past exploits, as presumably indicating what not only his real feelings but his true policy towards Philistia must be, however differently it might suit his present purpose to bear himself (comp. 1 Samuel 29:3-5). The danger which now threatened David must have been very great. In fact, to judge from Psalm 56:1, the Philistine lords must have actually "taken" him, to bring him before Achish, with a view to his imprisonment, if not his destruction. We are probably warranted in inferring that it was when thus led before the king, and waiting in the court before being admitted to the audience, that he feigned madness by scribbling on the doors of the gate, and letting his spittle fall upon his beard. The device proved successful. The Philistine lords with true Oriental reverence for madness as a kind of spiritual possession, dared not harm him any more; while Achish himself, however otherwise previously disposed (comp. 27:2, 3), would not have him in his house, under the apprehension that he might "rave against" him, and in a fit of madness endanger his life.

And as Psalm 56 described the feelings of David in the hour of his great danger, so Psalm 34 expresses those on his deliverance therefrom. Accordingly the two should be read in connection. Indeed the eight Psalms which date from the time of the persecutions by Saul (59, 7, 56, 34, 57, 52, 142, 54) are closely connected, the servant of the Lord gradually rising to full and triumphant anticipation of deliverance.

They all express the same trustfulness in God, the same absolute committal to Him, and the same sense of undeserved persecution. But what seems of such special interest, regarding, as we do, the history of David in its typical aspect, is that in these Psalms David's view is always enlarging, so that in the judgment of his enemies he beholds a type of that of the heathen who oppose the kingdom of God and its King (comp. for example, Psalm 56:7; 7:9; 59:5); thus showing that David himself must have had some spiritual understanding of the prophetic bearing of his history.

And now David was once more a fugitive — the twofold lesson which he might have learned being, that it needed no subterfuges to ensure his safety, and that his calling for the present was within, not outside the land of Israel. A comparatively short distance — about ten miles — from Gath runs "the valley of the terebinth," the scene of David's great combat with Goliath. The low hills south of this valley are literally burrowed by caves, some of them of very large dimensions. Here lay the ancient city of Adullam (Genesis 38:1; Joshua 12:15; 15:35, and many other passages), which has, with much probability, been identified with the modern Aid el Mia (Adlem). In the largest of the caves close by, David sought a hiding-place. What his feelings were either at that time, or later, in similar circumstances (1 Samuel 24), we learn from Psalm 57.

It has been well observed, that hitherto David had always remained within easy distance of Bethlehem. This would secure him not only the means of information as to Saul's movements, but also of easy communication with his own family, and with those who would naturally sympathize with him.

Adullam was only a few hours distant from Bethlehem, and David's family, who no longer felt themselves safe in their home, soon joined him in his new refuge. But not only they. Many there must have been in the troublous times of Saul's reign who were "in distress," oppressed and persecuted; many who under such misgovernment would fall "into debt" to unmerciful and violent exactors; many also, who, utterly dissatisfied with the present state of things, would, in the expressive language of the sacred text, "be bitter of soul." Of these the more active and ardent now gathered around David, first to the number of about four hundred, which soon increased to six hundred (23:13). They were not a band in rebellion against Saul. This would not only have been utterly contrary to David's constantly avowed allegiance and oft proved loyalty to Saul, but to the higher purpose of God. The latter, if we may venture to judge, seems to have been spiritually to fit David for his calling, by teaching him constant dependence on God, and by also outwardly training him and his followers for the battles of the Lord — not against Saul, but against Israel's great enemy, the Philistines; in short, to take up the work which the all-absorbing murderous passion of Saul, as well as his desertion by God, prevented him from doing. Thus we see once more how, in the Providence of God, the inward and the outward training of David were the result of circumstances over which he had no control, and which seemed to threaten consequences of an entirely different character. How in those times of persecution outlaws became heroes, and of what deeds of personal bravery they were capable in the wars of the Lord, we learn from the record of their names (1 Chronicles 12), and of some of their achievements (2 Samuel 23:13, etc. comp. 1 Chronicles 11:15, etc.).

But there were among them those nearest and dearest to David, his own aged father and mother, whose presence could only impede the movements of his followers, and whose safety he must secure. Besides, as such a band could not long escape Saul's notice, it seemed desirable to find a better retreat than the caves about Adullam. For this twofold object David and his followers now passed to the other side of Jordan. From the account of the war between Saul and Moab in 1 Samuel 14:47, we infer that the latter had advanced beyond their own territory across the border, and were now occupying the southern part of the trans-Jordanic country which belonged to Israel. This was within easy reach of Bethlehem. Accordingly David now went to Mizpeh Moab, the "outlook," mountain-height or "Tor" (as we might call it) of Moab, probably over against Jericho in the "Arboth of Moab" (Numbers 22:1; Deuteronomy 34:1, 8; Joshua 13:32), perhaps, as the name seems to indicate, on the fields of the Zophim (or outlookers), on the top of Pisgah (Numbers 23:14).

To the king of Moab, whose protection he could invoke in virtue of their descent from Ruth the Moabitess, he commended his father and mother, with the expressive remark, till he should know "what Elohim would do" unto him. He himself and his followers meantime entrenched on that "mountain-height," associated with the prophecy there delivered by Balaam concerning Israel's future.

It was impossible that such a movement on the part of David could long remain unknown. In two quarters it excited deep feelings, though of a very different character. It seems highly probable that the tidings reached the Naioth, and that it was from thence that Gad (afterwards David's "seer" and spiritual adviser, 2 Samuel 24:11-19.; 1 Chronicles 21:9, and the chronicler of his reign, 1 Chronicles 29:29) went to David by Divine commission.

But the stay in the land of Moab was not in accordance with the purpose of God. David must not flee from the discipline of suffering, and God had some special work for him in the land of Israel which Saul could. no longer do. In accordance with this direction, David left his entrenched position, recrossed the Jordan, and sought shelter in "the forest of Hareth," within the boundaries of Judah. But meantime Saul also had heard that "David had become known, and the men that were with him" (22:6).

Being aware of his position, he would secure his prey. A royal court is held at Gibeah. The king sits, as so often before, "under the tamarisk-tree on the height," his spear as scepter in his hand, and surrounded by all his officers of state, among them Doeg, the "chief of the herdsmen." Characteristically Saul seems now to have surrounded himself exclusively by "Benjamites," either because no others would serve him, or more probably because he no longer trusted any but his own clansmen. Still more characteristic is the mode in which he appeals to their loyalty and seeks to enlist their aid. He seems to recognize no motive on the part of others but that of the most sordid selfishness. Probably some of the words that had passed between Jonathan and David, when they made their covenant of friendship (20:42), had been overheard, and repeated to Saul in a garbled form by one of his many spies. That was enough. As he put it, his son had made a league with David, of which the only object could be to deprive him of his throne. This could only be accomplished by violence. Everyone was aware that David and his men then held a strong position. A conspiracy so fully organized must have been known to his courtiers. If they had no sympathy with a father betrayed by his own son, at least what profit could they as

Benjamites hope to derive from such a plot? It was to defend the courtiers from guilty knowledge of such a plot that Doeg now reported what he had seen and heard at Nob. David's was a conspiracy indeed, but one hatched not by the laity but by the priesthood; and of which, as he had had personal evidence, the high-priest himself was the chief abettor.

The suggestion was one which would only too readily approve itself to a mind and conscience like Saul's. There could be nothing in common between Saul and the ministers of that God Who by His prophet had announced his rejection and appointed his successor. A priestly plot against himself, and in favor of David, had every appearance of likelihood. It is only when we thus understand the real import of Doeg's account to the king, that we perceive the extent of his crime, and the meaning of the language in which David characterized it in Psalm 52. A man of that kind was not likely to shrink from any deed. Saul summoned Ahimelech and all his father's house to his presence. In answer to the charge of conspiracy, the priest protested his innocence in language the truth of which could not have been mistaken by any impartial judge.

But the case had been decided against the priesthood before it was heard. Yet, callous as Saul's men-at-arms were, not one of them would execute the sentence of death against the priests of Jehovah. It was left to the Edomite to carry out what his reckless malice had instigated. That day no fewer than eighty-five of the priests in actual ministry were murdered in cold blood. Not content with this, the king had "the ban" executed upon Nob. As if the priest-city had been guilty of idolatry and rebellion against Jehovah (Deuteronomy 13:15), every living being, both man and beast, was cut down by the sword. Only one escaped the horrible slaughter of that day. Abiathar, the son of Ahimelech, had probably received timely warning.

He now fled to David, to whom he reported what had taken place. From him he received such assurance of protection as only one could give who in his strong faith felt absolute safety in the shelter of Jehovah's wings. But here also the attentive reader will trace a typical parallel between the murder at Nob and that of the children at Bethlehem — all the more striking, that in the latter case also an Edomite was the guilty party, Herod the king having been by descent an Idumaean.

When Abiathar reached David, he was already on his way from the forest of Hareth to Keilah. Tidings had come to David of a Philistine raid against Keilah, close on the border — the modern Kilah, about six miles to the south-east of Adullam.

Keilah was a walled city, and therefore not itself in immediate danger. But there was plenty of plunder to be obtained outside its walls; and henceforth no threshing-floor on the heights above the city was safe from the Philistines. Here was a call for the proper employment of a band like David's. But his followers had not yet learned the lessons of trust which he had been taught. Although the expedition for the relief of Keilah had been undertaken after "inquiry," and by direction of the Lord, his men shrank from provoking an attack by the Philistines at the same time that they were in constant apprehension of what might happen if Saul overtook them. So little did they as yet understand either the source of their safety or the object of their gathering! What happened — as we note once more in the course of ordinary events — was best calculated to teach them all this. A second formal inquiry of the Lord by the Urim and Thummim, and a second direction to go forward, brought them to the relief of the city. The Philistines were driven back with great slaughter, and rich booty was made of their cattle.

But soon the danger which David's men had apprehended seemed really at hand. When Saul heard that David had "shut himself in by coming into a town with gates and bars," it seemed to him almost as if judicial blindness had fallen upon him, or, as the king put it: "Elohim has rejected him into my hand." So thinking, Saul rapidly gathered a force to march against Keilah. But, as we learn from the course of this narrative, each side was kept well informed of the movements and plans of the other. Accordingly David knew his danger, and in his extremity once more appealed to the Lord. It was not a needless question which he put through the Urim and Thummim, but one which was connected with God's faithfulness and the truth of His promises.

With reverence be it said, God could not have given up David into the hands of Saul. Nor did his inquiries of God resemble those by heathen oracles. Their main element seems to have been prayer. In most earnest language David spread his case before the Lord, and entreated His direction. The answer was not withheld, although, significantly, each question had specially and by itself to be brought before the Lord (23:11, 12).

Thus informed of their danger, David and his men escaped from Keilah, henceforth to wander from one hiding-place to another. No other district could offer such facilities for eluding pursuit as that large tract, stretching along the territory of Judah, between the Dead Sea and the mountains of Judah. It bore the general designation of "the wilderness of Judah," but its various parts were distinguished as "the wilderness of Ziph," "of Maon," etc., from the names of neighboring towns. In general it may be said of this period of his wanderings (ver. 14), that during its course David's head-quarters were on "mountain heights," whence he could easily observe the approach of an enemy, while "Saul sought him every day," but in vain, since "God gave him not into his hand."

The first station in these wanderings was the "wilderness of Ziph," on the outskirts of the town of that name, about an hour and three-quarters to the south-east of Hebron. South of it a solitary mountain-top rises about one hundred feet, commanding a full prospect of the surrounding country. On the other hand, anything that passed there could also easily be observed from below. It seems that this was "the mountain" (ver. 14), or, as it is afterwards (ver. 19) more particularly described, "the hill of Hachilah, on the south of the wilderness," where David had his principal station, or rather, to be more accurate, in "the thicket," or "brushwood," which covered its sides (vers. 15, 16).

It was thither that in the very height of these first persecutions, Jonathan came once more to see his friend, and, as the sacred text emphatically puts it, "strengthened his hand in God." It is difficult to form an adequate conception of the courage, the spiritual faith, and the moral grandeur of this act. Never did man more completely clear himself from all complicity in guilt, than Jonathan from that of his father. And yet not an undutiful word escaped the lips of this brave man. And how truly human is his fond hope that in days to come, when David would be king, he should stand next to his throne, his trusted adviser, as in the days of sorrow he had been the true and steadfast friend of the outlaw! As we think of what it must have cost Jonathan to speak thus, or again of the sad fate which was so soon to overtake him, there is a deep pathos about this brief interview, almost unequaled in Holy Scripture, to which the ambitious hopes of the sons of Zebedee form not a parallel but a contrast.

But yet another bitter experience had David to make. As so often in the history of the Church, and never more markedly than in the case of Him Who was the great Antitype of David, it appeared that those who should most have rallied around him were his enemies and betrayers. The "citizens" of Keilah would have given him up from fear of Saul. But the men of Ziph went further.

Like those who hypocritically pretended that they would have no other king but Caesar, they feigned a loyalty for which it is impossible to give them credit. Of their own accord, and evidently from hatred of David, they who were his own tribesmen betrayed his hiding-place to Saul, and offered to assist in his capture. It is pitiable to hear Saul in the madness of his passion invoking on such men "the blessing of Jehovah," and characterizing their deed as one of "compassion" on himself (23:21). But the danger which now threatened David was greater than any previously or afterwards. On learning it he marched still further southeast, where "the Jeshimon," or desert, shelves down into the Arabah, or low table-land. Maon itself is about two hours south-east from Ziph; and amidst the mountains between Maon and the Dead Sea on the west, we must follow the track of David's further flight and adventures. But meantime the plan which Saul had suggested was being only too faithfully carried out. Slowly and surely the men of Saul, guided by the Ziphites, were reaching David, and drawing the net around him closer and closer. Informed of his danger, David hastily "came down the rock," — perhaps the round mountain-top near Maon. It was high time, for already Saul and his men had reached and occupied one side of it, while David and his men retreated to the other.

The object of the king now was to surround David, when he must have succumbed to superior numbers. We are told that "David was anxiously endeavoring to go away from before Saul; and Saul and his men were surrounding David and his men to seize them." Almost had they succeeded — but that "almost," which as so often in the history of God's people, calls out earnest faith and prayer, only proves the real impotence of this world's might as against the Lord. How David in this danger cried unto the Lord, we learn from Psalm 54.

How God "delivered him out of all trouble," appears from the sacred narrative. Once more all is in the natural succession of events; but surely it was in the wonder-working Providence of God that, just when David seemed in the power of his enemies, tidings of an incursion by the Philistines reached Saul, which obliged him hastily to turn against them. And ever afterwards, as David or others passed through that "wilderness," and looked up the face of that cliff, they would remember that God is "the Helper" of His people — for to all time it bore the name "Cliff of Escape." And so we also may in our wanderings have our "cliff of escape," to which ever afterwards we attach this precious remembrance, "Behold, God is thine Helper."

CHAPTER 13: SAUL IN DAVID'S POWER AT EN-GEDI — THE STORY OF NABAL — SAUL A SECOND TIME IN DAVID'S POWER.
(1 SAMUEL 24-26)

WHEN Saul once more turned upon his victim, David was no longer in the wilderness of Maon. Passing to the north-west, a march of six or seven hours would bring him to En-gedi, "the fountain of the goat," which, leaping down a considerable height in a thin cascade, converts that desert into the most lovely oasis. In this plain, or rather slope, about one mile and a half from north to south, at the foot of abrupt limestone mountains, sheltered from every storm, in climate the most glorious conceivable, the city of En-gedi had stood, or, as it used to be called, Hazazon Tamar (the Cutting of the Palm-trees), perhaps the oldest place in the world (2 Chronicles 20:2). Through this town (Genesis 14:7) the hordes of Chedorlaomer had passed; unchanged it had witnessed the destruction of Sodom and Gomorrah, which must have been clearly visible from the heights above, where the eye can sweep the whole district far up the Jordan valley, and across the Dead Sea to the mountains of Moab. Quite close to the waters of that sea, on which the doom of judgment has ever since rested, a scene of tropical beauty and wealth stretched, such as it is scarcely possible to describe. Bounded by two perennial streams, between which the En-gedi itself makes its way, it must of old have been a little paradise; the plain covered with palm-trees, the slopes up the mountains with the choicest vineyards of Judaea, scented with camphire (Solomon Song 1:14). But all above was "wilderness," bare round limestone hills rising from two hundred to four hundred feet, burrowed by numberless caves, to which the entrance is sometime almost inaccessible. These were "the rocks of the wild goats," and here was the cave — perhaps that of Wady Charitun, which is said to have once given shelter to no less than thirty thousand men — where David sought safety from the pursuit of the king of Israel.

Wild, weird scenery this, and it reads like a weird story, when the king of Israel enters alone one of those caverns, the very cave in the farthest recesses of which David and his men are hiding. Shall it be life or death? The goal is within easy reach! They have all seen Saul coming, and now whisper it to David with bated breath, to rid himself for ever of his persecutor. The mixture of religion and personal revenge — the presenting it as "the day of which Jehovah had spoken unto him," is entirely true to Oriental nature and to the circumstances. Who would let such an opportunity pass? But it is not by our own hands that we are to be freed from our wrongs, nor is every opportunity to attain our aims, whatever they be, God-sent. There is ever the prior question of plain duty, with which nothing else, however tempting or promising of success, can come into conflict; and such seasons may be only those when our faith and patience are put on trial, so as to bring it clearly before us, whether or not, quite irrespective of all else, we are content to leave everything in the hands of God. And David conquered, as long afterwards his great Antitype overcame the tempter, by steadfast adherence to God's known will and ordinance. Stealthily crawling along, he cut off a corner from the robe which the king had laid aside. That was all the vengeance he took. It was with some difficulty that David had restrained his men. And now the king had left the cave to rejoin his followers. But still David's conscience smote him, as if he had taken undue liberty with the Lord's anointed. Climbing one of those rocks outside the cave, whence flight would have been easy, his voice startled the king. Looking back into the wild solitude, Saul saw behind him the man who, as his disordered passion had suggested, was seeking his life. With humblest obeisance and in most dutiful language, David told what had just happened. In sharp contrast with the calumnies of his enemies, he described the king's danger, and how he had cast from him the suggestion of his murder. Then bursting into the impassioned language of loyal affection, which had been so cruelly wronged, he held up the piece of the king's mantle which he had cut off, as evidence of the fact that he was innocent of that of which he was accused. But if so — if he had refused to avenge himself even in the hour of his own great danger, leaving judgment to God, and unwilling to put forth his own hand to wickedness, since, as the common proverb had it, "wickedness proceedeth from the wicked" — then, what was the meaning of the king's humiliating pursuit after him? Rather would he, in the conscious innocence of his heart, now appeal to Jehovah, alike for judgment between them two, and for personal deliverance, should these persecutions continue.

Words like these, of which the truth was so evident, could not but make their way even to the heart of Saul. For a moment it seemed as if the dark clouds, which had gathered around his soul and prevented the light penetrating it, were to be scattered. Saul owned his wrong; he owned the justice of David's cause; he even owned the lesson which the events of the past must have so clearly taught, which, indeed, his own persecution of David had, all unconsciously to himself, prophetically indicated, just as did the words of Caiaphas the real meaning of what was done to Jesus (John 11:49-52). He owned the future of David, and that in his hand the kingdom of Israel would be established; and all this not in words only, but practically, by insisting on a sworn promise that in that future which he foresaw, Oriental vengeance would not be taken of his house.

And yet David himself was not secure against the temptation to personal vengeance and to self-help, although he had resisted it on this occasion. The lesson of his own weakness in that respect was all the more needed, that this was one of the most obvious moral dangers to an ordinary Oriental ruler. But David was not to be such; and when God in His good Providence restrained him as he had almost fallen, He showed him the need of inward as well as of outward deliverance, and the sufficiency of His grace to preserve him from spiritual as from temporal dangers. This may have been one reason why the history of Nabal and Abigail is preserved in Holy Scripture. Another we may find in the circumstance that this incident illustrates not only God's dealings with David, but also the fact that even in the time of his sorest persecutions David was able to take upon himself the care and protection of his countrymen, and so, in a certain sense, proved their leader and king.

The whole story is so true to all the surroundings of place, time, and people, that we can almost portray it to ourselves. Samuel had died, mourned by all Israel. Although his work had long been finished, his name must always have been a tower of strength. He was the link which connected two very different periods, being the last representative of a past which could never come back, and seemed almost centuries behind, and also marking the commencement of a new period, intended to develop into Israel's ideal future. Samuel was, so to speak, the John the Baptist who embodied the old, and initiated the new by preaching repentance as its preparation and foundation. It was probably the death of Samuel which determined David to withdraw still farther south, to the wilderness of Paran, which stretched from the mountains of Judah far to the desert of Sinai.

Similarly our blessed Lord withdrew Himself after the death of John the Baptist. In the wilderness of Paran David was not only safe from pursuit, but able to be of real service to his countrymen by protecting the large flocks which pastured far and wide from the predatory raids of the wild tribes of the desert. It was thus (25:7, 15, 16) that David had come into contact with one whom we only know by what was apparently his by-name, Nabal, "fool" -an ominous designation in Old Testament parlance, where "the fool" represented the headstrong, self-willed person, who followed his own course, as if there were "no God" alike in heaven and on earth. And so he is described as "hard" — stubborn, stiff, — and "evil of doings" (ver. 3). His wife Abigail was the very opposite: "good of understanding, and fair of form." Nabal, as Scripture significantly always calls him was a descendant of Caleb. His residence was in Maon, while his "business" was in Carmel, a place about half an hour to the north-west of Maon. Here, no doubt, were his large cotes and folds, whence his immense flocks of sheep and goats pastured the land far and wide. It was the most joyous time for such a proprietor — that of sheep-shearing, when every heart would be open. A time of festivity this (ver. 36), which each would keep according to what was in him. And Nabal had cause for gladness. Thanks to the ever watchful care of David and his men, he had not suffered the slightest loss (vers. 15, 16); and the rich increase of his flocks crowned another year's prosperity. It was quite in the spirit of an Eastern chieftain in such circumstances, that David sent what would be a specially respectful embassy of ten of his men, with a cordial message of congratulation, in the expectation that at such a time some acknowledgment would be made to those who not only deserved, but must have sorely needed the assistance of a rich Judaean proprietor.

But Nabal received David's message with language the most insulting to an Oriental. The provocation was great, and David was not proof against it. Arming about four hundred of his men, he set out for Carmel, with the determination to right himself and take signal vengeance. Assuredly this was not the lesson which God had hitherto made David learn, nor that which He wished His anointed to teach to others. It was the zeal of the sons of Boanerges, not the meekness of Him Who was David's great Antitype. And so God kept His servant from presumptuous sin. Once more God's interposition came in the natural course of events. A servant who had overheard what had passed, and naturally dreaded the consequences, informed Abigail. Her own resolve was quickly taken.

Sending forward a present princely in amount, even in comparison with that which at a later period Barzillai brought to King David when on his flight from Absalom (2 Samuel 17:27-29), she hastily followed.

Coming down the hollow of a hill ("the covert of a hill"), she found herself of a sudden in the presence of David and his armed men. But her courage was not shaken. With humblest Oriental obeisance, she addressed David, first taking all the guilt on herself, as one on whom David would not stoop to wreak vengeance. Surely one like Nabal was not a fit object for controversy; and, as for herself, she had known nothing of what had passed.

But there were far weightier arguments for David's forbearance. Was it not evidently God's Providence which had sent her for a high and holy purpose? "And now, my lord, as Jehovah liveth, and as thy soul liveth, that (it is) Jehovah who has withheld thee from coming into blood-guiltiness, and from thy hand delivering thyself." This twofold sin had been averted. Such was her first argument. But further, was it not well to leave it to God — would not Jehovah Himself avenge His servant, and make all his enemies as Nabal — showing them to be but "Nabal," "fools" in the Scriptural sense, with all the impotence and ruin which this implied? It was only after having urged all this, that Abigail ventured to ask acceptance of her gift, offering it, as if unworthy of him, to David's men rather than to himself (ver. 27). Then returning to the prayer for forgiveness, she pointed David to the bright future which, she felt assured, was reserved for him, since he was not pursuing private aims, nor would he afterwards charge himself with any wrong in this matter. How closely all this tallied with her former pleas will be evident. In pursuance of her reasoning she continued: "And (though) a man is risen to pursue thee, and to seek thy soul, and (yet) the soul of my lord is bound up in the bundle of life with Jehovah thy God; and the soul of thine enemies shall He sling out from the hollow of the sling." Finally, she reminded him that when God had fulfilled all His gracious promises, this would not become a "stumbling-block" to him, nor yet be a burden on his conscience, that he had needlessly shed blood and righted himself.

Wiser speech, in the highest as well as in a worldly sense, than that of Abigail can scarcely be imagined. Surely if any one, she was fitted to become the companion and adviser of David. Three things in her speech chiefly impress themselves on our minds as most important for the understanding of this history. The fact that David was God's anointed, on whom the kingdom would devolve, seems now to have been the conviction of all who were godly in Israel. They knew it, and they expected it. Equally strong was their belief that David's present, as his future mission, was simply to contend for God and for His people. But most important of all was the deep feeling prevalent, that David must not try to right himself, nor work his own deliverance. This was a thoroughly spiritual principle, which had its foundation in absolute, almost childlike trust in Jehovah the living God, whatever might were arrayed against David, and however the probabilities might seem other to the outward observer. Viewed in this light, the whole contest between David and Saul would assume spiritual proportions. There was nothing personal now in the conflict; least of all, was it to be regarded as an attempt at rebellion against, or dethronement of Saul. The cause was altogether God's; only David must not right himself, but in faith and patience await the fulfillment of God's sure and steadfast promises. To have the matter thus set before him, was to secure the immediate assent of David's conscience. Recognizing the great spiritual danger from which he had just been delivered, he gave thanks to God, and then to the wise and pious woman who had been the instrument in His hand.

Meantime Nabal had been in ignorance alike of what had threatened him, and of what his wife had done to avert it. On her return, she found him rioting and in drunkenness. Not till next morning, when he was once more capable of understanding what had passed, did she inform him of all. A fit of impotent fury on the part of one who was scarcely sobered, resulted in what seems to have been a stroke of apoplexy. If this had been brought on by himself, the second and fatal stroke, which followed ten days later, is set before us as sent directly by God. It is not often that Divine vengeance so manifestly and so quickly overtakes evil-doing. David fully recognized this. Nor can we wonder, that on reviewing his own deliverance from spiritual danger, and the advice which had led to it, he should have wished to have her who had given it always by his side. In connection with this the sacred text also notes the union of David with Ahinoam of Jezreel, consequent probably on Saul's cruel and heartless separation between David and Michal, whom he gave to one Phalti, or Phaltiel (2 Samuel 3:15) of Gallim in Benjamin (Isaiah 10:30). Thus Saul himself had willfully and recklessly severed the last ties which had bound David to him.

Yet another bitter experience of betrayal and persecution was in store for David. Probably trusting to his new connection with two, no doubt, powerful families in the district — those of Ahinoam and of Abigail — David seems again to have advanced northwards from the wilderness of Paran. Once more we find David in the wilderness of Ziph — the most northern and the nearest to the cities of Judah. And once more the Ziphites were negotiating with Saul for his betrayal, and the king of Israel was marching against him with the three thousand men, who apparently formed the nucleus of his standing army.

Some years before, when betrayed by the Ziphites, David had on the approach of Saul retired to the wilderness of Maon, and been only preserved by tidings to Saul of a Philistine incursion. On yet another somewhat similar occasion, in the wilderness of En-gedi, David had had his enemy in his power, when Saul had entered alone a cave in which David and his men lay concealed. In this instance, however, the circumstances were different, alike as concerned the situation of Saul's camp, the location of David, the manner in which he came into contact with Saul, and even the communication which subsequently passed between them. The points of resemblance are just those which might have been expected: the treachery of the Ziphites, the means taken by Saul against David, the suggestion made to David to rid himself of his enemy, his firm resolve not to touch the Lord's anointed, as well as an interview between David and his persecutor, followed by temporary repentance. But the two narratives are essentially different. On learning that Saul and his army were encamped on the slope of the hill Hachilah, David and two of his bravest companions — Ahimelech, the Hittite, and Abishai, the son of Zeruiah, David's sister — resolved to ascertain the exact situation of the enemy. Creeping under cover of night through the brushwood, which as we know covered the sides of the hill (23:19), they found themselves soon where the camp of Israel lay open to them. As we imagine the scene, the three had gained the height just above the camp. Faithful as was the Hittite, and none more true or brave than he (comp. 2 Samuel 11:3, 6; 23:39), it was David's nephew Abishai, probably of the same age, who now volunteered to share with him the extremely perilous attempt of "going down" into the camp itself. But there was no murderous intent in the heart of David; rather the opposite, of proving his innocence of it. And so God blessed it. A deep sleep — evidently from the Lord — weighed them all down. In the middle, by the "waggons" of the camp, lay Saul, at his head the royal spear stuck in the ground, and a cruse of water beside him. Close by lay Abner, as chief of the host, to whom, so to speak, the custody of the king was entrusted — and all round in wide circle, the people. Once more comes the tempting suggestion to David. This time it is not his own hand, but Abishai's, that is to deal the blow. But what matters it: "For who has stretched out his hand against the anointed of Jehovah, and been unpunished? If Jehovah do not (literally, 'unless Jehovah') smite him [like Nabal], or his day be come and he die, or he go down into the war and be swept away — far be it from me, through Jehovah! — to stretch forth mine hand against Jehovah's anointed." And so David stayed the hand of his companion.

Noiselessly the two have removed the royal spear and the cruse from the side of Saul. They have crept back through the camp of sleepers, and through the brushwood, crossed the intervening valley, and gained a far-off height on the other side. Who dares break the king's slumber in the middle of his camp? But another ear than Abner's has heard, and has recognized the voice of David. It has gone right to the heart of Saul, as he learns how once more his life had been wholly in the power of him whom he has so unrelenting and so wickedly persecuted. Again he seems repentant, though he heeds not David's advice that, if these constant persecutions were the effect produced on his mind by the spirit of evil from the Lord, he should seek pardon and help by means of sacrifice; but if the outcome of calumnious reports, those who brought them should be regarded as sure of the Divine judgment, since, as he put it, "They drive me out this day, that I cannot join myself to the heritage of Jehovah, saying (thereby in effect): Go, serve other gods" (26:19). It is useless to follow the matter farther. Saul's proposal for David's return, and his promise of safety, were, no doubt, honestly meant at the time, just as are the sorrow and resolutions of many into whose consciences the light has for a time fallen. But David knew otherwise of Saul; and it marks an advance in his spiritual experience that he preferred committing himself to God rather than trusting in man.

CHAPTER 14: DAVID'S SECOND FLIGHT TO GATH — RESIDENCE AT ZIKLAG — EXPEDITION OF THE PHILISTINES AGAINST ISRAEL — SAUL AT JEZREEL — HE RESORTS TO THE WITCH AT ENDOR — APPARITION AND MESSAGE OF SAMUEL — DAVID HAS TO LEAVE THE ARMY OF THE PHILISTINES — CAPTURE OF ZIKLAG BY THE AMALEKITES — PURSUIT AND VICTORY OF DAVID.

(1 SAMUEL 27-30)

THE parting appeal of David sounds specially solemn when we remember that this was the last meeting of these two. Feeling that some day he might "fall into the hand of Saul," and that henceforth there was "no good for him," he resolved once more to seek shelter with King Achish at Gath.

His reception this time was very different from that on the former occasion. For years David had been treated by Saul as his avowed enemy. He came now not as a solitary fugitive, but at the head of a well-trained band of brave men, to place himself and them, as it would seem, at the disposal of Achish. He met a most friendly welcome, and for a time was located with his men in the royal city itself. This, of course, entailed restraints such as would have proved most irksome, if not impossible, to David. The pretext that the presence of such a large band under their own chieftain was scarcely becoming in the capital of his new royal master, furnished the plea for asking and obtaining another place of residence. For this purpose Ziklag was assigned to him — a city first belonging to Judah (Joshua 15:31), and afterwards to Simeon (Joshua 19:5), which lay close to the southern border of the land of Israel. Of course, the inference is fair that, at the time of which we write, it had been in the possession of the Philistines, and was probably deserted by its former inhabitants. No other place could have suited David so well. Whether we regard his raids against the heathen tribes, which was "his manner" during the whole year and four months that he was with the Philistines, as intended to repel their inroads into the territory of Israel, or else as incursions into heathen lands, the situation of Ziklag would afford him equal facilities. On every such occasion, as he returned laden with spoil, he took care to report himself at Gath, partly to disarm suspicion, and partly, no doubt, to secure the good will of Achish by giving him a large share of the booty. His reports may have been true to the letter — giving it a forced meaning, — but they were certainly untrue in spirit. But David never brought captives with him to Gath, who might have betrayed him, but always destroyed all who had witnessed his attacks.

If by means of these reported frequent successes in the land of Israel David secured the confidence of Achish, as one who had irretrievably broken with his own people, and if by the rich booty which he brought he besides obtained the favor of the Philistine, he was once more to experience that real safety was not to be gained by untruthfulness. Again there was to be war between the Philistines and Israel, this time on a larger scale than any since the first contest with Saul. It was but natural that Achish should have wished to swell his contingent to the army of the united Philistine princes by so large, well-trained, and, as he believed, trusty band as that of David. Of course, there was no alternative but to obey such a summons, although it must be admitted that the words of David, both on this occasion

(28:2), and afterwards, when dismissed the camp of the Philistines (29:8), are capable of two interpretations. Achish, however, took them in what seemed their obvious meaning, and promised in return ("therefore" — for that) to make David the chief of his body-guard. It need scarcely be told, what terrible anxieties this unexpected turn of events must have brought to David, or how earnestly he must have prayed and trusted that, at the right moment, some "way of escape" would be made for him.

The sacred narrative now carries us successively to the camp of Israel and to that of the Philistines. The battlefield was to be once more the Plain of Jezreel, where of old Gideon with his three hundred had defeated the hosts of Midian (Judges 7). A spot this full of happy, glorious memories; but, ah, how sadly altered were the circumstances! Gideon had been the God-called hero, who was to conquer in His might; Saul was the God-forsaken king, who was hastening to judgment and ruin. And each knew and felt it — Gideon when he was content to reduce his forces to three hundred men, and then crept down with his armor-bearer to hear the enemy foretell his own destruction; and Saul when viewing the host of the Philistines across the plain, "he was afraid, and his heart greatly trembled" (28:5), and when all his inquiries of the Lord remained without answer. It seems strange, and yet, as we think, it is most truthfully characteristic of Saul, that, probably after the death of Samuel, he displayed special theocratic zeal by a systematic raid upon all necromancy in the land, in accordance with Leviticus 19:31; 20:27; Deuteronomy 18:10, etc. Such outward conformity to the law of God, not only from political motives, but from those of such religiousness as he was capable of, seems to us one of the most striking psychological confirmations of the history of Saul.

The reason why the scene of battle was laid so far north, distant alike from the cities of the Philistine princes and from the residence of Saul, was, in all probability, that the Philistines now wished to obtain such undoubted supremacy in the north of Palestine as they seem to have virtually possessed in the south. A great victory in Jezreel would not only cut the land, so to speak, in two, but give them the key both to the south and to the north. With this view, then, the Philistines chose their ground. Where the great plain of Esdraelon shelves down to the Jordan it is broken in the east by two mountain-ranges. On the southern side of the valley, which is here about three miles wide, are the mountains of Gilboa, and at their foot, or rather spur, lies Jezreel, where the spring which gushes down is gathered into a pool of considerable size. On the northern side of the valley is Little Hermon, and at its foot the rich village of Shunem (the "twain rest"). Behind and to the north of Little Hermon runs another narrow branch of the plain. On its other side is the mountain where Endor lay amidst most desolate scenery; and in one of its many limestone caves was the scene of Saul's last interview with Samuel. Nor is it void of significance to us that Endor was but a few miles from Nazareth; for it is the close contiguity of these contrasting scenes which often sheds such lurid light upon events.

From his camp on the slopes of Gilboa and by the spring of Jezreel, Saul had anxiously watched the gathering hosts of Philistia on the opposite side at Shunem, and his heart had utterly failed him. Where was now the Lord God of Israel? Certainly not with Saul. And where was there now a David to meet another Goliath? Saul had successively "inquired of Jehovah" by all the well-known means, from the less to the more spiritual, but without answer. That alone should have been sufficient, had Saul possessed spiritual understanding to perceive its meaning. Had his been real inquiry of the Lord, he would have felt his desertion, and even now returned to Him in humble penitence; just as Judas, if his repentance had been genuine and true, would have gone out to seek pardon like Peter, instead of rushing in despair to self-destruction.

As the event proved, Saul did not really inquire of the Lord, in the sense of seeking direction from Him, and of being willing to be guided by it. Rather did he, if we may so express it, wish to use the Lord as the means by which to obtain his object. But that was essentially the heathen view, and differed only in detail, not in principle, from the inquiry of a familiar spirit, to which he afterwards resorted. Accordingly the latter must be regarded as explaining his former "inquiry," and determining its character. In this sense the notice in 1 Chronicles 10:14 affords a true and spiritual insight into the transaction. Already the utter darkness of despair had gathered around Saul. He was condemned: he knew it, felt it, and his conscience assented to it. What was to happen on the morrow? To that question he must have an answer, be it what it may. If he could not have it from God, he must get it somewhere else. To whom should he turn in his extremity? Only one person, sufficiently powerful with God and man, occurred to his mind. It was Samuel, — the very incarnation to him of Divine power, the undoubted messenger of God, the one man who had ever confronted and overawed him. It seems like fate which drives him to the very man who had so sternly, unrelentingly, and in the hour of his triumph, told him his downfall. But how was he to meet Samuel? By necromancy — that is, by devilry! The Divine through the anti-Divine, communication from on high by means of witchcraft: terrible contrasts these — combined, alas! in the life of Saul, and strangely connecting its beginning with its ending. But no matter; if it be at all possible, he must see Samuel, however he had parted from him in life. Samuel had announced his elevation, let him now come to tell him his fate; he had pushed him to the brow of the hill, let him show what was beneath. And yet who could say what might happen, or to what that interview might lead? For deep down in the breast of each living there is still, even in his despairing, the possibility of hope.

It is the most vivid description in Holy Scripture, next to that of the night of Judas' betrayal. Putting on the disguise of a common man, and only attended by two companions, Saul starts at dark. It was eight miles round the eastern shoulder of Hermon to Endor. None in the camp of Israel must know whither and on what errand the king has gone; and he has to creep round the back of the position of the Philistines, who lie on the front slope of Hermon. Nor must "the woman, possessor of an Ob" — or spirit by which the dead can be conjured up (Leviticus 20:27) — know it, that he who inquires of her is the one who "hath cut off those that have familiar spirits and the wizards out of the land."

It was night when Saul and his companions wearily reached their destination. They have roused the wretched impostor, "the woman, possessor of an Ob," and quieted her fears by promise that her nefarious business should not be betrayed. To her utter horror it is for once truth. God has allowed Samuel to obey Saul's summons; and, to be unmistakable, he appears, as he was wont in life, wrapped in his prophet's meil, or mantle. The woman sees the apparition, and from her description Saul has no difficulty in recognizing Samuel, and he falls in lowly reverence on his face.

During the whole interview between them the king remains on his knees. What a difference between the last meeting of the two and this! But the old prophet has nothing to abate, nothing to alter. There is inexpressible pathos in the king's cry of despair: "Make known to me what I shall do!" What he shall do! But Samuel had all his life-time made it known to him, and Saul had resisted. The time for doing was now past. In quick succession it comes, like thunderbolt on thunderbolt: "Jehovah thine enemy"; "Jehovah hath rent the kingdom out of thine hand, and given it to David"; "thy sins have overtaken thee!" All this

Saul knew long ago, although he had never realized it as now. And then as to his fate: to-morrow — defeat, death, slaughter, to Saul, to his sons, to Israel!

One by one, each stroke heavier than the other, they had pitilessly fallen on the kneeling king, weary, faint from want of food, and smitten to the heart with awe and terror; and now he falls heavily, his gigantic length, to the ground. The woman and Saul's companions had stood aside, nor had any heard what had passed between the two. But the noise of his fall brought them to his side. With difficulty they persuade him to eat ere he starts on his weary return to Jezreel. At last he yields; and, rising from his prostrate position, sits down on the divan, while they wait on him. But he has no longer speech, or purpose, or thought. As one driven to the slaughter, he goes back to meet his doom. It must have been early morning when once more he reached Gilboa — the morning of the dread and decisive battle.

The sacred narrative now turns once more to the Philistine host. The trysting-place for the contingents of the five allied "lords" or kings of the Philistines was at Aphek, probably the same as on a previous occasion (1 Samuel 4:1).

As they marched past, the division of Achish formed "the rear-ward." When the Philistine leaders saw David and his men amongst them, they not unnaturally objected to their presence. In vain Achish urged their faithfulness since they had "fallen away" to him. As it appeared to them, one who had in the past taken such a stand as David could never be trusted; and how better could he make his peace with his master than by turning traitor to the Philistines in the hour of their supreme need? And so, however reluctantly, Achish had to yield. David's remonstrance, couched in ambiguous language, was perhaps scarcely such (1 Samuel 29:8), but rather intended to make sure of the real views of Achish in regard to him. But it must have been with the intense relief of a realized God-given deliverance, that early next morning, ere the camp was astir, David and his men quitted its outskirts, where the rear-guard lay, to return to Ziklag.

It was the third day when the Hebrews reached their Philistine home. But what a sight greeted them here! Broken walls, blackened ruins, and the desolateness of utter silence all around! The Amalekites had indeed taken vengeance for David's repeated raids upon them (27:8). They had made an incursion into the Negeb, or south country, and specially upon Ziklag. In the absence of its defenders, the place fell an easy prey. After laying it waste, the Amalekites took with them all the women and children, as well as the cattle, and any other booty on which they could lay hands. It was a terrible surprise, and the first effect upon David and his men was truly Oriental (30:4). But it is both characteristic of David's followers, and indicates with what reluctance they must have followed him to Aphek, that they actually thought of killing David, as if he had been the author of that ill-fated expedition after Achish which had brought them such hopeless misery. It was bitter enough to have lost his own family, and now David was in danger of his life from the mutiny of his men. Had God spared him for this? On the very morning when they had broken up from Aphek, making almost forced marches to traverse the fifty miles to Ziklag, their homes had been utterly laid waste. Why all this? Did the Lord make him tarry, as Jesus did "beyond Jordan," till Lazarus had been three days dead? Never more than on occasion of extreme and seemingly hopeless straits did David prove the reality of his religion by rising to the loftiest heights of faith and prayer. The text gives a marked emphasis to the contrast: "But David strengthened himself in Jehovah his God." His resolve was quickly taken. The first thing was to inquire of the Lord whether he should pursue the Amalekites. The answer was even fuller than he had asked, for it promised him also complete success. The next thing was hasty pursuit of the enemy. So rapid was it, that when they reached the brook Besor, which flows into the sea to the south of Gaza, two hundred of his men, who, considering the state in which they had found Ziklag, must have been but ill-provisioned, had to be left behind.

They soon came on the track of the Amalekites. They had found an Egyptian slave, whom his inhuman master had, on the hasty retreat from Ziklag, left by the wayside to starve rather than hamper himself with the care of a sick man. Food soon revived him; and, on promise of safety and freedom, he offered to be the guide of the party to the place which, as he knew, the Amalekites had fixed upon as sufficiently far from Ziklag to permit them to feast in safety on their booty. A short-lived security theirs. It was the twilight — the beginning, no doubt, of a night of orgies — when David surprised them, "lying about on the ground," "eating and drinking, and dancing." No watch had been set; no weapon was in any man's hands; no danger was apprehended. We can picture to ourselves the scene: how David probably surrounded the camping-place; and with what shouts of vengeance the infuriated Hebrews fell on those who could neither resist nor flee. All night long, all the next day the carnage lasted. Only four hundred servant-lads, who had charge of the camels, escaped. Everything that had been taken by the Amalekites was recovered, besides the flocks and herds of the enemy, which were given to David as his share of the spoil. Best of all, the women and children were safe and unhurt.

It was characteristic of the wicked and worthless among the followers of David, that when on their return march they came again to those two hundred men who had been left behind "faint," they proposed not to restore to them what of theirs had been recovered from the Amalekites, except their wives and children. Rough, wild men were many among them, equally depressed in the day of adversity, and recklessly elated and insolent in prosperity. Nor is it merely the discipline which David knew to maintain in such a band that shows us "the skillfulness of his hands" in guiding them, but the gentleness with which be dealt with them, and, above all, the earnest piety with which he knew to tame their wild passions prove the spiritual "integrity," or "perfectness, of his heart" (Psalm 78:72). Many a wholesome custom, which ever afterwards prevailed in Israel, as well as that of equally dividing the spoil among combatants and non-combatants in an army (1 Samuel 30:24, 25), must have dated not only from the time of David, but even from the period of his wanderings and persecutions. Thus did he prove his fitness for the government long ere he attained to it.

Yet another kindred trait was David's attachment to friends who had stood by him in seasons of distress. As among his later servants and officials we find names connected with the history of his wanderings (1 Chronicles 27:27-31), so even now he sent presents from his spoil to "the elders" of the various cities of the South, where his wanderings had been, and who had proved "his friends" by giving him help in the time of need.

It may indeed have been that the south generally had suffered from the incursion of the Amalekites against Ziklag (30:1). But such loss could scarcely have been made up by "presents" from David. His main object, next to grateful acknowledgment of past aid, must have been to prepare them for publicly owning him, at the proper time, as the chosen leader of God's people, who would make "spoil of the enemies of Jehovah." At the proper time! But while these gifts were passing, all unknown to David, that time had already come.

CHAPTER 15: THE BATTLE ON MOUNT GILBOA — DEATH OF SAUL — RESCUE OF THE BODIES BY THE MEN OF JABESH-GILEAD — DAVID PUNISHES THE FALSE MESSENGER OF SAUL'S DEATH — DAVID KING AT HEBRON — ISH-BOSHETH KING AT MAHANAIM — BATTLE BETWEEN THE FORCES OF ABNER AND JOAB — ABNER DESERTS THE CAUSE OF ISH-BOSHETH — MURDER OF ABNER — MURDER OF ISH-BOSHETH.

(1 SAMUEL 31-2 SAMUEL 4)

BRIEF as are the accounts of the battle of Gilboa (1 Samuel 31; 1 Chronicles 10), we can almost picture the scene. The attack seems to have been made by the Philistines. Slowly and stubbornly the Israelites yielded, and fell back from Jezreel upon Mount Gilboa. All day long the fight lasted; and the darkness seems to have come on before the Philistines knew the full extent of their success, or could get to the sad work of pillaging the dead. Ill had it fared with Israel that day. Their slain covered the sides of Mount Gilboa. The three sons of Saul — foremost among them the noble Jonathan — had fallen in the combat. Saul himself had retreated on Gilboa. But the battle had gone sore against him. And now the enemy's sharpshooters had "found him" — come up with him. Thus the fatal moment had arrived: "Saul was sore afraid." But if he fell, let it at least not be by the hand of the Philistines, lest Israel's hereditary enemy "make sport" of the disabled, dying king.

Saul will die a king. The last service he asks of his armor-bearer is to save him from falling into Philistine hands by thrusting him through. But the armor-bearer dares not lift his sword against the Lord's anointed, and Saul plants his now otherwise useless sword on the ground, and throws himself upon it. The faithful armor-bearer follows his master's example. Soon all Saul's personal attendants have likewise been cut down (1 Samuel 31:6; comp. 1 Chronicles 10:6).

And now darkness stayed further deeds of blood. Before the morning light the tidings of Israel's defeat had spread far and wide. North of the valley of Jezreel, and even across the Jordan, which rolled close by, the people deserted the cities and fled into the open country, leaving their strongholds to the conquerors.

Meantime the plunderers were busy searching and stripping the dead in Jezreel and on Mount Gilboa. They found what they could scarcely have expected: the dead bodies of Saul and of his three sons. To strip them would have been comparatively little; but to add every insult, they cut off the heads of the king and of his sons, leaving the naked carcasses unburied. The gory heads and the bloody armor were sent round through Philistia, "to publish it in the houses of their idols, and among the people." Finally, the armor was distributed among the temples of the Ashtaroth (the Phoenician Venus), while the skull of Saul was fastened up in the great temple of Dagon.

But the Philistine host had not halted. They advanced to occupy the towns deserted by the Hebrews. The main body occupied Bethshan, the great mountain-fortress of Central Palestine, which from the top of a steep brow, inaccessible to horsemen, seemed to command not only the Jordan valley, but also all the country round. As if in utter scorn and defiance, they hung out on the walls of Bethshan the headless trunks of Saul and of his sons. And now night with her dark mantle once more covered these horrible trophies. Shall the eagles and vultures complete the work which, no doubt, they had already begun? The tidings had been carried across the Jordan, and wakened echoes in one of Israel's cities. It was to Jabesh-gilead that Saul, when only named but not yet acknowledged king, had by a forced night-march brought help, delivering it from utter destruction (1 Samuel 11). That had been the morning of Saul's life, bright and promising as none other; his first glorious victory, which had made him king by acclamation, and drawn Israel's thousands to that gathering in Gilgal, when, amidst the jubilee of an exultant people, the new kingdom was inaugurated. And now it was night; and the headless bodies of Saul and his sons, deserted by all, swung in the wind on the walls of Bethshan, amid the hoarse music of vultures and jackals.

But it must not be so; it cannot be so. There was still truth, gratitude, and courage in Israel. And the brave men of Jabesh-gilead marched all the weary night; they crossed Jordan; they climbed that steep brow, and silently detached the dead bodies from the walls. Reverently they bore them across the river, and ere the morning light were far out of reach of the Philistines. Though it had always been the custom in Israel to bury the dead, they would not do so to these mangled remains, that they might not, as it were, perpetuate their disgrace. They burned them just sufficiently to destroy all traces of insult, and the bones they reverently laid under their great tamarisk tree, themselves fasting for seven days in token of public mourning. All honor to the brave men of Jabesh-gilead, whose deed Holy Scripture has preserved to all generations!

It was the third day after the return of David and his men to Ziklag. Every heart must have been heavy with anxiety for tidings of that great decisive struggle between the Philistines and Saul which they knew to be going on, when all at once a messenger came, whose very appearance betokened disaster and mourning (comp. 1 Samuel 4:12). It was a stranger, the son of an Amalekite settler in Israel, who brought sad and strange tidings. By his own account, he had fled to Ziklag straight out of the camp of Israel, to tell of the defeat and slaughter of Israel, and of the death of Saul and of Jonathan. As he related the story, he had, when the tide of battle turned against Israel, come by accident upon Saul, who stood alone on the slope of Gilboa leaning upon his spear, while the Philistine chariots and horsemen were closing in around him. On perceiving him, and learning that he was an Amalekite, the king had said, "Stand now to me and slay me, for cramp has seized upon me for my life is yet wholly in me." On this the Amalekite had "stood to" him, and killed him, "for" — as he added in explanation, probably referring to the illness which from fear and grief had seized Saul, forcing him to lean for support on his spear — "I knew that he would not live after he had fallen; and I took the crown that was on his head, and the arm-band which was upon his arm, and I brought them to my lord — here!"

Improbable as the story would have appeared on calm examination, and utterly untrue as we know it to have been, David's indignant and horrified expostulation, how he had dared to destroy Jehovah's anointed (2 Samuel 1:14), proves that in the excitement of the moment he had regarded the account as substantially correct. The man had testified against himself: he held in his hand as evidence the king's crown and arm-band. If he had not murdered Saul, he had certainly stripped him when dead. And now he had come to David, evidently thinking he had done a deed grateful to him, for which he would receive reward, thus making David a partaker in his horrible crime. David's inmost soul recoiled from such a deed as murder of his sovereign and daring presumption against Jehovah, Whose anointed he was. Again and again, when defending precious life, Saul had been in his power, and he had rejected with the strongest energy of which he was capable the suggestion to ensure his own safety by the death of his persecutor. And that from which in the hour of his supreme danger he had recoiled, this Amalekite had now done in cold blood for hope of a reward! Every feeling would rise within him to punish the deed; and if he failed or hesitated, well might he be charged before all Israel with being an accomplice of the Amalekite. "Thy blood on thy head! for thy mouth hath testified upon thyself, saying, I have slain the anointed of Jehovah." And the sentence thus spoken was immediately executed.

It was real and sincere grief which led David and his men to mourn, and weep, and fast until even for Saul and for Jonathan, and for their fallen countrymen in their twofold capacity as belonging to the Church and the nation ("the people of Jehovah and the house of Israel," ver. 12). One of the finest odes in the Old Testament perpetuated their memory. This elegy, composed by David "to teach the children of Israel," bears the general title of Kasheth, as so many of the Psalms have kindred inscriptions. In our text it appears as extracted from that collection of sacred heroic poetry, called Sepher hajjashar, "book of the just." It consists, after a general superscription, of two unequal stanzas, each beginning with the line: "Alas, the heroes have fallen!" The second stanza refers specially to Jonathan, and at the close of the ode the head-line is repeated, with an addition, indicating Israel's great loss. The two stanzas mark, so to speak, a descent from deepest grief for those so brave, so closely connected, and so honored, to expression of personal feelings for Jonathan, the closing lines sounding like the last sigh over a loss too great for utterance. Peculiarly touching is the absence in this elegy of even the faintest allusion to David's painful relations to Saul in the past. All that is merely personal seems blotted out, or rather, as if it had never existed in the heart of David. In this respect we ought to regard this ode as casting most valuable light on the real meaning and character of what are sometimes called the vindictive and imprecatory Psalms. Nor should we omit to notice, what a German divine has so aptly pointed out: that, with the exception of the lament of Jabesh-gilead, the only real mourning for Saul was on the part of David, whom the king had so bitterly persecuted to the death — reminding us in this also of David's great Antitype, Who alone of all wept over that Jerusalem which was preparing to betray and crucify Him! The elegy itself reads as follows:

"The adornment of Israel on thy heights thrust through! Alas, the heroes have fallen! Announce it not in Gath, publish it not as glad tidings in the streets of Askelon, Lest the daughters of the Philistines rejoice, Lest the daughters of the uncircumcised jubilee! O mountains in Gilboa — no dew, nor rain upon you, nor fields of first-fruit offerings — For there defiled is the shield of the heroes, The shield of Saul, no more anointed with oil! From blood of slain, from fat of heroes The bow of Jonathan turned not backward, And the sword of Saul returned not void (lacking)! Saul and Jonathan, the loved and the pleasant, In their life and in their death were not parted — Than eagles were they lighter, than lions stronger! Daughters of Israel, over Saul weep ye, Who clad you in purple with loveliness, Who put jewels of gold upon your clothing! Alas, the heroes have fallen in the midst of the contest — Jonathan, on thy heights thrust through! Woe is me for thee, my brother Jonathan, — Pleasant wast thou to me exceedingly, More marvelous thy love to me than the love of women! Alas, the heroes have fallen — And perished are the weapons of war!" (2 Samuel 1:19-27.)

But the present was not a time for mourning only. So far as men could judge, there was no further necessity for David's exile. But even so he would not act without express Divine guidance. In answer to his inquiry by the Urim and Thummim he was directed to take up his residence in Hebron, where he was soon anointed king by his own tribe of Judah. As yet, however, and for the next seven and a half years, his rule only extended over that tribe. It is further evidence of the entire submission of David to the leading of Jehovah, and of his having fully learned the lesson of not seeking to compass his own "deliverance," that he took no steps to oppose the enthronement of Saul's son, however contrary this was to the Divine appointment; and that the contest which ultimately ensued originated not with David, but with his rival. On the contrary, David's first act as king of Judah was to send an embassy to Jabesh-gilead to express his admiration of their noble loyalty to Saul.

Nor does it detract from this mark of his generosity that, now their master was dead, he intimated his own elevation, to bespeak, if possible, their allegiance. The support of such men was well worth seeking. Besides, Jabesh-gilead was the capital of the whole of that district; and already the standard had there been set up of a rival, whose claims were neither founded on the appointment of God, nor on the choice of the people.

As we infer from the sacred narrative, there had been among the fugitives from the battle of Gilboa a son of Saul — whether the youngest or not must remain undetermined.

From the language of the text (2 Samuel 2:8), as well as from his subsequent history, he seems to have been a weak character — a puppet in the hands of Abner, Saul's uncle, whom that ambitious and unscrupulous soldier used for his own purposes. His original name, Esh-Baal, "fire of Baal" (1 Chronicles 8:33; 9:39), became in popular designation Ish-Bosheth, "man of shame," — Baal and Bosheth being frequently interchanged according to the state of popular religion (Judges 6:32; Jeremiah 11:13; Hosea 9:10). Even this may be regarded as indicating the popular estimate of the man. Immediately after the battle of Gilboa, Abner had taken him across the Jordan to Mahanaim, "the twain camp," where probably the broken remnants of Saul's army also gathered. The place was well chosen, not only from the historical remembrances attaching to the spot where angels' hosts had met Jacob on his return to the land of promise (Genesis 32:2), but also as sufficiently far from the scene of the recent war to afford safe shelter. Here Abner raised the standard of the Pretender to the throne of Israel; and, probably in the course of five and a half years, succeeded in gradually clearing the country from the Philistines, and subjecting it, with the exception of the territory of Judah, to the nominal rule of the "man of shame."

The first conflict between the armies of the rival kings was undoubtedly provoked by Abner. With all the forces at his disposal he marched upon Gibeon, primarily with the view of again establishing the royal residence at "Gibeah of Saul," but with the ulterior object of placing Ish-bosheth in the room of his father, and gradually pushing back David. Upon this, Joab advanced with the seasoned troops of David, to oppose his progress. The town of Gibeon was built on the slope of a hill overlooking a wide and fertile valley. On the eastern side of the hill deep down in a rock is a beautiful spring, the waters of which are drained into a large rectangular pool, about seventy-two feet long and forty-two feet wide (comp. also Jeremiah 41:12). South of this pool lay the army of Joab, north of it that of Abner. The two generals seem to have been previously acquainted (ver. 22); and perhaps Abner may from the first have had in his mind the contingency of having to make his peace with David. Be this as it may, the provocation to actual hostilities came once more from Abner. On his proposal, — perhaps with a view to decide the conflict by a kind of duel, instead of entering upon an internecine civil war — twelve young men from either side were to engage in a personal combat.

But such was the embitterment and determination of parties, that each one rushed on his antagonist, and, taking hold of him, buried his sword in his side; whence the spot obtained the name: "Plot of the sharp blades." This bloody and, in the event, useless "game" having proved indecisive, a fierce battle ensued; or rather, a rout of the Israelites, in which three hundred and sixty of them fell, as against nineteen of David's seasoned and trained warriors. The pursuit was only stopped when night had fallen, and Abner had rallied his scattered forces in a strong position on the top of a hill and then only at Abner's special request.

An incident in that day's pursuit is specially recorded for its bearing on the after-history. Of the three sons of Zeruiah, David's sister (1 Chronicles 2:16), — Abishai (1 Samuel 26:6), Joab, David's general-in-chief, and Asahel — the youngest was "light of foot as one of the roes in the field." Flushed with the fight, the youth singled out Abner, and followed him in his flight. After a little Abner, recognizing his pursuer, stood still. Probably the youth thought this meant surrender. But Abner, having ascertained that his pursuer was really Asahel, and deeming that his ambition would be satisfied if he carried away the armor of some enemy, bade him gratify his wish on one of the men-at-arms around. When the youth, bent on the glory of slaying Abner himself, nevertheless continued the pursuit, the captain once more stopped to expostulate. But neither the well-meant and kindly-spoken warning of Abner, nor the manifest discrepancy of fighting power between the two, could stay a lad intoxicated by perhaps a first success. To get rid of him, and almost in necessary self-defense, Abner now struck behind him with the butt-end of his lance, which was probably sharpened with a point, to be capable of being stuck in the ground (1 Samuel 26:7). Mortally wounded in "the abdomen," the lad fell, and soon "died in the same place." The sight of one so young and brave weltering in his blood and writhing in agony no doubt greatly increased the bitterness of that day's pursuit (ver. 23).

The battle of Gibeon seems to have been followed rather by a protracted state of war than by any other actual engagement between the forces of the two kings.

The general result is described as the house of Saul waxing weaker and weaker, and that of David stronger and stronger. Of both evidence appeared. The increasing political strength of David was shown, as usual among Eastern monarchs, by the fresh alliances through marriage into which he now entered. These would not only connect him with powerful families throughout the country, but prove to his subjects that he felt himself safe in his position, and could now in the Oriental fashion found a royal house. On the other hand, the dependence of Ish-bosheth upon Abner became constantly more evident and humiliating. At last the all-powerful general took a public step which in those days was regarded as implying an open claim to the succession to Saul's throne (comp. 2 Samuel 16:21; 1 Kings 2:21). Whether or not Abner had intended this when he took Rizpah, Saul's concubine, or merely wished to gratify his passion, with utter and marked disregard of the puppet whom it had suited his purpose to keep on the throne, Ish-bosheth at any rate resented this last and crowning insult. But Abner, who had no doubt for some time seen the impossibility of maintaining the present state of affairs (comp. ver. 17), was in no mood to brook even reproof. He broke into coarse invective, and vowed to Ish-bosheth's face that he would henceforth espouse the cause of David, and soon bring it to a successful issue. Nor did the wretched king even dare to reply.

If Ish-bosheth had regarded it as only the threat of an angry man, Abner at least was in full earnest. Negotiations with David were forthwith set on foot. But they met with a preliminary condition — right and proper not only in itself, but also from political considerations. It was a standing memento of David's weakness in the past, and a lasting disgrace, that his wife Michal should be parted from him, and continue the wife of another

— a mere subject of the kingdom. Besides, as the husband of Saul's daughter, and as recalling how he had obtained her hand, her restoration would place him on a manifest political vantage ground. Accordingly David sent Abner this message in reply: "Well, I will make a covenant with thee; only one thing I demand of thee, viz.: Thou shalt not see my face, unless thou before bringest Michal, the daughter of Saul, when thou comest to see my face." But it would have ill become David to address such a demand to Abner, except as all-powerful with Ish-bosheth, and therefore really responsible for his acts. The formal demand was made to Ish-bosheth himself, and grounded on David's rights. The son of Saul immediately complied — of course, under the direction of Abner, who himself executed the commission to fetch her from her present husband, and restore her to David. The publicity with which this was done — the husband being allowed to accompany her with his lamentations as far as the boundary of Judah — and the influential character of the embassy, as well as the act of restoration itself, must have given to the whole nation an idea of David's acknowledged position, and contributed to their speedy submission to his rule.

When Abner brought Michal to Hebron, at the head of an embassy of twenty men — whether sent by Ish-bosheth, or coming as a sort of representative deputation from Israel — he had, with characteristic energy, already taken all his measures. First he had assured himself of the co-operation of the tribal "elders," who had long been weary of a nominal rule which left them defenseless against the Philistines and others. After that he had entered into special negotiations with the tribe of Benjamin, which might naturally be jealous of a transference of royalty from themselves to Judah. Having secured the consent of all, he was able to offer to David the undivided allegiance of Israel. The king had favorably received Abner and his suite, and entertained them at a great banquet. Already the embassy was on its way back to accomplish its mission, when Joab and his men returned to Hebron from some raid, such as in the then circumstances of David might still be necessary for the support of the troops. On learning what had passed in his absence, he made his way to the king, and violently expostulated with him for not having acted treacherously towards his guest. Abner had come bent on treachery, and he ought not to have been allowed to escape. We can scarcely suppose that this pretense of zeal imposed upon any one, any more than afterwards, when he had murdered Abner, that of having acted as avenger of blood. In both instances his motives, no doubt, were envy, personal jealousy, and fear lest his position might be endangered. As David gave him no encouragement, he acted on his own responsibility, whether or not he used the name of David in so doing.

A swift messenger soon brought back Abner to Hebron. Joab, who had concerted his measures with Abishai, his brother (ver. 30), met the unsuspecting victim "in the gate;" and taking him aside from the pathway into the interior and darker roofed part, as if for some private communication, "slew" him by a wound in "the abdomen," similar to that by which Asahel had died.

As we understand it, the murderers would then turn round, and addressing the bystanders, declare that they were justified, since they had acted as "avengers of blood." But that such plea could not be urged in this instance must have been evident to all, since Abner's had been an act of self-defense, and certainly not intentional murder (comp. Deuteronomy 4:42, etc.; Joshua 20). Abner, however, represented a low type of Israelitish valor. If we were to credit his protestations (vers. 9, 10, 18) of desiring to carry out the Divine will in the elevation of David, we should, of course, have to regard him as having previously acted in conscious opposition to God, and that from the most selfish motives. But probably — put in an Oriental and Jewish fashion — it meant no more than the thousand protestations of "God wills it" and the "Te Deums" which in all ages of the world have covered human ambition with a garb of religiousness. But none the less foul and treacherous was Joab's deed, and it behooved David not only to express his personal abhorrence of it, but to clear himself of all suspicion of complicity. In this instance it was impossible for human justice to overtake the criminals. Probably public feeling would not have supported the king; nor could he at this crisis in his affairs afford the loss of such generals, or brave the people and the army. But David did all that was possible. Those whom human justice could not overtake he left in the hands of Divine vengeance to mete out the punishment appropriate to the inordinate desire after leadership which had prompted such a crime (ver. 29).

A public mourning was ordered, in which the murderers themselves had to take part. The king in his official character followed the murdered man to his burying, pronounced over him an appropriate elegy, and publicly announced his intention to fast, in token of personal mourning. From the remark added in the sacred text (ver. 37), it seems that such proofs of sincerity were requisite to counter-balance the suspicions otherwise excited by such an instance of treachery and deception in high places. To his own immediate surroundings — his "servants" (vers. 38, 39) — David spoke more unreservedly, lamenting the circumstances which still made him comparatively powerless in face of such reckless chiefs as the sons of Zeruiah.

But, on the other hand, increasing public confidence rewarded David's integrity of purpose. It was needed, if high-handed crime was to be suppressed in the land. Another glaring instance of the public demoralization consequent on Saul's long misrule soon occurred. The death of Abner had naturally the most discouraging effect, not only upon Ish-bosheth, but upon all his adherents. No one was now left of sufficient prominence and influence to carry out the peaceable revolution which Abner had planned. The present weak government could not long be maintained; and if Ish-bosheth died, the only representative of Saul's line left was a crippled child, Mephi-bosheth ("the exterminator of shame," or "of Baal"), the son of Jonathan, whose deformity had been caused by the nurse letting him fall when snatching him up for hasty flight on receiving tidings of the disastrous day at Jezreel.

Not even the most ardent partisan could have wished to see on the throne of Israel a child thus permanently incapacitated. But few could have been prepared for the tragedy which was so soon to put an end to all difficulties.

It seems that two of Ish-bosheth's "captains of bands," prompted, no doubt, by the hope of rich reward, had in the most deliberate and treacherous manner planned the murder of Ish-bosheth. They were brothers, from Beeroth, on the western boundary of Benjamin, but included in its territory (Joshua 18:25). Hence they were of the same tribe with Saul, which, of course, aggravated their crime. For some unexplained reason the Beerothites had fled en masse to Gittaim — perhaps, as has been suggested, on the occasion of Saul's slaughter of the Gibeonites (2 Samuel 21:1, 2). This, however, can scarcely be regarded as the motive of their crime.

Probably on pretense of superintending the receipt of what was necessary for the provisioning of their men, they entered the royal residence at the time when Ish-bosheth was taking the customary Eastern midday rest, made their way into his bed-chamber, stabbed him in his sleep in the abdomen, and cut off his head, to carry it to David as gory evidence of their deed.

The reception which they met was such as might have been expected. To the daring appeal of those interested murderers that they had been the instruments of Jehovah's vengeance upon Saul's wrongs to David, the king gave no further reply than to point to what had hitherto been the faith and experience of his heart and the motto of his life: "Jehovah liveth, Who hath redeemed my soul out of all adversity!" It needed not man's help, least of all the aid of crime. Never — not even in his darkest hour — had he either desponded, doubted, or sought to right himself. His strength, as his confidence, had lain in realizing Jehovah as the living God and his all-sufficient Savior. No other deliverance did he either need or seek. But as for this crime — had not his conduct to the lying messenger at Ziklag sufficiently shown his abhorrence of such deeds? How much more in regard to a murder so foul as this! Swift, sure, and signally public punishment was the only possible reply in such a case.

And thus at last, not by his own act, but through circumstances over which he had had no control, — allowed by Him Who gives full liberty to each man, though He overrules even the darkest deeds of the wicked for the evolving of good — David was left undisputed claimant to the throne of Israel. Faith, patience, and integrity were vindicated; the Divine promises to David had come true in the course of natural events — and all this was better far than even if Saul had voluntarily resigned his place, or Abner succeeded in his plans.

CHAPTER 16: DAVID ANOINTED KING OVER ALL ISRAEL — TAKING OF FORT ZION — PHILISTINE DEFEAT — THE ARK BROUGHT TO JERUSALEM — LITURGICAL ARRANGEMENTS AND INSTITUTIONS.

(2 SAMUEL 5, 6; 1 CHRONICLES 11-16)

THE cessation of the long-pending rivalry and the prospect of a strong monarchy under David must have afforded sincere relief and satisfaction to all the well-disposed in Israel. Even during the time when his fortunes were at the lowest, David had had constant accessions of valiant and true men from all tribes, not excluding Saul's tribe of Benjamin and the country east of the Jordan. Yet it implied no ordinary courage to face the dangers and difficulties of the life of an outlaw; no common determination to leave home and country in such a cause. The Book of Chronicles furnishes in this as in other instances most welcome notices supplemental to the other historical writings of the Old Testament.

Thus it gives us (1 Chronicles 12:1-22) the names of the leading men who joined David at different periods, with their tribal connection, and even helps us to guess what motives may have actuated at least some of their number. From these notices we learn that considerable accessions had taken place on four different occasions. When David was at Ziklag (vers. 1-7), he was joined by certain tribes-men ("brothers") of Saul (vers. 1-8), and by some men from Judah (vers. 4, 6, 7). While in the mountain-fastnesses, in the wilderness of Judah (1 Samuel 22-24), certain of the Gadites separated themselves unto him, "men of the army for war" — soldiers trained for war (ver. 8), "chief of the host" (not "captains of the host," ver. 14), "one to a hundred the least, and the greatest one to a thousand," who when breaking away from the army of Saul had not only crossed Jordan in the dangerous floodtime of early spring, but cut their way through those who would have barred it (ver. 15). A third contingent from Benjamin and Judah came during the same period (vers. 16-18). Their names are not mentioned; but they were headed by Amasai, probably another nephew of David — the son of Abigail, David's younger sister (1 Chronicles 2:16, 17). When challenged by David as to their intentions, Amasai had, under the influence of the Spirit, broken forth in language which showed the character of their motives (ver. 18). The last and perhaps most important contingent joined David on his road back to Ziklag, when dismissed from the armies of the Philistines. It consisted of seven chieftains of thousands of Manasseh, who gave David most valuable aid against the Amalekites.

If such had been David's position and influence in Israel even during Saul's lifetime, we can readily understand the rush of enthusiasm at his accession to the throne of a people once more united, now that there was no longer any rival claimant left. As they afterwards told David at Hebron, they all felt that he was their own, — just as Israel will feel when at last in repentant faith they will turn to their Messiah King; that in the past, even in Saul's life-time, he alone had been the victorious leader and chief of all; and that to him had pointed the express Divine promise as spoken through Samuel (1 Chronicles 11:3). And while the "elders of Israel" made a regular "covenant" with David, and anointed him king over Israel, hundreds and thousands of the men of war marched down to Hebron from the most remote parts of the country (1 Chronicles 12:23-40). Such enthusiasm had never before been witnessed. Not bidden to the war, but voluntarily they came, some bringing with them even from the northernmost parts of the land — from Issachar, Zebulun, and Naphtali — contributions in kind for the three days' popular feast which David's former subjects of Judah, and especially those around Hebron, were preparing in honor of this great and most joyous event. From both banks of the Jordan they came. Of course, we do not look for a large representation from Judah and Simeon (the latter being enclosed in the territory of Judah), since they were already David's, nor from the Levites, many of whom may previously have been in David's territory (1 Chronicles 12:24-26). Issachar was represented by two hundred of its most prominent public leaders, "knowing (possessing) understanding of the times, to know what Israel should do." Only the contingents from Ephraim and Benjamin were comparatively small, the former, owing either to the old tribal jealousy between Ephraim and Judah, or else from a real diminution in their number, such as had appeared even in the second census taken by Moses, while in the case of Benjamin it is sufficiently accounted for by the circumstance that "even till then the greatest part of them were keeping their allegiance to the house of Saul" (ver. 29).

Taking all these circumstances into account, the grand total of warriors that appeared in Hebron — 339,600 men, with 1222 chiefs, and so many of them from the other side Jordan, — afforded a truly marvelous exhibition of national unanimity and enthusiasm. And the king who was surrounded by such a splendid array was in the prime of his vigor, having just reached the age of thirty-seven and a half years (2 Samuel 5:5).

What a prospect before the nation! Well might they joy at the national feast which David gave in Hebron! Viewing this history in its higher bearing, and remembering the grounds on which the elders of Israel in Hebron based the royal claims of David, we venture to regard it as typical of Israel at last returning to their Savior-King. And surely it is not to strain the application, if thoughts of this feast at Hebron carry us forward to that other and better feast in the "latter days," which is destined to be so full of richest joy alike to Israel and to the world (Isaiah 25:6-10).

Surrounded by a force of such magnitude and enthusiasm, David must have felt that this was the proper moment for the greatest undertaking in Jewish history since the conquest of the land under Joshua. The first act of David's government must appropriately be the conquest of Israel's capital.

The city of the Jebusites must become truly Jerusalem — "the inheritance," "the abode" "of peace:" the peace of the house of David. The town itself had indeed already been taken immediately upon Joshua's death (Judges 1:8). But "the stronghold" on Mount Zion, which dominated the city, still continued to be held by "the Jebusites." Yet Jerusalem was almost marked out by nature to be Israel's capital, from its strength, its central position, and its situation between Benjamin and Judah. Far more than this, it was the place of which the Lord had made choice: to be, as it were, a guarded sanctuary within the holy land. So long as Zion was in possession of the Jebusites, as the original Canaanite "inhabitants of the land," the land itself could not be said to have been wholly won. Thither accordingly David now directed the united forces of his people. Yet such was the natural and artificial strength of Zion that "to say (express), David shall not come hither" (ver. 5), the Jebusites taunted him with what afterwards became a proverb, perpetuating among the people the fact that no conquest is too difficult for God and with God: "He will not come in hither, for even the blind and the lame shall drive thee away!" It was wise and right in David to take up this defiant taunt of the heathen, when he gave his men charge — perhaps directing them to scale the bare rock by the water-course, which may at that time have come down the brow of Zion: "Whoever smiteth Jebusites — let him throw (them) down the water-course: both 'the blind and the lame' who are hated of David's soul!"

At the same time no means were neglected of encouraging the leaders in the attack. As we learn from the Book of Chronicles (1 Chronicles 11:6), the leader who first scaled the walls was to be made general-in-chief. This honor was won by Joab, who had commanded David's separate army, before his elevation to the throne had united the whole host of Israel. And so, in face of the Jebusite boast, the impregnable fort was taken, and called "the City of David," — a lesson this full of encouragement to the people of God at all times. Henceforth David made it his residence. To render it more secure, "he built," or rather fortified, "round about from (fort) Millo and inwards," or, as in 1 Chronicles 11:8: "From the surrounding (wall) and to the surrounding," — that is, as we understand it: Zion, which had hitherto been surrounded by three walls, had now a fourth added on the north, reaching from Castle Millo (either at the north-eastern or at the north-western angle) to where the other wall ended. Similarly, Joab repaired the rest of the city walls (1 Chronicles 11:8).

What we have just related must, of course, not be taken as indicating a strict chronological succession of events. The building of these walls no doubt occupied some time, and many things occurred in the interval, which are related afterwards. Apparently the intention of the sacred historian was to complete his sketch of all connected with David's conquest of Zion and his making it the royal residence, not to write in chronological order. Hence we have also here notices of the palace which David built on Mount Zion, and of the help which Hiram, king of Tyre, gave him both in men and materials, and even of David's fresh alliances and of their issues, although the children were born at a much later period than this. As we understand it, soon after his accession, probably after the capture of Jerusalem and the final defeat of the Philistines, Hiram sent an embassy of congratulation to David, which led to an interchange of courtesies and to the aid which the king of Tyre gave in David's architectural undertakings.

Different feelings from those in Israel were awakened in Philistia by the tidings of David's elevation to the throne of united Israel, and of his conquest of the Jebusite fort. The danger to their supremacy was too real to be overlooked. On their approach, David retired to the stronghold of Zion. While the Philistines advanced unopposed as far as the valley of Rephaim, which is only separated by a mountain-ridge from that of Ben-Hinnom, David "inquired of Jehovah." So near had danger come, and so strongly did the king feel that he must take no step without Divine direction to avert it. For, placing ourselves on the standpoint of those times, this was the best, if not the only way of manifesting entire dependence on God's guidance — even to the incurring of what seemed near danger in so doing, and also the best if not the only way of teaching his followers much-needed lessons of allegiance to Jehovah, with all that religiously and morally followed from it.

The answer of the Lord conveyed promised assurance of help, and hence of victory. And in this light David afterwards described his triumph, exclaiming, "Broken in hath Jehovah upon mine enemies before me." To perpetuate this higher bearing of the victory, the spot was ever afterwards called "Baal-perazim" ("possessor of breaches"), — and from Isaiah 28:21, we know that the solemn import of the name never passed from memory. The victory and its meaning were the more notable that the Philistines had brought their gods with them to the battle, as Israel the Ark on a former occasion. Their idols were now burned by command of David, in accordance with Deuteronomy 7:5, 25. Yet a second time did the Philistines come up to Rephaim to retrieve their disaster. On this occasion also David was divinely directed — no doubt the more clearly to mark the Divine interposition: "Thou shalt not go up (viz., against them in front); turn thyself upon their rear, and come upon them from opposite the Bacha-trees. And when thou hearest the sound of marching in the tops of the Bacha-trees, then be quick, for then shall Jehovah go forth before thee to smite in the host of the Philistines." It was as David had been told; and the rout of the Philistines extended from Gibeon to the Gazer road, which runs from Nether Bethhoron to the sea.

Thus far for the political results of David's elevation, which are placed first in the "Book of Samuel," as dealing primarily with the political aspect of his kingdom, while in the Book of Chronicles, which views events primarily in their theocratic bearing, they are recorded after another of greatest importance for the religious welfare of the new kingdom. For the same reason also, the Book of Chronicles adds details not recorded in that of Samuel, about David's consultation with his chiefs, and the participation of the priests and Levites in what related to the removal of the ark of the Lord.

About seventy years had passed since the ark of Jehovah had stood in the Tabernacle, according to the express ordinance of God.

And now that Israel was once more united, not only in a political, but in the best and highest sense, and its God, appointed capital had at last been won, it was surely time to restore the ancient worship which had been so sadly disturbed. Nor could there be any question as to the location of the Ark. No other place fit for it but the capital of the land. For was it not the "ark of God" over which the Lord specially manifested His Presence and His glory to His people? — or, in the language of Holy Scripture (2 Samuel 6:2): "over which is called the Name, the NAME of Jehovah Zevaoth, Who throneth upon the cherubim." Much, indeed, had still to be left in a merely provisional state.

We cannot doubt that David from the first contemplated a time when the Lord would no longer dwell, so to speak, in tents, but when a stable form would be given to the national worship by the erection of a central sanctuary. But for the present it must remain — if in Jerusalem — yet in a "tabernacle." Nay, more than that, the tent which David would prepare would not be the tabernacle which Moses had made. This was in Gibeah, and there, since the murder of the priests at Nob, Zadok officiated, while Abiathar acted as high-priest with David. Neither of these two could be deposed; and so there must be two tabernacles, till God Himself should set right what the sin of men had made wrong. And for this, as we believe, David looked forward to the building of a house for the God of Israel. An undertaking of such solemn national importance as the transference of the Ark to Jerusalem must be that of the whole people, and not of David alone. Accordingly representatives from the whole land assembled to the number of thirty thousand, with whom he went to bring in solemn procession the Ark from Baalah of Judah, as Kirjath-Jearim ("the city of the woods.") also used to be called (Joshua 15:9; 1 Chronicles 13:6; comp. also Psalm 132:6).

One thing only David had omitted, but its consequences proved fatal. The act of David and of Israel was evidently intended as a return to the Lord, and as submission to His revealed ordinances. But if so, the obedience must be complete in every particular. Viewed symbolically and typically, all these ordinances formed one complete whole, of which not the smallest detail could be altered without disturbing the symmetry of all, and destroying their meaning. Viewed legally, and, so far as Israel was concerned, even morally, the neglect of any single ordinance involved a breach of all, and indeed, in principle, that of obedience and absolute submission to Jehovah, in consequence of which the people had already so terribly suffered. Once more we must here place ourselves on the stand-point of the stage of religious development then attained. For only thus can we understand either the grave fault committed by David, or the severity of the punishment by which it was followed. The arrangements which David had made for the transport of the Ark differed in one most important particular from those which God had originally prescribed. According to God's ordinance (Numbers 6) the Ark was only to be handled by the Levites — for symbolical reasons on which we need not now enter — nor was any other even to touch it (Numbers 4:15). Moreover the Levites were to carry it on their shoulders, and not to place it in a wagon. But the arrangements which David had made for the transport of the Ark were those of the heathen Philistines when they had restored it to Israel (1 Samuel 6:7, etc.), not those of the Divine ordinance. If such was the case on the part of the king, we can scarcely wonder at the want of reverence on the part of the people. It was a question of the safe transport of a sacred vessel, not of the reverent handling of the very symbol of the Divine Presence. It had been placed in a new cart, driven by the sons of Abinadab, in whose house the Ark had been these many years, while David and all Israel followed with every demonstration of joy, and with praise.

At a certain part of the road, by the threshing-floor of "the stroke" (Nachon, 2 Samuel 6:6; or, as in 1 Chronicles 13:9, Chidon, "accident"), the oxen slipped, when Uzzah, one of Abinadab's sons, took hold of the Ark. It scarcely needs the comment on this act, so frequently made, that Uzzah was a type of those who honestly but with unhallowed hands try to steady the ark of God when, as they think, it is in danger, to show us that some lesson was needed alike by the king and his people to remind them that this was not merely a piece of sacred furniture, but the very emblem of God's Presence among His people. It was a sudden and terrible judgment which struck down Uzzah in his very act before all the people; and though David was "displeased" at the unexpected check to his cherished undertaking, the more so that he must have felt that the blame lay with himself, he seems also to have learnt its lesson at least thus far, to realize, more than ever before, that holiness befitted every contact with God (2 Samuel 6:9).

The meaning of this judgment was understood by David. When three months later the Ark was fetched from where it had been temporarily deposited in the house of Obed-Edom, a Levite of Gath-Rimmon (Joshua 21:24; 19:45), and of that family of that Korahites (1 Chronicles 26:4; comp. Exodus 6:21), to whom the custody of the Ark was specially entrusted (1 Chronicles 15:18, 24), David closely observed the Divine ordinance. Of this, as indeed of all the preparations made by David on this occasion, we have, as might be expected, a very full account in 1 Chronicles 15:1-25. As the procession set forward a sacrifice of an ox and a fatling was offered (2 Samuel 6:13); and again when the Levites had accomplished their task in safety, a thank-offering of seven bullocks and seven rams was brought (1 Chronicles 15:26).

David himself, dressed as the representative of the priestly nation, in an ephod, took part in the festivities, like one of the people. It is a sad sign of the decay into which the public services of the sanctuary had fallen in the time of Saul, that Michal saw in this nothing but needless humiliation of the royal dignity. She had loved the warrior, and she could honor the king, but "the daughter of Saul" could neither understand nor sympathize with such a demonstration as that in which David now took part.

As she looked from her window upon the scene below, and mentally contrasted the proud grandeur of her father's court with what she regarded as the triumph of the despicable priesthood at the cost of royalty, other thoughts than before came into her mind alike as to the past and the present, and "she despised David in her heart."

The lengthened services of that happy day were past. David had prepared for the reception of the Ark a "tabernacle," no doubt on the model of that which Moses had made.

410

The introduction of the Ark into its "most holy place" was made the feast of the dedication of the new sanctuary which had been reared for its reception, when burnt-offerings and peace-offerings were brought. But there was more than this to mark the commencement of a new religious era. For the first time the service of praise was now introduced in the public worship of Israel.

Shortly after it was fully organized, as also the other ritual of the sanctuary (1 Chronicles 16). The introduction of fixed hymns of praise, with definite responses by the people (as in 1 Chronicles 16:34-36), marks the commencement of that liturgy which, as we know, was continued in the Temple, and afterwards in the Synagogues throughout the land. The grand hymn composed for this occasion was no doubt Psalm 24, as its contents sufficiently indicate. But besides we have in the Book of Chronicles (16:8-36), what must be considered either as a liturgical arrangement and combination of parts from other Psalms introduced at that time into the public worship, or else as a separate Psalm, parts of which were afterwards inserted into others. This question is, however, of little practical importance. In favor of the first view is the undoubted fact that the successive parts of the hymn in the Book of Chronicles occur in Psalm 55 (1-15), 46, 57 (1), and 56 (47, 48), and the circumstance that the expressions (1 Chronicles 16:4) "to record, and to thank, and to praise," mark a liturgical division and arrangement of the Psalms. The first of the three classes indicated, the Ascharah or "memorial" Psalms, were sung when meat-offerings were brought (Leviticus 2:2).

Psalm 38 and 70 in our Psalter may be mentioned as examples of this class. As to the second and third classes, we need only remark that Psalm 55 is the first of the Hodim, or Thank-Psalms, and Psalm 56 of the "Hallelujah," or "Praise" Psalms. Nor is it said that the hymn in Chronicles was actually sung in the form there indicated, the inference to that effect being derived from the words in italics in our Authorised Version (1 Chronicles 16:7). These are, of course, not in the Hebrew text, which has it: "On that day then gave" (appointed) "David first" (for the first time) "to thank Jehovah" (i.e. the service of song) "by the hand of Asaph and his brethren." On the other hand, however, the hymn in the Book of Chronicles is so closely and beautifully connected in its various parts, as to give the impression of one whole, parts of which may afterwards have been inserted in different Psalms, just as similar adaptations are found in other parts of the Psalter (comp., for example, Psalm 40:17, etc., with Psalm 70).

But, whatever may be thought of its original form, this "Psalm" of eight stanzas, as given in the Book of Chronicles, is one of the grandest hymns in Holy Scripture.

If the expression might be allowed, it is New Testament praise in Old Testament language. Only we must beware of separating the two dispensations, as if the faith and joy of the one had differed from that of the other except in development and form. From first to last the hymn breathes a missionary spirit, far beyond any narrow and merely national aspirations. Thus, in the fifth stanza (vs. 23-27), we have anticipation of the time when God's promise to Abraham would be made good, and all nations share in his spiritual blessing, — a hope which, in the sixth (28-30) and seventh stanzas (31-33), rises to the joyous assurance of Jehovah's reign over all men and over ransomed earth itself.

That this hymn is deeply Messianic, not only in its character but in its basis, needs no proof. In truth, we regard it and the earlier hymns of the same spirit, as that by the Red Sea (Exodus 15) and that of Hannah (1 Samuel 2:1-10), as forming links connecting the earlier with the later (prophetic) portions of the Old Testament, showing that, however gradually the knowledge may have come of the precise manner in which the promise would ultimately be fulfilled, the faith and hope of believers were, in substance, always the same. Nor, to pass from this to what to some may seem a comparatively secondary point, ought we to neglect noticing as an important advance, marked even by this Psalm, the establishment of a liturgical worship, apparent even in the introduction of a fixed hymnody, instead of occasional outbursts of sacred poetry, and by very distinct though brief liturgical formulas — the whole last stanza being, in fact, of that character.

The solemn services of the consecration ended, David dismissed the people, giving to each individual, probably for the journey homewards, needful provisions.

But in that most joyous hour David had once more to experience, how little sympathy he could expect, even in his own household. Although we can understand the motives which influenced Michal's "contempt" of David's bearing, we would scarcely have been prepared for the language in which she addressed him when, in the fullness of his heart, he came to bless his assembled household, nor yet for the odious representation she gave of the scene. Such public conduct on her part deserved and, in the circumstances, required the almost harsh rebuke of the king. The humiliation of the proud woman before man was ratified by her humiliation on the part of God: "Therefore Michal, the daughter of Saul, had no child unto the day of her death."

The placing of the Ark in the capital of Israel, thus making it "the city of God," was an event not only of deep national but of such typical importance, that it is frequently referred to in the sacred songs of the sanctuary. No one will have any difficulty in recognizing Psalm 24 as the hymn composed for this occasion. But other Psalms also refer to it, amongst which, without entering on details that may be profitably studied by each reader, we may mention Psalm 15, 68, 78, and especially Psalm 101, as indicating, so to speak, the moral bearing of the nearness of God's ark upon the king and his kingdom.

CHAPTER 17: DAVID'S PURPOSE OF BUILDING THE TEMPLE, AND ITS POSTPONEMENT — THE "SURE MERCIES" OF DAVID IN THE DIVINE PROMISE — DAVID'S THANKSGIVING.

(2 SAMUEL 7; 1 CHRONICLES 17)

THOSE who, with devout attention, have followed the course of this history, and marked in it that of the kingdom of God in its gradual unfolding, will feel that a point had now been reached when some manifestation of the Divine purpose, fuller and clearer than ever before, might be expected. As we look back upon it, not only the whole history, but every event in it, has been deeply significant, and fraught with symbolical and typical meaning. Thus we have marked how as each event, so to speak, kindled a light, which was reflected from the polished mirror of the Psalter, it seemed to throw its brightness far beyond its own time into that future on which the day had not yet risen. But even to the men of that generation what had taken place must have carried a meaning far beyond the present. The foundation of a firm kingdom in Israel, its concentration in the house of David, and the establishment of a central worship in the capital of the land as the place which God had chosen, must have taken them back to those ancient promises which were now narrowing into special fulfillment, and have brought into greater prominence the points in these predictions which, though still towering aloft, sprung out of what was already reached, and formed part of it. A never-ending kingdom, a never-passing king; a sanctuary never to be abolished: such were the hopes still before them in the world-wide application of the promises of which they already witnessed the national and typical fulfillment. These hopes differed, not in character, but only in extent and application, from what they already enjoyed. To use our former illustration, they were not other heights than those on which they stood, but only peaks yet unclimbed. These considerations will help us properly to understand the narrative of David's purpose to build a temple, and the Divine communication consequent upon it. For clearness' sake we first sketch the facts as stated in sacred history, and then indicate their deeper meaning.

To complete the history of the religious movement of that period, the sacred writers insert in this place the account of David's purpose to build a temple. The introduction to the narrative (2 Samuel 7:1), and the circumstance that at the time most if not all the wars mentioned in 2 Samuel 8 and 10 were past, sufficiently indicate that in this, as in other instances, the history is not arranged according to strict chronological succession. Still it must have taken place when David's power was at its zenith, and before his sin with Bathsheba. The king had been successful in all his undertakings. Victorious and world-famed, he inhabited his splendid palace on Mount Zion. The contrast between his own dwelling and that in which His ark abode to Whom he owed all, and Who was Israel's real King, was painfully great.

However frequent and unheeded a similar contrast may be in our days between the things of God and of man, David too vividly apprehended spiritual realities to remain contented under it. Without venturing to express a wish which might have seemed presumptuous, he told his feelings on this subject to his trusted friend and adviser, the prophet Nathan.

As might have been expected, Nathan responded by a full approval of the king's unspoken purpose, which seemed so accordant with the glory of God. But Nathan had spoken — as ancient writers note — from his own, though pious, impulse, and not by direction of the Lord. Oftentimes our thoughts, although springing from motives of real religion, are not God's thoughts; and the lesson here conveyed is most important of not taking our own impressions, however earnestly and piously derived, as necessarily in accordance with the will of God, but testing them by His revealed word, — in short, of making our test in each case not subjective feeling, but objective revelation.

That night, as Nathan was busy with thoughts of the great future which the king's purpose seemed to open, God spake to him in vision, forbidding the undertaking; or rather, while approving the motive, delaying its execution. All this time, since He had brought them up out of Egypt, God's Presence had been really among Israel; He had walked about with them in all their wanderings and state of unsettledness. Thus far, then, the building of an house could not be essential to God's Presence, while the "walking about in tent and dwelling" had corresponded to Israel's condition. Another period had now arrived. Jehovah Zevaoth had chosen David, and established his kingdom.

And in connection with it as concerned Israel (ver. 10) and David (ver. 11): "And I have appointed a place for My people Israel, and have planted it that it may abide in its place, and no more tremble; and that the children of wickedness" (malice) "may no more oppress it as at the first, and from the day when I appointed judges over My people Israel. And I give thee rest from all thine enemies, and Jehovah intimates to thee that a house will Jehovah make to thee."

Thus much for the present. As for the future, it was to be as always in the Divine arrangement. For God must build us a house before we can build one to Him. It was not that David was first to rear a house for God, but that God would rear one for David. Only afterwards, when all Israel's wanderings and unrest were past, and He had established the house of His servant, would the son of that servant, no longer a man of war (1 Chronicles 20:8; 28:3), but a man of peace, "Solomon," build the house of peace. There was inward and even outward congruity in this: a kingdom which was peace; a king the type of the Prince of peace; and a temple the abode of peace. This, then, was the main point: a promise alike to David, to Israel, and in regard to the Temple, that God would build David a house, and make his kingdom not only lasting, but everlasting, in all the fullness of meaning set out in Psalm 72. What followed will be best given in the words of Holy Scripture itself: "I shall be to him a Father, and he shall be to Me a son, whom, if he transgress, I will correct with the rod of men, and with stripes of the children of men; but My mercy shall not depart from him as I made it depart from Saul, whom I put away from before thee. And unfailing" (sure) "thy house and thy kingdom for ever before thee; and thy throne shall be established for ever!"

That this promise included Solomon is as plain as that it was not confined to him. No unprejudiced reader could so limit it; certainly no sound Jewish interpreter would have done so. For on this promise the hope of a Messianic kingdom in the line of David and the title of the Messiah as the Son of David were based. It was not only the Angel, who pointed to the fulfillment of this promise in the Annunciation to the Virgin (Luke 1:32, 33), but no one, who believed in a Messiah, would have thought of questioning his application. All the predictions of the prophets may be said to rest upon it. While, therefore, it did not exclude Solomon and his successors, and while some of its terms are only applicable to them, the fulfillment of this promise was in Christ. In this view we are not hampered but helped by the clause which speaks of human chastisements as eventual on sins in the successors of David. For we regard the whole history from David to Christ as one, and as closely connected. And this prophecy refers neither only to Solomon nor only to Christ; nor has it a twofold application, but it is a covenant-promise which, extending along the whole line, culminates in the Son of David, and in all its fullness applies only to Him. These three things did God join in it, of which one necessarily implies the other, alike in the promise and in the fulfillment: a unique relationship, a unique kingdom, and a unique fellowship and service resulting from both. The unique relationship was that of Father and Son, which in all its fullness only came true in Christ (Hebrews 1:5). The unique kingdom was that of the Christ, which would have no end (Luke 1:32, 33; John 3:35). And the unique sequence of it was that brought about through the temple of His body (John 2:19), which will appear in its full proportions when the New Jerusalem comes down out of heaven (Revelation 21:1-3).

Such was the glorious hope opening up wider and wider, till at its termination David could see "afar off" the dawn of the bright morning of eternal glory; such was the destiny and the mission which, in His infinite goodness, God assigned to His chosen servant. Much there was still in him that was weak, faltering, and even sinful; nor was he, whose was the inheritance of such promises, even to build an earthly temple. Many were his failings and sins, and those of his successors; and heavy rods and sore stripes were to fall upon them. But that promise never failed.

Apprehended from the first by the faith of God's people, it formed the grand subject of their praise, not only in Psalm 89, but in many others, such as Psalm 2, 45, 72, 110, 132, and continued the hope of the Church, as expressed in the burning language and ardent aspirations of all the prophets. Brighter and brighter this light grew, even unto the perfect day; and when all else seemed to fail, these were still "the sure mercies of David" (Isaiah 55:3), steadfast and stable; and at last fully realized in the resurrection of our Blessed Lord and Savior Jesus Christ (Acts 13:32-34).

It was significant that when David received, through Nathan, this Divine communication, "he went in," no doubt, into that "tabernacle," which was to be to him what the Pisgah-view of the land had been to Moses, and "remained" before Jehovah, uttering prayer, in which confession of unworthiness formed the first element, soon followed by thanksgiving and praise, and concluding with earnest entreaty. And such must all true prayer be — mingling humble confession with thanksgiving and with petition for the promised blessing.

CHAPTER 18: WARS OF DAVID — GREAT AMMONITE AND SYRIAN CAMPAIGN AGAINST ISRAEL — THE AUXILIARIES ARE DEFEATED IN TURN — THE CAPITAL OF MOAB IS TAKEN — EDOM SUBDUED — RECORD OF DAVID'S OFFICERS — HIS KINDNESS TO MEPHIBOSHETH.

(2 SAMUEL 8, 9; 1 CHRONICLES 18-20)

BY a fitting arrangement, the record of God's promise to establish the kingdom of David is followed by an account of all his wars, though here also the order is not strictly chronological. In fact, we have merely a summary of results, which is all that was necessary in a history of the kingdom of God — the only exception being in the case of the war with Ammon and their allies the Syrians, which is described in detail in 2 Samuel 10 and 11 because it is connected with David's great sin. As might be expected, the first war was with the Philistines, whom David subdued, taking "out of the hand of the Philistines the bridle of the mother" — that is, as we learn from 1Chronicles 18:1, the command of Gath, "the mother," or principal city of the Philistine confederacy — which henceforth became tributary to Israel.

The next victory was over the Moabites, who must have, in some way, severely offended against Israel, since the old friendship between them was not only broken (1 Samuel 22:3, 4), but terrible punishment meted out to them — the whole army being made to lie down, when two-thirds, measured by line, were cut down, and only one third left alive. It was, no doubt, in this war that Benaiah, one of David's heroes, "slew two lion-like men of Moab" (1 Chronicles 11:22).

The next contest, mentioned in 2 Samuel 8:3-6, evidently formed only an incident in the course of the great war against Ammon and its confederates, which is detailed at length in the tenth and eleventh chapters of 2 Samuel. From the number of auxiliaries whom the Ammonites engaged against Israel, this was by far the greatest danger which threatened the kingdom of David. As such it is brought before the Lord in Psalm 44 and 60, while the deliverance Divinely granted, with all that it typically implied concerning the future victory of God's kingdom, is gratefully celebrated in Psalm 68. In fact, Ammon had succeeded in girdling the whole Eastern frontier of the land with steel. Up in the far north-east rose Hadad-Ezer (Hadad, the sun-god, is help), and arrayed against Israel his kingdom of Zobah, which probably lay to the north-east of Damascus. Nor was he alone. With him were the forces of the Syrian (probably) vassal-territory, south of Hamath, between the Orontes and the Euphrates, of which Rehob (Numbers 13:21; Judges 18:28), or Beth-Rehob, was the capital. Descending still further south, along the northeastern frontier of Palestine, was the kingdom of Maacah (Deuteronomy 3:14), which joined in the war against Israel, as well as the men of Tob, who inhabited the territory between Syria and Ammon, where Jephthah had erewhile found refuge (Judges 11:5). Next we reach the territory of Ammon, from which the war originally proceeded. In the far south Moab had been only just subdued, while the Edomites made a diversion by overrunning the valley south of the Dead Sea — and a stubborn enemy they proved. Thus, as already stated, the whole eastern, northeastern, and south-eastern frontier was threatened by the enemy.

The occasion of this war was truly Oriental. Nahash, the king of the Ammonites, seems on some occasion, not otherwise known, to have shown kindness to David (2 Samuel 10:2). On his death, David, who never lost grateful remembrance, sent an embassy of sympathy to Hanun, the son and successor of Nahash. This the Ammonite princes chose to represent as only a device, preparatory to an attack on their capital, similar in character to that which so lately had laid Moab waste (8:2). There was something cowardly and deliberately provocative in the insult which Hanun put upon David's ambassadors, such as Orientals would specially feel, by shaving off the beard on one side of their face, and cutting off their long flowing dress from below up to the middle. It was an insult which, as they well knew, David could not brook; and Ammon accordingly prepared for war by raising, as we have described, all the border tribes as auxiliaries against Israel. A sum of not less than a thousand talents, or about 375,000 pounds, was spent on these auxiliaries (1 Chronicles 19:6), who amounted altogether to thirty-two thousand men — consisting of chariots, horsemen, and footmen — besides the one thousand men whom the king of Maacah furnished (2 Samuel 10:6; 1 Chronicles 19:6, 7).

Against this formidable confederacy David sent Joab, at the head of "all the host — the mighty men," that is, the choicest of his troops (2 Samuel 10:7). Joab found the enemy in double battle-array. The Ammonite army stood a short distance outside their capital, Rabbah, while the Syrian auxiliaries were posted on the wide unwooded plateau of Medeba (1 Chronicles 19:7), about fifteen miles south-west of Rabbah. Thus Joab found himself shut in between two armies. But his was not the heart to sink in face of such danger. Dividing his men into two corps, he placed the best soldiers under his brother Abishai, to meet a possible attack of the Ammonites, encouraging him with brave and pious words, while he himself, with the rest of the army, fell upon the Syrians. From the first the victory was his. When the Ammonites saw the flight of their auxiliaries, they retired within the walls of Rabbah without striking a blow. But the war did not close with this almost bloodless victory, although Joab returned to Jerusalem. It rather commenced with it. Possibly this may explain why only the second act in this bloody drama is recorded in the summary account given in 2 Samuel 8:3, etc., and in 1 Chronicles 18:4, etc. Combining these narratives with the fuller details in 2 Samuel 10 and 1 Chronicles 19, we gather that, on his defeat, or rather after his precipitate flight, Hadad-Ezer "went to turn again his hand at the river [Euphrates]," that is, to recruit his forces there (2 Samuel 8:3, in 1 Chronicles 18:3: "to establish his hand") — a statement which is further explained in 2 Samuel 10:16 and 1 Chronicles 19:16 by the notice, that the Syrian auxiliaries thence derived were placed under the command of Shobach, the captain of the host of Hadad-Ezer.

The decisive battle was fought at Helam (2 Samuel 10:17), near Hamath (1 Chronicles 18:3), and resulted in the total destruction of the Syrian host. No less than 1000 chariots, 7000 horsemen, and 20,000 footmen, were taken; while those who fell in the battle amounted to 700, or rather (according to 1 Chronicles 19:18) 7000 charioteers and horsemen, and 40,000 footmen (in 2 Samuel, "horsemen"). Shobach himself was wounded, and died on the field of battle.

David next turned against the Syrians of Damascus, who had come to the succor of Hadad-Ezer, slew 22,000 of them, put garrisons throughout the country, and made it tributary. But all the spoil taken in that war — notably the "golden shields," and the brass from which afterwards "the brazen sea, and the pillars and the vessels of brass," were made for the Temple (1 Chronicles 18:8) — was carried to Jerusalem. The immediate results of these victories was not only peace along the borders of Palestine, but that all those turbulent tribes became tributary to David. One of the kings or chieftains, Toi, the king of Hamath, had always been at war with Hadad- Ezer. On his complete defeat, Toi sent his son Hadoram to David to seek his alliance. The gifts which he brought, as indeed all the spoil of the war, were dedicated to the Lord, and deposited in the treasury of the sanctuary for future use.

But still the formidable combination against Israel was not wholly broken up. On the return of David's army from their victory over the Syrians, they had to encounter the Edomites (2 Samuel 8:13, 14), who had advanced as far as the "valley of salt," south of the Dead Sea.

The expedition was entrusted to Abishai, Joab's brother (1 Chronicles 18:12, 13), and resulted in the total rout of the enemy, and the garrisoning of the principal places in Edom by David's men; though, to judge by 1 Kings 11:5, 16, the operations took some time, and were attended with much bloodshed. The account just given of the wars of David appropriately closes with a notice of his principal officers of state, among whom we mark Joab as general-in-chief, Jehoshaphat as chancellor (magister memorioe), or recorder and adviser, Zadok as high-priest at Gibeon (1 Chronicles 16:39), and Jonathan as assistant of his father Abiathar (1 Kings 1:7, 42; 2:22-27) at Jerusalem, Seraiah as secretary of state, and Benaiah as captain of the body-guard — the Cherethi and Pelethi, or "executioners and runners" — while the king's sons acted as intimate advisers.

The record of this period of David's reign — indeed, of his life — would have been incomplete if the memory of his friendship with Jonathan had passed without leaving a trace behind. But it was not so. When he had reached the climax of his power, he made inquiry for any descendant of Saul to whom he might show "the kindness of God" for Jonathan's sake.

There is something deeply touching alike in this loving remembrance of the past, and in the manner of it, while David was at the zenith of his power, which shows his true character, and proves that success had not yet injured his better nature. There was but one legitimate scion of the royal house left — Mephibosheth, who bore in his lamed body the memorial of that sad day on Mount Gilboa. It is another bright glimpse into the moral state of the people that all this time the poor neglected descendant of fallen royalty should have found a home and support in the house of the wealthy chieftain Machir, the son of Ammiel, at Lodebar, near Mahanaim, the scene of Ishbosheth's murder (2 Samuel 4).

Yet another evidence was afterwards given of the worth and character of Machir. He had evidently known to appreciate David's conduct toward Mephibosheth, and in consequence become one of his warmest adherents, not only in the time of prosperity, but in that of direst adversity, when he dared openly to espouse David's cause, and to supply him in his flight with much needed help (2 Samuel 17:27-29).

But to return. The first care of the king was to send for Ziba, well known as a servant of Saul's — perhaps formerly the steward of his household. It is curious to note how, even after David assured him of his friendly intentions, Ziba on mentioning Mephibosheth, immediately told that he was "lame on his feet," as if to avert possible evil consequences. So strongly did the Oriental idea seem rooted in his mind, that a new king would certainly compass the death of all the descendants of his predecessor. Something of the same feeling appeared also in the bearing of Mephibosheth when introduced to David. But far other thoughts were in the king's heart. Mephibosheth was henceforth to be treated as one of the royal princes. His residence was to be at Jerusalem, and his place at the king's table while, at the same time, all the land formerly belonging to Saul was restored to him for his support. Ziba, whom David regarded as a faithful adherent of his old master's family, was directed, with his sons and servants, to attend to the ancestral property of Mephibosheth.

We love to dwell upon this incident in the history of David, which forms, so to speak, an appendix to the narrative of the first period of his reign, not merely for what it tells us of the king, but as the last bright spot on which the eye rests. Other thoughts, also, seem to crowd around us, as we repeat to ourselves such words as "the kindness of God" and "for Jonathan's sake." Thus much would a man do, and so earnestly would he inquire for the sake of an earthly friend whom he had loved. Is there not a higher sense in which the "for Jonathan's sake" can bring us comfort and give us direction in the service of love?

CHAPTER 19: SIEGE OF RABBAH — DAVID'S GREAT SIN — DEATH OF URIAH — TAKING OF RABBAH — DAVID'S SEEMING PROSPERITY — GOD'S MESSAGE THROUGH NATHAN — DAVID'S REPENTANCE — THE CHILD OF BATHSHEBA DIES — BIRTH OF SOLOMON.

(2 SAMUEL 11, 12)

THERE is one marked peculiarity about the history of the most prominent Biblical personages, of which the humbling lesson should sink deep into our hearts. As we follow their onward and upward progress, they seem at times almost to pass beyond our reach, as if they had not been compassed with the same infirmities as we, and their life of faith were so far removed as scarcely to serve as an example to us. Such thoughts are terribly rebuked by the history of their sudden falls, which shed a lurid light on the night side of their character — showing us also, on the one hand, through what inward struggles they must have passed, and, on the other, how Divine grace alone had supported and given them the victory in their many untold contests. But more than that, we find this specially exhibited just as these heroes of faith attain, so to speak, the spiritual climax of their life, as if the more clearly to set it forth from the eminence which they had reached. Accordingly, the climax of their history often also marks the commencement of their decline. It was so in the case of Moses and of Aaron, in that of David, and of Elijah. But there is one exception to this — or rather we should say, one history to which the opposite of this remark applies: that of our Blessed Lord and Savior. The climax in the history of His life among men was on the Mount of Transfiguration; and though what followed marks His descent into the valley of humiliation, even to the bitter end, yet the glory around Him only grew brighter and brighter to the Resurrection morning.

Once more spring-time had come, when the war against the Ammonites could be resumed. For hitherto only their auxiliaries had been crushed. The importance attached to the expedition may be judged from the circumstance that the ark of God now accompanied the army of Israel (2 Samuel 11:11). Again success attended David. His army, having in its advance laid waste every town, appeared before Rabbah, the strong capital of Ammon. Here was the last stand which the enemy could make — or, indeed, so far as man could judge, it was the last stand of David's last enemy. Henceforth all would be prosperity and triumph! It was in the intoxication of hitherto unbroken success, on the dangerous height of absolute and unquestioned power, that the giddiness seized David which brought him to his fall. It is needless to go over the sad, sickening details of his sin — how he was literally "drawn away of his lust, and enticed;" and how when lust had conceived it brought forth sin — and then sin, when it was finished, brought forth death (James 1:14, 15). The heart sinks as we watch his rapid downward course — the sin, the attempt to conceal it by enticing Uriah, whose suspicions appear to have been aroused, and then, when all else had failed, the dispatch of the murderous missive by Uriah's own hands, followed by the contest, with its foreseen if not intended consequences, in which Uriah, one of David's heroes and captains, who never turned his back to the foe (2 Samuel 23:39), fell a victim to treachery and lust.

It was all past. "The wife of Uriah" — as the text significantly calls Bathsheba, as if the murdered man were still alive, since his blood cried for vengeance to the Lord — had completed her seven days' hypocritical "mourning," and David had taken her to his house. And no worse had come of it. Her husband had simply fallen in battle; while the wife's shame and the king's sin were concealed in the harem. Everything else was prosperous. As the siege of Rabbah can scarcely have lasted a whole year, we assume that also to have been past. The undertaking had not been without serious difficulty. It had been comparatively easy to penetrate through the narrow gorge, and, following the "fish-stocked stream, with shells studding every stone and pebble," which made "Rabbah most truly 'a city of waters,'" to reach "the turfed plain," "completely shut in by low hills on every side," in which "the royal city" stood. This Joab took. But there still remained "the city itself," or rather the citadel, perched in front of Rabbah on "a round, steep, flat-topped mamelon," past which the stream flowed rapidly "through a valley contracted at once to a width of five hundred paces." As if to complete its natural defenses, on its other side were valleys, gullies, and ravines, which almost isolated the citadel.

But these forts could not hold out after the lower city was taken. Only it was a feat of arms in those days — and Joab, unwilling to take from the king the credit of its capture, sent for David, who in due time reduced it. The spoil was immense — among it the royal crown of Ammon, weighing no less than a talent of gold, and encrusted with precious stones, which David took to himself.

The punishment meted out to those who had resisted was of the most cruel, we had almost said, un-Israelitish character, not justified even by the terrible war which the Ammonites had raised, nor by the cruelties which they seem to have practiced against helpless Israelitish mothers (Amos 1:13), and savoring more of the ferocity of Joab than of the bearing of David — at least before his conscience had been hardened by his terrible sin. And so David returned triumphant to his royal city!

A year had passed since David's terrible fall. The child of his sin had been born. And all this time God was silent! Yet like a dark cloud on a summer's day hung this Divine sentence over him: "But the thing that David had done was evil in the eyes of Jehovah" (2 Samuel 11:27). Soon it would burst in a storm of judgment. A most solemn lesson this to us concerning God's record of our deeds, and His silence all the while. Yet, blessed be God, if judgment come on earth — if we be judged here, that we may "not be condemned with the world!" (1 Corinthians 11:32). And all this time was David's conscience quiet? To take the lowest view of it, he could not be ignorant that the law of God pronounced sentence of death on the adulterer and adulteress (Leviticus 20:10). Nor could he deceive himself in regard to the treacherous, foul murder of Uriah. But there was far more than this. The man whom God had so exalted, who had had such fellowship with Him, had sunk so low; he who was to restore piety in Israel had given such occasion to the enemy to blaspheme; the man who, when his own life was in danger, would not put forth his hand to rid himself of his enemy, had sent into pitiless death his own faithful soldier, to cover his guilt and to gratify his lust! Was it possible to sink from loftier height or into lower depth? His conscience could not be, and it was not silent. What untold agonies he suffered while he covered up his sin, he himself has told us in the thirty-second Psalm. In general, we have in this respect also in the Psalter a faithful record for the guidance of penitents in all ages — to preserve them from despair, to lead them to true repentance, and to bring them at last into the sunlight of forgiveness and peace.

Throughout one element appears very prominently, and is itself an indication of "godly sorrow." Besides his own guilt the penitent also feels most keenly the dishonor which he has brought on God's name, and the consequent triumph of God's enemies. Placing these Psalms, so to speak, in the chronological order of David's experience, we would arrange them as follows: Psalm 38, 6, 51, and 32 — when at last it is felt that all "transgression is forgiven," all "sin covered."

It was in these circumstances that Nathan the prophet by Divine commission presented himself to David. A parabolic story, simple, taken from every-day life, and which could awaken no suspicion of his ulterior meaning, served as introduction. Appealed to on the score of right and generosity, the king gave swift sentence. Alas, he had only judged himself, and that in a cause which contrasted most favorably with his own guilt. How the prophet's brief, sharp rejoinder: "Thou art the man" must have struck to his heart! There was no disguise now; no attempt at excuse or palliation. Stroke by stroke came down the hammer — each blow harder and more crushing than the other. What God had done for David; how David had acted towards Uriah and towards his wife — and how God would avenge what really was a despising of Himself: such was the burden of Nathan's brief-worded message. Had David slain Uriah with the sword of the Ammonites? Never, so long as he lived, would the sword depart from the house of David. Had he in secret possessed himself adulterously of Uriah's wife? Similar and far sorer evil would be brought upon him, and that not secretly but publicly. And we know how the one sentence came true from the murder of Amnon (2 Samuel 13:29) to the slaughter of Absalom (18:14), and even the execution of Adonijah after David's death (1 Kings 2:24, 25); and also how terribly the other prediction was fulfilled through the guilt of his own son (2 Samuel 16:21, 22).

The king had listened in silence, like one staggering and stunned under the blows that fell. But it was not sorrow unto death. Long before his own heart had told him all his sin. And now that the Divine messenger had broken through what had hitherto covered his feelings, the words of repentance sprang to his long-parched lips, as under the rod of Moses the water from the riven rock in the thirsty wilderness. They were not many words which he spoke, and in this also lies evidence of their depth and genuineness (comp. Luke 18:13) — but in them he owned two realities: sin and God. But to own them in their true meaning: sin as against God, and God as the Holy One, and yet God as merciful and gracious — was to have returned to the way of peace. Lower than this penitence could not descend; higher than this faith could not rise. And God was Jehovah — and David's sin was put away.

Brief as this account reads, we are not to imagine that all this passed, and passed away, in the short space of time it takes to tell it. Again we say: in this respect also let the record be searched of the penitential Psalms, that Old Testament comment, as it were, on the three days' and three nights' conflict, outlined in Romans 7:5-25, the history of which is marked out by the words "blasphemer," "persecutor," "injurious," and "exceeding abundant grace" (1 Timothy 1:13-16). For, faith is indeed an act, and immediate; and pardon also is an act, immediate and complete; but only the soul that has passed through it knows the terrible reality of a personal sense of sin, or the wondrous surprise of the sunrise of grace.

Assuredly it was so in the case of David. But the sting of that wound could not be immediately removed. The child who was the offspring of his sin must die: for David's own sake, that he might not enjoy the fruit of sin; because he had given occasion for men to blaspheme, and that they might no longer have such occasion; and because Jehovah was God. And straightway the child sickened unto death. It was right that David should keenly feel the sufferings of the helpless innocent child; right that he should fast and pray for it without ceasing; right even that to the last he should hope against hope that this, the seemingly heaviest punishment of his guilt, might be remitted. We can understand how all the more dearly he loved his child; how he lay on the ground night and day, and refused to rise or be comforted of man's comforts. We can also understand — however little his servants might — how, when it was all over, he rose of his own accord, changed his apparel, went to worship in the house of Jehovah, and then returned to his own household: for, if the heavy stroke had not been averted, but had fallen — his child was not gone, only gone before. And once more there came peace to David's soul. Bathsheba was now truly and before God his wife. Another child gladdened their hearts. David named him, symbolically and prophetically, Solomon, "the peaceful:" the seal, the pledge, and the promise of peace. But God called him, and he was "Jedidiah," the Jehovah-loved. Once more, then, the sunshine of God's favor had fallen upon David's household — yet was it, now and ever afterwards, the sunlight of autumn rather than that of summer; a sunlight, not of undimmed brightness, but amidst clouds and storm.

VOLUME 5: BIRTH OF SOLOMON TO REIGN OF AHAB

PREFACE

THE period of Israel's history treated in this Volume has a twofold special interest: political and religious. Beginning with the later years of David's reign, when the consciousness and the consequences of the great sin of his life had, so to speak, paralyzed the strong hand which held the reins of government, we are, first, led to see how in the Providence of God, the possibility of a great military world-monarchy in Israel (comp. Psalm 18:43-45) — such as those of heathen antiquity — was forever frustrated. Another era began with Solomon: that of peaceful development of the internal resources of the country; of rapid increase of prosperity; of spread of culture; and through friendly intercourse with other nations of introduction of foreign ideas and foreign civilization. When it is remembered that the building of the Temple preceded the legislation of Lycurgus in Sparta by about one hundred and twenty years; that of Solomon in Athens by more than four hundred years; and the building of Rome by about two hundred and fifty years, it will be perceived that the kingdom of Solomon presented the dim possibility of the intellectual, if not the political Empire of the world. What Jerusalem was in the high-day of Solomon's glory is described in a chapter of this history. But, in the Providence of God, any such prospect passed away, when, after only eighty years duration, the Davidic kingdom was rent into two rival and hostile states. Yet, although this catastrophe was intimated by prophecy — as Divine judgment upon Solomon's unfaithfulness — there was nothing either abrupt or out of the order of rational causation in its accomplishment. On the contrary, the causes of this separation lay far back in the tribal relations of Israel; they manifested themselves once and again in the history of the Judges and of Saul; made themselves felt in the time of David; appeared in that of Solomon; and only reached their final issue, when the difficult task of meeting them devolved upon the youthful inexperience and misguided folly of a Rehoboam. All this is fully explained in the course of this history. After their separation, the two kingdoms passed, in their relations, through three stages, the first one of hostility; the second one of alliance, which commenced with the reign of Jehoshaphat and of Ahab, and ended with the slaughter of the kings of Judah and Israel by Jehu; and the third again one of estrangement and of hostility. Of these three periods the first is fully traced, and the beginning of the second marked in the present Volume.

From the political we turn to the religious aspect of this history. It was indeed true that the empire of the world was to be connected with the Davidic kingdom (Psalm 2.) — but not in the sense of founding a great military monarchy, nor in that of attaining universal intellectual supremacy, least of all by conformity to the ways and practices of heathen worship, magic, and theurgy. The exaltation of Zion above the hills and the flowing of all nations unto it, was to be brought about by the going forth of the Law out of Zion, and of the Word of Jehovah from Jerusalem (Isaiah 2:2, 3). This — to confine ourselves to the present period of our history — had been distinctly implied in the great promise to David (2 Samuel 7.); it was first typically realized in the choice of Jerusalem as the City of God (Psalm 46; 48; 87.); and further presented in its aspect of peace, prosperity, and happiness in the reign of Solomon (Psalm 72.) to which the prophets ever afterwards pointed as the emblem of the higher blessings in the Kingdom of God (Micah 4:4; Zechariah 3:10, comp. with 1 Kings 4:25). But the great work of that reign, alike in its national and typical importance, was the building of the Temple at Jerusalem. This also has been fully described in the following pages.

But already other elements were at work. The introduction of heathen worship commenced with the decline of Solomon's spiritual life. After his death, the apostasy from God attained fearful proportions, partially and temporarily in Judah, but permanently in Israel. In the latter, from the commencement of its separate national existence under Jeroboam, the God-chosen Sanctuary at Jerusalem, and the God-appointed priesthood were discarded; the worship of Jehovah transformed; and by its side spurious rites and heathen idolatry introduced, until, under the reign of Ahab, the religion of Baal became that of the State. This marks the high-point of apostasy in Israel. The evolving of principles of contrariety to the Divine Covenant slowly but surely led up to the final destruction of the Jewish Commonwealth. But, side by side with it, God in great mercy placed an agency, the origin, character, and object of which have already been indicated in a previous Volume. The Prophetic Order may be regarded as an extraordinary agency, by the side of the ordinary economy of the Old Testament; and as intended, on the one hand, to complement its provisions and, on the other, to supplement them, either in times of religious declension or when, as in Israel, the people were withdrawn from their influences. Hence the great extension of the Prophetic Order in such periods, and especially in the kingdom of the ten tribes. But when, during the reign of Ahab, the religion of Jehovah was, so to speak, repudiated, and the worship of Baal and Astarte substituted in its place, something more than even the ordinary exercise of the Prophetic Office was required. For the prophet was no longer acknowledged, and the authority of the God, whose Messenger he was, disowned. Both these had therefore to be vindicated, before the prophetic agency could serve its purpose. This was achieved through what must be regarded, not so much as a new phase, but as a further development of the agency already at work. We mark this chiefly in the ministry of Elijah and Elisha, which was contemporary with the first open manifestation of Israel's national apostasy.

Even a superficial reader will observe in the ministry of these two prophets, as features distinguishing it from that of all other prophets, indeed, we might say, from the whole history of the Old Testament — the frequency and the peculiar character of their miracles. Three points here stand out prominently, their unwonted accumulation; their seeming characteristic of mere assertion of power; and their apparent purpose of vindicating the authority of the prophet. The reason and object of these peculiarities have already been indicated in our foregoing remarks. But in reference to the characteristic of power as connected with these miracles, it may be remarked that its exhibition was not only necessary for the vindication of the authority of the prophet, or rather of Him in Whose Name he spake, but that they also do not present a mere display of power. For it was always associated with an ultimate moral purpose in regard to the Gentiles or to Israel — the believing or the unbelieving among them; and in all the leading instances (which must rule the rest) it was brought about not only in the Name of Jehovah, but by calling upon Him as the direct Agent in it (comp. for the present Volume I Kings 17:4, 9, 14, 20- 22). Thus viewed, this extraordinary display of the miraculous appears, like that in the first proclamation of Christianity among the heathen, "for a sign, not to them that believe, but to them that believe not" (1 Corinthians 14:22) — as Bengel explains, in order that, drawn and held thereby, they might be made to listen.

But even so, some further remarks may here be allowed; not, indeed, in the way of attempted disquisition on what must always be a prime postulate in our faith, but as helps in our thinking. It seems to me, that miracles require for their (objective) possibility — that is, subjectively viewed for their credibility — only one postulate: that of the True and the Living God. It is often asserted, that miracles are not the traversing of the established, but the outcome of a higher order of things.

This, no doubt, must be metaphysically true; but practically it is only a hypothetical statement, since, admittedly, and, as the very idea of miracles implies, we know nothing of this higher nature or order of things. But may we not assert that a miracle does not seem so much an interference with the laws of Nature — of which at most we have only partial and empirical knowledge — as with the laws and habits of our own thinking concerning Nature. And if so, does not this place the question on quite another footing?

Given, that there is a God (be the seeming hypothetication forgiven!), and in living connection with His rational creatures — and it seems to follow that He must teach and train them. It equally follows, that such teaching must be adapted to their stage and capacity (power of receptiveness). Now in this respect all times may be arranged into two periods that of outward, and that of inward spiritual communication (of Law and Persuasion). During the former, the miraculous could scarcely be called an extraordinary mode of Divine communication, since men generally, Jews and Gentiles alike, expected miracles. Outside this general circle (among deeper thinkers) there was only a "feeling after God," which in no case led up to firm conviction. But in the second stage personal determination is the great characteristic. Reason has taken the place of sense; the child has grown to the man. The ancient world as much expected an argument from the miraculous as we do from the purely rational or the logically evidential. That was their mode of apprehension, this is ours. To them, in one sense, the miraculous was really not the miraculous, but the expected; to us it is and would be interference with our laws and habits of thinking. It was adapted to the first period; it is not to the second.

It would lead beyond our present limits to inquire into the connection of this change with the appearance of the God-man and the indwelling of the Holy Ghost in the Church. As we have shown in a previous Volume, under the Old Testament the Holy Spirit was chiefly known and felt as a power. The "still small voice" marks the period of transition.

"Prophetism" was, so to speak, the introduction of the "still small voice" into the world — first in a preparatory manner; in the fullness of time, as in all fullness, in the Christ; and finally as indwelling in the Church of God. These remarks will show what kind of questions are incidentally raised in the course of this history. Even in this respect the reader will have noticed progression in the successive Volumes of this Bible History. Otherwise also, it is hoped, he will mark it in these pages and in the notes, in the fuller and more critical treatment of all questions. A new feature here is the introduction of a few Jewish and Rabbinical notices, which may prove interesting and useful. In general, while I have endeavored to make my investigations thoroughly independent, and, so far as I could, original, it will, I trust, be also found that I have not neglected any sources of information within my reach. But above all, I would ever seek to keep steadily in view, as my main object, the practical and spiritual interest of this history. It all leads up to the Person of Christ, the Miracle of Miracles — the Miracle which gives meaning and unity to all others, and which is the truest evidence of them all. Thank God, we have sufficient and most firm historical ground for our faith in Him, as well as the inward teaching and the assurance of the Holy Ghost; sufficient, not indeed to supersede the necessity of faith, but to make that "blessed faith," so well grounded, so glorious, so joyous, and so transforming in its power, not only reasonable to us, but of obligatory duty to all men.

ALFRED EDERSHEIM.
LODERS VICARAGE, BRIDPORT Easter, 1880.

CHAPTER 1: JEWISH VIEW OF THE HISTORY OF DAVID — AMNON'S CRIME — ABSALOM'S VENGEANCE — FLIGHT OF ABSALOM — THE WISE WOMAN OF TEKOAH — ABSALOM RETURNS TO JERUSALEM — HIS CONSPIRACY — DAVID'S FLIGHT.

(2 SAMUEL 13-16)

IN studying the history of the Old Testament, every thoughtful Christian must feel that a special interest attaches to the views and interpretations of the ancient Synagogue. Too often they are exaggerated, carnal, and even contrary to the real meaning of Holy Scripture. But, on the other hand, there are subjects on which we may profitably learn from Jewish teaching. Among them are some of the opinions expressed by the Rabbis on the history and character of David. A brief review of these may be helpful, and serve both as retrospect of the past, and as preparation for the study of the closing years of his reign.

Considering the important part which David sustains in the history of Israel, the views expressed by the ancient Synagogue are, on the whole, remarkably free from undue partiality. But beyond this there is a shrewd discernment of real under apparent motives, and a keen appreciation of the moral bearing of actions. The bright side of David's character is dwelt upon his true humility, the affectionateness of his disposition, the faithfulness of his friendship, and, above all, his earnest heart-piety, which distinguished him not only from the monarchs of heathen nations, but from all his contemporaries, and made him for all time one of the heroes of faith.

On the other hand, his failings and sins are noted, and traced to self-indulgence, to rashness in arriving at conclusions, to suspiciousness in listening to every breath of slander, and even to a tendency to revengefulness, — all, we may observe, truly Oriental failings, the undisguised account of which is, of course, evidential of the truthfulness of the narrative. But what the Rabbis lay special stress upon is, that, while David kept indwelling sin in check, he failed in the full subdual, or rather in the moral renovation, of the heart. This led to his final and terrible sin. Of course, the Rabbis take a defective view of the case, since it would be more correct to reverse their statement. Nor should we omit to notice their conception of the higher aspects of his history. The typical bearing of his life is not lost sight of, and in every phase of it they point forward to "David's better Son." They also delight in marking throughout the overruling guidance of God, how the early training and history of David were intended to fit him for his calling; how, in Divine Providence, his failings and sins were, so to speak, ever reflected in their punishment, as, for example, his rashness in dividing the inheritance of Mephibosheth with his unworthy servant in the similar loss sustained by Rehoboam, David's grandson; how his life is full of deeper lessons; and how in the fifteenth Psalm he embodies in brief summary the whole spiritual outcome of the Law (this is noticed in Maccabees 24 a).

But of special interest in this history are the views taken of David's repentance, and of the consequences which followed from his great sin. David is here set before us as the model and ideal of, and the encouragement to, true repentance. In fact, tradition goes even further. It declares that the sin of Israel in making the golden calf and the fall of David were only recorded — it might almost seem, that they were only allowed — for the sake of their lessons about repentance. The former showed that, even if the whole congregation had erred and strayed, the door of mercy was still open to them; the latter, that not only for Israel as a whole, but for each individual sinner, however low his fall, there was assurance of forgiveness, if with true penitence he turned to God. The one case proved that nothing was too great for God to pardon; the other that there was not any one beneath His gracious notice. Be they many, or only one solitary individual, the ear of God was equally open to the cry of the repentant (comp. Av. Sar. 4. b, 5. a). The other point to which the Rabbis call attention is, that all the trials of David's later life, and all the judgments which overtook him and his house, might be traced up to his great sin, which, though personally pardoned, made itself felt in its consequences throughout the whole of his after-history (comp. especially Sanh. 107. a and b, where there are some interesting notices about David).

It cannot be doubted that there is deep truth in this view. For, although David was graciously forgiven, and again received into God's favor, neither he nor his government ever wholly recovered from the moral shock of his fall. It is not merely that his further history was attended by an almost continuous succession of troubles, but that these troubles, while allowed of God in judgment, were all connected with a felt and perceptible weakness on his part, which was the consequence of his sin. If the figure may be allowed, henceforth David's hand shook, and his voice trembled; and both what he did and what he said, alike in his own household and in the land, bore evidence of it.

As we reckon, it must have been about the twentieth year of his reign, when the sin of his son Amnon proved the beginning of a long series of domestic and public troubles.

In this instance also it was carnal lust which kindled the devouring flame. The gloss of the LXX. is likely to be correct, that David left unpunished the incest of Amnon with Tamar, although committed under peculiarly aggravating circumstances, on account of his partiality for him as being his first-born son. This indulgence on the part of his father may also account for the daring recklessness which marked Amnon's crime. The sentence of the Divine law upon such sin was, indeed, unmistakable (Leviticus 20:20:17). But a doting father, smitten with moral weakness, might find in the remembrance of his own past sin an excuse for delay, if not a barrier to action; for it is difficult to wield a heavy sword with a maimed arm.

Two years had passed since this infamous deed. But there was one who had never forgiven it. Absalom had not forgotten the day when his brave and noble sister, after having vainly offered such resistance as she could, driven with her shame from the door of her heartless brother, had brought back the tale of her disgrace, — her maiden-princess's "sleeved upper garment" rent, in token of mourning, her face defiled with ashes, her hand upon her head, as if staggering under its burden, and bitterly lamenting her fate. So fair had she gone forth on what seemed her errand of mercy; so foully had she been driven back!

These two years had the presence in his home of a loved sister, now "desolate" for ever, kept alive the remembrance of an irreparable wrong. The king had been "very wroth" — no more than that; but Absalom would be avenged, and his revenge should not only be signal, but overtake Amnon when least suspecting it, and in the midst of his pleasures. Thus Amnon's sin and punishment would, so to speak, be in equipoise. Such a scheme could not, however, be immediately carried out. It required time, that so all suspicion might be allayed. But then, as Absalom's plan of revenge was peculiarly Oriental, these long delays to make sure of a victim are also characteristic of the lands of still, deep passion. At the same time, the readiness with which Jonadab, Amnon's cousin (13:3) and clever adviser in wickedness, could suggest, before it was correctly known, what had taken place (vers. 32,

33), shows that, despite his silence, Absalom had not been able effectually to conceal his feelings. Perhaps the king himself was not quite without suspicion, however well Absalom had played his part. And now follows the terrible history. It is the time of sheep-shearing on Absalom's property, not very far from Jerusalem — a merry, festive season in the East. Absalom pressingly invites to it the king and his court, well knowing that such an invitation would be declined. But if the king himself will not come, at least let the heir-presumptive be there; and, if the king somewhat sharply takes up this suspicious singling out of Amnon, Absalom does not ask him only, but all the king's sons.

The consent has been given, and the rest of the story is easily guessed. Absalom's well-concerted plan; the feast, the merriment, the sudden murder; the hasty flight of the affrighted princes; the exaggerated evil tidings which precede them to Jerusalem; the shock to the king and his courtiers; then the partial relief on the safe arrival of the fugitives, followed by the horror produced as they tell the details of the crime — all this is sketched briefly, but so vividly that we can almost imagine ourselves witnesses of the scene. It was well for Absalom that he had fled to his maternal grandfather at Geshur. For all his life long the king could not forget the death of his firstborn, although here also time brought its healing to the wound. Absalom had been three years in Geshur — and "King David was restrained from going out after Absalom, because he was comforted concerning Amnon."

Great as Absalom's crime had been, we can readily understand, that popular sympathy would in large measure be on the side of the princely offender. He had been provoked beyond endurance by a dastardly outrage, which the king would not punish because the criminal was his favorite. To the popular, especially the Eastern mind, the avenger of Tamar might appear in the light of a hero rather than of an offender. Besides, Absalom had everything about him to win the multitude. Without any bodily blemish from head to foot, he was by far the finest-looking man in Israel. Common report had it that, when obliged once a year, on account of its thickness, to have his long flowing hair cut, it was put, as a matter of curiosity, in the scales, and found amounting to the almost incredible weight of twenty shekels. How well able he was to ingratiate himself by his manners, the after history sufficiently shows. Such was the man who had been left in banishment these three years, while Amnon had been allowed — so far as the king was concerned — to go unpunished!

Whether knowledge of this popular sympathy or other motives had induced Joab's interference, there seems no doubt that he had repeatedly interceded for Absalom; until at last he felt fully assured that "the heart of the king was against Absalom" (14:1).

In these circumstances Joab resorted to a not uncommon Eastern device. At Tekoah, about two hours south of Bethlehem, lived "a wise woman," specially capable of aiding Joab in a work which, as we judge, also commanded her sympathy. Arrayed in mourning, she appeared before the king to claim his interference and protection. Her two sons — so she said — had quarreled; and as no one was present to interpose, the one had killed the other. And now the whole family sought to slay the murderer!

True, he was guilty — but what mattered the "avenging of blood" to her, when thereby she would lose her only remaining son, and so her family become extinct? Would the death of the one bring back the life of the other — "gather up the water that was spilt"? Was it needful that she should be deprived of both her sons? Thus urged, the king promised his interference on her behalf. But this was only the introduction to what the woman really wished to say. First, she pleaded, that if it were wrong thus to arrest the avenging of blood, she would readily take the guilt upon herself (ver. 9). Following up this plea, she next sought and obtained the king's assurance upon oath, that there should be no further "destroying" merely for the sake of avenging blood (ver. 11). Evidently the king had now yielded in principle what Joab had so long sought. It only remained to make clever application of the king's concession. This the woman did; and, while still holding by the figment of her story (vers. 16, 17), she plied the king with such considerations, as that he was always acting in a public capacity; that lost life could not be restored; that pardon was God like, since He "does not take away a soul, but deviseth thoughts not to drive away one driven away;" and, lastly, that, to her and to all, the king was like the Angel of the Covenant, whose "word" was ever "for rest."

David could have no further difficulty in understanding the real meaning of the woman's mission. Accordingly, Joab obtained permission to bring back Absalom, but with this condition, that he was not to appear in the royal presence. We regard it as evidence of the prince's continued disfavor, that Joab afterwards twice refused to come to him, or to take a message to the king. It was a grave mistake to leave such a proud, violent spirit to brood for two years over supposed wrongs. Absalom now acted towards Joab like one wholly reckless — and the message which Joab finally undertook to deliver was in the same spirit. At last a reconciliation took place between the king and his son — but only outwardly, not really, for already Absalom had other schemes in view.

Once more we notice here the consequences of David's fatal weakness, as manifest in his irresolution and half-measures. Morally paralyzed, so to speak, in consequence of his own guilt, his position sensibly and increasingly weakened in popular estimation, that series of disasters, which had formed the burden of God's predicted judgments, now followed in the natural sequence of events. If even before his return from Geshur Absalom had been a kind of popular hero, his presence for two years in Jerusalem in semi-banishment must have increased the general sympathy. Whatever his enemies might say against him, he was a splendid man — every inch a prince, brave, warm-hearted, and true to those whom he loved — witness even the circumstance, told about Jerusalem, that he had called that beautiful child, his only daughter, after his poor dishonored sister (2 Samuel 14:27), while, unlike an Oriental, he cared not to bring his sons prominently forward.

Daring he was — witness his setting Joab's barley on fire; but an Eastern populace would readily forgive, rather like in a prince, what might almost be called errors on the side of virtue. And now Absalom was coming forward like a real prince! His state-carriage and fifty outrunners would always attract the admiration of the populace. Yet he was not proud — quite the contrary. In fact, never had a prince taken such cordial interest in the people, nor more ardently wished to see their wrongs redressed; nor yet was there one more condescending. Day by day he might be seen at the entering of the royal palace, where the crowd of suppliants for redress were gathered. Would that he had the power, as he had the will, to see them righted! It might not be the king's blame; but there was a lack of proper officials to take cognizance of such appeal-cases — in short, the government was wrong, and the people must suffer in consequence. As we realize the circumstances, we can scarcely wonder that thus "Absalom stole the hearts of the men of Israel."

How long this intrigue was carried on we cannot accurately determine, and only once more wonder at the weakness of the king who left it so entirely unnoticed. That the conspiracy which Absalom had so carefully prepared, though kept very secret, was widely ramified, appears from the circumstance, that, immediately on its outbreak, he could send "spies throughout all the tribes," to ascertain and influence the feelings of the people generally, and to bid his adherents, on a preconcerted signal, gather around him.

More than that, it seems likely that Ahithophel, one of David's privy councilors, and deemed the ablest of his advisers, had, from the first, been in the secret, and, if so, probably directed the conspiracy. This would explain the strange coincidence of Ahithophel's absence from Jerusalem at the time of the outbreak, and his presence at his native Giloh, not far from Hebron (Joshua 15:51). Nor is it likely that a man like Ahithophel would so readily have obeyed the summons of Absalom if he had been until then a stranger to his plans, and had not had good reason to expect success. And, indeed, if his advice had been followed, the result would have answered his anticipations.

The place chosen for the rising was Hebron, both on account of the facilities it offered for retreat in case of failure, and as the city where formerly (in the case of David) a new royalty had been instituted; perhaps also as the birthplace of Absalom, and, as has been suggested, because the transference of the royal residence to Jerusalem may have left dissatisfaction in Hebron. Absalom obtained the king's permission to go thither, on pretense of paying a vow made at Geshur. It was a clever device for entrapping two hundred influential persons from Jerusalem to invite them to accompany him, on pretext of taking part in the sacrificial feast. Arrived at Hebron, the mask was thrown off, and the conspiracy rapidly assumed most formidable proportions. Tidings of what had passed speedily reached Jerusalem. It was a wise measure on the part of the king to resolve on immediate flight from Jerusalem, not only to avoid being shut up in the city, and to prevent a massacre in its streets, but to give his adherents the opportunity of gathering around him. Indeed, in the hour of danger, the king seemed, for a brief space, his old self again. We can quite understand how, in David's peculiar state of mind, trials in which he recognized the dealings of God would rouse him to energy, while the even tenor of affairs left him listless. No weakness now — outward or inward! Prudence, determination, and courage in action; but, above all, a constant acknowledgment of God, self-humiliation, and a continuous reference of all to Him, marked his every step. In regard to this, we may here notice the progress of David's spiritual experience, marking how every act in this drama finds expression in the Book of Psalms. As Abraham perpetuated his progress through the land by rearing an altar unto Jehovah in every place where he sojourned, so David has chronicled every phase in his inner and outer life by a Psalm — a waymark and an altar for lone pilgrims in all ages. First, we turn to Psalms 41 and 45 — the former in which the designation Jehovah, the latter in which that of Elohim, prevails, — which become more full of meaning if (with Professor Delitzsch) we infer from them, that during the four years Absalom's plot was ripening, the king was partially incapacitated by some illness. These two Psalms, then, mark the period before the conspiracy actually broke out, and find their typical counterpart in the treachery of Judas Iscariot. Read in this light, these Psalms afford an insight into the whole history of this risings political as well as religious. Other two Psalms, 3 and 63, refer to David's flight; while the later events in, and the overthrow of the conspiracy, form the historical background of Psalms 61, 39, and 62.

When leaving Jerusalem in their flight, the king and his followers made a halt at "the far house." Besides his family, servants and officials, his body-guard (the Cherethi and Pelethi), and the six hundred tried warriors, who had been with him in all his early wanderings, accompanied him. In that hour of bitterness the king's heart was also cheered by the presence and steadfast adherence of a brave Philistine chieftain, Ittai, who had cast in his lot with David and with David's God. He had brought with him to Jerusalem his family (2 Samuel 15:22) and a band of adherents (ver. 20); and his fidelity and courage soon raised him to the command of a division in David's army (18:2).

It was winter, or early spring, when the mournful procession passed through a crowd of weeping spectators over the Kidron, to take the way of the wilderness that led towards Jericho and the Jordan.

At the foot of the Mount of Olives they again paused. Here the Levites, headed by Zadok the priest, put down the Ark, which had accompanied David, until the high-priest Abiathar, and the rest of the people who were to join the king, came up out of the city. They were wise as well as good words with which David directed the Ark of God to be taken back. At the same time he established communication with the city through the priests. He would wait by "the fords" of the wilderness until the sons of the two priests should bring him trustworthy tidings by which to guide his further movements.

It reads almost like prophecy, this description of the procession of weeping mourners, whom Jerusalem had cast out, going up "the ascent of the olive-trees," and once more halting at the top, "where it was wont to worship God!"

A little before, the alarming news had come that Ahithophel had joined the conspiracy. But now a welcome sight greeted them. Hushai, the Archite (comp. Joshua 16:2), David's friend and adviser, came to meet the king, and offered to accompany him. But the presence of unnecessary non-combatants would manifestly have entailed additional difficulties, especially if of the age of Hushai. Besides, a man like the Archite might render David most material service in Jerusalem, if, by feigning to join the conspirators, he could gain the confidence of Absalom, and so, perhaps, counteract the dreaded counsels of Ahithophel. Accordingly, Hushai was sent back to the city, there to act in concert with the priests.

Twice more David's progress was interrupted before he and his men reached Ayephim.

First it was Ziba, who, deeming this a good opportunity for securing to himself the covered property of his master, came on pretext of bringing provisions for the fugitives, but really to falsely represent Mephibosheth as engaged in schemes for recovering the throne of Israel amidst the general confusion. The story was so manifestly improbable, that we can only wonder at David's haste in giving it credence, and according to Ziba what he desired. Another and sadder interruption was the appearance of Shimei, a distant kinsman of Saul. As David, surrounded by his soldiers and the people, passed Bahurim, on the farther side of the Mount of Olives, Shimei followed on the opposite slope of the hill, casting earth and stones at the king, and cursing him with such words as these: "Get away! get away! thou man of blood! thou wicked man!" thus charging him, by implication, with the death, if not of Saul and Jonathan, yet of Abner and Ishbosheth. Never more truly than on this occasion did David act and speak like his old self, and, therefore, also as a type of the Lord Jesus Christ in similar circumstances (comp. Luke 9:52- 56). At that moment, when he realized that all which had come upon him was from God, and when the only hope he wished to cherish was not in human deliverance, but in God's mercy, he would feel more than ever how little he had in common with the sons of Zeruiah, and how different were the motives and views which animated them (2 Samuel 16:10). Would that he had ever retained the same spirit as in this the hour of his deepest humiliation, and had not, after his success, relapsed into his former weakness! But should not all this teach us, that, however necessary a deep and true sense of guilt and sin may be, yet if sin pardoned continueth sin brooded over, it becomes a source, not of sanctification, but of moral weakness and hindrance? Let the dead bury their dead, but let us arise and follow Christ and, "forgetting those things which are behind, and reaching forth unto those things which are before," let us "press toward the mark for the prize of the high calling of God in Christ Jesus" (Philippians 3:13, 14).

CHAPTER 2: AHITHOPHEL'S TWOFOLD ADVICE — HUSHAI PREVENTS IMMINENT DANGER — DAVID IS INFORMED, AND CROSSES THE JORDAN — THE BATTLE IN THE FOREST — DEATH OF ABSALOM — MOURNING OF DAVID — DAVID'S MEASURES — RETURN TO GILGAL — BARZILLAI AND JOAB AS REPRESENTATIVE MEN OF THEIR PERIOD — FEDERAL REPUBLICAN RISING UNDER SHEBA — MURDER OF AMASA — DEATH OF SHEBA.

(2 SAMUEL 16-20)

DAVID had not left the capital a moment too soon. He had scarcely quitted the city when Absalom and his forces appeared, and took possession of it. Hushai the Archite was one of the first to welcome him with feigned allegiance. There was a touch of boastful self-confidence about the manner in which the new king received his father's old counselor, which the experienced man of the world well knew how to utilize. By skillful flattery of his vanity, Absalom was soon gained, and Hushai obtained access to his counsels. Thus far everything had prospered with Absalom. Jerusalem had been occupied without a struggle; and the new king now found himself at the head of a very large force, though of wholly undisciplined troops. But Ahithophel at least must have known that, though David had fled, his cause was far from lost. On the contrary, he was at the head of veteran warriors, filled with enthusiasm for their leader, and commanded by the ablest generals in the land. Besides, account must also be taken of the reaction which would undoubtedly set in. The flush of confidence on the part of Absalom's raw levies, caused by success where no resistance had been offered, would pass away in measure as the real difficulties of their undertaking daily more and more appeared; while, on the other hand, sympathy with David, and adherents to his cause, would increase in the same proportion. In these circumstances even a much less sagacious adviser than Ahithophel, whose counsel was regarded in those days as if a man had inquired of the oracle of God, would have felt that Absalom's chief, if not his sole chance of success, lay in a quick and decisive stroke, such as should obviate the necessity of a protracted campaign. But first Ahithophel must secure himself, and, indeed all the adherents of Absalom.

Considering the vanity and folly of Absalom, of which his easy reception of Hushai must have afforded fresh evidence to Ahithophel, and David's well-known weakness towards his children, it was quite possible that a reconciliation might yet take place between the usurper and his father. In that case Ahithophel would be the first, the other leaders in the rebellion the next, to suffer. The great aim of an unscrupulous politician would therefore be to make the breach between father and son publicly and absolutely permanent. This was the object of the infamous advice which Ahithophel gave Absalom (2 Samuel 16:21, 22), though, no doubt, he represented it as affording, in accordance with Oriental custom, public evidence that he had succeeded to the throne. While recoiling with horror from this unnatural crime, we cannot but call to mind the judgment predicted upon David (2 Samuel 12:11, 12), and note how, as so often was the case, the event, supernaturally foretold, happened, not by some sudden interference, but through a succession of natural causes.

Having thus secured himself and his fellow-conspirators, Ahithophel proposed to select 12,000 men, make a rapid march, and that very night surprise David's followers, weary, dispirited, greatly outnumbered, and not yet properly organized. Had this advice been followed, the result would probably have been such as Ahithophel anticipated. A panic would have ensued, David fallen a victim, and with his death his cause been for ever at an end. But a higher power than the wisdom of the renowned Gilonite guided events. In the language of Holy Scripture, "Jehovah had appointed to defeat the good counsel of Ahithophel" (Samuel 17:14).

But, as first explained to Absalom and the council of Israelitish elders, Ahithophel's advice at once commended itself to their acceptance. Hushai seems not to have been present at that meeting. He was too prudent to intrude unbidden into the king's council-chamber. Besides, he had made arrangements for communicating with David before any measure of his enemies could have been executed. Just outside the city wall, by the "En-Rogel," "the Fuller's Fountain" — for they dared not show themselves in the city, the two young priests, Jonathan and Ahimaaz the swift-footed (2 Samuel 18:3), waited in readiness to carry tidings to David.

Although Absalom had followed Ahithophel's vile advice, by which no immediate danger was incurred, it was another thing to take so decisive a step as to risk the flower of his army in a night attack upon David. If Ahithophel had retired from the royal presence in the expectation of seeing his counsel immediately carried out, he was soon to find himself disappointed. Hushai was next sent for, and consulted as to the measure proposed by Ahithophel. It was easy for the old statesman to conjure up difficulties and dangers to one so inexperienced and so irresolute as Absalom, and still more, by means of unlimited flattery, to turn one so vain into another course. Absalom had only to speak, and all Israel would gather to him from Dan even to Beer-sheba, — they would light upon David like the dew upon the grass; or if he fled into a city, why, cart-ropes would suffice to drag it, to the smallest stone, into the nearest river! On the other hand, this was the worst time for attacking David and his men when they were desperate. The idea of a night surprise was altogether inadmissible, bearing in mind David's great experience in such warfare; while any mishap, however small, would be fatal to Absalom's cause. We scarcely wonder, even taking the merely rational view of it, that in such a council-chamber the advice of Hushai should have prevailed, although we recognize none the less devoutly, the Hand of God in ordering all. There was one, however, who did not deceive himself as to the consequences of this fatal mistake. Ahithophel knew, as if he had already witnessed it, that from this hour Absalom's cause was lost. His own course was soon and decisively chosen. He returned to his city, set his affairs in order, and, with the deliberate cynicism of a man who has lost all faith, committed that rare crime in Israel, suicide. Typical as the history of David is throughout, we cannot fail to see here also a terrible prefigurement of the end of him, who, having been the friend and companion of the Lord Jesus — perhaps regarded as the "wise adviser" among the simple disciples — betrayed his Master, and, like Ahithophel, ended by hanging himself (Matthew 27:5). Meanwhile, Hushai had communicated with the priests in Jerusalem. His counsel had, indeed, been adopted; but it was impossible to know what one so irresolute as Absalom might ultimately do. At any rate, it was necessary David should be informed, so as to secure himself against a surprise. A trusty maidservant of the priest carried the message to the young men by the "Fuller's Fountain." At the last moment their enterprise was almost defeated. A lad — probably one of those stationed to watch any suspicious movement — noticed their hurried departure in the direction of David's camp.

Happily, the young men had observed the spy, and got the start of those sent after them. It was not the first nor yet the last time that an Israelitish woman wrought deliverance for her people, when at Bahurim the two young priests were successfully hidden in an empty well, and their pursuers led astray (2 Samuel 17:18-20). And here we gladly mark how different from the present inmates of Eastern harems were the mothers, wives, and daughters of Israel, — how free in their social intercourse, and how powerful in their influence, the religious and social institutions of the Old Testament forming in this respect also a preparation for the position which the New Testament would assign to woman. But to return. Coming out of their concealment, the two priests reached the encampment safely, and informed David of his danger. Ere the morning light he and all his followers had put the Jordan between them and their enemies; and anything like a surprise was henceforth impossible.

It all happened as Ahithophel had anticipated. The revolution now changed into a civil war, of which the issue could not be doubtful. David and his forces fell back upon Mahanaim, "a strong city in a well-provisioned country, with a mountainous district for retreat in case of need, and a warlike and friendly population."

Here adherents soon gathered around him, while wealthy and influential heads of clans not only openly declared in his favor, but supplied him with all necessaries. We are inclined to regard the three mentioned in the sacred narrative (2 Samuel 17:27) as representative men; Shobi, of the extreme border-inhabitants, or rather foreign tributaries (comp. 2 Samuel 10:2); Machir, of the former adherents of Saul; and Barzillai, of the wealthy land-owners generally. With Absalom matters did not fare so well. Intrusting the command of his army to a relative, Amasa, the natural son of one Ithra, an Ishmaelite, and of Abigail, David's stepsister.

He crossed the Jordan to offer battle to his father's forces. These must have considerably increased since his flight from Jerusalem (comp. 2 Samuel 18:1, 2), though, no doubt, they were still greatly inferior in number to the undisciplined multitude which followed Absalom. David divided his army into three corps, led by Joab, Abishai, and Ittai — the chief command being entrusted to Joab, since the people would not allow the king himself to go into battle. The field was most skillfully chosen for an engagement with undisciplined superior numbers, being a thick forest near the Jordan, which, with its pitfalls, morasses, and entanglements, destroyed more of Absalom's followers than fell in actual contest. From the first the battle was not doubtful; it soon became a carnage rather than a conflict.

One scene on that eventful day had deeply and, perhaps, painfully impressed itself on the minds of all David's soldiers. As they marched out of Mahanaim on the morning of the battle, the king had stood by the side of the gate, and they had filed past him by hundreds and by thousands. One thing only had he been heard by all to say, and this he had repeated to each of the generals. It was simply. "Gently, for my sake, with the lad, with Absalom!"

If the admonition implied the existence of considerable animosity on the part of David's leaders against the author of this wicked rebellion, it showed, on the other hand, not only weakness, but selfishness, almost amounting to heartlessness, on the part of the king. It was, as Joab afterwards reproached him, as if he had declared that he regarded neither princes nor servants, and that it would have mattered little to him how many had died, so long as his own son was safe (2 Samuel 19:6). If such was the impression produced, we need not wonder that it only increased the general feeling against Absalom. This was soon to be brought to the test. In his pursuit of the rebels, one of Joab's men came upon a strange sight. It seems that, while Absalom was riding rapidly through the dense wood in his flight, his head had somehow been jerked in between the branches of one of the large spreading terebinths — perhaps, as Josephus has it (Ant. 7. 10, 2), having been entangled by the flowing hair. In this position the mule which he rode, perhaps David's royal mule — had run away from under him; while Absalom, half suffocated and disabled, hung helpless, a prey to his pursuers. But the soldier who first saw him knew too well the probable consequences of killing him, to be tempted to such an act by any reward, however great. He only reported it to Joab, but would not become his tool in the matter. Indeed, Joab himself seems to have hesitated, though he was determined to put an end to Absalom's schemes, which he must have resented the more, since but for his intervention the prince would not have been allowed to return to Jerusalem. And so, instead of killing, he only wounded Absalom with pointed staves, leaving it to his armor-bearers finally to dispatch the unhappy youth. His hacked and mangled remains were cast into a great pit in the wood, and covered by a large heap of stones. A terrible contrast, this unknown and unhonored criminal's grave, to the splendid monument which Absalom had reared for himself after the death of his sons! Their leader being dead, Joab, with characteristic love for his countrymen, sounded the rappel, and allowed the fugitive Israelites to escape.

But who was to carry to the king tidings of what had happened? Joab knew David too well to entrust them to any one whose life he specially valued. Accordingly, he sent a stranger, a Cushite; and only after repeated entreaty and warning of the danger, allowed Ahimaaz also to run with the news to Mahanaim. Between the outer and the inner gates of that city sat the king, anxiously awaiting the result of that decisive day. And now the watchman on the pinnacle above descried one running towards the city. Since he was alone, he could not be a fugitive, but must be a messenger. Soon the watchman saw and announced behind the first a second solitary runner. Presently the first one was so near that, by the swiftness of his running the watchman recognized Ahimaaz. If so, the tidings which he brought must be good, for on no other errand would Ahimaaz have come. And so it was! Without giving the king time for question, he rapidly announced the God-given victory. Whatever relief or comfort the news must have carried to the heart of David, he did not express it by a word. Only one question rose to his lips, only one idea of peace did his mind seem capable of contemplating, "Peace to the lad, to Absalom?"

Ahimaaz could not, or rather would not, answer. Not so the Cushite messenger, who by this time had also arrived. From his language — though, even he feared to say it in so many words — David speedily gathered the fate of his son. In speechless grief he turned from the two messengers, and from the crowd which, no doubt, was rapidly gathering in the gateway, and crept up the stairs leading to the chamber over the gate, while those below heard his piteous groans, and these words, oft repeated, "My son Absalom, my son! My son Absalom! Oh, would that I had died for thee! Absalom, my son — my son?"

That was not a joyous evening at Mahanaim, despite the great victory. The townsmen went about as if there were public mourning, not gladness. The victorious soldiers stole back into the city as if ashamed to show themselves — as if after a defeat, not after a brilliant and decisive triumph.

It was more than Joab could endure. Roughly forcing himself into the king's presence, he reproached him for his heartless selfishness, warning him that there were dangers, greater than any he had yet known, which his recklessness of all but his own feelings would certainly bring upon him. What he said was, indeed, true, but it was uttered most unfeelingly — especially remembering the part which he himself had taken in the death of Absalom — and in terms such as no subject, however influential, should have used to his sovereign. No doubt David felt and resented all this. But, for the present, it was evidently necessary to yield; and the king received the people in the gate in the usual fashion.

The brief period of insurrectionary intoxication over, the reaction soon set in. David wisely awaited it in Mahanaim. The country recalled the national glory connected with his reign, and realized that, now Absalom had fallen, there was virtually an interregnum equally unsatisfactory to all parties. It certainly was neither politic nor right on the part of David under such circumstances to employ the priests in secret negotiations with the tribe of Judah for his restoration to the throne. Indeed, all David's acts now seem like the outcome of that fatal moral paralysis into which he had apparently once more lapsed. Such, notably, was the secret appointment of Amasa as commander-in-chief in the room of Joab, a measure warranted neither by moral nor by military considerations, and certainly, to say the least, a great political mistake, whatever provocation Joab might have given. We regard in the same light David's conduct in returning to Jerusalem on the invitation of the tribe of Judah only (2 Samuel 19:14). Preparations for this were made in true Oriental fashion. The men of Judah went as far as Gilgal, where they had in readiness a ferry-boat, in which the king and his household might cross the river. Meantime, those who had cause to dread David's return had also taken their measures. Both Shimei, who had cursed David on his flight, and Ziba, who had so shamefully deceived him about Mephibosheth, went over Jordan "to meet the king." As David was "crossing," or, rather, about to embark, Shimei, who had wisely brought with him a thousand men of his own tribe, Benjamin — the most hostile to David — entreated forgiveness, appealing, as evidence of his repentance, to his own appearance with a thousand of his clansmen, as the first in Israel to welcome their king.

In these circumstances it would have been almost impossible not to pardon Shimei, though David's rebuff to Abishai, read in the light of the king's dying injunctions to Solomon (1 Kings 2:8, 9), sounds somewhat like a magniloquent public rebuke of the sons of Zeruiah, or an attempt to turn popular feeling against them. At the same time, it is evident that Shimei's plea would have lost its force, if David had not entered into separate secret negotiations with the tribe of Judah.

Ziba's motives in going to meet David need no comment. There can be little doubt that, well-informed as David must have been of all that had passed in Jerusalem, he could not but have known that the bearing and feelings of Mephibosheth had been the reverse of what his hypocritical servant had represented them (comp. 2 Samuel 19:24). All the more unjustifiable was his conduct towards the son of Jonathan.

Both the language of irritation which he used towards him, and the compromise which he attempted (19:29), show that David felt. though he would not own, himself in the wrong. Indeed, throughout, David's main object now seemed to be to conciliate favor and to gain adherents — in short, to compass his own ends by his own means, which were those of the natural, not of the spiritual man; of the Oriental, though under the influence of religion, rather than of the man after God's own heart. For, at the risk of uttering a truism, we must insist that there are only two courses possible — either to yield ourselves wholly to the guidance of the Holy Spirit, or else to follow our natural impulses. These impulses are not such as we may, perhaps, imagine, or suppose them to have become under the influence of religion. For the natural man always remains what he had been — what birth, nationality, education, and circumstances had made him. This consideration should keep us from harsh and, probably, erroneous judgments of others, and may likewise serve for our own warning and instruction.

Happily, this history also presents a brighter picture. It is that of the grand patriarchal chieftain, Barzillai, who had supported David in his adversity, and now came, despite the weight of his years, to escort the king over the Jordan. No reward or acknowledgment did he seek — in fact, the suggestion seemed almost painful. A good and true man this, happy in his independence, though not too proud to allow his son Chimham to go to court — all the more that he had nothing to gain by it. May we not legitimately infer, that his conduct was influenced not merely by loyalty to his earthly sovereign, but by the recognition of the higher spiritual truths, and the hope for Israel and the world, symbolized by the reign of David. For nearly eighty years Barzillai had watched in distant Rogelim the varying fortunes of his loved people. He remembered the time when Samuel was "judge;" he recalled the hope enkindled in the hearts of Israel when, after the brilliant exploit in his own Jabesh-gilead, Saul was proclaimed king. He had followed the waning glory of that same Saul — for far and wide are tidings carried in the East, told by watch-fires, and borne from home to home — until hope had almost died out in his soul. Then came the story of David, and increasingly, as he followed his career, or when some one would repeat one of those new Psalms — so different from the old war-songs in which Jewish deeds of valor had been recorded — ascribing all to Jehovah, and making man of no account, it all seemed to mark a new period in the history of Israel, and Barzillai felt that David was indeed God's Anointed, the symbol of Israel's real mission, and the type of its accomplishment. And at last, after the shameful defeat of Israel and the sad death of Saul, he had hailed what had taken place in Hebron. The capture of Jerusalem, the erection of a central sanctuary there, and the subjection of Israel's enemies round about, would seem to him bright links in the same chain. And though David's sad fall must have grieved him to the heart, it could never have influenced his views of Absalom's conduct, nor yet shaken his own allegiance. And now that David's reign, so far as its spiritual bearing was concerned, was evidently coming to a close — its great results achieved, its spiritual meaning realized — he would feel that nothing could undo the past, which henceforth formed part of the spiritual inheritance of Israel, or rather of that of the world at large. And so, in the spirit of Simeon, when he had witnessed the incipient fulfillment of Israel's hopes, Barzillai was content to "turn back again" to his own city, to die there, and be laid in the grave of his father and mother, who had lived in times far more troubled than his own, and had seen but "far off" that of which he had witnessed the happy accomplishment.

On the other hand, we may, at this stage of our inquiries, be allowed to place by the side of Barzillai another representative man of that period. If Barzillai was a type of the spiritual, Joab was of the national aspect of Judaism. He was intensely Jewish, in the tribal meaning of the word, not in its higher, world-wide bearing, only Judaean in everything that outwardly marked Judaism, though not as regarded its inward and spiritual reality.

Fearless, daring, ambitious, reckless, jealous, passionate, unscrupulous, but withal most loving of his country and people, faithful to, and, no doubt, zealous for his religion, so far as it was ancestral and national — Joab represented the one phase of Judaism, as Barzillai the other. Joab stands before us as a typical Eastern, or rather as the typical Eastern Judean. Nor is it without deep symbolical meaning, as we trace the higher teaching of history, that Joab, the typical Eastern Judaean, — may we not say, the type of Israel after the flesh? — should, in carrying out his own purposes and views, have at last compassed his own destruction.

David's difficulties did not end with the crossing of Jordan. On the contrary, they seemed rather to commence anew. He had been received by the tribe of Judah; a thousand Benjamites had come for purposes of their own; and probably a number of other tribesmen may have joined the king during his progress. But the tribes, in their corporate capacity, had not been asked to take part in the matter, and both David and Judah had acted as if they were of no importance. Accordingly, when the representatives of Israel arrived in Gilgal, there was fierce contention between them and the men of Judah about this unjustifiable slight — the men of Judah being the more violent, as usual with those who do a wrong.

It needed only a spark to set the combustible material on fire. A worthless man, one Sheba, a Benjamite, who happened to be there, blew a trumpet, and gave it forth to the assembled representatives of the tribes that, since they had no part in David, they should leave him to reign over those who had selected him as their king. It was just such a cry as in the general state of excitement would appeal to popular feeling. David soon found himself deserted by his Israelitish subjects, obliged to return to Jerusalem with only his own tribesmen, and threatened by a formidable revolution in front. To suppress the movement before it had time to spread and disintegrate the country by everywhere exciting tribal jealousies — such was David's first care on his return to Jerusalem, after setting his household in order (2 Samuel 20:3). But the fatal consequences of David's late conduct now appeared. True to his promise, he proposed to entrust to Amasa the command of the expedition against Sheba and what, to borrow a modern term, we may call the "Federal Republic." But, whether from personal incapacity, or, more probably, from the general want of confidence in, and dissatisfaction with, the new commander, Amasa did not even succeed in bringing together a force. As time was of the greatest importance, David felt himself obliged again to have recourse to Abishai, or rather, through him, to Joab. There was now no lack of trusty warriors, and the expedition at once moved northwards.

The forces, under the leadership of Abishai and Joab, had reached the great stone at Gibeon, when Amasa "came to meet them" from the opposite direction, no doubt, on his way to Jerusalem. Joab was, as usual, "girt with his armor-coat as a garment, and upon it the girdle of the sword, bound upon his loins, in its scabbard; and it [the scabbard] came out, and it [the sword] fell out."

Amasa seems to have been so startled by this unexpected appearance of a host with another leader as to have lost all presence of mind. He saw not the sword which Joab picked up from the ground, and now held low down in his left hand, but allowed his treacherous relative to take him by the beard, as if to kiss him, so that the sword ran into the lower part of his body. Probably Joab, while determined to rid himself of his rival, had adopted this plan, in the hope of leaving it open to doubt whether Amasa's death had been the result of accident or of criminal intention. Then, as if there were not time for delay, Joab and Abishai left the body weltering where it had fallen, and hastened on their errand.

It was a dreadful sight; and not all the urgency of the soldier whom Joab had posted by the dead or dying man could prevent the people from lingering, horror-stricken, around him. At last the body had to be removed. It had been left on the ground, probably alike as a mark of contempt and a warning to others not to provoke the jealousy of Joab. And now David's army was in full chase after Sheba and his adherents. They followed him through the whole land up to the far north among the fortresses by the Lake Merom, where he was at last tracked to Abel, or rather, Abel-Beth-maachah.

To this fortress Joab now laid siege. Its destruction, however, was averted by the wisdom of one of its women. Demanding speech of Joab from the city-wall, she reminded the general that the people of Abel had been famed, not for being rash in action, but rather wise and deliberate in counsel. Had Joab ever asked whether the town of Abel, which he was about to destroy, shared the views of Sheba, or took part in the rebellion? She, and, by implication, her fellow-citizens, were quite the contrary of turbulent conspirators. How, then, could Joab act so unpatriotically, so un-Jewishly, as to wish to destroy a city and a mother in Israel, and to swallow up the inheritance of Jehovah? And when Joab explained that it was not the destruction of a peaceable city, but the suppression of a rebellion which he sought, she proposed, as a speedy end to all trouble, that Sheba should be killed, and, in evidence of it, his head thrown over the wall. It was an easy mode of ridding themselves both of a troublesome visitor and of a terrible danger, — and the gory head cast at his feet convinced Joab that the rebellion was at an end, that he might retire from the city, dismiss his army, and return to Jerusalem. So ended the last rising against David — and, we may add, the political history of his reign.

CHAPTER 3: THE FAMINE — THE PESTILENCE — THE TEMPLE ARRANGEMENTS — DAVID'S LAST HYMN AND PROPHETIC UTTERANCE.

(2 SAMUEL 21-24; 1 CHRONICLES 21-27)

WITH the suppression of the federal revolution under Sheba, the political history of David, as related in the Second Book of Samuel, closes. Accordingly, the account of this, the second part of his reign, concludes, like that of the first (2 Samuel 8:16), with an enumeration of his principal officers (2 Samuel 20:23 to the end). What follows in the Second Book of Samuel (21-24), must be regarded as an Appendix, giving, first, an account of the famine which desolated the land (21:1-14), probably in the earlier part, and of the pestilence which laid it waste, probably towards the close of David's reign (24); secondly, some brief notices of the Philistine wars (21:15-22), and a detailed register of David's heroes (23:8-39), neither of which will require comment on our part; and, lastly, David's final Psalm of thanksgiving (22), and his last prophetic utterances (23:1-7). All these are grouped together at the end of the Second Book of Samuel, probably because it was difficult to insert them in any other place consistently with the plan of the work, which, as we have repeatedly noted, was not intended to be a biography or a history of David, chronologically arranged. Perhaps we should add, that the account of the pestilence was placed last in the book (24), because it forms an introduction to the preparations made for the building of the Temple by Solomon. For, as we understand it, no sooner had the place been divinely pointed out where the Sanctuary should be reared, than David commenced such preparations for it as he could make. And here the First Book of Chronicles supplements most valuable notices, not recorded in any other part of Scripture. From these we learn what David did and ordered in his kingdom with a view to the building of the Temple and the arrangement of its future services (1 Chronicles 22-29). We have thus four particulars under which to group our summary of what we have designated as the Appendix to the History of David, the famine; the pestilence; the Temple arrangements; and the last Psalm and prophecy of the king.

1. The Famine (2 Samuel 21:1-14). — There is not a more harrowing narrative in Holy Scripture than that connected with the famine which for three years desolated Palestine. Properly to understand it, we require to keep two facts in view. First, the Gibeonites, who, at the time of Joshua, had secured themselves from destruction by fraud and falsehood (Joshua 9:3, etc.), were really heathens — Hivites, or, as they are called in the sacred text, Amorites, which was a general designation for all the Canaanites (Genesis 10:16; 15:16; Joshua 9:1; 11:3; 12:8, etc.). We know, only too well, the character of the Canaanite inhabitants of the land; and although, after their incorporation with Israel, the Gibeonites must have been largely influenced for good, their habits of thinking and feeling would change comparatively little, — the more so because, as there would be few, if any, intermarriages between them and native Israelites, they would be left, at least socially, isolated. This will account for their ferocious persistence in demanding the uttermost punishment prescribed by the law.

The provisions of this law must be our second point of consideration. Here we have again to bear in mind the circumstances of the times, the existing moral, social, and national conditions, and the spiritual stage which Israel had then reached. The fundamental principle, laid down in Numbers 35, was that of the holiness of the land in which Jehovah dwelt among His people. This holiness must be guarded (ver. 34). But one of the worst defilements of a land was that by innocent blood shed in it. According to the majestic view of the Old Testament, blood shed by a murderer's hand could not be covered up — it was, so to speak, a living thing which cried for vengeance, until the blood of him that had shed it silenced its voice (ver. 33), or, in other words, until the moral equipoise had been restored. While, therefore, the same section of the law provided safety in case of unintentional homicide (vers. 10-29), and regulated the old practice of "avenging blood," it also protected the land against crime, which it would not allow to be compensated for by money (ver. 31). Hence the Gibeonites were strictly within the letter of the law in demanding retaliation on the house of Saul, in accordance with the universally acknowledged Old Testament principle of the solidarity of a family; and David had no alternative but to concede their claim. This is one aspect of the question. The other must be even more reverently approached. We can only point out how they who lived in those times (especially such as the Gibeonites) would feel that they might cry to God for vengeance, and expect it from the Just and True One; and how the sternest lessons concerning public breach of faith and public crimes would be of the deepest national importance after such a reign as that of Saul.

The story itself may be told in few sentences. For some reason unrecorded — perhaps in the excess of his carnal zeal, but certainly without sufficient grounds — Saul had made havoc among the Gibeonites, in direct contravention of those solemn engagements into which Israel had entered, and which up to that time had been scrupulously observed. When, afterwards, a famine desolated the land for three years, and David sought the face of Jehovah, he was informed that it was due to the blood-guilt which still rested on the house of Saul.

Upon this the king summoned the Gibeonites, and asked them what atonement they desired for the wrong done them, so that the curse which they had invoked might no longer rest on the inheritance of Jehovah. Their answer was characteristic. "It is not a matter to us of silver or of gold, in regard to Saul and his house, nor is it ours to put to death any one in Israel." "And he said, What say ye then? and I will do it for you." Then came the demand, made with all the ferocity and irony of which they were capable, that the blood-vengeance which they, as Gibeonites, did not venture to take, should be executed for them, and that seven of Saul's descendants should be handed over to them that they might be nailed to the cross — of course after they were dead, for so the law directed — as they termed it: "To Jehovah in Gibeah of Saul, the chosen of Jehovah."

Terrible as their demand was, it could not be refused, and the two sons of Rizpah, a foreign concubine of Saul, and five sons of Merab, Saul's eldest daughter, were selected as the victims. Then this most harrowing spectacle was presented.

From the commencement of the barley harvest in April until the early rains of autumn evidenced the removal of the curse from the land, hung those lifeless, putrescent bodies, which a fierce Syrian sun shriveled and dried; and beneath them, ceaseless, restless, was the weird form of Saul's concubine. When she lay down at night it was on the coarse hair-cloth of mourners, which she spread upon the rock; but day and night was she on her wild, terrible watch to chase from the mangled bodies the birds of prey that, with hoarse croaking, swooped around them, and the jackals whose hungry howls woke the echoes of the night.

Often has Judaea capta been portrayed as weeping over her slain children. But as we realize the innocent Jewish victims of Gentile persecution in the Middle Ages, and then remember the terrible cry under the Cross, this picture of Rizpah under the seven crosses, chasing from the slaughtered the vultures and the jackals, seems ever to come back to us as its terrible emblem and type.

"And it was told David what Rizpah, the daughter of Aiah, the concubine of Saul, had done. And David went [himself] and took the bones of Saul, and the bones of Jonathan his son, from the men of Jabesh-gilead, who had stolen them from the street of Bethshan, where the Philistines had hanged them, when the Philistines had slain Saul in Gilboa. and he brought up from thence the bones of Saul and the bones of Jonathan his son; and they gathered the bones of them that were crucified. And the bones of Saul and Jonathan his son buried they in the country of Benjamin in Zelah, in the sepulcher of Kish his father."

2. The Pestilence. — In regard to this event, it is of the greatest importance to bear in mind that it was sent in consequence of some sin of which Israel, as a people, were guilty. True, the direct cause and immediate occasion of it were the pride and carnal confidence of David, perhaps his purpose of converting Israel into a military monarchy. But this state of mind of their king was, as we are expressly told (2 Samuel 24:1), itself a judgment upon Israel from the Lord, when Satan stood up to accuse Israel, and was allowed thus to influence David (1 Chronicles 21:1). If, as we suppose, the popular rising under Absalom and Sheba was that for which Israel was thus punished, there is something specially corresponding to the sin alike in the desire of David to have the people numbered, and in the punishment which followed. Nor ought we to overlook another Old Testament principle evidenced in this history, that of the solidarity of a people and their rulers.

It seems a confirmation of the view, that the sin of David, in wishing to ascertain the exact number of those capable of beating arms, was due to carnal elation and pride, and that the measure was somehow connected with military ambition on his part, that both in 2 Samuel and in 1 Chronicles. This story follows an enumeration of the three classes of David's heroes, and of some of their most notable feats of arms.

The unwillingness of Joab and of the other captains, to whom the king entrusted the census, arose partly from the knowledge that such an attempt at converting all Israel into a large camp would be generally disliked and disapproved — a feeling with which he and his fellow-captains would, as Israelitish patriots, fully sympathize. But religious considerations also came in, since all would feel that a measure prompted by pride and ambition would certainly bring judgment upon the people (1 Chronicles 21:3). Remonstrance having been vain, the military census was slowly and reluctantly taken, the Levites being, however, excluded from it (Numbers 1:47-54), and the royal order itself recalled before the territory of Benjamin was reached. For already David's conscience was alive to the guilt which he had incurred. It was after a night of confession and prayer on the part of David, that Gad was sent to announce to him the punishment of his sin. For, the temporal punishment appropriately followed — not preceded — the confession of public sin. Left to choose between famine, defeat, and pestilence, David wisely and well cast himself upon the Lord, finding comfort only in the thought, which has so often brought relief to those who realize it, that, even when suffering for sin, it is well to fall into the hands of Jehovah. Nor was his unuttered hope disappointed.

The pestilence, terrible as it was in its desolations, was shortened from three days to less than one day, "from the morning to the time of the assembly," viz. for the evening sacrifice.

446

Meanwhile "David and the elders, clothed in sackcloth" (1 Chronicles 21:16), were lying on their faces in humiliation before the Lord. Significantly, it was as the Divine command of mercy sped to arrest the arm of the Angel messenger of the judgment, that he became visible to David and his companions in prayer. Already he had neared Jerusalem, and his sword was stretched towards it — just above Mount Moriah, at that time still outside the city, where Aravnah the Jebusite had his threshing-floor.

It was a fitting spot for mercy upon Israel, this place where of old faithful Abraham had been ready to offer his only son unto God; fitting also as still outside the city; but chiefly in order that the pardoning and sparing mercy now shown might indicate the site where, on the great altar of burnt-offering, abundant mercy in pardon and acceptance would in the future be dispensed to Israel. At sight of the Angel with his sword pointed towards Jerusalem, David lifted his voice in humblest confession, entreating that, as the sin had been his, so the punishment might descend on him and his household, rather than on his people. This prayer marked the beginning of mercy. By Divine direction, through Gad, David and they who were with him, went to Araunah to purchase the place thus rendered for ever memorable, in order to consecrate it to the Lord by an altar, on which burnt and peace-offerings were brought. And this was to be the site for the future "house of Jehovah God," and for "the altar of the burnt-offering for Israel" (1 Chronicles 22:1).

And God had both prepared and inclined the heart of the Jebusite for the willing surrender of the site for its sacred purposes. No doubt he was a proselyte, and probably (analogously to Rahab) had been an ally in the taking of Jerusalem under Joab. It seems that Araunah and his four sons, while busy in that threshing-floor, had also seen the figure of the Angel high above them, and that it had struck terror into their hearts (1 Chronicles 21:20). When, therefore, David and his followers came, they were prepared freely to give. not only the threshing-floor, but also all within it,11 if only Jehovah were pleased to accept the prayer of the king (2 Samuel 24:23). Thus most significantly, in its typical aspect, were Jew and Gentile here brought together to co-operate in the dedication of the Temple-site. It, no doubt, showed insight into Oriental character, though we feel sure it was neither from pride nor narrow national prejudice, that David refused to accept as a gift what had been humbly and, as we believe, heartily offered. But there was evident fitness in the acquisition of the place by money on the part of David, as the representative of all Israel. And as if publicly and from heaven to ratify what had been done, fire, unkindled by man, fell upon the altar and consumed the sacrifices (1 Chronicles 21:26). But from that moment the destroying sword of the Angel was sheathed at the command of God.

3. David's Temple arrangements. Since the Lord had, in His Providence, pointed out the place where the Sanctuary was to be reared, David, with characteristic energy, began immediate preparations for a work, the greatness of which the king measured by his estimate of Him for Whose service it was designed (1 Chronicles 22:5). It almost seems as if in these arrangements all David's former vigor had come back, showing where, despite his weaknesses and failings, the king's heart really was. Besides, the youth of his son and successor Solomon, and the consideration that probably no other monarch would wield such influence in the land as he had possessed, determined David not to neglect nor defer anything that he might be able to do. First, he took a census of the "strangers," and set them to prepare the stone, iron, and timber work.

His next care was to give solemn charge to Solomon concerning what was so much on his own heart. Recapitulating all that had passed, when he first proposed to "build an house unto the Name of Jehovah," he laid this work upon his son and God-appointed successor, as the main business of his reign. Yet not as a merely outward work to be done, but as the manifestation of spiritual religion, and as the outcome of allegiance to God and His law (1 Chronicles 22:6-12). Only such principles would secure true prosperity to his reign (ver. 13). For himself, he had "by painful labor" gathered great treasures, which were to be devoted to the building of the new Temple; and he had made all possible preparations for it. Finally, summoning "the princes of Israel, with the priests and the Levites" (1 Chronicles 23:1, 2), and presenting to them his son Solomon as successor in the kingdom, he entreated their co-operation with him in what was to be the great work of the future — making it not a personal, but a national undertaking, expressive of this, that they had "set heart and soul to seek Jehovah" their God (1 Chronicles 22:19).

It was in this solemn assembly of laity and priesthood that Solomon's succession was announced and accepted, and that the future organization of the Temple Services was determined and fixed.

A census of the Levites gave their number, from thirty years and upwards, at 38,000 men. Of these 24,000 were appointed to attend to the general ministry of the sanctuary (23:28-32), 6,000 to act as "officers and judges," 4,000 for instrumental music, and 4,000 as choristers — the latter (and probably also the former class) being subdivided into adepts, of which there were 288 (25:7), and learners (25:8). As all the Levites, so these 288 adepts or trained choristers were arranged by lot into twenty-four courses, a certain number of "learners" being attached to each of them. Each course of Levites had to undertake in turn such services as fell to them. Those who had charge of the gates were arranged into classes, there being altogether twenty-four posts in the Sanctuary in which watch was to be kept (1 Chronicles 26:1-19). Similarly, the priests, the descendants of Aaron, were arranged by lot into twenty-four courses for their special ministry (1 Chronicles 24:1-19). Lastly, the sacred text gives a brief account of the work of those 6000 Levites whom David appointed as "scribes and judges" (1 Chronicles 26:29-32), and of the final arrangement of the army, and of all the other public offices (1 Chronicles 27.).

4. David's last hymn and prophetic utterance (2 Samuel 22-23:2-7). — The history of David appropriately closes with a grand hymn, which may be described as alike the program and the summary of his life and reign in their spiritual aspect. Somewhat altered in language, so as to adapt it to liturgical purposes, it is inserted in our present Psalter as Psalm 18, to which we accordingly refer. This grand hymn of thanksgiving is followed — to use the language of an eminent German critic — by the prophetic testament of the king, in which he indicates the spiritual import and bearing of his kingdom.

If Psalm 18 was a grand Hallelujah, with which David quitted the scene of life, these his "last words" are the Divine attestation of all that he had sung and prophesied in the Psalms concerning the spiritual import of the kingdom which he was to found, in accordance with the Divine message that Nathan had been commissioned to bring to him. Hence these "last words" must be regarded as an inspired prophetic utterance by David, before his death, about the King and the Kingdom of God in their full and real meaning. The following is the literal rendering of this grand prophecy:

The Spirit of Jehovah speaks by me,
And His Word is on my tongue!
Saith the God of Israel,
Speaks to me the Rock of Israel:
A Ruler over man, righteous,
A Ruler in the fear of God -

And as the light of morning, when riseth the sun -
Morning without clouds -
From the shining forth out of (after) rain (sprouts
the green out of the earth!
For is not this my house with God?
Since an everlasting covenant He hath made with me,
Provided (prepared) in all things, and preserved (kept, watched over). -
Then, all my salvation and all good pleasure,
Shall He not cause it to spring forth?
And (the sons of) Belial, as thorns cast away are they all —
For they are not taken up in the hand
And the man who toucheth them,
Provides himself (lit., fills) with iron and shaft of spear,
And in fire are they utterly burned in their dwelling
(where they are).

CHAPTER 4: ADONIJAH'S ATTEMPT TO SEIZE THE THRONE — ANOINTING OF SOLOMON — GREAT ASSEMBLY OF THE CHIEFS OF THE PEOPLE — DYING CHARGE OF DAVID — ADONIJAH'S SECOND ATTEMPT AND PUNISHMENT — EXECUTION OF JOAB AND OF SHIMEI

(1 KINGS 1, 2; 1 CHRONICLES 23:1, 28-29)

THE history of David, as told in the Book of Chronicles, closes with an account of what, in its bearing on the theocracy, was of greatest importance, the public charge to Solomon in regard to the building of the Temple and the preparations for the work. On the other hand, the Book of Kings takes up the thread of prophetic history where the previous writers had dropped it. The birth of Solomon had been the beginning of the fulfillment of that glorious promise (2 Samuel 7:12-16), which gave its spiritual meaning and import to the institution of royalty in Israel. And the promises and the warnings embodied in that prediction form, so to speak, the background of the whole later history of the people of God.

Naturally, the first event recorded in this history is the formal installation of Solomon as the God-appointed successor of David (2 Samuel 7:12; 12:25; 1 Kings 8:20; 1 Chronicles 28:5-7). It was somewhat hastened by an incident which, like so many others that caused trouble in Israel, must ultimately be traced to the weakness of David himself. It has already been noticed, in the history of Amnon and in that of Absalom, to what length David carried his indulgence towards his children, and what terrible consequences resulted from it. Both Amnon and Absalom had died violent deaths. A third son of David, Chileab, whose mother was Abigail, seems also to have died. At least, so we infer from the silence of Scripture concerning him. These were the three eldest sons of David. The next in point of age was Adonijah the son of Haggith (2 Samuel 3:2-4). Like his elder brother, Amnon, he had been born in Hebron; like Absalom, he was distinguished by personal attractions. But he also, as Amnon and Absalom, had all his life been fatally indulged by David. In the expressive language of Holy Scripture, "his father had not made him sorry all his days, saying, Why hast thou done so?" (1 Kings 1:6.)

The consequence may be easily guessed. By right of primogeniture the succession to the throne seemed his. Why, then, should he not attempt to seize upon a prize so covered? His father had, indeed, sworn to Bathsheba that Solomon should be his successor (1 Kings 1:13, 30), and that on the ground of express Divine appointment; and the prophet Nathan (ver. 11), as well as the leading men in Church and State, not only knew (as did most people in the land), but heartily concurred in it. But what mattered this to one who had never learned to subject his personal desires to a higher will? This supposed Divine appointment of his younger brother might, after all, have been only a matter of inference to David, and Nathan and Bathsheba have turned it to account, the one because of the influence which he possessed over Solomon, the other from maternal fondness and ambition. At any rate, the prospect of gaining a crown was worth making an effort; and the more quickly and boldly, the more likely of success.

It must be admitted that circumstances seemed specially to favor Adonijah's scheme. David was indeed only seventy years old; but premature decay, the consequence of a life of exposure and fatigue, had confined him not only to his room (ver. 15), but to his bed (ver. 47). Such was his weakness, that the body had lost its natural heat, which could not be restored even by artificial means; so that the physicians, according to the medical views of those times, had advised bodily contact with a young, healthy subject. For this purpose Abishag, a fair maiden from Shunem, had been brought into the king's harem. In David's utter physical prostration, Adonijah might reckon on being able to carry on his scheme without interference from the king.

Indeed, unless David had been specially informed, tidings of the attempt would not even have reached his sick chamber until it was too late. The rebellion of Absalom had failed because David was in full vigor at the time, and so ably supported by Abiathar the priest and Joab the captain of the host. But Adonijah had attached these two to his interests. It is not difficult to understand the motives of Joab in trying to secure the succession for one who would owe to him his elevation, not to speak of the fact that the rival candidate for the throne was Solomon, the "man of peace," the pupil of Nathan, and the representative of the "religious party" in the land. But it is not so easy to account for the conduct of Abiathar, unless it was prompted by jealousy of Zadok, who officiated at Gibeon (1 Chronicles 16:39). As the latter was considered the principal Sanctuary (1 Kings 3:4), the high-priest who officiated there might have been regarded as entitled to the Pontificate, when the temporary dual service of Gibeon and Jerusalem should give place to the permanent arrangements of the Temple. If such was his motive, Abiathar may have also wished to lay the new king under personal obligations.

From such a movement — which took advantage first of the indulgence, and then of the illness of David; which compassed aims that every one would know to be equally contrary to the Divine appointment and the express declarations of the aged king; and in which the chief agents were an ambitious priest and an unscrupulous military chieftain, those who were faithful to their God or to their monarch would, of course, keep aloof. Adonijah knew this, and accordingly excluded such from the invitation to the feast, at which it had been arranged his accession to the throne should be proclaimed. In other respects his measures closely resembled those taken by Absalom. For some time previous to his attempt he had sought to accustom the people to regard him as their future king by assuming royal state (1 Kings 1:5).

At length all seemed ready. It is characteristic that, in order to give the undertaking the appearance of religious sanction, the conspirators prepared a great sacrificial feast. We know the scene, and we can picture to ourselves that gathering in the shady retreat of the king's gardens, under an over-arching rock, close by the only perennial spring in Jerusalem — that of the Valley of Kidron — which now bears the name of the "fountain of the Virgin," at that time the En-Rogel ("Spring of the Spy," or else "of the Fuller").

But a higher power than man's overruled events. To outward appearance the danger was indeed most urgent, the more so that it was not known in the palace. But already help was at hand. Nathan hastened to Bathsheba, and urged on her the necessity of immediate and decisive action. If Adonijah were proclaimed king, Solomon, Bathsheba, and all their adherents would immediately be put out of the way. In such circumstances court-ceremonial must be set aside; and Bathsheba made her way into the king's sick-chamber. She spoke respectfully but earnestly; she told him fully what at that very moment was taking place in the king's gardens; she reminded him of his solemn oath about the succession, which had hitherto determined her own conduct and that of Solomon's adherents; and, finally, she appealed to him as alone competent at this crisis to determine who was to be king. The interview had not terminated when, according to previous arrangement, Nathan was announced. He had come on the same errand as Bathsheba' to inform the king of what Adonijah and his adherents were doing, and that Solomon and the king's most trusted servants had been excluded from a feast, the object of which was not concealed. Had all this been done by direction of the king? If so, why had not he, so old and faithful a counselor, been informed that Adonijah was to be proclaimed successor to the throne?

With whatever weakness David may have been chargeable, he always rose to the requirements of the situation in hours of decisive importance, when either the known will of God or else the interests of his kingdom were in question. In this instance his measures were immediate and decisive.

Recalling Bathsheba, who had withdrawn during the king's interview with Nathan, he dismissed her with words of reassurance. Then he sent for Zadok, Nathan, and Benaiah, and gave them his royal command for the immediate anointing of Solomon as king over Judah and Israel. The scene is vividly portrayed in Scripture. The king's body-guard — the Cherethi and Pelethi — under the command of Benaiah, was drawn up in front of the royal palace. Soon a vast concourse of people gathered. And now the king's state-mule, richly caparisoned, was brought out. It was an unwonted sight, which betokened some great state event. Presently, the great news became known, and rapidly spread through the streets and up the bazaars, Solomon was about to be anointed king! The people crowded together, in hundreds and thousands, from all parts of the city. And now Solomon appeared, attended by Zadok the high priest, Nathan the prophet, and Benaiah the chief of the royal guard. The procession formed, and moved forward. To avoid collision with the party of Adonijah, it took an opposite or western direction to the valley of Gihon. Here, by authority and express command of David, Solomon was anointed king with the sacred oil by the joint ministry of the high priest and the prophet. The ceremony ended, the blast of the trumpets proclaimed the accession of the new monarch, and the people burst into a ringing shout, "God save King Solomon!" The enthusiastic demonstrations of joy were truly Eastern.

There were music of pipes and acclamations of the people, until the ground beneath seemed to rend with the noise. As the procession returned, the city rang with the jubilee, until it reached the royal palace, where King Solomon seated himself in solemn state on his father's throne, and received the homage of the court, while David gave public thanks that he had lived to see that day.

Meanwhile, out in the king's gardens, the strange shouts from the city had reached Adonijah and his guests. Joab had grown uneasy as he heard the well-known sound of the trumpet. The tidings traveled quickly, and already one was in waiting to explain its meaning. But it was not as Adonijah had hoped against hope. The son of Abiathar had come to inform the conspirators of what had just taken place in Gihon and in the royal palace. And now sudden terror seized those who had but lately been so confident in their feasting. Every one of the conspirators fled, foremost among them Adonijah; nor did he deem himself safe until he had reached the sacred precincts, and laid hold on the horns of the altar. This asylum he refused to quit, until Solomon had assured him by oath that his life would be spared — though on condition that his future conduct should give the king no cause for complaint.

The events just recorded, which are only briefly indicated in 1 Chronicles 23:1, were followed by a great assembly of the chief dignitaries in Church and State (1 Chronicles 28, 29.), when the accession of Solomon to the throne was formally confirmed, and he was anointed a second time (1 Chronicles 29:22). We remember, that similarly both Saul and

David were anointed a second time, on publicly receiving the homage of their subjects (1 Samuel 11:15; 2 Samuel 2:4; 5:3). It was in this great assembly that the aged king, speaking, as it were, from his death-bed, laid before his people the deepest wishes of his heart, and told his inmost thoughts concerning the character, the stability, and the object of royalty in Israel. Beginning with an evident reference to the great promise given to him and his house, David first solemnly owned, that the appointment to the royal office — more particularly his own election and that of Solomon as his successor — was of God as Israel's supreme King, and that the stability and welfare of the kingdom depended upon faithful allegiance to Jehovah, to which he accordingly admonished Solomon and the people (1 Chronicles 28:2-10).

Then, following further the line indicated in the covenant-promise, David pointed out that the grand object of his son's reign must be to build an house unto the LORD. This would be the initial typical fulfillment of that to which the prophetic promise pointed. So deeply had the king this work at heart, that he had already prepared all the plans for the Temple; and that he dedicated to this work the vast treasures which during his long reign he had accumulated, always with this great purpose in view (1 Chronicles 28:11-29:5). But this was not a work which Solomon either could or should undertake by himself. He must be supported in it by a willing people. And when the representatives of Israel in that great assembly readily and liberally promised of their substance, David seemed to feel that the work of his life was indeed done, and that God would now let "His servant depart in peace." The solemn and joyous eulogy, and the earnest prayer for his people, and for his son and successor on the throne, with which David dismissed this assembly, form a most appropriate close to his public career.

Gladly would we here end our record of David's life. But Scripture, in its truthful narration, calls us to witness yet another scene. We stand by the death-bed of David, and hear his last injunctions to his son and successor. At this time Solomon could not have been more than twenty years of age. Probably he was even younger. However wise and well-disposed, the temptations and difficulties of his position could not but awaken fears in the heart of his father, and that in proportion as he kept in view the terms of the Divine prediction concerning his house, with its warnings as well as its promises. In regard to matters Divine and spiritual, only one plain advice need he give to Solomon. Spiritual decidedness, faithfulness, and obedience to God, such simply were the means by which the promises given to David and his house would be inherited. But all the greater were the political dangers which beset the path of the youthful king, an unscrupulous military party, headed by Joab; a dissatisfied priestly faction, ready to plot and join any rebellious movement; and ill-suppressed tribal jealousies, of whose existence Shimei had, at a critical period, given such painful evidence. The leaders of two of these parties had long forfeited their lives; indeed, only the necessities of the time could have excused either the impunity with which Joab's treachery and his murder of Abner and Amasa had been passed over, or the indulgence extended to such conduct as that of Shimei. On the other hand, gratitude to such tried adherents in adversity as the family of Barzillai had proved, was alike dictated by duty and by policy. It was not, as some would have us believe, that on his death-bed David gave utterance to those feelings of revenge which he was unable to gratify in his lifetime, but that, in his most intimate converse with his son and successor, he looked at the dangers to a young and inexperienced monarch from such powerful and unscrupulous partisans. In these circumstances it was only natural that, before dying, he should have given to his son and successor such advice for his future guidance as his long experience would suggest; and similarly that, in so doing, he should have reviewed the chief dangers and difficulties which had beset his own path, and have referred to the great public crimes which, during his reign, had necessarily been left unpunished. The fact that, even before his death, an attempt had been made to elevate Adonijah to the throne, contrary alike to the known will of God and the appointment of David, and that the chief actors in this had been Joab and Abiathar, must have recalled the past to his mind, and shown him that the fire had been smoldering these many years, and might at any time burst into flame. But, however natural, and even lawful, such feelings on the part of David, it is impossible to read his parting directions and suggestions to Solomon without disappointment and pain. Truly, even the most advanced of the "children were in bondage under the elements of the world" (Galatians 4:3).

How far did the type fall short of the reality, and how dim and ill-defined were the foreshadowings of Him, "Who when He was reviled, reviled not again; when He suffered, He threatened not; but committed Himself to Him that judgeth righteously!"

And yet events soon proved that David's apprehensions had been only too well grounded. The aged king died, and was buried in his own "City of David," amidst the laments of a grateful nation, which ever afterwards cherished his memory (Acts 2:29). It seems that Adonijah, although obliged to submit to Solomon's rule, had not given up all hope of his own ultimate accession. The scheme which he conceived for this purpose lacked, indeed, the courage of open rebellion, but was characterized by the cunning and trickery of a genuine Oriental intrigue. To marry any of the late king's wives or concubines was considered in the East as publicly claiming his rights (2 Samuel 12:8; 16:21, 22). If such were done by a rival, it would be regarded as implying an insult to which not even the weakest monarch could submit without hopelessly degrading his authority in public opinion (2 Samuel 3:7). If Adonijah's primary object was to lower Solomon in public estimate, and that in a manner which he could neither resist nor resent, no better scheme could have been devised than that of his application for the hand of Abishag. By combined flattery and parade of his supposed wrongs and injuries, he gained the queen-mother as unconscious accomplice and even instrument of his intrigue. Any scruples might be set aside by the plea, that there could be no wrong in his request, since, in the strict sense, Abishag had neither been the wife nor the concubine of David. To punish with death so cunning and mean an intrigue can scarcely be called excessive severity on the part of Solomon. It was rather a measure necessary, if tranquillity was to be preserved in the land, all the more that, by his own admission, Adonijah still entertained the opinion that rightfully the kingdom was his, and that "all Israel set their faces on him that he should reign" (1 Kings 2:15).

Whether or not Abiathar and Joab were involved in this intrigue, is matter of uncertainty. At any rate an attempt so daring, and coming so soon after that in which these two had taken a leading part, called for measures which might prevent rebellion in the future, and serve as warning to the turbulent in Israel. That Joab felt conscious his conduct deserved the severest punishment, appears from the circumstance that he anticipated his sentence. On hearing of Adonijah's execution, he sought refuge within the sacred precincts of the Tabernacle. It would have been not only a dangerous precedent, but contrary to the express direction of the law (Exodus 21:12; Deuteronomy 19:11-13), to have allowed a criminal by such means to escape justice. However, it was not for his part in Adonijah's recent schemes that Joab now suffered the extreme penalty of the law, but for his former and still unpunished crimes, which his recent treasonable conduct seemed to bring afresh to view, just as some accidental ailment does a long latent fatal disease. As for Abiathar, in consideration of his office and former services to David, he was only removed from the

Pontificate, and banished to his ancestral property at Anathoth, the city of the priests. But Holy Scripture calls us to mark, how by the deposition of Abiathar the Divine prediction against the house of Eli (1 Samuel 2:31-36) was fulfilled, though in this instance also through a concurrence of intelligible causes.

There was now only one other left, who in heart and mind, as well as in popular opinion, belonged to the party opposed to the reigning house. That old offender, Shimei, was still at large, and enjoying ill-deserved safety. Had he during those years learned to respect the dynasty which he had once so wantonly insulted, or did he still consider it too weak to resent insubordination on his part? The question was soon to be decided; for Solomon now ordered Shimei to remain permanently within the bounds of Jerusalem, at the same time warning him that any infringement of this command, from whatever cause, would be punished by death. Shimei, who had probably expected a far more severe sentence, received with gratitude this comparatively slight restriction upon his liberty. He must have known that most Eastern monarchs would have acted towards him in a very different spirit. Besides, the restriction was not more irksome than that which limited the safety of an ordinary manslayer by the condition of his remaining within the bounds of the city of refuge. Nor was the command in itself unreasonable, considering the necessity of watching Shimei's movements, and the importance of convincing the people that a strong hand now held the reins of government. But whatever outward acquiescence Shimei had shown, he had no idea of yielding such absolute obedience as in his circumstances seemed called for. On the first apparently trivial occasion, Shimei left Jerusalem for the capital of Philistia without having sought the king's permission, and, upon his return, suffered the penalty which, as he well knew, had been threatened. By such measures of vigor and firmness "the kingdom was established in the hand of Solomon."

CHAPTER 5: SOLOMON MARRIES THE DAUGHTER OF PHARAOH — HIS SACRIFICE AT GIBEON — HIS DREAM AND PRAYER — SOLOMON'S WISDOM — SOLOMON'S OFFICERS AND COURT — PROSPERITY OF THE COUNTRY — UNDERSTANDING AND KNOWLEDGE OF THE KING.

(1 KINGS 3, 4, 2 CHRONICLES 1)

IT is remarkable how often seemingly unimportant details in the sacred narrative gain a fresh meaning and new interest if viewed in their higher bearing and spiritual import. Nor is such application of them arbitrary. On the contrary, we conclude that Scripture was intended to be so read. This is evident from the circumstance that it is, avowedly not a secular but a prophetic history, and that, being such, it is not arranged according to the chronological succession of events, but grouped so as to bring into prominence that which concerns the kingdom of God. This plan of Scripture history is not only worthy of its object, but gives it its permanent interest and application.

What has just been stated is aptly illustrated by the opening account of King Solomon's reign. Of course, no chronological arrangement could have been here intended, since the list of Solomon's officers, given in 1 Kings 4, contains the names of at least two of the king's sons-in-law (vers. 11,15), whose appointment must, therefore, date from a period considerably later than the commencement of his reign. What, then, we may ask, is the object of not only recording in a "prophetic history" such apparently unimportant details, but grouping them together irrespective of their dates? Without undervaluing them, considered as purely historical notices, we may venture to suggest a higher object in their record and arrangement.

This detailed account of all the court and government appointments serves as evidence, how thoroughly and even elaborately the kingdom of Solomon was organized — and by obvious inference, how fully God had made good in this respect His gracious promises to King David. But may we not go even beyond this, and see in the literal fulfillment of these outward promises a pledge and assurance that the spiritual realities connected with them, and of which they were the symbol and type, would likewise become true in the Kingdom of Him Who was "David's better Son?" Thus viewed, the Divine promise made to David (2 Samuel 7) was once more like a light casting the lengthening shadows of present events towards the far-off future.

The first event of national interest that occurred was the marriage of Solomon with the daughter of Pharaoh. It was of almost equal political importance to Egypt and to Palestine. An alliance with the great neighboring kingdom of Egypt might have seemed an eventuality almost unthought of among the possibilities of the new and somewhat doubtful monarchy in Israel. But, on the other hand, it may have been also of importance to the then reigning Egyptian dynasty (the 21st Time), which, as we know, was rapidly declining in authority.

To Israel and to the countries around, such a union would now afford evidence of the position and influence which the Jewish monarchy had attained in the opinion of foreign politicians. All the more are we involuntarily carried back in spirit to the period when Israel was oppressed and in servitude to Egypt. As we contrast the relations in the past and in the time of Solomon, we realize how marvelously God had fulfilled His promises of deliverance to His people. And here we again turn to the great promise in 2 Samuel 7, as alike instructive to Israel as regarded their present, and as full of blessed hope for their future. The time of the Judges had been one of struggle and disorganization; that of David one of war and conflicts. But with Solomon the period of peace had begun, emblematic of the higher peace of the "Prince of Peace." Thus viewed, the account of the prosperity of the land and people, as further evidenced by the wealth displayed in the ordinary appointments of the Court; by the arrangement of the country into provinces under officers for fiscal administration and civil government; and, above all, by the wisdom of Solomon, — who, while encouraging by example literature and study of every kind, chiefly aimed after that higher knowledge and understanding which is God-given, and leads to the fear and service of the Lord, — acquires a new and a spiritual meaning.

But to return to the sacred narrative. This marriage of Solomon with the daughter of Pharaoh — to which, from its frequent mention, so much political importance seems to have been attached — took place in the first years of his reign, although some time after the building of the Temple and of his own palace had commenced. Such a union was not forbidden by the law, nor was the daughter of Pharaoh apparently implicated in the charge brought against Solomon's other foreign wives of having led him into idolatry (1 Kings 11:1-7).

In fact, according to Jewish tradition, the daughter of Pharaoh actually became a Jewish proselyte. still, Solomon seems to have felt the incongruity of bringing her into the palace of David, within the bounds of which "the Ark of the Lord" appears to have been located (2 Chronicles 8:11), and she occupied a temporary abode "in the City of David," until the new palace of Solomon was ready for her reception.

But the great prosperity which, as we shall presently see, the country enjoyed during the reign of Solomon, was due to higher than merely outward causes. It was the blessing of the Lord which in this instance also made — rich that blessing which it was Solomon's chief concern to obtain. From the necessity of the case, Israel, and even Solomon, still worshipped on the ancient "high places."

Of these, the principal was naturally Gibeon — the twin height. For, right over against the city itself, on one of the two eminences ("mamelons") which gave it its name, the ancient Tabernacle which Moses had reared had been placed. Here Solomon, at the commencement of his reign, celebrated a great festival, probably to inaugurate and consecrate his accession by a public acknowledgment of Jehovah as the God of Israel. All the people took part in what was a service of hitherto unparalleled magnificence.

But something far better than the smoke of a thousand burnt-sacrifices offered in Israel's ancient Sanctuary, attested that the God, Who had brought Israel out of Egypt and led them through the Wilderness, still watched over His people. The services of those festive days were over, and king and people were about to return to their homes. As Solomon had surveyed the vast multitude which, from all parts of the country, had gathered to Gibeon, the difficulty must have painfully forced itself on him of wisely ruling an empire so vast as that belonging to him, stretching from Tiphsach (the Greek Thapsacus), "the fords," on the western bank of the Euphrates, in the north-east, to Gaza on the border of Egypt, in the southwest (1 Kings 4:24). The conquests so lately made had not yet been consolidated the means at the king's disposal were still comparatively scanty. tribal jealousies were scarcely appeased; and Solomon himself was young and wholly inexperienced. Any false step might prove fatal; even want of some brilliant success might disintegrate what was but imperfectly welded together. On the other hand, had Israel's history not been a series of constant miracles, through the gracious Personal interposition of the LORD? What, then, might Solomon not expect from His help?

Busy with such thoughts, the king had laid him down to rest on the last night of his stay in Gibeon. Ordinarily dreams are without deeper significance. So Solomon himself afterwards taught (Ecclesiastes 5:7); and so the spiritually enlightened among other nations, and the prophets in Israel equally declared (Job 20:8; Isaiah 29:7). And yet, while most fully admitting this (as in Ecclesiasticus 34:1-6), it must have been also felt, as indeed Holy Scripture teaches by many instances, that dreams might be employed by the Most High in the time of our visitation (Ecclesiasticus 34:6). So was it with Solomon on that night. It has been well remarked, that Adonijah would not have thus dreamed after his feast at En-rogel (1 Kings 1:9, 25), even had his attempt been crowned with the success for which he had hoped. The question which on that night the Lord put before Solomon, "Ask what I shall give thee?" was not only an answer to the unspoken entreaty for help expressed in the sacrifices that had been offered, but was also intended to search the deepest feelings of his heart. Like that of our Lord addressed to St. Peter, "Simon, son of Jonas, lovest thou Me?" it sounded the inmost depths of the soul. Such questions come, more or less distinctly, to us all, and that in every crisis of our lives. They may become fresh spiritual starting-points to us, seasons of greater nearness to God, and of spiritual advancement; or they may prove times of "temptation," if we allow ourselves to be "drawn away" and "enticed" of our own "lust."

The prayer of Solomon on this occasion once more combined the three elements of thanksgiving, confession, and petition. In his thanksgiving, acknowledgment of God mingled with humiliation; in his confession, a sense of inability with the expression of felt want; while his petition, evidently based on the Divine promise (Genesis 13:16; 32:12), was characterized by singleness of spiritual desire. For, in order to know what he sought, when so earnestly craving for "understanding," we have only to turn to his own "Book of Proverbs." And, as in the case of all whose spiritual aim is single, God not only granted his request, but also added to what He gave "all things" otherwise needful, thus proving that the "promise of the life that now is" is ever connected with that of the life "which is to come" (2 Timothy 4:8), just as in our present condition the soul is with the body. Perhaps we may put it otherwise in this manner. As so often, God extended the higher wisdom granted Solomon even to the lower concerns of this life, while He added to it the promise of longevity and prosperity — but only on condition of continued observance of God's statutes and commandments (1 Kings 3:14). Such gracious condescension on the part of the LORD called for the expression of fresh public thanksgiving, which Solomon rendered on his return to Jerusalem (1 Kings 3:15).

Evidence of the reality of God's promise soon appeared, and that in a manner peculiarly calculated to impress the Eastern mind. According to the simple manners of the times, a cause too difficult for ordinary judges was carried direct to the king, who, as God's representative, was regarded as able to give help to his people in all time of need. In such paternal dispensation of justice, there was no appeal to witnesses nor to statute-books, which indeed would have been equally accessible to inferior judges; but the king was expected to strike out some new light, in which the real bearings of a case would so appear as to appeal to all men's convictions, and to command their approval of his sentence. There was here no need for anything recondite — rather the opposite. To point out to practical common sense what was there, though unperceived until suddenly brought to prominence, would more than anything else appeal to the people, as a thing within the range of all, and yet showing the wise guidance of the king. Thus sympathy and universal trust, as well as admiration, would be called forth, especially among Orientals, whose wisdom is that of common life, and whose philosophy that of proverbs.

The story of the contention of the two women for the one living child, when from the absence of witnesses it seemed impossible to determine whose it really was, is sufficiently known. The ready wisdom with which Solomon devised means for ascertaining the truth would commend itself to the popular mind. It was just what they would appreciate in their king. Such a monarch would indeed be a terror to evil-doers, and a protection and praise to them that did well. It is probably in order to explain the rapid spread of Solomon's fame that this instance of his wisdom is related in Holy Scripture (1 Kings 3:28).

The prosperity of such a reign was commensurate with the fact that it was based upon the Divine promises, and typical of far greater blessings to come. The notices in 1 Kings 4 and 5 are strung together to indicate that prosperity by presenting to our view the condition of the Israelitish monarchy in the high-day of its glory. Wise and respected councilors surrounded the king.

The administration of the country was orderly, and the taxation not arbitrary but regulated. The land was divided, not according to the geographical boundaries of the "tribes," but according to population and resources, into twelve provinces, over each of which a governor was appointed. Among their number we find two sons-in-law of the king (4:11, 15), and other names well-known in the land (such as those of Baana, ver. 12, probably the brother of "the recorder," ver. 3, and Baanah, the son of Hushai, probably David's councilor, ver. 16). Had this policy of re-arranging the country into provinces been sufficiently consolidated, many of the tribal jealousies would have ceased. On the other hand, the financial administration, entrusted to these governors, was of the simplest kind. Apparently, no direct taxes were levied, but all that was requisite for the royal court and government had to be provided, each province supplying in turn what was required for one month. Such a system could not indeed press heavily, so long as the country continued prosperous; but with a luxurious court, in hard times, or under harsh governors, it might easily become an instrument of oppression and a source of discontent. From 1 Kings 12:4 we gather that such was ultimately the case. It need scarcely be added, that in each province the supreme civil government was in the hands of these royal officials; and such was the general quiet prevailing, that even in the extensive district east of the Jordan, which bordered on so many turbulent tributary nations, "one sole officer" (1 Kings 4:19) was sufficient to preserve the peace of the country.

Quite in accordance with these notices are the references both to the prosperity of Israel, and to the extent of Solomon's dominions (1 Kings 4:20, 21). They almost read like an initial fulfillment of that promise to Abraham, "Multiplying I will multiply thy seed as the stars of the heaven, and as the sand which is upon the sea shore; and thy seed shall possess the gate of his enemies" (Genesis 22:17).

And if, compared with the simplicity of Saul's and even of David's court, that of Solomon seems luxurious in its appointments, we must remember that it was intended to show the altered state of the Israelitish monarchy, and that even so the daily consumption was far smaller than at the court of the Persian monarchs in the high-day of their power and glory.

But the fame which accrued to the kingdom of Solomon from its prosperity and wealth would have been little worthy of the Jewish monarchy, had it been uncombined with that which alone truly exalteth a nation or an individual. The views of Solomon himself on this subject are pithily summed up in one of his own "Proverbs" (3:13, 14), "Happy is the man that findeth wisdom, and the man that causeth understanding to go forth; for merchandise (trading) with it, is better than merchandise with silver, and the gain from it than the most fine gold."

All this the "wise king" exemplified in his own person. God gave him "wisdom" not only far wider in its range, but far other in its character (Proverbs 1:7; 9:10)than that of the East, or of far-famed Egypt, or even of those deemed wisest in Israel, "and understanding exceeding much, and largeness of heart, even as the sand that is on the sea-shore" (1 Kings 4:29). Not satisfied with the idle life of an Eastern monarch, he set the example of, and gave encouragement to study and literature, the range of his inquiries extending not only to philosophy and poetry, but also to natural science in all its branches. It must have been a mighty intellectual impulse which proceeded from such a king; it must have been a reign unparalleled in that age, as well as among that people, which Solomon inaugurated.

CHAPTER 6: THE BUILDING OF SOLOMON'S TEMPLE — PREPARATIONS FOR IT — PLAN AND STRUCTURE OF THE TEMPLE, INTERNAL FITTINGS — HISTORY OF THE TEMPLE — JEWISH TRADITIONS.

(1 KINGS 5, 6, 7:13-51, 8:6-9; 2 CHRONICLES 2, 3, 4, 5:7-10)

WHILE Solomon thus wisely and in the fear of God ordered his government, and the country enjoyed a measure of prosperity, wealth, and power never before or afterwards attained, the grand work of his reign yet remained to be done. This was the building of an "house unto the Name of Jehovah God." We have already seen how earnestly David had this at heart; how fully it corresponded with the Divine promise; and how fitly its execution was assigned to Solomon as the great task of his reign, viewing it as typical of that of "David's greater Son." As might be expected, all outward circumstances contributed to further the work. Israel, as a nation, was not intended to attain pre-eminence either in art or science. If we may venture to pronounce on such a matter, this was the part assigned, in the Providence of God, to the Gentile world. To Israel was specially entrusted the guardianship of that spiritual truth, which in the course of ages would develop in all its proportions, until finally it became the common property of the whole world. On the other hand, it was the task assigned to that world, to develop knowledge and thought so as to prepare a fitting reception for the truth, that thus it might be presented in all its aspects, and carried from land to land in a form adapted to every nation, meeting every want and aspiration. This was symbolically indicated even in the building of Solomon's Temple. For, if that Temple had been exclusively the workmanship of Jewish hands, both the materials for it and their artistic preparation would have been sadly defective, as compared with what it actually became. But it was not so; and, while in the co-operation of Gentiles with Israel in the rearing of the Temple we see a symbol of their higher union in the glorious architecture of that "spiritual house built up" of "lively stones," we also recognize the gracious Providence of God, which rendered it possible to employ in that work the best materials and the best artificers of the ancient world.

For it was in the good Providence of God that the throne of Tyre was at the time occupied by Hiram, who had not only been a friend and ally of David, but to whom the latter had communicated his plans of the projected Temple-buildings. Indeed, Hiram had already furnished David with a certain proportion of the necessary materials for the work (1 Chronicles 22:4). The extraordinary mechanical skill of the Phoenicians — especially of the Sidonians — was universally famed in the ancient world. Similarly, the best materials were at their command. On the slopes of Lebanon, which belonged to their territory, grew those world-famed cedars with which the palaces of Assyria were adorned, and, close by, at Gebal (the ancient Byblos, the modern Jebeil) were the most skilled workmen (Ezekiel 27:9).

On the same slopes grew also the cypress, so suitable for flooring, its wood being almost indestructible, and impervious to rot and worms; while the Phoenician merchantmen brought to Tyre that "almug," "algum," or red sandal-wood which was so valued in antiquity (comp. 1 Kings 10:11)

461

The same skill as in the preparation of woodwork distinguished the Phoenician carvers, stone-cutters, dyers, modelers, and other craftsmen. To have at his disposal the best artificers of Phoenicia, and these under a trained and celebrated "master" (2 Chronicles 2:13, 14), must have been of immense advantage to Solomon. At the same time the extensive preparations which David had made rendered the work comparatively so easy, that the Temple-buildings, with their elaborate internal fittings, were completed in the short space of seven years (1 Kings 6:37, 38), while the later rearing of the king's palace occupied not less than thirteen years (1 Kings 7:1). But, although Solomon thus availed himself of Phoenician skill in the execution of the work, the plan and design were strictly Jewish, having, in fact, been drawn long before, in the time of King David.

The building of the Temple commenced in the second month ("Siv," "splendor" — the month of opening beauty of nature) of the fourth year of Solomon's reign, being the 480th from the Exodus (1 Kings 6:1).

But there was this peculiarity about the work, that no sound of ax, hammer, or chisel was heard on Mount Moriah while the Holy House was rising, day by day, in beauty and glory. As Jewish tradition has it, "The iron is created to shorten the days of man, and the altar to lengthen them; therefore it is not right that that which shortens should be lifted upon that which lengthens" (Midd. 3:4). The massive timber used was not merely prepared but dressed before it was brought to the sea, to be conveyed in floats to Joppa, whence the distance to Jerusalem was only about forty miles (1 Kings 5:9). Similarly, those great, splendid (not "costly," as in the Authorized Version) hewed stones (1 Kings 5:17), beveled at the edges, of which to this day some are seen in what remains of the ancient Temple-wall — the largest of them being more than thirty feet long by seven and a half high, and weighing above one hundred tons — were all chiseled and carefully marked before being sent to Jerusalem (1 Kings 6:7). An undertaking of such magnitude would require, especially in the absence of modern mechanical appliances, a very large number of workmen. They amounted in all to 60,000 Palestinians, who were divided into two classes. The first comprised native Israelites, of whom 30,000 were raised by a "levy," which, taking the census of David as our basis, would be at the rate of considerably less than one in forty-four of the able-bodied male population. These 30,000 men worked by relays, 10,000 being employed during one month, after which they returned for two months to their homes. The second class of workmen, which consisted of strangers resident in Palestine (1 Kings 5:15; 2 Chronicles 2:17,18), amounted to 150,000, of whom 70,000 were burden-bearers, and 80,000 "hewers in the mountains," or rather, as the expression always means, "stonecutters."

The two classes are carefully distinguished the Israelites being free laborers, who worked under the direction of Hiram's skilled men; while the others, who were the representatives of the ancient heathen inhabitants of Palestine, were really held to "bond-service" (1 Kings 9:20, 21; 2 Chronicles 2:17, 18; 8:7-9). The total number of men employed (160,000), though large, cannot be considered excessive, when compared, for example, with the 360,000 persons engaged for twenty years on the building of one pyramid (Pliny, Hist. Nat. 36. 12. apud Bahr u.s.) Over these men 3,300 officers were appointed (1 Kings 5:16), with 550 "chiefs" (1 Kings 9:23), of whom 250 were apparently native Israelites (2 Chronicles 8:10.) The number of skilled artificers furnished by Hiram is not mentioned, though probably the proportion was comparatively small. A very vivid impression is left on our minds of the transaction between the two kings.

When Hiram sent a friendly embassy to congratulate Solomon on his accession, the latter replied by another, which was charged formally to ask help in the building about to be undertaken. The request was entertained by Hiram in the most cordial manner. At the same time, bearing in mind Eastern phraseology, and that a Phoenician ally of David would readily recognize the God of Israel as a "national Deity," there is no reason for inferring, from the terms of his reply, that Hiram was personally a worshipper of Jehovah (1 Kings 5:7; 2 Chronicles 2:12). The agreement seems to have been, that Solomon would undertake to provide for the support of Hiram's men, wheat, barley, and oil, to the amount specified in 2 Chronicles 2:10; while, so long as building materials were required, Hiram charged for them at an annual rate of 20,000 measures of wheat, and twenty measures (about ten hogsheads) of "beaten oil," — that is, the best in the market, which derived its name from its manufacture, the oil being extracted by beating the olives before they were quite ripe (1 Kings 5:11). In regard to these terms, it should be remembered that Phoenicia was chiefly dependent on Palestine for its supply of grain and oil (Ezekiel 27:17; Acts 12:20). Lastly, the name of the "master-workman," whom Hiram sent, has also been preserved to us as Huram, or rather Churam, a man of Jewish descent by the mother's side (2 Chronicles 2:13, 14; comp. 1 Kings 7:14; 2 Chronicles 4:16). Even the completeness and entirely satisfactory character of these arrangements proved, that in this respect also "Jehovah gave Solomon wisdom, as He had promised him" (1 Kings 5:12).

Without entering into details, the general appearance and proportions of the Temple which Solomon built can be described without much difficulty.

The Temple itself faced east — that is to say, the worshippers entered by the east, and, turning to the Most Holy Place, would look west; while, if the veil had been drawn aside, the Ark in the innermost Sanctuary would have been seen to face eastwards. Entering then by the east, the worshipper would find himself in front of "a porch," which extended along the whole width of the Temple, — that is, twenty cubits, or about thirty feet — and went back a depth of ten cubits, or fifteen feet. The Sanctuary itself was sixty cubits (ninety feet) long, twenty cubits (thirty feet) wide, and thirty cubits (forty-five feet) high. The height of the porch is not mentioned in the Book of Kings, and the numeral given for it in 2 Chronicles 3:4, is evidently a copyist's error. Probably it rose to a height of about thirty cubits.

Of the total length of the Sanctuary, forty cubits were apportioned to the Holy Place, (which was thus sixty feet long, thirty wide, and forty-five high), and twenty cubits (thirty feet) to the Most Holy Place, which (1 Kings 6:20) is described as measuring twenty cubits (thirty feet) in length, width, and height. The ten cubits (fifteen feet) left above the Most Holy Place were apparently occupied by an empty room. Perhaps, as in the Temple of Herod, this space was used for letting down the workmen through an aperture, when repairs were required in the innermost Sanctuary. In that case the access to it would have been from the roof. The latter was, no doubt, flat.

The measurements just given apply, of course, only to the interior of these buildings. As regards their exterior we have to add not only the thickness of the walls on either side, and the height of the roof, but also a row of side-buildings, which have, not inaptly, been designated as a "lean-to." These side-buildings consisted of three tiers of chambers, which surrounded the Temple, south, west, and north — the east front being covered by the "porch." On the side where these chambers abutted on the Temple they seem to have had no separate wall. The beams, which formed at the same time the ceiling of the first and the floor of the second tier of chambers, and similarly those which formed the ceiling of the second and the floor of the third tier, as also those on which the roof over the third tier rested, were not inserted within the Temple wall, but were laid on graduated buttresses which formed part of the main wall of the Temple.

These buttresses receded successively one cubit in each of the two higher tiers of chambers, and for the roofing of the third, thus forming, as it were, narrowing steps, or receding rests on which the beams of the chambers were laid. The effect was that, while the walls of the Temple decreased one cubit in thickness with each tier, the chambers increased one cubit in width, as they ascended. Thus, if at the lowest tier the wall including the buttress was, say, six cubits thick, at the next tier of chambers it was, owing to the decrease in the buttress, only five cubits thick, and at the third only four cubits, while above the roof, where the buttress ceased, the walls would be only three cubits thick. For the same reason each tier of chambers, built on gradually narrowing or receding rebatements, would be one cubit wider than that below, the chambers on the lowest tier being five cubits wide, on the second six cubits, and on the third seven cubits. If we suppose these tiers with their roof to have been altogether sixteen to eighteen cubits high (1 Kings 6:10), and allow a height of two cubits for the roof of the Temple, whose walls were thirty cubits high (the total height, including roof, thirty-two cubits), this would leave an elevation of twelve to fourteen cubits (eighteen to twenty-one feet) for the wall of the Temple above the roof of "the chambers." Within this space of twelve to fourteen cubits we suppose the "windows" to have been inserted — south and north, the back of the Most Holy Place (west) having no windows, and the front (east) being covered by the "porch." The use of the "chambers" is not mentioned in the sacred text, but it seems more probable that they served for the deposit of relics of the ancient Tabernacle, and for the storage of sacred vessels, than that they were the sleeping apartments of the ministering priesthood. Access to these "chambers" was gained by a door in the middle of the southern facade, whence also a winding stair led to the upper tiers (1 Kings 6:8). The windows of the Temple itself, which we have supposed to have been above the roof of the "chambers," were with "fixed lattices" (1 Kings 6:4), which could not be opened, as in private dwellings, and were probably constructed, like the windows of old castles and churches, broad within, but mere slits externally.

While these protracted works were progressing, the LORD in His mercy gave special encouragement alike to Solomon and to the people. The word of the LORD, which on this occasion came to the king (1 Kings 6:11-13) — no doubt through a prophet, not only fully confirmed the promise made to David (2 Samuel 7:12, etc.), but also connected the "house" that was being built to the LORD with the ancient promise (Exodus 25:8; 29:45) that God would dwell in Israel as among His people. Thus it pointed king and people beyond that outward building which, rising in such magnificence, might have excited only national pride, to its spiritual meaning, and to the conditions under which alone it would fulfill its great purpose.

Thus far we have given a description of the exterior of the Temple. It still remains to convey some idea of its internal arrangements. If we may judge by the description of Ezekiel's Temple (Ezekiel 40:49), and by what we know of the Temple of Herod, some steps would lead up to the porch, which, as we imagine, presented the appearance of an open colonnade of cedar, set in a pavement of hewn stones, and supporting a cedar-roof covered with marble.

The most prominent objects here were the two great pillars, Jachin and Boaz, which Hiram cast by order of Solomon (1 Kings 7:15-22). These pillars stood, as we are expressly told, within "the porch" (1 Kings 7:21), and must have served alike architectural, artistic, and symbolical purposes. Added after the completion of the "House," perhaps for the better support of the roof of the "porch," their singular beauty must have attracted the eye, while their symbolical meaning appeared in their names. Jachin ("He supports"), Boaz ("in Him is strength"), pointed beyond the outward support and strength which these pillars gave, to Him on Whom not only the Sanctuary but every one who would truly enter it must rest for support and strength. Some difficulty has been experienced in computing the height of these pillars, including their "chapiters," or "capitals" (1 Kings 7:15-22), It seems most likely that they consisted of single shafts, each eighteen cubits high and twelve in circumference, surmounted by a twofold "chapiter" — the lower of five cubits, with fretted network depending, and ornamented with two rows of one hundred pomegranates; the higher chapiter four cubits high (1 Kings 7:19), and in the form of an opening lily. The symbolical significance of the pomegranate and of the lily — the one the flower, the other the fruit of the Land of Promise, and both emblematic of the pure beauty and rich sweetness of holiness — need scarcely be pointed out. If we compute the height of these pillars with their chapiters at twenty-seven cubits, we have three cubits left for the entablature and, the roofing of the porch ($18 + 5 + 4 + 3 = 30$).

"The porch," which (in its tablature) was overlaid with gold (2 Chronicles 3:4), opened into the Holy Place by folding doors, each of two leaves, folding back upon each other. These doors, which were the width of a fourth of the wall (1 Kings 6:33), or five cubits, were made of cypress-wood, and hung by golden hinges on door-posts of olive-wood. They were decorated with carved figures of cherubim between palm-trees, and above them opening flower-buds and garlands, the whole being covered with thin plates of gold, which showed the design beneath. Within the Sanctuary all the sacred furniture was of gold, while that outside of it was of brass.

In truth, the Sanctuary was a golden house. The floor, which was of cypress-wood, was overlaid with gold; the walls, which were paneled with cedar, on which the same designs were carved as on the doors, were covered with gold, and so was the ceiling. It need scarcely be said, how it must have glittered and shone in the light of the sacred candlesticks, especially as the walls were encrusted with gems (2 Chronicles 3:6). There were ten candlesticks in the Holy Place, each seven-branched, and of pure gold. They were ranged right and left before the Most Holy Place (1 Kings 7:49).

The entrance to the Most Holy Place was covered by a veil "of blue and purple, and crimson, and byssus," with "wrought cherubs thereon" (2 Chronicles 3:14). Between the candlesticks stood the "altar of incense," made of cedar-wood and overlaid with gold (1 Kings 6:20, 22; 7:48); while ten golden tables of shewbread (2 Chronicles 4:8) were ranged right and left. The implements necessary for the use of this sacred furniture were also of pure gold (1 Kings 7:49, 50).

Two folding-doors, similar in all respects to those already described, except that they were of oleaster wood, and not a fourth, but a fifth of the wall (= 4 cubits), opened from the Holy Place into the Most Holy. These doors we suppose to have always stood open, the entrance being concealed by the great veil, which the High-priest lifted, when on the Day of Atonement he went into the innermost Sanctuary.

Considerable difficulty attaches to a notice in 1 Kings 6:21, which has been variously translated and understood. Two interpretations here specially deserve attention. The first regards the "chains of gold before the Oracle," as chain-work that fastened together the cedar-planks forming the partition between the Holy and the Most Holy Place — somewhat like the bars that held together the boards in the Tabernacle. The other, which to us seems

465

the more likely, represents the partition boards between the Holy and the Most Holy Place, as not reaching quite to the ceiling, and this "chain-work" as running along the top of the boarding.

For some opening of this kind seems almost necessary for ventilation, for letting out the smoke of the incense on the Day of Atonement, and to admit at least a gleam of light, without which the ministrations of the High-priest on that day, limited though they were, would have been almost impossible. The only object within the Most Holy Place was the Ark overshadowed by the Cherubim. It was the same which had stood in the Tabernacle. But Solomon placed on either side of it (south and north) a gigantic figure of a Cherub, carved out of oleaster wood, and overlaid with gold. Each was ten cubits high; and the two, with their outspread wings, which touched over the Mercy-Seat, ten cubits wide. Thus, the two cherubim with their outspread wings reached (south and north) from one wall of the Sanctuary to the other (1 Kings 6:23-28). But, whereas the Mosaic Cherubim looked inwards and downwards towards the Mercy-Seat, those made by Solomon looked outwards towards the Holy Place, with probably a slight inclination downwards (2 Chronicles 3:13). Another notice has raised differences of opinion. From 1 Kings 8:8, we learn that the "staves" by which the Ark was carried were "drawn forward" ("lengthened," not "drawn out," as in the Authorized Version), so that their heads were visible from the Holy Place. As these "staves" were never to be drawn out (Exodus 25:15), and as all view of the interior of the Most Holy Place was precluded, this could only have been effected (as the Rabbis suggest) by drawing the staves forward, so that their heads would slightly bulge out on the veil. Of course this would imply that the staves faced east and west — not, as is generally supposed, south and north. Nor is there any valid objection to this supposition.

Descending from "the Porch," we stand in the "inner" (1 Kings 6:36) or "Court of the Priests" (2 Chronicles 4:9). This was paved with great stones, as was also the outer or "Great Court" (2 Chronicles 4:9) of the people. Within the "inner" or Priests' Court, facing the entrance to the Sanctuary, was "the altar of burnt-offering" (1 Kings 8:64), made of brass, and probably filled within with earth and unhewn stones. It was ten cubits high, and twenty cubits in length and breadth at the base — probably narrowing as it ascended, like receding buttresses (2 Chronicles 4:1).

Between the altar and the porch stood the colossal "sea of brass," five cubits high, and thirty cubits in circumference (1 Kings 7:23-26; 2 Chronicles 4:2-5). Its upper rim was bent outwards, "like the work of the brim of a cup, in the shape of a lily-flower." Under the brim it was ornamented by two rows of opening flower-buds, ten to a cubit. This immense basin rested on a pedestal of twelve oxen, three looking to each point of the compass. Its object was to hold the water in which the priests and Levites performed their ablutions. For the washing of the inwards and of the pieces of the sacrifices, ten smaller "lavers" of brass were provided, which stood on the right and left "side of the House" (1 Kings 7:38; 2 Chronicles 4:6). They were placed on square "bases," or, rather, wagons of brass, four cubits long and broad, and three cubits high, which rested on "four feet" (not "corners," as in the Authorized Version, 1 Kings 7:30) upon wheels, so as to bring them readily to the altar. Bearing in mind the height of the altar, this accounts for their being four cubits high (4 cubits for the laver itself). The sides of these wagons were richly ornamented with figures of lions, oxen, and cherubs, and beneath them were "garlands, pensile work."

Although it is not easy to make out all the other details, it seems that the tops of these "bases" or wagons had covers, which bulged inwards to receive the lavers, the latter being further steadied by supports ("undersetters" in the Authorized Version, or rather "shoulder-pieces"). The covers of the wagons were also richly ornamented. Lastly, in the Priests' Court, and probably within full view of the principal gate, stood the brazen scaffold or stand (2 Chronicles 6:13) from which King Solomon offered his dedicatory prayer, and which seems to have always been the place occupied in the Temple by the kings (2 Kings 11:14; 23:3). To this a special "ascent" led from the palace (1 Kings 10:5), which was, perhaps afterwards, roofed over for protection from the weather. The Priests' Court was enclosed by a wall consisting of three tiers of hewn stones and a row of cedar beams (1 Kings 6:36).

From the court of the priests steps led down to the "outer court" of the people (comp. Jeremiah 36:10), which was surrounded by a solid wall, from which four massive gates, covered with brass, opened upon the Temple-mount (2 Chronicles 4:9).

In this court were large colonnades and chambers, and rooms for the use of the priests and Levites, for the storage of what was required in the services, and for other purposes. The principal gate was, no doubt, the eastern (Ezekiel 11:1), corresponding to the "Beautiful Gate" of New Testament times. To judge by the analogy of the other measurements, as compared with those of the Tabernacle, the Court of the Priests would be 100 cubits broad, and 200 cubits long, and the Outer Court double these proportions (comp. also Ezekiel 40:27). Such, in its structure and fittings, was the Temple which Solomon built to the Name of Jehovah God. Its further history to its destruction, 416 years after its building, is traced in the following passages of Holy Scripture, 1 Kings 14:26; 15:18, etc.; 2 Chronicles 20:5; 2 Kings 12:5, etc.; 14:14; 15:35; 2 Chronicles 27:3; 2 Kings 16:8; 18:15, etc.; 21:4, 5, 7; 23:4, 7, 11; 24:13; 25:9, 13-17).

CHAPTER 7: DEDICATION OF THE TEMPLE — WHEN IT TOOK PLACE — CONNECTION WITH THE FEAST OF TABERNACLES — THE CONSECRATION SERVICES — THE KING'S PART IN THEM — SYMBOLICAL MEANING OF THE GREAT INSTITUTIONS IN ISRAEL — THE PRAYER OF CONSECRATION — ANALOGY TO THE LORD'S PRAYER — THE CONSECRATION — THANKSGIVING AND OFFERINGS.

(1 KINGS 8; 2 CHRONICLES 5-7:11)

AT length the great and beautiful house, which Solomon had raised to the Name of Jehovah, and to which so many ardent thoughts and hopes attached, was finished. Its solemn dedication took place in the year following its completion, and, very significantly, immediately before, and in connection with, the Feast of Tabernacles. Two questions, of some difficulty and importance, here arise. The first concerns the circumstance that the sacred text (1 Kings 7:1-12) records the building of Solomon's palace immediately after that of the Temple, and, indeed, almost intermingles the two accounts. This may partly have been due to a very natural desire on the part of the writer not to break the continuity of the account of Solomon's great buildings, the more so as they were all completed by the aid of Tyrian workmen, and under the supervision of Hiram. But another and more important consideration may also have influenced the arrangement of the narrative. For, as has been suggested, these two great undertakings of Solomon bore a close relation to each other. It was not an ordinary Sanctuary, nor was it an ordinary royal residence which Solomon reared. The building of the Temple marked that the preparatory period of Israel's unsettledness had passed, when God had walked with them "in tent and tabernacle" — or, in other words, that the Theocracy had attained not only fixedness, but its highest point, when God would set "His Name for ever" in its chosen center. But this new stage of the Theocracy was connected with the establishment of a firm and settled kingdom in Israel, when He would "establish the throne of that kingdom for ever" (compare 2 Samuel 7:5-16). Thus the dwelling of God in His Temple and that of Solomon in his house were events between which there was deep internal connection, even as between the final establishment of the Theocracy and that of David's royal line in Israel. Moreover, the king was not to be a monarch in the usual Oriental, or even in the ancient Western sense. He was to be regarded, not as the Vicegerent or Representative of God, but as His Servant, to do His behest and to guard His covenant. And this might well be marked, even by the conjunction of these two buildings in the Scripture narrative.

These considerations will also help us to understand why the Feast of the Dedication of the Temple was connected with that of Tabernacles (of course, in the year following). It was not only that, after "the eighth month," when the Temple was completed, it would have been almost impossible, considering the season of the year, to have gathered the people from all parts of the country, or to have celebrated for eight days a great popular festival; nor yet that of all feasts, that of Tabernacles, when agricultural labor was at an end, probably witnessed the largest concourse in Jerusalem.

But the Feast of Tabernacles had a threefold meaning. It pointed back to the time when, "strangers and pilgrims" on their way to the Land of Promise, Israel, under its Divine leadership, had dwelt in tents. The full import of this memorial would be best realized at the dedication of the Temple, when, instead of tent and tabernacle, the glorious house of God was standing in all its beauty, while the stately palace of Israel's king was rising. Again, the Feast of Tabernacles was essentially one of thanksgiving, when at the completion, not only of the harvest, but of the ingathering of the fruits, a grateful people presented its homage to the God to Whom they owed all, and to Whom all really belonged. But what could raise this hymn of praise to its loudest strains, if not that they uplifted it within those sacred walls, symbolical of God's gracious Presence as King in His palace in the midst of His people, whose kingdom He had established. Lastly, the Feast of Tabernacles — the only still unfulfilled Old Testament type — pointed forward to the time of which the present state of Israel was an initial realization, when the name of the LORD should be known far and wide to earth's utmost bounds, and all nations seek after Him and offer worship in His Temple. Thus, however viewed, there was the deepest significance in the conjunction of the dedication of the Temple with the Feast of Tabernacles.

But, as previously stated, there is yet another question of somewhat greater difficulty which claims our attention. To judge by the arrangement of the narrative, the dedication of the Temple (1 Kings 8) might seem to have taken place after the completion of Solomon's palace, the building of which, as we know, occupied further thirteen years (1 Kings 7:1). Moreover, from the circumstance that the second vision of God was vouchsafed "when Solomon had finished the building of the house of the LORD, and the king's house, and all Solomon's desire which he was pleased to do" (1 Kings 9:1), it has been argued, that the dedication of the Temple must have taken place immediately before this vision, especially as what was said to him seems to contain pointed reference to the consecration prayer of Solomon (1 Kings 9:3, 7, 8). But, even if that vision took place at the time just indicated, the supposed inference from it cannot be maintained.

For, although part of the sacred vessels may have been made during the time that Hiram was engaged upon Solomon's palace, it is not credible that the Temple should, after its completion, have stood deserted and unused for thirteen years. Nor are the arguments in favor of this most improbable assumption valid. The appeal to 1 Kings 9:1 would oblige us to date the dedication of the Temple even later than the completion of Solomon's palace, viz., after he had finished all his other building operations. As for the words which the LORD spake to Solomon in vision (2 Kings 9:3-9), although bearing reference to the Temple and the king's dedication prayer, they are evidently intended rather as a general warning, than as an answer to his petition, and are such as would befit the period of temptation, before Solomon, carried away by the splendor of his success, yielded himself to the luxury, weakness, and sin of his older age. From all these considerations we conclude that the Feast of the Dedication, which lasted seven days, took place in the seventh month, that of Ethanim, or of "flowing brooks," (the later Tishri), of the year after the completion of the Temple (eleven months after it), and immediately before the Feast of Tabernacles, which, with the concluding solemnity, lasted eight days.

The account of the dedication of the Temple may be conveniently ranged under these three particulars, the Consecration-Services, the Consecration-Prayer, and the Consecration-Thanksgiving and Festive Offerings. But before describing them, it is necessary to call attention to the remarkable circumstance that the chief, if not almost the sole prominent agent in these services, was the king, the high-priest not being even mentioned. Not that

Solomon in any way interfered with, or arrogated to himself the functions of the priesthood, but that, in the part which he took, he fully acted up to the spirit of the monarchical institution as founded in Israel. Solomon was not "king" according to the Saxon idea of cyning — cunning, mighty, illustrious, the embodiment of strength. According to the terms of the Covenant, all Israel were God's servants (Leviticus 25:42, 55; comp. Isaiah 41:8, 9; 44:1, 2, 21; 45:4; 49:3, 6; Jeremiah 30:10 and others). As such they were to be "a kingdom of priests" (Exodus 19:6) "the priest," in the stricter sense of the term, being only the representative of the people, with certain distinctive functions ad hoc. But what the nation was, as a whole, that Israel's theocratic king was pre-eminently the servant of the LORD (1 Kings 8:25, 28, 29, 52, 59). It was in this capacity that Solomon acted at the dedication of the Temple, as his own words frequently indicate (see the passages just quoted). In this manner the innermost and deepest idea of the character of Israel and of Israel's king as "the servant" of the LORD, became, so to speak, more and more individualized during the progress of the Old Testament dispensation, until it stood out in all its fullness in the Messiah — the climax of Israel and of Israelitish institutions — Who is the Servant of Jehovah. Thus we perceive that the common underlying idea of the three great institutions in Israel, which connected them all, was that of the Servant of Jehovah. The prophet who uttered the voice of heaven upon earth was the servant of Jehovah (comp., for example, Numbers 12:7, 8; Joshua 1:2; Isaiah 20:3, etc.).

So was the priest, who spake the voice of earth to heaven; and the king, who made heaven's voice to be heard on earth. That which gave its real meaning equally to this threefold function; downwards, upwards, outwards — was the grand fact that in each of them it was the Servant of Jehovah who was acting, or, in other words, that God was all in all. With these general principles in view we shall be better able to understand what follows.

1. The Consecration-Services (1 Kings 8:1-21). — These commenced with the transference of the Ark and of the other holy vessels from Mount Zion, and of the ancient Mosaic Tabernacle from Gibeon. The latter and the various other relics of those earlier services were, as we have suggested, placed in the chambers built around the new Sanctuary. In accordance with the Divine direction, the whole of this part of the service was performed by the Priests and Levites, attended by the king, "the elders of Israel, the heads of the tribes, and the princes (of the houses) of the fathers of Israel," who, as representatives of the people, had been specially summoned for the purpose. As this solemn procession entered the sacred courts, amidst a vast concourse of people, numberless offerings were brought. Then the Ark was carried to its place in the innermost Sanctuary. As the priests reverently retired from it, and were about to minister in the Holy Place, — perhaps to burn incense on the Golden Altar — "the cloud," as the visible symbol of God's Presence, came down, as formerly at the consecration of the Tabernacle (Exodus 40:34, 35), and so filled the whole of the Temple itself, that the priests, unable to bear "the glory," had to retire from their ministry.

But even here also we mark the characteristic difference between the Old and the New Dispensations, to which St. Paul calls attention in another connection (2 Corinthians 3:13-18). For whereas, under the preparatory dispensation God dwelt in a "cloud" and in "thick darkness," we all now behold "the glory of God" in the Face of His Anointed.

This was the real consecration of the Temple. And now the king, turning towards the Most Holy Place, filled with the Sacred Presence, spake these words of dedication, brief as became the solemnity, "Jehovah hath said, to dwell in darkness — Building, I have built an house of habitation to Thee, and a settling-place for Thy dwelling ever!" In this reference to what Jehovah had said, it would not be any single utterance which presented itself to Solomon's mind. Rather would he think of them in their connection and totality — as it were, a golden chain of precious promises welded one to the other, of which the last link seemed riveted to the solemnity then enacting. Such sayings as Exodus 19:9; 20:21; Leviticus 16:2; Deuteronomy 4:11; 5:22 would crowd upon his memory, and seem fully realized as he beheld the Cloudy Presence in the Holy House. Thus it is often not one particular promise or prophecy which is referred to when we read in Holy Scripture these words, "That it might be fulfilled," but rather a whole series which culminate in some one great fact (as, for example, in Matthew 2:15, 23). Nor should we forget that, when the king spoke of the Temple as God's dwelling for ever, the symbolical character alike of the manifestation of His Presence and of its place could not have been absent from his mind. But the symbolical necessarily implies the temporary, being of the nature of an accommodation to circumstances, persons, and times. What was for ever was not the form, but the substance — not the manner nor the place, but the fact of God's Presence in the midst of His people. And what is real and eternal is the Kingdom of God in its widest sense, and God's Presence in grace among His worshipping people, as fully realized in Jesus Christ.

When the king had spoken these words, he turned from the Sanctuary to the people who reverently stood to hear his benedictory "address." Briefly recounting the gracious promises and experiences of the past, he pointed to the present as their fulfillment, specially applying to it, in the manner already described, what God had said to David (2 Samuel 7:7, 8).

2. The Prayer of Consecration. — This brief address concluded, the king ascended the brazen pulpit-like platform "before the altar" (of burnt offering), and with his face, probably sideways, towards the people, knelt down with hands outspread in prayer (comp. 2 Chronicles 6:12, 13).

It seems like presumption and impertinence to refer in laudatory terms to what for comprehensiveness, sublimeness, humility, faith, and earnestness has no parallel in the Old Testament, and can only be compared with the prayer which our Lord taught His disciples.

Like the latter, it consists of an introduction (1 Kings 8:23-30), of seven petitions (the covenant-number, vers. 31-53), and of a eulogetic close (2 Chronicles 6:40-42). The Introduction sounds like an Old Testament version of the words "Our Father" (vers. 23-26), "which art in heaven" (vers. 27-30). It would be out of place here to enter into any detailed analysis. Suffice it to indicate the leading Scriptural references in it, as it were, the spiritual stepping-stones of the prayer and one or another of its outstanding points. Marking how a review of the gracious dealings in the past should lead to confidence in present petitions (comp. Matthew 21:22; Mark 11:24; James 1:6), reference should be made in connection with verses 23-26 to the following passages: Exodus 15:11; Deuteronomy 4:39; 7:9; Joshua 2:11; 2 Samuel 7:12-22; 22:32; Psalm 86:8. In regard to the second part of the Introduction (vers. 27-30), we specially note the emphatic assertion, that He, Whose Presence they saw in the cloud, was really in "heaven," and yet "our Father," who art upon earth. These two ideas seem carried out in it, (1) not as heathenism does, do we locate God here; nor yet will we, as carnal Israel did (Jeremiah 7:4; Micah 3:11), imagine that ex opere operato (by any mere deed of ours) God will necessarily attend even to His own appointed services in His house. Our faith rises higher — from the Seen to the Unseen — from the God of Israel to our Father; it realizes the spiritual relationship of children, which alone contains the pledge of His blessing; and through which, though He be in heaven, yet faith knows and addresses

Him as an ever-present help. Thus Solomon's prayer avoided alike the two extremes of unspiritual realism and of unreal spiritualism.

The first petition (vers. 31, 32) in the stricter sense opens the prayer, which in ver. 28 had been outlined, according to its prevailing characteristics, as "petition," "prayer for mercy" (forgiveness and grace), and "thanksgiving" (praise).

It is essentially an Old Testament "Hallowed be Thy Name," in its application to the sanctity of an oath as its highest expression, inasmuch as thereby the reality of God's holiness is challenged. The analogy between the second petition (vers. 33, 34) and that in the Lord's Prayer is not so evident at first sight. But it is none the less real, since its ideal fulfillment would mark the coming of the kingdom of God, which neither sin from within nor enemy from without could endanger. The references in this petition seem to be to Leviticus 26:3, 7, 14, 17; Deuteronomy 28:1-7, 15-25; and again to Leviticus 26:33, and 40-42, and Deuteronomy 4:26-28; 28:64-68, and 4:29-31; 30:1-5. The organic connection, so to speak, between heaven and earth, which lies at the basis of the third petition in the Lord's Prayer, is also expressed in that of Solomon (vers. 35, 36). Only in the one case we have the New Testament realization of that grand idea, or rather ideal, while in the other we have its Old Testament aspect. The references here are to Leviticus 26:19; Deuteronomy 11:17; 28:23, 24. At the same time the rendering of our Authorized Version (1 Kings 8:35): "When Thou afflictest them," should be altered to, "Because Thou humblest them," which indicates the moral effect of God's discipline, and the last link in the chain of true repentance.

The correspondence between the fourth petition in the Solomonic (vers. 37- 40) and in our Lord's Prayer will be evident — always keeping in view the difference between the Old and the New Testament standpoint. But perhaps verses 38-40 may mark the transition from, and connection between the first and second parts of the prayer. The fifth petition (vers. 41-43), which concerns the acceptance of the prayers of strangers (not proselytes), is based on the idea of the great mutual forgiveness by those who are forgiven of God, fully realized in the abolition of the great enmity and separation, which was to give place to a common brotherhood of love and service — "that all the people of the earth may know Thy Name, to fear Thee, as Thy people Israel." Here also we note the difference between the Old and the New Testament form of the petition — a remark which must equally be kept in view in regard to the other two petitions. These, indeed, seem to bear only a very distant analogy to the concluding portion of the Lord's Prayer. Yet that there was real "temptation" to Israel, and real "deliverance from evil" sought in these petitions, appears from the language of confession put into the mouth of the captives (ver. 47), which, as we know, was literally adopted by those in Babylon (Daniel 9:5; Psalm 106:6).

Here sin is presented in its threefold aspect as failure, so far as regards the goal, or stumbling and falling (in the Authorized Version "we have sinned"); then as perversion (literally, making crooked); and, lastly, as tumultuous rebellion (in the Authorized Version "committed wickedness"). Lastly, the three concluding verses (vers. 51-53)may be regarded either as the argument for the last petitions, or else as an Old Testament version of "Thine is the kingdom, and the power, and the glory." But the whole prayer is the opening of the door into heaven — a door moving, if the expression be lawful, on the two hinges of sin and of grace, of need and of provision.

3. The Consecration-Thanksgiving and Offerings. — To the prayer of Solomon, the descent of fire upon the great altar — probably from out the Cloudy Presence — which is recorded in 2 Chronicles 7:1, seems a most appropriate answer, (comp. Leviticus 9:24).

Little requires to be added to the simple account of what followed. Rising from his knees, the king turned once more to the people, and expressed the feelings of all in terms of mingled praise and prayer, basing them on such Scriptural passages as Deuteronomy 12:9, 10; Joshua 21:44, etc.; 23:14, and, in the second part of his address, on Leviticus 26:3-13; Deuteronomy 28:1-14. But it deserves special notice, that throughout (as Thenius has well remarked) the tone is of the loftiest spirituality. For, if the king asks for continued help and blessing from the Lord, it is for the express purpose "that He may incline our hearts to Him" (comp. Psalm 119:36; 141:4), "to keep His commandments" (1 Kings 8:58); and, if he looks for answers to prayer (ver. 59), it is "that all the people of the earth may know that Jehovah is God, and that there is none else" (ver. 60).

Lastly, we have an account of the vast number of festive offerings which Solomon and all Israel brought, and of the Feast of Tabernacles with which the solemn dedication-services concluded.

CHAPTER 8: THE SURROUNDINGS OF THE TEMPLE — DESCRIPTION OF JERUSALEM AT THE TIME OF SOLOMON — THE PALACE OF SOLOMON — SOLOMON'S FORTIFIED CITIES — EXTERNAL RELATIONS OF THE KINGDOM — INTERNAL STATE — TRADE — WEALTH — LUXURY — THE VISIT OF THE QUEEN OF SHEBA.

(1 KINGS 9, 10.; 2 CHRONICLES 7:11-9:28)

WE have now reached the period of Solomon's greatest worldly splendor, which, as alas! so often, marks also that of spiritual decay. The building of the Temple was not the first, nor yet the last, of his architectural undertakings. Mount Moriah was too small to hold on its summit the Temple itself, even without its courts and other buildings. Accordingly, as we learn from Josephus (Ant. 15. 11, 3), extensive substructures had to be reared. Thus, the level of the Temple-mount was enlarged both east and west, in order to obtain a sufficient area for the extensive buildings upon it. These rose terrace upon terrace — each court higher than the other, and the Sanctuary itself higher than its courts. We are probably correct in the supposition that the modern Mosque of Omar occupies the very site of the ancient Temple of Solomon, and that over the celebrated rock in it — according to Jewish tradition, the very spot where Abraham offered up Isaac — the great altar of burnt-offering had risen. Before the building of the Sanctuary itself could have been commenced, the massive substructures of the Temple must have been at least partially completed, although these and the outbuildings were probably continued during many years, perhaps many reigns, after the completion of the Temple.

The same remarks apply to another structure connected with the Temple, called "Parbar" (1 Chronicles 26:18). As already explained, the outer court of the Temple had four massive gates (1 Chronicles 26:13-16), of which the western-most opened upon "Parbar" or "Parvarim" (perhaps "colonnade"). This seems to have been an annex to the western side of the Temple, fitted up as chambers, stables for sacrificial animals, etc. (2 Kings 23:11, where our Authorized Version wrongly renders "Parvarim" by "suburbs"). From Parbar steps led down to the Tyropoeon, or deep valley which intersected the city east and west.

Although anything like an attempt at detailed description would here be out of place, it seems desirable, in order to realize the whole circumstances, to give at least a brief sketch of Jerusalem, as Solomon found, and as he left it. Speaking generally, Jerusalem was built on the two opposite hills (east and west), between which the Tyropoeon runs south-east and then south. The eastern hill is about 100 feet lower than the western. Its northern summit is Mount Moriah, which slopes down into Ophel (about 50 feet lower), afterwards the suburb of the priests. Some modem writers have regarded this as the ancient fort of the Jebusites, and as the site of the "City of David," the original Mount Zion. Although this is opposed to the common traditional view, which regards the western hill as Mount Zion, the arguments in favor of identifying it with the eastern hill seem very strong. These it would, of course, be impossible here to detail. But we may say that the history of David's purchase of the threshing-floor of Ornan the Jebusite (2 Samuel 24:16-24; 1 Chronicles 21:15-25)conveys these two facts, that the Jebusites had settlements on the western hill, and that David's palace (which, as we know, was in the City of David) was close by, only a little lower than Mount Moriah, since David so clearly saw from his palace the destroying Angel over the threshing-floor of Ornan. All this agrees with the idea, that the original stronghold of the Jebusites was on the slopes of Moriah and Ophel, and that David built his palace in that neighborhood, below the summit of Moriah.

Lastly, if the term "Mount Zion" included Moriah, we can understand the peculiar sacredness which throughout Holy Scripture attaches to that name. Be this as it may, the regular quarter of the Jebusites was on the western hill, towards the slope of the Tyropoeon, while the Jewish Benjamite quarter (the Upper City) was on the higher terrace above it (eastwards). Fort Millo was on the north-eastern angle of the Western City. Here King David had continued the wall, which had formerly enclosed the western hill northward and westward, drawing it eastward, so as to make (the western) Jerusalem a complete fortress (2 Samuel 5:9; 1 Chronicles 11:8). On the opposite (eastern) side of the Tyropoeon was the equally fortified (later) Ophel. Solomon now connected these two fortresses by enlarging Millo and continuing the wall across the Tyropoeon (1 Kings 3:1; 9:15; 11:27).

Without referring to the various buildings which Solomon reared, it may be safely asserted that the city must have rapidly increased in population. Indeed, during the prosperous reign of Solomon it probably attained as large, if not larger, proportions than at any time before the Exile. The wealthier part of the population occupied the western terraces of the west hill — the Upper City — the streets running north and south. The eastern slopes of the west hill were covered by "the middle city" (2 Kings 20:4, marginal rendering). It will have been noticed, that as yet only the southern parts of both the eastern and western hills of Jerusalem had been built over King Solomon now reared the Temple on Mount Moriah, which formed the northern slope of the eastern hill, while the increase of the population soon led to building operations on the side of the western hill opposite to it. Here the city extended beyond the old wall, north of "the middle city," occupying the northern part of the Tyropoeon. This was "the other" or "second part of the city" (2 Kings 22:14; 2 Chronicles 34:22; Nehemiah 11:9, the "maktesh" or "mortar" of Zephaniah 1:11). Here was the real business quarter, with its markets, "fishgate," "sheepgate," and bazaars, such as the "Baker Street" (Jeremiah 37:21), the quarters of the goldsmiths and other merchants (Nehemiah 3:8, 32), the "valley of the cheesemongers," etc. This suburb must have been soon enclosed by a wall. We do not know when or by whom the latter was commenced, but we have notices of its partial destruction (2 Kings 14:13; 2 Chronicles 25:23), and of its repair (2 Chronicles 32:5).

We have purposely not taken account of the towers and gates of the city, since what has been described will sufficiently explain the location of the great palace which Solomon built during the thirteen years after the completion of the Temple (1 Kings 7:1-12; 2 Chronicles 8:1). Its site was the eastern terrace of the western hill, probably the same as that afterwards occupied by the palace of the Asmonaeans (Maccabees) and of Agrippa II. The area covered by this magnificent building was four times that of the Holy House (not including its courts). It stood right over against the Temple. A descent led from the Palace into the Tyropoeon, and thence a special magnificent "ascent" (2 Chronicles 9:4) to the royal entrance (2 Kings 16:18), probably at the south-western angle of the Temple. The site was happily chosen — protected by Fort Millo, and looking out upon the Temple-Mount, while south of it stretched the wealthy quarter of the city. Ascending from the Tyropoeon, one would pass through a kind of ante-building into a porch, and thence into a splendid colonnade. This colonnade connected "the house of the forest of Lebanon," so called from the costly cedars used in its construction, with "the porch for the throne," where Solomon pronounced judgment (1 Kings 7:6, 7). Finally, there was in the inner court, still further west, "the house where Solomon dwelt," and "the house for Pharaoh's daughter," with, of course, the necessary side and outbuildings (1 Kings 7:8). Thus, the royal palace really consisted of three separate buildings. Externally it was simply of "costly stones" (ver. 9), the beauty of its design only appearing in its interior. Here the building extended along three sides. The ground-floor consisted of colonnades of costly cedar, the beams being fastened into the outer walls. These colonnades would be hung with tapestry, so as to be capable of being formed into apartments. Above these rose, on each side of the court, three tiers of chambers, fifteen on each tier, with large windows looking out upon each other. Here were the State apartments for court feasts, and in them were kept, among other precious things, the golden targets and shields (1 Kings 10:16, 17). Passing through another colonnade, one would next reach the grand Judgment- and Audience-halls, with the magnificent throne of ivory, described in 1 Kings 10:18-20; 2 Chronicles 9:17-19. And, lastly, the innermost court contained the royal dwellings themselves.

But this great Palace, the Temple, and the enlargement of Millo and of the city wall, were not the only architectural undertakings of King Solomon. Remembering that there were watchful foes on all sides, he either built or repaired a number of strong places. In the north, as defense against Syria, rose the ancient stronghold of Hazor (Joshua 11:13; Judges 4:2). The plain of Jezreel, the traditional battlefield of, as well as the highway into Palestine from the west and the north, was protected by Megiddo; while the southern approach from Egypt and the Philistine plain was guarded by Gezer, which Pharaoh had before this taken from the Canaanites and burnt, but afterwards given to his daughter as dowry on her marriage with Solomon. Not far from Gezer, and serving a similar defensive purpose, rose the fortress of Baalath, in the possession of Dan (comp. Josephus, Ant. 8, 6, 1). The eastern and northeastern parts of Solomon's dominions were protected by Tamar or Tadmor, probably the Palmyra of the ancients, and by Hamath-Zobah (2 Chronicles 8:4), while access to Jerusalem and irruptions from the north-western plain were barred by the fortification of Upper and Nether Bethhoron (1 Kings 9:15-19; 2 Chronicles 8:3-6).

Besides these fortresses, the king provided magazine-cities, and others where his chariots and cavalry were stationed — most of them, probably, towards the north. In all such undertakings Solomon employed the forced labor of the descendants of the ancient Canaanite inhabitants of Palestine, his Jewish subjects being chiefly engaged as overseers and officers in various departments (1 Kings 9:20-23). But even thus, the diversion of so much labor and the taxation which his undertakings must have involved were felt as a "grievous service" and "heavy yoke" (1 Kings 12:4), all the more that Solomon's love of building and of Oriental splendor seems to have rapidly grown upon him. Thus, once more by a natural process of causation, the inner decay marked by luxury led to the weakening of the kingdom of Solomon, and scattered the seeds of that disaffection which, in the days of his degenerate son, ripened into open rebellion. So true is it, that in the history of Israel the inner and the outer always keep pace. But as yet Solomon's devotion to the services of Jehovah had not lessened. For we read that on the great festivals of the year (2 Chronicles 8:12, 13) he was wont to bring numerous special offerings.

As regards the foreign relations of Solomon, reference has already been made (in ch. 5) to his marriage with the daughter of Pharaoh (1 Kings 3:1), which took place in the first years of his reign. In all likelihood this Pharaoh was one of the last rulers of the (21st) Tanite dynasty. We know that their power had of late greatly declined, and Pharaoh may have been glad to ally himself with the now powerful ruler of the neighboring country. On the new kingdom, however, such an alliance would shed great luster, especially in the eyes of the Jews themselves. The frequent references to Pharaoh's daughter show what importance the nation attached to this union. It may be well here again to note, that the Egyptian princess, who brought to her husband the dowry of an important border-fortress (Gezer), was not in any way responsible for Solomon's later idolatry, no Egyptian deities being named among those towards whom he turned (1 Kings 11:5-7).

Solomon's relations to Hiram, king of Tyre, at one time threatened to become less friendly than they had been at first, and afterwards again became. It appears that, besides furnishing him with wood, Hiram had also advanced gold to Solomon (1 Kings 9:11), amounting, if we may connect with this the notice in ver. 14, to 120 talents of gold, variously computed at £1,250,000 (Poole), £720,000 (S. Clarke), and £471,240 (Keil, whose estimate seems the most probable). We suppose it was in repayment of this sum that Solomon ceded to Hiram twenty cities in Northern Galilee, adjoining the possessions of Tyre. With these he might the more readily part, since the district was partially "Gentile" (Isaiah 9:1). But Hiram, who probably covered a strip of land along the coast, was dissatisfied with his new acquisition, and gave it the contemptuous designation of "the land of Cabul." The district seems, however, to have been afterwards restored to Solomon (2 Chronicles 8:2), no doubt on repayment of the loan and other compensation.

The later relations between Hiram and Solomon consisted chiefly in mercantile alliances. Although most writers regard the fleet which sailed to Ophir (1 Kings 9:27, 28) as identical with "the navy of Tarshish" (1 Kings 10:22), yet the names, the imports, as well as the regularity in the passages of the latter ("every three years"), and the express statement that its destiny was Tarshish (2 Chronicles 9:21) seem opposed to this view. Opinions are also divergent as to the exact location of Ophir, and the share which Hiram had in the outfit of this expedition, whether he only furnished sailors (1 Kings 9:27), or also the ships (2 Chronicles 8:28). In all probability the wood for these ships was cut in Lebanon by order of Hiram, and floated to Joppa, whence it would be transported by land (comp. 2 Chronicles 2:16) to Ezion-Geber and Elath, at the head of the Gulf of Akabah (the Red Sea), where the vessels would be built under the direction of Phoenician shipwrights. Upon the whole, it seems most likely that the Ophir whence they fetched gold was Arabia. The sacred text does not inform us whether these expeditions were periodical, the absence of such notice rather leading to the supposition that this was not the case, or at least that they were not continued. The total result of these expeditions was an importation of gold to the amount of 420 talents (according to Keil about 1 million sterling).

It was not only the prospect of such addition to the wealth of the country, but that this was the first Jewish maritime expedition — in fact, the first great national trading undertaking, which gave it such importance in public estimation that Solomon went in person to visit the two harbors where the fleet was fitting out (2 Chronicles 8:17). According to 1 Kings 10:11, the Phoenician fleet also brought from "Ophir" "precious stones" and "almug-trees," or sandal-wood, which King Solomon used for "balustrades" in the Temple, for his own palace, and for making musical instruments.

The success of this trading adventure may have led to another similar undertaking, in company with the Phoenicians, to Tartessus (Tarshish), the well-known great mercantile emporium on the south coast of Spain. The duration of such an expedition is stated in round numbers as three years; and the trade became so regular that afterwards all the large merchantmen were popularly known as "Tarshish-ships" (comp. 1 Kings 22:48; Psalm

48:7; Isaiah 2:16). The imports from Tarshish consisted of gold, silver, ivory, apes, and peacocks (1 Kings 10:22).

The two last-mentioned articles of import indicate the commencement of a very dangerous decline towards Oriental luxury. It has been well observed (by Ewald), that there was a moment in Israel's history when it seemed possible that David might have laid the foundation of an empire like that of Rome, and another when Solomon might have led the way to a philosophy as sovereign as that of Greece.

But it was an equally, if not more dangerous path on which to enter, and one even more opposed to the Divine purpose concerning Israel, when foreign trade, and with it foreign luxury, became the object of king and people. The danger was only too real, and the public display appeared in what the Queen of Sheba saw of Solomon's court (1 Kings 10:5), in the magnificence of his throne (vers. 19, 20), and in the sumptuousness of all his appointments (ver. 21). Two hundred large targets and three hundred smaller shields, all covered with beaten gold, hung around the house of the forest of Lebanon; all the king's drinking vessels, and all the other appurtenances for State receptions were of pure gold; the merchants brought the spices of the East into the country (ver. 15); while traders, importers, and vassal chiefs swelled the immense revenue, which in one year rose to the almost incredible sum of 666 talents of gold, which at the lowest computation amounts to upwards of 2 _ millions of our money, or only one million less than that of the Persian kings (Herod 3. 95).

Add to this the number of Solomon's chariots and horsemen, the general wealth of the country, and the importation of horses from Egypt, which made Palestine almost an emporium for chariots and horses; and it will not be difficult to perceive on what a giddy height king and people stood during the later years of Solomon's reign.

It was this scene of wealth and magnificence, unexampled even in the East, as well as the undisputed political influence and supremacy of the king, combined with the highest intellectual activity and civilization in the country, which so much astounded the Queen of Sheba on her visit to Solomon's dominions. Many, indeed, were the strangers who had been attracted to Jerusalem by the fame of its king (1 Kings 10:24). But none of them had been so distinguished as she, whose appearance was deeply symbolical of the glorious spiritual destiny of Israel (Psalm 72:10, 11; Isaiah 60:6), and indicative of the future judgment on the unbelief of those who were even more highly favored (Matthew 12:42; Luke 11:31). Sheba, which is to be distinguished from Seba, or Meroi in Ethiopia, was a kingdom in Southern Arabia, on the shores of the Red Sea, and seems to have been chiefly governed by Queens.

Owing to its trade, the population was regarded as the wealthiest in Arabia. It may have been that Solomon's fame had first reached the ears of the Queen through the fleet of Ophir. In consequence, she resolved to visit Jerusalem, to see, to test, and to learn for herself whether the extraordinary reports which had reached her were true. But, whatever may have specially influenced her to undertake so novel a pilgrimage, three things in regard to it are beyond question. She was attracted by the fame of Solomon's wisdom; she viewed that wisdom in connection with "the Name of Jehovah" (1 Kings 10:1); and she came to learn. What the higher import of this "wisdom" was, is explained by Solomon himself in Proverbs 3:14-18, while its source is indicated in Proverbs 2:4-6.

Thus viewing it, no event could have been more important, alike typically and in its present bearing on the ancient world. The Queen had come, scarcely daring to hope that Eastern exaggeration had not led her to expect more than she would find. It proved the contrary. Whatever difficulty, doubt, or question she propounded, in the favorite Oriental form of "riddles," "whatever was with her heart," "Solomon showed (disclosed to) her all her words" (the spoken and unspoken).

And here she would learn chiefly this, that all the prosperity she witnessed, all the intellectual culture and civilization with which she was brought into contact, had their spring above, with "the Father of lights." She had come at the head of a large retinue, bearing richest presents, which she left in remembrance and also in perpetuation of her visit — at least, if we may trust the account of Josephus, that the cultivation of balsam in the gardens of Jericho owed its origin to plants which the Queen had brought (Jos., Ant. 8. 6, 6). The notice is at least deeply symbolical. The spices of Sheba, so sweet and strong that, according to ancient accounts, their perfume was carried out far to sea, were to be brought to Jerusalem, and their plants to strike root in sacred soil (Psalm 72:10, 11; Isaiah 60:6). But now the balsam-gardens of Jericho, into which they were transplanted, are lying bare and desolate — for "the Queen of the South" hath risen up in judgment with that "generation;" and what further "sign" can or need be given to the generation that turned from Him Who was "greater than Solomon?"

CHAPTER 9: SOLOMON'S COURT — HIS POLYGAMY — SPREAD OF FOREIGN IDEAS IN THE COUNTRY — IMITATION OF FOREIGN MANNERS — GROWING LUXURY — SOLOMON'S SPIRITUAL DECLINE — JUDGMENT PREDICTED — SOLOMON'S ENEMIES: HADAD, REZON, JEROBOAM — CAUSES OF POPULAR DISCONTENT — AHIJAH'S PREDICTION OF THE DISRUPTION — JEROBOAM'S REBELLION AND FLIGHT INTO EGYPT — DEATH OF SOLOMON.

(1 KINGS 11)

GREATER contrast could scarcely be imagined than that between the state of Solomon's court and of the country generally, and the directions and restrictions laid down in Deuteronomy 17:16, 17 for the regulation of the Jewish monarchy. The first and most prominent circumstance which here presents itself to the mind, is the direct contravention of the Divine command as regarded the number of "princesses" and concubines which formed the harem of Solomon. Granting that the notice in Cant. 6. 8 affords reason for believing that the numerals in 1 Kings 11:3 may have been due to a mistake on the part of a copyist, still the sacred narrative expressly states, that the polygamy of Solomon, and especially his alliances with nations excluded from intermarriage with Israel, was the occasion, if not the cause, of his later sin and punishment.

While on this subject we may go back a step further, and mark (with Ewald) what sad consequences the infringement of the primitive Divine order in regard to marriage wrought throughout the history of Israel. It is undoubtedly to polygamy that we have to trace the troubles in the family of David; and to the same cause were due many of those which came on David's successors. If Moses was obliged to tolerate the infringement of the original institution of God, "the hardness of heart" which had necessitated it brought its own punishment, especially when the offender was an Eastern king. Thus the sin of the people, embodied, as it were, in the person of their representative, carried national judgment as its consequence.

But the elements which caused the fall of Solomon lay deeper than polygamy. Indeed, the latter was among the effects, as well as one of the further causes of his spiritual decline. First among these elements of evil at work, we reckon the growing luxury of the court. The whole atmosphere around, so to speak, was different from what it had been in the primitive times which preceded the reign of Solomon, and still more from the ideal of monarchy as sketched in the Book of Deuteronomy. Everything had become un-Jewish, foreign, purely Asiatic. Closely connected with this was the evident desire to emulate, and even outdo neighboring nations. Such wisdom, such splendor, such riches, and finally, such luxury, and such a court were not to be found elsewhere, as in the kingdom of which Jerusalem was the capital. An ominous beginning this of that long course of Jewish pride and self-exaltation which led to such fearful consequences. It is to this desire of surpassing other Eastern courts that the size of Solomon's harem must be attributed. Had it been coarse sensuality which influenced him, the earlier, not the later years of his reign, would have witnessed the introduction of so many strange wives. Moreover, it deserves special notice that the 700 wives of Solomon are designated as "princesses" (1 Kings 11:3). Without pressing this word in its most literal meaning, we may at least infer that Solomon courted influential connections with the reigning and other leading families of the clans around, and that the chief object of his great harem was, in a worldly sense, to strengthen his position, to give evidence of his wealth and power as an Eastern monarch, and to form promising alliances, no matter what spiritual elements were thus introduced into the country. Closely connected with all this was the rapidly growing intercourse between Israel and foreign nations. For one reason or another, strangers, whom Israel hitherto had only considered as heathens, crowded to Jerusalem. By their presence king and people would not only become familiar with foreign ideas, but so-called toleration would extend to these strangers the right of public worship, or rather, of public idolatry. And so strong was this feeling, that, although Asa, Jehoshaphat, Joash, and Hezekiah put an end to all idolatry, yet the high places which Solomon had built on the southern acclivity of the Mount of Olives remained in use until the time of Josiah (2 Kings 23:13), avowedly for the worship of those foreigners who came to, or were resident in, Jerusalem. Viewed in connection with what has just been stated, even the intellectual culture in the time of Solomon may have proved a source of serious danger.

All this may help us to form a more correct conception of the causes which led to the terrible decline in the spiritual history of Solomon, and this without either extenuating his guilt or, as is more commonly the case, exaggerating his sin. As Holy Scripture puts it, when Solomon was old, and less able to resist influences around, he so far yielded to his foreign wives as to build altars for their worship. This in the Scriptural and real sense was already to "go after Ashtoreth and Milcom" (1 Kings 11:5). But the sacred text does not state that Solomon personally "served them;" nor is there any reason for supposing that he either relinquished the service of Jehovah, or personally took part in heathen rites. To have built altars to "the abominations of the Gentiles," and to have tolerated, if not encouraged, the idolatrous rites openly enacted there by his wives, implied great public guilt.

In the language of Scripture, "Solomon's heart was not perfect with Jehovah his God;" he "did evil in the sight of Jehovah, and went not fully after Jehovah." His sin was the more inexcusable, that he had in this respect the irreproachable example of David. Besides, even closer allegiance to the LORD might have been expected from Solomon than from David, since he had been privileged to build the Temple, and had on two occasions received personal communication from the Lord, whereas God had never appeared to David, but only employed prophets as intermediaries to make known His good pleasure.

It need scarcely be said, that public sin such as that of Solomon would soon bring down judgment. As preparatory to it we regard that solemn warning, when the LORD a second time appeared in vision to Solomon (1 Kings 9:4-9). This being misunderstood or neglected, the actual announcement of judgment followed, probably through Ahijah. The terms of the sentence were terribly explicit. Solomon's kingdom would be rent from him, and given to his servant. Yet even so Divine mercy would accord a twofold limitation-the event foretold should not happen in the days of Solomon himself, and when it took place the kingdom should not be wholly taken away, but partially remain in his line. And this for the sake of David — that is, not from partiality for him, nor on account of any supposed superabundant merit, but because of God's promise to David (2 Samuel 7:14-16), and for God's own glory, since He had made choice of Jerusalem as the place where He would forever reveal His Name (1 Kings 9:3).

But although execution of the judgment was stayed, indications of its reality and nearness soon appeared. Once more we mark a succession of natural and intelligible causes, of which the final outcome was the fulfillment of the Divine prediction. It will be remembered that, of the two great wars in which David was involved after his accession, the most formidable was that against the hostile combination of tribes along the eastern boundary of his kingdom.

The distance, the character of the country, the habits of the enemy — the alliance of so many nationalities, their determination, and the stubborn resistance which they offered, made this a really great war. We know that the armies of David, under the leadership of Joab and Abishai, were victorious at all points (2 Samuel 8; 10; 1 Chronicles 19.). But, although the enemy may have been subdued and even crushed for a time, it was, in the nature of things, impossible wholly to remove the elements of resistance. In the far southeast, terrible, almost savage, vengeance had been taken on Edom (1 Chronicles 18:12).

From the slaughter of the people a trusty band of Edomites had rescued one of the youthful royal princes, Hadad (or Adad), and brought him ultimately to Egypt, where he met a hospitable reception from the then reigning Pharaoh — probably the predecessor of Solomon's father-in-law. If Pharaoh had at first been influenced by political motives in keeping near him one who might become a source of trouble to the growing Israelitish power, the young prince of Edom soon enlisted the sympathy and affection of his host (1 Kings 11:14-19). He married the sister of Tahpenes, the Gevirah, or queen dominant (principal) of Pharaoh's harem; and their child was acknowledged and brought up among the royal princes of Egypt.

When tidings of the death of David and afterwards of Joab reached Hadad, he insisted on returning to Edom, even against the friendly remonstrances of Pharaoh, who by this time would rather have seen him enjoying his peaceful retreat in Egypt than entering upon difficult and dangerous enterprises. But, although Hadad returned to his own country in the beginning of Solomon's reign, it was only towards its close — when growing luxury had enervated king and people — that his presence there became a source of trouble and anxiety. This we infer, not only from 1 Kings 4:24, but from such a notice as that in 1 Kings 9:26.

But in the extreme northeast, as well as in the far southeast, a dark cloud gathered on the horizon. At the defeat of Hadadezer by the troops of David (2 Samuel 8:3; 10:18) one of the Syrian captains, Rezon by name, had "fled from his lord." In the then disorganized state of the country he gradually gathered around him a band of followers, and ultimately fell back upon Damascus, of which he became king. The sacred text leads us to infer that, although he probably did not venture on open warfare with Solomon, he cast off the Jewish suzerainty, and generally "was an adversary" — or, to use the pictorial language of the Bible, "abhorred Israel."

Ill-suppressed enmity in Edom (far southeast), and more active opposition and intrigue at Damascus (in the northeast) — in short, the danger of a combination like that which had so severely taxed the resources of David, such, then, so far as concerned external politics, were the darkening prospects of Solomon's later years. But the terms in which Holy Scripture speaks of these events deserve special notice. We are told, that "Jehovah stirred up" or, rather, "raised up" these adversaries unto Solomon (1 Kings 11:14, 23). The expression clearly points to Divine Causality in the matter (comp. Deuteronomy 18:15, 18; Judges 2:18; 1 Samuel 2:35; Jeremiah 29:15; Ezra 34:23). Not, indeed, that the ambitious or evil passions of men's hearts are incited of God, but that while each, in the exercise of his free will, chooses his own course, the LORD overrules all, so as to serve for the chastisement of sin and the carrying out of His own purposes (comp. Psalm 2:1, 2; Isaiah 10:1-3).

But yet another and far more serious danger threatened Solomon's throne. Besides "adversaries" without, elements of dissatisfaction were at work within Palestine, which only needed favoring circumstances to lead to open revolt. First, there was the old tribal jealousy between Ephraim and Judah. The high destiny foretold to Ephraim (Genesis 48:17-22; 49:22-26) must have excited hopes which the leadership of Joshua, himself an Ephraimite (Numbers 13:8), seemed for a time to warrant. Commanding, perhaps, the most important territorial position in the land, Ephraim claimed a dominating power over the tribes in the days of Gideon and of Jephthah (Judges 8:1; 12:1). In fact, one of the successors of these Judges, Abdon, was an Ephraimite (Judges 12:13). But, besides, Ephraim could boast not only of secular, but of ecclesiastical supremacy since Shiloh and Kirjath-jearim were within its tribal possession. And had not Samuel, the greatest of the Judges, the one outstanding personality in the history of a decrepit priesthood, been, though a Levite, yet "from Mount Ephraim" (1 Samuel 1:1)? Even the authority of Samuel could not secure the undisputed acknowledgment of Saul, who was only too painfully conscious of the objections which tribal jealousy would raise to his elevation (1 Samuel 9:21). It needed that glorious God-given victory at Jabesh-Gilead to hush, under strong religious convictions, those discordant voices, and to unite all Israel in acclamation of their new king. And yet the tribe of Benjamin, to which Saul belonged, was closely allied to that of Ephraim (Judges 21:19-23). Again, it was the tribe of Ephraim which mainly upheld the cause of Ishbosheth (2 Samuel 2:9); and though the strong hand of David afterwards kept down all active opposition, no sooner did his power seem on the wane than "a man of Mount Ephraim" (2 Samuel 20:21) roused the tribal jealousies, and raised the standard of rebellion against him. And now, with the reign of King Solomon, all hope of tribal pre-eminence seemed to have passed from Ephraim. There was a new capital for the whole country, and that in the possession of Judah. The glory of the ancient Sanctuary had also been taken away. Jerusalem was the ecclesiastical as well as the political capital, and Ephraim had to contribute its wealth and even its forced labor to promote the schemes, to support the luxury, and to advance the glory of a new monarchy, taken from, and resident in, Judah!

But, secondly, the burden which the new monarchy imposed on the people must, in the course of time, have weighed very heavily on them (1 Kings 12:4). The building of a great national Sanctuary was, indeed, an exceptional work which might enlist the highest and best sympathies, and make the people willing to submit to any sacrifices. But this was followed by the construction of a magnificent palace, and then by a succession of architectural undertakings (1 Kings 9:15, 17-19) on an unprecedented scale. However useful some of these might be, they not only marked an innovation, but involved a continuance of forced labor (1 Kings 4:6; 5:13, 14; 11:28), wholly foreign to the spirit of a free people, and which diverted from their proper channels the industrial forces of the country. Nor was this all. The support of such a king and court must have proved a heavy demand on the resources of the nation (1 Kings 4:21-27). To have to pay enormous taxes, and for many long years to be deprived during so many months of the heads and the bread-winners of the family, that they might do what seemed slaves' labor for the glorification of a king, whose rule was every year becoming weaker, would have excited dissatisfaction even among a more enduring people than those tribes who had so long enjoyed the freedom and the privileges of a federated Republic.

It only needed a leader — and once more Ephraim furnished him. Jeroboam, the son of Nebat and of a widow named Zeruah, was a native of Zereda or Zererath (Judges 7:22), within the territory of Ephraim.

The sacred text describes him as a "mighty man of valor." His energy, talent, and aptitude pointed him out as a fit permanent overseer of the forced labor of his tribe. It was a dangerous post to assign to a man of such power and ambition. His tribesmen, as a matter of course, came to know him as their chief and leader, while in daily close intercourse he would learn their grievances and sentiments. In such circumstances the result which followed was natural. The bold, strong, and ambitious Ephraimite, "ruler over all the burden of the house of Joseph," became the leader of the popular movement against Solomon.

It was, no doubt, in order to foment the elements of discontent already existing, as well as because his position in the city must have become untenable, that "Jeroboam went out of Jerusalem" (1 Kings 11:29). When "the prophet Ahijah the Shilonite found him in the way," Jeroboam had already planned, or rather commenced, his revolt against Solomon. Himself an Ephraimite (from Shiloh), the prophet would not only be acquainted with Jeroboam, but also know the sentiments of his tribesmen and the views of their new leader. It was not, therefore, Ahijah who incited Jeroboam to rebellion by the symbolical act of rending his new garment in twelve pieces, giving him ten of the pieces, while those retained were emblematic of what would be left to the house of David.

Rather did he act simply as the Divine messenger to Jeroboam, after the latter had resolved on his own course. The event was, indeed, ordered of God in punishment of the sin of Solomon (vers. 11-13); and the intimation of this fact, with its lessons of warning, was the principal object of Ahijah's mission and message. But the chief actor had long before chosen his own part, being prompted, as Holy Scripture puts it, by a settled ambition to usurp the throne (1 Kings 11:37); while the movement of which he took advantage was not only the result of causes long at work, but might almost have been forecast by any observer acquainted with the state of matters. Thus we learn once more how, in the Providence of God, a result which, when predicted, seems miraculous, and is really such, so far as the Divine operation is concerned, is brought about, not only through the free agency of man, but by a series of natural causes, while at the same time all is guided and overruled of God for His own wise and holy purposes.

Indeed, closely considered, the words of the prophet, so far from inciting Jeroboam to rebellion against Solomon, should rather have deterred him from it. The scene is sketched in vivid outline. Jeroboam, in whose soul tribal pride, disgust at his work, contempt for the king, irrepressible energy, and high-reaching ambition, combined with a knowledge of the feelings of his tribesmen, have ripened into stern resolve, has left Jerusalem. The time for secret intrigue and dissimulation is past; that for action has arrived. As he leaves the hated city-walls — memorials of Ephraim's servitude — and ascends towards the heights of Benjamin and Ephraim, a strange figure meets him. It is his countryman from Shiloh, the prophet Ahijah. No salutation passes between them, but Ahijah takes hold of the new square cloth or upper mantle in which he has been wrapped, and rends it in twelve pieces. It is not, as usually, in token of mourning (Genesis 37:29; 44:13; 2 Samuel 13:19), though sadness must have been in the prophet's heart, but as symbol of what is to happen — as it were, God's answer to Jeroboam's thoughts. Yet the judgment predicted is not to take effect in Solomon's lifetime (1 Kings 11:34, 35); and any attempt at revolt, such as Jeroboam seems to have made (vers. 26, 40), was in direct contravention of God's declared will.

There were other parts of the prophet's message which Jeroboam would have done well to have borne in mind. David was always to "have a light before God" in Jerusalem, the city "which He had chosen to put His Name there" (1 Kings 11:36). In other words, David was always to have a descendant on the throne, and Jerusalem with its Temple was always to be

God's chosen place; that is, Israel's worship was to continue in the great central Sanctuary, and the descendants of David were to be the rightful occupants of the throne until He came Who was David's greater Son.

God had linked the Son of David with His City and the Temple, so that the final destruction of the latter marked the fulfillment of the prophecies concerning the house of David. Thus gloriously did the promise stretch beyond the immediate future, with its troubles and afflictions. Lastly, so far as regarded Jeroboam, the promise of succession to the kingdom of Israel in his family was made conditional on his observance of the statutes and commandments of God, as David had kept them (ver. 38). But Jeroboam was of far other spirit than David. His main motive had been personal ambition. Unlike David, who, though anointed king, would make no attempt upon the crown during Saul's lifetime, Jeroboam, despite the express warning of God, "lifted up his hand against the king." The result was failure and flight into Egypt.

Nor did Jeroboam keep the statutes and commandments of the LORD; and after a brief reign his son fell by the hand of the assassin (1 Kings 15:28). Lastly, and most important of all — the Messianic beating of the promise to David, and the Divine choice of Jerusalem and its Temple, were fatally put aside or forgotten by Jeroboam and his successors on the throne of Israel. The schism in the kingdom became one from the Theocracy; and the rejection of the central Sanctuary resulted, as might have been expected, in the establishment of idolatry in Israel.

Nor did King Solomon either live or die as his father David. A feeble attempt — perhaps justifiable — to rid himself of Jeroboam, and no more is told of him than that, at the close of a reign of forty years, he "slept with his fathers, and was buried in the city of David his father."

So far as we know, in that death-chamber no words of earnest, loving entreaty to serve Jehovah were spoken to his successor, such as David had uttered; no joyous testimony here as regarded the past, nor yet strong faith and hope as concerned the future, such as had brightened the last hours of David. It is to us a silent death-chamber in which King Solomon lay. No bright sunset here, to be followed by a yet more glorious morning. He had done more than any king to denationalize Israel. And on the morrow of his death, rebellion within the land; outside its borders — Edom and Syria ready to spring to arms, Egypt under Shishak gathering up its might; and only a Rehoboam to hold the rudder of the State in the rising storm.

CHAPTER 10: FAMILY OF SOLOMON — AGE OF REHOBOAM — HIS CHARACTER — RELIGIOUS HISTORY OF ISRAEL AND JUDAH — THE ASSEMBLY AT SHECHEM — JEROBOAM'S RETURN FROM EGYPT — REHOBOAM'S ANSWER TO THE DEPUTIES IN SHECHEM — REVOLT OF THE TEN TRIBES — THE REIGNS OF REHOBOAM AND OF JEROBOAM — INVASION OF JUDAH BY SHISHAK — CHURCH AND STATE IN ISRAEL — REHOBOAM'S ATTEMPT TO RECOVER RULE OVER THE TEN TRIBES — HIS FAMILY HISTORY — RELIGIOUS DECLINE IN ISRAEL, AND ITS CONSEQUENCES.

(1 KINGS 12; 14:21-23; 2 CHRONICLES 10-12)

STRANGE as it may seem, despite the multifarious marriages of the king, his alliances with neighboring nations, and his immense wealth, "the house of Solomon" was far from strong at the time of his decease. It may have been that Solomon left other sons besides Rehoboam, though it is strange that we find no notice of them, nor, indeed, of any child, except a casual remark about two of Solomon's daughters (1 Kings 4:11, 15). If other children survived him, their position must have been far less influential than that of the sons of David, nor does Rehoboam's succession appear to have been ever contested by any member of the family.

Rehoboam, or rather Rechavam ("he who enlargeth the people"), must have been very young at his accession. This we gather from the expression by which they "who had grown up with him" are described, and from the manner in which his son and successor, Abijah, characterized the commencement of his reign (2 Chronicles 13:7). There seems, therefore, considerable probability attaching to the suggestion, that the notice of his age at his accession — forty-one (1 Kings 14:21; 2 Chronicles 12:13) — is the mistake of a copyist, who in transcribing the figures misread the two letters ak — twenty-one — for am — forty-one. This supposition is strengthened by the fact that Rehoboam was not the son of the Egyptian princess, who seems to have been Solomon's first wife, but of Naamah, an Ammonitess; and we know that it was only after his religious decline (1 Kings 11:1) that Solomon entered upon alliances with "strange women," among whom Ammonitesses are specially mentioned.

Of the character of Rehoboam we know sufficient to form an accurate estimate. David had taken care to commit the upbringing of his son and successor to the prophet Nathan; and, so far as we can judge, the early surroundings of Solomon were such as not only to keep him from intimacy with light or evil associates, but to train him in earnest piety. But when Rehoboam was born, King Solomon had already entered upon the fatal path which led to the ruin of his race; and the prince was brought up, like any other Eastern in similar circumstances, with the young nobles of a court which had learned foreign modes of thinking and foreign manners. The relation between the aristocracy and the people, between the king and his subjects, had changed from the primitive and God-sanctioned to that of ordinary Eastern despotism; and the notions which Rehoboam and his young friends entertained, appeared only too clearly in the first act of the king's reign. In general, we gather that Rehoboam was vain, weak, and impulsive; ready to give up under the influence of fear what he had desired and attempted when he deemed himself secure. Firm religious principles he had not, and his inclinations led him not only towards idolatry, but to a form of it peculiarly dissolute in its character (1 Kings 14:23, 24; 2 Chronicles 11:f17; 12:1). During the first three years of his reign he remained, indeed, faithful to the religion of his fathers, either through the influence of the Levites who had gathered around him from all Israel — though even in this case his motives might be rather political than conscientious — or else under the impression of the outward consequences of his first great mistake. But this mood soon passed away, and when the state-reasons for his early adherence to the worship of Jehovah had ceased to be cogent, or he felt himself secure on his throne, he yielded, as we have seen, to his real inclinations in the matter.

Here, at the outset of the separate history of the kingdoms of Judah and Israel, it may be well to take a general view of the relation of these two divisions of the Jewish people to Jehovah, their King. That the sin of Israel was much deeper, and their apostasy from God much sooner and more fully developed than in the case of Judah, appears from the circumstance, that the Divine judgment in the banishment of the people from their land overtook Israel 123 years earlier than Judah. Yet at first sight it seems almost strange that such should have been the case.

Altogether, the period of the separate existence of the two kingdoms (to the deportation of the ten tribes under Shalmaneser, about 722 B.C.)extended over 253 years. During that time, thirteen monarchs reigned over Judah, and twenty over Israel — besides two periods of probable interregnum, or rather of anarchy in Israel. The religious history of the ten tribes during these two and a half centuries may be written in very brief compass. Of all the kings of Israel it is uniformly said, that they "walked in the ways of Jeroboam, the son of Nebat," except of Ahab and his two sons (Ahaziah and Joram), under whose reigns the worship of Baal became the established religion of the country. It follows, that there was not a single king in Israel who really served the LORD or worshipped in His Temple. On the other hand, there were at least five kings in Judah distinguished for their piety (Asa, Jehoshaphat, Uzziah, Jotham, and Hezekiah), while of the other eight, two (Joash and Amaziah) continued for a considerable, and a third (Rehoboam) for a short period their profession of the religion of their fathers. Four of the other five kings acquired, indeed, a terrible notoriety for daring blasphemy. Abijam, the son and successor of Rehoboam, adopted all the practices of his father during the last fourteen years of that monarch's reign. During the reign of Joram the worship of Baal was introduced into Judah; and we know with what terrible consistency it was continued under Ahaziah and Athaliah, the measure of iniquity being filled by Ahaz, who ascended the throne twenty years before the deportation of the ten tribes, when the doors of the Sanctuary were actually closed, and an idol-altar set up in the Temple court. But, despite all this, idolatry never struck its roots deeply among the people, and this for three reasons. There was, first, the continued influence for good of the Temple at Jerusalem; and in this we see at least one providential reason for the existence of a central Sanctuary, and for the stringency of the Law which confined all worship to its courts. Secondly, the idolatrous kings of Judah were always succeeded by monarchs distinguished for piety, who swept away the rites of their predecessors; while, lastly and most remarkably, the reign of the idolatrous kings was uniformly brief as compared with that of the God-fearing rulers. Thus, on a review of the whole period, we find that, of the 253 years between the accession of Rehoboam and the deportation of the ten tribes, 200 passed under the rule of monarchs who maintained the religion of Jehovah, while only during 53 years His worship was more or less discarded by the kings of Judah.

We repeat, it were a mistake to ascribe the separation of the ten tribes entirely to the harsh and foolish refusal of Rehoboam to redress the grievances of the people. This only set the spark to the inflammable material which had long been accumulating. We have seen how dissatisfaction had spread, especially in the northern parts of the kingdom, during the later part of Solomon's reign; how, indeed, a rising seems to have been actually attempted by Jeroboam, though for the time it failed. We have also called attention to the deep-seated tribal jealousy between Ephraim and Judah, which ever and again broke into open hostility Judges 8:1-3; 12:1-6; 2 Samuel 2:9; 19:42, 43). This, indeed, may be described as the ultimate (secondary) cause of the separation of the two kingdoms. And, if proof were required that the rebellion against Rehoboam was only the outcome of previously existing tendencies, we would find it even in the circumstance that the language used by the representatives of Israel, when renouncing the rule of Rehoboam, was exactly the same as that of Sheba when he raised against David the standard of what would be represented as the ancient federal Republic of Israel (2 Samuel 20:1 comp. with 1 Kings 12:16). Still more wrongful would it be to account for the conduct either of Israel or of Jeroboam, or even to attempt vindicating it, on the ground of the prophecy of Ahijah (1 Kings 11:29-39). The latter foretold an event in history, and explained the reason of what, in view of the promises to David, would otherwise have been unaccountable. But such prediction and announcement of judgment — even if known to the tribes — warranted neither their rebellion nor the usurpation of Jeroboam. It is, indeed, true that, as the Old Testament considers all events as directly connected with God, its fundamental principle being: Jehovah reigneth — and that not merely in a pseudo-spiritual, but in the fullest sense — this, as all other things that come to man, is ultimately traced up to the living God. So was the resistance of Pharaoh, and so are the sword, the pestilence, and the famine. For, all things are of Him, Who sendeth blessings upon His people, and taketh vengeance of their inventions; Who equally ruleth in the armies of heaven, and among the inhabitants of the earth; Who maketh the wrath of man as well as the worship of His people to praise Him; Who always doeth marvelously, whether He accomplish His purposes by direct interposition from heaven, or, as much more frequently, through a chain of natural causation, of which He holds the first, and man the last, link. This grand truth, as fully expressed and applied in the sublime language of Psalm 147, is the sheet-anchor of faith by which it rides out the storms of this world. Ever to look up straight to God, to turn from events and secondary causations to Jehovah as the living God and the reigning King, is that denial of things seen and affirmation of things unseen, which constitute the victory of faith over the world.

On the death of his father, Rehoboam seems to have at once, and without opposition, assumed the reins of government. His enthronement at Jerusalem implied the homage of Judah and its neighbor-tribe Benjamin. According to ancient custom, the representatives of the more distant tribes should have assembled at the residence of the king, when in a great popular assembly the royal dignity would be solemnly conferred, and public homage rendered to the new monarch (comp. 1 Samuel 11:15; 2 Samuel 2:4; 5:3; 1 Chronicles 29:22). But, instead of repairing to Jerusalem, the representatives of the ten tribes gathered at Shechem, the ancient capital of Ephraim, where important popular assemblies had previously been held (Joshua 8:30-35; 24:1-28), and the first claimant of royalty in Israel, Abimelech, had set up his throne (Judges 9:1-23). Only one meaning could attach to their choice of this place.

They had indeed come to make Rehoboam king, but only with full concessions to their tribal claims. All that they now required was an energetic leader. Such an one was to hand in the person of Jeroboam, who in the reign of King Solomon had headed the popular movement. After the failure of his attempt, he had fled into Egypt, and been welcomed by Shishak. The weak (21st Tanite) dynasty, with which King Solomon had formed a matrimonial alliance, had been replaced by the vigorous and martial rule of Shishak (probably about fifteen years before the death of Solomon). The rising kingdom of Palestine — allied as it was with the preceding dynasty — was too close, and probably too threatening a neighbor not to be attentively watched by Shishak. It was obviously his policy to encourage Jeroboam, and to support any movement which might divide the southern from the northern tribes, and thus give Egypt the supremacy over both. In point of fact, five years later Shishak led an expedition against Rehoboam, probably not so much for the purpose of humbling Judah as of strengthening the new kingdom of Israel.

The sacred text leaves it doubtful whether, after hearing of the accession of Rehoboam, Jeroboam continued in Egypt until sent for by the representatives of the ten tribes, or returned to Ephraim of his own accord. In any case, he was not in Shechem when the assembly of the Israelitish deputies met there, but was expressly sent for to conduct negotiations on their behalf.

It was a mark of weakness on the part of Rehoboam to have gone to Shechem at all; and it must have encouraged the deputies in their demands. Moderate as these sound, they seem to imply not only a lightening of the "heavy" burden of forced labor and taxation, but of the "grievous yoke" of what they regarded as a despotism, which prevented their free movements. It is on this supposition alone that we can fully account for the reply which Rehoboam ultimately gave them. The king took three days to consider the demand. First, he consulted Solomon's old advisers, who strongly urged a policy of at least temporary compliance. The advice was evidently ungrateful, and the king — as Absalom of old, and most weak men in analogous circumstances — next turned to another set of counselors. They were his young companions — as the text throughout contemptuously designates them: "the children (the boys) who had grown up with him." With their notions of the royal supremacy, they seem to have imagined that such dating attempts at independence arose from doubt of the king's power and courage, and would be best repressed if sternly met by an overawing assertion of authority. Rehoboam was not to discuss their demands, but to tell them that they would find they had to deal with a monarch far more powerful and far more strict than his father had been. To put it in the vain-glorious language of the Eastern "boy-counselors," he was to say to them, "My little finger is bigger than my father's hips. And now my father did lade upon you a heavy yoke, and I will add to your yoke; my father chastised you with whips [those of ordinary slaves], but I will chastise you with [so-called] 'scorpions'" — or whips armed with hooks, such as were probably used upon criminals or recalcitrants.

Grossly foolish as this advice was, Rehoboam followed it — the sacred writer remarking, in order to account for such an occurrence: "for the turn (of events) was from Jehovah, that He might perform His word which Jehovah spake by the hand of Ahijah the Shilonite to Jeroboam the son of Nebat."

The effect was, indeed, immediate. To the shout of Sheba's ancient war-cry of rebellion the assembly renounced their allegiance to the house of David, and the deputies returned to their homes. Rehoboam perceived his fatal error, when it was too late to retrieve its consequences. Even his attempt in that direction was a mistake. The king sent Adoram, the superintendent of the tribute and of forced labor — the two forming apparently one department of the king's dues — to arrange, if possible, matters with the rebellious tribes. But this seemed only like trifling with their grievances, and a fresh insult. The presence of the hated official called forth such feelings, that he was stoned, and Rehoboam himself narrowly escaped the same fate by flight to Jerusalem.

The rebellion of the ten tribes was soon followed by their formation into an independent kingdom. When, on their return from Shechem, the deputies made known the presence of Jeroboam, the tribes sent for him, and in a popular assembly appointed him king over all Israel. Still, it must not be thought that the whole land was absolutely subject to him. When thinking of monarchy in Palestine, it is always necessary to bear in mind the long-established and great municipal fights and liberties which made every city with its district, under its Elders, almost an independent state within the state. Accordingly, we find it chronicled as a note worthy fact (1 Kings 12:17), that King Rehoboam reigned over those Israelites who were settled in Judean towns — either wholly inhabiting, or forming the majority in them; while it is marked as a wise measure on the part of Rehoboam, that he distributed "his children throughout all the countries (districts) of Judah and Benjamin unto every fenced city" no doubt, with the view of making sure of their allegiance. It seems to have been otherwise within the domains of Jeroboam. From 2 Chronicles 11:13-16 we learn that, on the substitution by Jeroboam and his successors of the worship of the golden calves for the service of Jehovah, the old religion was disestablished, and the Levites deprived of their ecclesiastical revenues, the new priesthood which took their place being probably supported by the dues of their office, and, if we may judge from the history of Ahab (1 Kings 18:19), by direct assistance from the royal treasury. In consequence of these changes, many of the Levites seem to have settled in Judaea, followed perhaps by more or less extensive migrations of the pious laity, varying according to the difficulties put in the way of resorting to the great festivals in Jerusalem. It would, however, be a mistake to infer the entire exodus of the pious laity or of the Levites. But even if such had been the case, the feeling in the ancient Levitical cities would for some time have continued sufficiently strong to refuse allegiance to Jeroboam.

And here a remarkable document throws unexpected light upon our history. On the wall of the great Egyptian Temple of Karnak, Shishak has left a record of his victorious expedition against Judah. Among the conquests there named 133 have been deciphered — although only partially identified — while 14 are now illegible. The names ascertained have been arranged into three groups — those of Judean cities (the smallness of their number being accounted for by the erasures just mentioned); those of Arab tribes, south of Palestine; and those of Levitical and Canaanite cities within the territory of the new kingdom of Israel. It is the latter which here alone claim our attention.

Any conquest of cities within the territory of Jeroboam might surprise us, since the expedition of Shishak was against Judah, and not against Israel — indeed, rather in alliance with Jeroboam and in support of his new kingdom. Another remarkable circumstance is, that these Israelitish conquests of Shishak are all of Levitical or else of ancient Canaanite cities, and that they are of towns in all parts of the territory of the ten tribes, and at considerable distances from one another, there being, however, no mention of the taking of the intervening cities. All these facts point to the conclusion, to which we have already been directed on quite independent grounds, that the Levitical and ancient Canaanite cities within the territory of Jeroboam did not acknowledge his rule. This is why they were attacked and conquered by Shishak on his expedition against Judah, as virtually subject to the house of

David, and hence constituting an element not only of rebellion but of danger within the new kingdom of Israel. Before quitting this subject, these two remarks may be allowed, how wonderfully, and we may add, unexpectedly, documents of secular history — apparently accidentally discovered — confirm and illustrate the narratives of the Bible; and how wise, politically and religiously, how suited to the national life, were the institutions of the Old Testament, even when to our notions they seem most strange, as in the case of Levitical cities throughout the land. For, these cities, besides serving other most important purposes, formed also the strongest bond of political union, and at the same time the most powerful means of preserving throughout the country the unity of the faith in the unity of the central worship of Jehovah at Jerusalem. Thus national union and religious purity were bound up together, and helped to preserve each other.

But to return. On the elevation of Jeroboam to the new throne of Israel, Rehoboam made one more attempt to recover the lost parts of David's kingdom. He assembled an army of 180,000 men from Judah and Benjamin — the latter tribe having apparently become almost unified with Judah since the establishment of the political and religious capital in Jerusalem, through which ran the boundary-line between Judah and Benjamin. But the expedition was at its outset arrested by Divine direction through the prophet Shemaiah.

This abandonment of an expedition and dispersion of a host simply upon the word of a prophet, are quite as remarkable as the courage of that prophet in facing an army in such circumstances, and his boldness in so fully declaring as a message from Jehovah what must have been a most unwelcome announcement alike to king and people. Both these considerations are very important in forming an estimate, not only of the religious and political state of the time, and their mutual inter-relations, but of the character of, "Prophetism" in Israel. The expedition once abandoned was not again renewed, although throughout the reign of Rehoboam there were constant incursions and border-raids — probably chiefly of a predatory character — on the part of Judah and of Israel (1 Kings 14:30). The remaining notices of Rehoboam's reign concern the internal and external relations of Judah, as well as the sad religious change which passed over the country after the first three years of his rule. They are recorded, either solely or with much fuller details, in the Book of Chronicles (2 Chronicles 11:4 to 12:16). The first measure referred to is the building of fifteen fortresses, of which thirteen were in the land of Judah — Hebron forming, as it were, the center of theme and only two (Zorah and Aijalon) within the later possession of Benjamin.

They served as a continuous chain of forts south of Jerusalem, and to defend the western approaches into the country. The northern boundary was left wholly unprotected. From this it would appear that Rehoboam chiefly dreaded an incursion from Egypt, though it does not by any means follow that these fortresses were only built after the campaign of Shishak, which took place five years after the accession of Solomon's son.

The next notice concerns the family relations of Rehoboam. It appears that he had eighteen wives and sixty concubines (thirty, according to Josephus, Ant. 8. 10, 11), following in this respect the evil example of Solomon. Of his wives only two are named, his cousin Mahalath, the daughter of Jerimoth, a son of David (either the same as Ithream, 1 Chronicles 3:3, or the son of one of David's concubines, 1 Chronicles 3:9), and of Abihail, the daughter of Eliab, David's eldest brother; and Maachah, the daughter, or rather, evidently, the granddaughter of Absalom, through his only child, Tamar (2 Samuel 14:27; 18:18; comp. Jos. Ant. 8. 10, 11), who had married Uriel of Gibeah (2 Chronicles 13:2).

Maachah, named after her paternal great-grandmother (the mother of Absalom, 1 Chronicles 3:2), was the favorite of the king, and her eldest son, Abijah, made "chief among his brethren," with succession to the throne. As already noticed, Rehoboam took care to locate his other sons in the different districts of his territory, giving them ample means for sustaining their rank, and forming numerous and influential alliances for them. Altogether Rehoboam had twenty-eight sons and sixty daughters.

From these general notices, which must be regarded as referring not to any single period, but to the whole reign of Rehoboam, we pass to what, as regards the Scripture narrative, is the most important event in this history. The fact itself is told in fullest detail in the Book of Kings (1 Kings 14:22- 24); its punishment at the hand of God in the Book of Chronicles (2 Chronicles 12:2, 12).

After the first three years of Rehoboam's reign a great change seems to have come over the religious aspect of the country. Rehoboam and Judah did not, indeed, openly renounce the worship of Jehovah. On the contrary, we find that the king continued to attend the house of the LORD in royal state, and that after the incursion of Shishak there was even a partial religious revival (2 Chronicles 12:11, 12).

Still the general character of this period was, that "Rehoboam forsook the law of Jehovah, and all Israel with him," that "he did evil in that he did not set his heart on seeking Jehovah" (2 Chronicles 12:1, 14, lit.), and, lastly, that "Judah did the evil in the sight of Jehovah, and provoked Him to jealousy (viewing the relation between the LORD and Israel as one of marriage, Numbers 5:14) — more than anything which their fathers had done by their sins which they sinned" (1 Kings 14:22). These sins consisted in building Bamoth, or "high places," i.e., altars on every high hill, and setting up in every grove Mazzeboth, or memorial-stones and pillars dedicated to Baal, and Asherim, or trunks of trees dedicated to Astarte (with all the vileness which their service implied).

This idolatry was, indeed, not new in Israel — though it had probably not been practiced to the same extent. But in addition to this we now read of persons "consecrated" to the Syrian goddess, with the nameless abominations connected therewith. This form of heathen pollution was of purely Canaanite origin. As indicating the influence of the Canaanites upon Judah, it may perhaps be regarded as another evidence of the connection subsisting between Rehoboam and the ancient Canaanite cities within the territory of Israel.

The Divine punishment was not long withheld. Once more it came in the course of natural causation, through the political motives which influenced Shishak, and led him to support Jeroboam. In the fifth year of Rehoboam's reign Shishak marched a large army of Egyptians, Lybians, Sukkiim, ("tent-dwellers"? Arabs?), and Ethiopians, with 1,200 chariots" and 60,000 horsemen, into Judaea, and, after taking the fenced cities along his route, advanced upon Jerusalem, where Rehoboam and his army were gathered.

Once more the prophet Shemaiah averted a contest, which could only have ended in disaster. On showing them that the national danger, though apparently arising from political causes, was really due to their sin against Jehovah (2 Chronicles 12:2); and that it was needless to fight, since, as they had been God-forsaking, they were now God-forsaken (ver. 5) the king and his princes humbled themselves. Thereupon the LORD intimated through His prophet, that He would "grant them deliverance for a little while," on condition of their submitting to Shishak. The reason for this, "that they may know My service, and the service of the kingdoms of the countries," as well as the terms by which the promised deliverance was qualified, contained the most solemn warning of the ultimate consequences of apostasy. Yet the Divine forbearance continued other 370 years before the threatened judgment burst upon the nation. But at this time Jerusalem was spared. Voluntary submission having been made, Shishak entered the city, and contented himself with carrying away the treasures of the Temple and of the Palace, including among the latter the famous golden shields used by Solomon's body-guard on state occasions, for which Rehoboam now substituted shields of brass.

CHAPTER 11: POLITICAL MEASURES OF JEROBOAM — THE GOLDEN CALVES — THE NEW PRIESTHOOD AND THE NEW FESTIVAL — THE MAN OF ELOHIM FROM JUDAH — HIS MESSAGE AND SIGN — JEROBOAM STRUCK BY JEHOVAH AND MIRACULOUSLY RESTORED — INVITATION TO THE MAN OF ELOHIM — HEATHEN VIEW OF MIRACLES — THE OLD PROPHET — RETURN OF THE MAN OF ELOHIM TO BETHEL — JUDGMENT ON HIS DISOBEDIENCE — CHARACTER OF THE OLD PROPHET AND OF THE MAN OF ELOHIM — SICKNESS OF THE PIOUS CHILD OF JEROBOAM — MISSION OF HIS MOTHER TO AHIJAH — PREDICTED JUDGMENT — DEATH OF THE CHILD — REMAINING NOTICES OF JEROBOAM.

(1 KINGS 12:25-14:20)

FROM the history of Judah under Rehoboam, we turn to that of the newly-established kingdom of Israel, the record of which is only found in the Book of Kings (1 Kings 12:25 — 14:20). The first object of Jeroboam ("He shall increase the people") was to strengthen the defenses of his throne. For this purpose he fortified Shechem, the modern Nabiris — which he made his residence until he exchanged it for Tirzah (1 Kings 14:17) — and also the ancient Penuel (Genesis 32:30, 31; Judges 8:8), on the other side Jordan. As the latter place commanded the great caravan-route to Damascus and Palmyra, its fortification would serve the double purpose of establishing the rule of Jeroboam in the territory east of the Jordan, and of protecting the country against incursions from the east and northeast. His next measure, though, as he deemed it, also of a protective character, not only involved the most daring religious innovation ever attempted in Israel, but was fraught with the most fatal consequences to Jeroboam and to Israel. How deeply Israel had sunk appears alike from the fact that the king acted with the approbation of his advisers — no doubt the representatives of the ten tribes — and that the people, with the exception of the Levites and a minority among the laity, readily acquiesced in the measure. It implied no less than a complete transformation of the religion of Jehovah, and that for a purely political object.

The danger that, if the people regularly resorted to the great festivals at Jerusalem, their allegiance might be won back to their rightful king, who held rule in the God-chosen capital, was too obvious not to have occurred to a mind even less suspicious than that of an Oriental despot, who had gained his throne by rebellion. To cut off this source of dynastic and even personal peril, Jeroboam, with the advice of his council, introduced a complete change in the worship of Israel, In so doing, his contention would probably be, that he had not abolished the ancient religion of the people, only given it a form better suited to present circumstances — one, moreover, derived from primitive national use, and sanctioned by no less an authority than that of Aaron, the first High-priest. It was burdensome and almost impossible to go up to the central Sanctuary at Jerusalem. But there was the ancient symbol of the "golden calf," made by Aaron himself, under which the people had worshipped Jehovah in the wilderness.

Appealing, perhaps at the formal consecration of these symbols, to the very words which Aaron had used (Exodus 32:4), Jeroboam made two golden calves, and located them at the southern and the northern extremities of the territory of the ten tribes. This was the more easy, since there were both in the south and north "sacred" localities, associated in popular opinion with previous worship. Such in the extreme south was Beth-el — "the house of God and the gate of heaven" — consecrated by the twofold appearance of God to Jacob; set apart by the patriarch himself (Genesis 28:11-19; 35:1, 7, 9-15); and where of old Samuel had held solemn assemblies (1 Samuel 7:16). Similarly, in the extreme north Dan was a "consecrated" place, where "strange worship" may have lingered from the days of Micah (Judges 18:30, 31).

The setting up of the golden calves as the symbol of Jehovah brought with it other changes. An "house of Bamoth," or Temple for the high-place altars, probably with priests' dwellings attached, was reared. The Levitical priesthood was extruded, either as inseparably connected with the old worship, or because it would not conform to the new order of things, and a new priesthood appointed, not confined to any tribe or family, but indiscriminately taken from all classes of the people, the king himself apparently acting, in true heathen fashion, as Chief Pontiff (1 Kings 12:32, 33).

Lastly, the great Feast of Tabernacles was transferred from the 7 th to the 8th month, probably as a more suitable and convenient time for a harvest-festival in the northern parts of Palestine, the date (the 15 th) being, however, retained, as that of the full moon.

That this was virtually, and would in practice almost immediately become idolatry, is evident. Indeed, it is expressly attested in 2 Chronicles 11:15, where the service of the "Calves" is not only associated with that of the Bamoth, or high-place altars, but even with that of "goats" — the ancient Egyptian worship of Pan under the form of a goat (Leviticus 17:7).

It is true, the text does not imply, as our Authorized Version suggests, that the new priests were taken "from the lowest of the people." But the emphatic and more detailed repetition of the mode of their appointment (1 Kings 12:31, comp. 13:33), of which apparently the only condition was to bring an offering of one young bullock and seven rams (2 Chronicles 13:9), enables us to judge on what class of people the conduct of the religious services must soon have devolved.

A more daring attempt against that God-ordained symbolical religion, the maintenance of which was the ultimate reason for Israel's call and existence — so to speak, Israel's very raison d'etre — could not be conceived. It was not only an act of gross disobedience, but, as the sacred text repeatedly notes, a system devised out of Jeroboam's own heart, when every religious institution in Israel had been God-appointed, symbolical, and forming a unity of which no part could be touched without impairing the whole. It was a movement which, if we may venture so to say, called for immediate and unmistakable interposition from on high. Here, then, if anywhere, we may look for the miraculous, and that in its most startling manifestation. Nor was it long deferred.

It was, as we take it, the first occasion on which this new Feast of Tabernacles was celebrated, perhaps at the same time also the dedication of the new Temple and the inauguration of its services. Bethel was in festive array, and thronged by pilgrims — for no less a personage than the king himself was to officiate as Chief Pontiff on that occasion. Connecting, as we undoubtedly should do, the last verse of 1 Kings 12: with the first of chapter 13, and rendering it literally, we read that on this feast which he "made" (i.e. of his own devising) "to the children of Israel," the king "went up on the altar," that is, up the sloping ascent which led to the circuit around the altar on which the officiating priest stood. The sacrifices had already been offered, and their smoldering embers and fat had mingled with the ashes (1 Kings 13:3). And now the most solemn and central part of the service was reached. The king went up the inclined plane to the middle of the altar to burn the incense, when he was suddenly arrested, and the worshippers startled by a voice from among the crowd (comp. here the similar event in John 7:37). It was a stranger who spoke, and, as we know him, a Judaean, "a man of Elohim." He had come "in the word of Jehovah" (1 Kings 13:1) — not merely in charge of it, nor only in its constraining power, but as if the Word of Jehovah itself had come, and this "man of God" been carried in it to deliver the message which he "cried to the altar in the word of Jehovah" (ver. 2). It was to the spurious and rival altar that he spake, and not to the king — for it was a controversy with spurious worship, and King Jeroboam was as nothing before Jehovah.

That altar, and the policy which had reared it, would be shivered, the altar desecrated, and that by a son of David whereof he gave them immediate symbolic evidence that Jehovah had spoken by his mouth that day, by this "wondrous sight," that the altar would be rent, and the ashes laden with the fat of the sacrifices poured out.

Arrested by this uncompromising announcement from one whom he regarded as a daring fanatical intruder, the king turned quickly round, and stretching out his hand towards him, commanded, "Seize him!" But already a mightier Hand than King Jeroboam's was stretched out. Now, if ever, would Jehovah vindicate His authority, prove His Word, and show before all the people that He, Whose authority they had cast off, was the Living God. Then and there must it be shown, in the idol-temple, at the first consecration of that spurious altar, at the first false feast, and upon King Jeroboam, in the pomp of his splendor and the boastfulness of his supposed power (comp. here Acts 12:22, 23). The king had put forth his hand, but he could not draw it back, the Hand of the LORD held it. Some mysterious stroke had fallen upon him; and while he thus stood, himself a sign, the top of the altar suddenly parted, and the ashes, clogged and heavy with the fat of idol-sacrifices, poured out around him. No hand was stretched out to seize the "man of God". Nor was there need of it — the "man of God" had neither design nor desire to escape. Rather was it now the king's turn, not to command but to entreat. In the expressive language of the original, "And the king answered" (to the unspoken word of Jehovah in the stroke that had arrested his hand), and said, Soften now the Face of Jehovah thy God, and make entreaty on my behalf, and (or, that) "my hand shall return to me."

It was as he craved — for the prophecy and controversy were not with the king, but with the Altar. And all this had been only a sign, which had fulfilled its purpose, and would fulfill it still more, if the same Power that had appeared in the sudden stroke would again become manifest in its equally sudden removal. As for Jeroboam, Jehovah had no controversy with him then and there, nor indeed anywhere. The judgment of his sins would soon enough overtake him and his house. It might, indeed, seem passing strange that the king could now invite this "man of God" to his palace and table, and even promise him "a reward," if we did not bear in mind the circumstances of the times, and the heathen idea of miracles. To the heathen the miraculous, as direct Divine manifestation, was not something extraordinary and unexpected. Heathenism — may we not say, the ancient world? — expected the miraculous; and hence in those times God's manifestation by miracles might almost be designated not as an extraordinary, but, according to the then notions, as the ordinary mode of teaching. Moreover, heathenism regarded miracles as simply manifestations of power, and the worker of miracles as a magician, possessed of power —

the question being, whether the power of the deity whom he represented was greater than that of other gods, or not. It was, no doubt, in this light that Jeroboam regarded this "man of Elohim" the name Elohim itself expressing especially "power." This, as well as knowledge of the character of his own "prophets," and perhaps a secret hope that he might attach him to himself by a "reward," prompted the words of the king. He would do honor to the man of power, and, through him, to the deity whom he represented — perhaps even gain the man of God.

It need scarcely be said, that the mere fact of the "man of God" entering the king's palace and sharing his feast, probably a sacrificial idol-feast would not only have been contrary to the whole scope and spirit of his embassy, but have destroyed the moral effect of the scene enacted before the people. So, to mention a much lower parallelism is the moral effect of all Christian testimony, whether by word or life, annulled by every act of conformity to, and fellowship with the world (comp. Romans 12:1, 2). But in the present instance any danger of this kind had by anticipation been averted. God had given His messenger express command, neither to eat bread nor to drink water in that place, nor even to return by the way that he had come. These directions had, of course, a much deeper and symbolical meaning. They indicated that Bethel lay under the ban; that no fellowship of any kind was to be held with it; and that even the way by which the messenger of God had come, was to be regarded as consecrated, and not to be retraced.

In the discharge of the commission entrusted to him, the "man of God," who had "come in the word of Jehovah," was to consider himself as an impersonal being — till he was beyond the place to which, and the road by which he had been sent. Whatever view, therefore, we may take of his after-conduct, it cannot at least surprise us, that at that moment no earthly temptation could have induced him to accept the king's offer (1 Kings 13:8, 9).

Yet, as we think of it, the answer of the "man of God" seems to us disappointing. It is like that of Balaam to the messengers of Balak (Numbers 22:13, 18), and yet we know that all along his heart was with them, and that he afterwards yielded to their solicitations, to his own destruction. We would have expected more from the "man of God" than a mere recital of his orders — some expression of feeling like that of Daniel under analogous circumstances (Daniel 5:17). But, in repeating before all the people the express command which God had given him, the "man of God," like Balaam of old, also pronounced his own necessary doom, if he swerved from the injunction laid upon him. He had borne testimony — and by the testimony of his own mouth he must be content to be judged; he was quite certain of the command which God had laid upon him, and by that certainty he must abide.

And at first it seemed as if he would have done so. His message delivered, he left Bethel by another way than that which he had come. Among his astonished audience that day had been the sons of an old resident in Bethel, whose real character it is not easy to read.

In the sacred narrative he is throughout designated as Navi, or Prophet (literally: one who wells forth"), while the Divine messenger from Judah is always described as "man of Elohim" — a distinction which must have its meaning. On their return from the idol-temple, the eldest of his sons described to the old prophet the scene which they had witnessed. Inquiring from them what road the "man of God" had taken — which they, and probably many others had watched — he hastily rode after him, and overtook him.

The "man of Elohim" was resting under "the terebinth" — apparently a well-known spot where travelers were wont to unlade their beasts of burden, and to halt for shelter and repose (a kind of "Travelers' Rest"). Repeating the invitation of Jeroboam, he received the same answer as the king. There could be even less hesitation now, since the "man of God" had actually left Bethel, nor could he possibly have deemed it right to return thither. Upon this the old prophet addressed him as a colleague, and falsely pretended, not indeed that Jehovah, but that "an angel in the word of Jehovah," had directed him to fetch him back, when the other immediately complied. As the two sat at table in Bethel, suddenly "the word of Jehovah was upon the prophet who had brought him back." Because he had "resisted (rebelled against) the mouth of Jehovah, and not kept the commandment which Jehovah had commanded him," his dead body should not come into the sepulcher of his fathers.

Startling as such an announcement must have been, it would set two points vividly before him: his disobedience and his impending punishment — the latter very real, according to the views prevailing at the time (Genesis 47:30; 49:29; 50:25; 2 Samuel 19:37, etc.), although not implying either immediate or even violent death. It is very surprising to — us and indicative of the absence of the higher moral and spiritual elements — that this announcement was not followed by any expression of sorrow or repentance, but that the meal seems to have continued uninterrupted to the end. Did the old prophet seem to the other only under an access of ecstatic frenzy? Did the fact that he announced not immediate death blunt the edge of his message? Had disobedience to the Divine command carried as its consequence immediate spiritual callousness? Or had the return of the "man of God" to Bethel after all been the result of a deeper estrangement from God, of which the first manifestation had already appeared in what we have described as his strangely insufficient answer to Jeroboam's invitation and offer? These are necessarily only suggestions — and yet it seems to us as if all these elements had been present and at work to bring about the final result.

The meal was past, and the "old prophet" saddled his ass to convey his guest to his destination. But the end of the journey was never reached. As some travelers were passing that way, they saw an unwonted spectacle which must have induced them to hasten on their journey. Close by the roadside lay a dead body, and beside it stood the ass which the uhhappy man had ridden — both guarded, as it were, by the lion, who had killed the man, evidently by the weight of his paw as he knocked him down, without, however, rending him, or attempting to feed on his carcass. Who the dead man was, the travelers seem not to have known, nor would they, of course, pause by the road.

On passing through Bethel — which from the narrative does not seem to have been their ultimate destination, but the first station which they reached they naturally "talked in the town" about what they had just seen in its neighborhood. When the rumor reached the "old prophet," he immediately understood the meaning of all. Riding to the spot, he reverently carried home with him the dead body of the "man of God," mourned over, and buried him in his own sepulcher, marking the place by a monumental pillar to distinguish this from other tombs, and to keep the event in perpetual remembrance. But to his sons he gave solemn direction to lay him in the same tomb — in the rock-niche by the side of that in which the "man of God" rested. This was to be a dying testimony to "the man of God" that his embassy of God had been real, and that surely the "thing would be" (that it would happen) "which he had cried in the word of Jehovah against the altar which (was)at Bethel, and against all the Bamoth-houses which (are) in the cities of Samaria."

With this profession of faith in the truth of Jehovah's message, and in the power of the LORD certainly to bring it to pass at some future time, would the old prophet henceforth live. With it would he die and be buried — laying his bones close to those of the "man of God," sharing his grave, and nestling, as it were, for shelter in the shadow of that great

Reality which "the man of God" had cast over Bethel. So would he, in life and death, speak of, and cling to Jehovah — as the True and the Living God.

More than three hundred years later, and nearly a century had passed since the children of Israel had been carried away from their homes. Then it was that what, centuries before, the "man of God" had foretold, became literally true (2 Kings 23:15-18). The idol-temple, in which Jeroboam had stood in his power and glory on that opening day, was burned by Josiah; the Bamoth were cast down; and on that altar, to defile it, they gathered from the neighboring sepulchers the bones of its former worshippers, and burned them there. Yet in their terrible search of vengeance one monument arrested their attention. They asked of them at Bethel. It marked the spot where the bones of "the man of God" and of his host the "old prophet" of Samaria lay.

And they reverently left the bones in their resting-places, side by side — as in life, death, and burial, so still and for aye witnesses to Jehovah; and safe in their witness-bearing. But three centuries and more between the prediction and the final fulfillment: and in that time symbolic rending of the altar, changes, wars, final ruin, and desolation! And still the word seemed to slumber all those centuries of silence, before it was literally fulfilled. There is something absolutely overawing in this absence of all haste on the part of God, in this certainty of the final event, with apparent utter unconcern of what may happen during the long centuries that intervene, which makes us tremble as we realize how much of buried seed of warning or of promise may sleep in the ground, and how unexpectedly, but how certainly, it will ripen as in one day into a harvest of judgment or of mercy.

But too many questions and lessons are involved in this history to pass it without further study. Who was this "old prophet?" Was he a true prophet of Jehovah? And why did he thus "lie" to the destruction of the "man of God?" Again, why was such severe punishment meted out to the "man of God?" Did he deserve any for what might have been only an error of judgment? And why did his tempter and seducer apparently escape all punishment? To begin with the old "prophet" of Bethel — we do not regard him as simply a false prophet, whose object it was to seduce "the man of God," either from jealousy or to destroy the effect of his mission.

On the other hand, it seems equally incorrect to speak of him as a true prophet of God, roused from sinful conformity with those around by the sudden appearance of the Judean messenger of Jehovah, and anxious to recover himself by fellowship with "the man of God," even if that intercourse could only be secured by means of a falsehood.

Nor would we describe his conduct as intended to try the steadfast obedience of the "man of God." The truth seems to lie between these extreme opinions. Putting aside the general question of heathen divination, which we have not sufficient materials satisfactorily to answer, it is at least certain that not every Navi was a prophet of Jehovah. That God should have sent a message through one who was not His prophet, need not surprise us when we recall the history of Balaam. Moreover, it was peculiarly appropriate, that the announcement of guilt and punishment should come to the "man of God" through the person who had misled him by false pretense of an angelic command, and at the very meal to which the "man of God" should never have sat down. Again, it is evident that, from the moment he heard of the scene in the idol-temple, the "old prophet" believed in the genuineness and authority of the message brought to Bethel. Every stage in the history deepened this conviction, until at last it became, so to speak, the fundamental fact of his religious life, which must have determined his whole after-conduct. May it not have been that this "old Navi" was one of the fruits of the "Schools of the Prophets" — the prophetic order having apparently been widely revived during the later part of Solomon's reign? Settling in Bethel (as Lot in Sodom), he may have gradually lapsed into toleration of evil — as the attendance of his children in the idol-temple seems to imply — without, however, surrendering his character, perhaps his office of "Prophet," the more so as the service of Jehovah might be supposed to be only altered in form, not abolished, by the adoption of the symbol of the Golden Calves. In that case his immediate recognition of the "man of God," and his deepening conviction may be easily understood; his earnest desire to claim and have fellowship with a direct messenger of God seems natural; and even his unscrupulous use of falsehood is accounted for.

These considerations will help to show that there was an essential difference between him and "the man of God," and that the punishment which overtook the latter bears no possible relation to the apparent impunity of the "old prophet." That terrible judgment ought to be viewed from two different points, as it were, absolutely — from heaven downwards; and relatively to the person whom it overtook — from earth heavenwards. The most superficial consideration will convince, that, from the nature of the case, the authority of God must have been vindicated, and that by a patent and terrible judgment, if the object and meaning of the message which He had sent were not to be nullified. When "the man of God" publicly proclaimed in the temple the terms which God had prescribed, he pronounced his own sentence in case of disobedience. Besides, the main idea underlying the Divine employment of such messengers was that of their absolute and unquestioning execution of the exact terms of their commission. This essential condition of the prophetic office it was the more necessary to vindicate in Bethel, as also at the commencement of a period marked by a succession of prophets in Israel, who, in the absence of the God-ordained services, were to keep alive the knowledge of Jehovah, and, by their warnings and teaching, to avert, if possible, the catastrophe of national judgment which would overtake apostate Israel.

As regards "the man of God" himself, we have already noticed the increasing spiritual callousness, consequent upon his first unfaithfulness. But putting this aside, surely there never could have been any serious question in his mind as to his duty. By his own testimony, he had received express and unmistakable command of God, which Scripture again and again repeats, for the sake of emphasis; and his conduct should have been guided on the plain principle, that an obvious and known duty can never be set aside by another seeming duty. Besides, what evidence had he that an angel had really spoken to the "old prophet;" or even that his tempter was a "prophet" at all, or, if a prophet, acted in the prophetic spirit? All these points are so obvious, that the conduct of the "man of God" would seem almost incredible, if we did not recall how often in every-day life we are tempted to turn aside from the plain demands of right and duty by a false call in contravention to it. In all moral and spiritual questions it is ever most dangerous to reason, simple obedience and not argument is the only safe path (comp. here Galatians 1:8). One duty can never contravene another and the plainly known and clear command of God must silence all side-questions.

Viewing the conduct of the "man of God" as a fall and a sin, all becomes plain. He had publicly announced his duty, and he had publicly contravened it; and his punishment was, through the remarkable, though not miraculous, circumstances under which it overtook him, equally publicly known. Throughout the whole history there is, so to speak, a remarkable equipoise in the circumstances of his sin and of his punishment, as also in the vindication of God's authority.

And yet even so, the moral effect of God's message was apparently weakened through the sin of His messenger. So terribly fatal in their consequences are our sins, even when publicly punished. For it is scarcely possible to believe that, had it not been so, Jeroboam would "after this thing" have uninterruptedly continued his former course of defiance of the authority of God. But here the history also turns from Israel to its wretched king, and in a narrative of deepest pathos shows us at the same time the punishment of his sin, and the wonderful tenderness of God's dealings towards those who, in the midst of greatest temptations, have kept their hearts true to Him, and are preserved by His mercy from the evil to come. And most comforting is it to know that God has and keeps His own — even though it be in the family of a Jeroboam, and that true piety finds its respectful acknowledgment, even among a people so sunken as was Israel at that time.

If it were necessary to show how unhappiness and sin go hand in hand, the history about to be told would furnish ample evidence of it. The main reason of its insertion in the Biblical record is, of course, that it gave occasion to announce the Divine punishment upon the race of Jeroboam, as having traversed the fundamental condition on which the possibility of the new dynasty rested (1 Kings 11:38). At the same time, it seems also to cast an important side-light on the transaction between Ahijah the prophet and Jeroboam, when the former first announced to him his future elevation to the kingdom (1 Kings 11:29-39). Keil renders 1 Kings 14:7. "Thus saith Jehovah, the God of Israel: Therefore, because thou hast elevated thyself from amongst the people, and I have given thee ruler over My people Israel."

If this rendering is correct, it would imply that his elevation, or leadership of Israel, was in the first place entirely Jeroboam's own act, and that, having so elevated himself and assumed the leadership, God afterwards bestowed on him the rule to which he aspired, leaving for future trial the fitness of his race for the kingdom.

But, besides the higher Divine meaning of this history, it possesses also a deep human interest. It gives us a glimpse into the inner family life of the wretched king, as, divested of crown and purple, and having cast aside statecraft and religious falsehood, he staggers under a sore blow. For once we see the man, not the king, and, as each man appears truest, when stricken to the heart by a sorrow which no earthly power can turn aside. From Shechem the royal residence had been transferred to the ancient Canaanite city (Joshua 12:24) Tirzah, the beautiful (Cant. 6. 4), two hours to the north of Samaria, amidst cultivated fruit-and-olive-clad hills, up on a swelling height, with glorious outlook over the hills and valleys of rich Samaria.

The royal palace seems to have stood at the entering in of the city (comp. 1 Kings 14:17 with ver. 12). But within its stately apartments reigned silence and sorrow. Abijah, Jeroboam's son, and apparently the intended successor to his throne, lay sick. He seems like the last link that bound Jeroboam to his former better self. The very name of the child-Abijah, "Jehovah is my Father," or else "my Desire" — indicates this, even if it were not for the touching notice, that in him was "found a good thing towards Jehovah, the God of Israel, in the house of Jeroboam" (ver. 13) We can conceive how this "good thing" may have sprung up; but to keep and to cause it to grow in such surroundings, surely needed the gracious tending of the Good Husbandman. It was the one green spot in Jeroboam's life and home; the one germ of hope. And as his father loved him truly, so all Israel had set their hopes on him. Upon the inner life of this child — its struggles and its victories — lies the veil of Scripture silence; and best that it should be so. But now his pulses were beating quick and weak, and that life of love and hope seemed fast ebbing. None with the father in those hours of darkness — neither counselor, courtier, prophet, nor priest — save the child's mother. As the two kept sad watch, helpless and hopeless, the past, to which this child bound him, must have come back to Jeroboam. One event in it chiefly stood out: it was his first meeting with Ahijah the Shilonite. That was a true prophet — bold, uncompromising withal. With that impulse of despair which comes upon men in their agony, when all the delusions of a misspent life are swept away, he turned to the opening of his life, so full of hope and happy possibility, the ambition had urged him upon the path of reckless sacrifice of all that had been dearest and holiest; the unlimited possession had dazzled his sight and the sound of flattery deafened his ears. As to Saul of old on the eve of that fatal battle, when God and man had become equally silent to him, the figure of Samuel had stood out — that which to us might seem the most unlikely he could have wished to encounter — so now to Jeroboam that of Ahijah. Could he have wished to blot out, as it were, all that had intervened, and to stand before the prophet as on the day when first he met him, when great but not yet unholy thoughts rose within him? Had he some unspoken hope of him who had first announced to him his reign? Or did he only in sheer despair long to know what would come to the child, even though he were to learn the worst? Be this as it may, he must have word from Ahijah, whatever it might be.

In that hour he has no friend nor helper save the mother of his child. She must go, in her love, to the old prophet in Shiloh. But how dare she, Jeroboam's wife, present herself there? Nay, the people also must not know what or whither her errand was. And so she must disguise herself as a poor woman, carrying with her, indeed, as customary, a gift to the prophet, but one such as only the poorest in the land would offer. While alone and in humble disguise the wife of Jeroboam goes on her heavy embassy, across the hills of Samaria, past royal Shechem, Another has already brought her message to Shiloh. No need for the queen to disguise herself, so far as Ahijah was concerned, since age had blinded his eyes. But Jehovah had spoken to His aged servant, and charged him concerning this matter. And as he heard the sound of her feet within the door, he knew who his unseen visitor was, and addressed her not as queen but as the wife of Jeroboam. Stern, terrible things they were which he was commissioned to tell her; and with unswerving faithfulness and unbending truth he spake them, though his heart must have bled within him as he repeated what himself called "hard tidings."

All the more deeply must the aged prophet have felt them, that it was he who had announced to Jeroboam his future elevation. They concerned Jeroboam; but they also touched every heart-string in the wife and the mother, and must well nigh have torn each one of them as they swept across her. First: an uncompromising recital of the past, and a sternly true representation of the present — all glare, dazzle, and self-delusion dispelled, until it stood in naked reality before her.

Only two persons are in this picture, Jehovah and Jeroboam — all else is in the far background. That is enough; and now once in full sight of those two persons, the wife, the mother, must hear it all, though her ears tingle and her knees tremble. Not this child only, but every child, nay, every descendant, down to the meanest, whether it be child or adult — swept away: "And I will sweep out after the house of Jeroboam, as one sweepeth out dirt until it is quite gone" (1 Kings 14:10).

And not only this, but also horrible judgment; the carcasses of her children lying like carrion in street and on field, their flesh torn and eaten by the wild, unclean dogs that prowl about, or picked from their limbs by birds of prey who swoop round them with hoarse croaking.

Thus far for Jeroboam. And now as for the child that lay sick in the palace of Tirzah — it shall be in God's keeping, removed from the evil to come. As her feet touched the threshold of her doomed home, it would die. As it were, such heavy tidings shall not be brought within where he sleeps; its terrors shall not darken his bed. Before they can reach him, he shall be beyond their shadow and in the light. But around that sole-honored grave all Israel shall be the mourners, and God Himself wills to put this mark of honor upon His one child in that now cursed family. Lastly, as for apostate Israel, another king raised up to execute the judgment of God — nay, all this not merely in the dim future, but the scene seems to shift, and the prophet sees it already in the present.

Israel shaken as a reed in the water by wind and waves; Israel uprooted from their land, — cast away and, scattered among the heathen beyond the river, and given up to be trampled under foot. Such is the end of the sins of Jeroboam and of his people; such, in the bold figure of Scripture, is the sequel of casting Jehovah "behind their back." Of the further course of this history we know no more. The queen and mother went back, stricken, to her home; and it was as the prophet had told her from Jehovah. And this literal fulfillment would be to her for ever afterwards the terrible pledge of what was yet to come.

Nor do we read any more of Jeroboam. It almost seems as if Holy Scripture had nothing further to say of him, not even concerning his later and disastrous war with the son of Rehoboam (2 Chronicles 13:2-20). That is told in connection with the reign of the second king of Judah. Of Jeroboam we only read that he "reigned two and twenty years," that "he slept with his fathers," and that "Nadab his son reigned in his stead."

CHAPTER 12: ACCESSION OF ABIJAH — HIS IDOLATRY — WAR BETWEEN JUDAH AND ISRAEL — ABIJAH'S ADDRESS TO ISRAEL AND VICTORY — DEATHS OF JEROBOAM AND OF ABIJAH — ACCESSION OF ASA — RELIGIOUS REFORMATION IN JUDAH — INVASION BY ZERAH THE ETHIOPIAN — VICTORY OF ZEPHATHAH — AZARIAH'S MESSAGE TO THE ARMY OF ASA — GREAT SACRIFICIAL FEAST AT JERUSALEM — RENEWAL OF THE COVENANT WITH JEHOVAH.

(1 KINGS 15:1-15; 2 CHRONICLES 13-15)

JEROBOAM did not only survive Rehoboam, but he witnessed the accession of two other kings of Judah, Abijah and Asa. The reign of Abijah was very brief. Both in 1 Kings 15:2 and in 2 Chronicles 13:2 it is said to have lasted three years — an expression which must be understood according to this canon laid down by the Rabbis, that the commencement of a year in the reign of a king is to be reckoned as a full year. Thus, as Abijah ascended the throne in the eighteenth (1 Kings 15:1), and Asa in the twentieth (ver. 9) year of Jeroboam's reign, it follows that the former actually reigned only somewhat over two years. Two things are specially noticed concerning Abijah, his relation towards Jehovah (in 1 Kings 15:3- 5), and his relation to the kingdom of Jeroboam (2 Chronicles 13:2-20).

To begin with the former. It is stated that "he walked in all the sins of his father," and that "his heart was not perfect with Jehovah his God." These two statements are not explanatory of, but supplementary to, each other. We know that Rehoboam had not only followed the service of Jehovah (see, for example, 1 Kings 14:28), but that, by its side, a spurious worship had been tolerated, if not encouraged, which, in the view of Holy Scripture, was equal to idolatry. In this matter Rehoboam had not only followed the example of his father Solomon, during his later years, but greatly increased the evil which had then begun. A similar remark applies to the reign of Abijah, as compared with that of Rehoboam. That the idolatry of the reign of Rehoboam had grown both worse in character and more general in practice under that of Abijah, appears from the notices of the reformation instituted by his successor, Asa. The former circumstance is implied in the terms by which the idolatry of that period is described (2 Chronicles 14:3, 5), and by the circumstance that "the queen-mother" (Maachah, Abijah's mother and Asa's grandmother), who under Abijah held the official rank of Gevirah, "Queen" (the modern Sultana Valide), had made and set up "a horror for Asherah" — some horrible wooden representation, equally vile and idolatrous in its character.

Again, that idolatry had become more widely spread, and that its hold was stronger, we infer from the fact that, despite Asa's example, admonitions, and exertions (2 Chronicles 14:4, 5), "the high places did not cease" (1 Kings 15:14). This progressive spiritual decline under the reigns of Solomon, Rehoboam, and Abijah was so marked as to have deserved the removal of the family of David from the throne, had it not been for God's faithfulness to His covenant-promises (1 Kings 15:4, 5). But, although such was the state of religion, Abijah not only made loud profession of the worship of Jehovah, but even brought votive offerings to the Temple, probably of part of the spoil taken in war (1 Kings 15:15; comp. 2 Chronicles 13:16-19).

Concerning the relations of Judah to the neighboring kingdom of Israel, it may be said that the chronic state of warfare which had existed during the time of Rehoboam now changed into one of open hostilities. Two reasons for this may be given. Abijah was a much more vigorous ruler than his father, and the power of Egypt, on which Jeroboam relied for support, seems at that time to have decreased. This we gather, not only from the non-interference of Egypt in the war between Abijah and Jeroboam, but from the fact that, when Egypt at length sought to recover its lost ascendancy, it was under the rule of Zerah the Ethiopian (probably Osorkon II.), who was not the son, but the son-in-law, of the preceding monarch (2 Chronicles 14:9); and we know the fate that overtook the huge, undisciplined army which Zerah led.

The language of the sacred narrative (2 Chronicles 13:2, 3) implies, that the war between Judah and Israel was begun by Abijah. On both sides a levy of all capable of bearing arms was raised, though, so far as the numerical strength of the two armies was concerned, the response seems not to have been so universal in Judah as in Israel.

But perhaps the seeming discrepancy may be explained by the necessity of leaving strong garrisons in the south to watch the Egyptian frontier (comp. 2 Chronicles 14:9). The two armies met at the boundary of the two kingdoms, though, as we judge, within the territory of Israel. They camped in close proximity, only separated by Mount Zemaraim, a height to the east of Bethel and some distance north of Jericho, forming part of the ridge known as "Mount Ephraim," which stretched from the plain of Esdraelon southwards.

From this height Abijah addressed the army of Israel just before the battle began, in the hope of securing their voluntary submission, or at least weakening their resistance. Ignoring all that told against himself, Abijah tried to impress on his opponents that right was wholly on his side.

In language full of irony he set before them their weakness, as the necessary result of their apostasy from Jehovah, the God of their fathers, and of their adoption of a worship neither conformable to their ancient faith nor even respectable in the sight of men. Lastly, he loudly protested that, since Judah had gone to war under the leadership of Jehovah and in the manner appointed by Him, Israel was really fighting against Jehovah, the God of their fathers, and could not expect success. Whatever hollowness there may have been in this profession on the part of Abijah, it was at least the true war-cry of Israel which he raised. It found an echo in the hearts of his followers. In vain Jeroboam, by a cleverly executed movement, attacked Judah both in front and rear. The terror excited by finding themselves surrounded only led the people to cry unto Jehovah (2 Chronicles 13:14), and He was faithful to His promise (Numbers 10:9). The shout of the combatants mingled with the blast of the priests' trumpets, as Judah rushed to the attack. Israel fled in wild disorder, and a terrible carnage ensued. The fugitives were followed by the army of Judah, and Abijah recovered from Israel the border-cities, with the districts around them. In consequence of this victory the power of Jeroboam was henceforth on the wane, and that of Abijah in the ascendancy. Not long afterwards Jehovah struck Jeroboam, either suddenly or with lingering disease, of which he died. He had, however survived his rival, Abijah, for more than two years.

Abijah was succeeded on the throne of Judah by his son, Asa, probably at the time a boy of only ten or eleven years. This may in part account for his pious up-bringing, as, during his minority he would be chiefly under the official guardianship of the High-priest (comp. 2 Chronicles 22:12).

It also explains how a bold, resolute woman, such as Maachah, could still retain her official position as Gevirah, or "queen-mother," until, on attaining majority, the young king commenced his religious reformation. During the first ten years of Asa's reign the land had rest (2 Chronicles 14:1). While devoutly acknowledging the goodness of God in this, it is easy to understand the outward circumstances by which it was brought about. The temporary weakness of Egypt, the defeat of Jeroboam, and an alliance which Abijah seems to have contracted with Syria (2 Chronicles 16:3), as well as afterwards the rapid succession of rival dynasties in Israel, sufficiently explain it. For, during his long reign of forty-one years, Asa saw no fewer than seven kings ascend the throne of Israel.

The first work which Asa took in hand was a thorough religious reformation; his next, the strengthening of the defenses of the country. For this the temporary state of security prevailing offered a happy opportunity — "the land" being "still before them" — open and free from every enemy, though it was not difficult to foresee that such would not long be the case. And, as king and people owned that this time of rest had been granted them by Jehovah, so their preparations against future attacks were carried on in dependence upon Him. The period of trial came only too soon.

An almost countless Egyptian host, under the leadership of Zerah, the Ethiopian, swarmed into Judah. Advancing by the southwest, through the border of the Philistines, who, no doubt, made common cause with the Egyptians (2 Chronicles 14:14), they appeared before Mareshah (comp. Joshua 15:44).

This was one of the border fortresses which Jeroboam had built (2 Chronicles 11:8). The natural capabilities of the place and its situation, so near the southwestern angle of the country, and almost midway between Hebron and Ashdod, must have marked it as one of the most important strategical points in the Jewish line of defensive works against Philistia, or rather, against Egypt. About two miles north of Mareshah a beautiful valley debauches from between the hills.

This is the valley of Zephathah, where the relieving army of Asa, coming from the northeast, now took up its position. Here a decisive battle took place, which ended in the complete rout of the Egyptians. It has been well noted, that this is the only occasion on which the armies of Judah ventured to meet, and with success, either Egypt or Babylon in the open field (not behind fortifications).

On the only other occasion when a battle in the open was fought (2 Chronicles 25:20-24), it ended in the signal defeat of Judah. But this is only one of the circumstances which made the victory of Asa so remarkable. Although the battle-field (a valley) must have been unfavorable for handling so unwieldy a mass of soldiers and for deploying their war-chariots, yet the host of Egypt was nearly double that of Asa, and must have included well-disciplined and long-trained battalions. But, on the other hand, never before had a battle been fought in the same manner; never had there been more distinct negation of things seen and affirmation of things unseen — which constitutes the essence of faith — nor yet more trustful application of it than in Asa's prayer before the battle, "Is it not with Thee to help between the much (the mighty) relatively to no strength (in regard to the weak)?

Help us, Jehovah our God, for upon Thee do we put our trust; and in Thy name have we come (do we come) upon this multitude. O Jehovah, Thou art our God (the God of power, Elohim): let not man retain strength by the side of Thee (have power before Thee)!" Such an appeal could not be in vain. In the significant language of Holy Scripture, it was

"Jehovah" Who "smote" the Ethiopians, and "Asa and the people that were with him" only "pursued them." Far away to Gerar, three hours southeast from the border city, Gaza, continued the chase amidst unnumbered slain, and still the destroying sword of Jehovah was before His host (2 Chronicles 14:13), and His fear fell upon all the cities round about. To wrest the hostile cities of the Philistines and to carry away much spoil was only one sequence.

Henceforth Egypt ceased to be a source of terror or of danger, and full 330 years passed before its army was again arrayed against Judah. The occasion was too favorable not to have been improved.

Asa had entered on a course of right-doing, and the LORD, upon Whom he and his people had called, had proved a faithful and prayer-hearing God. If the religious reformation so happily begun, and the religious revival which had appeared, only issued in a thorough return to the LORD, the evil which had been in the far and near past and which threatened in the future, might yet be averted. The morrow of the great God-given victory seemed the most suitable time for urging this upon Judah. Accordingly, Azariah, the son of Oded, was Divinely commissioned to meet the returning victorious army of Asa, and to urge such considerations upon the people.

"The Spirit of Elohim" was upon him, and what he spake bore reference not only to the past and the present, but also to the future. Hence his message is rightly described as both "words" and "a prophecy" (2 Chronicles 15:8). Carefully examined, it contains alike an address and a prophecy. For it were a mistake to suppose, that the picture which Azariah drew of Israel's sin and its consequence in vers. 3, 5, 6 was only that of the far past in the time of the Judges, of the religious decline under Jeroboam and Abijah, or even of their future apostasy and its punishment. All these were included in what the prophet set before the people. And not only so, but his words extended beyond Judah, and applied to all Israel, as if the whole people were viewed as still united, and ideally one in their relation to the Lord. Accordingly, it deserves special notice, that neither in ver. 3 nor in ver. 5 any verb is used, as if to indicate the general application of the "prophecy." But its present bearing, alike as regarded Judah's sin and repentance, and God's judgment and mercy, was an earnest call to carry on and complete the good work which had already been begun (ver. 7).

And king and people hearkened to the voice of God through His prophet. Again and more energetically than before, the religious reformation was taken in hand. The idol "abominations" were removed, not only from Judah and Benjamin, but from the conquered cities of the north, and the great altar of burnt-offering in the Temple was repaired. The earnestness of this movement attracted the pious laity from the neighboring tribes, and even led those of Simeon (in the far south) who, apparently, had hitherto sympathized with the northern kingdom, as they shared their idolatry (comp. Amos 4:4; 5:5; 8:14), to join the ranks of Judah. At a great sacrificial feast, which the king held in Jerusalem, the solemn covenant into which Israel had originally entered with Jehovah (Exodus 24:3-8) was renewed, in repentant acknowledgment that it had been broken, and in believing choice of Jehovah as henceforth their God — just as it was afterwards renewed on two analogous occasions: in the time of Josiah (2 Kings 23:3; 2 Chronicles 34:31), and in that of Nehemiah (Nehemiah 10:28-39). The movement was the outcome of heart-conviction and earnest purpose, and consisted, on the one hand, in an undertaking that any introduction of idolatry should be punished by death (according to Deuteronomy 13:9), and, on the other, in an act of solemn national consecration to Jehovah.

To Asa, at least, all this was a reality, although, as regarded his subjects, the religious revival does not seem to have been equally deep or permanent (2 Chronicles 15:17). But the king kept his part of the solemn engagement. However difficult it might be, he removed "the Queen-mother" from her exalted position, and thus showed an example of sincerity and earnestness in his own household. And, in token of his consecration to Jehovah, he brought into His House alike those war-spoils which his father had, after the victory over Jeroboam, set apart as the portion for God, and what he himself now consecrated from the spoil taken in the war with Egypt. These measures were followed by a period of happy rest for the land — even to the twenty-fifth year of King Asa's reign.

CHAPTER 13: REIGN OF NADAB — HIS MURDER BY BAASHA — WAR BETWEEN JUDAH AND ISRAEL — BAASHA'S ALLIANCE WITH SYRIA — ASA GAINS OVER BEN-HADAD — PROPHETIC MESSAGE TO ASA — RESENTMENT OF THE KING — ASA'S RELIGIOUS DECLINE — DEATH OF ASA, DEATH OF BAASHA, REIGN OF ELAH — HIS MURDER BY ZIMRI — OMRI DETHRONES ZIMRI — WAR BETWEEN OMRI AND TIBNI — REBUILDING OF SAMARIA.

(1 KINGS 15:16-16:28; 2 CHRONICLES 16)

WHILE these things were going on in Judah, the judgment, which the LORD had, through Ahijah, pronounced upon Jeroboam and his house, was rapidly preparing. After an apparently uneventful reign of only two years, Nadab, the son and successor of Jeroboam, was murdered while engaged in the siege of Gibbethon (the Gabatha and Gabothane of Josephus). This border-city, on the edge of the plain of Esdraelon (not many miles southwest of Nazareth, and originally in the possession of Dan, Joshua 19:44), must have been of great importance as a defense against incursions from the west — to judge from the circumstance that not only Nadab but his successors sought, although in vain, to wrest it from the Philistines (comp. 1 Kings 16:15). No other event in the reign of Nadab is recorded.

"He walked in the way of his father, and in his sin," and sudden destruction overtook him. Baasha — probably the leader of a military revolution — murdered him, and usurped his throne. The first measure of the new king was, in true Oriental fashion, to kill the whole family of his predecessor. Although the judgment of God upon Jeroboam and his house, as announced by the prophet, was thus fulfilled, it must not for a moment be thought that the foul deed of Baasha was thereby lessened in guilt. On the contrary, Holy Scripture expressly marks this crime as one of the grounds of Baasha's later judgments (1 Kings 16:7). It is perhaps not easy, and yet it is of supreme importance for the understanding of the Old Testament, to distinguish in these events the action of man from the overruling direction of God. Thus when, after his accession, the prophet Jehu, the son of Hanani, was commissioned to denounce the sin, and to announce the judgment of Baasha, these two points were clearly put forward in his message. The sin of Baasha in the murder of Jeroboam's house, and the fact that his exaltation was due to the LORD (1 Kings 16:7; comp. ver. 2).

Baasha had sprung from a tribe wholly undistinguished by warlike achievements, and from a family apparently ignoble and unknown (1 Kings 16:2). His only claim to the crown lay in his military prowess, which the neighboring kingdom of Judah was soon to experience.

Under his reign the state of chronic warfare between the two countries once more changed into one of active hostility. From the concordant accounts in the Books of Kings and Chronicles (1 Kings 15:16-22; 2 Chronicles 16:1-6), we gather what was Baasha's object in this war, and what his preparations for it had been. It seems, that Asa's father, Ahijah, had formed an alliance with the rising power of Syria under Tabrimon ("good is

Rimmon"), with the view of holding Israel in check by placing it between two enemies — Syria in the north and Judah in the south.

This "league" was, as we infer, discontinued by Asa during the earlier part of his reign, when his confidence was more entirely placed in Jehovah his God. In these circumstances Baasha eagerly sought and entered upon an alliance with Syria. His primary object was to arrest the migration of Israelites into the kingdom of Judah, and the growing influence of Asa upon his own subjects, consequent, as we know, upon his great religious reformation (1 Kings 15:17). His secondary object was so to overawe Jerusalem, as virtually to paralyze the power of Judah. The invasion was at first successful, and Baasha penetrated as far as Ramah, about midway between Bethel and Jerusalem, thus obtaining command of the two roads which led from the north and the east to the Jewish capital. This, of course, implied not only the re-conquest of the towns which Abijah had taken from Israel (2 Chronicles 13:19; comp. also 15:8), but the complete isolation and domination of Jerusalem. Ramah was to be immediately converted into a strong fortress.

In these straits Asa seems to have forgotten the manner in which his former brilliant victory over Zerah had been obtained. Instead of relying wholly on Jehovah his God, he appears to have imagined that his former policy in regard to Syria had been a mistake. Like many who, on losing the first freshness of their faith, seek to combine trust in the LORD with what they regard as most likely means of worldly success, Asa entered into a new alliance with Ben-Hadad, purchasing it with the silver and gold treasured up in the Temple and in the royal palace.

He may have argued, that this did not imply a renunciation of his former allegiance to Jehovah; that he had no personal intercourse with Syria, which, indeed, was far separated from his dominions; that his was only a countermove to Baasha's schemes; and that a similar league had, during the reign of his father, proved eminently successful. But the result of an alliance so incongruous, and purchased in so dubious a manner, proved the beginning of spiritual declension and of little honor or real benefit to his country. Ben-Hadad was only too ready to entertain Asa's proposals. It could never have been his real policy to strengthen the neighbor-state of Israel, and to weaken that of Judah. On receiving the rich bribe, which made Judah virtually tributary to him, he broke his league with Baasha, and immediately invaded Israel, overrunning the northern territory, penetrating as far as the district of Chinneroth (Joshua 11:2; 12:3; 19:35), — which gave its name to the Lake of Gennesaret, — and occupying the land of Naphtali. This threatening danger in the north of his dominions obliged Baasha hastily to quit Ramah. Asa now summoned all Judah. The materials accumulated for the fortress of Ramah were removed, and used for building two new forts, Geba ("the height") and Mizpah ("the outlook") (comp. Joshua 18:24, 26; also Jeremiah 41:5-9). Both these cities lay within the territory of Benjamin, about three miles to the north of Ramah, in very strong positions, and commanded the two roads to Jerusalem.

But with the retreat of Baasha from Ramah, the troubles of Asa did not end; rather did they only then begin. When, alone and unaided, he had, in the might of Jehovah, encountered the hosts of Egypt, signal success had been his; peace and prosperity had followed; and God's prophet had been specially sent to meet the returning army with good and encouraging tidings. It was all otherwise now. Hanani the prophet was directed to meet Asa with a message of reproof and judgment; instead of, as formerly, peace, there would henceforth be continual warfare (2 Chronicles 16:9); and the alliance with Syria would prove neither to honor nor profit. On the other hand, even had his fears been realized, and the combined armies of Israel and Syria invaded Judah, yet if, instead of buying the alliance of Ben-Hadad, he had gone forward in the name of the LORD, victory such as that over the Ethiopians would again have been his (2 Chronicles 16:7). As it was, Asa had chosen a worldly policy, and by its issue he must abide. Henceforth it was no more Jehovah Who was arrayed against the might of man, but the contest would be simply one of cunning and strength, as between man and man (2 Chronicles 16:9).

Hanani had spoken, as all the prophets of Jehovah, fearlessly, faithfully, and only too truly. It was probably conviction of this which, in the unhumbled state of the king, kindled his anger against "the seer." Once more it might seem to Asa as not implying rebellion against God, only a necessary precaution against disunion and dissatisfaction among his own subjects, threatening to upset his political calculations and combinations, to use measures of severity against the prophet from which he would have shrunk at a former period of his reign. All the more requisite might these appear, since his unwelcome monitor evidently commanded the sympathies of an influential part of the community. But it was an unheard-of proceeding, which happily found imitation only in the worst times of Israel (1 Kings 22:,6-29; Jeremiah 20:2; 29:26; Acts 16:24), to put the prophet of the Load "in the house of stocks" on account of his faithfulness, and by a series of persecutions to oppress, and, if possible, crush those who sympathized with him.

Nor was this all. The fatal tendency which had showed itself in the Syrian alliance, and still more in the measures against Hanani and his sympathizers, continued and increased with the lapse of years. Two years before his death, Asa was attacked by some disease in his feet. In this "also" "he sought not Jehovah but in (by) the physicians."

It is not necessary to explain the blame which Holy Scripture evidently attaches to this, on the ground that these physicians were so called "medicine-men" (as among the heathen), nor to suppose that they used idolatrous or even superstitious means. The example of Hezekiah (2 Kings 20; 2 Chronicles 32:24) sufficiently shows, how one who fully trusted in the LORD would have felt and acted in these circumstances. On the other hand, Asa displayed in this instance the same want of practical religion as in his alliance with Syria — a state of mind which Bengel rightly characterizes as theoretical orthodoxy combined with practical atheism. And as formerly the prophet had summed up what Asa had no doubt regarded as the height of political wisdom in the curt, if somewhat harsh, criticism: "Thou hast acted stupidly over this" (2 Chronicles 16:9) — so might it have been said of him in this matter also. He had not sought Jehovah, but had sought in the physicians — and by the help which he had sought he must abide. He had not trusted in the supernatural, but applied to the natural and in the natural course of events his disease ended in death. It was not wrong to employ means, indeed such were used in the miraculous cure of Hezekiah (2 Kings 20:7), just as in the miraculous rescue of St. Paul's companions from shipwreck (Acts 27:23, 24, 43, 44). And, if one lesson more than another has been impressed on our minds in the course of this history, it is that of the use of natural means, in the ordinary and rational succession of events, for the accomplishment of supernatural and Divinely-announced purposes. But the error and sin of Asa consisted in seeking an object, however lawful and even desirable, in, by, and through secondary means, without first seeking Jehovah. Such conduct carried with it its natural result. For, what a man soweth, that — the very kind of grain — shall he also reap; just as, none the less, that we work for it (or perhaps have it supplied to our hands), but on the contrary, all the more because of it, we first pray, "Give us this day our daily bread," and then receive as directly from His hand the consecrated fruit of our labor.

There was the same sad consistency about Asa's death as in his life. He seems to have built him a special mausoleum in the city of David; and there they laid him in almost Egyptian pomp on a bed of spices, and burnt at his burying, whether for the first time in royal funerals, or according to a more ancient practice, a large quantity of costly spices and perfumes.

But in following the narrative of Holy Scripture, we have been really anticipating the course of this history. For, as previously stated, Asa not only outlived Baasha, but altogether saw eight kings on the throne of Israel. Baasha seems to have survived his defeat little more than a year. He was succeeded by his son Elah, in the twenty-sixth year of King Asa's reign. The rule of Elah lasted only two years, or, more exactly, part of two years. Baasha had set the example of military revolutions, in which the favorite of the soldiery ascended the throne by the murder of his predecessor, and the extirpation of all who might have rival claims to the crown. The precedent was a dangerous one; and henceforth the throne of Israel was occupied by a series of military adventurers, whose line did not extend beyond their immediate successors. The son of Baasha was a cowardly debauchee, who, forgetful even of the decorum of Eastern princes, indulged in orgies in the houses of his favorites, while his army was fighting before Gibbethon. He fell a victim to a court conspiracy. We know only two of the actors in it: Arza, the steward of the king's palace (or rather, his major-domo), in whose house Elah was drinking himself drunk, and the king's murderer and successor Zimri, who filled the post of chief over half his "chariots," or perhaps his cavalry. The reign of Zimri lasted only seven days, but they were stained by even more than the bloodshed usual on such occasions. For Zimri destroyed not only the family of his predecessor, but killed all the "blood-avengers" (relatives, kinsfolk), and even "the friends" of the late king.

Whether, as Josephus explains (Ant. 8. 12, 4), Zimri had chosen for his rebellion the moment when all the leading officers were in camp, or Omri himself was originally in the conspiracy, certain it is that the army was not disposed to acknowledge the new usurper. It immediately proclaimed their general Omri, and under his leadership marched back upon Tirzah. Zimri held out until the city was taken, when he retired into "the citadel of the king's palace," which he set on fire, perishing in its flames. But Omri had not at first undisputed possession of the throne.

For four years the people were divided between him and another pretender to the crown, Tibni, the son of Genath. At length Omri prevailed, and "Tibni died" — either in battle or, as Josephus seems to imply, (Ant. 8. 12, 5), by command of his rival.

Omri occupied the throne altogether twelve (or part of twelve) years. The first four of these passed in contests with Tibni. During the next two years he resided in Tirzah. After that he bought from Shemer for two talents of silver (about 780) the hill of Samaria. On this commanding position he built the new capital of Israel, which, according to the sacred text, he named Shomeron, after the former owner of the site.

But on other grounds it deserved to be called "watch-mountain," as the name may be rendered. Situated about the center of the land, six miles northwest of Shechem, it occupied a commanding hill, rising from a broad valley, and surrounded on all sides by mountains, through which there was only a narrow entrance from the west. The approach to the plateau on which Samaria stood is steep on all sides. Thus the site of the new capital, which was also distinguished by great beauty, was singularly adapted both for observation and defense. The country around was very rich, and the place well supplied with water. A more suitable spot could not have been chosen by monarch or general. This accounts for the continued importance of Samaria through all the varying fortunes of the country and its people.

The modern miserable village of Sebustiyeh (the ancient Sebaste), inhabited by less than one thousand people, which occupies the site of the once splendid city, where Omri, Ahab, and their successors held high court, contains but few remains of its ancient grandeur. But these are sufficiently remarkable.

The ancient Acropolis, or temple, palace, and citadel, seems to have stood on the western brow of the hill, and its site is still marked by the ruins of a most magnificent colonnade composed of graceful monoliths. The approach to the castle must have been by ascending terraces, which, no doubt, were covered with houses and palaces. Of these not a trace is left. Only on the topmost height — from which, westwards, the Mediterranean, and eastwards, across swelling mountains, a landscape of unrivaled beauty and fertility were full in view — a few broken and upturned pillars mark the site of the royal castle. The dynasties that reigned there have long been swept away; the people over whom they ruled carried into a captivity over which the veil of impenetrable mystery lies. Only the word of the LORD has stood firm and immovable. Of Nadab, of Baasha, of Elah, of Zimri, and of Omri, Scripture has only one and the same thing to say, that they walked in the way and in the sin of Jeroboam, the son of Nebat, "wherewith he made Israel to sin, to provoke Jehovah, the God of Israel, to anger." And over each and all did the same judgment sweep. And yet there were more grievous sins to follow, and more terrible judgments to come."

CHAPTER 14 — ASA AND JEHOSHAPHAT (3RD AND 4TH) KINGS OF JUDAH — AHAB (8TH) KING OF ISRAEL — ACCESSION OF AHAB — FURTHER RELIGIOUS DECLINE IN ISRAEL — POLITICAL RELATIONS BETWEEN ISRAEL AND JUDAH — ACCESSION OF JEHOSHAPHAT — AHAB'S MARRIAGE WITH JEZEBEL — THE WORSHIP OF BAAL AND ASTARTE ESTABLISHED IN ISRAEL — CHARACTER OF AHAB — RELIGIOUS REFORMS IN JUDAH — JEHOSHAPHAT JOINS AFFINITY WITH AHAB — MARRIAGE OF JEHORAM WITH ATHALIAH, AND ITS CONSEQUENCES.

(1 KINGS 16:29-33, 22:41-44; 2 CHRONICLES 17; 18:1, 2)

OMRI was succeeded on the throne of Israel by his son Ahab, in the thirty-eighth year of the reign of Asa, king of Judah. With the accession of Ahab a new period may be said to commence in the history of Israel, and this alike religiously and politically. In regard to the former, Omri had already prepared the way for further terrible progression in Israel's apostasy. In the language of Holy Scripture (1 Kings 16:25), he "did worse than all that were before him." Whatever the special "statutes" or ordinances in this respect which he introduced, they marked an era in the history of Israel's religious decline (Micah 6:16). But Ahab far out-distanced even his father's wickedness, first by entering into a matrimonial alliance with the vile dynasty of Ethbaal, and then by formally making the worship of Baal the established religion of Israel, with all of vileness and of persecution which this implied. In these circumstances, surely, we may look for extraordinary interposition on the part of Jehovah. For, with such a king and queen, and with a people, not only deprived of the Temple-services and the Levitical priesthood, but among whom the infamous rites of Baal and Astarte had become the established worship, ordinary means would manifestly have been in vain. Again and again had messengers sent from God spoken His Word and announced His judgments, without producing even a passing effect. It needed more than this, if the worship of Baal was to be effectually checked. Accordingly, this period of Israel's history is also marked by a great extension of the Prophetic order and mission. It was theirs to keep alive the knowledge of Jehovah in the land; theirs also to meet the gross and daring idolatry of king and people by a display of power which could neither be resisted nor gainsaid. Hence the unparalleled frequency of miracles, mostly intended to prove the vainness of idols as against the power of the Living God, the reality of the prophets' mission, and of the authority which the LORD had delegated to His messengers. Only thus could any effect be produced. It was an extraordinary period — and God raised up in it an extraordinary agency. We have already indicated that, in general, considering the notions and expectations of the times, miracles might almost be said to have been God's ordinary mode of teaching the men of that age. This holds specially true of the period now under consideration. Hence the unusual accumulation of the miraculous — and that chiefly in its aspect of power — as displayed by an Elijah and an Elisha, so far from seeming strange or unaccountable, appears eminently called for.

Politically speaking also, this was a period of great change. For, whereas hitherto the two kingdoms of Israel and Judah had been in a state of constant warfare, an alliance between them was now formed. At first, indeed, it seemed otherwise. As Ahab ascended the throne of Israel during the lifetime of Asa, the relations between the two kingdoms continued as before. And when, in the fourth year of King Ahab's reign, Jehoshaphat succeeded his father Asa (1 Kings 22:41), it appeared as if the prospect of an alliance between the sister-countries were more remote than ever. Jehoshaphat began his reign by strengthening the defenses of his country against Israel (2 Chronicles 17:1, 2). His religious measures were in the opposite direction from those of Ahab. Himself earnestly and decidedly pious, it is expressly stated that he walked "not after the doings of Israel." On the other hand, Ahab entered, probably at the beginning of his reign, into an alliance with the most wicked dynasty then in power, by marrying Jezebel, the daughter of Ethbaal (or Ithobalus, "Baal is with him").

Josephus has preserved to us the history of this royal family (Against Ap. 1. 18). It appears that Ethbaal was originally the High-priest of the great temple of Astarte in Tyre; that he murdered his king, and usurped the throne, which he occupied for thirty-two years; and that his dynasty continued for at least sixty-two years after his death. These notices will sufficiently explain the upbringing of Jezebel. A clever, strong, bold, and unscrupulous woman, she was by conviction a devotee to the most base and revolting idolatry which the world has ever known, combining with this the reckless contempt of the rights and consciences of others, and the utter indifference as to the means employed, which characterize the worst aspect of Eastern despotism. That she would hate the religion of Jehovah, and seek utterly to destroy — and, indeed, whatever would not bend to her imperious will; that she would prove the implacable foe of all that was pious or even free in Israel; and that she would not shrink from the wholesale murder of those who resisted or opposed her, follows almost as a matter of course. Yet, strange as it may sound, there is something grand about this strong, determined, bold woman, which appears all the more strikingly from its contrast with her husband. Jezebel was every inch a Queen — though of the type of the Phoenician Priest-King who had usurped the throne by murder.

The immediate consequence of this ill-fated union was, that the religion of Jezebel became the worship of the land of Israel. Ahab built in Samaria a temple to "the Baal" — the Sun-god (the producing principle in Nature) in which he erected not only an altar, but, as we gather from 2 Kings 3:2; 10:27, also one of those pillars which were distinctive of its vile services. As usual, where these rites were fully carried out, he also "made the Asherah" — Astarte, the Moon-goddess (the receptive principle in Nature) so that the Phoenician worship was now established in its entirety.

As we infer from later notices, there was a "vestry" attached to these temples, where special festive garments, worn on great occasions, were kept (2 Kings 10:22). Ahab — or perhaps rather Jezebel — appointed not less than 450 priests of Baal and 400 of Asherah, who were supported by the bounty of the queen (1 Kings 18:19; 22:6). The forced introduction of this new worship led to a systematic persecution of the prophets, and even of the openly professed worshippers of Jehovah, which had their complete extermination for its object (1 Kings 18:13; 19:10; 2 Kings 9:7). These measures were wholly due to the absolute power which Jezebel exercised over her husband. Left to himself, Ahab might have yielded to better influences (comp. 1 Kings 18:39-46; 20:13, etc.; 21:27-29). Altogether Ahab presents a strange, though by no means uncommon mixture of the good and the evil, the noble and the mean, issuing finally not in decision for God and what was right and true, but in the triumph of evil, to his own destruction and that of his race. For he possessed qualities which, if directed by the fear of God, might have made him even a great king. He was at times brave, even chivalrous (comp. for example 1 Kings 20:11, and even verse 32); royal in his tastes and undertakings (1 Kings 22:39; 2 Chronicles 18:2); and ready, under temporary emotion, to yield to the voice of conscience. But all this was marred by fatal weakness, selfishness, uncontrolled self-indulgence, an utter want of religion, and especially the influence of his wife, so that in the language of Holy Scripture he "sold himself to work wickedness in the sight of Jehovah," incited thereto by his wife Jezebel (1 Kings 21:25).

While these influences were at work in Israel, Jehoshaphat, encouraged by the blessing which rested on his kingdom, once more vigorously resumed the work of religious reformation in Judah (2 Chronicles 17:6-9). Not only did he take away the "high places and groves," but, in the third year of his reign, he sent five of his princes, accompanied by nine of the principal Levites and two priests, throughout the towns of Judah to teach the people the Law — no doubt the Pentateuch, of which they took with them an Authorized copy.

The actual instruction would unquestionably be committed to the priestly members of this commission (comp. Leviticus 10:11; Deuteronomy 17:8, 9), whilst the presence of the princes would not only secure the authority of the teachers and the efficiency of their work, but also be requisite for civil purposes, since the Law of Moses affected many of the social relations of life, and accordingly required for its enforcement the authority of the magistrates. Once more signal marks of the Divine approbation followed. Some of the Philistine chiefs rendered voluntary homage to Jehoshaphat; the Arab tribes, whom Asa had subdued during his pursuit of Zerah, the Ethiopian, again paid their tribute; new castles for the defense of the country were built, "store-cities" provided, and the various towns provisioned; while a large army was ready prepared, of which the five chiefs resided in Jerusalem, to be under the personal orders of the king.

It was in circumstances of such marked prosperity that Jehoshaphat "joined affinity with Ahab." The sacred text specially notes this (2 Chronicles 18:1), partly to show that Jehoshaphat had not even an excuse for such a step, and partly, as we think, to indicate that this alliance must, in the first place, have been sought by Ahab. The motives which would influence the King of Israel are not difficult to understand. The power of the country had been greatly weakened by Syria during the reign of Omri. Not only had Ben-Hadad possessed himself of a number of cities, both east (Ramoth-Gilead, for example) and west of the Jordan, but the country had become virtually subject to him, since he claimed even in the capital, Samaria, the right of having "streets," or rather "squares," that is, Syrian quarters of the town, which owned his dominion (comp. 1 Kings 20:34).

And now Ben-Hadad had been succeeded by a son of the same name, equally warlike and ambitious. In these circumstances it was of the utmost importance to Ahab to secure permanent peace on his southern or Judaean frontier, and, if possible, to engage as an active ally so powerful and wealthy a monarch as Jehoshaphat. On the other hand, it is not so easy to perceive the reasons which influenced the King of Judah. Of course he could not have wished to see the power of Syria paramount so close to his borders. Did he, besides, desire to have the long-standing (seventy years) breach between Judah and Israel healed? Had he a dim hope that, by the marriage of his son with the daughter of Ahab, the two realms might again be joined, and an undivided kingdom once more established in the house of David? Or did he only allow himself to be carried along by events, too weak to resist, and too confident to dread evil? We can only make these suggestions, since the sacred text affords no clue to this political riddle.

It was, as we reckon, about the eighth year of Jehoshaphat's reign, and consequently about the twelfth of that of Ahab, that Jehoram, the son of Jehoshaphat — then a lad of about fifteen or sixteen years — was married to Athaliah, the daughter of Ahab and Jezebel (2 Chronicles 21:6).

Jehoshaphat lived to see some of the bitter fruits of the rash and unholy alliance which he had sanctioned. Eight or nine years later, he went on that visit to Ahab which led to the disastrous war with Syria, in which Ahab himself perished (2 Chronicles 18.). Then followed the joint maritime expedition of Jehoshaphat and the son of Ahab, which ended in loss. But the worst was to come after the death of Jehoshaphat. His son and successor, the husband of Athaliah, introduced in Judah the idolatry of his wife, and brought shame and loss upon his people. The next occupant of the throne, the — son of Athaliah — followed the example of his father, and perished by command of Jehu. Lastly came the terrible tragedy of the wholesale murder of the royal princes by Athaliah, then her reign, and finally her tragic death.

It was not by means such as those which Jehoshaphat employed that good could come to Judah, the breach be healed between the severed tribes, the kingdom of David restored, or even peace and righteousness return to Israel. But already God had been preparing a new instrumentality to accomplish His own purposes. A Voice would be raised loud enough to make itself heard to the ends of the land; a Hand, strong enough not only to resist the power of Ahab and Jezebel, but to break that of Baal in the land. And all this not by worldly might or craftiness, but by the manifestation of the power of Jehovah as the Living God.

CHAPTER 15 — AHAB, (8TH) KING OF ISRAEL — REBUILDING OF JERICHO — THE MISSION OF ELIJAH — HIS CHARACTER AND LIFE — ELIJAH'S FIRST APPEARANCE — PARALLELISM WITH NOAH, MOSES, AND JOHN THE BAPTIST — ELIJAH'S MESSAGE TO KING AHAB — SOJOURN BY THE BROOK CHERITH — ELIJAH WITH THE WIDOW OF SAREPTA — THE BARREL OF MEAL WASTES NOT, NOR DOES THE CRUSE OF OIL FAIL — LESSONS OF HIS SOJOURN — SICKNESS AND DEATH OF THE WIDOW'S SON — HE IS MIRACULOUSLY RESTORED TO LIFE.

(1 KINGS 16:34-17)

WITH the enthronement of Ahab and Jezebel, the establishment of the worship of Baal as the state-religion, and the attempted extermination of the prophets and followers of the LORD, the apostasy of Israel had reached its high point. As if to mark alike the general disregard in Israel of the threatened judgments of God, and the coming vindication of Jehovah's Kingship, Holy Scripture here inserts a notice of the daring rebuilding of the walls of Jericho, and of the literal fulfillment of Joshua's curse upon its builder (1 Kings 16:34; comp. Joshua 6:26).

Indeed, the land was now ripe for the sickle of judgment. Yet as the long-suffering of God had waited in the days of Noah, so in those of Ahab; and as then the preacher of righteousness had raised the voice of warning, while giving evidence of the coming destruction, so was Elijah now commissioned to present to the men of his age in symbolic deed the alternative of serving Jehovah or Baal, with all that the choice implied. The difference between Noah and Elijah was only that of times and circumstances, the one was before, the other after the giving of the Law; the one was sent into an apostate world, the other to an apostatizing covenant-people. But there is also another aspect of the matter. On the one side were arrayed Ahab, Jezebel, Baal, and Israel — on the other stood Jehovah. It was a question of reality and of power, and Elijah was to be, so to speak, the embodiment of the Divine Power, the Minister of the Living and True God. The contest between them could not be decided by words, but by deeds. The Divine would become manifest in its reality and irresistible greatness, and whoever or whatever came in contact with it would, for good or for evil, experience its Presence.

We might almost say, that in his prophetic capacity Elijah was an impersonal being — the mere medium of the Divine. Throughout his history other prophets also were employed on various occasions, he only to do what none other had ever done or could do. His path was alone, such as none other had trodden nor could tread. He was the impersonation of the Old Testament in one of its aspects, that of grandeur and judgment — the living realization of the topmost height of the mount, which burned with fire, around which lightnings played and thunder rolled, and from out of whose terrible glory spake the Voice of Jehovah, the God of Israel. We have the highest authority for saying that he was the type of John the Baptist. But chiefly in this respect, that he lifted the ax to the root of the tree, yet, ere it fell, called for fruits meet for repentance. He was not the forerunner of the LORD, save in judgment; he was the forerunner of the King, not of the Kingdom; and the destruction of the state and people of Israel, not the salvation of the world, followed upon his announcement. A grander figure never stood out even against the Old Testament sky than that of Elijah. As Israel's apostasy had reached its highest point in the time of Ahab, so the Old Testament antagonism to it in the person and mission of Elijah. The analogy and parallelism between his history and that of Moses, even to minute details, is obvious on comparison of the two; and accordingly we find him, significantly, along with Moses on the Mount of Transfiguration.

Yet much as Scripture tells of him, we feel that we have only dim outlines of his prophetic greatness before us. By his side other men, even an Elisha, seem small. As we view him as Jehovah's representative, almost plenipotentiary, we recall his unswerving faithfulness to, and absolutely fearless discharge of his trust. And yet this strong man had his hours of felt weakness and loneliness, as when he fled before Ahab and Jezebel, and would fain have laid him down to die in the wilderness. As we recall his almost unlimited power, we remember that its spring was in constant prayer. As we think of his unbending sternness, of his sharp irony on Mount Carmel, of his impassioned zeal, and of his unfaltering severity, we also remember that deep in his heart soft and warm feelings glowed, as when he made himself the guest of the poor widow, and by agonizing prayer brought back her son to life. Such as this must have been intended by God, in His mercy, as an outlet and precious relief to his feelings, showing him that all his work and mission were not of sorrow and judgment, but that the joy of Divine comfort was his also. And truly human, full of intense pathos, are those days of wilderness-journey, and those hours on Mount Horeb, when in deepest sadness of soul the strong man, who but yesterday had defiantly met Ahab and achieved on Mount Carmel such triumph as none other, bent and was shaken, like the reed in the storm. A life this full of contrasts — of fierce light and deep shadows — not a happy, joyous, prosperous life; not one even streaked with peace or gladness, but wholly devoted to God, a bush on the wilderness-mount, burning yet not consumed. A life full of the miraculous it is and must be, from the character of his mission — and yet himself one of the greatest wonders in it, and the success of his mission the best attestation of, because the greatest of the miracles of his history. For, alone and unaided, save of God, he did conquer in the contest and he did break the power of Baal in Israel.

His first appearance, alike in the manner and suddenness of it was emblematic of all that was to follow. Of his birth and early circumstances, we know next to nothing. Josephus assumes (Ant. 8. 13, 2) that the Tishbah which gave him his name (1 Kings 17:1) lay on the eastern side of Jordan, in the land of Gilead; and some modern writers have found the name in the village of Tiseth, to the south of Busrah. But this view has been shown (by Keil) to be untenable. Even more fanciful is the suggestion, that the Hebrew expression means that he was "a stranger among the strangers of Gilead" — possibly a Gentile by birth. Most likelihood attaches to the generally received view, that his birthplace was the Tishbi in Upper Galilee (within the territory of Naphtali), known to us from apocryphal story (Tobit 1, 2, LXX) — and that, for some unascertained reason, he had migrated into Gilead, without, however, becoming one of its citizens. This the sacred text conveys by the expression, "Elijah the Tishbite from among the dwellers (strangers dwelling) in Gilead." Another inference as to his character may be drawn from his name Elijah: My God Jehovah! though it is scarcely necessary to say that he did not assume it himself.

With the same, or perhaps with even more startling unexpectedness and strangeness than that which characterized the appearance of John the Baptist — and with precisely the same object in it — Elijah suddenly presented himself in Samaria and before Ahab. It was, and intended to be — to adapt the figure of the Son of Sirach (Ecclesiasticus 48:1) like a fire that kindled suddenly, like a torch that blazed up in the still darkness of the night. There was, indeed, sufficient here to rouse the dullest mind. We can imagine the stern figure of the Tishbite, arrayed in an upper garment of black camel's hair — which henceforth seems to have become the distinctive garb of the prophets (Zechariah 13:4) — girt about his loins with a leathern girdle.

The dress betokened poverty, renunciation of the world, mourning, almost stern judgment, while the girdle, which, as the badge of office, was always the richest part of the dress, was such as only the poorest of the land wore. It was an unwonted sight, and, as he made his way up through the terraced streets of rich luxurious Samaria, its inhabitants would whisper with awe that this was a new prophet come from the wilds of Gilead, and follow him. What a contrast between those Baal-debauched Samaritans and this man; what a greater contrast still between the effeminate decrepit priests of Baal, in their white linen garments and high-pointed bonnets, and this stern prophet of Jehovah!

And now he had reached the height where palace and castle stand, and met Ahab himself, perhaps at the magnificent entrance to that splendid colonnade which overlooked such a scene of beauty and fertility. His message to the king was abrupt and curt, as became the circumstances — after all, only a repetition of Jehovah's denunciation of judgment upon an apostate people (Leviticus 26:19, etc.; Deuteronomy, 11:16, etc.; 28:23, etc.; comp. 1 Kings 8:35; Amos 4:7); but with this addition, that the cessation of dew and rain should last these years — whether many or few — "except" by his word.

This latter perhaps was intended to emphasize the impotence of Ahab's prophets and priests as against Jehovah. It was all most startling, the sudden, strange, wild apparition; the bold confronting of king and people there in Samaria; the announcement apparently so incredible in itself, and in such contrast to the scene of wealth and fruitfulness all around; the unexpected pronunciation of the name Jehovah in such a place; the authority which he pleaded and the power which he claimed — in general, even the terms of his message, "Lives Jehovah, the God of Israel, which I stand before His Face! If there be these years dew or rain, except by the mouth (the spoken means) of my word!"

What answer Ahab made, what impression it produced on him or his people, Holy Scripture, in its Divine self-consciousness and sublime indifference to what may be called "effect," does not condescend even to notice. Nay, here also silence is best — and the prophet himself must withdraw as suddenly as he had come, hide himself from human ken, not be within reach of question or answer, and let God work, alone and unseen. An absolute pause with that thunder-cloud overhead — unremoved and apparently unremovable — in presence of which man and Baal shall be absolutely powerless, such was the fitting sequence to Elijah's announcement.

Elijah's first direction was to the Wady Cherith — probably: east of the Jordan — one of those many wide water-courses which drain into the river of Palestine. In this wild solitude, like Moses, nay, like our LORD Himself, he was to be alone with God — - to plead for Israel, and to prepare for his further work. So long as water was left in the brook — for there is nothing needlessly miraculous, even in the story of Elijah — and so long as Jehovah had such strange provisioners as "the ravens" to act as His messengers — for there is nothing that is merely natural in this history, and the miraculous always appears by the side of the natural — the prophet would not want needed support.

In this also there were lessons of deepest significance to Elijah (compare as to God's strange messengers, Job 37:10; Psalm 78:23; Isaiah 5:6; Amos 9:3). When in the course of time the waters of Cherith failed, owing to the long drought, Elijah was directed to go to Zarephath (Sarepta, Luke 4:26), where God had "commanded" for him even a more strange provisioner than the ravens, a poor, almost famishing widow, and she a Gentile!

Here again everything is significant. Sarepta was not only a heathen city, outside the bounds of Israel, midway between Sidon and Tyre, but actually within the domains of Jezebel's father. The prophet, who was not safe from Jezebel in Israel, would be safe within Jezebel's own country; he for whom Ahab had so earnestly but vainly searched, not only throughout his own land, but in all neighboring countries (1 Kings 18:10), would be securely concealed in the land most hostile to Elijah's mission, and most friendly to Ahab's purposes. But there are even deeper lessons. It is only one of these, that, cast out of his own country and by his own people, God can find a safe refuge for His servant in most unlikely circumstances; and that, when faith seems to fail, where most we might have expected it, God will show that He has His own where least we would look for them. Again, the reference of our LORD to this history (Luke 4:25), shows these three things. That the entertainment of Elijah was a distinguishing honor conferred on the widow of Sarepta; that it proved of real spiritual benefit to her (as will be shown in the course of this history); and that it implied, that God had purposes of grace beyond the narrow bounds of Israel, unbelieving as it was — in the language of St. Paul, that He was not the God of the Jews only, but also of the Gentiles (Romans 3:29). May we not go a step farther, and see in this mission of Elijah to, and entertainment by a heathen widow, an anticipation at least of the announcement of that "Kingdom of God" in its world-wide bearing, which formed part of the message of his antitype, John the Baptist?

Once more the support of Elijah, though miraculous, was to be secured in the course of natural and easily intelligible events. Yet withal, as it had been Jehovah Who "commanded" the ravens, so it was He also Who "commanded" the widow of Sarepta, all unconscious as she was of it, to sustain Elijah.

But how should the prophet recognize her? He must go, trusting to God's direction, and, watching such natural indications as would appear, be guided to whither he was supernaturally sent. Arrived at the gate of Sarepta, he saw a widow, whose poverty was evidenced by her searching for a little brushwood. Was she the woman who would sustain him? There was a preliminary test ready to hand. She must have recognized the stranger by his dress as a prophet of Jehovah. Would she, the heathen, be willing to hold friendly communication with him? So he handed her the drinking-vessel which he had brought, with the request to interrupt her weary work in order to fetch him some water. Even this first test proved that God had, as of old (Genesis 24:12-21), and as afterwards (Luke 19:30-34; 22:9-12), by anticipation provided for His servant. And, assuredly, as ever, "the cup of cold water" given in the name of the LORD was soon to receive rich reward.

But there was yet another and a sharper test by which to ascertain whether she were the widow to whom Elijah was Divinely sent. If she would hold communion with a servant of Jehovah — did she truly believe in Jehovah Himself; and if so, was her faith such that she would venture her last means of support upon her trust in Him and in His word? To put it in another manner, heathen as she was, though thus far prepared, was there, if not activeness, yet receptiveness of faith in her, of sufficient capacity for such spiritual provision as that which was afterwards miraculously supplied for her temporal wants? This would be the last and decisive test. As she was going to fetch the water, without hesitating or murmuring at the interruption of the old, or at the imposition of the new task, Elijah arrested her with a request yet stranger and far harder than the first. She was evidently a poor widow, and we know from profane history that the famine, consequent on the want of rain in Israel, had also extended to Tyre. But when Elijah addressed to her what, even in these circumstances, would have seemed the modest request for "a morsel of the bread" in her hand — that is, in her possession — he could not have been aware of the terrible straits to which his future hostess was reduced.

It was not unwillingness to give even to a complete stranger part of her scanty provision, but that she had absolutely none left. Despair breaks down the barriers of reserve — at least to fellow-sufferers, and, as in this case, to fellow-believers. With the adjuration, "Lives Jehovah, thy God," which attested alike her knowledge of Elijah's profession and her own faith, she told how nothing but a handful of meal was left in the small Cad that held her provisions, and a little oil in her cruse. She had now come to gather by the highway a few sticks, with which to cook a last meal for herself and her child. After that they must lie down and die.

It is difficult to know which most to wonder at, Elijah's calmness, consistency, and readiness of faith, or the widow's almost incredible simplicity of trustfulness. Elijah was not taken aback; he did not hesitate to go on with the trial of his hostess to the end; least of all, was he afraid of the possible consequences. As in every real trial of our trust, there was first a general promise, and, on the ground of it, a specific demand, followed by an assurance to conquering faith ("the cad of meal shall not come to an end, nor the cruse of oil fail"). But, if it was as he told her, why this demand in its sharply trying severity: first, to use for Elijah part of the very little she had, and to bring it to him, and only after that to go back and prepare for herself and her son?

Needless, indeed, the trial would seem, except as a test of her faith; yet not a mere test, since if she stood it and inherited the promise, it would be such confirmation of it, such help and blessing to her — alike spiritually and temporally — as to constitute the beginning of a new life. And so it ever is; and therefore does every specific demand upon our faith stand between a general promise and a special assurance, that, resting upon the one, we may climb the other; and thus every specific trial — and every trial is also one of our faith — may become a fresh starting-point in the spiritual life.

And the widow of Sarepta obeyed. It requires no exercise of imagination to realize what her difficulties in so doing must have been. Did Elijah go back with her after she had brought him the cake, almost the last provision for herself and her child, — to watch as, with wonderment and awe, she prepared the first meal from her new store; or did he allow her to return home alone, perhaps wondering as she went whether it would be as the prophet had said, or whether perhaps she would never again see the Israelite stranger? One thing at least is clear, that this heathen woman, whose knowledge of Jehovah could only have been rudimentary and incipient, and who yet, at the word of a stranger, could give up her own and her son's last meal, because a prophet had bidden it, and promised her miraculous supply for the future, must have had the most simple childlike trustfulness in the God of Israel. What a lesson this, and how full of comfort, to Elijah! There was faith not only in Israel, but wherever He had planted its seed. Elijah had spread the wings of the God of Israel's promise (1 Kings 17:14), and this poor heathen had sought shelter under them.

There, almost hourly these many "days," the promise proved true, and, day by day, as when Israel gathered the manna in the wilderness, did an unseen Hand provide — and that not only for herself and her son, but for all "her household."

It was a constant miracle; but then we need, and we have a God Who doeth wonders — not one of the idols of the heathen, nor yet a mere abstraction, but the Living and the True

God. And we need in our Bible such a history as this, to give us the pledge of personal assurance, when our hearts well-nigh sink within us in the bitter trials of life — something which to all time may serve as evidence that Jehovah reigneth, and that we can venture our all upon it. And yet as great as this miracle of daily providing seems that other of the faith of the widow of Sarepta!

It was soon to be put to even greater trial — and, as before, not only she, but Elijah also, would learn precious lessons by it. "Days" (time)had passed in happy quiet since God had daily spread the table in the widow's home, when her son became ill. The sickness increased, until, in the language of the sacred text, "there was not left in him breath."

There is something in the immediate contact with the Divine, which, from its contrast, brings sin to our remembrance, and in consequence makes us feel as if it were impossible to stand unpunished before Him — until our thoughts of the Divine Holiness, which in this view seems as consuming fire, pass into the higher realization of the infinite love of God, which seeks and saves that which is lost (comp. Luke 5:8; also Isaiah 6:5). It was certainly not the wish that the prophet should be gone from her home, nor yet regret that he had ever come to it, which wrung from the agonized woman, as she carried to him her dead child in her bosom, these wild words, in which despair mingled with the consciousness of sin and the searching after the higher and better: "What have I to do with thee (what to [between] me and thee), man of the Elohim? Come art thou to me to bring to remembrance my sin, and (thus) to cause the death of my son?" The Divine, as represented by Elijah, having no commonality with her; its fierce light bringing out her sin, and her sin bringing down condign punishment — such were the only clearly conscious thoughts of this incipient believer — though with much of the higher and better, as yet unconsciously, in the background.

Elijah made no other answer than to ask for her son. He took him from her bosom, carried him to the Alijah (upper chamber) where he dwelt, and there laid him on his own bed. In truth, it was not a time for teaching by words, but by deeds. And Elijah himself was deeply moved. These "many days" had been a happy, quiet, resting time to him — perhaps the only quiet happy season in all his life. And as day by day he had been the dispenser of God's goodness to the widow and her household, and had watched the unfolding of her faith, it must have been a time of strengthening and of joy to his heart As St. Chrysostom has it: Elijah had to learn compassion in the house of the widow of Sarepta, before he was sent to preach to his own people. He learned more than this in that heathen home. Already he had learned that experience of faith, which, as St. Paul tells us, worketh a hope that maketh not ashamed (Romans 5:4, 5). But now it seemed as if it were all otherwise; as if he were only a messenger of judgment; as if his appearance had not only boded misery to his own people Israel, but brought it even upon the poor widow who had given him shelter. But it could not be so — and in the agony of prayer he cast this burden upon his God. Three times — as when the Name of Jehovah is laid in blessing on His people (Numbers 6:24, etc.),and as when the Seraphim raise their voice of praise (Isaiah 6:3), he stretched himself in symbolic action upon the child, calling upon Jehovah as his God, laying the living upon the dead, pouring his life, as it were, into the child, with the agony of believing prayer. But it was Jehovah Who restored the child to life, hearkening to the voice of His servant.

They are truly human traits, full of intense pathos, which follow — though also fraught with deep spiritual lessons. We can almost see Elijah as he takes down the child to his mother in that darkened room, and says to her only these words of deep emotion, not unmingled with loving reproof, "See, thy son liveth!" Words these, which our blessed

LORD has said to many a weeping mother when holding her child, whether in life or in death. And thus we can understand the words of the mother of Sarepta, and those of many a mother in like circumstances: "Now — thus — I know that a Man of Elohim thou, and that the Word of Jehovah in thy mouth is truth." She had learned it when first she received him; she had seen it day by day at her table; she had known it when God had answered her unspoken thought, her unuttered prayer, by showing that mercy and not judgment, love and forgiveness, not punishment and vengeance, were the highest meaning of His dealings.

The Rabbis see in this story an anticipation of the resurrection of the dead. We perceive this and more in it — an emblem also of the resurrection from spiritual death, a manifestation to Elijah and to us all, that "He quickeneth the dead, and calleth those things which be not as though they were" (Romans 4:17).

VOLUME 6: THE REIGN OF AHAB TO THE DECLINE OF THE TWO KINGDOMS

PREFACE

THE present Volume of this Bible History traces the period of the commencing decline alike in the kingdom of Israel and in that of Judah, although in the latter its progress was retarded by the gracious faithfulness of God in regard to the house of David, and by seasons of temporary repentance on the part of the people. The special interest of the period lies in this, that it was critical of the future of the nation. And of this its history also bears evidence in the more marked and direct — we had almost, said, realistic — interpositions, or, perhaps more correctly, self-manifestations on the part of the God of Israel: whether by more emphatic evidence of His constant Presence and claims, or in the more continuous mission and direct qualifications of the Prophets whom He commissioned.

This, as indicated in a previous Volume, accounts for the intensified miraculous character of that Biblical period — notably in connection with the history of Elijah and Elisha. For such prophetic mission was necessary, if in a crisis — when destruction, or at least severest judgment, was impending, or else national recovery, and with it great expansion of national influence — Israel was to be roused to a realization of the truth at issue, such as was, for example, presented by Elijah at the sacrifice on Mount Carmel. And not only as regarded that fundamental truth, but also its application to all the details of public and private life in Israel. In this, therefore, we find the rational vindication — we avoid the obnoxious designation, apologetic — of the otherwise strange, and certainly exceptional, manifestation of miraculous prophetic power in so many private as well as public affairs. In the state of Israel, and at that period, an Elijah and an Elisha were required, and, if required, their mission and their message must be thus evidenced: alike before all friends and against all gainsayers.

If, from this point of view, the application of the miraculous during this period, in private as well as in public concerns, is not, as some would have it, a retrogression, it marks in other and more important aspects a great progression — and that towards the perfectness of the New Testament. We must explain what we mean by a seeming retrogression. Very markedly the Old Testament history differs from all others, which in their earliest stages are legendary, in this, that whereas in them the miraculous is introduced in what may be called the prehistoric period, then speedily, almost abruptly, to cease; it is otherwise in that of the Old Testament. The patriarchal history (notably that of Isaac and Jacob) has comparatively less of the miraculous. It appears in the desert-history of new-born Israel, and on their entrance in the land. It disappears again in great measure, to reappear once more in manner altogether unprecedented at the period of which this Volume treats — that is, at a comparatively advanced time, when the history of Israel runs parallel to the trustworthy records of that of other nations as perpetuated on their monuments. Assuredly, this has its various lessons in regard to the credibility of the miraculous in the Old Testament. Most notably this, which, as before stated, marks that, which to some seems a retrogression, as a real progression: that the miraculous now stands with increasing clearness in direct connection with moral relationship towards God. So to speak: the miraculous inter-positions are now not so much for Israel as to Israel; not so much on behalf of Israel as such, but whether in judgment or in mercy, with direct reference and application to Israel's moral and spiritual condition. And this, as we have said, points to the perfectness of the New

Testament, in which the relation of God to each soul, as well as to the Church, and the spiritual condition of the soul, or of the Church: the outward and the inward, are correlative.

Thus, in the wider application, these miraculous elements in the history of Israel are themselves prophecies, of which the fulfillment is in Christ. Thus much must for the present suffice — the more so, as in the next Volume (which will conclude the Old Testament History) the opportunity will necessarily present itself for larger retrospect and wider survey. It only remains to add that the treatment of the subject in this Volume will be found in accordance with the progressive plan of this work, repeatedly indicated in previous Volumes. Alike the critical and exegetical notes will be found more frequent and more full, and the general treatment more detailed, and designed for more advanced readers. A new element in the present Volume is the light brought to bear on this period from the ancient monuments. We live in days when more attention than ever before is given to the critical study of the Old Testament; in days also when attacks are chiefly directed against the trustworthiness, the credibility, and, as it seems to us, the Divine Authority, in its true sense, of the Old Testament.

There are those, we will gladly believe, who can disjoint, and in logical connection with it, re-interpret the Old Testament, and yet retain their full faith in its direct Divine character, and in its preparation for the Christ. We must frankly confess that we are not of their number. There is, indeed, a general Divine character in the Old Testament, and a general preparation in it for the New, whatever historical views we may take of it, or whatever interpretations we may give of it. We would even advance beyond this, and say that Christ and Christianity have their absolute truth, quite irrespective of the Old Testament. But to us at least Jesus of Nazareth as the Christ is the direct outcome of the Old Testament, as well as its higher fulfillment: not only "a light to lighten the Gentiles," but, and even in this very respect also: "the glory of Thy people Israel."

ALFRED EDERSHEIM
8, Bradmore Road, Oxford:
1st November, 1885.

CHAPTER 1 — AHAB, KING OF ISRAEL — THREE YEARS' FAMINE IN ISRAEL — ELIJAH MEETS OBADIAH AND AHAB — THE GATHERING ON MOUNT CARMEL — THE PRIESTS OF BAAI — DESCRIPTION OF THEIR RITES — THE TIME OF THE EVENING SACRIFICE — ELIJAH PREPARES THE SACRIFICE — ELIJAH'S PRAYER — THE ANSWER BY FIRE — ISRAEL'S DECISION — SLAUGHTER OF THE PRIESTS OF BAAL- THE CLOUD NOT BIGGER THAN A MAN'S HAND — ELIJAH RUNS BEFORE AHAB TO JEZREEL.

(1 KINGS 18)

THREE and a half years had passed since the ban of Elijah had driven clouds and rain from the sky of Israel, and the dry air distilled no dew on the parched and barren ground (comp. Luke 4:25; James 5:17). Probably one of these years had been spent by the prophet in the retirement of Wadi Cherith; another may have passed before the widow's son was restored from death to life; while other eighteen months of quiet may have followed that event.

Surely, if ever, the terrible desolation which the prophet's word had brought upon the land must by this time have had its effect upon Israel. Yet we meet no trace of repentance in king or people: only the sullen silence of hopeless misery. What man could do, had been attempted, but had signally failed. As the want and misery among the people became more pressing, King Ahab had searched both the land and all neighboring countries for Elijah, but in vain (1 Kings 18:10), while Jezebel had wreaked her impotent vengeance on all the prophets of Jehovah on whom she could lay hands, as if they had been Elijah's accomplices, to be punished for what she regarded as his crime. If all the representatives of Jehovah were exterminated, His power could no longer be exercised in the land, and she would at the same time crush resistance to her imperious will, and finally uproot that hated religion which was alike the charter of Israel's spiritual allegiance and of civil liberty. Yet neither Ahab nor Jezebel succeeded. Though Elijah was near at hand, either in Ahab's dominions or in those of Jezebel's father, neither messenger nor king could discover his place of retreat. Nor could Jezebel carry out her bloody design. It affords most significant illustration of God's purpose in raising up "prophets," and also of the more wide sense in which we are here to understand that term, that such was their number, that, however many the queen may have succeeded in slaying, at least a hundred of them could still be hid, by fifties, in the limestone caverns with which the land is burrowed. And this, we infer, must have been in the immediate neighborhood of the capital, as otherwise Obadiah (the "servant of Jehovah"), the pious governor of Ahab's palace (comp. 1 Kings 4:6; 2 Kings 18:18; Isaiah 22:15), could scarcely have supplied their wants without being detected (1 Kings 18:4). Nor was Obadiah the only one in Israel who "feared Jehovah," though his position may have been more trying than that of others. As we know, there were still thousands left in Israel who had not bowed to Baal (1 Kings 19:18).

But there was at least one general effect throughout the land of this terrible period of drought. Every one must have learned that it had followed upon the announcement of Elijah; every one must have known what that announcement had been, with all concerning

Jehovah and His prophet that it implied; and, lastly, if no general repentance had taken place, every one must at least have been prepared for the grand decisive trial between God and Baal, which was so soon to take place. And still the weary days crept on as before; the sun rose and sank on a cloudless sky over an arid land; and there was no sign of change, nor hope of relief. It was summer. Jezebel had left the palace of Samaria, and was in her delicious cool summer-residence at Jezreel, to which more full reference will be made in the sequel (comp. 1 Kings 18:45, 46; and the inference from 1 Kings 21:2). But Ahab was still in Samaria, busy with cares, caused by the state of the land. This temporary absence of Jezebel explains not only Ahab's conduct, but how he went to meet Elijah, attempted no violence, and even appeared in person on Mount Carmel. So great was the strait even in Samaria itself, that the king was in danger of losing every horse and mule, whether for the public or his own service. To discover if any fodder were left in the country, the king and Obadiah were each to make careful survey of part of the land. Obadiah had not proceeded far on his mission, when the sight least expected — perhaps least desired — presented itself to his view. It was none other than Elijah, who had been Divinely directed to leave Sarepta and meet Ahab. As there is not anything in Holy Scripture without meaning and teaching, we may here mark, that, when this is assigned by the Lord as the reason for Elijah's mission: "I will send rain upon the ground" (1 Kings 18:1), it is intended to teach that, although it was Jehovah Himself (and not Elijah, as the Rabbis imagine) who held "the keys of the rain," yet He would not do anything except through His chosen messenger.

Obadiah could have no difficulty in immediately recognizing Elijah, even if he had not, as seems most likely, met him before. With lowliest reverence he saluted the prophet, and then received command to announce his presence to Ahab. But timid and only partially enlightened, although God-fearing, as Obadiah was, this was no welcome message to him. Ahab had so long and so systematically sought for Elijah, that Obadiah could only imagine the prophet had been miraculously removed from shelter to shelter, just in time to save him from being detected by the messengers of Ahab. In point of fact, we know that such was not the case; but those who have lost the habit of seeing God in the ordinary Providence of everyday life — as is the case with all who are conformed to the world — are too often in the habit of looking for things strange, or for miracles, and thus become at the same time superstitious and unbelieving. What — so argued Obadiah — if, after he had intimated Elijah's presence to the king, the prophet were once more miraculously removed? Would he not have to pay with his life for Elijah's escape; would not suspicious Ahab or bloodthirsty Jezebel wreak their vengeance on him as an abettor of the prophet? Most groundless fears these, as all which are prompted by the faint-heartedness of partially enlightened piety; and so Elijah hastened to assure him, not, as it seems to us, without a touch of pitying reproof. The meeting which followed between the king of Israel and the representative of Jehovah was characteristic of each. It is a mistake to suppose, as interpreters generally do, that the words with which Ahab accosted Elijah, "Art thou the one who troubleth Israel?" were intended to frighten the prophet by a display of authority.

Even Ahab could not have imagined that such would be their effect. It seems rather like an appeal. See what thou hast done; and what now? In truth, a man such as Ahab must have felt it difficult to know how to address the prophet. But Elijah was not, even momentarily, to be drawn into a personal controversy. With a sharp reproof, which pointed out that it was not he but the sin of Ahab and of his house which had brought trouble upon Israel, he directed the king to gather unto Mount Carmel the representatives of all Israel, as well as the 450 prophets of Baal and the 400 prophets of Astarte who enjoyed the special favor of the queen.

Putting aside for the moment the thought of the overruling guidance of God in the matter, it is not difficult to understand why Ahab complied with Elijah's direction. Naturally he could not have anticipated what turn matters would take. Certain it was that the land was in a terrible strait from which, if any one, Elijah alone could deliver it. Should he provoke him to fresh judgments by a refusal? What was there to fear from one unarmed man in presence of a hostile assembly? If Elijah could remove the curse, it was worth any temporary concession; if he refused or failed, the controversy with him would be easily settled, and that with popular approbation. Besides these, there may have been other secondary reasons for Ahab's compliance. As we have noticed, Jezebel was not then in Samaria; and Ahab may have felt that secret misgiving which is often the outcome of superstition rather than of partial belief. Lastly, he may at the moment have been under the influence of the overawing power of Elijah. It could scarcely have been otherwise in the circumstances.

That day Carmel witnessed one of the grandest scenes in the history of Israel. Three such scenes on mountain-tops stand out before the mind: the first on Mount Sinai, when the Covenant was made by the ministry of Moses; the second on Mount Carmel, when the Covenant was restored by the ministry of Elijah; the third on "the Mount of Transfiguration," when Moses and Elijah bare worshipful witness to the Christ in Whom and by Whom the Covenant was completed, transfigured, and transformed. In each case the scene on the Mount formed the high point in the life and mission of the agent employed, from which henceforth there was a descent, save in the history of Christ, where the descent to Gethsemane was in reality the commencement of the ascent to the Right Hand of God. Moses died and was buried at the Hand of God, Elijah went up with chariot of fire; Jesus died on the cross. Yet whereas from the mountain-top Moses and Elijah really descended, so far as their work and mission were concerned, the seeming descent of Jesus was the real ascent to the topmost height of His work and glory.

No spot in Palestine is more beautiful, more bracing, or healthful than Carmel, "the Park-like." Up in the northwest, it juts as a promontory into the Mediterranean, rising to a height of five hundred feet. Thence it stretches about twelve miles to the S.S.E., rising into two other peaks. The first of these, about four miles from the promontory, is not less than 1740 feet high. Still further to the south-east is a third peak, 1687 feet high, which to this day bears the name of El-Mahrakah, or "place of burning" (sacrifice).

This, there can scarcely be a doubt, was the place of Elijah's sacrifice. Let us try to realize the scene. On whichever side the mountain be ascended, the scene is one of unsurpassed beauty. The rich red soil, where not cultivated, is covered by a thick brushwood of luxurious evergreens. Not only flowering trees and delicious fragrant herbs, but all the flora of the North of Palestine seems gathered in this favored spot. So early as November, the crocus, narcissus, pink cistus, and large daisy are in bloom, and the hawthorn in bud. In spring, wild tulips, dark red anemones, pink phlox, cyclamen, purple stocks, marigolds, geranium, and pink, yellow, and white rock-roses make it bright with gay coloring. For numerous springs trickle along the foot of the mountain and fertilize the soil. Ascending to El-Mahrakah we catch glimpses of cliffs, which in some places descend sheer down to the plain. At last we reach a plateau where at the edge of a steep slope there is a perennial well, filled with water even in the driest season. Yet a little higher rises another plateau of rich soil, shaded by olives; and finally we reach the topmost peak, a semi-isolated knoll. This was the place of the two altars; that of Baal, and that ruined one of Jehovah restored by Elijah, and dating from before the building of the Temple, when such worship was lawful. On the plateau beneath, under the shade of the olives, full in view of the highest altar-peak, were on the one side Elijah, and on the other King Ahab, the priests of Baal, and the people. Yet a little lower was the well whence the water for Elijah's sacrifice was drawn. Some 1400 feet beneath, where the rapid descent is close to steep precipices and by sharp crags, rolls that "ancient river" Kishon, where the wild slaughter of the priests of Baal formed the closing scene in the drama of that day. But up on the topmost altar-height what an outlook! Westwards over Carmel and far to the sandhills around Caesarea; northwards, the Galilean hills, Lebanon and Hermon; eastwards, across the plain of Esdraelon, some six miles off, to Jezreel, — further away, to Shunem, Endor, Nain, Tabor, Nazareth, and even distant Gilead. A theater this truly befitting what was to be enacted on it.

Among those who on that day had gathered under the olives on that shady plateau just beneath the topmost peak, the four hundred priests of Astarte were not found. Whether they had shrunk from the encounter, or had deemed it inconsistent with the wishes of their spiritual patroness, the queen, to appear on such an occasion, certain it is that they were not with their four hundred and fifty colleagues of the priesthood of Baal. These must have been conspicuous amid king, courtiers, and the motley gathering from all parts of the land, by their white dresses and high pointed caps. Over against them, his upper garment of black camel-hair girt with a leathern girdle, stood the stern figure of the prophet; in the foreground was King Ahab. It was, indeed, a unique gathering, a wondrous array of forces, a day of tremendous import. To this Elijah had bidden king, priests, and people, and he left them not long in doubt of his object. First, he turned to the people with these words, which must have alike shown them their real condition and appealed to their judgment: "How long halt ye" (pass ye from one to the other) "as to the two opinions" (divisions, parties)?

If Jehovah be the Elohim — go after Him; but if the Baal, go after him! To an appeal so trenchantly true there could in the then condition of the public mind be no answer. Their very appearance on Mount Carmel was an attestation of this mental passing to and fro on the part of Israel — irrational, unsatisfactory, and self-condemnatory (Deuteronomy 6:4, etc.). But the question of Elijah also formed a most apt preparation for what was to follow. The two divided opinions were now to be brought to the test of truth; the two parties to measure their strength. Let Israel see and decide!

In the breathless silence that ensued upon this challenge Elijah now stood forward, and pointing to the white-robed crowd of priests over against him, he recalled to king and people that he and he only remained — that is, in active office and open profession — a prophet of Jehovah. Single-handed, therefore, he would go to the contest, if contest of power it were against that multitude. Power! They worshipped as God the powers of nature: let them then make trial on whose side the powers which are in nature were arrayed.

Let this be the test: the priests of Baal on their side, and he on his, would each choose a bullock and prepare it for sacrifice, but not kindle the fire beneath, "and it shall be the Elohim who shall answer by fire, He is the Elohim." A shout of universal assent greeted the proposal. In the circumstances it would be of the greatest practical importance that the futility of Baal-worship should be exhibited in the fullest manner. This explains the details of all that follows. Besides, after a whole day's vain appliance of every resource of their superstition, the grandeur of Jehovah's majestic interposition would also make the deeper impression. But although from Elijah's point of view it was important that the priests of Baal should first offer their sacrifice, the proposition was one to which no objection could be taken, since Elijah not only gave them the choice of the sacrificial animal, but they were many as against one. Nor could they complain so far as regarded the test proposed by Elijah, since their Baal was also the god of fire, the very Sun-god.

Now commenced a scene which baffles description. Ancient writers have left us accounts of the great Baal-festivals, and they closely agree with the narrative of the Bible, only furnishing further details. First rose a comparatively moderate, though already wild, cry to Baal; followed by a dance around the altar, beginning with a swinging motion to and fro.

The howl then became louder and louder, and the dance more frantic. They whirled round and round, ran wildly through each other's ranks, always keeping up a circular motion, the head low bent, so that their long dishevelled hair swept the ground. Ordinarily the madness now became infectious, and the onlookers joined in the frenzied dance. But Elijah knew how to prevent this. It was noon — and for hours they had kept up their wild rites. With cutting taunts and bitter irony Elijah now reminded them that, since Baal was Elohim, the fault it must lie with them. He might be otherwise engaged, and they must cry louder. Stung to madness, they became more frantic than before, and what we know as the second and third acts in these feasts ensued. The wild howl passed into piercing demoniacal yells. In their madness the priests bit their arms and cut themselves with the two-edged swords which they carried and with lances.

As blood began to flow the frenzy reached its highest pitch, when first one, then others, commenced to "prophesy," moaned and groaned, then burst into rhapsodic cries, accusing themselves, or speaking to Baal, or uttering incoherent broken sentences. All the while they beat themselves with heavy scourges, loaded or armed with sharp points, and cut themselves with swords and lances — sometimes even mutilated themselves — since the blood of the priests was supposed to be specially propitiatory with Baal.

Two more hours had this terrible scene lasted — and their powers of endurance must have been all but exhausted. The sun had long passed its meridian, and the time of the regular evening-sacrifice in the Temple of Jehovah at Jerusalem had come. From the accounts of Temple-times left us we know that the evening sacrifice was offered "between the evenings," as it was termed — that is, between the downgoing of the sun and the evening.

In point of fact the service commenced between two and three p.m. It must have been about the same time when Elijah began the simple yet solemn preparations for his sacrifice. Turning from the frantic priests to the astonished people, he bade them draw nigh. They must gather around him, not only in order to be convinced that no deception was practiced, but to take part with him, as it were, in the service. And once more Israel was to appear as the Israel of old in happier times, undivided in nationality as in allegiance to Jehovah. This was the meaning of his restoring the broken place of former pious worship by rolling to it twelve of the large pieces of rock that strewed the ground, according to the number of the tribes. And as he built the altar, he consecrated it by prayer: "in the name of Jehovah." Next, the soft crumbling calcareous soil around the altar was dug into a deep and wide trench. Then the wood, and upon it the pieces of the sacrifice were laid in due order. And now, at the prophet's bidding, willing hands filled the pitchers from the well close by. Once, twice, thrice he poured the water over the sacrifices, till it ran down into the trench, which he also filled. This, as we suppose, not merely to show the more clearly that the fire, which consumed the sacrifice in such circumstances, was sent from heaven, but also for symbolic reasons, as if to indicate that Israel's penitent confession was poured upon the offering.

And now a solemn silence fell on the assembly. The sun was going down, a globe of fire, behind Carmel, and covered it with purple glow. It was the time of the evening sacrifice.

But Jehovah, not Elijah, would do the miracle; the Hand of the living God Himself must be stretched out. Once more it was prayer which moved that Hand. Such prayer was not heard before — so calm, so earnest, so majestic, so assured, so strong. Elijah appeared in it as only the servant of Jehovah, and all that he had previously done as only at His Word: but Jehovah was the covenant-God, the God of Abraham, of Isaac, and of Israel, manifesting Himself as of old as the Living and True, as Elohim in Israel: the conversion of Israel to Him as their God being the great object sought for.

He had said it, and, as when first the Tabernacle was consecrated (Leviticus 9:24), or as when King Solomon (1 Chronicles 21:26; 2 Chronicles 7:1) brought the first offering in the Temple which he had reared to Jehovah, so now the fire of Jehovah leaped from heaven, consumed the sacrifice and the wood, enwrapped and burnt up the limestone rocks of which the altar was constructed, and with burning tongue licked up even the water that was in the trench. One moment of solemn silence, when all who had seen it fell in awe-stricken worship on their faces; then a shout which seemed to rend the very air, and found its echo far and wide in the glens and clefts of Carmel: "Jehovah, He the Elohim! Jehovah, He the Elohim!"

And so Israel was once more converted unto God. And now, in accordance with the Divine command in the Law (Deuteronomy 13:13; 17:2, etc.), stern judgment must be executed on the idolaters and seducers, the idol-priests. The victory that day must be complete; the renunciation of Baal-worship beyond recall. Not one of the priests of Baal must escape. Down the steep mountain sides they hurried them, cast them over precipices, those fourteen hundred feet to the river Kishon, which was reddened with their blood.

But up on the mountain-top lingered King Ahab, astonished, speechless, himself for the time a convert to Jehovah. He also was to share in the sacrifice; he was to eat the sacrificial meal. But it must be in haste, for already Elijah heard the sighing and low moaning of the wind in the forest of Carmel. Himself took no part in the feast. He had other bread to eat whereof they wot not. He had climbed the topmost height of Carmel out of sight of the king. None had accompanied him save his servant, whom tradition declares to have been that son of the widow of Sarepta who had been miraculously restored to life. Most fitting minister, indeed, he would have been in that hour. Once more it was agonizing prayer — not once, but seven times repeated.

At each break in it the faithful attendant climbed the highest knoll, and looked earnestly and anxiously over the broad expanse of the sea, there full in view. At last it had come — a cloud, as yet not bigger than a man's hand. But when God begins to hear prayer, He will hear it abundantly; when He gives the blessing, it will be without stint. Ahab must be up, and quick in his chariot, or the rain, which will descend in floods, will clog the hard ground, so that his chariot would find it difficult to traverse the six miles across the plain to the palace of Jezreel. And now as the foot of the mountain was reached, the heaven was black with clouds, the wind moaned fitfully, and the rain came in torrents. But the power of Jehovah was upon the Tishbite.

He girded up his loins and ran before the chariot of Ahab. On such a day he hesitated not to act as outrunner to the convert-king; nay, he would himself be the harbinger of the news to Jezreel. Up to the entrance of Jezreel he heralded them; to the very gate of Jezebel's palace he went before them, like the warning voice of God, ere Ahab again encountered his tempter. But there the two must part company, and the king of Israel must henceforth decide for himself to whom he will cleave, whether to Jehovah or to the god of Jezebel.

CHAPTER 2: DIFFERENT STANDPOINT OF THE OLD AND THE NEW TESTAMENT — ANALOGY BETWEEN ELIJAH AND JOHN THE BAPTIST — JEZEBEL THREATENS ELIJAH'S LIFE — THE PROPHET'S FLIGHT — HIS MIRACULOUS PROVISION — ANALOGY BETWEEN MOSES AND ELIJAH — ELIJAH AT MOUNT HOREB — WHAT DOEST THOU HERE, ELIJAH? — THE WIND, THE EARTHQUAKE, THE FIRE, AND THE STILL SMALL VOICE — THE DIVINE MESSAGE AND ASSURANCE TO ELIJAH — CALL OF ELISHA.

(1 KINGS 19)

UNSPEAKABLY grand as had been the scene on Mount Carmel, we instinctively feel that it was the outcome of the Old Testament. We cannot conceive it possible under the New dispensation. In so saying we do not so much refer to the ironical taunts which Elijah had addressed to the priests of Baal, when compassion, gentleness, and meekness might have seemed befitting, since it was necessary effectually to expose the folly as well as the sin of idolatry, and this was best done in such manner (comp. Isaiah 40:18, etc.; 41:7; 44:8-22; 46:5-11; Jeremiah 10:7, etc.). Nor do we allude only or mainly to the destruction of the priests of Baal. This was simply in obedience to the Old Testament Law, and was grounded alike on its economy and on the circumstances of the time.

Taking the lowest view, it was an act of necessary self-preservation, since the two religions could not co-exist, as the conduct of Jezebel had recently proved. But there is a higher view than this of the event. For the fundamental object of Israel's calling and existence — the whole typical import and preparatory purpose of the nation — was incompatible with even the existence of idolatry among them. Finally, there is this essential difference between the Old and the New Testament dispensation — that under the latter, religion is of personal choice, heart-willingness being secured by the persuasion of the Holy Ghost; while under the Old Testament (from its nature) religion was of Law. Religious liberty is a principle which necessarily follows from a religion of free choice, where God no longer addresses Himself to man merely, or mainly, with the authority of a general Law, but appeals to the individual conscience with the persuasion of a special invitation. Under the Old Testament, of which the fundamental principle was the sole Divine authority of Jehovah (Exodus 20:2, 3), idolatry was not only a crime, but a revolt against the Majesty of heaven, Israel's King, which involved the most fatal consequences to the nation. Yet even so, we repeat it, the scene on Mount Carmel could not have been enacted in New Testament times.

But while fully admitting this distinctive standpoint of the preparatory dispensation, it were a most serious mistake to forget that the Old Testament itself points to a higher and fuller manifestation of God, and never more distinctly than in this history of Elijah. Attention has already been called to the analogy between Elijah and John the Baptist. At this stage we specially recall three points in the history of the latter. It seems as if the Baptist had expected that his warning denunciations would be immediately followed either by visible reform, or else by visible judgment. But instead of this he was cast, at the instigation of Herod's wife, into a dungeon which he was never to leave; and yet judgment seemed to slumber, and the Christ made no movement either for the deliverance of His forerunner, or the vindication of his message. And, lastly, in consequence of this disappointment, spiritual darkness appears to have gathered around the soul of the Baptist. One almost feels as if it had been needful for such a messenger of judgment to become consciously weak, that so in the depression of the human the Divine element might appear the more clearly. And it was also good that it should be so, since it led to the inquiring embassy to Christ, and thus to a fuller revelation of the Divine character of the kingdom. The same expectation and the same disappointment are apparent in the history of Elijah on the morrow of the victory at Carmel. But they also led up to a fuller manifestation of the meaning and purpose of God. Thus we see how the Old Testament itself, even where its distinctive character most clearly appeared, pointed to that fuller and more glorious manifestation of God, symbolized, not by storm, earthquake, or fire, but by "the still small voice."

If Elijah had lingered in Jezreel in the hope that the reformation proclaimed on Mount Carmel would be followed up by the king, he was soon to experience bitter disappointment. There is, however, good reason for inferring that the impression then made upon the mind of Ahab was never wholly effaced. This appears not only from the subsequent relations between the king and prophets of the LORD (1 Kings 20), but even from his tardy repentance after the commission of his great crime (1 Kings 21:27-29). Indeed, it might almost seem as if, but for the influence of Jezebel upon the weak king, matters might at least temporarily have taken a different turn in Israel. But if such was the effect produced upon Ahab by the scene on Mount Carmel, we can understand that Jezebel's first wish must have been as soon as possible to remove Elijah from all contact with the king. For this purpose she sent a message, threatening the prophet with death within twenty-four hours. It need scarcely be said, that, if she had been so bold as really to purpose his murder, she would not have given him warning of it, and that the reference to twenty-four hours as the limit of his life must rather have been intended to induce Elijah to immediate flight. And she succeeded in her purpose — not, indeed, from fear on the part of the prophet, but from deep disappointment and depression, for which we may in some measure find even a physical cause in the reaction that must have followed on the day after Carmel.

Strange as it may seem, these felt weaknesses of men like Elijah come upon us with almost a sense of relief. It is not only that we realize that these giants of faith are men of like passions with ourselves, but that the Divine in their work is thereby the more prominently brought out. It deserves special notice that Elijah proceeded on his hasty journey without any Divine direction to that effect. Attended only by his faithful servant, he passed without pausing to the farthest boundary of the neighboring kingdom of Judah. But even that was not his final destination, nor could he in his then mood brook any companionship. Leaving his servant behind, he went into the wilderness of Paran. In its awful solitude he felt himself for the first time free to rest. Utterly broken down in body and in spirit, he cast himself under one of those wide-spreading brooms, which seemed as if they indicated that even in the vast, howling wilderness, the hand of the Great Creator had provided shelter for His poor, hardly bestead wanderers.

There is something almost awful in the life-and-death conflicts of great souls. We witness them with a feeling akin to reverence. The deep despondency of Elijah's soul found utterance in the entreaty to be released from work and suffering. He was not better than his fathers; like them he had vainly toiled; like them he had failed; why should his painful mission be prolonged? But not so must he pass away. Like Moses of old, he must at least gain distant view of the sweet land of beauty and rest. As so often, God in His tender mercy gave His beloved the precious relief of sleep. And more than that — he was to have evidence that even there he was not forsaken. An angel awakened him to minister to his wants. God careth for the body; and precious in His sight is not only the death, but also the felt need of His people. The same great Jehovah, Whose manifestation on Carmel had been so awful in its grandeur, condescended to His servant in the hour of his utmost need, and with unspeakable tenderness, like a mother, tended His weary child. Once more a season of sleep, and again the former heaven-given provision for the journey which he was to make — now in the guidance of God.

The analogy between Moses, as he through whom the Covenant was given, and Elijah, as he through whom the Covenant was restored, has already been indicated. There is, however, one great difference between the two. When Israel broke the Covenant which Moses was about to make, he pleaded for them with the most intense agony of soul (Exodus 33-34:9). When once more Israel broke the Covenant on the morrow of Carmel, Elijah fled in utter despondency of spirit. In both cases God granted light to His servants by such manifestation of Himself as gave deepest insight into His purposes of grace and anticipation of the manner in which they would be ultimately realized in all their fullness through Jesus Christ. And hence it was in this respect also fitting that Moses and Elijah should be with Jesus on the Mount of Transfiguration. But Elijah had not been like Moses; rather had he been like the children of Israel. And therefore, like them, must he wander for symbolic forty days in the wilderness, before liberty and light were granted, to learn the same lesson which God would have had Israel learn during their forty years of wandering. And so he came ultimately unto "the mount of God," to "the cave" — perhaps the very "clift of the rock" where Moses had first been permitted to hear the glorious revelation of what Jehovah was and of what He purposed.

It was a wondrous place in which to spend the night, and to hear amidst its silence the voice of Jehovah. The one question — afterwards repeated in different circumstances — "What doest thou here, Elijah?" was intended to bring his state of mind clearly to the consciousness of the prophet.

In tender mercy, no reproach was uttered, not even reproof of the rash request for release from seemingly hopeless, burdensome toil. But was it really hopeless? Did Elijah rightly apprehend God's final purpose in it; did he even know what in God's Providence would follow that seeming defeat of the prophet on the day after his great victory: how God would vindicate His cause, punish the rebellious, and take care of His own? What then had brought Elijah thither; what was his purpose in coming? Although the same question was twice asked and the same answer twice returned, it seems in each case to bear a somewhat different meaning. For the words of Elijah (vv. 10, 14) imply two things: an accusation against the children of Israel and a vindication of his own conduct in fleeing into the wilderness. The first of these seems to have been the meaning of his reply before the special manifestation of God (Romans 11:2, 3); the second, that after that revelation of God which the vision conveyed. This manifestation, so deeply symbolical, appears to us to have also wrought an entire change in the prophet.

The first question came to Elijah while still in the cave. As already stated, it elicited from him an accusation of His people, as if to appeal for vengeance to the LORD (Romans 11:2, 3) — "It is time for Thee to work, O LORD, for men have made void Thy Law" (Psalms

119:126)! Upon this Elijah was bidden to go forth out of the dark, narrow cave, and behold, as Jehovah passed by.

Not a word was spoken. But first burst "wind great and strong, rending mountains, shivering rocks before the face of Jehovah — not in storm Jehovah! And after the wind earthquake — not in earthquake Jehovah! And after the earthquake fire — not in fire Jehovah! And after the fire sound of soft silencing (audible gentle stilling)!"

Elijah could not but have understood the meaning of this. He knew it when, at the "sound of soft stilling," he wrapped his face in the mantle and came forth in most reverent attitude to stand before Jehovah (comp. Exodus 3:6; 33:20, 22; Isaiah 6:2). The storm which rends, the earthquake which shakes all to its foundations, the fire which consumes — these are but His messengers which at most precede His coming. But Jehovah Himself is not in them. When He cometh it is not in these, but in the gentle stilling of them. To learn this was a real, though not an expressed, answer to Elijah's despondency and to his accusing appeal against Israel, the more touchingly conveyed that, being indirect, like the answer of Jesus to the inquiry of the Baptist, it carried instruction but not rebuke. The mood of both was the same, their doubts, and the reply given to them. It was in effect, See what the LORD really is, purposes, and doeth; and learn reverently to bow and to adore. God is greater, higher, better than appears only in judgment: do thy work, and leave the result to Him — He will make it plain. And so, we suppose that, when after this manifestation the same question again came to Elijah, his answer was no longer in the spirit of accusation, but rather a statement of fact in vindication or explanation of his own presence on Mount Horeb.

With reverence be it said that, in the mood in which Elijah had come, no more fitting answer could have been made to him than this awful and glorious self-manifestation of Jehovah. If the LORD Himself had not been in the desolating messengers of terror, why should Elijah have expected it in the judgments which he was commissioned to execute? Nay, if Elijah himself had come forth to worship not in the storm, the earthquake, nor the fire, but had waited for the Presence of the LORD in the soft, gentle, stilling sound, why should he wonder if the revival of Israel's worship awaited a similar manifestation? But God would in the meantime take care of His own cause. The storm must burst from without on an unrepentant people: Hazael was to be anointed king of Syria, and foreign wars, more desolating than any that had preceded, would sweep over Israel. The earthquake would shake the house of Ahab to its foundations: and Jehu was to be appointed the minister of vengeance. That fire which Elijah had kindled would burn more brightly and fiercely: the mission of Elijah was to be continued in Elisha. To prepare all this was now the only work left for the aged and weary prophet. And in each case he did prepare it.

Elisha was called by the prophet himself. The destruction of the house of Ahab, which involved the elevation of Jehu, through whom it was accomplished, was distinctly announced to Ahab by Elijah in the field of Naboth (1 Kings 21:19, 21, 22); while the future power of Syria over Israel, which involved the elevation of Hazael, was similarly prophetically intimated (1 Kings 20:42) — as we conjecture from the expression "a certain man of the sons of the prophets" (1 Kings 20:35) — by direction of Elijah.

Yet one precious assurance, or rather visible token that Jehovah was still in Israel, in the voice of soft stilling, was granted to the prophet. All unknown to him God had even in corrupt Israel His own, a "remnant according to the election of grace" (Romans 11:2-5), a sacred covenant-number which could be counted by thousands — "still ones" in the land, who had never bent the knee to Baal nor kissed in worship the abominable image.

And yet further consolation was to be granted to the weary servant of the LORD. In each case the actual judgment was to be only intimated, not executed, through Elijah himself, or in his lifetime. But this comfort would he have, that, even in his lifetime, and while engaged in his mission, a yoke-fellow true in sympathy, ministry, and likeness of spirit, should attend him to make the burden seem easier to bear.

It was as had been told him. With a sense that his mission was well-nigh completed, and that what remained was chiefly to prepare Elisha for his work, the prophet turned again towards the land of Israel. As he proceeded on his way, nature itself must have seemed to reflect the gladsome revelation of stillness and peace which had been vouchsafed on Horeb. The abundant rain which had descended must have softened the long-parched fields. The country was putting on the garb of a new spring. Everywhere the work of the husbandman was resumed; herds and flocks were browsing in the meadows; busy hands were rapidly putting in the seed. Upwards he traveled along the rich Jordan valley, till, past the borders of Judah, he reached the ancient possession of Issachar. No more happy scene than on the fields of Abed Meholah, the "meadow of the dance," of which the very name seems to suggest the joyous time of rich harvest and the merry dances of the reapers. These fields, far as the eye could reach, were the possession of one Shaphat, and he was of those seven thousand who had not bent to Baal, as we infer even from the name which he had given to his son: Elisha, "the God of salvation," or better, "my God salvation." And now twelve yoke of oxen were ploughing up the land — eleven guided by the hands of servants, the twelfth, in good old Hebrew simple fashion, by the son of the owner of those lands.

With characteristic sparingness of detail the sacred text does not inform us whether Elijah had before known his successor, nor how he came now to recognize him. Suffice it, that he knew and called him, not in words, indeed, but by the unmistakable symbolic action of casting over him his prophet's mantle, as he passed. This was Elisha's first test. There was no absolute need for responding, nor yet for showing that he had understood an unspoken call, which could have offered so little to attract even one whose lot had been cast in circumstances much less happy than those of Elisha. But Elisha showed his inward and spiritual preparedness by at once responding to Elijah's call, with only this one request: to be allowed to take leave of his father and mother.

It was not stern rebuke nor reproof which prompted the reply of Elijah:" Go back, for what have I done to thee?" Precisely because he understood the greatness of the sacrifice which immediate obedience implied, would he leave Elisha entirely unswayed and free, and his service the outcome of his own heart's conviction and choice. Thus only could he be fitted for a calling which required such entire self-denial and self-sacrifice.

This further test also, which reminds us how our LORD set before intending followers the difficulties of their choice (Matthew 8:20) and before His disciples the absolute necessity of willing self-denial (Luke 14:26), did Elisha endure, as must every one who is to do service for God. It seems almost symbolic that the oxen with which he had been working, the yoke which bound them, and the wooden ploughshare which they had drawn, were now used to prepare the farewell-feast of Elisha. To forsake and give up all for the service of the LORD is only one lesson, which must be complemented, not so much by abandoning all of the past, as by consecrating to our new life-work all that we formerly had or did. Nor let us forget two other considerations, suggested by the history of Elisha's call. All personal decision for God, and all work undertaken for Him, implies a leave-taking and a forsaking of the old, which must "pass away" when "all things become new" (2 Corinthians 5:17). But this forsaking, though necessarily involving pain and loss, should not be sad — rather joyous, as leading through pain to real joy, and through seeming loss to real gain: a "feast," such as was the parting of Elisha from his home, and that of St. Matthew from his calling and friends.

Thus the end of the old will at the same time be the beginning of the new; the giving up of the former calling the first act of the new ministry. And however humble that ministry, or however indirectly it may seem to bear upon the LORD, it is really ministry of Him. Then, and for many years afterwards, Elisha did but "pour water on the hands of Elijah" (2 Kings 3:11) — yet from the moment that "he arose and went after Elijah" he was really, and in the judgment of God, "anointed to be prophet;" nor had he, nor needed he, other earthly consecration.

CHAPTER 3: GENERAL EFFECT OF ELIJAH'S MISSION — THE TWO EXPEDITIONS OF SYRIA AND THE TWOFOLD VICTORY OF ISRAEL-AHAB RELEASES BEN-HADAD — THE PROPHET'S DENUNCIATION AND MESSAGE

(1 KINGS 20)

BUT the mission of Elijah must also have had other and, in some respects, even more deep-reaching results than those with which God had comforted His servant in his deep dejection of spirit. Thus the "seven thousand" who had never bent the knee to Baal, must have been greatly quickened and encouraged by what had taken place on Carmel. Nay, it could not but have made lasting impression on King Ahab himself. Too self-indulgent to decide for Jehovah, too weak to resist Jezebel, even when his conscience misgave him, or directed him to the better way, the impression of what he had witnessed could never have wholly passed from his mind. Even if, as in the case of Israel after the exile, it ultimately issued only in pride of nationality, yet this feeling must ever afterwards have been in his heart, that Jehovah He was God — "the God of Gods" — and that Jehovah was in Israel, and the God of Israel.

It is this which explains the bearing of Ahab in the first wars with Ben-hadad of Syria.

It need scarcely be said that this monarch was not the same, but the son of him who during the reigns of Baasha (1 Kings 15:20) and Omri had possessed himself of so many cities, both east and west of the Jordan, and whose sovereignty had, in a sense, been owned within the semi-independent Syrian bazaars and streets of Samaria itself (1 Kings 20:34). To judge from various notices, both Biblical and on Assyrian monuments, this Ben-hadad had inherited the restless ambition, although not the sterner qualities of his father. The motives of his warfare against Ahab are not difficult to understand. It was the settled policy of Syria to isolate and weaken the neighboring kingdom of Israel. With this object in view, Ben-hadad IV. (the father of this king of Syria) had readily broken his league with Baasha, and combined with Asa against Israel.

But since the days of Omri the policy of both Israel and Judah had changed. Their former internecine wars had given place, first to peace, and then to actual alliance between the two kingdoms, cemented at last by the marriage of the son of Jehoshaphat with the daughter of Ahab (2 Chronicles 18:1; 2 Kings 8:18). To this cause for uneasiness to Syria must be added the close alliance between Israel and Tyre, indicated, if not brought about, by the marriage of Ahab with Jezebel. Thus the kingdom of Israel was secure both on its southern and western boundaries, and only threatened on that towards Syria. And the increasing prosperity and wealth of the land appear not only from the internal tranquillity that obtained during the thirty-six years of the reign of Ahab and his two descendants, but also from the circumstance that Ahab built so many cities, and adorned his capital by a magnificent palace made of ivory (1 Kings 22:39). Lastly, the jealousy and enmity of Ben-hadad must have been increased by his own relations to the great neighboring power of Assyria, which (as we shall see) were such as to make a dangerous alliance between the latter and Israel an event of political probability.

In these circumstances, Ben-hadad resolved to strike such a blow at Samaria as would reduce it to permanent impotence. At the head of all his army, and followed by thirty-two vassal kings, or probably rather chieftains, who ruled over towns with adjoining districts within the territory between the Euphrates and the northern boundary of Israel, he invaded Samaria.

He met with no opposition, for, as Josephus notes (Ant. 8. 14, 1), Ahab was not prepared for the attack. But even if it had been otherwise, sound policy would have dictated a retreat, and the concentration of the Israelitish forces behind the strong walls of the capital. This proved a serious check to the plans of Ben-hadad. The Syrian army laid, indeed, siege to Samaria, but the heat of the summer season, the character and habits of his allies, and even the circumstance that his own country seems to have been divided among a number of semi-savage chiefs, must have proved unfavorable to a prolonged warfare.

Ben-hadad might have succeeded if at the first onset he could have crushed the small, hastily-raised forces of Ahab by sheer weight of numbers. But the slow systematic siege of a well-defended city, into which Ahab had evidently gathered all the leading personages in his realm and all their wealth, must have appeared even to a boastful Oriental a doubtful undertaking, which might at any time be converted into a disaster by the sudden appearance of allies to Israel from Judah, Tyre, or perhaps even from Assyria.

It was probably shortly after the commencement of the siege of Samaria, that Ben-hadad sent envoys to demand in imperious terms the absolute submission of Ahab (1 Kings 20:2). At least so the latter seems to have understood it, when he declared his readiness to agree to his enemy's terms. But whether Ben-hadad had from the first meant more, or his insolence had grown with what he regarded as the necessities and fears of Ahab, the next day other heralds came from Ben-hadad, requiring in terms of extreme and wanton insult, not only the surrender of Ahab, but that of Samaria; and especially of the palaces of its nobility, for the avowed purpose of plunder. It was evident that Ben-hadad intended, not the surrender of Ahab, but the destruction ("evil") of the capital, and the ruin of the whole land (ver. 7). Possibly the apparently strange demand of Ben-hadad (ver. 6) may indicate a deeper scheme. To oblige Ahab formally to submit, would be of comparatively small, at most, of only temporary use.

On the withdrawal of Ben-hadad the hostility of Israel would, as experience had shown, once more break forth under Ahab, or some new military leader, and threaten Syria with the same or even graver danger than before. But if the spirit of the leaders could be crushed by having their substance taken from them, then the chiefs of the people would not only be detached from their native monarchy, which had proved powerless to protect them, but in future rendered dependent on Syria, and hence led to seek the favor of Ben-hadad, instead of giving their allegiance to their own Israelitish rulers.

But the scheme was foiled by the clumsy frankness of its avowal. Ahab summoned to his council the elders of Israel. He told them how on the previous day he had expressed to Ben-hadad his willingness to make absolute personal submission and surrender of all that he possessed — as Josephus, no doubt, correctly puts into his mouth — for the sake of their preservation and peace. But the new terms which Ben-hadad proposed involved the leaders of the people as well as himself, and meant ruin equally to them all. In these circumstances, "the elders" counselled the absolute rejection of the terms demanded. Their advice was ratified by a popular assembly (ver. 8). These measures of Ahab were wise. Besides, the bearing of Ben-hadad must have indicated even to a ruler less astute than Ahab, the weakness and folly of his opponent. And, instead of attacking the city, on the refusal of his terms, as he would have done had he been sure of his army, Ben-hadad now only sent a message of ridiculously boastful threatening, to which Ahab replied with calm dignity (vv. 10, 11).

Thus, for a time at least, Ahab seems in the school of adversity to have learned some of the lessons which his contact with Elijah might have taught him. Besides, it is only reasonable to suppose that both the composition of the force outside the city, and the utter demoralization of its leaders, were known in Samaria. A summer campaign in Palestine would have tried even the best disciplined troops. But the Syrian host contained a motley following of thirty-two Eastern chiefs, who probably had little other interest in the campaign than the hope of plunder. It was an army incoherent in its composition, and unwieldy from its very numbers. Hitherto their advance had been unchecked, and its progress, no doubt, marked by the desolation of the country along their straggling line of march. Their easy success would make them not only more reckless, but also unwilling to engage in serious fighting, especially in those hot and enervating days, when their leaders lay in the cool shadow of their booths, indulging in drunken orgies. It was a dissipated rabble, rather than an army.

Ben-hadad and his allies were engaged in a midday bout when the reply of Ahab to the Syrian challenge arrived. Received under such circumstances, we scarcely wonder that it provoked the order of Ben-hadad to make immediate preparation for an assault on the city. But in whatever these preparations consisted, — whether in the advance of siege engines, or amassing of the troops, they could scarcely have been very effective, since all the Syrian chiefs continued at their orgies, so that the hour of battle surprised them while incapacitated by intoxication (ver. 16). Matters were very different within Samaria. There a prophet appeared, to announce not only deliverance from the LORD, but to point its lesson in the contrast between the great multitude of the enemy, and the small number of Israel's host, by which they were to be defeated.

This, with the view of showing to Ahab and to Israel that He was Jehovah, the living Covenant God, Who gave the victory. Thus the teaching of Elijah on Mount Carmel was now to find its confirmation and application in national blessing. And that the influence of that scene had not been, as Elijah had feared, only temporary and transient, appears even from the presence of a prophet in Samaria, and from the whole bearing of Ahab.

He is neither doubtful nor boastful, but, as having learned the prophetic lesson, anxious to receive plain Divine direction, and to follow it implicitly. Apparently the land was parceled out among "princes of the shires," either hereditary chieftains of districts, or governors appointed by the king: an arrangement which throws further light on Ben-Hades' previously expressed purpose permanently to break the power of these leaders of Israel. These "princes of the shires" seem to have been each surrounded by a small armed retinue: "the young men" (comp. 2 Samuel 18:15). By these, numbering in all only 232 men, the victory over the great Syrian host was to be achieved. It only remained for Ahab to inquire, "Who shall commence the warfare?" For in such a victory the main condition would be exact conformity to all Divine directions, in order to show that all was of God, and to give evidence of the principle of faith on the part of the combatants.

Having received the direction that he was to begin the battle, Ahab lost no time. At midday — probably of the following day — when, as no doubt was well-known in Samaria, Ben-hadad and his thirty-two confederates were "drinking" themselves "drunk" in the booths, the 232 of the body-guard of the princes marched forth, followed by the 7000 men which formed the army of Israel. Although this number naturally reminds us of the 7000 who had not bent the knee to Baal, there is no need to regard it as referring to them, or (with the Rabbis) to "the true children of Israel." The precise number (232) of the body-guard points to an exact numeration, nor need we perhaps wonder if in the wonder-working Providence of God there was a striking coincidence between the number of the faithful and that of Israel's victorious host.

The same wonder-working Providence appears in the manner in which victory was granted. As so often, we mark the accomplishment of a result, miraculous when viewed by itself, yet, as regards the means, brought about in the order of natural causation. And thus we ever learn anew that, although too frequently we do not perceive it, we are constantly surrounded by miracles, since Jehovah is the living God; and that hence ours should be the faith of a constant expectancy. It reads as we might have expected in the circumstances, that, when Ben-hadad was informed that men had come out from Samaria, he commanded in his drunken conceit and boastfulness, they should not be attacked, but made captives and brought to him. It may have been that those who were sent to execute this command went not fully armed. At any rate they seem to have been quite unprepared for resistance; and when these 232 Israelitish soldiers cut down each a man, no doubt following it up by further onslaught, the Syrians might naturally imagine that this was only an advanced guard, which was intended to precede a sortie of the whole garrison of Samaria. A panic, not uncommon among Orientals, seized the unprepared and unmarshalled masses, whose officers the while lay drunken in the booths. The very number of the Syrians would make a formation or rally more difficult, while it would afterwards increase the confusion of what soon became an indiscriminate flight. At this moment King Ahab issued from Samaria with his whole army. Whether, as our present Hebrew text bears, the king struck at the war-horses and war-chariots of the enemy, with the view of capturing them, or, as the ancient Greek translators (the LXX.) seem to have read, he "took" them, — implying that there had not been time to harness the war-chariots when the Israelitish host was among them — the result would be the same. Ben-hadad, followed by a few horsemen, escaped by hasty flight, as the word used in the original conveys, on a "chariot-horse," showing how sore was the stress when the king was obliged hastily to escape on the first horse to hand.

If it were necessary to demonstrate the compatibility of direct Divine help, and of reliance upon it, with the most diligent use of the best means, the narrative which follows would show it. After this great victory the king and people might have indulged in outward, or still worse, in professedly religious security, to the neglect of what was plain duty. But the same prophet who before had announced Divine deliverance, now warned Ahab to gather all his forces, and prepare, for that — "at the turn of the year," that is, in the spring (comp. 2 Samuel 11:1), he might expect another attack from Syria. And to make best preparation for the coming danger, in obedience to the Divine word, would not supersede but presuppose faith, even as we shall work best when we feel that we have the Divine direction in, and the Divine blessing on, our undertakings.

It was as the prophet had told. It seems quite natural that the courtiers of Ben-hadad should have ascribed the almost incredible defeat of such an army to supernatural causes, rather than to the dissipation and folly of their king. They suggested that the gods of Israel were mountain-deities, and that the rout of Syria around mountainous Samaria had been due to this cause. But the result would be far different if the battle were waged in the plains, man against man, and not gods against men, ("but, on the other hand, we shall fight with them in the plain [see,] if we shall not be stronger than they!") The grounds of this strange suggestion must be sought partly in the notions of the heathen world, but also partly in the sin of Israel. The ancient heathen world worshipped not only gods on the heights, but gods of the heights, and the sin of Israel in rearing altars and chapels on "the high places" must have led to the inference that the national worship was that of mountain-deities.

Thus did Israel's disobedience bring also its temporal punishment. But to their general advice the courtiers of Ben-hadad added certain practical suggestions, to avoid the secondary causes to which they attributed their late defeat. The tributary "kings" were to be dismissed, and their places filled by governors. This would give not only unity to the army (comp. 1 Kings 22:31), but these officers, appointed by Ben-hadad himself, would naturally take a more personal interest in the cause of their king. And, instead of the former army, Ben-hadad was to raise one equal in numbers, but — as the text has it — "from those with thee" (thine own subjects).

In these well-conceived measures there was only one, but that a fatal, flaw. They proceeded on the supposition that the God of Israel was like one of the heathen deities. And this point was emphasized in the defeat of the Syrians, which was announced to Ahab by "a man of God," probably another than "the prophet" who had formerly been commissioned to him. But it deserves special notice that this message only came after the invasion of the Syrian host. Thus would the temptation be avoided of neglecting all ordinary preparations: faith would be tried, and also called forth; while, by this prediction, and from the disparity between Israel and the host of Syria, Israel would once more learn to recognize in this deliverance that Jehovah He was God.

The winter rains had ceased, and the spring wind and sun had dried the land. There was a fresh crispness in the air, and a bright light over the scene, when the immense Syrian host swarmed down into that historic battlefield of Israel, the great plain of Jezreel. We are carried back in imagination to the scene of Saul's last fatal defeat (1 Samuel 29:1), and beyond it to that of Gideon's glorious victory.

Once more the foe lay at Aphek, with his back against the hill on which probably the fortified city of that name stood, and facing the plain where it is broadest. As in imagination we travel southwards to the highlands, and to those mountains among which Samaria lies embosomed, we feel how literally Ben-hadad had acted on the suggestion of his servants to avoid a contest with the mountain-deities of Israel. It was the very time and place for Jehovah to show forth that great lesson which underlies and sums up all revelation. Of the Israelitish host we know not the numbers — only that, as they camped in two divisions on the opposite side of the valley, perhaps beneath the two spurs of the ridge that juts into the plain from the south-east, they seemed like two little flocks of kids — so small and weak, as compared with their enemies. For seven days the two armies lay observing each other. From the circumstance, specially mentioned in the text, that the Israelites had gone out "provisioned" (ver. 27, margin), and even from their camping in two divisions, we infer that the object of Ahab was to remain on the defensive, which, indeed, the inferiority of numbers rendered imperative. Besides, the Jewish position was most happily chosen. It barred the advance of the enemy, who could not move forward without first giving battle to Israel. The Syrians must have perceived the advantage of Ahab's position, with his back to the base of his operations, while the division of Israel into two camps might enable them to envelop their enemies if they attempted an advance, in which case the very size of the Syrian army would, from its unwieldiness, prove a serious difficulty. But the danger of idle delay in a hostile country, and in an Eastern warfare, was nearly as great. And so on the seventh day the attack was made — as we judge, by the Syrians. Their defeat was crushing. The great Syrian host of 100,000 was destroyed, and the men who either made their way from the battle-field to Aphek, or who had been left there as a garrison, experienced another and even more terrible calamity. While crowding into the gates, or else while occupying the ramparts, which had probably been hastily thrown up or strengthened, a wall fell upon 27,000 of their number.

Further defense being thus rendered impossible, the previous confidence of Ben-hadad gave place to abject fear. He fled from room to room — into the innermost chamber. His servants, who had formerly given such warlike counsel, now advised him to sue in most humble manner for his life, holding out the hope of the mercifulness of the kings of Israel of which they had heard. There is an ominous sound in this. The kings of Israel had never been distinguished for mercy. But they had only too often shown their sympathy with the heathen kingdoms around, and manifested a desire to make alliance with them, and to conform to their ways. Yet, even so, it is not easy to explain the conduct of Ahab when the Syrian envoys of Ben-hadad appeared before him, in true Eastern manner, with sackcloth on their loins and ropes round their necks, suing only for the life of him who now ostentatiously styled himself Ahab's "slave." It could scarcely have been due to weakness of character when Ahab broke into the almost joyous exclamation, "Is he yet alive?" Nor could it have been merely from kindness of disposition that he ostentatiously substituted: "he is my brother" for the designation, "thy slave Ben-hadad," used by the Syrian envoys. They were not slow to perceive the altered tone of the king. They favorably interpreted and laid hold on that which had come from him; and they said: "Thy brother Ben-hadad."

Presently, at Ahab's invitation, Ben-hadad himself was brought, and made to stand by the side of the king in his chariot — both in token of companionship and for more private conversation. In truth, nothing less than a treaty of alliance was in hand between them. Ben-hadad undertook to restore the towns which his father had taken from Ahab's father (in a warfare of which we have no other record) and to allow to Ahab the same rights and privileges as to having "streets," or rather "bazaars" — what in modern language would be called an Israelitish "factory" — in the Syrian capital, which Ben-Hades' father had possessed in Samaria; and with this covenant Ahab dismissed the Syrian king.

We have said that it is not easy to understand what motives could have prompted an act which, even politically, was a grave mistake. Was it flattered vanity on the part of Ahab, or sympathy with the heathen king, or part of his statecraft to secure, not only an ally, but a vassal on the northern flank of his kingdom, or all these combined? In any case he must have looked upon the victory over the Syrians in a manner far different from that in which it had been announced to him by the God who had wrought it. Ahab no longer thought of Jehovah; he inquired not as to His purpose or will. There was an ominous similarity between his conduct and that of Saul in regard to Agag (1 Samuel 15). Evidently, Ahab claimed to have himself gained the victory, and felt sure that in like circumstances — should Ben-hadad rebel — he would equally gain it once more. It was he, and not the LORD, who would shape and direct the destinies of Israel. Jehovah was only the national deity of that Israel of which Ahab was the king. And so the error of the Syrians was substantially repeated by Ahab, and the lesson which Jehovah would have taught by their defeat had to be learned anew by Israel and its king — this time in judgment.

This explains the commission with which God now charged one of "the sons of the prophets." We mark that the expression here occurs for the first time. It referred to those associations under the leadership of some prophet (hence sons of the prophets) which, in the decay of religious life in Israel, served such important purposes, alike for the preservation of religion, and in the execution of the Divine behests.

In fact, they would recall to Israel, what, as a nation, Israel had been destined to be, and ever keep it before them. Thus they represented, so to speak, ideal Israel in the midst of apostate Israel. To a member of this community it came "by the word of Jehovah" — that is, by direct command from Him — to confront Ahab with such a symbolic (or parabolic) presentation of his late conduct as would show it in its true light, and lead the king to pronounce sentence on himself. Thus only could a man like Ahab be convicted, if not convinced, of sin.

In the execution of this commission the "son of the prophet" went to one of his colleagues, and, telling him that it was "by the word of Jehovah," bade him "smite" him.

It was conduct not unlike that of Ahab when this behest was resisted by the prophet. Remembering these two things: that the person addressed was also a "son of the prophets," and that he had been informed that it was "by the word of Jehovah," we can understand the Divine judgment which so speedily overtook him when he was torn by a lion. For the fundamental idea, the very law, of prophetism was absolute, unquestioning obedience to the command of God. This was the lesson to be taught by these associations and their leaders, and it explains how sometimes exceeding strange things were given them to do in public, that so in the absoluteness of their obedience they might exhibit the absoluteness of God's authority. Hence not to have visited with signal judgment the disobedience of the prophet would have been not only to contravene the principle on which the whole prophetic institution rested, but also the very lesson and message which was to be conveyed to Ahab.

But what one "son of the prophets" had refused, another soon afterwards did. Then the "son of the prophets," now smitten till he was wounded, "disguised himself with a bandage upon his eyes," and waited for the king by the way.

The reason of his appearing as a wounded man was that he might appeal to the king with the more show of truth, and of claim upon his interference, as wounded in the fight. And a symbolism may also have been designed. For, as the prophet's conduct was intended to represent that of the king, it might be wished to anticipate this possible excuse of Ahab that the difficulty of his circumstances had rendered it not easy to retain Ben-hadad by the analogous case of a wounded man, who might have fair ground of excuse if he allowed his prisoner to escape.

The story which the wounded prophet told the king was to the effect that, while in the battle — and this is an important point, as intended to indicate that Ahab was only like a soldier engaged in a warfare in which God, and not the king of Israel, was the commander — one had turned aside and bidden him have safe custody of a captive, with this injunction: "If he be missed [viz., when the prisoners are mustered], thy life shall be for his life, or else thou shalt pay a talent of silver."

From the language we infer that the person who handed over the prisoner was represented as a superior officer; that the battle itself was ended, and that the captive was a very valuable prisoner, since such a price was set upon him. But while the pretended soldier "was busy here and there" — or, as it has been proposed to be read: "looked here and there" — the prisoner escaped. In these circumstances he appealed to the king that he might not be punished as threatened by his leader. The king had no hesitation how to decide. He told him that in recounting his story he had already pronounced sentence upon himself. Then the prophet, having removed the bandage from his eyes, so that the king recognized him, announced the application of the Divine parable. The war had been Jehovah's, not Ahab's, and Ben-hadad had been the "banned" of the Lord. "Because thou hast let go forth out of thine hand (custody) the man of my ban (compare Leviticus 27:29), therefore thy life shall be for his life, and thy people for his people."

The judgment pronounced was not only righteous, but alike the necessary sequence of God's dealings throughout this history, and of Ahab's bearing in it. And in the judgment the people as a whole must also share. For even if theirs had not been the same spirit as that which had prompted the conduct of Ahab, yet the public acts of rulers are those of the nation, and national sins are followed by national judgments. Ahab had been on his triumphant return to Samaria, there to receive the popular applause for his achievements, when, in presence of all his retinue, he was thus publicly confronted by the prophet's message. He now "went to his house much excited and angry." And this also casts further light both on what Ahab had done, and on what he was about to do.

CHAPTER 4: THE VINEYARD OF NABOTH — MURDER OF NABOTH — THE DIVINE MESSAGE BY ELIJAH — AHAB'S REPENTANCE.

(1 KINGS 21)

IT is significant that the words describing Ahab's state of mind on returning from Jezreel to Samaria after his unsuccessful negotiation with Naboth for his vineyard, are precisely the same as those formerly used in regard to the impression made on him by the prophet's message (1 Kings 20:43). On both occasions he "was much [and rebelliously] excited and angry." The identity of terms indicates identity of feelings. The same self-assertion, independence of God, and want of submissiveness which had led to his release of, and covenant with, Ben-hadad, and inspired feelings of rebellion and anger on hearing the Divine message, now prompted his resentment of Naboth's conduct.

The summer palace of Jezreel was the favorite retreat of King Ahab and Jezebel. The present somewhat marshy plain of Esdraelon, the almost bare mountains of Gilboa, and the miserable village which now occupies the site of Jezreel, and overlooks the ruins of Bethshan, can afford no adequate idea of what the place was in the days of Ahab and Jezebel and of their immediate successors. Then the mountains of Gilboa were richly wooded, and sweet springs brought freshness to the air and luxurious beauty to the vegetation of Jezreel, even as they carried fertility down into the great plain beneath, which in the summer light shimmered and trembled like a sea of golden corn. At the northern declivity of Gilboa, where it descends, steep and rocky, on a knoll about 500 feet high, stood Jezreel. Protected from the fierce southern sun by the delicious shade of Gilboa, that rises up behind, it looked — as suited to a summer-residence in the East — northwards, across the plain to the mountains of Galilee, to Tabor, and in the distance to snow-capped Hermon. The height descended into the valley of Jezreel, where a sweet spring rippled, and close by gathered into a pool. Eastwards, you would look down on Bethshan, and, across the deep depression of the Jordan valley, to the mountains on the other side, on which rested the blue and purple light. To the west you might sweep those fifteen miles to Mount Carmel, and perchance the westerly breeze might carry up the plain the fresh scent of the sea. Such was the Jezreel of Ahab and Jezebel — the nearest, the safest, the sweetest summer-retreat from Samaria.

On the east and south-east, where the hot limestone rock shelves into the valley beneath, are to this day wine-presses. They mark the neighborhood of where the vineyards of Jezreel must have been, among them that of Naboth. Right above was the royal palace, narrowed and cramped within the city walls, of which indeed it seems to have formed part. Manifestly it would be object of desire to acquire the land nearest to the palace, with the view of converting it into a garden. What such a garden might bear, and what sweet outlook on it could be enjoyed from the windows of the palace, may be judged from the lemon-groves still existing in the near neighborhood. But Naboth, the owner of the coveted piece of land, could not be tempted to part with it by the king's offer of either a better vineyard or an equivalent in money. It was the ancestral possession of the family of Naboth, and piety towards God combined with reverence for the memory of his fathers to forbid the unholy bargain. It is a healthy sign to find such stern assertion of principle so fearlessly uttered. Israel could not be wholly sunken in corruption and idolatry, so long as it numbered among its peasant-proprietors men like Naboth, nor could the service of Jehovah have left its households when even in Jezreel a burgher could appeal from the demands of an Ahab to the authority and law of his God. And it affords happy evidence of what the legislation of the Pentateuch had secured for Israel, that even in the worst times an Ahab dared not, like a heathen monarch, lay hands on Naboth, nor force him to surrender the inheritance of his fathers.

It is another mark of that self-willed and uncontrolled frame of mind which had determined the bearing of Ahab towards Ben-hadad, and then towards the prophet sent to rebuke him, that he could not brook the refusal of Naboth. It was utter and childish petulance, as well as unbridled selfishness, to act as he did on his return to Samaria. He turned his face to the wall and refused to eat bread. In Samaria at least all was submissive to his will — thanks to the strong hand of Jezebel. But, outside her sway, he was always encountered and opposed by Jehovah: now by His prophets, then by His worshippers. Here was a power which he dared not resist, yet to which he would not submit. But Jezebel shared neither the feelings nor the scruples of her husband. She dared what she would, and she would what she dared. She now spoke to the king as a strong unscrupulous woman to a weak and unprincipled man. She must have known what had prompted the refusal of Naboth — although it deserves notice that, in his account of what had passed, the king had studiously omitted all reference to it (ver. 6). Similarly, Ahab must have known that when Jezebel demanded the royal signet, with which official documents coming directly from the king were stamped, she must have had in view some scheme of violence. And often does it seem more convenient — certainly more easy- to remain in willful ignorance, than to learn what would call for our active resistance, or, in the absence of it, fill our conscience with uneasiness. And while remaining in willful ignorance, Ahab may have flattered himself that he had not incurred responsibility in the murder of Naboth.

The measures of Jezebel were at least plain and straightforward. The old Mosaic civil order still continued in Israel by which jurisdiction, even in matters of life and death, lay in the first instance with the "judges and officers" of a place (Deuteronomy 16:18). This local "senate," consisting partly of elected life-members, partly of what may be designated a hereditary aristocracy, might in times of corruption become subject to court influence, especially in a small royal borough such as Jezreel. Jezebel knew this only too well, and with a terrible frankness wrote to each member of that senate what would seem the king's directions. By these each recipient of the letter would become a fellow-conspirator, and each feel bound to keep the horrible secret. As if some great sin rested upon the city (comp. 1 Samuel 7:6), and, in consequence of it, some heavy judgment were to be averted, (2 Chronicles 20:2-4; Jeremiah 36:6, 9), the eldership of Israel gathered the people to a solemn fast. If it had been so, and some great sin had been committed or were even suspected, it would have been the duty of the city thus to purge itself of guilt or complicity. For according to the deep and true idea which underlay all the institutions of the Old Testament, there is solidarity (as it is called in modern language) between those whom God has placed side by side. There is solidarity between all the members of the human family — solidarity of curse and of blessing, of judgment and of promise, because all have sprung from a common stock. There is solidarity also in a city, since ten righteous men might have preserved Sodom from destruction; solidarity in a nation, since the sins or the piety of its rulers were returned in blessing or in judgment on the people — a solidarity which as it pointed back to a common ancestry, also pointed forward to the full and final realization of its inmost meaning in that great brotherhood of believers which Christ came to found. And hence it was that, when blood had been shed and the doer of the crime-remained unknown, the elders of the district had by a solemn act to clear themselves of the guilt (Leviticus 4:13, etc.; Deuteronomy 21:1-9), and that, as here, when a great crime was supposed to have been committed, all would humble themselves in fasting before they put away the evil-doer from among them.

In the assembly thus called Naboth was to be "set on high," not in order to assign him an honorable place, so as the more effectually to rouse public indignation when one so honored was convicted of such crime, nor yet to give the appearance of impartiality to the proceedings that were to follow. Evidently the fast had been appointed in humiliation for a sin as yet unknown to the people, and the assembly was called to set before them the nature of this crime. For this purpose Naboth was "set on high," as one incriminated before the elders, against whom witnesses were to rise, and on whom judgment was to be pronounced by the people of his own city. This explains (ver. 10) how these "two sons of Belial" who were to bear false testimony against Naboth were "set before him."

The sacred text only informs us that the two witnesses (comp. Deuteronomy 17:6, etc.; 19:15; Numbers 35:30) testified that Naboth had "blasphemed" — uttered blasphemous language against "God and the king." It is scarcely conceivable that Naboth should not have made some defense, nor that the people would have given so ready credence to such a charge against one so well known, if some colorable confirmation could not have been found for it. May it not have been that the refusal of the vineyard to Ahab had become known to the townsmen of Naboth, and that these two sons of Belial were suborned to say that Naboth had at the same time pronounced in their hearing a curse upon Ahab — perhaps also that he had uttered threats of resistance? Such a solemn curse would be regarded as an act of blasphemy, not only against the king, but primarily against God, Whose authorized representative the king was (comp. Exodus 22:28). But blasphemy against God was to be punished by stoning (Deuteronomy 13:10; 17:5).

As in all such cases, the punishment was immediately carried out, and apparently in Naboth's own vineyard, (Compare 1 Kings 21:19; 2 Kings 9:25,26.) where the witnesses would, according to our suggestion, have located the "blasphemy" spoken in reply to the request of the king. It is not necessary to suppose (as some commentators have done) that the property of a man stoned for such a crime was treated like that of one on whom the ban was pronounced, since in that case it would have been laid waste, not given to the king (Deuteronomy 13:16). But it was quite natural that the property of one who had been found guilty of high treason should be forfeited to the Crown. And so, when the elders of Jezreel informed Jezebel that Naboth was stoned, she could tell her royal husband to go and take possession of the vineyard that had been refused him for purchase by "the Jezreelite," since Naboth was dead.

There was bitter as well as haughty irony in the words of Jezebel, as if she had felt herself a queen whose wishes and commands were above all law, human or Divine, and could not be resisted by God or man (ver. 15). The text gives no indication that she had informed Ahab of the manner of Naboth's death; nor did the king make inquiry. But there was far more terrible irony of fact in what followed the words of Jezebel. On receiving the welcome tidings of Naboth's death, Ahab "rose up" to go and take possession of the coveted vineyard, — perhaps the very day after the judicial murder (comp. 2 Kings 9:26). But on that day Jehovah had bidden Elijah arise and meet Ahab with the Divine message, just as the king thought himself in secure possession of the fruit of his crime, as if there were no living God in Israel. We can picture to ourselves the scene. Ahab has come in his chariot from Samaria, apparently attended by his chief officers (2 Kings 9:25). Before entering his palace at Jezreel — on the way to it — he has reached the vineyard of Naboth. He is surveying with satisfaction his new possession, perhaps giving directions how it should be transformed into "a garden," when of a sudden there stands before him not one of the sons of the prophets, nor an ordinary seer, but the terrible figure of the Gileadite, with his burning eyes, clad in the rough cloak of black camel's hair, girt about with a leathern girdle. It must have recalled to Ahab his first apparition in the midst of Samaria, when the prophet had announced to his startled hearers the three years' drought, and then so suddenly and tracelessly vanished from sight.

And the last time he met the prophet had been on Mount Carmel; the last glimpse had been when through the blinding rain he saw the dark figure running before his chariot to the very gate of Jezreel, as if he had come to herald the triumph of Jehovah, and to bring back a new God-devoted king. That had been a weird sight of the prophet, through the storm; and it had been a short dim dream of Ahab's to make the scene on Mount Carmel a reality in Israel. With Jezebel came back to him the evil spirit of his "madness;" nay, it had even sought, or consented to, the destruction of him who but yesterday had visibly brought God's fire on the broken altar, and God's rain on the parched land.

And now he stood once more before him — Ahab knew only too well why. It was for briefest but unmistakable message. Its first sentence swept away all self-deception. It had not been Jezebel but Ahab who had killed. And now he had taken possession, as if there were not Jehovah in heaven, nor yet the eternal reflection of His Being, and the permanent echo of His speaking, in right and truth upon earth. Having thus not only wakened the conscience of Ahab, but vindicated the authority of Him in Whose Name he spoke, the next sentence of Elijah's message announced stern, strict, even literal retribution. The retort of Ahab we regard as a childish lament to the effect that Elijah, who had always been his personal enemy, had now at last "found him" in some actual sin, on which he might invoke Divine punishment.

It was an admission, indeed, in that moment of surprise, of his guilt and apprehension of the Divine punishment announced. But it conjoined with it this — if not in excuse, yet as a counter-charge — that Elijah was his personal enemy, and had lain in wait for the occasion to call down Divine judgment upon him. It was against this attempt to make it a merely personal controversy that Elijah's answer was directed (ver. 20). "I have found (not 'thee'), because thou hast sold thyself to work evil in the sight of Jehovah." What the prophet had spoken was not the outcome of personal enmity, nor was what had occurred the result of a sudden temptation or rash mood of the king, but of the whole direction of life which Ahab had deliberately chosen. And in this two elements were closely marked: that he had sold himself as a slave (Romans 7:14), so that he had no longer freedom of action, but had, as it were, to obey his master's behests; and that he had so sold himself, consciously or unconsciously, "to do the evil in the sight of Jehovah."

Accordingly, the judgment which Elijah announced was not merely personal to Ahab, as what he said about the dogs licking his blood; but it also struck his dynasty and doomed it to extermination for this twofold reason: "on account of the wrath which thou hast caused to go forth, and hast made Israel to sin." On the other hand, this general judgment should not take the place of personal punishment upon the doers of such a crime as the judicial murder of Naboth.

The dogs would "eat Jezebel at the wall of Jezreel," while a similar fate would overtake all the posterity of Ahab in the city (viz., of Samaria) or in the field. These must be regarded as personal judgments denounced on personal sins. This is also indicated by the intercalated remarks of the writer of the narrative (in verses 25, 26). But the actual punishment might be averted or modified by personal repentance, although not as regarded that pronounced on the national guilt in which the rule of Ahab had involved Israel.

If evidence of the truth of this narrative — and, as connected with it, of this whole history — were required, what is told in conclusion would furnish it. For a legendary story would not have represented Ahab as repenting and yet not renouncing his former courses. But this also is true to life. As formerly what he witnessed on Carmel, so now the words of Elijah went straight to Ahab's heart. He no longer disguised the truth from himself, nor sought to divert his mind by thoughts of personal animosity on the part of the prophet. It was against Jehovah that he had sinned, and before Jehovah he humbled himself. As a mourner he rent his clothes; as a penitent he wore sackcloth; as guilty he fasted; and as one staggering under a heavy load of grief and sin, he walked softly.

And all this publicly — in the sight of all men. It was fitting, if we may venture on the expression, and in accordance with God's previous declaration of judgment, that the living God Who had seen and avenged the crime done in secret should also acknowledge the repentance shown in public. Accordingly the word of Jehovah came once more to Elijah to declare that the personal repentance of the personal sin had brought remission of the personal punishment, though not of that denounced on the dynasty. The visible judgment, by which all were to perceive the retribution of God's justice, was delayed to the time of his son, and would have been delayed still further had he shown like repentance. But only delayed — for retribution must follow such open sin. And so the remembrance of it was kept up; and even this, in merciful warning to Ahab's son. But when the dogs licked up the blood of Ahab, as they washed the chariot stained with his gore, they recalled the yet unfulfilled judgment that hung like a dark cloud over the house of Ahab (1 Kings 22:38). But this was in Samaria, not in Jezreel, nor in the portion of Naboth, for, as the prophet had foretold, God brought not "the evil" itself, only its warning remembrance, in the days of Ahab. But on Jezebel would it descend with the terrible reality of a literal fulfillment.

CHAPTER 5 — AHAB AND AHAZIAH, (EIGHTH AND NINTH) KINGS OF ISRAEL. — JEHOSHAPHAT, (FOURTH) KING OF JUDAH. — THE VISIT OF JEHOSHAPHAT TO AHAB — THE PROJECTED EXPEDITION AGAINST RAMOTH-GILEAD — FLATTERING PREDICTIONS OF FALSE PROPHETS — MICAIAH — THE BATTLE OF RAMOTH-GILEAD — DEATH OF AHAB.

(1 KINGS 22; 2 CHRONICLES 18)

THE events told in the previous chapter were followed by a period of rest. Religiously, it might be described as one of approximation to the worship of Jehovah. But it might prove only the more dangerous on that account, as being the outcome of an attempted compromise where compromise was impossible. Evidence of this occurs to us alike from the summons and the bearing of those four hundred prophets whom Ahab called together, when requested by Jehoshaphat to inquire at "the word of Jehovah" as to the projected expedition against Ramoth-Gilead. Those four hundred could not have been "prophets of Baal," since the latter had been destroyed on Mount Carmel. Their bearing also widely differs from that of the prophets of Baal. Nor could they have been the four hundred "prophets of Asherah" [Astarte] — specially supported by Jezebel — who had been summoned to (1 Kings 18:19), but did not appear at, the decisive contest on Carmel (vers. 22, 26, 40). For, first, they were now summoned as professedly bringing "the word of Jehovah," that is, as prophesying in His Name.

Further, although they spoke at first of, Adonai (the Lord, ver. 6), yet afterwards (vers. 11, 12)they professed to announce what "Jehovah" would do, while Zedekiah their leader expressly referred to "the Spirit of Jehovah" as having gone from himself to Micaiah (ver. 24).

On the other hand, they must not be regarded as either true "prophets of Jehovah," or as "sons of the prophets." For from the first Jehoshaphat appears unwilling to recognize their authority. They were evidently not those whose guiding message he had originally wished (ver. 5), and in contrast to them he continued to ask for "a prophet of Jehovah" (ver. 7), upon which Ahab mentioned Micaiah (not one of those four hundred prophets) as one by whom "to inquire of Jehovah." Lastly, the four hundred false prophets are afterwards expressly designated, first, by the evil spirit, and then by Micaiah, not as those of Jehovah, but as those of Ahab (vers. 22, 23).

These considerations lead us to characterize the religious condition prevailing at the time as a debasement of the worship of Jehovah. Apparently these prophets professed to bring the word of Jehovah: yet they were only the lying prophets of Ahab. It seems not unlikely that Ahab may have restored the ancient rites instituted by Jeroboam, when Jehovah was professedly worshipped under the symbol of the golden calf that had brought Israel out of Egypt. This transformation of the religion of Israel has been fully described in another place. Such a form of worship would have the twofold recommendation, that, while it seemed a return from the service of Baal to that of Jehovah, it still left to Ahab, as king, the office and control of chief pontiff of the new religion (comp. 1 Kings 12:32, 33).

Indeed, it may have been in this sense also that the four hundred prophets were designated those of Ahab, just as they of Astarte may have been called those of Jezebel, because in her character as queen she was their high-priestess. And if these prophets were really priests of the worship originally instituted by Jeroboam, and now restored, it is only natural to suppose that they may have been formed into a prophetic association, after the mode and in imitation of the institution of the "sons of the prophets." Whether any connection between the two really existed at the time can scarcely be determined, although the angry speech of Zedekiah (ver. 24), the leader of the prophets of Ahab, seems to imply it.

And we can readily believe that in those degenerate days many of the "sons of the prophets" — perhaps even an association of them — may have lent themselves to this spurious worship of Jehovah. We can now realize the scene enacted before Ahab and Jehoshaphat. It is related in almost identical terms in the Books of Kings and of Chronicles (2 Chronicles 18:2-34). In the latter it is introduced, by an account of the circumstances which led up to the ill-fated expedition against Syria. We remember that eight or nine years previously, Jehoram, the son of Jehoshaphat, then a youth of about fifteen or sixteen, had been married to Athaliah, the daughter of Ahab and Jezebel.

So far as we know, the two monarchs had not personally met after that event. But when Israel, after the defeat of Ben-hadad, enjoyed a long period of peace, while Judah was in an equally prosperous condition (2 Chronicles 18:1), it was both natural and easy for the two monarchs whose families and kingdoms were so closely connected to arrange a personal interview. We may conjecture that the proposal had come from Ahab, nor are we probably mistaken in supposing that in this the Israelitish king had the scheme of an alliance against Syria in his mind. At any rate this would accord with that systematic intriguing and desire to form alliances which we have repeatedly noticed as characteristic of Ahab.

Jehoshaphat and his retinue were right royally received and entertained at Samaria. It was, surely, a strange thing to see a Davidic king of Judah on a visit to the capital of the rebel provinces, yet not more strange than that one of the decided religiousness of Jehoshaphat should consort with an Ahab. The consequences appeared only too soon. The Book of Chronicles uses the expression that Ahab "enticed" Jehoshaphat (2 Chronicles 18:2), while the Book of Kings only relates the circumstances that led to the formal alliance between them. Similarly we are not quite sure whether this "enticement" had preceded or followed the appeal of Ahab to "his servants," recorded in the Book of Kings (22:3).

But in all likelihood Ahab, who may have planned everything with a view to the project he had at heart, may have availed himself of the presence of all his chieftains to do honor to the king of Judah, to bring before them on some public occasion — perhaps at a banquet — the great grievance which Israel had against Syria. If our conjecture be correct, it would account both for Jehoshaphat's immediate and strange consent, and then for his hesitation and desire to ascertain the will of God in the matter.

The appeal which Ahab made, in the first place to his own officers, was about Ramoth-Gilead. Situated on the eastern bank of the Jordan — perhaps represented by the modern Es-Salt, and in that case pitched on a mountain-spur which far overlooks the country — it was a threatening outpost for Syria to occupy, whence they might not only watch Israel, but swoop across Jordan and up the valley to Jezreel, before even certain information of their advance could be brought to Israelitish headquarters. This city Ben-hadad had, under one or another pretext, not given up to Ahab, as by his treaty he had bound himself to do (1 Kings 20:34). We cannot wonder that Ahab should have desired to regain a place so important, and which, while in the possession of Syria, was a constant menace to him. But he should have remembered not only that the real blame rested with himself, but what the prophet had predicted as the punishment of his guilty folly in allowing Ben-hadad to escape (1 Kings 20:42). Accordingly he should not have taken such an expedition in hand without some express warrant from God. We are not told how the appeal to their patriotism was received by the officers of Ahab, but it was responded to by Jehoshaphat, to whom Ahab next addressed himself, in terms which sound terribly ominous, as we recall the word of the LORD in regard to the fate of any expedition of Ahab against Syria.

But, as already noted, other thoughts soon came to the king of Judah. He must have felt that he himself would never have entered on such an undertaking without the sanction of Jehovah. And in the present instance this seemed doubly needful. Yet, except as the expression of Jehoshaphat's tardy repentance, the proposal which he made to Ahab to "inquire at the word of Jehovah," seemed singularly inconsistent. He had entered into an alliance as regarded this special campaign; perhaps his hearty concurrence had decided the officers of Ahab; at any rate, it was — as the event proved — too late now to withdraw, whatever the word of Jehovah might be. In truth, it was only what may always be expected when those who serve and love the LORD allow themselves to be entangled in alliances with ungodly men, where one step leads to another, and one inconsistency involves the next, till at last we recoil when it is too late to withdraw, and the only thing consistent is to be inconsistent in owning God where His will can no longer be obeyed. But even this is good, for it is the first step to repentance. And though we must suffer the punishment of our folly, yet God will hear a Jehoshaphat in the disastrous battle, when he crieth to Him, and give gracious deliverance (2 Chronicles 18:31).

We are "in the void place in the entrance of the gate of Samaria" (1 Kings 22:10) — that is, in the open square before the gate. Two thrones have been set for the two kings, who appear arrayed in their royal robes. Before them is gathered the motley multitude of prophets.

Ahab puts the question, whether or not he (in Chron. "we") should go up to Ramoth-Gilead. And now the prophets — concerning whom we must not forget that they knew what saying of theirs would be "good" in the king's ears (1 Kings 22:13) — sway about in frenzied excitement. Here, there, everywhere rises the cry, "Go up, for the LORD will give it into the hand of the king." It was not only the unanimity of these four hundred men, but, no doubt, their appearance and bearing which made Jehoshaphat inquire whether, besides all these, there was not a prophet of Jehovah to be found in Samaria. From the answer of Ahab when mentioning the name of Micaiah: "I hate him, for he does not prophecy concerning me good, but only evil," and from the later direction to "one of the chamberlains," it has been inferred that Micaiah had lately been "prophesying" evil to the king — whether in answer to his inquiry, or directly commissioned of God — and that the prophet was at that moment a prisoner of Ahab. The latter point, indeed, seems quite established by verse 26, where Micaiah is ordered to be "taken back," or "returned" to custody.

Some points of interest for the understanding of this history may here be noted. It appears that the prophets of God delivered many more "prophecies" than are recorded in the Scriptures — and more especially, that Ahab was not left without warning. Further, it casts light on the true and the false prophets, that the latter were wont to declare what was pleasing to their employers ("good"); while the prophets of God faithfully delivered their message, whatever the consequences might be. And, lastly, it appears that the king regarded such message as the outcome of personal enmity towards himself. This is most instructive, as showing that men like Ahab took a purely heathen view of prophetism. As Balak had sought to influence Balaam, apparently in the belief that the soothsayer had power with God, and could at will direct or control His action, so Ahab imagined that what he called "good" or "evil" in the message was the result of either personal friendship or enmity. It was against this that Jehoshaphat protested (ver. 8, last clause), and not merely against the notion that Micaiah hated the king. Ahab yielded to Jehoshaphat, but the view which he had in advance presented of the motives and conduct of Micaiah must have blunted the edge of his words, alike to Ahab and to the people.

This explains the otherwise strange fact that his emphatic warning remained so entirely unheeded. It was, as we imagine, during the interval while Micaiah was being brought from his prison, that the leader of the false prophets indulged in a symbolical action. We can scarcely be mistaken in supposing that when Zedekiah rushed forward holding against his forehead two pointed pieces of iron, and exclaiming: "With these shalt thou push the Syrians, until they be consumed," he referred to the Divine promise by Moses in regard to Joseph (Deuteronomy 33:17).

"His horns, the horns of buffaloes: with them shall he push down the nations."

Here was the kingdom of Ephraim — the son of Joseph — and Ahab was the representative of that promise which was now about to have its fulfillment. Deeply interesting as this reference is, as showing the mixture of Old Testament religion and acknowledgment of God which, as we have seen, was combined in these prophets with that which was false, and opposed to Jehovah, it is also instructive as implying that the Book of Deuteronomy was not only existent at the time this history was originally recorded, but that its sayings — specially so far as they referred to Israel — must have thoroughly permeated the people.

If, as seems likely, the object of Zedekiah's symbolic action had been to impress on all present the certainty of his prediction, the arrival of Micaiah speedily changed the aspect of things. On the way, the official charged with bringing him from the prison had told Micaiah of the unanimous prediction of success by the four hundred prophets, and asked him to confirm it. We do not wonder at the emphatic reply which this elicited. If the prophetic office was to fulfill its Divine object, or, indeed, to be continued in Israel, it was needful to state distinctly that the prophet would, without fear or favor, simply deliver the message of Jehovah. And this, rather than irony, seems to have been also the reason why, in answer to Ahab's inquiry, Micaiah at first spoke in the same terms as the false prophets. Such a mechanical outward conformity to them could not have been misunderstood. It meant that Ahab did not really wish to have a message from Jehovah; that he had chosen his own path and his own guides in it. Ahab evidently understood him so, and, rendered bold by the scene which had been enacted, and by the apparent unwillingness, or, it might be, inability of Micaiah to interpose, he adjured him to speak only the truth in the name of Jehovah. Thus challenged, Micaiah could no longer hesitate. Indeed, after his first apparent confirmation of what the prophets had declared, as it were in chorus, his message would come with the more startling effect. We may also mark that it affords us yet further insight into the nature and origin of prophecy. When Micaiah said: "I saw all Israel scattered on the mountains, as sheep that have no shepherd; and Jehovah said, These have no masters, let them return every man to his house in peace," — the words represent, evidently, a vision; and that, not of something literally real, but as we might term it a parabolic vision.

It is in the same manner that we regard the next part of Micaiah's message. It must not be understood as declaring what really took place in heaven, but as a vision in which the prophet saw before him, as in a parable, the explanation and the higher Divine meaning of the scene that had just been enacted before the two kings, and the final sequence of it which he had just announced.

The points to be kept in view are: that the final judgment which would come to Ahab in his self-chosen campaign against Syria was of the LORD; nay, that the seductive influence of the prophets was part of the Divine judgment, and therefore of the Divine appointment — at least, in its permissive sense. Yet in all this Ahab's destruction would come through his own sin: being led to his ruin by those false prophets whom he had chosen, and by his unwillingness to hear the word of Jehovah, which he regarded as the outcome of personal hostility. Thus his destruction would be really due to his deliberate choice of a course in direct opposition to the Will of God. For these two elements are always combined in manner to us inexplicable, yet very really: the appointment of God and the free choice of man. And it was all the more necessary for Micaiah to state all this fully and fearlessly, since his first message had been interrupted by the peevish and false complaint of Ahab to Jehoshaphat, that it had happened as he had expected, since Micaiah would never prophesy aught but evil of him.

Thus viewed, there is a peculiar depth of meaning and a grandeur in the parabolic vision which Micaiah so vividly described. It would have carried conviction to all, if they had been open to it. The scene enacted in the open market-place of Samaria had its counterpart — its true spiritual reflex — in the great court of heaven. Instead of Ahab sitting on his throne surrounded by his own flattering prophets, and anticipating his victorious march upon Ramoth-Gilead, it was Jehovah, the God of truth, surrounded by all His host, who sat on His judgment-seat decreeing the destruction of the infatuated king. But as Ahab shall prepare his own destruction, so shall he also compass it. And this is quite in accordance with all God's dealings in mercy and judgment with Ahab. Ahab has disowned the LORD; he has now surrounded himself by these 400 prophets of falsehood to encourage himself and those with him in his undertaking. Be it, as he has chosen for himself; these prophets shall prophesy — yea, lies — and he will believe their smooth prophecy to the disregard of the Divine Will and warning, and so perish in his folly and rebellion. All this was so truthfully presented in the parabolic vision, and so pictorially set before those assembled, that at least Zedekiah, the leader of the false prophets, could have no doubt in the matter. However we may explain his ebullition of personal resentment in striking Micaiah, whether as a punishment or to put upon him a public affront, we can have no difficulty in understanding his words (ver. 24). If they sounded like a satirical reproof of Micaiah's presumption in arrogating to himself that he alone had really the Spirit of Jehovah, while all the others had not that inspiration — as if the Spirit of Jehovah had gone from him to Micaiah — they also convey to us yet another meaning. Zedekiah must have known that he had not a message from Jehovah, and he had imagined that Micaiah's prophecy would be as self-originated as had been his own.

But the words which he heard left on him no doubt that Micaiah had truly spoken from Jehovah, and the resentment at feeling that this was so, and that Micaiah, not himself, was the organ chosen by God, awakened within him feelings which found expression in angry words and still angrier deed. It was a spirit like that of Simon Magus — only intensified and manifested in manner congruous to Old Testament times. And this also explains the reply of Micaiah, which was directed against the words of Zedekiah. He should "see," quite perceive, the real difference between the true and the false prophet, when he would experience its results. Then, when his prediction would not only remain unfulfilled, but appear by the side of the warning of the true prophet, as having been false and misleading, would he in utter disgrace seek to hide himself from the sight of all men, and to escape that punishment of his crime which the survivors from the battle would no doubt inflict.

Not a few in that assembly must have understood the real meaning of the words of Zedekiah. But the majority would prefer to give them an interpretation more consonant with their mood, or at least more convenient. It might seem to them — to adopt the language of many among ourselves when inconvenient truth is in question — that the whole matter had now degenerated into a wrangle between opposing and rival theologians. At any rate, the time for all such talk had passed, and that for action come. Ramoth-Gilead was theirs; truly and fairly, by the law of God and of man, let theologians say what they pleased in exaltation of their respective schools and dogmas. And the two kings were united in an alliance against the Syrians that could not be unsuccessful: all was propitious, let them go up — make a sudden raid upon the stronghold, and take what was their own. And to mark how deeply he resented, and was able to punish what he regarded as an act of rebellion, Ahab ordered Micaiah to be taken back to the custody of Amon, the governor of the city. With him the name of Joash, the king's son, perhaps only a royal prince, was combined, probably in order to indicate that Micaiah was a state prisoner. And as such he was to be treated with special severity.

Thus far Ahab possessed the requisite power; but when he added: "Until I come in peace," he uttered a distinct challenge. To this, by whomsoever made — be he prince or private person, and howsoever made, whether in public or in private, or even in inward opposition to God's revealed truth, there is only this answer: "He that sitteth in the heavens shall laugh; the Lord shall have them in derision." But Micaiah could not allow it to pass unnoticed. The honor of Jehovah, Whose prophet he was, required the reply: "If thou comest at all in peace, Jehovah hath not spoken by me." And then, turning to the multitude around, he summoned them as witnesses between himself and the king.

We are not told what impression the scene had made upon Jehoshaphat. But we cannot help feeling that, in spite of his boastful language, it must have had a deep effect even upon Ahab. The expedition against Ramoth-Gilead would naturally follow as soon as possible after the popular assembly in Samaria. From the circumstance, that Jehu the prophet of the LORD delivered the Divine reproof against the alliance of Jehoshaphat with Ahab only after the return of the former from the Syrian campaign (2 Chronicles 19), we are inclined to infer that the king of Judah had not gone back to his own dominions before the joint march upon Ramoth-Gilead.

With this accords another impression derived from the narrative. The whole account of the battle, the apparently very subordinate part which Jehoshaphat played in it, as well as the absence of any reference to the army of Judah, and the solitary notice that Jehoshaphat returned to Jerusalem in peace (2 Chronicles 19:1), without any reference to his people — all convey the impression that Jehoshaphat had, without returning to Jerusalem, merely summoned a small Judaean contingent, so that his presence and aid — if known at all to the Syrians — were regarded as a very secondary element in the campaign. And when we compare this with the language of Jehoshaphat on entering into alliance with Ahab (1 Kings 22:4), and before he had heard the words of Micaiah, we feel that the contrast between his promises and performance must have been due to the prophetic warning which he had heard.

And as regards Ahab and his people we have similar indications of inward misgivings. It was the common practice for kings and leaders to go into battle in full array (comp. 2 Samuel 1:10).

When Ahab, therefore, made the strange proposal that Jehoshaphat alone should go in his royal robes, while he disguised himself, this must have been caused by apprehension of the Divinely threatened judgment, which after his usual manner he hoped to foil by astuteness. And if it be asked why in such case Jehoshaphat did not also disguise himself, the obvious answer is, that the Divine message had not threatened death to the king of Judah, and that, if both monarchs had so disguised themselves, it would have been virtually an announcement to their followers that they expected defeat, and the fulfillment of Micaiah's prophecy.

This is one side of the picture; the other is that presented from the Syrian camp. The military organization, introduced in the former campaign (1 Kings 20:24), now proved its efficiency. The "thirty and two captains" who commanded "the chariots" evidently formed the first line of attack. To them Ben-hadad gave special orders to direct their movements exclusively against the king of Israel, in the hope that, with his capture or death, alike the battle and the campaign would be ended.

The disguise of Ahab had almost defeated this plan. For when the Syrians pressed around the only chariot which bore one in royal apparel, in the belief that they fought with Ahab — and this also seems to imply that they were not aware of the presence of the king of Judah — Jehoshaphat "cried out," on which the Syrians, recognizing that it was not the voice of Ahab, desisted from the pursuit. It is impossible to determine whether Jehoshaphat had appealed to his pursuers, or called for the support of his men.

But the fact itself is of sufficient importance to be recorded alike in the Book of Kings and in that of Chronicles (2 Chronicles 18:31) and in precisely the same terms. But the writer of the Book of Chronicles, who tells this history from the standpoint of Judah, as in the Book of Kings it is related from that of Israel, adds that the providential deliverance which Jehoshaphat experienced was from Jehovah. It is scarcely necessary to add that this reflection is not in any way inconsistent with the briefer Israelitish record, nor implies divergent sources of information.

But the disguise of Ahab, so far from frustrating the judgment predicted, only served the more clearly to show the Divine agency in his destruction. As the battle continued, a man, "drew a bow in his simplicity" — that is, without taking aim at any definite person — when the arrow struck the king of Israel "between the joints and the breastplate," that is, where the cuirass which covered the breast met the jointed armor that protected the lower part of the body. Such a wound would, of necessity, be mortal, and the king directed the driver of the chariot to take him away from the fight. But the Syrians were unaware that the king of Israel had received his fatal wound. Thicker and hotter grew the fight, and the command of Ahab could not be obeyed. And all day long had he to be stayed in his chariot while his life was slowly ebbing away. It was a ghastly spectacle, the disguised king, mortally struck despite his disguise, now held up in his chariot, to continue against his will in the battle. Rarely has history so visibly and in every detail taught its Divine lessons. The sun was going down, and his slanting rays fell on the dying Ahab — more royal now than in his life. Presently the sound of battle was stilled, and the rest of darkness fell on the combatants.

But as the tidings spread of the death of their king, the people must have recalled the prophecy of Micaiah. And the very remembrance of it led to its literal fulfillment. For through the host ran the proclamation which scattered them as sheep that have not a shepherd: "Every man to his city, and every man to his own country."

While one prophecy was thus translated into fact, the knell of yet another was sounding in the hearing of the house of Ahab, had they but had ears to hear it. Through the darkness speeded the chariot that bore the dead body of Ahab, lying on its bloody bed. They reached Samaria, and there they buried their king. But the chariot full of his gore they took outside, to wash in the pool by the city. And, horrible to behold, in the pale moonlight the wild masterless dogs, which in the East prowl at night about the city-walls, lapped up the water mingled with gore which flowed out of the blood-dyed chariot as they washed it. And stranger and still more horrible, the red flood in large eddying circles mingled with the waters of the pool — that pool where "the harlots washed," — no doubt where Jezebel's priestesses of Astarte, the ministers of the worship of debauchery, nightly performed their semi-religious ablutions in that sacred fishpond, which here, as in all other places where the Syrian Astarte was worshipped, had been constructed and consecrated to the goddess.

What a coincidence, and how full of deepest significance! But did Ahab's successor not think of the blood of Naboth, and the curse which rested on Ahab, not only as the murderer of Naboth, but as he who had seduced Israel into idolatry and all sin? And did Jezebel not see in this red flood, in which her priestesses of the worship of impurity performed their sacred ablutions, a warning token of that judgment which was gathering, like a dark cloud, over her own head?

But as yet these judgments of the LORD slumbered. "So Ahab slept with his fathers, and Ahaziah his son reigned in his stead."

CHAPTER 6 — JEHOSHAPHAT, (FOURTH) KING OF JUDAH — THE REPROOF AND PROPHEY OF — JEHU — RESUMPTION OF THE REFORMATION IN JUDAH — INSTITUTION OF JUDGES AND OF A SUPREME COURT IN JERUSALEM — INCURSION OF THE MOABITES AND THEIR CONFEDERATES — NATIONAL FAST AND THE PRAYER OF THE KING — PROPHECY OF VICTORY — THE MARCH TO TEKOA — DESTRUCTION OF THE ENEMY — THE VALLEY OF BERAKHAH — RETURN TO JERUSALEM AND TO THE TEMPLE.

(2 CHRONICLES 19, 20:1-34)

BEFORE continuing the history of Israel, we turn aside to complete that of Jehoshaphat, king of Judah. It will be remembered that he had succeeded his father Asa in the fourth year of King Ahab's reign.

At that time Jehoshaphat was thirty-five years old; and as his reign lasted for twenty-five years (1 Kings 22:42; 2 Chronicles 20:31), it follows that he died at the age of sixty, which, when we consider the annals of the royal houses of Judah and Israel, must be considered a protracted life. A few other particulars are given us connected with Jehoshaphat's accession. Thus we learn that his mother's name was Azubhah, the daughter of Shilchi. Again, we gather how energetically he took in hand at the beginning of his reign the religious reformation commenced by his father Asa.

But the want of true sympathy on the part of his subjects prevented the full success of his measures. The idol-groves and heights, dedicated to Baal and Astarte, were indeed destroyed (2 Chronicles 17:6), but it was found impossible to abolish the corrupt worship of Jehovah celebrated on "the high places" (1 Kings 22:43; 2 Chronicles 20:33). Beyond these brief notices, the narrative in the Book of Kings only indicates that at that period there was no king in Edom, but that the country was ruled by a governor. This is manifestly stated in order to explain how the maritime expedition to Ophir could have been undertaken without provoking resistance on the part of Edom, in whose territory Ezion-Geber was situate. But the sacred text affords no information to account for this state of matters in Edom.

The scanty details about the reign of Jehoshaphat furnished in the Book of Kings — which deals mainly with the history of the northern kingdom — are supplemented in the Book of Chronicles. The compilers of the latter had evidently before them, amongst other sources of information, a prophetic history of that reign: "The Chronicles [or, the words] of Jehu, the son of Hanani, which are inserted in the book of the Kings of Israel" (2 Chronicles 20:34, comp. 1 Kings 22:45).

It was this Jehu, who, on the return of Jehoshaphat from the expedition against Ramoth-Gilead, announced to the king the Divine displeasure. Better than any other would he be acquainted with the spiritual declension in the northern kingdom, since it was he who had been sent to pronounce on Baasha, king of Israel, the judgment that should overtake him and his people for their apostasy (1 Kings 16:1, etc.). And who so fit to speak fearlessly to Jehoshaphat as the son of him who had formerly suffered imprisonment at the hands of Asa, the father of Jehoshaphat, for faithfully delivering his commission from God (2 Chronicles

16:7-10)? The message which he now brought was intended to point out the incongruity of Jehoshaphat's alliance with Ahab.

The punishment which the prophet announced as its sequence, came when the king experienced the effects of that other unholy alliance, in which Ammon and Moab combined against Judah (2 Chronicles 20). Again had Jehoshaphat to learn in the destruction of his fleet at Ezion-Geber (2 Chronicles 20:37) that undertakings, however well-planned and apparently unattended by outward danger, can only end in disappointment and failure, when they who are the children of God combine with those who walk in the ways of sin.

But in Jehoshaphat the warning of the prophet wrought that godly repentance which has not to be repented of Jehu had declared how God, in His condescension, acknowledged that "nevertheless there are good things found in thee" — and this, not merely as regarded his public acts in the abolition of open idolatry in his country, but also that personal piety which showed itself in preparing his own heart to seek after God. And now the sense of his late inconsistency led him all the more earnestly to show that he did not regard the religious condition of his late allies as a light matter. Once again he took in hand the religious reformation begun at the commencement of his reign. (2 Chronicles 17:7-10)

The account of the present movement is the more interesting that it furnishes proof of the existence of the Book of Deuteronomy at that time, long before the memoirs were written on which the Books of Chronicles are based. For, as we shall presently see, there are here constant references to the legislation in the Book of Deuteronomy, and that not pointedly and with a show of emphasis — such as we would have expected if Deuteronomy had been only lately invented or introduced — but in a manner which indicates a long admitted authority, so that its legislation had permeated the people, and its principles required only to be alluded to as something universally acknowledged, — not vindicated as something recently introduced. This line of argument, bringing out the undesigned evidences of the antiquity of the Mosaic legislation, seems to us to possess far more convincing force than much of the specious reasoning on the other side, which has of late been so confidently advanced. And while on this ground the reader should be warned against hastily adopting conclusions inconsistent with the assured truth of the Divine Word, he should also be encouraged to mark, in careful study, the many passages containing undesigned references, which are only intelligible on the supposition, not only of the existence, but of the long and generally acknowledged authority of the Mosaic legislation.

The reformation initiated by Jehoshaphat was carried out by him personally. For this purpose he traversed the country from its southern boundary (Beer-sheba) to its northern (Mount Ephraim). His main object was to "bring back" the people "to Jehovah, the God of their fathers." Partly in attainment of this, and partly to render the reformation permanent, he revised the judicial arrangements of the country, in strict accordance with the Deuteronomic Law. For, according to he Divine appointment, the judges in Israel were not only intended to pronounce sentences and to decide cases, but to guide and direct the people on all questions, civil and religious, and so to prevent the commission of sin or crime. The account given of the work of Jehoshaphat embraces these three points: the appointment of Judges; the principle underlying their authority; and the rule for its exercise.

As regards the first of these, we remember that the appointment of judges had been first proposed by Jethro (Exodus 18:21, 22), and then carried out by Moses (Deuteronomy 1:13,etc.) Such judges were now appointed for every "fenced city." This, not only because these places were the most important in the land, but in order to protect the administration of justice, and in accordance with the fundamental law in Deuteronomy 16:18.

As regards the principle on which their authority rested, the judges were to bear in mind that they were the representatives of the Great Judge, Whose aid was accordingly promised them (2 Chronicles 19:6) — and this also in accordance with the Deuteronomic statement: "for the judgment is God's" (Deuteronomy 1:17). From this it follows, as the practical rule, that in the administration of justice they were to be influenced by the fear of Jehovah, and not by fear of, nor favor for, man. And here we mark once more the implied reference to Deuteronomy 1:16, 17; 16:18-20.

Besides these provincial judges, Jehoshaphat appointed in Jerusalem a tribunal of appeal consisting of priests, Levites, and the chiefs of clans. With this mixed tribunal rested the final decision in all matters concerning religion and worship (2 Chronicles 19:8: "for the judgment of Jehovah;" and ver. 11: "in all matters of Jehovah"), as well as in civil and criminal cases (ver. 8: "in strifes;" ver. 11: "all the king's matters"). Moreover, it was their duty to warn, advise, and instruct in all doubtful cases, whether criminal, civil, or ecclesiastical, in which they were applied to either by the inferior judges or the people. As president of this mixed commission, Amariah, the high-priest, was appointed for ecclesiastical, and Zebadiah, the chief of the tribe of Judah, for civil cases.

And now that came to pass which had been predicted by the prophet in punishment of the alliance with Ahab. Happily, it found the people prepared by the religious revival which had passed over the land. As we infer from the tenor of the whole narrative, the Moabites, the Ammonites, and "with them certain of the Meunites," made an unexpected raid "from beyond the Sea" — that is, the Dead Sea — "from Edom."

They could come swooping round the southern end of the Dead Sea, or passing over by the southern ford, just opposite Engedi, the ancient Hazazon-tamar — probably the oldest city in the world. The name Engedi, "the spring of the goat," is derived from the manner in which its fertilizing spring seems to leap in its descent. The older name, Hazazon-tamar — either "rows of palms," or "the cutting of the palm-trees" — originated from the palms which once grew there in great luxuriance. But the site is now desolate, and where once palms flourished, and the most precious wine of Judaea was grown, only naked terraces shelve up the mountain-side. The plain or rather slope is described as extending about a mile and a half from north to south, being bounded on either side by a Wady with perennial water. Engedi touches the outrunners of the mountains of Judah.

Several hundred feet up the slope, about a mile and a half from the shore of the Dead Sea, the little streamlet which has given the place its name, dashes down in thin but high cataracts. Below these falls, and in the center of the plain, are the ruins which mark the site of the ancient city. As in the time of Abraham the Assyrian hordes (Genesis 14), so now these marauding invaders, had swarmed across — scarcely an army, rather a multitude of wild nomads. Along the plain, up the slope to the crest of the mountain, through the wadys, they crowded. It seemed a countless host, as their wild war-shouts resounded from hill-top and valley, or their dark forms covered the heights, whence they gazed across the wilderness towards the rich and coveted cities of Judah. So it seemed to the terrified fugitives, who brought exaggerated tidings of their numbers to Jehoshaphat. And only a distance of fifteen hours separated these plundering tribes from Jerusalem. Not a moment was to be lost. The first measure was to invoke the aid of the LORD. A fast was proclaimed throughout Judah — a day of humiliation for national sins and of prayer in the time of their great need (comp. Judges 20:26; 1 Samuel 7:6; Joel 2:15). Jehoshaphat himself took his place in the most prominent part of the temple, "before the new court" — either one newly constructed, or else renovated, and probably intermediate between "the great" or outer court, and "the court of the priests" (comp. 2 Chronicles 4:9). If so, it probably represented what at a later period was known as "the court of the women," and Jehoshaphat stood on the height afterwards covered by the steps leading up to the court of the priests, where the Levites who conducted the musical part of the temple-services were stationed. There, within sight and hearing of all, like Solomon of old, and as a true king, he represented and guided his people in their act of national humiliation and prayer. Ordinarily prayer did not form part of the symbolical temple-services. The latter could only be performed by the God-appointed priesthood. This, even on the lower ground that had others been allowed to intrude into these services, it would soon have led to the introduction of heathen rites. And of this there were only too many instances in the history of Israel. Never, except on such solemn occasions, was the voice of public prayer heard in the Temple, and the king did not intrude, but acted right kingly, when he now spake in name and on behalf of his people.

There could not have been a prayer of more earnest or realizing faith than that of Jehoshaphat. It began by the acknowledgment of Jehovah as the true and living God (v. 6), and as the Covenant-God, Who in fulfillment of His promises had given them the land (v. 7). In virtue of this twofold fact, Israel had reared the sanctuary (v. 8), and consecrated alike the Temple and themselves by solemnly placing themselves in the keeping of God, to the disowning of all other help or deliverance (v. 9). To this invocation at the dedication of the Temple (2 Chronicles 6:28-30) a visible response had been made when the fire came from heaven to consume the sacrifice, and the glory of Jehovah filled the house (2 Chronicles 7:1). On this threefold ground the prayer of Jehoshaphat now proceeded. A season of sore strait had now come, and they made their solemn appeal to God. Israel was in the right as against their enemies, who had neither pretext in the past for their attack, nor yet justification for it in the present. Nay, they had come against the possession of God which He had given to His people. It was His cause; they had no might of their own, but their eyes were upon the LORD (vers. 10-12).

When the Church, or individual members of it, can so believe and so pray, deliverance is at hand. But yet another act of faith was necessary. Theirs had been the faith of expectancy and of worship; it must now be that of work. As Israel stood in prayer before Jehovah, His Spirit came upon one of the ministering Levites, Jahaziel, a descendant of Mattaniah, perhaps the same as Nethaniah, a son of Asaph (1 Chronicles 25:2, 12). The message which he delivered from the LORD corresponded to every part of the prayer which had been offered. It bade them dismiss all fears — not because there was not real danger, but because the battle was Jehovah's. On the morrow were they to go forth to meet the enemy. But "it is not for you [it is not yours=ye need not] to fight in this [battle]: place yourselves, stand still, and see the salvation of Jehovah with you" (vers. 15-17). And humbly, reverently, did king and people bend before the LORD in the worship of praise and believing expectancy.

Early next morning they prepared to obey the Divine direction. It was to be a battle such as had never been witnessed since Jericho had fallen at the blast of the trumpets of the LORD when His Ark compassed its walls. And they prepared for it in such manner as host going to battle had never done. In the morning, as Judah marched out of the gate of Jerusalem, the king addressed to his people only this one command: to have faith — faith in their God, and in the word sent by His prophets. Thus should they be established. Then "he advised the people," and with one accord they appointed for their avant-guard the sacred Temple-singers, robed in their "holy array," who were to chant, as if marching in triumphal procession, the well-known words of worship: "Praise Jehovah, for His mercy endureth for ever" (comp. 2 Chronicles 7:3, 6).

If never before an army had so marched to battle, never, even in the marvelous history of Israel, had such results been experienced. Above Engedi the chalk cliffs rise 2000 feet above the Dead Sea, although even that height is still 2000 feet below the watershed. We have now reached the barren and desolate wilderness, known as that of Judah, which stretches southward to the mountains of Hebron, and northward to Tekoa. Innumerable wadys and broad valleys stretch between mountain crests, often of fantastic shape. It is a pathless wilderness, seamed by rocky clefts and caves. There, just past the cave where David had been in hiding from Saul, up the cliff Hazziz — perhaps the modern El Husasah — had the foe swarmed, and then deployed through the broad wady which leads towards Tekoa. Here, "at the end of the gully," would Israel descry them, see their defeat, yet not have to do battle for the victory.

And as on that bright day the host of Israel looked towards the ascent from Engedi, they caught sight of the enemy. At that moment as by a preconcerted signal they began to sing and to praise the LORD. Then a strange scene ensued. It were an entire misunderstanding of what Scripture designates as the agency of God, to apply to angelic combatants the words: "Jehovah set liers in wait [ambushments] against the children of Ammon, Moab, and Mount Seir."

For God Himself does that which happens in His all-overruling Providence, even though it come to pass in the orderly succession of natural events. There was no need of summoning angel-hosts. It is not only quite conceivable, but best explains the after-event, that a tribe of Edomites, kindred but hostile to that which had joined Ammon and Moab in their raid, should have lain in ambush in one of the wadys, waiting till the main body of the combatants had passed, to fall on the rear-guard, or probably on the camp followers, the women and children, and the baggage. They would calculate that long before the men in advance could turn upon them in those narrow defiles, they would have escaped beyond the reach of pursuit. And it is equally conceivable that when the attack was made the main body of the Ammonites and Moabites may have regarded it as a piece of treachery preconcerted between the clan of Edomites who were with them, and the kindred clan that lay in ambush. All this is quite in accordance with what might still take place among the Bedouins of those regions. But, in such circumstances, the Ammonites and Moabites would naturally turn to attack their treacherous allies, and thus the first scene in the strange drama of this internecine battle would be enacted. Mutual distrust once awakened, and passions kindled, we can easily understand how "every one helped to destroy another" — the havoc being probably increased by the peculiar character of the country, which here abounds in steep precipices and sudden rocky heights and descents.

While this strange battle was proceeding, Judah had advanced, to the sound of hymns of praise, beyond Tekoa, far as the last watch-tower, where usually an outlook was kept over the wilderness, so that timely tidings might be brought of any sudden raid by the wild tribes of the East. As "they looked unto the multitude," which they had erst descried in the dim distance, there was "not an escaping," no hasty flight, as in such circumstances might have been expected, and it seemed as if only dead bodies were left strewing the ground. Possibly the Judaeans had, on reaching the height of Tekoa, caught sight of the host, and then lost it again when descending into the wady.

When, on ascending once more, they stood at the watch-tower, they would see what formerly had been "a. multitude," now only dead bodies, nor could they, from the conformation of the district, discern any fugitives. It now only remained for Judah to seize the spoil of the battle in which Jehovah had gained the victory.

For three days the removal of the spoil continued. On the fourth, the host of Judah gathered in a valley, to the north-west of Tekoa, which from the solemn thanksgiving there made received the name of "Berakhah," "blessing," in the sense of praise and thanksgiving. It is deeply interesting to find that after the lapse of so many centuries this memorial of Jehovah's deliverance and of Jehoshaphat's and Judah's solemn thanksgiving still continues. Many masters have since held possession of the land: Assyrian, Roman, Moslem, Christian, and Turk: but the old name of the valley of blessing remains in the modern name Bereikut.

And from "the valley of blessing" Jehoshaphat and his people returned, as in procession, to the Temple, there again to praise the LORD, Who had, as ever, been faithful to His promise. And this gratitude of a believing people is one of the most true and beautiful results of the religious revival which Judah had experienced. It almost sounds like heaven's antiphon to Jerusalem's praise, when we read that "the terror of Elo-him" was upon all the kingdoms of the lands round about Judah, and that "his God" gave Jehoshaphat "rest round about."

CHAPTER 7 — JEHOSHAPHAT, (FOURTH) KING OF JUDAH, AHAZIAH AND (JEHORAM) JORAM, (NINTH AND TENTH) KINGS OF ISRAEL — THE JOINT MARITIME EXPEDITION TO OPHIR — AHAZIAH'S REIGN AND ILLNESS — THE PROPOSED INQUIRY OF BAAL-ZEBUB — THE DIVINE MESSAGE BY ELIJAH — ATTEMPTS TO CAPTURE THE PROPHET, AND THEIR RESULT — ELIJAH APPEARS BEFORE THE KING — DEATH OF AHAZIAH — ACCESSION OF JORAM — THE ASCENT OF ELIJAH — ELISHA TAKES UP HIS MANTLE.

(1 KINGS 22:48-2 KINGS 2:14; 2 CHRONICLES 20:35-27).

JEHOSHAPHAT saw two sons of Ahab ascend the throne of Israel. Of these Ahaziah immediately succeeded Ahab. Of his brief reign, which lasted two years, only two events are known: the first connected probably with the beginning, the second with the close of it. We judge that the attempted maritime expedition in conjunction with Jehoshaphat took place at the beginning of Ahaziah's reign — first, because the fitting out and the destruction of that fleet, and then the proposal for another expedition must have occupied two summers, during which alone such undertakings could be attempted; secondly, because it seems unlikely that Jehoshaphat would have entered into any alliance with an Ahaziah, except at the beginning of his reign. There was that connected with the death of Ahab which might readily influence a weak character like Jehoshaphat to think with hopefulness of the son of his old ally, since his accession had been marked by such striking judgments. Even the circumstance that Jezebel no longer reigned might seem promising of good. And, in this respect, it is significant that, with the death of Ahab, the ministry of Elijah passed into a more public stage, and was followed by the even more prominent activity of Elisha.

We remember the notice (1 Kings 22:47) that "there was then no king in Edom." However we may account for this state of matters, it was favorable for the resumption of that maritime trade which had brought such wealth to Israel in the reign of King Solomon (1 Kings 9:26-28). And there were not a few things in the time of Jehoshaphat that might recall to a Judaean the early part of Solomon's reign. Perhaps such thoughts also contributed to the idea of a joint expedition on the part of Judah and Israel. But it was a mode of re-union as crude and ill-conceived as that which had led to the alliance by marriage between the two dynasties, the state visit of Jehoshaphat to Ahab, and its political outcome in the expedition against Ramoth-Gilead. The story is briefly told in the book of Kings (1 Kings 22:48, 49), and one part of it more circumstantially in the Second Book of Chronicles (20:35-37). In the Book of Kings two expeditions are spoken of — the one actually undertaken, the other only proposed. Accordingly, only the first of these is recorded in Chronicles. It consisted of so-called Tarshish ships, which were to fetch gold from Ophir, setting sail from the harbor of Ezion-Geber, on the Red Sea, a port probably on the coast of South-eastern Arabia, although the exact locality is in dispute.

The ill-success of such an alliance with the wicked son of Ahab was announced (2 Chronicles 20:37) by Eliezer, the son of Dodavah — a prophet not otherwise mentioned. His prediction was verified when the allied fleet either suffered shipwreck or was destroyed in a storm. Jehoshaphat took the warning. When Ahaziah invited him to undertake a second expedition, in which (as seems implied in 1 Kings 22:49) Israelitish mariners were to take a leading part — perhaps because the former failure was ascribed in the north to the unskillfulness of the Judaeans — the proposal was declined.

The brief and inglorious reign of Ahaziah, the son and successor of Ahab, is said to have begun in the seventeenth year of Jehoshaphat, king of Judah, and to have lasted two years (1 Kings 22:51). There is apparently here a slight chronological difficulty (comp. 2 Kings 3:1), which is, however, explained by the circumstance that, according to a well-known Jewish principle, the years of reign were reckoned from the month Nisan — the Passover-month, with which the ecclesiastical year began — so that a reign which extended beyond that month, for however brief a period, would be computed as one of two years. Thus we conclude that the reign of Ahaziah in reality lasted little more than one year. The one great political event of that period is very briefly indicated, although fraught with grave consequences. From the opening words of 2 Kings — which, as a book, should not have been separated from 1 Kings — we learn that the Moabites, who, since the time of David, had been tributary (2 Samuel 8:2), rebelled against Israel after the death of Ahab.

It was probably due to the ill-health of Ahaziah that an attempt was not made to reduce them to obedience. For the king of Israel had fallen through "the lattice," or between the grating, probably that which protected the opening of the window, in the upper chamber.

In any case it seems unlikely that the fall was into the court beneath, but probably on to the covered gallery which ran round the court, like our modern verandahs. The consequences of the fall were most serious, although not immediately fatal. We cannot fail to recognize the paramount influence of the queen-mother Jezebel, when we find Ahaziah applying to the oracle of Baal-zebub in Ekron to know whether he would recover of his disease. Baal, "lord," was the common name given by the Canaanites, the Phoenicians, the Syrians (Aramaeans), and Assyrians to their supreme deity. Markedly it is never applied to God in the Old Testament, or by believing Israelites. Among the Canaanites (in Palestine) and the Phoenicians the name was pronounced Ba'al (originally Ba'l); in Aramaean it was Be'el; in Babylono-Assyrian Bel (comp. Isaiah 46:1; Jeremiah 50:2).

The Baal-zebub, worshipped in Ekron — the modern Akir — and the most north-eastern of the five cities of the Philistines, E.N.E. from Jerusalem, was the Fly God, who was supposed to send or to avert the plague of flies. Like the great Apollos, who similarly sent and removed diseases, he was also consulted as an oracle.

We should be greatly mistaken if we were to regard the proposed inquiry on the part of Ahaziah as only a personal, or even as an ordinary national sin. The whole course of this history has taught us that the reign of Ahab formed a decisive epoch in the development of Israel. The period between the murder of Nadab, the son of Jeroboam, and the accession of Omri, the father of Ahab, was merely intermediate and preparatory, the throne being occupied by a succession of adventurers, whose rule was only transitory. With Omri, or rather with his son Ahab, a new period of firm and stable government began, and politically it was characterized by reconciliation and alliance with the neighboring kingdom of Judah, and with such foreign enterprises as have been noticed in the course of this narrative. But even more important was the religious crisis which marked the reign of Ahab. Although Jeroboam had separated himself and his people from the Divinely ordered service of Jehovah, as practiced in Jerusalem, he had, at least in profession, not renounced the national religion, but only worshipped the God of Israel under the symbol of the golden calf, and in places where worship was not lawful. But Ahab had introduced the service of Baal and of

Astarte as the religion of the State. True, this progress in apostasy was in reality only the logical sequence of the sin of Jeroboam, and hence is frequently mentioned in connection with it in the sacred narrative. Nevertheless, the difference between the two is marked, and with Ahab began that apostasy which led to the final destruction of the northern kingdom, and to the trackless dispersion of the ten tribes. In this light we can understand such exceptional mission and ministry as those of Elijah and Elisha, such a scene as the call to decision on Mount Carmel, and such an event as that about to be related.

Viewed in this manner, the royal embassy sent to Ekron to consult "the fly god," was really a challenge to Jehovah, whose prophet Elijah was in the land, and as such it must bring sharpest punishment to all involved in it. It was fitting, so to speak, that, in contrast to the messengers of the earthly king, Jehovah should commission His angel, and through him bid His prophet defeat the object of Ahaziah's mission.

As directed, Elijah went to meet the king's messengers. His first words exposed — not for the sake of Ahaziah, but for that of Israel — the real character of the act. Was it because there was no God in Israel that they went to inquire of the "fly god" of Ekron? But the authority of Jehovah would be vindicated. Guilty messengers of an apostate king, they were to bring back to him Jehovah's sentence of death. Whether or not they recognized the stern prophet of Jehovah, the impression which his sudden, startling appearance and his words made on them was such that they at once returned to Samaria, and bore to the astonished king the message they had received.

It is as difficult to believe that the king did not guess, as that his messengers had not recognized him who had spoken such words. The man with the (black) hairy garment, girt about with a leathern girdle, must have been a figure familiar to the memory, or at least to the imagination, of every one in Israel, although it may not have suited these messengers — true Orientals in this also — to name him to the king, just as by slightly altering the words of the prophet they now sought to cast the whole responsibility of the mission on Ahaziah. But when in answer to the king's further inquiry, they gave him the well-known description of the Tishbite, Ahaziah at once recognized the prophet, and prepared such measures as in his short-sightedness he supposed would meet what he regarded as the challenge of Elijah, or as would at least enable him to punish the daring prophet.

We repeat, it was to be a contest, and that a public one, between the power of Israel's king and the might of Jehovah. The first measure of the king was to send to Elijah "a captain of fifty with his fifty." There cannot be any reasonable doubt that this was with hostile intent. This appears not only from the words of the angel in verse 15, but from the simple facts of the case. For what other reason could Ahaziah have sent a military detachment of fifty under a captain, if not either to defeat some hostile force and constrain obedience, or else to execute some hostile act? The latter is indeed the most probable view, and it seems implied in the reassuring words which the angel afterwards spoke to Elijah (v. 15).

The military expedition had no difficulty in finding the prophet. He neither boastfully challenged, nor yet did he fearfully shrink from the approach of the armed men, but awaited them in his well-known place of abode on Mount Carmel. There is in one sense an almost ludicrous, and yet in another a most majestic contrast between the fifty soldiers and their captain, and the one unarmed man whom they had come to capture. Presently this contrast was, so to speak, reversed when, in answer to the royal command to Elijah, as delivered by the captain, the prophet appealed to his King, and thus clearly stated the terms of the challenge between the two, whose commission the captain and he respectively bore. "And if a man of God I, let fire come down from heaven."

Terrible as this answer was, we can perceive its suitableness, nay, its necessity, since it was to decide, and that publicly and by way of judgment (and no other decision would have been suitable in a contest between man and God), whose was the power and the kingdom — and this at the great critical epoch of Israel's history. It is not necessary here to emphasize the difference between the Old and the New Testament — although rather in mode of manifestation than in substance — as we recall the warning words of our LORD, when two of His disciples would have commanded fire from heaven to consume those Samaritans who would not receive them (Luke 9:54). The two cases are not in any sense parallel, as our previous remarks must have shown; nor can we suppose the possibility of any parallel case in a dispensation where "the kingdom of God cometh not with observation" (Luke 17:20), "but in demonstration of the Spirit and of power" (1 Corinthians 2:4).

At the same time we must not overlook that the "captain and his fifty" were not merely unsympathetic instruments to carry out their master's behest, but, as the language seems to imply, shared his spirit.

Perhaps we may conjecture that if Elijah had come with them, he would, if unyielding, never have reached Samaria alive (comp. ver. 15). This hostile and at the same time contemptuous spirit appears still more clearly when, after the destruction of the first captain and his fifty by fire from heaven, not only a second similar expedition was dispatched, but with language even more imperious: "Quickly come down!" It could not be otherwise than that the same fate would overtake the second as the first expedition. The significance, we had almost said the inward necessity, of the judgment consisted in this, that it was a public manifestation of Jehovah as the living and true God, even as the king's had been a public denial thereof. It seems not easy to understand how Ahaziah dispatched a third — nay, even how he had sent a second company.

Some have seen in it the petulance of a sick man, or else of an Eastern despot, who would not brook being thwarted. Probably in some manner he imputed the failure to the bearing of the captains. And on the third occasion, the tone of the commander of the expedition was certainly different from that of his predecessors, although not in the direction which the king would have wished. It would almost seem as if the third captain had gone up alone — without his fifty (v. 13). In contrast to the imperious language of the other two, he approached the representative of God with lowliest gesture of a suppliant, while his words of entreaty that his life and that of his men should be spared indicated that, so far from attempting a conflict, he fully owned the power of Jehovah. Accordingly the prophet was directed to go with him, as he had nothing to fear from him. Arrived in the presence of the king, Elijah neither softened nor retracted anything in his former message. Ahaziah had appealed to the "fly-god" of Ekron, and he would experience, and all Israel would learn, the vanity and folly of such trust. "So he died according to the word of Jehovah which Elijah had spoken."

Ahaziah did not leave a son. He was succeeded by his brother Jehoram, or Joram, as we shall prefer to call him, to distinguish him from the king of Judah of the same name. Before entering on the history of his reign we must consider, however briefly, the history of Elijah and of Elisha, which is so closely intertwined with that of Israel.

The record opens with the narrative of Elijah's translation — and this not merely as introductory to Elisha's ministry, but as forming, especially at that crisis, an integral part of such a "prophetic" history of Israel as that before us. The circumstances attending the removal of Elijah are as unique as those connected with the first appearance and mission of the prophet. We mark in both the same suddenness, the same miraculousness, the same symbolic meaning. Evidently the event was intended to stand forth in the sky of Israel as a fiery sign not only for that period, but for all that were to follow. And that this history was so understood of old, appears even from this opening sentence in what we cannot help regarding as a very unspiritual, or at least inadequate, sketch of Elijah's ministry in the apocryphal book of Jesus the Son of Sirach (Ecclesiasticus 48:1): "Then stood up Elias the prophet as fire, and his word burned like a lamp." But while we feel that the circumstances attending his translation were in strict accordance with the symbolical aspect of all that is recorded in Scripture of his life and mission, we must beware of regarding these circumstances as representing merely symbols without outward reality in historic fact. Here the narrative will best speak for itself.

The rule of Ahaziah had closed with the judgment of the LORD pronounced through Elijah, and another reign not less wicked — that of Joram — had begun when the summons to glory came to the prophet of fire.

This latter was known, not only to Elijah himself, and to Elisha, but even to "the sons of the prophets." We do not suppose that Elisha, or still less "the sons of the prophets," knew that "Jehovah would cause Elijah to ascend in a storm-wind to heaven" — nay, perhaps Elijah himself may not have been aware of the special circumstances that would attend his removal. But the text (vers. 3, 5, 9) clearly shows that the immediate departure of Elijah was expected, while the language also implies that some extraordinary phenomenon was to be connected with it. At the same time we are not warranted to infer, either that there had been a special Divine revelation to inform all of the impending removal of Elijah, nor, on the other hand, that Elijah had gone on that day to each of the places where "the sons of the prophets" dwelt in common, in order to inform and prepare them for what was to happen.

As Holy Scripture tells it, the day began by Elijah and Elisha leaving Gilgal — not the place of that name between the Jordan and Jericho, so sacred in Jewish history (Joshua 4:19; 5:10), but another previously referred to (Deuteronomy 11:30) as the great trysting-place for the final consecration of the tribes after their entrance into the land of promise. We remember that Saul had gathered Israel there before the great defeat of the Philistines, when by his rash presumption the king of Israel had shown his moral unfitness for the kingdom (1 Samuel 13:12-15).

The town lay in the mountains to the south-west of Shiloh, within the territory of Ephraim. The site is now occupied by the modern village Filjilieh. A walk of eight or nine miles due south would bring them "down" to the lower-lying Bethel, whither, as Elijah said, God had sent him. Alike Gilgal and Bethel were seats of the sons of the prophets, and the two are also conjoined as centers of idolatry in prophetic denunciation (Hosea 4:15; Amos 4:4; 5:5).

Perhaps on that very ground the two were chosen for the residence of the prophets. The motive which induced Elijah to ask Elisha to leave him has been variously explained. We cannot persuade ourselves that it was from humility, or else because he doubted whether the company of Elisha was in accordance with the will of God — since in either case he would not have yielded to the mere importunity of his disciple. As in analogous cases, we regard it rather (Ruth 1:8, 11, 12; Luke 9:57-62; John 21:15-17), as a means of testing fidelity. There are occasions when all seems to indicate that modest and obedient retirement from the scene of prominent action and witness, perhaps even from the dangers that may be connected with it, is our duty. But he who would do work for the LORD must not stand afar off, but be determined and bold in taking his place, nor must he be deterred from abiding at his post by what may seem cross-Providences. Again, we cannot help feeling that the visit of Elijah to the schools of the prophets at Gilgal, Bethel, and Jericho, must have been intended as a test to them; while at the same time it was somehow connected with his approaching departure. This the sons of the prophets evidently perceived, in what manner we know not. But any formal leave-taking would seem entirely incongruous with Elijah's whole bearing — especially on that day; and it is inconsistent with the question to Elisha:" Knowest thou that Jehovah will take away thy master from thy head today?" The word "today" may, indeed, be taken in a more general sense, as equivalent to "at this time," but even so the question would have had no meaning if Elijah had come to say "farewell."

At each of these places, when Elijah and Elisha left it in company — in Gilgal, Bethel, and Jericho — the testing suggestion that Elisha should tarry behind, was repeated; on each occasion it was answered by the determined assertion that he would not leave his master. On each occasion also Elisha was met by the same question of those whose morbid curiosity, rather than intelligent interest, had been stirred, and on each he answered in manner to show how little inward sympathy there was between him and those who would have intruded themselves into the sanctuary of his soul. At last fifty of their number followed to view afar off — not to see how the two would cross the Jordan, but to observe what should happen. It need scarcely be added that, as in all similar attempts to see the Divine, they could not succeed in their purpose.

And now the two had gone down the bank of the Jordan, and stood by the edge of its waters. Elijah took off his loose upper garment, the symbol of his prophetic office, and wrapping it together as if to make it a staff (comp. Exodus 14:16), smote with it the waters. And lo, as when the Ark of God had preceded Israel (Joshua 4:23), the waters divided, and they passed over dry shod. Surely there could not have been more apt teaching for Elisha and for all future times, that the power of wonder-working rested not with the prophet individually, but was attached to his office, of which this rough raiment was the badge. The same truth was conveyed by what passed on the other side. There the reward — or, perhaps we should rather say, the result of his spiritual perseverance awaited Elisha. But although Elijah asked him to say what he should do for him before their parting, it was not his to grant the request. No one would imagine that Elisha's entreaty for a double measure of his master's spirit was prompted by the desire that his ministry should greatly surpass that of Elijah, although even in that case it would not be warrantable to attribute such a wish to anything like ambition. "Earnestly covet the best gifts," is a sound and spiritual principle; and Elisha might, without any thought of himself, seek a double portion of his master's spirit, in view of the great work before him. But perhaps it may be safer, although we make no assertion on the point, to think here of the right of the firstborn, to whom the law assigned a twofold portion (Deuteronomy 21:17). In that case Elisha would, in asking a double portion of his spirit, have intended to entreat the right of succession. And with this the reply of Elijah accords. Elisha had asked a hard thing, which it was not in any man's power to grant. But Elijah could give him a sign by which to know whether God designated and would qualify him to be his successor. If he saw it all, when Elijah was taken from him, then — but only then — would it be as he had asked.

Viewing Elisha's request in that light, we can have no difficulty in understanding this reply. And in general, spiritual perception is ever the condition of spiritual work. We do not suppose that if all the fifty sons of the prophets, who had followed afar off, had gathered around, they would have perceived any of the circumstances attending the "taking away" of

Elijah, any more than the prophet's servant at Dothan saw the heavenly hosts that surrounded and defended Elisha (2 Kings 6:14-17), till his eyes had been miraculously opened; or than the companions of St. Paul saw the Person or heard the words of Him Who arrested the apostle on the way to Damascus.

And as we think of it, there was special fitness in the sign given to Elisha. It is not stated anywhere in Holy Scripture that Elijah ascended in a fiery chariot to which fiery horses were attached — but that this miraculous manifestation parted between them two, as it were, enwrapping Elijah; and that the prophet went up in a storm-wind (2 Kings 2:11). The fiery chariot and the horses were the emblem of Jehovah of Hosts. To behold this emblem was pledge of perceiving the manifestation of God, unseen by the world, and of being its herald and messenger, as Elijah had been. Beyond the fact that Elijah so went up to heaven, and that the symbolic manifestation of Jehovah of Hosts was visible to Elisha — Holy Scripture does not tell us anything.

And it seems both wiser and more reverent not to speculate further on questions connected with the removal of Elijah, the place whither, and in what state he was "translated." If we put aside such inquiries, since we possess not the means of pursuing them to their conclusions — there is nothing in the simple Scriptural narrative, however miraculous, which transcends the general sphere of the miraculous, or that would mark this as so exceptional an instance that the ordinary principles for viewing the miracles of Scripture would not apply to it.

And Elisha saw it. As if to render doubt of its symbolic meaning impossible, the mantle, which was the prophet's badge, had fallen from Elijah, and was left as an heirloom to his successor. His first impulse was to give way to his natural feelings, caused alike by his bereavement and by veneration for his departed master, "My father, my father!" His next, to realize the great lesson of faith, that, though the prophet had departed, the prophet's God for ever remained: "The chariot of Israel, and the horsemen thereof!" We would suggest that the words, "And he saw him no more" (ver. 12), imply that he gave one upward look where Elijah had been parted from him, and where the fiery glow had now died out in the sky. Then, in token of mourning, he rent his clothes in two pieces, that is, completely, from above downwards. But while thus lamenting the loss of his loved master, he immediately entered on the mission to which he had succeeded, and that with an energy of faith, combined with a reverent acknowledgment of the work of his predecessor, which ought for all time to serve as a lesson to the Church. Bereavement and sorrow should not make us forget, rather recall to us, that Jehovah our God liveth; regret and a sense of loss should not dull, rather quicken us for work, in the name of God. Nor yet should the feeling that we have a call to work, dim our remembrance of those who have gone before us. We are all only servants successively taking up and continuing the task of those who have passed into glory; but he is our Master, Whose is the work, and Who liveth and reigneth for ever.

And so Elisha took up the mantle that had fallen from Elijah. It was not a badge of distinction, but of work and of office. With this mantle he retraced his steps to the bank of Jordan. One upward glance: "Where is Jehovah, the God of Elijah — even He?" spoken not in doubt nor hesitation, but, on the contrary, in assurance of his own commission from heaven, with all that it implied — and, as he smote the waters with the mantle of Elijah, they once more parted, and Elisha went over.

So shall the waters of difficulty, nay, the cold flood of death itself, part, if we smite in faith with the heaven-given garment; so shall the promise of God ever stand sure, and God be true to His Word; and so may we go forward undauntedly, though humbly and prayerfully, to whatever work He gives us to do.

CHAPTER 8 — ELISHA THE PROPHET — RETURN TO JERICHO — ACKNOWLEDGMENT BY THE SONS OF THE PROPHETS — HEALING OF THE WATERS OF JERICHO — JUDGMENT ON THE YOUNG MEN AT BETHEL — SETTLEMENT IN SAMARIA.

(2 KINGS 2:15-25)

THE history which now follows reads almost like a chronicle of Elisha. More correctly it may be described as the prophetic history of that period. With the removal of Elijah, Elisha had begun his ministry, the test of its reality having been the parting of the waters of Jordan. The next three incidents must be considered as preparatory to his prophetic activity; the first, as regarded his public acknowledgment by the sons of the prophets (2 Kings 2:15-18); the second and third that by the people, when Elisha publicly appeared as the instrument of God — in the one case, for mercy (vv. 19-22), in the other, for judgment (vv. 23, 24). Having thus established his authority, Elisha immediately afterwards assumed the place of God's representative in the affairs of Israel.

1. As we look more closely into it, a special significance attached to each of the three preliminary events just referred to. In the first it was seen that Elisha occupied precisely the same position of superiority as Elijah over the ordinary "sons of the prophets," as also the folly of their attempted interference in his work. Henceforth they would be unquestioning, obedient instruments of his behests, and this was the rightful position alike for them and as regarded the work of Elisha. According to our modern notions the circumstances may seem strange, but they are in agreement with the condition of the times and with the degree of spiritual understanding possessed even by the sons of the prophets. As Elisha returned alone, the "sons of the prophets," judging that the spirit of Elijah rested upon him, perhaps because they had watched as the waters of Jordan parted when he smote them — went to meet the prophet and to do him homage. And yet they began by urging a strange request — perhaps because notions such as they expressed were popularly entertained (as by Obadiah, 1 Kings 18:12) in regard to the influence of the Spirit on the prophets generally, or it may be only on the great prophet of fire. Or perhaps they imagined that Elijah might be in a trance or dead in some valley or on some mountain-height; or it may have been only from morbid curiosity to learn something more of what had happened. In any case their proposal marked an entire lack of spiritual understanding and sympathy.

There were fifty strong men among them, capable of enduring any fatigue, and equal to any work or burden. Might these not go to search whether peradventure the Spirit of Jehovah had not uplifted and then cast Elijah into some remote corner of that desolate and rocky region near Jericho?

To men who entertained such notions, it would have been impossible to communicate even what Elisha had witnessed, still less its predicted import to himself. Accordingly he contented himself with a simple negative to their request. And this should have taught them what was the first duty as well as qualification alike of a prophet and of the sons of the prophet: simple, unquestioning obedience. But, like many of us, in the process of our personal sanctification, they had to learn it by painful experience. Their insistence at last made him "ashamed," since it might seem as if he felt less concern for his master than they, and he yielded to their importunity.

When after three days' unavailing search they returned to Jericho, he reminded them of his first refusal — although for reasons which need not be repeated, he did not even then communicate to them what he had witnessed. But ever afterwards a spirit of willing submission to Elisha prevailed among the sons of the prophets.

2. The next requisite seemed to make such public manifestation of his prophetic authority as would secure for his message the faith and submission of the people. Besides, this was necessary in the contest with Baal, whose worship, if it had been finally established, would, so to speak, have denationalized Israel, even as it ultimately led to that banishment which has not yet been recalled. It was of absolute importance that the presence of Jehovah should appear, as it were, in a concrete form, through a living representative, who should be quick to bring blessing or judgment, and so to demonstrate what he proclaimed, in the only manner which the men of that time could understand. This may also in part explain why the mission of Elijah and Elisha differed in so many respects from that of the other prophets. And, as we farther consider it, we have evidence that it accomplished its purpose. We remember how once and again Ahab himself was arrested through the influence of Elijah. At first the reign of Ahaziah had seemed a return to the worst days of Ahab. But Elijah's announcement of his doom, together with the symbolic judgment on those two captains of fifty who had gone to capture the prophet, had had their effect.

Although Joram "wrought evil in the sight of Jehovah," it was "not like his father, and like his mother;" and we are expressly told that "he removed the pillar of Baal which his father had made" (2 Kings 3:2). This does not mean that he either destroyed the Temple of Baal, or even that pillar — perhaps we should rather call it a column or block. Probably all that was done was to remove this great memorial-pillar of Baal from the public position which it had occupied in the square, or in front, or in the gardens, of the palace, or else before the Temple of Baal, and to place it within the precincts of the latter (2 Kings 10:27). But even this implied that the worship of Baal was no longer the national religion — although the alternative was only between it and the worship instituted by Jeroboam. From this general estimate of the public influence exercised by the prophet, we turn to consider more fully the first miracle by which he established his prophetic authority — very significantly in an act of blessing. The men of Jericho interceded with Elisha — probably through their representatives — on behalf of their city. Every one might see how pleasant was its site: the very Paradise of Palestine, its rich soil basking under a tropical sun, yet shaded by palm, mulberry, and fig-trees, while the air was refreshed by perennial springs of bright water, and perfumed by the precious balsam-plants, the scent of which the wind would sometimes carry as far as out to sea. But all this luxuriance was marred by the character of the water. At a distance of about a mile from the ancient site of Jericho (not from the modern village which represents the ancient town), "there is a large and beautiful fountain of sweet and pleasant water," the so-called Ain-es-Sultan.

From its situation this must have furnished the water-supply for ancient Jericho, and hence have been the spring which Elisha healed, of which there is this farther confirmation that the other springs in the neighborhood are to this day mostly brackish. To this character of the water the inhabitants ascribed, and as it appears not without reason, the circumstance of the frequent miscarriages which alike diminished the population and the flocks.

Remembering the symbolic import of the mission of Elisha, as before explained, we should expect the prophet to give heed to so humble a complaint — for such it was, rather than a request. The means used were in accordance with the symbolic character of all else. The healing of the waters, although performed through the prophet, was the direct act of Jehovah (v. 21). Accordingly, as everything connected with the service of the LORD, the cruse to be used must be "new" (Numbers 19:2), dedicated to God alone. And the direct means of the "healing" was "salt," borne in this new cruse. Salt was added to everything offered, as being the emblem of incorruption, and hence of purification. And so they went up to the very spring of the waters, and there, not as of himself, but in the name of the LORD, Elisha "healed" the waters by a symbolic action, resembling that of Moses of old (Exodus 15:25).

Many lessons of deep significance are suggested by this miracle: most notably, how the salt borne in the new cruse when applied to the spring of the waters healed them — henceforth, completely, and for ever; and again, how in the healing three things were combined — the use of means (in themselves ineffectual), the word of the prophet, and the power of Jehovah. But most of all, does it help us to realize how God is a present help in time of trouble — if only we seek Him in the manner which He appoints.

3. Yet another attestation of Elisha's prophetic authority was needed. This time not in blessing, but in judgment — stern, quick, unrelenting. Those who despised his commission, or rather defied the power that was behind it, must learn in terrible experience its reality. And that this judgment at the beginning of Elisha's ministry was so understood, appears from this circumstance that his ministry never afterwards seems to have encountered active opposition.

Once more the prophet was pursuing his lonely way where last he had walked in company with his master. For it will be remembered, that the last station at which Elijah and Elisha tarried on their way to Jericho and the Jordan was Bethel. And this also is significant. As regards Elisha, because it must have called up most solemn thoughts, especially now when he was entering upon his work; and not less so as regarded the Bethelites who had last seen Elisha in company with Elijah just before his ascent. It did recall to them the last appearance among them of the two, but only to make mockery of the event connected with it. But this was to scoff alike at the dead and at the living prophet, and also at the great power of Jehovah. Thus it was really open defiance of God, all the more inexcusable that it was entirely unprovoked, and that it offended against the law of man almost as much as against that of God. For it was not only a breach of hospitality, but it discarded that reverence for authority specially of a religious kind, which has at all times been a characteristic feature in Eastern life.

Slowly had Elisha ascended those 3000 feet which lead up from the low plain of Jericho to the highlands where Bethel lies.

He was climbing the last height — probably up the defile of Wady Suweinit, where the hills above still bear marks of the extensive forest that once covered them — when he encountered a band of "young men," who, as the text seems to imply, had gone forth to meet him. They were not "little children" (according to our A.V.), but young men, as we infer from the use of the same expression in the case of Solomon (1 Kings 3:7), when he was about twenty years old, and the application of a similar, even stronger, designation to the youthful advisers of Rehoboam.

And their presence there meant a deliberate purpose. We have no means of ascertaining how they may have learned the approach of Elisha, or come to know that the great prophet, whom the fifty strong men had sought in vain, had "gone up," even although they may have attached to this only the vaguest notions. But as the taunt, "Baldhead," was undoubtedly a term of reproach, in whatever sense they may have used it, so the cry "Go up, go up!" with which they followed him, seems to us a mocking allusion to the ascent of Elijah.

In the spirit that prompted the words of Moses and Aaron (Exodus 16:6- 8), and of Peter (Acts 5:3, 4), not, we feel assured, in that of personal revenge, Elisha turned round and pronounced on them that doom which soon afterwards overtook them in a manner so strange that it seems to have been specially intended to attract public attention. For although the exceeding danger from bears, especially when irritated, is frequently referred to in Scripture, and the large number (forty-two) slain, not eaten, by the two she-bears, indicates how many youths had combined to go forth for the purpose of mocking Elisha, yet so extensive a calamity from such a cause was so unusual and must have spread such wide mourning as to draw universal attention to the ministry of Elisha.

We can scarcely suppose that Elisha tarried in Bethel. In pursuance of his object publicly to declare himself the successor of Elijah, he passed on to Mount Carmel, where Elijah had been during the latter part of his ministry, and thence returned to Samaria to be in readiness for his work.

CHAPTER 9 — JEHOSHAPHAT, (FOURTH) KING OF JUDAH — JORAM, (TENTH) KING OF ISRAEL — THE ALLIED EXPEDITION AGAINST MOAB — RECENT DISCOVERY OF "THE MOABITE STONE" — LESSONS OF ITS INSCRIPTION — THE MARCH THROUGH THE WILDERNESS OF EDOM — WANT OF WATER — INTERVIEW WITH ELISHA — DIVINE DELIVERANCE — DEFEAT OF MOAB AND ADVANCE OF THE ALLIES — THE SIEGE OF KIR-HARASETH — MESHA OFFERS UP HIS SON — WITHDRAWAL OF THE ALLIES.

(2 KINGS 3:5-27.)

THE first public act of Elisha's wider ministry is connected with an event of which the most strange and unlooked-for confirmation has been brought to light within the last few years. When in August, 1868, the Rev. F. Klein, of the Church Missionary Society, was traveling in Moab, his attention was directed by a friendly Sheik to a black basalt stone, about three feet ten inches in height, two feet in width, and fourteen and a half inches in thickness. The stone bore an inscription of thirty-four straight lines (about one and a quarter inches apart), which on learned investigation was found to be in the ancient Phoenician characters. The place where this memorial-stone, or column, was found was Diban, the ancient Dibon, the northern capital of Moab, north of the river Arnon. So far as can be judged from the shapeless mass of ruins (comp. Jeremiah 48:18) that cover the twin hills on which the ancient city had stood, surrounded by a wall, "it was quite within the old city walls; near what, we presume, was the gateway, close to where the road has crossed it." Whether it had originally stood there, is another and not easily answered question.

Before referring to the important evidence derived from this discovery, we shall in a few sentences, give the melancholy history of this stone. It may teach us a lesson about "our unhappy divisions." The unexpected discovery of this stone led, in the first place, to jealousies for its coveted possession among the European communities in Jerusalem. In the end, in their eagerness to make as much profit as was possible out of these contentions, the Arabs quarreled among themselves — and broke up the stone. Happily, most of the fragments have been secured, and some "squeezes" on paper had previously been taken, so that all the important parts of the inscription can be read, and have — with but slight variations — been interpreted by critics of different countries.

Perhaps it may be convenient here to put down such parts of the inscription as are of importance to our present purpose, adding afterwards brief comments in explanation. The inscription begins as follows (we mark the original lines): -

1. I Mesha am son of Chemoshgad, King of Moab, the

2. Dibonite. My father reigned over Moab thirty years and I reign-

3. ed after my father. And I erected this stone to Chemosh at Kirkha [a stone of]

4. [sa] lvation, for he saved me from all despoilers, and made me see my desire upon all my enemies, upon Om-

5. [r] i, king of Israel. He afflicted Moab many days, for Chemosh was angry with his count-

6. [r] y. His son succeeded him, and he also said, I will afflict Moab. In my days he said [Let us go]

7. And I will see my desire on him and his house. And Israel [said], I will destroy with an everlasting destruction. Now Omri took (had taken) the land

8. Medeba and.... occupied it.... the days of his son, forty years. And Chemosh [had mercy]

9. on it in my days, and I built Baal Meon, and made therein the tank, and I [built]

We cannot here continue this quotation, interesting as are the issues involved. What follows describes the reconquest by Mesha of various towns in the north of Moab, formerly occupied by Israel, their reconstruction and the dedication of captive women to "Ashtar-Chemosh" (Astarte-Chemosh), and of what are described as "vessels of Jehovah," to Chemosh — both at the taking of Nebo, in the northernmost part of Moab.

In lines 1-9, first clause of the inscription, Mesha relates the subjugation of Moab by Omri, the father of Ahab, and the deliverance of that country, which he ascribes to Chemosh. This we suppose to have been connected with the retreat of the allied armies from Kir-haraseth, and their evacuation of the country (2 Kings 3:25).

From all this we infer that the land of Moab, which had apparently recovered its independence during, or immediately after, the reign of Solomon, was, at least in part, reconquered by the warlike Omri. And from the list of towns which in other parts of the inscription Mesha mentions as having been retaken, we conclude that Omri had invaded Moab from the north, while afterwards the allied armies entered it from the south. Accordingly a number of places are named as such which the king of Israel had fortified and Mesha recaptured. All these towns are north of the Arnon. The deep gorge, and the rapid current of that river, would render its passage by a hostile army extremely difficult. Hence the invading army of Omri seems to have been arrested by that obstacle, and Jahaz, which lay north of the Arnon, is the most southern point mentioned in the inscription, as held and fortified by the king of Israel.

But while Northern Moab was thus occupied by Israel, the southern part of the country seems to have preserved its independence during the reign both of Omri and of Ahab. After the death of the latter, "Moab rebelled" (2 Kings 3:5), under the leadership of their brave king Mesha — a name which is connected with the word "deliverance." He styles his father Chemosh-Gad, which is a compound of the names of the two gods, Chemosh and Gad (the latter the god of fortune). The first intimation of the movement for the recovery of their independence seems to have been the sudden invasion of Judaea by Moab, in alliance with the Ammonites and a tribe of Edomites (2 Chronicles 20). Probably the Moabites had not yet felt themselves sufficiently strong for an attack on the Israelitish stronghold in Northern Moab, and accordingly resolved on making a raid across the undefended boundary of Judah, while at the same time they sought to combine into an anti-Israelitish alliance all the tribes along the eastern line of Palestine. We know that through the Divine help to Jehoshaphat, this expedition signally failed, while in the mutual slaughter which ensued the Edomite allies of Moab were the first to suffer. Hence, the projected anti-Israelitish league was not only broken up, but Edom was drawn into what seems to have been a Palestinian counter league, the pathetic story of which is connected with the so-called "Moabite stone." It is impossible to find words for the varied feelings which rise as we realize that after the lapse of 2,500 years a monumental stone should in such unexpected manner have been found to bear testimony to Holy Scripture, and especially to its record of that event from which

Mesha dates the recovery of the independence of Moab, — all the more that he ascribes the glory of it to Chemosh, his god.

When from the Moabite inscription we turn to the Biblical narrative, we learn that Mesha, like his predecessors, had been under heavy annual tribute to Israel, which was paid in kind. We read that he "was a sheepmaster." The extensive downs of Moab were covered by numberless flocks, and the tribute which he had to pay consisted of "a hundred thousand lambs, and a hundred thousand wethers — the wool." The wording in the original is not very clear, but as the term used for "lambs" generally designates "fed lambs," we conclude that if it is intended to convey that the wool formed the tribute, it must have been that of "the wethers," and that to this the hundred thousand fed lambs were added. It need scarcely be said that this tribute ceased when Mesha cast off the yoke of Israel.

The events previously related will sufficiently account for the anxiety of Jehoshaphat that the growing power of Moab should be checked, and a counter league formed effectually to oppose the common enemies of Palestine. As regards any religious scruples to an alliance with Israel, he may have argued that Joram was not like Ahaziah, nor even like Ahab (2 Kings 3:2), and that since God Himself had given such signal victory over Moab, a common invasion of their land might even be pleasing in His sight. We rarely fail to find a satisfactory or even a religious reason for doing that on which we set our hearts. But it does seem strange, that the answer which Jehoshaphat returned to the invitation of Joram to join him in the campaign against Moab should have been precisely the same as that which he had given on the disastrous occasion when Ahab asked him to go up against Ramoth-gilead (1 Kings 22:4). Perhaps, however, it was a common mode of expression in such circumstances, or else the sacred historian may have wished to emphasize the folly and wrong of Jehoshaphat's conduct by using the same terms as formerly in the unhappy alliance with Ahab. The plan agreed upon by the two monarchs was to make invasion of Moab from the south. This, not only in order to ensure the co-operation of the king of Edom, who had now joined the anti-Moabite league, and to protect their rear and their communications, but also for important strategic reasons. Northern Moab was, indeed, subject to Israel, but the Arnon marked the boundary, and no prudent commander would attempt to force such a position as the line of the Arnon in the face of a general like Mesha. On the other hand, by fetching "a seven days' compass," and advancing front the south and through Edom, alike their retreat was covered and supplies would be secured. And if Mesha could be drawn into the wilderness which separated Edom from Southern Moab, and belonged partly to the one, partly to the other country, the whole of Moab might be overrun, and the invading army from the south join hands with the Israelitish garrisons north of the Arnon.

But once more the incapacity, if not the treachery, of Edom defeated the plans of the allies. Mesha refused to be drawn into the wilderness of Edom. As we understand it, his army was posted on the Moabite side of the boundary, which is here formed by the Wady 'el Ahsa, while higher up it passes into the Wady Tufileh.

We suppose that it was here, or in some other dried-up wady close by, that the allies, who were now suffering from want of water, suddenly found themselves in presence of an enemy that swarmed the tangled brushwood and thicket around. Unable to cross the Wady and engage the enemy, who seemed ubiquitous, or to retreat into the wilderness, the position of the allies seemed, humanly speaking, hopeless.

It was in these circumstances that the grand difference in principle between the king of Israel and pious Jehoshaphat appeared, as it always does in seasons of trial and decision between the servants of the LORD and those of "strange gods." Joram could descry nothing but impending ruin, and his only thought concerning Jehovah was that He had brought the three kings together for their destruction. Jehoshaphat, though often and sadly failing through weakness of character, was yet true in the inmost direction of his heart. In his distress he instinctively turned to the LORD for guidance. His inquiry for a "prophet of Jehovah" brought out two facts of infinite comfort: that Elisha, known as the attendant of Elijah, was — no doubt by Divine direction — present in the camp; and that there was one in the following of the king of Israel — probably one of the superior officers — who knew of it, being evidently in sympathy with that which the prophet represented, as Obadiah had been in the days of Ahab (1 Kings 18:3).

We read that the three kings went to the tent of Elisha. This not merely from apprehension that he might refuse to come to them, nor yet from humility; but probably because they may have dreaded the effect upon the host of such words as formerly Micaiah had spoken in similar circumstances (1 Kings 22:17-28). The reception which this incongruous company of kings met at the hands of the prophet was certainly not encouraging. On the other hand, an appeal for help addressed to the prophet of Jehovah by the heathen king of Edom and the son of Ahab seemed to treat the prophetic office as if it had involved heathen magic and divination, just as Balak of old had sought to employ Balaam against Israel. To an appeal of such a character Elisha could not have listened; it should — as he told the king of Israel — be addressed to the prophets of Baal. How truly Elisha had judged Joram appears from his answer, when with almost incredible dullness, he once more urged — presumably as the reason for his coming — that Jehovah, the God of the prophet, and the old enemy of the house of Ahab, had brought these kings together for their destruction. With such an one it was impossible to argue, and the prophet turned from him to the king of Judah, for whose sake alone he would consent to continue the interview, or would seek the guidance and help of the LORD.

It has been assumed by a certain school of critics that when Elisha next called for a minstrel, it was to rouse in himself the prophetic faculty, or else that such was the common mode of producing prophetic inspiration. But for the latter assertion there is not a tittle of evidence, while, as regards the former, alike Biblical (1 Samuel 16:16) and heathen testimony go to prove that the purpose for which music was employed was to soothe, not to excite the mind.

It was not otherwise in the present instance. From the agitation of his interview with Joram Elisha was restored by the minstrel to quietness, and thus prepared for receiving the Divine communication. This was twofold: it gave promise of deliverance from the present straits and of complete victory over Moab. The people were directed to make the Wady full of pits — and then, without sound of wind, or sight of rain, would the Wady be filled with water, and the host set free from their present straits. But this was only preparatory. A complete victory would be granted to them, and in their victorious progress they would destroy all fenced cities and absolutely lay waste the enemy's country. It is not ours to vindicate the work of warfare here indicated, although not prescribed (v. 19).

It seems to be opposed to the express Divine direction in Deuteronomy 20:19, 20. In judging of it some considerations must, however, be kept in view. First and foremost we have to remember the spirit of the times. Nor is the time so far distant when a mode of warfare not very unlike this was common in an enemy's country. As a matter of fact, this mode of laying waste a hostile country seems to have been general at that time among all nations. Accordingly it is frequently represented on the Assyrian monuments, and referred to in classical writings.

It may be of interest here to recall two points which might otherwise be overlooked. It will be remembered that the inscription on the "Moabite stone" makes the following special reference to this mode of warfare: "In my days he said, [Let us go,] and I will see my desire on him and his house. And Israel (said), I will destroy with an everlasting destruction." Thus the Moabite stone to a certain extent bears testimony to the very words which Elisha had used. Again, it may be doubted whether, if Israel had not adopted this mode of warfare, the retreat of the allied army from Kir-haraseth would not have been followed by a most formidable Moabite invasion into Palestine. As it was, the repair of the havoc wrought in his country must have engaged all the energies of Mesha. And to this work of necessary restoration and recuperation the closing part of the Moabite inscription bears testimony.

We return to the narrative of what happened on the morrow of the interview with Elisha. As directed by the prophet, pits had been dug — as we imagine, either in the rear or along the sides of the camp of Israel, although we know too little of the actual circumstances to venture on any more detailed statement. However it may have been, the Divine prediction by Elisha was literally fulfilled. Once more it all happened in the orderly succession of events, while, if viewed by itself, the issue would seem, as in the highest sense it was, miraculous. And this indeed holds true of the record of most Biblical miracles, that they are the statement of effects, without the assignment or explanation of the causes that led up to them. In the present instance, it was no doubt a sudden storm that had burst in the mountains of Moab which sent a rush of water down the Wady by which Israel was camped. The prophetic historian, who loves to connect Jehovah's deliverance with the loved services of the sanctuary, reminds us that it was "when the meat-offering was offered," that "there came water by the way of Edom," — to disappear as suddenly as it had come, when the object had been served.

The Israelites in their camp had seen it, and hastened to quench their thirst. The Moabites also saw it, but to them it seemed as the eastern sun shone on the water in the pits, reddened as it was by the color of the soil, that they were gazing on pools of blood. Their late expedition into Judah suggested a ready explanation of the strange sight. Perhaps their superstition might lead them to imagine that Chemosh, of whose help we read so much in the Moabite inscription, had now granted to Moab a success precisely similar to that of Judah. The kings were destroyed — they had smitten one another: now, therefore, Moab to the spoil!

Meantime, the commanders of the allied army would naturally keep their men within their camp, so as to allow the disorderly rush of Bedawin, intent on spoil, to cross the Wady and approach them quite closely, before suddenly sallying forth to inflict indiscriminate slaughter. Mesha was too wary to risk another defeat of the same kind. He retreated before Israel, evacuating every fortified town, till he reached the stronghold of Kir-haraseth, where he resolved to make a final stand. The Jewish army slowly followed the retreating enemy, destroying every town and laying waste the country around. Their progress was arrested at the walls of Kir-haraseth. As we consider the situation of that fortress, we scarcely wonder that the allies found themselves unable to do more than harass the garrison by posting sharpshooters on the hills around ("the slingers went about it"), and attempt to reduce it by hunger. The position of Kir-Moab, "the fortress of Moab," (Isaiah 15:1), Kir-hareseth (Isaiah 16:7), Kir-haresh (Isaiah 16:7), or Kir-haraseth — for it bears all these names, which seem to mean "fortress of brickwork," — has been ascertained beyond reasonable doubt.

The Chaldee paraphrast designates it (Isaiah 15:1) Keraka deMoabh, which exactly answers to the modern name Kerak. A continuous ascent from the south, amidst Alpine scenery, leads up to Kerak, which lies 3,720 feet above the Mediterranean. From the last crest, whence there is a magnificent prospect far away, we look down into the "Wady of Kerak, some 1800 feet of nearly sheer precipice on the opposite side."

Along that Wady winds among rocks the road, so narrow that a few resolute men could hold it against an army. As the Wady widens, the ground is cultivated "with olives, figs, pomegranates, and a few vineyards and patches of corn." Soon Kerak itself is seen, towering high aloft. To reach it, we must first descend into the valley. Then an hour's climb up the opposite cliff brings the traveler to an arched tunnel of about eighty yards in length, through which he emerges into the city of Kerak.

The plateau on which the town stands is almost level, and measures from 800 to 1000 yards on each face of the triangle which the city forms, and of which the north-eastern side is the longest. Here, and to a less degree at the south-west angle, the plateau is connected with the heights which surround Kerak on every side. But everywhere else the town is cut off from the encircling range by "Wadies (in part) from 1000 to 1500 feet deep, with steeply scarped or else rugged sides." If we imagine this isthmus of rock, jutting into and rising above a sea of deep Wadies, itself surrounded by a broad wall with towers and other defenses, and crowned by a city to which there were only two entrances, each through a tunnel in the side of the cliff — we can form a picture of Kir-haraseth, as it appeared to the Jewish host that gazed on it from the heights around.

But although the allied army could not reduce the city, "the slingers" posted on the overlooking heights might inflict serious losses on the garrison. In fact, the place would soon have become untenable. In these circumstances Mesha endeavored, at the head of 700 swordsmen, to cut his way through the besieging army in the direction where the king of Edom was posted — either because this was the weakest point in the camp of the allies, or probably because he may have expected less resistance in that quarter. Driven back into the city, the frenzy of despair seized him. The idea underlying sacrifice was in heathen worship also that of substitution, though not as provided by the mercy of God, but in order to appease His wrath. It was not the infinite compassion and love of God which provided a ransom, but the despair of mercy and goodness that suggested such means as the last hope of expiation. Hence that which was nearest and dearest to a man was offered up to propitiate, if possible, a god who was not known to be full of compassion. And so the king of Moab now took his eldest son, who should have succeeded him on the throne, and in sight of besiegers and besieged offered him on the wall as a burnt offering. Thus would he conciliate Chemosh; thus also would he show his devotion to his country. It was a horrible, sickening spectacle, which made deepest impression on all onlookers — friend as well as foe. The undertaking on which Israel had engaged its allies became hateful to all — and the allied army retired from before Kir-haraseth. So ended the campaign against Moab.

CHAPTER 10 — THE MINISTRY OF ELISHA AS THE PERSONAL REPRESENTATIVE OF THE LIVING GOD IN ISRAEL — THE PROPHET'S WIDOW AND HER MIRACULOUS DELIVERANCE — THE SHUNAMMITE AND ELISHA — THE GOD-GIVEN CHILD — HIS DEATH AND RESTORATION TO LIFE — ELISHA AT GILGAL WITH THE "SONS OF THE PROPHETS" — "DEATH IN THE POT" AND REMOVAL OF THE HARM — THE MAN FROM BAAL-SHALISHA — GOD'S SUFFICIENT AND UNFAILING PROVISION FOR HIS OWN.

(2 KINGS 4)

THERE is something grand and truly characteristic of "prophetic history" when the Biblical narrative abruptly turns from the expedition against Moab, which, although so simply told, was of such deep and lasting political importance, to tell what reads like a summary of the prophetic activity of Elisha. It shows, on the one hand, how all events are regarded from the Divine point of view, while on the other hand, it helps us to understand the real meaning and purpose of the miraculous element in the ministry of Elisha, as designed to recall Israel to a realizing sense of the presence and power of Jehovah, and by such religious revival to avert imminent national judgment. Accidentally we obtain in the course of the narrative, interesting side-glimpses into private and public life in Israel, which generally confirm our confidence in the historic truth of what is related.

At the outset we may say that the impression which this history as a whole makes on us, is that it seems transferred or perhaps rather summarized, from some special narrative or work descriptive of the activity of Elisha. The incidents do not seem arranged in their strict chronological succession, but grouped according to their internal connection, so that an account of the more private activity of the prophet, as regards individuals, families, and communities, is followed by that of his public activity, in its bearing on Israel and Syria. Again, it is reasonable to suppose that all which is here recorded had not occurred exclusively during the reign of Joram, which lasted only twelve years (2 Kings 3:1). For as Elisha died during the reign of Joash (2 Kings 13:14), his ministry must have extended over four reigns, and lasted altogether about fifty-five or fifty-seven years. Hence there would be a blank of forty-five years in the narrative if all that is recorded of Elisha had taken place in the time of Joram. But the deepest lesson which the life and ministry of Elisha were intended to teach was to set forth, as against the dark background of coming judgment upon Israel's apostasy, the tender care, the sufficient provision, the ever-present help which the LORD would extend to His own servants and people.

The first narrative in this biographical sketch — as for want of better name we may term it — has somewhat inaptly been compared with the account of Elijah's miraculous provision for the widow of Sarepta (1 Kings 17:9-16).

On carefully comparing the two narratives, they will be seen to differ in every detail, except this, that in both instances the recipient of the benefit was a widow. But besides, the great object and meaning of the miracle at Sarepta was to be a prefiguration of the mercy and help to be extended to the Gentile world, with all of warning and teaching to Israel which this implied. Its counterpart, in the history of Elisha, would be the healing of

Naaman, rather than this narrative of Divine help granted to the impoverished widow of one of the sons of the prophets.

Josephus and some of the Rabbis have suggested that this widow had been the wife of that Obadiah who had provided shelter and food for the persecuted prophets in the reign of Ahab (1 Kings 18). But here also the only point of similarity between the two narratives is that the widow of the prophet pleads, in the words of Obadiah (1 Kings 18:12), that her husband "did fear Jehovah." The narrative bears that on the death of her husband, who had been one of the sons of the prophets, and (what is even more important) apparently well known to Elisha as one that feared Jehovah, the creditor had come to take her two sons as bondsmen. We know not through what adverse circumstances the family had been so far reduced; but we can readily believe that in those days faithfulness to Jehovah might lead to outward reverses, not to prosperity. And when he was removed who had been the support of his family by that daily labor, which evidently was not regarded as incompatible with his vocation as one of the "sons of the prophets," then "the creditor" seized on the sons of the widow. In so doing he availed himself of his legal right in the matter (Leviticus 25:39; comp. Matthew 18:25), although his action was unjustifiably harsh and selfish.

If in these circumstances the prophet had not given heed to the appeal of the widow, it would have implied either that he was not the living medium between God and His people, which he professed, or else that Jehovah was not the living and the true God in the sense in which Elisha had preached Him. With reverence be it said, the appeal to the prophet could no more have remained unanswered than a cry for help addressed to Christ in the days of His flesh.

A similar conclusion would be reached if, somewhat realistically, we were to transport this history into our own days. If a widow were, in like circumstances, to seek guidance and comfort, she would be pointed to the living God, and to His sure promise of help in all straits. But what is this when translated into concrete fact other than the miracle wrought at the intercession, or, if you please, at the instance, though not by the hands, of Elisha? And may we not say that, as regards the result, the same miracle is still daily enacted, though not in the same manner as regards the succession of events? In truth, the two worlds of the seen and unseen are not so wide apart as some imagine. To many of us the answer to the "Give us this day our daily bread," comes directly from heaven, and more than the daily bread, or the like of it, is assured to us in the realization of His daily and indirect help. And if in this history all this was exhibited in a concrete manner, it was required in the circumstances of the time and for the purposes of the mission of Elisha, although its lesson is to all time and to all men.

We mark, that in order to put aside any idea of direct agency in the matter on the part of the prophet, the miraculous help was not sent by the hands of Elisha, but connected so far as possible with some visible and ordinary means. It is in this manner that we explain the question of the prophet, what the widow had in her house. And when she replied, "Anointing oil," the promised help was connected with the use of it as a means.

The widow was directed to borrow empty vessels from all her neighbors, then to shut the door behind her and her sons, and to pour from what she had into those empty vessels, when the multiplying blessing of God would fill them. It would be difficult to imagine any symbol more full of meaning and instruction, alike in its general direction and in its details. It showed that God was a present help. His special blessing, given when needed directly and miraculously, would increase our scanty provision. Nor can we be mistaken in supposing that the direction to shut the door behind her and her sons was intended to enjoin not only reverent acknowledgment, but silent worship of God. And truly so ought we also, when seeking help from Him, ever to feel ourselves alone with Him, combining, like her of old, absolute trust in the promise of His Word with active obedience to His direction: doing what lies in us while praying; and praying while doing it. Lastly, it seems quite in accordance with what had passed that when all the borrowed vessels were full, and the oil had stayed, the widow should, before disposing of anything, have gone to the prophet for his direction, and, we may add, equally so that Elisha should have told her first to pay her creditor, and then to employ the rest towards the sustenance of herself and her sons.

The second narrative in this series of "the acts" of the prophet, transports us to the quiet of the village of Shunem, and the retirement of a pious Israelitish home. We know Shunem from our former history, but then it was associated with battle or else with scenes far different from those to which we are about to be introduced.

The modern Sulem is a wretched collection of mud-hovels. Except from its situation, it scarcely recalls the thriving, healthy, happy, agricultural village of old, as it seemed to look in sunny contentment over the rich plain of Esdraelon. It was in close contiguity to the summer palace of Jezreel, which was perched on the hill above, occupying a position equally beautiful and commanding. And despite its nearness to a corrupt court, there was quite another moral atmosphere about its homes. Shunem seems to have preserved something of the old Israelitish spirit, some of that purity, earnestness, impulsiveness, and we had almost said intenseness, which even long afterwards characterized Northern Palestine and the people of Galilee. A sturdy sense of independence (2 Kings 4:13), combined with reverent simplicity (verses 9, 10), warm home-affections (verses 16, 18, 20), earnest religiousness, and an unwavering spiritual faith (verses 23, 24, 28) — such are the ideas which we have learned to associate with Shunem. And the very physique of this population seems to have corresponded with this moral healthiness. Apparently Shunem was not only the home of wealthy men, but also of fair women, such as of the beautiful Abishag, King David's maiden wife (1 Kings 1:3), or the lovely Shulamite who ravished Solomon's heart (Cant. 6:13, etc.), and of the Shunammite of our present narrative.

We infer that at this time Elisha had been frequently passing between Samaria and what was probably his ordinary place of abode on Carmel.

The direct road from the one to the other place does not lead by Shunem, which lies somewhat farther to the east, at the south-western slope of "little Hermon," and on the opposite side of Esdraelon from Carmel, at a distance of about fifteen or twenty miles across the plain. But it so happened that on a certain occasion Elisha, "passed over [thus literally] to Shunem." According to good Israelitish custom, hospitality would be offered to him; but it was only what was becoming that such should have been extended to the prophet by the mistress of what seems to have been the "great" house at Shunem.

We infer that Elisha was at first unwilling to accept the invitation to the "great" house. Probably there were few such in the land where the prophet could have felt himself at home. But when he yielded to the urgent yet modest importunity of the Shunammite, he must soon have perceived that this was not only a pleasant place of rest on the journey, but one to which he might safely resort for refreshment of body and mind. We are too apt to apply our modern habits of thought and expression to the relationships of ancient times. Yet this may here be pointed out, that the manner in which the Shunammite marked Elisha as a "holy" man of God, indicates enlightened piety; the care with which she received him, affectionate regard; the provision which she made for his absolute privacy, unselfishness and reverence; and the circumstance (later alluded to) of her attendance on Elisha's religious instruction (v.

23), a certain spiritual relationship between them. And so it came that, after this first visit, "as oft" as Elisha "passed across" the plain of Esdraelon, "he turned aside" [and this also literally, since Shunem was not in the direct road] to enjoy the hospitality of the pious mistress of the "great" house at Shunem.

But the frequency of his visits, so far from inducing familiarity, only led to increased reverence on the part of the Shunammite. Her observation had led her to regard Elisha as not only far different from those who at that period may sometimes have passed as prophets, but even from ordinary sons of the prophets — even as a man of God distinguished by holiness. All this she urged on her husband as she proposed to make provision not only for his more proper entertainment, but for his complete privacy. In Palestine an outside stair led up from the road to the roof of the house, so that it was not necessary to pass through the interior of a dwelling. Part of the roof of the house she would now surround with walls, so making an "upper chamber" of it. This would give to the prophet at all times undisturbed, and, if he wished it, unobserved access to, and egress from, his lodging. This was indeed thoughtful, unselfish, and withal, respectful kindness and hospitality. The chamber thus provided, as well as the scanty furnishing of it, may seem to our modern notions very simple. Yet it implied the surrender by the family of the part of the house most appreciated in the East, while the furniture, however scanty according to our ideas, included not only more but better than was ordinarily found in the very simple sleeping apartments of Orientals. Evidently the object was to provide for a prolonged stay on the part of the prophet, and for his complete privacy, and, as appears from the context (v. 13), it included not only the prophet, but also his servant.

There was such delicacy about all this "trouble" with which the Shunammite had been "troubled" for him and his servant, that Elisha, who had at first been reluctant to accept any hospitality, now regularly availed himself of the provision for his comfort and retirement. It was only natural that he should have thought of some return to his hostess. Accordingly on one occasion he directed his servant Gehazi, whom we here meet for the first time, to inquire of the Shunammite what service he could render to her.

The suggestion: "Is there [ought] to be spoken for thee [is there occasion for it] to the king or the captain of the host?" indicates a somewhat insecure state of things, as well as a somewhat despotic order in the State when "the captain of the host" stands ominously near to the king. At the same time it also implies the existence of better relations between the monarch and the prophet, and so confirms the view formerly expressed that the ministry of Elijah and Elisha, attested at almost every stage by direct Divine manifestations, tended at least to arrest the progress of apostasy in Israel.

The answer of the Shunammite to Gehazi: "I dwell among my own people," manifests not only a true Israelitish spirit of frank independence, but reflects a favorable light on that district, which (as all other parts of the country) would be primarily under the rule of its own eldership.

What followed is most pictorially set forth. To the question of Elisha, what there was to be done for her, Gehazi, who certainly had keen worldly insight, replied: "Surely, she has no son, and her husband is old." It was only a suggestion, and in this respect also characteristic of Gehazi. But now, when it was not to be a favor asked of man, but wondrous mercy to be granted by God, Elisha spake to the Shunammite not through Gehazi but directly, giving her the promise of what under the Old Testament was regarded as bringing far deeper than merely a mother's joy.

And there is about her answer such air of genuineness, a mingling of hope with a not daring to expect, and withal such absence of any legendary embellishment, that we can almost imagine ourselves hearing her speak it, as she respectfully stands within the shadow of the door.

It was as Elisha had said, and the Shunammite became the joyous mother of a son. Since then years had passed, during which we have no record of Elisha's continued visits to the "great" house, now gladdened by the voice of a child. Perhaps he no longer, or at least, not so often, passed by; more probably Scripture, after its wont, is silent on that which is purely personal in the history. But the child had passed through five of the stages which Jewish affection, watching with special fondness the opening life, has successively marked by no less than nine designations. They are so interesting that we shall here put them down. The yeled ("born," "babe") had successively become a yonek, or suckling, and an olel, who, no longer satisfied with only this nourishment, asks for bread, then a gamel, or weaned one, and next a taph, one who clings to his mother.

And he had passed through this stage also, and was just entering on the stage designated by elem, becoming firm and strong. It was the time of harvest, and the child was going out to his father to the reapers, when the hot Eastern sun struck his head. At his cry of pain the father bade one of the servants carry the child back to his mother. All that long morning she pressed his aching head to her bosom, till when the mid-day sun shot down its arrows he lay still and dead in her arms. Not a cry of lament escaped that brave mother to tell them in the house of the terrible desolation that had swept over it. Her resolve was taken with the rapidity and unfailing certitude that comes of faith. To Elisha, or rather to Elisha's God! He had given; He could restore the child. In any case she would go with her complaint, not to man, but to the God of almighty help, and not rest satisfied with anything unless it came directly from Him.

It was quite in accordance with all this, and very significant, that in silence she carried her dead child to the prophet's chamber, and there laid him on the bed. Here let him rest, as it were, in keeping of the prophet's God, whose promise had first brought him, till, if ever, the prophet's God would again waken him. And so, like the prophet's widow when she received the Divine help, she shut the door. For, what had man to do with it? her appeal lay directly to God. But she must have been a strong as well as a good woman, strong also in faith, when she could so well keep her feelings under control that her husband had not even suspicion of aught amiss when she preferred the unusual request that one of the servants and one of the beasts of burden should be sent back from the field, that she might at once resort to the man of God. For it was neither New Moon nor Sabbath, when, as we are led to infer, the prophet was wont to give religious instruction, and people gathered around him, and perhaps came to Carmel from a considerable distance.

With a deprecating "Peace" — as it were, Pray let it be so — she waved aside the inquiry of the busy man. And, once her home behind her, she fully gave herself to what was before her. It was no longer a weak woman on whom the greatest earthly sorrow had descended, but one strong, resolute, bent on a great purpose, and wholly self-forgetful. As she had herself, no doubt for speed, seen to the saddling of the ass (v. 24), so she now bade the servant: "drive on, go; delay me not in my riding [hinder me not, keep me not back], unless I bid thee."

The sun must have been declining towards the west, when, after that ride of fifteen or twenty miles, she was nearing Carmel. From a bluff of the mountain the prophet had been watching the rider speeding in such haste across the plain, and recognized the Shunammite.

Although not Divinely informed, and therefore not Divinely assured of a happy issue, he must have known that only some great trouble to herself, her husband, or her child, would have brought her on that afternoon and in such manner. And so he sent Gehazi to meet her with an inquiry meant to reassure her, at least so far as his own interest and sympathy were concerned. But all the more that she so understood it, would she be neither detained by Gehazi, nor could she have opened her heart to him. Indeed, to have attempted telling her sorrow or her need to any man would have been to unfit her, in every sense, for telling it to the prophet. At sight of Elisha the strong woman for the first time gave way. She had reached the goal, and now in an agony of passion she threw herself at his feet and laid hold on them, as if in her despair she could not let him go without helping her. It was, as in Jacob's wrestling with the Angel, the mode of agonizing prayer suited to Old Testament times, when God and His help, and, indeed, most spiritual realities were presented in a concrete manner. From a spurious zeal for his master's honor, from false notions of what became, or did not become — the consequences of his utter want of spiritual insight and sympathy — Gehazi would have thrust her away. So would the multitude have silenced blind Bartimaeus, and even the disciples sent away the importunate Syrophenician woman (Matthew 15:23); and so do we in our mistaken notions of what is becoming or unbecoming too often hinder souls from personal contact with our LORD. But Elisha would not suffer Gehazi, for he knew that her soul was in anguish, although as God had not made him to know its cause, he was ignorant of what its issue would be.

It is this, we feel persuaded, which explains much in the conduct of Elisha — such as his first mission of Gehazi, which otherwise would seem strange, if not unintelligible. But surely never was Elisha more humbled than on the eve of the greatest miracle wrought by his hands; never did the poverty of his humanity, as merely an instrument in the hand of God, appear in more clear light than by the side of the help which Jehovah was about to send. And Elisha himself gave vent to these feelings when he spoke with such sorrow of Jehovah having hidden it from him, and not revealed it.

But this we may say, that never was legend so constructed. To every thoughtful reader such purely human traits of felt weakness and of ignorance not only of the future, but of the present and the past, must carry instructive conviction of the truth of this narrative, full of the miraculous though it be.

The first words which the Shunammite spoke to Elisha revealed the state of the case. They were not an entreaty of help; they contained not even a suggestion of it. And yet they were the strongest appeal that could have been made, since they laid hold on the faithfulness of God to His word and promise. The commission of the prophet to Gehazi to hasten on and lay Elisha's staff upon the face of the dead child seems at first difficult to understand. It is quite true that this was not an ordinary staff, but, as it were, the symbol of prophetic authority and rule, with all that this implied, like the staff of Moses (comp. here Exodus 4:17; 17:5, 9; Numbers 20:8, 9). But it is impossible to believe that Elisha expected either that the staff would restore life to the dead, or that Gehazi would be able to perform such a miracle; or, on the other hand, that Elisha acted under misapprehension, as Nathan had spoken to David when still uninstructed as to the will of God (2 Samuel 7:3, etc.); or else that the prophet could have imagined that the child was not really dead. Nor can we accept the suggestion sometimes made that Elisha had full well known Gehazi would not succeed, but had still sent him, in order to show — either to Gehazi, or to the Shunammite, or to Israel generally — that miracles were not magic, and that neither a Gehazi nor even a prophet's staff could produce them. It is difficult to use moderate language in rejecting suggestions which imply that Elisha had purposely employed what he knew to be useless measures in order to teach some abstract lesson, or that he could have done so at a moment of such agony and suspense. Kindred views in regard to God's dealings with us when under severe affliction are, indeed, too often entertained by Christians. They should give place to more enlightened conceptions of the character of God, and to a more simple and childlike faith in Him, Who afflicteth not willingly, but for our profit.

We feel convinced that the explanation of Gehazi's commission must be sought within the narrative itself. When Elisha dispatched his servant with his staff, it was with the intention that he should take his master's place. What afterwards determined him to go personally was the expressed resolve of the woman: "As Jehovah liveth, and as thy soul liveth, I will not leave thee [viz., behind; I will not go, nor yet go without thee]. Then he arose and went after her." All this seems in accordance with what has been previously stated. If, as Elisha expressed it with sorrow, Jehovah had not communicated to His servant what had happened in the house of the Shunammite, then the prophet was not only ignorant of the final issue, but left without any Divine commission in the matter. In these circumstances he would wait for such direction as might be indicated to him in the course of events. And he received it, clearly and unmistakably, through the expressed resolution of the Shunammite. Accordingly he immediately followed her. The previous mission of Gehazi may have been tentative and preparatory; and the laying of the prophet's staff on the face of the child perhaps symbolic of the arrestment of the progress of decay. Nor can there be difficulty in understanding the prophet's direction to Gehazi not to salute any one by the way, nor to return any salutation. It was intended not only to indicate the necessity of speed on what brooked no delay, and of avoiding any worldly distraction when on such an errand, but also to prevent all such publicity as to the matter in hand, as would have been the natural sequence of conversation, especially on the part of one like Gehazi (comp. here also Luke 10:4).

The narrative passes in silence over the long ride across Esdraelon to Shunem. Evening must have gathered on the deep blue summer sky, when the two at length neared the desolate home. Ere they came to it, Gehazi had met them with the report: "The lad is not awaked," — and this also is significant of Gehazi's thoughts about the matter. He had literally obeyed his master's behest, and laid the staff upon the face of the child, "but there was neither voice nor attending [on the part of the dead child]." But by this time, we dare not doubt it, Elisha knew what he had to do. Even if the Lord had been silent to him, he had already received sufficient direction (comp. here Exodus 14:15). What follows in the narrative (v. 32) is chiefly intended to set more clearly before us the reality of what now took place. Arrived in his chamber, the prophet shut the door upon himself and the dead child that lay on his bed. We have learned to understand the meaning of this act, which symbolically set forth being alone with God. As regards his prayer to Jehovah and the close personal contact with the dead child, Elisha followed, as from every point of view we would have expected, the example of his master, Elijah, when he recalled to life the widow's son at Sarepta (1 Kings 17:17, 24).

Differences in detail there are between the two narratives, such as will readily be noticed. But these are best accounted for by the difference both in the circumstances and character and mission of the two prophets. In any case they are not of importance. But alike the symbolism and the lessons of this history must be apparent to all.

First, as regards the Shunammite. We see in her a true and faithful Israelitish woman, who, in a time of general apostasy, owned Jehovah alike in her life and her home. Receiving a prophet, because of Him Who had sent him, because he was a holy man of God — and with humility and entire self-forgetfulness — she received a prophet's reward in the gift most precious to a Jewish mother, which she had not dared to hope for, even when announced to her. Then, when severely tried, she still held fast to her trust in the promise — strong even when weakest — once more self-forgetful, and following deepest spiritual impulse. And, in the end, her faith appears victorious — crowned by Divine mercy, and shining out the more brightly from its contrast to the felt weakness of the prophet. As we think of this, it seems as if a fuller light were shed on the history of the trials of an Abraham, an Isaac, or a Jacob; on the inner life of those heroes of faith to whom the Epistle to the Hebrews points us for example and learning (Hebrews 11), and on such Scripture-sayings as these: "Jehovah killeth, and maketh alive: He bringeth down to the grave, and bringeth up" (1 Samuel 2:6); "Know that Jehovah hath set apart him that is godly for Himself: Jehovah will hear when I call unto Him" (Psalms 4:3); or this: "All the paths of Jehovah are mercy and truth unto such as keep His covenant and His testimonies" (Psalms 25:10).

The last glimpse we have of the Shunammite in this narrative is when called by Elisha to receive back her living son, she bends in lowly reverence, and then silently retires (2 Kings 4:36, 37). When next we meet her, it is in circumstances of trial almost as great as that through which she had formerly passed. Once more she proves true, trustful, and brave; and once more is her faith crowned by mercy and deliverance.

Secondly, we think of the symbolical and typical teaching of this history. The Rabbis discuss the question, whether the dead child of the Shunammite could have Levitically defiled those who touched him.

This Pharisaic scruple deserves record for the significant answer it elicits: "The dead defileth, but the living does not defile." To us all this includes a meaning deeper than they could attach to it. The story speaks to us of Him through Whom "death is swallowed up in victory." As we think of Him Who, as God Incarnate, and as the Sent of the Father, is to us the Representative and the Prophet of God in a unique sense, we recall that it was not, as by Elijah or Elisha, through prayer and personal contact, but by the Word of His power that He raised the dead (Mark 5:39-42; Luke 7:13-15; John 11:43, 44). And beyond this we remember that "the hour.... now is, when the dead shall hear the Voice of the Son of God: and they that hear shall live"; and that "whosoever liveth and believeth" in Christ "shall never die" (John 5:25; 11:26).

Lastly, as regards the supernatural in this history, we fully admit that, as previously indicated, the history of Elijah and Elisha marks, so to speak, the high-point in the miraculous attestation of the mission of the prophets. But, by the side of it, there are so many elements of purely human interest, so many indications of human weakness, and so many details which would not have found a place in a legendary account (such as the fruitless mission of Gehazi), while, on the other hand, there is such unadorned simplicity about the whole narrative, and so much spiritual and typical teaching in it as to carry home almost instinctive conviction of the truth and reality of what is recorded.

Yet another, we might almost call it twofold, narrative taken from the history of Elisha's more private ministry claims our attention (2 Kings 4:38-44). It is instructive, as confirming the view that this whole section about Elisha's ministry is taken from a special work on the subject, that the scene is now laid at a considerable interval from the previous history, and at a time of famine (v. 38), which is only long afterwards described in connection with Elisha's prophecy (2 Kings 8:1). The prophet is once more at Gilgal — not that near

Jericho, but another Gilgal, close to Ebal and Gerizim, south-west of Shilo, and situated on a commanding plateau, 3,000 feet above the sea. Here a community of "the sons of the prophets" seems to have been settled (comp. 2 Kings 2:1). It is impossible to say whether Elisha was in the habit of visiting these settlements occasionally or at regular intervals, or else had come on purpose to share the poverty of the community at a time of exceptional distress. The former seems, however, the more likely, since we are told of "the sons of the prophets sitting before him," which, according to well-known Hebrew usage, means that Elisha was giving them instruction (comp. 2 Kings 6:1; Ezekiel 8:1; 14:1; 33:31; Zechariah 3:8; Acts 22:3).

While thus engaged the prophet directed that the usual humble meal should be prepared for the wants of his hearers. Even although it was a time of famine, yet the fare provided was so poor — and this, so far as the text informs us, not merely exceptionally, owing to the dearth — that our former impressions, derived from the straitened circumstances of the prophet's widow (4:1, 2), are fully confirmed. In truth, "the sons of the prophets" seem not only to have supported themselves by manual labor, but to have lived in the humblest manner. This willing submission to poverty and want from devotion to their work reflects the most favorable light on the institution to which they belonged. In the present instance one of their number was sent to gather "green esculents" to be seethed for pottage in the great pot in which their common meals were prepared. By some misadventure the person so sent brought among other herbage a very noxious fruit — probably the wild, or so-called "squirting" cucumber, which he had mistaken for the ordinary cucumber, one of the most common and favorite articles of food in the East.

The dangerous error was discovered after the meal had begun. An appeal to Elisha as the "man of God" brought speedy help. The symbolic meaning of casting "meal" into the pot was, that this was the ordinary and healthy food by which that which had been bitter and dangerous was now to be changed into palatable and nourishing diet. While the help Divinely brought by the prophet as the "man of God" was miraculous, it had, as we readily perceive, also a symbolic significance, the more so, that "the sons of the prophets" had, as disciples, been learning from Elisha. And thus did it become true in every sense: "Pour out for the people, that they may eat. And there was no harm in the pot."

Closely connected with this is the next event recorded. If the former showed how easily God could remove from the provision of His people that which was hurtful by the addition of that which in itself is nutritious and wholesome, the next event affords another instance how readily He can send unexpected provision to supply the wants of His servants. The lesson which it teaches is as old as that of Isaac's reaping an hundredfold of what he had sowed in Gerar at a time of famine (Genesis 26:12), and as true to all time, and to all God's servants, as it had been to the patriarch. In the present case, much needed help in their straits came to Elisha and to his companions from Baal-Shalisha, or Beth-Shalisha. We remember the district as connected with the history of Saul (1 Samuel 9:4): "the land of Shalisha," perhaps the "three valleys" land. It lay north of Lydda, in the plain of Sharon, and was not far distant from that Gilgal which we have described, and the location of which it confirms.

We know that the Lord directed the first-fruits to be given to the Priests and Levites (Numbers 18:13; Deuteronomy 18:4). This ordinance could not any longer be obeyed in the kingdom of Israel, since the Aaronic priesthood, for whose support it was destined, was not in office there. But the pious in Israel, to whom such contributions were not merely matter of obligation nor only of law, but who willingly offered to Jehovah, in acknowledgment of

His sovereignty and proprietary over the land, knew to observe the spirit, if they could no longer obey the letter, of the law. Accordingly this unnamed man from Baal-Shalisha brought, as is expressly stated, to the "man of God" "bread of the first-fruits, twenty loaves of barley and bruised ears of corn in his sack."

The provision supplied by the piety of this unnamed giver Elisha would, in the same spirit of devotion, have shared with those around him. But such conduct ill accorded with the spirit of Elisha's servant. Indeed, it may have been that this history was recorded to mark the character of Gehazi. In any case it was not in him at a time of dearth to dismiss the cares of the morrow by unselfish care for others. He would scarcely venture to state his views explicitly, but, adopting the more prudent course, contented himself with pointing out the apparent insufficiency of such provision for so large a company. It might, according to the pious intention of the donor, have supplied for some time the wants of the prophet, but to set it "before an hundred men" — probably a round number for the whole community — was to lose the real good that might be obtained, without an equivalent benefit to others. It needed the direct command of Elisha to secure his obedience. But Elisha did more. For the teaching not only of Gehazi, but of all, he added the promise, of which, indeed, this unexpected provision was an earnest, that, scanty as it might seem, this provision would not only suffice, but that there should be left over from it. And this, as we understand it, in the widest sense of constant and sufficient supply for all the wants of God's servants. For although this narrative is generally, and in a sense correctly, regarded as prefiguring the miraculous multiplication of the scanty provision with which our Lord fed the multitude (Matthew 14:19-21; John 6:9-13), yet the text does not here indicate any such miraculous increase of the food. But it does most emphatically indicate that Elisha was truly the prophet and servant of Jehovah; that his trust in his God was absolute and unwavering; and that, true to His promise, the Lord will always provide for His servants who look up unto Him. And this is the final lesson of this history to all time and to all men.

CHAPTER 11

Illustration and Confirmation of Biblical History from the Assyrian Monuments — The Deliverance of Syria through Naaman — Naaman's Leprosy and Journey to Samaria — Elisha's Message to Joram and to Naaman — Naaman's Healing and Twofold Request — Gehazi's Deceit and Conviction — Gehazi is struck with the Leprosy of Naaman.

(2 Kings 5.)

FROM the more private ministry of the prophet the Biblical narrative next passes to an account of his public activity. Very significantly, it was the means of bringing Israel once more into direct contact with their great enemy, Syria — this time, not in war, but in peace. And the bloodless victory which was achieved might have taught king and people how easily the LORD could turn the hearts of their adversaries, and by the manifestation of His goodness make them fellow-believers and fellow-worshippers with Israel. In this respect, the present history, as others in this section, is specially prefigurative of New Testament times.

As the narrative proceeds on the supposition of close relations between Israel and Syria — not otherwise mentioned in the Bible — and involves, at least indirectly, certain points of general interest, this seems a fitting opportunity for a brief summary of what recent discoveries of ancient monuments has taught us, not only confirmatory, but illustrative and explanatory of this period of Biblical history.

But in so doing we must keep some considerations in view by way of caution. For first, our knowledge of what may be called monumental history is as yet initial and fragmentary. Secondly, in any seeming discrepancy or slight divergence in details between the inscriptions on the monuments and the records of Jewish history, it seems neither reasonable nor safe to give absolute preference to the former. Jewish writers must have known their own history best, while, in their slight differences from the records on the monuments, we fail to discover any adequate motives on the part of the Jewish historians that could account for their falsifying facts. And, we need scarcely add, the same facts will assume different aspects when viewed from opposite sides. Again, it is admitted on all hands that there are manifest errors on the Assyrian monuments, and this on points where error is difficult, to account for. Thus, to mention one instance — on the Assyrian monuments, Jehu is designated as "the son of Omri," and that by the very monarch to whom he is both represented and described as bringing tribute. Further, we have to bear in mind that our knowledge of Jewish history is also fragmentary. The Old Testament does not profess to be a handbook of Jewish history. It furnishes prophetic or sacred history, which does not recount all events as they happened, nor yet always in their exact succession of time, but presents them in their bearing on the kingdom of God, of which it tells the history. Hence it records or emphasizes only that which is of importance in connection with it. Lastly, we must remember that the chronology of the Bible is in some parts involved in considerable difficulties, partly for the reasons just stated, partly from the different modes of calculating time, and partly also from errors of transcription which would easily creep into the copying of Hebrew numerals, which are marked by letters. Keeping in view these cautions, the neglect of which has led to many false inferences, we have no hesitation in saying, that hitherto all modern historical discoveries have only tended to confirm the Scripture narrative.

Turning to these extraneous sources for information on the earlier history of Judah and Israel under the Kings, we have here, first, the Egyptian monuments, especially those on the walls of the Temple of Karnak, which record the invasion of Judah and Jerusalem by Shishak, described in 1 Kings 14:25, 26, and 2 Chronicles 12. Pictorial representations of this campaign are accompanied by mention of the very names of the conquered Jewish cities.

But with the death of Shishak, the power of Egypt for a time decayed. In its stead that of Assyria reasserted itself. From that time onwards its monuments more or less continuously cast light on the history of Israel. Just as in the Biblical narrative, so in the Assyrian records of that time, Syria occupies a most important place. It will be remembered that that country had recovered its independence in the reign of Solomon, having been wrested by Rezon from the sovereignty of Judah (1 Kings 11:23-25). Thus far we perceive a general parallelism in the outlines of this history. But the Assyrian record leaves a strange impression on the mind, as we recall the importance of Omri, as having been the second if not the real founder of the Israelitish kingdom, the builder of its capital, and the monarch who gave its permanent direction alike to the political and the religious history of Israel. For the common designation for the land of Israel is "the land of Omri," "the land Omri," or "the land of the house of Omri." We regard it as a further indication of the political importance attached to that king when Jehu is designated as "the son of Omri." This could not have been from ignorance of the actual history, since the name of Ahab occurs on the monuments of Assyria, although (if correctly read) in a connection which does not quite agree with our ordinary chronology. Further illustration comes to us from the Assyrian monuments, both of certain phases in the Biblical history of Ahab, and of the explanatory words with which the account of Naaman's healing is introduced: "Now Naaman, captain of the host of the king of Syria, was a great man with his master, and honorable, because by him Jehovah had given deliverance unto Syria" (2 Kings 5:1).

Each of these statements requires some further explanation. As regards the history of Ahab, we note incidentally that the name Ethbaal (1 Kings 16:31) as that of a Sidonian king, occurs also on the Assyrian monuments, just as does Sarepta (1 Kings 17:9, 10), as being a Phoenician town, situate between Tyre and Sidon. But of greatest interest is it to learn from these monuments the political motives which prompted the strange and sudden alliance proposed by Ahab to Ben-hadad (a name amply confirmed by the monuments), after the battle of Aphek (1 Kings 20:26-34). In passing we may notice that in a fragmentary inscription of Asarhaddon, this Aphek, situated east of the lake of Galilee, and a little aside from the great road between Damascus and Samaria, is named as the border-city of Samaria.

Similarly, the mention of thirty-two kings allied with Ben-hadad in his campaign against Israel (1 Kings 20:1), is so far borne out by the Assyrian monuments, that in the campaigns of Assyria against Syria Ben-hadad is always described as fighting in conjunction with a number of allied Syrian princes.

From these inscriptions we also learn that the growing power of Assyria threatened to overwhelm — as it afterwards did — both Syria and the smaller principalities connected with it. A politician like Ahab must have felt the danger threatening his kingdom of Samaria from the advancing power of Assyria. If Ben-hadad had endeavored to strengthen himself by the subjugation of Samaria, Ahab, in the hour of his triumph, desired, by an alliance with the now humbled Ben-hadad, to place Syria as a kind of bulwark between himself and the king of Assyria. This explains the motive of Ahab, who had no real trust in the might and deliverance of Jehovah, but looked to political combinations for safety, in allowing to go out of his hand the man whom Jehovah "appointed to utter destruction" (1 Kings 20:42).

Another circumstance connected with the treaty of Aphek, not recorded in the Bible, and only known from the Assyrian monuments, casts light on this prophetic announcement of judgment to Ahab: "Therefore thy life shall be for his life, and thy people for his people." From the monuments we learn, in illustration of the alliance between Ben-hadad and Ahab, and of the punishment threatened upon it, that in the battle of Karkar, or Aroer, in which the Assyrian monarch Shalmaneser II. so completely defeated Syria, the forces of Ahab, to the number of not fewer than 2000 chariots and 10,000 men, had fought on the side of Ben-hadad. As we read of 14,000 or, in another inscription, of 20,500 of the allies as having been slain in this battle, we perceive the fulfillment of the Divine threatening upon that alliance (1 Kings 20:42).

At the same time we may also learn that many things mentioned in Scripture which, with our present means of knowledge, seem strange and inexplicable, may become plain, and be fully confirmed, by further information derived from independent sources.

The battle of Karkar was not the only engagement in which the forces of Syria met, and were defeated by, those of Assyria. It was fought in the sixth year of the reign of Shalmaneser. Another successful campaign is chronicled as having been undertaken in the eleventh year of the same reign, when Shalmaneser records that for the ninth time he crossed the Euphrates; and yet another, in the fourteenth year of his reign, when at the head of 120,000 men he crossed the river at its high flood. Two inferences may, for our present purpose, be made from these notices. The defeat of Ahab's forces, when fighting in conjunction with Ben-hadad, will account for the cessation of the alliance entered into after the battle of Aphek. Again, the repeated defeat of Ben-hadad by Assyria will explain how Ahab took heart of grace, and in company with Jehoshaphat undertook that fatal expedition against Ramoth-Gilead (1 Kings 22), in which literally the "life" of Ahab went for that of him whom, from short-sighted political motives, he had spared (1 Kings 20:42). Lastly, these repeated wars between Assyria and Syria, of which the Assyrian monarch would naturally only record the successful engagements, help us to understand the phrase by which Naaman, captain of the host of Syria, is introduced as he "by whom the LORD had given deliverance [perhaps "victory"] unto Syria" (2 Kings 5:1).

The expression just quoted seems to forbid the application of the words to the victory of Ben-hadad over Ahab, although the Rabbis imagine that the fatal arrow by which Ahab was smitten came from the bow of Naaman.

Accordingly we cannot (as most commentators do) mark this antithesis: that the conqueror of Israel had to come to Israel for healing. But the fact is in itself sufficiently remarkable, especially when we think of it in connection with his disease, which would have placed even an Israelite, so to speak, outside the pale of Israel. In striking contrast to the mention of the strength and bravery of Naaman, and of his exalted position, Scripture abruptly, without pause or copula of conjunction, records the fact: "a leper."

We need not pause to consider the moral of this contrast, with all of teaching which it should convey to us. Quite another lesson comes to us from an opposite direction. For we also learn from this history how, when our need is greatest, help may be nearest, and that, in proportion as we feel the hopelessness of our case, God may prepare a way for our deliverance. It was certainly so in this instance. Once more we mark the wonder-working Providence of God, Who, without any abrupt or even visibly direct interference, brings about results which, if viewed by themselves, must seem absolutely miraculous. And this, by means which at the time may have appeared most unpromising.

It must have been a crushing sorrow that came upon that Israelitish household, when the Syrian bands carried from it the little maiden whom we find afterwards waiting on Naaman's wife. Yet this was the first link in the chain of events which not only brought healing of body and soul to the Syrian captain, but anew proved alike to Jew and Gentile that there was a living God in Israel, who had placed there His accredited representative. Assuredly the most devoted affection could not have desired for a child a place of greater honor or usefulness than that which this Jewish maiden occupied in the household of the Syrian captain. What follows is told with utmost simplicity, and bears the impress of truth. For, it was only natural that this child should tell her mistress of the prophet in Samaria, or express the full confidence in his ability to recover her master of his leprosy. Similarly, it was only what we should have expected when her mistress repeated to her husband what the child had said, and perhaps equally natural on the part of Naaman to repeat this to his king, alike to obtain his leave for going to Samaria, and in such a manner as would be most likely to secure the desired result.

As heathens, and especially as Syrians, neither Naaman nor Ben-hadad would see anything strange in the possession of such magical powers by a prophet of Israel. Similarly, it was quite in accordance with heathen notions to expect that the king of Israel could obtain from his own prophet any result which he might desire. A heathen king was always the religious as well as the political chief of his people, and to command the services and obedience of his own prophet would seem almost a matter of course. It was for this reason that Ben-hadad furnished Naaman with a letter to the king of Israel. Hence also, imperious as the tone of the letter seems, it scarcely warranted the interpretation which the king of Israel — probably Joram — put upon it. What is reported of it in the sacred text (2 King 5:6) must, of necessity be regarded as only forming a part of the letter, stating its main object. On the other hand, we can quite understand that, from the Jewish point of view, Joram would speak of what he regarded as a demand that he himself should heal Naaman of his leprosy, as equivalent to requiring of him what God alone could do. His only it was to kill or to make alive (Deuteronomy 32:39; 1 Samuel 2:6), and leprosy was considered a living death (Numbers 12:12). As he communicated this strange behest to his attendants and advisers — presumably not in the presence of Naaman — it was not unnatural that Joram should regard it as a desire to find occasion of quarrel. The craven king of Israel rent his clothes, in token of deepest mourning — as if he had already seen his own and his people's destruction.

Some of the lessons suggested by the conduct of Joram may be of practical use. We mark first the cowardice of the man who gives way to despair before any danger has actually arisen. Yet there are not a few who tremble not before that which is real, but before fears which, after all, prove wholly groundless. It need scarcely be said how much good work, whether on the part of individuals or of the Church, has been hindered by apprehensions of this kind. The source of all lies, perhaps, not so much in disbelief as in non-belief, which is by far the commonest form of unbelief. Joram knew better and believed worse than the king of Syria — just as is sometimes the case with the children of God and the men of the world. He knew, as the Syrian did not, that God alone could give help; but he did not look for Divine help, as the Syrian, although in mistaken manner, had done. He had religion, but it stood him in no good stead; it was laid aside precisely when it was needed. He did not call to mind that there was a prophet in Israel, but in helpless terror rent his clothes. So we also, instead of immediately and almost instinctively resorting to God, too often forget Him till every other means has been exhausted, when we apply to Him rather from despair than from faith.

Reverently speaking, it would have been impossible for Elisha as "the man of God" to have been silent on this occasion. His message of reproof to the king: "Wherefore hast thou rent thy clothes?" and of confidence: "Let him come now to me, and he shall know that there is a prophet in Israel," is not one of self-assertion, but of assertion of God. It was a testimony and, let us add, a test alike for Israel and for the heathen world of the presence of the living and true God. Yet while viewing it in this grander application, we ought not to forget what confirmation it gave to the simple faith of that "little one" in the service of Naaman's wife. For God's dealings are most wide-reaching: they extend up to heaven, and yet embrace also the poorest of His people upon earth.

In accordance with the direction of the king, Naaman now betook himself "with his horses and his chariot" to the humble dwelling of Elisha, which, as we infer from verse 3, was in Samaria. Greater or more instructive contrast could scarcely be imagined. We know that Naaman had come to Samaria not only armed with a royal letter, almost imperious in its tone, and at the head of a great retinue, but bringing with him, as princely gifts for his expected healing, a sum of not less than ten talents of silver (computed at from 3000 pounds to about 3750 pounds), and six thousand pieces of gold (computed at from about 7500 pounds to about 9000 pounds), together with "ten changes of raiment," that is, of those festive suits which were so costly and so much valued in the East. Between this display and pomp and the humble waiting outside the lowly home of the prophet there was sufficient contrast. But it was unspeakably intensified when the prophet, without even seeing the Syrian captain, sent him this message: "Go and wash in Jordan seven times, and thy flesh shall come again to thee, and thou shalt be clean." We may at once say that the conduct of Elisha was not prompted by fear of defilement by leprosy, nor by a desire to mark the more clearly the miracle about to be performed, least of all by spiritual pride.

The spiritual pride of a Jew would have found other expression, and, in general, those who cherish spiritual pride are scarcely proof against such visits as this of Naaman. We cannot doubt that the bearing of Elisha was Divinely directed. One has said that it was dictated by the inner state of Naaman, as evinced by the manner in which he received the prophet's direction (ver. 11). Perhaps we should add (with another old writer), that Elisha would thus teach Naaman that neither his pomp nor his wealth was the cause of his healing, and also that help did not come from the prophet, as if such power were inherent in the prophet. The latter, indeed, would seem of chief importance in the teaching required by a heathen.

We can readily perceive how alike the manner and the matter of Elisha's direction would stir the indignation of Naaman. As Syria's captain he would naturally expect a different reception from the Israelitish prophet, and as a heathen, that Elisha would have used some magical means, such as to "move his hand up and down over the place," calling the while upon the name of Jehovah his God, and so heal him of his leprosy. And Naaman spoke both as a heathen and as a Syrian when he contemptuously compared the limpid waters of "Abana and Pharpar," a which transformed the wilderness around Damascus into a very paradise of beauty and riches, with the turbid flood of Jordan, if, indeed, healing were to be obtained by such means.

"So he turned, and went away in a rage." The reasoning by which Naaman had so nearly deprived himself of a benefit which would be to him as life from the dead, is substantially the same as that which leads so many to turn from the one remedy to which God directs them. The simple command of the Gospel to "Wash, and be clean," like the words of the prophet which had prefigured it, is still to the Jews a stumbling-block, and to the Greeks foolishness. The difficulty felt by Naaman is the same as that of so many in our days: the need of humiliation, and of faith in a remedy which seems so inadequate to the end. If washing be required, let it be in the Abana and Pharpar of our own waters, not in the turbid stream of Israel! But it is ever this humiliation of heart and simple faith in God's provision which are required for our healing.

"Except ye be converted, and become as little children, ye shall not enter into the kingdom of heaven" (Matthew 18:3). And so Naaman had to learn it. It was well that the relation between himself and his servants was so simple and affectionate ("my father"), that they could address him in terms of respectful expostulation, and so turn him from his rash purpose. For, often those around can see the true bearing of things far better than we. At the same time, we may also learn from the relation between Naaman and his servants how the faithful performance of ordinary duties may prepare the way for the reception of a higher blessing.

So it came to pass that instead of returning "in a rage" to Damascus, a leper, Naaman went down to Jordan. And as, obedient to "the saying of the man of God," he "dipped himself seven times in Jordan," "his flesh came again like unto the flesh of a little child, and he was clean." We can scarcely be mistaken in regarding the number seven as symbolic of the covenant (comp. also 1 Kings 18:43), and as also implying a trial of faith, since presumably the healing did not come till after the seventh washing. And now it appeared, by the effect produced, that Elisha had throughout sought the restoration not only of bodily health, but also the spiritual recovery of Naaman. Although not so bidden by the prophet, yet following the promptings of a renewed heart, like the grateful Samaritan in the Gospel (Luke 17:15), he returned to Elisha, and made such full acknowledgment of God — both negatively and positively — that it might have been said of it at that time: "I have not found so great faith, no, not in Israel" (Matthew 8:10). And he also showed, in such manner as he could, the evangelical fruits of gratitude, and of a new life direction. Of the first he gave evidence in his desire to offer a gift; of the second, in his request for "two mules' burden of earth." This, for the purpose of constructing an altar to Jehovah, as we infer from the expression of his resolve henceforth only to bring offerings unto the LORD.

Only very brief explanation seems necessary of Elisha's refusal to accept any gift from Naaman. For the prophets seem not unfrequently to have accepted such offerings (1 Samuel 9:7, 8; 1 Kings 14:3), and Elisha himself had only lately done so (2 Kings 4:42). But in the present instance it was of the utmost importance to show — in contradistinction to heathen soothsayers — that, as the prophet of God did not work miracles in his own power, nor by his own will, so he did it not for reward, and that the gift of God could not be purchased with money. Indeed, we can scarcely exaggerate the impression which the refusal of Elisha must have made both on the followers of Naaman and generally in Israel. One of the Fathers has here marked in the prophet's conduct the same principle which underlay the direction of our LORD when He sent out His disciples with this injunction: "Freely ye have received, freely give" (Matthew 10:8). Nor could Elisha be in doubt about the other request of Naaman. If in making his altar of earth according to the Divine direction (Exodus 20:24), he wished to use that of the land of Israel, it could not have been with the thought that the God of Israel could only be worshipped on Israelitish soil.

Any idea of Jehovah as a national Deity, bound to the soil of Israel, would have been in contradiction to his expressed conviction that there was "no God in all the earth but in Israel:" no national deities, but the One living and true God, Whose knowledge and manifestation were only in Israel. Nor would Elisha have given his sanction to what rested on so serious a mistake. But we can easily understand the feelings which prompted a desire to rear an Israelitish altar, not only in loving remembrance of the benefit received, but as congruous to the worship of Israel, to which his new faith had led him. It would be an outward expression of his inward faith, and would at the same time constantly proclaim throughout Syria that there was no other God than He of Israel, and no other worship than His.

And yet wider thoughts come to us. The Old Testament dispensation seems to enlarge as it has touch of the heathen world: it seems to break through its temporary bounds; it becomes universal in its application, and in its wide-hearted toleration loses its exclusiveness. Thus this incident also is prefigurative of New Testament times. For the implied sanction of Naaman's sacrifices — though probably only burnt and thank-offerings, — seems to carry us beyond the preparatory dispensation. On the other hand, it is evidence of this toleration when Elisha does not return a negative answer to the plea of Naaman — in which, however, an important alteration in the reading should be noted: "When my master goeth into the house of Rimmon to bow down there, and he leaneth on my hand, and I bow down in the house of Rimmon when he boweth down in the house of Rimmon — oh, let Jehovah forgive thy servant in this matter."

It will be noticed that according to this reading a sharp distinction is drawn — even although the terms used are the same — between the "bowing down" of Naaman, simply because his royal master leant on his arm, and the "bowing down" of the king of Syria for the purpose of worship. The very mention of this scruple by Naaman proved not only the tenderness of his enlightened conscience, but that he was not in any danger of conformity to heathen worship. And so, without specially entering on the matter, Elisha could bid him "go in peace."

But there was yet another and a sad sequel to this history. We have already had repeated occasion to notice the essential difference in spirit between the prophet and his servant. It now appeared in such manner as, if left unpunished, to have marred the work of Elisha. It seems difficult to understand how, with full knowledge of the great work just wrought, and of all that had passed, Gehazi could have taken up a position so different from that of his master. But, alas, there have been too many similar instances to make it appear quite strange. The character of Gehazi was in every respect the exact opposite of Elisha's. He was covetous, selfish, and narrow-minded. There is a striking contrast between the "As Jehovah liveth," with which Elisha prefaced his persistent refusal to receive aught of Naaman (ver. 16), and the same phrase in the mouth of Gehazi, as he resolved to "take somewhat" of "this Syrian" (ver. 20). To Gehazi it seemed that his master "had spared this Syrian" very needlessly and very foolishly, "in not receiving at his hands that which he brought." He could not see in what had passed anything higher than a transaction between man and man. It had been an act of romantic generosity, an unpractical display of mistaken principle, where every consideration — even nationality and religion — pointed in the other direction. At any rate, there was no reason why he should not act differently.

Naaman had pursued his journey a little distance, when he saw the servant of the prophet hastening after him. Showing to the servant honor similar to that which he would have paid to his master, the Syrian captain descended from his chariot to meet him. In answer to Naaman's anxious inquiry, Gehazi pretended a message from Elisha to the effect that two of the sons of the prophets had just come to him from Mount Ephraim, on which both Bethel and Gilgal were situated, and that he requested for them a talent of silver and two changes of garments. Probably we are to understand that these imaginary "sons of the prophets" were represented as having come in name of their respective communities, to crave help from Elisha. This would explain why Naaman should have urged Gehazi to "be pleased" — to "consent" — to take two talents (each from 300 pounds to 375 pounds). But for the hardening effect of sin, especially of lying and covetousness, Gehazi must have been touched by the evident simplicity of Naaman, and by that respectful courtesy which now would not allow the servant of the prophet, who had come on such a charitable errand, to be burdened with carrying the silver, but detailed two of his attendants for the purpose. Gehazi allowed them to come as far as "the hill," and then dismissed them, to prevent possible detection.

Having secreted the money in the house, Gehazi made his appearance before his master. To what he might have felt as a searching inquiry, "Whence, Gehazi?" he replied by a bold denial of having been absent from the house. Evidently Gehazi did not realize that the Jehovah Whom he had erst invoked, and before Whom Elisha stood, was the living and the true God. Taking up the very words of Gehazi, "Thy servant did not go," Elisha put it, "Did not my heart go?" and then set before him the whole scene as it had been present to his inward spiritual vision.

Then, setting forth the incongruity of such mean lying and self-seeking on such an occasion — when the glory of God should have been the sole thought and aim of a true Israelite, he pronounced upon him what must be felt a sentence of meet retribution. The Syrian had become an Israelite in heart and spirit, and he was healed of his leprosy in Israel's waters. The Israelite had become heathen in heart and spirit, and he and his were struck with the leprosy of the Syrian, whose money he had coveted for himself and his family. What each had sown, that did he reap. And this also was not only for just judgment, but for a testimony to God and to His servant.

CHAPTER 12: TWO WONDERFUL MANIFESTATIONS OF GOD'S PRESENCE WITH HIS PROPHET: THE INTERPOSITION ON BEHALF OF "THE SONS OF THE PROPHETS" BY THE BANKS OF JORDAN, AND THAT IN THE DELIVERANCE OF ELISHA AT DOTHAN — INFLUENCE OF ELISHA'S MINISTRY — GOD, THE EVER-PRESENT HELP AND DELIVERER IN TIMES OF DANGER — THE SYRIANS LED BLINDED INTO SAMARIA — THE CONDUCT OF THE KING AND OF THE PROPHET.

(2 KINGS 6:1-23.)

FOR a brief space the narrative turns again to the more private and personal ministry of Elisha. Or perhaps it may be more correct to say that the history which now follows is inserted in this connection, immediately after that of Gehazi, to show that as the unfaithful servant who did not realize the presence and help of Jehovah, received meet punishment, so would they who clung to the prophet in faith and with faithfulness experience the deliverance of God, and this, even in seemingly small matters, and, if need be, by extraordinary interposition. Thus the history of the miraculously restored ax would supplement and complement that of Gehazi's punishment — both teaching substantially the same lessons: only the one in their negative, the other in their positive aspect.

We have repeatedly noticed that the ministry of Elisha had its deep influence upon Israel, despite the corruption in Church and State. Perhaps one of the most pleasing evidences of this appears in the growing number of "the sons of the prophets." On a previous occasion (2 Kings 4:43) we found at Gilgal about one hundred assembled to listen to the instruction of Elisha. This would represent a large number in proportion to the small and, in parts, semi-heathen population of the northern kingdom — especially when we remember that there were similar communities at Bethel and at Jericho. It is probably among the latter that the present narrative is laid, and it shows that this community was so prosperous that their meeting-place no longer sufficed for their growing numbers.

It was this which led to the proposal of constructing another and larger place for their use by the banks of the Jordan. From the abundance of timber in the district it would be easy to provide accommodation sufficient for their simple wants. And the manner in which their proposal was worded (ver. 2) is peculiarly and graphically Eastern. Elisha not only assented to their project, but at their request consented to accompany and remain with them while engaged in their work. It need scarcely be said that this was not asked in order that the prophet might superintend their labors, but to have in their midst the loved master, whose very presence seemed to imply the Divine blessing, and whose words of instruction would secure it. In any case the whole narrative shows, on the one hand, the simplicity and earnestness of their faith, and, on the other, the poverty and humbleness of their outward circumstances.

Evidence of both was soon to appear. As they were engaged in felling the timber the ax-head of one of the workers became suddenly detached and fell into the water. His exclamation of distress addressed to Elisha, with this significant addition, that the ax had been "asked" or "entreated for," constituted an appeal to the prophet. It is of comparatively secondary importance, whether it had been so asked as a gift, or as a loan — though the former seems to us the meaning of the word.

What followed had best be recorded in a rigorously literal translation of the sacred text. "And the man of God said: Where has it fallen? And he showed him the place, and he [Elisha] cut off wood [a stick, piece of a tree], and put it in there [sent it], and he caused the iron to flow" — on which, the man, as directed by the prophet, "put in ["sent," the same word as before] his hand and took it." The first, but also the most superficial, impression on reading these words is that they do not necessarily imply anything miraculous.

Accordingly, both some of the Rabbis and certain modern interpreters have argued, either that the stick which had been cut off struck right into the hole of the ax-head and so brought it up, or else that the stick thrust under the ax had rendered it possible to drag it to land. But, to speak plainly, both these suggestions involve such manifest impossibilities, as hardly to require serious discussion. It is scarcely necessary to add that every such explanation is opposed equally to the wording and the spirit of the sacred text, which assuredly would not have recorded among the marvelous doings of the heaven-sent prophet a device, which, if it had been possible, could have been accomplished by any clever-handed person. There cannot be any doubt in the mind of every impartial man that Scripture here intends to record a notable miracle. On the other hand, there is nothing in the sacred text which obliges us to believe that the iron "did swim." In fact, the Hebrew word is never used in that sense. The impression left on our minds is that the iron which had sunk to the bottom was set in motion, made to float, probably, by some sudden rush of water. Beyond this we cannot go in our attempts to explain the manner in which this miraculous result may have been brought about.

But in another direction we can go much further. We recall what has previously been stated about the extraordinary character of the mission of Elijah and of Elisha, which accounts for a series of miracles in their history, unparalleled in the Old Testament, and, indeed, quite exceptional, being connected with what may be described as the decisive crisis in the religious history of the kingdom of Israel. If there was to be direct Divine interposition in order to recall Israel to their allegiance to Jehovah, it is evident that the religious state of the people, ripening for a judgment which history has shown to be irrevocable, would render necessary means that were extraordinary, even in the miraculous history of the Old Testament. And if the mission of the prophets was in itself an extraordinary means, chiefly necessitated by the condition of the people, these means now required to be intensified. Accordingly Elijah and Elisha were to be prophets of the prophets — if we may use the expression — in order that this great truth, which alone could have saved the people, might be presented in a concrete and most vivid manner; that Jehovah was the living and the true God, ever-present with His own, whether for blessing or in judgment. And this must be always kept in view when studying this history. Nay, is it not the great truth which should always be present to our minds, alike as the outcome of all history, the lesson of our experience, and the guide in our acting?

From this point of view much additional light is thrown on this particular event. Elisha, summoned to be among these poor, simple-hearted workers for God, could not have been deaf to their appeal, nor appeared helpless in presence of their felt need, however humble. Its very humbleness was only an additional reason for the Divine help. It would have been a contradiction in this special history, nay, in the history of Elisha generally, who seemed to embody the eternal presence of the living God among them. And as the man received back the lost ax-head — really to him a new ax-head, now to be used with a new ax-handle, it would teach him many lessons, not the least of them the constant care and provision of the God Whose messenger and representative the prophet was, and which extended as far as our need, however small and humble it might be.

Of this very truth, both Israel, as a nation, and their enemies, were presently to receive evidence, and that on a much larger scale. And this explains the next recorded event, without requiring us to regard it as having followed in strict chronological order on that just commented upon. The sacred text informs us that "the king of Syria was warring against Israel" — indicating rather a state of chronic warfare and marauding expeditions, such as are common in the East, than a regular campaign. In his consultation with his "servants" what place to occupy, there seems to have been a scheme to lay an ambush for the capture of the king of Israel, whether, as Josephus suggests (Ant. 9:4, 3), when Joram was on a hunting expedition, or else when he passed from one palace to another. But each time the prophet sent timely warning, and the king was wise enough to avoid the locality indicated, and, instead of passing that way, to send and obtain confirmation of what had been foretold him. As this happened repeatedly, the king of Syria suspected a traitor among his counselors, probably the more readily, that information of the king of Israel's projected movements must in every case have come to the Syrians from some confederate at the Israelitish court.

This explains how one of the servants of Ben-hadad — probably, one of those by whom these secret communications were carried on — could so readily point out that the information was conveyed by Elisha, whose prophetic knowledge compassed the inmost secrets of Syria's council-chamber.

It also explains how the residence of Elisha could be so readily ascertained, and an expedition planned and hastily carried out with the view of making him a prisoner. We have no difficulty in identifying the Dothan which was now the temporary residence of Elisha, and the object of Ben-Hades' attack. The spot still bears the old designation of Tell (hill) Dothan. The "twin wells" which gave it that name, are north and east of it. The place itself — about twelve miles north of Samaria, and a little to the south-west of Engannim — stands on a green hill, or enclosed upland basin, overlooking (to the north) one of the richest pasture-lands, the oblong plain of Dothan.

Here Joseph's brethren could find sufficient sustenance for their flocks when they had exhausted for a time the wider plain of Shechem (Genesis 37:17). Just below it, to the south, is the great caravan-route from Gilead to Sharon, and thence to Egypt, where those Midianites passed to whom Joseph was sold by his brethren. Dothan is surrounded by an amphitheater of hills; but northwards it looks out over the plain towards those defiles through which the Syrian host advanced that was to capture Elisha.

So far from being surprised at the array of "horses, and chariots, and a strong power," which Ben-hadad dispatched on this expedition, we feel that it is thoroughly in accordance with the heathen notions of power.

In the course of this narrative we have repeatedly met instances of this, and even the proposal to send fifty strong men for the rescue of Elijah (2 Kings 2:16) may be regarded as representing the influence of similar ideas in Israel. Besides, it might have been that the people would rise in defense of their prophet. Elisha knew all these preparations on the part of Ben-hadad; knew also, that during the night the city had been surrounded by the Syrians, so that, to the eye of man, there seemed no way of escape. But he rested quietly, for he also knew that "He that keepeth Israel neither slumbers nor sleeps." Nay, does it not seem as if the language of Psalms 121 quite specially described his experience, and as if he had been looking up to those "mountains" from whence his help was to come? And is it not often so in the experience of God's people, as if the wording of the Psalms were almost literally portraying alike what they feel and hope, and what happens to them?

It was early morning, and the servant of the prophet — not Gehazi now, but perhaps one of "the sons of the prophets" — went forth, it may be to make preparation for the return of his master from Dothan to his permanent home at Samaria (2 Kings 6:32).

This would throw light on the language which Elisha afterwards held to the Syrians (2 Kings 6:19). But when Elisha's servant saw the town surrounded by the Syrian host, his heart failed him, and he turned to his master with the despairing inquiry what they were to do. If our previous suggestion that they had intended leaving Dothan that morning be well founded, it is not necessary to suppose that the servant knew the expedition to have been especially destined against Elisha; but he would naturally feel that not only was their projected journey now impossible, but that his master and himself were in imminent danger from which there seemed no possibility of escape. What follows is both historically and symbolically of deepest importance. In answer to the prayer of Elisha the eyes of the young man were opened, and he beheld the height which overlooked Dothan — or else that on which it stood — full of horses and chariots of fire. Truly had Elisha said: "Fear not, for more they with us than they with them." It was not only the Divine answer to the Syrian challenge, and the manifestation of the Divine triumphant supremacy over the power of the enemy, but the revelation of the ever-present, watchful help of Him Whose angel "encampeth round about them that fear Him, and delivereth them" (Psalms 34:7; 55:18; 91:11). But although the vision was vouchsafed to the prophet's servant when his "eyes" were "opened" (Genesis 21:19; Numbers 22:31) — that is, a sight of objects granted him, which, in our present state, is preternatural — we regard it as none the less real. And this, though the appearance of "fire," which was the well-known symbol of the Divine manifestation (Exodus 24:17; 2 Kings 2:11; Psalms 1:3; Isaiah 29:6; Ezekiel 1:4, 27), and even the form of "chariots and horses" might be the human mode of presentation familiar to the Jewish mind (comp. also Psalms 104:3; Isaiah 66:15; Habakkuk 3:8). But we entertain no doubt of the real and constant, though by us unseen, presence of those angel-hosts, which alike the Old and the New Testament teach us to believe are the messengers of God's behests and ministering spirits to His saints. And this adds both solemnity and comfort to all our doing.

In view of this heavenly guard there could be no hesitation on the part of Elisha and his servant in carrying out what we have supposed to have been their original intention of returning to Samaria. And so the two went down to the Syrian host.

At the prayer of Elisha they were smitten, not with blindness but with blinding, so that, in the words of the Rabbis, "they saw, but they knew not." It was not, therefore, "a lawful stratagem" on his part, but literally true, when Elisha said to the Syrians who were about to make their way into Dothan: "This is not the way, and this is not the city; come after me, and I will bring you to the man whom you are seeking."

For Elisha was then on his way to his home at Samaria, nor could he who had just pointed his servant to the heavenly defense around them have been tempted to tell a lie in order to escape the threatened danger. His object was to show the Syrians that the God Whose prophet he was could not be contended with in such manner as they thought, nor His purposes frustrated. And not the Syrians only, but Israel also, would have practical proof that He was the living God when Elisha brought his blinded pursuers as his willing captives into Samaria.

It must have been a wonderful sight, alike to Syrians and Israelites, when, in answer to the prophet's prayer, the LORD once more "opened the eyes of the enemy," and they found themselves in the midst of Samaria. We can only indulge in conjecture, how, perhaps, Elisha had hurried on with the swiftest; how the watchman on the tower would have announced the approach of the strange band; how, although no marauding expedition would have been expected to make a raid upon Samaria, yet the royal troops would have mustered under the command of the king himself — and perhaps, as Josephus puts it, in his somewhat rationalistic account of the event, have surrounded the Syrians at the prophet's bidding; and, lastly, what terrible surprise followed when they discovered where they were. It is more important to mark how once more all acted in character. With an eagerness and a spiritual dullness characteristic of him, Joram would fain have slaughtered these captives of the LORD.

And with characteristic uprightness and large-hearted generosity, the prophet almost indignantly rebuked the spurious zeal and courage of the king: "Thou shalt not smite! Them whom thou hast made captives with thy sword and thy bow thou smitest."

It would have been unmanly to have done otherwise; Jehovah had not brought these blinded men there as His own captives to give the king of Israel an easy and a cruel triumph; nay, the whole moral purpose of this event, its very character, would have been changed, if the proposal of Joram had been carried out. And it was right royal treatment on the part of the Heavenly Conqueror's ambassador, when, at his bidding, they gave them a great meal, and then dismissed them to their master, to report how Jehovah made captives of the captors of His representative, and how He entertained and released His captives.

And what is right is also wise. We do not wonder to read that after this marauding bands of Syrians no longer made incursions into the land. But to us all there are many lessons here: not only of the unseen, but certain presence of our God and of His help; of rebuke to our groundless fears, and encouragement to go forward; but also as concerning the enemies of the people of God and our dealing with them. How often when they have surrounded Dothan, and deemed themselves certain of achieving their purpose, have they seemed blinded, and found themselves in the midst of Samaria. How many times have arguments and measures, which were thought certain of success against the truth or the people of God, ended in quite the opposite result. And lastly, should we not learn to deal with those whom not our own power, but God, has made helpless captives, not as if they were our personal enemies, but generously, while faithfully, although in meekness, instructing those who oppose themselves, if God peradventure will give them repentance to the acknowledging of the truth (2 Timothy 2:25)? For, as harsh or self-asserting bearing on the part of those who may defend the truth of God would tend to injure that cause, probably more than anything else, so assuredly would it be palpably and painfully incongruous. And yet — the LORD reigneth, and He will take care of His own work.

CHAPTER 13: SIEGE OF SAMARIA BY THE SYRIANS — TERRIBLE STRAITS AND TRAGEDY IN THE CITY — THE KING SENDS TO SLAY ELISHA, BUT ARRESTS HIS MESSENGER — ANNOUNCED DELIVERANCE AND JUDGMENT ON THE UNBELIEVING "LORD" — THE DISCOVERY BY THE FOUR LEPERS — FLIGHT OF THE SYRIANS — RELIEF OF SAMARIA — THE UNBELIEVING TRODDEN TO DEATH IN THE GATE.

(2 KINGS 6:24-7:20.)

THE sacred narrative now resumes the record of public events in Israel, although still in close connection with the ministry of Elisha, which at this crisis appears the primal factor in the history of the northern kingdom. Remembering that it is written from the prophetic standpoint, we do not here look for a strictly chronological arrangement of events, but rather expect to find them grouped according to the one grand idea which underlies this history.

It is impossible to determine what time may have intervened between the attempts and the expedition described in the last chapter and the open warfare against Samaria, the incidents of which we are about to relate. According to Josephus (Ant. 9:4, 4), it followed immediately — the narrative of those who had returned from Samaria having convinced Ben-hadad that any secret attempts upon the king of Israel were hopeless, and determined him to resort to open warfare, for which he deemed his army sufficient.

However that may be, he was soon to experience how vain were all such attempts when God was in defense of His people. And here the question naturally arises why such Divine interpositions should have been made on behalf of Israel. The answer is not difficult, and it will throw light upon the course of this history. Evidently, it was a period of comparative indecision, before the final attitude of the nation towards Jehovah was taken, and with it the ultimate fate of Israel decided. Active hostility to the prophet as God's representative and to the worship of Jehovah had ceased, and there were even tokens for good and of seeming return to the LORD. But, as events soon showed, there was not any real repentance, and what to a superficial observer might seem the beginning of a calm was only a lull before the storm. This interval of indecision, or token of pending decision, must be taken into account. The presence of the prophet in Israel meant the final call of God to Israel, and the possibility of national repentance and forgiveness. Every special interposition, such as those we have described, was an emphatic attestation of Elisha's mission, and hence of his message; and every deliverance indicated how truly and easily God could help and deliver His people, if only that were in them towards which the presence of the prophet pointed. And the more minute and apparently unimportant the occasions for such interposition and deliverance were, the more strikingly would all this appear. It is with such thoughts in our minds that we must study the history of the siege and miraculous relief of Samaria.

Ben-hadad was once more laying siege to Samaria (comp. 1 Kings 20). And to such straits was the city reduced that not only levitically unclean but the most repulsive kind of meat fetched a price which in ordinary times would have been extravagant for the most abundant supply of daintiest food, while the coarsest material for cooking it sold at a proportionally high rate. It must have been from want of provender for them that such beasts of burden as asses, so common and useful in the East, were killed. Even their number must have been terribly diminished (Comp. 2 Kings 7:13) when an ass's head would sell for eighty pieces of silver (variously computed at from 5 pounds to 8 pounds), and a "cab of doves' dung" — used when dried as material for firing — for five pieces of silver (computed at from 6/ to 10/).

If such were the straits to which the wealthier were reduced, we can imagine the sufferings of the poor. But only the evidence of those who themselves were actors in it could have made any one believe in the possibility of such a tragedy as that to the tale of which King Joram was to listen. While making the round of the broad city wall (the glacis), probably to encourage as well as to inspect the defenders of the city, and to observe the movements of the enemy, he was arrested by the cry for help of a frenzied woman. Probably too much accustomed to the state of famine and misery, the king uttered an ejaculation, indicative not only of the general distress prevailing in the city, but of his own state of mind. His words seem to imply that he felt Jehovah alone could give help, perhaps that he had some dim expectation of it, but that the LORD withheld from sending it for some reason for which neither king nor people were to blame.

As we view it in the light of his after-conduct (comp. vv. 31-33), King Joram connected the straits of Samaria with the prophet Elisha, — either they were due to his direct agency, or else to his failure to make intercession for Israel. Such ignorance of the spiritual aspect of God's dealings, even when they are recognized, together with an unhumbled state of heart, unwillingness to return to God, and the ascription of the evils befalling us to the opposite of their true cause, are only too common in that sorrow which Holy Scripture characterizes as "of the world," and working "death."

The horrible story which the woman told to the king was that she and another had made the agreement that each of them was successively to kill her son for a meal in which they two were to share; that the one had fulfilled her part of the bargain, but that, after partaking of the dreadful feast, the other had hidden her son. Whether or not the feelings of motherhood had thus tardily asserted themselves in the second mother, or whether, in the avarice of her hunger, she wished to reserve for herself alone the unnatural meal, matters not for our present purpose. But we recall that such horrors had been in warning foretold in connection with Israel's apostasy (Leviticus 26:29; Deuteronomy 28:53); that they seem to have been enacted during the siege of Jerusalem by Nebuchadnezzar (Lamentations 4:10); and lastly, that we have historical evidence of their occurrence during the last siege of Jerusalem by Titus (Jos. War, 6., 3, 4). Even if it had not reminded the king of the predicted Divine curse, such a tale could not have fallen on his ear, especially in existing circumstances, without exciting the deepest and strongest feelings. The story itself was sufficiently harrowing; but that a mother should, even in the madness of self-reproach, make public appeal to the king, that her neighbor should be kept to her part of the compact, revealed a state of matters and of public feeling which called for that universal mourning which the king, as head of the state, inaugurated, when almost instinctively "he rent his clothes." And so, too often, they that will not mourn for sin have to mourn for its consequences.

But as the people watched their king as, with rent clothes, he passed on his way, they took notice that he wore other token of mourning — that "he had sackcloth within upon his flesh." And yet, strange as it may seem, there is not any inconsistency between this and what immediately follows in the sacred narrative. There is no reason to doubt his outward penitence, of which this was the token — perhaps, alas, the main part. Nor do we require to suppose, as has been suggested, either that he had put on sackcloth in obedience to a general command of Elisha, or else that his anger against the prophet was due to the advice of the latter that Samaria should hold out in expectation of Divine deliverance, and that he (the king) had put on sackcloth in the belief that thereby he would secure the promised help. For similar conduct may still be witnessed as regards its spirit, although the outward form of it may be different. A man experiences the bitter consequences of his sinful ways, and he makes sincere, though only outward, repentance of them. But the evils consequent upon his past do not cease; perhaps, on the contrary, almost seem to increase, and he turns not within himself, for humiliation, but without, to what he supposes to be the causes of his misfortunes, perhaps often those very things which are intended ultimately to bring spiritual blessing to him. The sudden outburst of the king's anger against Elisha indicates that he somehow connected the present misery of Samaria with the prophet; and the similarity of his rash vow of Elisha's death with that of his mother Jezebel in regard to Elijah (1 Kings 19:2) would lead to the inference that Joram imagined there was a kind of hereditary quarrel between the prophets and his house. This, although he had but lately experienced personal deliverances through Elisha (2 Kings 6:9, 10). Perhaps, indeed, we may hazard the suggestion that one of the reasons for them may have been to show that the controversy was not with the members of the house of Ahab as such, but with them as alike the cause and the representatives of Israel's apostasy.

But the king's mood was fitful. The command to slay Elisha was immediately succeeded by another resolve, whether springing from fear or from better motives. He hastily followed the messenger whom he had sent, in order to arrest the execution of the sentence on which he had gone. Meanwhile the prophet himself had been in his house with the elders of the city — we can scarcely doubt, making very different application of the state of matters in Samaria than the king had done. We do not wonder that all that was happening should have been Divinely communicated to Elisha, nor yet that he should have described in such language the purposed judicial murder by Joram as characteristic of the son of Ahab and Jezebel. Plain and fearless as the words were, they would also remind the elders of the pending judgment against the house of Ahab. By direction of the prophet they who were with him now prevented the entrance of the king's messenger, who was so soon to be followed by the monarch himself. The words (ver. 33): "And he said, Behold this the evil is from Jehovah, why should I wait [hope] any longer?" were spoken by the king as he entered the presence of Elisha. They are characteristic of his state of mind. It was perhaps for this reason that the prophet apparently gave no heed of any kind to them. They only served to bring into more startling contrast the abrupt announcement which the prophet was commissioned to make. Alike in itself and in the circumstances of the city, it seemed to imply not only a miracle but an absolute impossibility. Yet the message was not only definite but solemnly introduced as "the word of Jehovah." It was to this effect, that about that time on the morrow, a seah (about a peck and a half of fine flour would be sold in the gate of Samaria, where the public market was held, for a shekel (about 2s. 7d.), and two seahs (about three pecks) of barley for the same price.

Such abundance as this would imply could not have been expected even in the most fruitful seasons. The words must have come with such surprise upon all, that only absolute faith in the prophet, or rather in the presence of Jehovah with him, could have secured credence for them. And is it not always so, whenever any real need of ours is brought face to face with a promise of God, — and are we not always tempted, in the weakness of our faith, either to minimize and rationalize God's promises, or else not to realize nor lay hold on them? Thus every promise is a twofold test: of His faithfulness — although only if we believe; and of our faith. And in that assembly there was at least one who did not hesitate to speak out his disbelief, even though the announcement had been solemnly made in the name of Jehovah, by one who had previously often earned a claim to credence, however incredible his predictions might have seemed. But this is the very test of faith — that the past never seems to afford a quite sufficient basis for it, but that it must always stretch beyond our former experience, just because it is always a present act, the outcome of a present life. And apart from the sneer which it conveyed, there was certainly reason in the retort of the adjutant, on whose hand the king leaned: (Comp. 2 Kings 5:18) "If Jehovah made windows in heaven, would this thing be?" But it needed not the direct sending of corn through windows made in the heavens. To the lessons of God's faithfulness to His promise there was now to be added, as counterpart, another of His faithfulness as regarded the threatened judgments upon unbelief. The officer who had disbelieved the announcement should see but not share in the good of its fulfillment.

As we transport ourselves into the circumstances, it must have been impossible to imagine any fulfillment of the prediction without the most direct Divine interposition. And yet it was only because they were ignorant of what would evolve that any miracle, in the sense in which we use that expression, seemed necessary. As they were so soon to learn, and as we understand it, all happened in the orderly and reasonable succession of events. But the miracle lies in the Divinely arranged concurrence of natural events, with a definite view to a Divine and pre-arranged purpose. And so — if we would only learn it — miracles are such, because we view God's doings from earth, and in the light of the present and the seen; miracles are the sudden manifestation of the ever-present rule of God; and, if we had but eyes to see and ears to hear, we are still and ever surrounded by miracles.

The means employed in the promised deliverance were as unexpected and strange as the deliverance itself. There were four lepers who, according to the law (Leviticus 13:46; Numbers 5:2), were kept outside the city, at the entrance to the gate.

In the straits to which Samaria was reduced, they could no longer expect even the scantiest provision which charity within the city might supply, or careful search without its walls might discover. In the alternative of certain starvation if they remained where they were, or possible death if they fell into the hands of the Syrians, they naturally chose the latter. As the twilight deepened into gloom, they started to carry out their purpose. As we understand it, they made a long circuit to approach the Syrian camp at its "uttermost part," that is, the part furthest from Samaria.

This would naturally be their best policy, as they would neither be observed from the city, nor by those in the camp of the enemy, who, as nearest to Samaria, might be expected to be most on the watch, while at the same time it might enable the lepers to present themselves as if they were not connected with the beleaguered. And this also allows sufficient time for the flight of the Syrians having taken place without being observed by the lepers, who probably had made a wide detour around the hills. For while they crept about the camp there was a strange movement within it. It is not necessary to suppose that the "noises of chariots," "of horses," and "of a great host," which the Syrians seemed to hear in the falling darkness, depended on a supernaturally caused illusion of their senses (comp. 2 Kings 6:19, 20); nor yet that the noise itself was supernaturally caused. Such noises are said to be occasionally heard in valleys shut in by mountains, and to have been popularly regarded as portending war.

The Syrians, at any rate, thought they heard the approach of relieving armies. Tribes from the great Hittite nation in the north, and bands, if not the armies of Egypt, had been hired against them by Joram, and were now simultaneously advancing on them from the north and the south. This would seem to explain how Samaria had held out amid such terrible straits. They had been looking for this succor all along. Terror peopled the night with the forms as well as the sounds of the dreaded host. We imagine that the panic began at the extremity of the camp. Presently they were in full flight, abandoning their horses, their asses, their tents, with all the provisions and treasures which they contained, and hastening to put Jordan between them and their imaginary pursuers.

When the four lepers reached the extremity of the Syrian camp, the fugitives were already far away. They listened, but heard not a sound of living men. Cautiously they looked into one tent, and finding it deserted, sat down to the untasted meal which lay spread, ate and drank, and then carried away, and hid what treasures they found. They entered the next tent, and found it similarly deserted. By the time they had carried away and hid its treasures also, it became quite evident to them that, for some unknown reason, the enemy had left the camp. It was, however, not so much the thought that this was a day of good tidings to Samaria, in which they must not hold their peace, as the fear that if they tarried till the morning without telling it, guilt would attach to them, that induced them hastily to communicate with the guard at the gate, who instantly reported the strange tidings. But so far from receiving the news as an indication that the prediction of Elisha was in the course of fulfillment, the king does not even seem to have remembered it. He would have treated the report as a device of the Syrians, to lure the people in the frenzy of their hunger outside the city gates. Foolish as the seeming wisdom of Joram was, there are only too many occasions in which neglect or forgetfulness of God's promise threatens to rob us of the liberty and blessing in store for us. In the present instance there were, happily, those among the king's servants who would put the matter to the test of experiment. From the few remaining troops, five horsemen and two chariots were to be dispatched to report on the real state of matters.

The rest is soon told. They found it as the lepers had informed them. Not only was the Syrian camp deserted, but all along the way to Jordan the track of the fugitives was marked by the garments and vessels which they had cast away in their haste to escape. And as the messengers came back with the tidings, the stream of people that had been pent up in the city gate poured forth. They "spoiled the tents of the Syrians." Presently there was abundance and more than that within Samaria. Once more market was held within the gate, where they sold for one shekel two sacks of barley, or else one sack of fine flour. And around those that sold and bought surged and swayed the populace. Presumably to keep order among them, the king had sent his own adjutant, the same "on whose hand" he had "leaned" when Elisha had made his prophetic announcement; the same who had sneered at its apparent impossibility. But it was in vain to seek to stem the torrent of the people. Whether accidentally or of purpose they bore down the king's adjutant, and trod him under foot in the gate. "And he died, as the man of God had said."

We mark at the close of this narrative the emphatic repetition of the circumstances connected with this event. For, assuredly, as it was intended to show the faithfulness of God in the fulfillment of His promise for good, so also that of the certain and marked punishment of unbelief. And both for the teaching of Israel, and, let us add, for that of all men, and in all ages.

CHAPTER 14 — CLOSE OF ELISHA'S PUBLIC MINISTRY: THE BEGINNING OF JUDGMENT — THE SHUNAMMITE ON HER RETURN FROM PHILISTIA RESTORED TO HER PROPERTY — ELISHA'S VISIT TO DAMASCUS — THE EMBASSY OF HAZAEL — PREDICTION OF FUTURE JUDGMENT THROUGH HIM — THE MURDER OF BEN-HADAD AND ACCESSION OF HAZAEL.

(2 KINGS 8:1-15.)

THE two narratives which follow that of the siege of Samaria may be characterized as in some sense supplementary to it. On the one hand, they mark the relations between Elisha and Joram; and on the other, those between the prophet and Syria. They also close what seems the more personal account of Elisha's activity. After that we have only an account of his death and burial (chap. 13.), drawn, as we suppose, from the same "memoirs" to which the whole of this series is due; the reference to Elisha's activity in the anointing of Jehu (chap. 9.) forming part of the more general history. Accordingly we again remind ourselves that what is about to be described must not be regarded as following in strict chronological succession what had preceded, but rather as in internal connection with it.

The first narrative introduces once more the Shunammite and her heaven-given, heaven restored son, although in circumstances far different from those in which we first knew them. Indirectly we learn and mark that the relations between the prophet and the family of Shunem had not ceased with the restoration of the child to life, although Holy Scripture has not preserved any record of such intercourse. And this also is instructive as regards Bible history. Further, we mark the affectionate interest of Elisha, and his care for the outward well-being of this family. Among the other dealings of God with Israel we learn that He "called for a famine" — a most emphatic expression (comp. Psalms 105:16; Haggai 1:11). This dearth was to last for seven out of the twelve years of Joram's reign. Before its commencement the prophet "had spoken" to the Shunammite, warning her to betake herself to any place outside the land of Israel where she might be able to secure a temporary home; and "the woman had arisen and done after the saying of the man of God." Although we have evidence that this famine pressed severely on the people (comp. 4:38), yet the advice of the prophet must have been determined by special circumstances. From the absence of any reference to him, it is probable that the Shunammite had lost her husband, and with him her mainstay in times of trouble and difficulty.

We are told that she went to the land of the Philistines — -probably as that nearest to her home, and at the same time least likely to suffer, both on account of its fertility and its easy communication with grain producing Egypt. When the predicted seven years of famine ended, the woman who, as the original expressly marks, had only gone "to sojourn as a stranger," returned to her home at Shunem. But here her faith, which had led her so literally to obey the words of the prophet, was to receive a rude shock. "Her house," to which so many loving and sacred memories attached, and "her land" — her own and her child's property — were occupied by strangers.

We remember the proud feeling of independence with which she had on a former occasion declined Elisha's offer to speak for her to the king (2 Kings 4:13), since she dwelt among her own people. But since then, and in the troubles connected with famine and Syrian invasion, times had sadly changed. And in the circumstances it seems scarcely less indicative of the Shunammite's independence of character, that she now appealed directly to the king, not for favor, but for justice. It was surely in the good providing of God, Who ordereth all things wisely and well, that the Shunammite addressed her appeal to the king just as he was talking with Gehazi, and the latter at his request was telling all the great things that Elisha had done. But we cannot infer from this conversation that their meeting occurred before the healing of Naaman, after which Gehazi was smitten with life-long leprosy, since, although lepers were banished from the cities, all intercourse with them was not prohibited, especially under such peculiar circumstances. On the other hand, it was evidently the period when the authority of the prophet with the king was at its highest, and hence either after the capture of the Syrians in Samaria (2 Kings 6:21), or, as we think, after the fulfillment of Elisha's prediction of the relief of Samaria, and the death of the disbelieving "lord." This would best accord with the present narrative. In any case, the appearance of the woman with her son during Gehazi's conversation would not only confirm its truth, but naturally augment the interest of the king in her complaint. And so he immediately ordered not only the restoration of her property, but a return, probably from the royal treasury, of the value of the produce of the land during the previous years. But to us and to all time this history is chiefly interesting as showing how the obedience of faith will, despite trials or appearances to the contrary, be met by the faithful care of the God of promise — and still further, how God will not allow the day of His people to set in trouble, but cause the light to break forth at eventide.

The second narrative in this history shows how the name and work of Elisha were known, not only in Israel, but beyond it, even in hostile Syria. This, after what we have already learned, cannot surprise us. Although there is not any express statement to that effect, we cannot but connect the journey of Elisha "towards Damascus," with the commission formerly given to Elijah to anoint Hazael king over Syria (1 Kings 19:15).

This may help us to understand that the Word of God has a wider than the barely literal application which so often tends to perplex the superficial reader. It also shows that its fulfillment may be delayed, and when made, come in other manner than was expected; and, lastly, that the prophets may for many years have borne about the painful secret of some trouble to come — forbearing to take any part till the moment for action, or rather for their obedience, was indicated to them from above.

It was, surely, not an accidental circumstance that when Elisha arrived in Syria Ben-hadad was on that sick-bed from which his treacherous servant intended he should never rise. For the prophet was not to come until all was ready and prepared for the deed by which Hazael would ascend the throne of Syria, that while in its sequences necessarily connected with the judgments foretold upon Israel, yet no part of the incentive to the crime could be imputed to the agency of the Divine messenger. Evidently, if Hazael had not intended to murder his master, and to pretend that he had died of his disease, the words of Elisha would have had no meaning, nor could they have suggested to him his crime.

On hearing of the near approach of the great prophet of Israel, Ben-hadad charged Hazael, probably his vizier or chief general, to meet Elisha, and inquire through him of Jehovah, whether he would recover from his sickness. After the manner of the time, Hazael went to meet the prophet with a present. We are not to understand that those forty camels which bore "of every good thing of Damascus," were literally fully laden. This magnifying of a present by distributing and laying it on a great many bearers or beasts of burden, is characteristic of the East, and is not uncommonly witnessed in our own days. Hazael delivered his master's message with unblushing hypocrisy. But Elisha had read his purpose, and replied in language which, while it unmasked, could never have suggested his murderous scheme: "Go, say to him, [viz. as thou intendest to do] Thou shalt surely live; howbeit Jehovah has shown me that he shall surely die." And as we recall the hypocritical words by which Hazael had tried to disguise his purpose and deceive the prophet, we feel that this was the most fitting answer to his pretended humility and care.

Yet this was only the beginning of what Elisha had to say to Hazael. "And he [Elisha] steadied his face, and set it till he [Hazael] was ashamed," when reading not only his inmost thoughts, but his future history also, the prophet burst into weeping. When Hazael inquired as to the reason of his tears, Elisha told the terrible cruelties which he knew the Syrian would perpetrate upon Israel. The mock humility of Hazel's answer: "But what is thy servant, the dog, that he should do this great thing?" reveals at least the spirit in which he contemplated such deeds against Israel. If Hazael had still thought to deceive Elisha, the announcement that God had shown to his prophet Hazael as king of Syria, must have convinced him that disguise was useless. Little more requires to be told. Hazael returned to his master, and gave him the lying assurance of recovery, as Elisha had foretold. Then as in his sore sickness Ben-hadad lay prostrate and helpless, Hazael laid upon his face a coverlet which had been soaked and made heavy with water. And so Ben-hadad died, and his murderer, whose crime remained probably unknown, ascended the throne.

The accession of Hazael was only part of the burden of judgment upon Israel which had been announced to Elijah. The other part was the usurpation of the throne of Israel by Jehu. With this twofold accession began the decay of the northern kingdom of Israel. Presently we shall read (10:32). "In those days Jehovah began to cut Israel short; and Hazael smote them in all the coasts of Israel," — a smiting which included the loss of the entire territory east of the Jordan. And we believe that it was to declare, perhaps to warn of, this judgment upon Israel, that Elisha was sent to Damascus, and made to have this interview with Hazael.

For Divine judgment cannot be arrested, though it may be deferred, and what Israel had sown when on the morrow of the decisive contest on Carmel it cast out Elijah, that would it reap, when, notwithstanding all mercies shown, the son of Ahab and Jezebel could order, though he dared not carry out, the execution of Elisha. They would have none of His prophets, however clearly their mission was attested of God; nay, rather, they would have none of that God Whose prophets Elijah and Elisha had been. And yet in faithfulness God would reveal the coming judgment to His servants, and through them to Israel.

But quite a peculiar feeling comes over us in these far-off islands of the West, when now, thousands of years after these events, we stand before the black obelisk on which this part of the history of ancient Assyria is recorded, and there read the names of Ben-hadad and of Hazael of Damascus — the former in connection with "Ahab of Jezreel," who was at one time his ally against Assyria; the latter, as humbly offering rich tribute to the king of Assyria, as also does Jehu, who is styled "the son of Omri" (the founder of the dynasty succeeding that of Omri). And here these histories commingle, and the records of the one will be found to throw welcome light upon those of the other.

CHAPTER 15 — JEHORAM AND AHAZIAH, (FIFTH AND SIXTH) KINGS OF JUDAH. JORAM, (TENTH) KING OF ISRAEL — ACCESSION OF JEHORAM — MURDER OF THE ROYAL PRINCES — INTRODUCTION OF THE SERVICE OF BAAL IN JUDAH — REVOLT OF EDOM — AND OF LIBNAH — THE WRITING FROM ELIJAH — INCURSION OF THE PHILISTINES AND OF ARAB TRIBES — SICKNESS, DEATH, AND BURIAL OF JEHORAM — STATE OF PUBLIC FEELING.

(2 KINGS 8:16-24; 2 CHRONICLES 21.)

THE tangled skein of Judaean and Israelitish history is now once more taken up. It is a period of fast-hastening judgment, luridly lit up by the horrors attending Diehard's accession to the throne of Israel, though retarded in Judah by the mercy of God towards the house of David, and the temporary repentance and return to Jehovah in the land.

The account in 2 Kings 8:16 introduces almost abruptly the accession of Jehoram to the throne of Judah, after the death of his father Jehoshaphat. It was probably for this reason, and because of the long gap between this and the previous historical notice about Judah (1 Kings 22:51), that the somewhat difficult explanatory clause (supposing it to be genuine) may have been inserted in 2 Kings 8:16: "And Jehoshaphat had been king of Judah." In 2 Kings 8 (vers. 16-24) the history of Judah and of the reign of Jehoram is given only in briefest outline. For details we must, as in other cases, turn to the Book of Chronicles (2 Chronicles 21.), whose narrative we now follow.

The historical notices with which the reign of Jehoram is introduced are almost identical in 2 Kings and 2 Chronicles. Both state that Jehoram was thirty-two years old at his accession, and that his reign lasted eight years. The Book of Chronicles connects, as usually, this accession with the death and burial at Jerusalem of the former king, while the Book of Kings marks that Jehoram ascended the throne of Judah "in the fifth year of Joram, the son of Ahab, king of Israel." And since the reign of the latter extended over twelve years (comp. 2 Kings 8:25), their rule must for seven years have been contemporaneous — that is, to within one year of the death of Joram of Israel.

Even more important is the notice given in the same words in the two narratives — quite prominently in the Book of Kings — to the effect that Jehoram "walked in the way of the kings of Israel, as did the house of Ahab: for the daughter of Ahab [Athaliah] was his wife: and he did the evil in the sight of Jehovah" (comp. 2 Chronicles 21:6). That notice explains alike the history of the reign of Jehoram and the hastening ruin of Judah. Nor can it have been without evil influence even upon Joram and Israel.

The fatal combination of political devices with earnest religion, which constituted the weakness of Jehoshaphat's reign, and led to his alliance with the house of Ahab, appeared also in his disposition regarding his children. Besides Jehoram, who as the eldest succeeded to the throne, he had left six sons.

For these he had — apparently during his lifetime — made not only ample provision in treasure, but assigned to them certain "fenced cities in Judah." This was to imitate the policy of Rehoboam (11:23), and, no doubt, with the same purpose of securing, in troublous times, the allegiance of the country districts and of their aristocracy, by assigning these "fenced cities" as residences to the royal princes. But in the present instance the device proved fatal to them. Jehoram had nothing to fear from his brother-in-law Joram — as Rehoboam had from Jeroboam.

But the semi-royal position of his brothers, supported — as it would almost seem — by intrigues of the chiefs of the local aristocracy, roused his fears. With the same unscrupulousness that characterized the house of Ahab and Jezebel, he rid himself of any possible rivals by the murder of all his brothers, and of their adherents among "the princes." And throughout, Diehard's reign was in accordance with its beginning. Following closely in the steps of the house of Ahab, he not only abolished all the pious ordinances and arrangements of his father, but actually rebuilt "the high places," which his grandfather Asa (17:3), and his father Jehoshaphat (17:6), had destroyed, and introduced the worship of Baal with all its abominations.

We cannot be mistaken in attributing a large share in these evil doings to Athaliah, although her name is not expressly mentioned. For, besides the repeated reference to the house of Ahab, we have the statement that his "brethren" of his "father's house were better" than Jehoram, which seems to imply that his special circumstances had made him different from the other members of Jehoshaphat's family, and also this — in our view, very significantly — that there came to him a writing from Elijah the prophet.

For, as there is not any other reference to Elijah throughout the Books of Chronicles, we infer that his activity had been confined to the northern kingdom, and that this solitary prophecy in regard to the kingdom of Judah must have been due to the connection of Jehoram with the house of Ahab, — or, to be more particular, to his marriage with Athaliah and her influence upon him. And we would date the composition of this "writing," or it may be its commission, shortly after that ill-fated union.

For it seems of quite secondary importance whether Elijah himself wrote this letter, with direction to have it delivered at the proper time to the husband of Athaliah, or else commissioned one of his disciples to write it in his name, when the circumstances of the case indicated it. And as regards this latter view, we remember that the direction to Elijah to anoint Hazael king of Syria, was executed six or seven years after the death of Ahab, that to anoint Jehu fourteen years after Ahab: in both cases, therefore, many years after the commission had been given (1 Kings 19:15, 16); in both cases also, not by Elijah himself, nor yet with precisely literal fulfillment of the commission given.

The "writing from Elijah" announced, for the public and personal sins of Jehoram, public and personal judgments. But even before that warning came from the dead prophet, with all the solemnity of a message straight from heaven, the judgment upon Judah had begun. Indeed, as the sacred writer remarks, it would have extended to the destruction of the whole family of Jehoram — and with it of the commonwealth of Israel -but for the gracious promise to David of the continuance of his house till his rule should merge in that of "David's greater Son" (2 Samuel 7:12, 13; 1 Kings 11:36).

Still most serious calamities befell the country, both in the east and in the west. In the south-east, Edom had for one hundred and fifty years been subject to Judah. It now rebelled. Josephus reports that the governor, whom Jehoshaphat had appointed, was murdered; while, from the prophecies of Joel (3:19), we infer that the rebellion was attended by a massacre of the Judaean settlers in Edom. From the account of the expedition against Edom — given with only slight variations in the Books of Kings and Chronicles — we learn that Jehoram started from Jerusalem with the host, and notably war-chariots; that he was surrounded by the Edomites, but that he and the captains of his chariots — representing the standing army — fought their way through the Edomites, while the people — that is, the probably undisciplined multitude that had followed Jehoram, fled to their homes.

Thus ended the brief campaign, with the permanent loss of Edom, which, except temporarily and for a short period (comp. 2 Kings 14:7, 22), did not again become subject to Judaea, till its subdual under the Maccabean prince Hyrcan, about a century before Christ. It afterwards returned to Palestine the terrible gift of a Herod.

Nor was Edom the only loss which the southern kingdom sustained. In the west, not far from the borders of Philistia, Libnah, the ancient Canaanitish royal, and afterwards a priest city, revolted (comp. Joshua 15:42; 12:15; 21:13).

Its site has not been localized with certainty, though it has, with some probability, been suggested that it is represented by the modern Tell-es- Safieh, somewhat to the south-east of Ascalon, and on the edge of the great Philistine plain. The hill on which the site stands was known in crusading times as "bright hill" (collis clarus), and the fort built upon it as "white garde" (Blanche Garde, alba specula or alba custodia). The name not only corresponds to the ancient Libnah, "whiteness," "sheen," but to the description of the place, as in its white sheen visible in all directions. If Libnah was at the time inhabited by priests, it may have been that Diehard's apostasy from the faith led to its revolt from his rule. This may have been prompted by the success of the rising in Edom, and the movement itself have been encouraged by the Philistines.

This view is supported by the account in the Book of Chronicles, that the Philistines, aided by certain Arab tribes from the neighborhood of Ethiopia — probably hired for the purpose — made an incursion into Judaea, and literally "clave it." We know sufficient of the fierceness of these Arabs "by the side of the Cushites," when their spirit is roused, to understand that Judah, divided and enfeebled, and under the rule of a Jehoram, could not withstand their onset. The invading host seems to have taken, if not Jerusalem itself, yet the place where the king and his household were; and they carried away with them what of the royal property they found, as well as the wives and sons of Jehoram, and indeed killed all the latter except the youngest, Jehoahaz, who, from some reason unknown, escaped death.

This was the beginning of that "great stroke" with which, as foretold in the writing from Elijah, Jehovah would smite Jehoram in his people, his children, his wives, and all his substance. For even this more public calamity had a personal character, since, as we read, "Jehovah stirred up against Jehoram the spirit" of these enemies; and very markedly their plunder was confined to the royal property. And when the second part of the threatened judgment befell the king, and that incurable internal disease attacked him of which he ultimately died, it seems difficult to understand how those who witnessed all this, and still more, they who succeeded him, could have maintained the same attitude as he towards Jehovah.

We can only account for it by the rooted belief that Jehovah was only a national deity, who was angry with those who forsook His service; but that the new deity, Baal, who had proved so mighty a god to the surrounding nations, would by and by take them under his protection. And as between the stern demands and the purity of the service of Jehovah, Who claimed of royalty absolute submission and simple stewardship and Who elevated all His people into a royal priesthood, and the voluptuous luxuriousness of the worship of Baal, who placed king and people in so very different a relationship to each other and to himself, rulers of the character of Jehoram or Ahaziah would not hesitate in their choice.

We have evidence that the ungodly rule of Jehoram was not popular in Judah. "He departed without being desired" by his people, nor did they make any burning of precious spices at his funeral, such as was customary at the obsequies of kings (comp. 2 Chronicles 16:14; Jeremiah 34:5). And although "they buried him in the city of David," yet "not in the sepulchers of the kings." If these notices seem to indicate a hostile popular feeling, the same inference comes to us from the unusual statement that "the inhabitants of Jerusalem made Ahaziah, his youngest son, king in his stead" (2 Chronicles 22:1).

It would probably be too much to conclude that there was opposition to the accession of one who must have been known to be like-minded with his father on the part of the Levite and Priest party, although the revolt of the priest city Libnah and the later activity of the high priest Jehoiada and of the Levites on behalf of Joash (22:11; 23) seem to point in that direction. But we cannot be mistaken in concluding that Ahaziah was placed on the throne by a faction in Jerusalem favorable to the new order of things. And it needs no elaborate argument to convince us that, alike religiously and politically, a regime must have been profoundly unpopular which had reversed the whole former order of things, was associated with the permanent loss of Edom, the defection of so important a center as Libnab, and the victorious incursions of Philistines and Arab bands. To these outward calamities must be added the paramount sway of a woman, such as the daughter of Ahab, and the remodeling of Judah after the pattern of Israel, which even mere patriots must have felt to be a most humiliating abdication of supremacy in favor of the northern kingdom. And in the history of the brief reign of Ahaziah, as well as in the later rising which resulted in the death of Athaliah, the existence of two parties in Judah must be kept in view; the one representing the corrupt court faction, the other the growing popular feeling in favor of return to the old order of things.

CHAPTER 16 — JORAM AND JEHU, (TENTH AND ELEVENTH) KINGS OF ISRAEL. AHAZIAH, (SIXTH) KING OF JUDAH — ACCESSION OF AHAZIAH — CHARACTER OF HIS REIGN — EXPEDITION OF JORAM AND AHAZIAH AGAINST HAZAEL AND TAKING OF RAMOTH-GILEAD — JORAM RETURNS WOUNDED TO JEZREEL — VISIT OF AHAZIAH — JEHU ANOINTED KING — RAPID MARCH ON JEZREEL — JORAM KILLED — PURSUIT AND DEATH OF AHAZIAH — JEZEBEL KILLED — FULFILLMENT OF THE DIVINE SENTENCE BY ELIJAH.
(2 KINGS 8:25-9:37; 2 CHRONICLES 22:1-9.)

THE brief reign of Ahaziah, or Jehoahaz (2 Chronicles 21:17) — for the names are precisely the same, the two words of which they are compounded being only reversed) — may be regarded as marking the crisis in the history alike of the northern and the southern kingdom. The young prince was twenty-two years old when he ascended the throne (2 Kings 8:26).

To say that he followed the evil example set by his father, would not express the whole truth. Holy Scripture designates his course as a walking "in the ways of the house of Ahab," explaining that his mother Athaliah a was his counselor, and that he was also influenced by the other members of that family. It was by their advice that he united with his uncle Joram in that expedition which ended in the death of the two kings, although there is no evidence that a Judaean army was actually joined to the forces of Israel.

We remember that fourteen years before, Jehoshaphat, the grandfather of Ahaziah, had joined Ahab in a similar undertaking, which had proved unsuccessful, and in which Ahab lost his life. We might wonder at the renewal of an attempt upon Ramoth-Gilead, when a man like Hazael occupied the throne of Syria; but the Assyrian monuments explain alike the expedition and its opening success. From these we learn that there was repeated war between Assyria and Hazael, in which, to judge from the number of Syrian war chariots captured (1121), the whole force of the country must have been engaged and exhausted. On another occasion we read of a war in which after a great victory an Assyrian monarch pursued his enemy from city to city, and even into the mountains, burning and destroying everything before him.

We may therefore conjecture that if Joram was not actually in league with Assyria — as Jehu afterwards was — the Israelitish king availed himself of the opportunity for an attack upon Ramoth-Gilead. In this he seems to have been successful (2 Kings 9:14), although he was wounded by the Syrians — as Josephus has it, by an arrow during the siege (Ant. 9:6, 1). Leaving Ramoth-Gilead, which he had taken, in the keeping of Jehu, his chief captain, Joram went back to the summer palace of Jezreel, to be healed of his wounds, both as nearer to the field of action, and because the court was there at the time.

It was to Jezreel that Ahaziah went to see his uncle, and during this fatal visit the "destruction" overtook him, which, as the writer of the Book of Chronicles notes, "was of God." It came together with that of Joram and the whole house of Ahab. The judgment which more than fourteen years before had been pronounced upon Ahab (1 Kings 21:21-24) had only been deferred till the measure of the guilt of his house was filled. And now the hour had come. In that awful vision on Mount Horeb, Elijah had received the commission to "anoint Jehu the son of Nimshi... to be king over Israel" (1 Kings 19:16), with special view to the work of punishment which he was to execute. The commission, which Elijah himself could not discharge, had devolved on Elisha; and, the proper time for its execution having arrived, the prophet now sent one of the "sons of the prophets" — a young man (9:4), possibly his personal attendant. As no doubt he literally obeyed the injunctions of his master, we shall best learn what these were by following the detailed account of what he actually said and did.

As directed by Elisha, he went to Ramoth-Gilead, carrying with him a vial, probably of holy oil, which the prophet had given him. Even this is significant. On his arrival he found, as so often in this history, all apparently arranged so as to carry out the special purpose of God. He had been told to "look out" Jehu, and here were all the captains of the host sitting together, probably in deliberation. Remembering that the chief command devolved on Jehu, it would not be difficult to single out the object of the young man's mission. He had only to say, "I have a word to thee, O captain," and Jehu as president would naturally answer. It was so; and on Jehu's inquiry to which of them the message was, the young prophet replied: "To thee, O captain."

The captains had been sitting in the great court, and Jehu now took his strange visitor "into the house," no doubt, as Elisha had directed, into "an inner chamber," one that opened out of another, where what passed between them could not be observed from the court. Here, without further explanation — for abruptness of delivery was part of the object in view, and indeed characteristic of the direct Divine message — the young man poured the oil on the head of Jehu, and stated the terms of his commission. It was in the name of "Jehovah, God of Israel," and on behalf of Israel, viewed as "the people of Jehovah" (2 Kings 9:6). This emphatic introduction of Jehovah marked the character of the work to which Jehu was called. He was now Divinely anointed king, to execute judgment on the house of Ahab, and to avenge at the hand of Jezebel the blood of the prophets, and of all the servants of Jehovah. And the whole house of Ahab was to perish like that of Jeroboam (1 Kings 14:10), and that of Baasha (1 Kings 16:3). But upon Jezebel would special personal judgment descend, commensurate to the terrible crime against Naboth, which she had planned and executed (1 Kings 21.). Thus would all men see that Jehovah was the living and true God; thus also would the loudest but also the last call to national repentance come to Israel, ere the storm of judgment burst over the land.

It is in this light that what seem from our point of view the horrible events of the beginning of Jehu's reign must be regarded. But then our point of view was not that of Israel at that time, and if the commencing judgment on national apostasy, and the final call to repentance which it implied, were to be effective, they must be suited to their, not to our, standpoint. Let it be remembered that the long ministry of Elijah and Elisha, with all the exceptionally direct and striking Divine interpositions connected with them, had passed without producing any appreciable effect on the people. The years of sudden famine, and its equally sudden cessation; the scene at the sacrifice on Carmel, as well as the prolonged public and private activity of Elisha, had apparently only wrought this result: that the great prophets came to be regarded as possessing some absolute power to influence the God of Israel (comp. 2 Kings 6:31; 8:4). A very different kind of ambassador was now to do God's behest and to execute His judgments, although perhaps just because he would do that for which he was called in his own wild Eastern manner, and in accordance with the spirit of the time.

It is in this sense that we can understand the Divine approbation conveyed to Jehu (2 Kings 10:30), even while feeling that the man himself and his modes of acting were contrary to God. And, indeed, this fact is distinctly brought out in the verse which follows the expression of the Divine approbation (ver. 31).

We have said that Jehu did his work as a Jehu, not as an Elisha, and in accordance with the spirit of his times. We may add that, as the experience of the past showed, no other mode would have been understood by Israel. It was a very dark night, and only the flashes of lightning and the flames of burning palaces which they had kindled could show what tempest of judgment had gathered in the sky. Yet even so might men have learned the possibility of brightness and calm with the sunrise of the morrow.

Returning to our history, we follow Elisha's messenger as, obedient to his directions, after having executed his commission, he opens the door and literally flees through the court where the assembled captains are in waiting for Jehu. He must not give explanations to any man; he must not be arrested nor questioned by any. His business was with Jehu — that done, alike in character with the Divine message, and even for the sake of its success, he must withdraw. And, although so widely differing in character, there is in this also a practical lesson for those who have some work to do for God. Let us avoid all mere talking, and, if we can, all explanation.

God's work will best explain itself, we cannot explain it. We must withdraw our personality as soon and as completely as may be; do the commission which we feel to be of God, and eschew in it saluting any man by the way (Luke 10:4). And so the young prophet would be outside the walls of Ramoth-Gilead, and on his way back to Samaria, when Jehu rejoined the "servants of his lord."

They must all have recognized the garb and appearance of one of "the sons of the prophets," and inferred that something of supreme importance was about to take place. For the proper understanding of this history it is necessary to bear in mind that it was possible to be opposed to the worship of Baal, and in favor of that of the God of Israel, without any personal or true religion. In point of fact, Jehu exterminated for the time alike the service and the servants of Baal, although he "took no heed to walk in the way of Jehovah, God of Israel, with all his heart; he departed not from the sins of Jeroboam, which made Israel to sin" (2 Kings 10:31).

It was the service of Baal which Ahab had initiated, while Jeroboam's worship of God under the symbol of the golden calf might be represented as the ancient Israelitish (in opposition to the Judaean and Levitic) service of the God of Israel. We can readily believe that there might be a large and influential national party in the northern kingdom, intensely opposed to the anti-Israelitish and foreign policy and ways in State and Church of the house of Ahab. And both from his antecedents (comp. 2 Kings 9:25, 26), and his subsequent conduct, we infer that Jehu was a leader — perhaps the leader — of this national party, which naturally would have many adherents throughout the country.

Quite consistent with this view is the deep interest taken by the captains in the mission of the young prophet to Jehu, and their readiness to take up his cause, even while at the same time the messenger was slightingly spoken of — just as men of the world might characterize such an one as a "mad" enthusiast. It is difficult to decide the reason of what seems the evasive answer first made by Jehu. But when perceiving by their interest the likelihood of their joining the national cause, he told them at least that part of the message which appointed him king over Israel.

If Jehu possessed the ferocity, he evidently had also the cunning of an Eastern. Perhaps he could scarcely have been prepared for the rapidity with which the military revolution was accomplished. The assembled captains took off their upper garments, and spread them, in token of homage, as a carpet "on the platform of the steps," that is, the steps which led up to a platform or balcony, and then, amidst the blast of trumpets, the usual signal at a coronation (1 Kings 1:39; 2 Kings 11:14), Jehu was proclaimed king.

The formal conspiracy against Joram, now hastily made, was immediately carried out. At the proposal of Jehu, the city gates were watched, lest any fugitive might bring tidings to Jezreel. Jehu himself, with Bidkar as his chief captain, in his chariot (ver. 25), and attended by a "multitude" (ver. 17) — no doubt, of horsemen — rapidly made his way to Jezreel. From incidental notices in the account (vers. 17, 30, 31) we gather that the royal palace formed part of the fortifications of the town, — perhaps, as in other places, that the palace was the only fortified part of Jezreel, the town straggling beyond, and lying, as it were, in the shelter of the palace fort, which would occupy the height. Thus the "watchman on the tower of Jezreel" would really hold that place of observation in the palace, and when "Jehu came to Jezreel," Jezebel could address him from a window above, as he "entered in at the gate."

From the knoll — about 500 feet high, forming a low spur of Mount Gilboa — on which Jezreel stands, two roads diverge, keeping close to Mount Gilboa. The one turns east and south, and then sharply round the corner at Beth-Shean; the other crosses the plain of Esdraelon, almost straight south to En-gannim ("the fount of the gardens," the modern Jenin), where the direct road leads to Samaria, but whence also we might turn off eastwards to Beth-Shean and the Jordan. It is almost needless to say that it was along the former of these roads that the watchman on the tower of Jezreel saw Jehu and his company advancing at "mad" haste. For miles they must have been visible on the road that led up to Beth-Shean. When the watchman announced their approach to the king, Joram, in his false security, directed that a single horseman should be sent to inquire what tidings they brought. As he reached Jehu, the rebel general imperiously bade him join his troop. This movement also the watchman observed and reported to Joram. If the dispatch of the first horseman may be understood, that of a second one seems in the circumstances little short of fatuity.

By the time the second messenger from Jezreel had obeyed the orders of Jehu and joined his companion, the troop was sufficiently near for the experienced eye of the watchman to recognize, not indeed the face of Jehu, but that the driving of the foremost chariot was like none other's than that of the bold, reckless chief captain of Israel's host. When the watchman reported it to the king, this would probably coincide with what had been his own idea from the first. A troop advancing from that direction could only have come from the army in Ramoth-Gilead — probably to bring tidings of some victory, or of the final retreat of the Syrians, or of proposals of peace. The announcement that it was Jehu himself would tend to confirm such anticipations. Accordingly Joram had his war chariot and that of Ahaziah hastily made ready, and the two kings went to meet Jehu.

As we descend from Jezreel on the road to Beth-Shean there are on the east and south-east of the city "rock-cut wine-presses on the rugged hills," marking no doubt where "the portion of Naboth" and his vineyard had been. It was here that the royal party encountered Jehu and his troop. To the light-hearted question of Joram, "Is it peace, Jehu?" such answer came as must at once and rudely have dispelled any illusions. "What! 'is it peace?' (until) so long as the whoredoms of Jezebel thy mother, and her witchcrafts, the many?" the former expression referring, as frequently, to idolatry (comp. Jeremiah 3:2, 3; Ezekiel 23:27); the latter to the enchantments and heathen rites practiced in connection with it. From which words we also learn that in popular opinion Jezebel exercised paramount influence over her son, and that the un-Israelitish rites prevalent were attributed to her.

With the short cry, "Deceit, Ahaziah!" Joram turned his horses' heads to flee into Jezreel, when Jehu, drawing his bow, sent the arrow with such strength between the shoulders of Joram that it passed out at his heart, and the king fell dead in his chariot. Then reminding his "adjutant" Bidkar of the burden or punitive sentence which Jehovah had in their presence laid upon Ahab, on the day they two had ridden behind the king as his attendants, when he had gone to take possession of the property of murdered Naboth, he commanded the body of Joram to be cast into that very plat of ground, "according to the word of Jehovah."

Meanwhile Ahaziah, perceiving the turn of matters, sought safety in flight. Leaving Jezreel aside, he turned sharp round the shoulder of Gilboa, and struck the direct road southwards: "fled the way of the Beth-Gan," which we regard as another name for En-gannim, the modern Jenin, at the southern end of the plain of Jezreel. Unwilling to allow his escape, Jehu, while himself preparing to enter Jezreel, gave rapid directions to pursue Ahaziah. "Him also smite — in the going up to Gur! which is by Ibleam." We can at least thus far identify "the going up to Gur," that the neighboring town of Ibleam has been localized in the modern Bir el Belemeh, south of En-gannim. It is here then that we must place the "ascent to Gur," where Jehu had expected, although mistakenly, that the pursuers might overtake the chariot of Ahaziah.

As we infer, the object of Ahaziah was to reach Megiddo in safety. That place has generally been located, but, as recently shown, erroneously, at the western edge of the plain of Jezreel, under Mount Carmel. In truth Megiddo lay in the opposite direction — south and east from Jezreel — being "the large ruin between Jezreel and Beth-shean, which still bears the name Mujedd'a." This location of Megiddo greatly helps the understanding of our narrative. As already stated, Ahaziah's hope was that in reaching Megiddo he would have not only out-distanced, but out-wearied his pursuers. And his purpose may have been to make his way to the Jordan, and along its eastern banks till he could cross into Judaea.

But in this hope, as we imagine, he was disappointed. Pursued to Megiddo, he fled to Samaria (2 Chronicles 22:9). The knowledge that the sons of Ahab were brought up in the houses of the principal men of the city (2 Kings 10:1) led him to expect that he might be able to hide for a time among the adherents of his grandfather. We know how little the loyalty of the nobles of Samaria was to be depended upon (2 Kings 10:1-7), and we do not wonder to read that Ahaziah was "caught" in Samaria, brought back to Megiddo, and there slain by order of Jehu. Nor does it seem strange that his body was given up to his servants to be taken to Jerusalem and buried there, as being a descendant of that Jehoshaphat "who sought Jehovah with all his heart." For the whole movement of Jehu was ostensibly for the purpose of abolishing the worship of Baal, and restoring that of Jehovah, the God of Israel.

We return to sketch, as briefly as we may, the closing hours of that day in Jezreel. Tidings of all that was passing had rapidly reached Jezebel. Her course was soon chosen. She knew she must die; and she would die as a princess of her race, and a queen. After the Oriental fashion, she put paint on her eyes, "and tired her head." Thus arrayed as a queen, she took her place at the window, awaiting the arrival of Jehu.

As he appeared, she called to him from above — taking up and adapting the word with which the messengers of Joram, and then the unfortunate king himself, had unsuspectingly greeted Jehu: "Is it peace? Zimri, murderer of his master!" The words were intended to remind Jehu of the fate of Zimri, whose reign lasted only seven days (1 Kings 16:9-19), perhaps to stir up feelings which would lead to a similar counter-revolution. Even if no other motive had been actuating him, self-preservation dictated quick and decisive action on the part of Jehu. Looking up, he exclaimed in his impatient way: "Who is on my side? Who?" and when some of the eunuchs immediately responded, Jezebel was, at his command, thrown from the window. Her blood bespattered the wall and the horses, and the chariot of Jehu, as he passed through the gate, crushed her mangled body.

And now King Jehu is at his royal banquet within the palace of the murdered princes. Was it statecraft, dictating regard for the Tyrian princess; or some pity for the fallen greatness of one who had died a proud queen; or a rising feeling that, for his own sake, a descendant of royalty should not be exposed to the extreme of popular contempt, which prompted him to give orders for the burial of Jezebel? But whatever his motives, the command came too late. Only the skull, the hands, and the feet of Jezebel were found; the rest had been food for those wild dogs which prowled about Jezreel. And if Jehu did not in his heart recognize the meaning and lessons of the terrible judgment which had fallen with such literality on the wretched queen, he at least declared and owned: "This is the word of Jehovah, which He spake by His servant Elijah the Tishbite." And so there was testimony in Israel for Jehovah and His Word in the judgments upon Ahab and his house — even as many centuries afterwards there was testimony of judgment for the Christ in the flames which consumed Jerusalem and its Temple.

CHAPTER 17 — JEHU, (ELEVENTH) KING OF ISRAEL. ATHALIAH, (SEVENTH) QUEEN OF JUDAH — MURDER OF THE "SONS" OF AHAB AND OF JORAM — DESTRUCTION OF THE ADHERENTS OF AHAB IN JEZREEL — MARCH ON SAMARIA — SLAUGHTER OF THE "BRETHREN" OF AHAZIAH — JEHONADAB THE SON OF RECHAB — MEANING OF THE RECHABITE MOVEMENT — THE FEAST OF BAAL AT SAMARIA — DESTRUCTION OF THE WORSHIPPERS — CHARACTER OF THE REIGN OF JEHU — DECLINE OF THE NORTHERN KINGDOM — COMMENCING DECLINE OF THE SOUTHERN KINGDOM.

(2 KINGS 10:2; 2 CHRONICLES 21:10; 24:17-26.)

WE have learned enough of this history to understand the seeming inconsistencies in the conduct of Jehu. Absolutely speaking, he was the instrument selected for executing the Divine punishment on the house of Ahab; and also in whose reign the national judgment upon Israel was to begin. Jehu himself clearly understood his mission as regarded the house of Ahab and the worship of Baal. But he accepted it as a national and, if the term may be used, a Jehovistic movement, without implying the necessity of true fear of the LORD, or of return to Him; and he carried it out as a Jehu. Alike as regarded his feelings and his methods, he was the instrument, not the servant of the LORD.

To such an one as Jehu even common prudence would have dictated to do what work he had, quickly, sharply, and completely. A dynasty that had extended over four reigns must have numbered many adherents, while on the other hand the demoralizing influence of the worship of Baal must have widely spread in the land. There was more than merely a mocking taunt in the reminder of Jezebel about the fate of Zimri. The mission as well as the rule of Jehu depended upon a rapid succession of measures which would alike anticipate the possibility of a counter-revolution, and render a return to the former state of things impossible. This explains the measures taken by the new king. Samaria was not only the capital, but a fortified city, where the main body of the standing army lay. Here, as we know, had been placed the "seventy sons of Ahab" — understanding the term in its wider sense, common in Hebrew, which included, besides the sons of Ahab, his grandsons, the children of Joram (comp. 2 Kings 10:3).

These royal princes of the house of Ahab were entrusted, some (in the Eastern fashion) for supervision, the younger for education to the "princes," — that is, the governor of the palace and the governor of the city (10:1, comp. 10:5) — to the "elders," and to certain prominent persons who had charge of them.

These officials in Samaria would embody the possibility of a counter-revolution, and to them Jehu addressed on the morrow of his entry into Jezreel what really amounted to a challenge, to declare themselves for the house of Ahab, or else to make submission to his rule. The motives which decided their choice (ver. 4) show that their inclination was in favor of the old regime, while their fears dictated submission to the usurper. So Jehu had judged wisely in forcing an immediate decision, without exposing himself by marching with his small troop against Samaria.

But this was not all. Neither their allegiance nor his rule was safe so long as any of the royal princes lived; and, indeed, their destruction was part of his work and mission. To have killed them himself would have been a doubtful expedient, which, even if successful, might have given rise to popular reaction, and at all events brought him ill-will, while it would have left free the hands of the adherents of Ahab. It was therefore, from his point of view, the wisest policy on receiving the submission of the leaders of Samaria to order them to kill all the royal princes and bring their heads to Jezreel. This would not only accomplish the primary object of Jehu, but, by making them participate in the crimes of his revolution, render any future movement against his rule impossible. At the same time the ghastly sight of those heads, sent to Jezreel by the chief representatives of the old regime, would offer an excellent opportunity for an appeal to the people.

When, therefore, next day the heads of the seventy princes were brought in baskets to Jezreel, he ordered them to be laid "at the entering in of the gate," where the blood of Jezebel had so lately bespattered the wall, and the chariot of the conqueror passed over her body. And in the morning Jehu, pointing to the gory heaps, could tell the people that not only himself, but all the chief personages under the late government, had part in the destruction of the house of Ahab; that those to whom they had been entrusted had chosen rather to slay these princes in cold blood than to take up their cause — that all had perished, and so the word spoken by the LORD through the great prophet Elijah had been fulfilled. Thus his rule and the slaughter of the house of Ahab had — as he put it — the support of all men and the sanction of God Himself.

It was now possible for Jehu to take possession of his capital without danger of opposition, and there to carry out his final measures against the old order of things. But before doing so he took care, so to speak, to secure his rear by killing all that had been connected with the house of Ahab in Jezreel, "all his great men," his friends, and his chief officials.

On his way to Samaria another tragedy was to be enacted. It was at a solitary place, in a locality which has not been ascertained, but which bore the name of "house of binding of the shepherds" — or, as the Chaldee Paraphrast calls it: "The house of assembly of the shepherds." Here, where evidently the roads from Jezreel and Jerusalem joined, Jehu and his followers met the forty-two princes, "the brethren of Ahaziah, king of Judah," who were going on a friendly visit to "the children of the king [Joram] and the children of the mistress," [lady-ruler, Gebhirah — evidently Jezebel].

So rapid had been the movements of Jehu, and so great was the fear of him, that tidings of what had passed in Israel had not traveled so far as to arrest the journey of the princes of Judah. Jehu's order was to "take them alive." Whether they offered resistance, or this was part of the original order of Jehu, certain it is that they were all killed "at the cistern of Beth-Eqed," into which their bodies were probably thrown.

As Jehu passed from the scene of slaughter he met a figure that seems strange and mysterious. "Jehonadab, the son of Rechab," who had come from Samaria to meet the new king, belonged to the Kenites (1 Chronicles 2:55). This tribe, which was probably of Arab nationality, appears so early as the days of Abraham (Genesis 15:19). Jethro, the father-in-law of Moses, belonged to it (Judges 1:16). Part at least of the tribe accompanied Israel into the Land of Promise (Numbers 10:29-32), and settled in the south of Judah (Judges 1:16), where we find them by-and-by mixed up with the Amalekites (1 Samuel 15:6). Another part of the tribe, however, seems to have wandered far north, where Jael, the wife of Heber the Kenite, slew Sisera on his flight from Barak (Judges 4:17, etc.; 5:24, etc.). Thus they appear to have occupied the extreme south and north of the country, and would even on that ground possess political importance. But what interests us more is their religious relationship to Israel. From the deed of Jael we infer that they were intensely attached to the national cause. Again, from the circumstance that Jehonadab, the son of Rechab — evidently the chief of the tribe — came from Samaria to meet Jehu, and from the anxiety which the latter displayed as to Jehonadab's views and intentions, as well as from the manner in which he treated him, we gather that the chieftain was a person of considerable political importance, while the invitation of Jehu: "Come with me, and see my zeal for Jehovah," shows that he and his tribe were identified with the service of Jehovah in the land. All this throws fresh light on the special injunction which from that time onward Jehonadab laid upon his tribe (Jeremiah 35:1-16). They were neither to build houses, nor to sow seed, nor to plant or have vineyards; but to dwell in tents, and so both to be and to declare themselves strangers in the land.

This rule, which the descendants of Rechab observed for centuries, must, from its peculiarity, have had a religious, not a political, bearing. It has with great probability been connected with Elijah, but the important question has not yet been mooted whether it originated before or after the occupation of Samaria by Jehu.

We believe the latter to have been the case, and it seems evidenced even by the circumstance that Jehonadab came from Samaria to meet Jehu. We suppose that the ministry of Elijah had made the deepest impression on Jehonadab and his tribe. The very appearance and bearing of the prophet would appeal to them, and his words seem as those of a second Moses. Earnestly they waited for the results of his mission and of that of Elisha. And when the word of Jehovah to and by Elijah was being fulfilled — Hazael made king of Syria, Jehu king of Israel, and the house of Ahab destroyed, root and branches — they would naturally turn to Jehu, in the hope that a national return to Jehovah would follow. It was a kind of Old Testament John the Baptist's hope of a kingdom of God. Feelings such as these prompted Jehonadab to go and meet Jehu, while the latter, knowing the deep impression which the Rechabite movement in favor of the reformation of Elijah had produced in the land, would be anxious to secure his public support, perhaps even — so strange and mixed are our motives — to gain his approbation. But what Jehonadab saw of Jehu must soon have convinced him that he was not one to carry out an Elijah-movement in its positive and spiritual aspect, however fitted an instrument he might be to execute Divine punishment. And so Jehonadab left Jehu to perpetuate in his own tribe the testimony of Elijah, by making them Nazarites for ever, thus symbolizing their dedication to God, and by ordering them to be conspicuously strangers in the land, thus setting forth their expectation of the judgments which Elijah had predicted upon apostate Israel.

We are now prepared to accompany Jehonadab, as after responding to Jehu's anxious challenge about his feelings toward him, he mounted Jehu's chariot to go with him and see his zeal for Jehovah. The first measure of the conqueror was to repeat in Samaria what he had done in Jezreel, and to kill all related to or connected with the family of Ahab. His next was, by a truly Eastern device, to seize and destroy the adherents of the religious rites introduced under the late regime. Although this was in fulfillment of his mission, it will be observed that it also afforded the best means of establishing his own rule, since the national worship of Baal was identified with the house of Ahab. Accordingly we imagine that when Jehu publicly announced that he meant to serve Baal even much more than Ahab, and proclaimed a solemn assembly for Baal, the gathering would be thoroughly representative. First, as we understand it, Jehu summoned all the prophets and priests of Baal, and "all his servants" — either the leading laity generally, or else those in Samaria itself — ostensibly to make preparation for his great sacrifice. Next, similar proclamation was made throughout the country. In both cases the object was to secure the attendance of all professed worshippers of Baal. On the day appointed, the courts of the Temple of Baal were thronged "from one opening to the other [the opposite]." To make the leaders of the new religion the more prominent, Jehu now directed that each of them should be arrayed in festive vestments, and then, to prevent any possible mistake, since some of the servants of Jehovah might have followed Jehu and Jehonadab to the house of Baal, he ordered, on his arrival, to search for and remove any worshippers of the LORD.

Neither of these measures would excite surprise, but would only be regarded as indications of Jehu's zeal, and his desire that the rites of Baal should not be profaned by the presence of strangers. The attendance of Jehonadab might seem strange; but he was in the train of the king whom he was known to have served, in whose company he had returned to Samaria, and with whom he had continued while he issued his mandates, and prepared for the feast of Baal. He might therefore be simply an adherent of Jehu, and now prepared to follow his lead.

The rest may be briefly told. As the sacrifices were offered Jehu surrounded the building with eighty of his trusted guards, who, on the given word of command, entered the building, threw down all they encountered, and penetrated into "the sanctuary of the house of Baal," where all who had been marked out to them were slaughtered. Then they brought out the wooden images and burnt them, while the large stone statue of Baal, as well as the Temple itself, were destroyed. And completely to desecrate the site, and mark the contempt attaching to it, Jehu converted it into a place for public convenience.

"Thus," as Scripture marks, "Jehu destroyed Baal out of Israel." Yet, as the cessation of idolatry after the return from the exile did not issue in true repentance towards God, nor in faith in the Messiah, so did not this destruction of Baal-worship lead up to the service of Jehovah. Rather did king and people stray farther from the LORD their God. Of the succeeding events in Jehu's reign, which lasted no less than twenty-eight years, no account is given in Scripture, except this notice, that "in those days Jehovah began to cut Israel short: and Hazael smote them in all the coasts of Israel; from Jordan eastward, all the land of Gilead, of the Gadites, and the Reubenites, and the Manassites, from Aroer, which is by the river Arnon, even Gilead and Bashan." And the Assyrian monuments throw farther light upon this brief record. They inform us about the wars of Hazael against Assyria, and they represent Jehu as bringing tribute to the king of Assyria. The inference which we derive is that Jehu had entered into a tributary alliance with the more powerful empire of Assyria against Hazael, and that when the latter had made his peace with Assyria, he turned against Jehu, and inflicted on Israel the losses thus briefly noticed in Scripture. Be this as it may, this at least is certain, that with the loss of the whole trans-Jordanic territory, the decline of the northern kingdom had commenced.

Nor was the state of matters more hopeful in the southern kingdom of Judah. The brief and bloody reign of Athaliah was, indeed, followed by the counter-revolution of Jehoiada, and the elevation of Joash to the throne. But the reformation then inaugurated was of short duration. After the death of Jehoiada, the worship of Jehovah was once more forsaken for that of "groves and idols, and wrath came upon Judah and Jerusalem for this their trespass" (2 Chronicles 24:18).

And although the LORD sent them prophets to bring them again unto the LORD, they not only would not give ear, but actually at the commandment of the king, and in the very house of Jehovah, shed the blood of Zechariah, which, according to Jewish legend, could not be wiped out, but continued to bubble on the stones, till the Assyrians entered and laid low the sanctuary thus profaned. And even before that, the army of Hazael, though greatly inferior in numbers, defeated that of Judah, desolated and despoiled the land, and laid siege to Jerusalem. The Syrian army was, indeed, bought off, but the hand of God lay heavy on the king. Stricken down by disease he was murdered in his bed by his own servants, and they the sons of strangers. Thus had inward and outward decline come to Judah also. And darker and yet darker gathered the clouds of judgment over a land and people which had "forsaken Jehovah, the God of their fathers."

VOLUME 7: FROM THE DECLINE OF THE TWO KINGDOMS TO THE ASSYRIAN AND BABYLONIAN CAPTIVITY

PREFACE

THE volume herewith introduced to the reader brings, according to the original plan of the series, this Bible History to a close. This circumstance naturally suggests a retrospect, however brief. In the Prefaces to preceding volumes, the chief characteristics of each period were successively sketched, and the questions indicated to which they gave rise, as well as the special points in respect of which the treatment of one part of this History differed from another. The period over which the present volume extends — that from the decline to the fall of the Kingdoms of Judah and Israel — can scarcely be said to have any distinguishing features of its own. It is the natural outcome and the logical conclusion of the history which had preceded. It means that this History, as presented in Holy Scripture, is one and consistent in all its parts; or, to put it otherwise, that what God had from the first said and done with reference to Israel was true. Thus, as always, even the judgments of God point to His larger mercies.

In two respects, however, this period differs from the others, and its history required a somewhat different treatment. It was the period during which most of the great prophets, whose utterances are preserved in the books that bear their names, lived and wrought, and over which they exercised a commanding influence. And never more clearly than in this period does it appear how the prophet, as the messenger of God, combined the twofold function of preaching to his own and, in a sense, to every future generation, and of intimating the wider purposes of God in the future. There is not in the prophetic utterances recorded any one series of admonitions, warnings, or even denunciations which does not lead up to an announcement of the happy prophetic future promised. In this respect prophecy has the same fundamental characteristic as the Book of Psalms, in which, whatever the groundnote, every hymn passes into the melody of thanksgiving and praise. This similarity is due to the fact that, in their Scriptural aspect, the progress of outward teaching and the experience of the inner life are ever in accordance. On the other hand, there is not in the prophetic writings any utterance in regard to the future which has not its root, and, in a sense, its starting point in the history of the time. The prophet, so to speak, translates the vernacular of the present into the Divine language of the future, and he interprets the Divine sayings concerning the future by the well-known language of the present. As between his teaching and his prediction, so between the history of the present and that of the future there is not a gap: they are one, because through both runs one unswerving purpose which gradually unfolds what from the first had been enfolded. And so history and prophecy also are one, because God is one. And so also, if we would rightly understand them, must we study not so much prophecies as isolated utterances, but as prophecy in its grand harmonious historical unity.

But apart from the considerations now offered, it must be evident to the most superficial observer how much and varied light the utterances of the contemporary prophets cast on the condition, the circumstances, and the history of the time in which they lived. Indeed, from their writings we obtain the most vivid account, not only of the moral and religious state of the people, and even of their manners, but of the moving springs and the real history of events. On the other hand, it must be equally evident how the history of the time illustrates not only the occasion but often the meaning of the prophetic utterances. And so the one helps the understanding of the other. But this circumstance has also naturally imposed on us the duty of studying the history of this period in connection with the various prophecies referring to it, to which, accordingly, constant reference will be found in the present Volume.

Another peculiarity of this period is that its history will be found inseparable from that of the great empires of the world — especially Assyria and Babylonia. Those who have followed the progress of Assyriological studies know how often and unexpectedly light has been cast on the history of the Old Testament by the information derived from the Assyrian monuments. But they equally know that this science is as yet almost in its infancy; that on some points connected with the Old Testament, the opinions of Assyriologists differ, or else have undergone change, while on others the information we possess may receive further confirmation, modification, or important addition. It will be understood that in these circumstances the preparation of the present volume has required special labor and care. I can only hope that it may serve to make clear the history of a period which without illustration both from the prophetic writings and the Assyrian records would be not a little difficult and complicated. Lastly, the twofold Index to the whole series, contributed by the industry of my daughter, will, it is believed, be helpful to the student.

Thus far as regards the present volume. And now it is with more than the common feelings of natural regret on bringing to a close a work which has engaged a writer more or less for a number of years, and on parting from a circle of readers, whom in the course of time he has come to regard as friends, that the concluding paragraphs of this Preface are written. The object in beginning this series was to make a fresh study of Old Testament history from the original text, with such help as was to be derived from the best criticism and from cognate sciences. And not only was it to follow the course of the outward history, describing it as accurately and fully as might be, but to reach beyond this to its spiritual and universal meaning to mark the unity, application, and unfolding of its underlying idea; and to point to its realization and completion in the kingdom of God. Briefly, the underlying idea of the Old Testament, in its subjective aspect, is that of "the Servant of the LORD." The history of the Old Testament in its progress to the New is that of the widening of the idea of the servant of the LORD into that of the kingdom of God. Lastly, its realization and completion is in the Christ and the Church of God. Unless, indeed, the Old Testament had this higher meaning and unity, it could not possess any permanent or universal interest, except from a historical point of view. It would not permanently concern mankind — no, nor even Israel, at least, in its present relation to the world. On the other hand, without it the New Testament would want its historical basis, and the historical Christ offer what would seem an absolutely unintelligible problem.

Such, then, has been the plan and conception of this Bible History. The readers in view were teachers, students, and generally the wider, educated and thoughtful public. Throughout, the desire has been not to ignore nor pass by difficulties or questions that might arise in the course of this History, but without always specially naming, rather to anticipate and remove or answer them by what seemed the correct interpretation of the narrative. How far this aim has been attained must be left to the judgment of others. This only may be truthfully said, that as difficulties have not in any case been consciously ignored, so their solution has not been sought by inventing an interpretation simply for the purpose of removing an objection. If it may seem that sometimes suggestions have been offered rather than positive statements made, it was because caution was felt to be not only in place but even part of necessary reverence.

But beyond all this there are wider questions connected with the Old Testament, which have, particularly of late, been prominently brought forward. In a work like the present it seemed specially desirable to avoid controversial matters, which, in any case, could not here be satisfactorily dealt with. And yet all reference to them could not be omitted. But on the most fundamental of them — that of the origin and date of the Pentateuch it may be well here to mark what appears an essential distinction. There is the widest difference between the question whether the Pentateuch — legislation is of Mosaic origin, and this other of the precise time when it, or any special part of it, may have been reduced to writing or redacted. The former is a question of principle, the latter one chiefly of literary criticism, and as such can have no absolute interest for general readers of the Bible.

On the first of these questions the present writer has not seen any reason for departing from the old lines of the Church's faith, but rather everything to confirm our adherence to them. Thus literary criticism may, and ought, in this, as in other matters, to continue its independent course of investigation without causing any misgivings to those who, on good and valid grounds, hold fast to the old truth concerning' Moses and the prophets' and the assured fact of their testimony to Christ. And the final result of all investigations can only be the confirmation and vindication of the faith of the Church.

In conclusion I have to thank the readers of this Bible History for their kindness, and the indulgence extended to me in completing this series. Any delay in it has been caused by literary engagements. To me, at least, it has afforded the refreshment of periodically returning to a loved work, while the marked advance in cognate studies tending to the illustration of this History has been of the greatest advantage during the progress of the Series. It only remains, with all humility, to offer the results of these labors to those who love the Old Testament, in the earnest hope that He in Whose service they were undertaken may graciously accept, and by His blessing further them, not only to the fuller knowledge, but to the spiritual understanding of His own Word.

ALFRED EDERSHEIM

6, CRICK ROAD, OXFORD,

July 21, 1887.

CHAPTER 1 — ATHALIA, (SEVENTH) QUEEN, AND JEHOASH, (EIGHTH) KING OF JUDAH — MURDER OF THE REMAINING PRINCES OF JUDAH BY ATHALIAH — RESCUE OF JEHOASH, AND HIS PRESERVATION IN THE TEMPLE — REIGN OF ATHALIAH — THE REVOLUTION INAUGURATED BY JEHOIADA — PROCLAMATION AND CORONATION OF JEHOASH — DEATH OF ATHALIAH — DESTRUCTION OF THE HOUSE OF BAAL — NEW SETTLEMENT IN CHURCH AND STATE.

(2 KINGS 11:1-20; 2 CHRONICLES 12:10-23:21.)

WITH the accession of Jehu and the destruction of the house of Ahab, and with the ill-fated alliance between the doomed race of Ahab and the descendants of David, the last period in the history of Israel and Judah's national decline had begun. The measure was not only full, but the Hand hitherto lifted in threatening was no longer stayed. We have reached a period of judgments, when each follows the other with only brief intermission. Of the events in Israel connected with the rebellion of Jehu, of the character of the religious changes introduced by him, and of the troubles and difficulties of the military monarchy which he founded, a detailed account has already been given. But the full sweep and import of these events will only be perceived as we mark their direct and indirect influence on the history of Judah.

The union between Jehoram, the son of Jehoshaphat, and Athaliah, the daughter of Ahab and Jezebel, had introduced apostasy, and brought calamity to the house of David. If the marriage had been planned from political motives, perhaps in the hope of an ultimate reunion of the two kingdoms, or at least with the expectation of a firm and close alliance between them, the result speedily showed the folly of attempting to achieve imaginary successes by subordinating principle to so-called policy.

Indeed, this is one of the lessons which throughout make the history of Israel typical of that of the Church, and in a sense of all history, and which constitute its claim to the designation of "prophetic." In it events move, so to speak, in step with the utterances of the God of Israel. No direct or sudden interference seems necessary; but in the regular succession of events, each deviation from Divine order and rule, each attempt to compass results by departure from God's law and word, brings with it, not success, but failure and ruin. From her entrance into her new home in Judah, to her seizure of its throne, Athaliah brought it only evil. Her very name, "Athaljah" ("Jehovah oppresseth"), seems significant. She possessed all the evil qualities of her mother Jezebel, without her queenly bearing and courage; all the cunning of her father, without any of his impulses towards good. Holy Writ marks that she was her son's "counselor to do wickedly" (2 Chronicles 22:3), and her influence for evil must have commenced in the previous reign of her husband, Jehoram. To the influence of "the house of Ahab" are expressly traced, both in the reign of Jehoram and in that of Ahaziah, the revival of idolatry (2 Kings 8:18, 27; 11:15; 2 Chronicles 22:3, 4); the desecration of the Temple of Jehovah (2 Chronicles 24:7), and those evil counselings (2 Chronicles 22:4)which brought such Divine judgments (2 Chronicles 21:13, 14, 16, 17; 22:7). To her, we cannot doubt, was due not only the slaughter of his "brethren," with which Jehoram stained the beginning of his reign (2 Chronicles 21:4), but the destruction by Jehu of so large a number of the remaining royal princes of Judah (2 Kings 10:13, 14; 2 Chronicles 22:7, 8). And if her murderous purpose on seizing the government had been wholly successful, the political union between the house of Ahab and that of Jehoshaphat would have ended in the extermination of the whole house of David.

There is not a scene in Jewish history more vividly depicted than that of Athaliah's seizure of the Jewish crown, and of her miserable end. It seems more than likely that on his ill-fated expedition to the court of Israel, Jehoram had entrusted the government of the kingdom to his mother, who had all along exercised such determining influence upon him.

We need not wonder, although we take notice of it, that the position of woman in Israel should have been so different from that generally assigned to her in the East. A nation which counted among its historical personages a Miriam, a Deborah, and an Abigail — not to speak of other well-known figures — must have recognized the dignity of woman. Nor can we here forget the influence respectively exercised by the mother of King Asa (1 Kings 15:13), by Jezebel, and by other queen-consorts or mothers.

When tidings successively reached Athaliah, first of the death of Ahaziah, and then of the murder of presumably the great majority of the royal princes, the thought would naturally suggest itself to such an ambitious and unscrupulous woman permanently to seize the reins of the government. Other motives may also have contributed to this resolve. She must have known that, despite all that had been done in the two previous reigns to denationalize Judah, her party formed only a small and unreliable minority even in the capital. Both in Jerusalem and throughout the country the great majority were, as events afterwards proved, opposed to the queen-mother, or at least attached to the old order in State and Church. The acknowledged and natural head of this party was the active and energetic high-priest, Jehoiada, the husband of Jehosheba or Jehoshabeath, the half-sister of the late King Ahaziah. And Athaliah must have felt that if, after the slaughter of the other princes by Jehu, a minor were proclaimed king, his guardianship and the government would naturally pass into other hands than hers.

In view of such possible dangers to herself, but especially for the realization of her own ambitious designs, the queen-mother resolved, in true Oriental fashion, on the slaughter of all that remained of the house of David. On its extinction there could no longer be any possible rival, nor yet any center around which an opposition could gather. It casts manifold light on the institution and the position of the priesthood, with its central national sanctuary in the capital, that at such a period the safety of the people ultimately rested with it. Evidently it must have been an institution of the highest antiquity; evidently, it must have formed part of the central life of Israel; evidently, it was from the first invested with all the dignity and influence which we associate with it in the Mosaic legislation; evidently, it was intended as, and did constitute, the religiously preservative and conservative element in the commonwealth, the guardian of Israel's religion, the rallying-point of civil rights and of true national life. Even the fact that in such a time the high-priest was wedded to the king's sister is significant.

From the general massacre of the royal house by Athaliah, Jehosheba had succeeded in rescuing an infant son of Ahaziah, Joash by name. Together with his nurse, he was for a short time concealed in "the chamber of beds," apparently that where the mattresses and coverlets of the palace were stored, and which would offer a very convenient hiding-place. Thence his aunt removed him to a still more safe retreat in the Temple, either one of the numerous chambers attached to the sanctuary, or, as seems most likely, to the apartments occupied by her husband and his family within the sacred enclosure, or closely joined to it.

So matters continued for six years, Joash probably passing for one of the children of the high-priest. During that time the plunder of the house of Jehovah and the transference of its dedicated things to the service of Baalim, which had been begun by the sons of Athaliah (2 Chronicles 24:7), must have been carried to its utmost extent. Naturally it would arouse a strong reaction on the part not only of those who held the foreign rites in abhorrence, but also of those who were opposed to the rule of the foreign queen who had murdered all that had remained of the family of David. In the seventh year of this misrule, Jehoiada "took courage," and organized a counter-revolution, in which all ranks in the State were equally represented.

If ever a movement of this kind was constitutional, it was that against the murderous usurper of the throne of David. The Book of Chronicles, while always relating events pre-eminently from the priestly and Levitical viewpoint, here furnishes some welcome details, apparently derived from the same original sources as the account in the Book of Kings, although omitted in the latter.

From the two accounts we infer that Jehoiada in the first place addressed himself to the five "captains of hundreds," or centurions, whose names are mentioned in 2 Chronicles 23:1. Apparently they commanded the five divisions of the royal bodyguard, which combined the designation Kari (equivalent to Kerethi) given in Davidic time to the corps, then consisting chiefly, if not entirely, of foreign (Philistian) auxiliaries, with the older (So in 1 Samuel 22:17) and more permanent name of "runners" (ratsim).

The account in the Book of Chronicles adds what in itself would seem most likely, that the military leaders distributed themselves through the country to secure the adhesion and co-operation of the heads of families and clans, and of the Levites. Manifestly it would be necessary to enlist the latter, since the central scene of the rising was to be the Temple. There the confederates met, probably at one of the great festivals, when the youthful prince was presented to them. As, no doubt, in the first instance the military leaders, so now the whole assembly bound themselves by a solemn oath to the undertaking, which primarily had only the proclamation of the new king for its object (comp. 2 Chronicles 23:3).

The differences, and even more the similarity, in the narratives of the event in the Books of Kings and Chronicles have suggested what to some appear discrepancies of detail. It is well to know that, even if these were established, they would not in any way invalidate the narrative itself, since in any case they only concern some of its minor details, not its substance. The most notable difference is that in the Book of Kings the plot and its execution seem entirely in the hands of the military; in Chronicles, exclusively in those of the priests and Levites. But in Chronicles also — and, indeed, there alone — the five military leaders are named; while, on the other hand, the narrative in the Book of Kings throughout admits the leadership of the priest Jehoiada. And even a superficial consideration must convince that both the priests and the military must have been engaged in the undertaking, and that neither party could have dispensed with the other. A revolution inaugurated by the high-priest in favor of his nephew, who for six years had been concealed in the Temple, and which was to be carried out within the precincts of the Sanctuary itself, could no more have taken place without the co-operation of the priesthood than a change in the occupancy of the throne could have been brought about without the support of the military power. And this leaves untouched the substance of the narrative in the two accounts, even if what we are about to suggest in the sequel should not seem to some a sufficient explanation of the part assigned respectively to the priesthood and the military in the two narratives.

Of this, at least, there cannot be any doubt, that the account in the Book of Kings deals with the operations assigned to the military. Briefly, they may be sketched as follows. As each of the "courses" into which the priesthood was divided relieved the other at the beginning of every Sabbath, so apparently also the royal bodyguard. The plan now agreed upon was, that the guard which was relieved should, instead of returning to their homes or barracks, march into the Temple, where the high-priest would furnish them with weapons from those that had formerly belonged to David, and which, no doubt, according to sacred custom, had been deposited in the sanctuary.

The sole object of that guard (2 Kings 11:7, 11) was in two divisions to surround the new king on either side, with orders to cut down any one who should try to penetrate their ranks, and to close around the person of the king in all his movements. Thus far for the guard that had been relieved. On the other hand, the relieving guard was to be arranged in three divisions. One of these was to form, as usually, the guard of the royal palace, so that the suspicions of Athaliah should not be aroused. The second division was to occupy the gate Sur, also called the "gate of the foundation" (2 Chronicles 23:5); while the third division was to be massed in "the gate behind the guard," the same as "the gate of the guard" (2 Kings 11:19), and which probably formed the principal access from the palace into the Temple. The object of all this was to guard the palace — not only to disarm suspicion, but for defense (2 Kings 11:5), and to ward off or bar any attempt on the part of adherents of Athaliah to possess themselves of the royal residence.

The importance of this will be understood, not only in case of a counter-revolution, but in view of the ancient custom of solemnly placing the king on the royal throne as the symbol of his accession to the government (1 Kings 1:35, 46), which it was intended to observe also on this occasion (2 Kings 11:19).

It must have been noticed that, minute and complete as these arrangements were, so far as regarded the defense of the new king and the guard of the royal palace against a sudden attack by the adherents of Athaliah, they left all the main gates of access to the Temple undefended against any eventuality. And yet it must have been quite as important to protect the Sanctuary from a hostile rush upon it, and to avert its profanation by a fight within its sacred precincts. It is on this ground that we deem it antecedently probable that provision should have been made for guarding the Temple itself, similar to that in regard to the king and the royal palace. But this would naturally devolve upon the Levites, as the regular custodians of the Temple, just as the military guard would as naturally have the immediate custody of the person of the king. And such participation on the part of the Levites seems otherwise necessarily implied in the circumstance that the rising was planned by the priesthood, and organized by them as well as by the military leaders. In all these circumstances it seems almost impossible to believe that an active part of some kind should not have been assigned to the Levites; that access to the Temple should either have been left unprotected; or that the guard of the Temple should have been entrusted to others than those who were its regular custodians.

These considerations leave no room to doubt the accuracy of the account given in the Book of Chronicles. Only as that in the Book of Kings details the arrangements for the safety of the king and the palace, so that in Chronicles records those made for the security of the Temple, which were entrusted to the Levites. Some other confirmatory particulars deserve attention. Thus we notice that although the account in Chronicles seems to imply that all the arrangements were in the hands of the Levites, yet when Athaliah was to be led to her doom, the order was given, not to the Levites, but to the military leaders, who were to bring her forth "within the ranks" (Sederoth). The verse is almost literally the same as in 2 Kings 11:15. The term which we have rendered "ranks" indicates an orderly arrangement, as of soldiers. It is used in 2 Kings 11:8 in reference to the military guard which was to surround the king, but not in designation of the wider compass of Levites, which, according to 2 Chronicles 23:7, was to be about the king. We therefore conclude that this division of Levites was to form an outer circle not only around the king, but also around his military guard. This also explains the difference in the directions given in 2 Kings 11:8 to the military guards to kill those who penetrated their "ranks," and in 2 Chronicles 23:7 to the Levites, to kill those who penetrated into the Temple. In other words, the Levites were to stand beyond the guards, and to prevent a hostile entrance into the Temple buildings; and if any gained their way through them to the ranks of the military, they were to be cut down by the guards. Thus the king was really surrounded by a double cordon — the military occupying the inner court around his person, while the Levites held the outer court and the gates.

The explanations just offered will, it is hoped, show that there is not any discrepancy between the accounts of this event in the Books of Kings and Chronicles. We can understand how in the latter the functions and localities are assigned to the Levites, which in the Book of Kings seem assigned to the military. Both had similar or kindred functions, and in close proximity to each other. Thus the two accounts are entirely compatible. In point of fact, they supplement each other, the writer of Chronicles, as usually, telling the part which the priesthood sustained in the national rising, while the writer of the Book of Kings simply relates the part taken by the secular power. Thus the one narrates what was specially done by the Levites, the other what by the military; yet each, as we have seen, also giving indications of the cooperation of the other actors. The whole question, however, is not of any real importance, although it may be well to state that the explanations which have been offered are substantially confirmed by the account given of the event by Josephus (Ant. ix. 7, 2).

The plan of Jehoiada and the leaders of the rising — or, as we may say, of the national party — was carried out in every particular. It is indicative of the general opposition to the new regime, as well as of the unpopularity of the queen, that the secret of the confederacy, although shared by so many, remained unknown to Athaliah. At the same time we must remember that they had bound themselves by an oath, on the keeping of which success depended that the priesthood was entirely under the control of its official chief; and that probably only a short time intervened between the league in the Temple (2 Kings 11:4; 2 Chronicles 23:3) and the execution of the plan agreed upon.

On the day appointed, both the military and the Levites were at their posts. The youthful king, who had been presented to the leaders at their first meeting in the Temple (2 Kings 11:4), was now formally introduced. Then the crown and the "testimony" were put upon him — the latter ceremony probably consisting in placing in his hands, rather than (as some have suggested) on his head, a copy of the Law, whether that referring to the duties of the king (Deuteronomy 17:18-20), or, more probably, the Law in a wider sense. Lastly, since the regular succession had been broken by the intrusion of Athaliah, the new monarch was anointed by Jehoiada and his sons, when, as was the custom, the people broke into demonstrations of joy, clapping their hands, and shouting, "Long live the king!"

However closely the secret had hitherto been kept, the acclamations of the guards and the people were heard in the palace, and the queen rushed into the Temple. Her access to it was not hindered by the military stationed in the palace, although (according to Josephus) her immediate bodyguard were prevented by the priests from following her into the Sanctuary. The sight which now met her eyes must at once have revealed to her the state of matters. On the elevated stand "at the entering in," probably to the court of the priests, usually occupied, at least on solemn occasions, by the king (2 Kings 23:3; 2 Chronicles 34:31), she saw the youthful prince, and beside him "the captains" and the Levites blowing their silver trumpets, while "the people of the land" greeted their new monarch.

According to the Biblical account, Athaliah rent her clothes and cried, "Conspiracy, conspiracy!" while Josephus adds that she called on those present to kill the young king. The appearance and attempted interference of the queen was the signal for her destruction. By direction of Jehoiada, she was led forth beyond the Temple between "the ranks" formed to prevent her escape or communication with possible adherents. Any who might attempt to follow her were to be immediately cut down, while Athaliah herself was to be killed beyond the bounds of the Sanctuary. It must have been close to it, where the stables communicated with the palace, that she met her fate.

While this was passing outside the Temple, Jehoiada completed the second part of the royal installation by a twofold solemn act, of which the first consisted in a covenant by which the new king and the people bound themselves to renewed allegiance to Jehovah; while by the second the king similarly bound himself to the people, no doubt to. rule in accordance with the law as laid down in the Book of Deuteronomy (2 Kings 11:17). The ancient God-appointed constitution in Church and State having thus been re-established, the new king was conducted in state to the palace by the principal entrance, and formally enthroned. It was probably only after this that the people proceeded to the house of Baal, wholly destroying it and its altars and images, and slaying Mattan, the priest of Baal. The religious reformation thus inaugurated was completed by the appointment of the officials required to superintend and carry on the orderly worship of the Temple — as we infer from 2 Chronicles 23:18, 19, in accordance with the arrangements originally made by David, but which had since fallen into desuetude. And the whole account of this religious revolution concludes with this significant record: "And all the people of the land rejoiced, and the city was in quiet."

CHAPTER 2 — JEHOASH, OR JOASH, (EIGHTH) KING OF JUDAH. JEHU, (ELEVENTH) KING OF ISRAEL — CHARACTER OF ATHALIAH, OF JEHOIADA, AND OF JOASH — LESSONS OF THIS HISTORY — EARLY REIGN OF JOASH — REPAIR OF THE TEMPLE — DEATH OF JEHOIADA — COUNTER-REFORMATION — MURDER OF ZECHARIAH — INVASION BY THE SYRIANS — CONSPIRACY AGAINST JOASH — MURDER OF THE KING.

(2 KINGS 12; 2 CHRONICLES 24.)

AS we look back on the events described in the preceding chapter, their deep meaning in this sacred history becomes increasingly apparent. The movement in the northern kingdom, which issued in the destruction of the house of Ahab and the elevation of Jehu, had been inaugurated by the prophets. It was speedily followed by another in Judah, under the leadership of the priesthood, which resulted in the dethronement of Athaliah and the accession of Joash. From the popular point of view, each of these movements represented a reaction against what was foreign and non-Israelitish in politics and in religion, and in favor of the ancient institutions in Church and State. And, surely, we cannot fail to perceive, from the higher point of view, the fitness that in the northern kingdom, where since the time of Jeroboam there was not any authorized priesthood (2 Chronicles 11:14), the prophets should, in a sense, have taken the lead in such a movement, nor that in Judah the Divinely-instituted priesthood should have sustained a similar part.

In truth, this was one of the higher purposes of the priestly office (Leviticus 10:10; Deuteronomy 33:10; Malachi 2:7). But what we are careful to mark is the light which this throws upon the Divinely-appointed institutions in Israel, especially in reference to the mutual relations of Church and State, and the influence for good of religion upon national life and civil liberty.

There is yet another aspect of these movements, alike as regards their short-lived success and their ultimate failure. They were a last Divine interposition in that downward course which led to the final judgments upon Israel and Judah. The people had fallen away from the Divine purpose of their national calling, and become untrue to the meaning of their national history. From this point of view the temporary success of these movements may be regarded as a Divine protest against the past. But they ultimately failed because all deeper spiritual elements had passed away from rulers and people. Nor is it otherwise than as those who, as it were, uttered this Divine protest that the prophets in the north and the priests in the south took so prominent a part in these movements. But with the vital aspect which would have given permanency to these movements, neither the military party in the north nor the majority in the south were in any real sympathy.

And still deeper lessons come to us. There is not a more common, nor can there be a more fatal mistake in religion or in religious movements than to put confidence in mere negations, or to expect from them lasting results for good. A negation without a corresponding affirmation — indeed, if it is not the outcome of it — is of no avail for spiritual purposes. We must speak, because we believe; we deny that which is false only because we affirm and cherish the opposite truth. Otherwise we may resist, and enlist unspiritual men, but we shall not work any deliverance in the land. "Jehu destroyed Baal out of Israel" (2 Kings 10:28), but "he departed not from the sins of Jeroboam, which made Israel to sin."

"And Joash did that which was right in the sight of Jehovah all the days of Jehoiada the priest" (2 Chronicles 24:2).

But "after the death of Jehoiada," "he and his people left the house of Jehovah, God of their fathers, and served groves and idols: and wrath came upon Judah and Jerusalem for this their trespass" (vers. 17, 18). And as if to mark this lesson the more clearly, the judgments alike upon Israel and upon Judah came to them through one and the same instrumentality — that of Hazael, king of Syria (2 Kings 10:32; 12:17, 18).

As regards the movement in the southern kingdom of Judah, Old Testament history does not present a nobler figure than that of Jehoiada, whether viewed as priest or patriot. Faithful to his religion, despite his connection with the house of Jehoram and the temptations which it would involve, he dared to rescue the infant prince and to conceal him for six years at the risk of his life. At that time he must have been upwards of a hundred years of age.

Even after six years of misrule, Jehoiada still seems most reluctantly to have taken the initiative against Athaliah, although from his custody of the infant-prince, no less than from his age and dignity, it naturally devolved upon him. In the language of the Book of Chronicles, he had to "take courage" for it. And when at last he acted, it was, to use a modern expression, in the most "constitutional" manner, as well as in the most earnest religious spirit. There cannot be doubt that the occupancy of the throne by Athaliah was not only an usurpation and a crime, but contrary to the law and constitution of the land. Yet in bringing about a change which was strictly legal, Jehoiada acted in the most careful manner, having first consulted with, and secured the co-operation of, all the estates of the realm. Similarly, the execution of the plan was entrusted to those to whom action in the matter naturally belonged; and if the high-priest marked the accession of the new king by a covenant between him and the people and Jehovah, he was at least equally careful to secure the constitutional rights and liberties of the people by another covenant between them and their sovereign. Lastly, in the period that followed, Jehoiada used his position and influence only in favor of what was best, and not at any time for lower or selfish purposes. To this record of his life we have to acid his activity in connection with the restoration of the Temple. We do not wonder that when he died at a patriarchal age, the unparalleled honor was accorded him of a burial not only in Jerusalem itself, where, according to tradition, there were no burying-places, but "in the city of David" and "among the kings," "because he had done good in Israel, and toward God and His house" (2 Chronicles 24:16).

But perhaps the most striking part in this history is the almost miraculous preservation of the infant prince Joash. This fulfillment of the Divine promise concerning the permanence of the house of David (2 Samuel 7:12- 16) must have impressed all those who believed in "the sure mercies of David." This the more, that during the six years of Joash's concealment, and when an Athaliah occupied the throne, it must have seemed to have entirely failed. The proclamation of the youthful scion of David in the Temple, the solemn religious covenant by which it was accompanied, and the happy reformation which followed, must have vividly recalled the ancient Divine promise, and directed the minds of all tree-hearted Israelites to the great goal in that Son of David in Whom all the promises were to be finally fulfilled. And for a time all seemed in accordance with the beginning of Joash's reign. It is only reasonable to suppose that during his minority, which would not have been so long as in the West, Jehoiada virtually, if not formally, acted as regent. In fact, the religious influence of the priest over the king continued "all his days, because [or since] Jehoiada the priest instructed him." If any doubt could attach to the meaning of this expression, it would be removed by the parallel notice that "Joash did that which was right in the sight of Jehovah all the days of Jehoiada the priest" (2 Chronicles 24:2).

His change after that is only too clearly evidenced by the murder of Zechariah, the son of Jehoiada, an event which has not been seriously called in question even by negative critics.

On the whole, it cannot be doubted that the great defect of the character and reign of Joash was a fatal weakness, such as that of his ancestor Ahab, probably due to want of stable, personal religious convictions. Under the guiding influence of Jehoiada, he "did that which was right;" yet even so he tolerated the worship of the people at the "high places." In view of his character, we must regard it as a specially wise act on the part of the high-priest to concern himself about the alliances of the young king, a circumstance which is specially noted in the Book of Chronicles (2 Chronicles 24:3).

Of his two wives, one (Jehoaddan) is mentioned as a native of Jerusalem; and from the age of her son, Amaziah, at his succession, we infer that he must have been born when his father, Joash, was twenty-two years of age (2 Chronicles 25:1).

But the most notable act of the reign of Joash was the restoration of the Temple. The need for it arose not so much from the age of the building, which had only been completed about a hundred and thirty years before, as from the damage done to it by the family of Athaliah, and the forcible appropriation for the service of Baalim of all that had been dedicated to the house of Jehovah (2 Chronicles 24:7). The initiative in the proposed restoration was taken by the king himself, although it is impossible to determine in what year of his reign. According to the original plan, the sum required for the work was to have been derived from "all the money of the consecrated;" that is, all the sacred offerings "brought into the house of Jehovah; the expression, "current money," meaning not coined money, which was not in use before the Exile, but silver weighed in certain proportions, for current payment to the workmen.

The sacred text further explains that this consecrated money was to be derived from two sources. from "the money of souls, after his estimation " — that is, the redemption money in case of vows, to be fixed according to the provisions of Leviticus 27:2, etc. — and from voluntary offerings. These sources of revenue the priests were to "take to themselves, every man of his acquaintance" (2 Kings 12:5), and with them to "repair the breaches of the house." The Book of Chronicles explains that this money was to be gathered by personal collection in all the cities of Judah. Considering that these contributions were mainly of the nature of voluntary offerings, like those once gathered for the Tabernacle (Exodus 35:21), such a mode of collection would appear the most suitable, especially in a time of religious revival following after a widespread religious decay.

The king had bidden the priests and Levites "hasten the matter" (2 Chronicles 24:5). But when, even in the twenty-third year of his reign, no satisfactory progress had been made with the needful repairs of the Temple, the king, with the consent of the priesthood, proceeded to make such alterations in the mode of collecting the money as virtually to place it in his own hands and those of the high-priest. It is not necessary to suppose that there had been defalcations on the part of the priesthood; indeed, the later arrangements are inconsistent with this idea. But we can quite understand that, besides the natural reluctance to collect from friends, the priests might find such calls interfering with the collection of their own revenues in the various districts; while the people would feel little confidence or enthusiasm in what was at best an irregular and disorderly mode of securing a great religious and national object. It was otherwise when the king and high-priest took the matter in hand. A chest for receiving voluntary contributions was placed at the entrance into the court of the priests, at the right side of the altar. A proclamation throughout the whole country, announcing a mode of collection identical with that when Moses had reared the Tabernacle in the wilderness, caused universal joy, and brought thousands of willing contributors. All the other arrangements were equally successful. When the chest was full, it was carried into the royal office, and opened in presence of the king's scribe and the high-priest or his representative, when the money was bound into bags and weighed to ascertain the exact amount. "And they gave the money that had been weighed into the hands of them that did the work [that is, them] that were appointed for the house of Jehovah," viz., to superintend the building operations. According to 2 Chronicles 24:12, these were Levites, and men of such trusted character that it was deemed unnecessary to require an account of their disbursements to the workmen whom they employed. The money was in the first place exclusively devoted to the repair of the Temple (2 Kings 12:13). But when this was completed, the rest was used for the purchase of sacred vessels for the service of the Sanctuary (2 Chronicles 24:14). And it is specially indicated, partly to show the liberality of the people, and partly the extent of the religious revival, that all these contributions in no way diminished the regular revenues of the priesthood (2 Kings 12:16).

We mark that the twenty-third year of Joash, when the king took in hand the hitherto neglected restoration of the Temple, was that in which, after Jehu's death, such great calamities befell the kingdom of Israel (see the next Chapter). In general, the accession of Jehu's son, his partial return to the service of the LORD), and afterwards the advance of Hazael into Israelitish territory, must all have had their influence on the state of matters in Judah. Shortly after the restoration of the Temple, Jehoiada died. The opportunity was seized by "the princes" to bring about a partial counter-reformation. It is only natural that the corruption of the last reigns should have had a demoralizing influence upon them. The moral rigor of the service of Jehovah would stand in marked contrast with the lascivious services of Asherah (Astarte — "groves" in the A.V.) and of idols, probably the sacred trees of Astarte, and the service of Baal connected therewith.

For the restoration of the latter, the "princes" humbly and earnestly petitioned the king. Joash yielded; and, although he is not charged in Holy Scripture with any act of personal idolatry, the sin which this involved brought its speedy judgment, and reacted on the whole later bearing of Joash.

It has sometimes been objected that so vital a change as this near the close of his reign seems difficult to understand. But the character of Joash, the removal of the paramount influence of Jehoiada, the growing power of the "princes" in the threatening hostilities from the north, and the circumstance that the king in the first place only permitted the proceedings of the corrupt aristocracy, sufficiently account for all that is recorded in the sacred narrative. On the other hand, there cannot be more instructive reading than to compare this later part of the history of Joash with that of Asa (1 Kings 15:9-24, and especially 2 Chronicles 14), which, although by way of contrast, seems almost a parallel to it.

The sanction given by the king to the introduction of idolatry in Judah soon brought, in the Divine order of things, its national punishment. But here also Divine mercy first interposed by admonitions and warnings sent through His prophets (2 Chronicles 24:19). Among these we have probably to include Joel, whose prophecies were probably uttered in the period of hopeful revival which characterized the first part of the reign of Joash. But now the warnings of the prophets were not only left unheeded: they called forth violent opposition. Still, prophets might be borne with because of their extraordinary mission and message. It was otherwise when the high-priest Zechariah, the son — or, rather, grandson — of Jehoiada, standing in his official capacity in the court of the priests, addressed the people gathered beneath in the lower court speaking in similar language, under the overpowering influence of the Spirit of God.

The princes and people conspired; and at the command of the king, unmindful not only of his duty to God, but even of the gratitude he owed to his former preserver and counselor, the grandson of Jehoiada was stoned to death "between the temple and the altar."

All things combined to mark this as a crime of no ordinary guilt, specially typical of what befell the last and greatest Prophet of Israel, the Christ of God. The death inflicted on Zechariah was that which the law had appointed for idolatry and blasphemy (Leviticus 20:2; 24:23). Thus the murderers of the high-priest, as those of Christ, unrighteously inflicted the punishment which was due to themselves. Again, in the one case as in the other, the crime was provoked by faithful admonitions and warnings sent directly of God. In both instances the crime was national, the rulers and people having equal part in it; in both, also, it was connected with the Temple, and yet the outcome of national apostasy. Lastly, in both instances the punishment was likewise national. Yet there is marked difference also. For, as Zechariah died, "he said, Jehovah, look upon it, and require it," while our Lord, when referring to this event as parallel to what was about to befall Him, implied no personal resentment when He uttered this prediction: "Behold your house is left unto you desolate." And yet further, unlike the words of Zechariah, those of Christ ended not with judgment, but with the promise of His return in mercy and the prospect of Israel's repentance (Matthew 23:39). Jewish tradition has preserved, although with many legendary additions, the remembrance of this national crime, fabling that the blood of the high-priest spilt on the Temple pavement could neither be wiped away nor be at rest, but was still bubbling up when more than two and a half centuries later Nebuzar-adan entered the Temple, till God in His mercy at last put it to rest after the slaughter of many priests.

The judgment predicted upon Judah was not long delayed. Joining together the notices in the Books of Chronicles and of Kings, we learn that exactly a year after the murder of Zechariah, Hazael, the king of Syria, made a victorious raid into Judah. We cannot be mistaken in connecting this with the expedition of the king of Damascus into the northern kingdom of Israel (2 Kings 13:3, 7, 22). Having conquered the territory east, and subjected that west of the Jordan, when Gilead specially suffered (Amos 1:3), Hazael seems next to have marched into Philistine territory, either for personal conquest or perhaps even at the request of the people. The latter seems suggested, as we shall see, alike by the siege and capture of Gath, and by the conjunction of the Philistine cities with Hazael in the prophecies of Amos (1:6-10; comp. also 6:2). These imply that the Philistine cities had been conspicuous by their traffic in the captives whom Hazael had taken in Judea.

The varying history of Gath deserves special notice. In the reign of Solomon it seems to have had a king of its own, although apparently under the suzerainty of Judea (1 Kings 2:39). During the reign of Rehoboam, the son and successor of Solomon, Gath is mentioned as one of the cities fortified for the defense of Judah (2 Chronicles 11:8). The suzerainty of Judah over Philistia seems to have continued up to the time of Jehoshaphat (2 Chronicles 17:11). We have no means of judging how the Egyptian expedition in the time of Asa affected the later condition of Philistia; but we know that in this, as in other hostile attacks upon Judah, the Philistines took an active part (2 Chronicles 21:16, 17). On all these grounds it seems likely that the native population of Gath, apparently the only city held by Judah, had called in the aid of the Syrians on their occupation of the kingdom of Israel, and that this had been the occasion for the siege of Gath by Hazael. From Gath to Jerusalem the distance is only about thirty miles, and the defeat of the Judean garrison in the Philistine fortress was naturally followed by an incursion of Judea proper. Although the Syrian force was numerically much inferior to that of Judah, the army of Joash was defeated with heavy losses. These notably included the destruction of those "princes" who had been leaders in the movement that ended in the murder of Zechariah. The Book of Chronicles (24:24) is careful to mark the hand of God in a defeat which formed so striking a contrast to the victory which the LORD had given to Asa with an army greatly inferior to his enemies (2 Chronicles 14:9, etc.) And yet this was only the beginning of judgment upon Joash. According to the account in the Book of Kings (2 Kings 12:18), Joash bought off the capture of his capital by handing to the conqueror all the hallowed things of the Temple and the treasures of the palace.

The withdrawal of the Syrian army, under conditions so disastrous and humiliating to Judah, was the signal for internal troubles. Joash lay sick and suffering, perhaps in consequence of wounds, in the castelated palace Millo (1 Kings 9:15), when he fell a victim to a palace conspiracy. Two of his servants murdered him as he lay in his bed. The Book of Chronicles traces his fate to the murder of "the son [grandson] of Jehoiada" — not, indeed, in the sense of this having been the motive of the conspirators, but as marking the real cause of his tragic end.

No doubt the conspiracy itself was due to the unpopularity which the king had incurred in consequence of the successive national disasters which marked the close of his reign. And even those who had most wished to see the sternness of Jehovah-worship relaxed in favor of the service of Baal must have felt that all the national calamities had been connected with the murder of Zechariah in the Temple, which they would impute to the king. Thus, not only religion, but superstition also, would be arrayed against Joash. Even his murder produced no revulsion in popular feeling. Joash was indeed buried "in the city of David," but "not in the sepulchers of the kings."

CHAPTER 3 — JOASH, (EIGHTH) KING OF JUDAH. JEHOASH, (TWELFTH AND THIRTEENTH) KINGS OF ISRAEL — ACCESSION OF JEHOAHAZ — CHRONOLOGY OF THE PERIOD — CHARACTER OF HIS REIGN — WARS WITH SYRIA — THE ASSYRIAN MONUMENTS — THE PRAYER OF JEHOAHAZ AND ITS ANSWER — RE-ARRANGEMENT OF THE TEXT — SPIRITUAL LESSONS OF THIS HISTORY — ACCESSION OF JEHOASH — THE DYNASTY OF JEHU AND REVERSAL OF THE POLICY OF AHAB — THE NEW RELATION TO THE PROPHETS — EXPLANATION OF IT — THE THREE FUNDAMENTAL PRINCIPLES IN THE BEARING OF THE PROPHETS — LAST INTERVIEW BETWEEN JEHOASH AND ELISHA — ITS LESSONS — THE MIRACLE AFTER ELISHA'S DEATH — VICTORIES OVER SYRIA.

(2 KINGS 13.)

THE reign of Joash, king of Judah, extended over the unusually long period of forty years. Acceding to the throne in the seventh year of Jehu, king of Israel, he survived not only that monarch and his son and successor, Jehoahaz, but also witnessed the accession of Jehoash. According to the Biblical text, Jehu was followed on the throne of Israel by Jehoahaz, his son, in the twenty-third, or more strictly speaking, in the twenty-first year of Joash, king of Judah.

His reign, which lasted seventeen years, was a period of incessant warfare with Syria, and of constant and increasing humiliation to Israel. The history is very briefly indicated in the Book of Kings, which is chiefly concerned in marking the deeper spiritual reasons for the disasters of Israel in the increasing apostasy of king and people.

But welcome light is thrown on the brief details of political history furnished in the Biblical account by what we read on the Assyrian monuments. It will be remembered that the Syrian conquest of Israelitish territory had begun during the reign of Jehu.

The Biblical notice of these successive conquests by Hazael (2 Kings 10:32, 33) is probably somewhat general, and not confined only to the time of Jehu. But the records on the Assyrian monuments show that Hazael was at war with the powerful empire of Assyria, defeated, and obliged to entreat peace under humiliating conditions. They also record that Jehu had paid tribute to the powerful king of Assyria — more strictly, that he had entered into a tributary alliance with that empire. When peace was concluded between Assyria and Hazael, the latter seems to have turned his whole force against the kingdom of Israel as allied to Assyria. By a series of victories, Hazael gradually possessed himself of the whole country east of the Jordan.

Thence, during the reign of Jehoahaz, he extended his conquests over the Israelitish territory west of the Jordan, till, in the judgment of God, the army of the king of Israel, gathered together in Samaria as the last stronghold, came to be reduced to,, fifty horsemen, ten chariots, and ten thousand footmen."

The rest — in the expressive language of Scripture — "the king of Syria had destroyed," "and made them as dust to trample upon" (lit. "to tread down") (2 Kings 13:7).

And we again mark, as indicated in the previous Chapter, that it was two years after the accession of Jehoahaz, viz., in "the three and twentieth year of King Jehoash" (2 Kings 12:6), during the full progress of the Syrian conquest of Israel, when the restoration of the Temple was begun. We can scarcely be mistaken in connecting this with a national reaction against what had taken place in the north, and with fear of judgments such as had overtaken Israel. Lastly, we should notice, in final explanation of the expedition of Hazael against Gath (2 Kings 12:17), which ultimately eventuated in a march upon Jerusalem, that the Assyrian monuments everywhere indicate a tributary dependence upon Assyria of the Philistine cities along the seacoast.

From this glimpse into the political history we turn to what throughout is the main object of the sacred writer, the indication of the religious causes which led up to these events. The Biblical text seems here somewhat involved, in part from the mixture of remarks by the writer with the historical notices extracted from existing documents. The following appears its real order. The usual notice (2 Kings 13:1) of the accession of Jehoahaz, and of the duration of his reign is followed by a general description of the character of that monarch (in ver. 2): as doing that which was evil in the sight of Jehovah, and continuing the wrongful religious institutions of Jeroboam. Then we have in ver. 3 a notice of the Divine punishment of these sins in the surrender of Israel to Hazael, king of Syria, and to Ben-Hadad, his son and successor. The following verse (ver. 4) marks the repentance and prayer of Jehoahaz, occasioned by these calamities, and God's gracious answer, although not in the immediate present (see vers. 22-25). Verses 5 and 6 form a parenthesis. Possibly it may begin with ver. 4. The reference to the wars of Ben-Hadad in ver. 3, which can only apply to the time of Jehoahaz, may be rather of a general character (see vers. 22 and 25).

In any case the continuous historical notices, or extracts, recommence with ver. 7, which describes the depressed condition of the kingdom under Jehoahaz, while vets. 8 and 9 record, in the usual form, the death of Jehoahaz and the accession of his son, Jehoash (or Joash). Thus, as already stated, vets. 5 and 6, if not also yet. 4, form an intercalated notice, telling on the one hand how God had heard the prayer of Jehoahaz by raising up "a savior" to Israel (ver. 5), and, on the other hand, how this gracious interposition did not really affect the spiritual state of Israel (ver. 6). They not only continued in the sins of Jeroboam, but "there stood the Asherah also in Samaria." This parenthetic notice must be considered as of a general character: "the savior" raised up being in the first place Jehoash (ver. 25), and finally and fully Jeroboam II. (2 Kings 14:25-27). Similarly the account of Israel's degenerate religious condition in 2 Kings 13:6 must be regarded as a general description, and not confined to either the reign of Jehoahaz, that of Jehoash, or that of Jeroboam II.

Lastly, the graphic expression, "the children of Israel dwelt in tents as beforetimes" (lit. "as yesterday and the third day") (the day before), is intended to recall the primitive happy days, the idea being that so thorough was the deliverance from the Syrians that Israel once more dwelt in perfect security as in olden times.

But the parenthesis in verses 5 and 6 is not the only one in this chapter. The brief notice in vers. 10-13 of the accession of Jehoash, the character of his reign, his death, and his succession by Jeroboam II., seems derived from the same historical record from which the equally brief previous account of Jehoahaz had been taken. It is followed in vers. 14-21 by a parenthetic account of what occurred in connection with the death of Elisha the prophet, derived, we would venture to suggest, from another source; perhaps a narrative of the lives and activity of Elijah and Elisha.

With this the writer connects (in verses 22-25)what really resumes and fully carries out the more summary remarks in vets. 4-6. Lastly, in chapter 14, the history of Jehoash — which had only been outlined in 13:9-13 — is taken up in detail and continued, and this in connection with the history of Judah, being perhaps derived from the annals of Judah, as the previous brief record may have been extracted from those of Israel.

Viewing this history from another and higher standpoint, we mark the readiness of the Lord in His mercy to listen to the entreaty of Jehoahaz, welcoming, as it were, every sign of repentance, and by His deliverance in response to it, encouraging a full return to Him, showing also that prosperity or disaster depended on the relation of the people towards Him. And assuredly no better evidence could be afforded us that even in our farthest decline we may still turn to God, nor yet that prayer — even by Jehoahaz, and in that state of Israel — shall not remain unanswered. Yet, though the prayer was immediately heard, as in the judgment pronounced upon Ahab (1 Kings 21:27-29), its immediate manifestation was delayed. These are precious practical lessons to all time, and the more valuable that they are in such entire accordance with God's dealings as declared in other parts of Revelation, exhibiting the harmony and inward unity of Holy Scripture. And even as regards the outward structure of this narrative, its very want of artistic connection only inspires us with greater confidence in its trustworthiness, as not concocted but apparently strung together from extracts of existing historical documents.

Jehoahaz was succeeded on the throne of Israel by his son Jehoash (or Joash), whose reign extended over sixteen years (2 Kings 13:10, 11). Religiously it was, like that of his father, marked by continuance in "the sins of Jeroboam, the son of Nebat." Indeed, as previously stated, this return to the religious policy of the founder of the northern kingdom, supplies the explanation of the administration of Jehu, and of the popular reaction against the house of Ahab which he represented and headed. Of this uniform policy we find an indication even in the name Jeroboam, which the son and successor of Jehoash bore. There was this other continuity also, that the monarchy founded by Jehu, originating in a military revolution, continued a military rule under his successors. This appears from the alliances with Assyria, from the continuous and finally successful wars with Syria during the whole of this dynasty, and lastly from the war with Amaziah, king of Judah (2 Kings 13:12). In this, as in the abolition of Ahab's religious institutions, we observe a reversal of the policy of the dethroned house. Nor can we be mistaken in ascribing to the latter cause the new friendly relations with the servants of Jehovah, and especially His prophets, which the new dynasty sought to inaugurate.

Almost the first act of Jehu had been to invite Jehonadab, the son of Rechab, to make public entry with him into Samaria, and to witness his zeal for Jehovah (2 Kings 10:16). Almost his first public measure had been the destruction of the temple of Baal, with its priests and worshippers (2 Kings 10:18-28). Even the slaughter of the descendants of Ahab and of the princes of Judah (2 Kings 13:4) might be imputed to the same motives — at least by a people in the religious condition of Israel. The same feelings may be traced in the repentant prayer of Jehoahaz (2 Kings 13:4), and lastly in the visit of Jehoash to the deathbed of Elisha (2 Kings 13:14).

It is another and a more serious question how the relation of these servants of Jehovah and especially of Elisha towards a dynasty stained by so many crime, and so unfaithful to the true service of the Lord, is to be explained. It certainly cannot be understood without taking several considerations into account. The situation was not simple, but complicated, and accordingly the motives influencing the conduct of the prophets were varied, and, if one-sidedly viewed, may for that very reason appear conflicting. These three considerations may, however, help us to understand their general bearing. First, the prophets were always only the executors of God's behests; they stood not in any independent personal relation to events or individuals. Secondly, the behests of God, and consequently the prophetic commission, whether as regarded judgment or deliverance, applied to acts and individual events, not to persons or lives.

Thirdly, the final object of all was, on the one hand, the vindication of Jehovah's dealings, and, on the other, the arresting of Israel's spiritual, and with it of their national decline. It was needful that signal judgments should sweep away Ahab and all connected with his ways, and Jehu was, in the circumstances of the time and in the state of the people, the most suitable instrument for it. Thus far, and thus far only, had his counter-revolution the countenance of the prophets. Again, it was in accordance with the Divine purpose of mercy that the first indication of any spiritual comprehension of God's judgments should be welcomed and encouraged.

Hence the prayer of Jehoahaz was heard; hence, also, and in further pursuance of the promise of deliverance, the interview between the king and the dying prophet, as well as the prediction of Jonah, the son of Amittai (2 Kings 14:25). Nor must we overlook in all this the human aspect of the question. The prophets were indeed first and foremost God's messengers; but they were also true patriots, and intensely national, and this not despite, but rather because of their office. Any national reaction, any possible prospect of national return to God, must have had their warmest sympathy and received their most hearty encouragement. In short, whenever they could, they would most readily range themselves on the side of their people and its rulers. They would co-operate whenever and in whatsoever they might; and only protest, warn, and denounce when they must. And a consideration alike of the bearing of Jehonadab (comp. Vol. VI., p. 210), and again of Elisha, must convince that as their co-operation was never withheld when it might be given, so it was never extended to that which was either wrong in itself or inconsistent with their spiritual mission.

If evidence were required of what has just been stated, it would be found in the last interview between Jehoash, the king of Israel, and Elisha. Forty-five years had elapsed since the anointing of Jehu, and as Elisha was grown up even during the reign of Ahab (1 Kings 19:19), he must have attained a very advanced age. Strange as it may seem, we have not any record of his public activity during the forty-five years that had passed since Jehu's accession. It is impossible to determine whether or not some of his recorded mighty deeds had been done during this lengthened period, although inserted in this history without regard to chronological order, having been extracted from a separate biographical rather than historical work. Or his activity may not have been of so public a character; or it may not have required record in the general history of Israel; or through him may have come the message to Jehu (2 Kings 10:30), and afterwards the impulse which led to the prayer of Jehoahaz.

Residing in Samaria, Elisha could not, even as regards his prophetic office, have fallen out of public view, since, on tidings of his last fatal illness, Jehoash at once hastened to his side.

Nor, on the other hand, could we imagine this history to have omitted all reference to the death of Elisha; nor yet that the prophet should have departed without some public admonition for good or pledge of Jehovah's near deliverance of Israel. Indeed, had it been otherwise, the victory over Syria, coming so long after the prayer of Jehoahaz, might have been imputed to the prowess of Jehoash, and not to the answer of God.

It would be difficult to imagine a more striking contrast than between the bearing of the youthful king of Israel and that of the aged dying prophet. Elisha is full of confidence and courage, while Jehoash is overwhelmed rather with concern than with grief at the impending death of the prophet, weeps "over his face," and addresses him: "My father, my father! the chariot of Israel, and the horsemen thereof!" The language is the same as that of Elisha himself on the removal of Elijah (2 Kings 2:12), but uttered in a spirit very different from his.

The king's was language of respectful affection, indeed, but also of unbelief, as if with the removal of Elisha's presence from amongst them the defense and might of Israel had ceased. Very different also from the bearing of Elisha when his master had been taken from him was that of Jehoash. Then the first act of Elisha had been one of faith that dared the utmost, when with the mantle fallen from his master's shoulders he smote the waters of Jordan, and they parted hither and thither. On the other hand, almost the first act of Jehoash in view of the departure of his master was one of unbelief, that in cowardice shrunk back, even within sound of the prophet's express directions and of the accompanying assurance of promised Divine help. So the same words have a very different meaning in the mouths of different persons, nor is there safety in any mere formula, however sacred or sanctioned. In this also the letter killeth, but the Spirit maketh alive.

Alike intrinsically, and in view of the condition of the king, as also for a lasting record to Israel, it was needful that the prophet should before his departure once more give emphatic testimony to Jehovah, emphatic confirmation also of His promise, and encouragement to Israel. So would his dying words become a permanent message to the people, and not only sum up and seal, but, so to speak, perpetuate his whole mission. It was in accordance with almost uniform prophetic custom (comp. 1 Kings 11:29- 32; Isaiah 20:2; Jeremiah 13:1; Ezekiel 4:1, and others), and also best suited to the condition of the king and the circumstances of the case, that this message should be joined to a symbolic act as its sign. It would be impossible to misunderstand it, when Elisha bade Jehoash take bow and arrows and put his hand upon the bow, while the prophet himself laid his hands upon that of the king. And when this had been done, the window towards the east was opened, or rather, its lattice removed, and the king at Elisha's command shot the arrow. Towards the east was Syria; in shooting the arrow thither, the king of Israel was acting at the direction, and with the symbolically assured helping Presence of the LORD. And so it meant: "An arrow of salvation [deliverance] of Jehovah [the deliverance being His] and an arrow of salvation from [against, over] Syria;" to which the prophetic promise was immediately added' "For thou shalt smite Syria in Aphek to destruction [complete annihilation]." The latter statement, it need scarcely be said, referred only to the Syrian host at Aphek, since this first was followed by other victories. But Aphek was a significant name, marking the locality where by Divine prediction and Divine help Israel had once before defeated the overwhelming might of Syria (1 Kings 20:26-30).

But the interposition of God, although direct, is not of the nature of magic. If any success granted by Him is to be complete, it implies moral conditions on our part. To put it otherwise: the full reception of God's benefits has for its condition full receptivity on the part of man. This was the meaning of Elisha's further behest to the king; this also the explanation of Jehoash's failure. The prophet bade him seize "the arrows" which he had already taken from the quiver, and "strike (that is, shoot, hit) towards the earth."

Instead of obeying fully and literally, or at least shooting five or six times, the king struck only thrice. It was a symbol he could not fully understand, and which therefore had not any real meaning for him. Of simple, unquestioning, and persevering obedience of faith he had not any conception. So far as his capacity reached he did obey. He may have dimly perceived that it meant the shooting at the enemy prostrate on the ground. But then "three times" indicated in ordinary Jewish parlance that a thing was completely and fully done (as in Exodus 23:17; Numbers 22:28, 32, 33; 24:10; 2 Kings 1:9-14), and three times he had "smitten." This also was symbolic of the king's moral incapacity for full deliverance. That at such a moment he should have failed in the test of faith and obedience, perhaps grown weary of what seemed meaningless in its continuation, and that this failure should have involved the delay of Israel's full deliverance, filled the prophet and patriot with holy indignation. It should be to him as he had done — only thrice, according to his obedience, but not to complete and final victory would Jehoash smite the Syrians.

We cannot help connecting the brief notice of the miracle after Elisha's death and burial with this interview between the king and the prophet. It was not as the king in his faint-heartedness had cried, or as Israel might have feared, that with the disappearance of the living prophet from among them "the chariot of Israel and the horsemen thereof" were gone. It was the God of the prophet, and not the prophet's god, that was Israel's defense and might. It needed not a living prophet — the same power which stood behind him in life could work deliverance through him after he was dead.

The main point was not the man, but his mission, and to it — that he was a prophets this miracle after his death gave the most emphatic attestation; such also as would both in itself and from its surrounding circumstances specially appeal to that time and generation. This, without overlooking its other possible symbolic application, seems to us its chief meaning.

It appears that "at the coming in of the year" — probably in the spring — after Elisha's burial, they were carrying a man to his burying, as was the wont, on an open bier. But lo, as the procession reached the last place of rest, one of those predatory Moabite bands, which, like the Bedawin of modern times, desolated the land, was seen swooping round to where the mourners were gathered. Only a hasty flight could save them from death or bondage. There was not time for hesitation. Rolling away the stone which barred the entrance, and opening the door of his sepulcher, they laid the dead man upon the bones of the prophet, and then hastily fled. But lo, life came again to the dead man by touch of the dead prophet — and "he stood on his feet," the only bring man in the silent home of the dead; safe in the sepulcher of Elisha from either flight or the Moabites. But whatever its immediate meaning, who can in this prophetic history refrain from thinking here of the life that comes from touch of the crucified Christ; of the raising of the young man carried at Nain on his bier to the burying; or even of the dim dawning of thoughts of a resurrection, the full blaze of whose light comes to us from the empty tomb on the Easter morning?

At its close the narrative again returns to what is its keynote (in vers. 4, 5). Again comes the record of the LORD'S compassion, of His faithful remembrance of the covenant with the Fathers, and of His merciful delay of that final punishment of Israel's sin which would sweep them far from their land. It was as God had promised. Hazael was dead. Once and again, nay three times, did Jehoash defeat Ben-hadad (III.), the son and successor of Hazael, and take from him those cities which had been captured in the reign of Jehoahaz.

But as from the rock-hewn sepulcher of Elisha came attestation of his Divine mission, so comes there to us from the monuments of Assyria confirmation of this defeat of Ben-hadad in fulfillment of Divine promise. For whereas his father is repeatedly referred to as a bold warrior even against the overwhelming might of Assyria, Ben-hadad (III.) is not even mentioned. This is most significant; evidently, his reign was smitten with weakness, and his power had been wholly broken.

CHAPTER 4 — AMAZIAH, (NINTH) KING OF JUDAH. JEHOASH, (THIRTEENTH) KING OF ISRAEL — ACCESSION OF AMAZIAH — CHARACTER OF HIS REIGN — MILITARY PREPARATIONS — THE HIRING OF ISRAELITISH MERCENARIES, WARNING OF THE PROPHET, AND DISMISSAL OF THE AUXILIARIES — "THE VALLEY OF SALT" — DEFEAT OF THE EDOMITES — MARCH UPON PETRA — DESCRIPTION OF PETRA — SLAUGHTER OF THE CAPTIVES — INTRODUCTION OF EDOMITE IDOLATRY — THE CHALLENGE OF AMAZIAH TO JEHOASH, AND HIS REPLY — DEFEAT OF JUDAH — CAPTURE AND PLUNDER OF JERUSALEM — CONSPIRACY AGAINST AMAZIAH — FLIGHT TO LACHISH — MURDER OF THE KING.

(2 KINGS 14:1-20; 2 CHRONICLES 25.)

IT has been well remarked that Jehoahaz of Israel had on his death left to his son and successor Jehoash, amidst the sore troubles of his country, this priceless inheritance the promised answer to his prayer. How largely his promise had already been fulfilled appears from a comparison of the condition to which Hazael had reduced the army of Israel in the time of Jehoahaz (2 Kings 13:7), with the three brilliant victories which Jehoash gained over Ben-hadad III. Nor were the military successes of Israel confined to foreign enemies. Jehoash proved as victorious against Judah as against Syria.

In the second year of the reign of Jehoash over Israel, Joash, king of Judah, was succeeded by his son Amaziah. The reign of that monarch, who ascended the throne at the age of twenty-five, extended over twenty-nine years. Its beginning was marked by a continuance of what on the whole might, as in the case of his father Joash, be characterized as doing that which was "right in the sight of Jehovah:" To this the Book of Kings adds, however, the qualification, "Yet not as David his father," which the Book of Chronicles explains by the expression, "not with a perfect heart."

In truth his religious bearing during that period was (as both the historical records note) like that of his father Joash, and included the toleration of worship and services in "the high places." But even this qualified adherence to the religion of his fathers did not continue during the latter part of his reign.

Ascending the throne after a palace-revolution to which his father had fallen victim (2 Kings 12:20, 21), it must have been some time before "the kingship [royal rule] was confirmed in his hand."

So soon as this first necessity was secured, he punished the authors of the late revolt by executing the murderers of his father. The sacred text especially notes that in so doing he spared their children, in conformity with the Mosaic law (Deuteronomy 24:16), which in this, as in so many other respects, differed from the common practice of ancient times.

But the promise of this good beginning failed only too soon. As one has aptly remarked, "with a perfect heart" Amaziah was only a soldier, and even this rather in the sense of a cruel and boastful Eastern monarch than of a wise or brave general. It seems not improbable that the successes of the king of Israel against Syria had awakened in Amaziah lust for military glory. For the attainment of this object he made preparations of the most extensive character. His first aim was again to reduce Edom to the vassalage which it had cast off during the reign of Jehoram (2 Kings 8:20-22).

In prospect of this expedition, he reorganized the forces of Judah, that had been shattered by the Syrians in the time of his father Joash (2 Chronicles 24:23, 24). From the account in 2 Chronicles 25:5, 6, he seems to have made a levy en masse, calling to arms the whole population capable of military service.

The national character of this measure appears even from the circumstance that the officers of the new army were first appointed according to the old arrangement of tribe, clans, and families (2 Chronicles 25:5), and that these chiefs then conducted the levy of the people. The grand total so called to arms appears large; but it is considerably smaller than that in the time of Abijah (2 Chronicles 13:3), in that of Asa (2 Chronicles 14:8), or in that of Jehoshaphat (2 Chronicles 17:14-8).

Besides raising a native Judaean army, Amaziah had recourse to the novel device of hiring 100,000 Israelitish mercenaries, at the enormous cost of 100 talents — presumably silver talents, amounting to about. 37,500 pounds of our money.

Such aid could only lead to defeat, since Jehovah was not with Israel. Of this even their hiring themselves out for a foreign warfare in which they were not in any wise concerned affords fresh evidence. Had Amaziah possessed spiritual insight, he would not have sought such help. As it was, "a prophet" was commissioned to warn him that if he went to battle relying on such aid he should surely succumb. God would show that He had power not only to help, but also to cast down. The answer of the king was characteristic. It indicated that while he rightly appraised the character of these mercenaries, he was chiefly concerned about the money which had been spent upon them.

The dignified reply of the man of God, pointing him upwards to Him who could give far more than this, at least silenced the king, and he dismissed his auxiliaries. But the matter ended not there. Disappointed, no doubt, of their hope of plunder and ravage, the Ephraimires returned to their homes "in burning anger" (2 Chronicles 25:10). Josephus, although telling the story with his usual embellishments, adds what seems a historical notice to the effect that these Israelites laid waste the land as far as Beth-horon, taking much cattle, and slaying 3,000 men (Ant. ix. 9, I). If this account be trustworthy, we can scarcely be mistaken in tracing to this the later war between Judah and Israel, with its disastrous consequences to Amaziah. If Amaziah had hitherto proved himself anything but what his name implied, "the strong one of Jehovah" [or perhaps, "Jehovah strengthens"], his true character was soon to appear, alike in his success and in his defeat. The dismissal of the Israelitish auxiliaries did not delay the preparations for the war. The south-eastern limit of "the land" may be roughly marked by the lower end of the Dead Sea., Here, east of the mountain of rock-salt (the Khashm Usdum), stretches southward that continuation of the Jordan-gorge (the Ghor) known as "the Valley of Salt" (the Sabkah). The valley, which extends about eight miles (about three hours), trends southwards to the white chalk cliffs, which rise 50 to 150 feet. They are formed from the debris washed down from the higher soil of the Arabah — here especially that part of "the plain" which stretches from Jericho downwards on both sides of the Jordan as far as the Elanitic Gulf of the Red Sea.

The "salt valley" itself formed the southern boundary of Judaea towards Edom. In its western and central parts it is wholly desolate, the clay soil being often flooded by the Dead Sea, and even the watercourses which traverse it being impregnated with the salt which encrusts the district. It is otherwise as regards the southern part of the valley, and especially the eastern, which is covered with vegetation, and where we still trace the sites of ancient towns. Here indeed we have an oasis that formed the ancient boundary between Edom and Moab.

In this "salt valley" had Joab, or rather Abishai, his brother, defeated Edom in the time of David (2 Samuel 8:13; 1 Chronicles 18:12, etc.), and here again did the Edomite army encounter the host of Amaziah. Although we know not the precise spot where the battle was fought, we may well suppose that it was in the southern part of the valley. The Edomites were within their own territory; their retreat would not be difficult, and, owing to the surrounding heights, comparatively safe. On the other hand, if the Judaean army had been beaten, it is not easy to imagine how any considerable remnant could have escaped, either by crossing the treacherous "valley," or by skirting it. Nevertheless the Edomite army was defeated, with a slaughter of 10,000 men, and the capture of other ten thousand.

The account in the Book of Kings (2 Kings 14:7) adds that the victorious Jewish army marched on to Sela, or Petra, where, according to 2 Chronicles 25:12, the wretched prisoners were "cast down from the height of Sela." Needless objection has been taken to the transport of prisoners over what is sometimes described as so long and difficult a journey.

Chiefly for this reason, the localization of the "Valley of Salt" has also been called in question. But if we suppose the battlefield to have been the southern part of the valley, these objections are removed. And obviously it would be the policy of the victorious army to penetrate into the heart of the conquered country, take its capital, and by an act of terrible vengeance to strike terror into the people.

It must have been a marvelous sight which met the Jewish host as they descended from the east into that surpassingly grand defile which opens into the so-called Wady Musa — the "Valley of Moses " — the site of the ancient, Sela, "rock " — better known by its later name of Petra. The "cleft," or Sik, which formed the only access to it, passes between perpendicular rocks of red sandstone, rising to a height of from 100 to 300 feet.

It follows the winding course of a torrent which rises in the mountains half an hour thence, at a spot said to be that where the rod of Moses had brought the water from the smitten rock. For an hour and a half we pass through this gorge, between rocky walls that "overlap and crumble and crack," their intervening heights "throughout almost as narrow as the narrowest part of the defile of Pfeffers." At the entrance we pass under an arch that spans the chasm. Our progress is along what had once been a paved way, where the torrent had been "diverted," "along troughs in the rocks, into a water-conduit for the city." Festoons of the caper-plant and wild ivy and oleanders fringe the road, which winds like a river, affording at every turn the surprise of new views. The cliffs are red — in the sunshine, scarlet; in the shadow, black. Then through a narrow opening, where the rocks here overarch, we find ourselves suddenly at a turn of the road in face of a temple, with its pale pink pillars, all hewn into the rock. For all here is rock — rock graves, streets of rock, rock dwellings, rock temples, rock monuments; gorgeous rocks, dull crimson streaked with purple, over which seem to flow ribbons of yellow and blue. Again the road narrows through the streets of tombs, till it passes into the bottom of the rock-enclosed hollow or valley, with its branching valleys of rocks. This is the site of Petra now a desolation, but once a city of splendor and wealth, the central station for the commerce from India.

For further description this is not the place. It was into the midst of all this wondrous glory of nature and wealth of man that the Jewish army marched with its ten thousand captives. There cannot be doubt that the victorious host plundered and laid waste Sela. This explains how Amos does not mention it, but only Bozrah (Amos 1:12), which seems to have become the capital of Edom.

Similarly, it is not named by the later prophets, except in Isaiah 16:1 and 42:11; and it only again emerges into importance in the fourth century before our era. But the most terrible scene yet remained to be enacted in the conquered city. We can scarcely be mistaken in supposing that the victors marched or drove their captives through its streets across to the western bank of the rivulet. There up the western cliffs mounts "a staircase" of broad steps "hewn out of the rocks." "High up in these cliffs, between two gigantic walls of cliff, stands a temple." It must be here, or on the cliffs above and around — or perhaps on the Acropolis somewhat to the south of it that we have to look for "the height of Sela" (2 Chronicles 25:12 — lit., "the top," or "head"), whence the ten thousand Edomite captives were hurled, their shattered limbs dashing from cliff and rock, and their mangled remains strewing the heights and covering the ground beneath. But as they that long afterwards laid waste Jerusalem changed its name to Aelia Capitolina, so did King Amaziah change that of Sela into Joktheel, "the subdued of God" (2 Kings 14:7). Yet neither the one nor the other name, given by man in his pride, did long continue.

It is a horrible, heart-sickening scene of history, so utterly un-Jewish in character that we can only account for its enactment by the state of moral degradation which the contemporary prophets Hosea and Amos describe in such vivid language. Yet another terrible inheritance, besides the guilt of this deed, did Judah bring back from the campaign against Edom. We can readily imagine how deeply the rock-city had impressed the mind of the king. But one of its chief features, which still first attracts the traveler, is the startling appearance and weird location of its temples. An Eastern mind, not religious, but superstitious, would readily come under the spell of these divinities whose temples were so weird and grand, so thoroughly in accord with nature around.

Be this as it may, on his return from Edom King Amaziah brought with him its idols, and did worship to them, although the notice of it in 2 Chronicles (25:14) seems to imply personal rather than national or public idolatry. None the less was Divine anger kindled against such a Jewish and Davidic king. In vain was Divine warning sent to him by "a prophet." The king replied by coarse sneers and threats, which, needless to say, so far from silencing the Divine messenger, only led to the announcement of near judgment. And the sacred narrative expressly marks the connection between this and the later conspiracy which cost the king his life (2 Chronicles 25:27).

Two characteristics which have so often impressed us in the course of this Divine history appear in this narrative also. For, first, the Divine decree, in this instance of judgment, was not immediately carried out, and to some it might seem to tarry. And, further, the execution of this decreed destruction came not in sudden or miraculous manner, but in what might be regarded as the natural course of events, through popular dissatisfaction at gratuitously provoked national disaster. Thus, however real the connection between the Divine agency and Amaziah's destruction, it would, on both the grounds above mentioned, require the eye of faith to perceive it. And this also is of permanent meaning: that the teaching of God is only to those who are capable of learning it.

It might almost seem as if the victory over Edom had infatuated the king and his council, filling them with unbounded self-confidence and overweening self-esteem. For, since they discarded God, was it not the prowess and might of Judah which had wrought the victory over Edom? Very significantly, the account of Judah's defeat by Israel in the Book of

Chronicles is introduced by the notice, "And the king took counsel." He had taunted the prophet as not being a counselor to the king, and the prophet had announced to him the counsel of God to his destruction. It would now appear how the king's own chosen counselors would themselves bring about this "counsel" of God.

As we have suggested, it is not unlikely that the war between Judah and Israel really grew out of the dismissal of the Israelitish auxiliaries from the host of Judah. This would be the more probable if the account of Josephus is trustworthy, that Amaziah had hired these soldiers directly from the king of Israel, and that on their return to their homes they had laid waste Judaean territory. And this would also better account for the challenge to fight which Amaziah, with advice of his council, addressed to Jehoash, king of Israel, than to view it as a demand for submission and return to obedience to the Davidic rule, which, according to Josephus, formed the burden of this message.

If the challenge of Amaziah was peculiarly Oriental and boastful in its tone, the reply of Jehoash equaled and even surpassed it in these respects. The allegory which he used about the "thorn" in Lebanon that had sought a family alliance with the cedar, meant that it was absolute folly on the part of Amaziah to regard himself as the equal of Jehoash.

Yet this was implied in his purpose of measuring himself with him. A contest between them! Why, a beast of the field in Lebanon passing over the thorn would crush it down. Then followed the mocking application of the simile:

"Thou hast indeed smitten Edom make thyself glorious [enjoy thy glory], and abide at home' why shouldest thou meddle with evil, that thou fall, thou and Judah with thee?" (2 Kings 14:10.)

The advice was sound, though extremely provocative to one in the mood of Amaziah. But Jehoash did not await his attack. Marching southwards, he met the Judaean army at Beth Shemesh, the south-eastern point in the ancient possession of Dan, close to the border of Philistia, situated in a beautiful valley only eight or nine hours west of Jerusalem. The battle was most disastrous for Judah. The army fled; Amaziah was taken prisoner; and the Israelitish host advanced unopposed to Jerusalem. Here they made a breach in the wall 400 cubits (or about 600 feet) wide, from the northern gate of Ephraim (or Benjamin, the present Damascus gate)to that in the north-west corner of the wall, where it runs southward.

Thus the city would be laid open towards the north, or the land of Israel. Josephus (Ant. ix. 9, 3) has it that Jehoash through this breach made triumphal entry into Jerusalem, carrying his royal prisoner with him. The victor plundered the Temple of what treasures it still contained in charge of one Obed-Edom. He also stripped the royal palace of its valuables, and taking with him "hostages" — probably from the chief nobles — returned to Samaria.

The war between Judah and Israel probably occurred quite near the close of the reign of Jehoash, king of Israel. As Amaziah of Judah reigned altogether twenty-nine years (2 Kings 14:2), and survived Jehoash for fifteen years (verse 17), we conclude that the Judaeo-Israelitish war had occurred in the fourteenth, and the Edomite war probably in the thirteenth, year of the reign of Amaziah. The fifteen years which followed after the death of Jehoash were full of trouble to the king of Judah. At last the general dissatisfaction, caused by the disasters of the war and the attempted introduction of foreign rites, culminated in a revolution at Jerusalem. Amaziah escaped to Lachish, in the low country of Judah (Joshua 15:33, 39), on the road from Hebron to Gaza.

Lachish has sometimes been erroneously identified with the present Tel-el-Hasi. Its more correct location seems to be, passing from Eleutheropolis [the Biblical Libnah] westwards to Ajlan, the ancient Eglon, whence at a distance of about forty-five minutes the ruins of Umm Lakis — the ancient Lachish are — reached.

As usually, the ancient city lay on the top of a hill. Among its ruins many cisterns are found. The country around is undulating, and two great wadys open on either side. Lachish was, as we know, strongly fortified (2 Chronicles 11:9); it was besieged by Sennacherib (2 Kings 18:14, 17; Isaiah 36:2); and could offer a stout resistance to Nebuchadnezzar (Jeremiah 34:7). In short, it was one of the strong fortresses towards Egypt, although, from the friable nature of the building materials, its ruins, as those of other similarly-constructed places, are not considerable. In the time of Solomon, Lachish had been one of the "chariot-cities," for which alike its situation near the Egyptian emporium of horses (1 Kings 9:19; 10:26-29), and the plentiful pasturage around, would specially fit it. From the prophecies of Micah (1:13), it appears to have been the first Judaean city to adopt the idolatrous worship of the northern kingdom, which thence passed into Jerusalem.

But the strong walls of Lachish could not afford security to Amaziah. The conspirators from Jerusalem followed the king, and his dead body was brought back to Jerusalem — perhaps in the very chariot in which he had made his escape. Yet even this circumstance, as well as his honorable burial with his royal ancestors, and the elevation to the throne of his son, "by all the people of Judah," indicate that although the discontent was not confined to the capital, yet the people generally were wholly averse to any change of dynasty, such as had characterized every revolution in Israel.

CHAPTER 5 — AZARIAH, OR UZZIAH, (TENTH) KING OF JUDAH. JEREBOAM II., (FOURTEENTH) KING OF ISRAEL

Accession of Azariah or Uzziah — Reign of Jeroboam II. — Restoration of Israelitish Territory — Political Causes and Divine Agency in these Successes — Corruption of the People — Scattered Historical Notices — New Phase in Prophecy — Its Characteristic — The two Prophets on the Boundary-line — Prophets of that Period: Joel, Amos, Hosea, Jonah.

(2 KINGS 14:21-29.)

IT would seem that a peculiar meaning attaches to the notice that all the people of Judah took Azariah, who was sixteen years old, and made him king instead of his father, Amaziah" (2 Kings 14:21). With the exception of the name, this statement is literally repeated in 2 Chronicles 26:1, indicating that the writers of the two books had copied it from the same historical record. But considering the youth of the new king on the death of his father, Amaziah, at the age of fifty-four (2 Kings 14:2), he could scarcely have been his eldest son. Probably there was, therefore, a special reason for his selection by the people. Possibly there may be some connection between it and the twofold name which he bears in Holy Scripture. In 2 Chronicles — written, as we may say, from the priestly point of view — the new king is always called Uzziah, while in the Book of Kings he is designated during the first part of his reign as Azariah, while one notices of the latter part of that period he appears as Uzziah (2 Kings 15:13, 30, 32, 34).

The usual explanations either of a clerical error through the confusion of similar letters, or that he bore two names, seem equally unsatisfactory. Nor is the meaning of the two names precisely the same — Azariah being "Jehovah helps;" Uzziah, "My strength is Jehovah." May it not be that Azariah was his real name, and that when after his daring intrusion into the sanctuary (2 Chronicles 26:16-20), he was smitten with lifelong leprosy, his name was significantly altered into the cognate Uzziah — "My strength is Jehovah" — in order to mark that the "help" which he had received had been dependent on his relation to the LORD.

This would accord with the persistent use of the latter name in 2 Chronicles — considering the view-point of the writer and with its occurrence in the prophetic writings (Hosea 1:1; Amos 1:1; Isaiah 1:1; 6:1; 7:1). And the explanation just suggested seems confirmed by the circumstance that although this king is always called Uzziah in 2 Chronicles, yet the Hebrew word for "help," which forms the first part of the name Azariah, recurs with marked emphasis in the account of the Divine help accorded in his expeditions (2 Chronicles 26:7, 13, 15).

At the accession of Uzziah (as we shall prefer to call him) the throne of Israel had been already occupied for fourteen years by Jeroboam II., the son and successor of that Jehoash who had inflicted such defeat on Amaziah of Judah (2 Kings 14:23). His exceptionally long reign extended over fifty-one years, being the longest of that of any Israelitish king."

Holy Scripture gives only the briefest sketch of outward events during that half-century in Israel. Religiously, it was marked by a continuance of the wrongful institutions of the founder of the Israelitish monarchy (Jeroboam I.). Politically, it was distinguished by the complete defeat of Syria, and the recovery of all the territory which had, in the most flourishing times of united Judah, been conquered by David or occupied by Solomon' in the language of the sacred text, "from the entering of Hamath unto the sea of the plain" (2 Kings 14:25).

Indeed, the conquests of Jeroboam seem to have extended even beyond this, and to the boundary of Moab (see Amos 6:14, where for "river of the wilderness," read "of the Arabah "). The Dead Sea unquestionably marked on that side the southern boundary originally of united Palestine, and afterwards of the trans-Jordanic kingdom of Israel, while the "entering in of Hamath" equally indicates the northern limits of the realm (Numbers 13:21; 34:8; Joshua 13:5; 1 Kings 8:65; 2 Chronicles 7:8; Amos 6:14). The precise locality designated as the "entering of Hamath," has not yet been accurately ascertained. But it must be sought in that broad rich plain, flanked towards the west by the Lebanon, and watered by the Orontes, which ascends for a distance of about eight hours from Homs to Hamah, the ancient Hamath the Great (Amos 6:2).

In all likelihood it is in this general sense that we are to understand what seems the parallel notice of these conquests (2 Kings 14:28):" Damascus and Hamath." The expression seems to refer to the whole of the broad plain just described the words bearing the same general meaning as when David is stated to have put garrisons in Syria of Damascus (2 Samuel 8:5, 6), and Solomon to have occupied Hamath (2 Chronicles 8:3, 4).

Here again welcome light comes to us from the monuments of Assyria. Thence we learn, on the one hand, that the kingdom of Israel was tributary to the king of Assyria, and, on the other, that that monarch conquered Damascus, took prisoner its king, who, having embraced his knees in submission, had to pay a ransom of 2,300 talents of silver, 20 of gold, 3,000 of copper, 5,000 of iron, together with garments of wool and linen, a couch and an umbrella of ivory, and other spoil numberless. The disastrous war of Syria with Assyria, and the tributary alliance of Israel with the latter, would sufficiently account for the conquests of Jeroboam II.

And yet here also there is a higher meaning. If, on the suggestion just made, the instrumentality used to bring about the victories of Jeroboam II. was not the direct help of Jehovah, but the prowess of Assyria, we ought to bear in mind that direct interposition on the part of the LORD in behalf of such a king could not have been expected. And yet, as noted in the sacred text (2 Kings 14:25), the promise of the LORD given through the prophet Jonah, the son of Amittai, was literally fulfilled — only in the natural course of political events. And the more clearly to mark the agency of God in what might seem the natural course of events, the connection between these successes and the original promise in 2 Kings 13:4, 5, is indicated in 2 Kings 14:26, as well as the higher meaning of all (in ver. 27).

It still remains to point out the strict accuracy of the Biblical account, alike as regards the prosperous internal condition of the land at that period (2 Kings 13:5), and the moral and religious decay of the people (2 Kings 13:6). If the victories of Jeroboam had, as on grounds of contemporary history seems likely, been gained in the early part of his reign, the rest of that long period was one of almost unprecedented wealth and prosperity, but also of deepest moral corruption. To both facts the contemporary prophets, Amos and Hosea, bear frequent witness — to the prosperity in such passages as Hosea 2:8; 12:9 [A.V. ver. 8]; Amos 3:15; 6:4-6; to the corruption, in many passages and in varied particulars.

A more terrible picture of religious degeneracy and public and private wickedness could scarcely be imagined than that painted by the prophets in this the most prosperous period of Israelitish history. Thus the goodness of God, misunderstood by an apostate people, which attributed all to its own prowess (see Amos 6:13), was only abused to further sin (Hosea 13:6). A people which could not be humbled by judgments, and to which every mercy became only the occasion for deeper guilt, was ripe for that final doom which the prophets predicted.

On some other points of interest scattered notices may here be put together. Firstly, Jeroboam II. was certainly the most warlike king and the most successful administrator of all who occupied the throne of Israel. Of this even the new registration in the re-conquered trans-Jordanic provinces affords evidence (1 Chronicles 5:11-17). Secondly, this history is another proof of how little real success could attend such a re-action against the foreign rites of the house of Ahab as that which had been initiated by Jehu. The worship of the golden calves speedily led to that on high places, and even to the restoration of the service of Baal (Hosea 2:13, 17; Amos 2:8; 4:4; 5:5; 8:14). Nay, Jeroboam and his priest at Bethel proceeded to actual persecution of the prophets of the Lord (Amos 7:10-17). Lastly, we may derive from a study of the prophetic writings much insight into the political relations of Israel and Judah at the time, more especially as regards Syria and Assyria.

But there is one subject which claims special attention. Even a superficial study must convince that from a religious point of view, and particularly as regards Israel's future and the great hope of the world entrusted to their keeping, we have now reached a new period. We are not now thinking of the general religious and moral decay, nor of the national judgment which was so soon to follow, but the other and wider aspect of it all. God's great judgments, when viewed from another point, are always seen to be attended with wider manifestations of mercy. It is never judgment only, but judgment and mercy — and every movement is a movement forward, even though in making it there should be a crushing down and a breaking down. Even here, so early in the history of the kingdom of God, the casting away of Israel was to be the life of the world. For with this period a new stage in prophecy begins. Hitherto the prophets had been chiefly God-sent teachers and messengers to their contemporaries — reproving, warning, guiding, encouraging. Henceforth the prophetic horizon enlarges.

Beyond their contemporaries who were hardened beyond hope of recovery, their outlook is henceforth on the great hope of the Messianic kingdom. They have despaired of the present: but their thought is of the future. They have despaired of the kingdom of Israel and of Judah; but the Divine thought of preparation that underlay it comes increasingly into prominence and clearer vision. The promises of old acquire a new and deeper meaning; they assume shape and outlines which become ever more definite as the daylight grows. It is the future, with Israel's Messiah-King to rule a people restored and converted, and an endless, boundless kingdom of righteousness and peace which in its wide embrace includes, reconciles, and unites a ransomed world, obedient to the LORD, which is now the great burden of their message, and the joyous assured hope of their thoughts. For doomed apostate Israel after the flesh, we have Israel after the spirit, and on the ruins of the old rises the new: a Jerusalem, a temple, a kingdom, and a King fulfilling the ideal of which the earthly had been the type. It is not meant that these prophets had not their message for the present also: to Israel and Judah, and to their kings, as well as regarding events either contemporary or in the near future. Had it been otherwise, they would not have been prophets to, nor yet understood by, their fellow-countrymen.

Besides, God's dealings and discipline with Israel still continued, and would of necessity continue — primarily to the coming of the Christ, and then beyond it to the final fulfillment of His purposes of mercy. Hence their ministry was also of the present, though chiefly in warning and announcement of judgment. But by the side of this despair of the present, and because of it, the ideal destiny of Israel came into clearer minds, the meaning of the Davidic kingdom, and its final spiritual realization in a happy future; and along with denunciations of impending judgment came the comfort of prophetic promises of the future.

Two points here specially present themselves to our minds. The first is, that with this period commences the era of written prophecy. Before this time the prophets had spoken; now they wrote, or — to speak more precisely — gathered their prophetic utterances and visions into permanent records. And, as connected with this new phase of prophetism, we mark that it is rather by vision and prediction than by signs and miracles that the prophets now manifested their activity. But the importance of written records of prophecy is self-evident. Without them, alike the manifestation and establishment of the Messianic kingdom in Israel and its spread into the Gentile world would, humanly speaking, have been impossible. Christianity could not have appealed to Messianic prediction as its spring, nor yet could the prophetic word of God have traveled to the Gentiles. With this yet a second fact of utmost interest seems intimately connected. On the boundary-line of the two stages of prophetism stand two figures in Jewish history: one looking backwards, Elijah; the other looking forwards, Jonah, the son of Amittai (2 Kings 14:25). Both are distinguished by their ministry to the Gentiles. Elijah, by his stay and ministry at Sarepta, to which might, perhaps, be added the ministry of Elisha to Naaman; Jonah, by that call to repentance in Nineveh which forms the burden of the prophetic book connected with his name while, on the other hand, his contemporary message to Jeroboam is apparently not recorded. Thus the great unfolding of prophecy in its outlook on the inbringing of the Gentiles was marked by symbolic events.

Without attempting any detailed account, the prophets of that period, and the contents of their writings, may here be briefly referred to. The earliest of them was probably Joel, "Jehovah is God" — a Judaean whose sphere of labor was also in his native country.

His "prophecy" consists of two utterances (1:2-2; 18; 2:19-3:21), couched in language as pure and beautiful as the sentiments are elevated. From the allusions to contemporary events (3:4-8, 19), as well as from the absence of any mention of Assyria, we infer that his ministry was in the time of Joash, king of Judah, and of the high-priest Jehoiada, — with which agree his temple-references, which indicate a time of religious revival. But here also we mark the wider Messianic references in chapters 2 and 3. The prophecies of Joel seem already referred to by Amos, "the burden-bearer" (comp. Amos 1:2; 9:13 with Joel 3:16, 18, 20). Amos himself was also a Judean, originally a "herdsman of Tekoa" (Amos 1:1; 7:14). But his ministry was in Israel, and during the latter part of Jeroboam's reign, after the accession of Uzziah (Amos 1:1). There in Bethel, where the false worship of Israel was combined with the greatest luxury and dissipation, the prophet was confronted by Amaziah, its chief priest. Although apparently unsuccessful in his accusations of political conspiracy against the prophet, Amos was obliged to withdraw into Judah (Amos 7:10-13). Here he wrote down his prophetic utterances, prefacing them by an announcement of coming judgment (Amos 1:2.) through a nation, evidently that very Assyria on which the confidence of Jeroboam had rested (comp. Amos 5:27; 6:14). Yet, amidst all his denunciations, Amos also looked forward to, and prophesied of the glorious Messianic kingdom (Amos 9:11-15). A third prophet of that period was Hosea, "help" — the Jeremiah of the northern kingdom, as he has been aptly designated. From certain allusions in his book we infer that he had been a native of the northern kingdom (Hosea 1:3; 6:10; comp. 7:8). His ministry was probably towards the end of the reign of Jeroboam, and extended to the rising of Shallum and of Menahem (comp. Hosea 6:8; 7:7). His prophecies give special insight into the political relations and dangers of the northern kingdom, and into the utter corruption of all classes. Frequent, too, are his references to Judah. Yet here also we mark the persistence of the outlook on the better Davidic kingdom (Hosea 3), with much concerning it scattered throughout his prophecies. Lastly, as yet another prophet of that period, we have again to refer to Jonah, the son of Amittai, a native of Gath-hepher, in the tribal possession of Zebulun, and therefore in the northern part of Israel.

Without entering on the critical questions connected with the story which forms the burden of the Book of Jonah, or discussing the precise date of its publication in its present form, a deep significance surely attaches to its association with the prophet contemporary of Jeroboam II.

It is not only that it points to a preaching of repentance to the Gentiles also, and to their ingathering with believing Israel into the family of God, but the circumstances of the time give it a special meaning. From apostate, morally sunken Israel, such as we have learned to know it from the descriptions of the prophets, Jonah, the very messenger who had announced coming deliverance to Jeroboam, turns by Divine commission to the Gentiles: to that great world-empire which was representative of them. And from this comes to us a fresh and deeper meaning in regard to the application of this history by our Lord (Matthew 12:39-41; 16:4; Luke 11:29-32). It had been "a wicked and adulterous generation" of old that had heard the prophecy of Jonah, and understood not the sign; nor was other sign to be given to it. So would it be to those who heard and saw the Christ, yet craved after other "sign" suited to their unbelief. None other than the sign of Jonah would be theirs — yet even this, "a sign" sufficient in itself (Matthew 12:40), a sign also not only of judgment, but of wider mercy (Matthew 12:41).

CHAPTER 6 — AZARIAH, OR UZZIAH, (TENTH) KING OF JUDAH — STATE OF JUDAH AT THE ACCESSION OF UZZIAH — ACCOUNT OF HIS REIGN IN THE BOOK OF KINGS — RE-OCCUPATION OF ELATH — RELIGIOUS CONDITION OF JUDAH — EXPEDITION AGAINST THE PHILISTINES AND NEIGHBORING TRIBES — OCCUPATION OF TRANS-JORDANIC TERRITORY — RESTORATION AND EXTENSION OF THE FORTIFICATIONS OF JERUSALEM — RE-ORGANIZATION — PROSPERITY OF THE COUNTRY — GROWING PRIDE AND CORRUPTION — THE SACRILEGE OF UZZIAH — HIS LEPROSY AND DEATH — JEWISH LEGENDS.

(2 KINGS 15:1-7; 2 CHRONICLES 26)

WHATEVER motives had determined the selection of Uzziah by all the people of Judah as successor to his murdered father (2 Kings 14:21), the choice proved singularly happy. To adapt the language of the prophet Amos (9:11), which, as mostly all prophetic announcements of the Messianic future, takes for its starting and connecting point reference to the present, easily understood, and hence full of meaning to contemporaries — Uzziah found, on his accession, "the tabernacle of David," if not "fallen" and in "ruins," yet with threatening "breaches" in it. Never had the power of Judah sunk lower than when, after the disastrous war with Israel, the heir of David was tributary to Jehoash, and the broken walls of Jerusalem laid the city open and defenseless at the feet of the conqueror. This state of things was absolutely reversed during the reign of Uzziah; and at its close Judah not only held the same place as Israel under the former reign, but surpassed it in might and glory.

There can be little doubt that Jeroboam II. retained the hold over Judah which his father Jehoash had gained; and this, not only during the fifteen years after his accession, in which Amaziah of Judah still occupied the throne, but even in the beginning of the reign of Uzziah. For "breaches" such as those that had been made are not speedily repaired, and Uzziah was, at his accession, a youth of only sixteen years (2 Kings 15:2). We therefore incline to the view that the otherwise unintelligible notice (2 Kings 15:1), that Uzziah acceded "in the twenty-seventh year of Jeroboam" bears reference to the time when he had shaken off the suzerainty of Jeroboam, and "began to reign" in the real sense of the term.

This would make the period of Judah's liberation the twenty-seventh after Jeroboam's accession, and the twelfth after the elevation of Uzziah to the throne, when that monarch was twenty-eight years of age.

Important though the reign of Uzziah was — chiefly from a political, but also from a religious point of view — the writer of the Book of Kings gives only a few and these the briefest notices of it. In fact, he may be said only to single out the leading characteristics of that period. As regards political events, he marks the beginning of the recovery of Judah's power in the occupation of the important harbor of Elath, and the rebuilding of that town (2 Kings 14:22). This, as we shall show reason for believing, probably in the early years of the accession of Uzziah.

As always, he records the age of the new king and the duration of his reign, as well as the name of his mother (2 Kings 15:2). If the suggestion previously made is correct, he also notices the exact time of the recovery of Judaean independence from Israel (2 Kings 15:1). Again, the religious character of this reign is described; while, lastly, the unhappy fate and end of the king are recorded, although without mention of what led to it. Manifestly the point of view in the Book of Kings is simply "prophetic" — not, as in Chronicles, priestly — and the writer hurries over events alike of a political and a personal character, to indicate what seems to him of main importance' the theocratic relation of the people to Jehovah.

The brief outline in the Book of Kings is amply filled up in that of Chronicles (2 Chronicles 26.). Here, also, the first event recorded is the taking of Elath. This important harbor, from which, as from the neighboring Ezion-Geber, Solomon had sent his fleet of traders to Ophir (1 Kings 9:26-28; 2 Chronicles 8:17, 18), lay on the north-eastern end of the Gulf of Akabah, and at present bears the same name. Of its ancient greatness only a tower remains for protection of the pilgrims to Mecca.

Around it are ruins and wretched hovels; but abundance of date-palms still betokens the former fertility. For half-an-hour beyond the town stretch, along the blue gulf, sands covered with beautiful shells; the view being finally shut off by granite and sandstone mountains. Such is the present aspect of "Eloth" (or Elath) "the strong trees." There can be little doubt that when in the days of Joram of Judah "Edom revolted" (2 Kings 8:20- 22), Elath recovered its independence. The conquest of Edom by Amaziah had apparently only extended as far as Petra, about half, way between the Dead Sea and Elath. In occupying it again and rebuilding it, Uzziah therefore completed the subjection of the country by his father. Such an expedition could not, in the state of Edom, have offered any real difficulty, however much its success must, after the late disasters, have raised the courage of Judah and inspired the people with confidence. These circumstances, as well as the place which the narrative occupies in the sacred text, lead us to infer that this was the first military undertaking of Uzziah, And, in view of his ultimate purpose as regarded Israel, the king would naturally begin with what was not only certain of success, but would also secure his rear in any future expedition. Nor was this all. A wide-reaching plan of national restoration would embrace the revival of commerce. And what prominence the new Tarshish mercantile marine held in public thought, and how it affected life in Judah in the days of Jotham, the successor of Uzziah, appears from the allusion in Isaiah 2:16.

As regards the religious condition of the country it is significant that, as the reign of former kings, so the present was characterized by a combination of doing "the right in the sight of Jehovah," with a continuance of "the high places," and their sacrifices and worship. It seems to indicate that this strange mixture in religion marked the highest point attained by the people. But even this qualified adherence to the worship of the Lord was only temporary, as the text explains: "in the days of Zechariah, who instructed him in the fear of God" (2 Chronicles 26:5). This prepares us alike for the later history of the king, and for what we shall learn of the condition of the people.

But the first or religious period of the reign of Uzziah was one of continuous and progressive prosperity. Although it is not possible to determine the precise chronological succession of events, it seems likely that the expedition against the Philistines soon followed that to the Red Sea. The object of it was finally to break up the great anti-Judaean confederacy which, in the days of King Jehoram, had wrought such havoc in Judah, after the successful revolt of Edom (2 Chronicles 21:8-10).

The defeat of Edom must have rendered this expedition also one of comparative ease. One by one the great Philistine cities fell; Gath, which, in the reign of Joash, had been wrested by Hazael of Syria, and made the starting-point of his incursion into Judah (2 Kings

12:17); Jabneh (Joshua 15:11), afterwards Jamnia, and about nine miles to the northeast of it, and three miles from the sea, Ashdod. It was probably owing to the importance of this strong town, which commanded the road from Egypt, that the sacred text specially mentions this district as one in which the king "built cities" (2 Chronicles 26:6). The general policy seems wisely to have been not to destroy nor depopulate the Philistine cities, but to render them harmless by breaking down their fortifications, and founding by their side throughout the Philistine territory, cities, inhabited no doubt by Juda~an colonists. And from Philistia the expedition naturally extended to, and reduced to submission, the Arab tribe to the south "in Gur-baal" and "the Meunim" (or Meunites).

We have now probably reached the period when either luxury and corruption had so demoralized Israel as to render it incapable of resisting the extending power of Judah, or else the government of Jeroboam II. had become paralyzed. For although the subdual of the Philistines and the other tribes to the south and south-east explains the statement that "the name" — here, presumably, the authority — of Uzziah "went to the going down into Egypt," more is implied in the notice that "the Ammonites gave gifts." This tribute imposed on Ammon evidently presupposes the occupation by Uzziah of the intervening trans-Jordanic territory belonging to Israel.

And its possession seems implied in the further notice (2 Chronicles 26:10), that the herds of Uzziah pastured "in the low country," that is, on the rich Philistine downs by the Mediterranean (1 Chronicles 27:28), and "in the plain," that is, on the wide grazing lands east of Jordan, in the ancient possession of Reuben (Deuteronomy 3:10; 4:43; and Joshua 13.).

But by far the most important undertaking of the reign of Uzziah was the restoration and the fortification of the northern wall of Jerusalem, which had been broken down in the time of Amaziah (2 Chronicles 25:23). Drawing an almost straight line along the north of the ancient city, Uzziah built three towers: "at the lower gate," in the north-western corner of the city, whence the wall slopes slightly southwards, and towards the west; at "the valley-gate," the present Jaffa gate; and lastly, at the opposite extremity of the northern wall (and again slightly south), to protect the so- called "horse gate" (Nehemiah 3:28; Jeremiah 31:40), where the northern wall forms to the east "a turning" or angle, whence it runs southwards (comp. Nehemiah 3:19, 20, 24, 25). Thus, as the "upper city" had, besides that just mentioned, not any other gate towards the west, nor yet any to the south, the entrance into the city was defended on the north, west, south, and at its north-eastern angle. Moreover, these forts were armed with new and powerful engines for projecting arrows and great stones upon any besieging host (2 Chronicles 26:15). Lastly, in accordance with all this, we read of a re-organization of the army, "according to the number of their enrollment (mustering) by the hand of Jeiel, the scribe, and Maaseiah, the officer (superintendent?), under the hand (direction) of Hananiah one of the king's captains" (2 Chronicles 26:11). The levy was again made in accordance with earliest national custom — although in even more systematic manner than before. Under two thousand six hundred "heads" or "chiefs of houses," "mighty men of valor," an army of not less than 307,500 men was gathered, and completely equipped by the king — the heavy infantry being furnished with shields, cuirasses, and helmets, the light infantry with bows and "stones for slings."

This specially indicates the completeness of the armament, which, this time, was not only furnished by the central authority, but with such care that even the slings and the stones generally picked up by the men were served out to the troops.

In these circumstances we do not wonder that the warlike fame of the king "went forth unto far," although we specially note how carefully the sacred text throughout emphasizes the Divine help extended to Uzziah in each part of his undertakings. Nor was the internal prosperity of the realm less marked. We have already seen how the reoccupation of Elath led to a revival of shipping and commerce which must have brought wealth to the country. Similarly, the king took a deep interest in agriculture. In the mountains of Judah the ancient terraces were repaired for the culture of the vine; in the more flat portions, as in the district of Carmel (1 Samuel 15:12; 25:2, 5), agriculture was carried on; whilst, alike in "the wilderness" of Judah, in "the low country" of the Philistine downs, and in the rich "plain" across the Jordan, numerous flocks and herds browsed — provision and security for the operations of "husbandry" being afforded by hewing out many cisterns and building watchtowers (2 Chronicles 26:10).

It has previously been stated that this was the flourishing period of prophetism in Israel. This perhaps the more, because now the last warning voices were raised among a people sunk in idolatry and corruption, and nigh to judgment. From the prophetic allusions the state of matters in Judah seems, at least during the first period of this reign, to have been somewhat better. But here also, alike owing to increasing prosperity and to success, "pride" and its resultant vices, soon became apparent (Amos 2:4; Hosea 5:5, 14; comp. also Isaiah 2:5, etc.; 3:12, 15; 7:10-13; 28:7-10).

This chiefly on the part of the king himself. In the expressive language of Holy Scripture, "when he was strong his heart was lifted up unto destruction" — that is, until he did that which was wrongful and destructive. Intolerant of any power in the land but his own, he sought to combine the chief functions of the priesthood with those of royalty.

The holiest service of the Temple was when the incense was offered on the golden altar within the Holy Place. It symbolized the offering of Israel's worship by the great High Priest. Regardless of the express Divine ordinance (Exodus 30:7, 27; Numbers 18:1-7), Uzziah penetrated into the Holy Place to arrogate to himself this holy function. In vain Azariah, "the chief priest" (2 Chronicles 26:17, 18), and with him eighty other brave men, no doubt priests of "the course" then on service, sought to arrest the king. Their remonstrance, really their warning, that the issue would be other than his pride had anticipated, only served to incite the wrath of the king. Such utter misunderstanding and perversion alike of the priestly functions in their deepest meaning, and of the royal office in its higher object — and that from motives of pride — must bring instant and signal judgment. While yet the censer with its burning coals was in his hand, and looks and words of wrath on his face and on his lips, in sight of the priesthood, he was smitten with what was regarded as pre-eminently and directly the stroke of God's own Hand (comp. Numbers 12:9, 10; 2 Kings 5:27). There, "beside the altar of incense," the plague-spot of leprosy appeared on his forehead.

Hastily the assembled priests thrust him, whom God had so visibly smitten, from the Holy Place, lest the presence of the leper should defile the sanctuary. Nay himself, terror-stricken, hastened thence. So the king, whose heart had been lifted up to the utter forgetfulness of the help hitherto given him by Jehovah until he dared the uttermost sacrilege, descended living into the grave in the very moment of his greatest pride. Till death released him he was a leper, dwelling outside the city, separated — "in a house of sickness " — or, as others have rendered the expression, with perhaps greater probability, in "a house of separation" (comp. Leviticus 13:46; Numbers 5:2; 2 Kings 7:3) Cut off from access to the house of the Lord, where he had impiously sought to command, and debarred from all intercourse with men, the kingdom was administered by Jotham, his son — for how long a period before the death of Uzziah it is impossible to determine. His punishment followed him even into the grave. For, although he was "buried with his fathers," it was "in the field of the burial which belonged to the kings," probably the burying ground of the members of the royal family; he was not laid in the sepulcher where the kings of Judah rested; "for they said, He is a leper."

Of the record of his deeds by Isaiah, to which the sacred text refers (2 Chronicles 26:2), no portion has been preserved. Although the activity of the prophet began during the reign of Uzziah (Isaiah 1:1; 6:1), yet, considering that it extended into that of Hezekiah, Isaiah must have been still young, when the leprous king died. Jewish legend has fabled much about the stroke that descended on the sacrilegious king. In his clumsy manner of attempting to account for the directly Divine by natural causes, Josephus connects the sudden leprosy of the king with that earthquake (Amos 1:1) of which the terrible memory so lingered in the popular memory as almost to form an era in their history (Zechariah 14:4, 5).

In that earthquake, which Josephus describes, he tells us: "a rent was made in the Temple, and the bright rays of the sun shone through it, and fell upon the king's face, insomuch that the leprosy seized upon him immediately." Other Jewish writers strangely identify the death of Uzziah referred to in Isaiah 6:1, with the living death of his leprosy, and the earthquake with the solemn scene there pictured. Yet this application of theirs is certainly true when they rank Uzziah with those "who attained not what they sought, and from whom was taken that which they had" (Ber. R. 20).

CHAPTER 7 — UZZIAH (TENTH), JOTHAM (ELEVENTH), AND AHAS, (TWELFTH) KING OF JUDAH. ZACHARIAH (FIFTEENTH), SHALLUM (SIXTEENTH), MENAHEM (SEVENTEENTH), PEKAHIAH (EIGHTEENTH),PEKAH (NINETEENTH) KING OF ISRAEL — ACCESSION AND MURDER OF ZACHARIAH — ACCESSION AND DEATH OF SHALLUM — ACCESSION OF MENAHEM — TAKING AND BACK OF TIPHSAH — ACCESSION AND VICTORIES OF PUL OR TIGLATH-PILESER II. OF ASSYRIA — TRIBUTE TO ASSYRIA — ACCESSION AND MURDER OF PEKAHIAH — MILITARY REVOLUTION AND ACCESSION OF PEKAH — AOOESSION AND REIGN OF JOTHAM IN JUDAH — SYRO-LSRAELITISH LEAGUE AGAINST JUDAH — ACCESSION OF AHAZ IN JUDAH — CHARACTER OF HIS REIGN — THE NEW IDOLATRY — CHANGES IN THE TEMPLE AND ITS WORSHIP.

(2 KINGS 15:8-16:18; 2 CHRONICLES 27, 28)

WHILE the kingdom of Judah was enjoying a brief period of prosperity, that of Israel was rapidly nearing its final overthrow. The deep-seated and wide corruption in the land afforded facilities for a succession of revolutions, in which one or another political or military adventurer occupied the throne for a brief period. In the thirteen or fourteen years between the death of Jeroboam II. and that of Uzziah, the northern kingdom saw no less than four kings (2 Kings 15:8-27), of whom each was removed by violence. In the thirty-eighth year of Uzziah, Jeroboam II was succeeded by his son Zachariah, the fourth and last monarch of the line of Jehu.

Holy Scripture here specially marks the fulfillment of Divine prediction (2 Kings 10:30), in the continuance of this dynasty "unto the fourth generation." Of his brief reign, which lasted only six months, we read that it was characterized by continuance in the sins of Jeroboam. A conspiracy by one Shallum, not otherwise known, issued, not in the private assassination, but in the public murder of the king.

So terribly had all bonds of society been loosened. The regicide occupied the throne for only one month. Menahem, whom Josephus describes as the general of Zachariah, advanced against Shallum from Tirzah, the ancient royal residence, and slew the usurper.

The assumption of the crown by Menahem seems to have met some resistance. At any rate, we read of an expedition of Menahem against a place called Tiphsah ("a ford"), which had refused to open its gates to him. The town and its surrounding district were taken, and Menahem took horrible vengeance on the population. The reign of Menahem, which, as regards religion, resembled that of his predecessors, lasted ten years. But it may truly be characterized as the beginning of the end. For with it commenced the acknowledged dependence of the northern kingdom upon Assyria, of which the ultimate outcome was the fall of Samaria and the deportation of Israel into the land of the conqueror.

Leaving aside, for reasons already indicated, questions of chronology, the Assyrian monuments enable us more clearly to understand the Biblical account of the relations

672

between Menahem and his eastern suzerain (2 Kings 15:19, 20). Thus we learn that after a period of decadence which may account for the independent progress of Jeroboam II., perhaps even for the occupation of Tiphsah by Menahem, a military adventurer of the name of Pul, apparently sprung from the lower orders, seized the crown of Assyria, and assumed the title of Tiglath-pileser II.

The first monarch of that name, five centuries earlier, had founded the power of Assyria, which was now to be re-established. In the very year of his accession he vanquished and impaled the king of Babylon, and henceforth himself assumed that title. Two years later he turned his armies to the west, and after a siege of three years took the Syrian city Arpad, in the neighborhood of Hamath, and not far from Damascus (comp. Isaiah 10:9, 36:19; 2 Kings 18:34; Jeremiah 49:23).

Without following his further military expeditions it may suffice to state that three years later (in the eighth year of his reign), he is described on the monuments as receiving the tribute of Menahem of Israel, among those of other vassal kings. The shattering of the power of the Syrian confederacy and the occupation of Hamath fully explain the Biblical notice of the advance of Pul or Tiglath-pileser II. into the northern kingdom. His progress was for the time arrested by the submission of Menahem, and his payment of an annual tribute of 1,000 talents of silver, or about 375,000 pounds, which the king of Israel levied by a tax of 50 shekels, or about. 6 pounds 5 shillings. on all the wealthier inhabitants of his realm. This would imply that there were 60,000 contributors to this tax, a large figure, indicating at the same time the wide prosperity of the country, and the extent of the burden which the tribute must have laid on the people. On these hard conditions Menahem was "confirmed" in "the kingdom" by the Assyrian conqueror Menahem was succeeded in the kingdom by his son Pekahiah, whose reign, of a character similar to that of his father, lasted only two years. He fell the victim of another military conspiracy headed by Pekah, the son of Remaliah, probably one of the captains of the king's bodyguard.

As we interpret the narrative (2 Kings 15:25), the king of Israel had surrounded himself with a bodyguard, such as that which of old had been formed by King David. The name of Pekahiah's father: "Menahem, the son of Gadi" (2 Kings 15:17), seems to indicate that he was descended from the tribe of Gad. It is therefore the more likely that this bodyguard had been raised from among his countrymen the Gileadites — those brave highlanders on the other side of Jordan who were famed as warriors (comp. Judges 11:1; 1 Chronicles 26:31). Thus the LXX. — perhaps after an old tradition — render, instead of "the Gileadites" of the Hebrew text, the 400, which reminds us of David's famous 600 (2 Samuel 15:18). This bodyguard we suppose to have been under the command of three captains, one of whom was Pekah, the leader of the rebellion. The other two: "Argob," so named from the trans-Jordanic district of Bashan (Deuteronomy 3:4), and "Arieh," "the lion" (comp. 1 Chronicles 12:8), fell, probably in defending the king. As we read it, Pekah, with fifty of the Gilead guard, pursued the king into the castle, or fortified part of his palace at Samaria, and there slew him and his adherents. The crime vividly illustrates the condition of public feeling and morals as described by the prophet Hosea (4:1, 2). The murderer of his master was not only allowed to seize the crown, but retained it during a period of thirty years.

This revolution had taken place in the last (the fifty-second) year of Uzziah. He was succeeded in Judah by his son Jotham, in the second year of Pekah, the son of Remaliah. Jotham was twenty-five years old when he ascended the throne, and his reign is said to have extended over sixteen years. But whether this period is to be reckoned from his co-regency

(2 Kings 15:5; 2 Chronicles 26:21), or from his sole rule, it is impossible to determine. And in this may lie one of the reasons of the difficulties of this chronology.

The reign of Jotham was prosperous, and only clouded towards its close. Both religiously and politically it was strictly a continuation of that of Uzziah, whose co-regent, or at least administrator, Jotham had been. According to the fuller account in the Book of Chronicles (2 Chronicles 27.), Jotham maintained in his official capacity the worship of Jehovah in His Temple, wisely abstaining, however, from imitating his father's attempted intrusion into the functions of the priesthood. Among the people the former corrupt forms of religion were still continued, and had to be tolerated. Naturally this corruption would increase in the course of time. Among the undertakings of the former reign, the fortifications of Jerusalem, the inward defense of the country, and its trans-Jordanic enlargement, were carried forward. As regards the first of these, the wall which defended Ophel, the southern declivity of the Temple-mount, was further built.

At the same time the sacred house itself was beautified by the rebuilding of the "higher" [or upper] gate on the north side of the Temple, where the terrace runs from which it derived its name. The "higher gate" opened from the "upper" [or inner] court — that of the priests — into the lower, which was that of the people (2 Kings 21:5; 23:12; 2 Chronicles 33:5). Each of these two courts was bounded by a wall. Probably the general ingress into the Temple was by the outer northern gate. Thence the worshippers would pass through the lower, outer, or people's court to the second wall that bounded the inner, upper, or priest's court, which extended around the Temple house.

Thus the worshippers, or at least those who brought sacrifices, would have to enter by this northern gate which Jotham rebuilt. As the inner or upper court lay on a higher level, we find that in the Temple of Ezekiel eight steps are said to lead up to it (Ezekiel 40:31, 34, 37), and such was probably also the case in the Temple of Solomon. Close to this "higher gate" — at the right hand, as you entered it — the chest for the collection of money for the Temple repairs had been placed by Jehoiada (2 Kings 12:9). Lastly, from its designation by Ezekiel (8:5), as "the gate of the altar," we infer that it formed the common access for those who offered sacrifices. Its later name of "new gate" was due to its reconstruction by Jotham, while the passages in which it is mentioned indicate that this was the place where the princes and priests were wont to communicate with the people assembled in the outer court (Jeremiah 26:10; 36:10).

Nor were the operations of Jotham confined to Jerusalem. "And cities he built in Mount Judah [the hill country], and in the forests [or thickets, where towns could not be built], castles [forts], and towns [no doubt for security]." To complete the record of that reign we add that the expedition of the previous reign against Ammon was resumed, and the Ammonites were forced to pay an annual tribute, not only of the produce of their fertile lands (10,000 Kor of wheat and as many of barley), but of a hundred talents of silver, or about. 37,500 pounds. But, as the sacred text implies (2 Chronicles 27:5), this tribute was only paid during three years.

In the fourth, probably the last year of Jotham's reign, it ceased, no doubt in consequence of the Syro-Israelitish league against Judah, which was apparently joined by the neighboring tribes who had hitherto been subject to Uzziah and Jotham. Lastly, of the internal condition of the country, of its prosperity, wealth, and commerce, but also of its luxury and its sins, a vivid picture has been left in those prophecies of warning judgment which form the opening chapters of the Book of Isaiah (chap. 1:5-6.).

Jotham himself only witnessed the approach of the calamities which were so soon to befall Judah. In the northern kingdom Pekah must have found himself in the midst of turbulent elements. Even if he had not to defend his crown against another pretender, the disorganized condition of the country, the necessity of keeping the people engaged in undertakings that would divert them from domestic affairs, as well as the obvious desirableness of forming foreign alliances to support his throne — perhaps even more ambitious plans — must have made the thirty years of this military usurper a period of sore trouble in Israel.

We catch only glimpses of it at the close of Jotham's reign. But our scanty information is to some extent supplemented by the Assyrian records. Holy Scripture simply informs us that "in those days Jehovah began to send against Judah Rezin, the king of Syria, and Pekah, the son of Remaliah" (2 Kings 15:37).

It is a majestic and truly prophetic mode of viewing events, thus to recognize in such a league as that of Rezin and Pekah the divinely-appointed judgment upon Judah. It is to pass from the secondary and visible causes of an event straight to Him Who over-rules all, and Who with Divine skill weaves the threads that man has spun into the web and woof of His dealings. In point of fact, the Syro-Israelitish league against Judah ultimately embraced not only the Ammonites, who refused to continue their tribute, but also the Edomites, the Philistines, and all the southern tribes lately reduced to subjection (2 Chronicles 28:17, 18).

As already stated, Jotham only witnessed the commencement of this great struggle, or else he was sufficiently strong still to keep in check what at first were probably only marauding expeditions. It was otherwise when his weak and wicked son Ahaz ascended the throne, in the seventeenth year of Pekah, the son of Remaliah (2 Kings 16:1). He was probably twenty-five years of age when he succeeded his father.

The sixteen years of his reign were in every sense most disastrous for Judah. As throughout this history, it is emphatically indicated that just as former successes had come from the help of the Lord, so now the real cause of Judah's reverses lay in their apostasy from God. From the first, and throughout, Ahaz "did not the right in the sight of the Lord." Nor should we omit to mark how the sacred text when describing each successive reign in Judah brings its religious character into comparison with that of David. This, not only because he was the founder of the dynasty, nor even because in him centered the Divine promise to the royal house of Judah, but from the strictly theocratic character of his public administration, which should have been the type for that of all his successors, even as Jeroboam's became that for the kings of Israel.

It is impossible to determine whether the varied idolatry described in 2 Chronicles 28:3, 4, characterized the beginning of Ahaz's reign, or was only gradually introduced during its course. More probably the latter was the case; and as the success of Syria was the avowed motive for introducing its gods into Judah, so that of Israel formed at least the pretext for walking "in the ways of the kings of Israel" (2 Chronicles 28:2). Indeed, there is not a single aspect from which the character of the king could have commanded either respect or sympathy. Unbelieving as regards the Lord and His power (Isaiah 7:11-13), he was nevertheless ready to adopt the most abject superstitions. By making "molten images for Baalim," he not only followed in the ways of the house of Ahab (1 Kings 16:32; 2 Kings 1:2; 3:2), but adopted the rites then practiced in Israel (Hosea 2:13; 13:1). Connected with these was the service of Moloch [or more correctly, Molech], who was only another form of Baal (comp. Jeremiah 19:3-6; 32:35). Alike, in the service of the one and the other, human sacrifices were offered: for which, indeed, Baal himself was supposed to have given a precedent.

But this was to revive the old Canaanitish and Phoenician worship, with all its abominations and all its defilements. The valley of Gihon, which bounds Jerusalem on the west, descends at its southern extremity into that of Hinnom, which in turn joins at the ancient royal gardens the valley of Kidron, that runs along the eastern declivity of the Holy City. There, at the junction of the valleys of Hinnom and Kidron, in these gardens, was Topheth — " the spitting out," or place of abomination — where an Ahaz, a Manasseh, and an Amon, sacrificed their sons and daughters to Baal-Moloch, and burnt incense to foul idols. Truly was Hinnom "moaning," and rightly was its name Gehinnom [valley of Hinnom — Gehenna], adopted as that for the place of final suffering.

And it is one of those strange coincidences that the hill which rises on the south side of this spot was that "potter's field," the "field of blood," which Judas bought with the wages of his betrayal, and where with his own, hands he executed judgment on himself. History is full of such coincidences, as men call them; nor can we forget in this connection that it was on the boundary-line between the reigns of Jotham and Ahaz that Rome was founded (in 752 B.C.), which was destined to execute final judgment on apostate Israel.

Nor was this all. Not only did Ahaz burn incense in that accursed place where he offered his own son as a burnt sacrifice to Baal-Moloch, but a similar idolatrous worship was offered on the high places, on the hills, and under every green tree (2 Chronicles 28:4; 2 Kings 16:4).

Thus, in regard to form — the many sanctuaries in opposition to the one place of worship — as well as to substance and spirit, there was direct contrariety to the institutions of the Old Testament. Indeed, it may not be without use here to mark that in the surroundings of Israel, exclusive unity of worship in one central temple, as against many sanctuaries, was absolutely necessary if a pure monotheism was to be preserved and the introduction of heathen rites to be avoided.

But the idolatry introduced by Ahaz was to be carried to all its sequences. A despotic edict of the king, while at Damascus, in singular contrast to the weakness displayed towards his foreign enemies, ordered a new altar for the Temple after the pattern sent to Jerusalem of one, no doubt devoted to an Assyrian deity, which he had seen in Damascus and approved. He was obeyed by a servile high-priest. When Ahaz returned to his capital sacrifices were offered by him on the new altar, probably thankofferings for his safe arrival.

This was only the beginning of other changes. It seems not unlikely that the king introduced in connection with the new altar the worship of the gods of Damascus (2 Chronicles 28:23, in connection with ver. 24). Certain it is that an exclusive place was assigned to it. Apparently Urijah, the priest, had originally set it at the rear of the old altar of burnt-offering, which stood "before the Lord," that is, "before the house," in other words, fronting the entrance into the sanctuary. But as this would have indicated the inferiority of the new altar, the king, on his return from Damascus, brought the two altars into juxtaposition. In the words of the sacred text (2 Kings 16:14): "And the altar, the brazen [one] a which [was] before Jehovah he brought near [placed in juxtaposition], from before the house [the sanctuary], from between the altar [the new Damascus altar] and the house of Jehovah, and he put it at the side of the altar [the new Damascus altar], northwards."

The meaning of this is that the brazen altar, which had hitherto faced the entrance to the sanctuary, eastwards, was now removed to the north side of the new altar, so that the latter became the principal, nay, the sole sacrificial altar. Accordingly, by command of the king, all sacrificial worship was now celebrated at this new heathen altar, the disposal of the old altar being left for further consideration.

The new place of sacrifice rendered other changes in the Temple furniture almost necessary. The old altar of burnt-offering was ten cubits, or about fifteen feet high (2 Chronicles 4:1). Hence there was an ascent to it, and a circuit around, on which the ministering priests stood. As the pieces of the sacrifice laid on the altar had to be washed, the "ten lavers of brass" for this purpose, which surrounded the altar, were placed on high "bases" or rather stands, so that the officiating priests could wash the sacrificial pieces without coming down from the circuit of the altar. The side pieces which formed the body of these stands were of brass, richly ornamented alternately with figures of lions and oxen with wreaths underneath them, and cherubim (comp. 1 Kings 7:27-40). For the new altar such high stands were no longer required, and accordingly Ahaz "broke away the sidepieces of the stands" [A. V. "cut off the borders of the bases"]. Similarly he lowered "the sea," by removing it from the pedestal of the "brazen oxen," and placing it on "a base of stone." Possibly the king may also have been influenced by a desire to make other use of these valuable pieces of Temple furniture than that for which they had been originally designed. At any rate they remained in the Temple till a later period (comp. Jeremiah 52:17-20).

It is more difficult to understand the import of the changes which King Ahaz made "on account of the king of Assyria" in "the covered Sabbath place," and "the entrance of the king, the outer one" (2 Kings 16:18). In our ignorance of the precise purpose or locality of these we can only offer such suggestions as seem in accordance with the language of the original. We conjecture that "the covered Sabbath place," or stand, "which they had built" — viz., since Solomonic times — was probably a place opening into the inner or priest's court, occupied by the king and his court when attending the services on Sabbaths and feast days. Connected with it would be a private "entrance" to this stand from, or through, the "outer" court (comp. Ezekiel 46:1, 2). We further conjecture that in view of a possible visit of, or in deference to, the king of Assyria, Ahaz now "turned the covered Sabbath place and the entrance of the king, the outer one, to the house of Jehovah," that is, that he removed both into the sanctuary itself, probably within the porch. We regard it as a further part of these alterations when, in 2 Chronicles 28:24, by the side of the notice, that Ahaz "broke up the vessels of the house of God," we find it stated that he "shut up the doors of the house of Jehovah." This implies that the services within the Holy Place were now wholly discontinued. Thus the worship would be confined to the sacrificial services at the new altar; while the transference into the Temple porch of the king's stand and of the entry to it, would not only bring them close to the new altar, but also assign to them a more prominent and elevated position than that previously occupied. We can readily understand that all such changes in the worship of Judah, and the pre-eminent position in it assigned to the king, would be in accordance with the views, the practice, and the wishes of the king of Assyria, however contrary to the spirit and the institutions of the Mosaic law.

After this we do not wonder to read that Ahaz "made him altars in every corner of Jerusalem," nor yet that "in every several city of Judah he made high places [bamoth] to burn incense unto other gods" (2 Chronicles 28:24, 25). What influence all this must have had on a people already given to idolatry will readily be perceived. Indeed, Holy Scripture only gives us a general indication of the baneful changes made in the public religious institutions of the country. Of the king's private bearing in this respect, we only catch occasional glimpses, such, for example, as in the significant later reference to "the altars" which he had reared "on the roof" of the Aliyah or "upper chamber" in the Temple, no doubt for the Assyrian worship of the stars (Jeremiah 19:13; Zephaniah 1:5).

CHAPTER 8 — AHAZ, (TWELFTH) KING OF JUDAH, PEKAH (NINETEENTH), HOSHEA, (TWENTIETH) KING OF ISRAEL — IMPORT OF THE CHANGES INTRODUCED BY AHAZ — PURPOSE OF THE SYRO-ISRAELITISH LEAGUE — TAKING OF ELATH, SUCCESS OF REZIN, AND VICTORY OF PEKAH — SIEGE OF JERUSALEM — APPEAL TO ASSYRIA — MESSAGE OF ISAIAH — WITHDRAWAL OF THE ALLIES — DANGER FROM ASSYRIA — THE PROPHET ODED AND LIBERATION OF THE JUDAEAN CAPTIVES — LESSONS OF IT — THE NAME SHEAR YASHUB — ASSYRIAN MARCH UPON ISRAEL — CAPTURE AND ANNEXATION OF NAPHTALI — FURTHER CAMPAIGN — TAKING OF SAMARIA — REVOLUTION, AND MURDER OF PEKAH — SUCCESSION OF HOSHEA — TRANSPORTATION OF ISRAELITES — SIEGE AND CAPTURE OF DAMASCUS — DEATH OF REZIN — CESSATION OF THE SYRIAN POWER.

(2 KINGS 15:29, 30; 16; 2 CHRONICLES 28)

A RELIGIOUS change so complete as that which has been described might seem incredible if it had been sudden, or we were left in ignorance of its deeper causes. In truth, it was no less than a systematic attempt to substitute a complicated heathenism for the religion of the Old Testament. If its institutions had any deeper spiritual import, everything in them must have been symbolic. Hence, every alteration would necessarily destroy the symmetry, the harmony, and with them the meaning of all. To substitute for the altar of burnt-offering one after the heathen pattern was not only to infringe on the Divinely prescribed order, but to destroy its symbolism. More than this, it was to interfere with, and in a sense to subvert, the institution of sacrifices, which formed the central part in the religion of Israel. Again, to close the doors of the Holy and Most Holy Places was to abolish what set forth Israel's fellowship with their Lord, His gracious acceptance of them, and His communication of pardon, light, and life.

The temple of Ahaz was no longer that of Jehovah, and the attempt to attach the old services to the new altar would only aggravate the sin, while it exhibited the folly of the king.

Even more strange seems the mixture of heathen rites which it was sought to introduce by the side of the perverted Temple ritual. It consisted of the worship of the Syrian deities, of Baalim, of Ashtoreth, of the host of heaven, and of Molech — in short, it combined Syrian, Phoenician, and Assyrian idolatry.

Yet in all this Ahaz found a servile instrument in the high priest Urijah (2 Kings 16:11-16). Assuredly the prophet's description of Israel's "watchmen" as "ignorant," "dumb dogs — loving to slumber," "greedy dogs," "insatiable shepherds," only bent on gain and steeped in vice, was true to the letter (Isaiah 56:10-12). And with this corresponds the same prophet's account of the moral and religious condition of the people (Isaiah 2:6-9; 5:7-23). In view of this, King Ahaz can only be regarded as the outcome of his time and the representative of his people. Accordingly the judgments announced in these prophecies of Isaiah read only as the logical sequence of the state of matters.

The account of these judgments comes to us equally from the Books of Kings and Chronicles, which here supplement one another, and especially from the prophecies of Isaiah, which in chapter 7 give the most vivid description of the condition of things. The Syro-Israelitish league had been formed at the close of the reign of Jotham (2 Kings 15:37), although its full effects only appeared when Ahaz acceded to the throne. In its development the confederacy embraced also the Edomites and Philistines, although probably at a later period — in all likelihood after the early victories of the Syrian and Israelitish armies (2 Chronicles 28:17, 18). The purpose of the two chief allies is easily understood. No doubt it was the desire of Syria and Israel, which Tiglath-pileser had so deeply humbled, to shake off the yoke of Assyria. And as, after a period of decadence, the Assyrian power had only lately been restored by the usurper Pul, a hope may have been cherished that a powerful league might huff Tiglath-pileser from his throne. But for this object it was necessary first to secure themselves against any danger from the south, especially as there is some indication in the Assyrian inscriptions of a connection existing between Judah and Assyria since the days of Uzziah.

In point of fact, the expedition was rather against Ahaz than against Judah, and we are distinctly informed that it was the purpose of the allies to depose the house of David, and to place on the throne of Judah a person of low origin, "the son of Tabheel," whose name indicates his Syrian descent (Isaiah 7:6).

It is only when realizing this purpose of making a full end of the house of David, with all the Messianic promises and hopes bound up with it, that we fully understand how it evoked, in the case of Ahaz, that most full and personal Messianic prediction of "the Virgin's Son" (Isaiah 7:14). Not only would their plan not "come to pass "(Isaiah 7:7), but looking beyond the unbelief and the provocations of an Ahaz (Isaiah 7:13), the Divine promise would stand fast. "The house of David" could not fail. For beyond the present was the final goal of promised salvation in Immanuel the Virgin-born And this was God's answer to the challenge of Rezin and of the son of Remaliah — His "sign" as against their plans: a majestic declaration also of His object in maintaining "the house of David," even when represented by an Ahaz. And when the hour of judgment came, it would be not by placing a Syrian king on the throne of David, but by carrying prince and people into a banishment which would open a new — the last — period of Israel's God-destined history.

But as tidings of the "confederacy," with its avowed purpose of taking all the strongholds and cities which commanded the defenses of Judah, and of setting up another king, reached "the house of David," in the poetic language of Isaiah, Ahaz' "heart shook, and the hearts of his people, as the trees of the forest shake before the wind" (Isaiah 7:2).

And in truth the success of the allies was such as to account for such feelings — at least on the part of an unbelieving and craven king. Joining together the narratives in the Books of Kings and Chronicles, we have first, in 2 Kings 16:5, a general account of the war — its purpose, beginning, and final failure. To this is added, in the next verse, a notice of the expedition of Rezin, in which he "restored Elath to Edom," when "the Edomites came to Elath," and continued to occupy it to the time of the writer. This brief account is supplemented in 2 Chronicles 28:5.

There we read of a twofold success of the allies — that achieved by Rezin, in consequence of which a great multitude of captives were carried to Damascus and a victory gained by Pekah. In all probability Rezin marched from Damascus through the trans-

Jordanic territory straight into the south of Judah, extending his march as far as the latest conquest of Judah, Elath. This was now restored to Edom.

Syria alone could scarcely have held such an isolated post, nor could it have been left in the rear in the hands of Judaeans. On the other hand, its restoration to Edom explains their active participation in the league (2 Chronicles 28:17). The text leaves it somewhat doubtful whether Rezin actually fought a pitched battle against a Judaean army, such as was evidently won by Pekah (2 Chronicles 28:6), or else the "smiting" of the Syrians spoken of in ver. 5 only referred in a more general sense to the losses inflicted on Judah by Rezin. As it is not likely that an army of Judah could have been opposed to Rezin, while another was dispatched against Pekah, we adopt the latter view.

While Rezin thus ravaged the south, Pekah attacked Israel from the north. In a pitched battle, no fewer than 120,000 Judaeans fell in one day.

Among the slain were Maaseiah, a royal prince, Azrikam, "prince of the palace" — probably its chief official, or major-domo — and Elkanah, "the second to the king" probably the chief of the royal council (comp. Esther 10:3). It is not easy to arrange the succession of events. But we conjecture that after the losses inflicted by Rezin in the south, and the bloody victory gained by Pekah in the north, the two armies marched upon Jerusalem, (2 Kings 16:5), with the object of deposing Ahaz. But from the strength of its late fortifications the undertaking failed of success. It was when Ahaz was thus pressed to the uttermost, and the Edomites and Philistines had actively joined the hostile alliance (2 Chronicles 28:17, 18), that two events of the gravest political and theocratic importance occurred. The first of these was the resolve of the king to appeal to Assyria for help, with abject submission to its ruler. The second was the appearance, the message, and the warnings of the prophet Isaiah (Isaiah 7; 8). As we understand it, their inability to take Jerusalem, and the knowledge that Ahaz had resolved to appeal to Tiglath-pileser, induced the kings of Syria and Israel to return to their capitals. Rezin carried probably at that time his captives to Damascus; while the Israelitish army laid the country waste, and took not only much spoil, but no less than 200,000 captives, mostly women and children ("sons and daughters") — as the sacred text significantly marks, to show the unprecedented enormity of the crime' "of their brethren" (2 Chronicles 28:8). Their ultimate fate will be told in the sequel.

We pass now to the second event referred to. While the fate of Judah was trembling in the balance, the prophet Isaiah was commissioned to go with his son, Shear Yashub to meet the king "at the end of the conduit of the upper pool, at the highway of the fuller's field" (Isaiah 7:3).

If this "upper pool" was (as seems most likely) the present Birket-el-Mamilla, the "dragon well" of Nehemiah 2:13, and "serpent's pool" of Josephus (War; V. 3, 2), it lay in the north-west of the city. The "pool," which is only a reservoir for rain-water, is partly hewn in the rock and lined with stone. From its eastern side an outlet channel or "conduit" opened, winding somewhat to the south of the Jaffa gate, eastwards into the city, where at present it debauches into "the Pool of the Patriarch" (the Hammam-el-Batrak), the Amygdalon [Tower] Pool of Josephus.

From the manner in which the locality is mentioned, we infer that the king was wont to pass that way, possibly on an inspection of the north-western fortifications. The prophet's commission to Ahaz was threefold. He was to admonish him to courage (Isaiah 7:4), and to announce that, so far from the purpose of the allies succeeding, Ephraim itself should, within a given time, cease to be "a people."

Lastly, he was to give "a sign" of what had been said, especially of the continuance of the house of David. This was, in contrast to the king's unbelief, to point from the present to the future, and to indicate the ultimate object in view — the birth of the Virgin's Son, Whose name, Immanuel, symbolized all of present promise and future salvation connected with the house of David.

The result was what might have been expected from the character of Ahaz. As, with ill-disguised irony, he rejected the "sign," implying that his trust was in the help of Assyria, not in the promise of God, so he persevered in his course, despite the prophet's warning. Yet it scarcely required a prophet's vision to foretell the issue, although only a prophet could so authoritatively, and in such terms, have announced it (Isaiah 7:17-8:22). Every Jewish patriot must have felt the wrong and humiliation, every clear-sighted politician have anticipated the consequences of calling in — and in such manner — the aid of Tiglath-pileser. For the terms on which Ahaz purchased it were the acknowledgment of the suzerainty of Assyria (2 Kings 16:7), and a present of the silver and gold in the Temple, the royal palace, and in the possession of the princes (2 Kings 16:8; 2 Chronicles 28:21.) If it led to the immediate withdrawal of Rezin and Pekah, yet the danger incurred was far greater than that avoided. And in 2 Chronicles 28:20 we read: "And Tiglath-pileser, king of Assyria, came against him [viz., against Ahaz], and distressed him, but strengthened him not." Although, even from its position in the text, this seems a general statement rather than the record of a definite event, yet some historical fact must underlie it.

Further reference will be made to it in the sequel. But, while we do not read of an expedition of Tiglath-pileser against Jerusalem, such may have been made, even if under the guise of a friendly visit.

And perhaps there may be some connection between this and the reported Temple alterations, "on account of the king of Assyria" (2 Kings 16:18). In any case Tiglath-pileset must have desired to extend his conquests further south than Samaria. He must have coveted the possession of such a city and fortress as Jerusalem; and the suzerainty so abjectly offered by. Ahaz would in his hands become a reality. In fact, the subjugation of Judea must have formed part of his general policy, which had the subjection of Egypt as its scope. And from 2 Kings 18:7, 14, 20, and Isaiah 36:5, we infer that from the time of Ahaz to that of Hezekiah the kingdom of Judah was actually both subject and tributary to Assyria.

An episode in the Syro-Israelitish war, hitherto only alluded to, still remains to be described. It will be remembered that the Israelitish victors had taken 200,000 prisoners. From the expressions used, we infer that these were brought to Samaria, not by the whole army — the majority having, after the Eastern manner, probably dispersed to their homes — but by a division, or armed escort, perhaps by those who formed the standing army. But even in Samaria God had not left Himself without a witness. "A prophet of Jehovah was there, whose name was Oded." As in the days of Asa, the prophet Azariah had met the victorious army of Judah on its return not with words of flattery, but of earnest admonition (2 Chronicles 15:1-7), so now this otherwise unknown prophet of Samaria. And his very obscurity, and sudden and isolated message, as well as its effect, are instructive of the object and character of prophetism. Only a prophet of the Lord could have dared, in the circumstances, to utter words so humiliating to Israel's pride, and so exacting in their demand. The defeat and loss of Judah had been in Divine punishment of sin, and would they now add to their own guilt by making slaves of the children of Judah and Jerusalem? Or did they presume to regard themselves as instruments of God's judgments, forgetful of the guilt which rested upon themselves? Nay, let them know that wrath was already upon them, alike for their sins, for this fratricidal war, and now for their purpose of enslaving their brethren — and let them set their captives free.

There is not the least reason for questioning the accuracy of this narrative, nor yet of that of the effectual intervention on behalf of the captives of four of the heads of houses in Ephraim, whose names have been handed down to honor.

The latter is a further confirmation of the historical character of the report. Indeed, even if it had not been recorded, we should have expected some such intervention. The more serious party in Israel, whether friends or foes of Pekah, must have disapproved of such an undertaking as that of their king. There had previously been wars between Israel and Judah; but never one in which Israel had joined a heathen power for the purpose of overthrowing the house of David, and placing on its throne a Syrian adventurer. It must have awakened every religious and national feeling; and the sight of 200,000 Judean women and children driven into Samaria, weary, footsore, hungry, and in rags, to be sold as slaves, would evoke not satisfaction, but abhorrence and indignation. It is to this that we understand the four princes to refer when speaking of the "trespass" already committed by this war, and warning against adding to it by retaining the captives as slaves. As we realize the scene, we do not wonder at the intervention of the princes, nor at the popular reaction when the words of the prophet roused them to full consciousness of their wrong. Nor, taking merely the political view of it, could princes or people have been blind to the folly of weakening Judah and entangling themselves in a war with Tiglath-pileser.

As so often in similar circumstances, the revulsion of popular feeling was immediate and complete. The spoil and the captives were handed over to "the princes;" those who had lately been prisoners were tenderly cared for as brethren and honored guests, and brought back to the Judean border-city Jericho. Without presuming to affirm that this episode was in the mind of our Lord when He spoke the parable of "the Good Samaritan," there is that in the bearing of these men who are expressed by names which reminds us of the example and the lessons in that teaching of Christ.

Another suggestion we would venture to make. It will be remembered that when Isaiah was directed to meet King Ahaz he was to go not alone, but accompanied by his son, Shear Yashub (Isaiah 7:3). The meaning of this evidently symbolical name is "A remnant shall return." May that name not have been a symbolic prediction of the episode just related, and intended to show how easily the Lord could give deliverance, without any appeal for help to Assyria?

If so, it casts still further light on the place occupied by symbolism, not only in the Old Testament, but in Hebrew, and in measure in all Eastern thinking. Symbolism is, so to speak, its mode of expression — the language of its highest thinking. Hence its moral teaching is in parables and proverbs; its dogmatics in ritual and typical institutions; while in its prophecy the present serves as a mirror in which the future is reflected. To overlook this constant presence of the symbolical and typical in the worship, history, teaching, and prophecy of the Old Testament is to misunderstand not only its meaning, but even the genius of the Hebrew people.

We turn once more to the course of this history to trace the results of Ahaz' appeal to Assyria as against Syria and Israel. Unfortunately, of the two groups into which the Assyrian inscriptions of that reign have been arranged, that which is chronological and also historically the most trustworthy has in important parts been destroyed or rendered illegible by a later monarch of a different dynasty (Esarhaddon).

Nevertheless we are able to gather a sufficiently connected history at any rate of twelve out of the eighteen years of the reign of Tiglath-pileser. Its beginning, and to the period of the taking of Arpad, has been described in the previous chapter. And thus much may be added generally, that "the picture of Tiglath-pileser derived from the Assyrian inscriptions entirely corresponds with what we know of him from the Bible.

Further, we learn that in Tiglath-pileser's expedition against the Syro-Israelitish league his first movement was against Israel and the smaller nations around Judah (2 Chronicles 28:17, 18). A brief account of the campaign against Israel is given in 2 Kings 15:29, 30, which we cannot help thinking is there out of its place.

But it correctly indicates, in accordance with the Assyrian inscriptions, the priority of the march against Israel to that upon Damascus, which is recorded in 2 Kings 16:9, and it seems also alluded to in 2 Chronicles 28:16, comp. ver. 17. From the Assyrian inscriptions we learn that Tiglath-pileser made an expedition against Philistia — that country being presumably named as the utmost western objective of a campaign which was equally directed against Samaria, the Phoenician towns, Edom, Moab, and Ammon, and even affected Judah. To the latter the notice in 2 Chronicles 28:20 may possibly bear reference.

Judging from the order of the conquered cities mentioned in the Assyrian inscriptions, Tiglath-pileser had left Damascus aside, and marched straight on the old Canaanitish towns at the western foot of Lebanon, which commanded the road to Palestine. Two of these are specially mentioned, Arka (Genesis 10:17), the modern Irka, about twelve miles north-east from Tripolis, and Zemar (Genesis 10:18), the modern Symra, the ancient Simyros.

After an unhappy break of two lines in the inscription, we next come upon the names of two of the cities which in 2 Kings 15:29 are described as taken by Tiglath-pileser, Gilead and Abel-beth-Maachah, with express notice of their situation in the land of Beth-Omri (Samaria), and of their having been added to the territory of Assyria. The inscription further states that Tiglath-pileser had set his own officials and governors over these districts. Thence the victorious expedition is traced as far as Gaza, whence no doubt, after having subjugated all the border-tribes to Northern Arabia, it returned to the land of "Beth-Omri." It is added that Tiglath-pileser carried away to Assyria all its inhabitants, with their chattels, and killed Pekah their king, appointing Hoshea in his place (2 Kings 15:30).

We do not fail to perceive in this record boastful exaggerations by the Assyrian monarch, since, although the revolution which cost Pekah his life (2 Kings 15:30) was no doubt occasioned by the victories of Tiglath-pileser, yet the Israelitish king fell by the hand of Hoshea, the leader of the rising. At the same time Hoshea was absolutely dependent on Assyria, to which he became tributary. On the Assyrian inscription the sum exacted from him is said to have amounted to ten talents of gold (67,500 pounds) and 1,000 talents of silver (375,000 pounds).

The list of the conquered Israelitish cities given in 2 Kings 15:29 enables us to follow the course of the campaign of Tiglath-pileset straight down from north to south, through Upper Galilee. The Assyrians took first Ijon, in the tribe of Naphtali (2 Chronicles 16:4), a place formerly conquered by Ben-hadad (1 Kings 15:20), probably the modern Tell Dibbin, on a hill in a "well watered" district, on the road from Damascus to Sidon. Thence the conquerors passed to Abel-beth-Maachah, "the meadow" of Beth-Maacah (a neighboring small Syrian district), also called Abel Mayim, "meadow of waters" (2 Chronicles 16:4), a considerable town, known to us from the clays of David (2 Samuel 20:18) and of Ben-hadad (1 Kings 15:20), situated about one and a half hours west-north-west from Dan. The next town occupied, Janoah (not that of Joshua 16:6), probably the modern Hunin, lay about midway between Abel-beth-Maachah and Kedesh, the place next captured. It was also in the possession of Naphtali — and indeed, to distinguish it from other places of the same name, was known as Kedesh-Naphtali, or Kedesh in Galilee (Joshua 20:7; 21:32; 1 Chronicles 6:76). This was one of the ancient Levitical cities, and the birthplace of Barak (Judges 4:6, 9). Although belonging to Upper Galilee, it was at the time of Christ held by the Tyrians (Jos. Wars, 2. 18, 1), whose territory here bounded with Galilee. It still retains its old name, and lies north-west of the marshes that surrounded Lake Merom. The other three names in 2 Kings 15:29 among the conquests of Tiglath-pileser seem those of districts rather than towns: Gilead, the later Gaulonitis, the northern portion of the trans-Jordanic district whixch Jeroboam II had only lately won back for Israel (2Kings 15:25); Galilee, in the more restricted sense of the term, that is: the northern part of it, or "Galilee of the Gentiles" (Isaiah 9:1; compare 1 Kings 9:11) — in short, "all the land of Nephtali."

The advance of Tiglath-pileser, marked by the occupation of those towns in a straight line from north to south, concerted Galilee and the adjoining trans-Jordanic district into an Assyrian province, which served as a basis for further operations. These terminated — perhaps after passing near or through Jerusalem — with the occupation of Samaria, where a revolution ensued, in which Pekah fell. He was succeeded by the leader of the rising, Hoshea, who became tributary to Assyria. The easier part of his undertaking accomplished, Tiglath-pileser turned his arms against Damascus. Here he met with a stubborn resistance. Holy Scripture only records (2 Kings 16:9) that Damascus was taken, Rezin killed, and the people carried captive to Kir — a district not yet certainly identified, but apparently belonging to Media (compare Isaiah 21:2; 22:6). It was thence that the Syrians had originally come (Amos 9:7), and thither they were again transported when their work in history was done (Amos 1:5).

Unfortunately, the Assyrian tablets which record this campaign are mutilated, that in which the death of Rezin was recorded being lost. But we learn that the siege of Damascus occupied two years; that Rezin was shut up in his capital, into which he had been driven; that not only was every tree in the gardens round Damascus cut down, but, in the language of the tablet, the whole land desolated as by a flood. With the capture of Damascus, the Damasco-Syrian empire, which had hitherto been a scourge for the punishment of Israel, came to an end. Henceforth it was only a province of Assyria. It is in the light of all these events that we have to read such prophecies as those in Isaiah 7 and the firs part of chapter 8.

The majestic divine calm of these utterances, their lofty defiance of man's seeming power, their grand certitude, and the withering irony with which what seemed the irresistible might of these two "smoking friebrands" is treated — all find their illustration in the history of this war. Such prophecies warrant is in climbing the heights of faith, from which Isaiah bids us to look, to where, in the dim distance the morning glow of the new Messianic day is seen to fill the sky with glory.

But in Damascus the conquered did Tiglath-pileser gather, as for an Eastern durbar, the vanquished and subject priunces. Thither also did King Ahaz go "to meet" the king of Assyria; and thence, as the outcome of what he had learned from prophecy and seen as its fulfillment in history, did this king of Judah send the pattern of the heathen altar to Jerusalem (2 Kings 16:10, 11). On the Assyrian monuments he is called Joachaz (Ja-u-ha-zi). But scared history would not join the name of the Lord with that of the apostate descendent of David. For all time it points at him the finger, "This is that King Ahaz" (2 Chronicles 28:22); and he sinks into an unhonored grave, "not into the sepulchers of the kings of Israel" (ver. 27). And yet other and still wider-reaching lessons come to us from this history.

CHAPTER 9 — HOSHEA, (TWENTIETH) KING OF ISRAEL — SUMMARY OF THIS HISTORY — ACCESSION OF HOSHEA — RELIGIOUS CHARACTER OF HIS REIGN — DEATH OF TIGLATH-PILESER AND ACCESSION OF SHALMANESER IV. — EXPEDITION INTO PALESTINE AND SUBMISSION OF HOSHEA — ATTEMPTED ALLIANCE OF ISRAEL WITH EGYPT — HOSHEA MADE A PRISONER — SIEGE OF SAMARIA — ACCOUNT OF IT IN THE ASSYRIAN INSCRIPTIONS — ACCESSION OF SARGON — CAPTURE OF SAMARIA — DEPORTATION OF ISRAEL — LOCALITIES OF THEIR EXILE — THE NEW COLONISTS OF SAMARIA AND THEIR RELIGION — LESSONS OF THIS HISTORY.

(2 KINGS 17)

THERE is a strange Jewish tradition to the effect that from the time when Reuben, Gad, and the half-tribe of Manasseh were deported, the observance of Jubilee years ceased (Arakh. 32 b; Fer. Shebh. 39 c; Fer. Gitt. 45 d).

Whatever of truth there may be in this notice, other peculiarities connected with this period are of such interest and importance in this history, alike retrospectively and prospectively, that we group them together in an orderly form before proceeding with our narrative.

When we turn to the first and most prominent factor in this history, Israel, we are impressed with this, that now, for the first time since the separation of the brother-nations, the northern kingdom had entered into a formal league against Judah with a heathen nation, and that its hereditary foe, Syria. And the significance of this fact deepens as we remember that the final object was not merely to conquer Judah, but to dethrone the house of David, and substitute for it a Syrian, presumably a heathen ruler. So forgetful had Israel become of its great hope, and of the very meaning of its national existence. For the first time also, at least in the Biblical record, does the Assyrian power now appear on the scene of Palestine, first to be bought off by Menahem (2 Kings 15:19, 20); then to be invoked by Ahaz, with the result of rendering Judah tributary, and finally of overthrowing Israel.

When we pass from Israel to Judah, we find that the country had now attained a state of national prosperity greater even than in the time of Solomon. But in its train had come luxury, vice, idolatry, and heathen thoughts and manners, to the utter corruption of the people. In vain did the prophets call to repentance (Joel 2:12-14; Isaiah 1:2-9, 16-20); in vain did they speak of nearing judgment (Micah 2:3; Isaiah 1:24; 3:1-8; 3:16- 4:1:5:5-to end); in vain seek to woo by promises of mercy (Micah 4:1-5; Isaiah 2:2-5). Priests and people boasted in an outward and formal observance of ritual ordinances, as if these were the substance of religion, and in this trust set lightly by the warning of the prophets (Isaiah 1:11- 15). In their overweening confidence as to the present, and their worldly policy as regarded the future, they brought on themselves the very evils which had been predicted, but from which they had deemed themselves secure. And so it came that a people who would not turn to their God while they might, had in the end this as their judgment of hardening, that they could no longer turn to Him (Isaiah 6:9-13).

Indeed, Judah had so declined that not only idolatry of every kind, but even the service of Molech — nay, witchcraft and necromancy, expressly denounced in the law (Deuteronomy 18:10-13), were openly practiced in the land (Isaiah 8:19). The Divine punishment of all this has already appeared in the preceding history. For if, at the beginning of the reign of Ahaz, Judah had attained its highest state of prosperity, it had sunk at its close to the lowest level yet reached. In truth all the three nations engaged in the war described in the previous chapter received meet punishment. The continuance of the northern kingdom was now only a question of time, and the exile of Israel had actually begun. Judah had become dependent on Assyria, and henceforth was only able fitfully and for brief periods to shake off its yoke, till it finally shared the fate of its sister-kingdom. Lastly, Syria ceased to exist as an independent power, and became a province of Assyria.

But in the history of the kingdom of God every movement is also a step towards the great goal, and all judgment becomes larger mercy. So was it on this occasion also. Henceforth the whole historical scene was changed. The prophetic horizon had enlarged. The falling away of Israel had become already initially the life of the world. The fullest predictions of the Person and work of the Messiah and of His universal kingdom date from this period. Even the new relations of Israel formed the basis for wider conceptions and spiritual progression. Those petty wars with Syria, Edom, Moab, Ammon, and Philistia, which had filled the previous history, now ceased to be factors in it, and Israel found itself face to face with the great world-power. This contact gave new form and shape to the idea of a universal kingdom of God, wide as the world, which had hitherto only been presented in dim outline, and of which only the germ had existed in the religious consciousness of the people. Thus in every respect this was the beginning of a new era, an era of judgment indeed, but also of larger mercy; an era of new development in the history of the kingdom of God; a type also of the final hardening of Israel in the rejection of their Messiah, and of the opening of the kingdom of heaven to all believers.

Hoshea, the son of Elah, the last king of Israel, ascended the throne in the twelfth year of Ahaz, king of Judah. His reign extended, at least nominally, over nine years (2 Kings 17:1). Of its religious character we have this brief notice, that "he did that which was evil in the sight of the Lord, but not as the kings of Israel that were before him." In the absence of details, we can only conjecture that this indicates decrease in the former active opposition to the worship of Jehovah. This seems implied in the circumstance that apparently no official hindrance was offered to the later invitation of Hezekiah to attend the Passover in Jerusalem (2 Chronicles 30:1-12). The Talmud has it that after the deportation of the golden calves to Assyria (Hosea 10:5, 6), Hoshea had abolished the military posts which since the time of Jeroboam 1. had been set to prevent Israelites from going up to the feasts at Jerusalem (Gitt. 88 a; Babh. Q. 121 b; comp. Seder O1. R. 22). Tiglath-pileser died probably five years after Ahaz had "met" him in Damascus. He was followed on the throne by Shalmaneser IV.

Although special records and inscriptions of his reign do not exist, we learn from fragmentary notices that in the third year of his reign the Assyrian monarch undertook expeditions against the west — presumably Phoenicia and Israel. Further light. comes to us from Josephus (Ant 9. 14, 2), who reproduces an extract from the historical work of Menander, itself derived from the Tyrian archives. Thence we learn that the Assyrian king invaded Phoenicia, and on the same occasion no doubt also Samaria, which was in league with it. As Shalmaneser was not a successful leader, we can easily understand that the allies may have cherished a hope that the heavy yoke of Assyria might be shaken off. But on the appearance of Shalmaneser Hoshea had to submit — in the language of Scripture, he "became his servant and rendered him tribute" (2 Kings 17:3).

Similarly, according to the Tyrian annals, most of the Phoenician cities seem to have surrendered or made terms with him, with the exception of Tyre, which held out for five years, and was only taken by Sargon, the successor of Shalmaneser. It is probably to this that the prophecy in Isaiah 23: refers. The Tyrian annals, and even the Assyrian inscriptions, mutilated as they are, lead us to regard this campaign as consisting of several expeditions into Phoenicia. This renders it difficult to know at what precise period the first submission of Hoshea was made.

It seems likely that the protracted resistance offered by Tyre may have encouraged the hope that Shalmaneser might after all prove unsuccessful against a powerful combination. Accordingly, Hoshea entered into negotiations with Seve, "the king of Egypt."

The king of Israel had good reason for looking hopefully to an alliance with this monarch. He was the first Pharaoh of the twenty-fifth Ethiopian dynasty. Under him Egypt, which before had been pressed in the north by the Assyrians and in the south by the Ethiopians, and suffered from internal dissensions, became strong, peaceful, and independent. This is not the place for details of a reign which was not only signally beneficial to his country, but elevated in character. Seve was too wise a monarch to be persuaded by the ambassadors, or seduced by the "presents" which Hoshea sent, into an active alliance with Israel against Assyria. The attempted "conspiracy" became known to Shalmaneser. He turned against Hoshea, who in the meantime had ceased to pay his tribute, seized and cast him into prison (2 Kings 17:4).

The further progress of this war is only briefly summarized in the Biblical record (2 Kings 17:5, 6), which is chiefly concerned with the issue of the struggle, and its spiritual import and lessons. It only relates that the siege of Samaria lasted three years; that at the end of them — that is, in the ninth (or last) year of Hoshea — the city was taken; and, lastly, that "Israel" was "carried away" to certain places which are mentioned. Happily, the Assyrian inscriptions enable us to fill up this bare outline. From them we learn that after the siege of Samaria had continued about two years, Shalmaneser was succeeded by Sargon, who took the city (after a siege of altogether three years) in the first year of his reign — that is, in the year 722 B.C.

Strictly speaking, the sacred text does not expressly attribute the capture of Samaria to Shalmaneser himself (comp. 2 Kings 17:6; 18:10, 11), although Sargon is not mentioned.

And for this silence, or even the ascription of this campaign wholly to Shalmaneser, there may be reasons, unknown to us, connected with the relation between Sargon and Shalmaneser, and the part which the former may have taken in the military operations or the conduct of the siege. Certain it is that Sargon was not the son of Shalmaneser, although apparently of princely descent — perhaps the scion of a collateral branch of the royal family. Nor do we know the circumstances of his accession — possibly in consequence of a revolution, easily accounted for by dissatisfaction with the king's failure both before Tyre and Samaria. In any case, the inscriptions distinctly inform us that Sargon captured Samaria, led away 27,280 of its inhabitants, took fifty chariots, leaving his subordinates to take the rest of the property found in the city, and appointing a governor, with the same tribute as Hoshea had paid.

Similarly, the Biblical account of the deportation of Israel into exile is supplemented and confirmed by the Assyrian records. The places to which they were carried are not indeed enumerated in the Assyrian inscriptions, but their location can mostly be ascertained.

"Halah" (or rather "Chalah"), the first place mentioned in 2 Kings 17:6, was, judging from its conjunction with "the river Chabor" and with "Gozan" (comp. 1 Chronicles 5:26), a district contiguous to them, called Chalcitis, where a mound called Gla may represent the city. There cannot be any doubt in regard to the other localities to which the Israelites were carried. They were "placed" "on the Chabor, the river of Gozan, and in the cities of the Medes."

"Gozan" — Gausanitis — the Assyrian Gu-za-nu, is a district in Mesopotamia traversed by the Chabor (Ass., Ha-bur), the "great" river, with "verdant banks," which springs near Nisibis, and is navigable long before it drains the waters of Gozan into the Euphrates. The last district mentioned lies east of the others. "Media" is the province stretching east of the Zagros Mountains, and north to the Caspian Sea, or rather to the Elbur mountain-chain, which runs parallel to its southern shore. Its "cities" had only lately been overrun by the Assyrian conqueror. In them the legendary book of Tobit still places these exiles (Tobit 1:14; 3:7).

The account of the Ten Tribes by Josephus adds little to our knowledge. He describes them as "an immense multitude, not to be estimated by numbers," and as located "beyond the Euphrates" (Ant. 11. 5, 2). Equally, if not even more vague, are the later references to them in 4 Esdras, and in Rabbinic writings. From all this we may infer that there was no longer any reliable historical information on the subject.

On another point, however, we have important information. We know that with these exiles went their priests (2 Kings 17:27), although not of Levitical descent (2 Chronicles 11:14). Thus the strange mixture of the service of the Lord and foreign rites must have continued. In the course of time the heathen elements would naturally multiply and assume greater prominence, unless, indeed, the people learned repentance by national trials, or from higher teaching. Of this there is not any evidence in the case of Israel; and if the footsteps of these wanderers shall ever be clearly tracked, we expect to find them with a religion composed of various rites, but prevailingly heathen, yet with memories of their historical past in traditions, observances, and customs, as well as in names, and bearing the marks of it even in their outward appearance.

On yet another point does the testimony of the Assyrian records confirm the Biblical narrative. From the inscriptions we learn that Sargon transported to Samaria, in room of the exiled Israelites, inhabitants of countries conquered by him. And when in 2 Kings 17:24 we read that these new colonists were "brought from Babylon, and from Cuthah, and from Ava and from Hamath, and from Sepharvaim," we recognize the names of places which, according to the Assyrian inscriptions, were conquered by Sargon, and whence, as was his wont, he deported the inhabitants.

From the inscriptions we further learn that these transportations were successive, and that even the earliest of them did not take place immediately on the removal of the Israelites. Thus we understand how lions, so numerous in Palestine at one time, but gradually diminished with the growth of the population, once more increased among the scanty and scattered settlers. The sacred historian recognizes in this the hand of the LORD.

And rightly so, since all who are in sympathy with things Divine must by the spiritual instinct of their new nature rise to the recognition of Him Who ruleth, and of Whose government and purposes all events are the unbidden means, and all men the unconscious, yet free, agents. But especially do we mark this realization of the eternal Presence of the living God as the distinguishing characteristic of Old Testament teaching, whose first and last utterance it is- "Jehovah reigneth."

But we have more than merely a general confirmation of the Biblical account. From the Assyrian records we learn that in the first year after his accession Sargon vanquished Merodach-Baladan of Babylon, and deported of the people to "Chatti," which is the designation for Syro-Palestine, inclusive of Samaria. Again, the Biblical expression "Babylon" includes besides the capital other cities of Babylon, and transportations from some of them to "the land of Beth Omri," or Samaria, are expressly recorded.

According to the inscriptions, these took place not only in the first but in other years, notably in the seventh after the accession of Sargon and the taking of Samaria. Among the cities mentioned as furnishing colonists, "Cuthah," which has been re-discovered in the modern Tell-Ibrahim, lay about fifteen miles north-east of Babylon. "Ava" has not yet been identified. Sepharvaim, or "the twin Sipar" (Sipphara), so called because the city was built on both banks of the Euphrates, has been recognized in the ruins of Abu-Habba, about twenty miles north of Babylon, where the celebrated Temple of the Sun has been laid bare. Lastly, Hamath is the well-known Syrian city which rebelled against Assyria under a king Jahubi'd, who was vanquished in the battle of Karkar, when Hamath was taken, and its people deported. The other cities mentioned in Scripture were conquered by Sargon at a later period, in his final wars against Merodach-Baladan, in the twelfth and thirteenth years after his accession (710, 709 B.C.). Hence the transportation of their inhabitants to Samaria must have been as many years after the taking of the capital of Israel.

As the sacred text informs us (2 Kings 17:25-33), the new colonists brought with them the worship of their national deities. Among these, "Succoth-benoth" — mentioned as the deity of "the men of Babylon" — is probably a corruption of the name of the well-known Babylonian goddess, Zir-banit, "She who gives seed [posterity]."

As the god of Cuth, "Nergal" is mentioned, and this is confirmed by the Assyrian inscriptions. Nergal seems to have been the lion-god represented by the colossal winged lions at the entrance to the palaces. Concerning "Ashima," the deity of Hamath, and Nibhaz and Tartak, the gods of the Avites, we possess not any definite information. On the other hand, "Adrammelech" ["Adar is king"] and Anammelech ["Anu is king"], the gods of Sepharvaim, represent well-known Assyrian deities. Adar (originally A-tar) means "father of decision."

In the inscriptions this god bears among others the designation of "lord of fire," which accords with the Biblical notice that the worshippers "burnt" to him "their children in fire." He is represented as a winged bull, with human head and a man's face. Anu was represented as a man clothed in the skin of a fish, culminating in a tiara. After the two supreme gods, Il and Asur, he occupied the first rank in the Triad [Anu, Bel, Nisroch]. He is also described as "the good god," and as "lord of the night." His female counterpart bore the name Anat or, Anatuv.

The perils which the new settlers experienced from the increase of wild beasts, which, in true heathen manner, they ascribed to their ignorance of "the manner of the God of the land," led to an appeal to the king. Entering into their views, Sargon dispatched to Samaria one of the priests who had accompanied Israel into exile. He settled in Bethel, the traditional metropolis of Israelitish worship, such as Jeroboam I. had remodeled it. And it was this corrupt form of Jehovah worship which he taught the new settlers. The result was a mixture of Israelitish truths, traditions, and corruptions, with the pagan rites which they had brought with them. Thus their new religion bore a strange similarity to the mixed new, partly Israelitish, partly foreign, population. And such, according to the writer of the Book of Kings, continued substantially the character of the religion of Samaria to his own days.

Yet another transportation of foreign colonists to Samaria seems to have taken place in the reign of Esar-haddon, or rather of his son — possibly in consequence of an attempted rising on the part of the Israelitish population (comp. Ezra 4:2, 10). But what most deeply impresses us in the Biblical narrative of these events is the spirit and manner in which at the close of Israel's national history the writer passes in review the leading characteristics. The Divine calling of Israel; their defection, rapidly growing into open idolatry; the warnings of the prophets sent to them, and their neglect; the hardening of heart, leading up to the utmost corruption in religion, morals, and life — such, with a brief reflection on Judah's kindred guilt and danger, is the summary presented to us of this history in its spiritual aspect. Scarcely on any other occasion does the sacred writer allow himself reflections of this kind. But they are appropriate, and almost needful, at the close of a history which relates events in their bearing on the kingdom of God, and views Israel as a nation called to be the servants and the messengers of the Lord. They explain the inner meaning of God's dealings in the past, and the deeper causes of a rejection and an exile which cannot end till Israel and Judah, no longer hostile nor separate, shall in one common repentance turn to seek Jehovah their God and the Son of David their King.

CHAPTER 10 — HEZEKIAH, (THIRTEENTH) KING OF JUDAH. HOSHEA, (TWENTIETH) KING OF ISRAEL — ACCESSION OF HEZEKIAH — POLITICAL CIRCUMSTANCES OF THE TIMES — RELIGION THE ONLY TRUE NATIONAL POLICY — THE POSITION OF ASSYRIA IN RELATION TO JUDAH — RELIGION THE CENTRAL PRINCIPLE OF HEZEKIAH'S REIGN — IDOLATRY ABOLISHED IN JUDAH — RESTORATION OF THE TEMPLE SERVICES — PURIFICATION OF THE TEMPLE — SERVICES OF RE. CONSECRATION — CELEBRATION OF THE PASS-OVER — INVITATION TO THE NORTHERN TRIBES — SUBSEQUENT FESTIVAL — RE-ARRANGEMENT OF THE TEMPLE-SERVICES — PROVISION FOR PRIESTS AND LEVITES — GENERAL INFERENCES — ACTIVITY OF HEZEKIAH IN REGARD TO THE CANON OF SCRIPTURE.

(2 KINGS 18:1-6; 2 CHRONICLES 29-31)

THERE is not a more striking instance of Divine mercy on the one hand, nor yet, on the other, of the personal character of religion even under the Old Testament, than that Ahaz should have been succeeded on the throne of Judah by Hezekiah. His name, "Strength of Jehovah," or, perhaps better, "God is might," was truly indicative of the character of his reign. In every respect — not only as regarded the king personally, but also in the results of his administration, as affecting his country and people — this period was in complete contrast to that which had immediately preceded it.

Hezekiah, the son of Ahaz, ascended the throne at the age of twenty-five, towards the close of the third year of Hoshea's reign in Israel.

He was therefore a witness of the events which befell Samaria. From a merely political point of view, the position of a king of Judah must have been one of no small difficulty. In the northern kingdom Pekah had sown the wind, and Hoshea would reap the whirlwind. The one had brought upon himself the might of Assyria; the other would ultimately lose crown and life in his attempts to shake off the yoke of the conqueror. And in his ruin would Israel be involved. Assyria was the paramount power, not only in Samaria, which was so soon to become a province of that empire, but in Judah also. For Ahaz had made himself tributary to it, and held his crown almost at the mercy of the great world-empire. And, as will appear in the sequel, Hezekiah himself was to feel the power of Assyria even before he came into actual conflict with it.

All this succession of evils, and those which were still to follow, were the consequences of the disbelief and unbelief of Ahaz. As he had discarded the religion of Jehovah, so he despised His Word. In the political circumstances of the country, the only alternative before him was either to trust in the Lord for deliverance, or else to surrender to a foreign power. Against the admonitions and warnings of the great prophet, who had assured him of Divine help, Ahaz had chosen the second alternative. His resolve was not only sin: it was folly. His short-sighted policy brought in another power whose domination could never afterwards be

693

permanently shaken off. Afterwards, when the kingdom of Israel came to an end, the two rival world-empires, Assyria and Egypt, stood face to face, only separated by little Judah — an object of ambition to both, a help to neither, yet whose subjection was absolutely necessary to Assyria, not only in view of its further projects, but even if previous conquests were to be preserved. And for an Assyrian monarch not to be successful was, as this history has shown, to lose crown and life.

So matters stood when Hezekiah ascended the throne. Of all the political combinations possible to him, he chose none. He returned to the point from which Ahaz had departed. His policy was not to have any policy, but to trust in the living God, to obey His Word, and to follow His guidance. His policy was his religion, and his religion was true policy. The only occasion on which he was tempted to deviate from it was at a later time, and it well-nigh proved fatal to him, as in the sequel it certainly did to his successors. Not that Hezekiah neglected to avail himself of political combinations as they arose. Indeed, this became the source of his danger. He may have argued that not to make use of the means placed within his reach was fatalism, not faith. In this he erred. Yet he did not put his trust in such alliances. He treated them rather as means for defensive, than as instruments sought for offensive purposes. The only real help which he sought was that of the living God.

Thus religion was the central principle of his reign and the secret of his success. The first act of his government was to abolish every kind of idolatry, whether of foreign or domestic origin. The "bamath," or "high places," were abolished; the matsebhoth, or stone pillars and statues erected for the worship of Baal, were broken down; and the Asherah, or wooden symbol of the lascivious worship of Astarte, was cut down. Nay, even the brazen serpent, which had apparently been preserved since the time of Moses, and had, no doubt in degenerate times, become almost an object of worship, was now destroyed, having received the appellation which, when made an idol, it deserved — Nechushtan, "brazen," a piece of brass (2 Kings 18:4).

In general, the sacred text describes Hezekiah as unequaled in religious earnestness and in conformity to the Divine law by any even of the pious kings that had preceded, or who succeeded him, and it places him on a level with "David his father." And this is fully vindicated by his abolition of even that form of Jehovah-worship on "heights" which Solomon, as well as Asa, Jehoshaphat, Jehoash, Amaziah, and Uzziah had tolerated (1 Kings 3:2;15:12, 14;22:43; 2 Kings 12:3; 14:4; 15:4, 35).

But the reformation initiated was not only negative, and Hezekiah restored the services of the Temple in their completeness and purity. From the detailed account in the Book of Chronicles, we learn that "the house of the Lord" had actually been closed (2 Chronicles 29:3, 7). By this we understand the closing of the Sanctuary itself, that is, of the holy and most holy places, since Ahaz continued to use the court of the priests, although for sacrifices at the heathen altar which he had reared. But now the doors of the Sanctuary were repaired, and once more thrown open. Then Hezekiah "gathered" the priests and Levites in "the wide place on the east," probably some well-known locality in the eastern part of the Temple-buildings (comp. Ezra 10:9; Nehemiah 8:1, 3, 16).

This for the purpose of calling upon them to sanctify themselves, and to remove the heathen abominations which had defiled the Temple. And with this object, the king made in their hearing an earnest review of the sinful past, with its consequent judgments, and a declaration of his purpose "to make a covenant with the Lord."

The response to his appeal was immediate and hearty. In the account of the work now taken in hand by representatives of the Levites they appear once more according to their ancient division into the three families of Kohath, Merari, and Gershon, as David had arranged their courses (1 Chronicles 23:6-23, comp. ver. 27). With these were conjoined as a special branch, probably on account of their pre-eminence (Numbers 3:30), the representatives of the house of Elizaphan, a chief of the Kohathites (Exodus 6:18). Next in the enumeration we find the representatives of the three ancient divisions of Levite musicians — the sons of Asaph, of Heman, and Jeduthun (comp. 1 Chronicles 25:1-6; 2 Chronicles 5:12).

While these heads of Levite houses gathered their brethren to do the work assigned to them, the priests similarly cleansed the inner part of the house, when the Levites flung the remnants of past heathen defilement into the brook Kidron. It marks the zeal with which the work was carried on that, begun on the first day of the first month of the first year of Hezekiah's reign — reckoning its ecclesiastical commencement from the month Nisan — it was completed on the sixteenth day.

Then the vessels which Ahaz had cast away were restored, viz., the altar of burnt-offering, the stands for the brazen lavers, and that for "the sea" (comp. 2 Kings 16:14, 17). The Temple having been thus purified, its services were recommenced with a grand function, when seven bullocks, seven rams, and seven lambs were offered for the congregation as burnt-offerings, and seven he-goats as sin-offerings (comp. Leviticus 4:14; Ezra 8:35).

In strict accordance with the Mosaic law, all the sacred functions were discharged by the Aaronic priesthood, with sprinkling of blood on the altar, and imposition of hands on the sacrifices, denoting their vicariousness (Leviticus 1:4; 4:4, 15, 24, and Leviticus 4:7, 18, 30; 5:9). But what specially distinguishes these services is that the sin-offerings were brought not only for Judah, but "for all Israel" (2 Chronicles 29:24), indicating alike the solidarity of "all Israel" as the congregation of the Lord, and the representative character of these sacrifices. And in accordance with the institution of David, the sacred strains from Levite instruments, and the inspired hymns of David and of Asaph, once more filled the Temple with the voice of melody and of praise, while the king, the princes of Judah, and the people responsively bowed their heads in lowly worship.

The more direct sacrificial offerings for the people were followed, at the king's suggestion, by thankofferings (comp. Leviticus 7:11, 16), also of a public character, to which "as many as were of upright heart" — probably they who had stood aloof from the idolatry of the previous reign — added burntofferings. As these thankofferings were brought by the congregation as a whole, the victims were not slain and flayed by the offerers, as was the case when brought by private individuals (Leviticus 1:5, 6); but this part of the service devolved on the priesthood, who called in, as in such case they might, the assistance of the Levites. When we remember that, besides the special "burnt-offerings" of individuals (70 bullocks, 100 rams, and 200 lambs), the "thankofferings" of the congregation amounted to no less than 600 oxen and 3,000 sheep (2 Chronicles 29:32, 33), we scarcely wonder that the priests alone should not have sufficed for the service. And as the text significantly marks, recalling the special defection of the priesthood, from the high-priest Urijah downwards (comp. 2 Kings 16:15), the number of priests who had as yet sanctified themselves was proportionally smaller than that of the more faithful Levites. "So the service of the house of Jehovah was established. And Hezekiah rejoiced and all the people, because of that which God had prepared to [for] the people [probably referring to their willing participation and contribution to these services], for the thing had come suddenly" [without long previous preparation] (2 Chronicles 29:35, 36).

What followed shows that, however sudden the impulse in this religious revival, it was neither transient nor superficial. Of all the festivals in Israel, the most solemn was that of the Passover. It commemorated Israel's national birthday as the redeemed of the Lord, and pointed forward to that better deliverance of which it was the emblem. Ordinarily this feast commenced on the evening of the 14th Nisan (Exodus 12:6, 8, and parallels). But in the present instance this was impossible. Not only had the cleansing of the Temple occupied till the 16th of the month, but a sufficient number of priests for the services had not yet sanctified themselves, while further time was required to make announcement of the Passover throughout all Israel. For, unlike the services at the reconsecration of the Temple, which seem to have been confined to the inhabitants of Jerusalem, this was to be observed as a great national festival. But it was possible to remove the difficulty thus arising. The law, while fixing the ordinary date of the Passover, had also made provision for an after-celebration of the feast on the corresponding day of the second month in cases of unavoidable hindrance (Numbers 9:6-13). This is one of the most instructive commendations on the character of the Mosaic law. It shows that the outward form was not of its essence, but was flexible and adaptable. Thus the law was not something rigidly outward and absolutely permanent, but gave indication of the possibility of an enlargement by a higher fulfillment of its spirit as distinguished from the mere letter. Hence such a provision seems like an unspoken pledge of a future transformation of the law, in accordance with the higher conditions and the wants of new circumstances. Lastly, it also affords a precedent and a warrant for such a change as that of the transference of the Sabbath from the close of the week to its beginning; from the day of rest to that of the Resurrection of Christ; from the memorial of the completion of the first creation to that of the second in the creation of the new heavens and the new earth, wherein dwelleth righteousness.

Of this legal provision of an after-Passover, Hezekiah resolved to avail himself. We mark as specially interesting in itself, and as foreshadowing great changes in the future political and ecclesiastical organization of Israel, that Hezekiah acted in this with the advice of "his princes and all the congregation in Jerusalem" (2 Chronicles 30:2). And yet more interesting is it to learn that the invitation to attend the Passover addressed by the king "and his princes" was sent not only to the cities of Judah, but to all Israel, "from Beersheba even to Dan." To this the text adds the retrospective notice that previous Paschal observances had been partial, not general: "for not in multitude [in large numbers] had they done it, as it is written" (2 Chronicles 30:5).

This brotherly invitation to the feast of Israel's birth and the common worship of their God and Redeemer was, so to speak, the answer which repentant Judah now made to that fratricidal war which Israel had so lately waged with the object of exterminating the kingdom of David. And the letters of the king and the princes bore such tender references to past sin and judgment, and to present national calamity, and breathed such a spirit of religious hope for the future, as almost to rise to the level of New Testament sentiment.

In spite of the mockery with which at least at first the invitation was received by the majority in what still remained of the northern kingdom, the final response was truly encouraging (comp. vers. 10, 18). In Judah it was both hearty and unanimous (2 Chronicles 30:12). From the other parts of the country "a multitude of people, even many," came from out of five of the tribes that still constituted the kingdom of Israel. For Naphtali had been annexed to Assyria, and Reuben and Gad been deported. The festival in Jerusalem was followed by a spontaneous national movement against idolatry.

For while the purification of the Temple had been a public act of reform initiated by the king, it was left to the people gathered in Jerusalem to remove the altars in the capital, whether in private houses or in more public places, which were the remnant of the idolatrous worship introduced by Ahaz (2 Chronicles 28:24).

The only drawback to the right observance of the Passover festivities was that many of the worshippers "were not sanctified." Accordingly the Levites had to offer for them the Paschal lamb, which, by the law, each offerer should have slain for himself and his house. This applied specially to those who had come from the northern kingdom (ver. 18). If, none the less, they were allowed to partake of the Paschal feast, this was a concession almost necessary in the circumstances, since otherwise theirs would not at all have been a Passover; and for this Hezekiah implored and obtained forgiveness from the Lord.

How deeply this revival had struck its roots appears from the voluntary resolve of the people to follow up the seven days of the Passover by other seven days of festivity. For the wants of the people during that time King Hezekiah and the princes made liberal provision (vers. 23, 24). It was at this time also that the removal of all traces of idolatry from the land, briefly noticed in 2 Kings 18:4, took place. This was effected, as the fuller account in the Book of Chronicles explains, by a spontaneous popular movement which extended beyond Judah to "Ephraim also and Manasseh" (2 Chronicles 31:1), although, as we may reasonably conjecture, only in districts from which the chief inhabitants had come to Jerusalem. Closely connected with the restoration of the Temple services were the arrangements now made for their orderly continuance. The "courses" of the priests and Levites were once more settled. The public sacrifices of the congregations — daily, Sabbatic, and festive — were provided by the king as his contribution. the "portion of his substance." The latter was indeed very large (comp. 2 Chronicles 32:27-29); but the number of sacrificial animals and other requisites furnished by the king according to the requirements of the law (Numbers 28, 29) was correspondingly great. It has been calculated to have amounted to "nearly 1,100 lambs, 113 bullocks, 37 rams, and 30 goats, besides vast quantities of flour, oil, and wine for the accompanying meat and drink-offerings."

For the personal support of the ministering priests and Levites nothing more was required than the re-enactment of the ancient provision of firstfruits, tithes, and firstlings (Exodus 23:19; Numbers 18:12, 21, etc.; Leviticus 27:30-33). These, together with "the tithe of dedicated things" (Leviticus 27:30; Deuteronomy 14:28), were now offered in such quantity as not only to suffice for the wants of the priesthood, but to leave a large surplusage, to the thankful joy and surprise of Hezekiah and the princes.

In answer to the king's inquiry the high-priest Azariah explained that the large store accumulated was due to the special blessing bestowed by the Lord on a willing and obedient people (2 Chronicles 31:5-10). The collection of this store began in the third month — that of Pentecost — when the wheat harvest was completed, and it ended in the seventh month — that of Tabernacles, which marked the close of the fruit harvest and of the vintage. And these contributions, or dues, came not only from Judah, but also from "the children of Israel" (ver. 6); that is, from those in the northern kingdom who had joined their brethren in returning to the service and the law of their Lord.

For the storage of these provisions, Hezekiah ordered that certain chambers in the Temple should be prepared, and he appointed officials, who are named in the sacred text, alike for the supervision and the administration of these stores (verses 11-19). Again and again it is noted with what "faithfulness" one and the other duty were discharged by each in the special department assigned to him (verses 12, 15, 18). The provision for the priesthood included not only those who were for the time actually on service in the Temple, but also the others in the priest cities, together with their wives and children, and lastly to those in the country districts around these cities (vers. 16-19).

These and all kindred arrangements were extended throughout all Judah. And the detailed account given of the religious activity of Hezekiah closes with the twofold notice that he "wrought the good, the right, and the truth before Jehovah his God;" and that in all he undertook, whether as matter of public or private religious arrangement, "he did it with all his heart, and prospered" (2 Chronicles 31:20, 21).

To the description of the reformation inaugurated by the piety of Hezekiah, it seems desirable to add some further particulars, either illustrative of the text or derived from other notices in Holy Scripture. As regards the trustworthiness of the account of the sacrificial worship in the restored Temple — that it was not of later invention, and designed to bear out the priestly institutions first enforced in the time of Ezra — we have to point to the important fact that the number of sacrifices and sin-offerings in the time of Hezekiah notably differs from that at the dedication of the Temple in the time of Ezra (comp. 2 Chronicles 29:21, 32 with Ezra 6:17). This, considering especially the symbolism of numbers, shows that the one account could not have been framed upon the other. It follows that the Mosaic institutions must have existed in and before the time of Hezekiah, and could not, as a certain school of critics contends, have originated with the priesthood at a much later period. Indeed, as we follow the present line of argument, by a comparison of the services in the time of Hezekiah with the Mosaic institutions to which they bear reference, the conviction grows upon us not only of the existence of the latter, but of their general acknowledgment, since, keeping in view the circumstances of the previous reign, it is impossible to suppose that all this could have been "invented" in the first year of Hezekiah's reign. And as connected with this we mark that not only were the liturgical services conformed to a previous model — the Davidic — but that the hymns chanted were in "the words of David and of Asaph the seer" (2 Chronicles 29:30). This seems not only to imply the existence at the time of Davidic and Asaphite psalms — the absence of any mention of other Psalm-collections here deserving special notice — but even to indicate some orderly collection of these Psalms in books. In short, it casts light on the beginning of the present arrangement of the Psalter in five books. It may well have been that, subject to later revision, the former collection of Psalms consisting, roughly speaking, of the two first books of Psalms (now Psalm 1-41; 42-72), was now enriched by the addition of a further collection — roughly speaking, the present third book of Psalms (Psalm 73-89), which in its present form begins with an Asaphite Psalm (Psalm 73), and has in succession eleven Psalms of the same authorship (Psalm 73-83).

But whatever our view, or more accurately, our conjectures, on this subject, there cannot at least be doubt that Hezekiah actively busied himself, under competent guidance, with the collection and arrangement of the existing sacred literature of Israel. This is expressly mentioned as regards a part of "the Proverbs of Solomon, which the men of Hezekiah, king of Judah, collected" (Proverbs 25:1).

And to this, as assuredly among the most important parts of Hezekiah's activity, the closing notice of his religious work done by him may also bear reference:

"And in every work that he began in the service of the house of God, and in the law, and in the commandments, to seek his God, he did it with all his heart, and prospered" (2 Chronicles 31:21).

CHAPTER 11 — HEZEKIAH (THIRTEENTH) KING OF JUDAH — OUTWARD EVENTS OF THE REIGN OF HEZEKIAH — VICTORY OVER THE PHILISTINES — LEAGUE AGAINST SARGON — ASSYRIAN ADVANCE AND SUBMISSION OF JUDAH — SENNACHERIB — THE ASSYRIAN INSCRIPTIONS THEIR ACCOUNT OF THE ASSYRIAN INVASION OF JUDAH — VICTORIES OF SENNACHERIB — ASSYRIAN MISREPRESENTATION OF EVENTS — THE BIBLICAL RECORD — WORKS IN DEFENSE OF JERUSALEM — THE VARIOUS SCRIPTURAL NARRATIVES OF THESE EVENTS — THE ASSYRIAN HOST BEFORE JERUSALEM — ITS LEADERS AND THE REPRESENTATIVES OF HEZEKIAH — THE CONFERENCE BETWEEN THEM.

(2 KINGS 18:7-19; 2 CHRONICLES 32:1-26; ISAIAH 36:, 37)

ALTHOUGH the beginning of Hezekiah's reign was mainly devoted to the first and most important task of religious reform, other matters of pressing necessity were not overlooked. The same wisdom which marked his restoration of the Temple services also guided his other administration, and the same happy results attended both. In fact, Hezekiah made use of the years of quiet to prepare against the troublous period which he must have felt to be at hand. And in the Book of Kings we have this general notice:

"And Jehovah was with him; in all to which he proceeded he prospered; and he rebelled against the king of Assyria and served him not" (2 Kings 18:7).

In truth, the relations between Hezekiah and the mighty world-empire of Assyria furnish the explanation of all the outward events of his reign. Of the first of these, the victory over the Philistines "unto Gaza," and the complete subjugation of their country, "from the tower of the watchmen to the fenced city" (2 Kings 18:8), it is impossible to fix the date. To judge from its position in the text, it seems to have taken place during the reign of Shalmaneser, before the accession of Sargon, by whom Samaria was taken. The apparent ill-success of Shalmaneser before Tyre may have rendered possible and encouraged such an undertaking on the part of Hezekiah. In any case, we have to bear in mind that Philistia, so important to Assyria as being the road to and from Egypt, always formed an objective point in the western expeditions of the "great kings," and that its cities seem to have been divided, some being disposed to make cause against Assyria, while others — notably Ashdod and Gaza, — together with Moab, Ammon, and Edom, were on the side of the eastern empire.

Thus the period of Shalmaneser's weakness was being utilized by Hezekiah, not only for his religious reformation, but for securing his flank in any future contest with Assyria, as well as for works of internal defense, to which reference will be made in the sequel.

The aspect of matters changed with the accession of Sargon. That monarch did not indeed feel himself strong enough immediately, after the taking of Samaria, to advance south against Egypt. Besides troubles nearer home, especially the subdual of Merodach Baladan, engaged his attention. But in the second year after his accession we find him engaged in a western expedition. In this campaign the rebellion of Hamath was crushed, and the great battle of Karkar won. But what most concerns our history is the expedition of Sargon against the hostile league formed by Seve of Egypt and Hanno, king of Gaza — as we conjecture a dependent of Hezekiah, who sympathized with, though he does not seem actually to have taken part in the anti-Assyrian combination. Sargon was completely successful. In the battle of Raphia the allies were defeated; Seve fled, and was allowed to make his peace by paying tribute, while Hanno was taken prisoner. On this occasion Hezekiah appears to have been called to account, and to have been obliged to make submission. An Assyrian inscription speaks of Sargon as "the subduer of Judah," though without any added mention of battle or triumph. From its date we conclude that it refers to something that had taken place during the expedition of Sargon against Seve and Hanno.

Sargon reigned altogether seventeen years. In the defective condition of the inscriptions, it is impossible to know for certain whether or not he was killed by an assassin. He was succeeded by his son Sennacherib, who, after a reign of twenty-four years, perished at the hands of his own sons (2 Kings 19:37).

The long period of rest between the second year of Sargon and the accession of Sennacherib had, no doubt, been employed by Hezekiah in further improving the condition of the country, possibly in strengthening the defenses of Jerusalem, and preparing for future eventualities (comp. 2 Kings 20:20; 2 Chronicles 32:5-30, and other passages). This is not the place to give a detailed account of the events of the reign of Sennacherib, as we learn them from the Assyrian inscriptions, except in so far as they bear on the narrative of Scripture. And even here we have to bear in mind that admittedly the inscriptions designedly give a false impression of what had really occurred in that war, in which Judaea was overrun and Jerusalem first besieged, and then a second time summoned to surrender. It will be more convenient to give the story of this expedition, in the first place, as told in the Assyrian records, before referring to the Biblical account.

We have many inscriptions of the time of Sennacherib, in Assyrian: Sin-ahi- irib, or Sin-ahi-ir-ba ('Sin,' the lunar god, 'gives many brethren') — famed also for strengthening and fortifying his capital, Nineveh ('Ninua'), and building there two magnificent palaces, one on each side of the river. Among the various memorials of his reign four inscriptions are of special importance.

Summarizing their contents, which vary only in details, we infer that, in the fourth year of Sennacherib's reign, another league had been formed of the principal Philistine and Phoenician cities of Judah and of the Egypto-Ethiopian empire, for the purpose of shaking off the domination of Assyria. So far as the first-named cities are concerned it comprised Sidon, Ascalon, and Ekron, the inhabitants of which city, probably at the beginning of the war, if not before it, sent Padi, their king, who was faithful to Assyria, in chains to Hezekiah, who cast him into prison. On the other side, Ammon, Moab, and Edom, together with a number of the coast-cities in "the west country" — notably, Ashdod and Gaza — remained faithful to Assyria. Tidings seem to have reached Sennacherib before the confederates had time to carry their plans into execution. The Assyrian army rapidly advanced. Elulaeus, king of Sidon, fled to Cyprus, and Ethobal was appointed in his place, while the cities along the route of the Assyrian conqueror either submitted to him or were taken. Sennacherib next advanced against Ascalon, and took it. Zidka, its king, and the royal family, were transported into Assyria; Sarludari, the son of the previous king, was appointed in his place; the whole country overrun and, like Sidon, made tributary. It was probably on his march from Acco to Ascalon — perhaps from Jaffa — that Sennacherib detached a corps into Judah, which took all the "fenced cities" thereof (comp. 2 Kings

18:13). The Assyrian inscriptions speak of the capture of forty-six fortified towns and of "innumerable castles and small places," of the transportation of 200, 150 of their captive inhabitants, men and women; of the taking of immense booty, and the annexation — probably only nominal, and, in any case, temporary — of the conquered districts to the domains of the small potentates on the sea-board, friendly to Assyria. It is to this expedition that Isaiah 10:28-34 refers, as indeed the whole prophecy in the tenth chapter of Isaiah applies to the war of Sennacherib against Judah.

Beyond Ascalon it was scarcely safe for Sennacherib to advance much further. The Egypto-Ethiopian army was expected in front; behind him, yet unconquered, was Ekron, and on his flank the strong fortress of Jerusalem, with the whole flower of the Judaean army and the hired auxiliaries to whom the Assyrian monuments refer. It was therefore a wise strategic movement on the part of Sennacherib to turn aside and lay siege to Lachish, the modern Umm Lakis.

It was still a continuation of his advance in the direction of Egypt, although a departure from the straight road to it, and it would oblige the Egyptian army to make a disadvantageous digression inland, thus removing it from the main basis of its operations. But in Lachish, Sennacherib also held a strong position both against Ekron and Jerusalem, the latter being at the apex of an isosceles triangle, of which Ekron and Lachish form the extremities of the base. Thus he would be able to turn upon either one or the other line converging upon Lachish, or else to move rapidly upon Gaza. On the other hand, Hezekiah, seeing the success of the Assyrian advance, and perhaps despairing of a timely approach of the Egyptian army, sought to make his peace with Sennacherib, and sent to Lachish the embassy and tribute of which we read in 2 Kings 18:14-16. It was, no doubt, on this occasion also that Hezekiah set at liberty the captive king of Ekron, according to the Assyrian records, and sent him to Sennacherib.

After this point the Assyrian inscriptions purposely become confused, and mix up a series of different events, with the evident intention of conveying a false impression and concealing the virtual, if not the actual, defeat of Sennacherib. As we infer from a comparison of the Assyrian account with the Biblical record, Sennacherib, who by that time must have been aware of the advance of an Egyptian army, detached a large division ("a great host") against Jerusalem, which, however, held out alike against the power and the threats of the Assyrian leaders (2 Kings 18:17-19:7).

Meantime the Egyptian host was approaching, and the Assyrian leaders returned, and found Sennacherib in Libnah, somewhere east of Lachish and north of Eleutheropolis. This probably before the battle which Sennacherib fought with the Egyptians at Altaku, on a parallel line between Jerusalem and Ekron. This indicates a further retreat of Sennacherib with his army. In much vainglorious language the Assyrian monarch claims a victory; but from the wording of the account, it is evident that the victory, if such it was, could only have been nominal, and was a real defeat. Instead, therefore, of turning upon Jerusalem, the Assyrians advanced against Ekron and took it, having already previously failed in their attempt to obtain the surrender of Jerusalem by a second message full of boastful and blasphemous threats (comp. 2 Kings 19:9-34). Then followed the destruction of the Assyrian host (ver. 35), and Sennacherib's return to Nineveh (ver. 36). On the Assyrian monuments nothing is said of these disastrous events, while Sennacherib boasts that he had shut up Hezekiah in his capital "as a bird in a cage," and the deputation and the tribute sent to Lachish are represented as if Hezekiah had dispatched them to Nineveh, implying a triumph of Assyrian arms and the final submission of Judah. The real course of events is, however, perfectly clear, and the accuracy of the Biblical account of Sennacherib's ignominious failure before Jerusalem and of his final retreat has been universally admitted.

With these facts before us, we turn to the "prophetic" narrative of them, in their spiritual import on the theocracy. As regards the history which we have been hitherto reading from the Assyrian monuments, the account in 2 Kings 18:13-19 keeps so parallel with what is written in Isaiah 36, 37, as similarly that in 2 Kings 20, with Isaiah 38 and 39 (with the exception of Hezekiah's hymn of praise, Isaiah 38:9-20), that a connection between the two is apparent. Whether either of them, and which, was derived from the other, are questions which have been differently answered by critics. Probably — for we are dealing in great measure with conjectures — both look back upon a common original, which, in the Book of Kings and in the prophecies of Isaiah, is presented respectively in a manner accordant with the spirit and object of each of those works.

It is another question whether this original account "in the Book of the Kings of Judah and Israel" was not written by the prophet Isaiah himself, as seems indicated in 2 Chronicles 32:32. In any case, the narrative in the Book of Chronicles, which, in accordance with its general spirit, so largely dwells on the Temple reformation of Hezekiah, seems an abbreviated summary of the two other accounts, although containing some notable peculiarities of its own.

The Biblical narrative opens with a brief reference to the first part of the campaign, when Sennacherib detached a corps which laid waste Judah and took the principal towns along the route (2 Kings 18:13; Isaiah 36:1). In 2 Chronicles 32:1-8, the various preparations are also noticed which Hezekiah had made, with advice of "his princes and mighty men," when he felt certain of the danger threatening Jerusalem.

First among them was the cutting off of the water-supply for a besieging army. To the west of Jerusalem runs from north to south the valley of Gihon. The rain-water and that coming from the hills around was stored in two pools, the upper (Isaiah 22:11 — the modern Birket Mamilla), and the lower (Isaiah 22:9 — the modern Pool of the Patriarch), which were connected by an open conduit.

As the upper pool lay outside the city walls}and would supply the wants of a besieging army, Hezekiah covered it in, and by an aqueduct brought its waters into a large reservoir or "lake," "between the two walls" of the upper and the lower city (Isaiah 22:11; comp. 2 Kings 20:20; 2 Chronicles 32:30). But some writers conjecture that in ancient times (although not at present) there may have been a spring or brook near the upper port, which Hezekiah also covered in, diverting its waters into the city (2 Chronicles 32:30). Further, he repaired all the walls that were broken down, "and raised (heightened) upon it (the) towers," and repaired (built?) "the other wall without" — probably that which inclosed the lower city — as well as "Millo, in the city of David," probably a strong tower with fortified buildings at the western side of the Tyropoeon, or Valley of Cheesemongers.

Similarly, arms of defense were prepared and officers appointed. Best of all, he gathered his men and captains, and encouraged them with the chief of all comforts, the assurance that Another, greater and stronger than all the might of Assyria, was with them, not "an arm of flesh," but Jehovah their God, to help them and to fight their battles.

When from this account we turn to the prophetic narrative in Isaiah 22, we feel that it had not been always so (ver. 11), but that through the admonitions of the prophet, what had been at first confidence in the strength of their defenses, became transformed into trust in the living God. Indeed, the prophet could not have sympathized with the whole previous policy of Hezekiah, which led up to the humiliating embassy to Lachish. But now he could bring them the assurance of Divine deliverance in that mood of spiritual repentance which was the outcome of his ministrations, and which appeared most fully during the siege of Jerusalem, and at the later summons for its surrender. We shall have to revert to this when telling of Hezekiah's bearing towards the ambassadors of Merodach-Baladan, who visited the Jewish capital before these events, probably some time before the commencement of this campaign.

The second event recorded in Scripture is the embassy of Hezekiah to Lachish, and the tribute there imposed upon him of "three hundred talents of silver and thirty talents of gold" (2 Kings 18:14-16). The impost, although not greatly differing from that which Menahem had to pay to Tiglath-pileser (2 Kings 15:19), was heavy, amounting in gold to 200,000 pounds, and in silver to 110,000 pounds and it necessitated the surrender of all the treasures in the Temple and the palace. It is remarkable that neither in the prophecy of Isaiah nor in the Book of Chronicles do we find any reference to the embassy of Hezekiah nor to the tribute which he sent. Probably both were viewed as the sequence of a course disapproved, which, however, had no real bearing on the events that followed, and which only because of their spiritual import, came within range of the object of the narrative.

The third event recorded in Holy Scripture is the detachment of the "great host" against Jerusalem, with all the events connected with it. Of this we have an account alike in the Book of Kings, in that of Chronicles, and in the prophecies of Isaiah.

The lead of the Assyrian expedition and the conduct of negotiations were entrusted to the "Tartan," which was the official title of the Assyrian commander-in-chief (comp. Isaiah 20:1), "the Rabh-Saris" — probably the translation of an Assyrian official title, which in Hebrew means "chief of the eunuchs" — and "the Rebh-Shakeh," apparently a Hebrew adaptation of Rab-sak, the Assyrian title of "chief captain," which repeatedly occurs on the monuments, and probably represents the second in command, or chief of the staff. We mark that appropriately the spokesman in summoning the city to surrender was not the general-in-chief, nor the chief eunuch (possibly the political officer), but the Rabh-Shakeh, or second in command.

The wisdom of Hezekiah's preparations, especially in depriving the Assyrians of the water supply, was soon apparent. For it was at that very place — the north-western angle of the city — that the strength of the Assyrian attack was delivered, and it was here, "by the conduit of the upper pool, which is in the highway of the fuller's field," that the three Assyrian leaders met the representatives of King Hezekiah, whom they had summoned to conference. Even had their spiritual preparation been less decisive, all must have felt there was something specially significant in the fact that a speech, such as that which the Rabh-Shakeh made, should have been delivered on the very spot where Isaiah had uttered God's message to Ahaz (Isaiah 7:3). It is impossible to determine at what period of the siege the conference between the two parties took place. But it was probably not long after the arrival of the besieging army. For, although the Rabh-Shakeh refers to the horrors of a protracted siege (2 Kings 18:27), his coarse language sounds rather like a threat of future than an indication of present straits. Besides, Jerusalem may have been shut up for some time before the actual siege, while in any case that free communication with the country must have been interrupted which was necessary for the supply of provisions to the capital. On the other hand, it was of the utmost importance to the Assyrians to gain possession of Jerusalem without delay, and so to set the besieging army free to operate against Egypt. Of two among the three representatives of Hezekiah — no doubt mentioned in the order of their rank (2 Kings 18:18) — we have some characteristic notices in Isaiah 22:15-22. From these we are led to conjecture that Shebna, "the scribe," or secretary — probably the chief private adviser of the king, and who may possibly have been of Syrian descent — was a man actuated by ambition and selfish motives, to whom the mistaken policy of Hezekiah's anti-Assyrian alliance may have been due.

On the other hand, we derive a correspondingly high impression concerning the first and chief representative of the king, Eliakim, the son of Hilkiah. He seems to have succeeded Shebna (comp. Isaiah 22:20, 21) in the office of major domo, which may be compared to that of the modern chef du cabinet, and as such probably stood nearest to the king. Possibly this transference of office may have been consequent on a change of political and religious views. Of Joab, the son of Asaph, the recorder or analyst, we know not anything farther, nor does he appear afterwards among them whom Hezekiah sent to the prophet Isaiah (2 Kings 19:1; Isaiah 37:2). His attendance on the present occasion was probably in his capacity of secretary of state.

Such were the representatives on the one side and the other, who on that eventful day met to set it clearly before Israel and before all men with whom was the might: whether with the arm of flesh, or with Jehovah; and whether or not the people had been right in resting themselves upon the words of Hezekiah, king of Judah (2 Chronicles 32:8).

CHAPTER 12 — HEZEKIAH, (THIRTEENTH) KING OF JUDAH.

Meaning and Lessons of the Account of the Assyrian Invasion.

(2 KINGS 18:17-19)

RARELY, perhaps, was there an occasion on which faith in the unseen was put to severer test than in the conference between the leaders of the Assyrian army and the representatives of King Hezekiah. What gave special point to the message which the Rabh-Shakeh addressed to the king of Judah was the deep sense of past inconsistency: that, as regarded the matter in hand, it had not always been with Judah as at present, and that in measure their present evil was the outcome of their wrong-doing. But there comes to us also for all time this precious lesson: that even where we have been utterly mistaken, if only we turn in repentance to our God, we may look for His help and deliverance in the new and better course on which we are entering, however we may have to suffer for past sin. For God remaineth faithful, however we may have erred and strayed from His ways.

It was only too true, as the Rabh-Shakeh said, that in rebelling against Assyria Hezekiah's confidence had been in Egypt; (compare chapters 9 and 11). Too true also, as even the experience of the past might have taught him, (compare chapters 9 and 11) that this was to trust in "the staff of a bruised reed" (comp. Isaiah 30:1-7).

Thus, assuredly, whether as regarded his plans or their proposed execution, it was "only word of the lips: counsel and strength for the war!" But in the second point which the Rabh-Shakeh urged lay the weakness of his cause and the strength of Hezekiah's position. Addressing himself to Hezekiah's adherents, he argued from the heathen point of view that since Hezekiah had abolished all the altars on the heights, and confined public religious worship to that in the Temple, he had not only forfeited any claim upon Jehovah, Whom he regarded as the Jewish national deity, but provoked Him to judgment. Accordingly, as on the one hand he had taunted Hezekiah with want of all means for resisting the power of his master, so on the other hand he now boldly claimed for the inroad of Assyria and its success, not only the approbation of, but even a mandate from Jehovah.

Alike politically and in its religious misrepresentations, the speech was well calculated to appeal to such a populace as that of Jerusalem. Hence also the representatives of Hezekiah requested the Rabh-Shakeh to communicate with them not in "Jewish" (that is, in Hebrew), as he had done, but in "Aramean," which, although the commercial language of Syria and Palestine, would not be understood by the common people.

The suggestion was haughtily rejected, and the Assyrian openly avowed that his object was not to negotiate with the king nor his representatives, but to produce a reaction among the besieged, whom he represented as reduced to the utmost straits. To them he now directly appealed. They were not to allow themselves to be deceived. Hezekiah would not be able to deliver them — viz., by the aid of Egypt — nor yet was this other pretension well-founded, that Jehovah would deliver them. Rather was it their wisdom to ignore the king, and make a treaty of submission to Assyria, in virtue of which, instead of their present misery, they might continue to enjoy undisturbed possession of their land till they could be transported into districts equally fertile with their own.

This bold avowal of the ultimate policy of Assyria must have marred an appeal otherwise cleverly contrived. But its effectiveness would be completely destroyed — at least with the pious in Israel — by the contemptuous reference to Jehovah, as if He were like the false gods of other nations, who in the past had been unable to deliver the lands of their worshippers from the might of Assyria.

It was an argument calculated, indeed, to influence heathens, to whom the question was as to the comparative power of gods, to be decided by outward results. But the very essence of Hebrew conviction lay in this, that there was none other God than Jehovah. It is this which constitutes the victory over that which is seen, but on which the men of the world ever deceive themselves in their ignorance of the power of a faith which is based on personal experience. And thus what in their view would seem the strongest argument in their appeal to "common sense" is in reality its refutation. It was in this spirit that the people on the wall of Jerusalem obeyed the injunction of Hezekiah, and answered not a word to the Assyrian.

It was wise and right in the representatives of Hezekiah to bring their report of this interview with clothes rent (2 Kings 8:37); wise and right also on the part of the king to share in this token alike of mourning and humiliation (compare 1 Kings 20:32; 2 Kings 6:30), as in a great public calamity. It identified Israel with its LORD, and made public recognition that every blasphemy of Him was a public crime and calamity, and hence a call to public mourning.

It was in such garb that the king went into the Temple to make his appeal to Jehovah. In this garb also did he send his former delegates to the Rabh-Shakeh, together with "the elders," probably the chief officials, of the now reformed priesthood, to Isaiah to bespeak his prayers.

By a proverbial expression he indicated that in the time of Israel's utmost agony they had not strength for deliverance, and were in danger of perishing. But since the words of the Assyrian were a challenge to God, He might "hear" them, and answer the "reproach" by a "rebuke;" therefore let Isaiah pray for the remnant still left. Strange as it may sound, the strength of this plea lay in the sense of felt weakness, which appeared in that the king called upon the prophet not to interpose, but to pray, and even so felt not secure of an answer even to the prophet's prayer, but rested his hope on the nature of the case.

There could not have been greater contrast than between the boastful confidence of the Assyrian in his might and the absolute submission of Hezekiah to the LORD); nor yet could prayer have been the outcome of clearer spiritual perception. Such prayer must have had its answer; and it came in the assurance that this very boastfulness of victory should give place to fear upon a rumor, and this confidence be laid low when "the great king" should "fall by the sword," and that "in his own land."

It was as had been said. The Rabh-Shakeh returned from his bootless expedition to his master, leaving, as we suppose, his army before Jerusalem. He found Sennacherib not at Lachish, but at Libnah, to which he had retreated probably on hearing of the advance of Tirhakah, the king of Ethiopia. As we have seen, Sennacherib gained indeed the victory of Altaku.

But it was a virtual defeat, which, with the failure to gain possession of Jerusalem, determined the final retreat of Sennacherib from Palestine. His circumstances must have made him most anxious to obtain the surrender of the Judaean capital. Accordingly, a second embassy had been dispatched to demand it — probably before the battle of Altaku, although after the approach of the Ethiopian army. This second summons was addressed to Hezekiah, and was in terms similar to those previously used, although it naturally contained no longer any reference to Egypt, and was also perhaps more directly challenging to the God of Israel (2 Kings 19:9-13).

It argues, in our view, a painful want not only of spiritual insight, but even of deeper sympathy, when certain modern critics depreciate the act of Hezekiah in going to the Temple to spread before Jehovah "the letters" of the Assyrian, either as mechanical or as evidence of a lower standpoint. It was not even symbolical, but, as Delitzsch has rightly designated it, a prayer without words — a sublime expression of faith, in entire accordance with what had preceded, and such as in certain events of our lives we might be disposed to imitate, at least in spirit. Still more strange does it seem to find the authenticity of the prayer with which Hezekiah accompanied this submission to the living God, questioned on the ground that the setting aside of all other gods as powerless, being the work of men's hands, and the exclusive acknowledgment of Jehovah were beyond the spiritual range of the time. Surely this is not only arbitrarily to displace the Scriptural records, but on the ground of it to construct a history of Israel, and then to judge events by this self-made standard.

It was only as we would have expected when Isaiah, in the name of his God, and as His representative, made response alike to the letter of the Assyrian and to the prayer of Hezekiah. His utterance consists, as has been rightly observed, of three parts.

In the first (vers. 21-28), the unconquered virgin daughter of Zion addresses to Sennacherib her Divine comment on his boasting; the second part (vers. 29-31) brings the Divine message to Hezekiah and to Judah; while the third (vers. 32-34) contains the prophetic announcement of the issue of this war. From the very outset we mark the attitude of lofty scorn in the contrast between the two adversaries, Sennacherib and the Holy One of Israel on high (ver. 22).

Then, in figurative language, the boast of the Assyrian is presented in vers. 23, 24, in each verse in its twofold aspect: as regarded what he claimed to have already done, and what he declared he would achieve in the future. There had been neither barrier nor resistance to him in the past; there could be no hindrance nor limitation to him in the future. All had been surmounted; all would be at his disposal. But, as against this boast of self-sufficiency, came the Divine question — here Israel's best answer — whether the great king had never "heard" — that is, whether it had never come to his knowledge, nor yet entered his mind — that all his past success had been of God's appointment, and he only the instrument of God's behest in executing pre-ordained judgments.

But since, so far from such acknowledgment of God, Sennacherib had raised himself against the LORD, he would experience alike his own helplessness and the Divine judgment. As a wild beast in the power of its captors, he would, like some of his own captives, be brought back the way which he had come (vers. 28, 29).

In its second part (vers. 30-32) the prophetic utterance turns from Sennacherib to Hezekiah and to Judah. We cannot fail to recognize the internal connection between this and the former utterance in Isaiah 7 in regard to the Syro-Israelitish invasion in the time of Ahaz. Once more we have "a sign" of the certainty of promised deliverance in an event as yet future. The absolute deliverance of Judah from the invasion of Assyria is guaranteed by this sign, that in the present year, when the ordinary operations of sowing had been interrupted, they would have sufficient for their support in that which sprang from the grains that had accidentally fallen out of the corn reaped at the former harvest. Similarly, as regarded the next year's harvest, for which it was impossible to make preparation, partly from the presence of the Assyrian army, and partly from the depopulation of the country, there would be sufficiency from the corn which sprang of itself (either on the old stems or from what dropped from unreaped ears). Lastly, in the third year, the ordinary agricultural operations would be resumed, because the Assyrian host would be gone without retaining occupation of the land, and because such as were left of the population would have returned to their homes from Jerusalem and the other fenced cities where they had sought refuge. Thus "the sign" lay in the promised certainty of their support through the Divine blessing on the land which Assyria boasted to have laid waste (vers. 23, 24).

Nor is it uncommon in fruitful districts of Palestine for a second harvest to spring from the ears of corn left standing in the fields. Thus the provision for their present wants, and that for the agricultural year on which they had already entered, coming to them through the direct blessing of God on a land over which the Assyrian claimed absolute power, would in those two years be a constant sign that the relation between Jehovah and Sennacherib was what had been told, and that they had not to fear any return of the enemy. And so would this prophetic "sign" — "natural" by the special blessing of God, but "supernatural" when viewed by itself — be alike for comfort and the strengthening of faith, but also for the constant exercise of it.

From another point of view also this prophetic utterance connects itself with the earlier prediction in Isaiah 7. Like the latter, it affords insight into the general character and structure of prophecy. Taking its departure from the present condition of things, it points to the full meaning of the prophecy, viewing it in its widening bearing, till in the dim distance it descries its fulfillment in what is the final goal of all prophecy — the Messianic kingdom. Thoughts of the growth of the seemingly scanty yet sufficient fruit left on the fields of Judah, but which in due time, when Judah was restored to quiet homes, would be followed by rich harvests, suggest the higher application to the "remnant escaped," which was yet again to "take root downward, and bear fruit upward." And with yet wider and final application (2 Kings 19:31) does it point forward to "the remnant" according to the election of grace, the faithful remnant, the true Israel (comp. Isaiah 4:2; 6:13; 10:20-23) in the Messianic day, when "the zeal of Jehovah of hosts" should "perform this" (Isaiah 9:7).

Lastly, the third part of Isaiah's utterance (vers. 32-34)is a direct prediction with reference to the threats of Sennacherib and the issue of this war.

Nor was the Divine judgment on Sennacherib long delayed. "In that night" "the angel of Jehovah" went forth to smite in the Assyrian host — probably that which still lay before Jerusalem — "all the mighty men of valor, and the leaders and captains" (2 Chronicles 32:21).

From 2 Samuel 24:15, 16, we are led to infer that, while the judgment was directly sent of God, the means employed was a pestilence. The number of victims amounted to not less than 185,000, although the text does not indicate, and there is certainly no reason for believing that they all fell in one night.

But to the sacred historian it seems from his prophetic view-point but as one unbroken scene in the great drama of judgment, and he pictorially describes it as a field of the slain, on which they looked as they "arose early in the morning." And so the Divine judgment completed what the turn which the campaign had taken had begun. It was only natural that Sennacherib should depart and return to his own land.

But the account in Holy Scripture in this also evidences its historical accuracy, that it describes him as dwelling "at Nineveh." For Sennacherib not only made this his permanent residence, fortified and converted it into his grand imperial fortress, but adorned it with two magnificent palaces.

There is one event in the history of Israel which the Divine judgment on Sennacherib and the deliverance of Judah must recall to every mind. It is Israel's miraculous deliverance at the time of the Exodus and of the destruction of the army of Pharaoh in the waves of the Red Sea (comp. Exodus 14:23-31). Then, as now, was the danger extreme, and it seemed as if Israel were defenseless and powerless before the mighty host of the enemy. Then, as now, was the word of the LORD clear and emphatic; then, as now, it was the night season when the deliverance was wrought; and then, as now, was it Israel's birth-time as a nation. For now, after the final transportation of Israel, did Judah stand forth as the people of the LORD, the inheritors of the promise, the representatives of the kingdom of God. As then, so now was Judah saved without drawing sword or bow, only by the interposition of the LORD. And so it has to all times remained by the side of the miracles of the Exodus as the outstanding event in the typical history of the people of God, perpetuated not only in the later non-canonical literature of Israel, but possibly forming the historical basis of Psalm 46, and more probably that of Psalm 75 and 76.

Yet other thoughts come to us — how the worldly policy of even a Hezekiah in forming alliances against Assyria was rebuked, and he learned in the school of affliction and humiliation to turn from all such help to God, and then obtained mercy; and how from the first Isaiah stood forth faithful in his warnings, and calm and unshaken in his confidence, the true prophet and representative of the LOAD. And yet beyond these lessons, which are to all times, comes to the Church and to every member of it the conviction that He who supernaturally, although by what we call natural means, once swept away the host of Egypt and again laid dead the proud warriors of Assyria, also watches with ever mindful care over the meanest of His creatures, so that not a sparrow can fall to the ground without His knowledge, nor yet any harm befall His people, nor earthly might overthrow His cause. For He of old is the living and the true God.

But as regarded Sennacherib himself, the Divine judgment seemed to slumber a long time. Yet, after many years' reign, it overtook him.

"As he was worshipping in the house of Nisroch his god, . . .[his sons] Adrammelech and Sharezer smote him with the sword, and they escaped into the land of Ararat. And Esarhaddon his son reigned in his stead."

CHAPTER 13 — HEZEKIAH, (THIRTEENTH) KING OF JUDAH —
DATE OF HEZEKIAH'S SICKNESS — ANNOUNCEMENT OF HIS
DEATH — THE PRAYER OF HEZEKIAH — THE DIVINE ANSWER —
MEANING AND LESSONS OF IT. — THE EMBASSY OF MERODACH-
BALADAN AND ITS OBJECT — RECEPTION OF THE ENVOYS BY
HEZEKIAH — THE PROPHET AND THE KING — PROPHECY OF
BABYLON.

(2 KINGS 20; ISAIAH. 38; 39)

THE narrative of Hezekiah's sickness and of the embassy of Merodach-baladan, which in an abbreviated form is also given in the Book of Isaiah (38:1-8, 21, 22; 39) must, on literary grounds and from its position in this history, be regarded as an appendix similar to that added to the account of David's reign in the closing chapters of the Second Book of Samuel.

Whether or not it was taken from a special and distinct record, or else inserted in this place in order not to break the continuity of a narrative which had a spiritual meaning and object of its own, it is certain that the events which it records could not have been posterior to the final departure of Sennacherib from the soil of Palestine.

After that there could not have been occasion for such anxiety in reference to the king of Assyria as to be met by the Divine promise in 2 Kings 20:6; nor could Hezekiah have shown such treasures to the ambassadors of Merodach-baladan, since he had previously stripped himself of them to Sennacherib (2 Kings 18:14- 16), nor yet from what we know of the history of Merodach-baladan could he then have sent such an embassy with the manifest purpose of an alliance against Assyria, nor, finally, would Hezekiah then have encouraged such overtures.

In these circumstances it is a question of historical interest, rather than of practical importance, whether the sickness of Hezekiah or rather the embassy of Merodach-baladan had been during the reign of Sargon or in that of Sennacherib, whether they had preceded the campaign of the former in Palestine, or that of the latter.

The text itself seems to point to the period immediately before the invasion of Sennacherib, since in the time of Sargon Jerusalem was not in such danger as is indicated in the reassuring promise given concerning it (ver. 6). But this is not all. On any theory, the numeral "fifteen" years in the promised addition to the spared life of Hezekiah (ver. 6), must have crept into the text by some mistake.

Admittedly, it would not synchronize with the period of Sennacherib's campaign; while on the other and it is certain that Sargon came into hostile contact with Hezekiah in the second year of his reign (that after the taking of Samaria), that is, in the sixth or seventh, scarcely in the eighth, year of Hezekiah's reign (2 Kings 18:10).

But fifteen years added to this would give at most twenty-two or twenty-three for the reign of Hezekiah, whereas we know that it lasted twenty-nine years (2 Kings 18:2) If, therefore, it is impossible to date the illness of Hezekiah and the embassy in the time of Sargon, we have to assign these events to the period immediately preceding the campaign of

Sennacherib in Palestine. It may have been that the number "fifteen," as that of the years added to the life of Hezekiah, had originally been a marginal remark.

With whomsoever it originated or however it passed into the text, the copyist, annotator, or editor, who regarded the fourteenth year of Hezekiah as that of Sennacherib's invasion (2 Kings 18:13), would naturally deduct this number from twenty-nine, the total of the years of Hezekiah's reign, and so arrive at the number fifteen as that of the years added to the king's life.

But, on the other hand, this also implies that in the view of this early copyist, annotator, or editor, the sickness of Hezekiah and the embassy of Merodach-baladan had immediately preceded the campaign of Sennacherib. The narrative itself offers no special difficulties. As Hezekiah lay sick the prophet Isaiah was directed to go and bid him set his house in order (2 Samuel 17:23), since his illness would terminate fatally.

The announcement was received by the king with the utmost alarm and grief. We have here to remember the less clear views entertained under the Old Testament, before the LORD by His coming and Resurrection had "brought life and immortality to light through the Gospel." Indeed, our own experience teaches the gradual unfolding of truth with our growing capacity for its perception. And any anticipation of fullest truth would neither have been in accordance with the character of the preparatory dispensation and the training under it, nor have done honor to the new Revelation which was to follow. Indeed, even now many of us learn slowly the joy of "departing," nor yet this without constant reference to that which is joined to it, the presence with the Lord, of which they of old knew not. Thus it was neither fatalism nor resignation to the inevitable, but faith, when they laid them down to sleep content with the assurance that sleeping or waking they were still with the LORD, and that it was well in this also to leave themselves implicitly in the hands of the covenant-keeping God. And so we can from every point of view understand it, that the Psalmist should have prayed, "O my God, take me not away in the midst of my days" (Psalm 102:24), and that Hezekiah "turned his face to the wall and prayed. . .and wept with great weeping."

For, assuredly, this being taken away in the midst of his days and of his work, would seem to him not only a mark of God's disfavor, but actual punishment. It is from this point of view, rather than as the expression of self-righteousness, that we regard the language of Hezekiah's plea. And apart from this there was not anything blameworthy either in the wish that his life should be spared, or in the prayer for it, although here also we cannot but mark the lower stand-point of those under the Old Testament. The prayer of Hezekiah, as for the present we simply note, was heard. Before Isaiah had passed "the middle city" he was Divinely directed to return to the king with the message that his request was granted, and to add to the promise of lengthened days the assurance of the safety of the kingdom of David and of Jerusalem in anticipation of those dangers which must have been foreseen as threatening the near future.

Thus far all had been as might have been looked for in the course of this history. But what followed suggests questions of the deepest importance. Isaiah had not only promised Divine healing, but that within the briefest period Hezekiah should once more go up to the Temple — no doubt to return thanks.

Yet he conjoined with this miraculous help the application of a common remedy, when he directed that a lump of figs should be laid on the boil. And as if still further to point the contrast, Hezekiah asked for "a sign" of the promise, and the prophet not only gave it, but allowed him a choice in that which from any point of view implied direct Divine interposition. For evidently Hezekiah asked for such "a sign" as would be a pledge to him of God's direct intervention on his behalf, while, on the other hand, the alternative proposed to him, that the shadow on the steps of the sun-clock of Ahaz, might either move forwards or backwards, forbids any natural explanation of it, such as that of a solar eclipse which Isaiah had either naturally or supernaturally foreknown. Hezekiah chose what to him seemed the more difficult, or rather the more inconceivable alternative — that of the shadow receding ten steps. And in answer to Isaiah's prayer, the "sign" desired was actually given.

It is not difficult to perceive the symbolical significance of this sign. As Isaiah had been commissioned to offer to Ahaz "a sign" of the promised deliverance, and to leave him the choice of it, "either in the depth or in the height above" (Isaiah 7:11), so here a similar alternative was presented to Hezekiah. As Ahaz in his trust in natural means and his distrust of Jehovah had refused, so Hezekiah in his distrust of natural means and trust of Jehovah asked for a sign. And lastly, even as Hezekiah had feared that his life-day would have ended in its mid-day hour, so now, when it was to be lengthened, did the falling shadow climb up again the ten steps to its mid-day mark.

But there are also deeper lessons to be learnt from this history. The change in the announcement of what was to befall Hezekiah, in answer to his prayer, is of eternal meaning. It encourages us "always to pray" — not excluding from the range of our petitions what are commonly called "things temporal." And yet the very idea of prayer also excludes any thought of the absolute certainty of such answer as had been primarily contemplated in the prayer. For prayer and its answer are not mechanically, they are morally connected, just as between Isaiah's promised sign and its bestowal, the prayer of the prophet intervened (2 Kings 20:11). As miracle is not magic, so prayer is not necessitarianism; and on looking back upon our lives we have to thank God as often for prayers unanswered as for prayers answered.

Yet another lesson connected with the change in the message which Isaiah was to bring to Hezekiah has been already noted by Jerome. There is widest bearing in this remark of his (on Ezekiel 33), that it does not necessarily follow because a prophet predicts an event that what he had predicted should happen. "For," as he adds, the prophet "did not predict in order that it might happen, but lest it should happen." And the immutability of God's counsels is not that of fatalism, but depends on the continuance of the circumstances which had determined them.

This may help us to understand another and in some respects more difficult question. Evidently alike the announcement of Hezekiah's untimely death and its revocation were determined by his relation towards God. This would in turn have its important bearing upon the conduct of the king in the coming Assyrian war, which concerned not only Hezekiah personally, but the whole Davidic line and the fate of Judah itself. But the lessons taught the king first by his danger and then by his restoration were precisely those which Hezekiah needed to learn if, obedient to the admonitions of Isaiah, and believing the promise of the LORD, he was consistently to carry out the will of Jehovah amidst the temptations and difficulties of the Assyrian invasion. This, not only because he had had experience of the truth of prophetic promise, but because he had learned, as he could not otherwise have been taught, that God answered prayer; that He was merciful and forgiving, and able to turn aside the most threatening danger, even at the extreme moment. In truth, what was afterwards witnessed in the deliverance of Jerusalem was on a large scale the same that Hezekiah himself had experienced in his healing. Thus the lessons of his recovery were intended as spiritual preparation for what was so soon to follow.

It still remains to refer more particularly to "the sign" itself on the sun-clock of Ahaz. From the circumstance that in the original account in the Book of Kings there is no mention of alteration in the relative position of the sun (as in the poetic quotation in Joshua 10:12, 13), but of a possible descent or ascent of the shadow, and that even this was to be only observable on the step-clock of Ahaz, we infer that, in the view of the writer, "the sign" was local, and hence could not have implied an interference with the regular order of Nature.

The Scriptural narrative conveys only that in that particular place something had occurred which made the shadow on the dial to retrograde, although at the same time we can have no hesitation in saying that this something was Divinely caused.

What this "something" of a purely local character was, we have not the means of ascertaining. Of the various suggestions most probability attaches to that of an extraordinary refraction of the sun-rays, which has been recorded to have produced similar phenomena in other places. If such Divine intervention be called a miracle, we demur not to the idea nor to the designation — though we prefer that of "a sign." But we add that, in a modified sense, Divine interpositions as signs to us are not so unfrequent as some people imagine.

The fame of Hezekiah's healing spread far and wide, with a rapidity not uncommon in the East. It reached a monarch who, especially at that time, was sorely in need of help, Divine or human. Few chapters in history suggest more interesting episodes than that of Merodach-baladan, who contended for the independence and supremacy and for the crown of Babylonia successively with Tiglath-pileser, Sargon, and Sennacherib — and who was by turns successful, vanquished, driven away and restored, and once more a fugitive. This is not the place to give such outline of his history as may be gathered from the notices of Berossus, the Chaldee historian, from the canon of Ptolemy, the Bible, and Assyrian inscriptions.

Suffice it here, that the date of his embassy to Hezekiah must have coincided with a brief period when at the beginning of Sennacherib's reign he once more occupied the throne of Babylonia for six months. It was only natural that in prospect of his conflict with Assyria he should have sought alliances in every quarter, and that the fame of Hezekiah's miraculous healing, of his great wealth and power — all no doubt exaggerated in Eastern fashion — should have induced him to send an embassy to Jerusalem. A diversion there, a possible confederacy against Assyria in the far west, such as was afterwards really formed, would have been of the greatest use to his cause. Equally natural was it, alike with reference to Assyria and to Hezekiah, that such an intention should not have been avowed, nor perhaps the possibility of an alliance formally discussed, till the ambassadors had been able to judge for themselves of the exact state of matters in Jerusalem. And so they went ostensibly to bring to Hezekiah congratulatory letters on his recovery, and "a present." But all parties including Sennacherib on the one side, and the prophet Isaiah on the other — understood the real object of the embassy.

All this fully explains the Biblical narrative. It is not necessary to suppose that the question of a treaty against Assyria was actually discussed between Hezekiah and the envoys of Merodach-baladan. Indeed, as this is not stated in Scripture, it seems unlikely that a treaty had been made or even proposed. In any case, it could not have been carried out, since long before it could have been acted upon Merodach-baladan was driven away. On the other hand, it seems equally clear that Hezekiah, however reticent he may have been, secretly favored the design of the embassy. It was with this view — to give practical evidence of his might — that "Hezekiah hearkened unto them, and shewed them all the house of his precious things, the silver, and the gold, and the spices, and the precious oil, and the house of his armor, and all that was found in his treasures; there was nothing in his house, nor in all his dominion, that Hezekiah shewed them not" (2 Kings 20:13).

It was a disingenuous device when Hezekiah, in answer to the questioning of Isaiah, sought to divert him by a reference to the "far country" whence the ambassadors had come, as if flattering to Jewish national pride, and implying the acknowledged supremacy of Jehovah's power. Such had not been the object of the prophet in asking about the country of these strangers. By eliciting that they had come from Babylon, he would indicate to Hezekiah that his inmost purpose in showing them all his treasures had been read. But to know it was to pronounce the Divine disapprobation of any such alliance against Assyria. This explains the severity of the punishment afterwards denounced upon Hezekiah for an offense which otherwise might have seemed trivial. But this had clearly appeared, that Hezekiah had not learned the lessons which his late danger and God-granted recovery were intended to teach; nor did he learn them otherwise than in the school of extreme anguish, after all his worldly policy had ended in defeat, his land been desolated, and the victorious host of Assyria laid siege to Jerusalem. And this seems to be the meaning of the reference in 2 Chronicles 32:25, 26, to the ungratefulness and the pride of the king after his miraculous recovery, as well as of this other notice (ver. 31), that in the matter of the ambassadors, God had left Hezekiah to himself, to try him, and "know all that was in his heart."

But with God there was not any changeableness. As afterwards Isaiah denounced the alliance with Egypt, so now he spoke the Divine judgment on the hoped-for treaty with Babylon. So far from help being derived from such alliance, Israel's future doom and misery would come from Babylon, and the folly of Hezekiah would alike appear and be punished in the exile and servitude of his descendants. Thus in the sequence of God this sowing of disobedience should be followed by a harvest of judgment. Yet for the present would there be "peace and continuance" — till the measure of iniquity was filled. And Hezekiah acquiesced in the sentence, owning its justice and grateful for its delay. Yet here also we perceive shortcoming. Hezekiah did not reach up to the high level of his father David in circumstances somewhat similar (2 Samuel 24:17), nor was his even the humble absolute submission of Eli of old (1 Samuel 3:18).

But as throughout this history Isaiah appeared as the true prophet of God by the consistency of his utterance of the Divine Will against all heathen alliances, by his resistance to all worldly policy, however specious, and even by his bearing on the twofold occasion which forms the subject of the present narrative, so did he now rise to the full height of his office. Never before had there been so unmistakable a prediction of the future as when Isaiah in the full height of Assyria's power announced that the world-empire of the future would not belong to it, but to vanquished Babylonia, and that Judah's judgment would not come from their present dreaded enemies, but from those who now had sought their alliance.

CHAPTER 14 — MANASSEH (FOURTEENTH), AMON (FIFTEENTH), KINGS OF JUDAH — POPULAR MOURNING FOR HEZEKIAH — ACCESSION OF MANASSEH — TEMPTATIONS AND CHARACTER OF THE KING — IDOLATRY AND CRUELTY OF HIS REIGN — MORAL STATE OF THE PEOPLE — PROPHETIC ANNOUNCEMENT OF JUDGMEN — SUPPLEMENTARY NARRATIVE IN THE BOOK OF CHRONICLES — ITS RELIABLENESS CONFIRMED BY THE ASSYRIAN INSCRIPTIONS — THE CAPTIVITY OF MANASSEH IN BABYLON — HIS REPENTANCE AND PRAYER — HIS RESTORATION TO JERUSALEM — SUPERFICIAL CHARACTER OF HIS REFORMATION — HIS DEATH — REIGN OF AMON.

(2 KINGS 21; 2 CHRONICLES 33)

WITH the death of Hezekiah, another and a strange chapter in Jewish history opens. When they buried him "in the ascent of the sepulchers of the sons of David," not only the inhabitants of Jerusalem — for the defense, adornment, and convenience of which he had done so much — but all Judah united to do him honor.

His reign, despite temporary reverses and calamities, had been prosperous for his country, and he left it in political circumstances far different from those when he had ascended the throne. Above all, his history might have been full of most important theocratic teaching to the people. If it was otherwise, we see in this only fresh evidence of that spiritual decay of which the prophets, in their description of the moral condition of the people, give so realistic a picture.

Manasseh was only twelve years old when he succeeded his father. According to our Western notions, he would have to be regarded as merely a child.

But in the East he would at that age have reached the most dangerous period of wakening manhood, before thought could have tempered willfulness, or experience set bounds to impulse. In such circumstances, to have resisted the constant temptation and incitement to gratify every will and desire, would have required one of strong moral fibber. But Manasseh was selfish and reckless, weak and cruel in his wickedness, and scarcely respectable even in his repentance. When the infant Jehoash acceded to the throne, he had the benefit of the advice of Jehoiada (2 Kings 12:2), and we know how his later and independent reign disappointed its early promise. But Manasseh had not any such guidance. The moral and religious corruption in his grandfather's reign, must, as we infer from the prophetic writings, be regarded as not only the outcome, but also partly the explanation of the measures of Ahaz. This condition of things could not have been effectually checked during Hezekiah's reign of twenty-nine years, especially amidst the troubles and the disorganization connected with the Assyrian invasion. In fact, we know that even among the intimate counselors of Hezekiah, there were those whom the prophetic word emphatically condemned (comp. Isaiah 22:15-19; 29:14-16; 30:1, 9- 14).

In these circumstances the sudden re-action and the "counter-reformation" of Manasseh's reign, in which he, apparently, carried the people with him, cannot appear altogether strange or surprising. Briefly, it was a kind of heathen ideal of religion in which various forms of national idolatry were combined. The corrupt mode of Jehovah-worship on "the heights" was restored. To this were added the Phoenician rites of Baal and Asherah, which Ahab had introduced in Israel, and the Assyro-Chaldean worship of the stars. All this was carried to its utmost sequences. In the Temple, on which Jehovah had put His thrice Holy Name, and which, as a firm and lasting abode in contrast to the Tabernacle, symbolized the permanence of His dwelling in the midst of Israel, and their permanence in the land, Manasseh built altars to the host of heaven, placing them in the outer and inner courts. Nay, in the sacred "house" itself, he set up the vilest of idols: "the graven image of the Asherah," whose worship implied all that was lascivious. Conjoined with this was the institution of a new priesthood, composed of them that had familiar spirits, and "wizards," while the king himself practiced divination and enchantment.

And as usual, together with all this, (Compare Deuteronomy 18:10, 11.) the service of Moloch, with its terrible rite of passing children through the fire, was not only encouraged by the example of the king (2 Kings 21:6; 2 Chronicles 33:6), but apparently came into general practice (2 Kings 23:10). Alike the extent and the shameless immorality of the idolatry now prevalent, may be inferred from the account of the later reformation by Josiah (2 Kings 23:4- 8). For, whatever practices may have been introduced by previous kings, the location, probably in the outer court of the Temple, of a class of priests, who, in their unnaturalness of vice, combined a species of madness with deepest moral degradation, and by their side, and in fellowship with them, that of priestesses of Astarte, must have been the work of Manasseh.

We know that some such abominations formed part of the religious rites, not only of the inhabitants of Canaan, but of the Babylonians.

On the other hand, we can scarcely avoid the inference that these forms of idolatry were chiefly encouraged for the sake of the vices connected with them. Thus it involved not only religious, but primarily moral degeneracy. Yet, as might be expected, there was also spiritual protest and a moral reaction against all this. Prophetic voices were heard announcing the near doom of a king and people more wicked than the Canaanites of old. But it is significant that the names of these Divine messengers are not mentioned here.

In truth, it was a time of martyrdom, rather than of testimony. There may be exaggeration in the account of Josephus, that Manasseh killed all the righteous among the Hebrews, and spared not even the prophets, but every day slew some among them (Ant. x. 3, 1); and only a basis of historical truth may underlie the Jewish tradition, which was adopted by the Fathers, that by command of Manasseh Isaiah was sawn asunder in a cedar-tree, in which he had found refuge. But Holy Scripture itself relates that Manasseh had filled Jerusalem "from end to end" with innocent blood.

As we have already marked, these sins were national, and this in a more special sense than merely the identification of a nation with its rulers and their public acts. As this condition of the people was not exceptional, but the outcome of a long course, so the Divine judgments were to be cumulative, extending back from the first beginning to the present stage of guilt (2 Kings 21:15). And commensurate not only with the sin of Israel, but with their utter unfaithfulness to the meaning and purpose of their calling, would be the coming evil.

In the figurative language of Scripture, the desolation of Jerusalem would be as complete as that of Samaria and of the house of Ahab — as it were, a razing to the ground, so that the builder might stretch over it the measuring line and apply the plummet, as if not anything had stood there (comp. Isaiah 34:11; Lamentations 2:8; Amos 7:7-9). Nay, Jerusalem would be thoroughly emptied and cleansed, as a dish that was wiped, and then turned upside down.

For Judah — the remnant of what had been the inheritance of God — would be cast off, and surrendered to their enemies for "a prey and a spoil" (2 Kings 21:12-14). Here the history of Manasseh abruptly breaks off in the Book of Kings, to be resumed and supplemented in that of Chronicles (2 Chronicles 33:11- 20). This in itself is noticeable, first, as casting fresh light on the "prophetic" character of the history as presented in the Books of the Kings, and, secondly, as attesting the historical value of those of Chronicles. In the Books of the Kings, the writer, or compiler, gives not the annals of a reign, nor the biographies of kings and heroes; but groups together such events as bear on the Divine issues of this history, in relation to the calling of Israel. This explains not only the brief summary of the longest reign in Judah or Israel — that of Manasseh, which lasted fifty-five years — but specifically the omission of what he had done for the defense of Jerusalem and Judah (2 Chronicles 33:14), as well as of his captivity, his repentance, return to his capital, and reformation. For these defenses of Judah were useless; the captivity of Manasseh was temporary; and his reformation was, as we shall see, only superficial. But rarely has the skepticism of a certain school of critics received more severe rebuke than in regard to the doubts which on internal grounds have been cast — and that not long ago — on the credibility of the narrative in 2 Chronicles 33:11- 20.

It was called in question for this reason, that, in view of the silence of the Book of Kings, there was not ground for believing that the Assyrians exercised supremacy in Judah — far less that there had been a hostile expedition against Manasseh; and because, since the residence of the Assyrian kings was in Nineveh, the reported transportation of Manasseh to Babylon (ver. 11) must be unhistorical. To these were added, as secondary objections, that the unlikely account of a king transported in iron bonds and fetters was proved to be untrustworthy by the still more incredible notice that such a captive had been again restored to his kingdom. Eminently specious as these objections may seem, they have been entirely set aside by the evidence from the Assyrian inscriptions, the preservation of whose testimony is here specially providential. Unfortunately, the lessons which might have been learned in regard to skepticism on "internal grounds" have had little influence.

Of the supremacy of Assyria over Judah in the time of Manasseh, there cannot be any doubt, notwithstanding the silence of the Book of Kings. In a list of twenty-two subject kings of "the land Chatti," in the reign of Esarhaddon, whom that monarch summoned, appears expressly the name of Minasi sar mat (ir) Jaudi, Manasseh, king of Judah.

But the capture of Manasseh by the Assyrian captains, and his deportation to Babylon, recorded in 2 Chronicles 33:11, seems to have taken place not in the reign of Esarhaddon, but in that of his successor, Asurbanipal (the Sardanapalus of classical writers), when his brother Samas-sum-ukln, the viceroy of Babylon, involved among other countries also Phoenicia and Palestine in his rebellion. And although the ordinary residence of Asurbanipal was in Nineveh, we have not only reason to believe that after his assumption of the dignity of king of Babylon, he temporarily resided in that city, but monumental evidence of it in his reception there of ambassadors with tributary presents. Lastly, we find the exact counterpart alike of this, that Manasseh was carried to Babylon with "hooks," and "bound in fetters," and then afterwards restored to his kingdom, in the Assyrian record of. precisely the same mode of deportation and of the same restoration by Asurbanipal of Necho of Egypt.

Holy Scripture tracing this restoration — not, as in the Assyrian inscription, to its secondary cause "the mercy of the king" — but to its real source, connects it with the repentance and prayer of Manasseh in his distress (2 Chronicles 33:12, 13). That in such circumstances the son of Hezekiah, with the remembrance of the Divine deliverance of his father in his mind, should have recognized the folly and guilt of his conduct, humbled himself, and prayed unto the LORD — seems so natural as scarcely to require confirmation.

Yet there is such, at least of his return to Jerusalem, in the historical notice of his additions to the fortifications of Jerusalem (2 Chronicles 33:14). And if his abolition of the former idolatry, and restoration of the service of Jehovah, seem not consistent with the measures that had afterwards to be adopted by his grandson Josiah, we have to remember that between them intervened the wicked reign of Amon; that Manasseh seems rather to have put aside than destroyed idolatry; and that the sacred text itself indicates the superficiality and incompleteness of his reformation (2 Chronicles 33:17).

The events just recorded must have taken place near the close of this reign, which extended over the exceptional period of fifty-five years. As Holy Scripture refers to his sins as extreme and permanent instance of guilt (2 Kings 23:26; 24:3; Jeremiah 15:4), so, on the other hand, Jewish tradition dwells upon the repentance of Manasseh and the acceptance of his prayer, as the fullest manifestation of God's mercy, and the greatest encouragement to repentant sinners. And, in truth, the threatened judgment upon Jerusalem was deferred for more than half a century. So it was in peace that Manasseh laid himself to sleep. He was buried in a garden attached to his palace, which popularly bore the name of "the garden of Uzza."

That the reformation made by Manasseh could only have been superficial, appears also from the record of the brief reign of his son and successor Amon. Indeed, some writers have seen a picture of that period in certain of the utterances of Zephaniah, although he prophesied during the reign of Josiah.

Amon was twenty-four years old at his accession, and his rule only lasted two years. It was marked by the resumption of the idolatry of Manasseh — apparently in an even aggravated form (2 Chronicles 33:23). A palace-conspiracy put an end to his life. As on a former occasion (2 Kings 14:20, 21), "the people of the land" secured the Davidic succession by proclaiming Josiah, the youthful son of Amen, heir to his throne.

CHAPTER 15 — JOSIAH, (SIXTEENTH) KING OF JUDAH — ACCESSION OF JOSIAH — HIS EARLY LIFE — ARRANGEMENT OF THE NARRATIVE — COLLECTION FOR REPAIR OF THE TEMPLE — THE REMNANT OF ISRAEL — CHARACTER OF THOSE EMPLOYED — THE REFORMATION NOT THE OUTCOME OF A GENERAL RELIGIOUS REVIVAL — TEMPLE REPAIRS — THE FINDING OF THE BOOK OF THE LAW — THE PROPHETESS HULDAH — THE ASSEMBLY AND COVENANT IN THE TEMPLE — DESTRUCTION OF THE EMBLEMS OF IDOLATRY IN JERUSALEM, JUDAH, AND IN THE NORTHERN TRIBAL POSSESSIONS — FULFILLMENT OF ANCIENT PROPHECY REGARDING BETHEL — THE GREAT PASSOVER IN JERUSALEM.

(2 KINGS 22; 23:1-23; 2 CHRONICLES 34; 35:1-19.)

JOSIAH was only eight years old when he succeeded to the royal dignity. As his extreme youth would withdraw him from the influences and temptations to which Manasseh had been exposed at his accession, so it must have necessitated the tutorship, or at least guidance, of men to whom, as generally venerated, a royal child would be entrusted. That such there were, we infer from the revival of prophecy, as represented by a Huldah, a Jeremiah, and a Zephaniah; from the notices we have of some whom we afterwards find surrounding the king; and, lastly, from the bearing of the priesthood under their chief Hilkiah.

Nor, indeed, could the lessons of the reign of Hezekiah, and even of that of Manasseh, have been wholly effaced during the brief rule of Amon. Such men as they, under whose auspices afterwards the reformation of Josiah was carried out, could have had no difficulty in showing the youthful king how the brightest memories of the royal house of Judah were associated with the names of David, Jehoshaphat, and Joash, Uzziah, and Hezekiah, and that the times of greatest national prosperity had been those of faithful and earnest allegiance to Jehovah and His service.

These are indeed mainly inferences; but they are grounded on the facts of this history, and explain them. Nor can we help thinking that even the early birth of an heir to the crown, implying as it does a royal marriage at the early age of thirteen, may here be of significance (comp. 2 Kings 22:1 with 23:36). But the whole history of Josiah's reign is of such importance, and it raises so many questions, that, for clearness' sake, it seems better to discuss separately its religious and its political aspect, so far as this is possible.

First and foremost in this reign stand the measures of religious reformation inaugurated by Josiah. These comprise the preliminary abolition of idolatry; the repair of the Temple; the discovery in it of the Book of the Law; the consequent national reformation by the king; and, lastly, the solemn national observance of the Passover. We have stated the events in the order of their time, and as given in the Book of Kings, from which the arrangement in the Book of Chronicles differs only in appearance. Each of these two accounts relates, with different circumstantiality, one or other of the events mentioned — in each case in accordance with the different view-point of the writers, to which reference has frequently been made. Thus the main topic in the Book of Kings is the religious reformation, alike in its positive aspect as regarded the Temple, the Law, and national Religion (2 Kings 22:3; 23:3), and in its negative aspect in the abolition of idolatry (2 Kings 23:4-20). On the other hand, the chronicler records at greatest length, and with fullest detail, the Paschal observance (2 Chronicles 35:1- 19), while he passes very briefly over what might appear as of graver importance (2 Chronicles 34:4-7).

This will explain what otherwise might have seemed a difficulty in the arrangement of the narrative. The account both in the Book of Kings and in Chronicles places the Temple restoration "in the eighteenth year of king Josiah." But in the former the record of the religious reformation begins with this event, while the chronicler prefaces it by a very brief summary of what had previously been done for the abolition of idolatry (2 Chronicles 34:3-7). That something of this kind must have preceded the restoration of the Temple seems evident. It cannot be supposed that a monarch like Josiah should for seventeen years have tolerated all that Amon had introduced, and then, in his eighteenth year, suddenly proceeded to the sweeping measures which alike the writers of Kings and of Chronicles narrate. It is, therefore, only reasonable to accept the statement of the latter, that "in the eighth year of his reign, while he was yet young" [in his sixteenth year — when presumably he commenced personally to administer the government], king Josiah "began to seek after the God of David his father," and that "in the twelfth year he began to purge Judah and Jerusalem" from their idolatry (2 Chronicles 34:3).

And then the chronicler, who, as we have stated, makes only briefest reference to the reformation described with such detail in 2 Kings 23:4-20, at once adds to the mention of the initial measures towards the abolition of idolatry a summary of what was finally done in that direction, after the restoration of the Temple and in consequence of the discovery of the Book of the Law (vers. 4-7). That such is really the purport of the narrative appears also from the reference at the close of the account of the Temple restoration in 2 Chronicles 34:33, which synchronizes with 2 Kings 23:4.

It was only natural that such preliminary measures as the chronicler relates should have been followed by, as indeed they must have stood in connection with, the restoration of the Temple and its services. This was done in the eighteenth year of Josiah's reign. Nearly two and a half centuries had passed since the former restoration by Joash (2 Kings 12:4-16), and the sacred building must have greatly suffered under the idolatrous kings, especially during the late reigns of Manasseh and Amon. As the restoration was naturally on the same lines with the previous one under Joash, the two accounts are necessarily similar. The collections for the Temple repairs, to which reference is made, must have begun some years previously (2 Kings 22:4) — perhaps so early as the eighth year of the king's reign. But what specially interests us is that contributions came not merely from Judah, but from the Israelitish inhabitants of what had been the kingdom of Israel (2 Chronicles 34:9). This indicates not only a religious movement among them, such as previously in the time of Hezekiah, (Compare 2 Chronicles 30:1, 18.) but that politically also the remnant of Israel in the land was drawn into a hopeful alliance with Judah. Yet further insight into the character of the reformation now begun comes from the history of some of those whom the king employed, either now or later, in connection with it. Foremost among them is Hilkiah, the high priest, the father or grandfather of Seraiah (1 Chronicles 6:13, 14; Nehemiah 11:11) who was high-priest at the time of the captivity (2 Kings 25:18), and an ancestor of Ezra (Ezra. 7:1). Again, chief among those whom Josiah sent to Hilkiah, was Shaphan the Scribe (2 Kings

22:3), the father of Gemariah, the protector of Jeremiah (Jeremiah 36:10, 19, 25), and grandfather of Micaiah (Jeremiah 36:20-13).

Of the personages afterwards mentioned 1 Kings 22:14), we have definite notices about Ahikam (the son of another Shaphan), who protected Jeremiah (Jeremiah 26:24), and was the father of Gedaliah (2 Kings 25:22); and about Achbor, the father of Elnathan, one of those among "the princes of Judah" who vainly endeavored to prevent the burning of the prophetic roll dictated to Baruch by Jeremiah (Jeremiah 36:12). Scanty as these notices are, they leave the impression that Josiah had surrounded himself with men embued, on the whole, with a true religious spirit.

This inference is the more important in view of the general state of the people. The whole history leads to the conviction that the reformation inaugurated by Josiah, although submitted to, and apparently shared in by the people, was not the outcome of a spiritual revival. It was a movement on the part of the king rather than of the nation. Of this we have only too much confirmation in the account which the prophets give of the moral and religious condition of the people, and of the evidently superficial and chiefly external character of the reformation.

And as we derive our knowledge of it from the pages of Jeremiah, we bear in mind that the beginning of his prophetic activity, in the thirteenth year of Josiah (Jeremiah 1:2), synchronized with the commencement of the reformatory movement. Thus we further understand why the changes inaugurated, however extensive, could not avert, as the prophetess Huldah announced, the Divine judgment from the nation, but only from their king (2 Kings 22:14-20). A reformation such as this could be but transient, and the people hastened only the more rapidly to their final apostasy.

It was during the extensive repairs in the Temple that a discovery was made of the greatest influence on the movement about to begin, and which has, especially of late, been connected with some important critical questions regarding the Pentateuch. As we read in Holy Scripture, the high priest Hilkiah informed "Shaphan the Scribe," that he had "found the book of the law (in 2 Chronicles 34:14: "the book of the law of the LORD, by the hand of Moses") in the house of the LORD" (2 Kings 22:8). This book Hilkiah gave to Shaphan. Its perusal led Shaphan not only to inform the king of it, but to read the book to him. On this Josiah "rent his clothes," in token of mourning for the guilt which Israel had incurred in their long absolute breach of its commandments.

Into the complicated questions, What was the exact compass of this special book (whether it comprised the whole Pentateuch, or what parts of it), and again, What was the date of this copy, and how it came to be found in the Temple — the present is not the place to enter. On some points, however, all sober-minded and reverent inquirers will be at one. Assuredly the finding of the book was not a fraud on the part of Hilkiah, nor yet the book itself a forgery, either by Hilkiah or any priest or prophet of that or the immediately preceding period.

Assuming, as there is every reason to do, that certainly it contained the Book of Deuteronomy, and probably also other portions, if not the whole, of the Law, we cannot imagine any reasonable motive on the part of the priesthood, and still less of the prophets, for the invention of such a book.

And plainly it must have been accepted and its genuineness attested by Jeremiah, who at that time had already been five years in the prophetic office. The further question of the precise contents of the book is both difficult of discussion and not of great practical importance. Irrespective of the time which the reading of the whole Pentateuch would have occupied (comp. here 2 Kings 23:2), the wording of Holy Scripture scarcely conveys in the first instance that the Book comprised the strictly historical portions of the Pentateuch (such as Genesis), but, as we expressly read, "the Book of the Covenant," and "the Book of the Law."

The latter expression leads us in the present case to think, first of all, of that aspect of the law which specially affected the people, and the breach of which entailed the national judgment that Huldah had announced, and the apprehension of which had caused such consternation to the king. If so, we should perhaps not have to think in the first place of those ritual ordinances found in the central portions of the Pentateuch, which are now commonly called the "Priest Code." These would chiefly affect the priesthood, nor perhaps could the people have followed with complete understanding the mere reading of their complicated ritual details. Besides, the previous history has furnished us with sufficient instances to show that, unlike the Law, the provisions and ordinances of the "Priest Code" must have been well known.

On the other hand, the main contents of the Book of the Law read in hearing of the people must have concerned the whole fundamental relation between Israel and Jehovah. Hence we conclude that it must have contained, besides the Book of Deuteronomy, at any rate those portions of the Pentateuch which related to the same all-important subject. Beyond these suggestions, which are necessarily in the nature of conjectures, we cannot here discuss this question. But on the main points we cannot have any hesitation. In Deuteronomy 31:25, 26, we find directions for depositing the Book of the Law in the innermost Sanctuary, as indeed might have been expected. That in the various troubles, when during many reigns the Mosaic law and order of worship were so often set aside, "the book" should have been removed and hidden by pious hands, and so for a time have become lost, can as little surprise us as its finding during the thorough repairs of the Temple.

And whatever the compass of this special book, the whole context shows, on the one hand, that it implies the embodiment of the Mosaic law in the Pentateuch, and, on the other, that the existence of that law was generally known and universally admitted as primitive, derived from the great Lawgiver himself, valid, and Divine.

We can now understand how, on hearing "the words of the Book of the Law," the king had "rent his clothes" and "sent to inquire of the LORD" both concerning himself. and his people. For such breach of the covenant and the law, as he now knew Israel to have been guilty of, must involve signal judgment. In the execution of the king's behest, they whom he sent, including the high-priest, addressed themselves to Huldah, "the prophetess," the wife of Shallum, "the keeper of the wardrobe," who "dwelt in Jerusalem, in the second town." This part of the city is also designated "the mortar" (Zephaniah 1:10, 11) — in the first place, probably, from its shape, being in the hollow of the valley, and surrounded by rising ground.

It probably formed the first addition to the old city which the increase of the population must have rendered necessary even in the time of Solomon.

It occupied the upper part of the Tyropoeon valley west of the Temple area, and north of "the middle city," and was the great business quarter, containing the markets, the bazaars, and homes of the industrial population. This may imply a comparatively humble outward position of "the prophetess." Why a Jeremiah or a Zephaniah should not have been sought — whether they were not in Jerusalem or from other reasons it is impossible to conjecture. But that such a deputation should have unhesitatingly addressed itself at such a crisis and in a matter so important to a woman, not only indicates the exceptional position which Huldah occupied in general opinion — by the side of and even above the two other Old Testament prophetesses, Miriam (Exodus 15:20) and Deborah (Judges 4:4) — but also casts light on the spiritual relations under the Old Testament, and on the religious conditions of the time.

Above all, it shows with what absolute freeness the Spirit of God selected the instruments which He employed in the execution of the Divine behests (comp. Joel 2:28, 29).

The plain and faithful words in which the prophetess announced the coming judgment (2 Kings 22:14-20) give a new and deeper meaning to the assembly of priests, prophets, and people from Jerusalem and from all parts of the land whom Josiah gathered to hear "the words of the book of the covenant which was found in the house of the LORD" (2 Kings 23:2).

Evidently in all that he did, the king was actuated by higher motives than merely the wish to avert punishment. In the Temple a solemn national "covenant" was made — no doubt, by the people expressing their assent to the law as binding upon them. In consequence of this, immediate measures were taken under the supervision of the high-priest and his subordinates (2 Kings 23:4) for the removal of all the emblems of idolatry which had defiled the Temple. The various "vessels made for Baal and for the Asherah, and for all the host of heaven" were burnt (comp. Deuteronomy 7:25; 12:3), "in the fields of Kidron, north-east of the city (comp. Jeremiah 31:40). Next, the Kemarim, or non-Levitical priesthood, that officiated whether at the high places, or at the various shrines of idolatry, were "put down." Thus the vile idol of Asherah was brought out from the sanctuary which it had desecrated, burnt by the brook Kidron, its ashes stamped to powder, and further to mark its profanation scattered over the common burying-place. Lastly, the houses erected in close proximity to the Temple itself, for the lowest form of frenzied heathen degradation, were broken down.

But these measures were not limited to the removal of idolatry from the Temple, and of the non-Levitical priesthood from office. Beside the Kemarim there were those of Levitical descent — Kohanim, or priests — who had celebrated an unlawful worship at the high places throughout Judah. These unworthy members of the priesthood were brought to Jerusalem and declared unfit for strictly priestly service in the Temple, although not deprived of what to many must have been the only means of subsistence.

At the same time any resumption of the former unlawful services was rendered impossible by the destruction of all the high places. Chief among these, as the common resort of those who passed in or came out of the city, were "the high places of the gates: that at the entrance of the gate of Joshua the governor of the city, [as well as] that at the left of a man, in the city-gate."

Similarly Topheth was permanently defiled. The sacred horses dedicated by previous kings to the sun, and perhaps used in processional worship, were "put away," and the sun-chariots burned. The altars, alike those on the roof of the Aliyah of Ahaz, and those set up by Manasseh in the two courts of the Temple, were broken down, their debris "made to run down from thence," and the dust of them cast into the Kidron.

Nor was this all. Outside Jerusalem, on the southern point of the Mount of Olives, there appear still to have been remains of even more ancient idolatry, which dated from the time of Solomon. These were now removed, and the places desecrated. And beyond Judah proper the movement extended throughout the ancient kingdom of Israel, even to the remotest northern tribal possession of Naphtali (2 Chronicles 34:6). This again affords indication of an approximation between the Israelitish inhabitants left in what had been the northern kingdom and Judah. And in the increasing weakness of the Assyrian empire, alike

Josiah and the Israelitish remnant may have contemplated a reunion and restoration under a king of the house of David. At any rate the rulers of Assyria were not in a condition to interfere in the affairs of Palestine, nor to check the influence which Josiah exercised over the northern tribes. On the other hand, we can understand that the measures against former idolatry should have been all the more rigorously carried out in the ancient Israelitish kingdom, which had so terribly suffered from the consequences of former apostasy (comp. 2 Kings 23:20). In Beth-el itself, the original seat of Jeroboam's spurious worship, not only was the altar destroyed, but the high place — that is, the sanctuary there — was burned, as also the Asherah, which seems to have taken the place of the golden call But as they proceeded further publicly to defile the altar in the usual manner by burning upon it dead men's bones, Josiah espied among the sepulchers close by — perhaps visible from where he stood — the monument of the prophet of old sent to announce, in the high-day of the consecration of that altar, the desolation which should lay it waste (comp. 1 Kings 13:1, 2).

But while they rifled the graves of an idolatrous people, they reverently left untouched the sepulcher which held the bones of the man of God from Judah, and by their side those of his host, the prophet of Beth el. And so literally did the judgment announced of old come to pass, that the bodies of the idol-priests were slain upon the altars at which they had ministered. And not only in Beth-el, but in the furthest cities of Samaria — as the chronicler graphically and pathetically puts it (2 Chronicles 34:6), "in their ruins round about" — was judgment executed, and even more severely than according to the letter of the Deuteronomic law (Deuteronomy 17:2- 5); for the representatives of the old idolatry were not only stoned, but slain "upon the altars."

It is with almost a sense of relief that we turn from scenes like these to the celebration of the Passover at Jerusalem by a people now at least outwardly purified and conformed to the Mosaic law. Of this festival, and the special mode of its observance, a full account is given in the Book of Chronicles (2 Chronicles 35:1-19). This only need here be said, that whether as regards the circumstances of king and people, or the manner of the Paschal observance, "surely there was not kept such a Passover from the days of the Judges that judged Israel, nor in all the days of the kings of Israel, nor of the kings of Judah" (2 Kings 23:22).

CHAPTER 16 — JOSIAH (SIXTEENTH), JEHOAHAZ (SEVENTEENTH), JEHOIAKIM (EIGHTEENTH), KINGS OF JUDAH — RETROSPECT — POLITICAL HISTORY — POSSIBLE REUNION OF JUDAH AND ISRAEL — THE FALL OF THE ASSYRIAN EMPIRE — INCURSION OF THE SCYTHIANS — REVOLT AND INDEPENDENCE OF BABYLONIA — THE EXPEDITION OF PHARAOH NECHO — RESISTANCE OF JOSIAH TO HIS PROGRESS — BATTLE OF MEGIDDO — DEATH AND BURIAL OF JOSIAH — APPOINTMENT, DEPOSITION, AND CAPTIVITY OF JEHOAHAZ — ACCESSION OF JEHOIAKIM — TRIBUTE TO EGYPT.

(2 KINGS 23:29-36; 2 CHRONICLES 35:20; 36:5.)

THE observant student of this history must have been impressed with the seemingly strange fact that, at the final crisis in the history of Judah, when that kingdom was hastening to its fall, monarchs of such opposite religious tendencies as Ahaz and Hezekiah, Amon and Josiah, should have succeeded one another. And it reflects most unfavorably on the moral and religious condition of the people that each reformation should, within so short a period, have been followed by a counter-reformation. On the other hand, it must be felt how gracious had been the divine dealing when, in succession to monarchs who, as we cannot but think, too truly represented the real state of the nation, pious kings were raised up, as if to give space for tardy repentance and recovery. Even the history of Manasseh would, in that sense, almost seem to have borne a symbolic meaning. But especially does the mind dwell on the administration of Josiah, with its very significant re-discovery and re-publication of the Law of Moses. As neither before nor after him was there any king whose heart was so "tender," and who so humbled himself before Jehovah (2 Kings 22:19), nor yet any who so "turned to Jehovah with all his heart, and with all his soul, and with all his might, according to all the law of Moses" (2 Kings 23:25) — so we must surely regard his upraising at that crisis, his bearing, and his rule as of direct Divine grace and interposition.

It is when taking into wider consideration these two facts — regarding the people and the king — that we fully understand the Divine sentence of judgment upon Jerusalem and Judah (2 Kings 23:26, 27), and the personal mercy extended to Josiah (2 Kings 22:20). We have been hitherto occupied with the most important measures of his reign — that public religious reformation which had as its necessary sequence the abolition of private idolatrous practices (2 Kings 23:24). But the political history of the time is also of deepest interest.

Reference has already been made to the approximation between Judah and the remnant of Israel left in the northern kingdom. All indications point to the inference that hopes were entertained, if not plans actually formed, of a possible re-union of the two kingdoms under the sway of Josiah. Thus, just as the independent existence of Judah was about to cease, the national prospects might seem to human view more promising than for centuries past. The disappointment of these hopes must have shown that, even as Israel had at the first held the land, not by the power of man, but by the Divine appointment, so would no combination, however hopeful, succeed in restoring what only the God of Israel could bestow. And this has its lessons for the future, as well as in the past.

It has already been stated that Assyria was no longer able to suppress any attempts at independent action in Palestine. Under the brilliant but cruel reign of Asurbanipal (the son of Ezar-haddon) Assyria had reached the highest point of its might; but with it also commenced the decay of the cumbrous empire. Its beginning may be dated from the rebellion of Sammughes (Saosduchin, i.e., Samul-sum-iskun), the brother of Asurbanipal and viceroy of Babylon. That rebellion was indeed crushed, and its author perished in the flames, the victor himself assuming the crown of Babylon. But already other forces were in the field. Elam-Persia, the latest conquest of Assyria, rose in rebellion. These armies were indeed vanquished in two or rather three wars; but from the east the Medes invaded Assyria. The attack was unsuccessful, and cost the Median king, Phraortes, his life. But over Western Asia and far down to Egypt the power of Assyria was lost. And from the north of the Black Sea, from the steppes of Russia, the Scythians swept down and overran the country to the shores of the Mediterranean, and down to the borders of Egypt. There Psammetichus succeeded in buying them off, and the majority of the barbarians returned northwards. Some writers have supposed that they came into conflict with Josiah, and that Jeremiah 4:5-6:30, as well as some of the utterances of Zephaniah, refer to this, and that the presence of the invaders was perpetuated in the later name of Scythopolis for Beth-Shean. But this is, to say the least, doubtful. When, after many years, the Medes succeeded in finally repelling the Scythians, Assyria was utterly exhausted, and the fall of Nineveh at hand.

But before that an event had taken place of special importance in the history of Judah. The decline of Assyria had naturally rekindled the hopes of Egypt, its rival for the empire of the ancient world. Hitherto it had always been worsted in the contests with Assyria. But now, Pharaoh-Necho (really Necho II.), the son of Psammetichus (the founder of the twenty-sixth, Saite dynasty), resolved to attack the Assyrian power. To us a special interest attaches to Necho, since he was the first to attempt joining the Red Sea with the Mediterranean, although he had finally to desist from the enterprise.

Circumstances seemed indeed favorable to the expedition of Necho against Assyria. Asurbanipal had on his death (probably in 626 B.C.) bequeathed to his successor or successors a very troubled heritage. In Babylonia Nabo-palassar appears (in 626 or 625) as nominally a viceroy, but virtually independent of Assyria.

The expedition of Necho, to which reference is made in 2 Kings 23:29, and at greater length in 2 Chronicles 35:20-25, was made in the year 609 B.C., or sixteen years after Nabopalassar had becotne ruler of Babylonia. In 2 Kings 23:29 the expedition is expressly described as against "the king of Assyria." But here a difficulty arises. According to some authorities the fall of Nineveh preceded or coincided with the accession of Nabo-palassar to the Babylonian throne in 626 B.C.

In that case the expedition of Necho would have been against the Babylonian monarch, who would have been designated "King of Assyria" as successor to that power. According to other authorities the fall of Nineveh would have to be placed between the years 609 and 606 B.C. As Asurbanipal seems to have still occupied the throne in 626 B.C., and as we read of two sieges of Nineveh, it appears most likely that this (the first) expedition of Necho was still literally against "the king of Assyria."

Avoiding a march through the land of Judah, the Egyptian army advanced along the ordinary route followed towards the East. At the slope of the hills which separate the low coast tract south of Carmel from the great plain of Esdraelon, its progress was barred by a Judaean army under Josiah, holding the strong position of Megiddo, the modern el-Lejjun, which commanded the valley of the Kishon (called in 1 (3) Esd. i. 27 that of Mageddo), and also access to the mountains of Samaria. It is not easy to form a definite opinion as to the motives which induced Josiah to attempt arresting the march of Necho. But probably he may have been influenced by those plans for the re-union of Israel and Judah to which reference has already been made. He may have thought that the danger to the independence of the new kingdom would be much greater if Necho succeeded in the object of his expedition than if matters continued as they were. Of the two powers which threatened Palestine — Egypt and Assyria — the former was, at that time, certainly more to be dreaded. Besides, had Josiah succeeded, he would have secured not only the gratitude of Assyria, but the virtual, if not the nominal independence of his kingdom.

It was in vain that Necho remonstrated with Josiah. In the remarkable message which his ambassadors were instructed to deliver (2 Chronicles 35:21), he probably did not refer to any special prophecies against Assyria, but rather to what he regarded as the general lesson which Josiah should derive from the history of Hezekiah, viewed in connection with subsequent events, as indicating the will of the God of Israel in regard to the destruction of Assyria.

But Josiah gave not heed to the warning. A decisive battle was fought on "the plain of Megiddo" (2 Chronicles 35:22). If the reading is correct that Josiah "disguised himself," we would almost be reminded of the similar device of Ahab (2 Chronicles 18:29).

But the precaution, if adopted, was useless. Mortally wounded by the archers, Josiah was lifted from his chariot, and probably expired on the way to Jerusalem (2 Kings 23:30), whither they carried him. He was buried in "his own sepulcher" — apparently in the new place of sepulcher prepared by Manasseh (2 Chronicles 35:24; comp. 2 Kings 21:18, 26). General and deep was the mourning in Jerusalem and Judah for good King Josiah. The prophet Jeremiah composed a "lament" for him, which, although now lost, seems to have been inserted in a special book of "Laments" mentioned by the Chronicler (35:25). Nay, his memory and the "lament" for him continued in Israel — and the memorial, if not some of the words, of it are preserved in Jeremiah 22:10, 18, and so late as in Zechariah 12:11.

In truth, the defeat of the Judean army and the death of Josiah, not only put an end to his great reformatory movement, and to the hopes of the possible re-union and recovery of Israel and Judah, but it sounded the knell of Jewish independence. Henceforth Judah was alternately vassal to Egypt or Babylonia. According to 1 Chronicles 3:15, Josiah had four sons, of whom the eldest, Johanan, seems to have died, either before his father or perhaps in the battle of Megiddo.

The other three, arranging them in the order of age, were Eliakim, afterwards called Jehoiakim; Shallum, afterwards called Jehoahaz; and Zedekiah. On the death of Josiah "the people of the land" made and anointed, as his successor, not the eldest royal prince, but his younger brother Shallum, who, on his accession, assumed the name Jehoahaz, "Jehovah holds up" (comp. 2 Kings 23:30, with Jeremiah 22:11, and 1 Chronicles 3:15).

From the fate which so speedily overtook him, we may infer that the popular choice of Jehoahaz was largely influenced by his opposition to Egypt. Of his brief reign of three months and, according to Josephus, ten days, we only know that "he did the evil in the sight of Jehovah." If Josephus also characterizes him as "impure in his course of life," this may refer to the restoration of the lascivious rites of his grandfather's reign.

Meantime, Necho had, after the battle of Megiddo, continued his march towards Syria. Thither, at Riblah (the modern Ribleh, on the Orontes) "in the land of Hamath," the victor summoned the new Jewish king.

On his arrival, Jehoahaz, who had been crowned without the leave of Necho, was put in bonds. Necho does not seem, on this occasion, to have pursued his expedition against Assyria. The great battle at Carchemish, to which the chronicler refers by anticipation (2 Chronicles 35:20), was fought on a second expedition, three years later, when the Egyptian army under Necho was defeated with great slaughter by Nebuchadnezzar, the son of Nabopalassar. This was after the fall of Nineveh, and when the Babylonian or Chaldean empire had taken the place of the Assyrian. But on the present occasion Necho seems to have returned, before encountering the Assyrians, into Egypt, whither "he brought" with him Jehoahaz, who died in captivity.

The Pharaoh appointed, in room of Jehoahaz, his brother Eliakim, who ascended the throne at the age of twenty-five, being two years older than Jehoahaz (2 Kings 23:31). After a not uncommon practice (Comp. Genesis 41:45; Ezra 5:14; Daniel 1:7), and to show how entirely the new king was his subject, Necho changed his name, Eliakim, into Jehoiakim — "Jehovah setteth up" — the selection of the name being probably determined by a regard for its effect upon the people. A tribute of 100 talents of silver and one talent of gold was imposed upon the land. This sum, so small as compared with the tribute formerly imposed by Tiglath-pileser on Menahem of Samaria (2 Kings 15:19), and that given to Sennacherib by Hezekiah (2 Kings 18:14), and amounting to only about 37,500 pounds in silver and 6,750 pounds in gold, affords evidence of the impoverishment of the country. After the example of Menahem of Samaria (2 Kings 15:20), Jehoiakim raised the tribute by a general tax upon the land. It was an ominous precedent to follow. But, to use the language of a great writer, the twenty-three years which elapsed between the decease of Josiah and the final deportation to Babylon, were only "the dying time" of the kingdom of Judah.

CHAPTER 17 — JEHOIAKIM (EIGHTEENTH), JEHOIACHIN (NINETEENTH), ZEDEKIAH (TWENTIETH), KING OF JUDAH — CHARACTER OF JEHOIAKIM'S REIGN — SKETCH OF THE HISTORY OF MEDIA — SKETCH OF THE HISTORY OF BABYLONIA — FALL OF NINEVEH — THE NEW BABYLONIAN EMPIRE — SECOND EXPEDITION OF NECHO — BATTLE OF CARCHEMISH — ADVANCE OF NEBUCHADNEZZAR — STATE OF THINGS IN JERUSALEM — PARTIAL SPOIL OF THE TEMPLE — RETURN OF NEBUCHADNEZZAR TO BABYLON — JEHOIAKIM FIRST PRISONER, THEN TRIBUTARY — REBELLION OF JEHOIAKIM — DEATH OF JEHOIAKIM AND ACCESSION OF JEHOIACHIN — SIEGE OF JERUSALEM — SURRENDER OF JEHOIACHIN — HIS FATE — FIRST DEPORTATION TO BABYLON — ACCESSION AND REIGN OF ZEDEKIAH — THE REBELLION OF ZEDEKIAH — ADVANCE OF NEBUCHADNEZZAR — SIEGE OF JERUSALEM — STATE OF MATTERS IN THE CITY — BRIEF RELIEF OWING TO THE ADVANCE OF AN EGYPTIAN ARMY — RESUMPTION OF THE SIEGE — CAPTURE OF PART OF THE CITY — FLIGHT AND CAPTURE OF ZEDEKIAH — THE SENTENCES AT RIBLAH — BURNING OF THE TEMPLE, DESTRUCTION OF THE CITY, AND DEPORTATION OF CAPTIVES — THE PROPHET JEREMIAH — APPOINTMENT OF GEDALIAH — THE COURT AT MIZPAH — MURDER OF GEDALIAH — PURSUIT AND FLIGHT OF THE MURDERERS — RETREAT INTO EGYPT — LAST PROPHECIES OF JEREMIAH — END OF THE EARTHLY DAVIDIC RULE — THE DESOLATE LAND KEEPS HER SABBATHS.

(2 KINGS 24, 25; 2 CHRONICLES. 36:5-END; WITH CORRESPONDING PASSAGES FROM THE BOOKS OF JEREMIAH AND OF EZEKIEL.)

The reign of Jehoiakim, which lasted eleven years, was in every respect most disastrous. In truth, it was the beginning of the end. The reformatory work of Josiah gave place to a restoration of the former idolatry (comp. 2 Chronicles 36:8). As in previous reigns, it was connected with complete demoralization of the people (comp. Jeremiah 7:9-15; 17:2; 19:4-9; Ezekiel 8:9-18). And this not only among the laity, high and low, but equally among the priests and prophets (comp. Jeremiah 23:9-14). All the louder rose the voices of the prophets' Jeremiah, Urijah, and Habakkuk. But their warnings were either unheeded and scorned, or brought on them persecution and martyrdom (2 Kings 24:4; Jeremiah 26:10, 11; and especially verses 20-23). Otherwise, also, it was a wretched government, characterized by public wrong, violence, oppression, and covetousness. While the land was impoverished, the king indulged in luxury, and built magnificent palaces, or adorned towns, by means of forced labor, which remained unpaid, and at the cost of the lives of a miserable enslaved people (Jeremiah 22:13-18; Habakkuk 2:9-17).

In these circumstances the crisis could not be long delayed. As previously stated, three years after his first expedition, Necho once more advanced against the rival empire in the east. There great changes had taken place. Nineveh had fallen under the combined assault of Nabopalassar, king of Babylonia, and Kyaxares, king of the Medes. Notices, however brief, of these events seem necessary for the more complete understanding of this history.

Media, by which name we understand the district in Asia reaching from south of the Caspian Sea, but east of the Zagros mountain, down to Elam (Susiana), seems to have been inhabited by a twofold population: the earlier settlers being of non-Arian, the later of Arian descent. Their history first emerges into clear light during the reign of Tiglath-pileser II., who incorporated into the Assyrian empire districts of Media, these conquests being continued by Sargon and Sennacherib. Media regained its independence during the reign of Asurbanipal (668-626, B.C.) when, as previously noted, Phraortes of Media made an unsuccessful inroad upon Assyria. His successor, Kyaxares (633-593, B.C.), in conjunction with Nabopalasar of Babylonia, put an end to the Assyrian empire and destroyed Nineveh. But the independence of Media did not long continue. Astyages, the successor of Kyaxares, was dethroned by Cyrus (in 558, B.C.), and his kingdom incorporated with Persia.

The other, and in this history more important factor in the destruction of the Assyrian empire, was Babylonia, which took its place. Babylonia, also known to us as "the land of the Chaldees," was bounded in the north by Armenia and Media as far as Mount Zagros; in the west by the Arabian desert; in the south by the Persian Gulf; and in the east by Elam (Susiana).

Its population was of twofold race. The earliest inhabitants were non-Semitic — the Accadians. To them the culture of the people is really due, and they were the inventors of the so-called cuneiform writing. To these inhabitants there joined themselves at any rate so early as in the third millennium before our era, Semitic immigrants, coming from Arabia. They occupied, in the first place, Southern Babylonia, in and around Ur, whence they gradually spread northwards, slowly gaining the mastery over the earlier nationality, but receiving the impress of its culture. These settlers were what we know by the name of the Chaldees. To the earlier history of Babylonia and its relations with Assyria, we have, so far as necessary for our present purpose, already adverted in connection with Merodach-baladan. Without here entering into the troubled period of the contests between Assyria (under Tiglath-pileser, Sargon, and Sennacherib) and Babylonia for its independence, we recall the rebellion of Saos-duchin, the brother of Asurbanipal, whom he had appointed viceroy of Babylon. After the suppression of that rising, and the death of Saosduchin, Asurbanipal himself assumed the crown of Babylon. But, as we have seen, his successors could not maintain the supremacy of Assyria. After the final defeat of the Scythians, the Medes, under Kyaxares, were advancing a second time against Assyria. The last king of that empire was purposing himself to make a stand against them. But Nabopalassar, instead of holding Babylonia for Assyria, had turned against it, and made common cause with the enemy, cementing the new alliance by the marriage of his son, Nebuchadnezzar, with Amytis, the daughter of Kyaxares. The two armies now marched against Nineveh, which made brave resistance. Saracus destroyed himself in the flames of his palace, and Nineveh was utterly laid waste.

With Nabopalassar, who founded the new Babylonian empire, began the period of the Chaldees — as they are chiefly known to us in Scripture. Here we may at once indicate that he was succeeded by his son, Nebuchadrezzar (or Nebuchadnezzar), and he in turn by his son, Evil-merodach, who, after two years' reign, was dethroned by his brother-in-law, Neriglissar. After four years (559-556, B.C.) Neriglissar was succeeded by his youthful son, Laborosoarchod. After his murder, Nabonidos (Nabunit, Nabunaid)acceded to the government, but after seventeen years' reign (555-539 B.C.) was dethroned by Cyrus. The eldest son of Nabonidos, and heir to the throne, was Belshazzar, whom we know from the Book of Daniel, where, in a not unusual manner, he is designated as the son, that is, the descendant of Nebuchadrezzar (Daniel 5:2, 11, 18). We infer that, while his father, Nabonidos, went to meet Cyrus, to whom he surrendered, thereby preserving his life, Belshazzar had been left as "king" in Babylon, at the taking of which he perished in the night of his feast, described in Holy Scripture.

From these almost necessary digressions we return to the Biblical history. It was three years after his first expedition that Pharaoh Necho once more turned his arms against the eastern empire. Even the direction of his march, as indicated by the battle fought at Carchemish, shows that the expedition was really intended against Assyria. But Nineveh had fallen, and the Egyptian army was encountered by the youthful heir to the new Babylonian empire, Nebuchadrezzar — in the inscriptions Nabukudurri-usur — "Nebo, protect the crown."

The Egyptian army was thoroughly defeated and followed by the victorious Nebuchadrezzar, who now recovered the Assyrian possessions in Western Asia, which had been lost in the previous reign. The date of this battle deserves special attention. For the victory of Carchemish (606 or 605 B.C.) was gained by the Babylonian army in the fourth year of Jehoiakim (Jeremiah 46:2), and it was in the same fourth year of his reign that Jeremiah made Baruch write in a book his prophetic denunciations of judgment (Jeremiah 36:1). The conjunction of these two events is deeply significant.

What followed can be easily understood. As Nebuchadrezzar advanced towards Palestine (2 Kings 24:1) — in the fifth year of the reign of Jehoiakim — the Jewish king, in abject fear, proclaimed a national fast (Jeremiah 36:9). Whether this was done from superstition, or for the sake of popular effect, or else in hope of conciliating the prophet and his adherents, certain it is that the professed repentance was hypocritical. The book of Jeremiah's prophecies, which Baruch had publicly read on that occasion, was cut in pieces by the king himself, and thrown on the fire (Jeremiah 36:22, 23). Jeremiah and Baruch only escaped imprisonment, if not death, by timely concealment. Nevertheless, Nebuchadrezzar appeared in Jerusalem. Jehoiakim, who would be regarded as a vassal of Egypt, was bound in fetters, with the intention of being carried to Babylon. This, however, was not done — perhaps because of the summons which rapidly recalled Nebuchadrezzar to Babylon. But the vessels of the temple were sent to Babylon, and placed, first in the victor's palace, and then in the temple of his god — probably Bel-Merodach or Belus (comp. 2 Kings 24:13; 2 Chronicles 36:6, 7; Jeremiah 35:11; 36:29-31; Daniel 1:2; and for the date also Jeremiah 25:1).

During the Syrian campaign of Nebuchadrezzar his father, Nabopalassar, had sickened. Tidings of his death now induced the heir to the crown speedily to return to Babylon, committing his Jewish, Phoenician, Syrian, and Egyptian captives, together with the spoil, to his subordinates (Jos. Ant. x. II, I).

Jehoiakim was allowed to remain for three years as a tributary to Babylonia (2 Kings 24:1). At the end of that time he rebelled. Nebuchadrezzar, who was probably detained by domestic affairs, left his punishment, in the first place, in the hands of his Chaldean garrisons, and of the old hereditary enemies who surrounded Judah. In the latter respect it is specially significant that the account in the Book of Kings attributes this to the direct agency of the Lord, in fulfillment of His purpose of judgment (2 Kings 24:2). The king of Egypt, who probably was not without share in the rebellion of Jehoiakim, did not venture to come to the aid of the land which was overrun by the enemy (2 Kings 24:7). In the midst of these troubles Jehoiakim died — perhaps by the hand of his assailants. The king who had wrought so much evil (2 Kings 24:4), and who had brought such misfortunes on his land, descended into the grave unmourned and unhonored (Jeremiah 22:18, 19; 36:30).

Jehoiakim was succeeded by his son, Jehoiachin ("Jehovah confirms"), a youth of eighteen years, who reigned for only three months and ten days (2 Chronicles 36:9).

He occupied the throne when Nebuchadrezzar himself appeared a second time on the soil of Palestine (2 Kings 24:11). It is impossible to determine whether what now happened was in punishment of the previous rebellion, or because the young king was guilty of similar intrigues with Egypt. From the indications in Holy Scripture we are led to suppose that the queen-mother, Nehushta ("the brazen"), the daughter of Elnathan, an influential prince of Jerusalem (2 Kings 24:8; Jeremiah 36:12, 25), had considerable share in the events of this brief reign. We infer this, on the one hand, from the connection of her father with Egypt (Jeremiah 26:22), and on the other from the pointed references to her and her fate (2 Kings 24:12; Jeremiah 13:18; 22:26; 29:2).

At first the siege of Jerusalem was entrusted to subordinate officers. But when the fall of the city seemed near Nebuchadnezzar himself appeared. Jehoiachin, together with the queen-mother, the court, the princes, and the leaders seem to have surrendered to the victor. The punishment inflicted on the city was of signal severity. All the treasures of the temple and the palace were carried away, the heavier furnishings of the sanctuary being cut in pieces.

Thus was the word of the Lord, long and often spoken, fulfilled (2 Kings 24:12, 13). The king himself, his mother, his wives, and all the officials, whether of the court, the state, or the army, were carried to Babylon. Nay, to make sure of the permanence of the conquest, "all Jerusalem" — in the sense of what made it the capital — and all who in any sense were "strong and apt for war" — who could either lead, or fight, or prepare the means for it — were carried into captivity. Their number is roughly stated as 11,000 (11,023[?] comp. Jeremiah 52:28), comprising 3,000 ranked as "princes" and leading citizens, 7,000 soldiers (10,000, 2 Kings 24:14), and 1,000 craftsmen, especially smiths (2 Kings 24:13-16).

Considering that the total population of Jerusalem at that time — including women and children — is only calculated at between 50,000 and 60,000 souls, only a sparse remnant can have been left behind — and that wholly composed of "the poorest sort of the people of the land." Among the captives was also the prophet Ezekiel (Ezekiel 1:1, 2; 40:1, comp. Jeremiah 29:1).

We may as well here relate the sequel of Jehoiachin's history. For thirty-seven years he lingered in a Babylonian prison. At the end of that period Evil-merodach ("the man of Merodach"), the son and successor of Nebuchadrezzar, showed him favor. Selected from out the other captive kings he was restored to rank, admitted to the royal table as one of the vassals at the court of the Babylonian monarch, and had a regular allowance assigned to him suited to the wants of his family and establishment. This continued till his death, the date of which is uncertain (2 Kings 25:27-30; Jeremiah 52:31, 34).

We now rapidly near the close of this history. On his departure from Jerusalem Nebuchadrezzar had, with singular generosity, appointed a king of the old Davidic lineage.

His choice had fallen on Mattaniah ("the gift of Jehovah"), whose name was changed into Zedekiah ("the righteousness of Jehovah").

The new king was the uncle of Jehoiachin, being the youngest son of Josiah by the same mother as Jehoahaz (comp. 2 Kings 23:31). The eleven years of his reign may be summed up in the brief formula which described that of Jehoiakim, as of so many others: "he did the evil in the sight of Jehovah." And significantly the sacred text adds: "For because of the anger of Jehovah did it come to pass in Jerusalem and in Judah, until He cast them out from His presence. And Zedekiah rebelled against the King of Babylon" (2 Kings. 24:20).

The "rebellion" of Zedekiah was the more culpable and aggravated that he had taken a solemn oath of fidelity to Nebuchadrezzar (2 Chronicles 36:13; Ezekiel 17:13). The precise circumstances which led up to his attempt at independence cannot be fully ascertained. Still there are sufficient indications to show the progress of what ultimately ended in open revolt.

The first care of the new king must have been to gather around him counselors and people. As all the most prominent and able men of Judah were in captivity, the task would in any circumstances have been one of extreme difficulty. In the present instance the measures taken seem to have been disastrous. The capital and the Temple were the scene of every idolatry (Ezekiel 8), while the administration of justice would appear to have been of the worst kind (Jeremiah 21:11, 12). It was not long before political intrigues began. Soon ambassadors from Edom, Moab, Ammon, Tyre, and Sidon, appeared at the court of Zedekiah — no doubt to deliberate about a combined movement against Babylonia (Jeremiah 27). Perhaps the contemplated rising was connected with troubles which Nebuchadrezzar had at that time to encounter in Elam (comp. Jeremiah 49:34-39). But all such hopes were doomed to speedy disappointment.

Zedekiah now deemed it prudent to send ambassadors to Babylon to assure his suzerain of his fidelity. The messengers also carried with them letters from Jeremiah to the exiles, who seem to have been in a state of restless expectation, probably due to the plans of Zedekiah (Jeremiah 29:1 and follow.). This was in the fourth year of Zedekiah (Jeremiah 28:1). How such hopes were fostered by false prophets appears from Jeremiah 28, which records the predictions of one Hananiah, and the Divine punishment which overtook him. The embassy to Babylon seems not to have appeased the suspicions of Nebuchadrezzar, and Zedekiah had to appear personally in Babylon (Jeremiah 51:59). This closes the first scene in the drama.

The next scene opens with fresh intrigues — this time chiefly with Egypt (Ezekiel 17:15-18) — probably through the numerous Judaean immigrants to that country (Jeremiah 24:8). Neighboring tribes, were, however, also implicated. Whether Zedekiah now deemed himself sufficiently strong with the help of Egypt, or else it was impossible any longer to conceal the plans of the allies, certain it is that he now openly rebelled (2 Kings 24:20). His punishment came quickly. Nebuchadrezzar advanced with his army, and pitched his camp at Riblah — significantly, the same place where Jehoahaz had been cast into bonds by Necho (2 Kings 23:33). Riblah remained the headquarters of the Babylonian army, as being a convenient point whence to operate against Palestine and Tyre on the one side, and on the other against Ammon and Moab (Ezekiel 21:19, 20, 22, 28; 26:1-7). Presently all Judaea was overrun. Indeed, it was entirely defenseless, with the exception of the fortified towns of Lachish, Azekah, and Jerusalem (Jeremiah 34:7). Against Jerusalem itself Nebuchadrezzar and his host now laid siege. This was on the tenth day of the tenth month of the ninth year of Zedekiah (2 Kings 25:1; Jeremiah 39:1).

In the city, the greatness of the danger gave rise to what might have seemed feelings of repentance, alternating, however, with opposite tendencies, as amidst the general stupefaction and helplessness one or the other party had the upper hand. In the midst of it all the king seemed as one utterly lost. At first all was energy. The useless houses which the kings and the nobles had reared, were thrown down, and their place and materials used for the defenses of the city (Jeremiah 33:4). It was a vain measure — and these defenses only became the graves of those who held them. Popular measures also were adopted. The king made a covenant with the people, and a solemn proclamation restored freedom to all of Hebrew nationality — men and women — whom previous exactions, violence, and unrighteousness had reduced to, or kept in, slavery (Jeremiah 34:8, 9). The "princes" sulkily submitted. But during the brief time that the Babylonians withdrew to meet the Egyptian army, they not only ignored what had been done, but once more reduced to bondage those who had so lately been set free (Jeremiah 34:10, 11).

As for Zedekiah himself, his conduct was characterized by that helpless perplexity and vacillation, which were the outcome of weakness and want of religious conviction. Deputations were sent to Jeremiah for inquiry of the LORD, and appeal to Him in name of past deliverances (Jeremiah 21:1, 2; 37:3). And yet, at the same time, the king imprisoned and maltreated the prophets. All this according as his nobles either opposed or protected Jeremiah. Yet when the prophet clearly set before the king the certain alternative of resistance and captivity, or else surrender and safety (Jeremiah 34:2-6, 38:17,18), Zedekiah could form no decision. Most characteristic of the situation is Jeremiah 38. As we read it, the king first yielded to his princes, who even ventured to charge the prophet with treacherous designs (Jeremiah 37:13), and Jeremiah was cast into a loathsome dungeon. Next, Zedekiah listened to intercessions on the other side, and Jeremiah was at least removed from the subterranean prison, where his feet had sunk in mire, and more humanely treated. Then the king actually sent for him and consulted him. Nay, he not only most solemnly swore to protect him, but seemed willing to follow his advice and surrender to the Chaldeans. But once more fear prevented his taking that step, notwithstanding the assurances of Jeremiah. In the end Zedekiah was even in fear that his nobles should hear of his conference with the prophet, and bade him give a different interpretation to their interview.

Meantime the siege was continuing, without hope of relief. Tyre suffered straits similar to those of Jerusalem, while Ammon, Moab, Edom, and the Philistines had not only withdrawn from the alliance, but were waiting to share in the spoil of Judah (Ezekiel 25). At length a gleam of hope appeared. An Egyptian army, under their King Hophra, the grandson of Necho, advanced through Phoenicia, and obliged the Chaldeans to raise the siege of Jerusalem (Jeremiah 37:5-7). The exultation and reaction in Jerusalem may be imagined — and it was probably in consequence of it that Jeremiah, who still predicted calamity, was cast into prison (ib. ver. 4). But the relief of Jerusalem was brief. The Egyptian army had to retire, and the siege of Jerusalem by the Chaldeans was resumed, and that under even more disadvantageous circumstances to the besieged. To the other calamities that of famine was now added (2 Kings 25:3). Of the horrors of that time Jeremiah has left a record in the Book of Lamentations (comp. i 19; ii. 11, 12, 20; iv. 3-10). The last resistance was soon overcome. On the ninth day of the fourth month [Tammuz], in the eleventh year of Zedekiah, the enemy gained possession of the northern suburb (2 Kings 25:4; Jeremiah 39:2, 3; 52:6, 7). Before the middle gate the Babylonian captains held a council of war (Jeremiah 39:2, 3). Then the king and all the regular army sought safety in flight during the darkness of the night (Jeremiah 39:4). As the Chaldeans held the northern part of the city, they fled southwards. Between the two walls, through the Tyropoeon, then out of the "fountain-gate," and through the king's garden, they made haste to gain the Jordan. But their flight could not remain unobserved. They were pursued and overtaken in the plains of Jericho. The soldiers dispersed in various directions. But the king himself and his household were taken captives, and carried to the headquarters at Riblah, where Nebuchadrezzar himself was at the time. Here Zedekiah was formally arraigned and sentence given against him. His daughters were set free, but his sons were slain before him. It was the last sight the king saw. His eyes were put out; he was bound hands and feet with double fetters of brass, and so carried to Babylon. (Compare 2 Kings 25:4-7; Jeremiah 4-7; 43:6; Ezekiel 12:12, 13.) There he died in ward (Jeremiah 52:11).

The remainder of this mournful tale is soon told. After the flight and capture of the king, the city could not long hold out. A month later, and on the seventh day of the fifth month (Ab) Nebuzar-adan ["Nebo gave posterity"] penetrated into the city.

The Temple was set on fire, as well as the king's palace. The whole city was reduced to ruins and ashes, and the walls which had defended it were broken down (2 Kings 25:9, 10). After three days the work of destruction was completed; and ever afterwards was the 10th (9th) of Ab mourned as the fatal day of Jerusalem's fall (Jeremiah 52:12; Zechariah 7:3, 5; 8:19).

"The rest of the people left in the city," and those who had previously passed to the enemy, together "with the remnant of the multitude," were carried away (2 Kings 25:11). We can scarcely be mistaken in regarding these captives as the chief part of the non-combatant population of Jerusalem and Judah.

The capture of Jerusalem found Jeremiah in prison for his faithfulness in announcing the coming ruin, and for warning his people of their impending fate. But the same faith and faithfulness led him there to yet loftier display of the prophetic character than even when bearing steadfast testimony amidst gainsaying, persecution, and suffering. In that prison, and in full view of the impending desolation, he announced, with the same firm faith as formerly the judgments upon Israel, not only the terrible doom that would overtake Babylon (Jeremiah 51:1), but also the certain restoration of Israel. And in sublime confidence of this event, he bought while in prison — in this also obedient to the Divine direction — fields in Anathoth, as it were in anticipation of the return of his people to their own land (Jeremiah 32:6-23). And beyond this did his rapt vision descry a better and spiritual restoration of Israel (Jeremiah 32:37-44). Assuredly, viewing the Prophet in the surroundings of his time and circumstances, it is not easy to understand how any one can fail to perceive either the sublime dignity of the prophetic office, or the Divine character of prophecy.

But the end has not yet been fully told. All of any value in the Temple that could be removed, either whole or when broken up, was taken to Babylon. As already stated, the general population of Jerusalem and of Judah were carried into captivity. Only the poorest in the land were left to be husbandmen and vine-dressers, so as not to leave the soil uncultivated — probably in expectation of a future colonization from Babylonia.

Lastly, signal punishment was dealt out to those who were regarded as ringleaders or as representative persons during the late rebellion. "Seraiah, the chief priest" (high priest), "Zephaniah, the second priest" (probably the substitute of the high priest), "and the three keepers of the door" — that is, the chiefs of the Levites who kept watch at the three Temple gates (Jeremiah 38:14), were brought before the court which sat at Riblah, and executed.

The same punishment as that of the Temple officials was meted out to the royal officers in the city — the chamberlain who had charge of the troops, five of the king's councilors, and the secretary of the general of the army. With these were executed sixty of the people of the land, either as prominent in the late rebellion, or as representing the people generally.

The civil administration of the country was entrusted by Nebuchadrezzar to Gedaliah, the son of Ahikam. The latter had held a high position in the reign of Josiah (2 Kings 22:12), and was even more distinguished for the piety and courage which saved the life of Jeremiah in the time of Jehoiakim (Jeremiah 26:24). The same adherence to the prophetic Word had induced Gedaliah to support the unpopular advice of submission to Nebuchadrezzar. Information of all that passed in the city would no doubt reach the camp of the Chaldeans, and it would be in consequence of what he had heard that Nebuchadrezzar appointed Gedaliah to his post. It was also this, as well as respect for the prophet and his office, which must have induced the king to give such charge about Jeremiah to Nebuzar-adan, his chief captain (Jeremiah 39:11-14; 40:1-4). The prophet was apparently set at liberty, but afterwards, by some mistake, carried with the other captives in chains to Ramah. Here the error was discovered, and Nebuzar-adan gave the prophet the choice of either going to Babylon, where all honorable provision should be made for him, or of settling in any part of the country. With true patriotic feeling, as well as in accordance with his prophetic work, Jeremiah chose to remain with the new Jewish governor, in order to support his authority, and to guide by his counsel the remnant of the people. But even this proved a thankless and a hopeless task. Gedaliah had taken up his residence in the ancient historic Mizpah.

Thither all that was left of Judah's representative men gathered, as also the wives, daughters, and children of the slain and the captives. Thither also came the fugitives who had sought safety in neighboring lands, as well as the remnants of the dispersed Jewish army. A court was being formed, and the governor was surrounded by a Chaldean and Jewish guard (Jeremiah 40:6-end; 41:3; 43:6). It even seems as if a kind of sanctuary had been set up (Jeremiah 41:5). For a brief time it appeared as if not only peace but a measure of prosperity were to be vouchsafed to the remnant of Judah. But once more all such hopes were disappointed. The rule of Gedaliah lasted only two months.

Chief among them who had come to him was Ishmael, the son of Nathaniah, himself of the seed royal. Partly in the hope of possessing himself of the government, to which his descent might lead him to aspire, and partly at the instigation of Baalis, the king of the Ammonites — who no doubt had purposes of his own in the matter — Ishmael put himself at the head of a gang of conspirators (comp. 2 Kings 25:25; Jeremiah 40:8- 16). In vain the generous Gedaliah was warned of his danger. Incapable of treachery himself, he would not believe in that of others, nor sanction measures of needful self-defense. Accordingly the plan of the conspirators was carried out. Gedaliah and all who were around him were massacred, and their dead bodies cast into the pit which, long before, Asa the king had made, for fear of Baasha, king of Israel (Jeremiah 41:1-9). Only ten men escaped slaughter by promises of rich supplies to the conspirators.

But even so the measure was not full. After his bloody success at Mizpah, Ishmael had carried away captive not only the women, but all the people, with the intention of passing over to the Ammonites. But when tidings of the crimes perpetrated reached Johanan, the son of Kareah, and the captains of the forces in the fields, who had formerly in vain warned Gedaliah of his danger (Jeremiah 40:13-16), they mustered to avenge the wrong. They pursued and overtook Ishmael at Gibeon. The captive Jews now made common cause with their deliverers, and Ishmael escaped with only eight followers into Ammon. But the faith of Johanan and his companions was not equal to the occasion. Afraid that the Chaldeans would avenge on them the treachery and slaughter at Mizpah, they drew off towards Egypt. With hypocritical pretense of a desire that Jehovah might through His prophet show them whither to go and what to do, they approached the prophet. Jeremiah was to inquire of the LORD — and they gave solemn promise implicitly to obey the voice of Jehovah. Yet all the time they had resolved to retire into Egypt. And so Jeremiah told them when he brought them the twofold message from his God, that they might dismiss all fear of the Chaldeans if they remained in the land; but that if they sought safety in Egypt, the sword of the conqueror, who would smite down their protector, should surely overtake them.

The warning was in vain. The message of Jeremiah was represented as only the outcome of his own and of Baruch's personal resentment; and the leaders of Judah carried the feeble remnant to Tahpanhes in Egypt — there yet again to hear the voice of the aged prophet, announcing the coming judgment on the country, where, in their unbelief and hard-heartedness, they had sought shelter (comp. Jeremiah 42 and 43).

So the last remnant of Judah had gone from the land. The Davidic rule had passed away, so far as merely earthly power was concerned. The Davidic kingdom to come would be wider, higher, deeper. It would embrace the brotherhood of man; it would reach up to heaven; it would root in righteousness, and peace, and joy in the Holy Ghost.

But over all the land would be desolateness and stillness. Yet was it a "stillness unto God." The land was keeping long-neglected silent Sabbath unto God' ten times, "to fulfill three-score and ten years." It was just about seventy years after the battle of Carchemish, which really decided the fate of Palestine and its subjection to Babylon, that, like the priests' silver trumpets at morn in the Temple, the voice of Cyrus announced the dawn of morning after the long night of exile, and summoned the wanderers from all lands to the threshold of their sanctuary (2 Chronicles 36:21-23). Again is the land keeping Sabbath.

And again is it "stillness unto God," till His Voice shall waken land and people, Whose are land and people, dominion and peace: till He shall come Who is alike the goal and the fulfillment of all past history and prophecy "a light to lighten the Gentiles, and the glory of Thy people Israel."

Made in the USA
Middletown, DE
03 October 2021